The
Princeton
Review

PrincetonReview.com

The Best
Northeastern Colleges

218 Select Schools
to Consider

By Robert Franek,
Tom Meltzer, Christopher Maier,
Julie Doherty, Erik Olson, Eric Owens,
Michael Palumbo, and Marissa Pareles

Random House, Inc.
New York

The Princeton Review, Inc.
111 Speen Street, Suite 550
Framingham, MA 01701
E-mail: bookeditor@review.com

ISBN 978-0-375-42992-7

Senior VP—Publisher: Robert Franek
Editors: Seamus Mullarkey, Laura Braswell
Production: Best Content Solutions, LLC
Production Editor: Kristen O'Toole

Printed in the United States of America on partially recycled paper.

9 8 7 6 5 4 3 2 1

ACKNOWLEDGMENTS

Each year we assemble an awe-inspiringly talented group of colleagues who work together to produce our guidebooks; this year is no exception. Everyone involved in this effort—authors, editors, data collectors, production specialists, and designers—gives so much more than is required to make *The Best Northeastern Colleges* an exceptional student resource guide. This new edition gives prospective college students what they really want: The most honest, accessible, and pertinent information about the colleges they are considering attending.

My sincere thanks go to the many who contributed to this tremendous project. I know our readers will benefit from our collective efforts to collect the opinions of current students at the outstanding schools we profile. A special thank you goes to our authors, Tom Meltzer, Julie Doherty, Eric Owens, Anne DeWitt, Kristen O'Toole, Adam Davis, and Mukul Bakhshi, for their dedication in pouring through tens of thousands of surveys to produce the campus culture narratives of each school profiled. Very special thanks go to Seamus Mullarkey and Laura Braswell for their editorial commitment and vision. A warm and special thank you goes to our Student Survey Team, Andrea Kornstein, Adrinda Kelly, Abe Koogler and Steven Aglione, who continue to work in partnership with school administrators and students alike. My continued thanks go to our data collection pros, Ben Zelevansky and David Soto, for their successful efforts in collecting and accurately representing the statistical data that appear with each college profile. The enormousness of this project and its deadline constraints could not have been realized without the calm presence of our production partner, Scott Harris. Scott and his team's many years of dedication, focus, and most important, careful eyes, continue to delight and remind me of what a pleasure it is to work together on this project each year. Special thanks also go to Jeanne Krier, our Random House publicist, for the dedicated work she continues to do on this book and the overall series since its inception. Jeanne continues to be my trusted colleague, media advisor, and friend. I would also like to make special mention of Tom Russell and Nicole Benhabib, our Random House publishing team, for their continuous investment and faith in our ideas. Last, I thank my TPR Partner Team, Scott Kirkpatrick, Michael Bleyhl, Paul Kanarek, Robin Staley, Brian Healy and Tom Modero for their confidence in me and my content team and for their commitment to providing students the resources they need to find the right fit school for them. Again, to all who contributed so much to this publication, thank you for your efforts; they do not go unnoticed.

Robert Franek
Senior VP—Publisher
Lead Author—The Best Northeastern Colleges:
218 Select Schools to Consider

Contents

PART 1: INTRODUCTION

GETTING INTO THE BEST NORTHEASTERN COLLEGES

This is a guide to the Northeast's 218 most academically outstanding institutions, so it's no surprise that many of them may be selective in their admissions. If you're like any one of the 2 million (and growing!) high school students who apply to college each year, you're probably wondering what admissions officers at these schools are looking for in an applicant. What exactly does it take to get into a selective college? To be sure, high grades in challenging courses are just the beginning. To get into most of the colleges in this book, you will need to:

- Earn high grades.

- Enroll in challenging courses.

- Prepare for the SAT or the ACT, and SAT Subject Tests.

- Polish your writing skills.

- Plan ahead for those letters of recommendation you'll need by establishing great relationships with your teachers and advisors.

- Focus on activities, community service, and/or after-school or summer employment that show commitment over a long period of time and allow you to demonstrate leadership skills.

Here's a brief primer in what you should be doing year by year in high school to prepare yourself for admission to *your* "best fit" college. For a detailed guide on how you can make the most of your high school years and segue those experiences into a successful college application, check out our book: *The Road to College: The High School Student's Guide to Discovering Your Passion, Getting Involved, and Getting Admitted.* Pick it up at www.princetonreviewbooks.com.

FRESHMAN YEAR

It's easier to finish well in high school if you start off that way. Concentrate on your studies and work hard to earn good grades. Get to know your teachers and ask for their help if you are having trouble in a subject (or even if you just really enjoy it and want to learn more): They'll most certainly want to help you do your best. Odds are, there is an honor roll at your school: Make it a goal to get on it. And if your grades are so good that you qualify for membership in the National Honor Society, pat yourself on the back and don't think twice about accepting the invitation to join.

Make it a point to meet your guidance counselor to begin thinking about colleges you may be interested in and courses and admission tests they require. Also work on building your vocabulary to get an early start on prepping for the SAT and ACT. Sign up for the Princeton Review's Vocab Minute on PrincetonReview.com.

READ A GOOD BOOK!

Your vocabulary and reading skills are key to doing well on the SAT and ACT. You can do some early prep for both tests by reading good books. Here are some fiction and non-fiction books we love by great authors you may not have encountered before.

- *The Curious Incident of the Dog in the Night-Time: A Novel* by Mark Haddon
- *A Heartbreaking Work of Staggering Genius* by Dave Eggers
- *Life of Pi* by Yann Martel
- *Reading Lolita in Tehran* by Azar Nafisi
- *White Teeth* by Zadie Smith

For extra practice building your vocabulary, check out our *Word Smart* books. Full of mnemonic tricks, they make learning even the toughest vocabulary a breeze.

SOPHOMORE YEAR

As a sophomore, you'll need to stay focused on your studies. You'll also want to choose one or more extracurriculars that interest you. Admissions officers look favorably on involvement in student government, student newspaper, varsity sports, and community service. But don't overload your schedule with activities just to rack up a long list of extracurriculars that you hope will impress admissions officers. Colleges would much rather see you focus on a few worthwhile extracurriculars than divide your time among a bunch of different activities that you're not passionate about. If you didn't earn strong grades during your freshman year, start doing so this year. Scope out the Advanced Placement course offerings at your school. You'll want to sign up for as many AP courses as you can reasonably take, starting in your junior year. Admissions officers will want to see that you've earned high grades in challenging classes. Our test-prep series, *Cracking the AP*, can help give you a leg up on passing the AP exams and gaining college credit while in high school.

Your sophomore year is when you'll have an opportunity to take the PSAT. Given every October, the PSAT is a shortened version of the SAT. It is used to predict how well students may do on the SAT, and it determines eligibility for National Merit Scholarships. While your PSAT scores won't count until you retake the test in your junior year, you should approach this as a test run for the real thing. Check out our book, *Cracking the PSAT/NMSQT* for more info. It has two full-length practice tests and tips on how to score your best on the test.

WHAT SHOULD YOU DO THIS SUMMER?

Ahhh, summer. The possibilities seem endless. You can get a job, intern, travel, study, volunteer, or do nothing at all. Our Princeton Review book, *The Road to College*, has great suggestions for summer projects. Here are a few ideas to get you started:

- **Go to College**: No, not for real. However, you can participate in summer programs at colleges and universities at home and abroad. Programs can focus on anything from academics (stretch your brain by taking an intensive science or language course) to sports to admissions guidance. This is also a great opportunity to explore college life firsthand, especially if you get to stay in a dorm.

- **Prep for the PSAT, SAT, or ACT**: So maybe it's not quite as adventurous as trekking around Patagonia for the summer or as cool as learning to slam dunk at basketball camp, but hey, there's nothing adventurous or cool about being rejected from your top-choice college because of unimpressive test scores. Plus, you'll be ahead of the game if you can return to school with much of your PSAT, SAT, and ACT preparation behind you.

- **Research Scholarships**: College is expensive. While you should never rule out a school based on cost, the more scholarship money you can secure beforehand, the more college options you will have. You'll find loads of info on financial aid and scholarships (including a scholarship search tool) on our site, PrincetonReview.com.

JUNIOR YEAR

You'll start the year off by taking the PSAT in October. High PSAT scores in your junior year will qualify you for the National Merit Scholarship competition. To become a finalist, you also need great grades and a recommendation from your school.

Make sure your grades are high this year. When colleges look at your transcripts they put a heavy emphasis on junior year grades. Decisions are made before admissions officers see your second-semester senior-year grades, and possibly before they see your first-semester senior-year grades! It's critical that your junior-year grades are solid.

During your junior year, you'll probably take the SAT or ACT test for the first time. Most colleges require scores from one of these tests for admission and/or scholarship award decisions. Plan to spend 3–12 weeks preparing for the tests. The SAT is comprised of Math, Critical Reading, and Writing sections. Colleges will see your individual section scores and your composite score, but generally they'll be most concerned with your composite score.

More and more students are opting to take the ACT in addition to, or instead of, the SAT. Most colleges accept the ACT in lieu of the SAT. The ACT has an English, Reading, Math, and Science section, plus the optional Writing section. (Some schools require the essay, so be sure to ask before you take the test.) One great advantage of the ACT is that you can take the test several times and choose what scores to send. If you take the SAT several times, all your scores are sent to the colleges. If you're not sure which test to take, first make sure that all the schools to which you're applying accept both tests. If your chosen schools do accept both scores, visit PrincetonReview.com to take a free assessment test that will help you identify whether the ACT or SAT is better for you.

ACT or SAT?

Not sure which test to take? First make sure that all the schools to which you're applying accept both tests (nearly all colleges now do so, but it's best to check). Then take the test on which you do better. Visit PrincetonReview.com to take a free assessment test that will help you identify whether the ACT or SAT is better for you. We also have a new book on this very subject: *ACT or SAT? Choosing the Right Exam for You*. More and more students are opting to take the ACT in addition to, or instead of, the SAT. No matter which test you end up taking, you should plan to spend 3–12 weeks preparing for the tests.

Most highly selective colleges also require you to take three SAT Subject Tests in addition to the SAT or ACT. If you have SAT Subject Tests to take, plan now. You can't take the SAT and SAT Subject Tests on the same day. The Princeton Review can help with all the standardized tests you will need to take throughout high school. Log on to PrincetonReview.com for more info about our classes and study guides.

Also take time during your junior year to research colleges, and, if possible, visit schools high on your "hopes" list. When researching colleges, you'll want to consider a variety of factors besides whether or not you can get in, including location, school size, majors or programs offered that interest you, and cost and availability of financial aid. It helps to visit schools because it's the best way to learn whether a school may be right for you. If you can schedule an interview with an admissions officer during your visit, it may help him or her discover how right *you may be* for the school.

SENIOR YEAR

It's time to get serious about pulling everything together for your applications. Deadlines will vary from school to school, and you will have a lot to keep track of, so make checklists of what's due when. If you're not happy with your previous SAT scores, you should take the October SAT. If you still need to take any SAT Subject Tests, now's the time.

If you have found the school of your dreams and you're happy with your grades and test scores, consider filing an Early Decision application. Many selective colleges commit more than half of their admissions spots to Early Decision applicants. To take this route, you must file your application in early November. By mid-December, you'll find out whether you got in—but there's a catch. If you're accepted Early Decision to a college, you must withdraw all applications to other colleges. This means that your financial aid offer might be hard to negotiate, so be prepared to take what you get.

Regardless of which route you decide to take, have a backup plan. Make sure you apply to at least one safety school—one that you feel confident you can get into and afford. Another option is to apply Early Decision at one school, but apply to other colleges during the regular decision period in the event that you are rejected from the early decision college.

When you ask teachers to write recommendations for you, give them everything they need. Tell them your application deadline and include a stamped, addressed envelope, or directions on how to submit the recommendation online, and be sure to send them a thank-you note after you know the recommendation was turned in. Your essay, on the other hand, is the one part of your application you have total control over. Don't repeat information from other parts of your application. And by all means, proofread! You'll find tips from admissions officers on what they look for (and what peeves them the most) about college applicants' essays in our book, *College Essays That Made a Difference*.

In March/April, colleges will send you a decision from the admissions office regarding your admission or rejection. If you are admitted (and you applied for financial aid) you'll also receive a decision from the financial aid office detailing your aid award package. The decision from the financial aid office can sometimes be appealed. The decision from the admissions office is almost always final. If you are wait-listed, don't lose hope. Write a letter to the college expressing how much you'd still like to attend the school and include an update on your recent activities. When colleges admit students from wait lists, they almost always give preference to students who have made it clear that they really want to attend.

It's important to wait until you've heard from all of the colleges you've applied to before making your final choice. May 1 is when you'll need to commit to the lucky college that will have you in its freshman class. We know how exciting but stressful that decision can be. If you're having a difficult time choosing between two colleges, try to visit each of them one more time. Can you imagine yourself walking around that campus, building a life in that community, and establishing friendships with those people? Finally, decide and be happy. Don't forget to thank your recommenders and tell them where you'll be going to school. Some of the best times of your life await!

26 Tips for Getting Financial Aid, Scholarships and Grants, and for Paying Less for College

by Kalman A. Chany, author of *Paying for College Without Going Broke*
(Random House/Princeton Review Books)

Getting Financial Aid

1. Learn how the aid process works. The more and the sooner you know about the process, the better you can take steps to maximize your aid eligibility.

2. Apply for financial aid no matter what your circumstances. Some merit-based aid can only be awarded if the applicant has submitted financial aid application forms.

3. Don't wait till your child is accepted to apply for financial aid. Do it when applying for admission.

4. Complete all the required aid applications. All students seeking aid must submit the FAFSA (Free Application for Federal Student Aid); other forms may also be required. Check with each college to see what's required and when.

5. Get the best scores you can on the SAT or ACT. They are used not only in decisions for admission but also financial aid. If your scores and other stats exceed the school's admission criteria, you are likely to get a better aid package than a marginal applicant.

6. Apply strategically to colleges. Your chances of getting aid will be better at schools that have generous financial aid budgets. (Check the "Best Value Colleges" list and Financial Aid Ratings for schools in this book and on princetonreview.com.)

7. Don't rule out any school as too expensive. A generous aid award from a pricey private school can make it less costly than a public school with a lower sticker price.

8. Take advantage of education tax benefits. A dollar saved on taxes is worth the same as a dollar in scholarship aid. Look into Coverdells, education tax credits, and loan deductions.

Scholarships and Grants

9. Get your best possible score on the PSAT: It is the National Merit Scholarship Qualifying Test and also used in the selection of students for other scholarships and recognition programs.

10. Check your eligibility for grants and scholarships from your state. Some (but not all) states will allow you to use such funds out of state.

11. Look for scholarships locally. Find out if your employer offers scholarships or tuition assistance plans for employees or family members. Also look into scholarships from your church, community groups, and high school.

12. Look for outside scholarships realistically: they account for less than 5% of aid awarded. Research them at princetonreview.com or other free sites. Steer clear of scholarship search firms that charge fees and "promise" scholarships.

PAYING FOR COLLEGE

13. Start saving early when the student is an infant. Too late? Start now. The more you save, the less you'll have to borrow.

14. Invest wisely. Considering a 529 plan? Compare your own state's plan which may have tax benefits with other states' programs. Get info at savingforcollege.com.

15. If you have to borrow, first pursue federal education loans (Perkins, Stafford, PLUS). Avoid private loans at all costs.

16. Never put tuition on a credit card. The debt is more expensive than ever given recent changes to interest rates and other fees some card issuers are now charging.

17. Try not to take money from a retirement account or 401(k) to pay for college. In addition to likely early distribution penalties and additional income taxes, the higher income will reduce your aid eligibility.

PAYING LESS FOR COLLEGE

18. Attend a community college for two years and transfer to a pricier school to complete the degree. Plan ahead: Be sure the college you plan to transfer to will accept the community college credits.

19. Look into "cooperative education" programs. Over 900 colleges allow students to combine college education with a job. It can take longer to complete a degree this way but graduates generally owe less in student loans and have a better chance of getting hired.

20. Take as many AP courses as possible and get high scores on AP exams. Many colleges award course credits for high AP scores. Some students have cut a year off their college tuition this way.

21. Earn college credit via "dual enrollment" programs available at some high schools. These allow students to take college level courses during their senior year.

22. Earn college credits by taking CLEP (College-Level Examination Program) exams. Depending on the college, a qualifying score on any of the 33 CLEP exams can earn students three to 12 college credits. (See Princeton Review's *Cracking the CLEP-9th Edn.*)

23. Stick to your college and your major. Changing colleges can result in lost credits. Aid may be limited/not available for transfer students at some schools. Changing majors can mean paying for extra courses to meet requirements.

24. Finish college in three years if possible. Take the maximum number of credits every semester, attend summer sessions, and earn credits via online courses. Some colleges offer three-year programs for high-achieving students.

25. Let Uncle Sam pay for your degree. ROTC (Reserve Officer Training Corps) programs available from U.S. Armed Forces branches (except the Coast Guard) offer merit-based scholarships up to full tuition via participating colleges in exchange for military service after you graduate.

26. Better yet: Attend a tuition-free college. Check out the 11 institutions in the "Tuition-Free Honor Roll" list in our book, *The Best 373 Colleges*.

How and Why We Produce This Book

This book is modeled after our bestselling guidebook, the *Best 373 Colleges*. When we published the first edition of *Best Colleges* in 1995, there was a void in the world of college guides (hard to believe, but true!). No publication provided college applicants with statistical data from colleges that covered academics, admissions, financial aid, and student demographics along with narrative descriptions of the schools *based on comprehensive surveys of students attending them*. Of course, academic rankings of colleges had been around for some time. They named the best schools on hierarchical lists, from 1 to 200 and upwards, some in tiers. Their criteria factored in such matters as faculty salaries, alumni giving, and peer reviews (i.e., what college administrators thought of the schools that, in many cases, they competed with for students). But no one was polling students at these terrific colleges about their experiences on campus—both inside and outside the classroom. We created our first *Best Colleges* guide to address that void. It was born out of one very obvious omission in college guide publishing and two very deep convictions we held then and hold even more strongly today:

- **One:** The key question for students and parents researching colleges shouldn't be *"What college is best, academically?"* The thing is, it's not hard to find academically great schools in this country. (There are hundreds of them, and many of them are concentrated in the Northeast.) The key question—and one that is truly tough to answer—is *"What is the best college for me?"*

- **Two:** We believe the best way for students and parents to know if a school is right—and ultimately best—for them is to visit it. Travel to the campus, get inside a dorm, audit a class, browse the town, and—most importantly—talk to students attending the school. In the end it's the school's customers—its students—who are the real experts about the college. Only they can give you the most candid and informed feedback on what life is really like on the campus.

Fueled by these convictions, we worked to create a guide that would help people who couldn't always get to the campus nonetheless get in-depth campus feedback to find the schools best for them. We culled an initial list of 250 academically great schools, based on our own college knowledge and input we got from 50 independent college counselors. We gathered institutional data from those schools and we surveyed 30,000 students attending them (about 120 per campus on average). We wrote the school profiles featured in the book, incorporating extensive quotes from surveyed students, and we included in the book more than 60 ranking lists of top 20 schools in various categories based on our surveys of students at the schools. In short, we designed a college guide that did something no other guide had done: It brought the opinions of a huge number of students at the nation's top colleges to readers' doorsteps.

The success of *Best Colleges* prompted us to publish the first edition of *Best Northeastern Colleges* in 2003. Our goal was to raise awareness of academically excellent but lesser-known colleges for those looking to study within the Northeastern United States. Many of the schools within these pages are nationally competitive institutions of higher learning; we therefore also include profiles of them in the *Best 373 Colleges*. An important difference between this book and the *Best 373 Colleges*, however, is that we do not include any ranking lists.

But why are some of the outstanding schools in this book *not* included in *Best 373 Colleges*? For one or both of two possible reasons. First, it may be because—at this time—they have a regional, rather than a national, focus. That is, they draw their students primarily from the state in which they are located or from bordering states. A second possible reason is that—again, at this time—they have not met the rigorous standards for inclusion in *Best 373 Colleges*. Is that

meant as a snub to the schools that didn't make it into *Best 373 Colleges*? Absolutely not. There are more than 3,500 institutions of higher learning in the United States, and the *Best 373 Colleges* profiles the top 10 percent, academically, of those schools. *Best Northeastern Colleges,* on the other hand, offers student opinion-driven information on all of the top colleges in eleven states and the District of Columbia. The 11 states are: Connecticut, Delaware, Maine, Maryland, Massachusetts, New Hampshire, New Jersey, New York, Pennsylvania, Rhode Island, and Vermont.

To determine which schools will be included in each edition, we don't use mathematical calculations or formulas. Instead we rely on a wide range of quantitative and qualitative input. Every year we collect data from nearly 2,000 colleges for our *Complete Book of Colleges* and our web-based profiles of schools. We visit colleges and meet with scores of admissions officers and college presidents. We talk with hundreds of high school counselors, parents, and students. Colleges also submit information to us requesting consideration for inclusion in the book. As a result, we are able to maintain a constantly evolving list of colleges to consider adding to each new edition of the book. Any college we add to the guide, however, must agree to allow its students to complete our anonymous student survey. (Sometimes a college's administrative protocols will not allow it to participate in our student survey; this has caused some academically outstanding schools to be absent from the guide.) Finally, we work to ensure that our book features a wide representation of colleges by environment, character, and type. It includes public and private schools, historically black colleges and universities, men's and women's colleges, science- and technology-focused institutions, nontraditional colleges, highly selective schools, and some with virtually open-door admissions policies.

Our student survey for the book is a mammoth undertaking. In the early years, our surveys were conducted on campuses and on paper, but the launch several years ago of our online survey (http://survey.review.com) has made it possible for students to complete a survey anytime and anywhere. In fact, 99 percent of our student surveys are now completed online. A few schools prefer the old-fashioned paper survey route; in those instances we work with the administration to hire a campus representative (usually a student) to set up shop in one or more highly trafficked areas of the campus where students can stop and fill out the survey.

Each school in *Best Northeastern Colleges* is surveyed *at least* once every three years. The reality is that unless there's been some grand upheaval or administrative change on campus, there's little change in student opinion from one year to the next; shifts only tend to emerge in a third or fourth year (as surveyed students leave or matriculate). Thus, each year we target a third of the campuses in the book for resurveying. We resurvey colleges more often than that if colleges request it (and we can accommodate the request) or if we believe it is warranted for one reason or another. Online surveys submitted by students outside of a school's normal survey cycle and independent of any solicitation on our part are factored into the subsequent year's ratings calculations. In that respect, our surveying is a continuous process.

All colleges and universities whose students we plan to survey are notified about the survey through our administrative contacts at the schools. We depend upon them for assistance either in notifying the student body about the availability of the online survey via e-mail or, if the school opts for a paper version of the survey, in identifying common, high-traffic areas on campus at which to survey. The survey has more than 80 questions divided into four sections: "About Yourself," "Your School's Academics/Administration," "Students," and "Life at Your School." We ask about all sorts of things, from "How many out-of-class hours do you spend studying each day?" to "How do you rate your campus food?" Most questions offer students a five-point grid on which to indicate their answer choices (headers may range from "Excellent" to "Awful"). Eight questions offer students the opportunity to expand on their answers with narrative comment. These essay-type responses are the sources of the student quotations that appear in the school profiles.

Once the surveys have been completed and responses stored in our database, every college is given a score (similar to a grade point average) for its students' answers to each question. This score enables us to compare students' responses to a particular question from one college to the next. We use these scores as an underlying data point in our calculation of the ratings that appear in the profile headers and "Stats" section. Once we have the student survey information in hand, we write the college profiles. Student quotations in each profile are chosen because they represent the sentiments expressed by the majority of survey respondents from the college; or, they illustrate one side or another of a mixed bag of student opinion, in which case there will also appear a counterpoint within the text. We do not select quotes for their extreme nature, humor, or unique perspective.

Our survey is qualitative and anecdotal rather than quantitative. In order to guard against producing a write-up that's off the mark for any particular college, we send our administrative contact at each school a copy of the profile we intend to publish prior to its publication date, with ample opportunity to respond with corrections, comments, and/or outright objections. In every case in which we receive requests for changes, we take careful measures to review the school's suggestions against the student survey data we collected and to make appropriate changes when warranted.

For this year's edition, on average, we surveyed 120 students per campus, though that number varies depending on the size of the student population. Whether the number of students we survey at a particular school is 100 or 1,000, on the whole we have found their opinions to be remarkably consistent over the years. What is most compelling to us about how representative our survey findings are is this: We ask students who take the survey—after they have completed it—to review the information we published about their school in the previous edition of our book and to grade us on its accuracy and validity. Year after year we've gotten high marks: This year, 81 percent of students said we were *right on*.

All of the institutions in this guide are academically terrific in our opinion. Not every college will appeal to every student, but that is the beauty of it. These are all very different schools with many different and wonderful things to offer.

We hope you will use this book as a starting point (it will certainly give you a snapshot of what life is like at these schools) but not as the final word on any one school. Check out other resources. Visit as many colleges as you can. Talk to students at those colleges—ask what they love and what bothers them most about their schools. Finally, *form your own opinions* about the colleges you are considering. At the end of the day, it's what *you* think about the schools that matters most, and that will enable you to answer that all-important question: *"Which college is best for me?"*

HOW THIS BOOK IS ORGANIZED

Each of the colleges and universities in this book has its own two-page profile. To make it easier to find and compare information about the schools, we've used the same profile format for every school. Look at the sample pages below:

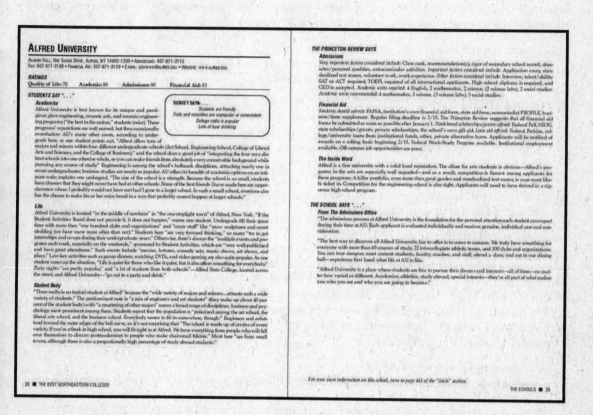

Each spread has several components. First, at the very top of the profile you will see the school's address, telephone and fax numbers for its admissions office, the telephone number for its financial aid office, and its website and/or e-mail address. Next, you will find the school's ratings in four categories: Quality of Life, Academics, Admissions Selectivity, and Financial Aid. We compile the ratings based on the results from our student surveys and/or institutional data we collect from school administrators. These ratings are on a scale of 60–99 If a 60* (60 with an asterisk) appears as any rating for any school, it means that the school reported so few of the rating's underlying data points by our deadline that we were unable to calculate an accurate rating for it. In such cases the reader is advised to follow up with the school about the specific measures the rating takes into account. Be advised that because the Admissions Selectivity Rating is a factor in the computation that produces the Academic Rating, a school that has **60*** (60 with an asterisk) as its Admissions Selectivity Rating will have an Academic Rating that is lower than it should be. Also bear in mind that each rating places each college on a continuum for purposes of comparing colleges within *this edition only*. Since our ratings computations may

change from year to year, it is invalid to compare the ratings in this edition to those that appear in any prior or future edition.

The profile header is followed by a "Survey Says . . ." bubble and "Academics," "Life," and "Student Body" sections, which are based primarily from student survey responses for that particular college. Then comes the "Admissions" section, which includes information on how the school's admissions office weighs the different components of your application; followed by the "Inside Word" on admissions, academics, life, or demographics at that school; "Financial Aid" application pointers; and an institution-authored message under the title "From the Admissions Office." Finally, at the end of the profile is the page number on which the school's statistical data appears. Here's an explanation of each profile section:

Contact Information
Includes the school's address, admissions phone and fax numbers, financial aid phone number, admissions e-mail address, and website.

Quality of Life Rating
On a scale of 60–99, this rating is a measure of how happy students are with their lives outside the classroom. To compile this rating, we weighed several factors, all based on students' answers to questions on our survey. They included the students' assessments of: their overall happiness; the beauty, safety, and location of the campus; comfort of dorms; quality of food; ease of getting around campus and dealing with administrators; friendliness of fellow students; and the interaction of different student types on campus and within the greater community.

Academic Rating
On a scale of 60–99, this rating is a measure of how hard students work at the school and how much they get back for their efforts. The rating is based on results from our surveys of students and institutional data we collect from administrators. Factors weighed included how many hours students reported that they study each day outside of class, and the quality of students the school attracts as measured by admissions statistics. We also considered students' assessments of their professors' teaching abilities and of their accessibility outside the classroom.

Admissions Selectivity Rating
On a scale of 60–99, this rating is a measure of how competitive admission is at the school. This rating is determined by several factors, including the class rank of entering freshmen, test scores, and percentage of applicants accepted. By incorporating these factors (and a few others), our admissions selectivity rating adjusts for "self-selecting" applicant pools. The University of Chicago, for example, has a very high admissions selectivity rating, even though it admits a surprisingly large proportion of its applicants. This is because Chicago's applicant pool is self-selecting; that is, nearly all the school's applicants are exceptional students.

Financial Aid Rating
On a scale of 60–99, this rating is a measure of the financial aid the school awards and how satisfied students are with the aid they receive. It is based on school-reported data on financial aid and students' responses to the survey question, "If you receive financial aid, how satisfied are you with your financial aid package?"

Survey Says . . .
Our "Survey Says" list, located under the ratings on each school's two-page spread, is based entirely on the results of our student surveys. In other words, the items on this list

are based on the opinions of the students we surveyed at those schools (*not* on any quantitative analysis of library size, endowment, etc.). These items reveal popular or unpopular trends on campus for the purpose of providing a snapshot of life on *that campus only*. The appearance of a Survey Says item in the sidebar for a particular school does *not* reflect the popularity of that item relative to its popularity amongst the student bodies at other schools. Some of the terms that appear on the Survey Says list are not entirely self-explanatory; these terms are defined below.

Different types of students interact: We asked students whether students from different class and ethnic backgrounds interacted frequently and easily. When students' collective response is "yes," the heading "Different types of students interact" appears on the list. When the collective student response indicates there are not many interactions between different students from different class and ethnic backgrounds, the phrase "Students are cliquish" appears on the list.

No one cheats: We asked students how prevalent cheating is at their school. If students reported cheating to be rare, the term "No one cheats" shows up on the list.

Students are happy: This category reflects student responses to the question "Overall, how happy are you?"

Students are very religious *or* **Students aren't religious:** We asked students how religious students are at their school. Their responses are reflected in this category.

Diverse student types on campus: We asked students whether their student body is made up of a variety of ethnic groups. This category reflects their answers to this question. This heading shows up as "Diversity lacking on campus" or "Diverse student types on campus." It does not reflect any institutional data on this subject.

Students get along with local community: This category reflects student responses to a question concerning how well the student body gets along with residents of the college town or community.

Career services are great: New to the book last year, this category reflects student opinion on the quality of career/job placement services on campus. This heading shows up as "Career services are great."

Academics, Life, and Student Body

This section shares the straight-from-the-campus feedback we get from the school's most important customers: The attending students. The section summarizes the opinions of freshman through seniors we've surveyed and it includes direct quotes from scores of those students. When appropriate, it also incorporates statistics provided by the schools. The Academics section describes how hard students work and how satisfied they are with the education they are getting. It also often tells you which programs or academic departments students rated most favorably and how professors interact with students. Student opinion regarding administrative departments also works its way into this section. The Life section describes life outside the classroom and addresses questions ranging from "How comfortable are the dorms?" to "How popular are fraternities and sororities?" In this section, students describe what they do for entertainment both on-campus and off, providing a clear picture of the social environment at their particular school. The Student Body section will give you the lowdown on the types of students the school attracts and how the students view the level of interaction among various groups, including those of different ethnic, socioeconomic, and religious backgrounds. All quotations in these

sections are from students' responses to open-ended questions on our survey. We select quotations based on the accuracy with which they reflect overall student opinion about the school as conveyed in the survey results.

Admissions

This section lets you know which aspects of your application are most important to the admissions officers at the school. It also lists the high school curricular prerequisites for applicants, which standardized tests (if any) are required, and special information about the school's admissions process (e.g., Do minority students and legacies, for example, receive special consideration? Are there any unusual application requirements for applicants to special programs?).

The Inside Word

This section gives you the inside scoop on what it takes to gain admission to the school. It reflects our own insights about each school's admissions process and acceptance trends. (We visit scores of colleges each year and talk with hundreds of admissions officers in order to glean this info.) It also incorporates information from institutional data we collect and our surveys over the years of students at the school.

Financial Aid

Here you'll found out what you need to know about the financial aid process at the school, namely what forms you need and what types of merit-based aid and loans are available. Information about need-based aid is contained in the financial aid sidebar. This section includes specific deadline dates for submission of materials as reported by the colleges. We strongly encourage students seeking financial aid to file all forms—federal, state, and institutional—carefully, fully, and on time. Check out our annually updated book, *Paying for College Without Going Broke*, for advice on completing the forms and strategies for getting the most financial aid possible.

From the Admissions Office

This section is the school's chance to speak directly to you about the key things they would like you to know about their institution. For schools that did not respond to our invitation to supply text for this space, we excerpted an appropriate passage from the school's catalog, web site, or other admissions literature. For this section, we also invited schools to submit a brief paragraph explaining their admissions policies regarding the SAT (especially the Writing portion of the exam) and the SAT Subject Tests. We are pleased that nearly every school took this opportunity to clarify its policies as we know there has been some student and parent confusion about how these scores are evaluated for admission.

For More Information

We refer you to the page number in our school statistics section where you can find detailed statistical information for the particular school you're reading about.

SCHOOL STATISTICS

This section, located in the back of the book, contains various statistics culled from our student surveys and from questionnaires school administrators fill out. Keep in mind that not every category will appear for every school, since in some cases the information is not reported or not applicable.

ALFRED UNIVERSITY

CAMPUS LIFE

Fire Safety Rating	60*
Green Rating	72
Type of school	private
Environment	rural

STUDENTS

Total undergrad enrollment	1,971
% male/female	51/49
% from out of state	35
% live on campus	67
% African American	4
% Asian	2
% Caucasian	64
% Hispanic	2
% international	3

ACADEMICS

Calendar	semester
Student/faculty ratio	12:1
Profs interesting rating	85
Profs accessible rating	84
Most common reg class size	10–19 students
Most common lab size	fewer than 10 students

MOST POPULAR MAJORS
business/commerce
ceramic sciences and engineering
fine/studio arts

SELECTIVITY

# of applicants	2,577
% of applicants accepted	70
% of acceptees attending	26
# of early decision applicants	53
% accepted early decision	83

FRESHMAN PROFILE

Range SAT Critical Reading	440–610
Range SAT Math	500–620
Range ACT Composite	22–27
Minimum paper TOEFL	550
Minimum computer TOEFL	213
% graduated top 10% of class	18
% graduated top 25% of class	48
% graduated top 50% of class	85

DEADLINES

Early decision Deadline	12/1
Notification	12/15
Regular Priority	2/1
Notification	rolling
Nonfall registration?	yes

FINANCIAL FACTS

Annual tuition	$25,246
Room and board	$11,174

Required fees	$850
Books and supplies	$900
% frosh rec. need-based scholarship or grant aid	74
% UG rec. need-based scholarship or grant aid	73
% frosh rec. non-need-based scholarship or grant aid	44
% UG rec. non-need-based scholarship or grant aid	39
% frosh rec. need-based self-help aid	66
% UG rec. need-based self-help aid	66
% frosh rec. any financial aid	92
% UG rec. any financial aid	90
% UG borrow to pay for school	83
Average cumulative indebtedness	$23,292

462 ■ THE BEST NORTHEASTERN COLLEGES

If a school has completed each and every data field (and not all do), the headings will appear in the following order:

Fire Safety Rating
On a scale of 60–99, this rating measures how well prepared a school is to prevent or respond to campus fires, specifically in residence halls.

We asked schools several questions about their efforts to ensure fire safety for campus residents. We developed the questions in consultation with the Center for Campus Fire Safety (www.campusfire.org). Each school's responses to eight questions were considered when calculating its Fire Safety Rating. They cover:

1. The percentage of student housing sleeping rooms protected by an automatic fire sprinkler system with a fire sprinkler head located in the individual sleeping rooms.

2. The percentage of student housing sleeping rooms equipped with a smoke detector connected to a supervised fire alarm system.

3. The number of malicious fire alarms that occur in student housing per year.

4. The number of unwanted fire alarms that occur in student housing per year.

5. The banning of certain hazardous items and activities in residence halls, like candles, smoking, halogen lamps, etc.

6. The percentage of student housing fire alarm systems that, if activated, result in a signal being transmitted to a monitored location, where security investigates before notifying the fire department.

7. The percentage of student housing fire alarm systems that, if activated, result in a signal being transmitted immediately to a continuously monitored location which can then immediately notify the fire department to initiate a response.

8. How often fire safety rules-compliance inspections are conducted each year.

Schools that did not report answers to any of the questions receive a Fire Safety Rating of 60* (60 with an asterisk). The schools have an opportunity to update their fire safety data every year and will have their fire safety ratings recalculated and published annually. You can also find Fire Safety Ratings for the *Best Northeastern Colleges* (and several additional schools) in our *Complete Book of Colleges,* 2011 Edition.

Green Rating
We asked all the schools we collect data from annually to answer a number of questions that evaluate the comprehensive measure of their performance as an environmentally aware and responsible institution. The questions were developed in consultation with ecoAmerica, a research and partnership-based environmental nonprofit that convened an expert committee to design this comprehensive rating system, and cover: 1) whether students have a campus quality of life that is both healthy and sustainable; 2) how well a school is preparing students not only for employment in the clean energy economy of the 21st century, but also for citizenship in a world now defined by environmental challenges; and 3) how environmentally responsible a school's policies are.

Each school's responses to ten questions were considered when calculating its Green Rating. They cover:

1. The percentage of food expenditures that go toward local, organic, or otherwise environmentally preferable food.

2. Whether the school offers programs including free bus passes, universal access transit passes, bike sharing/renting, car sharing, carpool parking, vanpooling, or guaranteed rides home to encourage alternatives to single-passenger automobile use for students.

3. Whether the school has a formal committee with participation from students that is devoted to advancing sustainability on campus.

4. Whether new buildings are required to be LEED Silver certified or comparable.

5. The schools overall waste diversion rate.

6. Whether the school has an environmental studies major, minor or concentration.

7. Whether the school has an 'environmental literacy' requirement.

8. Whether a school has produced a publicly available greenhouse gas emissions inventory and adopted a climate action plan consistent with 80% greenhouse gas reductions by 2050 targets.

9. What percentage of the school's energy consumption, including heating/cooling and electrical, is derived from renewable resources (this definition included 'green tags' but not nuclear or large scale hydro power).

10. Whether the school employs a dedicated full-time (or full-time equivalent) sustainability officer.

Colleges that did not supply answers to a sufficient number of the green campus questions for us to fairly compare them to other colleges receive a Green Rating of 60*. The schools have an opportunity to update their green data every year and will have their green ratings re-calculated and published annually.

Affiliation
Any religious order with which the school is affiliated.

Environment
Whether the campus is located in an urban, suburban, or rural setting.

Total undergrad enrollment
The total number of degree-seeking undergraduates who attend the school.

"% male/female" through "# countries represented"
Demographic information about the full-time undergraduate student body, including male-to-female ratio, ethnicity, and the number of countries represented by the student body. Also included are the percentages of the student body who are from out of state, attended a public high school, live on campus, and belong to Greek organizations.

Calendar
The school's schedule of academic terms. A "semester" schedule has two long terms, usually starting in September and January. A "trimester" schedule has three terms, one usually beginning before Christmas and two after. A "quarterly" schedule has four terms, which go by very quickly: the entire term, including exams, usually lasts only nine or ten weeks. A "4/1/4" schedule is like a semester schedule, but with a month-long term in between the fall and spring semesters. (Similarly, a 4/4/1 has a short term following two longer semesters.) When a school's academic calendar doesn't match any of these traditional schedules, we note that by saying "other." For schools that have "other" as their calendar, it is best to call the admissions office for details.

Student/faculty ratio
The ratio of full-time undergraduate instructional faculty members to all undergraduates.

Profs interesting rating
On a scale of 60–99, this rating is based on levels of surveyed students' agreement or disagreement with the statement: "Your instructors are good teachers."

Profs accessible rating

On a scale of 60–99, this rating is based on levels of surveyed students' agreement or disagreement with the statement: "Your instructors are accessible outside the classroom."

% profs teaching UG courses

This category reports the percentage of professors who teach undergraduates and distinguishes between faculty who teach and faculty who focus solely on research.

% classes taught by TAs

This category reports the percentage of classes that are taught by TAs (teaching assistants) instead of regular faculty. Many universities that offer graduate programs use graduate students as teaching assistants. They teach undergraduate courses, primarily at the introductory level.

Most common lab size; Most common regular class size

Institutionally reported figures of the most commonly occurring class size for regular courses and for labs/discussion sections.

Most popular majors

The three majors with the highest enrollments at the school.

% of applicants accepted

The percentage of applicants to whom the school offered admission.

% of acceptees attending

The percentage of those who were accepted who eventually enrolled.

accepting a place on wait list

The number of students who decided to take a place on the wait list when offered this option.

% admitted from wait list

The percentage of applicants who opted to take a place on the wait list and were subsequently offered admission. These figures will vary tremendously from college to college, and should be a consideration when deciding whether to accept a place on a college's wait list.

of early decision applicants

The number of students who applied under the college's early decision or early action plan.

% accepted early decision

The percentage of early decision or early action applicants who were admitted under this plan. By the nature of these plans, the vast majority who are admitted ultimately enroll. (See the early decision/action description that follows in this section for more detail.)

Range/Average SAT Verbal, Range/Average SAT Math, Range/Average SAT Writing

The average and the middle 50 percent range of test scores for entering freshmen. Don't be discouraged from applying to the school of your choice even if your combined SAT scores are 80 or even 120 points below the average, because you may still have a chance of getting in. Remember that many schools value other aspects of your application (e.g., your grades, how good a match you make with the school) more heavily than test scores.

Minimum TOEFL
The minimum test score necessary for entering freshmen who are required to take the TOEFL (Test of English as a Foreign Language). Most schools will require all international students or non-native English speakers to take the TOEFL in order to be considered for admission.

Average HS GPA
The average grade point average of entering freshman. We report this on a scale of 1.0–4.0 (occasionally colleges report averages on a 100 scale, in which case we report those figures). This is one of the key factors in college admissions.

% graduated top 10%, top 25%, top 50% of class
Of those students for whom class rank was reported, the percentage of entering freshmen who ranked in the top tenth, quarter, and half of their high school classes.

Early decision/action deadlines
The deadline for submission of application materials under the early decision or early action plan.

Early decision, early action, priority, and regular admission deadlines
The dates by which all materials must be postmarked (we'd suggest "received in the office") in order to be considered for admission under each particular admissions option/cycle for matriculation in the fall term.

Early decision, early action, priority, and regular admission notification
The dates by which you can expect a decision on your application under each admissions option/cycle.

Nonfall registration
Some schools will allow incoming students to matriculate at times other than the fall term, which is the traditional beginning of the academic calendar year. Other schools will allow you to register for classes only if you can begin in the fall term. A simple "yes" or "no" in this category indicates the school's policy on nonfall registration.

Annual in-state tuition
The tuition at the school, or for public colleges, the cost of tuition for a resident of the school's state. Usually much lower than out-of-state tuition for state-supported public schools.

Annual out-of-state tuition
For public colleges, the tuition for a nonresident of the school's state. This entry appears only for public colleges, since tuition at private colleges is generally the same regardless of state of residence.

Room & board
Estimated annual room and board costs.

Books and supplies
Estimated annual cost of necessary textbooks and/or supplies.

% frosh receiving need-based aid
The percentage of all degree-seeking freshmen who applied for financial aid, were determined to have financial need, and received any sort of aid, need-based or otherwise.

% UG receiving need-based aid
The percentage of all degree-seeking undergrads who applied for financial aid, were determined to have financial need, and received any sort of aid, need-based or otherwise.

Nota Bene: The statistical data reported in this book, unless otherwise noted, was collected from the profiled colleges from the fall of 2009 through the spring of 2010. In some cases, we were unable to publish the most recent data because schools did not report the necessary statistics to us in time, despite our repeated outreach efforts. Because the enrollment and financial statistics, as well as application and financial aid deadlines, fluctuate from one year to another, we recommend that you check with the schools to make sure you have the most current information before applying.

To all of our readers, we welcome your feedback on how we can continue to improve this guide. We hope you will share with us your comments, questions, comments, and suggestions. Please contact us at Editorial Department, Princeton Review Books, 111 Speen St., Framingham, MA 01701, or e-mail us at bookeditor@review.com. Good luck!

GLOSSARY

ACT: Like the SAT but less tricky—the ACT tests stuff you actually learned in the classroom. Most schools accept either SAT or ACT scores; if you consistently get blown away by the SAT, consider taking the ACT instead of (or in addition to) the SAT.

APs: Advanced Placement courses are essentially college-level courses offered in various high schools that culminate in the Advanced Placement Examinations each May. Students who obtain a minimum score on their AP exams may be awarded college credit or placement out of intro-level courses in the subject area. Excellent deal, no matter how you cut it!

College-prep curriculum: 16 to 18 academic credits (each credit equals a full year of a high school course), usually including: 4 years of English, 3 to 4 years of social studies, and at least 2 years each of science, mathematics, and foreign language.

Common Application: A general application form used by nearly 300 colleges and universities. Students who complete the Common Application save on time and mental frenzy, but may be required to submit application supplements to schools.

Core curriculum: Students at schools with core curricula must take a number of required courses, usually in such subjects as world history, Western civilization, writing skills, and fundamental math and science.

CSS/Financial Aid PROFILE: The College Scholarship Service PROFILE, an optional financial aid form required by some colleges in addition to the FAFSA.

Direct Lender: Direct Lending schools participate in the Direct Lending Program (see "Direct Loan Program").

Direct Loan Program: With this federal educational loan program, funds are lent directly by the U.S. Government through the school's financial aid office, with no need of a private lender such as a bank. If the college only participates in the (William D. Ford) Direct Loan Program, the borrower must obtain any Stafford, PLUS, or GradPLUS loan through this program, though one can use a private alternative loan program for any additional non-federal funding.

Distribution or general education requirements: Students at schools with distribution requirements must take a number of courses in various subject areas, such as foreign language, humanities, natural science, and social science. Distribution requirements do not specify which courses you must take, only which types of courses.

Early Decision/Early Action: Early decision is generally for students for whom the school is a first choice. The applicant commits to attending the school if admitted; in return, the school renders an early decision, usually in December or January. Early action is similar to early decision, but less binding; applicants need not commit to attending the school and in some cases may apply early action to more than one school. Early decision and early action policies of a few of the most selective colleges in the country have changed quite dramatically recently. It's a good idea to call the school and get full details if you plan to pursue one of these options.

FAFSA: Stands for the Free Application for Federal Student Aid. This is a financial aid need analysis form written by the U.S. Department of Education. This form is required for virtually all students applying to colleges for financial aid. Some colleges also require that applicants complete other aid application forms (such as the CSS/Financial Aid PROFILE or the college's own form) to be considered for financial aid.

Greek system, Greeks: Fraternities and sororities.

Humanities: The branches of knowledge concerned with human art and culture. These include such disciplines as art history, drama, English, foreign languages, music, philosophy, and religion.

Merit-based grant: A scholarship (not necessarily covering the full cost of tuition) given to students because of some special talent or attribute. Artists, athletes, community leaders, and academically outstanding applicants are typical recipients.

Natural sciences: The branches of knowledge concerned with the rational study of the universe using the rules or laws of natural order. These include such disciplines as astronomy, biology, chemistry, genetics, geology, mathematics, physics, and zoology.

Need-based grant: A scholarship (not necessarily covering the full cost of tuition) given to students because they would otherwise be unable to afford college. Student need is determined on the basis of the FAFSA. Some schools also require the CSS PROFILE and/or institutional applications to determine a student's need.

Priority deadline: Some schools will list a deadline for admission and/or financial aid as a "priority deadline," meaning that while they will accept applications after that date, all applications received prior to the deadline are assured of getting the most thorough, and potentially more generous, appraisal possible.

RA: Residence assistant (or residential advisor). Someone, usually an upperclassman or graduate student, who supervises a floor or section of a dorm, usually in return for free room and board. RAs are responsible for enforcing the drinking and noise rules.

SAT: A college entrance exam required by many schools; most schools will accept either the ACT or the SAT.

SAT Subject Tests: Subject-specific exams administered by the Educational Testing Service (the same folks who do the SAT). These tests are required by some, but not all, colleges.

Social sciences: The branches of knowledge which emphasize the use of the scientific method in the study of the human aspects of the world. These include such disciplines as anthropology, economics, geography, history, international studies, political science, psychology, and sociology.

Work-study: A federally funded financial aid program that provides assistance to students by subsidizing their wages for on-campus and off-campus jobs. Eligibility is based on need.

PART 2: THE SCHOOLS

ADELPHI UNIVERSITY

LEVERMORE HALL, ROOM 110, SOUTH AVENUE, GARDEN CITY, NY 11530 • ADMISSIONS: 516-877-3050
FAX: 516-877-3039 • E-MAIL: ADMISSIONS@ADELPHI.EDU • WEBSITE: WWW.ADELPHI.EDU

RATINGS
Quality of Life: 75   Academic: 72·   Admissions: 81   Financial Aid: 62

STUDENTS SAY "..."

Academics

This "relatively small school" in Garden City, New York offers an impressively wide range of programs and majors (such as an Honors College, School of Business, and School of Nursing), as well as "generous" financial aid. Though most students commute to campus, the school tries hard to create a "beautiful environment that cultivates leadership and growth"

and encourages "close-knit attention to students." The small campus makes transport between buildings easy, and the facilities are always being improved. "I know that when I step on campus and walk through the beautiful grounds that my mood will lift. The positive atmosphere is really great," says one content student. The administration is "great and very accessible" and has designed an educational system that rewards the students who take advantage of opportunities by letting them "help shape the University setting and create their own overall experiences." In other words, "Get involved and study hard, and you'll love this campus!!!"

Those who do study here speak highly of their professors. For the most part, the majority of students find their professors to be "incredibly accommodating and enthusiastic," though some think "there are a few teachers [who] should retire and let someone else who can remember the subject teach." Overall, most feel their professors are "good instructors providing students with useful knowledge preparing them for their careers." A few students complain that there are "too many general education requirements," but once these are completed, the academic ball really gets rolling. The class registration system and financial aid offices are also cited as needing some work, but Adelphi's "small classes get you more one-on-one time with the teachers."

Life

Since Adelphi is mainly attended by commuters, the place is "a ghost town on the weekends;" however, some students do live in dorms, and fraternities and sororities do exist. "I find campus life OK. It's not its extremely fun, but it's not totally boring," says one junior. The classic dorm room hangout is popular among residents, and the school does provide shuttles to Target, the nearby mall, train stations, and other places, not to mention the ease with which one can get to New York City via the train. Recently, there has been a push to increase school spirit and activity, and "it has been working." During the week, the dry campus offers tons of organizations and clubs, recreational facilities, and campus activities such as "parties, battle of the bands, comedy shows, theatrical shows, and constant commotion (good commotion) in the University Center." "Getting jobs on campus is a little difficult" for those looking to work near their classes.

Student Body

Pretty much overwhelmingly, the typical student at Adelphi is "from Long Island and commutes back and forth to school," though there are a lot of different backgrounds (including a sizable number of international students) "that contribute to the University's diversity." "Students tend to stick with their own groups" but are very friendly with each other, and most join a minimum of one club or organization on top of their classes, "obtaining a good balance of labor and leisure." Some commuter students wish that club hours were more standard or earlier in the night, to allow for greater participation. There are many atypical students, and "there is a place for everyone to feel connected to the school no matter what religion, race, gender, or sexual orientation—the student only needs to look harder to find these places."

THE PRINCETON REVIEW SAYS

Admissions

Very important factors considered include: Rigor of secondary school record. *Important factors considered include:* Class rank, application essay, academic GPA, standardized test scores, character/personal qualities, extracurricular activities, talent/ability, volunteer work. *Other factors considered include:* Alumni/ae relation, first generation, interview, level of applicant's interest, work experience. ACT with Writing component required. TOEFL required of all international applicants. High school diploma is required and GED is accepted. *Academic units recommended:* 4 English, 3 mathematics, 3 science, 2 foreign language, 4 social studies, history, English, math, science, or foreign language.

Financial Aid

Students should submit: FAFSA, state aid form. The Princeton Review suggests that all financial aid forms be submitted as soon as possible after January 1. *Need-based scholarships/grants offered:* Federal Pell, SEOG, state scholarships/grants, private scholarships, the school's own gift aid, United Negro College Fund. *Loan aid offered:* Federal Perkins, Federal Nursing, other, New York HELP Program (private alternative). Applicants will be notified of awards on a rolling basis beginning 2/15. Federal Work-Study Program available. Institutional employment available. Off-campus job opportunities are good.

The Inside Word

Students with strong grades, community service and average test scores are likely to be a good match for Adelphi. Those who don't meet the admissions requirements but are deemed to have academic potential may enroll in Adelphi's General Studies Program. Conversely, candidates in the top 15 percent of their classes who achieve SAT scores of 1250 or higher are encouraged to apply to its honors program.

THE SCHOOL SAYS "..."

From The Admissions Office

"Adelphi University is a vibrant intellectual and creative community. Since 1896, our students have benefited from an academically rich and globally relevant education. We offer eight distinct schools-the College of Arts and Sciences, the Derner Institute for Advanced Psychological Study, the Ruth S. Ammon School of Education, University College, Honors College, and the Schools of Business, Nursing, and Social Work-that share one vision of excellence. Adelphi professors are distinguished leaders and pioneers in their fields. Our small classes and low student/faculty ratio allow for innovative learning with accessible teachers. We know that knowledge is acquired both inside the classroom and beyond it. Our more than 80 clubs and organizations offer opportunities to meet and connect with students with similar interests. Adelphi's numerous study abroad opportunities and global internships are a hallmark of our commitment to think globally and act locally. We put your professional goals in reach with a broad range of paid internships and community partnerships to prepare you for the demands of your career or graduate study. Adelphi's home in Garden City, NY is the best of both worlds. The lush 75-acre campus is a sustainable green environment, with state-of-the art research performance, residential, and recreational facilities. Beyond the campus, New York City is a short train or car ride away. Whether you're a nurse, a biologist, a dancer, or psychologist, you will receive a highly personalized, comprehensive, and unparalleled education."

For even more information on this school, turn to page 461 of the "Stats" section.

ALBRIGHT COLLEGE

PO Box 15234, Thirteenth and Bern Streets, Reading, PA 19612-5234 • Admissions: 800-252-1856
Fax: 610-921-7729 • E-mail: ADMISSION@ALBRIGHT@.EDU • Website: WWW.ALBRIGHT.EDU

RATINGS
Quality of Life: 65   Academic: 81   Admissions: 79   Financial Aid: 77

STUDENTS SAY "..."

Academics

Albright College's motto is "A different way of thinking," and students tell us that it's not just an empty slogan. Rather, this principle "is truly evident, in a positive way, in all aspects" of an Albright education "including the academic options, clubs and organizations, campus living, and social aspects." Interdisciplinary study is central to Albright's academic philosophy; one junior majoring in soci-

> **SURVEY SAYS . . .**
> *Great computer facilities*
> *Athletic facilities are great*
> *Frats and sororities dominate social scene*
> *Theater is popular*
> *Student government is popular*

ology tells us that "I have been able to relate theater and sociology within the same semester, which is something I could have never pictured before." Students thrive or fail here to the extent that they can embrace the Albright approach. Those who love it appreciate "the interdisciplinary nature of each class" and insist that "if you come to Albright and come to believe in Albright's principles, you will have the opportunity to exceed any imaginable expectations in social life, academics, athletics, and any other endeavor that you wish to be a part of." Those who don't may conclude that "Albright costs at least twice what a state school does and doesn't offer anything more than you would find at a state school," although to do so they'd have to ignore the "small classes where you can feel comfortable answering or asking questions." Most classes are "discussion—rather than lecture-based, which makes for a much better learning environment!" Albright also boasts "great facilities. The new gym, the Shumo Center, is state of the art, and now Albright is making renovations on other buildings that will make the campus even better."

Life

Life at Albright "is relaxing and fun," with students focused on schoolwork during the week and on the "plenty of things to do on and around campus" on the weekends. This includes "'experience events' that the school sets up," which can be "anything from comedians to educational lectures to plays. You have to attend sixteen experience events by the end of your sophomore year." Other options include "Greek life (date parties, formals, philanthropic activities), athletics, shopping (mall, outlets, King of Prussia, which is about 60 minutes from campus), Reading Phillies and Royals games" and taking advantage of "sports recreation facilities nearby (rock climbing, laser tag, water parks, mini golf)." Also, "The college actually plans trips to locations that are further than we want to drive, like New York City. There are always things going on in Philadelphia, and if you want to go, you can find others who want to, too." Despite all these options, "there is quite a bit of alcohol on campus, although there's plenty to do for those who don't want to drink." While some city folks may find life here a bit to slow, many here believe that "you will not be bored unless you allow yourself to be."

Student Body

Albright's academic approach attracts students who "value being unique and following your own path. We are able to fit together, because we respect and reward individuality." Most are "very involved and full of school spirit," and "everyone is very open and friendly," but "there are still many cliques." These include "the Greeks, the artists, the jocks and cheerleaders, the 'gangstas,' the Asians, and the shy folk. The cliques are most apparent in the cafeteria, however outside of the dining hall all the groups do mesh and interact." Undergrads here tend to be "either really career-minded or really socially minded." Socially minded men take note: "Females outnumber males" by a substantial margin.

Admissions

Very important factors considered include: Rigor of secondary school record. *Important factors considered include:* Class rank, application essay, academic GPA, recommendation(s), standardized test scores, character/personal qualities. *Other factors considered include:* Alumni/ae relation, extracurricular activities, talent/ability, volunteer work, work experience. SAT or ACT or test optional interview required; high school diploma is required and GED is accepted. *Academic units required:* 4 English, 2 mathematics, 3 science, (1 science labs), 2 foreign language, 2 social studies, 1 history, 2 academic electives. *Academic units recommended:* 4 English, 3 mathematics, 4 science, (2 science labs), 3 foreign language, 2 social studies, 2 history, 2 academic electives.

Financial Aid

Students should submit: FAFSA. The Princeton Review suggests that all financial aid forms be submitted as soon as possible after January 1. *Need-based scholarships/grants offered:* Federal Pell, SEOG, state scholarships/grants, private scholarships, the school's own gift aid. *Loan aid offered:* Federal Perkins, other, private educational loans. Applicants will be notified of awards on a rolling basis beginning 2/14. Federal Work-Study Program available. Institutional employment available. Off-campus job opportunities are good.

The Inside Word

Albright is a small school with a 70+ percent acceptance rate, so you can expect a close, sympathetic reading of your application here. Admissions officers are looking for reasons to accept you. Give them that reason. Counter poor test scores or mediocre high school grades with a killer essay, enthusiastic recommendations, and a list of extracurricular experiences that promises you will contribute something of value to the Albright campus community.

THE SCHOOL SAYS "..."

From The Admissions Office

"**Academics:** Founded in 1856, Albright College is recognized as a national leader in interdisciplinary study. Nearly half of our students opt for combined or interdisciplinary majors . . . while still graduating in 4 years. Last year, students chose 143 different combinations of majors—from art/biology and psychology/business to education/theater and sociology/Latin American studies. But whether students select one major or combine fields, Albright's faculty work closely with students to create experiences that reflect individual talents, interests, and career goals.

"**Atmosphere**: Albright College is renowned for its openness and warmth. Students who visit Albright rate it as one of the friendliest small liberal arts colleges anywhere. Albright students have a strong sense of community based on friendliness, tolerance, and mutual support. These are the common ties that bind the community and make Albright an easy place for students to be heard and have an impact.

"**Outcomes:** An Albright education is designed to help students develop their individual voices and visions and become skilled problem solvers and communicators. Albright graduates leave with the knowledge, skills, and confidence to succeed.

"**Location:** The Albright campus is located 1 hour west of Philadelphia in a tree-lined suburb of Reading, Pennsylvania, a metropolitan area of 250,000.

"**Scholarships and Financial Aid:** Albright is pledged to help make its education affordable. This is evident in Albright's inclusion in Barron's *Best Buys in College Education* and in our generous need-based financial aid awards and numerous merit scholarships (ranging from $5,000 per year to full tuition)."

For even more information on this school, turn to page 461 of the "Stats" section.

ALFRED UNIVERSITY

ALUMNI HALL, ONE SAXON DRIVE, ALFRED, NY 14802-1205 • ADMISSIONS: 607-871-2115
FAX: 607-871-2198 • FINANCIAL AID: 607-871-2159 • E-MAIL: ADMWWW@ALFRED.EDU • WEBSITE: WWW.ALFRED.EDU

RATINGS
Quality of Life: 78   Academic: 80   Admissions: 80   Financial Aid: 83

STUDENTS SAY "..."

Academics

Alfred University is best known for its unique and prestigious glass engineering, ceramic arts, and ceramic engineering programs ("the best in the nation," students insist). These programs' reputations are well earned, but they occasionally overshadow AU's many other assets, according to undergrads here; as one student points out, "Alfred offers tons of majors and minors within four different undergraduate schools (Art School, Engineering School, College of Liberal Arts and Sciences, and the College of Business)," and the school does a good job of "integrating the four very distinct schools into one cohesive whole, so you can make friends from absolutely every conceivable background while pursuing any course of study." Engineering is among the school's hallmark disciplines, attracting nearly one in seven undergraduates; business studies are nearly as popular. AU offers its breadth of academic options on an intimate scale; explains one undergrad, "The size of the school is a strength. Because the school is so small, students have chances that they might never have had at other schools. Some of the best friends I have made here are upperclassmen whom I probably would not have met had I gone to a larger school. In such a small school, everyone also has the chance to make his or her voice heard in a way that probably cannot happen at larger schools."

> **SURVEY SAYS . . .**
> *Students are friendly*
> *Frats and sororities are unpopular or nonexistent*
> *College radio is popular*
> *Lots of beer drinking*

Life

Alfred University is located "in the middle of nowhere" in "the one-stoplight town" of Alfred, New York. "If the Student Activities Board does not provide it, it does not happen," warns one student. Undergrads fill their spare time with more than "one hundred clubs and organizations" and "crazy stuff" like "snow sculptures and secret sledding (we have snow more often than not)." Students here "are very forward thinking," so many "try to get internships and co-ops during their undergraduate years." Otherwise, there's always the "multiple events and programs each week, especially on the weekends," sponsored by Student Activities, which are "very well-publicized and have great attendance." Such events include "movies, lectures, comedy acts, music shows, art shows, and plays." Low-key activities such as group dinners, watching DVDs, and video gaming are also quite popular. As one student sums up the situation, "Life is quiet for those who like it quiet, but it also offers something for everybody." Party nights "are pretty popular," and "a lot of students from both schools"—Alfred State College, located across the street, and Alfred University—"go out to a party and drink."

Student Body

"There really is no typical student at Alfred" because the "wide variety of majors and minors...attracts such a wide variety of students." The predominant note is "a mix of engineers and art students" (they make up about 40 percent of the student body) with "a smattering of other majors" across a broad range of disciplines, business and psychology most prominent among them. Students report that the population is "polarized among the art school, the liberal arts school, and the business school. Everybody seems to fit in somewhere, though." Engineers and artists tend toward the outer edges of the bell curve, so it's not surprising that "The school is made up of crazies of every variety. If you're a freak in high school, you will fit right in at Alfred. We have everything from people who will fall over themselves to discuss postmodernism to people who make chain-mail bikinis." Most here "are from small towns, although there is also a proportionally high percentage of study abroad students."

THE PRINCETON REVIEW SAYS

Admissions

Very important factors considered include: Class rank, recommendation(s), rigor of secondary school record, character/personal qualities, extracurricular activities. *Important factors considered include:* Application essay, standardized test scores, volunteer work, work experience. *Other factors considered include:* Interview, talent/ability. SAT or ACT required; TOEFL required of all international applicants. High school diploma is required, and GED is accepted. *Academic units required:* 4 English, 2 mathematics, 2 science, (2 science labs), 2 social studies. *Academic units recommended:* 4 mathematics, 3 science, (3 science labs), 3 social studies.

Financial Aid

Students should submit: FAFSA, institution's own financial aid form, state aid form, noncustodial PROFILE, business/farm supplement. Regular filing deadline is 3/15. The Princeton Review suggests that all financial aid forms be submitted as soon as possible after January 1. *Need-based scholarships/grants offered:* Federal Pell, SEOG, state scholarships/grants, private scholarships, the school's own gift aid. *Loan aid offered:* Federal Perkins, college/university loans from institutional funds, other, private alternative loans. Applicants will be notified of awards on a rolling basis beginning 2/15. Federal Work-Study Program available. Institutional employment available. Off-campus job opportunities are poor.

The Inside Word

Alfred is a fine university with a solid local reputation. The allure for arts students is obvious—Alfred's programs in the arts are especially well regarded—and as a result, competition is fiercest among applicants for these programs. A killer portfolio, even more than great grades and standardized test scores, is your most likely ticket in. Competition for the engineering school is also tight. Applicants will need to have thrived in a rigorous high school program.

THE SCHOOL SAYS "..."

From The Admissions Office

"The admissions process at Alfred University is the foundation for the personal attention each student can expect during their time at AU. Each applicant is evaluated individually and receives genuine, individual care and consideration.

"The best way to discover all Alfred University has to offer is to come to campus. We truly have something for everyone with more than 60 courses of study, 22 intercollegiate athletic teams, and 100 clubs and organizations. You can tour campus; meet current students, faculty, coaches, and staff; attend a class; and eat in our dining hall—experience first hand what life at AU is like.

"Alfred University is a place where students are free to pursue their dreams and interests—all of them—no matter how varied or different. Academics, athletics, study abroad, special interests—they're all part of what makes you who you are and who you are going to become."

For even more information on this school, turn to page 461 of the "Stats" section.

ALLEGHENY COLLEGE

OFFICE OF ADMISSIONS, MEADVILLE, PA 16335 • ADMISSIONS: 800-521-5293
FAX: 814-337-0431 • FINANCIAL AID: 800-835-7780 • E-MAIL: ADMISS@ALLEGHENY.EDU • WEBSITE: WWW.ALLEGHENY.EDU

RATINGS
Quality of Life: 75   Academic: 89   Admissions: 90   Financial Aid: 85

STUDENTS SAY "..."

Academics

Allegheny College "allows students to follow a very unique path by encouraging distribution within majors and minors." Indeed, the school requires students to declare both a major and a minor concentration outside their major division of knowledge (e.g., natural science majors must minor in a humanities or social science discipline), a requirement that undergraduates say "pushes students to achieve more than they ever thought." Likewise, a mandatory research-based senior project in one's major field of study makes for a "challenging" academic experience. One student says the school is so tough that "it over-prepares us for the 'real world,'" and that toughness helps give the school its "amazing reputation for a higher standard of learning." Pre-meds are especially drawn by the school's success in placing graduates in better medical schools; the psychology and English departments also earn students' praises. Allegheny goes the extra mile on service; professors "are always available when you need help or someone to talk to," the college president "is always walking around campus talking to the students," and the career services office "is excellent," offering "all forms of out-of-class learning in a central location. A student can go there to find out about internships, community service, or international services (studying abroad)." All of those combined elements explain why students tell us that "Allegheny College is the perfect place to get a well-rounded education and a jump start on your career after graduation."

> **SURVEY SAYS . . .**
> Lab facilities are great
> Athletic facilities are great
> Career services are great
> School is well run
> Students are friendly
> Students are happy
> Student government is popular

Life

Allegheny academics are demanding, so "students are often found in the library studying and/or other various areas on the campus during the weekdays. We take our studies very seriously and spend a lot of time getting our work done." Weekends, however, "are filled with various activities held on campus and usually sponsored by the school or random parties at off-campus houses." Some brag that "There are infinite things to do on campus. There is always an event going on, or a play, or a dance, or many other possibilities." Greek life is fairly big on campus, and the school's alcohol policy "is pretty moderate. The college treats us like adults who can make our own decisions." Students add that "We aren't one of those schools where drinking is the only thing to do. We run around and sled in the snow, go to movies (Tuesday is only $5!), go out to eat in town, see concerts, etc." It's fortunate that campus is so busy because hometown Meadville is a small town that "doesn't offer much" in the way of diversions. The weather isn't so hot either; "The school is located near Lake Erie, so there is a lot of precipitation throughout the year....Slush builds up, and students, faculty, and visiting families must leap across snowdrifts in order to access the sidewalks."

Student Body

The typical student at Allegheny "is white, middle-class, and prepared to learn." Many are "extremely devoted to both their schoolwork and involvement in extracurricular activities," and they "'overload' [on] credits every semester while taking on leadership position after leadership position." "Those who go Greek" and the "tree-loving hippie liberals" are among the more conspicuous groups at Allegheny, but "There are all types here. Qualities that most students have are intelligence and openness to new ideas. We do have people that look quite strange sometimes, but people are nice to them. We have so many groups that even the crazy art kids who have colored hair and don't wear shoes find their niche and interact positively with sorority girls who always wear heels."

THE PRINCETON REVIEW SAYS

Admissions

Very important factors considered include: Class rank, academic GPA, rigor of secondary school record. *Important factors considered include:* Recommendation(s), standardized test scores, character/personal qualities, extracurricular activities, interview, level of applicant's interest. *Other factors considered include:* Application essay, alumni/ae relation, first generation, geographical residence, racial/ethnic status, talent/ability, volunteer work, work experience. SAT or ACT required; ACT with Writing component recommended. TOEFL required of all international applicants. High school diploma is required, and GED is accepted. *Academic units required:* 4 English, 3 mathematics, 3 science, 2 foreign language, 3 social studies, 1 academic electives.

Financial Aid

Students should submit: FAFSA. The Princeton Review suggests that all financial aid forms be submitted as soon as possible after January 1. *Need-based scholarships/grants offered:* Federal Pell, SEOG, state scholarships/grants, private scholarships, the school's own gift aid, Federal Academic Competitiveness Grant, National SMART Grant, Veterans Educational Benefits, Yellow Ribbon Program. *Loan aid offered:* Direct Subsidized Stafford, Direct Unsubsidized Stafford, Direct PLUS, Federal Perkins, other, private loans from commercial lenders. Applicants will be notified of awards on a rolling basis beginning 3/1. Federal Work-Study Program available. Institutional employment available. Off-campus job opportunities are excellent.

The Inside Word

Not everybody accepted to Allegheny was a stellar high-school student—about three out of four undergrads here graduated in the top 25 percent of their high school class—but the typical admit here has solid high school grades in a demanding curriculum and above-average standardized test scores. Extras count; admissions officers take the time to get to know applicants' full profiles and may find compelling evidence in recommendations or extracurricular experiences to mitigate less-than-optimal grades and/or test scores.

THE SCHOOL SAYS "…"

From The Admissions Office

"Being innovative, collaborative, creative, analytical and inventive: these are the traits so in demand in today's global marketplace. Discovering and developing these traits happens best when students pursue unusual combinations of majors and minors. This is the Allegheny culture.

We're proud of our beautiful campus and cutting-edge technologies, and we know that our professors are leading scholars who pride themselves even more on being among the best teachers in the United States. Yet it's our students who make Allegheny the unique and special place that it is. Allegheny attracts students with unusual combinations of interests, skills and talents. How do we characterize them? Although it's impossible to label our students, they do share some common characteristics. You'll find an abiding passion for learning and life, a spirit of camaraderie, and shared inquiry that spans across individuals as well as areas of study. You'll see over and over again such a variety of interests and passions and skills that, after a while, those unusual combinations don't seem so unusual at all.

"Allegheny is not for everybody. If you've noticed that when life gives you a choice between two things, you're tempted to answer both or simply yes; if you start to get excited because you sense there is a college willing to echo the resounding yes, then we look forward to meeting you."

For even more information on this school, turn to page 462 of the "Stats" section.

AMERICAN UNIVERSITY

4400 MASSACHUSETTS AVENUE, NORTHWEST, WASHINGTON, DC 20016-8001 • ADMISSIONS: 202-885-6000
FAX: 202-885-1025 • FINANCIAL AID: 202-885-6100 • E-MAIL: AFA@AMERICAN.EDU • WEBSITE: WWW.AMERICAN.EDU

RATINGS
Quality of Life: 98   Academic: 84   Admissions: 91   Financial Aid: 87

STUDENTS SAY "..."

Academics

American University exploits its Washington, D.C. location—that facilitates a strong faculty, prestigious guest lecturers, and "a wealth of internship opportunities"—to offer "incredibly strong programs" in political science and international relations. "The poli-sci kids are all going to be president one day, and the international studies ones are all going to save the world," a student insists. The school of

> **SURVEY SAYS . . .**
> *Career services are great*
> *Students love Washington, DC*
> *Great off-campus food*
> *Low cost of living*
> *Political activism is popular*

communications also excels, and the school works hard to accommodate "interdisciplinary majors and the opportunities associated with studying them," which include "taking advantage of the resources of the city. The school values learning out of the classroom as much as learning in the classroom." As you might expect from a school with a strong international relations program, "AU's study abroad program is one of the best." Although AU "does not have the automatically recognizable prestige of nearby Georgetown," that's not necessarily a drawback; on the contrary, "The administration and professors go out of their way to ensure a great academic experience," in part because the school is trying to "climb in the rankings and gain recognition as one of the nation's top universities." However, AU is still "not the place for science majors," and some concede that "the university could improve programs in other fields, aside from its specialties in international studies, public affairs, business, and communication."

Life

"The greatest strength of AU is the activity level both politically and in the community," students tell us, noting that during the most recent election the campus "was a proxy holy war...Whether it was signs in windows, talk in the class or in the hallways, T-shirts, or canvassing in Metro-accessible Virginia, students on both sides took November 4 religiously." As one student explains, "Let's put it this way: A politician who comes to campus is likely to draw about 90 percent of the student population [and] an AU basketball game, about nine [percent]." Students get involved in the community through "campus outreach by student-run organizations," which many see as "the school's greatest asset." The typical undergrad is "incredibly engaged and active...Students seek internships in every line of work, becoming actively involved in a field of interest before graduation." When it's time to relax, "Washington, D.C. offers limitless opportunities to explore." Many "enjoy partying and hanging out off-campus and on campus (even though AU is a 'dry campus')," but there are also "a lot of people who don't drink and have a very good time just using what D.C. has to offer: museums, restaurants, parks, cinemas, theaters, and shops." As one student sums it up: "The city is the school's greatest resource. You will never run out of things to do in Washington."

Student Body

AU attracts a "liberal, non-religious" crowd that "tends to be very ideologically driven." "Liberals run the show," most here agree, although they add that "Plenty of students don't fit this mold, and I've never seen anyone rejected for what they believe." The campus "is very friendly to those with alternative lifestyles (GLBT, vegetarian, green-living, etc.)," but students with more socially conservative inclinations note that "while AU boasts about the many religious groups on campus, there is still a general antipathy toward piety, especially Christianity." The perception that some departments outshine others is reflected in the way students perceive each other; one says, "You have the political studies know-it-alls, the international studies student who thinks he is going to save the world, the artsy film/communication students, and the rest [who] are unhappy students who couldn't get into George Washington or Georgetown."

THE PRINCETON REVIEW SAYS

Admissions

Very important factors considered include: Academic GPA, rigor of secondary school record, standardized test scores, level of applicant's interest. *Important factors considered include:* Application essay, recommendation(s), extracurricular activities, volunteer work. *Other factors considered include:* Alumni/ae relation, character/personal qualities, first generation, geographical residence, racial/ethnic status, talent/ability, work experience. SAT Subject Tests recommended; SAT or ACT required; ACT with Writing component required. TOEFL required of all international applicants. High school diploma is required, and GED is accepted. *Academic units required:* 4 English, 3 mathematics, 3 science, (2 science labs), 2 foreign language, 2 social studies, 3 academic electives. *Academic units recommended:* 4 English, 4 mathematics, 4 science, 3 foreign language, 4 social studies, 4 academic electives.

Financial Aid

Students should submit: FAFSA, and the CSS Financial Aid Profile. Regular filing deadline is 2/15. The Princeton Review suggests that all financial aid forms be submitted as soon as possible after January 1. *Need-based scholarships/grants offered:* Federal Pell, SEOG, state scholarships/grants, private scholarships, the school's own gift aid. Various academic merit scholarships are awarded by the Undergraduate Admissions Office. Most scholarships do not require a separate application and are renewable for up to three years if certain criteria are met. *Loan aid offered:* William P. Ford Stafford Direct, Federal Perkins, and PLUS. Applicants will be notified of awards on or about 4/1. Federal Work-Study Program available. Institutional employment available. Off-campus job opportunities are excellent.

The Inside Word

American asks applicants to indicate their intended field of study. Those selecting one of American's hallmark disciplines—e.g., political science, international studies, communications—will have the highest hurdles to clear. No one cruises into American. However, despite strong competition from other area powerhouses, American sees a strong applicant pool that allows it to be very selective.

THE SCHOOL SAYS "..."

From The Admissions Office

"American University is located in the residential "Embassy Row" neighborhood of Washington, D.C. Nestled among embassies and ambassadorial residences, AU's campus offers a safe, suburban environment with easy access to Washington's countless cultural destinations via the Metrorail subway system. A global center of government, Washington D.C. stands unmatched in academics, professional, and cultural resources. AU's faculty includes scholars, journalists, artists, diplomats, authors, and scientists. Combining a liberal arts core curriculum with in-depth professional programs, academics at AU provide the necessary balance between theoretical study and hands-on experience. Our Career Center will work with you to enhance this experience with access to unique internship opportunities available only in Washington. Combine this with our diverse national and international student body and our world-class study abroad program, and AU can open up a world of possibilities."

For even more information on this school, turn to page 462 of the "Stats" section.

AMHERST COLLEGE

Campus Box 2231, PO Box 5000, Amherst, MA 01002 • Admissions: 413-542-2328
Fax: 413-542-2040 • Financial Aid: 413-542-2296 • E-mail: admissions@amherst.edu • Website: www.amherst.edu

RATINGS
Quality of Life: 94   Academic: 97   Admissions: 99   Financial Aid: 93

STUDENTS SAY "..."

Academics

With just over 1,700 students, Amherst College "has a strong sense of community born of its small size" that goes hand-in-hand with an atmosphere that "encourages discussion and cooperation." Many here are quick to praise the "fantastic" professors and "supportive" administration. "Professors come here to teach," says one undergrad, "not just to do research." The "enriching" academics are bolstered by the "dedicated" faculty, but slackers be warned: You must be

> **SURVEY SAYS . . .**
> *No one cheats*
> *School is well run*
> *Dorms are like palaces*
> *Campus feels safe*
> *Low cost of living*
> *Musical organizations are popular*

"willing to sit down and read a text forward and backward and firmly grasp it" as "skimming will do you no good." Besides having "easily accessible" professors, some students also appreciate that "registration is done by paper" as "it forces you to talk to your advisor." Another student notes that "I'm amazed at how easy it is to sit down for a casual lunch with anyone in the administration without there having to be a problem that needs to be discussed." Indeed, most here agree that "the support for students is as good as anyone could expect." However, some mention that despite the "administration, staff, and faculty" being "accessible and receptive to student input on every level," the "realities of running a small school in this economic climate mean a lot of suggestions won't be acted upon any time soon." Nevertheless, Amherst's alumni have a solid track record when it comes to obtaining postgraduate degrees—so much so that some think of the college "as prep school for grad school."

Life

While students at Amherst are "focused first and foremost on academics, nearly every student is active and enjoys life outside of the library." "There's a club or organization for every interest" here, and students assure us that if there isn't one that you're interested in, "the school will find the money for it." Students also praise the "awesome" dorms (some say they're "as spacious, well-maintained, and luxurious as many five-star hotels"), for being "designed to facilitate social interaction." Coincidentally, the dorms tend to serve as the school's social hub, particularly since Greek organizations were banned back in 1985. Amherst makes up for the lack of frat houses with "a number of socials put on by student government and I-Club (International Club) that are held throughout the year at bars downtown." And don't worry if you don't have a car since these events "have free buses that transport students to and from the bars." Some bemoan that the town of Amherst is "incredibly small" and doesn't feature much in the way of fun. Others take solace in "the many eateries in town that feature lots of ethnically diverse foods" and "go to sporting events." And since Amherst is part of the Five Colleges consortium, there's "an extended social life to be had," however "not that many people go out of their way to experience it." For those who like liquor with their extracurricular activities, most "drink on campus instead of off campus" thanks to some "huge apartment parties."

Student Body

Traditionally, the student body at Amherst has been known by the "stereotype of the preppy, upper middle class, white student," but many here note that the school is "at least as racially diverse as the country and more economically diverse than people think." That's not to say that the college doesn't have "a sizeable preppy population fresh from East Coast boarding schools," but overall students here report that "Diversity—racial, ethnic, geographic, socioeconomic—is more than a buzzword here." The campus is also "a politically and environmentally conscious" place, as well as a "highly athletic one." The school's small size "means that no group is isolated and everyone interacts and more or less gets along." Others, however, aren't as convinced about the student body's unity. "There is definitely a divide in the student body," says one undergrad. "The typical Amherst student is either an extremely quiet, bookish nerd or a lumbering, backward-baseball-cap-wearing jock." That said, the school is filled with "open-minded, intellectually passionate, and socially conscious critical thinkers." As one student puts it, "Most students—even our most drunken athletes and wild party-goers—are concerned about learning and academics."

Admissions

Very important factors considered include: Application essay, academic GPA, recommendation(s), rigor of secondary school record, standardized test scores, character/personal qualities, extracurricular activities, first generation, talent/ability. *Important factors considered include:* Class rank, alumni/ae relation, volunteer work. *Other factors considered include:* Geographical residence, state residency, work experience. SAT and SAT Subject Tests or ACT required; ACT with Writing component recommended. TOEFL required of all international applicants. High school diploma or equivalent is not required. *Academic units recommended:* 4 English, 4 mathematics, 3 science, (1 science labs), 4 foreign language, 2 social studies, 2 history.

Financial Aid

Students should submit: FAFSA, CSS/Financial Aid PROFILE, noncustodial PROFILE, business/farm supplement. Income documentation submitted through college. The Princeton Review suggests that all financial aid forms be submitted as soon as possible after January 1. *Need-based scholarships/grants offered:* Federal Pell, SEOG, state scholarships/grants, private scholarships, the school's own gift aid. *Loan aid offered:* Direct Subsidized Stafford, Direct Unsubsidized Stafford, Direct PLUS, Federal Perkins, college/university loans from institutional funds. Applicants will be notified of awards on or about 4/1. Federal Work-Study Program available. Institutional employment available. Off-campus job opportunities are excellent.

The Inside Word

Membership certainly has its benefits at Amherst College. For the price of entry to this school students also gain entrance to the prestigious Five Colleges consortium, which allows enrolled students to take courses for credit at no additional cost at any of the four participating consortium members (Hampshire College, Mount Holyoke College, Smith College, and the University of Massachusetts—Amherst). And this deal isn't just confined to the classroom: Students can use other schools' libraries, eat meals at the other cafeterias, and participate in extracurricular activities offerred at the other schools. And don't worry about how you'll get there—your bus fare is covered, too.

THE SCHOOL SAYS "…"

From The Admissions Office

"Amherst College looks, above all, for men and women of intellectual promise who have demonstrated qualities of mind and character that will enable them to take full advantage of the college's curriculum....Admission decisions aim to select from among the many qualified applicants those possessing the intellectual talent, mental discipline, and imagination that will allow them most fully to benefit from the curriculum and contribute to the life of the college and of society. Whatever the form of academic experience—lecture course, seminar, conference, studio, laboratory, independent study at various levels—intellectual competence and awareness of problems and methods are the goals of the Amherst program, rather than the direct preparation for a profession.

"Applicants must submit scores from the SAT plus two SAT Subject Tests. Students may substitute the ACT with the Writing component."

For even more information on this school, turn to page 463 of the "Stats" section.

ARCADIA UNIVERSITY

450 SOUTH EASTON ROAD, GLENSIDE, PA 19038 • ADMISSIONS: 215-572-2910 • FAX: 215-572-4049
E-MAIL: ADMISS@ARCADIA.EDU • WEBSITE: WWW.ARCADIA.EDU

RATINGS
Quality of Life: 74   Academic: 75   Admissions: 80   Financial Aid: 76

STUDENTS SAY "..."

Academics

SURVEY SAYS . . .
Students are friendly
Frats and sororities are unpopular or nonexistent
Theater is popular

Arcadia University near Philadelphia is "a gem in suburbia" that offers "a global learning experience." "Arcadia's all about study abroad" and the program is "huge." Regardless of major, "almost everyone at Arcadia" spends some time globetrotting. Destinations for "semesters, summers, or even community service trips" include China, South Africa, New Zealand, Ireland, and South Korea. Also, "freshman preview is an amazing, once-in-a-lifetime opportunity" that allows first-year students to spend a week in England, Scotland, or Spain. (Preview for transfer students is in Italy). Back on campus, "there are small class sizes, which make learning so easy." The "usually accessible" professors "genuinely care about their students and the subject that they teach." A host of excellent majors includes a "very hands-on" education program. Arcadia is "a good art school," too. Theater is particularly strong. Some students say that Arcadia is "good for science majors." Others disagree: "Arcadia is okay for science majors," they say, "but not a great place."

Life

This campus "in the suburbs of Philadelphia" is "beautiful." "Arcadia has a friggin' castle," observes a senior. "Enough said." Socially, "everyone knows everyone" and the "unnecessary drama" can occasionally feel like "a glorified high school." Cultural events are abundant. "The dance club (Knight Club) is very popular." "In the fall, we have Mr. Beaver, which is a male mock beauty pageant," explains a senior. It's "always fun." Thursday nights are the big party nights and "as big as a Friday or Saturday night" at other places. On the whole, though, "Arcadia is fairly low key" and "very far from a party school." There's no Greek system and the festivities that do occur "don't get very rowdy." Ordering pizza and watching movies is a "favorite pastime." Many students love the social scene. "This is exactly what I wanted from my school," declares a junior. Others complain about "weekend nothingness." They note that Arcadia has a large commuter population and a reputation as "a suitcase college." Of course, that term has a slightly different connotation here. "There are a huge number of students who are studying abroad," relates a sophomore. "At Arcadia, you get your typical college party life overseas." Also, the train station is "right down the street" from campus. The "20-minute train ride into Philly" is "great for weekend trips or anything fun."

Student Body

"Most students" here are "pretty friendly" and come from middle class backgrounds. There are also "a good number of international students." Commuter students make up twenty percent of the population, and women noticeably outnumber men. "There are more squirrels than boys on campus," laments one female. "If you run into a guy, he is most likely a jock or gay." Indeed, Arcadia boasts "a highly tolerant campus" and a "very strong" gay community. There are also lots of "artsy" types who are "very outside the social norm." Other students are "ridiculously nerdy." Of course, there are plenty of perfectly normal people here, too. "You know: the ones that throw on sweats and leave their hair elegantly disheveled because that's the look these days." For the most part, though, "everyone has their own style." "There seems to be a higher ratio of weird people here at Arcadia than in the regular world."

THE PRINCETON REVIEW SAYS

Admissions

Very important factors considered include: Academic GPA, rigor of secondary school record. *Important factors considered include:* Class rank, application essay, recommendation(s), standardized test scores, extracurricular activities. *Other factors considered include:* Alumni/ae relation, character/personal qualities, interview, talent/ability, volunteer work, work experience. SAT or ACT required; ACT with Writing component required. TOEFL required of all international applicants. High school diploma is required and GED is accepted. *Academic units recommended:* 4 English, 3 mathematics, 3 science, (3 science labs), 2 foreign language, 2 social studies, 2 history.

Financial Aid

The Princeton Review suggests that all financial aid forms be submitted as soon as possible after January 1. Off-campus job opportunities are good.

The Inside Word

Solid grades and test scores should get you admitted to Arcadia without much of a problem, although the admissions staff will take the time to make sure you're a good fit. Note that you have to audition if you want to major in acting and submit a portfolio for art programs.

THE SCHOOL SAYS "..."

From The Admissions Office

"Arcadia University is a top-ranked private university in metropolitan Philadelphia and a national leader in study abroad. The 2009 Open Doors report ranks Arcadia University first in the nation among master's universities in the percentage of undergraduate students studying abroad. Arcadia University promises a distinctively global, integrative and personal learning experience that prepares students to contribute and prosper in a diverse and dynamic world. As a student at Arcadia University, your education expands beyond the classroom. Our study abroad programs, international faculty, and global vision of education combine to create an environment that affords you a world of opportunities. Our College of Global Studies offers study abroad opportunities at some of the top universities and sites around the world, and students have the opportunity to study at 100 programs in 16 countries, including England, France, Scotland, Wales, Ireland, Northern Ireland, Australia, China, Greece, India, Italy, South Africa, Spain, Tanzania, New Zealand and Germany."

"Freshmen at Arcadia have the unique opportunity to spend spring break in London, Scotland or Spain for $495. The London/Scotland/Spain Preview Program introduces students to overseas study and travel. Students may choose from more than 60 different undergraduate programs and 15 graduate degrees. Our 13:1 student/faculty ratio enables students to work closely with faculty for academic advising, research, and publication activities."

For even more information on this school, turn to page 463 of the "Stats" section.

THE ART INSTITUTE OF BOSTON AT LESLEY UNIVERSITY

700 BEACON STREET, BOSTON, MA 02215-2598 • ADMISSIONS: 617-585-6700 • FAX: 617-437-1226
E-MAIL: ADMISSIONS@AIBOSTON.EDU • WEBSITE: WWW.AIBOSTON.EDU

RATINGS
Quality of Life: 73   **Academic:** 85   **Admissions:** 81   **Financial Aid:** 64

STUDENTS SAY ". . ."

Academics

The Art Institute of Boston at Lesley University is a small, private, and "very hands-on" school that offers majors in fine art, illustration, photography, graphic design, animation, and art history. The sophisticated facilities here include a well-stocked printmaking studio, a clay lab with several kilns, a

wood shop, an impressive collection of photography equipment, and computer labs for design and animation. Graduation requirements include a wide array of liberal arts requirements and a sequence of foundational art courses. Art-related courses are reportedly "very long and intense." Students here greatly appreciate that "Every professor at AIB is a working professional." And though "teaching methods can be haphazard at times," the faculty is generally full of "enthusiastic" and "insanely talented" artists who "have a love for their craft." As one student explains, "They teach artists how to improve their art and how to ready themselves for the real world." "One-on-one interaction" is common thanks to an "intimate environment" that "fosters close relationships and connections to job opportunities after graduation." "Some things like registration are confusing," though, and the administration can be hit-or-miss, ranging from "always having its doors open" to needing "to get it together."

Life

The facilities on AIB's tiny campus are "open well past regular hours" and students here, as you might expect, spend a pretty good chunk of their time making art. Traditional clubs and extracurricular activities are very sparse. Students "use the city as their campus." Boston is "a great environment for art students" and, really, every other kind of student. It would be hard to find a better college town anywhere. "The area is packed with students," observes a junior. "AIB practically sits in the backyard of Fenway Park." The location allows students here to take full advantage of the city without the hassle of a car. Cheap restaurants are everywhere. "Bars and music venues are extremely popular." Drinking is certainly possible. Drugs are here, too, but "heavy users never last." "The lifestyle is what you choose it to be," explains a sophomore. "There are plenty of kids who want to party and there are plenty of kids who want to sit in and watch movies in pajamas."

Student Body

With a description like "smoke-loving," it seems fair to say that tobacco is in anything but short supply here. Otherwise, "the only thing every student shares in common is a passion for the visual arts and a desire to create it." The budding professional artists at AIB are "a nice eclectic mix of strangeness and normality." There are "creative and rebellious types." You'll find "the suffering artist" and "pretentious art school stereotypes who think pictures of empty places are really deep and important." "Some of us have tons of piercings," says a freshman. Others dress very fashionably. One student calls AIB "scenester heaven." "Most people are comfortable expressing their individuality and being who they are" and "everyone seems to get along just fine." However, "people generally stick to the friends they made freshman year in their own major and very rarely are able to branch out."

THE PRINCETON REVIEW SAYS

Admissions

Very important factors considered include: Academic GPA, rigor of secondary school record. *Important factors considered include:* Class rank, application essay, recommendation(s), standardized test scores, character/personal qualities, extracurricular activities, interview, talent/ability. *Other factors considered include:* Alumni/ae relation, first generation, geographical residence, level of applicant's interest, racial/ethnic status, volunteer work, work experience. SAT or ACT required; ACT with Writing component required. TOEFL required of all international applicants. High school diploma is required and GED is accepted. *Academic units required:* 4 English. *Academic units recommended:* 4 English, 1 mathematics, 1 science, 1 foreign language, 2 social studies, 2 history, 2 academic electives, 2 studio art.

Financial Aid

Students should submit: FAFSA. The Princeton Review suggests that all financial aid forms be submitted as soon as possible after January 1. *Need-based scholarships/grants offered:* Federal Pell, SEOG, state scholarships/grants, private scholarships, the school's own gift aid. *Loan aid offered:* Direct Subsidized Stafford, Direct Unsubsidized Stafford, Direct PLUS, Federal Perkins, state loans. Applicants will be notified of awards on a rolling basis beginning 2/15. Federal Work-Study Program available. Institutional employment available. Off-campus job opportunities are excellent.

The Inside Word

High school grades are important at AIB. Keep in mind that you'll have to take several general education courses here. Your standardized test scores will be considered as well. However, this is an art school, so the portfolio that you submit is most likely the thing that is going to make or break your application.

THE SCHOOL SAYS "..."

From The Admissions Office

"At AIB, art is it. We have all gravitated here because of AIB's creative energy.

"At AIB, you really do join a community of serious artists. You will find a close-knit group who will push and prod and sometimes annoy you to get you to do your best. That's AIB, intimate, supportive, populated by students and teachers who will tell you when your work is phenomenal or especially when your perspective is flat or your concept is trite. To become a working artist you need that honesty.

"AIB's teachers are good. They know how to cajole and push you into fulfilling all your wild potential. Our teachers truly want to be at AIB—for its positive energy and its inquisitive, imaginative students. Both great artists and great teachers, AIB faculty are working professionals, successful artists, designers, and innovators.

"Though AIB is an art school through and through, it is also one of four schools within Lesley University, a multi-site liberal arts university based in Cambridge. Located just across the Charles River from Boston, AIB and Lesley College students live in residence halls and join clubs/activities together. Unlike at most independent art schools, Lesley University opens up the world of liberal arts to AIB students and offers the many benefits a large, urban university has to offer (your parents will be reassured).

"AIB graduates go out into the real world with the skills needed to get a job in their field. With an AIB degree, your opportunities will be limitless."

For even more information on this school, turn to page 564 of the "Stats" section.

Assumption College

500 Salisbury Street, Worcester, MA 01609-1296 • Admissions: 888-882-7786 • Fax: 508-799-4412
E-mail: admiss@assumption.edu • Website: www.assumption.edu

RATINGS
Quality of Life: 73   **Academic:** 79   **Admissions:** 77   **Financial Aid:** 77

STUDENTS SAY "..."

Academics

Assumption College is a Catholic school in the greater Boston area, offering liberal arts and pre-professional majors to a small student population of just more than 2,000 undergraduates. Relying on both practical instruction and academic expertise, "the professors at Assumption College are very qualified individuals whose goal is to educate students and prepare them for the future. They are not just trying to feed students information but also stimulate thought and discussion." Expectations are high, and "academics can be challenging, but are mostly manageable as long as you put in the time." Fortunately, "the size of the school allows for a large amount of personal attention," and professors, "go above and beyond the call of duty to make sure you get the best education they can offer." Undergrads admit that there are some professors whose courses are less interesting than others; however, they universally praise the faculty's commitment to its students. A freshman details, "The professors, at least 80% of the time, are excellent lecturers. There are almost no lectures, which are not accompanied by productive discussions."

SURVEY SAYS . . .
Lab facilities are great
Great computer facilities
Frats and sororities are unpopular or nonexistent
Student government is popular
Lots of beer drinking
Hard liquor is popular

Life

Assumption is a Catholic school, so "religion is prominent and there are good programs for religious students. However, if you are not religious it isn't shoved down your throat or forced on you." A largely residential campus, "there is a good sense of community here, especially within the residence halls and clubs." Off-campus, in the surrounding town of Worcester, you'll find "a lot of restaurants and bars that students frequent, as well as a lot of good shopping." While freshmen cannot have cars on campus, "the school has a deal with YellowCab called 'safe ride.' As long as you have your school ID you can get a ride back to campus for $4 only after dark." Students admit, "Drinking is definitely a large part of the culture here." However, they also reassure us that "many people don't drink." For those who prefer a mellower social schedule, "bingo is a favorite activity on campus, and many students are involved in Campus Ministry." In addition, students spend time at "sporting events, comedians, open mic nights, bingo, or just hanging out in a friend's room."

Student Body

A studious, friendly, and social group, Assumption students are generally described as "hard workers, committed, driven, and smart." Outside of their studies, "the typical student gets involved, whether it be sports, student government, academic clubs, or an on-campus job." The majority of Assumption students come from "a suburban, white, upper-middle-class background. There aren't many who deviate from this norm, but those who do manage to fit in well enough." In addition, Assumption students seem to partake in an unwritten preppy dress code. A junior chides "Assumption was once described to me as a walking J. Crew ad, which is basically true." However, students reassure us that Assumption is committed to acceptance; "If you are a minority or not into preppy clothing, you are treated the same and respected for your differences."

THE PRINCETON REVIEW SAYS

Admissions

Very important factors considered include: Application essay, academic GPA. *Important factors considered include:* Recommendation(s), rigor of secondary school record, interview, level of applicant's interest, volunteer work. *Other factors considered include:* Class rank, standardized test scores, alumni/ae relation, character/personal qualities, extracurricular activities, first generation, racial/ethnic status, talent/ability, TOEFL required of all international applicants. High school diploma is required and GED is accepted. *Academic units required:* 4 English, 3 mathematics, 2 science, 2 foreign language, 2 history, 5 academic electives.

Financial Aid

Students should submit: FAFSA. Regular filing deadline is 2/1. The Princeton Review suggests that all financial aid forms be submitted as soon as possible after January 1. *Need-based scholarships/grants offered:* Federal Pell, SEOG, state scholarships/grants, private scholarships, the school's own gift aid. *Loan aid offered:* Direct Subsidized Stafford, Direct Unsubsidized Stafford, Direct PLUS. Applicants will be notified of awards on a rolling basis beginning 2/16. Federal Work-Study Program available. Institutional employment available. Off-campus job opportunities are good.

The Inside Word

Assumption takes the "personal qualities" of its applicants into consideration, looking closely at candidates' co-curricular activities, leadership experiences, and commitment to community service. Essays and letters of recommendation, both required, are also considered important indicators of character. Spend some extra time on the non-academic part of your application, and choose your recommenders carefully.

THE SCHOOL SAYS "..."

From The Admissions Office

"Assumption College, founded in 1904, is the fourth-oldest Catholic college in New England. Assumption combines academically rigorous programs in the liberal arts, the sciences and professional studies grounded in the Catholic intellectual tradition. These programs enable students to cultivate the academic skills and personal values they need to meet the demands of a constantly changing world.

"At Assumption, we believe that a college education should develop and enrich the formation of the spirit and heart as well as the intellect. We value those moments of transformation that make our students more insightful and enlightened—moments that occur not only in the classroom or the lab, but also on the playing field or the stage, in a residence hall, or volunteering in the community.

"We believe that each of our students has the ability to make a positive difference in the world. To that end, our faculty and staff instruct, counsel and inspire students to help them become compassionate leaders, effective problem solvers, and fulfilled, productive adults.

"Assumption's 185-acre campus in Worcester, Massachusetts, combines easy access to New England's second largest city with the beauty, comfort, and security of a residential neighborhood. The college offers a state-of-the-art Science Center, a new Information Technology Center, a new multi-sport athletic field, and guarantees on-campus housing options (including four new residence halls opened since 2000) for all four years."

For even more information on this school, turn to page 464 of the "Stats" section.

BABSON COLLEGE

MUSTARD HALL, BABSON PARK, MA 02457-0310 • ADMISSIONS: 800-488-3696 • FAX: 781-239-4006
FINANCIAL AID: 781-239-4219 • E-MAIL: UGRADADMISSION@BABSON.EDU • WEBSITE: WWW.BABSON.EDU

RATINGS

Quality of Life: 87   Academic: 85   Admissions: 93   Financial Aid: 90

STUDENTS SAY ". . ."

Academics

Babson is a school well suited to the age of specialization. Its business is business; if you're looking for a well-regarded undergraduate degree in business, Babson can serve your needs because the school "offers multiple opportunities for students to gear their own educations" to develop "a complete set of management skills." As one student puts it, "When I took a quick look at the curriculum, I was positive

> **SURVEY SAYS . . .**
> *Great computer facilities*
> *School is well run*
> *Diverse student types on campus*
> *Campus feels safe*
> *Low cost of living*

whatever I wanted to study in business could be found" at Babson. The school is best known for its emphasis on entrepreneurship; all freshmen must undertake the school's Foundations in Management and Entrepreneurship immersion course, during which undergrads create their own startups. Those who choose to pursue the field further can jockey for space in E-Tower, a "community of 21 highly motivated entrepreneurs chosen to live together" and immerse themselves in all things entrepreneurial (similar housing options are available for students in, among others, finance and green business). Internship opportunities are abundant thanks to the school's reputation and proximity to Boston, providing students "a hands-on experience of how things work in the real world." Professors "want nothing more than to see their students learn and do well. Many...refer to themselves as 'pracademics' because they have had such amazing real-world experience from which they can draw on in the classroom. From executives of Fortune 500 companies to entrepreneurs who own multi-million dollar companies, the knowledge of professors at Babson is only rivaled by their desire to see students do well." Career placement services here "are really strong."

Life

Babson is in the "perfect location," "near Boston but not in it." One student explains: "We are not in the busy city life on a daily basis, but we are able to get into Boston very easily, whether it's driving, taking the T, or the Babson Shuttle that drops you off right in the center of Fanueil Hall." (The shuttle runs only on weekends.) Campus life, once considered subpar, "is definitely a lot better. [Student government] sponsors and hosts many events throughout the months to keep students entertained and involved," including "Knight Parties, where there are monthly dance parties in one of our large auditoriums" and "spring, winter, and fall weekend, where they have entertainment and bands come to the school. This year we even had Jimmy Fallon come for a comedy concert in the fall—the show was packed; it was standing room only." Students report that "A favorite hangout on a Thursday night is the pub, where there is entertainment and food. Babson [provides] supervised drinking for those of legal drinking age." The school's numerous student-run clubs "are very motivated, providing diverse and educating events" such as mixers and symposia.

Student Body

"It is hard to pin-point a typical student, as Babson is so diverse," but the common thread is that "we all view business as a primary, shared strand that can link our interests and passions in order to help us make a difference in the world." Babson "is an international college. Outside of our library, there is a flag tree where the flags of different students represented on our campus are flown to show our diversity. We have students from about 64 different countries," and students "learn from each others' differences. It is one of the great pieces of knowledge we are able to pick up at Babson." The "dominant domestic students will be the preppy white boy and girl who treat their designer clothes like aprons," while "international students are mostly of Indian and Hispanic descent who do not refrain from displaying their wealth," all supplemented by "a small population of students that are swimming in personal debt to attend Babson or could never place a foot on the campus if it weren't for their financial aid."

THE PRINCETON REVIEW SAYS

Admissions

Very important factors considered include: Application essay, academic GPA, recommendation(s), rigor of secondary school record, standardized test scores, character/personal qualities. *Important factors considered include:* Class rank, extracurricular activities. *Other factors considered include:* Alumni/ae relation, first generation, geographical residence, interview, level of applicant's interest, racial/ethnic status, state residency, talent/ability, volunteer work, work experience. SAT or ACT required; SAT and SAT Subject Tests or ACT recommended; ACT with Writing component required. TOEFL required of all international applicants. High school diploma is required, and GED is accepted. *Academic units recommended:* 4 English, 4 mathematics, 4 science, (3 science labs), 4 foreign language, 2 social studies, 2 history, 1 pre-calculus.

Financial Aid

Students should submit: FAFSA, CSS/Financial Aid PROFILE, noncustodial PROFILE, business/farm supplement. Federal tax returns, W-2s, and Verification Worksheet. Regular filing deadline is 2/15. The Princeton Review suggests that all financial aid forms be submitted as soon as possible after January 1. *Need-based scholarships/grants offered:* Federal Pell, SEOG, state scholarships/grants, the school's own gift aid. *Loan aid offered:* Federal Perkins, state loans. Applicants will be notified of awards on or about 4/1. Federal Work-Study Program available. Institutional employment available. Off-campus job opportunities are good.

The Inside Word

Babson's national profile is ascending quickly, resulting in a substantial uptick in the number of applications received each year. Expect admissions standards to rise in accordance. The school considers writing ability a strong indicator of preparedness for college; proceed accordingly.

THE SCHOOL SAYS "..."

From The Admissions Office

"Nationally recognized as a Top 20 Business Program and the #1 school in entrepreneurship for 13 years, Babson College defines entrepreneurship education for the world. Our learning concepts provide students with the ability to adapt to ever-changing business environments, the experience to hit the ground running upon graduation, and the know-how to discover opportunities that will create economic and social value everywhere. We believe, as do our graduates and their employers, in the value of an integrated approach combined with experiential education. As a business school where one-half of the classes are in liberal arts, Babson emphasizes creativity, imagination, and risk-taking as essential to learning the foundation of business.

"Babson's close-knit community provides students with the opportunity to form close relationships with faculty and staff. An average class size of 29 and student/faculty ratio of 14:1 allow faculty to serve as role models and mentors committed to helping our students grow. With more than 90 percent holding a doctoral degree, these accomplished business executives, authors, entrepreneurs, scholars, researchers, and artists bring an intellectual diversity and real-world experience that adds depth to Babson's programs. Most importantly, faculty members teach 100 percent of the courses.

"At Babson, students receive a world-class education that is innovative and creative, yet practical. They study business, learn about leadership, and undertake a transformative life experience preparing them to create an authentic, powerful brand of success. Our students make friends, find mentors, and develop long-lasting relationships that will thrive long after graduation."

For even more information on this school, turn to page 465 of the "Stats" section.

BARD COLLEGE

OFFICE OF ADMISSIONS, ANNANDALE-ON-HUDSON, NY 12504 • ADMISSIONS: 845-758-7472
FAX: 845-758-5208 • FINANCIAL AID: 845-758-7526 • E-MAIL: ADMISSION@BARD.EDU • WEBSITE: WWW.BARD.EDU

RATINGS

Quality of Life: 65   Academic: 93   Admissions: 96   Financial Aid: 88

STUDENTS SAY "..."

Academics

Students come to Bard seeking "a liberal arts college with a left-leaning student body of creative thinkers who are all actively interested in political and social activism and learning/academia for its own sake," and "we find it," they tell us. Those yearning for "an atmosphere of curious individuals striving for knowledge," a place where "there are intelligent discussions both inside and outside the classroom" will find a home at this small liberal arts school

> **SURVEY SAYS . . .**
> *Lots of liberal students*
> *No one cheats*
> *Students aren't religious*
> *Campus feels safe*
> *Frats and sororities are unpopular or nonexistent*
> *Political activism is popular*

in the scenic Hudson Valley. All students start their educations here building a solid grounding, starting with a three-week orientation and intensive communication and research workshop, followed by the year-long freshman seminar that is a survey of history's "great ideas." As one student observes, "The curriculum at Bard is set up to give students a broad foundation of knowledge," a foundation they get to test when completing their senior project in their final year. As at many elite small schools, "The administration and professors are amazingly accessible. A simple e-mail can get you an appointment with the dean of students, and the professors encourage students to ask for help or to discuss any ideas they may have." Students aren't coddled, however; writes one, "One reason that the school doesn't run as 'smoothly' [as other schools] is that this place isn't about handing life's jewels to everyone. All the students must put some effort into their work to get the real payoff. It's a bit like real life in that manner." As one student puts it, "Bard, more than any other school, is what you make of it. If you wish to make a big splash, the school will provide you with the proper equipment (large boulders, diving boards, etc.). It is up to you, though, to take advantage of it."

Life

Bard "has a gorgeous campus," and undergrads "take full advantage of that when the weather is warm. Blithewood, our Italian-style gardens, is often full of students picnicking and playing Frisbee, and elsewhere on campus most trees have at least one student reading, or perhaps playing an instrument, in the shade. Other popular pastimes/attractions include the on-campus art museum, the waterfall, and many winding, hilly hiking trails that snake around Blithewood and along the Hudson River." The campus hosts a rich cultural life; the "student-run entertainment space—a converted auto garage known as SMOG—holds many fantastic music shows (both student bands and musical guests), as well as the very popular themed dance parties," and "Art is everywhere. Students frequently have the opportunities to see world-class performances by the American Symphony Orchestra for free or for a mere $5." All this activity makes up for the fact that "the campus is a little isolated," as does the fact that "shuttles run to nearby towns rather frequently." Undergrads tell us that "This is not a beer-pong school. Rather than the norm being the stereotypical frat-style college party, many 'parties' are just friends sitting together; drinking boxed wine; listening to jazz or indie rock; and discussing philosophy, art, current events, etc." When they need to get away, "Many kids go to New York City for the weekends."

Student Body

"Bard is a safe haven for all hipsters, serious intellectuals, artists, and dreamers," so it should come as no surprise that "Everyone at Bard was atypical in high school, and consequently it's difficult to classify anyone as either typical or atypical. Students here are brilliant, enthusiastic, passionate, and genuinely different." They tend to be "very passionate about their specific interests and work hard to manifest them in the community," with "an unbelievable sensitivity to the subtleties of, and a passion for, language." "It's 'cool' to be intellectual, artistic, and well-read" here, and "'hipster' fashion is in style." Occasionally some "do try to be a little too philosophical, and some kids can border on pretentious or self-righteous, but most are absolutely amazing people with fascinating backgrounds."

THE PRINCETON REVIEW SAYS

Admissions

Very important factors considered include: Application essay, academic GPA, recommendation(s), rigor of secondary school record, character/personal qualities, extracurricular activities, talent/ability. *Important factors considered include:* Volunteer work, work experience. *Other factors considered include:* Class rank, standardized test scores, alumni/ae relation, first generation, geographical residence, interview, level of applicant's interest, racial/ethnic status, religious affiliation/commitment, state residency. TOEFL required of all international applicants. High school diploma is required, and GED is accepted. *Academic units recommended:* 4 English, 4 mathematics, 4 science, (3 science labs), 4 foreign language, 4 social studies, 4 history.

Financial Aid

Students should submit: FAFSA, CSS/Financial Aid PROFILE, state aid form, noncustodial PROFILE, business/farm supplement. Regular filing deadline is 2/15. The Princeton Review suggests that all financial aid forms be submitted as soon as possible after January 1. *Need-based scholarships/grants offered:* Federal Pell, SEOG, state scholarships/grants, private scholarships, the school's own gift aid. *Loan aid offered:* Federal Perkins, other, loans from institutional funds (for international students only). Applicants will be notified of awards on or about 4/1. Federal Work-Study Program available. Institutional employment available. Off-campus job opportunities are good.

The Inside Word

Bard receives more than enough applications from students with the academic credentials to gain admission, so the school has the luxury of focusing on matchmaking. The goal is to find students who can handle the independence allowed here and who will thrive in an intellectually intensive environment. The school requires two application essays; expect both to be very carefully scrutinized by the admissions office.

THE SCHOOL SAYS "..."

From The Admissions Office

"An alliance with Rockefeller University, the renowned graduate scientific research institution, gives Bardians access to Rockefeller's professors and laboratories and to places in Rockefeller's Summer Research Fellows Program. Almost all our math and science graduates pursue graduate or professional studies; 90 percent of our applicants to medical and health professional schools are accepted.

"The Globalization and International Affairs (BGIA) Program is a residential program in the heart of New York City that offers undergraduates a unique opportunity to undertake specialized study with leading practitioners and scholars in international affairs and to gain internship experience with international-affairs organizations. Topics in the curriculum include human rights, international economics, global environmental issues, international justice, managing international risk, and writing on international affairs, among others. Internships/tutorials are tailored to students' particular fields of study.

"Student dormitory and classroom facilities are in Bard Hall, 410 West Fifty-Eighth Street, a newly renovated 11-story building near the Lincoln Center District in New York City.

"Bard College does not require SAT scores to be submitted for admissions consideration. Students may choose to submit scores, and, if submitted, we will consider them in the context of the overall application. "

For even more information on this school, turn to page 465 of the "Stats" section.

BARD COLLEGE AT SIMON'S ROCK

84 ALFORD ROAD, GREAT BARRINGTON, MA 01230 • ADMISSIONS: 413-528-7312 • FAX: 413-528-7334
FINANCIAL AID: 413-528-7297 • E-MAIL: ADMIT@SIMONS-ROCK.EDU • WEBSITE: WWW.SIMONS-ROCK.EDU

RATINGS
Quality of Life: 86   Academic: 98   Admissions: 90   Financial Aid: 88

STUDENTS SAY ". . ."

Academics

Bard College at Simon's Rock is a tiny, "rigorous," and "unique" bastion of the liberal arts and sciences that allows high-school-aged students "the opportunity to start their college careers and broaden their academic horizons a bit earlier than is orthodox." At Simon's Rock, you can enroll after completing tenth or eleventh grade. "I wasn't learning anything in high school," explains an art history major. "Simon's Rock recognizes that and provides you with another option." There's a Lower College and an Upper College. (Students in

> **SURVEY SAYS . . .**
> *Class discussions encouraged*
> *No one cheats*
> *Athletic facilities are great*
> *Students aren't religious*
> *Campus feels safe*
> *Frats and sororities are unpopular or nonexistent*
> *Political activism is popular*

the Lower College are the ones who would otherwise be in high school.) Both colleges offer an incredible amount of freedom to design your own course of study. There are more than 40 majors. The arts programs are "very strong." Students in the engineering program can spend three years at Simon's Rock and then two years at Columbia University. Several outstanding study-abroad opportunities send students to places such as Istanbul, Ghana, Oxford, and the Sorbonne in Paris. Many people "only stay here two years," long enough to earn an associate's degree. After that, they transfer to a more traditional college. However, you can also stick around at SRC to get your bachelor's degree. Either way, "the academic expectations are formidable." Coursework is "challenging" and "requires a lot of time input out of class." There's quite a bit of reading. Seniors must complete a self-designed thesis. Classes are small—the average size is a mere 10 students—and they are filled with "engaging" discussion. "Simon's Rock professors are generally very supportive and understanding." They provide "up-close and personal attention" and "go out of their way to be available out of the classroom."

Life

The "gorgeous" campus here can be "a bit of a bubble" and, at times, "small to the point of claustrophobia," but students promise that there is much to do. There's "a large number of clubs for the size of the school," and "new clubs and interests are always forming." "The athletic center is top-notch." Winters are hard, but "the spring is pure glory." Hikes "in the beautiful woods" are common, weather permitting. Equally common is "just hanging out." Often, students will "simply sit around talking about random stuff, ranging from the weather to Marx." "Most of campus smokes." "Drugs and alcohol are a major form of recreation and stress relief." However, the party scene is "relatively low-key." Often, it's "sneaking around under night skies" to darkened party spots. Students also emphasize that it is "possible to have fun and attend parties without being pressured" into consuming anything you'd rather avoid. The "very small town" of Great Barrington is a little less than two miles away. "Befriending car-endowed people is a good skill." Without or without wheels, though, "there is very little to do off campus." Simon's Rock is "isolated" in the Berkshire Mountains of "rural" western Massachusetts, roughly in "in the middle of nowhere." On the plus side, New York City and Boston are reasonably easy to reach. Older students frequently make treks to those cities on the weekends.

Student Body

For the students here, "Simon's Rock is a blissful release from the institutional hell of high school." Students come here from 40 or so states. They are "brilliant and creative" and "excited to learn." "Lots of people come from their high school used to being the smartest person in the room," explains one student, "and then they realize that, wow, there are lots of really smart people here, and now you have someone to talk to about serious stuff." Students describe themselves as "strong individuals who lean toward nonconformity." They are "a little misunderstood." They "tend to be liberal," and they are "very aware and educated in current politics." "Some people are very, very androgynous." "Many are artists." Many are "hippies." Many are artists and hippies. Ultimately, Simon's Rock is filled with "kids who think outside the box." "Most people walk to their own beat." "Brightly dyed hair, body piercings, tattoos, girls with buzz cuts, guys in skirts, and crazy clothing ensembles are SRC trademarks."

THE PRINCETON REVIEW SAYS

Admissions

Very important factors considered include: Application essay, recommendation(s), rigor of secondary school record, character/personal qualities, interview, talent/ability. *Important factors considered include:* Class rank, academic GPA, level of applicant's interest. *Other factors considered include:* Standardized test scores, alumni/ae relation, extracurricular activities, first generation, racial/ethnic status, volunteer work, work experience. TOEFL required of all international applicants. High school diploma or equivalent is not required. *Academic units recommended:* 2 English, 2 mathematics, 2 science, (1 science labs), 2 foreign language, 2 social studies, 2 history.

Financial Aid

Students should submit: FAFSA, CSS/Financial Aid PROFILE, business/farm supplement, Parent and Student Federal Taxes/Federal Verification Worksheet. The Princeton Review suggests that all financial aid forms be submitted as soon as possible after January 1. *Need-based scholarships/grants offered:* Federal Pell, SEOG, state scholarships/grants, private scholarships, the school's own gift aid. *Loan aid offered:* Federal Perkins, state loans, other, alternative educational loans. Applicants will be notified of awards on a rolling basis beginning 4/15. Federal Work-Study Program available. Institutional employment available. Off-campus job opportunities are good.

The Inside Word

Because Simon's Rock boasts healthy application numbers, it is in a position to concentrate on matchmaking. To that end, admissions officers seek students with independent and inquisitive spirits. Applicants who exhibit academic ambition while extending their intellectual curiosity beyond the realm of the classroom are particularly appealing. Successful candidates typically have several honors and advanced placement courses on their transcripts, as well as strong letters of recommendation and well-written personal statements.

THE SCHOOL SAYS "..."

From The Admissions Office

"Simon's Rock is dedicated to one thing: To allow bright, highly motivated students the opportunity to pursue college work leading to the AA and BA degrees at an age earlier than our national norm.

"Simon's Rock College of Bard will accept either the SAT or the ACT with or without the Writing component."

For even more information on this school, turn to page 466 of the "Stats" section.

BARNARD COLLEGE

3009 BROADWAY, NEW YORK, NY 10027 • ADMISSIONS: 212-854-2014 • FAX: 212-854-6220
FINANCIAL AID: 212-854-2154 • E-MAIL: ADMISSIONS@BARNARD.EDU • WEBSITE: WWW.BARNARD.EDU

RATINGS
Quality of Life: 99   **Academic:** 95   **Admissions:** 97   **Financial Aid:** 95

STUDENTS SAY "..."

Academics

Life is lived in the fast lane at Barnard, an all-women's liberal arts college partnered with Columbia University that
incorporates "a small school feel with big school resources
and incorporates both campus and city life." Nestled in the
Morningside Heights neighborhood of Manhattan on a
gated (main) campus, the school maintains an "independent spirit" while providing a "nurturing environment," and

its partnership with a larger research university gives it the
"best of both worlds" and affords its students the opportunities, course options, and resources that many colleges
don't have.

The academic experience at Barnard is simply "wonderful," according to the students. Teachers here are "experts
in their field" and "value their positions as both teachers and mentors," to the extent "they make you want to
stay on Barnard's campus for class and not take classes at Columbia." "I've never been in an environment where
there is such a reciprocal relationship between students wanting to learn and be challenged and professors wanting to teach and help," says a junior. Though underclassmen typically aren't able to get into as many of the small
classes (the process of which "is a nightmare"), one student claims that "some of the best classes I've had have
been in large lecture halls." The administration gets thumbs-up nearly across the board for their accessibility and
compassion for students. Deans are always available to students wanting to meet, and the alumni network and
career services are singled out for their efficacy. "Every time there is an issue on campus that students care about
or an event that has happened, we get e-mails and town-hall style meetings devoted to discussing the issues."
"Barnard is New York—busy, exciting, full of opportunity," says one student.

Life

Not much goes on around campus, to the chagrin of a few, but as one freshman puts it, "Why stay on campus
when you're in New York?" Students take advantage of the resources available to them in New York City, from
Broadway shows and Central Park to museums and restaurants; "The possibilities are endless," and "make it
impossible to stick to a budget." Theater and a capella are also very big here, and many students are involved with
clubs and organizations at Columbia, sometimes even dominating them. There are some complaints that facilities
and dorms are "crumbling." There are some complaints that facilities and dorms are "crumbling," but the recently opened Diana Center building has fast become a hub of student activities, including studying, learning, socializing, dining, and relaxing. "Life at Barnard is probably 60–75% academic and around 25–40% free."

Student Body

Even though it's all women here, Barnard is "the anti-women's college," as "very, very few students are here for
the single-sex education"—they're here for the academics and New York. There's a definite liberal slant on campus, and these "usually politically savvy," "very cultured," "energetic and motivated" women are "ambitious
and opinionated," with career and leadership goals at the top of their agenda. "Barnard students are not lazy"
and have no problems booking their days full of study and activities. Most here learn to "fit into the mad rush"
very quickly and take advantage of their four short years. Although quite a few students are from the tri-state
area and the majority are white, "there is still a sense of diversity" thanks to a variety of different backgrounds,
both cultural and geographical; there's also a "tiny gay community" that seems easily accepted.

THE PRINCETON REVIEW SAYS

Admissions

Very important factors considered include: Academic GPA, recommendation(s), rigor of secondary school record, standardized test scores, character/personal qualities, extracurricular activities. *Important factors considered include:* Application essay, talent/ability, volunteer work. *Other factors considered include:* Class rank, alumni/ae relation, first generation, geographical residence, interview, level of applicant's interest, racial/ethnic status, work experience. SAT and SAT Subject Tests or ACT required; ACT with Writing component required. TOEFL required of all international applicants. High school diploma or equivalent is not required. *Academic units recommended:* 4 English, 3 mathematics, 3 science, (2 science labs), 3 foreign language.

Financial Aid

Students should submit: FAFSA, institution's own financial aid form, CSS/Financial Aid PROFILE, state aid form, noncustodial PROFILE, business/farm supplement, federal income tax returns. Regular filing deadline is 2/1. The Princeton Review suggests that all financial aid forms be submitted as soon as possible after January 1. *Need-based scholarships/grants offered:* Federal Pell, SEOG, state scholarships/grants, private scholarships, the school's own gift aid. *Loan aid offered:* Federal Perkins, state loans, college/university loans from institutional funds. Applicants will be notified of awards on or about 3/31. Federal Work-Study Program available. Institutional employment available. Off-campus job opportunities are excellent.

The Inside Word

As at many top colleges, early decision applications have increased at Barnard—although the admissions standards are virtually the same as for their regular admissions cycle. The college's admissions staff is suprisingly open and accessible for such a highly selective college with as long and impressive a tradition of excellence. The admissions committee's expectations are high, but their attitude reflects a true interest in who potential students are and what's on their minds. Students have a much better experience throughout the admissions process when treated with sincerity and respect—perhaps this is why Barnard continues to attract and enroll some of the best students in the country.

THE SCHOOL SAYS "..."

From The Admissions Office

"Barnard College is a small, distinguished liberal arts college for women that is partnered with Columbia University and located in the heart of New York City. The college enrolls women from all over the United States, Puerto Rico, and the Caribbean. More than 30 countries, including France, England, Hong Kong, and Greece, are also represented in the student body. Students pursue their academic studies in more than 40 majors and are able to cross register at Columbia University.

"Applicants for the entering class must submit scores from the SAT Reasoning Test and two SAT Subject Tests of their choice or the ACT with the Writing component."

For even more information on this school, turn to page 466 of the "Stats" section.

BATES COLLEGE

23 CAMPUS AVENUE, LEWISTON, ME 04240-9917 • ADMISSIONS: 207-786-6000 • FAX: 207-786-6025
FINANCIAL AID: 207-786-6096 • E-MAIL: ADMISSIONS@BATES.EDU • WEBSITE: WWW.BATES.EDU

RATINGS
Quality of Life: 86　　　Academic: 93　　　Admissions: 95　　　Financial Aid: 94

STUDENTS SAY "..."

Academics

"You will not find it hard to gain access to resources" at Bates
College, a small school in Maine that "tries to be unique in
the homogeneous world of New England's small liberal arts
colleges by weaving together academics with real world
experience." First-year seminars, mandatory senior theses,
service-learning, and a range of interdisciplinary majors are

> **SURVEY SAYS . . .**
> *Students are friendly*
> *Great food on campus*
> *Frats and sororities are unpopular or nonexistent*
> *Student publications are popular*

part of the academic experience. About two-thirds of the students here study abroad at some point before graduation. "Research and internship opportunities" are absurdly abundant. A fairly unusual 4-4-1 calendar includes two
traditional semesters and an "incredible" five-week spring term that provides really cool opportunities. Examples
include studying marine biology on the Maine coast, Shakespearean drama in England, or economics in China and
Taiwan. The "brilliant, accessible, and friendly" faculty does "whatever it takes to actually teach you the material
instead of just lecturing and leaving." "The professors at Bates are here because they are passionate about their field
and want to be teaching," explains a politics major. "I have never met so many professors who are willing to dedicate endless time outside of class to their students," gushes a psychology major. Course selection can be sparse, but
the "regularly available" administration is "responsive to student concerns" as well.

Life

"The library is the place to be during the week because everyone is there." The academic workload is reportedly substantial, but "it is entirely manageable and does not restrict you from participating in athletics, clubs, or
just having some down time." Parties are common on the weekends, and students "stand mashed up against
everyone else in the keg line." There's a great college radio station—91.5 on your FM dial—and many students
get involved. "Bates also has a lot of traditions that students get excited about." In the winter during Puddle
Jump, just for instance, Batesies who feel especially courageous can take the plunge into the frigid water of Lake
Andrews. Otherwise, "dances, comedians, and trivia challenges are shockingly well attended because there's not
a whole lot else to do." The biggest social complaint here centers on the surrounding area. It's the kind of place
where "you wouldn't want to be walking alone at 3 in the morning." Also, relations between Batesies and local
residents are reportedly strained. "The interaction between the town and college is relatively minimal," relates a
junior. When students feel they just have to get away, they can "hit up the nearby ski slopes." The great outdoors
is another option. Bates rents "tents, sleeping bags, kayaks, climbing gear, stoves, vans—really anything you
want for outdoor fun." Also, Boston and some smaller cities such as Freeport and Portland are easily accessible.

Student Body

Students tell us that "Bates needs to improve its ethnic diversity." Most of the students here are white. In the last
three years, however, the percentage of students who identify as Asian, African, Native, and/or Latino/a American
has increased. "Your typical Batesie owns at least two flannel shirts" and "likes to have fun on the weekends." There
are "a lot of jocks," and some "take the sports teams here way too seriously." Students here call themselves "down
to earth" yet "intellectually driven." They enjoy "participating in academics, sports, and clubs." They "love the outdoors." However, this campus is "eclectic," and "Bates students are by no means monolithic in character." "We have
everyone from the prep-school spoiled brat to the hippie environmentalist, from people with all different gender
and sexual preferences and orientations to the former or current goth," observes a junior. "There are dorks, brains,
goof-offs, and class clowns." There are "plenty of kids who apparently haven't found the dorm showers," too.
"There are few, if any, cliques on campus." "Crossing boundaries" is quite common. "There are different groups but
none of them are exclusive in any way." "Even those who do not fit into any specific social group are widely accepted" (with the possible exception of the people who "plain suck").

Admissions

Very important factors considered include: Class rank, application essay, academic GPA, recommendation(s), rigor of secondary school record, character/personal qualities, extracurricular activities, interview, level of applicant's interest, talent/ability. *Other factors considered include:* Standardized test scores, alumni/ae relation, first generation, geographical residence, racial/ethnic status, state residency, volunteer work, work experience. TOEFL required of all international applicants. High school diploma is required, and GED is not accepted. *Academic units required:* 4 English, 3 mathematics, 3 science, (2 science labs), 2 foreign language, 3 social studies. *Academic units recommended:* 4 English, 4 mathematics, 4 science, (3 science labs), 4 foreign language, 4 social studies.

Financial Aid

Students should submit: FAFSA, CSS/Financial Aid PROFILE, noncustodial PROFILE. Regular filing deadline is 2/1. The Princeton Review suggests that all financial aid forms be submitted as soon as possible after January 1. *Need-based scholarships/grants offered:* Federal Pell, SEOG, state scholarships/grants, private scholarships, the school's own gift aid. *Loan aid offered:* Federal Perkins, state loans. Applicants will be notified of awards on or about 4/1. Federal Work-Study Program available. Institutional employment available. Off-campus job opportunities are good.

The Inside Word

While holding its applicants to lofty standards, Bates strives to adopt a personal approach to the admissions process. Officers favor qualitative information and focus more on academic rigor, essays, and recommendations than GPA and test scores. The school seeks students who look for challenges and take advantage of opportunities in the classroom and beyond. Interviews are strongly encouraged—candidates who opt out may place themselves at a disadvantage.

THE SCHOOL SAYS "..."

From The Admissions Office

"Bates College is widely recognized as one of the finest liberal arts colleges in the nation. The curriculum and faculty challenge students to develop the essential skills of critical assessment, analysis, expression, aesthetic sensibility, and independent thought. Founded by abolitionists in 1855, Bates graduates have always included men and women from diverse ethnic and religious backgrounds. Bates highly values its study-abroad programs, unique calendar (4-4-1), and the many opportunities available for one-on-one collaboration with faculty through seminars, research, service-learning, and the capstone experience of senior thesis. Co-curricular life at Bates is rich; most students participate in club or varsity sports; many participate in performing arts; and almost all students participate in one of more than 110 student-run clubs and organizations. More than two-thirds of alumni enroll in graduate study within 10 years.

"The Bates College Admissions Staff reads applications very carefully; the high school record and the quality of writing are of particular importance. Applicants are strongly encouraged to have a personal interview, either on campus or with an alumni representative. Students who choose not to interview may place themselves at a disadvantage in the selection process. Bates offers tours, interviews, and information sessions throughout the summer and fall. Drop-ins are welcome for tours and information sessions. Please call ahead to schedule an interview.

"At Bates, the submission of standardized testing (the SAT, SAT Subject Tests, and the ACT) is not required for admission. After two decades of optional testing, our research shows no differences in academic performance and graduation rates between submitters and nonsubmitters."

For even more information on this school, turn to page 467 of the "Stats" section.

BENNINGTON COLLEGE

OFFICE OF ADMISSIONS AND FINANCIAL AID, BENNINGTON, VT 05201 • ADMISSIONS: 800-833-6845
FAX: 802-440-4320 • FINANCIAL AID: 802-440-4325 • E-MAIL: ADMISSIONS@BENNINGTON.EDU • WEBSITE: WWW.BENNINGTON.EDU

RATINGS
Quality of Life: 84   **Academic:** 96   **Admissions:** 89   **Financial Aid:** 76

STUDENTS SAY ". . ."

Academics

Bennington caters to students who want maximum control over their academic endeavors; all students here participate in the Plan Process, "which allows students to create their own course of study." Here's how it works: "Either a student devises his own personalized set of requirements, or [the requirements] are recommended by a 'plan committee' of usually three faculty members personally assigned to each student." The idea is to "leave up to the student the chance to connect ideas and classes that would normally be left out of a core curriculum," and unsurprisingly, students here love it—for many it is the primary reason they choose to attend Bennington. The Field Work Term internship program is another compelling factor. This "seven-week internship term in the winter" gives students "the ideal opportunity to connect with professionals in our areas of interest and learn what you are (and what you aren't) interested in pursuing" while also building a resume. The social sciences, humanities, and performing/creative arts are strongest here, but students insist that the hard sciences are also "strong...and more popular than one might think for a small 'alternative' liberal arts school." Bennington professors "range from being very available to ridiculously available," and "most are extremely active and respected in their fields, and all are willing to meet outside of class and help a motivated student find professional connections."

> **SURVEY SAYS . . .**
> *Lots of liberal students*
> *Class discussions encouraged*
> *Students aren't religious*
> *Dorms are like palaces*
> *Low cost of living*
> *Intercollegiate sports are unpopular or nonexistent*
> *Frats and sororities are unpopular or nonexistent*
> *Theater is popular*

Life

Bennington undergrads are "very focused on work. All students share a passion for what they are doing," to the extent that "The class doesn't end when we leave the classroom. Discussions often continue, and people are always taking about their classes and their work." Because Bennington is a small school "people are generally friendly and very interested in one another and their work," and because the campus "is a little isolated" "there isn't much to do off-campus," so students must be "good at entertaining themselves." Fortunately, "There is always plenty to do on campus. Sometimes there are too many events to choose from: dance concerts, plays, readings, themed parties, art openings, and many more events, on campus and off." Some party intensely "to blow off some steam" because "we all work so exceedingly hard," but most here agree the situation is under control; students can't ignore academics for too long because "with the way our academic system works, you can be kicked out for getting too many C's." When they need to get away, undergrads "are most likely to take day trips to nearby Brattleboro and Williamstown, each of which are very close and offer all sorts of diversions."

Student Body

"Self-motivated, voraciously curious, and open to growth," the typical Bennington student "is very devoted to his work and personally invested in creating something meaningful with [his] time. A stereotype for the general student body could be 'indie kid,' but that doesn't quite fit because the students here have a broader awareness of disciplines and interests outside of their own due to the cross-disciplinary nature of [the] studies." To some, it seems that "Everyone here is a total nerd: art nerd, science nerd, lit nerd, language nerd, math nerd, drama nerd, dance nerd. Nerds of all shapes, types, and aesthetic genres." They are "the type of people who would rather dance in polyester or read a book than go to a basketball game." There are "probably fewer than a handful of republicans on campus, and there are definitely no Abercrombie & Fitch sweatshirts around."

THE PRINCETON REVIEW SAYS

Admissions

Very important factors considered include: Application essay, academic GPA, recommendation(s), rigor of secondary school record, class rank, character/personal qualities, extracurricular activities, interview, talent/ability. *Other factors considered include:* Standardized test scores, alumni/ae relation, first generation, geographical residence, level of applicant's interest, racial/ethnic status, volunteer work, work experience. TOEFL required of all international applicants. High school diploma is required, and GED is accepted. *Academic units recommended:* 4 English, 4 mathematics, 3 science, 2 foreign language, 4 social studies, 4 history.

Financial Aid

Students should submit: FAFSA, institution's own financial aid form, CSS/Financial Aid PROFILE, noncustodial PROFILE, student and parent federal tax returns and W-2s. Regular filing deadline is 2/15. The Princeton Review suggests that all financial aid forms be submitted as soon as possible after January 1. *Need-based scholarships/grants offered:* Federal Pell, SEOG, state scholarships/grants, private scholarships, the school's own gift aid. *Loan aid offered:* Direct Subsidized Stafford, Direct Unsubsidized Stafford, Direct PLUS, college/university loans from institutional funds. NOTE: College/university loans from institutional funds for International students only. Applicants will be notified of awards on or about 4/1. Federal Work-Study Program available. Institutional employment available. Off-campus job opportunities are good.

The Inside Word

Bennington students need to be academically accomplished, driven, and self-directed in order to handle the academic freedom granted by the curriculum. The admissions office seeks all these qualities in applicants and, because of the school's prestige, typically finds them in all admitted students. A campus visit isn't required but is strongly recommended as an excellent way to demonstrate your interest in the school and to provide admissions officers with the personal contact they prefer in evaluating candidates.

THE SCHOOL SAYS "..."

From The Admissions Office

"The educational philosophy of Bennington is rooted in an abiding faith in the talent, imagination, and responsibility of the individual; thus, the principle of learning by practice underlies every major feature of a Bennington education. We believe that a college education should not merely provide preparation for graduate school or a career, but should be an experience valuable in itself and the model for lifelong learning. Faculty, staff, and students at Bennington work together in a collaborative environment based upon respect for each other and the power of ideas to make a difference in the world. We are looking for intellectually curious students who have a passion for learning, are willing to take risks, and are open to making connections.

"Submission of standardized test scores (the SAT, SAT Subject Tests, or the ACT) is optional."

For even more information on this school, turn to page 467 of the "Stats" section.

BENTLEY UNIVERSITY

175 FOREST STREET, WALTHAM, MA 02452-4705 • ADMISSIONS: 781-891-2244 • FAX: 781-891-3414
FINANCIAL AID: 781-891-3441 • E-MAIL: UGADMISSION@BENTLEY.EDU • WEBSITE: WWW.BENTLEY.EDU

RATINGS
Quality of Life: 89   **Academic:** 80   **Admissions:** 90   **Financial Aid:** 85

STUDENTS SAY ". . ."

Academics

"If you're looking to work in business in the Boston area, desire a beautiful campus, state-of-the-art trading room, and technologically advanced university, Bentley University is the place for you," one student assures us. Bentley is known for its business program, and many students cite the program's excellent reputation as their reason for choosing to attend college here, as well as strong career services and professional internship opportunities.

> **SURVEY SAYS . . .**
> Great computer facilities
> Athletic facilities are great
> Career services are great
> Dorms are like palaces
> Campus feels safe
> Low cost of living

Students are pleased with Bentley's abilities to create a "career-bound student while instilling the importance of liberal studies," and to "prepare you and help you earn a job with all the technical and educational background you need." They also "love that most of the professors have worked outside of academia and can bring...real-world experience and examples to the classroom." Professors are "great role models and have had a lot of experience in the business world," and "all professors hold office hours, and they are all responsive to e-mail and phone messages." "Class sizes are capped at 35, which gives students a solid relationship with each professor," and "a lot of classes are discussion-based and force you to think about real-world applications." Some students note that classes can be challenging, but that "many of the departments have tutoring labs available for students at all levels." The administration also receives high marks: It is "truly concerned with students' wants," "engaging and open to new ideas," and "very communicative."

Life

Bentley students study hard and are "very business-like" during week, so they use weekends to blow off a little steam. Many seek fun in the local sports teams (Red Sox, Patriots, and Celtics), local bars on Moody Street, and regular shuttles into Cambridge (Boston is also easily accessible via public transportation). "This university really strikes a great balance of fun and work." While students are happy to have a city like Boston nearby, with its "bars, historical sites, theatres, restaurants, clubs, etc.," there is plenty of activity on campus, too, and "entertainment is limitless." "Students are extremely involved at Bentley." "Most students participate in more than one club, and many hold administrative positions in the club. These clubs lead to not only good friends but also networking opportunities." "Many people participate in very competitive intramural sports." Bentley does have a Greek system, though frat houses are located off campus.

Student Body

A typical student at Bentley "is an intelligent, white New Englander." Moreover, they are "very driven and know what they want to do with their life," and they "know how to have a good time and balance that with schoolwork." "On the surface, most students appear to be the same: serious business students working all the time," and they are "involved in a few extracurriculars." However, look beneath the surface and you will notice a significant international population and "a lot of atypical students" who "fit in with the rest of the students perfectly." Some students say they think the majority of their peers come from wealth, but most feel that Bentley is fairly balanced: "While walking through campus, you may see tons of individuals driving expensive cars or walking to class dressed to the nines, [but] you will also encounter people driving inexpensive cars and walking to class dressed in sweats."

Admissions

Very important factors considered include: Academic GPA, application essay, recommendation(s), rigor of secondary school record, standardized test scores. *Important factors considered include:* Character/personal qualities, extracurricular activities, level of applicant's interest, volunteer work. *Other factors considered include:* Class rank, alumni/ae relation, first generation, geographical residence, interview, racial/ethnic status, state residency, talent/ability, work experience. SAT or ACT required; ACT with Writing component required. TOEFL required of all international applicants. High school diploma is required, and GED is accepted. *Academic units recommended:* 4 English, 4 mathematics, 3 science, (3 science labs), 3 foreign language, 3 social studies, 2 additional English, mathematics, social or lab science, foreign language.

Financial Aid

Students should submit: FAFSA, CSS/Financial Aid PROFILE, noncustodial PROFILE, business/farm supplement, Federal Tax Returns, including all schedules for parents and student. Regular filing deadline is 2/1. The Princeton Review suggests that all financial aid forms be submitted as soon as possible after January 1. *Need-based scholarships/grants offered:* Federal Pell, SEOG, state scholarships/grants, private scholarships, the school's own gift aid. *Loan aid offered:* Federal Perkins, state loans. Applicants will be notified of awards on a rolling basis beginning 3/25. Federal Work-Study Program available. Institutional employment available. Off-campus job opportunities are good.

The Inside Word

If you have a bunch of electives available to you senior year, you may think that choosing business classes is the best way to impress the Bentley admissions office. Not so; the school would prefer you take a broad range of challenging classes—preferably at the AP level—in English, history/social sciences, math, lab sciences, and foreign language. The school enjoys a sizable applicant pool, so you'll need solid grades and test scores to gain admission.

THE SCHOOL SAYS "..."

From The Admissions Office

"Bentley University, a leader in business education, is dedicated to preparing a new kind of business leader, one with the deep technical skills, broad global perspective and the high ethical standards required to make a difference in an ever-changing world. Bentley infuses its advanced business curriculum with the richness of a liberal arts education, providing students with relevant, practical, and transferable skills—precisely what they need to succeed and pursue their passions in life. Bentley also offers a double major in business and liberal studies, allowing students to graduate with a well-rounded skill set that makes them stand out to future employers. Concepts and theories learned in the classroom come alive in hands-on, high-tech learning laboratories such as the Financial Trading Room, Center for Marketing Technology, and Media & Culture Labs and Studio. Ethics and social responsibility are woven throughout the school's curriculum, making the Bentley Service-Learning Program one of the top-ranked in the U.S. Students choose from numerous athletic, social, and cultural opportunities, including 27 countries for study abroad. Students develop skills and build their resume through internships with leading companies. State-of-the-art athletic and recreation facilities complement 23 varsity teams in Division I & II, plus extensive intramural and recreational sports programs. Boston and Cambridge are minutes from campus and are rich resources for internships, job opportunities, cultural events, and social life."

For even more information on this school, turn to page 467 of the "Stats" section.

BOSTON COLLEGE

140 COMMONWEALTH AVENUE, DEVLIN HALL 208, CHESTNUT HILL, MA 02467-3809 • ADMISSIONS: 617-552-3100
FAX: 617-552-0798 • FINANCIAL AID: 800-294-0294 • E-MAIL: UGADMIS@BC.EDU • WEBSITE: WWW.BC.EDU

RATINGS
Quality of Life: 93   **Academic:** 89   **Admissions:** 97   **Financial Aid:** 94

STUDENTS SAY ". . ."

Academics

Students praise the strong academics, the competitive athletic teams, the lively social scene, and the premium location that all combine to create a remarkable all-around college experience at Boston College. For many, though, BC's greatest asset is the "strong spiritual presence [that] shows how positive an influence religion can have on one's life." Don't worry; "they don't try to make anybody be Catholic" here. Rather, the school "simply reflects the Jesuit ideals of community, spirituality, and social justice," and these ideals

> **SURVEY SAYS . . .**
> *Students love Chestnut Hill, MA*
> *Campus feels safe*
> *Everyone loves the Eagles*
> *Frats and sororities are unpopular or nonexistent*
> *Student publications are popular*
> *Student government is popular*
> *Hard liquor is popular*

pervade both the curriculum and the academic community. True to the Jesuit ideal of "educating the entire person," BC requires a thorough core curriculum "including philosophy, theology, and language requirements," rounded out by "strong [but optional] programs, such as internships and studying abroad." Beyond the core curriculum, "BC offers something for everyone. If you go here, you are with business students, nursing students, education majors, and arts and science majors." Even though this is a fairly large school, students insist that "you never feel like a number here. Yes, you have to be independent and seek out your professors. But when you do seek them out, you get incredible individualized attention." One undergrad sums it up like this: "BC's strength is a mix of everything. It may not be an Ivy League school in academics or win national championships everywhere in NCAA athletics, but it is a 'jack of all trades' when it comes to academics, athletics, art, and social activity."

Life

There is a "real spirit of volunteerism and giving back to the community [that] is one of BC's greatest strengths," many students here tell us, reporting that "there are about a million volunteer groups on campus, as well as a bunch of immersion trips to different places, the most renowned of which is the Appalachia group trip." Students here "really care about the world outside of Chestnut Hill. In a way, even the notion of studying abroad has turned into a question of 'How can I help people while there?' BC's Jesuit mission is contagious." Not all extracurricular life at BC is so altruistic, however; students here love to have fun in "the greatest location of any college ever! We are on the T [train], so we can get into the city of Boston whenever we like, but we are in suburbia, so we can relax without all of the gimmicks of city life." Undergrads love to explore Boston, a city with "tons of great museums, historical sights, restaurants, and a lot of great concerts," that also happens to be "such a big college town. It's easy to meet kids that go to BU, Harvard, Emerson, Northeastern, or any of the other universities in the area." Closer to campus, BC has "great sports. The ice hockey team is consistently ranked high nationally," and students turn out to support their Eagles in both men's and women's athletics.

Student Body

Boston Magazine once described the BC student body as "a J. Crew catalog with a slight hangover," and while students protest that "there are a number of students who do not conform to such a vision of the student body," they also admit that "there are a lot of preppy people at our school. Girls usually wear skirts and Uggs (unless it's freezing out, but it has to be very, very cold), and boys usually wear jeans and T-shirts or collared cotton shirts." And yes, "the typical BC student is white, Catholic, usually from the Northeast, [and] probably had family who went to BC," but with 9,000 undergrads, "We have students from all sorts of backgrounds, religions, sexual orientations." BC students tend to be extremely ambitious; they are "those super-involved people in high school who were three-season team captains, class presidents, and straight-A students. [They] have carried over that focus and determination into college."

Admissions

Very important factors considered include: Academic GPA, rigor of secondary school record, standardized test scores. *Important factors considered include:* Class rank, application essay, recommendation(s), alumni/ae relation, character/personal qualities, extracurricular activities, religious affiliation/commitment, talent/ability, volunteer work. *Other factors considered include:* First generation, racial/ethnic status, work experience. SAT and SAT Subject Tests or ACT required; ACT with Writing component required. TOEFL required of all international applicants. High school diploma is required, and GED is accepted. *Academic units recommended:* 4 English, 4 mathematics, 4 science, (4 science labs), 4 foreign language, 4 social studies.

Financial Aid

Students should submit: FAFSA, CSS/Financial Aid PROFILE, noncustodial PROFILE, business/farm supplement. The Princeton Review suggests that all financial aid forms be submitted as soon as possible after January 1. *Need-based scholarships/grants offered:* Federal Pell, SEOG, state scholarships/grants, private scholarships, the school's own gift aid. *Loan aid offered:* Federal Perkins, Federal Nursing, state loans. Applicants will be notified of awards on or about 4/1. Federal Work-Study Program available. Institutional employment available. Off-campus job opportunities are good.

The Inside Word

BC is one of many selective schools that eschew set admissions formulae. While a challenging high school curriculum and strong test scores are essential for any serious candidate, the college seeks students who are passionate and make connections between academic pursuits and extracurricular activities. The application process should reveal a distinct, mature voice and a student whose interest in education goes beyond the simple desire to earn an A.

THE SCHOOL SAYS "..."

From The Admissions Office

"Boston College students achieve at the highest levels with honors including two Rhodes scholarship winners, nine Fulbrights, and one each for Marshall, Goldwater, Madison, and Truman Postgraduate Fellowship Programs. Junior Year Abroad and Scholar of the College Program offer students flexibility within the curriculum. Facilities opened in the past 10 years include: the Merkert Chemistry Center, Higgins Hall (housing the Biology and Physics departments), three new residence halls, the Yawkey Athletics Center, the Vanderslice Commons Dining Hall, the Hillside Cafe, and a state-of-the-art library. Students enjoy the vibrant location in Chestnut Hill with easy access to the cultural and historical richness of Boston.

"Boston College requires freshman applicants to take the SAT with writing (or the ACT with the writing exam required). Two SAT Subject Tests are required; students are encouraged to take Subject Tests in fields in which they excel."

For even more information on this school, turn to page 468 of the "Stats" section.

BOSTON UNIVERSITY

121 BAY STATE ROAD, BOSTON, MA 02215 • ADMISSIONS: 617-353-2300 • FAX: 617-353-9695
FINANCIAL AID: 617-353-2965 • E-MAIL: ADMISSIONS@BU.EDU • WEBSITE: WWW.BU.EDU

RATINGS
Quality of Life: 83   **Academic:** 85   **Admissions:** 94   **Financial Aid:** 83

STUDENTS SAY "..."

Academics

Boston University shrugs off the dichotomy that generally separates public and private institutions, offering both the diversity and choice that only a large school can, while also offering the friendliness, security, and personal attention you'd expect from a pricey, private college. The key to BU's success is the varied yet close-knit academic departments: "Boston University is a huge institution full of opportunities to learn and experience the city, but it's also made up of small academic and extracurricular communities that offer students a home away from home." A junior adds, "BU has so many choices when it comes to majors and classes that I find myself struggling to pick just four classes a semester." In addition to coursework, "internship and study-abroad opportunities are easily accessible," and there are "dual-degree and MA/BA opportunities within our many colleges and schools." Despite their prestigious names and careers, "Professors at BU are here to teach, not to research. Students are their primary concern, and that shows through their work." Outside of class, professors "have office hours, but are more than happy to meet if that doesn't match with my schedule," one student shares. When it comes to the nuts and bolts of administering this stellar educational experience, students should be mindful that BU is "a large university with tons of offices" so it can be "difficult to quickly get an answer to a pressing question." At the same time, "The administration does not stay in their offices; they are readily accessible and easy to converse with." Of particular note, the "Dean of Students...is a great resource on campus and is actively working to participate in events with the students."

Life

Academics come first at Boston University, but social life is a close second. With an urban campus located "in the heart of Boston," students love heading off campus and "exploring places like Chinatown, Quincy Market, the North End, and Boston Common." If you want to mix and mingle with other undergraduates, there's no better atmosphere: "Whether it is on our campus or across the river at Harvard or across town at Northeastern, there is always some kind of social event to attend." On campus, dorms are comfortable, cafeteria food is good, and "there are 525 clubs and organizations that are constantly meeting." Of particular note, "There is a great community service center, which offers many different programs that cater to your schedule." While many students spend their free time in the city, campus activities at BU include such sundry offerings as "free concerts at our own mini club, BU Central, or the laser light show at the BU Beach." In addition, "the different culture clubs at BU will occasionally host themed dances...which are fun and a great opportunity to learn about the culture of your fellow peers." Sports enthusiasts on campus are plentiful—especially when it comes to BU's champion ice hockey team—and "students with the sports pass, which is normally included in tuition...can even pick up hockey tickets for free and just enjoy the game."

Student Body

Set in one of the world's best college towns, you'll meet kids "from all over America and all over the globe" at Boston University. At the same time, BU draws "a lot of people from the Northeast coast, and especially from the Boston area," who already know and love the city. Size and diversity make the social experience inclusive and accepting: "There are no real stigmas or cliques on campus because everyone is so diverse." No matter how unique your interests, you're sure to find like minds: "There are an amazing amount of clubs that meet every night of the week—including quidditch, astronomy, camping, religious/ethnic clubs, and many, many more." In fact, many students tell us, "We have such a large student body that there really is someone for everyone here." At the same time, academics are priority number one for most students. A current student explains, "BU is so diverse, but one thing that so many people have in common is a drive to succeed. Grades are competitive and students are driven to succeed, not only in school but also in internships."

THE PRINCETON REVIEW SAYS

Admissions

Very important factors considered include: Rigor of secondary school record. *Important factors considered include:* Class rank, application essay, academic GPA, recommendation(s), standardized test scores. *Other factors considered include:* Alumni/ae relation, character/personal qualities, extracurricular activities, first generation, geographical residence, level of applicant's interest, racial/ethnic status, state residency, volunteer work, work experience. SAT and SAT Subject Tests or ACT required; ACT with Writing component required. TOEFL required of all international applicants. High school diploma is required, and GED is accepted. *Academic units required:* 4 English, 3 mathematics, 3 science, (3 science labs), 2 foreign language, 3 social studies. *Academic units recommended:* 4 English, 4 mathematics, 4 science, (4 science labs), 4 foreign language, 4 social studies.

Financial Aid

Students should submit: FAFSA, CSS/Financial Aid PROFILE, noncustodial PROFILE. Regular filing deadline is 2/15. The Princeton Review suggests that all financial aid forms be submitted as soon as possible after January 1. *Need-based scholarships/grants offered:* Federal Pell, SEOG, state scholarships/grants, private scholarships, the school's own gift aid. *Loan aid offered:* Direct Subsidized Stafford, Direct Unsubsidized Stafford, Direct PLUS, Federal Perkins, state loans. Applicants will be notified of awards on a rolling basis beginning in late March. Federal Work-Study Program available. Institutional employment available. Off-campus job opportunities are excellent.

The Inside Word

At Boston University, your academic performance in high school is the single most important factor in an admissions decision. Competitive applicants are those who pursued the most challenging curriculum available at their school. Admissions requirements vary depending on the school or program to which you apply (though students are welcome to apply "undeclared"), so prospective students should check the school's website.

THE SCHOOL SAYS "..."

From The Admissions Office

"Boston University (BU) is a private teaching and research institution with a strong emphasis on undergraduate education. We are committed to providing the highest level of teaching excellence, and fulfillment of this pledge is our highest priority. Boston University has 10 undergraduate schools and colleges offering more than 250 major and minor areas of concentration. Students may choose from programs of study in areas as diverse as biochemistry, theater, physical therapy, elementary education, broadcast journalism, international relations, business, and computer engineering. BU has an international student body, with students from every state and more than 100 countries. In addition, opportunities to study abroad exist through more than 70 semester-long programs, spanning more than 26 countries on six continents.

"BU requires freshman applicants to take the SAT and two SAT Subject Tests. Students are encouraged to take subject tests in fields in which they excel. Students may submit the results of the ACT in lieu of the SAT and SAT Subject Tests."

For even more information on this school, turn to page 468 of the "Stats" section.

BOWDOIN COLLEGE

5000 COLLEGE STATION, BRUNSWICK, ME 04011-8441 • ADMISSIONS: 207-725-3100 • FAX: 207-725-3101
FINANCIAL AID: 207-725-3273 • E-MAIL: ADMISSIONS@BOWDOIN.EDU • WEBSITE: WWW.BOWDOIN.EDU

RATINGS
Quality of Life: 99   **Academic:** 98   **Admissions:** 98   **Financial Aid:** 99

STUDENTS SAY "..."

Academics

> **SURVEY SAYS . . .**
> *School is well run*
> *Great food on campus*
> *Dorms are like palaces*
> *Low cost of living*

Bowdoin students lavish praise on their prestigious small school, celebrating the "range and rigor" of the academic programs, the beautiful Maine setting, and the "vibrant group of faculty and students." They even love the cafeteria food! A classic liberal arts school, the academic curriculum at Bowdoin is "very challenging, discussion-oriented, and [it] demands creativity from the students." Despite the school's small size, you'll find a "varied and interesting course selection" within its more than 35 major and minor programs. In addition, students "have the ability to self-design classes and majors" and to participate in "some of the best undergraduate research opportunities liberal arts schools have to offer." According to their adoring students, Bowdoin professors are "extremely intelligent, well-spoken, and effective teachers," who are also "very enthusiastic about their work and welcome students to chat or ask questions one-on-one." At Bowdoin, "Professors put their students first and always make time to meet, whether to talk about a paper, or for coffee, or both." "Academics are highly rigorous," and major programs are typified by "challenging courses with professors who expect a high level of work." Fortunately, the "environment is very laid-back," and students are usually "competitive with themselves but not competitive with others." A current senior adds, "Academically, Bowdoin is very challenging, but I've loved having to put in my best effort to do well. It's good to be challenged!" Throughout the faculty and administration, "student opinions are highly valued and sought out." The school's popular president "invests a significant amount of time in us, the students," and "The first-year deans...make it a point to meet with each first-year student one-on-one, preferably in the first semester."

Life

College life is incredibly comfortable for Bowdoin undergraduates. On this pretty Maine campus, "freshmen dorms are very luxurious," and "facilities are great, including new athletic fields and [a] new fitness center." Cafeteria food gets rave reviews, and the dining services department is "excellent about listening to student opinions and promoting sustainability." A senior admits, "I will probably never eat this well again in my life." While there aren't any fraternities and sororities at Bowdoin, "There are social houses, where many sophomores, juniors, and (some) seniors live. These former Greek houses put on multiple events each week, from themed parties with several kegs, to coffee houses, movies, and discussions with professors." "Work hard, play hard" is a popular mantra on campus, and "There are always multiple parties going on Thursday, Friday, and Saturday nights." Alternately, "Getting outside and exploring Maine is very popular with our outdoorsy student body." In surrounding Brunswick, students enjoy "amazing restaurants and coffee shops on and around Maine Street." In addition, "Portland is 30 minutes away and is a great city with lots of resources." Echoing the sentiments of many happy Bowdoin students, a satisfied sophomore tells us, "I wish I could stay in college forever."

Student Body

You'll meet a lot of "wealthy, athletic, New Englanders" at Bowdoin College. In fact, students joke that, "Everyone seems to be from a small town right outside Boston." Those outside the dominant demographic admit that there seems to be "a divide between the typical New England kid and the 'diverse' kids, who come from other states are less well-off, or are racially diverse." However, "students here work really hard to create a community that is open and accepting," and the majority of students have "no trouble fitting in." On that note, "Bowdoin students truly are nice. We often marvel at how there do not seem to be mean or unfriendly people here." Student athletes are common, and "around 70 percent of the campus is involved in some kind of sport," from intramurals to the outing club. Nonetheless, academics are top priority: "No matter if they are a theater kid or hockey player, everyone can be found in the library during the week." In addition to schoolwork, Bowdoin students are "always passionate about something, be it music, rock-climbing, or volunteer work."

Admissions

Very important factors considered include: Class rank, application essay, academic GPA, recommendation(s), rigor of secondary school record, character/personal qualities, extracurricular activities, talent/ability. *Important factors considered include:* Standardized test scores, alumni/ae relation, first generation. *Other factors considered include:* Geographical residence, interview, racial/ethnic status, state residency. TOEFL required of all international applicants. High school diploma is required, and GED is not accepted. *Academic units recommended:* 4 English, 4 mathematics, 4 science, (3 science labs), 4 foreign language, 4 social studies.

Financial Aid

Students should submit: FAFSA, CSS/Financial Aid PROFILE, noncustodial PROFILE, business/farm supplement. Regular filing deadline is 2/15. The Princeton Review suggests that all financial aid forms be submitted as soon as possible after January 1. *Need-based scholarships/grants offered:* Federal Pell, SEOG, state scholarships/grants, private scholarships, the school's own gift aid. *Loan aid offered:* Federal Perkins, state loans Applicants will be notified of awards on or about 4/5. Federal Work-Study Program available. Institutional employment available. Off-campus job opportunities are good.

The Inside Word

Many students feel instantly at home on the Bowdoin campus. A current freshman reports, "Bowdoin was a great fit for me on paper, and I fell in love with the campus and student body when I visited." A senior agrees, "I had visited over 20 colleges, and they all start to look the same academically, but Bowdoin stood out because of the people." During the admissions process, prospective students can schedule a tour and personal interview with admissions staff or a Bowdoin senior. If it's a fit, the school offers the option to apply early decision.

THE SCHOOL SAYS "..."

From The Admissions Office

"A Bowdoin education is best summed up by 'The Offer of The College':"

> To be at home in all lands and all ages;
> To count Nature a familiar acquaintance,
> And Art an intimate friend;
> To gain a standard for the appreciation of others' work
> And the criticism of your own;
> To carry the keys of the world's library in your pocket,
> And feel its resources behind you in whatever task you undertake;
> To make hosts of friends...
> Who are to be leaders in all walks of life;
> To lose yourself in generous enthusiasms
> And cooperate with others for common ends—
> This is the offer of the college for the best four years of your life."

Adapted from the original 'Offer of the College'
by William DeWitt Hyde
President of Bowdoin College 1885–1917"

For even more information on this school, turn to page 469 of the "Stats" section.

BRANDEIS UNIVERSITY

415 SOUTH STREET, MS003, WALTHAM, MA 02454 • ADMISSIONS: 781-736-3500 • FAX: 781-736-3536
FINANCIAL AID: 781-736-3700 • E-MAIL: SENDINFO@BRANDEIS.EDU • WEBSITE: WWW.BRANDEIS.EDU

RATINGS
Quality of Life: 80   **Academic:** 90   **Admissions:** 97   **Financial Aid:** 77

STUDENTS SAY "..."

Academics

"Strong academics and an activist spirit" imbue Brandeis University, where "quirk and politically and socially aware students actually [go] to classes they really have a desire to attend," because they care "about learning both inside and outside the classroom, about other people, and about the world around us." No touchy-feely granola institution, Brandeis is "a top research university" as well as "a strong liberal arts school," and its students are serious about the

SURVEY SAYS ...
No one cheats
Students are friendly
Campus feels safe
Musical organizations are popular
Student publications are popular
Political activism is popular

future: "If you're thinking about business, law, or medical school, you'll fit right in with the pack" here. Brandeis' independent undergrads love that the "curriculum is flexible and allows you to do what you want." One explains: "The core curriculum is only composed of eight categories, which makes it easy for students to jump into classes of their interest, rather than get tied up in general or required courses. Not to mention that those eight requirements are incredibly flexible: I took Intro to 3D Animation last semester for my science requirement!" Brandeis' impressive academics "encourage [students] to think outside of the box and try new things," an approach that jibes with the "overall intellectual" environment created by students and faculty. Because "Brandeis is primarily an undergraduate institution," students don't feel that they need to compete with grad students for their professors' attention. "The fact that I can have such close contact on a daily basis with such incredibly talented individuals is something that occasionally astounds me," one undergrad writes.

Life

"There is definitely a strong campus life" at Brandeis, where "there is always something going on." Campus activity "is diverse. One Saturday you might go to a party and then the next day you might play a board game with your friends until three in the morning; or a concert one night and an art history lecture the next night." As one student puts it, "There are people who go out and party hard all week, [and] there are people who stay in on weekend nights to do work. The truth is Brandeis is a place where just about anyone can find someone like them." Students place a premium on creativity; fortunately, "there is always something creative to do." Undergrads "ice skate, dance, sing in an a cappella group, perform in a play, play a club or intramural sport, work on campus, have an internship off campus," or simply hang out in the campus coffeehouse located in "a replica of a Scottish castle." The Brandeis Shuttle allows students to "go into Boston on the weekends...the average student makes it to Boston once or twice a month" in order to "see a movie, have a meal, go to a museum or Quincy Market, [and] go to bars or clubs (only if you're over 21...Boston is strict)." Hometown Waltham isn't half bad either; we're told that "the food is great and there's a movie theater, bars, and Lizzy's Ice Cream" nearby.

Student Body

"There is no 'typical student' except that generally people are driven and creative," Brandeis undergrads tell us. Most here "are passionate about something and have many interests, though those interests are varied." Students tend to be "involved in a variety of activities" that include "community service or a peace group of some sort." Most are "probably double-majoring;" are "into dance, singing, or a musical band of some sort;" and have "frequent contact with leaders, administrators, and faculty." They're also likely to be "quirky...the reason they come to Brandeis is because they're drawn to these qualities....What other university would host a silent dance in their Campus Center where everyone's listening to their own iPod?" As one student sums up, "The typical student is studious, liberal, and passionate. Also Jewish. But not EVERYONE is Jewish. There are atypical students, but the great thing about Brandeis is that we don't care if you're different. If you're a good person who has something interesting to offer, [someone] will be your friend."

THE PRINCETON REVIEW SAYS

Admissions

Very important factors considered include: Class rank, academic GPA, rigor of secondary school record, standardized test scores, character/personal qualities. *Important factors considered include:* Application essay, recommendation(s), extracurricular activities, level of applicant's interest, talent/ability, volunteer work, work experience. *Other factors considered include:* Alumni/ae relation, first generation, geographical residence, interview, racial/ethnic status. SAT or ACT required; ACT with Writing component required. TOEFL required of all international applicants. High school diploma is required, and GED is accepted. *Academic units recommended:* 4 English, 4 mathematics, 4 science, (2 science labs), 4 foreign language, 4 social studies.

Financial Aid

Students should submit: FAFSA, CSS/Financial Aid PROFILE, noncustodial PROFILE, business/farm supplement. The Princeton Review suggests that all financial aid forms be submitted as soon as possible after January 1. *Need-based scholarships/grants offered:* Federal Pell, SEOG, state scholarships/grants, private scholarships, the school's own gift aid. *Loan aid offered:* Direct Subsidized Stafford, Direct Unsubsidized Stafford, Direct PLUS, Federal Perkins, state loans, college/university loans from institutional funds. Federal Work-Study Program available. Institutional employment available. Off-campus job opportunities are fair.

The Inside Word

Brandeis used to be considered the "safety school" for kids who hoped to gain admission to at least one of the Ivies. That was back when Brandeis was accepting three-quarters of its applicants, but those days are long gone. Admissions standards have risen at all top schools, and Brandeis is no exception: If you expect to get in here, you've got your work cut out for you. Your application should give evidence of both the ability and enthusiasm to handle demanding academics. A clear demonstration of writing ability will also help a lot.

THE SCHOOL SAYS "…"

From The Admissions Office

"Education at Brandeis is personal, combining the intimacy of a small liberal arts college and the intellectual power of a large research university. Classes are small and are taught by professors, 98 percent of whom hold the highest degree in their fields. They give students personal attention in state-of-the-art resources, giving them the tools to succeed in a variety of postgraduate endeavors.

"This vibrant, freethinking, intellectual university was founded in 1948. Brandeis University reflects the values of the first Jewish Supreme Court Justice Louis Brandeis, which are passion for learning, commitment to social justice, respect for creativity and diversity, and concern for the world.

"Brandeis has an ideal location on the commuter rail nine miles west of Boston; state-of-the-art sports facilities; and internships that complement interests in law, medicine, government, finance, business, and the arts. Brandeis offers generous university scholarships and need-based financial aid that can be renewed for four years.

"Brandeis requires that students send official scores for the SAT or ACT with Writing. Students for whom English is not their first language should take the TOEFL (Test of English as a Foreign Language)."

For even more information on this school, turn to page 469 of the "Stats" section.

BROWN UNIVERSITY

PO Box 1876, 45 Prospect Street, Providence, RI 02912 • Admissions: 401-863-2378 • Fax: 401-863-9300
Financial Aid: 401-863-2721 • E-mail: admission_undergraduate@brown.edu • Website: www.brown.edu

RATINGS
Quality of Life: 97   Academic: 95   Admissions: 99   Financial Aid: 95

STUDENTS SAY "..."

Academics

Known for its somewhat unconventional (but still highly regarded) approaches to life and learning, Brown University remains the slightly odd man out of the Ivy League, and the school wouldn't have it any other way. The school's willingness to employ and support different, untested methods such as the shopping period, the first two weeks of the semester where anyone can drop into any class in order to "find out if it's something they're interested in enrolling in," or the *Critical Review*, a student publication that produces reviews of courses based on evaluations from students who have completed the course, is designed to treat students "like an adult" through "freedom and choice." This open-minded environment allows them "to practice passion without shame or fear of judgment," the hallmark of a Brown education. Even if students do find themselves exploring the wrong off-the-beaten path, "there are multitudes of built-in support measures to help you succeed despite any odds." Even grades are a non-issue here, "except amongst paranoid premeds."

Professors are mostly hits with a few misses, but there are "amazing professors in every department, and they're not hard to find;" it's just "up to students to find the teaching styles that work for them." "Academics at Brown are what you make of them," and even though students are diligent in their academic pursuits and feel assured they're "getting a wonderful education with the professors," most agree that their education is "really more about the unique student body and learning through active participation in other activities." The administration gets cautiously decent reviews for their accessibility and general running of the school, but it also gets scolded for getting "distracted by the long term." The president, however, is absolutely loved by students for being "an incredible person with a great vision for the school."

Life

Thinking—yes, thinking—and discussing take up a great deal of time at Brown. "People think about life, politics, society at large, global affairs, the state of the economy, developing countries, animals, plants, rocket science, math, poker, each other, sex, sexuality, the human experience, gender studies, what to do with our lives, etc.," says a senior anthropology major. "Most people here don't go home that often," and like any school, "there are people who go out five nights a week and people who go out five nights a semester." "Alcohol and weed are pretty embedded in campus life," and most parties are dorm room events, even though partying "never gets in the way of academics or friendship. If you don't drink/smoke, that's totally cool." There's also plenty of cultural activities, such as indie bands, student performances, jazz, swing dancing, and speakers. Themed housing (art house, tech house, interfaith house) and co-ops are also popular social mediators.

Student Body

It's a pretty unique crowd here, where "athletes, preps, nerds, and everyone in between come together" because they "love learning for the sake of learning, and [they] love Brown equally as much." "The 'mainstream' is full of people who are atypical in sense of fashion, taste in music, and academic interests," says a junior. Unsurprisingly, everyone here's "very smart," as well as "very quirky and often funny," and "a great amount are brilliant and passionate about their interests;" "most have interesting stories to tell." People here are "curious and open about many things," which is perhaps why sexual diversity is a "strong theme" among Brown interactions and events. The overall culture "is pretty laid-back and casual," and "most of the students are friendly and mesh well with everyone."

THE PRINCETON REVIEW SAYS

Admissions

Very important factors considered include: Rigor of secondary school record, character/personal qualities, level of applicant's interest, talent/ability. *Important factors considered include:* Class rank, application essay, academic GPA, recommendation(s), standardized test scores, extracurricular activities. *Other factors considered include:* Alumni/ae relation, first generation, geographical residence, interview, racial/ethnic status, state residency, volunteer work, work experience. SAT and SAT Subject Tests or ACT required; ACT with Writing component required. TOEFL required of all international applicants. High school diploma is required, and GED is not accepted. *Academic units required:* 4 English, 3 mathematics, 3 science, (2 science labs), 3 foreign language, 2 history, 1 academic electives. *Academic units recommended:* 4 English, 4 mathematics, 4 science, (3 science labs), 4 foreign language, 2 history, 1 visual/performing arts, 1 academic electives.

Financial Aid

Students should submit: FAFSA, CSS/Financial Aid PROFILE, noncustodial PROFILE. Regular filing deadline is 2/1. The Princeton Review suggests that all financial aid forms be submitted as soon as possible after January 1. *Need-based scholarships/grants offered:* Federal Pell, SEOG, state scholarships/grants, private scholarships, the school's own gift aid. *Loan aid offered:* Direct Subsidized Stafford, Direct Unsubsidized Stafford, Direct PLUS, Federal Perkins, college/university loans from institutional funds. Applicants will be notified of awards on or about 4/1. Federal Work-Study Program available. Institutional employment available. Off-campus job opportunities are excellent.

The Inside Word

The cream of just about every crop applies to Brown. Gaining admission requires more than just a superior academic profile from high school. Some candidates, such as the sons and daughters of Brown graduates (who are admitted at virtually double the usual acceptance rate), have a better chance for admission than most others. Minority students benefit from some courtship, particularly once admitted. Ivies like to share the wealth and distribute offers of admission across a wide range of constituencies. Candidates from states that are overrepresented in the applicant pool, such as New York, have to be particularly distinguished in order to have the best chance at admission. So do those who attend high schools with many seniors applying to Brown, as it is rare for several students from any one school to be offered admission.

THE SCHOOL SAYS "..."

From The Admissions Office

"Founded in 1764, Brown is a private, coeducational, Ivy League university in which the intellectual development of undergraduate students is fostered by a dedicated faculty on a traditional New England campus.

"Applicants will be required to submit results of the SAT Reasoning Test and any two SAT Subject Tests (except for the SAT Subject Test Writing). Students may substitute any SAT tests with the ACT with the Writing component."

For even more information on this school, turn to page 470 of the "Stats" section.

BRYANT UNIVERSITY

1150 DOUGLAS PIKE, SMITHFIELD, RI 02917 • ADMISSIONS: 401-232-6100 • FAX: 401-232-6741
FINANCIAL AID: 401-232-6020 • E-MAIL: ADMISSIONS@BRYANT.EDU • WEBSITE: WWW.BRYANT.EDU

RATINGS
Quality of Life: 80   Academic: 76   Admissions: 88   Financial Aid: 80

STUDENTS SAY "..."

Academics

There are liberal arts programs at Bryant University, but business is the top draw here. A wealth of programs in accounting, finance, marketing, and management has earned Bryant a reputation far and wide as "a business-driven institution that blends the academic and the real world." The placement rate for internships and meaningful jobs after graduation is "very high," thanks to a loyal alumni base and an "excellent" career center that offers a ton of personalized services. "During interview season, I had interviews every day, which led to second interviews, which led to multiple job offers," boasts an accounting major. Students also rave about their cutting-edge campus technology. Academically, we hear students complain about "too many PowerPoint presentations" and "an excessive amount of group work," but "classes are always small" and professors are "always available." Many professors are "obsessed with their jobs" and "pride themselves on seeing their students succeed." They are "good at teaching but even better at providing real working knowledge and examples." Others, however, could definitely improve "when it comes to the fundamentals of teaching and being able to effectively communicate the subject matter." The part-time faculty is especially "hit-or-miss." Despite some complaints about registration and limited course offerings, Bryant's "very friendly" and "approachable" administration generally ensures that things "flow smoothly." Red tape is rare.

> SURVEY SAYS ...
> Great computer facilities
> Great library
> Athletic facilities are great
> Career services are great
> Campus feels safe
> Lots of beer drinking
> Hard liquor is popular

Life

"Life at Bryant is the typical college experience." Most undergrads choose to live on this clean, "beautiful," and modern campus "all four years," and there's "a great sense of community." The "intense" academic workload means that weekdays can be "stressful." Nevertheless, students at Bryant are "very involved" in "massive amounts of extracurriculars." "The athletic facilities are great," and many students participate in both intramurals and varsity sports. Students are in charge of most of the activities on campus, and they put on a lot of events. The "fun social scene" typically begins on Thursday. "Parties are generally all on campus," and "most people get really drunk on the weekends." An assortment of harder stimulants is also popular. "If you want to do drugs, you will be able to find them," suggests one student. "At the same time, if you want nothing to do with drugs, you will never see them." The surrounding town of Smithfield "has nothing to do," but "a short drive into Providence" leads to "great food, bars, clubs, and shopping." For more serious urban life, students can always head up to Boston as well.

Student Body

"Students at Bryant are very similar, with similar goals and objectives in mind." There's kind of a "common mold" here of "health-conscious" suburbanites "from the Northeast" who have "aspirations to make good sums of money after entering the job market." "The administrators and teachers are pretty much the most liberal people on campus," explains a senior. "We are a relatively conservative school." During the week, these "competitive" (occasionally "cutthroat") "business leaders of tomorrow" are "hardworking and diligent." Preppy attire dominates, and "clothes often seem to be a big deal." "It is not unusual to see students in suits," but only "when they have presentations or interviews, not just for the hell of it." On the weekends, students tend to be "typical party kids." "There definitely are students who deviate" from the norm, but there aren't many and they "don't fit in as well." Some students contend that this place is "diverse economically." Others tell us that "the typical student is white, middle -to upper-middle-class." Ethnic diversity is "rather low," and minority students "tend to stick together." International students do, too. In fact, the whole campus is "very cliquey." With more than 56% of students involved in more than 80 clubs and organizations on campus, there is something for everyone at Bryant. It's important to be involved, as some students note, "If you're not involved in a sport, or Greek life, or another group, then your social life will be limited to your small group of friends."

THE PRINCETON REVIEW SAYS

Admissions

Very important factors considered include: Academic GPA, rigor of secondary school record. *Important factors considered include:* Class rank, application essay, recommendation(s), standardized test scores. *Other factors considered include:* Alumni/ae relation, character/personal qualities, extracurricular activities, first generation, geographical residence, interview, level of applicant's interest, racial/ethnic status, state residency, talent/ability, volunteer work, work experience. SAT or ACT required; TOEFL required of all international applicants. High school diploma is required, and GED is accepted. *Academic units required:* 4 English, 4 mathematics, 2 science, (2 science labs), 2 foreign language, 2 history. *Academic units recommended:* 4 English, 4 mathematics, 3 science, (2 science labs), 3 foreign language, 3 history.

Financial Aid

Students should submit: FAFSA. Regular filing deadline is 2/15. The Princeton Review suggests that all financial aid forms be submitted as soon as possible after January 1. *Need-based scholarships/grants offered:* Federal Pell, SEOG, state scholarships/grants, private scholarships, the school's own gift aid. *Loan aid offered:* Direct Subsidized Stafford, Direct Unsubsidized Stafford, Federal Perkins, privately funded education loans. Applicants will be notified of awards on or about 3/24. Federal Work-Study Program available. Institutional employment available. Off-campus job opportunities are fair.

The Inside Word

If you're a solid student you should meet little trouble getting into Bryant. The university's admissions effort has brought in qualified applicants from across the country, but the heaviest draw remains from New England. Students attending Bryant will receive a strong education that integrates business and the arts and sciences. You will benefit from the precious connections in the corporate world offered through Bryant's career services.

THE SCHOOL SAYS "..."

From The Admissions Office

"Bryant is a four-year, private university in New England where students build knowledge, develop character, and achieve success—as they define it. In addition to a first-class faculty, state-of-the-art facilities, and advanced technology, Bryant offers stimulating classroom dynamics; internship opportunities at more than 350 companies; 70-plus student clubs and organizations; varsity, intramural, and club sports for men and women; and many opportunities for community service and leadership development. Bryant is the choice for individuals seeking the best integration of business and liberal arts, utilizing state-of-the-art technology. Bryant offers degrees in actuarial mathematics, applied mathematics and statistics, applied economics, applied psychology, business administration, communication, global studies, history, information technology, international business, literary and cultural studies, politics and law, and sociology.

"A cross-disciplinary academic approach teaches students the skills they need to successfully compete in a complex, global environment. Students can pursue one of 27 minors in business and liberal arts, and 80 areas of study. Bryant's rigorous academic standards have been recognized and accredited by NEASC and AACSB International. Bryant's international business program is a member of CUIBE, the Consortium for Undergraduate International Business Education. Technology is a fundamental component of the learning process at Bryant. Every entering freshman is provided with a Thinkpad® laptop for personal use. Students exchange their laptop for a new one in their junior year, which they will own upon graduation.

"Bryant University is situated on a beautiful 420-acre campus in Smithfield, Rhode Island. The campus is only 15 minutes away from the state capital, Providence; 45 minutes from Boston; and 3 hours from New York City. Bryant requires that enrolling students take the SAT or the ACT (Writing section not required)."

For even more information on this school, turn to page 470 of the "Stats" section.

BRYN MAWR COLLEGE

101 NORTH MERION AVENUE, BRYN MAWR, PA 19010-2899 • ADMISSIONS: 610-526-5152
FAX: 610-526-7471 • FINANCIAL AID: 610-526-5245 • E-MAIL: ADMISSIONS@BRYNMAWR.EDU • WEBSITE: WWW.BRYNMAWR.EDU

RATINGS

Quality of Life: 97   Academic: 97   Admissions: 95   Financial Aid: 94

STUDENTS SAY "..."

Academics

Bryn Mawr College is "a community of women scholars" that offers "an amazing, intense, multifaceted," and "pretty tough" academic experience. Coursework "can be stressful, especially around midterms and final times, but in the end it's worth it." The faculty is mostly stellar. "One of the main things I love about Bryn Mawr is the personal relationships formed over the years with the professors," boasts a chem-

istry major. "Anywhere you go to school you will have some bad teachers and some boring classes, and Bryn Mawr is no exception," relates a junior, "but overall I have been extremely impressed with and challenged by the classes I have taken at my college." The highly popular administration is "here for the students' success." "Bryn Mawr is an extremely autonomous place where students are given a lot of freedom to do as they please." "If you need something and you go to the right people, you can pretty much make it happen." Additionally, students can take courses at nearby Haverford, Swarthmore, and Penn. And upon graduation, Mawrters can take advantage of a loyal network of alumnae who "are doing amazing things and have a really strong connection to the school."

Life

Bryn Mawr's "absolutely beautiful" campus is "ensconced in collegiate Gothic arches." The dorms are gorgeous, and the food is "delicious." It's all a little slice of heaven—except for the "bleak" athletic facilities. Neat traditions at Bryn Mawr include Hell Week, which allows first-year students to bond with everyone else, and May Day, an entire day of catered picnics, live music, and hanging out on the greens, which always involves a Maypole dance, a Robin Hood play, and a late-night screening of *The Philadelphia Story* (starring BMC alum Katherine Hepburn). "These traditions are unique, intimate experiences that bring the whole school together and make you feel proud to be a Mawrter," explains a junior. When students aren't basking in the warm glow of ritual, they "love to study, study, study," but other activities are plentiful. "There is always something to do on campus, whether it's a student theater production, an a cappella concert, an improv group show, movies being shown, outside groups coming to perform, speakers coming to campus, you name it," says a senior. Sports and dance are big extracurricular activi-ties, too. Mawrters drink "more than you'd think for an allegedly quiet, nerdy women's college," but "Bryn Mawr's party scene is more of an intimate-friends-over-to-your-room type of deal." Trips to Swarthmore, Villanova, or Haverford provide "plenty of chances to interact with the opposite sex, if that's what you're after." "There are tons of great restaurants, music venues, galleries, and shopping all within minutes of campus," as well, and nearby Philadelphia offers more urban recreation.

Student Body

Many students say that diversity "is one of the things that makes Bryn Mawr stand out." Others say that students looking for diversity "may not find it here." Whatever the case, "Bryn Mawr is a bunch of brilliant women." They are "nerdy, ambitious, driven, talented" people who "can occasionally be over-competitive" and are "swamped with work yet thriving on it." "We all came into Bryn Mawr with a background in leadership, and all intend to leave Bryn Mawr as future leaders in our respective fields," asserts a junior. It's definitely a left-leaning crowd. "A lot of students at Bryn Mawr are adamant about being politically correct to the point that it begins to become annoying." "Contrary to popular belief, Bryn Mawr isn't a haven for lesbians," though "homosexuality is com-mon and visible." Socially, there is a variety of types of people at the school—from awkward, socially uncomfort-able people to very outgoing, social butterflies" to "mud-splattered" rugby players. "Some of us fly that freak flag high and proud," declares a senior. However, "there are plenty of average girls who look at *Cosmo*," too.

THE PRINCETON REVIEW SAYS

Admissions

Very important factors considered include: recommendation(s), rigor of secondary school record. *Important factors considered include:* application essay, academic GPA, character/personal qualities, extracurricular activities. *Other factors considered include:* class rank, standardized test scores, alumni/ae relation, first generation, geographical residence, interview, racial/ethnic status, talent/ability, volunteer work, work experience. Bryn Mawr offers a unique "Test Flexible" policy. SAT and SAT Subject Tests or ACT or a combination of SAT Subject Tests and AP Exam Scores required; TOEFL required of all international applicants. High school diploma is required, and GED is accepted. *Academic units required:* 2 academic electives. *Academic units recommended:* 4 English, 3 mathematics, 2 science, (1 science labs), 3 foreign language, 2 social studies, 2 history.

Financial Aid

Students should submit: FAFSA, CSS/Financial Aid PROFILE, business/farm supplement, statement of earnings from parents' employer. Regular filing deadline is 3/1. The Princeton Review suggests that all financial aid forms be submitted as soon as possible after January 1. *Need-based scholarships/grants offered:* Federal Pell, SEOG, state scholarships/grants, the school's own gift aid, Federal Academic Competitiveness Grant (ACG), Federal National Science and Mathematics to Retain Talent Grant (SMART). *Loan aid offered:* Federal Perkins. Applicants will be notified of awards on or about 3/23.

The Inside Word

Bryn Mawr's student body is among the academically best in the nation. Outstanding preparation for graduate study draws an applicant pool that is well prepared and intellectually curious.

THE SCHOOL SAYS "..."

From The Admissions Office

"Bryn Mawr's extraordinary academics, vibrant and diverse community, and focus on global leadership prepare students to challenge convention and take their places in the world. Every year 1,300 women from around the world gather on the College's historic campus to study with leading scholars, conduct advanced research, and expand the boundaries of what is possible. A Bryn Mawr woman is defined by a rare combination of personal characteristics: an intense intellectual commitment; a purposeful vision of her life; and a desire to make a meaningful contribution to the world. Consistently producing outstanding scholars, Bryn Mawr is ranked among the top ten of all colleges and universities in percentage of graduates who go on to earn a Ph.D., and is considered excellent preparation for the nation's top law, medical and business schools. More than 500 students collaborate with faculty on independent projects every year, and to augment an already strong curriculum, students may choose from more than 5,000 courses offered through nearby Haverford and Swarthmore colleges, as well as the University of Pennsylvania.

"Minutes outside of Philadelphia and only two hours by train from New York City and Washington, D.C., Bryn Mawr is recognized by many as one of the most stunning college campuses in the United States.

"Note: Bryn Mawr has initiated a "Test Flexible" admissions policy, which sets a new standard _or the use of AP exam scores at Bryn Mawr. See the website for full details: www.brynmawr.edu/admissions/test_policy.shtml."

For even more information on this school, turn to page 470 of the "Stats" section.

BUCKNELL UNIVERSITY

FREAS HALL, LEWISBURG, PA 17837 • ADMISSIONS: 570-577-1101 • FAX: 570-577-3538
FINANCIAL AID: 570-577-1331 • E-MAIL: ADMISSIONS@BUCKNELL.EDU • WEBSITE: WWW.BUCKNELL.EDU

RATINGS
Quality of Life: 81   **Academic:** 92   **Admissions:** 96   **Financial Aid:** 94

STUDENTS SAY ". . ."

Academics

> **SURVEY SAYS . . .**
> *Athletic facilities are great*
> *Low cost of living*
> *Frats and sororities dominate social scene*

Bucknell University delivers the quintessential East Coast college experience, with a balanced combination of "great academics, a liberal arts education, beautiful campus, sterling reputation, and a great social scene." At this prestigious small school, instruction is top notch because "teachers are all interested in their subject matter and are always willing to let class discussion take its course." If you need extra help or just some words of advice, "professors are incredibly available. They will always drop whatever they are doing to take as much time as is needed to help a student." In fact, "you get so close to some teachers that you baby-sit their kids or have meals with them." Bucknell offers a challenging yet non-competitive environment, where "students are always willing to help a classmate who is struggling, which is a rare characteristic on today's elite campuses." Additionally, Bucknell's excellent facilities and ample co-curricular opportunities—including a "fantastic" overseas program—complement the undergraduate experience. A senior adds, "I've had the opportunity to do research, and this is one of the best experiences I've had at Bucknell." The school runs well, and there is "very little red tape" holding up administrative functions—a rarity in the world of higher education. Bucknell staff members are "always willing to help you," and the administration is generally student-oriented.

Life

An idyllic place to work and live, the Bucknell campus is "gorgeous," and when the weather is nice, "people are always playing football on the quad or reading textbooks on benches with their Ray-Bans on." Whether you like cinema, chess, or soccer, "there are over 130 clubs and organizations, so there is something for everyone." In addition, "Fitness in general is very popular here," and "many students will go to the gym in their free time." While student interests may vary, there is one uniting factor: "Greek life is really big on campus," and the party scene is hopping. A current student elaborates, "Weekends are when the books are tossed on the shelf and every student on campus...hightails it to various fraternity parties." That said, students acknowledge that Greek life isn't for everyone. One student reassures us that while "Greek life is definitely a visible part of the social life at Bucknell," it's "not the only option," and "it's not necessary to go Greek in order to have a social life here." Whether affiliated or not, students may choose to "attend university-sponsored movie showings or go to the theater downtown, watch a movie with friends in our hall lounge, go to the 7th Street Cafe for a smoothie, or go to other university-sponsored events, like concerts." In downtown Lewisburg, students enjoy "all types of little shops and restaurants, as well as one of the only original art deco movie theaters left in the country." If you want to take a break from the "bubble," "Bucknell also provides plenty of opportunities to get off campus with trips to NYC, D.C., local hockey games, skiing areas, and other events."

Student Body

While there are exceptions to any rule, Bucknell students are predominantly "white, upper-middle class, and from the Northeast." Attracting many likeminded recruits, Bucknellians are "rich but never flashy, classic preppy, intellectual, driven, friendly, social, and very active." Bucknell undergraduates also claim to be a particularly attractive set. Says one, "Our school seems to defy nature with the number of beautiful people on campus." On the whole, most Bucknell undergraduates "find a good balance between school and social life, and they are often dedicated to extracurriculars." Greek life is huge, and many undergraduates "party as hard as they study." However, academics are always first priority, and "a student who skips class on a regular basis is very rare." On this small Pennsylvania campus, "there really isn't a lot of diversity," and a student jokes, "It looks like we go to school at a country club." Still, "the school works hard to bring minority students and international students here through various scholarship programs."

THE PRINCETON REVIEW SAYS

Admissions

Very important factors considered include: Class rank, application essay, academic GPA, rigor of secondary school record, standardized test scores, character/personal qualities, talent/ability. *Important factors considered include:* Recommendation(s), extracurricular activities, level of applicant's interest, volunteer work, work experience. *Other factors considered include:* Alumni/ae relation, first generation, geographical residence, racial/ethnic status, religious affiliation/commitment. SAT or ACT required; ACT with Writing component required. TOEFL required of all international applicants. High school diploma is required, and GED is accepted. *Academic units required:* 4 English, 3 mathematics, 2 science, 2 foreign language, 2 social studies, 2 history, 1 academic electives. *Academic units recommended:* 4 English, 4 mathematics, 3 science, 4 foreign language, 2 social studies, 2 history, 1 academic electives.

Financial Aid

Students should submit: FAFSA, CSS/Financial Aid PROFILE, noncustodial PROFILE. Regular filing deadline is 1/1. *Need-based scholarships/grants offered:* Federal Pell, SEOG, state scholarships/grants, private scholarships, the school's own gift aid, Federal ACG Grant, Federal SMART. *Loan aid offered:* Federal Perkins. Applicants will be notified of awards on or about 4/1. Federal Work-Study Program available. Institutional employment available. Off-campus job opportunities are poor.

The Inside Word

Admission to Bucknell is competitive, and admissions officers will cast a keen eye on the quality of your application, including your performance in a hopefully rigorous secondary school curriculum, as well as your SAT or ACT test scores. The university is interested in assessing both your aptitude for college-level study in general and your ability to contribute to the Bucknell experience, in particular. It's wise to learn a bit about Bucknell before applying: Bucknell's supplement to the Common Application asks you to explain why the school is a good fit for you.

THE SCHOOL SAYS "..."

From The Admissions Office

"Bucknell combines the personal experience of a small liberal arts college with the breadth and opportunity typically found at larger research universities. With a low student/faculty ratio, students gain exceptional hands-on experience, working closely with faculty in an environment enhanced by first-class academic, residential, and athletic facilities. Together, the College of Arts and Sciences and the College of Engineering offer 56 majors and 65 minors. Learning opportunities permeate campus life in and out of the classroom and across the disciplines. For example, engineering students participate in music ensembles, theater productions, and poetry readings, while arts and sciences students take engineering courses, conduct scientific research in the field, and produce distinctive creative works. Students also pursue their interests in more than 150 organizations and through athletic competition in the prestigious Division I Patriot League. These activities constitute a comprehensive approach to learning that teaches students how to think critically and develop their leadership skills so that they are prepared to make a difference locally, nationally, and globally."

For even more information on this school, turn to page 471 of the "Stats" section.

CALIFORNIA UNIVERSITY OF PENNSYLVANIA

250 UNIVERSITY AVENUE, CALIFORNIA, PA 15419 • ADMISSIONS: 724-938-4404 • FAX: 724-938-4564
FINANCIAL AID: 724-938-4415 • E-MAIL: INQUIRY@CUP.EDU • WEBSITE: WWW.CUP.EDU

RATINGS
Quality of Life: 71   Academic: 67   Admissions: 73   Financial Aid: 75

STUDENTS SAY ". . ."
Academics

California University of Pennsylvania is an "affordable," medium-sized public school in the western part of the Keystone State that "gets students ready to have careers." Among the "variety of majors," students praise the art and nursing programs. The "top-notch" College of Education also has "an excellent reputation." Many classrooms are

> **SURVEY SAYS . . .**
> *Great computer facilities*
> *Students are friendly*
> *Dorms are like palaces*
> *Everyone loves the Vulcans*

"state of the art." "Smaller" class sizes are "really good for interaction." "Questions don't go unanswered," "and the professors actually can remember your name." The mostly "dedicated and helpful" faculty here is generally popular as well. "Some are horrible," particularly in the general education courses. Overall, the professors "are pretty decent," though. "They really seem to care about your success," comments a physics major. The administration at Cal U is "very involved" and typically "reliable." "They seem to be doing an okay job," estimates an education major, "except for the parking situation." "Frustration during registration" can also be a problem.

Life

Everybody loves the swanky, "massive," and otherwise "awesome" "suite-style" residence halls at Cal U. The fact that each suite has its own bathroom is another "huge plus." "The dorm rooms are the best I've ever seen," gloats a junior. In addition to the sweet accommodations, students at Cal U enjoy a "very beautiful campus" "nestled near the Monongahela River." There are "many new buildings and facilities." The landscaping is "just phenomenal," and everything is "within walking distance." Students differ concerning the social atmosphere. The majority loves it, citing "tons and tons of clubs" and a reasonably noticeable Greek system. "A lot of people party and what not," they point out. "Intramurals are popular," and the intercollegiate teams (called the Vulcans, incidentally) tend to have "amazing success," "dominating in Division II sports." Other students contend that the campus has "no spirit," though, and they complain that "you have to make your own fun" at Cal. "There is not much to do on campus or off," one senior says. "Most people usually go home during the weekends." There is universal agreement that the "small town" surrounding campus is "very boring." "If you like a rural setting or a place where you can feel safe and not worry about loud noises, lots of people, and that sort of thing," advises a sophomore, "then you'd definitely enjoy yourself here." Students who long for a more urban milieu can always head to Pittsburgh, less than an hour away.

Student Body

Virtually everyone at Cal U is from Pennsylvania. They tend to come from "middle- to low-income" families. Many are "paying for school themselves" and "holding down one or more jobs while attending." There is a large contingent of commuters and nontraditional students who "kind of just go to school and go home or to work." "Many older and middle-aged individuals come here to either start as undergrads or to further their educations." Cal students describe themselves as "responsible," "very friendly," and "pretty accepting." There are some "over-the-top achievers," but "students here typically have average to above-average intelligence." There is "a plethora of athletes." "Preppy" is probably the overwhelming stereotype, but you'll find "the occasional rebel" and a smattering of various styles. "Everyone fits in somewhere," promises a junior.

THE PRINCETON REVIEW SAYS

Admissions

Very important factors considered include: Class rank, rigor of secondary school record, standardized test scores. *Other factors considered include:* application essay, recommendation(s), extracurricular activities, interview, talent/ability, work experience. SAT or ACT required; TOEFL required of all international applicants. High school diploma is required and GED is accepted. *Academic units required:* 4 English, 3 mathematics, 1 science, (1 science labs), 2 social studies, 2 history, 6 academic electives, 1 arts and humanities. *Academic units recommended:* 4 English, 3 mathematics, 1 science, (1 science labs), 2 foreign language, 2 social studies, 2 history, 6 academic electives, 1 arts and humanities.

Financial Aid

Students should submit: FAFSA. The Princeton Review suggests that all financial aid forms be submitted as soon as possible after January 1. *Need-based scholarships/grants offered:* Federal Pell, SEOG, state scholarships/grants, private scholarships, the school's own gift aid. *Loan aid offered:* Federal Perkins Applicants will be notified of awards on a rolling basis beginning 4/1. Federal Work-Study Program available. Institutional employment available. Off-campus job opportunities are good.

The Inside Word

It's not difficult to get admitted to Cal U, and decisions are made very much by the numbers. If you have standardized test scores at or slightly below average and decent high school grades, you shouldn't have a problem.

THE SCHOOL SAYS "..."

From The Admissions Office

"California University, a proud member of the Pennsylvania State System of Higher Education, has a mission to build character and careers. Character education is a part of every classroom, lived in every residence hall and on every playing field. Career building is an ongoing, four-year process. Students participate in hands-on learning and research, and gain invaluable real-world experience through co-ops and internships. Cal U's unique Career Advantage Program provides a checklist for career success beginning with the freshman year and continuing through graduation.

"Each bachelor's degree requires a minimum of 120 semester hours of credit including a general education requirement of 51 credits. An honors program provides an opportunity for an enhanced educational experience to students who meet the criteria.

"All classes are taught by teaching faculty members. The student/faculty ratio is 20:1. Doctorates are held by more than 74 percent of the full-time faculty.

"Cal U is recognized as a leader in providing premiere student living options. Two locations, the lower and the upper campus, provide students with the Suite Life, a whole new experience in university living."

For even more information on this school, turn to page 472 of the "Stats" section.

CARNEGIE MELLON UNIVERSITY

5000 FORBES AVENUE, PITTSBURGH, PA 15213 • ADMISSIONS: 412-268-2082 • FAX: 412-268-7838
FINANCIAL AID: 412-268-2068 • E-MAIL: UNDERGRADUATE-ADMISSIONS@ANDREW.CMU.EDU • WEBSITE: WWW.CMU.EDU

RATINGS
Quality of Life: 70   Academic: 99   Admissions: 97   Financial Aid: 78

STUDENTS SAY "..."

Academics

CMU is an academic powerhouse that "pushes [students] to a much greater level of understanding." Undergrads are quick to reason that this is due to "outstanding faculty who are extremely passionate about their fields of study." Of course, this passion "transfers to rigorous and interesting courses." Indeed, "one definitely develops an excellent work ethic by attending this institution." A bio and psych double-major concurs stating, "Every student works hard: It is unavoidable." Fortunately, he goes on to say, "I have never had any trouble accessing any of my professors. They are quick to answer e-mails and are more than willing to meet with you outside of class and office hours." The university "offers a huge variety of top-ranked programs, such as the business school, the engineering school, the computer science school, and the music and drama departments." Naturally this "makes it easy to take a variety of classes but still get a quality education." And as one student puts it, "At the end of the day knowledge is oozing from my pores. I love it!" One senior did reveal that signing up for class can be a hassle because "the registration system is pretty much from the '80s." However, he did assure us that the administration is aware of the issues and "working on it." Overall, students are fairly happy with the "accessible" administration. One happy sophomore shares that those on the faculty "listen to students' requests and move to make changes on campus accordingly." And a computer science major sums up by stating, "The administration is helpful when you need it and never too intrusive."

Life

Though undergrads at Carnegie Mellon are "very focused on their education and their [future] careers" many students are still able to strike "a balance." Indeed, one senior assures us that he and his peers "know how to have fun too." Students in need of a study break can find distraction in a myriad of campus events. The residential staff (residential assistants and faculty advisors) often host activities like "movie nights, stressball crafting, and snowball fights." Additionally, undergrads can participate in anything from "intramural sports teams, to building racing vehicles [and] designing computer games." Performances from the many "a capella and drama groups" are also well attended. Though one junior admits that "we're not big partiers comparatively," plenty of students "do go to frat parties on the weekend." And many undergrads revel in CMU traditions, such as carnival when "classes are cancelled for two days, and week-long parties occur." Impressively, "public transportation is free for Carnegie Mellon students" making Pittsburgh highly accessible. The city offers a number "of museums to visit," and "the Waterfront, where there's great shopping, a movie theater, and various restaurants are only a bus ride away." Finally, those who are 21 can take advantage of "the vast number of bars, lounges, and clubs in the area."

Student Body

Carnegie Mellon seems to attract "focused, intelligent" students who are "ambitious, goal-oriented" and "maybe a little too smart for [their] own good." In short, the university is "a utopia for nerds." And while this might mean you'll encounter a few "socially awkward" peers, one sophomore assures us that it's "a very comfortable, friendly environment." Though a number of undergrads proclaim that there's "no typical student," there are "two common types—the artsy student and the total computer geek." Don't be misled however, these kids can't easily be pigeonholed. "Some are engineers, some are actors, some are scientists, and some are writers." "Everyone is unique and interesting." Indeed, quick to praise their "quirky" and "well-rounded" fellow students, many undergrads here greatly appreciate the fact that people "are passionate about a variety of subjects." Impressively, "Students are not only ethnically and religiously diverse, but every person here has some unique or interesting characteristic." Moreover, "everyone is really accepting of students that are different than them." And as a content chemical engineering major shares, "everyone finds their place."

THE PRINCETON REVIEW SAYS

Admissions

Very important factors considered include: Class rank, academic GPA, rigor of secondary school record, standardized test scores. *Important factors considered include:* Application essay, recommendation(s), alumni/ae relation, character/personal qualities, extracurricular activities, first generation, interview, level of applicant's interest, racial/ethnic status, talent/ability, volunteer work, work experience. SAT Subject Tests required; SAT or ACT required; ACT with Writing component required. TOEFL required of all international applicants. High school diploma is required, and GED is accepted. *Academic units required:* 4 English, 4 mathematics, 3 science, (3 science labs), 2 foreign language, 3 academic electives. *Academic units recommended:* 4 English, 4 mathematics, 3 science, (3 science labs), 2 foreign language, 4 academic electives.

Financial Aid

Students should submit: FAFSA, institution's own financial aid form, parent and student federal tax returns, parent W-2 forms. Regular filing deadline is 5/1. The Princeton Review suggests that all financial aid forms be submitted as soon as possible after January 1. *Need-based scholarships/grants offered:* Federal Pell, SEOG, state scholarships/grants, private scholarships, the school's own gift aid. *Loan aid offered:* Federal Perkins. Applicants will be notified of awards on or about 3/15. Federal Work-Study Program available. Institutional employment available. Off-campus job opportunities are good.

The Inside Word

Don't be misled by Carnegie Mellon's acceptance rate. Although relatively high for a university of this caliber, the applicant pool is fairly self-selecting. If you haven't loaded up on demanding courses in high school, you are not likely to be a serious contender. The admissions office explicitly states that it doesn't use formulas when making decisions. That said, a record of strong academic performance in the area of your intended major is key.

THE SCHOOL SAYS "..."

From The Admissions Office

"If you're looking for an intellectual environment that blends academic and artistic richness with classroom innovation, explore Carnegie Mellon. Consistently ranked as a top-25 institution, Carnegie Mellon is world-renowned for its unique approach to education and research. Left-brain and right-brain thinking unite within our collaborative culture, and is the foundation of learning at Carnegie Mellon."

"As a student, you will acquire a depth and breadth of knowledge while sharpening your problem-solving, critical thinking, creative and quantitative skills. You will develop sound critical judgment, resourcefulness and professional ethics through a collaborative and hands-on education. As a graduate, you will be one of the innovative leaders and problem-solvers of tomorrow."

"While a Carnegie Mellon education is marked by a strong focus on fundamental and versatile problem-solving skills in a particular discipline, your talents and interests don't remain confined to one area. The university respects academic diversity and provides opportunities for you to explore more than one field of study. Carnegie Mellon consists of seven colleges (six undergraduate): Carnegie Institute of Technology (engineering), College of Fine Arts, College of Humanities and Social Sciences (combining liberal arts education with professional specializations), Tepper School of Business, Mellon College of Science, the School of Computer Science, and the Heinz College. Here, music, molecular science, acting, analysis, opera and organic chemistry weave in and out of the lives and minds of Carnegie Mellon students on a daily basis."

"The university's 150-acre main campus is located in the Oakland area of Pittsburgh, five miles from downtown."

For even more information on this school, turn to page 472 of the "Stats" section.

THE CATHOLIC UNIVERSITY OF AMERICA

CARDINAL STATION, WASHINGTON, DC 20064 • ADMISSIONS: 202-319-5305 • FAX: 202-319-6533
FINANCIAL AID: 202-319-5307 • E-MAIL: CUA-ADMISSIONS@CUA.EDU • WEBSITE: WWW.CUA.EDU

RATINGS
Quality of Life: 70   Academic: 73   Admissions: 84   Financial Aid: 83

STUDENTS SAY "..."

Academics

At The Catholic University of America, strong academic programs are infused with "the values and traditions of conservative Catholicism, including service to the community, family, and Catholic morality." For students seeking a spiritual atmosphere, CUA is a "great learning environment where your faith can grow exponentially." However,

"Contrary to popular belief, students do not attend this school based on its religious affiliation." Instead, the "intimate class sizes," generous scholarship packages, and fantastic location lure many top students to this small school. At CUA, academic opportunities (such as overseas studies) are plentiful, and courses are tough but manageable. A current student shares, "I am challenged, and will leave college feeling empowered with the skills needed to succeed in whatever career path I choose." No matter what your major, there are "required religion courses" woven into the curriculum. Students tell us, "The emphasis on classical philosophy for all majors really teaches students how to think in complex ways." While not every professor is unilaterally adored, most "are well-organized and truly knowledgeable about the subject...they teach." Instructors "really care about the individual, and you are definitely not just a number to them." Depending on your perspective, you might describe the school's administration as "an oppressive regime that allows no fun," or you might characterize them as a friendly group of student-oriented individuals who are "strict but fair." Either way, things tend to "run smoothly" on the CUA campus, despite the fact that there are some "communication issues" between administrative departments.

Life

Offering a range of clubs and activities, an active campus ministry, varied social events, and varsity sports, life at CUA is a "good mix of spirituality and fun." "There is a huge spirit [of] community service and giving back" at CUA, and many students are involved in volunteer work with Catholic charities. In fact, "CUA is located in a section of D.C. dubbed 'Little Vatican.' The large number of Catholic organizations in the immediate area provides ample opportunities for spiritual development and self-discovery." In addition to faith-based activities, the surrounding city is a great jumping off point for culture and recreation. In their spare time, students "go to concerts, museums, parks, [and] political rallies" in surrounding D.C., or they enjoy eating in some of the "amazing restaurants in the area." Given the propitious location, it is not surprising that "a lot of students are interested in politics and become active in political groups." Come the weekend, CUA is a "bit of a party school," and "most people go out to the bars at night on Thursdays, Fridays, and Saturdays for fun." More than 70 percent of CUA students live on campus, which they describe as a "quiet oasis located amidst a bustling metropolis."

Student Body

With its distinctive personality and cosmopolitan location in Washington, D.C., CUA tends to attract students from a similar background. On this small campus, undergraduates are predominately "white, upper-middle-class [and] Catholic," and almost "every student is either from New York, Massachusetts, or ROP (Right Outside Philly)." Most characterize the community as lacking diversity, telling us that, "Aside from drama and architecture students, the majority of the undergrads do not stick out." CUA has a "strong Catholic identity" and a good portion of students are "extremely religious." At the same time, "There are a decent number of non-Catholics at the school, as well as kids from other countries and cultures." With academics, as with religion, some students are more committed to their studies than others. A current student elaborates, "Half the students are very religious or academic, while the other half are less interested in academics and more interested in fun activities."

THE PRINCETON REVIEW SAYS

Admissions

Very important factors considered include: Academic GPA, recommendation(s), rigor of secondary school record, standardized test scores, character/personal qualities, level of applicant's interest, volunteer work. *Important factors considered include:* Application essay, extracurricular activities, first generation, interview, talent/ability. *Other factors considered include:* Class rank, alumni/ae relation, racial/ethnic status, work experience. SAT Subject Tests recommended; SAT or ACT required; ACT with Writing component required. TOEFL required of all international applicants. High school diploma is required, and GED is accepted. *Academic units recommended:* 4 English, 3 mathematics, 3 science, (1 science labs), 2 foreign language, 4 social studies, 1 fine arts or humanities.

Financial Aid

Students should submit: FAFSA, Alumni and Parish Scholarship Applications if appropriate. The scholarship deadlines are 11/15 for Early Action and 2/15 for Regular Decision. The Princeton Review suggests that all financial aid forms be submitted as soon as possible after January 1. *Need-based scholarships/grants offered:* Federal Pell, SEOG, state scholarships/grants, private scholarships, the school's own gift aid. *Loan aid offered:* Direct Subsidized Stafford, Direct Unsubsidized Stafford, Direct PLUS, Other. Applicants will be notified of awards on a rolling basis beginning 4/1. Federal Work-Study Program available. Institutional employment available. Off-campus job opportunities are good.

The Inside Word

The Catholic University of America offers a non-binding Early Action program, as well as regular admission. A student's academic record and test scores are important elements in an admissions decision, as is a history of service in his or her school or community. If it sounds like a fit, prospective students can get a feel for life at CUA during an "open house" day, when they are invited to attend mass, meet with the deans, take a tour, and eat lunch on campus.

THE SCHOOL SAYS "..."

From The Admissions Office

"The Catholic University of America's friendly atmosphere, rigorous academic programs, and emphasis on time-honored values attract students from all 50 states and more than 80 foreign countries. Its 193-acre, tree-lined campus is only 10 minutes from the Capitol building. Distinguished as the national university of the Catholic Church in the United States, CUA is the only institution of higher education established by the U.S. Catholic bishops; however, students from all religious traditions are welcome. "CUA offers undergraduate degrees in more than 80 major areas in eight schools of study. Students enroll into the School of Arts and Sciences, Architecture, Nursing, Engineering, Music, Philosophy or Professional Studies. Additionally, CUA students can concentrate in areas of preprofessional study including law, dentistry, medicine, or veterinary studies.

"With Capitol Hill, the Smithsonian Institution, NASA, the Kennedy Center, and the National Institutes of Health among the places students obtain internships, firsthand experience is a valuable piece of the experience that CUA offers.

Numerous students also take the opportunity in their junior year to study abroad at one of Catholic's 17 country program sites. Political science majors even have the opportunity to do a Parliamentary Internship in either England or Ireland. With the campus just minutes away from downtown via the Metrorail rapid transit system, students enjoy a residential campus in an exciting city of historical monuments, theaters, festivals, ethnic restaurants, and parks.

"Matriculating students should submit the SAT Subject Test: Foreign Language exam if they plan to continue studying that language at CUA."

For even more information on this school, turn to page 473 of the "Stats" section.

CENTRAL CONNECTICUT STATE UNIVERSITY

1615 STANLEY STREET, NEW BRITAIN, CT 06050 • ADMISSIONS: 800-832-3200 • FAX: 862-832-2295
E-MAIL: ADMISSIONS@CCSU.EDU • WEBSITE: WWW.CCSU.EDU

RATINGS
Quality of Life: 63   Academic: 63   Admissions: 71   Financial Aid: 68

STUDENTS SAY ". . ."

Academics

Central Connecticut State University is an "affordable," medium-sized school with a host of "good academic programs." The school of education is particularly notable. There are solid study abroad options. Opportunities for undergraduate research are ample, "especially in the sci-

ences." CCSU's campus is "beautifully landscaped" but "a few of the buildings need overhauling." The library in particular "could use an aesthetic lift." One student also suggests that "desks should be thrown into Long Island Sound." The faculty receives mixed reviews. "We have some great professors," says an education major. "There are also some that are not so great." "My professors are excellent," says a music education major. "They really know their subject." Other professors "have cool jobs" and bring real world experience to night classes. Some profs "are just here for the benefits," though. Foreign professors with thick accents in math, science, and tech classes also cause "misunderstanding and confusion." The small class sizes at CCSU "make it easier to have one-to-one communication" with professors. Many faculty members are "very accessible" and "may even allow you to make house calls if necessary." Others are "not that reachable." A few students laud the top brass. To others, the administration seems "distant" and "mostly disorganized." "Each department is very different," observes a sophomore.

Life

"The campus at CCSU is a nice size. It's not too big but not too small either." "The cafeteria food is disgusting," though. "I refuse to eat in the dining hall most days," says a junior. Socially, CCSU is "really a commuter school." "For fun, people either go to the student center to hang out or go out with friends to either other dorm rooms or apartments nearby," says a freshman. "There are movie nights on Wednesdays and activity nights every Thursday in the student center." Thursday is also the "big party night." After that, a whole lot of students head home for the weekend. If you stick around, "weekends are awful." "If you're thinking of coming here and are from out of state, I would reconsider unless you're pretty outgoing," cautions a junior. Students who stick around "tend to go off campus to do stuff." Without question, "having a car helps." Surrounding towns and the bright lights of nearby Hartford provide some decent options for weekend fun.

Student Body

"The typical student is a commuter." "Most students are middle-class Connecticut residents who are coming here because it's cheap and nearby," says a junior. There is "a wide range of minority students" on campus. "The diversity is great," enthuses a sophomore. "It's a very welcoming atmosphere." "Everyone fits in one way or another" but cliques are common. "Generally, the athletes hang out with the athletes; minorities hang out with minorities; etc." A lot of students have "many things aside from classes going on, like a job." CCSU is also something of a haven for nontraditional and older students. "It is very appropriate for working professionals."

Admissions

Very important factors considered include: Rigor of secondary school record. *Important factors considered include:* Class rank, academic GPA, standardized test scores. *Other factors considered include:* Application essay, recommendation(s), extracurricular activities, geographical residence, interview, racial/ethnic status, talent/ability, SAT required; TOEFL required of all international applicants. High school diploma is required and GED is accepted. *Academic units required:* 4 English, 3 mathematics, 2 science, (1 science labs), 2 social studies, 1 history. *Academic units recommended:* 3 foreign language.

Financial Aid

Students should submit: FAFSA, business/farm supplement. Regular filing deadline is 9/15. The Princeton Review suggests that all financial aid forms be submitted as soon as possible after January 1. *Need-based scholarships/grants offered:* Federal Pell, SEOG, state scholarships/grants, the school's own gift aid. *Loan aid offered:* Direct Subsidized Stafford, Direct Unsubsidized Stafford, Direct PLUS, Federal Perkins Applicants will be notified of awards on a rolling basis beginning 3/15. Federal Work-Study Program available. Institutional employment available. Off-campus job opportunities are good.

The Inside Word

The admissions process at CCSU is extraordinarily straightforward. If your SAT scores approach average and your high school grades in serious coursework aren't atrocious, you should be fine.

THE SCHOOL SAYS "…"

From The Admissions Office

"Selected as one of the 'Great Colleges for the Real World' and honored as a 'Leadership Institution' by the Association of American Colleges and Universities, CCSU stands as a national example of quality undergraduate education. Offering more than 100 majors in 82 fields of study in its four schools, CCSU also provides a wide array of special curricular opportunities to enrich learning.

"As exemplified in the university's slogan, 'Start with a dream. Finish with a future!' CCSU is committed to preparing students for success in whatever field they choose. The Offices of Career Services and Cooperative Education provide interesting career-related work experience plus opportunities to make connections with hundreds of participating employers. Nearly 70 percent of participating students are offered permanent, career-starting positions with their co-op employers upon graduation.

"CCSU's campus is attractive, with new and renovated buildings adding to the classic collegiate 'look' of its historical architecture. Academic buildings feature state-of-the-art, fully networked 'smart classrooms.' A newly renovated and expanded student center provides lounges, conference and game rooms, dining and information services, a bookstore, and a range of other support services. With 120 student clubs and organizations covering a broad spectrum of interests, there is a wealth of opportunities to meet new people, broaden horizons, and develop leadership skills. Athletics are a big part of campus life; and students enjoy a state-of-the-art fitness center with training rooms, a swimming pool, a track, and tennis and basketball courts. And CCSU's 18 Division I sports teams provide exciting opportunities to play or watch."

For even more information on this school, turn to page 473 of the "Stats" section.

CHATHAM UNIVERSITY

WOODLAND ROAD, PITTSBURGH, PA 15232 • ADMISSIONS: 412-365-1290 • FAX: 412-365-1609
E-MAIL: ADMISSIONS@CHATHAM.EDU • WEBSITE: WWW.CHATHAM.EDU

RATINGS
Quality of Life: 98   Academic: 79   Admissions: 77   Financial Aid: 82

STUDENTS SAY "..."

Academics

A small, all-women's college within a university of 2,200 students, Chatham University seeks to create "an empowering environment for women who strive to be leaders in today's world," and, according to most students, the school accomplishes its mission. With 600-plus undergraduates, the school is "so small it's really easy to get to know everyone. Not only do you feel personally connected to campus, but it opens a lot of doors. If there's something that you want to add, attend, dislike, etc., you feel very comfortable asking faculty, staff, students or administration to make changes!"

> **SURVEY SAYS . . .**
> Athletic facilities are great
> Different types of students interact
> Students get along with local community
> Students love Pittsburgh, PA
> Great off-campus food
> Dorms are like palaces
> Campus feels safe
> Frats and sororities are unpopular or nonexistent

These small class sizes also allow "tons of faculty-student interaction. I had a meltdown where I got really behind in classes and my profs found me, talked me through it and helped me make a plan for getting back on track. I didn't even ask for their help, they just cared enough to do that." The administration could definitely "use a little bit of an improvement" in terms of asking for and implementing student input, but are respected by students for the most part. That said, many students here appreciate that the Chatham experience culminates in a thesis project that "affords an excellent opportunity to truly develop ourselves in a more mature academic format."

Life

Chatham is located in Pittsburgh's Shadyside neighborhood, "a residential area where mansions and trees surround most of the campus." The campus offers "a break from the city" without being "completely secluded from the bulk of things" because "Chatham is just a block away from Walnut Street in Shadyside, where all the fun shopping and dining is," as well as "Squirrel Hill on the other side of campus, which is a great place to browse." Best of all, the college "is located near a lot of major universities" that provide "great things to get involved with off-campus with other area college students. If partying is what you're interested in, it's easy to find, but for those of us who don't party, we have our fun, too." Non-party options include "an abundance of organizations to get involved with and activities to partake in." As well as concerts, "hanging out at one another's apartments, going to gallery crawls, and going to on campus events or events at other nearby campuses." Many students also hold jobs off-campus.

Student Body

Chatham caters to women primarily from the Western Pennsylvania region, but within that distinction, there's plenty of room for diversity on all fronts, as "the student body really is kind of a potpourri." Chatham has "lots of foreign students who are on top of all of their work, and a good solid section of leftist, queer, or queer friendly students to keep things interesting;" indeed, there is a wide range of nationality and sexual orientation represented here, and the "open-minded" crowd is "loud and like to fight for equal rights." That diversity extends to students' interests: "Walking around campus you will find people who are really interested in art, but they are best friends with someone interested in politics and math. Everyone just fits in." Students here tend to be "politically, environmentally, and socially conscious" women who "care about gender, race, and sexual-orientation issues."

THE PRINCETON REVIEW SAYS

Admissions

Very important factors considered include: Rigor of secondary school record. *Important factors considered include:* Application essay, academic GPA. *Other factors considered include:* Class rank, recommendation(s), standardized test scores, alumni/ae relation, character/personal qualities, extracurricular activities, interview, level of applicant's interest, talent/ability, volunteer work, work experience. TOEFL required of all international applicants. High school diploma is required and GED is accepted. *Academic units required:* 4 English, 2 mathematics, 2 science, 3 Social Science. *Academic units recommended:* 4 English, 3 mathematics, 3 science, 2 foreign language, 3 social science.

Financial Aid

Students should submit: FAFSA. The Princeton Review suggests that all financial aid forms be submitted as soon as possible after January 1. *Need-based scholarships/grants offered:* Federal Pell, SEOG, state scholarships/grants, private scholarships, the school's own gift aid, United Negro College Fund *Loan aid offered:* Federal Perkins Applicants will be notified of awards on a rolling basis beginning 2/15. Federal Work-Study Program available. Institutional employment available. Off-campus job opportunities are good.

The Inside Word

Chatham's single-sex demographic turns off some potential undergraduates. As a result, Chatham presents women a unique opportunity for admittance to a fine liberal arts college. The location has its benefits as well. Cooperative learning programs provide access to nine colleges and universities in Pittsburgh, including UPitt and Carnegie Mellon.

THE SCHOOL SAYS "..."

From The Admissions Office

"Chatham University prepares students from around the world to develop solutions to some of the world's biggest challenges. Every Chatham student - women in Chatham's historic women's residential college, and men and women in Chatham's graduate programs-receives a highly individualized, experiential educational experience that is informed by Chatham's strong institutional commitment to globalism, the environment and citizen leadership. Founded in 1869, Chatham University includes the Shadyside Campus, with Chatham Eastside and the historic 39-acre Woodland Road arboretum; and the 388-acre Eden Hall Campus north of Pittsburgh.

"Knowing that building relationships is important for first-year students, Chatham created its First-Year Student Sequence. This distinctive program introduces students to the Chatham community and Pittsburgh's dynamic culture, both in and out of the classroom. Many Chatham students take advantage of opportunities for experiential learning, including internships, practica, service-learning and study abroad. With an increased focus on early internships, many students experience more than one before they graduate. Opportunities for study abroad are numerous, and vary from short term trips with faculty to summer, semester- and year-long experiences. Belize, Egypt, Spain, Costa Rica, Ireland, Russia, and the Netherlands are recent locations of student and faculty trips.

"All first-year students receive HP tablet computers which are integrated into course work and can access our wireless campus network. Chatham's undergraduate student/faculty ratio is 10:1, which ensures greater interaction between students and faculty.

"Undergraduate students may earn both their bachelor's and master's degrees from Chatham in as few as five years through the Accelerated Graduate Program, or through a partnership with Carnegie Mellon University's H. John Heinz III School of Public Policy."

For even more information on this school, turn to page 474 of the "Stats" section.

CHESTNUT HILL COLLEGE

9601 GERMANTOWN AVENUE, PHILADELPHIA, PA 19118-2693 • ADMISSIONS: 215-248-7001 • FAX: 215-248-7082
FINANCIAL AID: 215-248-7182 • E-MAIL: CHCAPPLY@CHC.EDU • WEBSITE: WWW.CHC.EDU

RATINGS
Quality of Life: 81   **Academic:** 79   **Admissions:** 72   **Financial Aid:** 73

STUDENTS SAY ". . ."

Academics

Based on the "principles of the Sisters of St. Joseph," who founded the school, the purpose of attending Chestnut Hill College is "receiving a 'holistic education.'" That is, students are expected to "to grow in knowledge and in spirituality" during their tenure here. To that end, students are exposed to a wide range of subjects through a core curriculum. Students have mixed feelings about these core classes.

> **SURVEY SAYS . . .**
> Students are friendly
> Students love Philadelphia, PA
> Great off-campus food
> Frats and sororities are unpopular or nonexistent
> Student government is popular

Whereas some students believe that the core classes really make them "well rounded individuals," others complain that that roundedness comes at a cost: "In core classes/general education courses, the teachers are less knowledgeable than other professors and are often first-year teachers and stumble on their own words." Still, overall, students feel "the full-time profs here are excellent." "They actually remember your name and genuinely care about you. To them you are their student and not just a name on the roster sheet." However, "Sometimes the adjuncts aren't too good." Concerning how hard they are expected to work, students feel that "It's not a competitive school, but the academics are challenging." As far as the administration goes, students don't offer very many kind words. Some say that "The registrar is sometimes not quite on the ball," and others "wish financial aid was run more efficiently." Other students offer more generalized critiques: The "administration is inept, unaccountable, and seem to be blind-folded half the time;" "They basically give you a run around."

Life

"Chestnut Hill College is located on the border of Philadelphia, so there is plenty to do when you step off campus." You can catch "either the Chestnut Hill west or east train into Center City. From there, you can get anywhere. You can also catch the R5 in Ambler (5 miles away) and go up towards Doylestown. You have this safe country, old time feel with the Chestnut Hill area, but you are minutes from anything you could ever want for entertainment." Within the Chestnut Hill area itself students go "down Germantown Ave. for fun. There are a lot of great shops and places to eat on the avenue." "There is also a mall and a movie theater nearby and many campus organizations hold events on campus." The social crossroads of campus is the piazza, where students are almost always hanging out "regardless of how cold it is, and joking around." Because of the school's strict alcohol policies, students also "go off campus to parties whether at a different college or someone's house." The general vibe amongst undergraduates is that there is a time for work and a time for play: "On weeknights, we have heavy workloads, but on Thursday to Sunday we have fun." Students' biggest complaint about living conditions at Chestnut Hill concerns the on-campus fare. Simply put, "the caf food is horrible."

Student Body

The typical student at Chestnut Hill is "between the ages of 18–23," "middle-class," and from the East Coast, most probably from "from the Tri-State area." He or she is "goal-oriented" and "focused," but also "very outgoing, friendly and willing to help just about anybody." This person is "involved in campus affairs" and "does a lot of volunteer work" but "could be of any ethnicity." Because of the small size of the school, "everyone knows everyone." In general, the school has a "laid back atmosphere; you can wear sweatpants and a hoodie and not worry" that you will be judged for your sartorial slovenliness. "There are a few atypical students but there does not seem to be any prejudice or discrimination towards them."

THE PRINCETON REVIEW SAYS

Admissions

Very important factors considered include: Application essay, rigor of secondary school record. *Important factors considered include:* Academic GPA, recommendation(s), standardized test scores, character/personal qualities, extracurricular activities, interview. *Other factors considered include:* Class rank, alumni/ae relation, level of applicant's interest, talent/ability, volunteer work, work experience. SAT or ACT required; TOEFL required of all international applicants. High school diploma is required and GED is accepted. *Academic units recommended:* 4 English, 3 mathematics, 3 science, 2 foreign language, 4 social studies.

Financial Aid

Students should submit: FAFSA. Regular filing deadline is 4/15. The Princeton Review suggests that all financial aid forms be submitted as soon as possible after January 1. *Need-based scholarships/grants offered:* Federal Pell, SEOG, state scholarships/grants, private scholarships, the school's own gift aid. *Loan aid offered:* Federal Perkins Applicants will be notified of awards on a rolling basis beginning 1/31. Federal Work-Study Program available. Off-campus job opportunities are good.

The Inside Word

Admissions officers rank high school transcript and personal essays as the most important factors in determining who gets into Chestnut Hill. Some extra sweat invested into those personal essays could help an applicant overcome less-than-impressive standardized test scores. A good interview can also help a lot here.

THE SCHOOL SAYS "..."

From The Admissions Office

"Chestnut Hill College provides students with an opportunity for the highest quality education needed to achieve personal and professional success. We offer 30 majors and 39 minors that can lead to countless career opportunities. Over 82 percent of our faculty possess the highest degree in their field. They are professors who share a love for learning and readily make themselves available outside of class. There are also opportunities to study abroad and create individualized majors.

"College is much more than declaring a major or cramming for finals. Joining others who share your passion is an ideal way to expand your horizons and build on your classroom education. At Chestnut Hill College there are over 25 organizations devoted to a variety of student interests—everything from the biology club to Amnesty International. There are also 14 NCAA Division II teams, with plans to expand the number of sports offered. If your sports pursuits are of an individual nature, you can go horseback riding, mountain biking in Fairmount Park, or Rollerblading from the Philadelphia suburbs to the art museum.

"At Chestnut Hill College, we pride ourselves on our philosophy of holistic education. We believe that a curriculum should go beyond the lecture hall, off the reading list, and out of the library. It should emphasize growth of the whole person not only through a liberal arts education but also through an exciting social life, a healthy spiritual life, and a well-rounded active life, therefore exposing students to the best college has to offer."

For even more information on this school, turn to page 474 of the "Stats" section.

CITY UNIVERSITY OF NEW YORK—BARUCH COLLEGE

UNDERGRADUATE ADMISSIONS, ONE BERNARD BARUCH WAY BOX H-0720, NEW YORK, NY 10010
ADMISSIONS: 646-312-1400 • FAX: 646-312-1361 • E-MAIL: ADMISSIONS@BARUCH.CUNY.EDU • WEBSITE: WWW.BARUCH.CUNY.EDU

RATINGS
Quality of Life: 73   Academic: 71   Admissions: 90   Financial Aid: 68

STUDENTS SAY ". . ."

Academics

Baruch College consists of three schools, and although its School of Arts and Sciences and School of Public Affairs are both fine, it's the Zicklin School of Business that garners nearly all the attention here (as well over three-quarters of the student body). Zicklin offers a "very demanding business-oriented program that provides a great education in an overcrowded environment" where "it's very easy to get lost," but just as easy for go-getters to access "unparalleled internships, career, and networking opportunities to major global companies' headquarters." Because New York City is a worldwide finance capital, Baruch's connections and internships provide "a gateway to the world of finance," and it is for this reason—as well as for the fact that "tuition is about one-fourth what it is at NYU," making it "the best college value in New York City"—that students flock to Baruch. Students warn that you must be willing to "put 110 percent into your studies and take advantage of the NYC network and Starr Career Development Center" to reap all available benefits here. Those who make the effort will discover a career office that "works tirelessly to prepare its students for the working world. Not only do they offer workshops on how to make yourself an attractive candidate, they also offer counseling and even resumé reviews to make sure your resume is perfect, as well as mock interviews that help you analyze your strengths and weaknesses as an interviewer."

> **SURVEY SAYS . . .**
> Great computer facilities
> Great library
> Diverse student types on campus
> Different types of students interact
> Students love New York, NY
> Student publications are popular
> Very little drug use

Life

Baruch has no campus, just a collection of six buildings scattered over four city blocks. Most of the action centers around the 17-story Newman Vertical Campus facility, which is "beautiful" but "does not offer a lot of things to do" between classes. Furthermore, the mostly residential area surrounding the school offers "few places you can hang out at, especially when you have huge breaks between classes." Although the building is fairly new, "the escalators almost never work," and the elevators "are always as packed as the commute on the train." Many here grumpily opt for the stairway. School-related extracurriculars are hampered by the lack of a "real campus" and by the fact that many students are commuters who work part time. Some get involved in community service and/or major-related clubs and organizations, but anyone coming here for a traditional college experience will be sorely disappointed. However access to New York City, for most, more than compensates for this drawback.

Student Body

The "hard-working" student body at Baruch could well be "the most diverse university in the country." It's the sort of place where "You can eat samosas on Tuesday, mooncakes on Wednesday, and falafel on Thursdays for free because of all the cultural events that are held." Students brag that "hundreds of countries are represented in our student body" and note that "The one common thread would be we are mostly business-oriented and have jobs/internships outside of school." While students get along well in class, outside the classroom they can be "very cliquey." One student explains, "If you know people from your high school, you stick with them; if you're a foreign student you stick with others from your home country. Otherwise you get the cold shoulder." Because "the school puts tremendous pressure on grades," most students are "extremely stressed."

THE PRINCETON REVIEW SAYS

Admissions

Very important factors considered include: Academic GPA, rigor of secondary school record, standardized test scores. *Important factors considered include:* Application essay, recommendation(s). *Other factors considered include:* Class rank, alumni/ae relation, character/personal qualities, extracurricular activities, interview, talent/ability, work experience. SAT or ACT required; TOEFL required of all international applicants. High school diploma is required, and GED is accepted. *Academic units required:* 4 English, 3 mathematics, 2 science, (2 science labs), 2 foreign language, 4 social studies. *Academic units recommended:* 4 mathematics, 2 foreign language, 1 academic electives.

Financial Aid

Students should submit: FAFSA, state aid form. Regular filing deadline is 4/30. The Princeton Review suggests that all financial aid forms be submitted as soon as possible after January 1. *Need-based scholarships/grants offered:* Federal Pell, SEOG, state scholarships/grants, the school's own gift aid, City merit scholarships. *Loan aid offered:* Direct Subsidized Stafford, Direct Unsubsidized Stafford, Direct PLUS, Federal Perkins. Applicants will be notified of awards on a rolling basis beginning 4/1. Federal Work-Study Program available. Institutional employment available. Off-campus job opportunities are excellent.

The Inside Word

Baruchs business school greatly upgrades the school's profile in its hallmark academic field. Admissions have grown steadily more competitive since, especially for students seeking undergraduate business degrees. Today, Baruch receives nearly 10 applications for every slot in its freshman class. Your math scores on standardized tests count more heavily here than verbal scores.

THE SCHOOL SAYS "..."

From The Admissions Office

"Baruch College is in the heart of New York City. As an undergraduate, you will join a vibrant learning community of students and scholars in the middle of an exhilarating city full of possibilities. Baruch is a place where theory meets practice. You can network with city leaders; secure business, cultural, and nonprofit internships; access the music, art, and business scene; and meet experts who visit our campus. You will take classes that bridge business, arts, science, and social policy, learning from professors who are among the best in their fields.

"Baruch offers 23 majors and 62 minors in three schools: the School of Public Affairs, the Weissman School of Arts and Science, and the Zicklin School of Business. Highly qualified undergraduates may apply to the Baruch College Honors program, which offers scholarships, small seminars and honors courses. Students may also study abroad through programs in more than 30 countries.

"Our seventeen-floor Newman Vertical Campus serves as the college's hub. Here you will find the atmosphere and resources of a traditional college campus, but in a lively urban setting. Our classrooms have state-of-the-art technology, and our library was named the top college library in the nation. Baruch also has a simulated trading floor for students who are interested in Wall Street. You can also enjoy a three-level athletics and recreation complex, which features a 25-meter indoor pool as well as a performing arts complex. The College just introduced a residence hall opportunity for undergraduates on Manhattan's vibrant Lower East Side in a newly built building at 101 Ludlow Street. The first residents will move in this August, before classes begin.

"Baruch's selective admission standards, strong academic programs, and top national honors make it an exceptional educational value."

For even more information on this school, turn to page 475 of the "Stats" section.

CITY UNIVERSITY OF NEW YORK—BROOKLYN COLLEGE

2900 BEDFORD AVENUE, BROOKLYN, NY 11210 • ADMISSIONS: 718-951-5001
FINANCIAL AID: 718-951-5051 • E-MAIL: ADMINGRY@BROOKLYN.CUNY.EDU • WEBSITE: WWW.BROOKLYN.CUNY.EDU

RATINGS

Quality of Life: 63   **Academic:** 63   **Admissions:** 88   **Financial Aid:** 95

STUDENTS SAY ". . ."

Academics

Brooklyn College "is the perfect representative of Brooklyn as a borough and [of] success in the community," an institution that, like its home borough, "educates its students in an environment that reflects diversity, opportunity (study abroad, research, athletics, employment), and support."

> **SURVEY SAYS . . .**
> *Great computer facilities*
> *Great library*
> *Diverse student types on campus*
> *Very little drug use*

"Lauded as one of the best senior colleges in CUNY" and boasting "a beautiful campus," Brooklyn College entices a lot of bright students looking for an affordable, quality, undergraduate experience as well as some attracted by the school's relatively charitable admissions standards. It's easier to get in here than to stay in; Brooklyn College is "an academically challenging and rigorous school" that "feels a lot more competitive than one would anticipate." Professors "are fabulous" and "really passionate about the subjects that they teach and their students' career paths," although there are some "grumpy and nasty professors" that might best be avoided. Students are especially sanguine about special programs here, such as the various honors programs, in which "you will meet tons of highly intelligent people. Honors classes boast very good in-class discussions and highly vibrant, enthusiastic students. Non-honors classes are more run-of-the-mill but still very good academically." The school also works hard to provide "constant and innumerable job opportunities available to students and the Magner Center, which helps students find jobs and internships, and [to] help them prepare for the real world through resume writing workshops [and] job interview workshops." There are also "many financial awards available."

Life

"Apart from all the clubs and athletics on campus, most people come for class and then leave" at Brooklyn College because "we are a commuter school with no dorms, so it has to be this way. All social activities happen off campus." There are "pretty nice places to hang out around campus for the occasional coffee," and "there are a lot of student organization and a lot of activities done to help enhance student life on campus," but the "immediate surroundings of the Brooklyn College campus are generally not where you would want to stay for hours," and "on weekends the campus usually is dead." That said, "The campus is quite beautiful, and the quad during spring time is usually a nice place to sit and relax." Furthermore, "New York City hotspots are a 20- to 40-minute [subway] ride away," and Brooklyn itself is "a great place to live" where "there are always fun things happening."

Student Body

"The typical student at Brooklyn College is hard-working, from the NY metro area, and a commuter" (the last because there are no residence halls here). Many "hold part-time jobs and pay at least part of their own tuition, so they are usually in a rush because they have a lot more responsibility on their shoulders than the average college student." Like Brooklyn itself, "The student body is very diversified," with everyone from "an aspiring opera singer to quirky film majors to single mothers looking for a better life for their children," and so "no student can be described as being typical. Everyone blends in as normal, and little segregation is noticed (if it exists)." Students here represent more than 100 nations and speak nearly as many languages. There are even students "that come from Long Island to North Carolina, from Connecticut to even Hong Kong."

THE PRINCETON REVIEW SAYS

Admissions

Very important factors considered include: Academic GPA, rigor of secondary school record, standardized test scores. SAT or ACT required; TOEFL required of all international applicants. High school diploma is required, and GED is accepted. *Academic units recommended:* 4 English, 3 mathematics, 3 science, 3 foreign language, 4 social studies, 4 academic electives.

Financial Aid

Students should submit: FAFSA, state aid form. The Princeton Review suggests that all financial aid forms be submitted as soon as possible after January 1. *Need-based scholarships/grants offered:* Federal Pell, SEOG, state scholarships/grants, private scholarships, the school's own gift aid. *Loan aid offered:* Direct Subsidized Stafford, Direct Unsubsidized Stafford, Direct PLUS, Federal Perkins. Applicants will be notified of awards on a rolling basis beginning 5/1. Federal Work-Study Program available. Institutional employment available. Off-campus job opportunities are excellent.

The Inside Word

Brooklyn College does not set the bar inordinately high; students with less-than-stellar high school records can receive a chance to prove themselves here. Once they get in, though, they'd better be prepared to work; Brooklyn College typically loses about 20 percent of its freshman class each year, and six-year graduation rates rarely exceed 50 percent. Getting into Brooklyn College is one thing; surviving its academic challenges is a whole other thing entirely.

THE SCHOOL SAYS "..."

From The Admissions Office

"Brooklyn College, a premier public liberal arts college founded in 1930. For the last five years it has been designated as one of "America's Best Value Colleges" by the Princeton Review and, in 2009, was cited as one of the top 50 Best-Value Public Colleges in the nation.

"Respected nationally for its rigorous academic standards, the college has increased both the size and academic quality of its student body. It takes pride in such innovative programs as its award-winning Freshman Year College; the Honors Academy, which houses six programs for high achievers; and the core curriculum. Its School of Education is ranked among the top twenty in the country. Brooklyn College's strong academic reputation has attracted an outstanding faculty of nationally renowned teachers and scholars. Among the awards they have won are Pulitzers, Guggenheims, Fulbrights, and National Institutes of Health grants.

"The student body consists of more than 16,000 undergraduate and graduate students who represent the ethnic and cultural diversity of the borough. The College's accessibility by subway or bus allows students to further enrich their educational experience through New York City's many cultural events and institutions. In recent years, student achievements have been acknowledged with Rhodes, Fulbright, and Truman Scholarships and an Emmy Award.

"The Brooklyn College campus, considered to be among the most beautiful in the nation, is in the midst of an ambitious program of expansion and renewal. The dazzling library is the most technologically advanced educational and research facility in the CUNY system and we are building a student residence hall off-campus and expects to open for the fall 2010 semester. The West Quad Building, a state-of-the-art student services and physical education facility, opened in fall 2009. Ground will be broken soon for a new performing arts center, followed in the coming years with a new science complex."

For even more information on this school, turn to page 475 of the "Stats" section.

CITY UNIVERSITY OF NEW YORK—HUNTER COLLEGE

695 PARK AVENUE, NEW YORK, NY 10021 • ADMISSIONS: 212-772-4000 • FAX: 212-650-3336
FINANCIAL AID: 212-772-4820 • E-MAIL: ADMISSIONS@HUNTER.CUNY.EDU • WEBSITE: WWW.HUNTER.CUNY.EDU

RATINGS
Quality of Life: 66   **Academic:** 68   **Admissions:** 85   **Financial Aid:** 78

STUDENTS SAY "..."

Academics

New Yorkers seeking "a superb learning environment for the independent and self-motivated" should check out Hunter College, a school that offers "a great education at an affordable price." A "serious academic environment" where "learning is taken very seriously" and "most people know exactly what they want and are going for it with full determination" create "an amazing energy" at Hunter, an energy that feeds off the diverse New York student body.

> **SURVEY SAYS . . .**
> Diverse student types on campus
> Different types of students interact
> Students get along with local community
> Students love New York, NY
> Political activism is popular
> Very little drug use

"Hunter is all about bringing people from all different parts of the world together in one place to learn from one another and to be exposed to almost every subject imaginable to help one find their true calling in life," one student reports. The New York location also gives Hunter access to many top academics; many professors here "teach at other, more expensive, universities. Throughout my Hunter career, I have had professors who also teach at NYU, Hofstra, Cooper Union, and Yale! So it really is quite the bargain." "Crowded" classes mean students need to "take matters in their own hands" if they "want to succeed and graduate in four years," but those who seek connections tell us that "despite the heavy loads they take on, professors are always available for individual attention, and they help you through anything you ask." Tight budget constraints leave students wishing they "had more resources in terms of books, facilities, and more technology in the classrooms, but that has less to do with the school than it does with state funding." Accounting, education, media production, and psychology all earn high marks at Hunter.

Life

Hunter College "is mostly a commuter school," and as a result "students interact mostly on campus in between classes." "Making friends can be difficult, but definitely not impossible," one student explains. The school "encourages student interaction through student government-run parties and other student-run activities," and undergraduates "have our favorite spots on campus where we know we'll always run into someone. Usually we will go out for coffee or food before, in between, or after classes." The school facility is compact with no outdoor campus to speak of, but there are still "a lot of places for students to hang out: outside, on the bridges, in the cafeteria. We make the most of the space we have." Undergraduates typically "do their own thing and don't really judge or think about others," which makes for a copacetic campus but also means "it is difficult to have a real college experience." Most students don't mind because "off campus is New York City, so there is always tons to be done," including "going out to eat, walking around Manhattan, shopping," and taking in "the best nightlife in the world."

Student Body

Hunter College is "extremely diverse in almost every sense of the word." Ethnic, religious, gender preference, and political diversity are all in evidence. "Our population is as diverse as New York," one student aptly observes. Undergraduates are even diverse in age; as one undergraduate observes, "The average age for a Hunter student is, I believe, 25. That alone opens up the spectrum of atypical students." What they share in common is that so many have "something to contribute, an experience that can be shared somewhere where others can learn from it. Everyone exchanges their experiences, allowing Hunter students to be some of the most open-minded, understanding people I believe New York City, and even the rest of the country, has to offer." Students tend to be "very liberal and outspoken." Women outnumber men by a two-to-one margin.

THE PRINCETON REVIEW SAYS

Admissions

Very important factors considered include: Application essay, academic GPA, rigor of secondary school record, standardized test scores. SAT or ACT required; TOEFL required of all international applicants. High school diploma is required, and GED is accepted. *Academic units required:* 2 English, 2 mathematics, 1 science, (1 science labs). *Academic units recommended:* 4 English, 3 mathematics, 2 science, 2 foreign language, 4 social studies, 1 visual/performing arts, 1 academic electives.

Financial Aid

Students should submit: FAFSA, state aid form. The Princeton Review suggests that all financial aid forms be submitted as soon as possible after January 1. *Need-based scholarships/grants offered:* Federal Pell, state scholarships/grants, the school's own gift aid. *Loan aid offered:* Direct Subsidized Stafford, Direct Unsubsidized Stafford, Direct PLUS, Federal Perkins, state loans, college/university loans from institutional funds, CUNY Student Assistance Program(CUSTA), Aide for Part-Time-Study (APTS), SEEK. Applicants will be notified of awards on a rolling basis beginning 5/15. Federal Work-Study Program available. Institutional employment available. Off-campus job opportunities are fair.

The Inside Word

Hunter admissions officers are inundated with more than 30,000 applications each year. There's no way the admissions office can get through all those applications without applying some cutoffs and formulas; although these aren't made public, a look at the stats for the most recent incoming class will give you some idea of what grades and test scores you'll need to be admitted here. Rolling admissions mean early application is pretty much a must here; programs fill up fast as a result of Hunter's solid reputation and bargain-basement tuition. Applications to the Macaulay Honors College must be submitted by December 15.

THE SCHOOL SAYS "..."

From The Admissions Office

"Located in the heart of Manhattan, Hunter offers students the stimulating learning environment and career-building opportunities you might expect from a college that's been a part of the world's most exciting city since 1870. The largest college in the City University of New York, Hunter pulses with energy. Hunter's vitality stems from a large, highly diverse faculty and student body. Its schools—Arts and Sciences, Education, the Health Professions, and Social Work—provide an affordable first-rate education. Undergraduates have extraordinary opportunities to conduct high-level research under renowned faculty, and many opt for credit-bearing internships in such exciting fields as media, the arts, and government. The college's high standards and special programs ensure a challenging education. The Block Program for first-year students keeps classmates together as they pursue courses in the liberal arts, pre-health science, pre-nursing, premed, or honors. A range of honors programs is available for students with strong academic records, including the highly competitive tuition-free Hunter CUNY Honors College for entering freshmen and the Thomas Hunter Honors Program, which emphasizes small classes with personalized mentoring by outstanding faculty. Qualified students also benefit from Hunter's participation in minority science research and training programs, the prestigious Andrew W. Mellon Minority Undergraduate Program, and many other passports to professional success.

"Applicants for the entering class are required to take either the SAT or the ACT."

For even more information on this school, turn to page 475 of the "Stats" section.

CITY UNIVERSITY OF NEW YORK—QUEENS COLLEGE

65-30 KISSENA BOULEVARD, FLUSHING, NY 11367 • ADMISSIONS: 718-997-5000 • FAX: 718-997-5617
FINANCIAL AID: 718-997-5101 • E-MAIL: ADMISSIONS@QC.EDU • WEBSITE: WWW.QC.EDU

RATINGS
Quality of Life: 79   Academic: 72   Admissions: 60   Financial Aid: 70

STUDENTS SAY "..."

Academics

"A great education at an affordable price" could easily be the mantra of Queens College. A stalwart of New York City's university system, Queens offers "an amazingly diverse campus" and a "warm, welcoming" atmosphere. Largely a "commuter" school, undergrads here can choose from "a wide variety of classes," although, as one psych

major warns, "they can close out quickly." Despite the fact that "the workload can be quite heavy at times," undergrads speak glowingly of their "understanding" professors who constantly "push you to reach your full potential." They are "extremely intelligent and personable," and they are always "willing to meet with students outside of the classroom to discuss anything and everything." One ecstatic senior goes as far as saying, "I feel like I am around close relatives." However, other students do fret over "the high turnover" among faculty and worry that this can "make it difficult to form meaningful academic connections." Praise also extends to administrators who "always make an effort to connect with students and are always very open and willing to talk." Indeed, even though there's "a lot of bureaucracy," undergrads still find them to be "very down-to-earth" and "approachable." As a media studies major expounds, "Students and administrators host town hall meetings numerous times throughout the semester in order to exchange ideas on how to make the campus a better place."

Life

Some undergrads at Queens College lament that, because of the commuter culture, "There isn't much interaction between the students on campus." They simply "go to class and then go home." However, one content freshman insists, "There are so many activities to attend and clubs to join. You just need to get involved." Indeed, the college offers everything from "literary magazines, newspapers, and radio [to] student government." There are also plenty of opportunities for the altruistically inclined. As a media studies major shares, "I am deeply involved in a growing movement of students that are getting active in the community. We host charity drives, distribute food and clothes to the homeless, and [advocate for] a greener campus." The college also recently opened its first dormitory, which has been a definite boon to campus life. One happy resident tells us, "The Summit is amazing. It's fun to hang around there or sit on the Quad on a nice day and do homework/talk with friends." Fortunately, "There is a nice atmosphere on campus, and it feels safe and comfortable for both commuters and residents." The surrounding area offers plenty of great dining options, especially "Chinese food and Kosher restaurants, depending on which way you walk." And of course, Manhattan is "very close and easily accessible." Students frequently head into the city "to go clubbing, out to eat, or hit the bars and museums."

Student Body

As a finance major shares, "Flushing is one of the most ethnically diverse cities in the United States and the demographics of the school reflect that." Certainly, diversity is a buzzword around the Queens campus, and the college attracts many "Jewish, Asian, and Hispanics students." An impressed sophomore goes further, "There is no typical student at Queens College. If you can name a language, it's spoken here. If you name a country, someone has ethnic ties to it. There are students of all races, sexual orientations, ethnicities, and genders at Queens who live together in harmony." A speech pathology major observes, "Every time I walk through campus, I feel as if I am trekking through the seven continents." Most of these "easy-going," "unassuming," and "liberal" undergrads find common ground in their desire "to get a good education" with an "inexpensive" price tag. As one media studies major sums up, "The school has so many clubs that everyone finds a way to fit in with their own niche groups."

THE PRINCETON REVIEW SAYS

Admissions

Very important factors considered include: Academic GPA, rigor of secondary school record, standardized test scores. SAT Subject Tests recommended; SAT or ACT required; TOEFL required of all international applicants. High school diploma is required, and GED is accepted. *Academic units required:* 4 English, 3 mathematics, 2 science, (2 science labs), 3 foreign language, 4 social studies. *Academic units recommended:* 3 science, (3 science labs).

Financial Aid

Students should submit: FAFSA, institution's own financial aid form, state aid form. The Princeton Review suggests that all financial aid forms be submitted as soon as possible after January 1. *Need-based scholarships/grants offered:* Federal Pell, SEOG, state scholarships/grants, private scholarships, the school's own gift aid. *Loan aid offered:* Direct Subsidized Stafford, Direct Unsubsidized Stafford, Direct PLUS, Federal Perkins. Applicants will be notified of awards on a rolling basis beginning 3/1. Federal Work-Study Program available. Institutional employment available. Off-campus job opportunities are good.

The Inside Word

Minority enrollment has declined at CUNY in the past several years, partially as a result of changes to admissions criteria and stiffer competition for minority applicants. The school would love to boost its numbers, meaning that qualified minority students could be able to finagle a pretty nice financial aid package here, making an already economical situation even more affordable.

THE SCHOOL SAYS "..."

From The Admissions Office

"At Queens College, you will engage the world of ideas with faculty and students from the world over, prepare for your career, and enjoy the many activities our beautiful, 77-acre campus has to offer. And with the August 2009 opening of The Summit—our new residence hall—you'll find a place to enjoy everything that comes with a college residential experience.

"Since 1937, we've provided a premier liberal arts education to talented students. From graduate and undergraduate degrees, a variety of honors and pre-professional programs to research and real-work internship opportunities, you'll find countless ways to realize your potential under the guidance of our award-winning, dedicated faculty. We offer nationally recognized programs—such as our Aaron Copland School of Music—in many fields. And we're also the ideal choice for aspiring teachers, preparing more future educators than any college in the tri-state area.

"Located only minutes from Manhattan, our campus boasts a traditional quad overlooking the skyline. You'll find a stimulating and welcoming environment here, with a bustling student union, an impressive arts center, and opportunities to participate in dozens of clubs and sports. (We're the only City University of New York college to participate in Division II.) Campus-wide wi-fi, computer kiosks, and cybercafes keep you informed and in touch. And best of all, as part of CUNY, we can offer all this at an affordable cost. To apply for fall 2011, submit your application online along with your SATs comprising Critical Reading, Writing, and Math."

For even more information on this school, turn to page 476 of the "Stats" section.

CLARK UNIVERSITY

950 MAIN STREET, WORCESTER, MA 01610 • ADMISSIONS: 508-793-7431 • FAX: 508-793-8821
FINANCIAL AID: 508-793-7478 • E-MAIL: ADMISSIONS@CLARKU.EDU • WEBSITE: WWW.CLARKU.EDU

RATINGS
Quality of Life: 71   Academic: 84   Admissions: 91   Financial Aid: 91

STUDENTS SAY ". . ."

Academics

Clark University is a "vibrant," "left-wing" liberal arts school in Worcester, Massachusetts. There are "good research opportunities" and standout offerings in psychology, geography, and the hard sciences. Clark also offers an accelerated, one-year Master's program in several majors at no extra charge. Coursework is "hard but doable." "I am challenged but not burned out," reports an English major.

> **SURVEY SAYS . . .**
> Lots of liberal students
> No one cheats
> Students are friendly
> Frats and sororities are unpopular or nonexistent
> Political activism is popular

"Overall, you'll get a lot out of Clark if you're willing to work for it." "The small size is very comfortable and welcoming" and "Class discussions are often interesting and enlightening." Professors are generally "committed to facilitating their students' education." "Most get very enthusiastic when teaching." "I've never had a class here with a sage on a stage who just stands behind a lectern and reads from their lecture notes without making eye contact," reports a government major. "My professors have always been available outside of class for help," adds a business major. However, there are also some "utter bores" who "really don't seem to know what they are teaching." The range of classes is "limited" as well. "There is not much variety" and popular courses "fill up fast." Views of the administration are very mixed. Some students call management "nondescript." Others contend that Clark's bureaucracy "rivals some small countries." Still others insist that the brass is "very visible and accessible" and "tries to listen to what the students want."

Life

Some buildings on Clark's "pretty compact" campus are "falling apart." Some classrooms are "kind of crappy." "The food leaves something to be desired," too. "Please send frozen dinners," begs a sophomore. Socially, there's a community feel. Many students are involved in community service and various kinds of activism. "Politics play a huge role." "Every student here believes strongly in something, which makes for an interesting campus." "There aren't big turnouts" at athletic events. "Students are actually more likely to attend a lecture on refugees from Rwanda than a basketball game," predicts a senior. "Many students hang out in small groups in their dorms, suites, or apartments." "There's a substance-free scene." There's also "plenty of weed and alcohol with dabbles here and there into harder drugs." "Clark isn't a major party school," though. "People here like to be mellow." "The area around the school isn't the greatest" but some students tell us that Worcester is "a perfectly good place to go to school." "Nightlife off campus is fun," they say, and "there are so many restaurants, it's ridiculous." Also, the "extremely active" Colleges of Worcester Consortium allows students to attend classes and events at several nearby schools. Others students complain that "the city of Worcester is depressing and gloomy at best." "It's unfortunate that Clark is where it is," laments one Clarkie. When students want to escape, Boston isn't too far.

Student Body

"If you couldn't find your niche in high school, you will probably find it at Clark," advises a junior. "It is kind of a haven for the awkward and slightly awkward." Clarkies are an "eclectic" "collection of independent minds." "There's a little of everything." "You can carve your own path here without being a loner." Conservatives are "accepted with curiosity" but most students are "socially conscious" types who "scream their bleeding liberal hearts out at any given cause of the week." Clark also "has an artsy feel." "Hipsteresque," "groovy people" who "dress sloppily in expensive clothes" are numerous. Jocks are here but they are "in the vast minority." "The closet-rich hippie" is not uncommon. However, many students tell us that Clark's flower-power reputation is unwarranted. "Sure, there are maybe a token five students who don't wear shoes, don't shower as often as most people would like, and own bongos," asserts a sophomore, "but three of them are posers anyway." You'll find "various sexual orientations" at Clark but ethnic diversity is pretty limited. There is a strong contingent of Jewish students and a large population of "filthy rich" international students but little in the way of traditionally underrepresented minorities.

THE PRINCETON REVIEW SAYS

Admissions

Very important factors considered include: Academic GPA, recommendation(s), rigor of secondary school record, standardized test scores, character/personal qualities. *Important factors considered include:* Application essay, extracurricular activities, talent/ability, volunteer work. *Other factors considered include:* Class rank, alumni/ae relation, first generation, geographical residence, interview, level of applicant's interest, racial/ethnic status, work experience. SAT or ACT required; TOEFL required of all international applicants. High school diploma is required, and GED is accepted. *Academic units recommended:* 4 English, 3 mathematics, 3 science, (2 science labs), 2 foreign language, 2 social studies, 2 history.

Financial Aid

Students should submit: FAFSA, CSS/Financial Aid PROFILE, noncustodial PROFILE. Regular filing deadline is 1/15. The Princeton Review suggests that all financial aid forms be submitted as soon as possible after January 1. *Need-based scholarships/grants offered:* Federal Pell, SEOG, state scholarships/grants, the school's own gift aid. *Loan aid offered:* Direct Subsidized Stafford, Direct Unsubsidized Stafford, Direct PLUS, Federal Perkins, state loans. Applicants will be notified of awards on or about 3/31. Federal Work-Study Program available. Institutional employment available. Off-campus job opportunities are good.

The Inside Word

Clark is surrounded by formidable competitors, and its selectivity suffers because of it. Most B students will encounter little difficulty gaining admission. Given the university's solid academic environment and access to other member colleges in the Worcester Consortium, it can be a terrific choice for students who are not up to the ultra-competitive admission expectations of "top-tier" universities.

THE SCHOOL SAYS "…"

From The Admissions Office

"Clark University prepares students to make a meaningful difference in a world hungry for change.

"Our vibrant intellectual life is an outgrowth of a dedicated faculty who are as passionate about teaching and mentoring as they are about generating new knowledge. As undergraduates, Clark students have an array of opportunities to not only study with award-winning researchers but also to work at their side in pursuit of solutions to pressing global problems.

"This approach to education—learning through inquiry—is just one of the three distinguishing features of a Clark education. The other two are making a difference and experiencing diverse cultures. Each permeates campus life in many ways: through rigorous academic courses, independent projects, internships and other educational experiences; through research and social action, both locally and globally; and through interactions with the dynamic members of the Clark community and study-abroad experiences. Students also have the possibility of earning a bachelor's and master's degree in five years, with the fifth year is tuition free.

"Clark's status as a small research university grounded in the liberal arts, its urban location, and its tradition of community partnerships place Clark students in an ideal position to breathe life into the University's motto, "Challenge convention, change our world."

"Clark requires that students submit scores from the SAT. Students will be judged by their performance in Critical Reading and Math; Clark does not look at the results of the Writing section."

For even more information on this school, turn to page 476 of the "Stats" section.

CLARKSON UNIVERSITY

PO Box 5605, Potsdam, NY 13699 • Admissions: 315-268-6479 • Fax: 315-268-7647
Financial Aid: 315-268-7699 • E-mail: admissions@clarkson.edu • Website: www.clarkson.edu

RATINGS
Quality of Life: 62   Academic: 68   Admissions: 86   Financial Aid: 79

STUDENTS SAY ". . ."

Academics

A "demanding," "hands-on," and "absolutely innovative" academic environment is the big draw at tech-heavy Clarkson University in the "frozen wasteland" of northern New York. The hard sciences and business programs "are growing," although Clarkson is still best known as an "engineering school." For engineers, "Clarkson is all about preparing you for the ridiculous amount of work you will get in the real world by giving you an even more ridiculous amount of work." Outstanding programs for business majors include entrepreneurship and supply chain manage-

ment. Classroom discussion is generally rare here and the faculty gets wildly mixed reviews, which is pretty normal wherever techies congregate. Some professors are "super friendly" and "willing to meet outside of their office hours." "Others couldn't teach at elementary schools" and are "more interested in their own research than their classes." Opinions concerning the administration also vary. Some students call management "very visible" and "truly concerned about student life," others strongly disagree." "I feel like they market to get students in," vents a senior, "and then really drop the ball." We would be remiss if we did not also add that a few students consider Clarkson's library to be "worthless." Opportunities "for co-ops, internships, and jobs" are a great feature. "Companies love to hire future employees" here.

Life

"There's nothing to do" in "extremely rural" Potsdam. "Don't come here if you like the city," advises a senior. "There is a bittersweet relationship between the students and Clarkson," adds a freshman. The "dreary" campus is full of "atrocious" "concrete buildings," the food is "horrible," the "overcrowded" dorms "could use some updating," and winters are "cold and desolate." On the plus side, the students here are "fairly tight knit." "It's a small campus with small classes in a small town" explains a junior, "so people get a chance to develop meaningful relationships." Also, the Adirondack Mountains are "very close" and "a lot of the students" enjoy the outdoors. If you like ice hockey, it's "the most popular thing on campus." The team here is a Division I powerhouse, and home games "bring the whole school together" "We show so much school spirit it's like the other team's fans aren't there," vaunts a first-year student. Business majors (and others) reportedly have "copious amounts of free time." For the engineers, though, grading can be "merciless," and "downtime is a luxury." It's "very hard to achieve good grades but rewarding when you do." Weekend life at Clarkson ranges from a popular Greek life to students who "just stay in their dorms all day and night" playing videogames.

Student Body

Overall, Clarkson students are "something of a nerdy crowd." "The typical student is a nerdy white guy," observes a senior. "It's mostly white males" "looking to get managerial and high-end engineering jobs" here. "There are many athletes" and plenty of business majors with "gelled hair." "The only people I have my nerdy classes with are other nerdy white guys." "Pretty much everyone looks the same from an outsider's view," agrees a sophomore. "Diversity has a different meaning at Clarkson," adds a junior. "What type of a techie are you?" Students describe themselves as "very smart," "hardworking," and "generally ambitious." A large contingent is "friendly" and outgoing. The "socially awkward" "quiet kid in high school" who "doesn't understand hygiene" is also here in spades. Clarkson's "horrible ratio of men to women" makes for a "miserable sausage fest," at least according to many males. Meanwhile, women have their own complaints. "It's hard to find a good looking guy," laments a senior. "There is a saying: 'although the odds are good, the goods are odd.'" "If you take out most of the antisocial engineering boys, the ratio becomes closer to 50:50." Other students claim that the ratio is "improving" and note that "SUNY Potsdam isn't far."

Admissions

Very important factors considered include: Academic GPA, rigor of secondary school record. *Important factors considered include:* Class rank, recommendation(s), standardized test scores, extracurricular activities, volunteer work. *Other factors considered include:* Application essay, alumni/ae relation, character/personal qualities, first generation, level of applicant's interest, talent/ability, work experience. SAT Subject Tests recommended; SAT or ACT required; TOEFL required of all international applicants. High school diploma is required, and GED is accepted. *Academic units required:* 4 English, 3 mathematics, 3 science. *Academic units recommended:* 4 mathematics, 4 science.

Financial Aid

Students should submit: FAFSA, state aid form. The Princeton Review suggests that all financial aid forms be submitted as soon as possible after January 1. *Need-based scholarships/grants offered:* Federal Pell, SEOG, state scholarships/grants, private scholarships, the school's own gift aid, HEOP. *Loan aid offered:* Direct Subsidized Stafford, Direct Unsubsidized Stafford, Direct PLUS, Federal Perkins, college/university loans from institutional funds, other, private/alternative loans. Applicants will be notified of awards on a rolling basis beginning 3/19. Federal Work-Study Program available. Institutional employment available. Off-campus job opportunities are excellent.

The Inside Word

Clarkson's acceptance rate is too high for solid applicants to lose much sleep about gaining admission. Serious candidates should interview anyway. If you are particularly solid and really want to come here, it could help you get some scholarship money. Women and minorities will encounter an especially friendly admissions committee.

THE SCHOOL SAYS "..."

From The Admissions Office

"Clarkson University is New York State's highest ranked small research institution. Located in Potsdam, New York, in the foothills of the northern Adirondack mountains, Clarkson is the institution of choice for 3,000 enterprising, high-ability students from diverse backgrounds who embrace challenge and thrive in a rigorous, highly collaborative learning environment.

"Clarkson's programs in engineering, business, the sciences, liberal arts, and health sciences emphasize team-based learning as well as creative problem solving and leadership skills. Clarkson is also on the leading edge of today's emerging technologies and fields of study offering innovative, boundary-spanning degree programs in engineering and management, digital arts and sciences, and environmental science and policy, among others.

"At Clarkson, students and faculty work closely together in a supportive, friendly environment. Students are encouraged to participate in faculty-mentored research projects from their first year, and to take advantage of co-ops and study abroad programs. Our collaborative approach to education translates into graduates in high demand; our placement rates are among the highest in the country. Alumni experience accelerated career growth. One in seven alumni are already a CEO, president, or vice president of a company.

"Applicants are required to take the ACT with Writing section optional or the SAT. We will use the student's best scores from either test. SAT Subject Tests are recommended but not required."

For even more information on this school, turn to page 477 of the "Stats" section.

COLBY COLLEGE

4800 MAYFLOWER HILL, WATERVILLE, ME 04901-8848 • ADMISSIONS: 207-872-3168 • FAX: 207-872-3474
FINANCIAL AID: 207-872-3168 • E-MAIL: ADMISSIONS@COLBY.EDU • WEBSITE: WWW.COLBY.EDU

RATINGS
Quality of Life: 83   Academic: 92   Admissions: 95   Financial Aid: 95

STUDENTS SAY "..."

Academics

> **SURVEY SAYS . . .**
> *Great food on campus*
> *Dorms are like palaces*
> *Frats and sororities are unpopular or nonexistent*

This small, close-knit liberal arts college draws praise from students for its rigorous but caring approach to academics. It's a place where devoted professors "invite students to dinner" and learning happens "for learning's sake." Small classes are one of Colby's biggest draws. "Professors are always willing to go the extra mile," one student says. A senior adds, "Over the course of my time at Colby I've been to at least six different professors' houses for departmental events, class dinners, and group discussions." Professors get high grades for their teaching and accessibility, which together foster a "love for learning" in undergraduates. As one student dryly notes, "Waterville, Maine is not the country's academic capital, so the professors that choose to be at Colby are here to teach, not to use the facilities." This dedication to academics can make Colby an intense place to go to school, and students here aren't "afraid to work hard and study." In addition, students must not only complete their major requirements but also fulfill a hefty load of distribution requirements to graduate. The popular "Jan Plan" allows students to pursue focused course work, independent study or internships during an intensive 4-week term in January. While the administration "works hard to keep students happy and entertained," some feel that their needs are "occasionally ignored in favor of the everlasting quest to turn Colby into a small Ivy."

Life

"Friends and a sense of community drive life at Colby," one senior writes. Students live together in coed, mixed-class dorms. Everything centers around the campus, which is "constructed on a gorgeous wooded hill near the Kennebec River in central Maine." Since "there isn't a ridiculous amount to do" in these self-contained environs, "Colby works hard to fill the day with countless events, lectures, discussions, and concerts. People can study hard, party, take advantage of the beautiful outdoors, and most do all three." A student notes that "the size of the school is perfect: On any given day, I could see five friends or acquaintances (and countless familiar faces!) on my way to class." This makes for a friendly atmosphere as "it's easy to start up a conversation with pretty much anyone. When the great outdoors beckons, students answer the call by hiking in autumn and spring, skiing in winter, and participating in traditional outdoor sports like football. A senior explains, "People like to unwind after our incredibly stressful weeks with movies, skiing, and partying." The "alcohol-centered social scene" usually takes place at small dorm parties or at the few local pubs.

Student Body

While the prototypical Colby student may be "white and from 20 minutes outside of Boston," undergrads are quick to point out that their "campus is very open to diversity and ready to embrace it." Students single out the administration for "doing a great job of bringing in a more diverse student population." One student explains that "more and more international students and urban kids are coming through programs like the Posse Scholarship." A junior adds, "We have students here that dress in business suits and bow ties while others walk around in capes." Most students, however, settle for the more general description of "preppy students who enjoy the outdoors and enjoy having a good time." That said, students report that "there's pretty much a place for everyone somewhere at Colby; chances are you'll find people both very similar to you in interests, background, etc. and people who are completely the opposite." One student elaborates, explaining that despite all differences, "the one word I'd use to describe a Colby student is friendly."

Admissions

Very important factors considered include: Rigor of secondary school record, character/personal qualities. *Important factors considered include:* Class rank, application essay, academic GPA, recommendation(s), standardized test scores, extracurricular activities, racial/ethnic status, talent/ability. *Other factors considered include:* Alumni/ae relation, first generation, geographical residence, interview, level of applicant's interest, state residency, volunteer work, work experience. TOEFL required of all international applicants. High school diploma or equivalent is not required. *Academic units recommended:* 4 English, 3 mathematics, 2 science, (2 science labs), 3 foreign language, 2 social studies or history.

Financial Aid

Students should submit: FAFSA, CSS/Financial Aid PROFILE, business/farm supplement, either CSS Profile or institutional application, and tax returns to finalize aid offers. Regular filing deadline is 2/1. The Princeton Review suggests that all financial aid forms be submitted as soon as possible after January 1. *Need-based scholarships/grants offered:* Federal Pell, SEOG, state scholarships/grants, private scholarships, the school's own gift aid. *Loan aid offered:* Direct Subsidized Stafford, Direct Unsubsidized Stafford, Direct PLUS, Federal Perkins, state loans, college/university loans from institutional funds, other, alternative loans. Applicants will be notified of awards on or about 4/1. Federal Work-Study Program available. Institutional employment available. Off-campus job opportunities are poor. Colby does not include college loans as part of its aid packages.

The Inside Word

Colby continues to be both very selective and successful in converting admits to enrollees, which makes for a perpetually challenging admissions process. Currently, only 34 percent of applicants are accepted, so hit those books and ace those exams to stand a fighting chance. One thing that could set you apart from the pack? An interest in travel. Two-thirds of Colby students study abroad—in fact, for some degrees it's required.

THE SCHOOL SAYS "..."

From The Admissions Office

"Colby is one of only a handful of liberal arts colleges that offer world-class academic programs, leadership in internationalism, an active community life, and rich opportunities after graduation. Set in Maine on one of the nation's most beautiful campuses, Colby provides students a host of opportunities for active engagement, in Waterville or around the world. The Goldfarb Center for Public Affairs and Civic Engagement connects teaching and research with current political, economic, and social issues at home and abroad. Recently Colby replaced loans in its financial aid packages with grants, which don't have to be repaid, making it possible for students to graduate without college-loan debt. Students' access to Colby's outstanding faculty is extraordinary, and the college is a leader in undergraduate research and project-based learning. The college has won awards for sustainable environmental practices as well as one of the first Senator Paul Simon Awards for Internationalizing the Campus.

"The challenging academic experience at the heart of Colby's programs is complemented by a vibrant community life and campus atmosphere featuring more than 100 student-run organizations, more than 50 athletic and recreational choices, and numerous leadership and volunteer opportunities.

"Colby graduates succeed. They find their places at the best medical schools and research universities, the finest law and business programs, top financial firms, in the arts, government service, social service, education, and nonprofit organizations, and they are inspired leaders in their communities.

"Applicants must submit scores from the SAT, or SAT Subject Tests in three different subject areas. The choice of which test(s) to take is entirely up to each applicant. The optional ACT Writing Test is recommended."

For even more information on this school, turn to page 477 of the "Stats" section.

COLGATE UNIVERSITY

13 OAK DRIVE, HAMILTON, NY 13346 • ADMISSIONS: 315-228-7401 • FAX: 315-228-7544
FINANCIAL AID: 315-228-7431 • E-MAIL: ADMISSION@MAIL.COLGATE.EDU • WEBSITE: WWW.COLGATE.EDU

RATINGS
Quality of Life: 90　　Academic: 96　　Admissions: 97　　Financial Aid: 98

STUDENTS SAY ". . ."

Academics

Colgate University, "the epitome of a work-hard, play-hard school," provides "a rigorous academic environment, an outstanding student and faculty population, and an abundance of social opportunities" to its "preppy," "intelligent-but-not-nerdy" student body. Students report that "Colgate is academically strong in the humanities, such as political science, English, psychology, and economics" and "also has good natural sciences programs that are enhanced by the new science building," a $56.3 million structure that houses 40 research labs, 13 teaching labs, and a teaching/research greenhouse. All students here must complete a set of general education requirements that "force you to look beyond your major work," sometimes leading to discovery of new, unanticipated areas of interest. "It is not uncommon for students to double major in two vastly different departments" as a result of their gen-ed experiences, students tell us. Colgate's size and location foster community-building; the "administration and faculty don't just work at Colgate, but live Colgate. In this way, they are dedicated to your education and create a passionate, hands-on, and inspiring place to learn," translating into "great opportunities to research with great professors and be in leadership positions." The workload is tough here; "at the end of a semester you may have four final exams and 80 pages of writing to do, but that absolutely won't stop you from going out on Friday night. (Saturday night too. And Wednesday night. Maybe Monday also.)"

Life

Colgate students take pride in the fact that they can handle both demanding academics and a bustling party scene. "The daytime is for work, nighttime (except Tuesday) is for fun," explains one student. "If you know where to look, you can find a party five days a week and definitely on weekends." Some warn that "The social/party scene around here can get a bit frustrating for some girls at times. If you like to be in serious relationships, Colgate is going to be a whole different ballgame for you…mostly the students here are interested in hook-ups," but by and large student feedback on the party scene is positive. Greek life "makes up a lot of the social scene, but the school itself provides many opportunities open to the entire campus that are generally very well attended," including "banquets, sports events, movies, etc." Colgate football and hockey are "extremely popular;" the school is "Division I in athletics, which is unique for a small liberal arts school. This aspect brings a lot of school spirit and adds to the sense of community here." There's "not much to do in Hamilton" other than "three main bars and The Jug," the latter being a "legendary" "bar/mosh pit that underclassmen go to after making the long trek from the dorms up on campus into town."

Student Body

"When looking from the surface, Colgate students don't appear diverse" because of the "undeniable majority of white students all in Uggs and Oxfords," but "although most students dress alike, there are great discussions in and out of the classroom because each Colgate student is actually very different from the next once you have the opportunity to talk to them." Even so, just about everyone here concedes that "this is a very preppy campus." Students tend to be "very laid-back, but in that perfectly groomed, 'I just rolled out of bed looking this good' kind of way." They are also "passionate about something. Everyone has her own thing to enjoy. It could be a recreational club, a dance group, a community service group, an academic or research project, a student club, etc. You find that a lot of Colgate students are active members in one way or another."

THE PRINCETON REVIEW SAYS

Admissions

Very important factors considered include: Class rank, academic GPA, rigor of secondary school record. *Important factors considered include:* Application essay, recommendation(s), standardized test scores, character/personal qualities, extracurricular activities, talent/ability. *Other factors considered include:* Alumni/ae relation, first generation, geographical residence, racial/ethnic status, volunteer work, work experience. SAT or ACT required; TOEFL required of all international applicants. High school diploma is required, and GED is accepted. *Academic units required:* 4 English, 3 mathematics, 3 science, (2 science labs), 3 foreign language, 3 social studies. *Academic units recommended:* 4 English, 4 mathematics, 4 science, (3 science labs), 4 foreign language, 4 social studies.

Financial Aid

Students should submit: CSS/Financial Aid PROFILE, noncustodial PROFILE. Regular filing deadline is 1/15. The Princeton Review suggests that all financial aid forms be submitted as soon as possible after January 1. *Need-based scholarships/grants offered:* Federal Pell, SEOG, state scholarships/grants, private scholarships, the school's own gift aid. *Loan aid offered:* Federal Perkins. Applicants will be notified of awards on or about 4/1. Federal Work-Study Program available. Institutional employment available. Off-campus job opportunities are fair.

The Inside Word

As at many colleges, Colgate admissions caters to some long-established special interests. Athletes, minorities, and legacies (children of alumni) are among those who benefit from more favorable review. Wait-listed students, take note—about three percent of students on the waitlist wind up admitted to the school.

THE SCHOOL SAYS "..."

From The Admissions Office

"Students and faculty alike are drawn to Colgate by the quality of its academic programs. Faculty initiative has given the university a rich mix of learning opportunities that includes a liberal arts core, 51 academic concentrations, and a wealth of Colgate faculty-led, off-campus study programs in the United States and abroad. But there is more to Colgate than academic life, including more than 180 student organizations, athletics and recreation at all levels, and a full complement of living options set within a campus described as one of the most beautiful in the country. A new center for community service builds upon the tradition of Colgate students interacting with the surrounding community in meaningful ways. Colgate students become extraordinarily devoted alumni, contributing significantly to career networking and exploration programs on and off campus. For students in search of a busy and varied campus life, Colgate is a place to learn and grow."

For even more information on this school, turn to page 478 of the "Stats" section.

COLLEGE OF THE ATLANTIC

105 EDEN STREET, BAR HARBOR, ME 04609 • ADMISSIONS: 800-528-0025 • FAX: 207-288-4126
FINANCIAL AID: 207-288-5015 • E-MAIL: INQUIRY@ECOLOGY.COA.EDU • WEBSITE: WWW.COA.EDU

RATINGS
Quality of Life: 93   **Academic:** 90   **Admissions:** 87   **Financial Aid:** 88

STUDENTS SAY "..."

Academics

The College of the Atlantic takes a unique approach to academics. All undergrads "major in Human Ecology," an
interdisciplinary philosophy that addresses environmental
and social issues. While there are distribution requirements, a sophomore ensures us that "those are easy to fulfill" and asserts that "all other classes are elective."
Unfortunately, due to COA's small size, "most classes are
[only] offered every other year." Therefore, if a particular
course sparks your interest, you "need to jump on the

> **SURVEY SAYS . . .**
> *Lots of conservative students*
> *No one cheats*
> *Students aren't religious*
> *Great food on campus*
> *Low cost of living*
> *Intercollegiate sports are unpopular or nonexistent*
> *Frats and sororities are unpopular or nonexistent*

[opportunity]." The intimate size does have plenty of advantages however. Undergrads here seem to unanimously agree that "COA is a very close-knit community" where "inter-personal relationships with staff, faculty, and administration" flourish. Students eagerly sing the praises of their professors: "an eclectic and brilliant
group of people" who are "extremely accessible." And this availability isn't limited to normal workday hours.
One junior told us that it's quite common for professors "to give out their home phone numbers." Though
friendly and supportive, professors don't let their students slack off. While the workload "varies from class to
class" it's most definitely "not light." Luckily, these "self-motivated" undergrads happily embrace their assignments. As one impressed freshman sums up, "For students in search of a school that will challenge them, [COA]
is an excellent place."

Life

Though COA students are often "swamped with reading and homework" there is always "time to have fun."
Hometown Bar Harbor is a place "that is booming with tourists in the summer and pretty much dead in the
winter." While undergrads frequent a few local hangouts, they mostly "make our own fun." Students can often
be found playing "hockey on the pond" or "pick-up games of soccer," hosting "spontaneous midnight poetry
readings," "tobogganing at the golf course," or throwing "dance parties in the art gallery." There's even the
occasional "sword fight in the library." COA's location is an outdoor enthusiast's dream, and students are quick
to take advantage of the school's proximity to Acadia National Park. Opportunities abound to "hike, bike [and]
go out on the ocean" and "snowshoe/ski in the winter." The small population helps to ensure a "strong sense
of community," and undergrads are always content with attending a potluck and simply enjoying "philosophical conversations that last until early morning." There is a party scene, but "alcohol does not dominate social
life at all." Finally, the school also hosts a variety of activities "such as concerts, open mics, and hiking trips."

Student Body

Undergrads at the College of the Atlantic readily acknowledge that many people assume they're "all tree-hugging hippies" who always wear "Birkenstocks and tie dye." And while there are plenty of "outdoorsy" types,
students are quick to assert that many of their peers shatter this stereotype. Though the majority might categorize themselves as "atypical," most everyone is "compassionate, kind, and aware." Passion is another common
attribute, and one freshman gushes, "Everyone is incredibly cool and into something, whether it be poetry, fighting climate change, dance, whales [or] organic farming...everyone wants to improve the lives of others." With
such a politically aware student body, COA is a bastion for liberal, left-leaning undergrads. Indeed, this sentiment is punctuated by a sophomore who exclaims, "I think there are about two Republicans in the whole school."
That being said, "The college [has] a very egalitarian outlook, [and] everyone is equal and equally valued." While
the majority of COA undergrads are "white [and] middle-class," the college manages to attract "a lot of international students through the Davis Scholarship Program," ensuring a diversity of experience and opinion.

THE PRINCETON REVIEW SAYS

Admissions

Very important factors considered include: Application essay, recommendation(s), rigor of secondary school record. *Important factors considered include:* Class rank, academic GPA, character/personal qualities, extracurricular activities, interview, talent/ability, volunteer work, work experience. *Other factors considered include:* Standardized test scores, alumni/ae relation, first generation, geographical residence, level of applicant's interest, racial/ethnic status, state residency. TOEFL required of all international applicants. High school diploma is required, and GED is accepted. *Academic units required:* 4 English, 3 mathematics, 2 science, (2 science labs), 0 foreign language, 2 social studies. *Academic units recommended:* 4 mathematics, 3 science, 2 foreign language, 2 history, 1 academic electives.

Financial Aid

Students should submit: FAFSA, institution's own financial aid form, noncustodial PROFILE, business/farm supplement. Regular filing deadline is 2/15. The Princeton Review suggests that all financial aid forms be submitted as soon as possible after January 1. *Need-based scholarships/grants offered:* Federal Pell, SEOG, state scholarships/grants, private scholarships, the school's own gift aid. *Loan aid offered:* Federal Perkins. Applicants will be notified of awards on or about 4/1. Federal Work-Study Program available. Off-campus job opportunities are good.

The Inside Word

As applicants might expect, admissions standards at College of the Atlantic are somewhat atypical. The school covets students who carve their own intellectual courses rather than follow a conventional academic path. Students at COA are expected to bring strong ideas and values to the classroom, and applicants are assessed accordingly. Essays and interviews are where you can make your mark. Of course, the college's integrated approach also means you should have a well-rounded secondary school record. Candidates should also demonstrate a kinship with the philosophy of human ecology.

THE SCHOOL SAYS "..."

From The Admissions Office

"College of the Atlantic is a small, intellectually challenging college on Mount Desert Island, Maine. We look for students seeking a rigorous, hands-on, self-directed academic experience. Come for a visit, and you will begin to understand that COA's unique approach to education, governance and community life extends throughout its structure. Resolutely value centered and interdisciplinary—there are no departments and no majors, COA sees its mission as preparing people to become independent thinkers, to challenge conventional wisdom, to deal with pressing global change—both environmental and social—and to be passionately engaged in transforming the world around them into a better place.

"College of the Atlantic does not require standardized testing as part of the application process. Learning and intelligence can be gauged in many ways; standardized test scores are just one of many measures. If an applicant chooses to submit standardized test scores for consideration, the SAT, SAT Subject Tests, or ACT scores are all acceptable."

For even more information on this school, turn to page 478 of the "Stats" section.

COLLEGE OF THE HOLY CROSS

ADMISSIONS OFFICE, ONE COLLEGE STREET, WORCESTER, MA 01610-2395 • ADMISSIONS: 508-793-2443
FAX: 508-793-3888 • FINANCIAL AID: 508-793-2265 • E-MAIL: ADMISSIONS@HOLYCROSS.EDU • WEBSITE: WWW.HOLYCROSS.EDU

RATINGS
Quality of Life: 70   **Academic:** 95   **Admissions:** 96   **Financial Aid:** 92

STUDENTS SAY ". . ."

Academics

> **SURVEY SAYS . . .**
> *Frats and sororities are unpopular or nonexistent*
> *Student government is popular*
> *Lots of beer drinking*
> *Hard liquor is popular*

The College of the Holy Cross is a smallish, "rigorous" Jesuit school "that does an incredible job of giving its students a very broad education [and] preparing them with the tools for the real world." Every student must complete a broad liberal arts curriculum. Regardless of your major, you'll take courses in history, literature, religion, philosophy, foreign language, math, science, and art. In additional, all first-year students take part in full-year seminars that are heavy on intellectual development. There's an array of exciting and often exotic study abroad options. The semester in Washington, D.C. receives a lot of praise. Internship programs are also abundant, and students also have access to a "large and strong alumni network." "Holy Cross alums are insane" about their old alma mater, and they love to hire the latest batch of graduates. "The emphasis here is on teaching and learning, not research," and the academic atmosphere is intense. "At Holy Cross, the professors will keep you busy throughout the week." "Classes are hard," warns a biology major. Good grades are hard to come by. "You have to work your tail off to just get an A–." At the same time, students love their "caring" and "amazing" professors, and they point out that small class sizes provide opportunities for meaningful faculty-student interaction. Profs are "very accessible outside the classroom," too. In fact, they "almost force you to get to know them." "If you show interest and work hard, you will do well," concludes an English major.

Life

There's "a lively social scene" on this "beautiful" hilltop campus. There are more than 80 clubs and organizations, and virtually everyone is "active in something, whether it be a varsity team, intramurals, student government, clubs, the newspaper, theater, or music." Studying is also an exceedingly common pastime. "The libraries and study rooms are often packed with students at night." On the weekends, however, "Holy Cross is a very big party school." "Although I would not consider Holy Cross to be the most outrageously fun school," relates a senior, "the student body at Holy Cross likes to drink." "People work hard during the week, and they like to let loose and have fun." Parties generally occur "in dorm rooms or at nearby off-campus housing." "Bars are popular," too, and usually "cheap." Students are also quick to call our attention to the fact that there is plenty to do on the weekends besides drinking. "If that's not your scene, there are so many other things to do," reports one student. There is everything "from going to plays, to sporting events, dances, karaoke, and stand-up comedians—all right here on campus." The food is probably the biggest complaint we hear. "Stick to the pasta," recommends a senior. The surrounding city of Worcester is home to "great" grub, but it's kind of sketchy otherwise. Luckily, "trips to Boston and Providence are extremely feasible, and the school has free buses to these locations on the weekends."

Student Body

Holy Cross is a "remarkably" welcoming campus. "This is the most friendly campus you will ever step foot on," claims a senior. You can find students from just about every state, but the majority tends to come from New England and the mid-Atlantic states. Students tend to be Catholic, though there are certainly plenty of people with different religions and with no religion at all. "Religion is not a major issue" here, really. Atypical students exist, and they "fit in just fine," but most of the undergraduate population at HC does kind of fit a certain mold. "The typical student is upper-middle-class, white, somewhat preppy, and athletic." That student is "smart," "hardworking," and probably "from the suburbs." "If you dress really preppy all the time, party hard on the weekends, and study in the rest of your remaining time, this is the school for you."

THE PRINCETON REVIEW SAYS

Admissions

Very important factors considered include: Class rank, academic GPA, recommendation(s), rigor of secondary school record, interview. *Important factors considered include:* Application essay, character/personal qualities, extracurricular activities, level of applicant's interest. *Other factors considered include:* Standardized test scores, alumni/ae relation, first generation, geographical residence, racial/ethnic status, talent/ability, volunteer work, work experience. TOEFL required of all international applicants. High school diploma is required, and GED is accepted. *Academic units recommended:* 4 English, 4 mathematics, 4 science, (2 science labs), 4 foreign language, 2 social studies, 2 history.

Financial Aid

Students should submit: FAFSA, CSS/Financial Aid PROFILE, noncustodial PROFILE, business/farm supplement, parent and student federal tax returns. Regular filing deadline is 2/1. The Princeton Review suggests that all financial aid forms be submitted as soon as possible after January 1. *Need-based scholarships/grants offered:* Federal Pell, SEOG, state scholarships/grants, private scholarships, the school's own gift aid. *Loan aid offered:* Direct Subsidized Stafford, Direct Unsubsidized Stafford, Direct PLUS, Federal Perkins, Other, MEFA. Applicants will be notified of awards on or about 4/1. Federal Work-Study Program available. Institutional employment available. Off-campus job opportunities are fair.

The Inside Word

Admission to Holy Cross is competitive; therefore, a demanding high school course load is required to be a viable candidate. The college values effective communication skills—it thoroughly evaluates each applicant's personal statement and short essay responses. Interviews are important, especially for those applying early decision. Students who graduate from a Jesuit high school might find themselves at a slight advantage.

THE SCHOOL SAYS "..."

From The Admissions Office

"When applying to Holy Cross, two areas deserve particular attention. First, the essay should be developed thoughtfully, with correct language and syntax in mind. That essay reflects for the Board of Admissions how you think and how you can express yourself. Second, activity beyond the classroom should be clearly defined. Since Holy Cross [has only] 2,800 students, the chance for involvement/participation is exceptional. The board reviews many applications for academically qualified students. A key difference in being accepted is the extent to which a candidate participates in-depth beyond the classroom—don't be modest; define who you are.

"Standardized test scores (i.e., SAT, SAT Subject Tests, and ACT) are optional. Students may submit their scores if they believe the results paint a fuller picture of their achievements and potential, but those students who don't submit scores will not be at a disadvantage in admissions decisions."

For even more information on this school, turn to page 479 of the "Stats" section.

THE COLLEGE OF NEW JERSEY

PO Box 7718, Ewing, NJ 08628-0718 • Admissions: 609-771-2131 • Fax: 609-637-5174
Financial Aid: 609-771-2211 • E-mail: ADMISS@VM.TCNJ.EDU • Website: WWW.TCNJ.EDU

RATINGS
Quality of Life: 94   **Academic:** 88   **Admissions:** 93   **Financial Aid:** 68

STUDENTS SAY "..."

Academics

The College of New Jersey, "a small, liberal arts, state school that offers, to the best of its abilities, everything that a private school offers," earns plaudits from a student body that understands just what a great deal the school represents. "Many of my friends had well above 1300 SAT scores and got into very prestigious schools such as Georgetown, NYU, Columbia, and Villanova, but chose TCNJ because of its unbeatable cost," explains one student, who warns that the school is "no joke" academically and notes that even those aforementioned friends "are constantly studying and find no cake-walk when it comes to classes." Students benefit from "up-to-date facilities" including "an amazing library" and solid career services. Most impressive, however, is the small-school service students here receive; professors "clearly have their students' best interests in mind," and the administration is not only "amazingly helpful" but also solicitous of student opinion; "Whenever a position opens up in a department, the students are encouraged to attend lectures by prospective candidates and offer their input," one student writes. No wonder undergrads insist that TCNJ is "a smaller school that is a bargain for its quality of education."

> **SURVEY SAYS ...**
> *Great library*
> *School is well run*
> *Students are friendly*
> *Low cost of living*
> *Students are happy*
> *Student publications are popular*

Life

With "a beautiful campus, great location, top-notch faculty, the newest technology, an interested student body, and competitive sports teams," TCNJ really "is the total package." There "are a lot of things going on on-campus for people to get involved in," including "clubs and intramural sports that people commonly do for fun." The student center "offers games, and there are always performances going on," and "there are tons of student organizations and club teams." Although "People are generally the Abercrombie or Hollister type" here, "you don't have to be athletic or involved at all to be popular at TCNJ. It's completely acceptable to just hang out with people doing nothing constructive." The off-campus party scene "is fine," and "many people "attend the fraternity parties offered on Tuesdays, Fridays, and Saturdays," but "There is not much to do once you leave campus unless you have a car," and one student notes "some of the surrounding areas are a little sketchy." Further afield things get better, as "our school is a 15-minute drive from Princeton and 45 minutes outside of Philly."

Student Body

"You can find any personality type at TCNJ," students tell us, from "your typical jocks who love to party" to "extremely conservative kids who haven't missed a Sunday mass since getting here" and "a few hippie types and everything in between. Whatever your social circle, you're bound to fit in." What they share in common is that most are "smart, dedicated people who care about their education very much," "were in the top 15 percent of their high school class," and "are willing to push themselves to do better in school." While "everyone has different interests, inside the classroom there is never an intellectual differentiation between those in the Medieval Club and those in Greek life. I think everyone is atypical in his own way, and this is a great place for everyone to be able to find a niche." And while "the typical student at TCNJ is white and middle-upper-class to upper class," the school also hosts a solid population of students of "different faiths and ethnicities."

THE PRINCETON REVIEW SAYS

Admissions

Very important factors considered include: Class rank, rigor of secondary school record, standardized test scores, extracurricular activities, volunteer work. *Important factors considered include:* Application essay, recommendation(s), character/personal qualities, geographical residence, state residency, talent/ability. *Other factors considered include:* Academic GPA, alumni/ae relation, first generation, level of applicant's interest, racial/ethnic status, work experience. SAT or ACT required; TOEFL required of all international applicants. High school diploma is required, and GED is accepted. *Academic units required:* 4 English, 3 mathematics, 3 science, (2 science labs), 2 foreign language, 2 social studies. *Academic units recommended:* 4 English, 3 mathematics, 3 science, (3 science labs), 3 foreign language, 3 social studies.

Financial Aid

Students should submit: FAFSA. Regular filing deadline is 10/1. The Princeton Review suggests that all financial aid forms be submitted as soon as possible after January 1. *Need-based scholarships/grants offered:* Federal Pell, SEOG, state scholarships/grants, private scholarships, the school's own gift aid. *Loan aid offered:* Federal Perkins, Federal Nursing Applicants will be notified of awards on a rolling basis beginning 6/1. Federal Work-Study Program available. Institutional employment available. Off-campus job opportunities are excellent.

The Inside Word

The College of New Jersey accepts nearly half of all applicants, but that figure is deceiving; this is a self-selecting applicant pool; those with no chance of acceptance simply don't bother. Admissions are as competitive as you'd expect at a school that offers state residents a small-college experience and a highly respected degree for bargain-basement prices. Competition among biology majors has grown especially fierce; applications must be in by January 1 rather than February 15, and biology majors' applications are not processed on a rolling basis.

THE SCHOOL SAYS "…"

From The Admissions Office

"The College of New Jersey is one of the United States' great higher education success stories. With a long history as New Jersey's preeminent teacher of teachers, the college has grown into a new role as educator of the state's best students in a wide range of fields. The College of New Jersey has created a culture of constant questioning—a place where knowledge is not merely received but reconfigured. In small classes, students and faculty members collaborate in a rewarding process: As they seek to understand fundamental principles, apply key concepts, reveal new problems, and pursue new lines of inquiry, students gain a fluency of thought in their disciplines. The college's 289-acre tree-lined campus is a union of vision, engineering, beauty, and functionality. Neoclassical Georgian Colonial architecture, meticulous landscaping, and thoughtful design merge in a dynamic system, constantly evolving to meet the needs of TCNJ students. About half percent of TCNJ's entering class will be academic scholars, with large numbers of National Merit finalists and semifinalists. More than 400 students in the class received awards from New Jersey's Outstanding Student Recruitment Program. The College of New Jersey is bringing together the best ideas from around the nation and building a new model for public undergraduate education on one campus…in New Jersey!

"The College of New Jersey will accept the SAT as well as the ACT with or without the Writing component."

For even more information on this school, turn to page 479 of the "Stats" section.

COLUMBIA UNIVERSITY

535 WEST 116TH STREET, NEW YORK, NY 10027 • ADMISSIONS: 212-854-2521 • FAX: 212-894-1209
FINANCIAL AID: 212-854-3711 • E-MAIL: UGRAD-ADMISS@COLUMBIA.EDU • WEBSITE: WWW.STUDENTAFFAIRS.COLUMBIA.EDU/

RATINGS
Quality of Life: 94   **Academic:** 96   **Admissions:** 99   **Financial Aid:** 97

STUDENTS SAY ". . ."

Academics

Nestled in Manhattan's upper west side neighborhood and "at the crossroads of the world," Columbia's campus "itself is an inspiration and a motivation to push and to excel academically." While being "one of the world's great research universities," the school still manages to feel "closer to a liberal arts college than a gigantic mega-school." Students are drawn to this "first rate intellectual oasis" for its "holistic education" and "rich, historic Columbia core curriculum," which "surveys the humanities and the sciences" and "serves as a knowledge base as well as the connecting thread to all Columbia students." Another boon is the "high quality" of "thought-provoking" and "brilliant and successful" professors who are "truly invested in teaching the things they love to their students" but who "will not hold your hand or check up on you." "It is very, very difficult to get an A here, but it's difficult to do too much worse as well." Using a "tough love" approach, Columbia "believes in treating its students like adults" and pushes them toward "independence and self sufficiency" while providing "amazing resources in fields of networking, research, and internships" that will make everyone "a better citizen of the world." Although students acknowledge that Columbia's administration "truly cares about its students and the health of the school," many wish to improve the school's bureaucracy, which is "notoriously difficult to deal with."

> **SURVEY SAYS . . .**
> Great library
> Diverse student types on campus
> Students love New York, NY
> Great off-campus food
> Campus feels safe
> Students are happy
> Student publications are popular
> Political activism is popular

Life

"Columbia is as cosmopolitan and entertaining as New York City," sums up one satisfied student. Provided with "the best of both worlds," students often take advantage of their "secluded and idyllic green" campus' prime location, which gives them "unparalleled access to all the resources of the greatest city in the world." Another student boasts that attending Columbia gives you an "easy pass to the city, whether you are visiting museums for free with a flash of your ID or seeing your application pushed to the front when applying for amazing internships." The majority of students "venture downtown at least once a week to see a Broadway show, go to a concert or museum, or just explore." For those who are not tempted by the "free admission to over 30 museums in New York" or "a meal or dessert in Chinatown or Little Italy," there are plenty of "campus clubs and activities, including the fraternity and sorority scenes or on-campus parties." With a campus that "caters to every single person that comes through its doors," Columbia is "like being in a really rich agar" where students can pursue whatever they are interested in from "engaging in intellectual conversation" to "getting involved in politics through student groups on campus to continuing (or discovering) a love for the arts by being a part of a musical ensemble."

Student Body

A "diverse community of serious thinkers who also know how to have fun," Columbia students describe themselves as "bookworms" who are "cynical but enthusiastic" as well as "very politically active and liberal." With "driven" people "from distinct backgrounds, distinct ideologies, distinct everything," Columbia students list the school's diversity as one of its strengths, but one student cautions that "the diversity could use less of a leftist bias." "Extremely smart and interested in learning for its own sake," a "typical" Columbia student "has strong views but is willing to discuss and change them." Columbia students are also "more intense than those you might find at other schools," points out one student. Indeed, during exam season it's not uncommon to see students "bring sleeping bags and cases of Red Bull to the library." Despite this intensity, there is "a minimal amount of ill-intended competition," and "nobody is scrutinized for being different or pressured to be anything they are not."

THE PRINCETON REVIEW SAYS

Admissions

Very important factors considered include: Class rank, application essay, academic GPA, recommendation(s), rigor of secondary school record, standardized test scores, character/personal qualities. *Important factors considered include:* Extracurricular activities, talent/ability. *Other factors considered include:* Alumni/ae relation, geographical residence, interview, racial/ethnic status, volunteer work, work experience. SAT and SAT Subject Tests or ACT required; ACT with Writing component required. TOEFL required of all international applicants. High school diploma is required, and GED is accepted. *Academic units recommended:* 4 English, 4 mathematics, 4 science, (4 science labs), 4 foreign language, 4 history, 4 academic electives.

Financial Aid

Students should submit: FAFSA, CSS/Financial Aid PROFILE, noncustodial PROFILE, parent and student income tax forms. Regular filing deadline is 3/1. The Princeton Review suggests that all financial aid forms be submitted as soon as possible after January 1. *Need-based scholarships/grants offered:* Federal Pell, SEOG, state scholarships/grants, private scholarships, the school's own gift aid. *Loan aid offered:* Federal Perkins, other, Alternative loans. Applicants will be notified of awards on or about 4/1. Federal Work-Study Program available. Institutional employment available. Off-campus job opportunities are excellent.

The Inside Word

Earning an acceptance letter from Columbia is no easy feat. Applications to the university continue to rise, and many great candidates are rejected each year. Admissions officers take a holistic approach to evaluating applications; there's no magic formula or pattern to guide students seeking admission. One common denominator among applicants is stellar grades in rigorous classes and personal accomplishments in non-academic activities. Admissions officers are looking to build a diverse class that will greatly contribute to the university.

THE SCHOOL SAYS "..."

From The Admissions Office

"Columbia maintains an intimate college campus within one of the world's most vibrant cities. After a day exploring New York City you come home to a traditional college campus within an intimate neighborhood. Nobel Prize–winning professors will challenge you in class discussions and meet one-on-one afterward. The core curriculum attracts intensely free-minded scholars, and connects all undergraduates. Science and engineering students pursue cutting-edge research in world-class laboratories with faculty members at the forefront of scientific discovery. Classroom discussions are only the beginning of your education. Ideas spill out from the classrooms, electrifying the campus and Morningside Heights. Friendships formed in the residence halls solidify during a game of Frisbee on the South Lawn or over bagels on the steps of Low Library. From your first day on campus, you will be part of our diverse community.

"Columbia offers extensive need-based financial aid and meets the full need of every student admitted as a first-year with grants instead of loans. Parents with calculated incomes below $60,000 are not expected to contribute any income or assets to tuition, room, board and mandatory fees and families with calculated incomes between $60,000 and $100,000 and with typical assets have a significantly reduced contribution. To support students pursuing study abroad, research, internships and community service opportunities, Columbia offers the opportunity to apply for additional funding and exemptions from academic year and summer work expectations. A commitment to diversity—of every kind—is a long-standing Columbia hallmark. We believe cost should not be a barrier to pursuing your educational dreams."

For even more information on this school, turn to page 480 of the "Stats" section.

CONNECTICUT COLLEGE

270 MOHEGAN AVENUE, NEW LONDON, CT 06320 • ADMISSIONS: 860-439-2200 • FAX: 860-439-4301
FINANCIAL AID: 860-439-2200• E-MAIL: ADMIT@CONNCOLL.EDU • WEBSITE: WWW.CONNCOLL.EDU

RATINGS
Quality of Life: 83   Academic: 95   Admissions: 95   Financial Aid: 91

STUDENTS SAY ". . ."

Academics

"Warm environment" doesn't always refer to the weather at Connecticut College, a close-knit school in eastern Connecticut. It refers to an environment that encourages students "to get out and experience the world," and "prepares them for life in the 'real world' as a grad." The school's relatively small size allows students to get to know

one another well and affords "a large variety of academic opportunities" to each one—a far cry from the waiting-list mentality that often overtakes larger universities. Numerous resources are provided to help with academics, such as a writing center, language lab, a career services office, internship and study-abroad programs, and the school's unique certificate programs. Students also all adhere to the school's Honor Code, which "instills a sense of self-awareness and self-governance among the student body." The student government garners a high level of respect from the body at large, and there is a feeling that it "really enacts change on campus and in the New London community."

Classes are "engaging and interesting," which makes for a smooth transition from high school to college, and "professors are available inside and outside of the classroom." Indeed, professors' personal touches are the most highly sung aspect of Conn College life, and students rave over having "more than just a teacher-student relationship, but rather a person-person relationship" with their teachers. Most professors go by their first names, and are "down-to-earth people who place themselves at the same level as their students." "I am constantly learning and enthralled in class," says a senior art history major.

Life

Students without cars have trouble getting off campus, which doesn't matter as "there is basically nothing to do in New London." However, the city does have a few distractions like museums and restaurants and happens to be "perfectly located right in between New York City and Boston," with a train station conveniently located downtown. The vast majority of people live on campus, so dorms are "great social houses" in which people leave their doors open and are interested in getting to know their neighbors. When the weather is nice, going to the beach and hanging out on the green is very popular, and when it's not, students are given free-rein to start their own clubs and to volunteer with local organizations. People work hard during the week, but Thursdays and Saturdays are the big days to let loose. Everyone stays on campus on the weekends, and the school organizes plenty of things to do, such as theme dances, movies, a capella shows, and "Friday Night Lives" where up-and-coming bands come and play a concert for students.

Student Body

"People are just nice" at Conn College, and friends aren't hard to come by." Most people here are highly involved in the social and academic atmosphere of the school, play a sport, and are "open-minded and involved in a variety of activities." "For better or worse, people are unapologetically themselves…it is a unique quality about Conn that makes it both wonderful and unbearable at times," says one student. The typical student is from "right outside of Boston, New York, Connecticut, or any other New England state." There "is not a particularly diverse student body at Conn," though life experiences and interests of the students make it so that the perceived diversity is "truly immense." "Generally, students are wealthy" and "uncommonly good-looking." There "are a few academic superstars but, for the most part, students are on the same page academically." The school has many international students and study-abroad options to promote academic and personal diversity.

THE PRINCETON REVIEW SAYS

Admissions

Very important factors considered include: Class rank, academic GPA, rigor of secondary school record, character/personal qualities. *Important factors considered include:* Application essay, recommendation(s), extracurricular activities, interview, racial/ethnic status, talent/ability, volunteer work, work experience. *Other factors considered include:* Alumni/ae relation, first generation, geographical residence, level of applicant's interest, religious affiliation/commitment, state residency. Submission of standardized test scores (SAT, SAT II, ACT) is optional. TOEFL required of all international applicants. High school diploma is required, and GED is accepted.

Financial Aid

Students should submit: FAFSA, CSS/Financial Aid PROFILE, noncustodial PROFILE, business/farm supplement, federal tax returns; personal, partnership, and Federal W-2 statements. Regular filing deadline is 2/1. The Princeton Review suggests that all financial aid forms be submitted as soon as possible after January 1. *Need-based scholarships/grants offered:* Federal Pell, SEOG, state scholarships/grants, the school's own gift aid. *Loan aid offered:* Direct Subsidized Stafford, Direct Unsubsidized Stafford, Direct PLUS, Federal Perkins. Applicants will be notified of awards on or about 4/1. Federal Work-Study Program available. Institutional employment available. Off-campus job opportunities are good.

The Inside Word

Connecticut College is the archetypal selective New England college, and admissions officers are judicious in their decisions. Competitive applicants will have pursued a demanding course load in high school. Admissions officers look for students who are curious and who thrive in challenging academic environments. Since Connecticut College has a close-knit community, personal qualities are also closely evaluated, and interviews are important.

THE SCHOOL SAYS "..."

From The Admissions Office

"Chartered in 1911, Connecticut College was founded in the spirit of political and social equality, self-determination, and shared governance. The college seeks students who are not only smart and intellectually curious, but who also bring a wide range of life experiences and perspectives that enable this spirit to endure within the College community. The College's near century-old Honor Code defines campus life and is observed by all students, faculty, and staff. The Honor Code inspires students to challenge themselves and their peers to see the world from diverse perspectives, to remain receptive to new ideas and experiences, and, by instilling a sense of mutual respect, to consider how their actions and education may ultimately better the common good. Ninety-nine percent of students live on campus. There is no Greek system. Dozens of clubs represent the students' numerous activist, volunteer, spiritual, creative, or athletic interests.

"The College offers more than 50 majors and minors and a series of interdisciplinary learning centers. All classes and labs are taught by professors. Students participate in the NCAA Division III New England Small College Athletic Conference (NESCAC.) The College is nationally known for pioneering environmental initiatives, including commitments to renewable energy, and career and internship placement. The College has been called a "college with a conscience" by the Princeton Review for fostering social responsibility and public service and is one of the top sending schools for both Teach for America and The Peace Corps. In the past three years, thirteen Connecticut College students have been awarded Fulbright Scholarships and three students have been awarded Goldwater Scholarships."

For even more information on this school, turn to page 480 of the "Stats" section.

THE COOPER UNION FOR THE ADVANCEMENT OF SCIENCE AND ART

30 COOPER SQUARE, NEW YORK, NY 10003 • ADMISSIONS: 212-353-4120 • FAX: 212-353-4342
FINANCIAL AID: 212-353-4130 • E-MAIL: ADMISSIONS@COOPER.EDU • WEBSITE: WWW.COOPER.EDU

RATINGS
Quality of Life: 79   Academic: 91   Admissions: 99   Financial Aid: 92

STUDENTS SAY ". . ."

Academics

One of the coolest things about The Cooper Union is that there is no tuition. The school "offers a full-tuition scholarship to everyone who is accepted." We hasten to add, though, that room and board (in New York City), books and supplies, and various fees add up to quite a bit each year. There is a mandatory core curriculum here in the humanities and social sciences but, so far as majors go, programs in engineering, art, and architecture are the only options on the menu. Cooper is "one of the best schools for what it does in the coun-

try." "It is a school where the students can really go crazy and learn a lot." "Classes are small," and "professors are more than willing to give extra help outside of class." However, it's "not for the weak of heart." The "very visceral and involving" academic experience is "hell." The pace is "exhaustive and murderous." "Cooper Union: where your best just isn't good enough," muses a civil engineering major. Cooper is about "hours of study, neglect of personal life," and generally "working your ass off." And "the work you put in does not necessarily reflect in your grades." "I have never worked so hard in my life and probably never will," speculates a junior, but "as long as you can get through it, you're set for life." Complaints among students here include "worthless" adjunct professors, lab equipment "could be upgraded," "the administration is sometimes difficult to approach" and "scheduling is always weird." Nonetheless, management "mostly meets the students' needs, with minor mishaps."

Life

"There is no meal plan" at Cooper, and the lodging situation is harsh. "There is only housing guaranteed for first-year students and since Manhattan is a very expensive place to live, it becomes a problem after that." "Everyone is extraordinarily busy," comments a fine-arts major. "School is life and there's no way around it." For the architecture students, life is "nothing except architecture in radical explorations and expressions." For engineers, "Cooper is about selling your soul for four years." Art students sometimes "take time off because it's hard to be creative every minute." "The intense workload gives little break for fun." There are "many extracurricular programs" but the urban fare of New York City consumes most free time. The surrounding East Village is full of funky shops, cheap eateries, theaters, bars, and live music venues; subways can whisk students throughout the five boroughs at any time of day. "Drinking with friends is a great and sometimes necessary way to decompress" but for most students, "ruthlessly sucking on booze" is a very occasional thing. "We are not a party school," says a sophomore. "We get to campus in the morning, and leave late at night." "Cooper isn't for everybody," advises a senior. "If you need excessive guidance or prefer an exclusive, well-defined campus structure, you won't be happy here."

Student Body

Diversity here is simply dreamy. Cooper's overwhelming male population is exceptionally ethnically diverse, and "everyone is very different from everyone else." "The student body is teeming with sensitive and excitable minds, which caters to an unbridled sense of adventure and exploration." These "really ridiculously smart" students have "incredible, raw talent." Personalities "range from your seemingly typical frat jock to your genius who knows everything but how to socialize." Cooper students are very often "hardcore" and come in three stereotypes. "The art kids all wear the same 'unique' clothing and smoke a lot," and they're "definitely more free-spirit, social people." "The engineers are either playing video games or saying sad jokes that only other engineers would understand." And "the architecture students can be a mixture of both, or anywhere in between, but they are hard to catch because all they do is work all the time." These three groups of students "don't mix so much" and sometimes there are rivalries. "The battle is like the Cold War, mostly sent in written messages on bathroom walls but no direct actions. It's benign in nature and just for amusement."

THE PRINCETON REVIEW SAYS

Admissions

Very important factors considered include: Academic GPA, rigor of secondary school record, standardized test scores, level of applicant's interest, talent/ability. *Important factors considered include:* Application essay, character/personal qualities, extracurricular activities. *Other factors considered include:* Class rank, recommendation(s), first generation, interview, racial/ethnic status, volunteer work, work experience. SAT or ACT required; ACT with Writing component recommended. TOEFL required of all international applicants. High school diploma is required, and GED is accepted. *Academic units required:* 4 English, 1 mathematics, 1 science, 1 social studies, 1 history, 8 academic electives. *Academic units recommended:* 4 English, 4 mathematics, 4 science, (3 science labs), 2 foreign language, 4 social studies.

Financial Aid

Students should submit: FAFSA, CSS/Financial Aid PROFILE. Regular filing deadline is 6/1. The Princeton Review suggests that all financial aid forms be submitted as soon as possible after January 1. *Need-based scholarships/grants offered:* Federal Pell, SEOG, state scholarships/grants, private scholarships, the school's own gift aid. *Loan aid offered:* Federal Perkins, college/university loans from institutional funds. Applicants will be notified of awards on or about 6/1. Federal Work-Study Program available. Institutional employment available. Off-campus job opportunities are excellent.

The Inside Word

It's ultra-tough to get into The Cooper Union. There are typically more than 3,000 applicants vying for fewer than 300 slots. Not only do students need to have top academic accomplishments, but they also need to be a good fit for Cooper's offbeat milieu.

THE SCHOOL SAYS "…"

From The Admissions Office

"Each of Cooper Union's three schools, architecture, art, and engineering, adheres strongly to preparation for its profession and is committed to a problem-solving philosophy of education in a unique, scholarly environment. A rigorous curriculum and group projects reinforce this unique atmosphere in higher education and contribute to a strong sense of community and identity in each school. With McSorley's Ale House and the Joseph Papp Public Theatre nearby, Cooper Union remains at the heart of the city's tradition of free speech, enlightenment, and entertainment. Cooper's Great Hall has hosted national leaders, from Abraham Lincoln to Booker T. Washington, from Mark Twain to Samuel Gompers, from Susan B. Anthony to Betty Friedan, and more recently, President Bill Clinton and Senator Barack Obama.

"In fall of 2009 we opened the doors of our new academic building. Designed by Pritzker Prize–winning architect, Thom Mayne, the new building was designed to enhance and encourage more interaction between students in all three schools.

"We're seeking students who have a passion to study our professional programs. Cooper Union students are independent thinkers, following the beat of their own drum. Many of our graduates become world-class leaders in the disciplines of architecture, fine arts, design, and engineering.

"For art and architecture applicants, SAT scores are considered after the home test and portfolio work. For engineering applicants, high school grades and the SAT and SAT Subject Test scores are the most important factors considered in admissions decisions. Currently, we do not use the Writing section of the SAT to assist in making admissions decisions. We expect to reconsider that policy as more data is available in the near future."

For even more information on this school, turn to page 480 of the "Stats" section.

CORNELL UNIVERSITY

410 THURSTON AVENUE, ITHACA, NY 14850 • ADMISSIONS: 607-255-5241 • FAX: 607-255-0659
FINANCIAL AID: 607-255-5145 • E-MAIL: ADMISSIONS@CORNELL.EDU • WEBSITE: WWW.CORNELL.EDU

RATINGS
Quality of Life: 88   **Academic:** 92   **Admissions:** 98   **Financial Aid:** 96

STUDENTS SAY "..."

Academics

"Any person, any study." Thus goes the motto of Cornell University, located in rural, cold upstate New York. The school consists of seven different undergraduate colleges, all of which have "differing focuses and missions that are somehow unified and work together pretty cohesively." These smaller schools, including the well-known Hotel School and

> **SURVEY SAYS ...**
> *Great computer facilities*
> *Great library*
> *Great food on campus*
> *Student publications are popular*

College of Agricultural and Life Sciences, allow students to "receive all the benefits of a smaller college with the access, excitement, and opportunity provided by a large university." However, "You have to strongly believe in what you're studying and why you're studying it so as not to be freaked out by others who are in different majors and colleges." Though Cornell "may seem awfully large," students say it makes finding a close-knit community incredibly easy and "constantly challenges you to do better."

No matter what major you choose, Cornell offers "rigorous" academics, where "it takes a lot of hard work to succeed, but the resources are there for you to do so." The administration "makes huge attempts to be transparent," often using student panels for advice, though there's still some red tape clinging to a few processes (such as class registration). Class sizes range from small to large, but professors remain "incredible" and attentive across the board, though the size of the school (about 14,000 undergrads) often means you have to be proactive in seeking out help. "If you show genuine interest, [faculty] are more than excited to help you." Many are also focused on their research, which can be distracting, but it also provides students with plenty of opportunities to work with the academic bigwigs themselves. "Just the other day in one of my biology classes, my professor was going over a very important topic and just added in, 'Yeah, I came up with this,'" says a student.

Life

"Cornell is about studying hard, being involved in many activities, and always doing more than the average person can handle, all while still having a social life and partying hard," says a senior. "Work hard, work harder, stress hard, play hard," says another senior about the resounding ethos that makes for a "nice balance" of life. There's also a natural progression for students as they become upperclassmen—living in the dorms and drinking at parties or frat houses is quite popular for freshmen and sophomores, while upperclassmen often find apartments and outside venues for weekend entertainment. There are always "a variety of activities that do not include drinking" on offer, including "a capella concerts, movie nights, special speakers and discussions, and sports games."

Hometown Ithaca offers a farmers' market, restaurants, bars, and a movie theater. On campus, extracurricular offerings abound, and "it's not too hard to find something that interests everyone"—there's even an origami club—and the majority of students choose to join multiple organizations. On top of all that Ithaca offers, the school's northeast location also allows for "access to great weekend and break destinations like New York City and Washington, D.C."

Student Body

With such a large student body, "there is always a niche that any individual can fall into." Sure enough, the school's size and Ivy League status make it "a largely diverse and exciting bubble" where there is an abundance of "athletes or frat/sorority people," but at the same time, "you have a large group of students who do other activities." "We have our nerdy engineers, our outgoing hoteliers, our hipster art students, [and] our hard-core dairy farmers," brags one proud student. A "strong work ethic" seems to be the unifying thread among Cornell's diverse student body, as all students are "very focused on performing well in the classroom." "Most everyone has a secret nerdiness inside them that actually adds to their 'coolness,'" explains one. The different schools tend to naturally group together more frequently, so that each quad "has its own vibe," but "everyone is very friendly and approachable." Basically, "when you come here, you become the typical Cornellian."

Admissions

Very important factors considered include: Application essay, academic GPA, recommendation(s), rigor of secondary school record, standardized test scores, extracurricular activities, talent/ability. *Important factors considered include:* Class rank. *Other factors considered include:* Alumni/ae relation, character/personal qualities, first generation, geographical residence, interview, racial/ethnic status, state residency, volunteer work, work experience. SAT or ACT required; ACT with Writing component required. TOEFL required of all international applicants. High school diploma or equivalent is not required. *Academic units required:* 4 English, 3 mathematics. *Academic units recommended:* 3 science, (3 science labs), 3 foreign language, 3 social studies, 3 history.

Financial Aid

Students should submit: FAFSA, institution's own financial aid form, CSS/Financial Aid PROFILE, noncustodial PROFILE, business/farm supplement, prior year tax forms. Regular filing deadline is 1/2. The Princeton Review suggests that all financial aid forms be submitted as soon as possible after January 1. *Need-based scholarships/grants offered:* Federal Pell, SEOG, state scholarships/grants, private scholarships, the school's own gift aid. *Loan aid offered:* Direct Subsidized Stafford, Direct Unsubsidized Stafford, Direct PLUS, Federal Perkins, college/university loans from institutional funds. Applicants will be notified of awards on or about 4/1. Federal Work-Study Program available. Institutional employment available. Off-campus job opportunities are fair.

The Inside Word

Gaining admission to Cornell is a tough coup regardless of your intended field of study, but some of the university's seven schools are more competitive than others. If you're thinking of trying to "backdoor" your way into one of the most competitive schools—by gaining admission to a less competitive one, then transferring after one year—be aware that you will have to resubmit the entire application and provide a statement outlining your academic plans. It's not impossible to accomplish, but Cornell works hard to discourage this sort of maneuvering.

THE SCHOOL SAYS "..."

From The Admissions Office

"Cornell University, an Ivy League school and land-grant college located in the scenic Finger Lakes region of central New York, provides an outstanding education to students in seven small to midsize undergraduate colleges: Agriculture and Life Sciences; Architecture, Art, and Planning; Arts and Sciences; Engineering; Hotel Administration; Human Ecology; and Industrial and Labor Relations. Cornellians come from all 50 states and more than 100 countries, and they pursue their academic goals in more than 100 departments. The College of Arts and Sciences, one of the smallest liberal arts schools in the Ivy League, offers more than 40 majors, most of which rank near the top nationwide. Applied programs in the other six colleges also rank among the best in the world. "Other special features of the university include a world-renowned faculty; 4,000 courses available to all students; an extensive undergraduate research program; superb research, teaching, and library facilities; a large, diverse study-abroad program; and more than 800 student organizations and 36 varsity sports. Cornell's campus is one of the most beautiful in the country; students pass streams, rocky gorges, and waterfalls on their way to class. First-year students make their home on North Campus, a living-learning community that features a special advising center, faculty-in-residence, a fitness center, and traditional residence halls as well as theme-centered buildings such as Ecology House. Cornell University invites applications from all interested students and uses the Common Application exclusively with a short required Cornell Supplement. Students applying for admissions will submit scores from the SAT or ACT (with writing). We also require SAT Subject Tests. Subject test requirements are college-specific."

For even more information on this school, turn to page 481 of the "Stats" section.

DARTMOUTH COLLEGE

6016 McNUTT HALL, HANOVER, NH 03755 • ADMISSIONS: 603-646-2875 • FAX: 603-646-1216
FINANCIAL AID: 603-646-2451 • E-MAIL: ADMISSIONS.OFFICE@DARTMOUTH.EDU • WEBSITE: WWW.DARTMOUTH.EDU

RATINGS
Quality of Life: 91   **Academic:** 94   **Admissions:** 99   **Financial Aid:** 93

STUDENTS SAY ". . ."

Academics

"Hogwarts + Disneyland = Dartmouth," a student at this prestigious Ivy League institution writes, reflecting the widely held perception of Dartmouth College as an intellectual amusement park, a place where academic and extracurricular life intertwine to create "a tight-knit community dedicated to scholarship, creativity, intellectualism, and the well-rounded individual." While "academic interests vary widely" across campus, the school's "interdisciplinary approach...allows students from all different majors to be able to engage in analytical discussions on issues from the depiction of women and gender roles in science fiction, to the marginalization of the bottom billion in the international political economy, to nostalgia resulting from rural to urban relocation in the age of globalization." Central to this approach is the D-Plan, Dartmouth's quarterly academic calendar "where students take about three classes at a time for ten weeks." Students love it, telling us, "It gives you great flexibility to go abroad and secure fantastic off-term internships and volunteer opportunities." Students typically take advantage of the opportunities; as one explains, "Dartmouth is really big on the 'Dartmouth experience,' which basically means trying to do the most awesome things that you can fit into four years as an undergrad. This means that about two-thirds of undergrads, regardless of major, study abroad at least once. Everyone uses their 'off terms' to either try to save the world by volunteering or doing research if they're not doing some high-profile internship."

Life

Life at Dartmouth "is always busy...after attending classes in the morning, we run from meetings to debates to the library and finally to Frat Row. It is a relentless, fast-paced cycle, but it is so unbelievably fun and rewarding." "Greek life dominates" the Dartmouth campus, where student involvement in the Greek system approaches a whopping 50 percent, although one student notes that "once you get to know the Greek scene, it becomes apparent that it's unique and very welcoming and much more low key than at other schools." For those wondering, "Yes, Dartmouth is the school upon which Animal House was based....we do party a lot, but the mentality is definitely work hard, play hard." Dartmouth has an active drama and dance scene, and "a capella is particularly popular." Students like to stay active: "We throw a Frisbee on the green, hike through the mountains, play hockey on Occom Pond, play tennis, ski at the Skiway," and "sled on cafeteria trays" to burn off extra energy. "A strong sense of school spirit" is fueled by the college's "rich traditions," like "running around a giant bonfire hundreds of times." No matter what they're into, "no one leaves campus on weekends because no one wants to miss a weekend at Dartmouth."

Student Body

The quintessential Dartmouth undergraduate is "athletic, sociable, and very active within the community inside and outside of Dartmouth." "The binding element of the typical Dartmouth student is passion," one student tells us. "Whether it is academics or the environment, students are committed to an area of interest and try to contribute to that field." "There is a ton of diversity," one undergrad reports. "Through my friends I can interact and get a taste of Ghana, Trinidad, and Japan; what it means to be a Sikh, Jew, Buddhist, or Christian; how it feels to be a homosexual or transsexual; what it's like to live below the poverty line or miles above it." Wonder what they all share in common? "Everyone here is exceptional."

THE PRINCETON REVIEW SAYS

Admissions

Very important factors considered include: Class rank, application essay, academic GPA, recommendation(s), rigor of secondary school record, standardized test scores, character/personal qualities, extracurricular activities. *Important factors considered include:* Talent/ability, volunteer work. *Other factors considered include:* Alumni/ae relation, first generation, geographical residence, interview, racial/ethnic status. SAT or ACT and two subject tests required; ACT with Writing component required. TOEFL required of all international applicants. High school diploma or equivalent is not required. *Academic units recommended:* 4 English, 4 mathematics, 4 science, 3 social studies, 3 history.

Financial Aid

Students should submit: FAFSA, CSS/Financial Aid PROFILE, noncustodial PROFILE, business/farm supplement. Current W-2 or Federal Tax Returns. Regular filing deadline is 2/1. The Princeton Review suggests that all financial aid forms be submitted as soon as possible after January 1. *Need-based scholarships/grants offered:* Federal Pell, SEOG, state scholarships/grants, private scholarships, the school's own gift aid. *Loan aid offered:* Federal Perkins, college/university loans from institutional funds. Applicants will be notified of awards on or about 4/2. Federal Work-Study Program available. Institutional employment available. Off-campus job opportunities are excellent.

The Inside Word

Dartmouth doesn't have any problem attracting qualified applicants. On the contrary, this elite institution receives many, many more applications from fully qualified hopefuls than the school can possibly accommodate. As a result, many students who meet all the qualifications to attend Dartmouth are turned away every year because there simply isn't room for them. Dartmouth reviews applications holistically, meaning your best shot is to compile an application that paints a compelling portrait. Some special talent, life experience, or personal trait may be your ticket in, if Dartmouth thinks it will enhance the education of your classmates.

THE SCHOOL SAYS "…"

From The Admissions Office

"Do something great, be ambitious, and aspire to change the world." This advice comes from Dr. Jim Yong Kim, who is the President of Dartmouth College and also an internationally recognized physician and humanitarian who founded Partners in Health and served as the Director of the Department of HIV/AIDS at the World Health Organization.

"With its focus on undergraduate education and a flexible year-round academic calendar that encourages travel and research, Dartmouth is uniquely positioned to help students pursue their interests, prepare for a career and make an impact on the world. All classes are taught by members of the faculty, over 1,000 students per year pursue independent study for credit, and almost two-thirds of students participate in study abroad programs. On campus, students participate in nearly 400 student organizations, including 34 intercollegiate varsity teams, over 40 different community service projects, and more than 50 performing groups. Dartmouth's hometown of Hanover offers an active political scene, a vibrant arts community, and unparalleled outdoors and recreational opportunities (including our own ski mountain!).

"To help all Dartmouth students take advantage of the "Dartmouth Experience," the College practices need-blind admission for all applicants, meets the full demonstrated need for all admitted students, and offers free tuition and no loan requirements for all students whose annual family incomes are below $75,000.

"Dartmouth's admissions process is designed to identify students who will thrive in a challenging and flexible academic environment, who value community, and who will take advantage of the College's undergraduate focus."

For even more information on this school, turn to page 481 of the "Stats" section.

DELAWARE VALLEY COLLEGE

700 EAST BUTLER AVENUE, DOYLESTOWN, PA 18901-2697 • ADMISSIONS: 215-489-2211
FAX: 215-230-2968 • E-MAIL: ADMITME@DEVALCOL.EDU • WEBSITE: WWW.DEVALCOL.EDU

RATINGS
Quality of Life: 73   Academic: 71   Admissions: 77   Financial Aid: 76

STUDENTS SAY ". . ."

Academics

Delaware Valley College is a small Pennsylvania school that offers an array of majors, many in agricultural and animal sciences. As one undergraduate puts it, "If a person wants to get into the farming business, [conduct] lab work, or [do] just about anything to do with working or training animals, this is the place to go. We have two barns of horses on campus, cows, sheep, llamas, a small animal facility that has mice, rats, guinea pigs, hamsters, gerbils, lizards, snakes, fish, and dogs and our own greenhouse on campus." Thanks to the school's "connections to the Philadelphia Zoo," and amenities like "barns right on campus," many undergraduates feel that one of the "greatest strengths of Delaware Valley is the hands-on experience that all majors get." In addition, "the required employment program lets students work in their field of study." Undergraduates extol professors who are "very knowledgeable and easily accessible," saying classes are "wonderfully taught." Coursework is challenging but manageable; "Some of the professors are very hard and expect a lot of work, but they are also very fair and are always available for out-of-class help."

<aside>
SURVEY SAYS . . .

Students are friendly
Students get along with local community
Students love Doylestown, PA
Great off-campus food
Campus feels safe
Everyone loves the Aggies
Student government is popular
Political activism is unpopular or nonexistent
Lots of beer drinking
</aside>

Life

At DelVal, the "small population allows for more student involvement in every aspect of collegiate life." In addition to classes, "Most students have jobs and hobbies" and, on the weekends, "There are many events held on campus like dances, karaoke nights, comedians, bingo, and game nights that are open to the whole campus." In addition, "There is a lot of open space for games of football, ultimate Frisbee, catch, and soccer." People "watch movies, go down to the barns, go to the gym, or just hang out" in their spare time. In addition, the school provides "many opportunities for students to take trips off-campus," and hometown Doylestown "is a very interesting place to visit and walk around in for a day." "People mostly go home on the weekends," so "sometimes it seems like the campus is empty." Since the campus empties out on Fridays, "Thursdays are a very popular night to socialize with friends." On Thirsty Thursdays, "most of the campus goes out and parties and drinks." If you don't live in the area but still want to take a weekend excursion, "the Septa [Philadelphia and the surrounding region's rail system] can take him or her right into Philly."

Student Body

Because of DelVal's focus on agricultural and animal sciences, the school attracts many "people who have spent most of their lives living on a farm." However, students report that there are also a lot of students from urban backgrounds here, too—specifically, many students hail "from the city of Philadelphia." The combination of urban and rural can be unique: "To sum up, students here can differentiate a Jersey cow from a Brown Swiss, then give directions to a hot spot in Philly." While "most students are either into farming or animals (or both)," the school's "growing business department and an awesome athletics teams," do add to the student diversity. Concerning ethnic diversity, students report a "very homogenous student body" that is "predominantly white" and "conservative." While "It's easy to meet people and make friends," "cliques tend to form easily." One undergrad observes: "The cliques are obvious: There are the southern farmers, the northern farmers, the future vets, the horse girls, and everyone else who is here to play football."

THE PRINCETON REVIEW SAYS

Admissions

Very important factors considered include: academic GPA, standardized test scores. *Important factors considered include:* Class rank, rigor of secondary school record, interview. *Other factors considered include:* Application essay, recommendation(s), alumni/ae relation, character/personal qualities, extracurricular activities, level of applicant's interest, talent/ability, volunteer work, work experience. SAT or ACT required; ACT with Writing component recommended. TOEFL required of all international applicants. High school diploma is required and GED is accepted. *Academic units required:* 3 English, 2 mathematics, 2 science, (1 science labs), 2 social studies, 6 academic electives.

Financial Aid

Students should submit: FAFSA, state aid form. Regular filing deadline is 4/1. The Princeton Review suggests that all financial aid forms be submitted as soon as possible after January 1. *Need-based scholarships/grants offered:* Federal Pell, SEOG, state scholarships/grants, private scholarships, the school's own gift aid. *Loan aid offered:* Federal Perkins, other, Alternative Loans. Applicants will be notified of awards on a rolling basis beginning 2/1. Federal Work-Study Program available. Institutional employment available.

The Inside Word

Delaware Valley considers a variety of factors when making admissions decisions, chief among them are GPA and standardized scores. The school has a rolling admissions policy so students are advised to apply as early as possible, especially those considering the more popular majors. Candidates interested in Del Val's strong agricultural program should bring solid science marks to the table.

THE SCHOOL SAYS "..."

From The Admissions Office

"Delaware Valley College is one of the safest colleges in the U.S. Although it is a small, private institution, it offers many of the programs found at a large land grant institution. The college is located in Doylestown, Pennsylvania, convenient to most of the region's attractions. The college's athletic teams compete in the NCAA Division III Middle Atlantic conference. Merit scholarships ranging from $9000 to $15,000 are available to qualified students. Last year the college awarded over $16,000,000 in scholarships to its students, making a private education affordable to its students. Many of the college's students are involved in athletics and/or one or more of the over 50 clubs or campus organizations."

For even more information on this school, turn to page 482 of the "Stats" section.

DICKINSON COLLEGE

PO Box 1773, Carlisle, PA 17013-2896 • Admissions: 717-245-1231 • Fax: 717-245-1442
Financial Aid: 717-245-1308 • E-mail: admit@dickinson.edu • Website: www.dickinson.edu

RATINGS
Quality of Life: 78   **Academic:** 87   **Admissions:** 93   **Financial Aid:** 90

STUDENTS SAY "..."
Academics

Dickinson College is a "quintessential small liberal arts school" in a "small town in central Pennsylvania." The big draw here is an "aggressive" global focus. "Dickinson has completely followed through on all of their promises of a campus that supports international experiences," says a sociology major. Courses "have a strong focus on international issues." Studying abroad "fits seamlessly into the curriculum" and is "a huge deal." "Dickinson has exceptional study-abroad programs everywhere in the world." The administration is sometimes "preoccupied with rising in the ranks and improving superficial perceptions" of the school but Dickinson's president is insanely popular. He "has weekly office hours." "From the president down, the faculty and administrators make themselves available." "Any complaint is heard and listened to, not just brushed off." The academic atmosphere here is "difficult but doable." Classes are small. "Students do not often skip, as professors do take note." The "completely accommodating" faculty receives high marks. "They are good teachers, passionate about their subjects, and it is very easy for students to develop strong out-of-the-classroom relationships with their professors," says an international business major. "I can honestly say I've only had one professor who I didn't consider high quality," adds one junior.

Life

"The campus is beautiful," observes a senior at Dickinson. "On a nice day, it can take your breath away." It's also "overloaded with clubs and organizations." During the week, "there is a lot to do if you're willing to do it, and a lot of it is college sponsored." There is a "consistently full schedule of lectures." There are plenty of arts-related events. "All the different cultural clubs have a dinner every semester." "Intramural sports are a big deal." "The gym is in constant use." "Greek life is really big at Dickinson" as well. "On the weekends, the majority of people get nice and drunk." Drugs are not uncommon, either. Students who don't party are here too, "trying desperately to make their own fun." There's also "a lot of drama" on campus. "We like to call it Dickinson High," one student admits. The "dull" surrounding town is "not a social mecca." "I love art museums, live music, and cultural diversity," says a senior. "Carlisle does not have any of that." "There is nothing to do in Carlisle unless you are 21 and can get into the bars, where the most exciting thing to do is drink and maybe dance with a nice townie." "If you don't mind small towns, you'll be fine," advises a junior, "but big city people should look elsewhere for their college experience unless they're tired of the rat race."

Student Body

"The most glaring trait of the student body is that it is mostly white," says one student though others claim that "there are tons of international students," and the "growing" Posse Program brings minority students to campus. Still, as a first-year student relates, "the school is not as diverse as some of us would want it to be." Overall, "there is a lot of homogeneity." Most students here are "socially oriented" and come from somewhere on the East Coast or in the mid-atlantic states. "Many students are very rich and have no problem spending copious amounts of money." "The parking lots are filled with Jeep Grand Cherokees, Saabs, and BMWs." Other students receive "sweet financial aid deals," though. Academically, Dickinsonians "range anywhere from overzealous to apathetic," but the vast majority "can usually balance a full academic load with an active and rich social life." "The typical student at Dickinson is very preppy. The girls are gorgeous, and the guys look like they are straight out of a J. Crew catalog, and everyone is also really athletic." "Finding the oddballs can be difficult." Cliques are common, and "the campus is quite split between Greek life and non-Greek life."

THE PRINCETON REVIEW SAYS

Admissions

Very important factors considered include: Academic GPA, rigor of secondary school record, extracurricular activities, talent/ability, volunteer work. *Important factors considered include:* Class rank, recommendation(s), standardized test scores, alumni/ae relation, work experience. *Other factors considered include:* Application essay, character/personal qualities, first generation, geographical residence, interview, level of applicant's interest, racial/ethnic status, state residency. SAT or ACT recommended; TOEFL required of all international applicants. High school diploma is required, and GED is accepted. *Academic units required:* 4 English, 3 mathematics, 3 science, (2 science labs), 2 foreign language, 2 social studies, 2 academic electives. *Academic units recommended:* 3 foreign language.

Financial Aid

Students should submit: FAFSA, CSS/Financial Aid PROFILE, state aid form, noncustodial PROFILE. Regular filing deadline is 2/1. The Princeton Review suggests that all financial aid forms be submitted as soon as possible after January 1. *Need-based scholarships/grants offered:* Federal Pell, SEOG, state scholarships/grants, private scholarships, the school's own gift aid. *Loan aid offered:* Federal Perkins, college/university loans from institutional funds. Applicants will be notified of awards on or about 3/20. Federal Work-Study Program available. Institutional employment available. Off-campus job opportunities are good.

The Inside Word

Dickinson's admissions process is typical of most small liberal arts colleges. The best candidates for such a place are those with solid grades and broad extracurricular involvement—the stereotypical "well-rounded student." Admissions selectivity is kept in check by a strong group of competitor colleges that fight tooth and nail for their cross-applicants.

THE SCHOOL SAYS "..."

From The Admissions Office

"College is more than a collection of courses. It is about crossing traditional boundaries, about seeing the inter-relationships among different subjects, about learning a paradigm for solving problems, about developing critical thinking and communication skills, and about speaking out on issues that matter. Dickinson was intended as an alternative to the 15 colleges that existed in the U.S. at the time of its founding; its aim, then as now, was to provide a "useful" education whereby students would 'learn by doing' through hands-on experience and engagement with the community, the region, the nation, and the world. And this is truer today than ever, with workshop science courses replacing traditional lectures, fieldwork experiences in community studies in which students take oral histories, and 13 study centers abroad in nontourist cities where students, under the guidance of a Dickinson faculty director, experience a true international culture. Almost 53 percent of the student body study abroad, and a total of 58 percent study off campus, preparing them to compete and succeed in a complex global world.

"Applicants wishing to be considered for academic scholarships are required to submit scores from either the SAT or ACT, but Dickinson does not require results from either test for admission."

For even more information on this school, turn to page 482 of the "Stats" section.

DREW UNIVERSITY

36 MADISON AVENUE, MADISON, NJ 07940-1493 • ADMISSIONS: 973-408-3739 • FAX: 973-408-3068
FINANCIAL AID: 973-408-3112 • E-MAIL: CADM@DREW.EDU • WEBSITE: WWW.DREW.EDU

RATINGS
Quality of Life: 77   Academic: 84   Admissions: 86   Financial Aid: 79

STUDENTS SAY "..."

Academics

For 15 years, Drew University was practically synonymous with Tom Kean, the popular university president who had previously served as Governor of New Jersey. Kean's prominence brought lots of regional and national attention to this small school, to the great benefit of students and the university alike. His departure ruffled some feathers, but

> **SURVEY SAYS ...**
> *Frats and sororities are unpopular or nonexistent*
> *Theater is popular*
> *Student publications are popular*
> *Political activism is popular*

Drew seems to have weathered the transition. The plans for expansion (which were started under Kean) have resulted in new majors in Business Studies and Environmental Studies and Sustainability. New scholarships for students who volunteer in their communities for high school are in the works as well. The vast majority of students here continue to extol this "small school with a beautiful campus and prime location" near New York City. The school's location allows students to take advantage of "programs such as Wall Street Semester and United Nations Semester, as well as field trips to theaters on Broadway and art museums." Students also tell us that location affords "awesome job opportunities in the surrounding areas." Students praise the curriculum's liberal arts focus that ensures "that everyone gets exposed to at least a little bit of every other subject before they leave." Drew's "small class sizes allow for the difficulty of the classes to be manageable," and students say "every professor wants to know your name by the end of the semester." While students acknowledge that "Drew is a school that's in the midst of finding and creating its unique identity," they also don't feel any imperative to rush the process. In fact, they tell us that Drew is "one of the best schools in New Jersey when it comes to education," just as it is.

Life

Drew's small size, coupled with the fact that "there are so many clubs, organizations, and sports teams to join" encourages student participation in extracurricular activities. One student opines: "With a school so small, I doubt that anyone who graduates does not have a leadership position in something." An active performing arts program means that there is "lots of involvement in the arts," among students including theater, musical performances, a capella, and student art exhibits." Drew "is not a party school per se" but "for people who do like to party, it's very easy because the alcohol policy is like the world's most un-enforced thing." More often, when students want a wild night they "simply hop on the train a block away and head for Morristown or New York for an evening or weekend," or "when the weather is conducive" they might "take a trip with a few friends down to the beach." Hometown Madison is "adorable" with "a small-town atmosphere." On the downside, "there isn't much to do in town," but with New York City "right around the corner," that's hardly a make-or-break problem.

Student Body

Drew "caters to a lot of wealthy kids from Dirty Jerz (New Jersey)," students who "live within a few hours of campus and have the opportunity to travel home if they choose to, although it does not at all feel like a 'suitcase school.'" Despite this trend, "There is a very wide variety of students at Drew—all different races, ethnicities, and backgrounds." The student body includes "tons of theater kids" as well as "your typical jocks." (One student observes that "there is definitely a division between jocks and everyone else at this school—not that our sports teams are even good.") Students tell us that "Drew is a reach school for some and a safety for others, so there are very, very brilliant students here, while others...not so much." Women outnumber men by a healthy 3-to-2 ratio.

THE PRINCETON REVIEW SAYS

Admissions

Very important factors considered include: Academic GPA, rigor of secondary school record, talent/ability. *Important factors considered include:* Application essay, recommendation(s), extracurricular activities, interview, level of applicant's interest. *Other factors considered include:* class rank, standardized test scores, alumni/ae relation, character/personal qualities, first generation, geographical residence, racial/ethnic status, volunteer work, work experience. ACT with Writing component recommended. TOEFL required of all international applicants. High school diploma or equivalent is not required. *Academic units recommended:* 4 English, 3 mathematics, 2 science, 2 foreign language, 2 social studies, 2 history, 3 academic electives.

Financial Aid

Students should submit: FAFSA. Regular filing deadline is 2/15. The Princeton Review suggests that all financial aid forms be submitted as soon as possible after January 1. *Need-based scholarships/grants offered:* Federal Pell, SEOG, state scholarships/grants, private scholarships, the school's own gift aid. *Loan aid offered:* Federal Perkins, state loans. Applicants will be notified of awards on or about 4/1. Federal Work-Study Program available. Institutional employment available. Off-campus job opportunities are fair.

The Inside Word

Drew University gives applicants the option of submitting a graded writing sample in place of standardized test scores. If the goal was to attract more applicants, all we can say is: mission accomplished. Drew now draws almost 5,400 applicants. The profile of the average admitted student, oddly, hasn't changed; instead, Drew seems to be attracting more applications from those who see the school as a safety.

THE SCHOOL SAYS "..."

From The Admissions Office

"At Drew, great teachers in small classes are transforming the undergraduate learning experience. With a commitment to civic engagement, nurturing leadership skills and mentoring, Drew Professors make educating undergraduates their top priority. With a spirit of innovation, they bring the most distinctive modes of experiential learning into and beyond the Drew classroom. The result is a stimulating and a challenging education that connects the traditional liberal arts and sciences to the community, to the workplace, and to the world. New programs in Business, Public Health, Environmental Science, and new Honors and Civic Scholar Programs complement innovative programs like the Drew International Seminars and NYC semesters focused on Wall Street, the UN, museums, and theaters.

"Drew University is a test optional school; it accepts the SAT, the ACT or, a graded high school research paper. The Selection Committee will consider the highest Verbal, Math, and Writing scores individually in its evaluation of candidates for admission. A student's transcript is considered to be the most important factor during the application process."

For even more information on this school, turn to page 483 of the "Stats" section.

DREXEL UNIVERSITY

3141 CHESTNUT STREET, PHILADELPHIA, PA 19104 • ADMISSIONS: 215-895-2400 • FAX: 215-895-5939
FINANCIAL AID: 215-895-2535 • E-MAIL: ENROLL@DREXEL.EDU • WEBSITE: WWW.DREXEL.EDU

RATINGS
Quality of Life: 84   Academic: 76   Admissions: 87   Financial Aid: 73

STUDENTS SAY ". . ."

Academics

If you survive Drexel University's challenging undergraduate curriculum, "you are going to graduate ready for the real world," students at this engineering and business powerhouse assure us. Offering 70 tough academic majors, "an innovative engineering and business school," and an "awesome co-op program," Drexel "really prepares students to be

the future workforce." Be warned, however, that courses are fast-paced, and "Drexel really pushes its students to the limit with its tight 10-week schedule." Fortunately, "professors are educated and prepared enough to help students get through every task." Even in large lecture courses (and first-year students should expect a few), "The professors are available and willing to help if you reach out to them." At the same time, researching your classes before registration is a must because "professors greatly vary. Some courses you'd be better off teaching yourself, and some professors are great." Through the school's excellent co-op program, students in every field are matched with "a full-time job for six months" (with the possibility of up to 18 months of work experience in total.) This unparalleled experience gives students "the opportunity to gain experience in their field while providing them with a competitive edge upon graduation." When it comes to the school's management, students admit that, "Oftentimes the administration is too concerned with 'the big picture' and forgets to attend to the needs of individuals as opposed to the school as a whole." However, "If you can look past the constant construction and bureaucratic red tape, you'll see that Drexel is one of the most forward-thinking universities out there right now."

Life

Drexel students are busy, ambitious, and career-minded—and proud of it. At this bustling school, "students go on co-op, they max out on class credits, and many work outside jobs either with former co-op companies or with other employers." With the exception of Greek affiliates and athletes, "most students live off campus after their freshman year," and through co-op and work, students are "integrated into the adult world with grown-up problems and consequences." In this way, the Drexel experience "forces you in to the adult world a couple years before most people"—a challenge, as well as an advantage. When they aren't working, studying, or interning, "students may join an intramural league or another such club," watch movies, or work out at the campus recreation center, a "state-of-the-art facility." The campus is located just "five minutes from downtown Philadelphia," so Drexel students take advantage of all the "great things to do in the city, from shopping, to great eateries, to museums, and other cultural activities." In particular, "Phillies games are really popular...and Drexel does a really, really good job of hooking students up with student-discounted tickets with great seats." Back on campus, "Our basketball's fan base—the DAC pack—actively encourages people to come out to basketball games, and there's great school spirit." In addition, "there's always a party going on Thursday night through Saturday"—not to mention constant parties at the Penn State campus across the street.

Student Body

Hard-working and practical, the typical student at Drexel is "focused on their career and takes school seriously." Drexel's hardworking undergraduates admit, "It's part of the campus culture to be stressed out. If you're not stressed then you're not working hard enough." Despite the demanding curriculum, "more often than not, students will help each other on assignments." Demographically, "many students are from suburbs in Pennsylvania, New Jersey, and New York," though there is also a "large international presence" on campus—principally from Asia and the Middle East. On this male-dominated campus, "girls are steadily evening out the percentages, but in any class it is clear they are outnumbered." While you cannot easily classify the student body, Drexel is home to large populations of "international students, athletic students, design students, Greek-life students, and many more types of people." While there is "little mixing of social groups" outside the classroom, there are "a lot of unique people here, so everyone can find their niche."

THE PRINCETON REVIEW SAYS

Admissions

Very important factors considered include: Class rank, academic GPA, rigor of secondary school record, standardized test scores. *Important factors considered include:* Application essay, recommendation(s), character/personal qualities. *Other factors considered include:* Alumni/ae relation, extracurricular activities, first generation, interview, level of applicant's interest, talent/ability, volunteer work, work experience. SAT or ACT required; TOEFL required of all international applicants. High school diploma is required, and GED is accepted. *Academic units required:* 3 mathematics, 1 science, (1 science labs). *Academic units recommended:* 1 foreign language.

Financial Aid

Students should submit: FAFSA. The Princeton Review suggests that all financial aid forms be submitted as soon as possible after January 1. *Need-based scholarships/grants offered:* Federal Pell, SEOG, state scholarships/grants, private scholarships, the school's own gift aid, United Negro College Fund. *Loan aid offered:* Federal Perkins, Federal Nursing, college/university loans from institutional funds. Applicants will be notified of awards on a rolling basis beginning 3/15. Federal Work-Study Program available.

The Inside Word

Drexel enjoys a strong applicant pool. More than 60 percent of freshmen were in the top 25 percent of their high school class. The school operates an early application program for the Westphal College of Media Arts and Design. Top incoming students from all disciplines are also eligible for the A.J. Drexel Scholarship.

THE SCHOOL SAYS "..."

From The Admissions Office

"Drexel has gained a reputation for academic excellence since its founding in 1891. In 2006, Drexel became the first top-ranked doctoral university in more than 25 years to open a law school. Its main campus is a 10-minute walk from Center City Philadelphia. Students prepare for successful careers through Drexel's prestigious experiential education program—The Drexel Co-op. Alternating periods of full-time, professional employment with periods of classroom study, students can earn an average of $14,000 per six-month co-op. At any one time, about 2,000 full-time undergraduates are on co-op assignments. Drexel integrates science and technology into all 70 undergraduate majors. Students looking for a special challenge can apply to one of 14 accelerated degree programs including the BS/MBA in business; BA/BS/MD in medicine; BA/BS/JD in law; BS/MS or BS/PhD in engineering; BS/MS in information technology; and BS/DPT in physical therapy.

"Pennoni Honors College offers high achievers unique opportunities. Students Tackling Advanced Research (STAR) allows qualified undergraduates to participate in a paid summer research project, and the Center for Civic Engagement matches students with community service opportunities. Students in any major can take dance, music, and theater classes offered through Drexel's performing arts programs.

"Drexel's study-abroad program allows students to spend a term or more earning credits while gaining international experience. Adventurous students can also enjoy co-op abroad. Locations include London, Costa Rica, Prague, Rome, and Paris. The admissions office invites prospective students to schedule a campus visit for a first-hand look at all Drexel offers."

For even more information on this school, turn to page 483 of the "Stats" section.

DUQUESNE UNIVERSITY

600 FORBES AVENUE, PITTSBURGH, PA 15282 • ADMISSIONS: 412-396-5000 • FAX: 412-396-5644
FINANCIAL AID: 412-396-6607 • E-MAIL: ADMISSIONS@DUQ.EDU • WEBSITE: WWW.DUQ.EDU

RATINGS
Quality of Life: 80   Academic: 74   Admissions: 82   Financial Aid: 82

STUDENTS SAY "..."

Academics

> SURVEY SAYS . . .
> *Athletic facilities are great*
> *Students love Pittsburgh, PA*
> *Low cost of living*

Cosmopolitan yet caring, you get the best of both worlds at Duquesne University. Located in the heart of downtown Pittsburgh, this Catholic school unites "the diversity and opportunities of an urban university with the community and comfort of a small liberal arts college." "Well respected in the Pittsburgh area," health fields are particularly strong at Duquesne. "The physician assistant program is world-renowned and selective," while pharmacy students say it is unique to find such a "good pharmacy program [at] a smaller university." The music school also receives ample praise and benefits from studio teachers who are "some of the best in the world." Regardless of the specific program, "Professors are eager to really engage with students and are available for extra support whenever you need it." Course work can be challenging, yet "The school wants [its] students to do well, and it offers many different services to aid in this." In fact, "every department offers free tutors" to help students make the grade. On the flip side, the school's academic advisors often fall short, and many students struggle to schedule classes and meet graduation requirements. A music student admits, "One semester I was not even a full-time student because my advisor failed to schedule three of my classes!" Fortunately, the majority of the school's staff is accessible, visible, and friendly; "The administrators, the professors, and the school ministers can be seen walking around campus. All of them have been known to stop and talk to groups of students around the school."

Life

Located "on a very pretty, secluded campus in the middle of downtown Pittsburgh," students at Duquesne love their school's location, just steps outside a city with "a rich cultural district and an even better nightlife." During the week, "life at school consists of going to classes, spending many hours at the library, and going to Starbucks for social interactions." During the weekend, things get more exciting. Thanks to "the free campus buses that shuttle students to the Oakland and South Side areas on Friday and Saturday nights," students enjoy "bars, movie theaters, concerts (big names and locals), and tons of restaurants." While the Duquesne campus is dry, "Many people go out on the weekends, typically to parties on the south side or at the University of Pittsburgh." In addition, "Students also attend a lot of sporting events, including the Pittsburgh Steelers and Penguins, Duquesne games and Pitt games." If you don't feel like straying too far from home, the school manages a campus club called Nite Spot, "where they show movies that haven't come out on DVD yet, have bizarre activities like pillow-making that actually turn out to be really fun, and dance lessons." Another popular hangout is the Power Center—the "nicest facility on campus"—where "the exercise equipment is new and the classes are free."

Student Body

From Greek organizations to the table tennis club, "many of the students at Duquesne are very involved in campus organizations and service-oriented activities." At the same time, students are "driven to succeed" academically, and "show up to every class with his or her work complete." "Well mannered and well dressed," Duquesne students don their best duds to go to lecture, and "the majority of people look like they just walked out a fashion catalogue." Students admit the school is not particularly diverse, and "the typical student at Duquesne is white, from the Pittsburgh area (or at least Pennsylvania), and Catholic." However, "Not all of the student body has Catholic values, and I have found that the student body doesn't push their own values onto anyone else." With 5,800 undergraduates, "the school is big enough that you can meet a lot of different people, but small enough that you have a sense of community by being able to see people you know anywhere you go on campus." Still, most students divide into smaller cliques, and "unless you join a frat or sorority, making a large networked group of friends is difficult."

THE PRINCETON REVIEW SAYS

Admissions

Very important factors considered include: Application essay, academic GPA, recommendation(s), rigor of secondary school record, standardized test scores. *Important factors considered include:* Class rank, character/personal qualities, extracurricular activities, interview, talent/ability, volunteer work. *Other factors considered include:* Alumni/ae relation, first generation, level of applicant's interest, racial/ethnic status, work experience. SAT or ACT required; ACT with Writing component required. High school diploma is required, and GED is accepted. *Academic units recommended:* 4 English, 2 mathematics, 2 science, 2 foreign language, 2 social studies, 4 academic electives.

Financial Aid

Students should submit: FAFSA, institution's own financial aid form. Regular filing deadline is 5/1. The Princeton Review suggests that all financial aid forms be submitted as soon as possible after January 1. *Need-based scholarships/grants offered:* Federal Pell, SEOG, state scholarships/grants, private scholarships, the school's own gift aid, United Negro College Fund. *Loan aid offered:* Federal Perkins, Federal Nursing, other, Private alternative loans. Applicants will be notified of awards on a rolling basis beginning 3/1. Federal Work-Study Program available. Institutional employment available. Off-campus job opportunities are good.

The Inside Word

Duquesne requires all prospective students to complete a college preparatory curriculum in high school; however, there is no minimum GPA required for admission, nor minimum test scores. Nonetheless, a student's academic record and test scores are the only two factors considered in awarding merit scholarships.

THE SCHOOL SAYS "..."

From The Admissions Office

"Duquesne University was founded in 1878 by the Holy Ghost Fathers. Although it is a private, Roman Catholic institution, Duquesne is proud of its ecumenical reputation. Duquesne University's attractive and secluded campus is set on a 49-acre hilltop ('the bluff') overlooking the large corporate metropolis of Pittsburgh's Golden Triangle. It offers a wide variety of educational opportunities, from the liberal arts to modern professional training. Duquesne is a medium-sized university striving to offer personal attention to its students in addition to the versatility and opportunities of a true university. A deep sense of tradition is combined with innovation and flexibility to make the Duquesne experience both challenging and rewarding. The Palumbo Convocation/Recreation Complex features a 6,300-seat arena, home court to the university's Division I basketball team; racquetball and handball courts; weight rooms; and saunas. Extracurricular activities are recognized as an essential part of college life, complementing academics in the process of total student development. Students are involved in nearly 100 university-sponsored activities, and Duquesne's location gives students the opportunity to enjoy sports and cultural events both on campus and in the city. There are six residence halls with the capacity to house 3,538 students."

For even more information on this school, turn to page 484 of the "Stats" section.

Eastern Connecticut State University

83 Windham Street, Willimantic, CT 06226 Admissions: 860-465-5286 • Fax: 860-465-5544
Financial Aid: 860-465-5205 • E-mail: admissions@easternct.edu • Website: www.easternct.edu

RATINGS
Quality of Life: 71   Academic: 78   Admissions: 69   Financial Aid: 65

STUDENTS SAY ". . ."

Academics

Otherwise known as "Connecticut's public liberal arts school," Eastern Connecticut State University offers many of the conveniences of a private-school education, at an affordable in-state price. "A smaller school with smaller classes," ECSU's "thorough liberal arts curriculum" is conducted within a "comfortable learning environment." Among the faculty, there is "refreshing" variety: "Each professor has their own way of teaching, but each of them manages to make class interesting and engaging." More importantly, "The professors seem to be very knowledgeable and loaded with extensive experience in their specific field." In most majors, the workload is "challenging but not overbearing." If you do get bogged down, "The professors, for the most part, want to see their students succeed and are very understanding when it comes to personal needs." Moreover, a student adds, "I went to the academic advisement center and I was amazed about how fast I was helped, and it actually made a positive difference in my work." Some students dislike the school's advising system, explaining, "All advisors are also professors who have very little time to spare." The school recently hired four full-time advisors to help address this isssue. While the president is often seen walking around campus or attending student events, "the administration stays more behind the scenes and [is] less accessible than professors."

> **SURVEY SAYS . . .**
> *Low cost of living*
> *Frats and sororities are unpopular or nonexistent*

Life

Although 40 percent of Eastern students commute to school, those who live on campus say, "Most students are very happy with their residence halls, the food on campus, [and] events on campus." For daily doses of recreation, "The residence halls offer activities such as billiards or ping pong, while there is a well-updated and oft-used gym right on campus." "Attending sporting events is popular" with the athletic student body, and "There are always activities going on such as movies, parties, crafts, music, [and] comedians. You will never be bored at this school." For a change of pace, "The town around campus [Willimantic] offers many excellent venues for food and entertainment, with live music in many places." Socially, "there is no Greek system" at ECSU and the "school is strictly a dry campus." Therefore, "most people go off-campus to party," often visiting "a few local bars" within walking distance. Generally considered a "suitcase school," weekends are quiet at Eastern, and "By 4 o'clock Friday, nearly half of the school has left to go home."

Student Body

Eastern boasts an "outgoing and enthusiastic" student population. Among the school's 4,000-plus full-time undergraduates, most are "active in the campus community by participating in clubs and activities," and many also take part in community service projects. Academically, "There is a large portion of students who are very focused on their schoolwork and [are] constantly using the library or computer lab to do their work." On the other hand, some students "only give minimal amounts of effort in order to pass classes." "The average student is white and middle class," though there are "many different races, socioeconomic statuses, and all sexual orientations" on campus. Personality-wise, "Everyone is very different, from athletes (which can be further split up into soccer, basketball, [and] lacrosse players) to RAs, to biology majors." Overall, however, "students are casual and friendly," and "If someone is different they are accepted and everyone listens to their ideas."

THE PRINCETON REVIEW SAYS

Admissions

Very important factors considered include: Class rank, standardized test scores, talent/ability. *Important factors considered include:* Academic GPA, recommendation(s), rigor of secondary school record, level of applicant's interest. *Other factors considered include:* application essay, character/personal qualities, extracurricular activities, interview, volunteer work, work experience. SAT or ACT required; TOEFL required of all international applicants. High school diploma is required and GED is accepted. *Academic units required:* 4 English, 3 mathematics, 2 science, (1 science labs), 2 foreign language, 2 social studies, 3 history.

Financial Aid

Students should submit: FAFSA. The Princeton Review suggests that all financial aid forms be submitted as soon as possible after January 1. *Need-based scholarships/grants offered:* Federal Pell, SEOG, state scholarships/grants, private scholarships, the school's own gift aid. *Loan aid offered:* Federal Perkins. Federal Work-Study Program available. Institutional employment available. Off-campus job opportunities are excellent.

The Inside Word

Students ranked within the top half of their high school class stand a good chance of admission to Eastern. Test scores and personal recommendations are important factors in ECSU's admissions decision. Through the "New England Regional Student Program," residents of Maine, Rhode Island, Massachusetts, New Hampshire, and Vermont are eligible for reduced tuition and fees in select academic programs.

THE SCHOOL SAYS "..."

From The Admissions Office

"Eastern's admissions staff encourages motivated students who are interested in a quality, affordable liberal arts education to apply for admission. Eastern's admission committee evaluates all applications under the same criteria with emphasis placed on the applicant's prior academic performance in high school and demonstrated commitment to community service and active engagement. Admission decisions are made on a rolling basis. Students are encouraged to apply as early as possible but no later than May 1 for the fall semester. Information sessions and campus tours are offered daily. Prospective students are strongly encouraged to visit to learn first-hand why Eastern is recognized as the best public liberal arts university in Connecticut."

For even more information on this school, turn to page 484 of the "Stats" section.

ELIZABETHTOWN COLLEGE

LEFFLER HOUSE, ONE ALPHA DRIVE, ELIZABETHTOWN, PA 17022 • ADMISSIONS: 717-361-1400
FAX: 717-361-1365 • E-MAIL: ADMISSIONS@ETOWN.EDU • WEBSITE: WWW.ETOWN.EDU

RATINGS
Quality of Life: 88　　**Academic: 83**　　**Admissions: 86**　　**Financial Aid: 82**

STUDENTS SAY ". . ."

Academics

Elizabethtown College in central Pennsylvania offers a broad core curriculum and "very small" classes. "This semester I have class sizes ranging from five to 23 people," comments a biotechnology major. "It's really nice to hear your professors call you by name during class, or even if they

see you on campus." Study abroad programs in more than two dozen countries are popular as well. "I have studied abroad in Australia and China," brags a senior. On Etown's "aesthetically appealing campus," "most professors are very good teachers. As you will find everywhere, some are not the greatest, but the tutors [in the Learning Services department] can help with those courses." "I've taken courses in various departments and they are all fabulous instructors and just great people in general," gloats a happy psychology major. "They really take an interest not just in your school work, but are eager to know about your personal life and are willing to do anything to help you succeed." Some students call the management "arrogant and aloof." Others aren't so harsh. "Overall, the administration is incompetent even though they mean well," proposes a senior.

Life

"Etown is a nice place," says a senior. "The intimacy of the college really stands out." It's also "very safe." There's an "integrity policy" that students take seriously. You can leave your valuables most anywhere and "they will be there when you return." Also, Elizabethtown's motto is "Educate for Service" and a laudable amount of volunteerism goes on. Many students think "the dorms could be improved," though. There is also disagreement about the quality of student life. "I would warn people to prepare to have a car and go off campus on weekends if they want something interesting to do," advises a dissatisfied junior. Other students contend that extracurricular involvement is high. Student-run organizations "really put a lot of effort into making sure there are on-campus activities," they say. "Life at Etown is never dull. There are always things to do on the weekend or during the week—everyone is very involved in activities on and off campus." "The students who are disappointed with their time here are those who expect the *Animal House*, large state-school experience." Though drinking definitely happens on this campus, the atmosphere is "rarely thrust in your face." There are no fraternities or sororities. Instead, athletic teams "basically sustain the social life" with house parties. Road trips to Harrisburg and Lancaster are frequent and Hershey is only a few miles north. When the wind is right, the campus "sometimes smells like chocolate."

Student Body

"To sum it up quite simply," says a senior, "Etowners are nice people." They are "down to earth" kids "with diverse interests and spunk." "Geographically, most students are from the Mid-Atlantic area, especially Pennsylvania and New Jersey." They tend to come from a "Christian background." The school is "affiliated with the Church of the Brethren" (which is sort of comparable to the Quaker and Mennonite churches). "You don't see a lot of religious activity on campus, though." Elizabethtown is home to "very typical 18–22 year olds" "from the suburbs." "Most students are a little on the preppy side." "There aren't too many rebels" and "there are barely any atypical students." The gay population is "freakishly small." A solid smattering of international students "adds a diverse element" but ethnic minorities are scarce. "Looking around, you will see mostly white students." "I wish we had more diversity here," hankers a freshman.

Admissions

Very important factors considered include: Rigor of secondary school record. *Important factors considered include:* Class rank, recommendation(s), standardized test scores, interview, racial/ethnic status, volunteer work. *Other factors considered include:* Application essay, alumni/ae relation, character/personal qualities, extracurricular activities, geographical residence, religious affiliation/commitment, state residency, talent/ability, work experience. SAT or ACT required; TOEFL required of all international applicants. High school diploma is required and GED is accepted. *Academic units required:* 4 English, 3 mathematics, 2 science, (2 science labs), 2 foreign language, 2 social studies, 2 history. *Academic units recommended:* 4 English, 4 mathematics, 4 science, (3 science labs), 2 foreign language, 2 social studies, 2 history, 2 academic electives.

Financial Aid

Students should submit: FAFSA, institution's own financial aid form, Federal Tax Records. The Princeton Review suggests that all financial aid forms be submitted as soon as possible after January 1. *Need-based scholarships/grants offered:* Federal Pell, SEOG, state scholarships/grants, private scholarships, the school's own gift aid. *Loan aid offered:* Federal Perkins, state loans. Applicants will be notified of awards on a rolling basis beginning 3/1.

The Inside Word

The Admissions Office at Elizabethtown strongly encourages you to tell "what experiences are uniquely yours and how [they] will distinguish you from other applicants." The popular occupational therapy and allied health programs fill quickly, so if you are interested in these options, apply early.

THE SCHOOL SAYS "…"

From The Admissions Office

"The most important aspect of the admissions program is to admit graduates of Elizabethtown. The entire focus of the admissions process is determining if a student is a good fit for Elizabethtown and if Elizabethtown is a good fit for the student. We pride ourselves on our 'conversational interviews' as a way to set students at ease so that we can discover their potential to contribute to our community. Applicants are assessed in three areas: academic fit, co-curricular fit, and social fit. Integrity, diversity, academic excellence, and a commitment to services are qualities that are highly valued.

"Elizabethtown distinguishes its educational experience by blending a high standard of scholarship with four signature attributes: educating students in a relationship-centered learning community, fostering in students international and cross-cultural perspectives, complementing classroom instruction with experiential-learning opportunities, and preparing students for purposeful lives and meaningful work. This year, the college will graduate two NCAA Postgrad scholars. The college is also one of a few small, regional colleges to have recently graduated a Rhodes Scholar. The campus visit will set Elizabethtown apart from other places as you experience the beautiful campus and new buildings for business and science, mathematics and engineering, and newly renovated athletic facility."

For even more information on this school, turn to page 485 of the "Stats" section.

ELMIRA COLLEGE

ONE PARK PLACE, ELMIRA, NY 14901 • ADMISSIONS: 607-735-1724 • FAX: 607-735-1718
E-MAIL: ADMISSIONS@ELMIRA.EDU • WEBSITE: WWW.ELMIRA.EDU

RATINGS

Quality of Life: 65   Academic: 79   Admissions: 84   Financial Aid: 77

STUDENTS SAY ". . ."

Academics

"Elmira College is all about school spirit," students agree, pointing to the ubiquitous octagons (the official school shape) and purple everything ("Our school color is every-where: the rugs, the walkways, the soap in the bathrooms, the rock salt in winter...the punch for special occasions"). The ever-present school spirit is something a fact that many here find appealing, and a few feel is "a little ridiculous."

> **SURVEY SAYS . . .**
> Low cost of living
> Everyone loves the Soaring Eagles
> Frats and sororities are unpopular or nonexistent
> Lots of beer drinking
> Hard liquor is popular

Undoubtedly the school is best suited to those who long to immerse themselves in community-building tradi-tions. It also helps if they enjoy co-curricular requirements like the Encore Program (students must attend eight performing arts productions each term during freshman and sophomore years) and community service (60 hours during freshman year). Other unique curricular features here include a required Saturday morning writ-ing class for freshmen (generally resented, although some appreciate how it keeps freshmen from going home on weekends) and a six-week short term in April and May called Term III, it's "devoted to travel, field experi-ence, research, independent study, and innovative courses." Students call it "the best thing ever." Elmira "is best known for its nursing and education programs." Business and the sciences are also popular.

Life

The city of Elmira "does not give too much to the students. Sure, there are places to eat, mini-malls, and bigger malls, but that can get old. How many times can a college student go out to eat? We're not made of money and can't afford that every week, never mind every night!" Worse still, some here feel the city is "sketchy and unsafe." Others counter "the idea that Elmira is 'sketchy' depends on where your hometown is "says one stu-dent." My hometown is a big city, so this area seems really tame to me." Fortunately, "Elmira College knows this" about its hometown and compensates. "Every weekend they set up some comedian or band to come and play." In addition, campus life provides "athletic events all week and movies every weekend, usually ones that were in theaters and are very popular! All in all, there's a lot to do for a small college." Although EC "does not have any fraternities or sororities, people still find lots of ways to get connected. Partying on weekends is com-mon, but it's not rampant. You can choose not to take part in it and avoid it easily."

Student Body

"There are a lot more females than males at Elmira College," but students tell us "that is slowly changing" as the school pursues diversity more aggressively. Similarly, "the black community is on the rise" here although it still remains quite small. Minority representation arrives mostly in the form of "a rather large international student population." Elmira "loves collecting valedictorians and salutatorians, giving them huge financial aid so they can brag about the ridiculous percentages," thus many here were high achievers in high school. "About half of the population participates in sports of some kind at some level, be it varsity, junior varsity, or intramural." There is also "a large gay community" on campus, and students report the environment is "GLBT friendly."

Admissions

Very important factors considered include: Class rank, academic GPA, rigor of secondary school record, character/personal qualities. *Important factors considered include:* Application essay, recommendation(s), standardized test scores, extracurricular activities. *Other factors considered include:* Alumni/ae relation, first generation, geographical residence, interview, level of applicant's interest, racial/ethnic status, talent/ability, volunteer work, work experience. SAT or ACT required; TOEFL required of all international applicants. High school diploma is required and GED is accepted. *Academic units required:* 4 English, 3 mathematics, 3 science, (2 science labs), 3 social studies, 1 history, 2 academic electives. *Academic units recommended:* 2 foreign language.

Financial Aid

Students should submit: FAFSA, state aid form. State aid forms if applicable (NY, VT, RI). Regular filing deadline is 6/30. The Princeton Review suggests that all financial aid forms be submitted as soon as possible after January 1. *Need-based scholarships/grants offered:* Federal Pell, SEOG, state scholarships/grants, private scholarships, the school's own gift aid. *Loan aid offered:* Federal Perkins, college/university loans from institutional funds, other, GATE Student Loan; private alternative loans. Applicants will be notified of awards on a rolling basis beginning 2/1. Federal Work-Study Program available. Institutional employment available. Off-campus job opportunities are good.

The Inside Word

Matchmaking is an important factor in Elmira admissions. The staff has a good idea of who will succeed here and attempts to fashion incoming classes accordingly. Enthusiasm for Elmira is a big part of the equation, meaning an overnight campus visit can impact your chances quite positively.

THE SCHOOL SAYS "..."

From The Admissions Office

"Elmira College remains rooted in the liberal arts and sciences, enriching its students' inquiry and analysis of their world, communication skills, and civic and ethical responsibility. The college also requires every student to complete a career-related internship, knowing this hands-on experience helps 98 percent of June graduates secure jobs in their desired field of employment or enter graduate or professional school by Labor Day each year. More than one-third of the student body studies abroad with Elmira College professors during the 6-week spring term. The college's 12:1 student/faculty ratio allows the academic experience to be both rigorous and individualized. No classes are taught by teaching assistants. Committed to the residential college experience, on-campus housing is guaranteed all 4 years for undergraduates. Elmira College alumni are loyal, offering internships for students and demonstrating unwavering commitment through giving generously of their time, professional expertise, and financial resources."

For even more information on this school, turn to page 485 of the "Stats" section.

EMERSON COLLEGE

120 BOYLSTON STREET, BOSTON, MA 02116-4624 • ADMISSIONS: 617-824-8600 • FAX: 617-824-8609
FINANCIAL AID: 617-824-8655 • E-MAIL: ADMISSION@EMERSON.EDU • WEBSITE: WWW.EMERSON.EDU

RATINGS
Quality of Life: 91   Academic: 82   Admissions: 94   Financial Aid: 82

STUDENTS SAY "..."

Academics

God help the future Wall Streeters who somehow find themselves members of the student body at Emerson, a big happy
group of "creative people" who come together to share their
passions ("whether it be on the stage, the page, the big screen
or the small"), and learn more about their own mediums of
self-expressions via collaboration with diverse individuals.
The focus on the more creative side of communication and
the arts, provides "a community that (usually) understands
what an artist needs to thrive and grow." "People come to

Emerson knowing exactly what they want to do, and then [they] do that thing all out for four years," says a sophomore. According to its students, Emerson "brings creativity and ingenuity to the arts and communication unlike
any other school in the country." Although those who attend the school are more than aware that most of their fellow students might be "part of the next generation of America's starving artists (unless you're a marketing or CSD
major)," the school does a tremendous job of offering each student a "specialized career-oriented experience," no
matter how non-traditional the career path.

The excellent student-teacher ratio means personal attention that goes beyond just office hours, which translates
into a lot of time spent with people who are "practicing professionals in their respective fields." The largest classroom at Emerson can accommodate only about 70 students, so lectures (if a student even has any) "are only about
50 students large," and one must "be prepared to do most of your learning outside of the classroom in projects."
Design and technology majors in particular get a good deal of hands-on experience. While there can be "a little
too much red tape around some of the administrative aspects of Emerson," one student claims that "there is no
other school I have encountered where one would feel more easily acknowledged and listened to by professors."

Life

The drive to succeed in such competitive industries means "a majority of students are busier than the average professional" and "don't really sleep," which is not surprising, considering all of the rehearsals, film shoots, concerts,
and organization meetings seemingly required of Emerson life. The school is located right in the heart of downtown Boston, and many admit that it can be hard to concentrate with Boston Common right across the street and
the realization that "you live in a city, not a campus bubble." After junior year "most people live off campus,"
which is where most parties are also hosted; although there's a fair share of partying for those who are interested,
"students are more inclined to have an 80's costume and dance party than a frat bash." For those who resist the
lure of the cafés, theaters, bars, and performances, plain old-fashioned silliness in the dorms seems equally as
exciting, "like coloring or old video games or children's books—everyone just wants to have fun."

Student Body

Around Boston, "an Emerson student can be spotted from a mile away," not because they all look alike, but
because they all look so different (although "if you wanted to peg Emerson students as the artsy young adults
with an offbeat fashion-forward style and a cigarette in one hand and Starbucks in the other, it wouldn't be hor-
ribly inaccurate"). Almost all students find a common thread in a love of the arts, which often results in a unifying ambition amongst "people wanting to 'make it' in their field." One film student remarks that Emerson is
filled with what she refers to as "my 'type' of people." This "friendly, eclectic, and fun" group of students leans
pretty far to the left politically, and there is a large gay community at Emerson. There seems to be one student in
every class that "can be pretentious and annoying," but these souls are in the minority. Overall, Emersonians are
a "very accepting community" of driven individuals.

Admissions

Very important factors considered include: Academic GPA, standardized test scores. *Important factors considered include:* Class rank, application essay, recommendation(s), rigor of secondary school record, character/personal qualities, extracurricular activities, talent/ability. *Other factors considered include:* Alumni/ae relation, first generation, geographical residence, racial/ethnic status, volunteer work, work experience. SAT or ACT required; ACT with Writing component required. TOEFL required of all international applicants. High school diploma is required, and GED is accepted. *Academic units required:* 4 English, 3 mathematics, 3 science, 3 foreign language, 3 social studies. *Academic units recommended:* 4 English, 3 mathematics, 3 science, 3 foreign language, 3 social studies, 4 academic electives.

Financial Aid

Students should submit: FAFSA, CSS/Financial Aid PROFILE, noncustodial PROFILE, business/farm supplement. Tax Returns. The Princeton Review suggests that all financial aid forms be submitted as soon as possible after January 1. *Need-based scholarships/grants offered:* Federal Pell, SEOG, state scholarships/grants, private scholarships, the school's own gift aid. *Loan aid offered:* Federal Perkins, state loans. Applicants will be notified of awards on or about 4/1. Federal Work-Study Program available. Institutional employment available. Off-campus job opportunities are excellent.

The Inside Word

Expect your living situation to be made easier by recent developments on Emerson's campus. The Max Mutchnick Campus Center, named in recognition of the substantial gift made by the Emerson alumnus and co-creator/executive producer of *Will & Grace*, is an 185,000-square-foot building that features a gym, offices, and residence hall. This facility, combined with the new Paramount Center residence hall and renovation of the Colonial Theatre (which also features dorm rooms), means nearly three quarters of the students will be able to live on campus and indulge in affordable rent.

THE SCHOOL SAYS "..."

From The Admissions Office

"Founded in 1880, Emerson is one of the premier colleges in the country for communication and the arts. Students may choose from more than two-dozen undergraduate and graduate programs supported by state-of-the-art facilities and a nationally renowned faculty. The campus is home to WERS-FM, the oldest noncommercial radio station in Boston; the historic 1,200-seat Cutler Majestic Theatre; and *Ploughshares*, the award winning literary journal for new writing.

"Located on Boston Common in the heart of the city's Theatre District, the campus is walking distance from the Massachusetts State House, Chinatown, and historic Freedom Trail. More than half the students reside on-campus, some in special learning communities such as the Writers' Block and Digital Culture Floor. There is also a fitness center, athletic field, and new gymnasium and campus center.

"Emerson has nearly 80 student organizations and performance groups as well as 15 NCAA teams, student publications, and honor societies. The College also sponsors programs in Los Angeles and Washington, D.C.; study abroad in the Netherlands, Taiwan, and Czech Republic; and course cross-registration with the six-member Boston ProArts Consortium.

"Students have access to outstanding facilities, including sound treated television studios, digital editing and audio post-production suites. An 11-story performance and production center houses a theatre design/technology center, makeup lab, and costume shop. There are seven programs to observe speech and hearing therapy, a professional marketing focus group room, and digital newsroom, and new performance development center with a sound stage, scene shop, black box, and film screening room."

For even more information on this school, turn to page 485 of the "Stats" section.

EUGENE LANG COLLEGE—THE NEW SCHOOL FOR LIBERAL ARTS

65 WEST ELEVENTH STREET, NEW YORK, NY 10011 • ADMISSIONS: 212-229-5665 • FAX: 212-229-5355
FINANCIAL AID: 212-229-8930 • E-MAIL: LANG@NEWSCHOOL.EDU • WEBSITE: WWW.LANG.EDU

RATINGS
Quality of Life: 71   **Academic:** 83   **Admissions:** 85   **Financial Aid:** 72

STUDENTS SAY ". . ."

Academics

Eugene Lang College is an "unconventional," highly urban school with few academic requirements where courses have "really long poetic titles" and professors "go by their first names." "Lang is about small classes in a big city," summarizes a writing major. There's a "rich intellectual tradition" and, no matter what your major, an "interdisciplinary curriculum." "At Eugene Lang, you have the freedom to pursue your artistic or intellectual direction with absolute freedom,"

> **SURVEY SAYS . . .**
> *Lots of conservative students*
> *Class discussions encouraged*
> *Athletic facilities need improving*
> *Students aren't religious*
> *Students love New York, NY*
> *Great off-campus food*
> *Intercollegiate sports are unpopular or nonexistent*

says a philosophy major. However, "students who are uncomfortable in a city and who are not excited about learning for learning's sake should not come to this school." Lang's "clueless," "incredibly bureaucratic" administration is hugely unpopular. The "approachable" and monolithically "radical" faculty is a mixed bag. "Seventy-five percent of the professors are pure gold, but the 25 percent who are not really are awful." "Lang's greatest strength (other than location) is its seminar style of teaching," explains a first-year student. "I've yet to be in a class with more then 15 people." Students say their class discussions are phenomenal. "The students, however, at times can be somewhat draining." "All the teachers are highly susceptible to being led off on long tangents" and some "are too gentle and not comfortable shutting down wandering or irrelevant conversation." Juniors and seniors can take classes at several schools within the larger university (including Parsons The New School for Design and Mannes College The New School for Music). "So if Lang's ultra-liberal, writing-intensive seminars are too much," notes an urban studies major, "you can always take a break." Internships all over Manhattan are common, too.

Life

There are "great talks given on campus every week by a wide variety of academics on almost every social issue imaginable." Otherwise, "Lang is the anti-college experience." "There is very little community" on this speck of a campus on the northern end of Greenwich Village. "Space and facilities are limited." "There is no safe haven in the form of a communal student space" except for "a courtyard of a million cigarette butts." Certainly, "you aren't going to have the traditional college fun" here. On the other hand, few students anywhere else enjoy this glorious level of independence. "Life at Eugene Lang is integrated completely with living in New York City," and "you have the entire city at your fingertips." When you walk out of class, "you walk out into a city of 9 million people." There are dorms here, but "most students have apartments," especially after freshman year. For fun, Lang students sometimes "hang around other students' apartments and smoke pot." Many "thoroughly enjoy the club scene." Mostly though, "people band into small groups and then go out adventuring in the city" where "there is always something to do that you've never done, or even heard of, before."

Student Body

"Lang offers the kids with dreadlocks and piercings an alternative place to gather, smoke, and write pretentious essays." It's "overrun with rabid hipsters." "Cool hair" and "avant-garde" attitudes proliferate. So do "tight pants." "Every student at Lang thinks they are an atypical student." "There is a running joke that all Lang students were 'that kid' in high school," says a senior. "Shock is very popular around here," and "everyone fits in as long as they are not too mainstream." "It's the normal ones who have the trouble," suggests a sophomore. "But once they take up smoking and embrace their inner hipster, everything's cool." "There are a lot of queer students, who seem to be comfortable." "We're really not all that ethnically diverse," admits a first-year student. There are "less affluent kids due to great financial aid," and there is a strong contingent of "trust-fund babies" and "over-privileged communists from Connecticut." "Most students are wealthy but won't admit it," says a senior. "To be from a rich family and have it be apparent is a cardinal sin." "Most students are extremely liberal and on the same wavelength politically." "Conservative kids are the freaks at our school. Left is in. But having a Republican in class is so exciting," suggest a senior. "We can finally have a debate."

THE PRINCETON REVIEW SAYS

Admissions

Very important factors considered include: Application essay, academic GPA, recommendation(s), rigor of secondary school record. *Important factors considered include:* Standardized test scores, character/personal qualities, interview, level of applicant's interest, volunteer work. *Other factors considered include:* Class rank, alumni/ae relation, extracurricular activities, first generation, geographical residence, talent/ability, work experience. SAT or ACT required; TOEFL required of all international applicants. High school diploma is required, and GED is accepted. *Academic units required:* 4 English. *Academic units recommended:* 3 mathematics, 3 science, 2 foreign language, 3 social studies, 2 history.

Financial Aid

Students should submit: FAFSA, state aid form. The Princeton Review suggests that all financial aid forms be submitted as soon as possible after January 1. *Need-based scholarships/grants offered:* Federal Pell, SEOG, state scholarships/grants, private scholarships, the school's own gift aid. *Loan aid offered:* Federal Perkins. Applicants will be notified of awards on a rolling basis beginning 3/1. Federal Work-Study Program available. Institutional employment available. Off-campus job opportunities are excellent.

The Inside Word

The college draws a very self-selected and intellectually curious pool. Those who demonstrate little self-motivation will find themselves denied. It would be a terrible idea to blow off the interview here.

THE SCHOOL SAYS "..."

From The Admissions Office

"Eugene Lang College offers students of diverse backgrounds an innovative and creative approach to a liberal arts education, combining the stimulating classroom activity of a small, intimate college with the rich resources of a dynamic, urban university—The New School. The curriculum at Lang is challenging and flexible. Small classes, limited in size to 18 students, promote energetic and thoughtful discussions, and writing is an essential component of all classes. Students can earn a bachelor's degree in Liberal Arts by designing their own program of study within one of 14 interdisciplinary areas in the arts, social sciences, and humanities. Lang also offers bachelor's degrees in the Arts (pending New York State approval), Culture and Media, Economics, Education Studies, Environmental Studies (pending New York State approval), History (pending New York State approval), Philosophy, and Psychology. Students have the opportunity to pursue a five-year BA/BFA or BA/MA with other programs offered at the university. Lang's Greenwich Village location puts many of the city's cultural treasures—museums, libraries, music venues, theaters, and more—at your doorstep."

For even more information on this school, turn to page 486 of the "Stats" section.

FAIRFIELD UNIVERSITY

1073 NORTH BENSON ROAD, FAIRFIELD, CT 06824 • ADMISSIONS: 203-254-4100 • FAX: 203-254-4199
FINANCIAL AID: 203-254-4125 • E-MAIL: ADMIS@MAIL.FAIRFIELD.EDU • WEBSITE: WWW.FAIRFIELD.EDU

RATINGS
Quality of Life: 75   **Academic:** 80   **Admissions:** 89   **Financial Aid:** 77

STUDENTS SAY "..."

Academics

Study amongst the trees of the "breathtaking campus" at Fairfield University, a competitive mid-sized school with a Division I basketball team and Jesuit ideals. A stalwart of the preppy New England college scene, the school has wealth and is definitely "image conscious," but financial aid packages are said to be super for students in need." Fairfield's extremely rigorous and time-consuming core courses ensure that students receive a well-rounded education, and the small enrollment assures students small class

> **SURVEY SAYS . . .**
> *Great library*
> *Diversity lacking on campus*
> *Great off-campus food*
> *Frats and sororities are unpopular or nonexistent*
> *Student publications are popular*
> *Lots of beer drinking*
> *Hard liquor is popular*

sizes once they move beyond the mandatory curriculum. The school's Connecticut location is just an hour away from New York City, which provides a plethora of work-study and internship possibilities for the students. This is especially convenient for students in Fairfield's notably strong nursing and business programs, the latter of which is taught by a faculty mostly comprised of current and ex-professionals.

Though students are generally happy here, thanks to an involved student government and a high quality of life, many wish that there was "more school spirit" amongst the student body. The "Leviathan" administration has not curried much favor with students, with the Registrar, Career Planning and the Division of Student Affairs receiving singular complaints. Complaints of inefficacy and bureaucracy abound, and the various offices "act in distinct bubbles, with one hand not knowing what the other is doing." Opinions of professors are at the opposite end of the spectrum, as most find almost all their teachers "extremely engaging" and "wonderful people." "They actually read your essays and provide constructive criticism," says a student. "Professors have been amazing, inspiring, accessible, and have defined my time at Fairfield," says another.

Life

Not surprising for a school with an "ideal party location on the beaches of the Long Island Sound, only an hour north of New York City by train," students here like to drink. Although all go to "most of the classes," they know that they "must leave time for going out on Tuesdays, Thursdays, and the weekend," making Fairfield "the opposite of a suitcase school." "Weekends are usually for partying, whether it's a townhouse party or a party down at the beach." There are some great bars in town, too. This isn't to say that hedonism completely rules the school; many students remain very active in student activities and service organizations, and for those who don't want to party, the late-night programming "offers tons of activities and trips almost every Thursday, Friday, and Saturday night." The student government organizes many of these events, as well as trips into the city for Broadway performances, comedy shows, and sporting events.

Student Body

Almost everyone hails from the Northeast at this "homogenous, preppy school" with "generally very intelligent" students. Pockets run pretty deep amongst students, which leads some of this "Ugg wearing, blond haired, Seven for All Mankind-wearing" crowd to "think they're God's gift to mankind." There are plenty of "more mellow, normal folks" here, and even though "it doesn't take much" to be considered an atypical student, those who are usually "find their own niche and have no problems living their lives the way they wish." The school is attempting to increase this diversity—minority enrollment has increased in the past years, and there's a "growing gay and lesbian population."

THE PRINCETON REVIEW SAYS

Admissions

Very important factors considered include: Application essay, academic GPA, recommendation(s), rigor of secondary school record. *Important factors considered include:* Character/personal qualities, extracurricular activities, first generation, interview, talent/ability, volunteer work, work experience. *Other factors considered include:* Class rank, standardized test scores, alumni/ae relation, geographical residence, racial/ethnic status, TOEFL required of all international applicants. High school diploma is required, and GED is not accepted. *Academic units required:* 4 English, 3 mathematics, 2 science, (2 science labs), 2 foreign language, 2 social studies, 2 history, 1 academic electives. *Academic units recommended:* 4 English, 4 mathematics, 3 science, (2 science labs), 4 foreign language, 2 social studies, 2 history, 1 academic electives.

Financial Aid

Students should submit: FAFSA, CSS/Financial Aid PROFILE, noncustodial PROFILE, business/farm supplement. Regular filing deadline is 2/15. The Princeton Review suggests that all financial aid forms be submitted as soon as possible after January 1. *Need-based scholarships/grants offered:* Federal Pell, SEOG, state scholarships/grants, private scholarships, the school's own gift aid, Federal Nursing Scholarships. *Loan aid offered:* Federal Perkins, Federal Nursing, other, alternative loans. Applicants will be notified of awards on or about 4/1. Federal Work-Study Program available. Institutional employment available. Off-campus job opportunities are good.

The Inside Word

Steady increases in the number of admission applications has nicely increased selectivity in recent years. Fairfield's campus and central location, combined with improvements to the library, campus center, classrooms, athletic facilities, and campus residences, make this a campus worth seeing.

THE SCHOOL SAYS "…"

From The Admissions Office

"Fairfield University welcomes students of unique promise into a learning and living community that will give them a solid intellectual foundation and the confidence they need to reach their individual goals. Students at Fairfield benefit from the deep-rooted Jesuit commitment to education of the whole person—mind, body, and spirit, and our admission policies are consistent with that mission. When considering an applicant, Fairfield looks at measures of academic achievement, students' curricular and extracurricular activities, their life skills and accomplishments, and the degree to which they have an appreciation for Fairfield's mission and outlook. In keeping with its holistic review process, Fairfield is test optional for undergraduate students seeking admission for the fall of 2010 and beyond. Students who decide not to submit SAT or ACT scores will be required to write an additional essay and are encouraged to participate in an admission interview.

"Fairfield University students are challenged to be creative and active members of a community in which diversity is encouraged and honored. With its commitment to education for an inspired life, Fairfield has developed a unique educational model to ensure that students receive the guidance they need to reach their fullest potential. The integration of living and learning is at the heart of a Fairfield education through students' participation in living and learning communities, vocational exploration, civic engagement, and finally, discernment of how they want to put their gifts and education to work in the world. As a result of this holistic model of education, Fairfield graduates are highly successful in gaining admission to selective graduate schools, while others achieve satisfying careers. A signification achievement for the university is that 55 Fairfield graduates have been tapped as Fulbright scholars since 1993."

For even more information on this school, turn to page 486 of the "Stats" section.

FORDHAM UNIVERSITY

441 EAST FORDHAM ROAD, THEBAUD HALL, NEW YORK, NY 10458 • ADMISSIONS: 718-817-4000
FAX: 718-367-9404 • FINANCIAL AID: 718-817-3800 • E-MAIL: ENROLL@FORDHAM.EDU • WEBSITE: WWW.FORDHAM.EDU

RATINGS
Quality of Life: 79   Academic: 84   Admissions: 92   Financial Aid: 75

STUDENTS SAY ". . ."

Academics

Fordham University—"the Jesuit school located in the capital of the world"—"offers a sense of community and a true college experience within the hustle and bustle" of New York City. Noteworthy majors include the performing arts and "an exceptional business program." There's also an "excellent honors program" and "a pretty good library." Another perk at Fordham are the "vast and exciting opportunities" for internships, which are abundant and "heavily encouraged." Students here tell us that they receive "a broad and holistic liberal arts education," thanks in large part to a "strict" and "extensive" core curriculum with a "somewhat large number of degree requirements." Classes are "small," and the "incredibly accessible" professors "love what they do." "Each of my professors has made me interested in their subject, even if I was only taking the class out of requirement," relates a finance major. "I get the impression that they are genuinely interested in what the students think." "I do not think I have ever had a really *bad* professor," adds an English major. Be warned, though: "The grade differentiation between some professors for the same class is absurd." It pays to ask around before registering. Opinion concerning the administration is decidedly split. Some students tell us that management is "friendly and approachable." "You can drop anyone an e-mail and expect a response back," proponents say. Critics pan the staff for an "overall lack of collaborative spirit" and gripe that the red tape is "fairly annoying."

Life

Fordham is two schools in one. There's the school's long-established location in Rose Hill, a "beautiful, Gothic, green" college campus complete with a "huge lawn" that is "located in an oasis in the middle of the Bronx," adjacent to "the original Little Italy" and its "amazing Italian food." There's also another, smaller campus at Lincoln Center in the heart of Manhattan. The big complaint here is the on-campus grub, which ranges from "pretty bad" to "prison-grade gruel." "Honestly," asks a mystified first-year student, "what is this stuff?" Otherwise, students are quite happy. Size-wise, Fordham is "just small enough that you'll see people you recognize whenever you walk around, but just large enough that it's always different people." "Life at Fordham is busy," explains a junior. "Obviously, we are all here for the academics, and that is a big focus for everyone but, additionally, almost all students are involved in activities on and off campus." There are "extracurriculars for every taste." "People love to play intramural sports." Fordham is big on community service as well, and "There are so many ways to get involved with volunteering." Students also spend a lot of time just soaking up all the "extensive and vibrant culture" "that New York City has to offer on any given day." "The choices of things to do here are endless." "Students often spend a lot of time in bars," and it's possible to "party four or sometimes five times a week." However, parties are usually "kept under control." Fordham students are more serious than not. They "know when to put their academic well-being before" a good time.

Student Body

"Students fit into two main groups at Fordham: East Coast prep or NYC hipster." Many students graduated from private high schools somewhere on the East Coast. It's generally an "upper-middle-class," "hardworking" crowd. "Dress is stylish." Fashions are especially trendy among the more artsy "urbanites" at Lincoln Center. However, "There is room here for every kind of person imaginable because, after all, this is New York." Students at Fordham "get along very well and tend to dabble in a variety of clubs and programs." Students "tend to socialize in smaller groups," but "stereotypical cliques, like you would classify in high school, don't really apply here." "The Catholic culture contributes to a willingness to suspend typical political labels in exchange for a deeper look at the moral and social issues of our day," reflects a senior. "Everyone finds their niche."

THE PRINCETON REVIEW SAYS

Admissions

Very important factors considered include: Class rank, rigor of secondary school record, standardized test scores. *Important factors considered include:* Application essay, recommendation(s), character/personal qualities, extracurricular activities, talent/ability. *Other factors considered include:* Alumni/ae relation, first generation, geographical residence, racial/ethnic status, volunteer work, work experience. SAT Subject Tests recommended; SAT or ACT required; ACT with Writing component recommended. TOEFL required of all international applicants. High school diploma is required, and GED is accepted. *Academic units required:* 4 English, 3 mathematics, 3 science, 2 foreign language, 2 social studies, 2 history, 6 academic electives. *Academic units recommended:* 4 English, 4 mathematics, 4 science, 3 foreign language, 2 social studies, 2 history, 6 academic electives.

Financial Aid

Students should submit: FAFSA, CSS/Financial Aid PROFILE, noncustodial PROFILE, business/farm supplement. Regular filing deadline is 2/1. The Princeton Review suggests that all financial aid forms be submitted as soon as possible after January 1. *Need-based scholarships/grants offered:* Federal Pell, SEOG, state scholarships/grants, private scholarships, the school's own gift aid. *Loan aid offered:* Federal Perkins. Applicants will be notified of awards on or about 4/1.

The Inside Word

Applicants to Fordham are required to indicate whether they are applying to the Rose Hill campus in the Bronx or the Lincoln Center campus in Manhattan. If you want to enroll in the College of Business Administration, you must specify that, too. Admission criteria vary by school, but all are very competitive. Graduation from a Catholic high school—particularly a prestigious one on the East Coast—is always a plus.

THE SCHOOL SAYS "…"

From The Admissions Office

"Fordham University offers a distinctive, values-centered educational experience that is rooted in the Jesuit tradition of intellectual rigor and personal attention. Located in New York City, Fordham offers to students the unparalleled educational, cultural and recreational advantages of one of the world's greatest cities. Fordham has two residential campuses in New York—the tree-lined, 85-acre Rose Hill campus in the Bronx, and the cosmopolitan Lincoln Center campus in the heart of Manhattan's performing arts center. The University's state-of-the-art facilities and buildings include one of the most technologically advanced libraries in the country. Fordham offers a variety of majors, concentrations and programs that can be combined with an extensive career planning and placement program. More than 2,600 organizations in the New York metropolitan area offer students internships that provide hands-on experience and valuable networking opportunities in fields such as business, communications, medicine, law and education.

"Applicants are required to take SAT or the ACT with the Writing section. SAT Subject Tests are recommended but not required."

For even more information on this school, turn to page 487 of the "Stats" section.

FRANKLIN & MARSHALL COLLEGE

PO Box 3003, Lancaster, PA 17604-3003 • Admissions: 717-291-3953 • Fax: 717-291-4381
Financial Aid: 717-291-3991 • E-mail: admission@fandm.edu • Website: www.fandm.edu

RATINGS
Quality of Life: 72   **Academic:** 91   **Admissions:** 94   **Financial Aid:** 86

STUDENTS SAY ". . ."

Academics

Franklin & Marshall is widely regarded as a school that "prepares students well for law school and medical school," along with retaining "a stellar reputation in graduate school admissions departments," but there's more to F&M than a bunch of high-strung future doctors and lawyers. True, the school has earned a reputation as a pre-professional powerhouse through its "intense workload" and "very difficult grading structure," conditions that some see as necessary in order to provide "an environment for

intense personal and academic growth and development of the skills necessary to achieve well-rounded success in life." But F&M also boasts "amazing departments in German, economics, history, government...and geology/environmental science," among others. And in all areas—not just in the high-profile sciences and business—the school ensures that "independent research, especially for upperclassmen, is a vital part of the academic experience" and that "there are enough resources that can be accessed to make good grades more easily attainable," the "demanding" workload notwithstanding. Close student-teacher relationships help make the experience; professors here "are by far the greatest thing about this school. If you're interested in doing something, you can always find a professor or other staff member who would love to help you."

Life

"There is a grind at F&M" during the week, "not a bad one, but you have to be ready for it. Everyone takes his role as a student here very seriously: class, library, meetings, more class, more library, extracurriculars. Most students follow this itinerary during the week." Weeknight respites come in the form of "concerts, movies, amazing lectures, and other things to break up the schedule." For most, weekends "are a good time to relax and drink and forget about all of the work that has been done and still needs to be done in the week to come," so "most students like to go to one or more of the numerous fraternity parties or they may go to a party in someone's room or apartment." And "If you aren't into the drinking scene or the partying scene on campus"—and some students here aren't—"you can go to Ben's Underground, which is an alcohol-free, student-run club. Students can go to play pool or see comedians. It's really a nice facility to use and open all week." Also, "athletics are fairly popular for a Division III school, and the orchestra draws as well." Hometown Lancaster offers "a bunch of art galleries, really good cafés, an old opera house that has great plays, and a concert venue that has pretty big-name bands play." However, by the time most students are juniors, "Lancaster and the frat scene get old, so older students take to the local bars and sometimes take road trips to...Philadelphia or Washington, D.C."

Student Body

F&M is "an extremely preppy school, and many designers are flashed all around campus. Students are not afraid to show that they have money, but they are never in your face about it." Not everyone here is a slave to fashion. "You have students that do not get all dressed up for class that just wear sweats and sweatshirt," says a student. Along with those students "from boarding schools or expensive private schools," you'll find "a handful of international students, a smaller handful of minority students, and a few 'townies.' Everyone finds a niche, though." The small campus sometimes feels smaller because students can be cliquish; undergrads here "can be broken into many groups: frats, sororities, specific athletic groups, similar interests (arts, music, etc.)."

THE PRINCETON REVIEW SAYS

Admissions

Very important factors considered include: Class rank, academic GPA, rigor of secondary school record, character/personal qualities. *Important factors considered include:* Application essay, recommendation(s), standardized test scores, extracurricular activities, interview, talent/ability, volunteer work. *Other factors considered include:* alumni/ae relation, geographical residence, level of applicant's interest, racial/ethnic status, work experience. TOEFL required of all international applicants. High school diploma is required, and GED is accepted. *Academic units required:* 4 English, 3 mathematics, 2 science, (2 science labs), 2 foreign language, 1 social studies, 2 history, 1 visual/performing arts. *Academic units recommended:* 4 mathematics, 3 science, (3 science labs), 4 foreign language, 3 social studies, 3 history.

Financial Aid

Students should submit: FAFSA, CSS/Financial Aid PROFILE, noncustodial PROFILE, business/farm supplement. Regular filing deadline is 2/15. The Princeton Review suggests that all financial aid forms be submitted as soon as possible after January 1. *Need-based scholarships/grants offered:* Federal Pell, SEOG, state scholarships/grants, private scholarships, the school's own gift aid. *Loan aid offered:* Federal Perkins, college/university loans from institutional funds. Applicants will be notified of awards on or about 4/1. Federal Work-Study Program available.

The Inside Word

Applicants who feel that their standardized test scores do not accurately reflect their abilities may opt to omit them from their applications, in which case they must instead include two recent (junior or senior year) graded papers, preferably from a humanities or social science course. Since F&M is a school that requires a significant amount of writing from its students, there could hardly be a better way to demonstrate your qualifications to attend than with the written word.

THE SCHOOL SAYS "…"

From The Admissions Office

"Franklin & Marshall students choose from a variety of fields of study, traditional and interdisciplinary, that typify liberal learning. Professors in all of these fields are committed to a common purpose, which is to teach students to think, speak, and write with clarity and confidence. Whether the course is in theater or in physics, the class will be small, engagement will be high, and discussion will dominate over lecture. Thus, throughout their four years, beginning with the First-Year Seminar, students at Franklin & Marshall are repeatedly invited to active participation in intellectual play at high levels. Our graduates consistently testify to the high quality of an F&M education as a mental preparation for life."

For even more information on this school, turn to page 487 of the "Stats" section.

FRANKLIN W. OLIN COLLEGE OF ENGINEERING

OLIN WAY, NEEDHAM, MA 02492-1245 • ADMISSIONS: 781-292-2222 • FAX: 781-292-2210
FINANCIAL AID: 781-292-2364 • E-MAIL: INFO@OLIN.EDU • WEBSITE: WWW.OLIN.EDU

RATINGS

Quality of Life: 99 **Academic:** 99 **Admissions:** 99 **Financial Aid:** 97

STUDENTS SAY "..."

Academics

Revered for its "tight-knit community, rigorous academics, project-based learning, and ingenuous approach to education," Franklin W. Olin College of Engineering "bridges the gap between a traditional engineering education and [the] real world." On this campus of 300 undergraduates where "smart" and "quirky" are the norm, "Students [are] eager to be challenged academically and faculty gladly deliver that challenge." "Learning is doing" at Olin, and students laud the

"innovative curriculum" for its "small classes," "hands-on approach," and "group-focused learning." "Olin believes in Renaissance engineers, " and allows "students to pursue passions beyond engineering." Though classes are "wickedly challenging," students say they "bond around the difficulty." The focus on "experiential education" and "entrepreneurial implementation" provides students with "the ability to help design the curriculum and the school culture." Professors are "one of the best—if not the best—part of Olin," and are frequently described as "always available, always knowledgeable, [and] always approachable." Students note that even the higher-ups go by a first name basis: "You can regularly chat with the president at lunch." The kicker? Every enrolled student receives a half-tuition scholarship. Students with additional demonstrated need are awarded grants (no loans).

Life

At Olin, the spirit of hands-on collaboration transcends the classroom. This "tight-knit community of eager learners and tinkerers" thrives on a spirit of "innovation and initiative." "Small, quirky, and somewhat in a bubble, but full of amazing adventures and opportunities," Olin is all about "bringing together amazing people to build twenty-first century engineers." "People work hard, but they also know how to play hard, take breaks, and have fun." Though students say that there are "boatloads of work," in general life at Olin is "intense and fun." "There's also a lot going on, like Nerf wars, tyrannosaurus dodge ball, experimental baking, pickup soccer, zombie video games, auditorium movie screenings, midnight dump raids, elevator dance parties, themed hall parties, etc." A typical day includes everything from "watching a movie" to a "midnight bike expedition." Located a stone's throw from Beantown, Olin students "go into Boston" on the weekends. Students here thrive on the spirit of "carpe diem," a phrase that has now become an "e-mail list to which almost all students subscribe." "Students send out these carpes about anything and everything that others might find interesting or fun." The facilities aren't too shabby either. Each room comes with "its own fridge, microwave, freezer, and bathroom/shower."

Student Body

"Olin is a place where intelligent, motivated students can explore their interests both in engineering and in life as a whole." One student breaks the student body down into this simple formula: "Take the nation's top engineering students, mix with awesome personalities, add a dash of amazing resources, shake vigorously." When it comes to describing the typical student, there is no status quo. "There are all sorts of people at Olin. Some of us avoid homework by discussing metaphysics and ethics. Others watch old episodes of *Firefly*.... Some people read books in their spare time." The commonality? "Students care about their educations," and "everyone takes their own paths." Though students say they "may make geeky jokes," "People don't act like socially stunted nerds." "Passionate, intelligent, witty, [and] exceedingly interesting," "The typical student at Olin is atypical, whether that means having a hidden talent in unicycle fire juggling, a passion for writing musicals, an obsession with velociraptors, or a tendency to make pancakes at three in the morning every Thursday." Their own biggest fans, students say, "Every student at Olin is interesting enough that you want to sit down and talk to them for hours." "We think about pretty much everything from quantum physics to Obama's healthcare reform to *Speedracer* to what's for dinner." As innovative and diverse as their curriculum, Olin students "are straight, gay, Jewish, nerdy, partiers, gamers, rich, poor, and encompass all other social groups."

THE PRINCETON REVIEW SAYS

Admissions

Very important factors considered include: Application essay, academic GPA, recommendation(s), rigor of secondary school record, character/personal qualities, extracurricular activities, level of applicant's interest, talent/ability. *Important factors considered include:* Class rank, standardized test scores, racial/ethnic status, volunteer work. *Other factors considered include:* First generation, geographical residence, interview, state residency, work experience. SAT Subject Tests required; SAT or ACT required; High school diploma or equivalent is not required. *Academic units recommended:* 4 English, 4 mathematics, 3 science, (3 science labs), 2 foreign language, 2 social studies, 2 history, 1 calculus, 1 physics.

Financial Aid

Students should submit: FAFSA. The Princeton Review suggests that all financial aid forms be submitted as soon as possible after January 1. *Need-based scholarships/grants offered:* Federal Pell, SEOG, private scholarships, the school's own gift aid. Applicants will be notified of awards on a rolling basis beginning 4/1. Institutional employment available.

The Inside Word

Not many colleges can boast that they are filled with students who turned down offers from the likes of MIT, Cal Tech, and Carnegie Mellon, but Olin can. Olin is unique among engineering schools in that the admissions office really looks for more than just brains. Things like social skills and eloquence are taken extremely seriously here. Students who exhibit creativity, passion, and an entrepreneurial spirit are favored over their less adventurous peers. Reclusive geniuses seeking four years of technical monasticism will be at a disadvantage in the application pool.

THE SCHOOL SAYS "..."

From The Admissions Office

"Every enrolled student receives a half-tuition scholarship. Students with additional demonstrated need are awarded grants (no loans).

"The selection process at Olin College is unique to college admission. Each year a highly self-selecting pool of approximately 900 applicants is reviewed on traditional selection criteria. Approximately 270 finalists are invited to one of three Candidates' Weekends in February and March. These candidates are grouped in to five-person teams for a weekend of design-and-build exercises, group discussions, and interviews with Olin students, faculty, and alumni. Written evaluations and recommendations for each candidate are prepared by all Olin participants and submitted to the faculty admission committee. The committee admits about 170 candidates to yield a freshman class of 85. The result is that the freshman class is ultimately chosen on the strength of personal attributes such as leadership, cooperation, creativity, communication, and their enthusiasm for Olin College.

"A waiting list of approximately 20 is also established. All wait-list candidates who are not offered a spot in the class may defer enrollment for 1 year-with the guarantee of the Olin Scholarship. Wait-list students are strongly encouraged to do something unusual, exciting, and productive during their sabbatical year.

"Students applying for admission are required to take the SAT (or the ACT with the writing section). Olin College also requires scores from two SAT Subject Tests: math (level 1 or 2) and a science of the student's choice."

For even more information on this school, turn to page 488 of the "Stats" section.

THE GEORGE WASHINGTON UNIVERSITY

2121 I STREET NORTHWEST, SUITE 201, WASHINGTON, D.C. 20052 • ADMISSIONS: 202-994-6040
FAX: 202-994-0325 • FINANCIAL AID: 202-994-6620 • E-MAIL: GWADM@GWIS2.CIRC.GWU.EDU • WEBSITE: WWW.GWU.EDU

RATINGS

Quality of Life: 94   **Academic:** 85   **Admissions:** 96   **Financial Aid:** 92

STUDENTS SAY ". . ."

Academics

Get ready for "hands-on learning in an environment unlike any other" at George Washington University, where a location "four blocks away from the White House, down the street from the State Department, and near nearly all world headquarters" means "connections and opportunity" for undergraduates. Students call it "the perfect place to study international affairs" and praise the "amazing journalism program," the excellent political communications major, the political science program ("What political science major would pass up the chance to go toe-to-toe with protestors every week at the rallies outside the White House and Congress?"), the sciences (benefiting from the region's many research operations), and other departments too numerous to name. As one student puts it, "GW is a place where everyone can find their niche. Whether you are a politically active campaign volunteer, a hip-hop dancer, or a future Broadway actor, there is a place for you at GW." The school places a premium on hiring "professors of practice," teachers who "are either currently working in their field or just retired to teach." The faculty includes "former ambassadors, governors on the Federal Reserve Board, and CNN correspondents." These instructors emphasize "a balance between theory and practice that provides a foundation of knowledge and pragmatism from which students can feel prepared to enter any sector of work after school." The resulting education "gets students prepared for post-college life through an emphasis on internships and career-focused classes," putting "a lot of emphasis on acclimation to the real world."

Life

"Life at GW is about independence," students report. "There are no real cafeterias" on campus, "You have to rely on your own feet for transportation, and there is very little regulation in dorms." As a result, "There is little school spirit, but that fact alone seems to tie everyone together." The campus isn't entirely dead; there are frat parties ("which are hard to attend for non-member males and easy to attend for women"), the "occasional dorm-room party, which is usually small," and "apartment parties off campus" for upperclassmen. Campus organizations offer all sorts of events, and the school hosts a veritable who's who of guest speakers on a regular basis. Students love the school's Midnight Monument Tour, held "during the warmer parts of the year," during which "students walk the five blocks to the National Mall at 2 A.M. and tour the monuments. It is an awesome experience." Still, most students prefer to spend free time exploring D.C. on their own. The city provides "so much to do...it's overwhelming: monuments, free museums, fairs, every major sports franchise, and lots of student specials on the above things." D.C.'s upscale Georgetown neighborhood is nearby for "shopping, dining, seeing movies, etc.," while culturally diverse Adams Morgan is great for shopping, ethnic dining, and live music.

Student Body

"GW students are often stereotyped as spoiled and wealthy Northeastern kids," and while quite a few students here concede that there's some basis for the stereotype, most would also add that "white, preppy, fraternity/sorority members" who "like nice labels on their clothing" neither define nor dominate the campus population. "The reality is that there's tremendous diversity here of all stripes—geographic, religious, political, racial, and intellectual," with "students from dozens of countries and all 50 states." "GW is truly a national and even international school," one student writes. "I love walking out of the library and hearing conversations happening in a half-dozen languages." The school has always been a popular destination for Jewish students. There is also "a huge LGBT group on campus, with very little discrimination." Nearly everyone here is "incredibly driven," "combining classes with an internship, maybe a sport, and usually a few extracurriculars."

THE PRINCETON REVIEW SAYS

Admissions

Very important factors considered include: Academic GPA, rigor of secondary school record. *Important factors considered include:* Class rank, application essay, recommendation(s), standardized test scores, extracurricular activities, interview, talent/ability, volunteer work. *Other factors considered include:* Alumni/ae relation, character/personal qualities, first generation, geographical residence, level of applicant's interest, racial/ethnic status, work experience. SAT or ACT required; TOEFL required of all international applicants. High school diploma is required, and GED is not accepted. *Academic units required:* 4 English, 2 mathematics, 2 science, (1 science labs), 2 foreign language, 2 social studies. *Academic units recommended:* 4 English, 4 mathematics, 4 science, 4 foreign language, 4 social studies.

Financial Aid

Students should submit: FAFSA, CSS/Financial Aid PROFILE. Regular filing deadline is 2/1. The Princeton Review suggests that all financial aid forms be submitted as soon as possible after January 1. *Need-based scholarships/grants offered:* Federal Pell, SEOG, state scholarships/grants, the school's own gift aid. *Loan aid offered:* Federal Perkins. Applicants will be notified of awards on a rolling basis beginning 3/24. Federal Work-Study Program available. Institutional employment available. Off-campus job opportunities are excellent.

The Inside Word

With almost 20,000 applications to process annually, GW could be forgiven if it gave student essays only a perfunctory glance. The school insists, however, that essays are carefully reviewed. Take note and proceed accordingly. If you thought the economic downturn would diminish interest in this pricey institution, think again: In 2009–2010, applications were up three percent over the previous year. That's part of a larger trend at GW, where application rates have surged throughout the past decade. This school is only getting more popular, so applicants should be prepared to bring their A-game.

THE SCHOOL SAYS "..."

From The Admissions Office

"At GW, we welcome students who show a measure of impatience with the limitations of traditional education. At many universities, the edge of campus is the real world, but not at GW, where our campus and Washington, D.C. are seamless. We look for bold, bright students who are ambitious, energetic, and self-motivated. Here, where we are so close to the centers of thought and action in every field we offer, we easily integrate our outstanding academic tradition and faculty connections with the best internship and job opportunities of Washington, D.C. A generous scholarship and financial assistance program attracts top students from all parts of the country and the world.

"Students applying should send SAT or ACT scores. We will use those scores that best work to the student's advantage. Applicants to the BA/MD, IEMP, and BA/JD programs are required to submit scores for SAT Subject Tests. "

For even more information on this school, turn to page 488 of the "Stats" section.

GEORGETOWN UNIVERSITY

THIRTY-SEVENTH AND P STREETS NORTHWEST, WASHINGTON, D.C. 20057 • ADMISSIONS: 202-687-3600 • FAX: 202-687-5084
FINANCIAL AID: 202-687-4547 • WEBSITE: WWW.GEORGETOWN.EDU

RATINGS
Quality of Life: 84   **Academic:** 90   **Admissions:** 98   **Financial Aid:** 94

STUDENTS SAY " . . . "

Academics

This moderately sized elite academic establishment stays true to its Jesuit foundations by educating its students with the idea of "cura personalis," or "care for the whole person." The "well-informed" student body perpetuates upon itself, creating an atmosphere full of vibrant intellectual life, that is "also balanced with extra-curricular learning and development." "Georgetown is…a place where people work very, very hard without feeling like they are in direct competition," says an international politics major. Located in Washington,

> **SURVEY SAYS . . .**
> Students love Washington, DC
> Great off-campus food
> Students are happy
> Frats and sororities are unpopular or nonexistent
> Student publications are popular
> Political activism is popular
> Lots of beer drinking

D.C., there's a noted School of Foreign Service here, and the access to internships is a huge perk for those in political or government programs. In addition, the proximity to the nation's capital fetches "high-profile guest speakers," with many of the most powerful people in global politics speaking regularly, as well as a large number of adjunct professors who, either are currently working in government, or have retired from high-level positions.

Georgetown offers a "great selection of very knowledgeable professors, split with a good proportion of those who are experienced in realms outside of academia (such as former government officials) and career academics," though there are a few superstars who might be "somewhat less than totally collegial." Professors tend to be "fantastic scholars and teachers" and are "generally available to students," as well as often being "interested in getting to know you as a person (if you put forth the effort to talk to them and go to office hours)." Though Georgetown has a policy of grade deflation, meaning "A's are hard to come by," there are "a ton of interesting courses available," and TAs are used only for optional discussion sessions and help with grading. The academics "can be challenging or they can be not so much (not that they are ever really easy, just easier);" it all depends on the courses you choose and how much you actually do the work. The school administration is well-meaning and "usually willing to talk and compromise with students," but the process of planning activities can be full of headaches and bureaucracy, and the administration itself "sometimes is overstretched or has trouble transmitting its message." Nevertheless, "a motivated student can get done what he or she wants."

Life

Students are "extremely well aware of the world around them," from government to environment, social to economic, and "Georgetown is the only place where an argument over politics, history, or philosophy is preceded by a keg stand." Hoyas like to have a good time on weekends, and parties at campus and off-campus apartments and townhouses "are generally open to all comers and tend to have a somewhat networking atmosphere; meeting people you don't know is a constant theme." With such a motivated group on such a high-energy campus, "people are always headed somewhere, it seems—to rehearsal, athletic practice, a guest speaker, [or] the gym." Community service and political activism are particularly popular, as is basketball. Everything near Georgetown is in walking distance, including the world of D.C.'s museums, restaurants, and stores, and "grabbing or ordering late night food is a popular option."

Student Body

There are "a lot of wealthy students on campus," and preppy-casual is the fashion de rigueur; this is "definitely not a 'granola' school," but students from diverse backgrounds are typically welcomed by people wanting to learn about different experiences. Indeed, everyone here is well-traveled and well-educated, and there are "a ton of international students." "You better have at least some interest in politics or you will feel out-of-place," says a student. The school can also be "a bit cliquish, with athletes at the top," but there are "plenty of groups for everybody to fit into and find their niche," and "there is much crossover between groups."

THE PRINCETON REVIEW SAYS

Admissions

Very important factors considered include: Class rank, application essay, academic GPA, recommendation(s), rigor of secondary school record, standardized test scores, character/personal qualities, talent/ability. *Important factors considered include:* Extracurricular activities, interview, volunteer work. *Other factors considered include:* Alumni/ae relation, geographical residence, racial/ethnic status, state residency, work experience. SAT Subject Tests recommended; SAT or ACT required; TOEFL required of all international applicants. High school diploma is required, and GED is accepted. *Academic units recommended:* 4 English, 2 mathematics, 1 science, 2 foreign language, 2 social studies, 2 history.

Financial Aid

Students should submit: FAFSA, CSS/Financial Aid PROFILE, noncustodial PROFILE, business/farm supplement. Tax returns. Regular filing deadline is 2/1. The Princeton Review suggests that all financial aid forms be submitted as soon as possible after January 1. *Need-based scholarships/grants offered:* Federal Pell, SEOG, state scholarships/grants, private scholarships, the school's own gift aid. *Loan aid offered:* Federal Perkins, Federal Nursing, other, alternative loans. Applicants will be notified of awards on or about 4/1. Federal Work-Study Program available. Institutional employment available. Off-campus job opportunities are excellent.

The Inside Word

It was always tough to get admitted to Georgetown, but in the early 1980s Patrick Ewing and the Hoyas created a basketball sensation that catapulted the place into position as one of the most selective universities in the nation. There has been no turning back since. GU gets almost 10 applications for every space in the entering class, and the academic strength of the pool is impressive. Virtually 50 percent of the entire student body took AP courses in high school. Candidates who are wait-listed should hold little hope for an offer of admission; over the past several years Georgetown has taken very few off their lists.

THE SCHOOL SAYS "…"

From The Admissions Office

"Georgetown was founded in 1789 by John Carroll, who concurred with his contemporaries Benjamin Franklin and Thomas Jefferson in believing that the success of the young democracy depended upon an educated and virtuous citizenry. Carroll founded the school with the dynamic Jesuit tradition of education, characterized by humanism and committed to the assumption of responsibility and action. Georgetown is a national and international university, enrolling students from all 50 states and over 100 foreign countries. Undergraduate students are enrolled in one of four undergraduate schools: the College of Arts and Sciences, School of Foreign Service, Georgetown School of Business, and Georgetown School of Nursing and Health Studies. All students share a common liberal arts core and have access to the entire university curriculum.

"Applicants must submit scores from SAT or the ACT. SAT Subject Tests can also be recommended."

For even more information on this school, turn to page 489 of the "Stats" section.

GETTYSBURG COLLEGE

ADMISSIONS OFFICE, EISENHOWER HOUSE, GETTYSBURG, PA 17325-1484 • ADMISSIONS: 717-337-6100 • FAX: 717-337-6145
FINANCIAL AID: 717-337-6611 • E-MAIL: ADMISS@GETTYSBURG.EDU • WEBSITE: WWW.GETTYSBURG.EDU

RATINGS
Quality of Life: 89   **Academic:** 96   **Admissions:** 95   **Financial Aid:** 96

STUDENTS SAY ". . ."

Academics

> **SURVEY SAYS . . .**
> *Athletic facilities are great*
> *Great food on campus*
> *Low cost of living*

Personal and intellectual growth is at the heart of the Gettysburg College experience. Students eagerly praise the school's "friendly, community-oriented atmosphere," and competent, caring professors. "The faculty takes a developed interest in the students' academics and successes, [and] the campus offers countless opportunities for leadership, self-discovery and the like." In fact, first-year students are surprised to find that "By the first day, the professor knows each student by name and why they're taking the class." With uniformly small class sizes and an emphasis on discussion in the classroom, "professors at Gettysburg make sure that students understand why they are learning the things that they are, and there is a lot of emphasis put on putting 'theory into practice' outside of the classroom." "Many professors go above and beyond, making themselves available to aid students." A current student shares, "My Intro to Chemistry professor would be at the Science Center until 11 P.M. before an exam, helping everyone study." Academic opportunities—such as the "amazing study-abroad program"—are ample at Gettysburg. Plus, as an exclusively undergraduate institution, Gettysburg "allows for opportunities (i.e., research, publications) that many do not get" at larger universities. In this "nurturing environment," the "administration knows students by name" and even the "registrar, transportation services, off-campus studies, and library staff are lovely and do everything they can to help you." In particular, "President Riggs (a Gettysburg alum and former faculty member) is a phenomenal community leader and makes a sincere effort to connect with students, faculty, and staff."

Life

Enthusiastic and overcommitted, most students at Gettysburg are pursuing "a major and a minor or a double major, and a majority are involved in at least several college organizations (whether it's a community service group, sports team or Greek organization)." With so much on their plate, it is no surprise that "the students at Gettysburg buckle down and work hard" during the week. Socially, "Life at Gettysburg is very Greek-oriented," and, come the weekend, "frat hopping" is "popular on this campus." Not your style? No worries: Greek life may be "huge" on campus, "however, that does not mean that that is the only thing to do." For students looking for alternate activities, the school hosts "movie nights, plays, and musical performances." Many students also "love going to our theme parties and Happy Hours at the Attic, our on-campus nightclub," while others "get together with friends and watch movies or go out for coffee." For a relaxing respite, "The surrounding area and town is beautiful, so one of my favorite things to do is just walk around out on the battlefields or through town." In addition, "People also like to get off campus traveling to bigger city areas like Baltimore, Harrisburg, D.C., and even Philly and New York City."

Student Body

Academics come first at Gettysburg, where "The student body is extremely intelligent and motivated and serious about their work." When they aren't studying, "Gettysburg's student body is very involved" in the school and local community, and "Volunteering is very popular." "Each student—in one way or another—takes part in community service during their time at Gettysburg." Demographically, "Most of the student body is...middle class, white, and from the Northeast." And, lest we forget, the Gettysburg student body is also well known for its uniform "tendency to wear preppy clothes." A current student elaborates, "Open up a J. Crew magazine and find the most attractive models in it and you have a typical Gettysburg College student." While some say the student body has a "cookie cutter" feel to it, others remind us that "While Gettysburg has a reputation for being mostly white, upper-class students, there is diversity all around if you are willing to open up your eyes and see it."

THE PRINCETON REVIEW SAYS

Admissions

Very important factors considered include: Class rank, academic GPA, recommendation(s), rigor of secondary school record. *Important factors considered include:* Application essay, standardized test scores, character/personal qualities, extracurricular activities, interview, talent/ability, volunteer work. *Other factors considered include:* Alumni/ae relation, first generation, geographical residence, level of applicant's interest, racial/ethnic status, work experience. SAT or ACT recommended; TOEFL required of all international applicants. High school diploma is required, and GED is accepted. *Academic units required:* 4 English, 3 mathematics, 3 science, (3 science labs), 3 foreign language, 3 social studies, 3 history. *Academic units recommended:* 4 English, 4 mathematics, 4 science, (4 science labs), 4 foreign language, 4 social studies, 4 history.

Financial Aid

Students should submit: FAFSA, CSS/Financial Aid PROFILE, business/farm supplement. Regular filing deadline is 2/15. The Princeton Review suggests that all financial aid forms be submitted as soon as possible after January 1. *Need-based scholarships/grants offered:* Federal Pell, SEOG, state scholarships/grants, private scholarships, the school's own gift aid. *Loan aid offered:* Federal Perkins, college/university loans from institutional funds. Applicants will be notified of awards on or about 3/26. Federal Work-Study Program available. Institutional employment available. Off-campus job opportunities are excellent.

The Inside Word

Prospective Gettysburg students can register for an account on the school's website to view Gettysburg events in their area or connect with students on campus. To really get a feel for Gettysburg, however, many students say a campus visit is a must. If you're lucky enough to gain admission to this competitive liberal arts school, a campus visit might be just the thing to seal the deal.

THE SCHOOL SAYS "..."

From The Admissions Office

"Four major goals of Gettysburg College to best prepare students to enter the real world, include: first, to accelerate the intellectual development of our first-year students by integrating them more quickly into the intellectual life of the campus; second, to use interdisciplinary courses combining the intellectual approaches of various fields; third, to encourage students to develop an international perspective through course work, study abroad, association with international faculty, and a variety of extracurricular activities; and fourth, to encourage students to develop (1) a capacity for independent study by ensuring that all students work closely with individual faculty members on an extensive project during their undergraduate years and (2) the ability to work with their peers by making the small group a central feature in college life.

"Gettysburg College strongly recommends that freshman applicants submit scores from the SAT. Students may also choose to submit scores from the ACT (with or without the Writing component) in lieu of the SAT."

For even more information on this school, turn to page 489 of the "Stats" section.

GORDON COLLEGE

255 GRAPEVINE ROAD, WENHAM, MA 01984-1899 • ADMISSIONS: 866-464-6736 • FAX: 978-867-4682
E-MAIL: ADMISSIONS@HOPE.GORDON.EDU • WEBSITE: WWW.GORDON.EDU

RATINGS

Quality of Life: 91   **Academic:** 85   **Admissions:** 84   **Financial Aid:** 76

STUDENTS SAY ". . ."

Academics

The motto of Gordon College is "Freedom within a framework of faith." For the uninitiated, that translates to "a liberal arts education through a Christian perspective." It's delivered through "engaging professors who share the same passion for Christ and change in the world" that the students here have. In addition to being "great teachers," professors are also "highly skilled, intelligent, accessible, and caring." "Even in big lecture classes, they invite you to have lunch with them and try to learn all their students' names. If a professor's office hours aren't accessible for a student, they are happy to make time for him or her, and they are always available via e-mail." "The teachers expect much out of you, but when you are done with a class you are a master in the field. Even the core curriculum is incredibly straining, but intellectually rewarding." One caveat: "Some of the adjunct teachers are not really that great." "Gordon's administration runs a tight ship, but does not always listen to the opinions of the students when making decisions." That's just fine with many students, though, who coo that "Our administrators are really invested in Gordon's mission, and they really care about students." "Facilities could be better, but they are building new structures, like our new science center, to improve the quality." Several academic programs have their promoters here, but the music department is the object of special praise.

> **SURVEY SAYS . . .**
> Athletic facilities are great
> Students are very religious
> Students get along with local community
> Campus feels safe
> Frats and sororities are unpopular or nonexistent
> Very little drug use

Life

"Life here is fairly quiet." "The week consists mostly of going to class, studying, the gym, and occasional movies and Bible studies." Weekends can also be slow. "We usually manage to entertain ourselves fairly well, though. There are plenty of movies going on all around campus in people's rooms." When they want to get off-campus for fun, "people often go into Boston as we are quite close." "There are numerous museums, exhibits, shows, concerts, restaurants, and games to see there. Many people also enjoy going to one of the many beaches that surround our campus." "There is a lot of school spirit around the sports teams, especially because there are several other rival colleges nearby that we play against often." There are also "a wide variety of extra-curricular activities" for students to join. "There are some party people but not many." "Unfortunately, the 'party group' and the 'Bible group' don't connect much." Not surprisingly, given the religious affiliation of the school, a spiritual vibe pervades the campus, "we enjoy worshipping and getting into deep intellectual conversations about God and existence." "The cafeteria food could be improved," and "Some of the older dorms could be remodeled." Students would also like the school to expend some more resources "providing more ways for students without cars to get off campus."

Student Body

The typical Gordon College student is a "white," "preppy," "middle class, evangelical Christian." She grew up in a "suburban" setting, and is "most likely from the New England area." She was "either home-schooled or went to a private Christian school." Temperamentally, she is "academically focused and hard-working," "involved with either athletics or music," and she "loves the Lord." It is not out of the ordinary for students to "meet their future spouse on campus and get married their senior year." There are "not many international students, or students with different ethnic backgrounds," which leads one student to sum up the student body in both a positive and negative sense, depending on your perspective (i.e., whether the term "Good Shepherd" has meaning for you): "The word sheep sometimes comes to mind—white, fluffy, followers."

THE PRINCETON REVIEW SAYS

Admissions

Very important factors considered include: Application essay, academic GPA, recommendation(s), rigor of secondary school record, standardized test scores, character/personal qualities, extracurricular activities, interview, religious affiliation/commitment. *Important factors considered include:* Class rank, talent/ability. *Other factors considered include:* Alumni/ae relation, racial/ethnic status, volunteer work, work experience. SAT or ACT required; ACT with Writing component required. TOEFL required of all international applicants. High school diploma is required and GED is accepted. *Academic units required:* 4 English, 2 mathematics, 2 science, (1 science labs), 2 foreign language, 2 social studies, 5 academic electives. *Academic units recommended:* 3 mathematics, 3 science, (3 science labs), 4 foreign language, 3 social studies.

Financial Aid

Students should submit: FAFSA Regular filing deadline is 3/1. The Princeton Review suggests that all financial aid forms be submitted as soon as possible after January 1. *Need-based scholarships/grants offered:* Federal Pell, SEOG, state scholarships/grants, private scholarships, the school's own gift aid. *Loan aid offered:* Federal Perkins, state loans, college/university loans from institutional funds. Applicants will be notified of awards on a rolling basis beginning 4/15. Federal Work-Study Program available. Off-campus job opportunities are good.

The Inside Word

Interviews are required at Gordon, presumably so admissions officers can gauge candidates' readiness for the rigorous curriculum and high level of religious commitment. Students interested in studying social work must meet a second, more rigorous set of admissions requirements in addition to general requirements. Prospective music and theater majors must audition as part of their application, and prospective art majors must submit a portfolio for faculty review. The high admit rate here is somewhat misleading, as a look at the high yield percentage and the lifestyle expectations of the college should make clear.

For even more information on this school, turn to page 490 of the "Stats" section.

GOUCHER COLLEGE

1021 DULANEY VALLEY ROAD, BALTIMORE, MD 21204-2794 • ADMISSIONS: 410-337-6100
FAX: 410-337-6354 • FINANCIAL AID: 410-337-6141 • E-MAIL: ADMISSIONS@GOUCHER.EDU • WEBSITE: WWW.GOUCHER.EDU

RATINGS
Quality of Life: 87   **Academic:** 88   **Admissions:** 84   **Financial Aid:** 78

STUDENTS SAY ". . ."

Academics

A "small, East Coast, liberal arts school, with a tremendous history," Goucher College provides a "global education" best embodied in the motto "Learn for yourself, learn to be yourself, enjoy yourself, respect everyone else and you will succeed." Located on a "beautiful campus right outside a

> **SURVEY SAYS . . .**
> *Great food on campus*
> *Low cost of living*
> *Frats and sororities are unpopular or nonexistent*

big city," students say the "intimate size is what is apparent about Goucher through and through." With a "socially informed" student body of self-motivated learners and thinkers, academics at Goucher are about "owning your education." As one student notes, "What you get out of your Goucher experience is directly related to what you put into it." Innovative thinkers flock here for "the openness of the student body, political nature of the institution, and the required study-abroad program." Students say Goucher is a "very creative place" where "importance is placed on academics as well as the arts." "Easily accessible and ready to talk about anything and everything, while providing incredible insight and tools for students to investigate their own questions," professors "are what make Goucher great." As one student observes, academics at Goucher are all about "pushing myself beyond my old boundaries and really discovering what I am capable of and who I am." Assignments tend to focus on "challenging you to make your own opinions on a topic and testing them." Though some students feel they "could get rid of the administration for the most part," others note that while "The administration can be a little hands-off, you can access who you need to when it comes down to it. " In principle, Goucher is "a place where one feels comfortable to talk to anyone, even the president of the college." "The professors are always available. Many will give you their home phone numbers or eat lunch with you."

Life

"Goucher is about living to learn and having fun in the process." An "eclectic yet tight-knit community," with a focus on "activism and global citizenship," "Goucher strives to represent, explore, and respect all aspects of humanity." Not typically known as a party school, parties on campus "tend to be low key, in people's rooms or apartments." Students say that the absence of fraternities and sororities "really helps to minimize [the] pressure of drinking." As studying abroad is required, it is "a major topic of conversation and a major source of student unity." In addition, there are "lots of school-sponsored events, such as speakers, plays, [and] small-name bands." As one student notes, "We've had everyone from [Karl Rove] to Tuvan Throat Singers to Paul Rusesabagina (the man Hotel Rwanda was based on), to an amazing group of poets called the Elephant Engine High Dive Revival, just this year alone. " On campus, "There's a kind of coffee house/pub/general hang out spot called the Gopher Hole where there are often dance parties, poetry slams, and other…fun activities always happening." Hometown Towson boasts "terrific restaurants, a concert venue, a movie theater, art galleries, quirky shops," [and] a large and modern mall. "When campus starts to feel a little small…there is a free shuttle that runs into Baltimore."

Student Body

A haven for liberal-minded, independent thinkers with a flair for unique hobbies and interests, students jokingly say that Goucher is "a place where students who never 'fit in' in high school come and find each other," "zombies and pirates included." The typical Goucher student is "socially, politically, emotionally, and internationally aware." "Everyone's a little weird, and most of them [are] very intelligent." When asked to give a composite picture, students paint the average Goucher student as "18 to 20 years old, female, liberal-minded, and very strong-headed." "We're a group of feminists, hippies, oddballs, geeks, hvz players, and intellectuals, with the occasional soccer player thrown in." Another notes, "I can walk down Van Meter highway at any given time and see a group of lacrosse boys on the way to the SRC, the Pirate Club selling cupcakes in front of Pearlstone, or kids hanging out in front of the library." "There's a group for everyone at Goucher."

Admissions

Very important factors considered include: Academic GPA, rigor of secondary school record. *Important factors considered include:* Application essay, recommendation(s), talent/ability. *Other factors considered include:* Class rank, standardized test scores, alumni/ae relation, character/personal qualities, extracurricular activities, first generation, geographical residence, interview, level of applicant's interest, racial/ethnic status, state residency, volunteer work. TOEFL required of all international applicants. High school diploma is required, and GED is accepted. *Academic units required:* 4 English, 3 mathematics, 2 science, 2 foreign language, 3 social studies, 2 academic electives. *Academic units recommended:* 4 English, 4 mathematics, 3 science, 4 foreign language, 3 social studies, 2 academic electives.

Financial Aid

Students should submit: FAFSA, CSS/Financial Aid PROFILE, noncustodial PROFILE, business/farm supplement. Regular filing deadline is 2/1. The Princeton Review suggests that all financial aid forms be submitted as soon as possible after January 1. *Need-based scholarships/grants offered:* Federal Pell, SEOG, state scholarships/grants, private scholarships, the school's own gift aid. *Loan aid offered:* Federal Perkins, college/university loans from institutional funds. Applicants will be notified of awards on a rolling basis beginning 4/1. Federal Work-Study Program available. Institutional employment available. Off-campus job opportunities are excellent.

The Inside Word

Although there is a test-optional admissions policy, Goucher accepts the ACT with Writing in lieu of the SAT, and SAT Subject Tests are required for an applicant to be considered for merit funding. Goucher's high admit rate masks a self-selecting applicant pool; you cannot gain acceptance here without a solid high school transcript and test scores.

THE SCHOOL SAYS "…"

From The Admissions Office

"Through a broad-based arts and sciences curriculum and a groundbreaking approach to study abroad, Goucher College gives students a sweeping view of the world. Goucher is an independent, coeducational institution dedicated to both the interdisciplinary traditions of the liberal arts and a truly international perspective on education. The first college in the nation to pair required study abroad with a special travel stipend of $1,200 for every undergraduate, Goucher believes in complementing its strong majors and rigorous curriculum with abundant opportunities for hands-on experience. In addition to participating in the college's many study abroad programs (including innovative 3-week intensive courses abroad alongside traditional semester and academic year offerings), many students also complete internships and service-learning projects that further enhance their learning.

"The college's almost 1,500 undergraduate students live and learn on a tree-lined campus of 287 acres just north of Baltimore, Maryland. Goucher boasts a student/faculty ratio of just 9:1, and professors routinely collaborate with students on major research projects—often for publication, and sometimes as early as students' first or second years. The curriculum emphasizes international and intercultural awareness throughout, and students are encouraged to explore their academic interests from a variety of perspectives beyond their major disciplines.

"A Goucher College education encompasses a multitude of experiences that ultimately converge into one cohesive academic program that can truly change lives. Students grow in dramatic and surprising ways here. They graduate with a strong sense of direction and self-confidence, ready to engage the world—and succeed—as true global citizens."

For even more information on this school, turn to page 490 of the "Stats" section.

GREEN MOUNTAIN COLLEGE

One College Circle, Poultney, VT 05764-1199 • Admissions: 802-287-8000
Fax: 802-287-8099 • Financial Aid: 802-287-8210 • E-mail: admiss@greenmtn.edu • Website: www.greenmtn.edu

RATINGS

Quality of Life: 75   **Academic:** 79   **Admissions:** 74   **Financial Aid:** 78

STUDENTS SAY ". . ."

Academics

"Small," "incredibly progressive" Green Mountain College in rural Vermont "does the environmental, green thing" throughout its curriculum. "A strong liberal arts program" includes four mandatory core courses that relate in way or another to the environment. Interdisciplinary block courses allow students to focus on one ecological topic. GMC gets

> **SURVEY SAYS . . .**
> *Students are friendly*
> *Low cost of living*
> *Frats and sororities are unpopular or nonexistent*

more than half of its electricity from Vermont dairy farms. The pride and joy of the campus is a "fossil fuel-free" and generally "kick-ass" farm that "gives students firsthand experience in agriculture and subsistent farming." There's a barn "packed with animals." "We grow delicious, organic produce," notes an environmental studies major. Reviews of the academic experience here are generally positive. There is a wealth of opportunities for "hands-on learning," internships, and studying abroad. Unique majors include adventure recreation and resort management. There's also the progressive program, which allows students to chart their own academic course. "Professors go by their first names." A few are "absolutely awful," but most are "a joy to have in class." They are "very approachable" and active in the larger community. "I love going to a bluegrass concert and seeing my stats professor playing banjo," gushes a happy first-year student.

Life

"Green Mountain is all about environmentalism, skiing, the outdoors, and the Grateful Dead." Maple trees "cover the campus." There are several "very pretty buildings," too. In keeping with its environmentally sustainable ethos, a LEED Gold Certified residence hall was completed in fall of 2009. Socially, "life is laid-back." "Everybody pretty much knows everybody." "During the winter, the weather is harsh," but both fall and spring are pleasant. "It is amazing to go outside when it is nice out to see rugby, Frisbee, volleyball, music circles, and music coming from all different dorms," observes a junior. "There is a river right behind the college, and it's a popular hangout spot," adds a senior. "People swim during the day and have bonfires at night." "There is a lot of partying" as well. Campus activities include "concerts, contra-dances, dinners, parties, and much more." The "isolated" hamlet of Poultney has "little to offer beyond small-town New England charm." "The closest city, Rutland, isn't that big and is a half hour away." The area is "scenic," though, and it's a nature lover's paradise. "There are ski hills in every direction," and the College "runs trips almost every weekend to do outdoor activities such as kayaking, rock climbing, hiking, etc."

Student Body

"The typical student is white and from New England." That student is also a "tree-loving" "outdoors type" who "has long hair." Individuality is "deeply embraced" here. "Our school population consists mainly of people who would be atypical at other schools," explains a senior. However, most students are "left-wing liberals" who are "environmentally aware." "If you have a different point of view, it can be overwhelming." "Future activists" proliferate. There are "many vegetarians and vegans." On the whole, Green Mountain's student population is "a conglomeration of hippies and ski bums." Students are "sixties-oriented in fashion, lifestyle, food choices, and personality." Even the rare preppy students "seem to be able to embrace their inner hippie." "At times, it's like a time warp."

THE PRINCETON REVIEW SAYS

Admissions

Very important factors considered include: Application essay, academic GPA, rigor of secondary school record, character/personal qualities. *Important factors considered include:* Class rank, recommendation(s), extracurricular activities, interview, volunteer work. *Other factors considered include:* Standardized test scores, level of applicant's interest, talent/ability, work experience. SAT or ACT recommended; TOEFL required of all international applicants. High school diploma is required, and GED is accepted. *Academic units required:* 4 English, 3 mathematics, 3 science, (2 science labs), 2 foreign language, 3 social studies, 1 history, 5 academic electives. *Academic units recommended:* 4 mathematics, 4 science, 3 foreign language, 3 social studies, 2 history.

Financial Aid

Students should submit: FAFSA, CSS/Financial Aid PROFILE, noncustodial PROFILE. The Princeton Review suggests that all financial aid forms be submitted as soon as possible after January 1. *Need-based scholarships/grants offered:* Federal Pell, SEOG, state scholarships/grants, private scholarships, the school's own gift aid. *Loan aid offered:* state loans, other, alternative loans. Applicants will be notified of awards on a rolling basis beginning 1/1.

The Inside Word

It's a holistic process here, which is fabulous news if your academic record thus far is less than stellar. Standardized test scores are optional. Only send yours if they are good. Don't miss the interview. Pay meticulous attention to the essay. Take advantage of the opportunity to supplement your application with additional materials. Also, note that financial aid is ample.

THE SCHOOL SAYS "..."

From The Admissions Office

"Green Mountain College is a liberal arts college that's been on the forefront of sustainability education since 1995, when we introduced our Environmental Liberal Arts general education program. The College's list of awards and citations for sustainability initiatives continues to grow. In 2007 Green Mountain College earned a Campus Sustainability Leadership Awards from the Association for the Advancement of Sustainability in Higher Education (AASHE), and GMC was one of three schools to receive the Sustainable Endowments Institute's 2009 Sustainability Innovator Award.

"While we are proud of our national recognition for sustainability, three quarters of our students do not major in environmental studies, but rather select a liberal arts major that they are passionate about- education, business, art, psychology, biology, etc. The student body is united by a sense of social responsibility and penchant for service, not by a commitment to environmentalism. Diversity thrives at Green Mountain College.

"GMC's working farm is a special attraction for students from all majors. It provides a visible model of sustainability and produces a significant quantity of food for the College community. Students can also major in Sustainable Agriculture and Food Production and/or earn 12 credits over the summer in Farm Life Ecology, a 'field and table intensive.'

"We award scholarships for academic merit, service, leadership, creative arts, and environmental advancement at the time of admission, so students should submit evidence of these activities with their application for admission. The College guarantees graduation in four years for students who meet a few minimum requirements."

For even more information on this school, turn to page 491 of the "Stats" section.

GROVE CITY COLLEGE

100 CAMPUS DRIVE, GROVE CITY, PA 16127-2104 • ADMISSIONS: 724-458-2100 • FAX: 724-458-3395
FINANCIAL AID: 724-458-2163 • E-MAIL: ADMISSIONS@GCC.EDU • WEBSITE: WWW.GCC.EDU

RATINGS
Quality of Life: 78   Academic: 80   Admissions: 92   Financial Aid: 62

STUDENTS SAY ". . ."

Academics

Students see the world from a "Christian viewpoint in a safe atmosphere" at Grove City, a college in Pennsylvania that offers "conservative libertarian Christianity applied to a serious Western liberal arts curriculum." As one student puts it, "we are a school that celebrates the trinity of Jesus, C.S. Lewis, and Ronald Reagan." Students here "serve God while working their butts off" in academically rigorous classes designed to give "a good education based on biblical values" through the integration of faith in both the curriculum and college life. Administration makes it a point to be available to the students; the president of the college has weekly time set apart when students can personally talk with him. Still, campus living can sometimes get complicated, as "rules at Grove City are not always enforced as they say, and some rules exist that are not written anywhere." Class registration is "one of the most stressful things EVER!" The campus itself is beautiful, and the school "does a great job with keeping it up," but parking is both expensive and far away. Since the average class size at GCC is relatively small, the classroom is "definitely a student-friendly setting." Though many have a couple of teachers they've been unhappy with, all are very satisfied with both what the professors give them and ask of them. Professors have extremely high expectations for their students and "have challenging tests and a lot of work," but they "truly care about you and are open to students asking questions and talking to them about work or anything else outside of class." "They are committed to learning and mastering all areas of human endeavor for the glory of God," says a student. The school's excellent job placement rate and "reasonable price" are just a few more of the many reasons students choose to come here.

Life

Activities abound at Grove City, with "excellent" intramurals topping the popularity list, and "a million and one" clubs. "I am involved in Clowns for Christ, Life Advocates (a pro-life group), and the Grove City Democrats," says a busy student. A favorite activity on campus is Warriors, which is an hour of worship once a week. This dry campus is "not exactly a party school or one where weekend life is traditionally 'hopping.'" On weekends, students typically hang out in their friends' rooms and watch movies or go to dances. The rules here are quite strict—there are "inter-visitation rules proscribing which hours males and females may be on male and female halls"—so students do "fun but non-illegal things" in their spare time. Many agree that the school could stand to "[rein] in campus safety." No one is a big fan of the town itself, but Pittsburgh is only an hour or so away. There are also, thankfully, "good restaurants within 15 or 20 minutes," since the school "could improve drastically in quality of food provided." All students live on campus and must have meal plans. "I'd have to say that the most fun is making up your own fun," says a student. One "could stop and have a deep conversation with a perfect stranger, and it would be normal," and indeed, "you hear many conversations about religious issues."

Student Body

No doubt about it—the typical student here is "white, middle- to upper-class, and very religious." Many of these "Grovers" were home-schooled. As for atypical students and minorities, well, "there aren't a lot," but they do manage to find each other. Diversity here could definitely use some TLC—a large number of students wish that the school would "[bring] in people who are not all the same." Still, most people are "friendly and helpful," and "there is rarely an interpersonal conflict." Studies tend to be a center of focus here, and the "library is constantly crowded with students working hard to keep up." They all "work together in order to achieve a diploma instead of believing they have to compete with each other." "Everyone on campus is over-committed. Coming to Grove City, you basically admit to and crave being stressed beyond belief," says an elementary education major.

Admissions

Very important factors considered include: Application essay, academic GPA, rigor of secondary school record, standardized test scores, character/personal qualities, interview, level of applicant's interest, religious affiliation/commitment. *Important factors considered include:* Recommendation(s), extracurricular activities, geographical residence. *Other factors considered include:* Class rank, alumni/ae relation, first generation, racial/ethnic status, state residency, talent/ability, volunteer work, work experience. SAT or ACT required; TOEFL required of all international applicants. High school diploma is required, and GED is accepted. *Academic units recommended:* 4 English, 3 mathematics, 3 science, (2 science labs), 3 foreign language, 2 social studies, 2 history.

Financial Aid

Students should submit: Institution's own financial aid form Regular filing deadline is 4/15. The Princeton Review suggests that all financial aid forms be submitted as soon as possible after January 1. *Need-based scholarships/grants offered:* State scholarships/grants, private scholarships, the school's own gift aid. *Loan aid offered:* State loans, other, private loans. Applicants will be notified of awards on or about 3/26. Institutional employment available. Off-campus job opportunities are good.

The Inside Word

Admission to Grove City has become very competitive, and any serious contender will need to hit the books. While a rigorous class schedule is a given, admissions officers also closely assess character and personal qualities. GCC is steeped in Christian values, and the school seeks students who will be comfortable in such an environment. As such, interviews and recommendations hold significant weight.

THE SCHOOL SAYS "..."

From The Admissions Office

"A good college education doesn't have to cost a fortune. For decades, Grove City College has offered a quality education at costs among the lowest nationally. Since the 1990s, increased national academic acclaim has come to Grove City College. Grove City College is a place where professors teach; you will not see graduate assistants or teacher's aides in the classroom. Our professors are also active in the total life of the campus. More than 100 student organizations on campus afford opportunity for a wide variety of cocurricular activities. Outstanding scholars and leaders in education, science, and international affairs visit the campus each year. The environment at GCC is friendly, secure, and dedicated to high standards. Character-building is emphasized and traditional Christian values are supported.

"There is a fresh spiritual vitality on campus that touches every aspect of your college life. In the classroom we don't shy away from discussing all points of view, however we adhere to Christ's teaching as relevant guidance for living. Come and visit and learn more."

For even more information on this school, turn to page 491 of the "Stats" section.

HAMILTON COLLEGE

198 COLLEGE HILL ROAD, CLINTON, NY 13323 • ADMISSIONS: 800-843-2655 • FAX: 315-859-4457
FINANCIAL AID: 800-859-4413 • E-MAIL: ADMISSION@HAMILTON.EDU • WEBSITE: WWW.HAMILTON.EDU

RATINGS
Quality of Life: 84   Academic: 97   Admissions: 97   Financial Aid: 96

STUDENTS SAY ". . ."

Academics

A small, liberal arts school, Hamilton College "runs smoothly" with "top-notch" professors who are "very committed,
passionate, and genuinely caring." The close student-faculty
relationships are a distinguishing characteristic of Hamilton.
One junior who chose Hamilton for its "small class size and

> **SURVEY SAYS . . .**
> *Lab facilities are great*
> *Great computer facilities*
> *Athletic facilities are great*
> *School is well run*

opportunity to really establish a relationship with the professors" described the accessibility of the professors
as "AMAZING." A graduating senior tells us, "My professors have inspired me to take on my education as a
truly personal and important aspect of my life, even after I complete my formal education." One student comments on how Hamilton is a leader in teaching effective writing and persuasive speaking: "Hamilton challenges
me to improve my writing each and every day, regardless of the class...writing is a central aspect." Though the
"extraordinary focus on writing" is paramount at Hamilton, the school also offers a "strong science program."
The science curriculum emphasizes "undergraduate research" and a recently built, state-of-the-art science facility provides students with ample "research opportunities." Students also love Hamilton's distinct open curriculum. The "lack of distribution requirements" gives students the freedom to make their own educational
choices and to select classes that reflect their unique interests. With "no required curriculum...it's nice to know
that you're not wasting any time and are taking the classes that you really want [and] need to."

Life

A "picturesque oasis of academia" Hamilton makes students feel like the fact that they are "isolated away from
city noise and bustle, but close enough to an urban area to be connected." The closest major city is Syracuse,
located about an hour's drive from campus, and the school "organizes trips to New York City regularly."
Hamilton is a "small town," but students agree that though Hamilton "is in the middle of nowhere" it does not
mean it is lacking in things to do. In fact, says one student, "that's far from the truth." During the week, "the
pressure is on," and life at Hamilton is "academically oriented" with everyone working hard and "little time to
play." At week's end, students are ready to "have as much fun as possible," and the focus turns to "various fraternity or sorority parties and any athletic events going on." Students tell us, "Greek life is popular but not
threatening" and "provides much of the party life on-campus." Most Greek events are "open to the campus"
but foster a "very inclusive social environment." The campus "accommodates students so that everyone is able
to get together and have fun." Students agree that there is "something to do for everyone." Hamilton boasts a
long list of student-run clubs and teams, active intramural leagues, "incredible athletic and workout facilities,"
a "pretty decent" 9-hole golf course, and "miles of trails for skiing, snow-shoeing, and jogging." Winters tend
to be quite long, "so curling up with a blanket and a movie in a dorm room is always popular."

Student Body

If you are looking for a school "where you hold doors for people" and "greet friends, acquaintances, and even
professors" while walking around campus, Hamilton may be just the place for you. Students are enthusiastic
about the "tight-knit community" of students and professors on campus. One student tells us, "There's such a
great sense of community. Everyone is friendly, intelligent, and driven without being overly competitive."
Students find that Hamilton provides a great opportunity to attend an "elite liberal arts school" where "students will want to help you instead of compete against you." One freshman tells us that the student body at
Hamilton was "frighteningly friendly." While Hamilton "doesn't exactly have a wealth of diversity," the "student body is very inclusive." The majority of Hamilton students are "very preppy, white, and upper-class," but
"everyone and anyone can find their niche" and still be "respected as an individual by the community at large."
Overall, students at Hamilton have "diverse interests" and are often involved on campus in a variety of ways.
When it comes to the environment, politics, or any other current events, students tell us, "It's the most aware
group of people I've ever met."

THE PRINCETON REVIEW SAYS

Admissions

Very important factors considered include: Class rank, academic GPA, rigor of secondary school record. *Important factors considered include:* Application essay, recommendation(s), standardized test scores, character/personal qualities, extracurricular activities, interview. *Other factors considered include:* Alumni/ae relation, first generation, geographical residence, level of applicant's interest, racial/ethnic status, talent/ability, volunteer work, work experience. SAT and SAT Subject Tests or ACT required; TOEFL required of all international applicants. High school diploma is required, and GED is accepted. *Academic units recommended:* 4 English, 3 mathematics, 3 science, 3 foreign language, 3 social studies.

Financial Aid

Students should submit: FAFSA, institution's own financial aid form, CSS/Financial Aid PROFILE, state aid form, noncustodial PROFILE, business/farm supplement. Regular filing deadline is 2/8. The Princeton Review suggests that all financial aid forms be submitted as soon as possible after January 1. *Need-based scholarships/grants offered:* Federal Pell, SEOG, state scholarships/grants, private scholarships, the school's own gift aid. *Loan aid offered:* Federal Perkins, college/university loans from institutional funds. Applicants will be notified of awards on or about 4/1. Federal Work-Study Program available. Institutional employment available.

The Inside Word

Similar to any prestigious liberal arts schools, Hamilton takes a well-rounded, personal approach to admissions. They rely heavily on academic achievement and intellectual promise, but in a mission to create a talented and diverse incoming class, admissions officers also strive to attain a complete, accurate profile of each candidate. The admissions team at Hamilton is adamant about interviews either on or off campus with alumni volunteers. Serious applicants may want to polish up their interview skills as students who decline to interview put themselves at a competitive disadvantage.

THE SCHOOL SAYS "..."

From The Admissions Office

"As a national leader for teaching students to write effectively, learn from one another, and think for themselves, Hamilton produces graduates who have the knowledge, skills, and confidence to make their own voices heard on issues of importance to them and their communities.

"A key component of the Hamilton experience is the college's open, yet rigorous, liberal arts curriculum. In place of distribution requirements that are common at most colleges, Hamilton gives its students freedom to choose the courses that reflect their unique interests and plans. Faculty advisors assist students in planning a coherent and highly individualized academic program. In fact, close student-faculty relationships at Hamilton are a distinguishing characteristic of the college, but ultimately students at Hamilton take responsibility for their own future. Part of that future includes a lifelong relationship with the college. Hamilton alumni are exceptionally loyal and passionate supporters of their alma mater. That support manifests itself through internships, speaking engagements, job-shadowing opportunities, and financial donations.

"The intellectual maturity that distinguishes a Hamilton education extends to the application process. Students are free to choose which standardized tests to submit, based on a specified set of options, so that those who do not test well on the SAT or ACT may decide to submit the results of their AP or SAT Subject Tests. The approach allows students the freedom to decide how to present themselves best to the Committee on Admission."

For even more information on this school, turn to page 492 of the "Stats" section.

HAMPSHIRE COLLEGE

ADMISSIONS OFFICE, 893 WEST STREET, AMHERST, MA 01002 • ADMISSIONS: 413-559-5471
FAX: 413-559-5631 • FINANCIAL AID: 413-559-5484 • E-MAIL: ADMISSIONS@HAMPSHIRE.EDU • WEBSITE: WWW.HAMPSHIRE.EDU

RATINGS
Quality of Life: 84   **Academic:** 90   **Admissions:** 89   **Financial Aid:** 92

STUDENTS SAY ". . ."

Academics

Undergrads come to Hampshire College "seduced by the prospect of designing [their] own program of study." The school offers students "a self-designed curriculum" facilitated by "close relationships with professors, small classes, and the great combination of communal living and individualism that a true Hampshire student embodies." A "divisional system," with a student's academic career consisting of three divisions, imposes some sense of order. Division I "is first-year requirements and such," while "Divisions II and III constitute the core of your time. That's when you focus down upon the areas that interest you more than the rest of the school." Undergrads explain that "in class, students learn as a group in discussions or hands-on activities (few lectures, no tests), while outside of class one focuses on independent projects (research, reading, writing, art-making)." The experience culminates in a 'Division III,' an all-consuming year-long senior thesis project "that allows students to become excited and completely invested" while "producing a unique product at the end of the year." Students "receive evaluations instead of grades, which we feel is a much more productive system." While Hampshire "is very small," which might limit students' choices, "it belongs to the Five Colleges consortium," a group that includes the massive University of Massachusetts—Amherst. With the course offerings of five colleges available to them, Hampshire students can "take any course we could dream of."

Life

"Life at Hampshire seems extremely spontaneous," so "while one minute we may be complaining of boredom, the next we may start doing something fun and exciting. We are normally very good at entertaining ourselves." "Usually what people do is just hang out with a small group of friends," and "there is partying on the weekends," although "parties here consist generally of 50 people or less, never the roaring, dangerously wild parties that are often found at colleges." Parties often take place in the "mods," apartment-style housing favored by upperclassmen, where students "throw a lot of sweaty dance parties where hippies, scenesters, and geeks all grind up against each other." Also, "live music is very common" on and around campus, "drum circles and random games of Frisbee are unavoidable," and "going to the nearby towns of Amherst or Northampton isn't bad." Students can also choose from "tons of clubs, from Spinsters Unite! to the Red Scare Ultimate Frisbee Team, [or] Students for a Free Tibet to Excalibur, which is the sci-fi and fantasy club. You can even take yoga, karate, or tai chi classes. There are parties all the time for those who like that kind of thing, and movies, video games, clubs, and playing in the forest or on the farm for those who don't." There are also "five colleges in the area to hang out at. Enough said."

Student Body

"Picture all the various groups of misfits in high school" and you'll have a picture of the students at Hampshire, a place where "Nonconformity is so normal it's almost conformist to be nonconformist. You can't say 'the kid with the dreadlocks' because the person would reply with 'Which one?'" Undergrads assure us that "Hampshire is really open to any type of student." Though there many different types of students on campus, all students have "at least one serious and one kitschy academic or extracurricular pursuit. Those who identify as male are usually bearded and wear plaid." The common threads among students: "They are all interesting. They all have talents, stories, and are just plain interesting to be around. They are full of creativity and life and seem to really enjoy where they are." They also tend to be "socially conscious, left-wing, and artistic. We are fond of do-it-yourself philosophies, from [magazines] to music and film production to designing ecologically sustainable communities." One student warns, "this is not a good school for fundamentalist Christians."

> **SURVEY SAYS . . .**
> Lots of liberal students
> Class discussions encouraged
> No one cheats
> Students aren't religious
> Great off-campus food
> Frats and sororities are unpopular or nonexistent
> Political activism is popular

THE PRINCETON REVIEW SAYS

Admissions

Very important factors considered include: Application essay, character/personal qualities. *Important factors considered include:* Recommendation(s), rigor of secondary school record, extracurricular activities, level of applicant's interest, talent/ability. *Other factors considered include:* Class rank, academic GPA, alumni/ae relation, interview, racial/ethnic status, volunteer work, work experience. TOEFL required of all international applicants. High school diploma is required, and GED is accepted. *Academic units required:* 4 English, 3 mathematics, 2 science, (2 science labs), 2 foreign language, 2 history. *Academic units recommended:* 4 English, 4 mathematics, 4 science, (2 science labs), 4 foreign language, 4 history.

Financial Aid

Students should submit: FAFSA, CSS/Financial Aid PROFILE, noncustodial PROFILE. The Princeton Review suggests that all financial aid forms be submitted as soon as possible after January 1. *Need-based scholarships/grants offered:* Federal Pell, SEOG, state scholarships/grants, private scholarships, the school's own gift aid. *Loan aid offered:* Direct Subsidized Stafford, Direct Unsubsidized Stafford, Direct PLUS, Federal Perkins. Applicants will be notified of awards on or about 4/1. Federal Work-Study Program available.

The Inside Word

Hampshire's admissions policies are the antithesis of formula-based practices. Officers want to know the individual behind the transcript, and personal characteristics hold substantial weight in the admissions decision. Demonstrating discipline and an independent and inquisitive spirit may just carry more weight than a perfect 4.0. Writing is pivotal to a Hampshire education, and applicants must put considerable thought into their personal statements. They will be read carefully.

THE SCHOOL SAYS "…"

From The Admissions Office

"The Admissions Committee focuses its selection process on fit over formula. Because all majors at Hampshire are personalized, it is important that you have the passion and ambition requisite to negotiate your education with faculty advisors. Hampshire seeks students who have elected to challenge themselves in high school and demonstrate a genuine passion for learning."

"In addition to the Common Application, Hampshire's supplement asks questions that are meant to reveal more about you as a thinker, learner, and community member. An analytical essay gives the Admissions Committee a sense of your ability to ask complex questions, think critically, synthesize information, and formulate original conclusions. The Admissions Committee welcomes examples of work, whether that be scientific or creative. Personal interviews are valued and strongly encouraged."

"At Hampshire, you will personalize your major. You will gain a strong foundation in the liberal arts and learn the skills to create new knowledge in virtually any chosen field of study. The process of personalizing majors requires a highly personalized, intensive connection with faculty advisors; faculty begin as teachers and mentors and become colleagues and collaborators. As a Hampshire student, you will be able to take courses at four other neighboring colleges for free-and you will have a limitless range of opportunities to engage in outside-the-classroom real-world experiences. Hampshire's program will give you the skills and confidence to create knowledge and accomplish great things as a graduate."

For even more information on this school, turn to page 492 of the "Stats" section.

HARTWICK COLLEGE

PO Box 4020, Oneonta, NY 13820-4020 • Admissions: 888-427-8925 • Fax: 607-431-4138
E-mail: admissions@hartwick.edu • Website: www.hartwick.edu

RATINGS
Quality of Life: 69   **Academic:** 74   **Admissions:** 70   **Financial Aid:** 76

STUDENTS SAY ". . ."

Academics

Hartwick College is a small liberal arts school in upstate New York with a broad core curriculum, notable offerings in nursing and music education, and "a very strong biology program." Another highlight is the Pine Lake Environmental Campus, "a natural classroom of woodlands" that is "an amazing retreat to either relax or study in." Hartwick also boasts a January term, aka "one month of

intense study" for internships and "very interesting" classes. "Study abroad opportunities for J-Term are pretty great" as well, and tons of students spend their Januaries in places "all around the world." "Small class sizes are a plus" and "students can do double or even triple majors if they are so inclined." Professors are "easily approachable." As far as teaching goes, "some professors are wonderful, some are horrible." Most students agree that despite a few bad apples, there are some "amazing teachers" here. "They really try to interact with the students and make sure they are learning," says a political science major. The administration can be "iffy," but for the most part it's "very friendly and involved." Hassles are few. "Things get done so much faster here than at bigger schools," notes an economics major.

Life

Hartwick's campus in the foothills of the Catskill Mountains boasts "great scenery," but it's extremely hilly. The stairs that students must climb to get to class are reportedly "awful." Many students also complain about the grub. "The food here is so bad that fast-food quickly becomes a delicacy," gripes a sophomore. Socially, this campus is "close-knit." "Hartwick is often referred to as Hartwick High School because of how small the school is and how much drama goes on," confides a senior. Student organizations are abundant and "really easy" to start. Many students participate in various musical groups. "A large portion of the student population participates in either varsity or intramural sports," and the "highly respected" men's soccer team is "a big thing around here." "The school puts on a lot of clean-fun type of activities each week," notes a senior. "Attendance is moderate, but it's nice to have the option." Alternatively, "there are always parties." While the Greek system is "not as glorified as it is at other colleges," frats still dictate "much of the social scene." Also, "Oneonta is a bar town" and there is no lack of drinking establishments. Otherwise, though, Oneonta is "just in the middle of nowhere" and has little to offer. "I was hoping for a cuter, artsier town," laments a freshman.

Student Body

The vast majority of the student population is from the state of New York and virtually everyone here receives at least some financial aid. Nevertheless, students report that "upper-middle class yuppie offspring" and "unfriendly, rich snobs" who "do little work and party often" make up a sizeable contingent. Also, "jock-types" are "overwhelming" in numbers. In this mix you'll also find some "free spirits," "nature lovers," "tech kids," and "a lot of academics" as well. "Fitting in is not hard for most people." "There are many social circles and it's not hard to find your own little niche." However, "the jocks and the eccentrics" often don't mix well and "Hartwick students tend to stay in cliques."

THE PRINCETON REVIEW SAYS

Admissions

Very important factors considered include: Rigor of secondary school record. *Important factors considered include:* Class rank, academic GPA, recommendation(s). *Other factors considered include:* Application essay, standardized test scores, alumni/ae relation, character/personal qualities, extracurricular activities, first generation, geographical residence, interview, level of applicant's interest, racial/ethnic status, state residency, talent/ability, volunteer work, work experience. TOEFL required of all international applicants. High school diploma is required and GED is accepted. *Academic units recommended:* 4 English, 3 mathematics, 3 science, (2 science labs), 3 foreign language, 2 social studies, 2 history.

Financial Aid

Students should submit: FAFSA. The Princeton Review suggests that all financial aid forms be submitted as soon as possible after January 1. *Need-based scholarships/grants offered:* Federal Pell, SEOG, state scholarships/grants, private scholarships, the school's own gift aid. *Loan aid offered:* Federal Perkins, Federal Nursing. Applicants will be notified of awards on or about 3/15. Federal Work-Study Program available. Institutional employment available. Off-campus job opportunities are good.

The Inside Word

The acceptance rate is high at Hartwick, and students with average grades and test scores will have no problem gaining admission. If you're serious about Hartwick and your grades and test scores are mediocre or worse, opting for an interview is a really good idea.

THE SCHOOL SAYS "..."

From The Admissions Office

"The foundation of a Hartwick education is learning by doing. Students are actively involved in learning, whether it's managing a 'virtual' business, engaging in transcultural nursing in Jamaica, or designing and building environmentally friendly houses on the college's Pine Lake campus. Many Hartwick students conduct research with their professors, sometimes resulting in students coauthoring articles for journals in their disciplines. This hands-on learning helps 96 percent of graduating seniors find jobs or enter graduate or professional school within 6 months of graduation. Another program unique to Hartwick that leads to the high placement rate is MetroLink. This award-winning annual program takes students to New York, Boston, and Washington, DC for a week-long experience in 'shadowing' professionals in those cities. Established Metrolink sites include the Boston Red Sox, Saatchi & Saatchi advertising, the Bronx Zoo, the FBI, and the Smithsonian Institution. Recent full-semester internships have included the National Baseball Hall of Fame, the New York Mets, John Hancock Insurance, the U.S. Congress, and many others."

For even more information on this school, turn to page 492 of the "Stats" section.

HARVARD COLLEGE

BYERLY HALL, 8 GARDEN STREET, CAMBRIDGE, MA 02318 • ADMISSIONS: 617-495-1551 • FAX: 617-495-8821
FINANCIAL AID: 617-495-1581 • E-MAIL: COLLEGE@FAS.HARVARD.EDU • WEBSITE: WWW.FAS.HARVARD.EDU

RATINGS
Quality of Life: 88   **Academic:** 99   **Admissions:** 99   **Financial Aid:** 99

STUDENTS SAY ". . ."

Academics

Those who are lucky enough to attend this legendarily "beautiful, fun, historic and academically alive place" in Cambridge, Massachusetts, find a "dynamic universe" that has the ability to both inspire and intimidate, and to open up a portal to an "amazing irresistible hell," plus about a billion opportunities beyond that. Needless to say, it's "very difficult, academically," but the school "does a good job of watching over its freshmen through extensive advising programs." Those that are not willing to go after what

SURVEY SAYS . . .
Lab facilities are great
Great computer facilities
Great library
Diverse student types on campus
Students love Cambridge, MA
Student publications are popular
Political activism is popular

they want—classes, positions in extracurriculars, jobs, etc.,—do not gain access to the vast resources of the university. With such a definitive grouping of intelligent people, there does tend to be "latent competition." Nobody is cut-throat in classes, but "people find ways to make everything (especially clubs and even partying) competitive." Still, this is a good thing, and one student claims his experience to be "rewarding beyond anything else I've ever done." "It is impossible to 'get the most out of Harvard' because Harvard offers so much," says another. As at any school, "some professors are better than others," but for the most part, the "the brightest minds in the world" here are "incredible" and "every so often, fantastic," and "the level of achievement is unbelievable." says a student. Harvard employs a lot of Teaching Fellows (TFs) for the larger lecture classes, so "you do have to go to office hours to get to know your big lecture class professors on a personal level," but "this is not a deterrent." The administration can be "waaaaay out of touch with students" and "reticent to change," and there are more than a few claims of bureaucracy, but many agree it has the students' best interests at heart.

Life

Most students have resolved their study habits by the time they get to Harvard, so "studying becomes routine, and there is a vibrant social atmosphere on campus and between students and the local community." In Cambridge and Boston, there's always something to do, whether it's "go see a play, a concert, hit up a party, go to the movies, or dine out." The new pub on campus is an excellent place to hang out and see people, "especially if you want to play a game of pool or have a reasonably priced drink," drinking also occurs on weekends at parties or at Harvard's finals clubs, though it is by no means a prevalent part of social life here. In addition to school-sponsored events such as panels and film screenings, the number of student organizations is staggering. "Basically, if you want to do it, Harvard either has it or has the money to give to you so you can start it," says a student. "Boredom does not exist here. There are endless opportunities and endless passionate people to do them with." During freshman year, the school organizes a lot of holiday/special event parties for people to get to know one another, and conversations are rarely surface-level and "often incorporate some sort of debate or interesting/important topic."

Student Body

Everyone is here to achieve, and this makes for a very common, and broad mold of a typical student. As one junior computer science major succinctly puts it: "Works really hard. Doesn't sleep. Involved in a million extracurriculars." People here have nothing but the highest opinion of their fellow students, and when it comes to finding the lowest common denominator, it's that "everyone is great for one reason or another." However, all of these virtuosos are down-to-earth, and there are also a lot of well-rounded kids "who aren't geniuses but are pretty good at most things." Admitting the best of the best makes for quite a diverse campus, and "there is a lot of tolerance and acceptance at Harvard for individuals of all races, religions, socio-economic backgrounds, life styles, etc."

THE PRINCETON REVIEW SAYS

Admissions

Factors considered include: Application essay, academic GPA, recommendation(s), rigor of secondary school record, standardized test scores, alumni/ae relation, character/personal qualities, extracurricular activities, first generation, geographical residence, interview, racial/ethnic status. SAT or ACT required; ACT with Writing component required. High school diploma or equivalent is not required. *Academic units recommended:* 4 English, 4 mathematics, 4 science, 4 foreign language, 3 social studies, 2 history.

Financial Aid

Students should submit: FAFSA, CSS/Financial Aid PROFILE, tax forms through IDOC. Regular filing deadline is 2/1. The Princeton Review suggests that all financial aid forms be submitted as soon as possible after January 1. *Need-based scholarships/grants offered:* Federal Pell, SEOG, state scholarships/grants, private scholarships, the school's own gift aid. *Loan aid offered:* Direct Subsidized Stafford, Direct Unsubsidized Stafford, Direct PLUS, Federal Perkins, college/university loans from institutional funds. Applicants will be notified of awards on or about 4/1. Federal Work-Study Program available. Institutional employment available. Off-campus job opportunities are excellent.

The Inside Word

It just doesn't get any tougher than this. Candidates to Harvard face dual obstacles—an awe-inspiring applicant pool and, as a result, admissions standards that defy explanation in quantifiable terms. Harvard denies admission to the vast majority, and virtually all of them are top students. It all boils down to splitting hairs, which is quite hard to explain and even harder for candidates to understand. Rather than being as detailed and direct as possible about the selection process and criteria, Harvard keeps things close to the vest—before, during, and after. They even refuse to admit that being from lesser populated states like South Dakota is an advantage. Thus the admissions process does more to intimidate candidates than to empower them. Moving to a common application seemed to be a small step in the right direction, but with the current explosion of early decision applicants and a super-high yield of enrollees, things are not likely to change dramatically.

THE SCHOOL SAYS "…"

From The Admissions Office

"The admissions committee looks for energy, ambition, and the capacity to make the most of opportunities. Academic ability and preparation are important, and so is intellectual curiosity—but many of the strongest applicants have significant, non-academic interests and accomplishments, as well. There is no formula for admission, and applicants are considered carefully, with attention to future promise.

"Freshman applicants may submit the SAT. The ACT with Writing component is also accepted. All students must also submit three SAT Subject Tests of their choosing."

For even more information on this school, turn to page 493 of the "Stats" section.

HAVERFORD COLLEGE

370 West Lancaster Avenue, Haverford, PA 19041 • Admissions: 610-896-1350 • Fax: 610-896-1338
Financial Aid: 610-896-1350 • E-mail: admitme@haverford.edu • Website: www.haverford.edu

RATINGS
Quality of Life: 96   **Academic:** 98   **Admissions:** 98   **Financial Aid:** 92

STUDENTS SAY "..."

Academics

"The academic experience is nothing less than stellar" at Haverford. "The classroom is an incredible place where I have been intellectually pushed beyond what I believed possible." The work load can be "intense," but "professors are always available and willing to help," and there is "a

support system to help you...composed of students and faculty." Everyone raves about the accessibility of professors. "I have the cell phone number or house number of all my professors. An incredible number of professors live on or within a block of campus and regularly invite students over for tea or dinner." Some students note the lack of research opportunities, but most "love how we have access to Bryn Mawr, Penn, and Swarthmore. The schools really work together to provide a wide range of courses." Haverford is known for its honor code, which "really works, and we actually do have things like closed-book, timed, take-home tests. I honestly don't know of anyone that who ever cheated." The administration also receives high marks. "There is a lot of discourse between the administration and the students," and "the deans...are pretty receptive to student opinions." Though a few students feel "the degree of transparency between the administration and students has dropped in recent years," the "administration does a good job of keeping us informed about important news," and the president holds weekly office hours.

Life

The academic demands of Haverford keep its students focused. "In general, students go to class, participate in extracurriculars, and do homework all day Monday through Thursday." "Students are very active on campus," "with classes, work, on-campus jobs, volunteering, running clubs, and acting on administrative committees." "People are very oriented toward social justice, and overall, our student body is very aware." "Conversations at meals consist of discussions on political issues, scientific breakthroughs, etc." "But that doesn't mean people don't know how to have fun," students assure us. "There are a ton of concerts, a capella shows, student theater, movies, dinners, dances, sponsored events in Philly." "While students here do party," many note and there's no pressure to drink, and plenty of students don't. There is easy access to public transportation, and students say "it's nice to have Philadelphia so close—the music scene is amazing." At the same time, "a lot of people never leave campus because there is so much to do there." Thursday and Saturday are the nights to party, owing to the athletic teams' schedules, and there's not much of a bar scene. Most socializing is on campus, and school-sponsored events are well-attended. "Every weekend night there are at least three options—a music show, an improv show, a movie, or games." It seems Haverford students never really disengage from the classroom, though "Don't be surprised if you witness a discussion about someone's senior thesis next to a keg-stand."

Student Body

Many students describe themselves as a little "nerdy" or "quirky," but in the best possible way. "For the most part, Haverfordians are socially awkward, open to new friends, and looking for moral, political, [or] scholarly debate." The honor code draws a particular type of student—"don't choose to go here if you're not dedicated to the ideas of trust, concern, and respect and to making sure we are a well-run community." Most are "liberal-minded" and "intellectual" and "want to save the world after they graduate."

Admissions

Very important factors considered include: Application essay, academic GPA, recommendation(s), rigor of secondary school record, character/personal qualities, extracurricular activities. *Important factors considered include:* Class rank, standardized test scores, talent/ability, volunteer work, work experience. *Other factors considered include:* Alumni/ae relation, first generation, geographical residence, interview, level of applicant's interest, racial/ethnic status. SAT Subject Tests required; SAT or ACT required; ACT with Writing component recommended. TOEFL required of all international applicants. High school diploma or equivalent is not required.

Financial Aid

Students should submit: FAFSA, CSS/Financial Aid PROFILE, noncustodial PROFILE, business/farm supplement, CSS College Board Noncustodial Parents' Statement is required (not the Noncustodial supplement). Regular filing deadline is 1/31. The Princeton Review suggests that all financial aid forms be submitted as soon as possible after January 1. *Need-based scholarships/grants offered:* Federal Pell, SEOG, state scholarships/grants, the school's own gift aid. *Loan aid offered:* Federal Perkins. Applicants will be notified of awards on or about 4/1. Federal Work-Study Program available. Institutional employment available. Off-campus job opportunities are good.

The Inside Word

Haverford's applicant pool is an impressive and competitive lot. Intellectual curiosity is paramount, and applicants are expected to keep a demanding academic schedule in high school. Additionally, the college places a high value on ethics, as evidenced by its honor code. The admissions office seeks students who will reflect and promote Haverford's ideals.

THE SCHOOL SAYS "..."

From The Admissions Office

"Haverford strives to be a college in which integrity, honesty, and concern for others are dominant forces. The college does not have many formal rules; rather, it offers an opportunity for students to govern their affairs and conduct themselves with respect and concern for others. Each student is expected to adhere to the honor code as it is adopted each year by the Students' Association. Haverford's Quaker roots show most clearly in the relationship of faculty and students, in the emphasis on integrity, in the interaction of the individual and the community, and through the college's concern for the uses to which its students put their expanding knowledge. Haverford's 1,100 students represent a wide diversity of interests, backgrounds, and talents. They come from public, parochial, and independent schools across the United States, Puerto Rico, and 38 foreign countries. Students of color are an important part of the Haverford community.

"Haverford College requires that all applicants submit the results of the SAT exam or the ACT with the optional Writing test. Two SAT Subject Tests are required."

For even more information on this school, turn to page 493 of the "Stats" section.

HOBART AND WILLIAM SMITH COLLEGES

639 SOUTH MAIN STREET, GENEVA, NY 14456 • ADMISSIONS: 315-781-3472 • FAX: 315-781-3471
FINANCIAL AID: 315-781-3315 • E-MAIL: HOADM@HWS.EDU • WEBSITE: WWW.HWS.EDU

RATINGS
Quality of Life: 70   **Academic:** 88   **Admissions:** 87   **Financial Aid:** 91

STUDENTS SAY ". . ."

Academics

"Students come before all else" at tiny, upstate Hobart and William Smith, a pair of associated single-sex colleges that share a campus, faculty, and administration, yet remain very distinct in their identities, combining to make the academic and social lives of the students as varied and interesting as possible. While "there aren't always tons of options" for classes, "there are lots of interesting choices offered for such a small school." This "liberal arts education with a flair" also

places a strong emphasis on studying abroad as a part of a student's education. Tuition can be a workout for some however there are many grants offered. Students are enthralled with the school, from the "beautiful, green campus" offering "a small slice of New England stuck in upstate New York" to the "unrivalled experience."

The "vibrant" professors have "diverse viewpoints," and though "you have to learn to adapt to different teaching styles," they treat students with complete respect, so "the academic experience is more in the vein of colleagues." Everyone here is happy with their academic experience, and even though there's an occasional dud, "for every professor who seems mediocre, there's two more who are absolute gems of teaching ability." "I have had professors invite me to office hours, send me internship opportunities, discuss my career goals, and even invite me to their houses for dinner," says another. As for higher up, the raves are similar. The administration works very hard to accommodate everyone on campus and "is usually successful at it." This success is partly due to the coordinate system, which allows for separate deans for both Hobart and William Smith, granting "more individual attention to the students." They will "get to know you and will stop on the sidewalk and have a chat whenever they see you." However, students do wish the administration was a little less strict in its policies and enforcement.

Life

Life in general is pretty hectic, but students are "very good at balancing school and socializing."Most kids always stay busy with their school work, but "really let loose on the weekends." Bars, frat parties, and campus parties can all occur in the same night, and the school offers "a very positive program" called Safe Rides, which provides late-night van rides. Geneva is a beautiful town, but it's no NYC. The cold winter months can be endless, and the rural location means students "make their own fun here," whether through tray-sledding, barbequing, or skinny-dipping, and it "kind of works out better." On nice days, the quad acts as a hub of student life, when students "bring horse shoes, Frisbees, footballs, baseballs, and blankets and just spend the day together." There's also skiing, malls and outlets for shopping, and a wildlife refuge not too far away. Without a nearby big urban center, students are "continuously immersed in campus life and happenings," and most are very happy with the offerings from the school and campus groups. Community service is very popular here, as well.

Student Body

"Preppy white person" seems to encapsulate most everyone's perception of the student body, with "Polo, L.L.Bean, Lily Pulitzer & Lacoste everywhere." A lot of students come from affluent backgrounds, but in recent years, thanks to scholarships and opportunity programs, there's a significant number of international students and minority students and "they blend in seamlessly." there are "rich kids and alternative types melting all together in a pretty good harmony," sums up a student. People "usually get along with each other regardless of being typical or not," partially due to the rampant involvement in student organizations and groups. With fewer than 2,000 people in the student body, there's not much mystery left after a couple of years, when "you can walk to class and recognize at 90 percent of the people you see," but the general pervading friendliness of the school as a whole means that "there is a happy niche here for everyone."

THE PRINCETON REVIEW SAYS

Admissions

Very important factors considered include: Rigor of secondary school record. *Important factors considered include:* Class rank, application essay, academic GPA, recommendation(s), standardized test scores, character/personal qualities, extracurricular activities, volunteer work, work experience. *Other factors considered include:* Alumni/ae relation, first generation, geographical residence, interview, level of applicant's interest, racial/ethnic status, talent/ability. SAT or ACT required; ACT with Writing component required. TOEFL required of all international applicants. High school diploma is required, and GED is accepted. *Academic units required:* 4 English, 3 mathematics, 3 science, (2 science labs), 2 foreign language, 2 social studies, 2 history, 2 academic electives. *Academic units recommended:* 3 foreign language, 3 social studies, 4 academic electives.

Financial Aid

Students should submit: FAFSA, CSS/Financial Aid PROFILE, state aid form, noncustodial PROFILE, parent's and student's tax returns. Regular filing deadline is 2/1. The Princeton Review suggests that all financial aid forms be submitted as soon as possible after January 1. *Need-based scholarships/grants offered:* Federal Pell, SEOG, state scholarships/grants, private scholarships, the school's own gift aid. *Loan aid offered:* Federal Perkins. Applicants will be notified of awards on or about 4/1. Federal Work-Study Program available. Institutional employment available. Off-campus job opportunities are good.

The Inside Word

Applicants to the academic side of Seneca Lake's scenic shore should know that HSW likes to see a student who embraces a challenge. They recommend that hopefuls prepare themselves for a rigorous college curriculum by taking at least two years of a foreign language and a couple of AP courses for good measure.

THE SCHOOL SAYS "..."

From The Admissions Office

"Hobart and William Smith Colleges seek students with a sense of adventure and a commitment to the life of the mind. Inside the classroom, students find the academic climate to be rigorous, with a faculty that is deeply involved in teaching and working with them. Outside, they discover a supportive community that helps to cultivate a balance and hopes to foster an integration among academics, extracurricular activities, and social life. Hobart and William Smith, as coordinate colleges, have an awareness of gender differences and equality and are committed to respect and a celebration of diversity.

"Freshman applicants are required to take either the ACT with or without the optional Writing portion or the SAT. Their highest composite score will be used in admissions decisions. Students are encouraged to submit results of any SAT Subject Test they have taken."

For even more information on this school, turn to page 494 of the "Stats" section.

HOFSTRA UNIVERSITY

ADMISSIONS CENTER, BERNON HALL, HEMPSTEAD, NY 11549 • ADMISSIONS: 516-463-6700
FAX: 516-463-5100 • FINANCIAL AID: 516-463-6680 • E-MAIL: HOFSTRA@HOFSTRA.EDU • WEBSITE: WWW.HOFSTRA.EDU

RATINGS
Quality of Life: 64   Academic: 78   Admissions: 87   Financial Aid: 66

STUDENTS SAY ". . ."

Academics

> SURVEY SAYS . . .
> *Low cost of living*

Hofstra University, "the most prestigious private university on Long Island," according to students, is "large enough to feel part of something big but small enough to feel a sense of community." Students say the size is just right, providing "admirable" class sizes that "are perfect for nurturing relationships with professors." Hofstra undergraduates are especially bullish on the undergraduate business program and the communications and broadcast journalism programs. The latter are "anchored by [an]…award-winning radio station" and numerous other "opportunities to get hands-on experience in various aspects of broadcast [journalism]." All programs benefit from the school's proximity to New York City, which affords not only "top-notch…guest speakers and lecturers to the university" but also abundant "career-making connections to [your chosen] profession through internships and opportunities." Students also love Hofstra's music and theater programs, but most students look toward more reliably remunerative professions. As one student puts it, "This school is about successfully preparing its students for their professional careers as effectively and efficiently as possible." The rewards here are especially great for go-getters. One student explains, "Hofstra provides all of the opportunities that a college student can ask for," but "Many students don't take advantage of them, so it allows relatively easy access to some amazing programs if you have the drive."

Life

Hofstra "is generally considered a party school," students concede, "but it is easy to avoid that if you want to." Many students "go to the bars and pubs that are around college campus" to blow off steam, or "if not, they make parties at their dorms when their RA is away and invite people over to play beer pong." Greek organizations on campus are "really enjoyable," hosting "fundraisers and activities," not to mention the occasional house party. For those seeking alternatives, "There are several malls and movie theaters nearby, the train station is 10 minutes away, and it's only about a half hour ride into NYC, and Nassau Coliseum is also right next door so there are always concerts and events. Jones Beach is also very close and popular when [the weather] is nice." The Student Center Theater shows "popular films that are out of the theaters but not yet released on DVD almost every weekend." College sporting events are less popular—"Our teams aren't great," one student concedes—and the school recently dropped its football program to save money. Hometown Hempstead "is a bit of a bust." Not only is there "nothing to do" in town, but students perceive it as "an area of depression and crime….The campus itself is generally quite safe, but that safety does not extend very far past the limits of the campus." Fortunately, safer destinations are nearby and easily accessible by car or public transportation.

Student Body

You will certainly find examples of the Long Island stereotype here, kids who are into "buying expensive brands that display their logo on their clothing," sport "fake tans, fake hair, and fake personalities," and are "primarily concerned with drinking, getting laid, and finishing their business degrees." But while these may be the most conspicuous students on campus at Hofstra, they hardly make up the entire student body. Opinions differ on whether they are "only a slight majority" or an even smaller percentage, but most here agree that there's plenty of room for everyone. One student explains that "As Hofstra positions itself as a national institution, geographic diversity as well as non-traditional student populations have grown." Another adds, "There is a sizable group of atypical students who hang out with the other atypical students like themselves." Their ranks include "the free-spirited hippies, the metal heads, the guys who just like sports but don't play, and the people who are actually here to study. They fit in because this minority (albeit it's a big one) all acts similarly."

THE PRINCETON REVIEW SAYS

Admissions

Very important factors considered include: Class rank, application essay, academic GPA, recommendation(s), rigor of secondary school record, standardized test scores. *Important factors considered include:* Character/personal qualities, extracurricular activities, interview, talent/ability. *Other factors considered include:* Alumni/ae relation, geographical residence, level of applicant's interest, racial/ethnic status, volunteer work, work experience. SAT Subject Tests recommended; ACT with Writing component required. TOEFL required of all international applicants. High school diploma is required, and GED is accepted. *Academic units required:* 4 English, 3 mathematics, 3 science, (1 science labs), 2 foreign language, 3 social studies. *Academic units recommended:* 4 mathematics, 4 science, (2 science labs), 3 foreign language, 4 social studies.

Financial Aid

Students should submit: FAFSA, state aid form. The Princeton Review suggests that all financial aid forms be submitted as soon as possible after January 1. *Need-based scholarships/grants offered:* Federal Pell, SEOG, state scholarships/grants, private scholarships, the school's own gift aid, ACG & SMART. *Loan aid offered:* Federal Perkins, college/university loans from institutional funds. Applicants will be notified of awards on a rolling basis beginning 3/1. Federal Work-Study Program available. Institutional employment available. Off-campus job opportunities are excellent.

The Inside Word

Hofstra is aggressive about filling its incoming class as quickly as possible, offering two rounds of early action and rolling admissions. This is a process that favors those who apply early, so you'd do well to get your application in here as soon as possible.

THE SCHOOL SAYS "..."

From The Admissions Office

"Hofstra is a university on the rise. When you step onto campus you feel the energy and sense the momentum of a university building a national reputation as a center for academic excellence.

"At Hofstra, you'll find an outstanding faculty dedicated to teaching, and small classes, averaging just fewer than 20 students. Outside the classroom, you'll find a multitude of study abroad options, a vibrant extracurricular life, and amazing internship opportunities and cultural experiences in nearby New York City.

"The Hofstra campus—so beautiful it is recognized as an arboretum—features new and cutting-edge teaching facilities. At Hofstra, you will share your classrooms and residence halls with students from nearly every U.S. state and more than 70 countries.

"Students applying for admission may submit either SAT or ACT scores, and an essay is required. The admission team at Hofstra realizes that each applicant is unique and gives each one individual attention."

For even more information on this school, turn to page 494 of the "Stats" section.

HOOD COLLEGE

401 ROSEMONT AVENUE, FREDERICK, MD 21701 • ADMISSIONS: 301-696-3400 • FAX: 301-696-3819
E-MAIL: ADMISSIONS@HOOD.EDU • WEBSITE: WWW.HOOD.EDU

RATINGS
Quality of Life: 85   **Academic: 82**   **Admissions: 80**   **Financial Aid: 83**

STUDENTS SAY "..."

Academics

Students enjoy "a broad and productive education combined with a relaxed and fun campus life" at Hood College, a small private liberal arts college. "Known for its education major," as well as for strong programs in biology, economics, and mathematics, Hood features "great overall academics" rein-forced by small class sizes that facilitate a "wonderful" learn-

> **SURVEY SAYS . . .**
> *Lab facilities are great*
> *Students get along with local community*
> *Students love Frederick, MD*
> *Frats and sororities are unpopular or nonexistent*

ing environment and the "easy flow" of discussion. Students caution that "most of the classes are moderately dif-ficult and the level of conversation and debate is usually top-notch. If you like to reason, debate, and create well-rounded arguments, this is the place for you." Professors "will go as far as inviting you over for dinner to discuss a project, mourn a loss, or just to give advice," and administrators are "engaging and enjoyable." One student exclaims, "They are the reason I call my college 'my Hood, my home.' The administration will go as far as hugging a homesick freshman or making us all breakfast-for-dinner the night before finals!" On the downside, "classes that are required for graduation aren't always offered when they are needed," which is a common problem at small schools.

Life

Hood is located in Frederick, a town of 60,000 "near Washington, D.C., Baltimore, and Annapolis, which all provide great urban environments for having fun." Downtown Frederick is "right off campus" and "provides good food, shopping, and socializing" as well as opportunities to "explore old historic buildings." The one drawback is that "Frederick still shuts down pretty early at night, so most of us have to get inventive if we want to have fun after 9 p.m. off campus. We'll end up playing flashlight tag or going on scavenger hunts through town in the dark." On campus "the school always provides something for us to do," including "New York day-trips, movie night when they pay for our tickets to see the movie of our choice, and tons of free activities for weekend fun." There are also traditions "such as Policies for Dollars, Handel's Messiah May Madness, Hood Ball, Vespers, and Holiday Dinner just to name a few," all of which "are an important part of what makes Hood so special." Even so, many students "leave for the weekend, so usually by lunchtime on Friday it's pretty empty."

Student Body

"Nobody is the same at Hood," one student reports, but "if you had to pinpoint a 'typical' student it would prob-ably either be a white, politically moderate girl majoring in psychology or a tall, jock-like guy who's majoring in biology or chemistry. But really, even they are only a small percentage of our population." Another agrees that Hood students "are a small but very diverse group. There are students who have every possible religious, political, racial and sexual affiliation." Hood is home to "a lot of foreign exchange students and a lot of special-needs...They all make Hood such a rich environment...we're like a big family."

Admissions

Very important factors considered include: Academic GPA, rigor of secondary school record. *Important factors considered include:* Standardized test scores. *Other factors considered include:* Class rank, application essay, recommendation(s), alumni/ae relation, extracurricular activities, first generation, interview, level of applicant's interest, SAT or ACT required; TOEFL required of all international applicants. High school diploma is required and GED is accepted. *Academic units required:* 4 English, 3 mathematics, 3 science, (2 science labs), 2 foreign language, 2 social studies, 1 history, 1 academic electives. *Academic units recommended:* 4 mathematics.

Financial Aid

Students should submit: FAFSA. The Princeton Review suggests that all financial aid forms be submitted as soon as possible after January 1. *Need-based scholarships/grants offered:* Federal Pell, SEOG, state scholarships/grants, private scholarships, the school's own gift aid. *Loan aid offered:* Direct Subsidized Stafford, Direct Unsubsidized Stafford, Direct PLUS, Federal Perkins. Applicants will be notified of awards on a rolling basis beginning 2/15. Federal Work-Study Program available. Institutional employment available. Off-campus job opportunities are good.

The Inside Word

After years of growth in its applicant pool (subsequent to going fully coed in 2003), the numbers have finally started to level off at Hood College. Despite a lopsided male-female ratio, the male minority receives no preferential treatment here. Applicants of both genders were admitted to the class of 2011 at an identical rate.

THE SCHOOL SAYS "..."

From The Admissions Office

"Hood College has experienced several changes in recent years. Student enrollment has increased, yet classes remain small and students have ample opportunity to meet with faculty outside of class for advising, discussion, and individual research projects. The college opened its new science and technology center in 2002, with state-of-the-art laboratories designed specifically for biology, biochemistry, chemistry, and environmental science. Both the classroom (average class size is 14) and the extracurricular environment focus on active student learning. Hood students also develop and practice critical-thinking skills in every class and every campus activity. Along with the obvious social and cultural advantages of Hood's proximity to Washington, D.C. and Baltimore, students have an abundant array of internships in government and industry. On campus, students have the opportunity to get involved in numerous clubs, activities, and organizations from community service, literary, and artistic groups to intramurals and NCAA Division III intercollegiate sports. About one-third of Hood's students compete in 19 varsity athletic teams, and several Hood teams are multi-year champions in their respective sports. Hood's lively and involved student body is diverse, including more than one-fifth who are students of color."

For even more information on this school, turn to page 495 of the "Stats" section.

HOUGHTON COLLEGE

PO Box 128, Houghton, NY 14744 • Admissions: 800-777-2556 • Fax: 585-567-9522
E-mail: admission@houghton.edu • Website: www.houghton.edu

RATINGS

Quality of Life: 87   Academic: 83   Admissions: 85   Financial Aid: 76

STUDENTS SAY ". . ."

Academics

Houghton College, "a small Christian liberal arts school" that is "a particularly good choice for those looking into music, the sciences, and ministry," offers students "an academically challenging experience complemented by a Christian atmosphere and dedication to creating scholar servants." A small student body and a remote location mean the entire community is "connected through many

> **SURVEY SAYS . . .**
> *Students are very religious*
> *Students get along with local community*
> *Low cost of living*
> *Frats and sororities are unpopular or nonexistent*
> *Very little drug use*

activities and classes....We get to know our professors as well as our fellow students." It also "allows for quite a bit of discussion in class (the average class size is 21 students). This is a valuable part of my education, since I have learned so much not just from professors' lectures but also from fellow students as we digest information and discuss its application to life and faith." Outstanding disciplines include biology (featuring "impressive equipment for a small college" and allows many professors to "design their own labs for students, sometimes writing a lab book solely for use at Houghton"), a "great equestrian program," and solid programs in music and education. Students report "many juniors and seniors take advantage of independent study options, where they can pursue an academic interest one-on-one with a professor." Study-abroad programs also attract many students who, as a result of their experiences, become "very interested in going out and getting involved in global issues affecting the world's population."

Life

Houghton is located in a remote area that, depending on your perspective, is either "beautiful...with many things going on" or "boring." Some simply appreciate how the seclusion leaves them "able to concentrate on school and not worry about going shopping or partying." Others note "Houghton offers a wide variety of groups and organizations to be involved with, ranging from rock climbing and paddle sports to Student Government and Evangelicals for Social Activism to Gadfly. Life at Houghton is never dull and there are always people around willing to talk over a cup of coffee or try anything fun, crazy, and exciting." Undergrads also "play a lot of sports, go to sporting events, watch movies, and come up with random ways to have fun." "A lot of our out-of-class time, however, is spent doing homework," says a student. Whatever 'typical' party scene exists here is "hidden from the general population" because "alcohol, illegal drugs, and sexual promiscuity" are all banned (and could result in expulsion).

Student Body

"Houghton is made up mostly of white Protestant students," reports a student, with more than "10 percent...having lived a majority of their lives overseas." Many are "the stereotypical born-again Christians" who "grew up in the church; many with parents who worked in some capacity with in the church." Most are "from New York or Pennsylvania," and "as a result they can go home any weekend they want," leaving "students from farther away...feeling stranded on an isolated campus." Locals are "used to the weather" (i.e. cold winters), while "other students may not be so content with the location." At a nearly two-to-one clip, "Houghton has more females than males."

THE PRINCETON REVIEW SAYS

Admissions

Very important factors considered include: Academic GPA, religious affiliation/commitment. *Important factors considered include:* Class rank, application essay, recommendation(s), rigor of secondary school record, standardized test scores, character/personal qualities. *Other factors considered include:* Alumni/ae relation, extracurricular activities, interview, level of applicant's interest, racial/ethnic status, talent/ability, volunteer work, work experience. SAT or ACT required; TOEFL required of all international applicants. High school diploma is required and GED is accepted. *Academic units recommended:* 4 English, 3 mathematics, 2 science, (2 science labs), 2 foreign language, 1 social studies, 2 history.

Financial Aid

Students should submit: FAFSA. The Princeton Review suggests that all financial aid forms be submitted as soon as possible after January 1. *Need-based scholarships/grants offered:* Federal Pell, SEOG, state scholarships/grants, private scholarships, the school's own gift aid. *Loan aid offered:* Federal Perkins. Applicants will be notified of awards on a rolling basis beginning 3/15. Federal Work-Study Program available. Institutional employment available. Off-campus job opportunities are poor.

The Inside Word

Houghton is not for everyone. The curriculum and the student body are deeply committed to evangelical Christianity, and anyone not 100 percent on board with this won't likely feel comfortable here. Admissions officers know this and will give special consideration to those who, in their view, are "good fits" for the college.

THE SCHOOL SAYS "..."

From The Admissions Office

"Since 1883, Houghton College has provided a residential educational experience that integrates high-quality academic instruction with the Christian faith. Houghton is selective in admission, attracting a very capable student body from 25 countries and 40 states. The college receives widespread national recognition for the quality of its student profile, faculty, and facilities. Enrolling 1,200 full-time students, Houghton is located on a beautiful 1,300-acre campus in western New York. The college's campus includes a 386-acre equestrian center as well as cross-country and downhill ski trails. Houghton's campus combines classic-style architecture with state-of-the-art technology and facilities, including a campus-wide computer network and wireless Internet access. Houghton's traditional liberal arts curriculum offers more than 40 majors and programs. Numerous study abroad programs are available, including Houghton's own offerings in the Tanzania, Eastern Europe, and London. The First-Year Honors Program offers highly qualified students the opportunity to study in England or central europe during the second semester of their first year with 25 of their peers and two Houghton faculty members. There is a strong pre-professional orientation, with 30 to 35 percent of graduates moving on to graduate or professional school upon graduation. Houghton alumni can be found teaching at 175 colleges and universities around the United States and abroad."

For even more information on this school, turn to page 495 of the "Stats" section.

HOWARD UNIVERSITY

2400 SIXTH STREET NORTHWEST, WASHINGTON, DC 20059 • ADMISSIONS: 202-806-2700 • FAX: 202-806-4462
FINANCIAL AID: 202-806-2800 • E-MAIL: ADMISSION@HOWARD.EDU • WEBSITE: WWW.HOWARD.EDU

RATINGS
Quality of Life: 65   **Academic:** 78   **Admissions:** 88   **Financial Aid:** 64

STUDENTS SAY ". . ."

Academics

SURVEY SAYS . . .
Career services are great
Students are happy
Frats and sororities dominate social scene
College radio is popular
Student publications are popular
Student government is popular
Political activism is popular

Howard University, which students proclaim as "the Mecca of black education," has a storied history and an excellent location (ideal for students seeking internships and post-graduation job placements) to "prepare students for the future through academic integrity and social enterprise." Recruiters flock to the Howard campus, in part because "academically, Howard is very strong" and in part because "the university has connections all across the country. Howard does a great job of bringing those connections to campus," in part because of the perception that "organizations are forced to come here to employ their minority quotas." Undergrads here report that "The academic experience largely depends on what you major in. If you're going for African-American studies, business or dentistry you'll get what you've paid for." The presence of a college of medicine (and its affiliated hospital) bolsters offerings in life sciences and premedical studies as well. Students caution that "facilities are outdated and need a major technological and physical update," and "the administration needs some work." Though students say "there are great, qualified people in places of high authority," many feel that the administration at large is "not transparent in the decision making process." Some add, they can be "very disorganized, and you must be extremely patient to deal with the entire financial aid process." However, students universally agree that "the professors at Howard are the best! They truly care about their students, and they want everyone to succeed."

Life

"We always, always, always have something going on" on the "very active" Howard campus. There are "hundreds of organizations that tailor to any needs you can think of," and students are "very active politically and socially, so there are rallies and there are parties. Each and every extreme is met with its opposite here." There's "always somewhere to go" on campus, "whether it be the Punchout Cafe to hang with your friends, Power Hall to relax, study and work with your friends, to 'the yard' to chill and people watch, [or] to the gym to work out. If you are isolated on Howard's campus it is because you choose to be." The world awaiting off campus is even more active. As one student explains, "There is so much to do in the Washington, D.C. area that there is rarely any room for boredom. Georgetown, Chinatown, and Pentagon City are just a few of the places that students go." Adams Morgan is another popular destination. No need to bring a car here. "Everything we would want to go to is Metro-accessible so there's no problem moving about D.C. as if we've lived here our whole lives." Fun is typically confined to weekends, as "Many of us work very hard during the week. Sunday through Thursday, we stay on campus and focus on getting schoolwork done and attending any organizational meetings or events."

Student Body

The typical Howard student "is African American with a deep desire toward success." Undergrads are "extremely serious about their career goals and their academic achievement," and "very involved in political activism, campus organizations, and community." Although nearly all black, the student population "is extremely diverse. I sit in classes with people from Spain, England, Trinidad and Tobago, South Africa, Nigeria, Alaska, etc." Students "come from all walks of life. You can find people with different religious beliefs, ethnic origins, and sexual preferences. There are students with interests in every field imaginable. Howard represents the black world."

THE PRINCETON REVIEW SAYS

Admissions

Very important factors considered include: Class rank, rigor of secondary school record, standardized test scores. *Important factors considered include:* Recommendation(s), character/personal qualities. *Other factors considered include:* Application essay, alumni/ae relation, extracurricular activities, talent/ability, volunteer work, work experience. SAT or ACT required; ACT with Writing component required. TOEFL required of all international applicants. High school diploma is required, and GED is accepted. *Academic units required:* 4 English, 2 mathematics, 2 science, 2 foreign language, 2 social studies, 2 history. *Academic units recommended:* 4 English, 3 mathematics, 4 science, (2 science labs), 2 foreign language, 2 social studies, 2 history, 4 any other academic courses counted towards graduation.

Financial Aid

Students should submit: FAFSA. Regular filing deadline is February 15. The Princeton Review suggests that all financial aid forms be submitted as soon as possible after January 1. *Need-based scholarships/grants offered:* Federal Pell, SEOG, ACG, SMART, TEACH, state scholarships/grants, private scholarships, the school's own gift aid, Federal Nursing Scholarships. *Loan aid offered:* Direct Subsidized Stafford, Direct Unsubsidized Stafford, Direct PLUS, Federal Perkins, Federal Nursing. Applicants will be notified of awards on a rolling basis beginning 4/1. Federal Work-Study Program available. Institutional employment available. Off-campus job opportunities are excellent.

The Inside Word

A large applicant pool and graduation rate of those who enroll is a combination that adds up to selectivity at Howard. The school is willing to give applicants a pass on standardized test scores if their high school records indicate seriousness about, and the ability to handle, advanced study.

THE SCHOOL SAYS "…"

From The Admissions Office

"Since its founding, Howard has stood among the few institutions of higher learning where blacks and other minorities have participated freely in a truly comprehensive university experience. Thus, Howard has assumed a special responsibility in preparing its students to exercise leadership wherever their interests and commitments take them. Howard has issued approximately 111,233 degrees, diplomas, and certificates to men and women in the professions, the arts and sciences, and the humanities. The university has produced and continues to produce a high percentage of the nation's African American professionals in the fields of medicine, dentistry, pharmacy, engineering, nursing, architecture, religion, law, music, social work, education, and business. There are more than 10,036 students from across the nation and approximately 85 countries and territories attending the university. Their varied customs, cultures, ideas, and interests contribute to Howard's international character and vitality. More than 1,598 faculty members represent the largest concentration of black scholars in any single institution of higher education.

"All applicants who have never been to college are required to submit scores from either the SAT or the ACT (with the Writing component)."

For even more information on this school, turn to page 496 of the "Stats" section.

INDIANA UNIVERSITY OF PENNSYLVANIA

216 PRATT HALL, INDIANA, PA 15705 • ADMISSIONS: 724-357-2230 • FAX: 724-357-6281
FINANCIAL AID: 415-357-2218 • E-MAIL: ADMISSIONS_INQUIRY@GROVE.IUP.EDU • WEBSITE: WWW.IUP.EDU

RATINGS
Quality of Life: 66   Academic: 67   Admissions: 69   Financial Aid: 70

STUDENTS SAY ". . ."

Academics

"An affordable school that has something to offer everyone," Indiana University of Pennsylvania (IUP) serves up "excellent academic programs" that are "academically challenging but not impossible if you make an honest effort." "Music, nursing, and education are the school's greatest strengths," one student says. Others laud the "fantastic fine arts program;" IUP's "very good College of Business;" and

> **SURVEY SAYS . . .**
> Great computer facilities
> Frats and sororities dominate social scene
> Student publications are popular
> Lots of beer drinking
> Hard liquor is popular

solid programs in theater, mathematics, chemistry, criminology, and English. Students here enjoy "awesome professors" who are "concerned with [students'] welfare and academic growth," and the students find their teachers "ridiculously easy to get into contact with—no need to make an appointment." The vast majority of students here are firmly focused on their post-graduation earning potential; they tell us that the school "is about learning to be the best at your career in the future." Students with higher intellectual and academic ambitions usually find their way into the Robert E. Cook Honors College, which "teaches students to think critically, participate in cultural events, and take active roles in the global community." The program has "fewer than 100 students in the freshman class, which means that we can have very small classes. Our professors know who we are and are able to give us more individual attention than would be possible with a larger group."

Life

Indiana, Pennsylvania, is the kind of town John Mellencamp would sing about— small, working-class, but not without its charms or bars. In fact, some claim the town "has a lot to offer kids to do. Malls, skating rinks, restaurants, movie theaters, ice hockey rinks, sports events, and campus events keep most of the students busy." Others aren't so sure; one writes, "Indiana is a small town with little to do, especially in the winter, when we get a lot of snow," which is why "people drink," and "when we aren't drinking, we think about the next time we will be drinking." Students concede that "Sometimes IUP gets a bad rap being known as a party school," but they point out that "college is all what you make it. The academic programs are exceptional," and those students "who want no alcohol/drugs involved in their college life whatsoever" will find options available to them, including trips to town, "movies and games," and "outdoor activities when the weather is nice." The school also boasts a "good selection of clubs" that provide a quick way "to meet people." If you need a taste of city life, "Pittsburgh is an hour away by car" and has "lots to do."

Student Body

Most IUP undergrads "are from the surrounding small towns," which are "predominantly white," but the school remains "more diverse" than the region (although "less diverse than U.S. Census percentage numbers") by drawing from other areas, including the city of Pittsburgh. Students describe the population as "very mixed," affording "the opportunity to interact with more people" than they would at "many other colleges." "No matter what your interest is, it wouldn't be too hard to find someone that you can share this interest with," one student tells us. Students view themselves as "down-to-earth" and pragmatic; as one explains, "This is the kind of school where intellectual growth is not the primary concern; it seems as if people are interested in getting a degree to get a better job...The few that are here for intellectual growth and enlightenment suffer from an apathetic community."

THE PRINCETON REVIEW SAYS

Admissions

Very important factors considered include: Academic GPA, standardized test scores. *Important factors considered include:* Rigor of secondary school record. *Other factors considered include:* Class rank, application essay, recommendation(s), extracurricular activities. SAT or ACT required; TOEFL required of all international applicants. High school diploma is required and GED is accepted. *Academic units recommended:* 3 English, 3 mathematics, 3 science, 2 foreign language, 3 social studies.

Financial Aid

Students should submit: FAFSA. The Princeton Review suggests that all financial aid forms be submitted as soon as possible after January 1. *Need-based scholarships/grants offered:* Federal Pell, SEOG, state scholarships/grants, private scholarships, the school's own gift aid, United Negro College Fund. *Loan aid offered:* FFEL Subsidized Stafford, FFEL Unsubsidized Stafford, FFEL PLUS, Federal Perkins, other, private alternative loans. Applicants will be notified of awards on a rolling basis beginning 3/15. Federal Work-Study Program available. Institutional employment available. Off-campus job opportunities are good.

The Inside Word

IUP serves a dual mission: to provide low-cost higher education to as broad a range of students as possible and to maintain rigorous academic standards. Accordingly, admissions aren't as competitive here as they are at other top schools; students with above-average secondary school records and average or better standardized test scores are likely admits here. Once in, middling students better be prepared to step up their game, or they will soon find themselves on their way out the door.

THE SCHOOL SAYS "..."

From The Admissions Office

"At IUP, we look at each applicant as an individual, not as a number. That means we'll review your application materials very carefully. When reviewing applications, the admissions committee's primary focus is on the student's high school record and SAT scores. In addition, the committee often reviews the optional personal essay and letters of recommendations submitted by the student to help aid in the decision-making process. We're always happy to speak with prospective students. Call us toll-free at 800-422-6830 or 724-357-2230 or e-mail us at admissions-inquiry@iup.edu.

"Students applying for admission are required to take the SAT or ACT."

For even more information on this school, turn to page 496 of the "Stats" section.

IONA COLLEGE

715 North Avenue, New Rochelle, NY 10801 • Admissions: 914-633-2502 • Fax: 914-633-2642
E-mail: admissions@iona.edu • Website: www.iona.edu

RATINGS
Quality of Life: 82   **Academic:** 73   **Admissions:** 87   **Financial Aid:** 64

STUDENTS SAY ". . ."

SURVEY SAYS . . .
Great computer facilities
Great library
Low cost of living

Academics

A "small, diverse, private, Catholic [college], with a large commuter population," Iona College is known for "its proximity to New York City" and its "quality of education," all delivered in a picturesque suburban setting. In many ways, students say Iona features "the best of both worlds with the suburbs down the street in one direction and downtown city in the other." Iona's "beautiful, quiet" New Rochelle campus "has that New England feeling to it" but offers big city opportunities. Students at Iona feel like they are "getting the most for [their] money." Many flock to the school for its excellent business school and generous scholarships. Iona combines "a great commute," "a beautiful, loving campus," and a "warm, welcoming attitude." Professors at Iona can be hit or miss. As one student says, "I found that the professors that taught me my major were professional and well-organized. The professors teaching the core classes were mediocre at best." Overall, Iona "is about academic achievement while also improving the social life of its students and preparing them for the outside world." These qualities make it a gem which stays in the family: "Both my parents and some of my relatives attended Iona and they loved it."

Life

The "super friendly students," "safe private campus," and close proximity to "the country's greatest city" (only an "easy train ride away"), all make Iona a great choice for commuters and residents alike. This "small, close-knit community" is comprised of motivated individuals who are "always eager to reach out to others and help them in order to make a difference." With Manhattan only a 20 minute ride away on the Metro North commuter railroad, students take full advantage of the opportunity "to go to New York City" for a night out on the town. During the week, students tend to stay on campus and enjoy "hanging out in the dorm rooms with a bunch of people." Though "the underclass dorms are dry," for those of age there is liquid diversion in the area: "A lot of the students like to go out to the bars, right by Iona, known as Beechmont and Spectators." If that's not your speed, students say there is "always some kind of a house party going on somewhere over the weekend." The school is "constantly improving and advancing the campus," a mission in which they invite students to take part; "There are many leadership positions available to students, with the offer of creating new clubs and organizations that do not [currently] exist." Nearby entertainment includes "The Westchester Mall and the Galleria."

Student Body

Iona's community "is one of the most diverse communities out there." "Whether commuters or dorm students everyone seems to get along," and many are "part of an organization or club on campus." Though the typical student tends to be "a white, Christian person, usually who comes from an Irish or Italian background" and "is from Westchester County," students say "There is a mix of many different groups. Every person will find a group to fit in with and all groups get along well with each other." In fact, diversity is exactly what makes Iona distinct. "Many people from different social [and] ethnic...groups make up what we call our 'home away from home.'"

THE PRINCETON REVIEW SAYS

Admissions

Very important factors considered include: Academic GPA, rigor of secondary school record. *Important factors considered include:* Class rank, application essay, standardized test scores, character/personal qualities, interview. *Other factors considered include:* Recommendation(s), alumni/ae relation, extracurricular activities, first generation, geographical residence, level of applicant's interest, talent/ability, volunteer work, work experience. SAT or ACT required; TOEFL required of all international applicants. High school diploma is required and GED is accepted. *Academic units required:* 4 English, 3 mathematics, 2 science, (2 science labs), 2 foreign language, 1 social studies, 1 history, 1 academic electives. *Academic units recommended:* 4 mathematics, 3 science, 2 social studies, 2 history, 3 academic electives.

Financial Aid

Students should submit: FAFSA, institution's own financial aid form, state aid form. Regular filing deadline is 4/15. The Princeton Review suggests that all financial aid forms be submitted as soon as possible after January 1. *Need-based scholarships/grants offered:* Federal Pell, SEOG, state scholarships/grants, private scholarships, the school's own gift aid. *Loan aid offered:* Federal Perkins, other, alternative loans. Applicants will be notified of awards on a rolling basis beginning 12/20. Federal Work-Study Program available. Institutional employment available. Off-campus job opportunities are good.

The Inside Word

With 2,800 full-time undergraduates, Iona offers a private, comprehensive, four-year Catholic education in a diverse community. For transfer students with twenty or more college credits at the time of application, the admissions cut-off is a 2.5 cumulative GPA at the college level. For students with fewer than twenty-four college credits at the time of application, high school GPA and standardized test scores are weighed more heavily.

THE SCHOOL SAYS "..."

From The Admissions Office

"Students appreciate Iona on a number of levels: They find the academic programs challenging and supportive; they enjoy the large number of organized and individual activities, and they love being close to New York City for the internships and social opportunities it provides.

"Iona has a beautiful, green, 35-acre campus in New Rochelle, New York, just 20 minutes from Manhattan. Students use mass transportation to take advantage of New York City for social and educational opportunities, including internships at some of the world's most recognized institutions.

"After Iona, our graduates continue to excel: 76 percent of our graduates go on to pursue graduate or professional studies and gain acceptance at the world's most prestigious graduate schools (Harvard, Yale, Johns Hopkins, Oxford, University of Chicago). Iona alumni also excel in the workplace, currently heading global industries (New York Stock Exchange, NASDAQ, AOL, American Express, Terex, AFL-CIO) and provide our students with a network of internship opportunities and our graduates with employment opportunities.

"We invite you to schedule a visit to Iona College and experience our campus in person. You can 'Spend-A-Day' and sample what it's like to be a college student—sit in on a class or seminar, have lunch in the dining commons or café, tour the residence halls, student union and brand-new library, among others. Call (800) 231-IONA today to schedule your visit or speak to an admissions counselor."

For even more information on this school, turn to page 496 of the "Stats" section.

ITHACA COLLEGE

100 JOB HALL, ITHACA, NY 14850-7020 • ADMISSIONS: 607-274-3124 • FAX: 607-274-1900
FINANCIAL AID: 607-274-3131 • E-MAIL: ADMISSION@ITHACA.EDU • WEBSITE: WWW.ITHACA.EDU

RATINGS
Quality of Life: 81   **Academic:** 80   **Admissions:** 83   **Financial Aid:** 87

STUDENTS SAY ". . ."

Academics

If you don't know whether you'd be happier at a small school or a large university, Ithaca College offers the best of both worlds. With just more than 6,400 undergraduates, Ithaca College is "not so big that you get lost, but not so small that you have a lack of opportunities." The school offers 100 major programs, with instructors who "are enthusiastic and genuinely interested in the subject matter and the students." A senior tells us, "In the end they become more mentors or friends than professors. We call them by their first names, and they take note of what's happening in our lives outside the classroom." Ithaca College was originally founded as a Music Conservatory, and their music programs continue to have an excellent reputation, as does the Park School of Communications. More than 1,000 Ithaca undergraduates are pursuing majors within the communications field, doling out praises for their strong and practical education. A senior enthuses, "We run radio and television stations, newspapers, [and] ad campaigns. We make films! We try to make a mini-real world so that we are super prepared for real life." Not everyone has contact with the school's administration; those who do say that they are "more than willing to work with you and give you respect." A junior attests, "I am a member of Student Government, and thus far the administration has really valued the opinions and ideas of the students." While the town of Ithaca's natural beauty is universally touted, on campus "some buildings are a little dated."

> ### SURVEY SAYS . . .
> *Great off-campus food*
> *Low cost of living*
> *Frats and sororities are unpopular or nonexistent*
> *College radio is popular*
> *Theater is popular*
> *Student publications are popular*

Life

Ithaca is a great place to get the full college experience. Residential life helps to forge a strong bond between undergraduates, as "all students live on campus for the first three years." In their free time, almost every student takes part in extracurricular clubs, sports teams, or campus activities. Off campus, Ithaca is a bustling college town with plenty of student-oriented attractions. In their free time, "a lot of people enjoy what is offered in the town of Ithaca. The commons has a large variety of restaurants and shops, and the farmer's market is amazing!" Due to the natural beauty of the region, "going hiking in the gorges is also very popular, especially in the warmer months." At the same time, students warn us that, "the weather here is usually very gloomy; sun is very rare past November." When the snow begins to fall, "a good amount of the population enjoys skiing and snowboarding" and, students admit, partying becomes a more popular activity. In general, however, partying is just one of the many options available to IC students; life at Ithaca is well rounded, multifaceted, and fulfilling. A senior agrees, "People here focus on everything from school work to parties to political issues. There really is a good balance."

Student Body

Getting involved in the community is second nature to most Ithaca students. A junior explains, "The typical student has a cause: some issue that they are passionate about and will devote much of their in-class study and extracurricular activities to—from gender issues, to LGBT issues, to race, to sustainability and the environment." Of particular note, "many students here are concerned about their environmental impact. There are a lot of clubs and classes centered around environmental awareness and education." Nearly 45 percent of the student population comes from the state of New York, and "the general student population is similar in background." However, students repeatedly reassure us that, "while Ithaca College is not the most diverse school, it prides itself on making everyone feel welcome and accepted. We are a community, and no one gets left out." Students acknowledge the existence of cliques, but they reassure us that, "unlike high school, you are not limited to being friends with the ones who are just like you. Everyone interacts and gets to know each other."

Admissions

Very important factors considered include: Academic GPA, rigor of secondary school record, standardized test scores. *Important factors considered include:* Class rank, application essay, recommendation(s), character/personal qualities, extracurricular activities, talent/ability. *Other factors considered include:* Alumni/ae relation, first generation, level of applicant's interest, volunteer work, work experience. SAT or ACT required; ACT with Writing component required. TOEFL required of all international applicants. High school diploma is required, and GED is accepted. *Academic units required:* 4 English, 3 mathematics, 3 science, 2 foreign language, 4 social studies, 1 academic electives.

Financial Aid

Students should submit: FAFSA, CSS/Financial Aid PROFILE. The Princeton Review suggests that all financial aid forms be submitted as soon as possible after January 1. *Need-based scholarships/grants offered:* Federal Pell, SEOG, state scholarships/grants, private scholarships, the school's own gift aid. *Loan aid offered:* Federal Perkins, Other, alternative loans. Applicants will be notified of awards on a rolling basis beginning 2/15. Federal Work-Study Program available. Institutional employment available. Off-campus job opportunities are good.

The Inside Word

Ithaca College brings the personal touch to the admissions process, offering one-on-one admissions counseling to prospective students during the application process or after acceptance to the college. Admissions is selective, with roughly 12,000 applicants for just 1,600 first-year spots, and 49 percent of incoming freshman held a spot in the top 15 percent of their high school class.

THE SCHOOL SAYS "..."

From The Admissions Office

"Ithaca College was founded in 1892 as a music conservatory, and it continues that commitment to performance and excellence. Its modern, residential 750-acre campus, equipped with state-of-the-art facilities, is home to the Schools of Business, Communications, Health Sciences and Human Performance, Humanities and Sciences, and Music and our new Division of Interdisciplinary and International Studies. With more than 100 majors—from biochemistry to business administration, journalism to jazz, philosophy to physical therapy, and special programs in Washington, D.C.; Los Angeles; London; and Australia—students enjoy the curricular choices of a large campus in a personalized, smaller school environment. And Ithaca's students benefit from an education that emphasizes active learning, small classes, collaborative student-faculty research, and development of the whole student. Located in central New York's spectacular Finger Lakes region in what many consider the classic college town, the college has 25 highly competitive varsity teams, more than 130 campus clubs, two radio stations, and a television station, as well as hundreds of concerts, recitals, and theater performances annually.

"Students applying for admission must have official scores from either the SAT or the ACT with the Writing section sent to Ithaca College by the testing agency. The college will also consider results of SAT Subject Tests, if submitted."

For even more information on this school, turn to page 497 of the "Stats" section.

JOHNS HOPKINS UNIVERSITY

3400 NORTH CHARLES STREET/140 GARLAND, BALTIMORE, MD 21218 • ADMISSIONS: 410-516-8171
FAX: 410-516-6025 • FINANCIAL AID: 410-516-8028 • E-MAIL: GOTOJHU@JHU.EDU • WEBSITE: WWW.JHU.EDU

RATINGS

Quality of Life: 77   **Academic:** 89   **Admissions:** 98   **Financial Aid:** 91

STUDENTS SAY ". . ."

Academics

Johns Hopkins University has a reputation as an academic powerhouse, one that its undergrads wholeheartedly affirm. Although the university offers "a pretty intense environment" with "really rigorous" classes, all of this is made bearable by professors are "concerned with the individual student" and "extremely approachable, even in [an] organic chemistry class of 300 students." Indeed, "They enjoy being in the classroom and sharing what they know. Each is passionate about their area of study and eager to share it with students who are equally as enthusiastic." A satisfied senior echoes these praises, saying, "All the professors that I've encountered at Hopkins recognize that learning should be fun and thought-provoking. Their lectures or discussions engage students to think about the materials in a different way and pursue further outside study." "Engage" is the operative word here, as undergrads are "treated as though they are participants in their respective academic fields, not just 'students'." However, as one senior cautions, "There's very little grade inflation, and you work hard for the grade you get." Praise also extends to the administration, which students describe as "caring to a fault, willing to help, and generally highly interested in the undergraduate experience." As one junior sums up, "It's clear that our professors and deans genuinely care about the students, as evidenced by their attendance at student fundraisers, fraternity scholarship events, and even plays and a cappella concerts. They want students to learn about anything that interests them, but they want students to grow as people too, and it's astonishing how high their success rate is in that regard."

Life

Life at Hopkins is "certainly based around work." Indeed, most undergrads are diligent students "who put work over everything else." This is a school where "people care about what they study" and it's not uncommon to see fellow students "stay up all night debating philosophy, politics or the theory of evolution." Sound a little intense? No worries: One junior assures us that "there's never a dull moment at Johns Hopkins: You just have to step outside your room and look for five seconds." Another senior confirms, "There's always something cool going on around campus, whether it's from the world of entertainment (like Will Ferrell coming to speak) or academia." There are numerous "free on-campus movies, plays, dance, and a cappella performances" to take in along with "the BEST lacrosse team in America" and "incredibly competitive [Division III] sports like soccer and water polo." And with roughly a quarter of the student body involved in fraternities and sororities, Greek life offers a "tremendous social outlet." Fortunately, when students get bored on campus, they can always explore hometown Baltimore for entertainment options. The city offers "movie theaters, malls, shopping centers, a TON of restaurants, a good music scene, and proximity to D.C., clubs, and other colleges. Many undergrads can frequently be found hanging out by the Inner Harbor or the nearby Towson Mall.

Student Body

While it might be difficult to define the typical Hopkins undergrad, the vast majority are "hardworking and care about their GPAs, and will do what they can to get the grades they want." Thankfully, many are also "balance artists; they are able to balance schoolwork, extracurricular activities, jobs, and a social life without getting too bogged down or stressed." Though students "are competitive in the sense that they all want to do well," that competitiveness is never adversarial. One junior declares, "I have found that there is an incredible mutual respect that permeates the student body, one that allows engineers to discuss poetry with English majors, sees historians present at astronomy lectures, and gets linguists to help lacrosse players study for French tests, all while reserving judgment upon each other." A sophomore continues, "I've never been someplace where there are so many diverse interests. As clichéd as it may sound, there truly is a niche for everyone."

THE PRINCETON REVIEW SAYS

Admissions

Very important factors considered include: Academic GPA, recommendation(s), rigor of secondary school record, character/personal qualities. *Important factors considered include:* Class rank, application essay, standardized test scores, extracurricular activities, talent/ability, volunteer work, work experience. *Other factors considered include:* Alumni/ae relation, first generation, geographical residence, interview, racial/ethnic status, state residency. SAT or ACT required; SAT and SAT Subject Tests or ACT recommended; ACT with Writing component required. TOEFL required of all international applicants. High school diploma or equivalent is not required. *Academic units recommended:* 4 English, 4 mathematics, 4 science, 4 foreign language, 2 social studies, 2 history.

Financial Aid

Students should submit: FAFSA, CSS/Financial Aid PROFILE, noncustodial PROFILE, business/farm supplement. current year federal tax returns. Regular filing deadline is 3/1. The Princeton Review suggests that all financial aid forms be submitted as soon as possible after January 1. *Need-based scholarships/grants offered:* Federal Pell, SEOG, state scholarships/grants, private scholarships, the school's own gift aid. *Loan aid offered:* Direct Subsidized Stafford, Direct Unsubsidized Stafford, Direct PLUS, Federal Perkins, college/university loans from institutional funds. Applicants will be notified of awards on or about 4/1. Federal Work-Study Program available. Institutional employment available. Off-campus job opportunities are good.

The Inside Word

Top schools like Hopkins receive more and more applications every year and, as a result, grow harder and harder to get into. With more than 16,000 applicants, Hopkins has to reject numerous applicants who are thoroughly qualified. Give your application everything you've got, and don't take it personally if you don't get a fat envelope in the mail.

THE SCHOOL SAYS "…"

From The Admissions Office

"The Hopkins tradition of preeminent academic excellence naturally attracts the very best students in the nation and from around the world. The admissions committee carefully examines each application for evidence of compelling intellectual interest and academic performance as well as strong personal recommendations and meaningful extracurricular contributions. Every applicant who matriculates to Johns Hopkins University was found qualified by the admissions committee through a 'whole person' assessment, and every applicant accepted for admission is fully expected to graduate. The admissions committee determines whom they believe will take full advantage of the exceptional opportunities offered at Hopkins, contribute the most to the educational process of the institution, and be the most successful in using what they have learned and experienced for the benefit of society.

"Freshman applicants may take either the SAT or the ACT with Writing component. For those submitting SAT scores, submitting scores from three SAT Subject Tests is recommended."

For even more information on this school, turn to page 497 of the "Stats" section.

JUNIATA COLLEGE

ENROLLMENT OFFICE, 1700 MOORE ST., HUNTINGDON, PA 16652 • ADMISSIONS: 877-586-4282
FAX: 814-641-3100 • FINANCIAL AID: 814-641-3142 • E-MAIL: ADMISSION@JUNIATA.EDU • WEBSITE: WWW.JUNIATA.EDU

RATINGS

Quality of Life: 80   Academic: 86   Admissions: 89   Financial Aid: 80

STUDENTS SAY "..."

Academics

Juniata College has catapulted from regional to national status in the past decade on the strength of its great natural science programs, housed in the 88,000-square-foot, state-of-the-art Von Liebig Center for Science (VLCS). Students tell us while Juniata "is centered around a very tough but rewarding science program," science is hardly the only game in town. The "business, theatre, and education departments are strong, too." Another student explains, "Other departments are beginning to receive support from trustees and alumni now that VLCS is complete. Several buildings will be undergoing renovations to allow for the expansion of the humanities and social sciences." Business, in particular, seems likely to receive a lot of attention as it is among the school's most popular disciplines. Undergrads tout JC's "great entrepreneurial program...where all students are encouraged to start their own businesses and some are given start-up cash." Education is also popular. Students appreciate they are "given a practicum their first semester freshman year," meaning "if they don't like being in the classroom, they can change their major right away." "At most other schools, you have to wait until your junior year to get some classroom experience, [in your major]" says a student. Other perks of a Juniata education include the prominence of the study-abroad program and the (Program of Emphasis) where, "students are afforded the option to create their own major which allows us to explore many possibilities that would otherwise be restricted by a designated major."

Life

Juniata "is located in Huntingdon, Pennsylvania, which is a tiny town in the middle of nowhere, 30 minutes south of State," so "needless to say, there is not a lot to do off campus." Fortunately, "the Juniata Activities Board (JAB) brings numerous acts to campus including comedians, musicians, hypnotists, [and] magicians." The campus also hosts "various weekend parties, but they normally don't happen until Saturday nights because a large population of the student body is active in athletics with games either Friday night or Saturday afternoon." Since Juniata "doesn't have any Greek societies," students compensate by being "active in many clubs, including the Agriculture Club, Health Occupations Students of America, student government, the Equine club, and the Student Alumni Association." Otherwise, quiet fun ("video games and movie watching are very popular") dominates. One student explains, "The people who are dissatisfied with Juniata were definitely expecting something else, usually something more along the lines of Penn State."

Student Body

Juniata "is notoriously middle-class and Caucasian" with "very few minority students." Diversity arrives in the form of "a vast number of international students, both in semester and year-long exchange programs. The international presence at Juniata does a lot for class debate, and often opens the eyes of otherwise typically American students to the perspectives of those from other nations." Undergrads here "work hard for their grades. They want to excel. Basically, they're motivated and determined to succeed in the real world," to the point they often "choose to do homework and study above most other activities." Ultimately, "a typical student is really studious and really cares about their education. Everyone is able to find their own clique in which they fit into and feel comfortable."

THE PRINCETON REVIEW SAYS

Admissions

Very important factors considered include: Application essay, academic GPA, recommendation(s), rigor of secondary school record, standardized test scores, character/personal qualities. *Important factors considered include:* Extracurricular activities, first generation, interview, talent/ability, volunteer work. *Other factors considered include:* Alumni/ae relation, geographical residence, level of applicant's interest, racial/ethnic status, state residency. SAT or ACT recommended; TOEFL required of all international applicants. High school diploma is required, and GED is accepted. *Academic units required:* 4 English, 3 mathematics, 3 science, (2 science labs), 2 foreign language, 1 social studies, 3 history. *Academic units recommended:* 4 English, 4 mathematics, 4 science, 2 foreign language, 1 social studies, 3 history.

Financial Aid

Students should submit: FAFSA. Regular filing deadline is 3/1. The Princeton Review suggests that all financial aid forms be submitted as soon as possible after January 1. *Need-based scholarships/grants offered:* Federal Pell, SEOG, state scholarships/grants, private scholarships, the school's own gift aid. *Loan aid offered:* Federal Perkins, college/university loans from institutional funds. Applicants will be notified of awards on a rolling basis beginning 2/28. Federal Work-Study Program available. Institutional employment available. Off-campus job opportunities are good.

The Inside Word

As at many traditional liberal arts schools, the admissions process at Juniata is a personal one. Applications are scoured for evidence the student is committed to attending Juniata and to remaining there for the full four years. The school is best known for its premedical programs, meaning applicants to these programs will have the highest hurdles to clear.

THE SCHOOL SAYS "..."

From The Admissions Office

"Juniata's unique approach to learning has a flexible, student-centered focus. With the help of two advisors, more than half of Juniata's students design their own majors (called the "Program of Emphasis" or "POE"). Those who choose a more traditional academic journey still benefit from the assistance of two faculty advisors and interdisciplinary collaboration between multiple academic departments.

"In addition, all students benefit from the recent, significant investments in academic facilities that help students actively learn by doing. For example, the new Halbritter Performing Arts Center houses an innovative theater program where theater professionals work side-by-side with students. The Sill Business Incubator provides $5,000 in seed capital to students with a desire to start their own business. The LEEDS-certified Shuster Environmental Studies Field Station, located on nearby Raystown Lake, gives unparalleled, hands-on study opportunities to students. And the von Liebig Center for Science provides opportunities for student/faculty research surpassing those available at even large universities.

"As the 2003 Middle States Accreditation Team noted, 'Juniata is truly a student-centered college. There is a remarkable cohesiveness in this commitment—faculty, students, trustees, staff, and alumni, each from their own vantage point, describe a community in which the growth of the student is central.' This cohesiveness creates a dynamic learning environment that enables students to think and grow intellectually, to evolve in their academic careers, and to graduate as active, successful participants in the global community.

"Freshman applicants may submit the SAT (or the ACT with the Writing component). We will use their best scores from either test. "

For even more information on this school, turn to page 498 of the "Stats" section.

KEENE STATE COLLEGE

229 MAIN STREET, KEENE, NH 03435 • ADMISSIONS: 603-358-2276 • FAX: 603-358-2767
E-MAIL: ADMISSIONS@KEENE.EDU • WEBSITE: WWW.KEENE.EDU

RATINGS
Quality of Life: 80   **Academic:** 70   **Admissions:** 72   **Financial Aid:** 71

STUDENTS SAY "..."

Academics

"Keene State College is a great liberal arts school in a pictur-esque New England town" that is "really great for education majors." There are almost 40 other majors to choose from, though, and "the academic experience as a whole is generally good." "The physical campus is almost entirely new." "Classrooms are spacious, attractive, and comfortable." A few professors are "dull" and "just suck at teaching." However, "the majority of professors love what they do, and that's reflected in their teaching style." Students receive "lots of individual attention." "Here you are a person and not a number," promises a junior. "My profes-sors are always more than willing to meet with me whenever I need to," gloats an education major. "They are extremely accessible and helpful." "The administration is always there when you have a question" as well. There's "very little bureaucracy" and everything "flows nicely."

Life

According to students the "gorgeous" and "relaxing" campus at Keene State is the perfect size. "The campus is small enough I can randomly run into my friends, but big enough that if I need space, it's there," says a soph-omore. For many students, "life consists of a lot of studying." "A lot of work gets done Sunday through Thursday." If you want, you can "slack off immensely," though, and still get by. Sports are popular and there is a "wide variety" of clubs and activities. There is also a smattering of Greek life. "The weekend party scene is great." Students here have been known to get "drunk and rowdy." The bar scene is lively. "A lot of the sports teams have houses, so they sometimes throw open parties" as well. The "friendly" surrounding hamlet of Keene "is quintessentially New England," complete with an "awesome main street" and several "unique stores and restaurants." Each year, "thousands of jack-o-lanterns" line the streets for the big pumpkin festival in town and there is a big gourd-carving free-for-fall called Pumpkin Lobotomy on the quad. Further afield, there's "Mount Monadnock to climb" and outdoor activities galore.

Student Body

"There is undoubtedly a lack of ethnic diversity here." "A lot of the kids are from New Hampshire" but a sig-nificant percentage comes from others states around the region. "Many students at Keene State seem to be from Connecticut." "The typical student at Keene State is white and preppy or a jock." "There are definitely some students who've come here for the school's regional reputation as a party school." There are "some hipster types." "There are very many crunchy, earthy students" as well. "Everyone drinks coffee." KSC is home to "very few bookworms or nerds." You'll occasionally see kids with "funky-colored hair and mohawks," but it's definitely not the norm. "There [are] cliques, but there aren't armored walls" between them. "You have your core group of friends, but most groups are totally willing to expand and diversify," notes one student.

THE PRINCETON REVIEW SAYS

Admissions

Very important factors considered include: Rigor of secondary school record. *Important factors considered include:* Application essay, academic GPA, recommendation(s), standardized test scores. *Other factors considered include:* Class rank, alumni/ae relation, character/personal qualities, extracurricular activities, first generation, level of applicant's interest, racial/ethnic status, talent/ability, volunteer work, work experience. SAT or ACT required; ACT with Writing component recommended. TOEFL required of all international applicants. High school diploma is required and GED is accepted. *Academic units required:* 4 English, 3 mathematics, 3 science, 2 social studies, 2 academic electives.

Financial Aid

Students should submit: FAFSA. Regular filing deadline is 3/1. The Princeton Review suggests that all financial aid forms be submitted as soon as possible after January 1. *Need-based scholarships/grants offered:* Federal Pell, SEOG, state scholarships/grants, private scholarships, the school's own gift aid. *Loan aid offered:* Federal Perkins, college/university loans from institutional funds. Federal Work-Study Program available. Institutional employment available. Off-campus job opportunities are excellent.

The Inside Word

Keene State is a safety school for many applicants with aspirations of attending flagship universities throughout New England. Keene State takes the time to look at your admissions application, primarily in an effort to justify admitting otherwise substandard candidates. The gatekeepers here want to invite you in; all you have to do is give them a good reason.

THE SCHOOL SAYS "..."

From The Admissions Office

"Keene State College is known as a moderately selective school with retention rates that look more like those of a selective school. We are proud that the quality of our applicants continues to increase each year, and we regularly cross applications with competitive flagship universities throughout New England.

"Students considered for admission to Keene State College are expected to have completed a competitive program of study in high school. Our 19 percent increase in applications in the past two years has given us the opportunity to become more selective and to close applications to nonresident students by March 1 – a month earlier than our usual deadline. The average GPA for a student entering Keene State College has consistently remained slightly above 3.0 (in academic courses) for the past five years. Admission to Keene's college-wide honors program is more competitive, with a minimum GPA of 3.25 and cumulative SAT scores of 1050.

"Our applicants' average scores on the SAT verbal and math sections show a slight increase this year compared to recent years, with average scores of 508 verbal and 512 math. Also, as our students have mentioned, Keene State College takes pride in developing the fullest potential of students who enter not only as learners but as good citizens. More than 60 percent of our students are involved in community service. The College's recognition with distinction on President Bush's Honor Roll for Service is a tribute to our students' engagement in the world."

For even more information on this school, turn to page 498 of the "Stats" section.

King's College

133 North River Street, Wilkes-Barre, PA 18711 • Admissions: 570-208-5858
Fax: 570-208-5971 • E-mail: admissions@kings.edu • Website: www.kings.edu

RATINGS
Quality of Life: 73   Academic: 73   Admissions: 75   Financial Aid: 72

STUDENTS SAY ". . ."

Academics

King's College is a small Catholic liberal arts school in northeastern Pennsylvania. There are 35 majors and ten pre-professional programs. "The business school and the education program are both great strengths." The five-year physician assistant program is "fantastic" as well. The administration is "unorganized" but "very accessible." The president "lives in a dorm hall," for example. "Small class sizes" are reportedly a plus. Professors get to "know you on a personal level." While a few faculty members "couldn't teach a first-grade class," most of them are "200 percent passionate" and "committed to helping you understand the things they teach." They "genuinely care about your life" and are "always willing to help." "I've had an amazing academic experience," gushes a business major. The Office of Career Planning is another "great asset." Internship opportunities abound, and some "99 percent" of all King's newly minted alumni find jobs within six months of graduation. The limited course selection is the big academic complaint here. "Many of the classes offered, particularly in the sciences, are only offered once every other year," laments a biology major.

Life

The atmosphere at King's is "very friendly and inviting." "You can walk across campus, and half of the people you pass are either acquaintances or friends," observes a senior. "It's rare to see anyone sitting alone at lunch." "There are your typical cliques," and "everyone sort of has their own little group." "Extracurricular activities are very popular, and almost everyone is involved in at least one." "King's students are highly involved with community service activities," notes a sophomore. Many play an intercollegiate sport, too. Some students grumble that King's "could have more activities and things to do around campus." Others tell us the school is "always sponsoring some kind of event." There are "great trips at cheap prices" to New York City and the ski mountains nearby. There is "daily Mass," of course. Also, "there are always impromptu soccer and Frisbee games on campus, plus snowball fights." "The bars around campus are very popular," and "partying is a common occurrence," but events are usually "low key." The surrounding town of Wilkes-Barre "has a lot" to offer, but there's not much "within walking distance." The campus is "near a bad part of town" that is "usually not extremely welcoming."

Student Body

King's College is "decidedly non-diverse," especially ethnically. Most students hail from "Pennsylvania, New Jersey and New York." "There are a lot of commuter students" from the local area. There's a solid contingent of nontraditional students, too. You'll see some "hicks" and some "students from wealthy families" but the crowd here is "mostly middle class." Virtually everyone gets at least some financial aid. Students are "generally Catholic" and largely "career oriented." They describe themselves as "very friendly" "and easy to talk to." "Academically, about half are the overachiever-go getter type," says a senior, "and the [rest] are your average hang-out-and-maybe-get-an-education-along-the-way type." "Many of the students are athletes, but very few act like a typical jock." Most everyone is "typical looking." Think "sweatpants and a hoodie." However, you will see a smattering of "punks, goths, and theater kids" as well.

THE PRINCETON REVIEW SAYS

Admissions

Very important factors considered include: Class rank, academic GPA, rigor of secondary school record. *Important factors considered include:* Application essay, Standardized test scores, character/personal qualities. *Other factors considered include:* Recommendation(s), alumni/ae relation, extracurricular activities, interview, volunteer work, work experience. SAT or ACT recommended; ACT with Writing component recommended. TOEFL required of all international applicants. High school diploma is required and GED is accepted. *Academic units required:* 4 English, 3 mathematics, 3 science, (2 science labs), 2 foreign language, 3 social studies, 1 history. *Academic units recommended:* 4 English, 4 mathematics, 4 science, (2 science labs), 4 foreign language, 3 social studies, 1 history, 2 computer science, 2 academic electives.

Financial Aid

Students should submit: FAFSA, institution's own financial aid form. The Princeton Review suggests that all financial aid forms be submitted as soon as possible after January 1. *Need-based scholarships/grants offered:* Federal Pell, SEOG, state scholarships/grants, private scholarships, the school's own gift aid. *Loan aid offered:* Subsidized Direct Loans. Unsubsidized Direct Loans, Direct Parent PLUS Loans, Federal Perkins, other, Private Loans. Applicants will be notified of awards on a rolling basis beginning 3/1. Federal Work-Study Program available. Institutional employment available. Off-campus job opportunities are fair.

The Inside Word

The admit rate is reasonably high at King's College. Class rank is much more important here than it is some other places, but decent grades in a serious college-prep curriculum should get you admitted. Standardized test scores are not required. Only send yours if they are good.

THE SCHOOL SAYS "..."

From The Admissions Office

"King's offers students personal attention, a welcoming atmosphere and a challenging liberal arts education taught by a dedicated faculty that prepares its graduates for a successful future.

"King's is a Catholic college operated in the tradition of the Holy Cross Congregation with a small urban campus that is within driving distance of several large cities. Founded in 1946 with a mission to teach first generation college students from working-class families, 40 percent of the College's current enrollment are the first in their families to earn bachelor's degree. Alumni satisfaction is also reflected in the significant number of graduates whose children attend King's." "The personalized attention King's students receive (student/faculty ratio of 13:1) and the quality of the College's academic programs directly contribute to the fact that 99 percent of its graduates are employed or attending graduate school within six months after graduation.

"A tangible sense of community exists at King's, evident in the College's nationally recognized service program, the high percentage of student participation in more than 50 campus clubs and organizations and the fact that almost half of King's students participate in some form of athletics.

"More than 70 percent of students who attend King's graduate from the College, which means the Admissions staff know how to select young people who will thrive here. With regard to financial aid, more than 95 percent of incoming first-year students receive financial assistance. For 2008–09 academic year, the average financial package for first-year students accounted for 64 percent of full-time tuition costs."

For even more information on this school, turn to page 499 of the "Stats" section.

KUTZTOWN UNIVERSITY OF PENNSYLVANIA

ADMISSIONS OFFICE, 15200 KUTZTOWN ROAD, KUTZTOWN, PA 19530-0730 • ADMISSIONS: 610-683-4060
FAX: 610-683-1375 • E-MAIL: ADMISSION@KUTZTOWN.EDU • WEBSITE: WWW.KUTZTOWN.EDU

RATINGS
Quality of Life: 69   Academic: 66   Admissions: 71   Financial Aid: 84

STUDENTS SAY "..."

Academics

SURVEY SAYS . . .
Athletic facilities are great
Diverse student types on campus
Lots of beer drinking
Hard liquor is popular

Over the years, Kutztown University has developed a reputation as a place where students can receive a small-school education at state-school prices. And while the prices aren't changing much ("It's really inexpensive!" students assure us), the size of the school is. Undergrads tell us that "Kutztown is expanding. The largest state-school residence hall in Pennsylvania opened here last fall...The academic side of campus is straying from the 'classroom' style buildings [the addition of] with lecture halls (capacity 175 per room)." Students tell us that "The growth of the school has definitely taken away its appeal," The situation isn't likely to change. For those who can abide the burgeoning population, Kutztown offers a number of appealing programs. Education programs are strong, as is the College of Visual and Performing Arts. Science and nursing programs are gaining strength, with students informing us that "Interestingly enough, the hard sciences at this 'liberal arts' school are very thorough and the programs prepare the students for great successes in their careers."

Life

Kutztown students are a studious and focused lot and "during the week it's [about] academics." Of course they also have their share of fun; the school sponsors a slate of activities including, "guest speakers, plays, concerts, comedians, movies, casino night, bingo, and other fun events." Additionally, "many students go to parties in town throughout the week." Fortunately, various organizations sponsor regular trips to New York City and Washington, D.C., and to professional sporting events in Philadelphia. Students with cars occasionally seek out fun in nearby Reading and Allentown. However, many students do tend to "go home on the weekends." One student explains, "KU is what they call a suitcase school. When it comes to 3:00 on Friday afternoon, there is traffic backed up throughout the entire campus."

Student Body

KU is home to "preppy teachers, laid-back students, and crazy art students" who "all get along because we respect each other and always learn something new about other people. It's more fun when everyone is different." Geographically, the campus is not so diverse; KU is "filled with students from the surrounding towns, and nearly everyone knows each other from their high school," although it should be noted that the school's location "near several urban centers" draws "rural, suburban and urban students equally, with the diversity and opportunities anticipated by this mixture of students." The school also has a substantial population of nontraditional students.

THE PRINCETON REVIEW SAYS

Admissions

Very important factors considered include: Class rank, rigor of secondary school record, standardized test scores. *Other factors considered include:* Academic GPA, recommendation(s), character/personal qualities, extracurricular activities, geographical residence, interview, racial/ethnic status, state residency, talent/ability, volunteer work, work experience. SAT or ACT required; TOEFL required of all international applicants. High school diploma is required and GED is accepted. *Academic units recommended:* 4 English, 4 mathematics, 4 science, 2 foreign language, 4 social studies.

Financial Aid

Students should submit: FAFSA. The Princeton Review suggests that all financial aid forms be submitted as soon as possible after January 1. *Need-based scholarships/grants offered:* Federal Pell, SEOG, state scholarships/grants, private scholarships, the school's own gift aid *Loan aid offered:* Federal Perkins Applicants will be notified of awards on a rolling basis beginning 3/30. Federal Work-Study Program available. Institutional employment available. Off-campus job opportunities are fair.

The Inside Word

The profile of an incoming class at Kutztown pretty well matches the profile of the average college-bound high school student. More than one-third of incoming students graduated in the bottom half of their class, so it's fair to say that solid candidates should face little challenge gaining entry.

THE SCHOOL SAYS "…"

From The Admissions Office

"In a recent independent survey, 94 percent of students and recent alumni rated their education at Kutztown University as excellent or good in regard to their overall college experience, the quality of instruction they received, and the quality of the faculty. Kutztown offers excellent academic programs through its undergraduate Colleges of Liberal Arts and Sciences, Visual and Performing Arts, Business, and Education and through its graduate studies program. A wide range of student support services complements the high-quality classroom instruction.

"In addition, Kutztown students have the advantage of a well-rounded program of athletic, cultural, and social events. At Kutztown, there are clubs, organizations, and activities to satisfy nearly every taste. Currently, 9,614 full-time and part-time students are enrolled at the university. About half of the full-time undergraduates live in residence halls; the rest live at home or in apartments in nearby communities.

"Kutztown University's attractive 325-acre campus includes a mix of old and new buildings, including stately Old Main, the historic building known to generations of Kutztown's students; Golden Bear Village West, a modern townhouse complex; the Student Union Building, the Academic Forum and the recently renovated Sharadin Arts building.

"The university's graduate program awards the Master of Science, Master of Art, Master of Education, Master of Business Administration, Master of Library Science, Master of Public Administration, and Master of Social Work degrees."

For even more information on this school, turn to page 499 of the "Stats" section.

LA ROCHE COLLEGE

9000 BABCOCK BOULEVARD, PITTSBURGH, PA 15237 • ADMISSIONS: 412-536-1272 • FAX: 412-847-1820
E-MAIL: ADMISSIONS@LAROCHE.EDU • WEBSITE: WWW.LAROCHE.EDU

RATINGS
Quality of Life: 77   Academic: 71   Admissions: 70   Financial Aid: 86

STUDENTS SAY ". . ."

Academics

A small, Catholic school in suburban Pittsburgh, La Roche College "integrates liberal arts and professional education in creative ways." Offering more than 50 degree programs in a range of diverse fields (like nursing, accounting, graphic design, and real estate), the La Roche College education is highly practical, providing its students with "all the tools needed to succeed" in the real world. Thanks to a low enrollment and uniformly small class sizes, "students get a lot of individualized attention" from their instructors.

Described as both "attentive" and "caring," professors treat "students as more than just students, but as individual learners." If you are struggling in a class, "It is easy to make an appointment with your professors and meet with them every week." In addition, "La Roche has great tutoring programs as well as a [Writing Center] to help the students succeed." While this private school comes with a high price tag, "[it offers] great scholarships and lots of financial aid" to qualified students, which helps take the sting out of the tuition check. Students say the administration still has plenty of room for improvement: "There are a lot of problems as far as classes and budget and the overall way in which La Roche is run."

Life

With just more than 1,200 full-time undergraduates, "Life at La Roche is very laid back." On this small campus, "everyone knows everyone" and it only "takes about five minutes to walk to class" from the dorms. Students assure us that "If you are willing to be involved, you will never be bored." At La Roche, there are over 30 student groups and an active intramural sports program, as well as 12 varsity men's and women's teams. Alcohol is prohibited on campus, but, students admit that "people still drink" from time to time. Even so, a party "never gets out of control" at La Roche, and most students prefer to "hang out with…friends, study together, [and] go out to eat" in their free time. When they want a break from the school's "lovely and spacious campus," students really appreciate their location on the outskirts of Pittsburgh. With this "amazing city at your fingertips," a fun night on the town is only a short drive away. On that note, "you better hope you have a car to get off campus," because "everyone goes home" on the weekend.

Student Body

On this small campus, the majority of students are Pittsburgh locals, and about half are commuters. The college also attracts international students from almost 50 countries worldwide, creating an "academic and social community where everyone is accepted as they are." Friendliness is the common denominator among the La Roche student body, and most students describe their classmates as "very nice and well-rounded individuals." A current student attests, "Being a transfer student myself, I've seen the environment of other college campuses, and I can honestly say that I have never seen such a diverse group of students interacting so seamlessly."

THE PRINCETON REVIEW SAYS

Admissions

Very important factors considered include: Academic GPA, standardized test scores. *Important factors considered include:* Level of applicant's interest. *Other factors considered include:* Application essay, recommendation(s), rigor of secondary school record, character/personal qualities, interview, talent/ability, volunteer work, SAT or ACT required; high school diploma is required and GED is accepted. *Academic units required:* 4 English, 3 mathematics, 3 science, (2 science labs), 3 social studies, 3 history. *Academic units recommended:* 4 English, 3 mathematics, 3 science, 1 foreign language, 3 social studies.

Financial Aid

Students should submit: FAFSA. Regular filing deadline is 5/1. The Princeton Review suggests that all financial aid forms be submitted as soon as possible after January 1. *Need-based scholarships/grants offered:* Federal Pell, SEOG, state scholarships/grants, private scholarships, the school's own gift aid. *Loan aid offered:* Federal Perkins, other, private loans. Applicants will be notified of awards on a rolling basis beginning 3/1. Federal Work-Study Program available. Institutional employment available. Off-campus job opportunities are excellent.

The Inside Word

La Roche accepts students on a rolling basis and admissions decisions are rendered with blessed efficiency; it usually takes just 10 to 14 days for the admissions committee to review an application. While it is always best to apply early in the admissions cycle, you can submit your application as late as August 15 for the fall semester. If you want to speak directly to an admissions officer, their names, telephone numbers, and e-mail addresses are listed on the school's website.

THE SCHOOL SAYS "..."

From The Admissions Office

"La Roche College is a private, Catholic, co-educational college located just minutes from Pittsburgh on 40 acres of wooded suburban sprawl. With a 12:1 faculty/student ratio, we make sure you aren't simply a face in the crowd - you are someone who is valued as an active member of the campus community.

"La Roche students may choose from 50 majors and programs - ranging from nursing and other health sciences to history, criminal justice, business and interior design. In fact, La Roche offers the top 10 career majors chosen by college students today.

"Outside the classroom, you'll find your place among any of the more than 30 student clubs and organizations. Or maybe you'll be part of our athletics and intramurals program. La Roche offers 12 NCAA Division III men's and women's sports (part of the Allegheny Mountain Collegiate Conference), as well as several junior varsity sports programs.

"The college offers apartment-style residence hall suites, equipped with a refrigerator and a microwave, a private bathroom, Internet and cable television access, and free laundry facilities. You also may choose to live off campus in any of several apartment complexes near La Roche.

"La Roche offers an affordable private education made possible by generous financial aid; the average package is about $13,000 per student, and 94% of our students receive financial aid. In addition, La Roche provides many scholarship opportunities, as well as federal loans and grants."

For even more information on this school, turn to page 500 of the "Stats" section.

LAFAYETTE COLLEGE

118 MARKLE HALL, EASTON, PA 18042 • ADMISSIONS: 610-330-5100 • FAX: 610-330-5355
FINANCIAL AID: 610-330-5055 • E-MAIL: ADMISSIONS@LAFAYETTE.EDU • WEBSITE: WWW.LAFAYETTE.EDU

RATINGS
Quality of Life: 81   **Academic:** 91   **Admissions:** 94   **Financial Aid:** 93

STUDENTS SAY ". . ."

Academics

Lafayette College is "a small liberal arts college" that is "especially strong in engineering and physical sciences." There are "very cool" undergraduate research opportunities. Career services "are also phenomenal" and "an excellent alumni network" provides abundant career and internship opportunities. The "efficient, helpful, and very accessible" administration "generally listens to the comments of the students" and does "a great job of keeping the school running smoothly." The biggest academic complaint at Lafayette is that the range of courses offered in a typical semester is too narrow. The classes offered tend to be "small" and "difficult." "You must study," reports an economics major. "Not every professor is the greatest." "There is the occasional professor who makes you want to tear your hair out." On the whole, though, Lafayette's professors are "really knowledgeable and really do care about how you do and what you take out of the class." "I feel like I get a lot of individual attention," says a chemical engineering major. "Professors will explain difficult material until you understand," relates a math major, " and not just say it once and look at you like you're stupid if you still don't understand." Outside of class, faculty members typically remain "extremely available" and "beg you to talk to them and meet with them."

> **SURVEY SAYS . . .**
> Lab facilities are great
> Great computer facilities
> Athletic facilities are great
> Career services are great
> School is well run
> Campus feels safe

Life

Lafayette is located on a hill above Easton, Pennsylvania. The "gorgeous," "scenic" campus is full of "picturesque North Eastern college-like buildings." A few dorms "are in desperate need of renovation," though, and the "repetitive" food is "not that great tasting." Socially, Lafayette is reportedly "very homey." "At almost any social gathering, there will be people you know." The "amazing" sports center is "a very popular spot." "Lafayette is a very athletic school and most students participate in either varsity athletics or in a club or intramural sport," explains a sophomore. In the fall, "football games are extremely spirited." The annual contest against rival Lehigh "is attended by basically the whole student body." Beyond sports, many students tell us "there is always something to do on campus." "Everyone is really involved," they say. There are "a capella concerts, comedians, movies, and club-sponsored activities." A "multitude of speakers" visit campus. There's "a broad range" of religious groups. Other students contend "there should be more to do." "I have not experienced the outpouring of entertainment at the school," grumbles a freshman. Whatever the case, "the party scene is really fun." The frats and various sports teams throw parties "Wednesday through Saturday nights" and many students participate. However, many others don't. "Half the campus considers Lafayette a party school and the other half doesn't know what school the first half is talking about," suggests a junior.

Student Body

Lafayette is a haven for "well-rounded," "preppy," "smart jocks," and "your classic white rich kid" "from New York, New Jersey, or Pennsylvania." "There is certainly a mold," admits a senior. "Everyone is pretty similar." "Collar-popping" suburbanites are everywhere. "Crazy-colored hair and facial piercings are not really something you see," observes a first-year student. "You will see a lot of smiling and door-holding," though. Students take pride in the "incredibly friendly" vibe at Lafayette. Many students are "hard-partying" types. There are also "the kids who live in the library 20 hours a day." Most students fall somewhere in the middle. "People like to have a good time but they are also serious about their work and are genuinely interested in their area of study." "Both conservatives and liberals" will find soul mates at Lafayette but many students are "almost completely apathetic" when it comes to politics. Some students "have a snobby attitude," but others either don't flaunt their wealth or don't come from money at all. "We're not all running around with iPhones and Fendi bags," says a sophomore. Ethnic diversity is pretty minimal. "There are a few minority and foreign students but they hang out with each other in their own little cliques."

THE PRINCETON REVIEW SAYS

Admissions

Very important factors considered include: Academic GPA, rigor of secondary school record. *Important factors considered include:* Class rank, application essay, recommendation(s), standardized test scores, character/personal qualities, extracurricular activities, talent/ability. *Other factors considered include:* Alumni/ae relation, first generation, geographical residence, interview, level of applicant's interest, racial/ethnic status, volunteer work, work experience. SAT Subject Tests recommended; SAT or ACT required; ACT with Writing component required. TOEFL required of all international applicants. High school diploma or equivalent is not required. *Academic units recommended:* 4 English, 3 mathematics, 2 science, (2 science labs), 2 foreign language, 5 academic electives.

Financial Aid

Students should submit: FAFSA, CSS Profile, and/or Non-Custodial Profile by 1/15 for regular decision. Tax data must be submitted via College Board's IDOC service by 3/15. The Princeton Review suggests that all financial aid forms be submitted as soon as possible after January 1. *Need-based scholarships/grants offered:* Federal Pell, SEOG, state scholarships/grants, and school's own gift aid. *Loan assistance offered:* Direct Subsidized and Unsubsidized Loans, Direct PLUS, and Federal Perkins. Federal Work Study and on-campus employment opportunities are also available. Applicants will be notified of awards on or about 4/1.

The Inside Word

Applications are reviewed three to five times and evaluated by as many as nine different committee members. In all cases, students who continually seek challenges and are willing to take risks academically win out over those who play it safe to maintain a high GPA.

THE SCHOOL SAYS "..."

From The Admissions Office

"Lafayette offers academic choices as broad and diverse as universities many times our size. Students and alumni say our curriculum-with extraordinary breadth and depth for an undergraduate college-is a key strength.

"At Lafayette, education is a dynamic and engaged process-not passive. Students are encouraged to cross traditional academic boundaries to connect and integrate knowledge from different fields in the humanities, social sciences, natural sciences, and engineering and to work together to approach intellectual challenges and wider-world problems from multiple perspectives.

"Our approach is active and global, working in communities locally, nationally, and internationally. Global opportunities range from faculty-led semester programs to concentrated interim session courses to international service projects. Students who experience immersion in international settings or work in student-faculty teams to address global challenges have an advantage in advanced studies and employment after they graduate. These experiences are vital for citizenship and leadership in an increasingly interconnected, globalized world.

"Lafayette is a vibrant environment in which to explore and grow. With more than 250 clubs and activities-including the arts, Division I sports, and community service, to name just a few-students have many ways to balance work and play, develop leadership skills, and have fun. And because of our location, just 70 miles from New York City, Lafayette offers significant opportunities to connect with prominent leaders in many fields who visit campus and to take advantage of the major artistic, cultural, and financial centers of the Eastern United States."

For even more information on this school, turn to page 501 of the "Stats" section.

LANCASTER BIBLE COLLEGE

PO Box 83403, 901 Eden Road, Lancaster, PA 17608 • Admissions: 717-560-8271 • Fax: 717-560-8213
E-mail: admissions@lbc.edu • Website: www.lbc.edu

RATINGS
Quality of Life: 86 **Academic:** 88 **Admissions:** 77 **Financial Aid:** 74

STUDENTS SAY "..."

Academics

"Lancaster Bible College is all about preparing young men and women to build God-honoring relationship[s] and to serve God and others through professional ministries, church ministries, and everyday life encounters," students here tell us. As its name might suggest, LBC offers a "teaching program with a strong biblical emphasis." Aside from its specialized focus, what sets LBC apart from most schools is the student body's almost unanimous appreciation of the faculty and administration. Professors are "very educated in their topics and experienced in fields relating to those topics;" they also "really care about the students

> **SURVEY SAYS ...**
> *Students are very religious*
> *Students get along with local community*
> *Dorms are like palaces*
> *Students are happy*
> *Frats and sororities are unpopular or nonexistent*
> *Political activism is unpopular or nonexistent*
> *Very little beer drinking*
> *Very little hard liquor*
> *Very little drug use*

and are willing to go the extra mile for them." Administrators do "a fabulous job of communicating their vision to the students. They often spend time with students by eating in the cafeteria, attending chapel, or just being readily available." As one satisfied junior writes: "All of the staff and faculty at my school are usually available to help and talk to students outside the classroom. I have a few professors I talk to about personal issues, and I know that they pray for me."

Life

Students at LBC "study toward the goal of knowing God more," and their "lives reflect this devotion to God." "Everyone is involved in some kind of service, whether that is helping a YMCA or interning at a church." Add "classes," "chapel," and, for many, "on-campus jobs," and one might envision a relatively Spartan existence for LBC undergrads. This, however, is not the case: "Most students are very anxious to have fun and enjoy their college years," a sophomore tells us. Fun entails "a lot of active things," such as "tak[ing] walks," "ice skating at Clipper Stadium," "working out in the gym," and "playing intramural sports such as dodgeball and Ultimate Frisbee," or "three-on-three basketball." Students say that "going to sports games to support our teams [is] very popular here, too." When they tire themselves out, undergrads enjoy "just hanging out playing pool and watching movies," and love exploring hometown Lancaster, which "has a wide variety of restaurants and other things to do." Music fans appreciate that "a lot of time on the weekends there will be a concert going on in the chapel"—often by a well-known Christian musician—"and as students we get in free or [at a] discount."

Student Body

"Because students at LBC are all Bible majors along with their specific majors, most have a desire to be in some [type] of church ministry, whether it be full-time or part-time, after their graduation." Undergrads here tend to "come from a conservative background"; are already "familiar with Christianity and the Bible"; and fall somewhere between "moderate" and "zealous in faith and Christian living." They're also typically "Caucasian," though "There are a few African Americans and Asians" on campus. An undergrad describes the situation this way: "There isn't a variety of diversity on our campus, but those of a different background are definitely loved and cared for." Another student adds: "We all share the common bond of Christ and are, therefore, like one big family." While students "who don't seem to care much about Christ" are still "embraced," they are "somewhat separated, possibly because of their own goals."

THE PRINCETON REVIEW SAYS

Admissions

Very important factors considered include: Application essay, recommendation(s), rigor of secondary school record, standardized test scores, character/personal qualities, religious affiliation/commitment. *Important factors considered include:* Extracurricular activities. *Other factors considered include:* Interview, talent/ability, volunteer work, SAT or ACT required; ACT with Writing component recommended. TOEFL required of all international applicants. High school diploma is required and GED is accepted.

Financial Aid

Students should submit: FAFSA, state aid form. The Princeton Review suggests that all financial aid forms be submitted as soon as possible after January 1. *Need-based scholarships/grants offered:* Federal Pell, SEOG, state scholarships/grants, private scholarships, the school's own gift aid, Office of Vocational Rehabilitation Blindness and Visual Services Awards. *Loan aid offered:* Federal Perkins, other, alternative loans. Applicants will be notified of awards on a rolling basis beginning 3/1. Federal Work-Study Program available. Institutional employment available. Off-campus job opportunities are good.

The Inside Word

LBC works extra hard to make sure that the students it admits are a good fit with its specialized academic and social environment. Applicants are required to write a 500-word autobiography that should touch upon their conversion, church experiences, and reasons for wanting to attend LBC. Of the three required references, one must come from a pastor and another must come from a Christian friend.

THE SCHOOL SAYS "…"

From The Admissions Office

"At Lancaster Bible College, you'll discover:

- We believe in training ministry leaders. We believe in educating service-minded scholars like you to serve as ministry leaders in professional positions throughout the globe. Our alumni serve as pastors, worship leaders, counselors, business leaders, college presidents, teachers, missionaries, coaches, and school administrators—here and abroad—and we are just warming up.

- We believe in helping students to fulfill their dreams. We believe in making it a reality for young scholars like you to serve at their best through a premier Bible college education, and we back it up with financial aid. Every year we raise more than $1.5 million to help fund our students' educations.

- We believe in community. From your first visit to LBC through graduation day, you will be amazed at how many faculty homes you're invited into, how many one-on-one conversations you'll have, and just how tight this community of care really is. You'll see and feel why campus friendliness finishes at the top of our student surveys.

You see, at LBC, we believe that students who want to serve the Lord are the world's greatest hope. If you're that kind of student, we want you to be a part of this place we call home—because we believe in you!"

For even more information on this school, turn to page 501 of the "Stats" section.

LEBANON VALLEY COLLEGE

101 NORTH COLLEGE AVENUE, ANNVILLE, PA 17003-6100 • ADMISSIONS: 717-867-6181
FAX: 717-867-6026 • E-MAIL: ADMISSION@LVC.EDU • WEBSITE: WWW.LVC.EDU

RATINGS

Quality of Life: 79   **Academic:** 79   **Admissions:** 81   **Financial Aid:** 80

STUDENTS SAY "..."

Academics

Undergrads at Lebanon Valley College attribute a great academic experience to "professors that...really get to know you and are very willing to offer advice and guidance." As one freshman expounds, "Professors are not only interested in expanding your knowledge of your particular topic but also of expanding you as a person." LVC students are held to high standards "especially in the science fields," and many agree that this leads to a "challenging but rewarding" education. Students laud the music department stating it "places a great emphasis on personal development as a musician." The vast majority also heap praise on the administration noting they are "very good at listening to the students and helping them to succeed." A number of undergrads are also quick to highlight the fact that even the president "has an open-door policy" and can be seen "frequently walking around campus or eating in the dining hall."

> **SURVEY SAYS . . .**
> *Lab facilities are great*
> *Athletic facilities are great*
> *Students are friendly*
> *Low cost of living*
> *Students are happy*

Life

By and large, students agree that "life at Lebanon Valley is pretty laid-back." Though it is "set in the country," LVC is "near enough to larger towns and cities so as not to feel isolated." Fortunately, the campus is generally buzzing with activity, be it the "comedians who come on Friday nights" or the regular "Saturday night dances." Additionally, since "music is big" at LVC, "many students participate in the bands/orchestras/choirs and also form their own bands or perform in theater." While undergrads admit there are definitely students "who like to party," one grateful freshman stresses "there is no pressure to drink." Students tend to venture off-campus quite a bit, often heading "to the local cafés or to the diner outside of town to hang out with friends and get a bite to eat." There is also a "small movie theater in town that offers discounts to students." The college itself sponsors a myriad of weekend trips with destinations such as "New York, Washington, and King of Prussia." Finally, for those undergrads who want to indulge their sweet tooth, "Hershey Park is only eight miles away."

Student Body

On the surface, you might easily categorize LVC undergrads. "You have your student athletes, your student band members, and student actors," but many stress that "there is a group for everyone on campus." Indeed, "there are very few loners." Students readily assert that their peers are "very friendly" and always "willing to lend a hand." While the college may not appear "ethnically diverse at a glance," a freshman assures us that "diversity and acceptance are stressed by various on-campus awareness groups." And while "students are fairly similar to each other in many ways, nearly everyone embraces the differences among us, and those who are different have no problem finding others who feel or think similarly to them."

Admissions

Very important factors considered include: Class rank, rigor of secondary school record. *Important factors considered include:* Academic GPA, character/personal qualities, extracurricular activities, interview, level of applicant's interest, talent/ability. *Other factors considered include:* Application essay, recommendation(s), standardized test scores, alumni/ae relation, first generation, geographical residence, racial/ethnic status, state residency, volunteer work, work experience. TOEFL required of all international applicants. High school diploma is required and GED is accepted. *Academic units required:* 4 English, 3 mathematics, 2 science, 2 foreign language, 1 social studies. *Academic units recommended:* 3 science, (2 science labs), 3 foreign language, 2 history.

Financial Aid

Students should submit: FAFSA, institution's own financial aid form. The Princeton Review suggests that all financial aid forms be submitted as soon as possible after January 1. *Need-based scholarships/grants offered:* Federal Pell, SEOG, state scholarships/grants, private scholarships, the school's own gift aid. *Loan aid offered:* Federal Perkins. Applicants will be notified of awards on a rolling basis beginning 3/1. Federal Work-Study Program available. Institutional employment available. Off-campus job opportunities are good.

The Inside Word

Lebanon Valley looks primarily at high school grades and curriculum. If you're a B student in the top half of your class, the school's website reports, you have a very good chance of gaining admittance. Students in the top 30 percent of their graduating class are eligible for generous scholarships.

THE SCHOOL SAYS "..."

From The Admissions Office

"Lebanon Valley College encourages applications from students who have taken a challenging college-prep program in high school and performed well. Typical successful applicants have had 3 years of science, 3 of math, and 2 of a foreign language, in addition to English and social studies. While high school grading systems vary widely, we look for applicants to have at least a B average and rank in the top half of their class. Our outstanding, nationally recognized scholarship program complements this process. The college offers scholarships worth up to 50 percent of the value of tuition to students accepted for admission who ranked in the top 30 percent of their high school class. The scholarships are based on the class rank decile, with awards of one-quarter tuition going to those in the third decile, one-third to those in the second decile, and one-half to those in the top 10 percent of their class. Though optional for admission to the college, standardized test scores give students from high schools that do not provide a class rank access to the scholarships; during the interview process, the college provides an opportunity for students with a minimum combined SAT critical reading and math score of 1100 to apply for these scholarships. Admission decisions for each class are made on a rolling basis beginning in mid-October. Students offered admission are also informed of their scholarship award based on class rank information received on the high school transcript. Students whose class rank improves during their senior year will be considered for an increased award."

For even more information on this school, turn to page 502 of the "Stats" section.

LEHIGH UNIVERSITY

27 MEMORIAL DRIVE WEST, BETHLEHEM, PA 18015 • ADMISSIONS: 610-758-3100 • FAX: 610-758-4361
FINANCIAL AID: 610-758-3181 • E-MAIL: ADMISSIONS@LEHIGH.EDU • WEBSITE: WWW.LEHIGH.EDU

RATINGS
Quality of Life: 71   Academic: 89   Admissions: 97   Financial Aid: 90

STUDENTS SAY "..."

Academics

SURVEY SAYS . . .
Great library
Students are happy
Frats and sororities dominate social scene
Student publications are popular
Lots of beer drinking
Hard liquor is popular

The main thing students at Lehigh University in Bethelehem, Pennsylvania seem to share is a general love for the school and its entire way of life, as evidenced by the "amazing" alumni base that returns to the school frequently (and provides for good networking). Despite rigorous academics, Lehigh "maintains a substantial social scene," and "work hard, play hard is not just a saying here—it's the lifestyle." Students have "to work for grades, they are not just given out," and outside of the classroom, there's a strong emphasis on experimental learning and real-world applications. The engineering and business programs are particularly strong here, as are the international relations and biology departments. Though tuition is dear, new financial aid policies have been put into place and "the school lives up to its academic reputation...You definitely get your money's worth at the end of the day." The level of instruction here is "top-notch," and "the classes aren't necessarily a drag to go to." Teaching becomes better" as students begin to take more and more upper-level classes. Instructors "are always available and want to help you out," and they "really try to have a positive relationship with all of the students." Still a few professors seem to be more interested in their research than their teachings. "For my Folktales and Fairytales class, we were invited to the professor's house to tell stories around her fireplace," says a senior. The administration "does not take into account student opinion as well as it could," and many students wish it was more transparent in its reasoning for changes (especially concerning the recent crackdown on partying, the surest way to get a Lehigh student up in arms), but most students are satisfied with the level of accessibility.

Life

Unless you have a car, there really isn't much to do in the immediate surrounding area. The school does provide a shuttle to some common off-campus destinations and the town is home to many festivals throughout the year. On campus, studying takes up most weeknights, and though there are events "here and there," "drinking is king at Lehigh" and "Greek life is everything." "It's party hard, work hard. We have all the Ivy League rejects who are crazy competitive combined with crazy parties. What's better?" asks a sophomore. Though the jury is out as to how crucial drinking is to Lehigh social life, "the school provides a lot of alcohol-free activities such as game night, comedians, movie nights, etc.," and there is "plenty of socializing" through sports, student organizations, and plain old hanging out. "Even kids who are obsessed with video games won't just sit and play alone in their rooms. They'll find others with the same interest and do so together," says a student. "There are tons of ways to get involved on campus and have a good time, you just have to get creative," says another.

Student Body

It's a "white and preppy" world at Lehigh, where most students come from the Northeast and the typical student's economic background can be described as "appreciates the finer things in life." People here "like to look good" and "tend to dress up for classes very often." There are still "a few splashes of ethnicity" here, and while there used to be a lot of pressure to fit that specific mold, now "there are a lot of different types of students. It's a friendlier campus." The school has actually seen a rise in enrollment by students from underrepresented backgrounds in recent years, and continues to try and build diversity. Socially, there are three types of students at Lehigh: "those who are Greek, those whose friends are Greek, and those who have no friends." The final group is in the extreme minority, as "it isn't hard to find a friend at Lehigh," and even the atypical students "usually just connect with each other." Ever the balanced bunch, Lehigh students "recognize the scholastic opportunity that Lehigh provides but also thrive on the party scene."

THE PRINCETON REVIEW SAYS

Admissions

Very important factors considered include: Recommendation(s), rigor of secondary school record. *Important factors considered include:* Application essay, standardized test scores, character/personal qualities, extracurricular activities, level of applicant's interest, talent/ability, volunteer work. *Other factors considered include:* Class rank, academic GPA, alumni/ae relation, first generation, geographical residence, racial/ethnic status, work experience. SAT or ACT required; ACT with Writing component required. TOEFL required of all international applicants. High school diploma or equivalent is not required. *Academic units required:* 4 English, 3 mathematics, 2 science, (2 science labs), 2 foreign language, 2 social studies, 3 academic electives.

Financial Aid

Students should submit: FAFSA, CSS/Financial Aid PROFILE, noncustodial PROFILE, business/farm supplement. Regular filing deadline is 2/15. The Princeton Review suggests that all financial aid forms be submitted as soon as possible after January 1. *Need-based scholarships/grants offered:* Federal Pell, SEOG, state scholarships/grants, private scholarships, the school's own gift aid, United Negro College Fund *Loan aid offered:* Federal Direct Subsidized Loans, Federal Direct Unsubsidized Loans, Federal Direct PLUS Loans, Private Educational Alternative Loans. Applicants will be notified of awards on or about 3/30. Federal Work-Study Program available. Institutional employment available. Off-campus job opportunities are good.

The Inside Word

Lots of work at bolstering Lehigh's public recognition for overall academic quality has paid off. Liberal arts candidates will now find the admissions process to be highly selective. Students without solidly impressive academic credentials will have a rough time getting in regardless of their choice of programs, as will unenthusiastic, but academically strong candidates who have clearly chosen Lehigh as a safety.

THE SCHOOL SAYS "..."

From The Admissions Office

"Lehigh University is located 50 miles north of Philadelphia and 75 miles southwest of New York City in Bethlehem, Pennsylvania, where a cultural renaissance has taken place with the opening of more than a dozen ethnic restaurants, the addition of several boutiques and galleries, and Lehigh's Campus Square residential/retail complex. Lehigh combines learning opportunities of a large research university with the personal attention of a small, private college, by offering an education that integrates courses from four colleges and dozens of fields of study. Students customize their experience to their interests by tailoring majors and academic programs from more than 2,000 courses, carrying a double major, or taking courses outside their college or major field of study. Lehigh offers unique learning opportunities through interdisciplinary programs such as the Integrated Degree in Engineering, Arts, and Sciences and Computer Science and Business. You'll learn from and work alongside faculty who are leaders in their field and bring the latest knowledge and newest discoveries to classrooms, laboratories, and workshops to enhance your educational experience and give you real-world exposure. Investigation, innovation, and global exploration will drive your educational experience at Lehigh. Here, we share a common set of core values: integrity and honesty, equitable community, academic freedom, intellectual curiosity, and leadership. Lehigh's vibrant campus life offers many social and extracurricular activities. Choose from 150 clubs and organizations, in which over 60 percent of undergraduates participate.

"Lehigh requires students to submit scores from the SAT. Students may also take the ACT with the Writing portion in lieu of the SAT. SAT Subject Tests are recommended but not required."

For even more information on this school, turn to page 502 of the "Stats" section.

LE MOYNE COLLEGE

1419 SALT SPRINGS RD., SYRACUSE, NY 13214-1301 • ADMISSIONS: 315-445-4300
FAX: 315-445-4711 • E-MAIL: ADMISSION@LEMOYNE.EDU • WEBSITE: WWW.LEMOYNE.EDU

RATINGS

Quality of Life: 73   Academic: 71   Admissions: 80   Financial Aid: 75

STUDENTS SAY "..."

Academics

A small Jesuit school in the suburbs of Syracuse, Le Moyne College is distinguished by its close-knit community atmosphere. A "small, academically challenging, but supportive school," Le Moyne maintains a top-notch teaching staff and a bulletin full of "interesting, intelligent, [and]

> **SURVEY SAYS . . .**
> *Low cost of living*
> *Frats and sororities are unpopular or nonexistent*
> *Very little drug use*

engaging classes." Professors are "out of this world," and "the overall academic experience is one of the highest caliber, which constantly challenges the student to go further and achieve an understanding of the subject at hand, not just a completion of the assignment." With few exceptions, professors are "very accessible and approachable, always willing to lend an extra academic hand," and class sizes are uniformly small. Students generally say the academic programs are "challenging, without being too stressful" and the professors and staff "emphasize hard work, but also emphasize having a positive attitude." Administrators "keep up with student needs, but also run the school in an efficient and conservative manner."

Life

Providing a nice mix of curricular challenges and extracurricular diversions, "the environment here at Le Moyne is conducive to learning, but it is also a great place to come and have a good time." On campus, "there is always a lot going on to keep students busy and out of trouble. There are comedians, small bands, and even bingo nights." Taking advantage of the school's pretty campus, "people are out on the grass playing ultimate Frisbee, playing football, basking in the summer sun," or, during the snowy months, "all bundled up inside with each other, in a comfortable place." In fact, during their down time, "many times students end up just hanging out in each other's dorm rooms or in the student lounges located all over campus." Parties are a popular weekend pastime. However, "fun can mean drinking for some people, but it is not the main focus here," one student says. "It is easy to find something to do and people to hang out with no matter what you're into."

Student Body

Within the cohesive Le Moyne community, there is a little bit of something for everyone. No matter who you are, "there is always a place to fit in, whether it be in the science lab, the Performing Arts Center, or in any of our clubs that hold weekly discussions on important issues to college kids like race, sexuality, and the desire to succeed and make a difference." Despite the disparate interests and personalities, an accepting and friendly attitude permeates the campus culture. A current undergraduate explains, "Many students are very politically interested and involved. Many are very set on their academics. We have athletes drama kids. What they all have in common is their friendliness and approachability." Many students come to Le Moyne directly from a Catholic high school, but there are "students of different religious groups" as well. In addition, many students are "very civic-minded at my school and participate in a lot of activities around town."

Admissions

Very important factors considered include: Academic GPA, rigor of secondary school record. *Important factors considered include:* Class rank, application essay, recommendation(s), standardized test scores, extracurricular activities, interview, talent/ability, work experience. *Other factors considered include:* Alumni/ae relation, character/personal qualities, geographical residence, level of applicant's interest, state residency, volunteer work, SAT or ACT required; TOEFL required of all international applicants. High school diploma is required and GED is accepted. *Academic units required:* 4 English, 3 mathematics, 3 science, 3 foreign language, 4 social studies. *Academic units recommended:* 4 mathematics, 4 science, (3 science labs).

Financial Aid

Students should submit: FAFSA, institution's own financial aid form, state aid form. The Princeton Review suggests that all financial aid forms be submitted as soon as possible after January 1. *Need-based scholarships/grants offered:* Federal Pell, SEOG, state scholarships/grants, private scholarships, the school's own gift aid. *Loan aid offered:* Federal Perkins. Applicants will be notified of awards on or about 3/15. Federal Work-Study Program available. Institutional employment available. Off-campus job opportunities are excellent.

The Inside Word

To be considered for admission to Le Moyne College, high school students must present a strong high school transcript, which includes four years of English and three to four years of college preparatory math, foreign language, social science, and natural science. Prospective students can register online for a weekend campus tour, and they may request the opportunity to eat in a dining hall, sit in on classes, and schedule an admissions interview. Le Moyne also assigns an admissions counselor to each prospective student, depending on that student's geographical region.

THE SCHOOL SAYS "…"

From The Admissions Office

"As a Le Moyne College student, you'll be equipped with the intellectual skills necessary to succeed in the world, and the will to use your abilities to promote a more just society.

"At the heart of the Le Moyne experience is the 470-year-old Jesuit tradition characterized by a commitment to learning in all of its forms. We encourage students to ask questions, think deeply and to look beyond the apparent. You will learn how to think for yourself—and about others—and in the process build a foundation for a rewarding life.

"Le Moyne offers a supportive and close-knit community in which to explore your potential. With more than 30 majors, you'll find a course of study that fits you—delivered in small classes by faculty who know you by name. In preparation for life's next step, the classroom experience is supplemented by valuable internship, challenging research, service learning projects, and exciting study-abroad opportunities.

"Of course, there's more to the college experience than academics. In addition to being a great place to learn, Le Moyne is also a great place to call home! As a student, you can take part in a wide variety of campus activities—from athletics to student organizations to the arts—or you can just enjoy hanging out with your friends. From dances to Dolphy Day (Google that one), the Le Moyne experience lets you have fun while forming friendships.

"During your time at Le Moyne, you'll grow intellectually, spiritually and socially as you are recognized for who you are—and who you can become."

For even more information on this school, turn to page 501 of the "Stats" section.

LESLEY COLLEGE AT LESLEY UNIVERSITY

LESLEY COLLEGE, 29 EVERETT STREET, CAMBRIDGE, MA 02138 • ADMISSIONS: 617-349-8800
FAX: 617-349-8810 • E-MAIL: LCADMISSIONS@LESLEY.EDU • WEBSITE: WWW.LESLEY.EDU

RATINGS

Quality of Life: 73   **Academic:** 78   **Admissions:** 81   **Financial Aid:** 66

STUDENTS SAY ". . ."

Academics

Lesley College is a school on the move, with a new library, fitness center, and a campus expansion that includes recently completed suite-style dorms. As a result of the many changes, the school is "growing in size and expanding a ton," yet professors and administrators have managed to maintain "a really personal experience". Required internships mean that the Lesley experience "is all about hands-on

> **SURVEY SAYS . . .**
> *Students get along with local community*
> *Students love Cambridge, MA*
> *Great off-campus food*
> *Frats and sororities are unpopular or nonexistent*
> *Student government is popular*

learning and trying out the professional field that you want to work in." Students call this experience "the greatest strength of Lesley." The emphasis on experiential learning suits Lesley's academic strengths in art therapy, business management, education, and psychology (amongst others). The curriculum is "very socially conscious, very human-services focused," serving well the "artists, activists, athletes, hippies, and oddballs who come to the People's Republic of Cambridge in a surprising (not perfect) show of unity to engage in left-wing coursework and extracurricular activities." Undergrads warn us that "The Lesley style is not for everyone. We do papers, and we have discussions. We write reflectively. This can get old for some seniors and is not a learning style that everyone can appreciate. However, for those of us that chose Lesley for that reason it is a spectacular way to learn, and it is also very fitting for our people-focused majors."

Life

Lesley is "a really fun school, but not a party school." The school provides "lots of activities on campus to entertain students (comedians, movie nights, dances, and such). Lesley genuinely cares about keeping students entertained." The school's location "in an extremely convenient part of Cambridge.... It is safe and close to both Harvard Square and Porter Square," which means "Your options are endless, thanks to public transportation!" Boston offers "clubs and an amazing music scene" as well as political rallies and, of course, "Red Sox and Celtics and Bruins games." An active intercollegiate athletic program occupies one segment of the student body, while others immerse themselves in the arts; writes one student in the latter group, "The theatre program is increasing quite a bit, so we have much more performance arts programs, considering the size of our school." Undergrads also participate in "a fair amount of political and environmental discussion and concern."

Student Body

"Atypical is typical" at Lesley, where students constitute "a really, really diverse group. Half of Lesley University is comprised of the Art Institute of Boston. All of the undergrads live together, and everyone seems to get along really well whether they go to AIB or LC. There are students from different socioeconomic groups, different sexual orientations; it's a real mix." The school's active athletic program means there are lots of jocks here, and "The athletes are pretty close because we spend so much time together, but we're definitely not divided from the rest of the student body like at some schools. I feel like we do a really good job mixing it up overall. Pretty much everyone here has a major that involves helping people or changing the world in some way, I think that brings us together a lot."

Admissions

Very important factors considered include: Academic GPA, rigor of secondary school record. *Important factors considered include:* Class rank, application essay, recommendation(s), standardized test scores, character/personal qualities, extracurricular activities, interview, talent/ability, volunteer work. *Other factors considered include:* Alumni/ae relation, first generation, geographical residence, level of applicant's interest, racial/ethnic status, work experience. SAT or ACT required; ACT with Writing component required. TOEFL required of all international applicants. High school diploma is required and GED is accepted. *Academic units required:* 4 English, 3 mathematics, 3 science, (2 science labs), 1 social studies, 1 history, 4 academic electives. *Academic units recommended:* 4 English, 4 mathematics, 4 science, (2 science labs), 2 foreign language, 2 social studies, 2 history, 2 visual/performing arts recommended for some programs in art or expressive therapies.

Financial Aid

Students should submit: FAFSA. The Princeton Review suggests that all financial aid forms be submitted as soon as possible after January 1. *Need-based scholarships/grants offered:* Federal Pell, SEOG, state scholarships/grants, private scholarships, the school's own gift aid. *Loan aid offered:* Direct Subsidized Stafford, Direct Unsubsidized Stafford, Direct PLUS, Federal Perkins, state loans Applicants will be notified of awards on a rolling basis beginning 2/15. Federal Work-Study Program available. Institutional employment available. Off-campus job opportunities are excellent.

The Inside Word

Lesley College seeks students who "desire to impact the world around them." Commitment to social justice is just at least as important as academic credentials here. You can't just talk a good game; your extracurricular activities should show that you've acted on your principles. Demonstrated success in a college prep high-school curriculum is also important.

THE SCHOOL SAYS "…"

From The Admissions Office

"Lesley College prepares men and women for careers and lives that make a difference, providing students with the skills and knowledge to make a positive difference and create hope. Central to this mission is a commitment to broad liberal arts preparation, career-focused field placements and internships, and true integration of theory and practice.

"Lesley College combines the advantages of an intimate learning community with all of the academic and co-curricular resources of a large university. That includes access to the professionals and programs of the Art Institute of Boston at Lesley, and a wide-ranging array of graduate programs and academic centers. The Lesley campus is steps away from bustling Harvard Square, in the heart of America's premier college town. The exciting cultural and educational resources of the Boston area are not just an added social benefit to college life; involvement in the community is an important aspect of the Lesley undergraduate experience. With over 30 clubs and organizations and Division III athletics, it's easy to be a part of something."

"Lesley graduates are creative problem solvers, highly qualified professionals, confident lifelong learners, and engaged citizens, active in their workplaces and communities. They believe individuals, working collaboratively, can make a difference. Whether they choose to enter professional fields or pursue graduate studies, their undergraduate experiences at Lesley prepare them for leadership and success in the "real" world; and our 95% job placement rate proves it. In classrooms, human service settings, government, nonprofit organizations and corporations, the environment, and the arts, Lesley graduates are working daily to improve the lives of others and the world around them.

"Come see for yourself how we are waking up the world, schedule your visit today."

For even more information on this school, turn to page 503 of the "Stats" section.

LIM COLLEGE

12 EAST FIFTY-THIRD STREET, NEW YORK, NY 10022 • ADMISSIONS: 212-752-1530 • FAX: 212-750-3432
E-MAIL: ADMISSIONS@LIMCOLLEGE.EDU • WEBSITE: WWW.LIMCOLLEGE.EDU

RATINGS

Quality of Life: 77   **Academic:** 70   **Admissions:** 70   **Financial Aid:** 60

STUDENTS SAY ". . ."

Academics

A "small school, specializing in the business of fashion,"
students say LIM College provides them "with the knowledge and experience needed to succeed in the fast-paced,
business world of fashion, and they do this through industry professionals in the perfect setting: New York City!"
Lauded for its "hands-on experience, small classes, job
placement, and experienced and knowledgeable teachers,"
LIM College is "the best place to learn about business and

fashion as one." In fact, LIM College is the only college in the U.S. to focus exclusively on business and fashion.
Students attribute the "high percentage of students that receive jobs right out of college" to the focus LIM places
on its required internship. Some note, "The professors are a hit or miss. You either get really good teachers or
people that worked in the industry and have experience but [are] not experienced in teaching." However, others say it's all about finding the gems: "Some professors are amazing and really want you to succeed. They will
help you with connections." In terms of the top brass, students note "a slight break in communication between
students and the administration because there is no solid system put into place." However, most feel their "academic experience at LIM College has been good with some bumps along the way."

Life

With a campus located in the heart of New York City, LIM students say "everything [is] at our disposal."
Though the school is a dry campus with a zero tolerance policy, "people generally go out to bars or clubs" if
they feel the need to let loose. In general students "love to party and go out and socialize." Though some say
that "it is difficult to meet different people because the campus is [in] New York City and there are a lot of commuters," others say that the Manhattan "culture of food, museums, and sights" makes up for any lack of on-
campus community. In addition, "LIM does do a great job of having dry campus activities that all students can
enjoy." Always on the cutting edge of trends in both the business and design end of the industry, "when a LIM
College student takes their studies serious then his [or] her time is consumed with school work, internships and
jobs." Saturdays are "usually the only time throughout the week...to breathe and have fun."

Student Body

"The typical LIM student loves fashion" and is "hard-working for the most part." Destined to cut their teeth in
the fast-paced world of the New York fashion industry, "They want to succeed in school, work/internships, and
in life. They know what they want for their future and go after it." Though largely female, "There are a few guys
who make up a small percentage of the student population." Some students lament that the average student is
"wealthy and from the tri-state area," which can lead to "cliques." However, others feel that for the most part
students at LIM are "artsy, diverse, and accepted by everyone." "Everyone is unique and expresses themselves
in different ways."

Admissions

Very important factors considered include: Academic GPA, interview, SAT or ACT required, level of applicant's interest. *Important factors considered include:* Class rank, application essay, recommendation(s), rigor of secondary school record, alumni/ae relation, character/personal qualities, extracurricular activities, talent/ability, volunteer work, work experience. *Other factors considered include:* Geographical residence, racial/ethnic status, state residency, Activity Sheet; TOEFL required of all international applicants. High school diploma is required and GED is accepted.

Financial Aid

Students should submit: FAFSA, institution's own financial aid form. The Princeton Review suggests that all financial aid forms be submitted as soon as possible after January 1. *Need-based scholarships/grants offered:* Federal Pell, SEOG, state scholarships/grants, private scholarships, the school's own gift aid. *Loan aid offered:* Direct Subsidized Stafford, Direct Unsubsidized Stafford, Direct PLUS. Applicants will be notified of awards on a rolling basis beginning 2/15. Federal Work-Study Program available. Institutional employment available. Off-campus job opportunities are excellent.

The Inside Word

When assessing applications, LIM looks for a B average in high school course work and strong standardized test scores. It does, however, accept some applicants who don't reach those benchmarks. Students in this camp should consider the school's new early action option; you'll need to get your application materials in by November 15, but you'll get a decision by December 15.

THE SCHOOL SAYS "..."

From The Admissions Office

"LIM College, Where Business Meets Fashion, has been educating fashion's future leaders for more than 70 years. Situated in midtown Manhattan, in the heart of the fashion industry, LIM College takes full advantage of its prime New York City location and believes that the most powerful way to learn is to harvest experience from industry professionals. From day one, LIM College incorporates real-world experience into a unique hands-on curriculum.

"With majors in Fashion Merchandising, Marketing, Management, and Visual Merchandising, an excellent student to faculty ratio, and an average class size of 18, LIM College understands the value of personal attention. LIM College is dedicated to preparing its students for success in the fashion and related industries, and with a career placement rate of more than 90 percent, LIM College alumni move forward and upward into exciting careers.

"LIM College's highly regarded faculty, a diverse group of industry professionals and educators, bring the business of fashion into the classroom. An advisory board comprised of top-level fashion business executives also counsels the College on the latest developments in retail, manufacturing, product development, public relations, marketing, publishing, and visual merchandising.

"LIM College students are immediately exposed to the fashion industry through field trips, a guest lecture series, and two 5-week, full-time internships. And in their senior year, students also complete a Co-op, an entire semester of full-time work in the industry along with a capstone project that incorporates aspects of all four years of their LIM College education."

For even more information on this school, turn to page 500 of the "Stats" section.

Loyola University in Maryland

4501 North Charles Street, Baltimore, MD 21210 • Admissions: 410-617-5012 • Fax: 410-617-2176
Financial Aid: 410-617-2576 • Website: www.loyola.edu

RATINGS
Quality of Life: 94   Academic: 86   Admissions: 88   Financial Aid: 97

STUDENTS SAY ". . ."

Academics

A Jesuit school in suburban Baltimore, Loyola University Maryland "seeks to develop the whole person—intellectually, emotionally, socially, and spiritually." Jesuit values are stressed through the school's "well-rounded curriculum, encouraging participation in community service, and teaching values in diversity both on and off campus." Across the board, students say the Loyola faculty is comprised of

> **SURVEY SAYS . . .**
> Athletic facilities are great
> School is well run
> Dorms are like palaces
> Frats and sororities are unpopular or nonexistent
> Student government is popular

accomplished scholars and talented teachers. A senior shares, "Professors are the best part about Loyola. They love their subjects and their students, and make class interesting with their enthusiasm." When it comes to academic or personal matters, "the professors at Loyola are so caring it almost seems unnatural. They will go out of their way to make sure you understand material and always have their door open after class discussions." What's more, the academic experience is characterized by small class sizes and ample discussion. A sophomore offers, "I could not be happier with my academic experience at Loyola. Even the biggest classes are small enough to facilitate close interaction with the professors." Outside the classroom, academic opportunities abound, and "professors encourage us to become part of the department through research or work-study programs." Likewise, the "administration cares deeply about fostering growth outside of the classroom." A senior attests, "As a three-year member of the student government association at Loyola I have always been impressed with the openness of the administration and their willingness to work for the best interests of the students."

Life

Despite the demands of coursework, you'll get the full college experience at Loyola University Maryland. Outgoing and social, most Loyola undergraduates are "motivated to achieve a balance between academic success and the social benefits of college." In the admiring words of one junior, "The typical student at Loyola is genius at time management. They find a way to get to the gym at least three times a week, go out at least three times week, and pull off above a 3.0 GPA every semester." However, Loyola students never lose track of their educational priorities, telling us, "The social life is very important here, but in all honesty, academics come first." In addition to hitting the off-campus bars, there are many attractions in the surrounding city of Baltimore. A sophomore reports, "For fun, my friends and I go out to eat in Baltimore, head to Towson mall, and go to the movies or concerts. Baltimore has a lot to offer to the college student." There are also plenty of extracurricular activities, clubs, and organizations at school, and "Loyola goes to great lengths to develop a sense of community across the campus." On that note, day-to-day life is easygoing and pleasant on Loyola's pretty campus. Happily, campus housing is top-notch, and "many students live in suites or apartments, and can thus cook their own food in their own kitchens."

Student Body

Loyola tends to admit outgoing and well-rounded students who want to benefit from all the academic, extracurricular, and social aspects of college life. On the whole, students "care deeply about their education and realize they are here to learn. But they also enjoy themselves and are not too uptight." Considering the fact that Loyola is a private, Jesuit college on the East Coast, it's not surprising that "the average student comes from the greater Philadelphia, New Jersey, and New York area (although that seems to be changing) and ranges in economic background from middle- to upper-class." You'll find a shared affinity for Ugg boots and The North Face apparel on the Loyola campus, and "the majority of students are preppy." Even so, you can't judge a book by its cover. A sophomore tells us, "Everyone seems like they may be a typical 'Loyola Girl' but when you look deeper you find that these people are unique and diverse." No matter what your background or interests, "there are enough clubs and a wonderful student life on campus that atypical students find their place and become as much a part of Loyola as typical students."

THE PRINCETON REVIEW SAYS

Admissions

Very important factors considered include: Application essay, recommendation(s), rigor of secondary school record, character/personal qualities. *Important factors considered include:* Class rank, alumni/ae relation, extracurricular activities, first generation, talent/ability, volunteer work. *Other factors considered include:* Academic GPA, standardized test scores, geographical residence, interview, level of applicant's interest, racial/ethnic status, work experience. TOEFL required of all international applicants. High school diploma is required, and GED is accepted. *Academic units required:* 4 English, 3 mathematics, 3 science, 3 foreign language, 2 social studies, 2 history. *Academic units recommended:* 4 English, 4 mathematics, 4 science, 4 foreign language, 3 social studies, 3 history, 1 visual/performing arts, 1 computer science.

Financial Aid

Students should submit: FAFSA, CSS/Financial Aid PROFILE, noncustodial PROFILE, business/farm supplement. Regular filing deadline is 2/15. The Princeton Review suggests that all financial aid forms be submitted as soon as possible after January 1. *Need-based scholarships/grants offered:* Federal Pell, SEOG, state scholarships/grants, private scholarships, the school's own gift aid. *Loan aid offered:* Direct Subsidized Stafford, Direct Unsubsidized Stafford, Direct PLUS, Federal Perkins, college/university loans from institutional funds. Applicants will be notified of awards on or about 4/1. Federal Work-Study Program available. Institutional employment available. Off-campus job opportunities are good.

The Inside Word

Grades are more important than standardized test scores in the admissions process at Loyola. Your junior and senior grades are particularly critical. The content of the courses you've taken weighs fairly heavily, too. Obviously, harder courses look better. If your standardized test scores aren't awful and your high school GPA is the equivalent of a B-plus or better, it is extremely likely you will get admitted here. If your GPA is more like a B, your odds are still pretty good. If your academic profile is a little thin, definitely take advantage of the opportunity to interview.

THE SCHOOL SAYS "..."

From The Admissions Office

"To make a wise choice about your college plans, you will need to find out more. We extend to you these invitations. Question-and-answer periods with an admissions counselor are helpful to prospective students. An appointment should be made in advance. Admission office hours are 9:00 A.M. to 5:00 P.M., Monday through Friday. College day programs and Saturday information programs are scheduled during the academic year. These programs include a video about Loyola, a general information session, a discussion of various majors, a campus tour, and lunch. Summer information programs can help high school juniors to get a head start on investigating colleges. These programs feature an introductory presentation about the college and a campus tour."

For even more information on this school, turn to page 503 of the "Stats" section.

LYCOMING COLLEGE

700 COLLEGE PLACE, WILLIAMSPORT, PA 17701 • ADMISSIONS: 570-321-4026 • FAX: 570-321-4317
E-MAIL: ADMISSIONS@LYCOMING.EDU • WEBSITE: WWW.LYCOMING.EDU

RATINGS
Quality of Life: 75   Academic: 78   Admissions: 78   Financial Aid: 75

STUDENTS SAY ". . ."

Academics

Lycoming College is one of the ever-shrinking group of selective undergraduates-only liberal arts and sciences institutions in the United States, which is a fact it touts proudly in its promotional literature. Students recognize the benefits of the school's approach, extolling the "school's focus on a student-centered liberal arts education" and professors who "truly care about the students and do whatever

they can to ensure the students are getting the education they are paying for." Strong programs in biology, chemistry, business, sociology, archaeology, and English stand out among the 34 majors offered. With only 1,500 undergrads and favorable student-teacher ratio, Lycoming can provide "small class sizes, so we really get a chance to develop good relationships with the faculty. All of our professors know us by name, and they are more than willing to help us with the material outside of class. They even invite us to picnics and dinners at their homes! In the labs, we get hands-on experience that isn't possible at a larger school." The school's size also allows administrators to "try to get to know the students, inviting us to meetings where they interview people for new positions (e.g. director of security), to meetings with the mayor, and to talk about the school." Students also appreciate Lycoming's history of "great job placement" and its reputation with graduate schools.

Life

Lycoming College "has a very active student body," with most students involved in sports and/or clubs. "It is almost a guarantee that if you look out your window you will see groups of students on the quad playing ball, reading under the trees, having snowball fights or sledding down the hill on cafeteria trays," one student observes. On the weekends "everyone stays here, and there is always something going on, from sporting events to campus movies," as "The Campus Activities Board (CAB) does a great job of providing entertainment on campus, with prerelease movies every weekend as well as movies on the campus TV station." Five fraternities and sororities mean "There's generally a party if that's what you're into." Many here feel that "Williamsport is a small town and...that there's nothing to do outside of the college," but "This is untrue. Williamsport actually has a relatively active art, music, and entertainment scene (for a small town)."

Student Body

Lycoming may "remind you of one big high school," particularly a "typical preppy, white, middle- to upper-middle-class" high school. As in high school, students tend to break down into predictable social sets; "There are the Greeks, jocks, and artistic groups, and then everyone else finds a group pretty easily." While "Lycoming is extremely uniform in terms of race/social demographics, the student body is quite diverse in terms of interests and personalities. Because Lycoming offers a few unique programs—archaeology, creative writing, and a lacrosse team, to name a few—the school attracts a wide range of students." Most here "are involved in several clubs and sports" and "hold some type of leadership position in at least one."

THE PRINCETON REVIEW SAYS

Admissions

Very important factors considered include: Rigor of secondary school record. *Important factors considered include:* Class rank, application essay, academic GPA, recommendation(s), standardized test scores, interview, racial/ethnic status. *Other factors considered include:* Alumni/ae relation, character/personal qualities, extracurricular activities, first generation, geographical residence, level of applicant's interest, talent/ability, volunteer work, work experience. SAT or ACT recommended; TOEFL required of all international applicants. High school diploma is required and GED is accepted. *Academic units required:* 4 English, 3 mathematics, 3 science, (2 science labs), 2 foreign language, 4 social studies, 3 history, 2 academic electives. *Academic units recommended:* 4 English, 4 mathematics, 4 science, (2 science labs), 4 foreign language, 4 social studies, 4 history, 2 academic electives.

Financial Aid

Students should submit: FAFSA, institution's own financial aid form. The Princeton Review suggests that all financial aid forms be submitted as soon as possible after January 1. *Need-based scholarships/grants offered:* Federal Pell, SEOG, state scholarships/grants, private scholarships, the school's own gift aid. *Loan aid offered:* Federal Perkins, college/university loans from institutional funds. Applicants will be notified of awards on a rolling basis beginning 3/1. Federal Work-Study Program available. Institutional employment available. Off-campus job opportunities are good.

The Inside Word

Admissions at Lycoming are competitive but hardly cutthroat. High school students with a B average and above-average standardized test scores should clear all admissions hurdles with little difficulty. Athletes, minority students, and others who add diversity and value to the campus will get more slack; so too will marginal applicants who make clear that Lycoming is their first choice. An interview and campus visit are useful in this regard.

THE SCHOOL SAYS "…"

From The Admissions Office

"At a time when many colleges have tried to become all things to all people, Lycoming has chosen to remain a traditional, undergraduate, residential, liberal arts college. What makes Lycoming different is the way it chooses to deliver its curriculum—in small classes taught by highly credentialed, well-seasoned, full-time professors. 'It's how we teach, not what we teach that is special here,' says Professor Robert Larson, chair of the faculty. 'It's the way we respond to questions, the comments we write on papers, and the way we interact with students outside the classroom that makes this school so appealing.' Staying true to who we are is the reason we've been in business since 1812."

For even more information on this school, turn to page 504 of the "Stats" section.

MANHATTANVILLE COLLEGE

2900 PURCHASE STREET, ADMISSIONS OFFICE, PURCHASE, NY 10577 • ADMISSIONS: 914-323-5124
FAX: 914-694-1732 • E-MAIL: ADMISSIONS@MVILLE.EDU • WEBSITE: WWW.MVILLE.EDU

RATINGS

Quality of Life: 95   **Academic:** 78   **Admissions:** 80   **Financial Aid:** 82

STUDENTS SAY ". . ."

Academics

"Helpful and easy-to-reach" professors, "very involved" administrators, and "close proximity to New York City" (although still far enough from its "pollution and distractions") all contribute to the "close and supportive community" that is Manhattanville College. Students here have the "unbelievable" opportunity to "exchange ideas" with professors who have "studied in the best universities in the world. There are so many distinguished professors here, ranging from experts in world religions, to former ambassadors in the United Nations. Almost all of them are well-known in their areas of study." Better still, nearly all "are approachable" and "offer office hours and are always there when they are supposed to be." Further help is available through "the Supplemental Instructor Program, which provides free extra help in math, history, and science courses." Mville (as it is affectionately called by its students) places a lot of emphasis on experiential learning, and the school's location is an asset in that regard. Not only is Mville close to the myriad of internship opportunities of the megalopolis next door, but "We [also] have tons of corporations literally in our neighborhood, like MasterCard, IBM, MBIA, [and] JPMorgan" that bring "plenty of internships." A "good education program" and "strong programs in psychology and marketing" are among the standouts here. Many undergrads appreciate the fact that "Manhattanville College reaches out to people with no money to pay for school," although they acknowledge the drawbacks. "The school doesn't accept enough people who can pay for school and, therefore, the school does not make money. And then we the students pay for that" through service shortages and class cancellations.

Life

"There is not too much to do on campus" at Manhattanville, "and the school's campus is pretty small so you cannot really explore the grounds too much," students warn. "Many people commute, so the campus is basically dead at night and on weekends," and what socializing might occur is at least in some instances hampered by "the very strict residence assistants and residence directors" who battle on-campus partying. As a result, most students seek fun "in nearby White Plains, a small city filled with different restaurants, malls, Wal-Mart-type places, and a huge movie theater. People also go into New York City for fun, as our Valiant Express bus takes people into the city every weekend, and shuttles go to and from White Plains every day." On-campus options include "lots of interest groups and activities that one can join," and "a game room with different things like billiards and ping-pong." Finally, "the students here have a lot of school spirit, so there is always a great turnout for games." Men's and women's basketball and men's hockey are among the popular draws.

Student Body

"The diversity at Manhattanville is enormous," students report. "Although the school is fairly small, there are people from all over the world." One student observes, "Sometimes I feel like I'm in the minority as a non-Spanish speaker, which is interesting." Undergrads tend to hang with their own; "Dominicans sit with Dominicans, Puerto Ricans with Puerto Ricans, misfits with misfits, artists with artists, jocks with jocks. At Manhattanville the stereotypical personalities are clumped together by habit and for the most part tend to gravitate toward one another, with minor glimpses of interaction with other groups." Regardless of any cliques, "all of the students at the school are extremely cordial. Since it is such a small school, you get to know everyone's face." Undergrads here generally "are not the type of people who are very academically competitive with one another, want to change the world, or have super-high goals for their future. What they may lack in ambition they make up for in kindness. There are a few students here who work very hard and want to go to a great graduate school, or have a great job, and do everything they can to get all A's. They fit in just as well as everyone else because almost all the students here are very accepting and good-natured."

Admissions

Very important factors considered include: Rigor of secondary school record. *Important factors considered include:* Application essay, recommendation(s), extracurricular activities, interview. *Other factors considered include:* Alumni/ae relation, character/personal qualities, geographical residence, talent/ability, volunteer work, work experience. TOEFL required of all international applicants. High school diploma is required, and GED is accepted. *Academic units required:* 4 English, 3 mathematics, 2 science, 2 social studies, 5 academic electives.

Financial Aid

Students should submit: FAFSA, state aid form. Regular filing deadline is 3/1. The Princeton Review suggests that all financial aid forms be submitted as soon as possible after January 1. *Need-based scholarships/grants offered:* Federal Pell, SEOG, state scholarships/grants, private scholarships, the school's own gift aid. *Loan aid offered:* Direct Subsidized Stafford, Direct Unsubsidized Stafford, Direct PLUS Applicants will be notified of awards on a rolling basis beginning 3/1. Federal Work-Study Program available. Institutional employment available. Off-campus job opportunities are excellent.

The Inside Word

Applicants demonstrating middle-of-the-road academic achievement will most likely find themselves with an acceptance letter from Manhattanville. The school does seek "good fits," however and frequently attempts to assess compatibility with a candidate interview. The college still seeks to achieve greater gender balance, so male candidates enjoy a slightly higher admission rate than female candidates. In addition to meeting regular admissions requirements, students who wish to pursue a degree in fine arts or performing arts must present a portfolio or audition, respectively.

THE SCHOOL SAYS "..."

From The Admissions Office

"Manhattanville's mission—to educate ethically and socially responsible leaders for the global community—is evident throughout the college, from academics to athletics to social and extracurricular activities. With 1,600 undergraduates from 59 nations and 39 states, our diversity spans geographic, cultural, ethnic, religious, socioeconomic, and academic backgrounds. Students are free to express their views in this tight-knit community, where we value the personal as well as the global. Any six students with similar interest can start a club, and most participate in a variety of campus wide programs. Last year, students engaged in more than 23,380 hours of community service and social justice activity. Study-abroad opportunities include not only the most desirable international locations, but also a semester-long immersion for living, studying, and working in New York City. In the true liberal arts tradition, students are encouraged to think for themselves and develop new skills—in music, the studio arts, on stage, in the sciences, or on the playing field. With more than 50 areas of study and a popular self-designed major, there is no limit to our academic scope. Our Westchester County location, just 35 miles north of New York City, gives students an edge for jobs and internships. Last year, the men's and women's ice hockey teams were ranked #1 in the nation for Division III."

For even more information on this school, turn to page 504 of the "Stats" section.

MARIST COLLEGE

3399 NORTH ROAD, POUGHKEEPSIE, NY 12601-1387 • ADMISSIONS: 845-575-3226 • FAX: 845-575-3215
E-MAIL: ADMISSIONS@MARIST.EDU • WEBSITE: WWW.MARIST.EDU

RATINGS
Quality of Life: 76   Academic: 79   Admissions: 90   Financial Aid: 70

STUDENTS SAY "..."

Academics

Marist College, "a smaller private school in a nice area with a great campus life," offers a surprising range of options to its largely career-minded student population. The school is home to "a very good business school;" "a good criminal

> **SURVEY SAYS . . .**
> *Great computer facilities*
> *Low cost of living*

justice department;" "a reputable teacher education program;" and "great concentrations in teaching, communications, and fashion." All departments benefit from the school's "unique partnership with IBM," which translates into "very advanced computer technology and Web services. Our online library is very extensive and extremely helpful for research papers and projects." Similarly, students appreciate the school's vigorous efforts to place them in meaningful internships. One student explains: "The internship departments have directors in each major, and a great many opportunities are made available to students for internships during both the academic year and the summer months. There is even staff on campus to go over your resumé with you and make sure it is properly formatted and has all of the necessary information in it for potential employers to review when you apply for an internship." The school's location, "about an hour and a half from New York City," is key to the success of the internship program. Students also love the "intensive study-abroad program," through which they "can go almost anywhere in the world for the same price as a semester at Marist."

Life

With "breathtaking views of the Hudson River" and "a great campus complete with nature trails and a riverfront park," Marist College offers an idyllic setting in which to pursue a college degree. Students tell us that campus life "pretty much has something for everyone: campus organizations based around race/heritage, Greek organizations, service, sports, performing arts, and co-curricular organizations. Students have many opportunities to build their social networks." Many here "are extremely concerned with life after college, and therefore many engage in activities and internships that will give them more experience in their careers." They still find time for fun, though. Campus-based diversions include "comedians, bands, hypnotists, singers, and speakers [who] come every week to give performances for the students," while off-campus life includes forays into hometown Poughkeepsie ("the school is about seven minutes from the Galleria Mall, which has a big selection of stores") or nearby historic Hyde Park; trips to New York City are most likely to occur on the weekend, since the city is about 90 minutes away (the trip, however, only requires "an extremely easy train ride to the middle of the city"). Poughkeepsie has an active nightclub and bar scene, students tell us.

Student Body

"A typical Marist student is from New York, New Jersey, or Connecticut;" is "middle- to upper-middle-class;" and has "a good background education and social skills." Undergrads here "display a hard work ethic in class while taking the initiative to become involved with student-run clubs, activities, and sports," but students aren't especially driven by academics for their own sake; they simply want to "get their work done and have a good time while getting great grades." Many here "tend to be politically conservative, but a lot of students just don't have an interest in politics. Also, Marist does not have the hipster crowd." The school was once a Catholic school, and although it is now officially nondenominational, vestiges of its old identity are evident in the student body; "most students are Catholic," one student reports, "but religious diversity is increasing bit by bit" as the years pass.

Admissions

Very important factors considered include: Academic GPA, rigor of secondary school record. *Important factors considered include:* Class rank, application essay, recommendation(s), character/personal qualities, extracurricular activities, geographical residence, state residency, talent/ability, volunteer work, work experience. *Other factors considered include:* Alumni/ae relation, level of applicant's interest, racial/ethnic status. TOEFL required of all international applicants. High school diploma is required, and GED is accepted. *Academic units required:* 4 English, 3 mathematics, 3 science, (2 science labs), 2 foreign language, 2 social studies, 1 history, 2 academic electives. *Academic units recommended:* 4 mathematics, 4 science, (3 science labs), 3 foreign language.

Financial Aid

Students should submit: FAFSA, institution's own financial aid form. Regular filing deadline is 5/1. The Princeton Review suggests that all financial aid forms be submitted as soon as possible after January 1. *Need-based scholarships/grants offered:* Federal Pell, SEOG, state scholarships/grants, private scholarships, the school's own gift aid. *Loan aid offered:* Federal Perkins, other, alternative loans. Applicants will be notified of awards on a rolling basis beginning 3/15. Federal Work-Study Program available. Institutional employment available. Off-campus job opportunities are excellent.

The Inside Word

About one-quarter of its most recent incoming class graduated outside the top 25 percent of their high school class. Those lacking academic bona fides will have to make it up in other areas, however; evidence of leadership, ability to contribute to the life of the campus (e.g. artistic or athletic skill), an interesting background that will add diversity to classroom discussion, or a similar distinguishing trait will be needed to make up for a middling academic record.

THE SCHOOL SAYS "…"

From The Admissions Office

"Marist is a 'hot school' among prospective students. We are seeing a record number of applications each year. But the number of seats available for the freshman class remains the same, about 950. Therefore, becoming an accepted applicant is an increasingly competitive process. Our recommendations: keep your grades up, participate in community service both in and out of school, and exercise leadership in the classroom, athletics, extracurricular activities, and your place of worship. We encourage a campus visit. When prospective students see Marist—our beautiful location on a scenic stretch of the Hudson River, the quality of our facilities, the interaction between students and faculty, and the fact that everyone really enjoys their time here—they want to become a part of the Marist College community. We'll help you in the transition from high school to college through an innovative first-year program that provides mentors for every student. You'll also learn how to use technology in whatever field you choose. We emphasize three aspects of a true Marist experience: excellence in education, community, and service to others. At Marist, you'll get a premium education, develop your skills, have fun and make lifelong friends, be given the opportunity to gain valuable experience through our great internship and study abroad programs, and be ahead of the competition for graduate school or work."

For even more information on this school, turn to page 505 of the "Stats" section.

MARLBORO COLLEGE

PO BOX A, SOUTH ROAD, MARLBORO, VT 05344 • ADMISSIONS: 802-258-9236 • FAX: 802-257-4154
FINANCIAL AID: 802-257-4333 • E-MAIL: ADMISSIONS@MARLBORO.EDU • WEBSITE: WWW.MARLBORO.EDU

RATINGS

Quality of Life: 82   **Academic:** 99   **Admissions:** 93   **Financial Aid:** 87

STUDENTS SAY ". . ."

Academics

Marlboro College is all about giving students "the freedom to pursue their own interests and study what they want." Here, undergrads design their own junior and senior curricula, then pursue them in one-on-one tutorials with professors. The process, known here simply as "The Plan," culminates in a substantial senior thesis. The goal is to "learn how to think critically and find the resources you need in the course of completing a dissertation-level project," and

undergrads here "wouldn't settle for anything less in their academic pursuits." Freshmen and sophomores complete more traditional-style courses, albeit in smaller classrooms and with a greater-than-usual focus on writing and discussion. The size of the school—just more than 300 undergraduates attend—is sometimes a hindrance. One student observes that, "Since there is generally only one professor per field, it is a bit disappointing to realize that there can only be a limited number of classes offered per semester." "Too often a student will reach the final year when his/her Plan sponsor goes on sabbatical and a replacement is not hired in time or hired at all. This presents a problem: Does the student leave the college until their professor returns, or does the student switch Plan sponsors, potentially altering the focus of their work so much they dislike what they're doing?" Despite these issues, "professors are very receptive and try to accommodate individual interests as best they can." Most here feel these are reasonable costs to bear in order to pursue "independent, difficult, intellectually stimulating work inside a student-centered and directed curriculum."

Life

Marlboro is "a little school on top of a hill" with Brattleboro, the closest town, "about a half hour away," so "life is pretty intensely focused on the campus." "While we do make the trip to Brattleboro fairly often, most of our time is spent 'on the hill,'" says one student. Students "study a lot, but there is also a lot of hanging out, mainly in small impromptu ways." They "like to debate about philosophy, politics, and religion." Fun "is found in the 300 acres that surround the college: skiing, hiking, long walks in an apple orchard, broomball (a hippie version of hockey), soccer, etc." Trips to Brattleboro are pleasant because it's "an arts town." Students occasionally travel to Massachusetts college towns Amherst and Northampton for concerts or shopping and "frequently classes take field trips to NYC or Boston." Many get involved in grassroots political organization, both on campus and off.

Student Body

The typical Marlboro student "wouldn't fit quite right anywhere else: academically driven, maybe a little nerdy, politically vocal, and looking for a laid-back environment. There is no atypical student at Marlboro, because we all would have been atypical someplace else." Personality types run the gamut, including "hippie environmentalists, geeks and gamers, theater kids, artists, and so on and so forth and every combination thereof. We're underrepresented in the jock and beauty queen categories, but that doesn't seem to bother anybody." Everyone here, we're told, "is extremely passionate about their own little academic niche, and furthermore each person is one of the smartest people you will ever meet." The school is home to "a large gay population and a few transgender students," but "there are a lack of minority students, [and] Republicans."

Admissions

Very important factors considered include: Application essay, academic GPA, rigor of secondary school record, character/personal qualities. *Important factors considered include:* Extracurricular activities, interview. *Other factors considered include:* Class rank, recommendation(s), standardized test scores, alumni/ae relation, first generation, geographical residence, level of applicant's interest, state residency, talent/ability, volunteer work, work experience. TOEFL required of all international applicants. High school diploma is required, and GED is accepted. *Academic units recommended:* 4 English, 3 mathematics, 3 science, (1 science labs), 3 foreign language, 3 social studies, 3 history, 3 academic electives.

Financial Aid

Students should submit: FAFSA. Regular filing deadline is 3/1. The Princeton Review suggests that all financial aid forms be submitted as soon as possible after January 1. *Need-based scholarships/grants offered:* Federal Pell, SEOG, state scholarships/grants, private scholarships, the school's own gift aid. Applicants will be notified of awards on a rolling basis beginning 3/15. Federal Work-Study Program available. Institutional employment available. Off-campus job opportunities are fair.

The Inside Word

Don't be misled by Marlboro's acceptance rate—this is not the type of school that attracts many applications from students unsure of whether they belong at Marlboro. Most applicants are qualified both in terms of academic achievement and sincere intellectual curiosity. The school seeks candidates "with intellectual promise, a high degree of self-motivation, self-discipline, personal stability, social concern, and the ability and desire to contribute to the College community." These are the qualities you should stress on your application.

THE SCHOOL SAYS "..."

From The Admissions Office

"Marlboro College is distinguished by its curriculum, praised in higher education circles as unique; it is known for its self-governing philosophy, in which each student, faculty, and staff has an equal vote on many issues affecting the community; and it is recognized for its 60-year history of offering a rigorous, exciting, self-designed course of study taught in very small classes and individualized study with faculty. Marlboro's size also distinguishes it from most other schools. With 300 students and a student/faculty ratio of 8:1, it is one of the nation's smallest liberal arts colleges. Few other schools offer a program where students have such close interaction with faculty, and where community life is inseparable from academic life. The result, the self-designed, self-directed Plan of Concentration, allows students to develop their own unique academic work by defining a problem, setting clear limits on an area of inquiry, and analyzing, evaluating, and reporting on the outcome of a significant project. A Marlboro education teaches you to think for yourself, articulate your thoughts, express your ideas, believe in yourself, and do it all with the clarity, confidence, and self-reliance necessary for later success, no matter what postgraduate path you take."

For even more information on this school, turn to page 505 of the "Stats" section.

MARYLAND INSTITUTE COLLEGE OF ART

1300 WEST MOUNT ROYAL AVENUE, BALTIMORE, MD 21217 • ADMISSIONS: 410-225-2222 • FAX: 410-225-2337
E-MAIL: ADMISSION@MICA.EDU • WEBSITE: WWW.MICA.EDU

RATINGS
Quality of Life: 74   Academic: 92   Admissions: 91   Financial Aid: 71

STUDENTS SAY ". . ."

Academics

Small, "prestigious" Maryland Institute College of Art specializes in "turning promising talent into undeniable skill." Majors here include an "incredible painting program" and "one of the best" illustration programs in the country. While MICA obviously focuses on art, there's also a respectable array of required liberal arts and art history courses and a thorough foundational curriculum. "The school makes sure everyone has a strong foundation...so that, for example, even a photo major will still be at least decent at drawing." Extensive internship opportunities and a throng of study abroad options are other perks. Classes are "wonderfully small" and often "very long." "The workload is quite heavy." "It is insanely time-consuming to be a student here." "Everyone works their [butts] off and complains about it," says an illustration major, "but we all really love what we do." The faculty at MICA is largely comprised of "actual artists living and working in the real world." There are "really exceptionally amazing teachers and horrifyingly bad ones." For the most part, though, professors are "dedicated" and "readily available" outside of class. "They challenge students on an individual basis and critique with expert eyes." The administration is "a little disorganized." "They take forever to get back to you on any issue," gripes an exasperated senior.

Life

This "tiny, urban campus" boasts "exceptionally nice" dorms. There is "no rah-rah school spirit" and very little in the way of traditional college life. Basically, "people have art on the mind 24/7." "Studio work is very demanding" and takes up huge chunks of time. Students definitely let loose when they have a chance, though. "There's a lot of drinking," and "a lot of house parties with loud music and bad beer." "Hardly a weekend goes by [when] there isn't a sweaty warehouse party with killer dance music." More mellow fare is also abundantly available. "Groups of friends get together at each other's houses a lot." Gallery openings and independent theater and film showings are popular. Trips to New York City and the District of Columbia are fairly common. The surrounding city of Baltimore is "charming for some, terrifying for others." Critics point out that the neighborhood bordering the north of the campus is "a rough place." Devotees of the city insist that it has "unique and interesting restaurants" and "an excellent music scene." "It's an exciting place to live right now," says a sophomore.

Student Body

Students here are "passionate," "hardworking, ambitious," "incredibly observant," and usually "very liberal." Many come from "wealthy suburban" enclaves on the East Coast. They are "very fashionable." Many "go to class looking runway-ready." There are "droves of hipsters" who get "most of their clothes at Urban Outfitters and the rest at the thrift store." Beyond that, this population is hard to classify. MICA is full of "oddballs" who "were the misfits at their high school." "The whole campus is basically atypical students." "There are so many atypical students that they become typical." "Strange haircuts" are customary. "There really is no way to stand out by being weird." Socially, MICA is "very cliquey." "You can tell what major kids are just by looking at their clothes," maintains a senior. "Every department has a clique."

THE PRINCETON REVIEW SAYS

Admissions

Very important factors considered include: Academic GPA, rigor of secondary school record, level of applicant's interest, talent/ability. *Important factors considered include:* Class rank, application essay, standardized test scores, extracurricular activities, interview. *Other factors considered include:* Recommendation(s), alumni/ae relation, character/personal qualities, racial/ethnic status, volunteer work. SAT or ACT required; TOEFL required of all international applicants. High school diploma is required and GED is accepted. *Academic units required:* 4 English, 2 mathematics, 2 science, (1 science labs), 4 social studies, 3 history, 6 academic electives, 2 studio art, 4 studio art recommended, 1 art history recommended. *Academic units recommended:* 4 English, 3 mathematics, 3 science, 4 social studies, 4 history, 5 studio art, 4 studio art recommended, 1 art history recommended.

Financial Aid

Students should submit: FAFSA, institution's own financial aid form. Regular filing deadline is 2/15 for new students and 3/1 for transfer and returning students. The Princeton Review suggests that all financial aid forms be submitted as soon as possible after January 1. *Need-based scholarships/grants offered:* Federal Pell, SEOG, state scholarships/grants, private scholarships, the school's own gift aid. *Loan aid offered:* Federal Perkins Applicants will be notified of awards on or about 4/10. Federal Work-Study Program available. Institutional employment available. Off-campus job opportunities are excellent.

The Inside Word

Test scores, grades, and letters of recommendation all matter here, but your portfolio is the make-or-break piece of the application. A portfolio that demonstrates talent and originality can mitigate many other shortcomings; a weak portfolio will torpedo an otherwise exemplary application.

THE SCHOOL SAYS "..."

From The Admissions Office

"Maryland Institute College of Art attracts some of the most talented, passionate, and serious visual art and design faculty and students in the world. The college is a universe of artists, designers, and scholars who celebrate the creative process, the majesty of the arts, and the mind-expanding pursuit of knowledge. To maintain this community of artists, admission is highly competitive. Successful applicants are men and women who have made a commitment to art, and demonstrated this commitment by developing a serious portfolio of artwork. In selecting from among the many outstanding applications we receive for a limited number of places, MICA's Admission Committee considers a comprehensive set of factors. Central to our evaluations are the artistic and academic qualifications of our candidates, but we also consider extracurricular activities and achievements, art experience beyond required classroom instruction, and personal qualities. The portfolio is the most meaningful indicator of serious artistic commitment, ability, and potential to succeed in MICA's rigorous studio environment. Your artwork reflects your visual sensitivity, intellectual curiosity and creativity, motivation and self-discipline, and previous experience in the visual arts. Portfolios are evaluated on an individual basis, in the context of the specific educational background and experiences of each applicant. Our evaluation of your academic performance is determined by grades, level of classwork, test scores, and class rank. The required essay is also seriously considered."

For even more information on this school, turn to page 506 of the "Stats" section.

MARYWOOD UNIVERSITY

Office of Admissions, 2300 Adams Avenu, Scranton, PA 18509 • Admissions: 570-348-6234
Fax: 570-961-4763 • Financial Aid: 866-279-9663 • E-mail: yourfuture@marywood.edu • Website: www.marywood.edu

RATINGS
Quality of Life: 69   Academic: 71   Admissions: 79   Financial Aid: 60

STUDENTS SAY "..."

Academics

Marywood University is a small Catholic university that offers a wide range of undergraduate majors and pre-professional programs, from art therapy and music performance to physician assistant and interior design. Marywood University consists of four colleges and a School of Architecture. No matter what you choose to study, the intimate classroom environment is the strength of a Marywood education. A freshman explains, "Through class discussions, I feel that I am truly learning and absorbing the material, as opposed to other schools where teachers dictate or lecture for hours." Academic programs are "challenging but not overwhelming," and "the professors do everything in their power to help their students learn and be able to apply that knowledge to real life." At the same time, personal accountability is vital. Teachers know you by name, and "small class sizes get you extra attention but also make it obvious if you skip class." If you are looking to take a wide range of classes, Marywood is not the best option, as most majors have extensive course requirements, and it can be difficult to get a spot in classes outside your declared department. On the other hand, "Marywood is awesome if you know exactly what you want to do. It has some excellent programs and combines them with general humanities classes."

> **SURVEY SAYS . . .**
> *Lots of liberal students*
> *Athletic facilities are great*
> *Low cost of living*
> *Frats and sororities are unpopular or nonexistent*
> *Very little drug use*

Life

When they aren't in the library, Marywood students enjoy college life through "on-campus events, movies, bowling, house parties, and just hanging out in the lounges." School spirit surges during the school's sporting events, and "students get excited about the basketball games as well as the women's soccer games." Even though Marywood is a dry campus, you can always take "a trip down to Scranton University for party life (if that's what you're into)." When it comes to the surrounding city, "a lot of people complain that there is nothing to do around Scranton, but you just have to know where to look." In fact, "there is a lot of good shopping, movie theaters, restaurants, bars and clubs" in Scranton, and some nightclubs permit entry to age 18 and up. If you are willing to take a trip outside the city, "the spring and fall are a great time to go on hikes or enjoy the outdoor attractions" and, in the winter, "there is a ski resort close by."

Student Body

Well-rounded, friendly, and studious, the typical Marywood undergraduate "does well in class, works out at the gym, is involved with clubs, and is surrounded by many friends." Most undergraduates at Marywood are "young, white, middle-class" students from New York, New Jersey, and Pennsylvania, though the campus also attracts "students from all over the world, all different religions." Within the college community, you'll find "art lovers in our art field and sport lovers in our new gym, movie watchers in the Madonna Hall Movie Theater and dancers in our new dance studio. There are sorority girls always looking to add new girls to the Zeta Phi Delta and coffee drinkers at the many coffee spots on campus." Fortunately, all students "fit in as one big friendly community." A freshman shares, "Life at college is very safe and relaxing. People are free to make their own choices and [are] encouraged to have their own opinions."

THE PRINCETON REVIEW SAYS

Admissions

Very important factors considered include: Class rank, academic GPA, rigor of secondary school record, standardized test scores, character/personal qualities. *Important factors considered include:* Application essay, recommendation(s), interview, talent/ability. *Other factors considered include:* Extracurricular activities, level of applicant's interest, volunteer work. SAT or ACT required; TOEFL required of all international applicants. High school diploma is required, and GED is accepted. *Academic units required:* 4 English, 2 mathematics, 1 science, (1 science labs), 3 social studies, 6 academic electives,.

Financial Aid

Students should submit: FAFSA. The Princeton Review suggests that all financial aid forms be submitted as soon as possible after January 1. *Need-based scholarships/grants offered:* Federal Pell, SEOG, state scholarships/grants, private scholarships, the school's own gift aid, Federal Nursing Scholarships. *Loan aid offered:* Federal Perkins, state loans, other, private alternative loans. Applicants will be notified of awards on a rolling basis beginning 2/15. Federal Work-Study Program available.

The Inside Word

After you have applied to Marywood, you can participate in their "College for a Day" program, which gives prospective students an inside look at university life, from the classroom to the cafeteria. Marywood reviews applications on a rolling basis, and therefore, you should apply as early as possible. Once a prospective student has submitted all of the application materials, the admissions department will usually make a decision within two or three weeks.

THE SCHOOL SAYS "…"

From The Admissions Office

Marywood University is a comprehensive, Catholic university with just over 2,206 full-time and part-time men and women undergraduates and 1,300 graduate students on campus. There are over 90 undergraduate programs to choose from, many offering graduate components or even doctoral degree programs, if desired. Established in 1915, the university today houses 1,000 undergraduate resident students on a national award-winning campus considered one of the most beautiful in the northeast. In recent years, the university has made $100 million in improvements to campus, including new athletics, residence hall and dining facilities, and one of the finest studio arts facilities in the northeast. Marywood offered the first doctoral degree programs in the Northeastern Pennsylvania region. Of our full-time faculty members, 85% hold the most advanced degrees in their field. Our faculty members are grounded in professional practice and skilled in the art of teaching, and are highly respected practitioners, industry professionals, and visionary educators.

"Marywood operates on a rolling admissions basis. High school seniors are encouraged to submit their application for admission before March 1. Students applying for federal and state financial aid should submit the Free Application for Federal Student Aid (FAFSA) by February 15. At Marywood, you will discover that a top-notch private college experience is more affordable than you ever dreamed. In fact, 98 percent of our first-time students receive financial assistance in the form of scholarships, grants, loans, and work-study programs."

For even more information on this school, turn to page 506 of the "Stats" section.

MASSACHUSETTS INSTITUTE OF TECHNOLOGY

77 MASSACHUSETTS AVENUE, CAMBRIDGE, MA 02139 • ADMISSIONS: 617-253-4791
FAX: 617-253-1986 • FINANCIAL AID: 617-253-4971 • E-MAIL: ADMISSIONS@MIT.EDU • WEBSITE: WWW.MIT.EDU

RATINGS
Quality of Life: 87   **Academic:** 97   **Admissions:** 99   **Financial Aid:** 96

STUDENTS SAY ". . ."

Academics

Massachusetts Institute of Technology, the East Coast mecca of engineering, science, and mathematics, "is the ultimate place for information overload, endless possibilities, and expanding your horizons." The "amazing collection of creative minds" includes enough Nobel laureates to fill a jury box as well as brilliant students who are given substantial control of their educations; one explains, "The administration's attitude toward students is one of respect. As soon as you come on campus, you are bombarded with

choices." Students need to be able to manage a workload that "definitely push[es you] beyond your comfort level." A chemical engineering major elaborates: "MIT is different from many schools in that its goal is not to teach you specific facts in each subject. MIT teaches you how to think, not about opinions but about problem solving. Facts and memorization are useless unless you know how to approach a tough problem." Professors here range from "excellent teachers who make lectures fun and exciting" to "dull and soporific" ones, but most "make a serious effort to make the material they teach interesting by throwing in jokes and cool demonstrations." "Access to an amazing number of resources, both academic and recreational," "research opportunities for undergrads with some of the nation's leading professors," and a rock-solid alumni network complete the picture. If you ask "MIT alumni where they went to college, most will immediately stick out their hand and show you their 'brass rat' (the MIT ring, the second most recognized ring in the world)."

Life

At MIT "It may seem…like there's no life outside problem sets and studying for exams," but "there's always time for extracurricular activities or just relaxing" for those "with good time-management skills" or the "ability to survive on [a] lack of sleep." Options range from "building rides" (recent projects have included a motorized couch and a human-sized hamster wheel) "to partying at fraternities to enjoying the largest collection of science fiction novels in the United States at the MIT Science Fiction Library." Students occasionally find time to "pull a hack," which is an ethical prank, "like the life-size Wright brothers' plane that appeared on top of the Great Dome for the one-hundredth anniversary of flight." Undergrads tell us that "MIT has great parties—a lot of Wellesley, Harvard, and BU students come to them," but also that "there are tons of things to do other than party" here. "Movies, shopping, museums, and plays are all possible with our location near Boston. There are great restaurants only [blocks] away from campus, too…From what I can tell, MIT students have way more fun on the weekends than their Cambridge counterparts [at] Harvard."

Student Body

"There actually isn't one typical student at MIT," students here assure us, explaining that "hobbies range from building robots and hacking to getting wasted and partying every weekend. The one thing students all have in common is that they are insanely smart and love to learn. Pretty much anyone can find the perfect group of friends to hang out with at MIT." "Most students do have some form of 'nerdiness'" (like telling nerdy jokes, being an avid fan of *Star Wars*, etc.), but "contrary to MIT's stereotype, most MIT students are not geeks who study all the time and have no social skills. The majority of the students here are actually quite 'normal.'" The "stereotypical student [who] looks techy and unkempt…only represents about 25 percent of the school." The rest include "multiple-sport standouts, political activists, fraternity and sorority members, hippies, clean-cut business types, LARPers, hackers, musicians, and artisans. There are people who look like they stepped out of an Abercrombie & Fitch catalog and people who dress in all black and carry flashlights and multi-tools. Not everyone relates to everyone else, but most people get along, and it's almost a guarantee that you'll fit in somewhere."

Admissions

Very important factors considered include: Character/personal qualities. *Important factors considered include:* Class rank, academic GPA, recommendation(s), rigor of secondary school record, standardized test scores, extracurricular activities, interview, talent/ability. *Other factors considered include:* Application essay, alumni/ae relation, first generation, geographical residence, racial/ethnic status, volunteer work, work experience. SAT or ACT required; ACT with Writing component required. High school diploma or equivalent is not required. *Academic units recommended:* 4 English, 4 mathematics, 4 science, 2 foreign language, 2 social studies.

Financial Aid

Students should submit: FAFSA, CSS/Financial Aid PROFILE, noncustodial PROFILE, business/farm supplement, parent's complete federal income tax returns from prior year and W-2s. Regular filing deadline is 2/15. The Princeton Review suggests that all financial aid forms be submitted as soon as possible after January 1. *Need-based scholarships/grants offered:* Federal Pell, SEOG, state scholarships/grants, private scholarships, the school's own gift aid. *Loan aid offered:* Direct Subsidized Stafford, Direct Unsubsidized Stafford, Direct PLUS, Federal Perkins, college/university loans from institutional funds. Applicants will be notified of awards on or about 4/1. Federal Work-Study Program available. Institutional employment available. Off-campus job opportunities are excellent.

The Inside Word

MIT has one of the nation's most competitive admissions processes. The school's applicant pool is so rich it turns away numerous qualified candidates each year. Put your best foot forward and take consolation in the fact that rejection doesn't necessarily mean that you don't belong at MIT, but only that there wasn't enough room for you the year you applied. Your best chance to get an edge: Find ways to stress your creativity, a quality that MIT's admissions director told *USA TODAY* is lacking in many prospective college students.

THE SCHOOL SAYS "…"

From The Admissions Office

"The students who come to the Massachusetts Institute of Technology are some of America's—and the world's—best and most creative. As graduates, they leave here to make real contributions—in science, technology, business, education, politics, architecture, and the arts. From any class, many will go on to do work that is historically significant. These young men and women are leaders, achievers, and producers. Helping such students make the most of their talents and dreams would challenge any educational institution. MIT gives them its best advantages: a world-class faculty, unparalleled facilities, and remarkable opportunities. In turn, these students help to make the institute the vital place it is. They bring fresh viewpoints to faculty research: More than three-quarters participate in the Undergraduate Research Opportunities Program, developing solutions for the world's problems in areas such as energy, the environment, cancer, and poverty. They play on MIT's 41 intercollegiate teams as well as in its 50+ music, theatre, and dance groups. To their classes and to their out-of-class activities, they bring enthusiasm, energy, and individual style."

For even more information on this school, turn to page 506 of the "Stats" section.

MERRIMACK COLLEGE

OFFICE OF ADMISSION, AUSTIN HALL, NORTH ANDOVER, MA 01845 • ADMISSIONS: 978-837-5100
FAX: 978-837-5133 • E-MAIL: ADMISSION@MERRIMACK.EDU • WEBSITE: WWW.MERRIMACK.EDU

RATINGS
Quality of Life: 73   **Academic:** 73   **Admissions:** 79   **Financial Aid:** 89

STUDENTS SAY "..."

Academics

SURVEY SAYS . . .
Students are friendly
Students get along with local community
Campus feels safe
Lots of beer drinking
Hard liquor is popular

Merrimack students report a "very satisfying" academic experience, enhanced by "professors that are brilliant, energetic, and easily approachable both in and out of the classroom." One impressed sophomore notes, "My professors have gotten to know me on a personal level, and some stay in touch even when I'm no longer enrolled in any of their classes." Importantly, they "work with you to examine your future goals and guide you on the right path." Additionally, undergrads applaud the "small class sizes," which encourage "heavy debate with professors and fellow students." While students are quick to praise their time in the lecture halls, opinions are mixed when it comes to the administration. Though a junior assures us that "administrators are easy to work with when solving issues and agendas," others claim dealing with them is a "headache" and a "waste." Fortunately, change is expected as Merrimack recently welcomed the arrival of a new president.

Life

Though Merrimack students must hit the books during the week, they readily push academics aside once the weekend rolls around. The athletic undergrads "love the sports here at Merrimack" and many are involved in intramurals such as "flag football and ski club." Social activities tend to focus around dorm life as they are "very conducive to having people over to hang out and have fun, from having a few drinks to sitting around watching TV to having large parties." And one sophomore adds, "On weekends, most people just go to on-campus parties in the senior apartments." Of course "Merrimack offers a wide range of opportunities for students, and there is always something to do." These school sponsored activities range from comedians and bands to speakers such as "the cast members of MTV's *Real World*." Students do complain that hometown "North Andover and the surrounding area is too quiet for someone looking to have fun after 9 P.M. because everything closes down." And while there are a number of local dining options, "the area is very expensive making it hard to go out to eat." Those in search of some urban action can take advantage of Merrimack's proximity to Boston, and many students do take the occasional weekend trip.

Student Body

Many admit that Merrimack isn't the most diverse of colleges, defining the majority as "white, upper-middle class, and Christian." Indeed, a sophomore boldly states that "Merrimack is a school of Abercrombie & Fitch models." That said, many undergrads are "friendly and like to get involved on campus." And a knowledgeable senior promises that his peers are "easy to get along with." Merrimack students like to be active, and athletes "make up a surprisingly large part of the student body." Despite the school maintaining Catholic affiliation "the average student is not that spiritually involved." The relatively small student population leads to a strong community feeling, and "by senior year...you have talked to most of the people in your class."

Admissions

Very important factors considered include: Application essay, academic GPA, rigor of secondary school record, class rank, application essay. *Important factors considered include:* Class rank, recommendation(s), character/personal qualities, talent/ability. *Other factors considered include:* Alumni/ae relation, extracurricular activities, interview, level of applicant's interest, volunteer work, work experience. TOEFL required of all international applicants. High school diploma is required and GED is accepted. *Academic units required:* 4 English, 3 mathematics, 3 science, (3 science labs), 2 foreign language, 1 social studies, 1 history, 3 academic electives. *Academic units recommended:* 4 English, 4 mathematics, 4 science, (4 science labs), 3 foreign language, 2 social studies, 2 history, 3 academic electives.

Financial Aid

Students should submit: FAFSA, noncustodial PROFILE, business/farm supplement. Sibling Verification. Regular filing deadline is 2/1. The Princeton Review suggests that all financial aid forms be submitted as soon as possible after January 1. *Need-based scholarships/grants offered:* Federal Pell, SEOG, state scholarships/grants, private scholarships, the school's own gift aid. *Loan aid offered:* Federal Perkins, state loans, college/university loans from institutional funds, other, alternative loans. Applicants will be notified of awards on or about 3/31. Federal Work-Study Program available. Off-campus job opportunities are good.

The Inside Word

Applicants should seriously consider applying to Merrimack through the early action program. The program is non-binding, and early action candidates not granted early action will still receive full consideration for the fall term. Merrimack College only accepts the Common Application for first-year applicants. A short supplement is also required.

THE SCHOOL SAYS "…"

From The Admissions Office

"Merrimack College is a four-year, independent, Catholic college grounded in the liberal arts and guided by the teachings of St. Augustine. The College offers undergraduate degrees in business, education, engineering, liberal arts and science, as well as master of education degree programs. Merrimack's contemporary academic approach of fusing liberal arts with professional education means students become engaged and ready to make critical, moral, and informed decisions of thought, communication, and action in their own lives and in service to others. What makes Merrimack distinctive is that 'active learning' is our educational philosophy and a call to action. Students learn by doing—not only in the classroom and the laboratory, but also in the field and in the real world. Located on a suburban setting just 25 miles north of Boston, Massachusetts, Merrimack offers a strong cooperative education program for all majors, undergraduate research opportunities, and extensive service-learning experiences that promote social responsibility. Students at Merrimack have unparalleled opportunities for an education that extends far beyond campus. Merrimack's 2,000 students represent 28 states and 17 countries; nearly 80 percent live on campus."

For even more information on this school, turn to page 507 of the "Stats" section.

MESSIAH COLLEGE

ONE COLLEGE AVENUE, GRANTHAM, PA 17027 • ADMISSIONS: 717-691-6000 • FAX: 717-796-5374
E-MAIL: ADMISS@MESSIAH.EDU • WEBSITE: WWW.MESSIAH.EDU

RATINGS
Quality of Life: 86   **Academic:** 81   **Admissions:** 88   **Financial Aid:** 73

STUDENTS SAY ". . ."

Academics

Messiah College, a small evangelical liberal arts school just outside Harrisburg, "is a place where Christian theology meets real life, individuals encounter true community, intense scholarship is connected to fervent faith, and where students stop 'doing' and start 'becoming.'" Students come here for a "Christ-centered education" but appreciate that "it is not 'cookie cutter Christianity'—you are forced to think outside your comfort zone and the 'box.' Professors stretch you and you have to really think about what you believe and why." This "community of thinkers, not regurgitators" pursues "stringent academics" in nursing, engineering, education, English, and religious studies. Students here also benefit from a "great study abroad program" that is "easily accessible, easy to pursue, and goes to so many countries!" The school also embodies "a strong concern for social justice and environmental issues" that manifests itself in service as well as "discussions of homelessness, poverty, and other injustices" across the campus. Best of all, "There are plenty of resources to help with homework (including tutoring), there are plenty of places to go to do homework, and there are state-of-the-art labs. Messiah has all a student needs."

Life

"Life is pretty laid back" at Messiah "since we live in a rural area," says one student. Most students here are "very outdoors-oriented: Frisbee, especially ultimate Frisbee, football, soccer, recreational sports, hiking, and rock climbing are popular." Men's and women's soccer games pull big crowds here. "Our men's soccer team won the National Championship for the past three years, and both the men and women usually make it to the Final Four," explains one student. Messiah works hard to bring entertainment to campus and over the past few years performers here have included Bob Dylan, Nickel Creek, Feist, Copeland, Regina Spektor, and Jars of Clay. No wonder "Messiah has been called 'the concert Mecca' of central Pennsylvania." But while some here assure us that "There are lots of places to hang out with other students to have fun" such as the new Student Union ("a great place to go with friends to get something to eat and to hang out") and the dorms ("People have fun by getting together to watch movies and play video games with friends."), some urban transplants tell us "this is a very hard adjustment to make. I'm in the boonies, and I hate it."

Student Body

Students at Messiah tend to be "socially and environmentally aware or even active—they care about the school and local community, and they seek to be involved in service locally, nationally, and abroad." Most are "white Christians from the Northeast," but "there are also quite a few international students," and even, surprisingly, "a few atheists." As at many religious schools, Messiah offers "a not-very-welcoming environment for students of other sexual orientations. Rather than really confront these issues, they are typically glossed over or ignored." Words like "sheltered" and "naïve" pop up frequently in students' descriptions of their peers, but many report that "there's actually a lot of diversity in terms of how people grew up."

THE PRINCETON REVIEW SAYS

Admissions

Very important factors considered include: Class rank, academic GPA, recommendation(s), rigor of secondary school record, standardized test scores, character/personal qualities, extracurricular activities, religious affiliation/commitment, talent/ability. *Important factors considered include:* Application essay, volunteer work. *Other factors considered include:* Alumni/ae relation, interview, level of applicant's interest, racial/ethnic status, work experience. TOEFL required of all international applicants. High school diploma is required and GED is accepted. *Academic units required:* 4 English, 2 mathematics, 2 science, (2 science labs), 2 foreign language, 2 social studies, 4 academic electives. *Academic units recommended:* 4 English, 3 mathematics, 3 science, (3 science labs), 2 foreign language, 2 social studies, 2 history, 4 academic electives.

Financial Aid

Students should submit: FAFSA. The Princeton Review suggests that all financial aid forms be submitted as soon as possible after January 1. *Need-based scholarships/grants offered:* Federal Pell, SEOG, state scholarships/grants, private scholarships, the school's own gift aid. *Loan aid offered:* Direct Subsidized Stafford, Direct Unsubsidized Stafford, Direct PLUS, Federal Perkins, Federal Nursing. Applicants will be notified of awards on a rolling basis beginning 3/15. Federal Work-Study Program available. Institutional employment available. Off-campus job opportunities are good.

The Inside Word

Don't test well? If you're in the top 20 percent of your high school graduating class, you can opt to submit a graded writing sample in place of your standardized test scores. And good news for those schooled outside of school: Messiah is "homeschool friendly," with more than 150 students who were homeschooled during their senior year (and many more who were homeschooled at some point in their education).

THE SCHOOL SAYS "..."

From The Admissions Office

"Messiah College is a place where education involves a student's intellect, character, and Christian faith. Students receive a superb higher education and also discover a higher calling as they prepare for lives of service, leadership, and reconciliation.

"As a community of learners, Messiah gives academics a high priority. More than 2,900 students from 39 states and 28 countries receive a thorough liberal arts foundation and pursue their choice of more than 50 liberal or applied majors.

"Messiah students learn in many settings. Whether they are involved in student government, a national championship–quality athletic team, or a community-service project, students apply what they have learned. Co-curricular activities and organizations provide a laboratory for testing values and convictions. These opportunities for character development at Messiah are as diverse as the students who bring their gifts and abilities. The 20 intercollegiate athletic teams, academic clubs, student publications, the radio station, music and theater ensembles, and leadership development programs are just a few of the opportunities available.

"For the person of faith, rigorous intellectual study demands a similar response from the heart. Messiah College faculty and administration mentor students toward spiritual maturity. Students explore their faith while asking the difficult questions of life.

"Interested students should visit during their sophomore or junior year of high school either individually or during one of the various open house events. Applications for admission are considered on a rolling basis."

For even more information on this school, turn to page 507 of the "Stats" section.

MIDDLEBURY COLLEGE

THE EMMA WILLARD HOUSE, MIDDLEBURY, VT 05753 • ADMISSIONS: 802-443-3000 • FAX: 802-443-2056
FINANCIAL AID: 802-443-5158 • E-MAIL: ADMISSIONS@MIDDLEBURY.EDU • WEBSITE: WWW.MIDDLEBURY.EDU

RATINGS
Quality of Life: 99   **Academic:** 99   **Admissions:** 98   **Financial Aid:** 95

STUDENTS SAY ". . ."

Academics

Home to "smart people who enjoy Aristotelian ethics and quantum physics, but aren't too stuck up to go sledding in front of Mead Chapel at midnight," Middlebury College is a small, exclusive liberal arts school with "excellent foreign language programs" as well as standout offerings in environmental studies, the sciences, theater, and writing. Distribution requirements and other general requirements ensure that a Middlebury education "is all about providing students with a complete college experience including excellent teaching, exposure to many other cultures, endless opportunities for growth and success, and a challenging (yet relaxed) environment." Its "small class size and friendly yet competitive atmosphere make for the perfect college experience," as do "the best facilities of a small liberal arts college in the country. The new library, science center, athletic complex, arts center, and a number of the dining halls and dorms have been built in the past 10 years." Expect to work hard; "it's tough, but this is a mini-Ivy, so what should one expect? There is plenty of time to socialize, and due to the collaborative atmosphere here, studying and socializing can often come hand in hand. The goal of many students here is not to get high grades" but rather "learning in its purest form, and that is perhaps this college's most brightly shining aspect." The collaborative atmosphere is abetted by the fact that "admissions doesn't just bring in geniuses, they bring in people who are leaders and community servants. Think of the guy or girl in your high school whom everybody describes as 'so nice'…that's your typical Middlebury student."

Life

"This high level of involvement in everything translates into an amazing campus atmosphere" at Middlebury, where "most people are very involved. There is a club for just about everything you can imagine, and if you can imagine one that hasn't yet been created, you go ahead and create it yourself." With great skiing and outdoor activity close by, "Almost everyone is athletic in some way. This can translate into anything from varsity sports to intramural hockey (an extremely popular winter pastime!). People are enthusiastic about being active and having fun." Because the school "is set in a very small town, there aren't too many (if any) problems with violence, drugs, [or] crime. It's the ideal college town because of its rural setting, in that there are no real distractions other than those that are provided within the college campus." Of course, the small-town setting also means that "the only real off-campus activity is going out to eat at the town's quaint restaurants or going to the one bar in town," but fortunately "when it comes to on-campus activities, Middlebury provides the student population with tons of great events. Everything from classy music concerts to late-night movies and dance parties can be found as a Midd-supported activity. The student activity board does a fabulous job with entertaining the students virtually every day."

Student Body

"The typical [Middlebury] student is athletic, outdoorsy, and very intelligent." The two most prominent demographics are "very preppy students (popped collars)" and "extreme hippies." One undergrad explains: "The typical students are one of two types: either 'Polo, Nantucket red, pearls, and summers on the Cape,' or 'Birks, wool socks, granola, and suspicious smells about them.' A lot of people break these two molds, but they often fall somewhere on the spectrum between them." There's also "a huge international student population, which is awesome," but some international students, "tend to separate out and end up living in language houses." There's also "a really strong theater/artsy community" here. One student notes, "Other than a few groups, everyone mingles pretty well. We're all too damn friendly and cheerful for our own good."

THE PRINCETON REVIEW SAYS

Admissions

Very important factors considered include: Class rank, academic GPA, rigor of secondary school record, character/personal qualities, extracurricular activities, talent/ability. *Important factors considered include:* Application essay, recommendation(s), standardized test scores, racial/ethnic status. *Other factors considered include:* Alumni/ae relation, first generation, geographical residence, interview, level of applicant's interest, volunteer work, work experience. SAT and SAT Subject Tests or ACT required; High school diploma or equivalent is not required. *Academic units recommended:* 4 English, 4 mathematics, 3 science, (3 science labs), 4 foreign language, 3 social studies, 2 history, 1 academic electives, 1 fine arts, music, or drama.

Financial Aid

Students should submit: FAFSA, CSS/Financial Aid PROFILE, noncustodial PROFILE. Regular filing deadline is 2/1. The Princeton Review suggests that all financial aid forms be submitted as soon as possible after January 1. *Need-based scholarships/grants offered:* Federal Pell, SEOG, state scholarships/grants, private scholarships, the school's own gift aid. *Loan aid offered:* Federal Perkins, college/university loans from institutional funds. Applicants will be notified of awards on or about 4/1.

The Inside Word

Middlebury gives you options in standardized testing. The school will accept either the SAT or the ACT or three SAT Subject Tests, (the three must be in different subject areas, however). Middlebury is extremely competitive; improve your chances of admission by crafting a standardized test profile that shows you in the best possible light.

THE SCHOOL SAYS "…"

From The Admissions Office

"The successful Middlebury candidate excels in a variety of areas including academics, athletics, the arts, leadership, and service to others. These strengths and interests permit students to grow beyond their traditional 'comfort zones' and conventional limits. Our classrooms are as varied as the Green Mountains, the Metropolitan Museum of Art, or the great cities of Russia and Japan. Outside the classroom, students informally interact with professors in activities such as intramural basketball games and community service. At Middlebury, students develop critical-thinking skills, enduring bonds of friendship, and the ability to challenge themselves.

"Middlebury offers majors and programs in 45 different fields, with particular strengths in languages, international studies, environmental studies, literature and creative writing, and the sciences. Opportunities for engaging in individual research with faculty abound at Middlebury."

For even more information on this school, turn to page 508 of the "Stats" section.

MISERICORDIA UNIVERSITY

301 LAKE STREET, DALLAS, PA 18612 • ADMISSIONS: 570-674-6264 • FAX: 570-675-2441
E-MAIL: ADMISS@MISERICORDIA.EDU • WEBSITE: WWW.MISERICORDIA.EDU

RATINGS

Quality of Life: 83   Academic: 78   Admissions: 77   Financial Aid: 74

STUDENTS SAY ". . ."

Academics

"Misericordia is all about the health science majors," and given the school's well-regarded programs in nursing, physical therapy, and medical imaging it's easy to see why. Misericordia also boasts solid offerings in business and education, but it's truly the health sciences that grab most of the attention (and most of the students; one in three here graduate with a degree in the health sciences). Students warn that the programs "are very challenging" and that "the coursework is rigorous," but that "it all adds up in the end" to a highly marketable degree. "Hands-on experience taught by professionals in the field," resources that "are becoming increasingly more and more advanced in technology and equipment," and a dedicated faculty ("Many of our professors, even the part-time [teachers], stay late [and] come in on their days off...just to help even one student that is struggling.") are the hallmarks of a Misericordia education. All of this results in "a friendly, caring environment" that promotes success. Students also praise the school's "programs for internships and studying abroad," which they report "are becoming more and more important and popular."

Life

Life is "peaceful and relaxed" on the Misericordia campus. Some find it too peaceful, telling us that "there really are not things to do on the weekends." As a result, "a lot of students go home," and "the ones that stay here don't push for things to do...they just complain." The Office of Student Activities does its best, hosting "different activities throughout the year and on the weekend as much as they can. We have had mind readers, comedians, game nights, etc." The school also "offers programs to go white-water rafting, hiking, paddling, camping, and rock climbing." Sporting events draw decent crowds, and there are off-campus parties. Though hometown Dallas can be sleepy, "there's a lot to do" in nearby Wilkes-Barre, which "has two colleges" and so "is much more of a college town than Dallas." "Shuttle services go to the surrounding cities," making a car less of a necessity than at other schools.

Student Body

"The typical student is a white female" at Misericordia; students note that "the female-to-male ratio is very high." Undergrads tend to be "hard-working, dedicated, and committed to the four charismas that define our school: service, justice, hospitality, and mercy." "Despite your outward appearance, the person in front of you will always hold the door for you. That's just Mis students," undergrads here assure us. The school "is populated almost entirely by Caucasian, upper-middle-class students. While there is some socioeconomic diversity, there is little to no racial diversity, nor is there a strong LGBT community in any way."

THE PRINCETON REVIEW SAYS

Admissions

Very important factors considered include: Academic GPA, rigor of secondary school record. *Important factors considered include:* Class rank, standardized test scores. *Other factors considered include:* Application essay, recommendation(s), character/personal qualities, extracurricular activities, interview, racial/ethnic status, volunteer work, work experience. SAT or ACT required; TOEFL required of all international applicants. High school diploma is required and GED is accepted. *Academic units required:* 4 English, 4 mathematics, 4 science, 4 social studies.

Financial Aid

Students should submit: FAFSA, institution's own financial aid form Regular filing deadline is 5/1. The Princeton Review suggests that all financial aid forms be submitted as soon as possible after January 1. *Need-based scholarships/grants offered:* Federal Pell, SEOG, state scholarships/grants, private scholarships, the school's own gift aid, Federal Nursing Scholarships. *Loan aid offered:* Federal Perkins, Federal Nursing, state loans. Applicants will be notified of awards on a rolling basis beginning 3/15. Federal Work-Study Program available. Institutional employment available. Off-campus job opportunities are good.

The Inside Word

Prospective health sciences students have a higher hurdle to clear than do others at Misericordia. The good news is that Misericordia is set up to take a relatively large number of health sciences students; about one in three here graduate with a degree in the field. If your high school science grades aren't solid, be prepared to explain how that will change when you get to Misericordia.

THE SCHOOL SAYS " . . . "

From The Admissions Office

"Caring, motivated students get the attention they deserve and the quality education they seek. Although we're at a record level for undergraduate enrollment, classes are still kept small, often with as few as 10 students in advanced areas. Overall, the student/faculty ratio is 3:1, ensuring personalized attention. Students choose from 31 majors in three colleges. Some of the majors in high-demand careers include nursing, physical therapy, occupational therapy, biology (premed and pre-vet), and speech-language pathology as well as education, business, and sport management. And, MU offers a Guaranteed Career Placement program (GPP) that says MU will assure you a paid internship if you are not working in your chosen field or in graduate school within six months of earning your degree.

"We know you'll be challenged here; but at MU, you'll also find a supportive environment, one of the best in the nation. The National Survey of Student Engagement (NSSE) shows that our students perform better academically and are more satisfied. In fact, 91 percent of our freshmen found their overall experience to be good or excellent, so we know you'll feel right at home.

"At Misericordia, education also means socialization. We believe that there is life outside of the classroom and that those experiences are an integral part of a college education. MU has two-dozen clubs and social organizations. The Student Government Association sponsors a multitude of activities throughout the year, focused on student fun and involvement. As a Division III school, Misericordia competes in the Middle Atlantic Corporation (MAC) Freedom Conference. We currently have 20 men's and women's varsity sports."

For even more information on this school, turn to page 508 of the "Stats" section.

MOLLOY COLLEGE

1000 HEMPSTEAD AVENUE, ROCKVILLE CENTRE, NY 11570 • ADMISSIONS: 516-678-5000
FAX: 516-256-2247 • E-MAIL: ADMISSIONS@MOLLOY.EDU • WEBSITE: WWW.MOLLOY.EDU

RATINGS
Quality of Life: 62   **Academic:** 71   **Admissions:** 79   **Financial Aid:** 68

STUDENTS SAY "..."

Academics

At Molloy College, "a decently priced private school," students "love the small class sizes," and "Molloy is a close-knit school where students receive individual attention from professors." As with any school, "most people think about getting through their internships, assignments and finals." Located on Long Island in a town that's a "40-minute train ride from the city and 20-minute car ride from the beach," many of the students also appreciate Molloy's proximity to home. Another major draw is the "excellent nursing program" with professors "who really know what they are talking about since they are nurses with years of experience under their belts." Students also come to Molloy for other "strong major programs such as…education, criminal justice, and social work." Molloy's professors are "always accessible," and the administration "is constantly looking to improve life on campus." Though, a small school can mean "less of a variety of elective classes for students to choose from," students like that the smaller size of Molloy translates to a more "cozy campus." Also, it's easy to navigate as "everything is pretty much right there." Within this "warm and personal environment," the professors "are willing to help you accomplish [your] goals."

> **SURVEY SAYS ...**
> *Low cost of living*
> *Frats and sororities are unpopular or nonexistent*
> *Very little beer drinking*
> *Very little drug use*

Life

For some students, Molloy is "the small-knit community" that makes you "feel at home." At the traditional commuter college, students would like more parking options and are looking forward to the day when Molloy has more student lounges and builds dorms, but in the near future, "they do have plans to build dorms, so they're improving." In fact, the first dorm is expected in 2011, along with a major new student center. Still at Molloy, "weekends are pretty quiet," but when class is in session, students hang around "the Anselma room" "to eat lunch and do homework." Also, "many people enjoy going out for dinner or to a bar/lounge," and the student government "puts on many cool events for students to enjoy." Student athletes enjoy life at Molloy, "being on a team…makes you feel more connected [and] gives you confidence," and other students enjoy their role as spectators and "hang out for sports."

Student Body

"Your average commuter student…attends class and then drives home or straight to work," which can make making friends somewhat challenging, but one student says the simplest way to connect is simple, just "stick around after classes." Others recommend that students looking for a social outlet: "Join a club or organization." Some students feel that Molloy is "a continuation of high school" and "a little clique-y" as "most majors stick together," but others feel differently; "most students are involved in club activities or sports, but all in all, the majority of students are friendly." At Molloy, "there are students of all ages, and they interact differently," but "students who are working parents" "fit in well." Many students also share altruistic leanings and are "very dedicated to community service."

THE PRINCETON REVIEW SAYS

Admissions

Very important factors considered include: Academic GPA, rigor of secondary school record, standardized test scores. *Other factors considered include:* Class rank, application essay, recommendation(s), extracurricular activities, interview, talent/ability, volunteer work, work experience. SAT or ACT required; ACT with Writing component required. TOEFL required of all international applicants. High school diploma is required and GED is accepted. *Academic units required:* 4 English, 3 mathematics, 3 science, 3 foreign language, 4 social studies. *Academic units recommended:* 4 English, 4 mathematics, 4 science, 3 foreign language, 4 social studies.

Financial Aid

Students should submit: FAFSA, state aid form Regular filing deadline is 5/1. The Princeton Review suggests that all financial aid forms be submitted as soon as possible after January 1. *Need-based scholarships/grants offered:* Federal Pell, SEOG, state scholarships/grants, private scholarships, the school's own gift aid, Federal Nursing Scholarships. *Loan aid offered:* Federal Perkins, Federal Nursing. Applicants will be notified of awards on a rolling basis beginning 2/1. Federal Work-Study Program available. Off-campus job opportunities are good.

The Inside Word

Molloy looks for applicants who have completed core coursework in high school, but students who have not will still have their applications reviewed individually. Applicants can submit SAT or ACT scores. Acceptances are based on rolling admissions, and individual schools, like nursing majors or nuclear medicine majors, may have additional requirements in addition to what Molloy requires for general admission.

THE SCHOOL SAYS "..."

From The Admissions Office

"Molloy College is committed to the idea that education has the power to transform lives, for both our students and our community. Conveniently located in Rockville Centre, Long Island, Molloy offers students a unique, multidimensional educational experience. Our faculty is accomplished, yet approachable, leading small classes where students are encouraged to think critically and explore creatively.

"Whether it's participating in a music ensemble, writing for a campus publication, or serving as a student government representative, Molloy has something for each and every student. Through our Global-Learning Program, students study abroad in such exotic and enriching destinations as India, Thailand, France, Spain, Italy, and even Australia. For those who choose to combine sports with scholastic success, Molloy offers a number of winning programs while competing in the East Coast Conference of NCAA Division II.

"Molloy students have many exciting opportunities to "fast track" their careers. With dual bachelor's/master's degree programs in Accounting, Business Management, Criminal Justice, Education, and Music Therapy, Molloy students can complete a dual degree in five years. Students are also encouraged to become involved in a variety of Molloy-sponsored service projects.

"By reaching out to our students and our communities, Molloy has built a rich and diverse educational environment over the past 50+ years. One of the most affordable private colleges on Long Island, Molloy College helps students develop that all-important confidence, that strong, "I will" attitude that enables them to succeed in their careers, and more importantly, to make a difference in our world. For more information, call 516.678.5000 ext. 6230."

For even more information on this school, turn to page 509 of the "Stats" section.

MONMOUTH UNIVERSITY

ADMISSION, MONMOUTH UNIVERSITY, 400 CEDAR AVENUE, WEST LONG BRANCH, NJ 07764-1898
ADMISSIONS: 732-571-3456 • FAX: 732-263-5166 • E-MAIL: ADMISSION@MONMOUTH.EDU • WEBSITE: WWW.MONMOUTH.EDU

RATINGS
Quality of Life: 76   Academic: 72   Admissions: 79   Financial Aid: 68

STUDENTS SAY ". . ."

Academics

Monmouth University is "not a large university, but not a tiny one," the sort of place where you "can hang out with friends one day and meet a whole new crowd the next." It's big enough to qualify as "a diverse school with good academics, recognized extracurriculars, and impressive athletics," yet small enough that "students really get to build great academic relationships with their professors and get

> **SURVEY SAYS . . .**
> Great computer facilities
> Students love West Long Branch, NJ
> Great off-campus food
> Campus feels safe
> Hard liquor is popular

the attention and education that they need and deserve." Standout departments include communications, business (where most of the professors "have worked for companies prior to teaching so they have a lot of insight"), education, music, criminal justice, and premedical sciences. In all disciplines students must complete "an internship program—what we call the experiential education requirement—that really sets up students for life after college. Many of the students get hired by the people for whom they intern." If there's a drawback here, it's that the student body carries too much dead weight, such as students who "have no interest" in anything but the nearby beach and thus threaten to transform the school into "a post-high school country club." However, "for a student willing to commit himself, Monmouth is a great school. At the same time, it is easy for a student to get by doing marginal work. Basically, you get out of it what you put into it."

Life

Life at Monmouth University "is a totally unique experience for each person. Some people go home every weekend and hate it; others choose to get involved and love it. Personally, I chose the latter choice and couldn't be happier about it." One student reports, "when I'm not endlessly slaving away over my senior thesis, you can find me (or any student my age, really) spending time on the beach, shopping, enjoying my wonderful apartment in Pier Village, or frequenting any one of the local bars." The party scene is not what it once was here; one student reports that "Monmouth somehow still has the reputation as a 'party school,' which was true around 10 years ago, but not anymore." Students warn, "The MU police are extremely strict about alcohol consumption. Most parties on campus are busted by RAs or the police." As a result, "off-campus parties are popular. Not a lot of people go home on the weekends, but a good number go to different schools around here." Alternatively, "there is lots of nightlife around the area: Long Branch, Seaside Park, Sayreville, Red Bank, Belmar, etc. Lots of dance clubs allow girls 18 and over in with a small cover charge on select days of the week." Finally, "students often take weekend trips into the city (either New York or Philadelphia) by train or by car" when they want to get off campus.

Student Body

There's a lot of conspicuous wealth at Monmouth in the form of "various expensive cars in the parking lots" and "designer clothes and bags." Students are typically "very trendy," "extremely image-conscious," and "beautiful and very materialistic." Students "are very in tune with the latest fashion and technology trends." They tend to come from "New Jersey; Pennsylvania; or Staten Island or Long Island, New York. We are all from the suburbs and probably have the same family income." Monmouth's proximity to the beach attracts "many skaters and surfers" as well as "a lot of relaxed people."

THE PRINCETON REVIEW SAYS

Admissions

Very important factors considered include: Academic GPA, rigor of secondary school record, standardized test scores. *Important factors considered include:* Extracurricular activities, volunteer work, work experience. *Other factors considered include:* Application essay, recommendation(s), alumni/ae relation, character/personal qualities. SAT or ACT required; ACT with Writing component required. TOEFL required of all international applicants. High school diploma is required, and GED is accepted. *Academic units required:* 4 English, 3 mathematics, 2 science (1 science lab), 2 history, 5 academic electives. *Academic units recommended:* 2 foreign language, 2 social studies.

Financial Aid

Students should submit: FAFSA. Applications processed on a rolling basis. The Princeton Review suggests that all financial aid forms be submitted as soon as possible after January 1. *Need-based scholarships/grants offered:* Federal Pell, SEOG, state scholarships/grants, private scholarships, the school's own gift aid, Federal Nursing Scholarships. *Loan aid offered:* Direct Subsidized Stafford, Direct Unsubsidized Stafford, Direct PLUS, Federal Perkins, state loans, college/university loans from institutional funds, other, alternative loans. Applicants will be notified of awards on a rolling basis beginning 2/15. Federal Work-Study Program available. Institutional employment available. Off-campus job opportunities are good.

Inside Word

B students with slightly above-average SAT or ACT scores should find little impediment to gaining admission to Monmouth. The school's national stature is on the rise, resulting in a more competitive applicant base, but Monmouth must still compete with many heavy hitters for top regional students.

THE SCHOOL SAYS "…"

From The Admissions Office

"Monmouth University offers a well-rounded but bold academic environment with plenty of opportunities— personal, professional, and social. Monmouth graduates are poised for success and prepared to assume leadership roles in their chosen professions, because the university invests in students beyond the classroom.

"Monmouth emphasizes hands-on learning, while providing exceptional undergraduate and graduate degree programs. There are programs for medical scholars, honors students, marine scientists, software engineers, teachers, musicians, broadcast producers, and more. Faculty members are lively participants in the education of their students. These teacher/scholars, dedicated to excellence, are often recognized experts in their fields. Students may be in a class with no more than 35 students (half of Monmouth's classes have fewer than 21 students) learning from qualified professors who know each student by name.

"Monmouth recognizes its students are the energy of its campus. The Monmouth community celebrates student life with cultural events, festivals, active student clubs, and organizations that reflect the school's spirit. Athletics play a big part in campus life. A well-established member of the NCAA Division I, Monmouth athletics is a rising tide supported by some of the best fans in the Northeast.

"The president of Monmouth University, Paul G. Gaffney II, believes the reputation of the university starts with the achievements and successes of its students. At Monmouth, students find the support and guidance needed to make their mark in the world."

For even more information on this school, turn to page 509 of the "Stats" section.

MOORE COLLEGE OF ART & DESIGN

TWENTIETH STREET AND THE PARKWAY, PHILADELPHIA, PA 19103-1179 • ADMISSIONS: 215-965-4014 • FAX: 215-568-3547
E-MAIL: ENROLL@MOORE.EDU • WEBSITE: WWW.MOORE.EDU

RATINGS
Quality of Life: 73   Academic: 82   Admissions: 77   Financial Aid: 68

STUDENTS SAY "..."

Academics

"Moore is all about giving women in the arts the technical skill and empowerment to lead and succeed in their professional careers," students here say. "The small size of the school" and "the all-women experience" are a big draw, as are "great employment opportunities through the very active career center." While some students say "academic

> ### SURVEY SAYS . . .
> *Students love Philadelphia, PA*
> *Intercollegiate sports are unpopular or nonexistent*
> *Intramural sports are unpopular or nonexistent*
> *Frats and sororities are unpopular or nonexistent*

teachers can be hit-or-miss," students almost unanimously agree their "studio teachers are out of this world." These "real artists" facilitate "hands-on learning," and "go out of their way to write recommendations [and] help find jobs," and "are truly there because they love to teach and enjoy their students." Students warn, however, "The work is hard and if you don't keep up, it's even harder to pull yourself out of the hole." Opinion of the administration is mixed: "We need a better food service, more studios, nicer classrooms," a piqued sophomore declares. A more even-handed student avers: "When it comes to individual problems or concerns, they are usually very helpful."

Life

"Don't plan on having much of a life during the school year," Moore students warn. Schoolwork looms large in their lives to the point that one has "nightmares about school and unfinished projects." Less-stressed students take a more organic view of their course load. "The work is diverse and challenging," a 3-D design major writes. "Every day I am opening up my creative self and finding out where it is I want to be in the art world." When students don't have homework, which, they caution, is not often, they "do lots of things. They go out and drink, go to open galleries, go to parties, draw on sidewalks with chalk, and just hang out." There are also "plenty of leisure activities organized by the administration or other students, such as movie nights, relaxation therapy nights (usually toward finals time), trips out and around the Philadelphia area, [and] shopping trips."

Student Body

"The group of women who make up Moore's student body is so diverse for such a small community that I could never pinpoint a stereotypical Moore girl," a sophomore writes. "Each girl is very unique in personality and creativity." Students tell us there are "many different cultures and sexual orientations represented" on campus. While some say "you can tell the design students from the art students," "most art students dress down to go to class and are ready to get dirty and work into their art," while "the design students usually dress up to go to class and are a bit more trendy and appearance-conscious"—students across the board agree "it's an art school, we are all atypical." What's the quality that binds Moore students? "They are up for the challenge," a senior writes. A freshman adds, "We are all a little wacky, especially around finals and big project times."

THE PRINCETON REVIEW SAYS

Admissions

Very important factors considered include: Academic GPA, rigor of secondary school record, standardized test scores, character/personal qualities, interview, level of applicant's interest, talent/ability. *Important factors considered include:* Application essay, recommendation(s), extracurricular activities. *Other factors considered include:* Class rank, volunteer work, work experience. SAT recommended; TOEFL required of all international applicants. High school diploma is required and GED is accepted.

Financial Aid

Students should submit: FAFSA. The Princeton Review suggests that all financial aid forms be submitted as soon as possible after January 1. *Need-based scholarships/grants offered:* Federal Pell, SEOG, state scholarships/grants, private scholarships, the school's own gift aid *Loan aid offered:* Federal Perkins, other, alternative loans. Applicants will be notified of awards on a rolling basis beginning 2/15. Federal Work-Study Program available. Off-campus job opportunities are good.

The Inside Word

In lieu of submitting a traditional portfolio with their application, Moore applicants may attend the school's Summer Art and Design Institute (SADI), a four-week program in portfolio development and basic art skills, upon completion of their junior or senior year of high school. Applicants who wish to be considered for SADI must submit a sample of their artwork and a written request to the school's Director of Admissions.

THE SCHOOL SAYS "…"

From The Admissions Office

"Moore College of Art & Design offers 10 arts and design majors leading to a Bachelor of Fine Arts degree. Choose to major in textile design, fashion design, fine arts (with a 2D or 3D emphasis), graphic design, illustration, art education, art history, interior design, curatorial studies and photography and digital arts.

"Each BFA program is designed to nurture students' creative talents and give them the hands-on technical and professional skills essential to building a successful career in fine arts, design, art history, and art education.

"Learn from award-winning, professionally active faculty who bring real-world knowledge and expertise into the classroom, and encourage excellence, exploration, and self-expression. Problem solving, critical thinking, self-confidence, risk taking and creativity all are stressed throughout the BFA curriculum, with the goal of preparing students for lifelong learning and leadership in their chosen field.

"We encourage you to call our admissions office. We are all very excited to hear from you and to assist you throughout the admissions process. Admissions counselors are available to speak with you during regular business hours. We invite you to come visit our campus to experience firsthand the uniqueness of an education at Moore College of Art & Design, which is the best way to find out if it is the right place for you."

For even more information on this school, turn to page 510 of the "Stats" section.

MORAVIAN COLLEGE

1200 MAIN ST., BETHLEHEM, PA 18018 • ADMISSIONS: 800-441-3191 • FAX: 610-625-7930
FINANCIAL AID: 610-861-1330 • E-MAIL: ADMISSIONS@MORAVIAN.EDU • WEBSITE: WWW.MORAVIAN.EDU

RATINGS
Quality of Life: 83   **Academic:** 83   **Admissions:** 79   **Financial Aid:** 74

STUDENTS SAY "..."

Academics

For those students seeking a place where "everybody knows your name," take a look at Moravian College, a tiny school in eastern Pennsylvania that offers the "liberal arts experience," using a "well-rounded education to mold a well-rounded individual." This "outwardly modest institution" disguises a solid academic environment that is "more geared toward learning rather than just getting good grades on tests," which, combined with the cozy community feel of the surroundings, provides the "perfect peaceful atmosphere for studying and socializing." One student, commenting on the school's relatively low weekend retention rate, describes the school as "Camp Moravian—a lot of people may go home, but those who stay behind have a lot more fun."

> **SURVEY SAYS . . .**
> Great computer facilities
> Great library
> Low cost of living
> Students are happy

For the most part, Moravian's "fairly forgiving" professors "are engaging and provide students with challenging questions concerning the real world." Their availability and willingness to help students understand the material gets praise all around, as does their demeanor; more than one student tells of being invited into a teacher's home for dinner. "Students are able to get the individual attention they need," says one. However, this doesn't mean that there aren't a few points that need to be worked on: "All of my professors are intelligent, but not all of them are meant to be teachers," says one freshman. A few students express some discontent with the administration's level of involvement, but the "college president is a regular fixture on campus," and he "can be seen eating in the student café or sitting on a bench outside the academic building." Though most find the registration process "archaic," the academic advising system helps keep students on track in their course selection.

Life

With such a small undergrad enrollment, students get to know each other's business pretty easily and quickly, and most see this as a positive thing, listing "the chance for strong relationships" as one of the school's greatest strengths. Hanging out with friends, video games, and cards seems to be a pretty big part of relaxing at Moravian, and "there are a lot of different groups and clubs on campus that also plan activities for the rest of the student body to be part of." Almost everything necessary to amuse oneself in this "safe and nurturing environment" is "within walking distance," making it easy to go check out the events offered by the school, such as "movies every week and comedians a few times a semester," and Moravian runs Friday mall trips for those needing supplies. The soccer field and basketball arena are located in the center of the campus, "which makes it easy to attend the home games," and the school has such a wonderful music program that "the recitals are worth checking out, even if you're not a music major." A Greek scene is present on campus but not in an overwhelming way, so that "if you are looking for a party, you can find one. If you are not into the party scene, that's fine."

Student Body

"I'm not going to lie, Moravian's a very white school," confesses a student. Most of the students are from "Pennsylvania, New Jersey, or New York" and come from middle-to-upper-class homes, though "not many people question the economic situations of others." There is, at least, some diversity at Moravian (the "Multicultural Club is one of the best clubs on campus"), and the students that make up this "close-knit community" are a "very open group of people" in how they relate to atypical students. Since there is a separate campus devoted to art and music, there tends to be a fair number of "artsy" students on the south campus to balance out the healthy portion of student athletes that populate mainly the north campus.

THE PRINCETON REVIEW SAYS

Admissions

Very important factors considered include: Class rank, academic GPA, rigor of secondary school record, alumni/ae relation, character/personal qualities. *Important factors considered include:* Application essay, recommendation(s), standardized test scores, extracurricular activities, first generation, level of applicant's interest, racial/ethnic status, talent/ability, volunteer work. *Other factors considered include:* geographical residence, interview, work experience. SAT or ACT required; ACT with Writing component required. TOEFL required of all international applicants. High school diploma is required, and GED is accepted. *Academic units required:* 4 English, 3 mathematics, 3 science, (2 science labs), 2 foreign language, 4 social studies. *Academic units recommended:* 4 mathematics, 3 foreign language.

Financial Aid

Students should submit: FAFSA, Moravian College Financial Aid Application, CSS/Financial Aid PROFILE. Regular filing deadline is 3/15. The Princeton Review suggests that all financial aid forms be submitted as soon as possible after January 1. *Need-based scholarships/grants offered:* Federal Pell, SEOG, state scholarships/grants, the school's own gift aid. *Loan aid offered:* Federal Perkins. Applicants will be notified of awards on or about 4/1.

The Inside Word

Moravian is a small liberal arts school with all the bells and whistles. Applicants will find a pretty straightforward admissions process—solid grades and test scores are required. Counselors will look closely to find the extras—community service, extracurricular activities—that make students stand out from the crowd. Moravian has many programs that should not be overlooked, including music, education, and the sciences.

THE SCHOOL SAYS "..."

From The Admissions Office

"Founded in 1742, Moravian is proud of its history as one of the oldest and most respected liberal arts colleges. Students find a supportive environment for self-discovery and academic achievement that nurtures their capacity for leadership, lifelong learning, and positive societal contributions. Moravian enrolls students from a variety of socioeconomic, religious, racial, and ethnic backgrounds. Providing a highly personalized learning experience, the College offers opportunities for students to direct their education toward individual and professional goals. Students are encouraged to collaborate with faculty on original research, pursue honors projects, independent work, internships, and field study. Moravian recently produced 7 Fulbright scholars, a Goldwater scholar, a Rhodes finalist, a Truman Scholarship finalist, and 3 NCAA postgraduate scholars.

"Facilities range from historic to modern, with a $20 million academic complex featuring current educational technology, at the heart of the Main Street Campus. The College recently completed a new residence hall on its historic Hurd Campus. The $25 million project houses approximately 230 students, contains classrooms, and other learning spaces that support the academic and co-curricular mission of the College. The Leadership Center fosters student leadership qualities and skills. Moravian encourages the complete college experience for mind, body, and spirit. Its robust varsity sports program has produced nationally ranked women's softball and track teams, and All-American student athletes—including several Olympic hopefuls—in many sports. Athletes complete on a state-of-the-art synthetic multi-sport field and the eight-lane Olympic track."

For even more information on this school, turn to page 510 of the "Stats" section.

MOUNT HOLYOKE COLLEGE

50 COLLEGE STREET, SOUTH HADLEY, MA 01075 • ADMISSIONS: 413-538-2023 • FAX: 413-538-2409
FINANCIAL AID: 413-538-2291 • E-MAIL: ADMISSIONS@MTHOLYOKE.EDU • WEBSITE: WWW.MTHOLYOKE.EDU

RATINGS
Quality of Life: 88　　**Academic:** 98　　**Admissions:** 95　　**Financial Aid:** 97

STUDENTS SAY "..."

Academics

Mount Holyoke "is a rigorous all women's college that prepares its students to become the leaders of tomorrow by
encouraging them to pursue their passions in a safe, comfortable, and challenging environment," undergrads at this
small, prestigious, liberal arts school tell us. Biology, chemistry, the humanities, and international studies are among
the strong suits of the school; in nearly all disciplines, professors "are highly respected in their fields, many of them
being very prominent figures among their respective academic communities" who are also "very kind; excited to

impart their knowledge; very, very accessible outside of class; and willing to spend a lot of time helping individual students." They aren't pushovers, though; "Despite their overall generosity, they hold every student to a very
high academic standard (no grade inflation here), and the material covered in each course is always challenging
and of high academic caliber." Students may supplement their curricula with classes at other area colleges through
the Five College Consortium, but they do say that the consortium is "very underused."

Life

"People are very focused on their academics, sometimes too much so" at Mount Holyoke, and "Much of our time
is dedicated to class work." Undergrads typically find time for the "fabulous traditions that help to define"
school life, such as "milk and cookies in the evening (a snack put out by dining services at 9:30 on school nights)
and class colors and mascots." Otherwise, "Mount Holyoke life is what you make of it. We are an all women's
college, but that doesn't mean you are going off to a convent. It is easy to have a social life through the Five
College Consortium, and it is easy to go into Boston or New York." Also, "people are active in clubs and sports,
and they hang out in the common areas or on the green with friends," and "there are many on-campus events,
such as speakers, movie screenings, etc. to keep anyone busy." The campus itself "is so beautiful...between the
foliage, the classic brick buildings, and the well kept landscape of the college, I was in love!" Off-campus life
offers "movie theaters and restaurants, as well as parties at the other four colleges." Hometown South Hadley
"is admittedly not the most happening town ever (to put it mildly)," but Amherst and Northhampton—which
are "great for eating, shopping, and anything else imaginable"—"are only a free bus ride away."

Student Body

The Mount Holyoke student body "is extremely diverse, from ethnicity to race to religion to sexual orientation to
individual interests. However, the community works as a whole because of the common interest in academics and
openness of the students who attend." If there is a "typical" student, it's one who "is female and academically
motivated," undergrads tell us. Students are also typically "very aware of world issues, politically active, and
open-minded," "very concerned about grades and jobs," and, perhaps, "overly politically correct." Among the
subpopulations that stand out, "The most visible opposites are the 'pearls and cardigans,' the 'Carhartts and
piercings' types, and the hippies. There are a ton of people, however, who are somewhere in between those."

THE PRINCETON REVIEW SAYS

Admissions

Very important factors considered include: Class rank, application essay, academic GPA, recommendation(s), rigor of secondary school record. *Important factors considered include:* Character/personal qualities, extracurricular activities, first generation, interview, talent/ability, volunteer work, work experience. *Other factors considered include:* Standardized test scores, alumni/ae relation, geographical residence, level of applicant's interest, racial/ethnic status, TOEFL required of all international applicants. High school diploma is required, and GED is accepted. *Academic units recommended:* 4 English, (3 science labs), 3 history, 1 academic electives.

Financial Aid

Students should submit: FAFSA, CSS/Financial Aid PROFILE, noncustodial PROFILE, business/farm supplement. Regular filing deadline is 3/1. The Princeton Review suggests that all financial aid forms be submitted as soon as possible after January 1. *Need-based scholarships/grants offered:* Federal Pell, SEOG, state scholarships/grants, private scholarships, the school's own gift aid. *Loan aid offered:* Direct Subsidized Stafford, Direct Unsubsidized Stafford, Direct PLUS, Federal Perkins, state loans, college/university loans from institutional funds. Applicants will be notified of awards on or about 4/1. Federal Work-Study Program available. Institutional employment available. Off-campus job opportunities are fair.

The Inside Word

Mount Holyoke has seen a 30 percent increase in the size of its applicant pool in the last decade, allowing what was already a selective institution to become a highly selective one. Matchmaking is a significant factor here; strong academic performance, well written essays, and an understanding of and appreciation for "the Mount Holyoke experience" will usually carry the day.

THE SCHOOL SAYS "..."

From The Admissions Office

"The majority of students who choose Mount Holyoke do so simply because it is an outstanding liberal arts college. After a semester or two, they start to appreciate the fact that Mount Holyoke is a women's college, even though most Mount Holyoke students never thought they'd go to a women's college when they started their college search. Students talk of having 'space' to really figure out who they are. They speak about feeling empowered to excel in traditionally male subjects such as science and technology. They talk about the remarkable array of opportunities—for academic achievement, career exploration, and leadership—and the impressive, creative accomplishments of their peers. If you're looking for a college that will challenge you to be your best, most powerful self and to fulfill your potential, Mount Holyoke should be at the top of your list.

"Submission of standardized test scores is optional for most applicants to Mount Holyoke College. However, the TOEFL is required of students for whom English is not their primary language, and the SAT Subject tests are required for homeschooled students."

For even more information on this school, turn to page 511 of the "Stats" section.

MUHLENBERG COLLEGE

2400 WEST CHEW STREET, ALLENTOWN, PA 18104-5596 • ADMISSIONS: 484-664-3200 • FAX: 484-664-3234
FINANCIAL AID: 484-664-3175 • E-MAIL: ADMISSION@MUHLENBERG.EDU • WEBSITE: WWW.MUHLENBERG.EDU

RATINGS
Quality of Life: 78   Academic: 86   Admissions: 94   Financial Aid: 91

STUDENTS SAY ". . ."

Academics

A small, liberal arts school with a decidedly friendly touch, Muhlenberg College encourages a spirit of community between students, faculty, and staff. Muhlenberg professors are "warm, willing to talk, and really nice," giving students the confidence, resources, and opportunities they seek in an undergraduate education. A senior enthuses, "If you take

> **SURVEY SAYS . . .**
> Athletic facilities are great
> Students are friendly
> Low cost of living
> Theater is popular

advantage of it, you can get close with your professors, do independent work, and pave your own way in preparation for whatever you want to eventually do or become." A student in the pre-medical program adds, "The science classes are very difficult, but there are a lot of resources, such as workshops, tutoring, recitations, and meeting with the professor personally." While academics are challenging, they aren't so rigorous student don't have time for a well-balanced lifestyle. A junior explains, "Muhlenberg allows me to take a full course load each semester while still giving me time to have a job, have a social life, and be connected with the organizations with which I want to be affiliated, in a comfortable and close-knit setting." Things tend to run smoothly, and "the administrators have reached a balanced approach where they are not visible in everyday activities but are clearly in control." At the same time, many students say they've had the opportunity to brush elbows with the school's top administrators. A freshman remembers, "I couldn't believe it when, during the first week of classes, President Helm sat down with my friends and me at brunch and asked us how our first week was going."

Life

Academics are taken seriously, but personal life and extracurricular activities are also an important part of the experience at Muhlenberg College. A sophomore explains, "Academically, Muhlenberg can be rigorous at times, depending on what you place on yourself, but activities outside the classroom are also given a lot of emphasis, so it's not like all you're ever doing is studying." On campus, students participate in intramural sports, attend campus events, or join student clubs. In addition, "all of the sports teams have games nonstop." In dorms, in the suites, in the fraternity houses, or off-campus, "parties are commonplace on the weekends." At the same time, students reassure us "partying happens very often on and off campus, but it is rarely out of control like on bigger campuses." A senior adds, "People definitely work hard here, but then we let loose on the weekends. Saturdays aren't big study days, but Sunday nights in the library are packed." Although first-year students are not allowed to have cars, "there's a shopping center within walking distance," as well as "a shuttle service that will drive students to any place in Allentown, such as the bowling alley, movies, mall, ice skating rink, mini golf, and restaurants." At the same time, students remind us Allentown doesn't offer a multitude of social options for college students. For more cosmopolitan options, the school's location between New York and Philadelphia is unbeatable.

Student Body

Muhlenberg is a patently "friendly campus" where everyone finds a niche and "people smile at you as you walk by them." The overwhelming majority of undergraduates hail from middle-class, suburban families in New Jersey, Long Island, or Pennsylvania, creating a "fairly homogeneous" student body. Preppy is the dominant dress code, though there is also a big group of "artsy, theater-type students" who come to participate in the school's excellent theater program. Fortunately, "the Muhlenberg community is extremely accommodating to all types of students," and varying interests and lifestyles are represented and accepted. A student attests, "Typical students are usually white and middle-class, however, there is a great amount of diversity with people of different religious backgrounds, social backgrounds, and sexual orientations." Adds another, "At first glance we appear to be a very homogeneous campus, but upon closer inspection and by personal experience, it is clear the student body is diverse and is very accepting of that diversity."

THE PRINCETON REVIEW SAYS

Admissions

Very important factors considered include: academic GPA, rigor of secondary school record. *Important factors considered include:* application essay, recommendation(s), standardized test scores, character/personal qualities, extracurricular activities, interview, talent/ability. *Other factors considered include:* class rank, alumni/ae relation, first generation, level of applicant's interest, racial/ethnic status, volunteer work, work experience. ACT with Writing component recommended. TOEFL required of all international applicants. High school diploma is required, and GED is accepted. *Academic units required:* 4 English, 3 mathematics, 2 science, 2 foreign language, 2 history. *Academic units recommended:* 4 English, 4 mathematics, 3 science, 4 foreign language, 2 social studies, 3 history,

Financial Aid

Students should submit: FAFSA, institution's own financial aid form, CSS/Financial Aid PROFILE, noncustodial PROFILE Regular filing deadline is 2/15. The Princeton Review suggests that all financial aid forms be submitted as soon as possible after January 1. *Need-based scholarships/grants offered:* Federal Pell, SEOG, state scholarships/grants, private scholarships, the school's own gift aid. *Loan aid offered:* Federal Perkins, Other, Private. Applicants will be notified of awards on or about 4/1. Federal Work-Study Program available. Institutional employment available. Off-campus job opportunities are excellent.

The Inside Word

Muhlenberg College accepts only the Common Application and does not require any supplemental essays, unless you are applying early decision. Muhlenberg is also part of a growing group of colleges that do not require SAT scores or other standardized tests for admission. Students who do not submit test scores are required to appear for an admissions interview and to submit a graded essay from their junior or senior year in high school.

THE SCHOOL SAYS "..."

From The Admissions Office

"Listening to our own students, we've learned that most picked Muhlenberg mainly because it has a long-standing reputation for being academically demanding on one hand but personally supportive on the other. We expect a lot from our students, but we also expect a lot from ourselves in providing the challenge and support they need to stretch, grow, and succeed. It's not unusual for professors to put their home phone numbers on the course syllabus and encourage students to call them at home with questions. Upperclassmen are helpful to underclassmen. 'We really know about collegiality here,' says an alumna who now works at Muhlenberg. 'It's that kind of place.' The supportive atmosphere and strong work ethic produce lots of successes. The premed and pre-law programs are very strong, as are programs in theater arts, English, psychology, the sciences, business, and accounting. 'When I was a student here,' recalls Dr. Walter Loy, now a professor emeritus of physics, 'we were encouraged to live life to its fullest, to do our best, to be honest, to deal openly with others, and to treat everyone as an individual. Those are important things, and they haven't changed at Muhlenberg.'

"Students have the option of submitting SAT or ACT scores (including the Writing sections) or submitting a graded paper with teacher's comments and grade on it from junior or senior year and interviewing with a member of the admissions staff."

For even more information on this school, turn to page 511 of the "Stats" section.

NAZARETH COLLEGE

4245 EAST AVENUE, ROCHESTER, NY 14618-3790 • ADMISSIONS: 585-389-2860 • FAX: 585-389-2826
E-MAIL: ADMISSIONS@NAZ.EDU • WEBSITE: WWW.NAZ.EDU

RATINGS
Quality of Life: 93   **Academic:** 83   **Admissions:** 84   **Financial Aid:** 74

STUDENTS SAY "..."

Academics

Nazareth College is "a very personalized school" in the suburbs, "about 10 miles from downtown Rochester, New York." "Education is a huge degree program" and there are quite a few physical therapy and nursing majors. Naz is also great for theater and music. "All of their productions are always spectacular," gushes a sophomore. "I constantly feel like I'm watching a Broadway show whenever I go see one." The academic pace is reasonable. "I would say that our academic program is rigorous but not mental-illness inducing," suggests an English literature major. "I count this as a strength." "Most of the professors are a lot of fun, and they try to make classes interesting. Plus, they take the time to get to know you personally, which is great." "Professors care about how you are doing," declares a nursing major. "You are not just a number." Course selection is limited but classes are wonderfully small. "The administration loves student feedback" and receives generally glowing reviews. Nazareth's president frequently walks around campus and greets students. "I think Naz is doing a fine job," proffers a sophomore.

Life

Students here enjoy an "absolutely gorgeous" campus. The residence halls "are very comfortable and quite spacious," and they offer free laundry machines. Socially, there is no Greek system, but the student activities council does a fantastic job of having activities planned." Some of these activities are "lame events," but many are widely attended. Intramural and varsity sports are also reasonably big. The surrounding town is a little hamlet right on the Erie Canal "with fun shops and places to eat." "Pittsford, as a town, is very safe and very nice to walk around in," says one student. However, if you attend Nazareth, you probably want to bring a vehicle with you. "Everyone has a car. It's like a requirement," warns a sophomore. "If you want to find a party, you (usually) can." Older students often frequent the bars and clubs of downtown Rochester for fun. However, "some weekends are slow," and "Nazareth is definitely not a big party school." Road trips are common. "Nazareth isn't really far from anywhere, which makes other colleges, towns, and locations easy to access." Some students also go home on more than a few weekends.

Student Body

"The typical student at Nazareth is a white girl from suburbia"—usually somewhere around Buffalo, Rochester, or Syracuse. Students at Naz are "concerned about their grades." "The same kids you see drunk on Saturday night at the bars are the kids working hard in the library all Sunday." They are a little on the cliquey side but "very friendly," too. "There are a few jerks, but nobody likes them, anyway," says one student. "Students here tend to be very liberal." "There are many preppy and sports-oriented people." "There are a lot of artsy and intellectuals," too. "And there are, of course, your weirdoes, but that's normal." There is apparently a notable contingent of gay males as well, "though more straight men are attending as they realize that they have a big sea to fish in."

Admissions

Very important factors considered include: class rank, application essay, academic GPA, recommendation(s), rigor of secondary school record. *Important factors considered include:* Character/personal qualities, extracurricular activities, geographical residence, interview, level of applicant's interest, racial/ethnic status, state residency, talent/ability, volunteer work, work experience. *Other factors considered include:* Standardized test scores if submitted (Nazareth is test-optional), alumni/ae relation, first generation, TOEFL required of all international applicants. High school diploma is required, and GED is accepted. *Academic units required:* 4 English, 3 mathematics, 3 science, (2 science labs), 3 foreign language, 3 social studies. *Academic units recommended:* 4 English, 4 mathematics, 4 science, 4 foreign language, 4 social studies.

Financial Aid

Students should submit: FAFSA. Priority filing deadline is 2/15. The Princeton Review suggests that all financial aid forms be submitted as soon as possible after January 1. *Need-based scholarships/grants offered:* Federal Pell, SEOG, state scholarships/grants, private scholarships, the school's own gift aid. *Loan aid offered:* Federal Perkins. Applicants will be notified of awards on a rolling basis beginning 2/1. Federal Work-Study Program available. Institutional employment available. Off-campus job opportunities are excellent.

The Inside Word

Admissions Officers at Nazareth College are looking for candidates who will enhance the college community as a whole. This means that a special talent in athletics, music, the arts, or leadership areas counts; it can be especially helpful to candidates whose academic records are less than exemplary.

THE SCHOOL SAYS "..."

From The Admissions Office

"Growing interest in Nazareth—applications have grown 25 percent in five years—is a result of many factors. New facilities have increased and improved academic, performing arts, residential, and athletic spaces. Major offerings now include music/business, international business, communication and rhetoric, and music theatre. Nazareth has worked diligently to keep tuition at $5,000 less than the New York State average for private colleges. Our track record is strong—retention and graduation rates exceed national averages; 75 percent of our students participate in a career-related internship with 93 percent of them citing this a very worthwhile experience; and 93 percent of our students are employed or in graduate school within one year of graduation. The College has produced 12 Fulbright scholars and six faculty Fulbrights, in the past decade alone, along with two Thomas R. Pickering Graduate Foreign Affairs Fellowships. The Center for International Education has developed more opportunities for our students to study abroad and for international students to study at Nazareth. With civic engagement and service learning as hallmarks of the Nazareth experience, 91 percent of undergrads participate in community service while at Nazareth. A proactive approach to campus security and state-of-the-art emergency notification system places Nazareth ahead of the curve regarding student safety. Student athletes, veterans of conference and national championships, have one of the highest graduation rates among NCAA Division III institutions. The Nazareth College Arts Center brings an international roster of performing art companies to campus, and provides high-quality facilities for student productions."

For even more information on this school, turn to page 511 of the "Stats" section.

NEUMANN COLLEGE

ONE NEUMANN DRIVE, ASTON, PA 19014 • ADMISSIONS: 610-558-5616 • FAX: 610-558-5652
E-MAIL: NEUMANN@NEUMANN.EDU • WEBSITE: WWW.NEUMANN.EDU

RATINGS
Quality of Life: 78   **Academic:** 70   **Admissions:** 73   **Financial Aid:** 82

STUDENTS SAY ". . ."

> **SURVEY SAYS . . .**
> *Different types of students interact*
> *Students get along with local community*
> *Frats and sororities are unpopular or nonexistent*

Academics

Neumann College, a small Catholic school outside of Philadelphia, specializes in providing undergraduates with "a personalized educational atmosphere based on Christian beliefs and moral values." The curriculum "emphasizes respect for individuals, concern for the environment, and social responsibility." Students praise "the service-learning that is stressed because this is a Franciscan school." As a result, "the volunteer opportunities and events held on this campus are remarkable." So, too, are academic offerings in nursing, education, communications, and criminal justice, as well as "one of the best" sports management programs in the region. No matter what you study here, you're sure to find "every professor and administrator in the Neumann College community is so friendly and very approachable." In particular, Neumann "is great for students who do not want huge lecture classes" that might be more common at bigger schools. Professors "go the extra mile to help in any way," and "the Academic Resource Center offers free tutoring in all subjects."

Life

You'll find a "quiet environment" at Neumann. The campus is dry, and residence halls are "strict with alcohol," so there are "no big parties" on campus. Students admit, "it does get a little boring"—so much so that many of "those living on campus leave on the weekends." Others head to "parties off campus" or simply enjoy "hanging out with friends" in the dorms. The Student Activities Board "offers a good amount of events for students to have some fun on campus," including novelty nights, dances, and black-light volleyball. Hockey games are also extremely popular. "There are shuttles to the rink for games," so students don't have to worry about driving or parking. In addition, "the school provides transportation to the malls and other places." Still, many here feel "having a car is a must" because "there is not much to do in the immediate area surrounding the college." There is, however, "a lot to do within a 15- to 30-minute drive off campus" including "three malls, a number of movie theaters, clubs, [and] bars."

Student Body

"Most of Neumann's population"—two-thirds, to be precise—"is girls." The same proportion of the school belongs to the Roman Catholic Church, and "a lot of the students here are religious." Men and non-Catholics need not worry about fitting in here, though. At Neumann, "Everyone is friendly and gets along." There is a 16 percent minority population, a sizable non-traditional student group, and, as the years pass, "the campus is growing more and more diverse." Fortunately, "It's easy to make friends," and a friendly vibe pervades the school. It's the kind of place where "students hold doors open for you. Even if you are steps away from the door, they wait until you get there."

Admissions

Very important factors considered include: Recommendation(s), rigor of secondary school record, extracurricular activities, talent/ability. *Important factors considered include:* Class rank, standardized test scores, alumni/ae relation, character/personal qualities, interview, level of applicant's interest. *Other factors considered include:* Application essay, racial/ethnic status, religious affiliation/commitment, volunteer work, SAT or ACT required; TOEFL required of all international applicants. High school diploma is required and GED is accepted. *Academic units required:* 4 English, 2 mathematics, 2 science, 2 foreign language, 2 social studies, 4 academic electives. *Academic units recommended:* 4 English, 2 mathematics, 3 science, 2 foreign language, 2 social studies, 4 academic electives.

Financial Aid

Students should submit: FAFSA. The Princeton Review suggests that all financial aid forms be submitted as soon as possible after January 1. *Need-based scholarships/grants offered:* Federal Pell, SEOG, state scholarships/grants, private scholarships, the school's own gift aid, Federal Nursing Scholarships. *Loan aid offered:* Direct Subsidized Stafford, Direct Unsubsidized Stafford, Direct PLUS, Federal Nursing. Applicants will be notified of awards on a rolling basis beginning 3/1. Federal Work-Study Program available. Off-campus job opportunities are excellent.

The Inside Word

Neumann College delivers an environment that fosters personal and academic development. The admissions team seeks students who will take advantage of this setting and tends to favor applicants who demonstrate a high degree of potential. The ideal candidate desires a learning experience based on Catholic tenets.

THE SCHOOL SAYS "…"

From The Admissions Office

"Neumann College offers the ideal educational setting. As a small college, it provides students with the personal attention and support they seek. Dedicated faculty teach and assist our students in developing their thinking, writing, communication, and technical skills. As a Catholic college in the Franciscan tradition, Neumann College supports the spiritual, social, and athletic development of students. Neumann College's academic majors most often include experiential components, allowing students to blend classroom study and real work experiences. Neumann College graduates are well on their way to career advancement, having benefited from a tailored curriculum, personal advisement, support, and field experiences that offer them the competitive edge. Freshmen begin career exploration right away through the Academic Resource and Career Counseling Center.

"Campus life is a real strength of Neumann College. Three new suite-style residence halls are home to almost 800 residents. Residence halls are totally wired. Designed to offer the advantage of living in a community while supporting privacy and independence, the living-learning centers combine academic space and recreational, health, and fitness facilities all under one roof. Two modern dining facilities offer a variety of meal plans including a late-night serving at 10 P.M.

"There's always plenty to do at Neumann. The advantages of nearby Philadelphia and a variety of on-campus activities and programs fill the student's schedule. Neumann College offers 15 intercollegiate sports (NCAA), 6 performing arts groups, and dozens of student clubs and organizations. Students planning for college are always invited to visit and see Neumann College firsthand."

For even more information on this school, turn to page 512 of the "Stats" section.

NEW JERSEY INSTITUTE OF TECHNOLOGY

UNIVERSITY HEIGHTS, NEWARK, NJ 07102 • ADMISSIONS: 973-596-3300 • FAX: 973-596-3461
FINANCIAL AID: 973-596-3480 • E-MAIL: ADMISSIONS@NJIT.EDU • WEBSITE: WWW.NJIT.EDU

RATINGS

Quality of Life: 61   **Academic:** 69   **Admissions:** 81   **Financial Aid:** 77

STUDENTS SAY ". . ."

Academics

> **SURVEY SAYS . . .**
> *Diverse student types on campus*
> *Low cost of living*
> *Very little drug use*

Mathematics, science, technology, and architecture offerings all shine at New Jersey Institute of Technology. The school is a "leader in the field of technology in the Tri-State Area" whose public school pricing allows students to "graduate without the bank owning our first-borns, which is a definite plus," says a student. As is the case at many prestigious tech-oriented schools, "The professors are generally hired for research rather than teaching ability, [so] there are some who cannot teach, and they aren't that great at grading assignments or handing back papers either." The demanding undergraduate curriculum means "you have to be serious about studies if you are choosing NJIT. There is no time for fun and games." Students groan about the demands made on them but also recognize the benefits. "NJIT is an intense academic university that allows students to be prepared for the working world," explains one architect. Another plus of studying at NJIT is "how well the students interact, especially during exam time. Seniors help juniors, who help sophomores, who help freshman. It's helpful when someone who has taken the courses you're taking at the moment can put things into perspective and give you hints about what may be on the test."

Life

NJIT is "not the best school socially, but few engineering schools are," students concede. Since "a lot of classes give amazing amounts of homework, it is hard to have a normal social life. Most nights are spent doing homework late, then getting a few hours of fun before passing out." Extracurricular life has improved recently with the addition of new recreation facilities; one student notes, "The game room has been improved, with pool tables, bowling, and arcades, and a much-needed pub on campus." NJIT also boasts "a pretty good gym to work out in, and a brand-new soccer field." Undergrads note optimistically that "our team sports are all performing better, and the students are starting to feel a sense of competition building. There are plenty of parties on Thursday nights on campus, organized by frats or clubs," and, of course, "possibilities are endless because New York City is minutes away." Affordable public transportation opens the door to "major league sports, world-class museums, and theater." Hometown Newark, although much maligned by students and locals, offers "great food and restaurants less than half a mile away from campus, in the Ironbound section." Students do appreciate how the "small classes and campus make a 'small-town' atmosphere during the semester," though offset against the school's urban environs.

Student Body

"There are two types of students at NJIT," writes one undergrad, elaborating: "The first are the ones who are involved with athletics, clubs, organizations, and other things. The others are the antisocial ones. These people stay in their dorms and play computer games all day." How many of each category populate this campus? One student offers some pertinent data: "Class attendance dropped 32 percent the day *Halo 2* came out." Like the region surrounding it, "NJIT is a total melting pot; the mix of ethnic backgrounds of students is diverse." While many say the various groups interact well, just as many others describe the student body as "clusters of ethnic groups isolated from each other." Because of curricular demands, "Everyone is pretty smart. But you also have the very smart people." When asked in what ways his school could stand to improve, one succinct information technology student wrote "girls!" reflecting a sentiment running through much of the student body. The male/female ratio is about 4:1.

THE PRINCETON REVIEW SAYS

Admissions

Very important factors considered include: Class rank, rigor of secondary school record, standardized test scores. *Important factors considered include:* academic GPA. *Other factors considered include:* Application essay, recommendation(s), alumni/ae relation, character/personal qualities, extracurricular activities, geographical residence, interview, level of applicant's interest, racial/ethnic status, religious affiliation/commitment, state residency. SAT or ACT required; TOEFL required of all international applicants. High school diploma is required, and GED is accepted. *Academic units required:* 4 English, 4 mathematics, 2 science, (2 science labs). *Academic units recommended:* 2 foreign language, 1 social studies, 1 history, 2 academic electives.

Financial Aid

Students should submit: FAFSA. Regular filing deadline is 5/5. The Princeton Review suggests that all financial aid forms be submitted as soon as possible after January 1. *Need-based scholarships/grants offered:* Federal Pell, SEOG, state scholarships/grants, private scholarships, the school's own gift aid. *Loan aid offered:* Direct Subsidized Stafford, Direct Unsubsidized Stafford, Direct PLUS, Federal Perkins, state loans, college/university loans from institutional funds. Applicants will be notified of awards on a rolling basis beginning 12/20. Federal Work-Study Program available. Institutional employment available. Off-campus job opportunities are good.

The Inside Word

NJIT is a great choice for students who aspire to technical careers but don't meet the requirements for better-known and more selective universities. To top it off, it's a pretty good buy.

THE SCHOOL SAYS "..."

From The Admissions Office

"Talented high school graduates from across the nation come to NJIT to prepare for leadership roles in architecture, business, engineering, medical, legal, science, and technological fields. Students experience a public research university conducting nearly $90 million in research that maintains a small-college atmosphere at a modest cost. Our attractive 45-acre campus is just minutes from New York City and less than an hour from the Jersey shore. Students find an outstanding faculty and a safe, diverse, and caring learning and residential community. NJIT's academic environment challenges and prepares students for rewarding careers and fulltime advanced study after graduation. The campus is computing-intensive. NJIT is a Top 50 Best Value College, according to The Princeton Review

"Students applying for admission to NJIT may provide scores from either the SAT or the ACT. Writing sample scores will not be used for admission purposes, but are used for placement in first-year courses. SAT Subject Test scores are not required for any major."

For even more information on this school, turn to page 512 of the "Stats" section.

NEW YORK UNIVERSITY

22 WASHINGTON SQUARE NORTH, NEW YORK, NY 10011 • ADMISSIONS: 212-998-4500 • FAX: 212-995-4902
FINANCIAL AID: 212-998-4444 • E-MAIL: ADMISSIONS@NYU.EDU • WEBSITE: WWW.NYU.EDU

RATINGS
Quality of Life: 78   Academic: 81   Admissions: 96   Financial Aid: 81

STUDENTS SAY "..."

Academics

"Location, location, location" in "the most amazing city on earth," along with "great facilities" and "top-notch faculty," makes New York University an excellent choice for those seeking "an untraditional college experience" in "a paradise for the independent and motivated." With more than 20,000 students and 11 distinct schools offering more than 230

> ### SURVEY SAYS . . .
> Students love New York, NY
> Great off-campus food
> Low cost of living
> Theater is popular

undergraduate degrees, NYU "is about diversity. Students are from all over the world; they come from different cultures, and they have different talents and interests. Similarly, NYU offers endless opportunities for students, no matter what their interests or ambitions are." The school offers voluminous opportunities to participate in research, pursue an internship, or begin a career in the arts (although "you have to be active and willing to find these opportunities"). Given the school's size, many students are "actually quite surprised by the accessibility of both the faculty and administration." Although "this is not the kind of school where students really get to know all of their teachers, as it is unlikely that a student will have a professor more than once," those who make the effort report that "It is so easy to meet with [professors] outside of class, and I still get e-mails from professors about internships, jobs, and scholarship recommendations." Many here also tout the "great study abroad programs."

Life

"Living in New York City is the biggest part of going to school at New York University," NYU students agree. The school's New York City campus is located in the heart of Greenwich Village, one of the city's major nightlife destinations, so "there is always something to do at any hour of the day," usually within walking distance of the school. One student reports, "Every weekend there are tons of things to do, both at NYU and in New York City. NYU really takes advantage of its location, so a lot of the programming provided by residence life or the student resource center is engaging you in the city that has become your new home." Living in the Big Apple means that "On any given day you can go to a museum, concert, sporting event, or theater performance…and a lot of the times, NYU will foot the bill if you go to an event in the city with your RA or with a club." The location also provides plenty of internship opportunities, which is good because "The vast majority of students at NYU are interested in interning and finding jobs through that gateway." The school has no campus per se; it surrounds Washington Square Park, a busy public square where students love to relax when the weather is accommodating.

Student Body

"There is no typical student at NYU," where an undergraduate student body of more than 20,000 and a broad range of academic interests ensure a broad demographic. "Each school at NYU attracts a different group," students tell us. "The Tisch School of the Arts attracts a very out-there group of actors and the like," while the Stern Business School "has a massive population of Asians and Indians." "Hipsters are pretty pervasive throghout all schools except Stern," although "every school has people who break those stereotypes. [Even so,] few students can find ways to not fit in because of the huge number of students" at the university. Throughout NYU, "Students tend to be incredibly motivated and ambitious." Students insist that "it is also important to note that NYU students are very accepting of each other's differences," an important factor at a school that brings together "students of all different backgrounds, ethnicities, and gender identities and makes them coexist within the university."

THE PRINCETON REVIEW SAYS

Admissions

Very important factors considered include: Application essay, academic GPA, recommendation(s), rigor of secondary school record, standardized test scores, extracurricular activities, talent/ability. *Important factors considered include:* Class rank, alumni/ae relation, character/personal qualities, first generation, geographical residence. *Other factors considered include:* Racial/ethnic status, volunteer work, work experience. Test score submission options include an SAT Reasoning Test score; an ACT (with Writing Test) score; three SAT Subject Test scores; or three AP Exam scores. TOEFL required of all international applicants. High school diploma is required, and GED is accepted. *Academic units required:* 4 English, 3 mathematics, 3 science, 2 foreign language, 4 history. *Academic units recommended:* 4 English, 4 mathematics, 4 science, 3 foreign language, 4 history.

Financial Aid

Students should submit: FAFSA, state aid form, Early Decision applicants may submit an institutional form for an estimated award. Regular filing deadline is 2/15. The Princeton Review suggests that all financial aid forms be submitted as soon as possible after January 1. *Need-based scholarships/grants offered:* Federal Pell, SEOG, state scholarships/grants, private scholarships, the school's own gift aid. *Loan aid offered:* Federal Perkins, Federal Nursing. Applicants will be notified of awards on a rolling basis beginning 4/1. Federal Work-Study Program available. Institutional employment available. Off-campus job opportunities are excellent.

The Inside Word

Undergraduates may apply to only one of NYU's undergraduate schools and colleges. Those applying to the Silver School of Social Work; Steinhardt School of Culture, Education, and Human Development; the Tisch School of the Arts; or the Preston Robert Tisch Center for Hospitaility, Tourism, and Sports must indicate an intended major on their application (those applying to the College of Arts and Sciences or the Stern School of Business may indicate that they are undecided on their major). This is different from the application process at most schools and obviously requires some forethought. Remember that this is a highly competitive school; if your application does not reflect a serious interest in your intended area of study, your chances of gaining admission will be diminished.

THE SCHOOL SAYS "..."

From The Admissions Office

"New York University (NYU) is unlike any other U.S. institution of higher education in the world. When you enter NYU, you become part of a close-knit community that combines the nurturing atmosphere of a small- to medium-sized college with the myriad offerings and research opportunities of a global, urban university. The energy and resources of New York City serve as an extension of our Washington Square campus, providing unique opportunities for research, internships, and job placement. In addition, NYU welcomes students to its new honors college in Abu Dhabi in fall 2010. With thousands of undergraduate course offerings and over 230 areas of study from which to choose, you can explore and develop your intellectual and professional passions from your very first semester. Along with this extraordinary range of courses and programs, each of our schools offers a strong liberal arts foundation, introducing you to the traditions of scholarship and inquiry that are the keys to success at NYU and throughout life. NYU's intellectual climate is fostered by a faculty of world-famous scholars, researchers, and artists who teach both undergraduate and graduate courses. In addition, an integral element of the NYU academic experience is our study abroad programs. NYU offers ten international academic centers for study abroad—in Berlin, Buenos Aires, Florence, Ghana, London, Madrid, Paris, Prague, Shanghai, and Tel Aviv, along with the complete branch campus in Abu Dhabi."

For even more information on this school, turn to page 513 of the "Stats" section.

NIAGARA UNIVERSITY

BAILO HALL, OFFICE OF ADMISSIONS, NIAGARA UNIVERSITY, NY 14109 • ADMISSIONS: 800-462-2111 • FAX: 716-286-8710
E-MAIL: ADMISSIONS@NIAGARA.EDU • WEBSITE: WWW.NIAGARA.EDU

RATINGS
Quality of Life: 71   **Academic:** 73   **Admissions:** 76   **Financial Aid:** 87

STUDENTS SAY "..."

Academics

A medium-sized Catholic college in the Vincentian tradition, Niagara University offers a range of manageable, interesting, and practical majors programs, enhanced by a highly supportive and student-oriented atmosphere. In the classroom, "professors here don't simply stand up and lec-

> **SURVEY SAYS ...**
> *Low cost of living*
> *Everyone loves the Purple Eagles*
> *Very little drug use*

ture; they give you an experience that will take you the step above the rest." Most importantly, small class sizes promote "discussion-based and hands-on activities that allow students to be a part of the learning process." In fact, "the classes are more like learning communities," in which professors strive to "engage students about topics that interest them." Mentors as well as instructors, "professors are usually available during the week to chat or talk about class. And they encourage us to talk about other things, like jobs or graduate school." Additionally, the educational program at Niagara emphasizes ethics and service. All undergraduates are required to take philosophy and religion courses, designed to "help shape us into better people and help us understand what the real world is going to be all about." In most cases, it is this holistic approach that sets Niagara apart. A senior shares, "I've grown in so many ways, and my professors have always been around to help push just a little bit harder than I was willing to push myself. It sounds cliché, but knowing they believe and want the best for me helps me believe and want the best for me."

Life

For most students, life at Niagara is "fast-paced and full of activity." Beyond academics, there are a multitude of clubs and student groups, including "the poetry society, outdoors club, diversity club, and intramural sports." In particular, "the newspaper and the theater are wildly popular," and "the campus ministry program is huge on community service, as there are many opportunities, even to serve on week-long trips." With competitive Division I sports, "most social activities at Niagara are centered around athletics," and school pride is vibrant across the community. Many students hail from the surrounding region, and therefore, "a good portion of student tends to go home for the weekend." Others head to Canada to party, or take advantage of the "great hiking trails around the Niagara River Gorge."

Student Body

Niagara is a Catholic college, and Vincentian values infuse the academic and extracurricular programs. Even so, "most students and teachers are pretty open-minded," and the community welcomes all faiths and upbringings. Located near the U.S.-Canada border, most Niagara students come from towns within "a three-hour radius" of campus. While there are "not a lot of unique or different kids," the environment is accepting. A first-year student explains, "I don't think that this is the most diverse campus, but it definitely has a very welcoming atmosphere. With its foundations on Vincentian beliefs, doing well by others is a key goal here at Niagara." When it comes to hobbies and pastimes, you'll find a "diverse set of interests" on the NU campus, and with "so many clubs and organizations on campus, there is bound to be one you can fit into." Overall, Niagara students describe their classmates as "friendly, helpful, intelligent, understanding, and committed to their studies."

THE PRINCETON REVIEW SAYS

Admissions

Very important factors considered include: Rigor of secondary school record. *Important factors considered include:* Recommendation(s), standardized test scores, interview. *Other factors considered include:* Class rank, application essay, alumni/ae relation, character/personal qualities, extracurricular activities, talent/ability, volunteer work, SAT or ACT required; TOEFL required of all international applicants. High school diploma is required and GED is accepted. *Academic units required:* 4 English, 2 mathematics, 2 science, 2 foreign language, 2 social studies, 4 academic electives.

Financial Aid

Students should submit: FAFSA, state aid form. The Princeton Review suggests that all financial aid forms be submitted as soon as possible after January 1. *Need-based scholarships/grants offered:* Federal Pell, SEOG, state scholarships/grants, private scholarships, the school's own gift aid. *Loan aid offered:* Direct Subsidized, Direct Unsubsidized, Direct PLUS, Federal Perkins, Federal Nursing, state loans, college/university loans from institutional funds. Applicants will be notified of awards on a rolling basis beginning 3/1. Federal Work-Study Program available. Off-campus job opportunities are excellent.

The Inside Word

Niagara University offers more than 50 major programs, including pre-professional preparation in pre-dental, pre-law, pre-medical, pre-pharmacology, pre-pharmacy, and pre-veterinary. Students who have not chosen a major may apply for entry into the school's Academic Exploration Program. Admissions decisions are made on a rolling basis until the class is filled.

THE SCHOOL SAYS "..."

From The Admissions Office

"Educating students in mind, body, heart, and soul has been synonymous with a Niagara education since it was founded by the Vincentian Fathers and Brothers in 1856. As the oldest Vincentian University in the United States, Niagara University has a rich Catholic heritage that traces back to St. Vincent de Paul. Today, a Niagara education is an ideal balance of challenging academic programs and a close-knit campus community where professors and administrators care about you. Through active and integrative learning, our curriculum is designed to prepare students to assume leadership roles in their careers and communities.

"Nationally and internationally accredited programs in education, business and hospitality management round out the numerous majors offered in arts and sciences. With service learning (community service) woven into every degree program, it's no wonder that NU was named, once again, to the President's Higher Education Community Service Honor Roll with Distinction.

"The campus is located in the suburbs of Lewiston, New York, just three miles north of the world-famous Niagara Falls. Nearby metropolitan areas include Buffalo, New York and Toronto, Canada. This affords our students an opportunity to experience the sights and sounds of the western New York region.

"But most importantly, Niagara graduates are successful. Our most recent survey found that within six months of graduation, 96 percent of our students landed a job and 59 percent were attending graduate school. This is well above the national average."

For even more information on this school, turn to page 513 of the "Stats" section.

NORTHEASTERN UNIVERSITY

360 HUNTINGTON AVENUE, 150 RICHARDS HALL, BOSTON, MA 02115 • ADMISSIONS: 617-373-2200
FAX: 617-373-8780 • FINANCIAL AID: 617-373-3190 • E-MAIL: ADMISSIONS@NEU.EDU • WEBSITE: WWW.NEU.EDU

RATINGS
Quality of Life: 88　　**Academic:** 79　　**Admissions:** 93　　**Financial Aid:** 68

STUDENTS SAY "..."

Academics

Northeastern "is all about mixing classroom-based instruction with real-world experience" via a robust, justly renowned co-op program (which places students in real-life major-related internships and jobs for up to 18 months) that provides "meaningful work and life experience" to nearly all undergraduates. While some may quibble co-op "isn't the best thing for all majors, only those oriented toward business, journalism, communications, engineering, some sciences, and architecture," most here insist "the co-op program is Northeastern's bragging right" and "without any doubt the school's greatest strength." As one student explains, "Experiences on co-op lead to better discussion and learning in the classroom as professors tackle real-world applications of their subjects with the knowledge that we have been there before, rather than stay in the theoretical realm." "Northeastern students have some of the strongest post-college resumés in the nation" as a result of their co-op experiences. As you might expect, Northeastern's strengths lie in such solidly pre-professional programs as business, health services, engineering, and computer and information sciences. Students caution it's the type of school "where you get in what you put out...If you sit around and complain about not getting a good job and not having much help from advisors or professors, it's probably because you didn't try very hard. If you put in the effort, you will find many, many people are willing to do a great deal to help you succeed, and doors will fly open to ensure your success, and you'll meet a lot of great people (classmates and faculty) and make a lot of friends along the way."

Life

"There is always something to do, either on campus or around the city" at Northeastern, and understandably so; the school is located in Boston, perhaps the nation's preeminent college town. Boston affords "unlimited amounts of things to do like shopping, walking around, movies, etc." Boston is especially accommodating to those older than 21, since "there are plenty of bars to enjoy" all across town. For sports fans, "Fenway Park and the TD Banknorth Garden are a short distance away for athletic games," and "Matthews Arena, home of Husky hockey and the men's basketball team," are nearby. On campus, Greek life "is on the rise," and "Greeks...are extremely involved on campus, planning service events, educational speakers or fun events, such as bringing former Red Sox players or popular comedians to campus." Extracurricular clubs "including but not limited to sports, newspaper, religious groups, social awareness, diversity groups, and more" are widely available to students. "The campus has much to offer as far as recreation from an ice rink to multiple gym facilities. It also has a large student center, multiple outdoor quads, and dorm activities. There is never a dull moment on campus, there is always something to do."

Student Body

"Because of our highly attractive location, there is no 'typical' Northeastern student," undergrads here insist, informing us "students come from the local Boston neighborhoods, ivy towns in Connecticut, countries around the world and cities across the country." The university's "wide range of courses to study" further ensures "a wide range of students" on campus. Finally, the school's large population practically ensures a diverse mix, as evidenced by the "250 or so clubs ranging from anime to the Caribbean Student Organization, from fraternities to a gay/lesbian/transsexual organization. You find virtually every race/gender/religious/political type of people here, and they all fit in and generally get along." The enticement of co-op, of course, means most everyone here is "looking to obtain a solid education and prepare themselves for the working world." You won't find a lot of ivory-tower intellectuals here.

THE PRINCETON REVIEW SAYS

Admissions

Very important factors considered include: Academic GPA, rigor of secondary school record. *Important factors considered include:* Application essay, recommendation(s), standardized test scores, character/personal qualities, extracurricular activities, first generation, talent/ability, volunteer work. *Other factors considered include:* Class rank, alumni/ae relation, geographical residence, interview, racial/ethnic status, state residency, work experience. SAT or ACT required; ACT with Writing component required. TOEFL required of all international applicants. High school diploma is required, and GED is accepted. *Academic units required:* 4 English, 3 mathematics, 3 science, (2 science labs), 2 foreign language, 3 social studies, 2 history. *Academic units recommended:* 4 mathematics, 4 science, (4 science labs), 4 foreign language.

Financial Aid

Students should submit: FAFSA, CSS/Financial Aid PROFILE. The Princeton Review suggests that all financial aid forms be submitted as soon as possible after January 1. *Need-based scholarships/grants offered:* Federal Pell, SEOG, state scholarships/grants, private scholarships, the school's own gift aid. *Loan aid offered:* Direct Subsidized Stafford, Direct Unsubsidized Stafford, Direct PLUS, Federal Perkins, Federal Nursing, state loans. Applicants will be notified of awards on a rolling basis beginning 3/15. Federal Work-Study Program available. Institutional employment available. Off-campus job opportunities are excellent.

The Inside Word

With more than 34,000 applicants each year, Northeastern admissions officers must wade through an ocean of applications in order to select the incoming class. The volume requires that much of the early winnowing be strictly numbers-based the school has too many applicants with decent test scores and high school grades to bother with substandard candidates. Those who make the first cut should receive a more personalized review that includes a close look at essays, extracurriculars, and recommendations. A campus visit couldn't hurt.

THE SCHOOL SAYS "…"

From The Admissions Office

"Northeastern students take charge of their education in a way you'll find nowhere else, because a Northeastern education is like no other. Our students don't just take class: They take class further, integrating their coursework with real-world experiences-professional co-op placements, research, study abroad, and community service. Northeastern's dynamic of academic excellence and experience means that our students are better prepared to succeed in the lives they choose. On top of that, they experience all of this on a beautifully landscaped, 73-acre campus in the heart of Boston, where culture, commerce, civic pride, and college students from around the globe are all a part of the mix."

For even more information on this school, turn to page 514 of the "Stats" section.

PACE UNIVERSITY

ONE PACE PLAZA, NEW YORK, NY 10038 • ADMISSIONS: 212-346-1323 • FAX: 212-346-1040
E-MAIL: INFOCTR@PACE.EDU • WEBSITE: WWW.PACE.EDU

RATINGS
Quality of Life: 72   **Academic:** 70   **Admissions:** 75   **Financial Aid:** 71

STUDENTS SAY ". . ."

Academics

Reflecting an emphasis on career-building and practical education, Pace University's undergraduate programs are split between two campuses in New York City and Westchester County. For students looking to get their feet wet in the real world, the Pace experience couldn't be bet-

> **SURVEY SAYS . . .**
> *Diverse student types on campus*
> *Students love New York, NY*
> *Great off-campus food*

ter: "The opportunities in New York City are endless," and the school's "co-op department is amazingly good at finding jobs and internships" for students and recent grads. In the classroom, professors "do well integrating their real-world experience into their lessons and encourage discussion from the students." In many departments—especially the well-loved theater major—instructors are "absolutely phenomenal in connecting with students" and many professors "provide amazing opportunities that lead to building a resume as well as a future job." Teaching can be "hit or miss," and you won't know "whether or not you will be getting a decent or outstanding professor" until the first day of class. However, you can avoid pitfalls if you "do research before you register for a class." Unfortunately, "the professors are far more accessible than the administration," which students say is "reluctant to take—and slow to act—on student requests." Among the improved facilities and services students would like to see on campus, a "better library" and an upgrade to the "old, rusty weight room" are at the top of the list.

Life

"Whether [it's]…restaurants, theatrical performances, clubs, Times Square, museums, parks, shopping, or simply exploring the city," you will never be bored in the city that never sleeps. Students on Pace's Manhattan campus boast, "New York City is our campus," and "Most students just spend their days here exploring, everything from concerts to art shows and architecture." That also means that most students "spend their free time off campus, which detracts somewhat from the school's sense of community." Those looking for a more traditional college experience might prefer Pace's Westchester campus, located in a pleasant "suburban setting" and perfect for students who want "to be near NYC but not live there." Westchester students say they get together for "parties and social gatherings all the time," and often head out to "local bars around Pleasantville." With two campuses, you can literally get the best of both worlds at Pace. In fact, a current student tells us she "started off at Westchester to get the 'ideal' college setting, [and] will be taking classes and living on the city campus my final year to experience city life."

Student Body

"Pace is like a miniature version of the city"—that would be New York—and you'll meet people "from all walks of life" on campus. Encompassing every extreme, a Pace student might be "a liberal, gay, Vietnamese-American reading the Wall Street Journal or a conservative, straight, Jewish white kid from Yonkers playing the cello in the hallway." On both the Westchester and New York City campuses, students hail from all over the United States—as well as many foreign countries—though the majority come from "Westchester county, upstate New York, and Long Island, with some scattered students from Massachusetts, Connecticut, and Philadelphia." Considering the school's location, it is not surprising that your typical undergraduate is "a fast paced, get-in-and-get-out type of person that loves New York City," and many are "involved in an organization or Greek life, or is an athlete." While "everyone's idea of fun differs," students agree that "our school environment is very friendly," and most students fit in easily.

Admissions

Very important factors considered include: Rigor of secondary school record, standardized test scores. *Important factors considered include:* Class rank, academic GPA. *Other factors considered include:* Application essay, recommendation(s), alumni/ae relation, character/personal qualities, extracurricular activities, talent/ability, volunteer work, work experience. SAT or ACT required; TOEFL required of all international applicants. High school diploma is required and GED is accepted. *Academic units required:* 4 English, 3 mathematics, 2 science, (2 science labs), 2 foreign language, 1 social studies, 2 history, 2 academic electives. *Academic units recommended:* 4 English, 4 mathematics, 2 science, (2 science labs), 3 foreign language, 2 social studies, 3 history, 2 academic electives.

Financial Aid

Students should submit: FAFSA, state aid form. The Princeton Review suggests that all financial aid forms be submitted as soon as possible after January 1. *Need-based scholarships/grants offered:* Federal Pell, SEOG, state scholarships/grants, private scholarships, the school's own gift aid, Federal Nursing Scholarships, endowed and restricted scholarships and grants. *Loan aid offered:* Direct Subsidized Stafford, Direct Unsubsidized Stafford, Direct PLUS, Federal Perkins, Federal Nursing Applicants will be notified of awards on a rolling basis beginning 2/25. Off-campus job opportunities are good.

The Inside Word

Academics, community involvement, and extracurricular activities are among the most important factors in an admissions decision at Pace. Students must also submit standardized test scores (either the SAT or the ACT.) For nursing and theater majors, application deadlines are earlier, and theater majors must schedule an audition in addition to submitting application materials.

THE SCHOOL SAYS "…"

From The Admissions Office

"Pace University blends a wide choice of high-quality professional education with a liberal arts curriculum that teaches critical and independent thinking. For more than 100 years, Pace has provided practical experiences that prepare students for significant careers. Pace students thrive on the opportunities and challenges of the New York metropolitan area.

"Pace's 13,000 diverse undergraduate and graduate students from across the U.S. and 123 countries have a choice of campuses four blocks from Wall Street in New York City or in suburban Westchester County. More than 90 percent of first-year students receive financial aid. Classes average 20 students.

"Nearly 40 percent of Pace undergraduates live on campus, participating in 90 clubs and student organizations (and in Westchester, in Division II sports).

"More than 450 companies come to Pace to find their next generation of talent, and the University's co-op and internship program is the largest of its kind in the metropolitan area. Students find work with Fortune 500 companies like IBM, Citigroup, Verizon, Deloitte, Goldman Sachs, and at institutions like the Argonne National Laboratory. More The Pace Career Advisory Network provides connections to 500-plus alumni who want to help others succeed.

"Pace University successfully challenges its students to lift their lives and prospects to new levels. "There is greatness within us all," reads a poster on the downtown New York City campus, "sometimes you just need the right opportunity to find it. Welcome to Pace University."

For even more information on this school, turn to page 514 of the "Stats" section.

PENNSYLVANIA STATE UNIVERSITY—UNIVERSITY PARK

201 SHIELDS BUILDING, UNIVERSITY PARK, PA 16802-3000 • ADMISSIONS: 814-865-5471
FAX: 814-863-7590 • FINANCIAL AID: 814-865-6301 • WEBSITE: WWW.PSU.EDU

RATINGS
Quality of Life: 98   Academic: 77   Admissions: 92   Financial Aid: 63

STUDENTS SAY ". . ."

Academics

Pennsylvania State University "offers an amazing education [and] a sense of community, family, and pride," its students tell us, and while students appreciate the "hundreds of classes to choose from (you can literally take any class you could ever dream of)" and the "endless opportunities for academic and personal growth," it's the "amazing sense of pride and tradition" that truly captivates most. As one student explains, "It's about…the feeling you get even when you come back to visit 20 years later. Once you're a Penn Stater, you're always a Penn Stater. You don't get the same feeling anywhere else. Believe me, I've looked." With "strong academics in the sciences, engineering, and business," PSU has the means to educate the go-getters of tomorrow, then help them find jobs through "a very strong alumni base" that students tell us is "the largest dues-paying alumni association in the world." Academics are "incredible," with "innumerable opportunities to connect with administrators and professors, although it is up to the student to take advantage of them." Online course management services "make keeping up to date in your classes really easy." All these options and opportunities have students bragging that PSU is "a Public Ivy." One with way better football.

> **SURVEY SAYS . . .**
> *Low cost of living*
> *Everyone loves the Nittany Lions*
> *Student publications are popular*

Life

"Once the weekend arrives it's either party time or rest-up time" at Penn State, and students tell us that "it's usually party time." "Fraternities are very popular at Penn State for first-year students, and apartments and house parties go well with the upperclassmen." Students also tout University Park's "many places to go out to dinner" ("people go out to eat a lot!"), and close proximity to a "Target, Wal-Mart and movie theaters that can all be accessed by cheap buses that run on campus." In addition, students can attend "a ton of concerts that come through State College because the Bryce Jordan Center is the biggest arena between Pittsburgh and Philadelphia" and "free events sponsored by the Student Programming Association." "Almost every weekend there is a student group performing on campus, whether it be comedy, singing, or acting," one student reports. And then there's Nittany Lion football. As one student puts it, "Football is a way of life here." Many students are also active in philanthropy; THON, the school's annual dance marathon, is "the largest student-run philanthropy in the world, raising money for pediatric cancer research."

Student Body

PSU is a big school with lots of different types of students, but there is definitely a predominant look on campus, which is "sweatpants and T-shirts. We like to be comfortable, relaxed, but always school spirited." Indeed, your typical PSU undergrad is "a diehard football fan" with "a plethora of pride for the school and lion." About one-quarter of the student body originates from outside Pennsylvania ("there's a large number of students from New Jersey"), with the majority of Keystone State natives coming "usually from either the Philadelphia or Pittsburgh area" as well as representing "middle-class white kids from central Pennsylvania." Whatever their geographical roots, the typical PSU undergrad "is someone who works hard during the week [and] is involved in activities on campus, but definitely wants to have a good time once the weekend comes." As one student puts it, "The libraries and study areas on campus are always packed but so are the streets downtown on weekends."

Admissions

Very important factors considered include: Academic GPA, standardized test scores. *Important factors considered include:* Rigor of secondary school record. *Other factors considered include:* Class rank, application essay, recommendation(s), alumni/ae relation, character/personal qualities, extracurricular activities, talent/ability, volunteer work, work experience. SAT or ACT required; ACT with Writing component required. TOEFL required of all international applicants. High school diploma is required, and GED is accepted. *Academic units required:* 4 English, 3 mathematics, 3 science, 2 foreign language, 3 social studies.

Financial Aid

Students should submit: FAFSA. The Princeton Review suggests that all financial aid forms be submitted as soon as possible after January 1. *Need-based scholarships/grants offered:* Federal Pell, SEOG, state scholarships/grants, private scholarships, the school's own gift aid. *Loan aid offered:* Direct Subsidized Stafford, Direct Unsubsidized Stafford, Direct PLUS, Federal Perkins, college/university loans from institutional funds, other, private loans. Applicants will be notified of awards on a rolling basis beginning 3/1. Federal Work-Study Program available. Institutional employment available. Off-campus job opportunities are good.

The Inside Word

High school GPA is by far the most important factor in PSU admissions. According to the school's website, high school grades account for two-thirds of the final admissions decision. Standardized test scores, class rank, extracurricular activities, and other factors make up the remaining one-third. PSU admits on a rolling basis. Given this school's popularity with Pennsylvania residents, applicants would do well to get their applications in as early as possible.

THE SCHOOL SAYS "…"

From The Admissions Office

"Unique among large public universities, Penn State combines the over-35,000-student setting of its University Park campus with 20 academically and administratively integrated undergraduate locations—small-college settings ranging in size from 600 to 3,400 students. Each year, more than 60 percent of incoming freshmen begin their studies at these residential and commuter campuses, while nearly 40 percent begin at the University Park campus. The smaller locations focus on the needs of new students by offering the first two years of most Penn State baccalaureate degrees in settings that stress close interaction with faculty. Depending on the major selected, students may choose to complete their degree at University Park or one of the smaller locations. Your application to Penn State qualifies you for review for any of our campuses. Your two choices of location are reviewed in the order given. Entrance difficulty is based, in part, on the demand. Due to its popularity, the University Park campus is the most competitive for admission.

"Freshman applicants may submit the results from the SAT or the ACT with the Writing Component. The Writing portions of these tests will not necessarily be factored into admission decisions."

For even more information on this school, turn to page 514 of the "Stats" section.

POLYTECHNIC UNIVERSITY—BROOKLYN

Six Metrotech Center, Brooklyn, NY 11201-2999 • Admissions: 718-260-3100 • Fax: 718-260-3446
E-mail: admitme@poly.edu • Website: www.poly.edu

RATINGS
Quality of Life: 65   Academic: 72   Admissions: 92   Financial Aid: 88

STUDENTS SAY "..."

Academics

Polytechnic University—Brooklyn is a private, "commuter-based engineering school in New York City" that boasts "rigorous" engineering, mathematics, and computer science programs. Be warned: Poly is "boot camp for engineers." As such, "Schoolwork and exams are crazy," and academic success "requires a lot of hard work, diligence, and a good attitude." On the bright side, "As long you work hard and study hard, you can achieve great things." "Professors are hit-or-miss," "the good professors are awesome" and "extremely educated in their field," "The bad ones are really bad." Due to the school's international faculty, students often complain that, "the language barrier between the student and the professor is difficult at times." Class sizes are "usually small," and professors are "always willing to see you and help you one-on-one." Students, however, are generally down on the "very unhelpful" administration, saying they are "not unified" and "blow through money."

Life

While the "school is not very good looking," the Poly campus has seen steady improvement in recent years. "Dorms are now right on campus," and "the main academic building has been renovated and expanded." It feels a lot like a "brand-new school." Overall, though, "life on campus is not that exciting," primarily because "the typical student at Poly will study nothing less than 3.5 hours a day." Campus clubs and organizations "aren't too popular," though many people enjoy "poker or table tennis tournaments" and videogames. In addition, "Most students are commuters, so there isn't as much of a social scene as there should be." For students who live on campus, "There's a fair amount of drinking," and many "gather in the student lounge or in their respective major lounge and just relax and laugh." While life at school is a bit serious, don't forget that "Poly is located in New York City" and "only a few minutes away from Manhattan, a goldmine for nightlife, food, and activities." A mere 15-minute stroll leads to the Brooklyn Bridge and great Manhattan neighborhoods like Little Italy and Chinatown.

Student Body

Drawing students from surrounding New York City and more than 50 countries worldwide, Poly is an "ethnically diverse" yet generally accepting community. On this small campus, "Everyone is different, yet this difference makes it easy to connect with others." Observes a sophomore, "kids are very diverse, with many interests and different backgrounds...as a foreigner, I [feel] like the entire world met in one place." However, students gripe there are "very few women" from any countries. You'll meet plenty of "stereotypical nerds," many of whom "stick to themselves and their laptops." You'll also find handful of "popular and trendy people" who are "involved in lots of activities." In fact, "The only real common thread is an interest in technology." "Most students are serious about their studies; they have to be to survive here."

THE PRINCETON REVIEW SAYS

Admissions
Very important factors considered include: Rigor of secondary school record, standardized test scores. *Important factors considered include:* Class rank. *Other factors considered include:* Application essay, recommendation(s), interview, SAT or ACT required; TOEFL required of all international applicants. High school diploma is required and GED is accepted. *Academic units required:* 4 English, 4 mathematics, 4 science, 3 social studies, 2 academic electives. *Academic units recommended:* 2 foreign language.

Financial Aid
Students should submit: FAFSA, institution's own financial aid form, CSS/Financial Aid PROFILE, state aid form. The Princeton Review suggests that all financial aid forms be submitted as soon as possible after January 1. *Need-based scholarships/grants offered:* Federal Pell, SEOG, state scholarships/grants, private scholarships, the school's own gift aid, United Negro College Fund. *Loan aid offered:* Federal Perkins, college/university loans from institutional funds, other, alternative loans. Applicants will be notified of awards on a rolling basis beginning 2/15. Off-campus job opportunities are excellent.

The Inside Word
Most successful applicants to Polytechnic boast strong standardized test scores and a challenging secondary school transcript chock-full of math and science classes. Poly promises a demanding 4 years but makes it worth your while—all graduates are guaranteed a job within 6 months of graduation.

For even more information on this school, turn to page 515 of the "Stats" section.

PRINCETON UNIVERSITY

PO BOX 430, ADMISSION OFFICE, PRINCETON, NJ 08544-0430 • ADMISSIONS: 609-258-3060
FAX: 609-258-6743 • FINANCIAL AID: 609-258-3330 • WEBSITE: WWW.PRINCETON.EDU

RATINGS
Quality of Life: 99   Academic: 99   Admissions: 99   Financial Aid: 99

STUDENTS SAY ". . ."

Academics

An Ivy League institution with a singular focus on under-graduate study (and one of the best engineering schools in the Ivy League" to boot), Princeton University upholds every ounce of its reputation, according to students. With top-notch, "endless" resources at each student's disposal, terrific financial aid packages (no student loans!), and a centuries-old reputation, the school provides the "academic and social opportunity of a lifetime," all within the goth-ic walls of a beautiful, enclosed New Jersey campus. "Princeton is all about learning; every second is an educational experience," one student says. Though the academics can be "grueling," they're also well worth the effort, and work is "never assigned without a reason. [There is] no busywork." The administration's ongoing effort to curb grade inflation means that competition does exist at Princeton, although it's mainly competition with one's self— "discovering the drive and focus to spend time for your academic classes and extracurriculars" is the one of the hardest parts of being a student here. "Princeton is full of opportunities to further your interests, but only if you actively take a role," says a sophomore. Still, students are all supportive of continuing the Princeton tradition of excellence, and the "strong student body" allows for "better class discussions and more meaningful projects." There's no question that the professors (who teach all of the classes) here are all-stars in their fields. "We're using textbooks that they wrote and studying theories that they developed," says a student. "In my biology for non-science majors class, my Nobel-prize winning professor personally taught me how to use a microscope! If that's not passion for teaching, I don't know what is!" says another. The administration has fans in most students; while there are "regular tiffs" with the administration over some aspects of school life (one suggests that "less administrative intervention could improve the school"), those in charge (especially within the school's residential colleges) are "very friendly, accessible, and helpful in resolving student-life issues."

Life

Even though Princetonian lives are lived out mostly on campus, tiny Princeton is "the perfect distance" from NYC, Philadelphia, and some beautiful beaches for those students who do choose to pop out for a bit. Everyone is constantly busy, not just with the large amounts of work but "with a range of extracurricular activities from athletics to dance groups." Princeton's unique "eating clubs"—10 social clubs that are housed in off-campus mansions and that upperclassmen can join and enjoy the right to eat, "hang out, relax, study, party, and every-thing in between" keep most partying ("once or twice a week") in a safe setting amongst fellow students. There is, however, somewhat of a divide "between students who spend time at eating clubs (80 percent or so) and students who choose to abstain from partying and prefer to study." Most of the clubs are "very accessible" to all students for events, and "it's nice to have the social scene localized to one [place close to] campus, because everyone always knows where the parties will be." One student refers to a popular saying on campus, "Academics, social life, and sleep: pick two."

Student Body

The typical Princetonian has a work-hard/play-hard mentality—working very, very hard on weeknights, but "willing to put down their books to party on the weekends." Students tend to get "absorbed" in their work at crunch times. Though not even close to a majority, there is definitely a segment of the population that "holes up in their rooms" to study, in direct contrast to the "social" student that one typically meets around campus. This bunch of "competitive, brilliant" students has a mix of typical and atypical and no real problem reconciling the two, though students would like to see diversity increase even further than it has in recent years. "From star athletes to musical prodigies to academic powerhouses, everyone brings something different to the table," says a student. This driven group "thinks about how to be successful in their lives after Princeton, and [they] plan accordingly."

Admissions

Very important factors considered include: Class rank, application essay, academic GPA, recommendation(s), rigor of secondary school record, standardized test scores, character/personal qualities, talent/ability. *Important factors considered include:* Extracurricular activities. *Other factors considered include:* Alumni/ae relation, first generation, geographical residence, interview, racial/ethnic status, volunteer work, work experience. SAT or ACT required; ACT with Writing component required. TOEFL required of all international applicants. High school diploma or equivalent is not required. *Academic units recommended:* 4 English, 4 mathematics, 4 science, (2 science labs), 4 foreign language, 2 social studies, 2 history, 1 visual/performing arts.

Financial Aid

Students should submit: FAFSA, institution's own financial aid form. The Princeton Review suggests that all financial aid forms be submitted as soon as possible after January 1. *Need-based scholarships/grants offered:* Federal Pell, SEOG, state scholarships/grants, private scholarships, the school's own gift aid. *Loan aid offered:* Federal Perkins, college/university loans from institutional funds. Applicants will be notified of awards on or about 4/1. Federal Work-Study Program available. Institutional employment available. Off-campus job opportunities are good.

The Inside Word

Princeton is much more open about the admissions process than the rest of their Ivy compatriots. The admissions staff evaluates candidates' credentials using a 1–5 rating scale, common among highly selective colleges. Princeton's recommendation to interview should be considered a requirement, given the ultracompetitive nature of the applicant pool. In addition, three SAT Subject Tests are required.

THE SCHOOL SAYS "…"

From The Admissions Office

"Methods of instruction [at Princeton] vary widely, but common to all areas is a strong emphasis on individual responsibility and the free interchange of ideas. This is displayed most notably in the wide use of preceptorials and seminars, in the provision of independent study for all upperclass students and qualified underclass students, and in the availability of a series of special programs to meet a range of individual interests. The undergraduate college encourages the student to be an independent seeker of information and to assume responsibility for gaining both knowledge and judgment that will strengthen later contributions to society.

Princeton offers a distinctive financial aid program that provides grants, which do not have to be repaid, rather than loans. Princeton meets the full demonstrated financial need of all students—domestic and international—offered admission. More than half of Princeton's undergraduates receive financial aid.

"All applicants must submit results for both the SAT as well as SAT Subject Tests in three different subject areas."

For even more information on this school, turn to page 516 of the "Stats" section.

PROVIDENCE COLLEGE

RIVER AVENUE AND EATON STREET, PROVIDENCE, RI 02918 • ADMISSIONS: 401-865-2535 • FAX: 401-865-2826
FINANCIAL AID: 401-865-2286 • E-MAIL: PCADMISS@PROVIDENCE.EDU • WEBSITE: WWW.PROVIDENCE.EDU

RATINGS
Quality of Life: 65   **Academic:** 78   **Admissions:** 93   **Financial Aid:** 76

STUDENTS SAY ". . ."

Academics

"Governed by the thought of St. Thomas Aquinas," Providence College is "a tight-knit community of well-rounded, charismatic, and intelligent kids" benefiting from "a definite emphasis on a Catholic intellectual approach to the world." Nowhere is that approach more evident then in PC's "well-rounded core curriculum," one student writes. The cornerstone of the curriculum is the Development of Western Civilization course sequence, "a great asset to the school" that "produces students who have an awareness of the West's cultural heritage." Outside of the core, students flock to business and marketing, premedical studies, and education programs; a "great political science program" is also popular among students. Students report that "PC is full of wonderful professors, very genuine people who want to share their knowledge…and help their students to become thoughtful and conscientious adults." Likewise, their classmates "are caring individuals who are…willing to go the extra-mile for their peers." The result is a "sense of community—the smaller campus and student body mean that you see familiar faces every day, definitely something that comforts new students" and encourages them to participate in the life of the campus. As one student sums up, "PC in a nutshell is thinking about Kant, Hegel, or Dostoevsky, listening to Taylor Swift, making life-long relations[hips] and getting involved in student-run clubs."

Life

Life at PC can get a bit "monotonous during the week" when students "are engrossed in their work," but campus life "changes dramatically when the weekend arrives." "Most everyone likes to party Thursday, Friday, and Saturday night (and some even during the week)," with a typical night starting at a bar. Seniors usually "go to McPhail's, the on-campus bar") and ending at a party in off-campus houses "after the bars close." Basketball and hockey games "are big school events," and many students are "very involved in clubs, some of the most popular being Student Congress, Friars Club, Board of Programmers, and Board of Multicultural Student Affairs." Intramurals are also "very popular at PC." Students love venturing out into hometown Providence, "a great city with so many options." "There is a great mall about 10 minutes from campus with a movie theater and an Imax," as well as "great restaurants" and "a lot of other colleges in the area." Getting to these places is "easy," "as PC students can take the RIPTA bus for free with their student ID card." While most here like to have fun, most also know when to stop. "Whenever I visit the library it is full, and I hardly find a place to sit, and this is not because the library is too small," one student warns.

Student Body

The Providence College population is largely "white and Catholic from New England, New York, or New Jersey." There is "not a great amount of diversity" in this "preppy," "sheltered" crowd of kids. "Everyone is the same," one student cautions. "Girls all have Vera Bradley bags, [and] every student has a North Face jacket." Students tend to be "very focused on their academics while remaining highly involved in extracurricular activities and volunteerism" and very career-minded; most "will probably work in the business world upon graduation." The number of international students here "is quite small," but they "fit in perfectly with the rest of the American students," according to one international student.

Admissions

Very important factors considered include: Academic GPA, recommendation(s), rigor of secondary school record. *Important factors considered include:* Application essay, character/personal qualities, extracurricular activities. *Other factors considered include:* Class rank, standardized test scores, alumni/ae relation, first generation, geographical residence, level of applicant's interest, racial/ethnic status, state residency, talent/ability, volunteer work, work experience. TOEFL required of all international applicants. High school diploma is required, and GED is not accepted. *Academic units required:* 4 English, 4 mathematics, 3 science, (2 science labs), 3 foreign language, 2 social studies, 2 history. *Academic units recommended:* 4 English, 4 mathematics, 4 science, (2 science labs), 3 foreign language, 2 social studies, 2 history.

Financial Aid

Students should submit: FAFSA, CSS/Financial Aid PROFILE, business/farm supplement. Regular filing deadline is 2/1. The Princeton Review suggests that all financial aid forms be submitted as soon as possible after January 1. *Need-based scholarships/grants offered:* Federal Pell, SEOG, state scholarships/grants, private scholarships, the school's own gift aid, Federal Academic Competitive Grant/Smart Grant. *Loan aid offered:* Direct Subsidized Stafford, Direct Unsubsidized Stafford, Direct PLUS, Federal Perkins. Applicants will be notified of awards on or about 4/1. Federal Work-Study Program available. Institutional employment available. Off-campus job opportunities are good.

The Inside Word

Few schools can claim a more transparent admissions process than Providence College. The admissions section of the school's website includes a voluminous blog authored by the assistant dean of admissions. Surf on over to http://blogs.targetx.com/providence/ScottSeseske/ and learn everything you could possibly want to know about the how, what, when, and why of Providence admissions. Providence has a test-optional policy, meaning applicants are not required to submit standardized test scores.

THE SCHOOL SAYS "..."

From The Admissions Office

"Infused with the history, tradition, and learning of a 700-year-old Catholic teaching order, the Dominican Friars, Providence College offers a value-affirming environment where students are challenged on every level—body, mind, heart, and soul. Providence College offers 50 majors leading to baccalaureate degrees in business, education, the sciences, arts, and humanities. Our faculty is noted for a strong commitment to teaching. A close student/faculty relationship allows for in-depth classwork, independent research projects, and detailed career exploration. While noted for the physical facilities and academic opportunities associated with larger universities, Providence also fosters personal growth through a small, spirited, family like atmosphere that encourages involvement in student activities and athletics.

"Submission of standardized test scores is optional for students applying for admission. This policy change allows each student to decide whether they wish to have their standardized test results considered as part of their application for admission. Students who choose not to submit SAT or ACT test scores will not be penalized in the review for admission. Additional details about the test-optional policy can be found on our website at Providence.edu/testoptionalpolicy."

For even more information on this school, turn to page 516 of the "Stats" section.

QUINNIPIAC UNIVERSITY

MOUNT CARMEL AVENUE, 275 MOUNT CARMEL AVENUE, HAMDEN, CT 06518 • ADMISSIONS: 203-582-8600
FAX: 203-582-8906 • E-MAIL: ADMISSIONS@QUINNIPIAC.EDU • WEBSITE: WWW.QUINNIPIAC.EDU

RATINGS
Quality of Life: 78   Academic: 80   Admissions: 86   Financial Aid: 65

STUDENTS SAY ". . ."

Academics

> SURVEY SAYS . . .
> *Low cost of living*
> *Hard liquor is popular*

Quinnipiac University, "a professional school with the goal of educating its students to succeed in the future," boasts excellent programs in business, communications, and the health sciences, especially in those for nursing, physician's assistant, and physical and occupational therapy. Undergrads insist that QU's physical therapy program "is the best in the region." "The structure of the PT program is so well thought out that each class is working off the other in helping me get a education and actually learn the material," one student reports. Students in all health science fields appreciate QU's regional cache, especially when it comes time to apply to graduate school or to find a job. Communications and journalism majors get plenty of hands-on experience in the school's "full green-screen room as well as editing, media production, and journalist rooms." The departments produce "lively student television programming (news, sports, a game show, a travel show, and soon a cooking show), an excellent student newspaper, and an eclectic student radio station." Future teachers also find a happy home at QU; the school offers "a great five-year teaching program" that confers both a BA and a masters. "It's excellent preparation for teachers," one student tells us. By developing a number of hallmark programs, QU has elevated its national profile considerably, and students approvingly observe that the school "is focused on growing and becoming a school on the rise. There have been a lot of improvements on campus and [administrators] actually are interested in the students' opinions."

Life

According to most students, QU is your prototypical 'work-hard, play-hard' school. As one undergrad explains, "I spend Monday through Thursday doing loads of homework/studying, and as soon as Friday comes, it's time to party. Almost everyone on campus drinks, and a lot of people take the shuttles to bars and clubs." But while "drinking is definitely the students' most popular activity," it's hardly the only option. "When there is a men's ice hockey game, a lot of people get tickets and attend," students report, and basketball is also popular (both teams play in "a beautiful new arena"). QU offers a number of dry options, and "a lot of students stay sober and still have a great time with their friends or at school-sponsored events." Those looking "for quieter activities" can avail themselves of "the movie theater, bowling allies, and a ton of restaurants in Hamden, North Haven, and New Haven." The campus itself "is consistently described as a country club, and it's not far from the truth. The dorms as well as the campus are gorgeous."

Student Body

"The typical 'Quinnipiac Girl' (yes we say that here)," according to one student, "is very fashion-forward and is from Long Island. She is always in designer clothing, and in the winter she wears Uggs, tight leggings, and a North Face jacket carrying either a really nice, leather Coach bag or a Vera Bradley bag. The typical boy is also from Long Island and is Italian. He also wears fashion clothing." It's easy to dismiss these students as "mostly spoiled [and] rich" at first glace, but students caution against doing that. Says one, "Once you realize that's not everyone, and you actually get involved in the school, you realize the people at QU are amazing! It's a great place to be." True, some bad apples have generated "negative "press due to several racial incidents on campus" in recent years, "but that does not reflect the majority of students at QU," many here assure us. If anything, "students tend to be naive about other ethnicities because the majority of people at Quinnipiac are Caucasian" and "very sheltered."

THE PRINCETON REVIEW SAYS

Admissions

Very important factors considered include: Academic GPA, rigor of secondary school record. *Important factors considered include:* Class rank, application essay, standardized test scores. *Other factors considered include:* Recommendation(s), alumni/ae relation, character/personal qualities, extracurricular activities, interview, level of applicant's interest, racial/ethnic status, talent/ability, volunteer work, work experience. SAT or ACT required; ACT with Writing component recommended. TOEFL required of all international applicants. High school diploma is required, and GED is accepted. *Academic units required:* 4 English, 3 mathematics, 3 science, (2 science labs), 2 foreign language, 2 social studies, 4 years of science and math req. in PT, OT, Nursing and PA. *Academic units recommended:* 4 English, 4 mathematics, 4 science, (3 science labs), 2 foreign language, 3 social studies.

Financial Aid

Students should submit: FAFSA, CSS/Financial Aid PROFILE. Students applying during 2010–2011 for the spring 2011 or fall 2011 semesters will need to provide the CSS Profile. The Princeton Review suggests that all financial aid forms be submitted as soon as possible after January 1. *Need-based scholarships/grants offered:* Federal Pell, SEOG, state scholarships/grants, private scholarships, the school's own gift aid, Federal Nursing Scholarships. *Loan aid offered:* Direct Subsidized Stafford, Direct Unsubsidized Stafford, Direct PLUS, Federal Perkins, Federal Nursing, state loans Applicants will be notified of awards on a rolling basis beginning 2/15. Federal Work-Study Program available. Institutional employment available. Off-campus job opportunities are excellent.

The Inside Word

Quinnipiac admits students on a rolling basis, a process that favors those who get their applications in early. Programs in physical therapy, nursing, and physician assistant are quite competitive. The school strongly recommends that those seeking spots in these programs apply no later than early November.

THE SCHOOL SAYS "…"

From The Admissions Office

"Quinnipiac today is 'three settings, one university', with an undergraduate population growing to 6500, many of whom remain at QU for the ever expanding graduate programs, and a continuing focus on our core values: academic excellence, a student oriented environment and a strong sense of community.

"The Mount Carmel campus, the academic home to all undergraduates with traditional, suite and apartment housing for freshmen and sophomores, is 250 acres in a stunning setting adjacent to Sleeping Giant state park. The nearby 250 acre York Hill campus is home to juniors and seniors in apartments with breathtaking views, a lodge style student center, covered parking, and the TD Bank sports center with twin arenas for hockey and basketball. The 100 acre North Haven campus, just 4 miles distant, is the home to graduate programs in Health Sciences, and Education, and a soon to be developed Medical School (est. opening 2013/2014).

"Academic initiatives such as the honors program, 'writing across the curriculum', QU seminar series, extensive internship experiences, study abroad opportunities and a highly regarded emerging leaders student-life program form the foundation for excellence in business, communications, health sciences, nursing, education, liberal arts and law.

"State of the art facilities include the Financial Technology Center, HD fully digital production studio, extensive health science labs, recreation and sports fields and arenas. More than 90 student organizations, 19 Division I teams, community service, student publications, and a strong student government offer a variety of outside-of-class experiences. "

For even more information on this school, turn to page 516 of the "Stats" section.

RAMAPO COLLEGE OF NEW JERSEY

505 RAMAPO VALLEY ROAD, MAHWAH, NJ 07430 • ADMISSIONS: 201-684-7300 • FAX: 201-684-7964
E-MAIL: ADMISSIONS@RAMAPO.EDU • WEBSITE: WWW.RAMAPO.EDU

RATINGS
Quality of Life: 79   **Academic:** 73   **Admissions:** 89   **Financial Aid:** 68

STUDENTS SAY "..."

Academics

Ramapo College of New Jersey is a smallish, public, career-oriented liberal arts school on the fringes of northern New Jersey's suburban sprawl. "The classes are small" and students call Ramapo "a great bargain." Business programs are particularly "excellent." Some students like the "hands-on

> **SURVEY SAYS . . .**
> *Great computer facilities*
> *Athletic facilities are great*
> *Dorms are like palaces*

experience" they gain from the required experiential learning components of the curriculum. Other students call experiential learning "a big waste of time and effort." "While watching movies or attending seminars may seem nice to fulfill the requirement, the forced nature of it has irritated many a student," explains an accounting major. The faculty at RCNJ is all over the place. Some professors "have a passion for teaching." They're "dedicated to their students" and "very accessible." "The great professors will blow you away," promises a business major. However, other professors are "dull and incomprehensible." Student opinion really varies when it comes to the administration. "Ramapo runs fairly smoothly," contends an education major. Others disagree. "The school's administration is slightly lacking in terms of service towards their students, but I would assume that is the case in most schools."

Life

Ramapo's campus is "very clean" and "in a beautiful and quiet location." "The gym is really nice" and the rooms in the newer residence halls are "huge" and "extremely comfortable." There are "many extracurricular options" and the school "does try to plan things." However, "school spirit is definitely lacking" and "unless you join a club or activity early on, it is very hard to get to know people." The basic problem is that "too many people go home on the weekends." "It's a suitcase college," laments a junior. "It is completely empty here on a Saturday night." Greek life provides an outlet for students who join frats and sororities but "the college goes a little overboard" with "ridiculously strict and severe" alcohol and drug policies. As a result, it's "hard to have fun and party like a normal college kid." Surrounding Mahwah is a "grim town" and "having a car on campus is essential to avoid feeling cut off from the world." If you have wheels, a handful of malls are "within 20 minutes" and there's "an absolutely gorgeous hiking area" just down the road. If you enjoy more urban pursuits, New York City is also reasonably close. "I go often," proclaims a sophomore.

Student Body

Except for the solid contingent of international students, virtually everyone here is "New Jersey born and bred." Many students are "preppy" and most "come off as put-together," and are "white, upper middle-class suburbans." Commuters, nontraditional students, and "transfers from community college" make up a good percentage of the student population. Though there are a few girls with "the latest Ugg boots," wearing "Hollister," "make-up and sidebangs," it's mostly "lots of jeans and hoodies" and "hats with pre-frayed brims" at Ramapo, and many students describe themselves as "laid back." The campus tends to be "very clique oriented." "Eating in the cafeteria is almost like eating in a high school cafeteria all over again," observes a junior.

THE PRINCETON REVIEW SAYS

Admissions

Very important factors considered include: Class rank, academic GPA, rigor of secondary school record, standardized test scores. *Important factors considered include:* Application essay, recommendation(s), extracurricular activities, talent/ability. *Other factors considered include:* Alumni/ae relation, geographical residence, state residency, volunteer work, work experience. SAT required; ACT with Writing component recommended. TOEFL required of all international applicants. High school diploma is required and GED is accepted. *Academic units required:* 4 English, 3 mathematics, 3 science, (2 science labs), 2 foreign language, 3 social studies, 3 academic electives.

Financial Aid

Students should submit: FAFSA. The Princeton Review suggests that all financial aid forms be submitted as soon as possible after January 1. *Need-based scholarships/grants offered:* Federal Pell, SEOG, state scholarships/grants, private scholarships, the school's own gift aid, Federal Nursing Scholarships, Federal TRIO Grant. *Loan aid offered:* Direct Subsidized Stafford, Direct Unsubsidized Stafford, Direct PLUS, Federal Perkins, state loans. Applicants will be notified of awards on a rolling basis beginning 4/1. Federal Work-Study Program available. Institutional employment available. Off-campus job opportunities are good.

The Inside Word

Ramapo's location in North Jersey and proximity to New York City is a perfect combination for many students. Virtually all the students here graduated in the top half of their high school classes and admission is moderately competitive. If you haven't slacked off in college prep courses and your standardized test scores are decent, you shouldn't have much of a problem gaining entry.

THE SCHOOL SAYS "..."

From The Admissions Office

"Students admitted to Ramapo College for Fall 2007 had an average SAT score of 1160 and ranked in the top 20 percent of their graduating class. Applications to the freshman class were the highest in the history of the college; admission was offered to fewer than half (45 percent) of the freshman applicants. Ramapo students come from all 21 counties in New Jersey as well as 17 states and more than 52 countries. Ninety percent of freshmen and about 60 percent of all full-time students live on campus, for a total of 2,929 residential students.

"Ranked a top pick, regional Top Public Universities, Ramapo College of New Jersey is sometimes mistaken for a private college. This is, in part, due to its unique interdisciplinary academic structure, its size of around 5,700 students, and its pastoral setting. Ramapo offers bachelor's degrees in the arts, business, humanities, social sciences, and the sciences as well as in professional studies, which include pre-law, premed, nursing, and social work. In addition, the college offers courses that make students eligible to obtain teacher certification at the elementary and secondary school levels.

"Undergraduate students choose to concentrate their studies in one of five schools: Anisfield School of Business; American and International Studies; Contemporary Arts; Theoretical and Applied Science; and Social Science and Human Services. Of the 700 course offerings and 40 academic programs, the most popular are business administration, communication arts, psychology, nursing, and biology."

For even more information on this school, turn to page 517 of the "Stats" section.

REGIS COLLEGE

235 WELLESLEY STREET, WESTON, MA 02493-1571 • ADMISSIONS: 781-768-7100 • FAX: 781-768-7071
E-MAIL: ADMISSION@REGISCOLLEGE.EDU • WEBSITE: WWW.REGISCOLLEGE.EDU

RATINGS
Quality of Life: 71   **Academic:** 75   **Admissions:** 71   **Financial Aid:** 68

STUDENTS SAY "..."

Academics

Regis College is "a small, Catholic liberal arts college" in the suburbs of Boston. The highlights of this "terrific institution" include "rigorous academics," "small classes," and a "close-knit" and "very diverse" student population. The "excellent nursing program" is "very popular." The "welcoming" administration is "always available." "Here at Regis, if you have a problem, there is always someone that can help you," promises a senior. The "extremely supportive and encouraging" professors are "very knowledgeable in their subject areas." "As with anywhere, you will have your teachers who suck" but most professors "really care about their students" and "really enjoy getting to know each student on a personal level." "I have been blessed to have met several very inspiring professors," says a happy junior. "They give you so much attention in and out of the classroom." Regis has been going through something of a transition since going coed, though "The typical student is female because it was an all-women's college until recently."

> **SURVEY SAYS...**
> Diverse student types on campus
> Students love Weston, MA
> Campus feels safe
> Frats and sororities are unpopular or nonexistent
> Musical organizations are popular
> Very little drug use

Life

Regis boasts a "quiet," "calm," and "beautiful" campus "in a great area" 12 miles from Boston. It's "small enough so everyone knows everyone else" and there is a real sense of community. "The students value that community and are sentimental about school traditions." "A lot of students participate in some type of sport." Student organizations "try very hard to hold activities on weekends that appeal to students," though most "go home," which can make for a "low-fun atmosphere." Otherwise, "Students spend time with friends during the week while attending classes" and there's a "nice swimming pool." One student notes that "Regis has become almost a commuter school." "The campus is deserted on the weekend." A shuttle is available for students who want to venture off campus, but "Having a car is almost necessary." "For fun many people leave campus and go to other schools for parties." Of course, "the city of Boston" provides an endless array of things to do.

Student Body

"Almost anyone can fit in and have a wonderful experience at Regis," reports a junior. "Regis has been trying hard to diversify its student population, and that shows here on campus." "A wide variety" of "social, ethnic, and socioeconomic groups" call this campus home. "There is a huge range of ethnic groups," says a student. While there are "people from all over the world who speak many different languages," the "typical student is your 'typical' student." The undergrads at Regis report that they are "friendly," "talkative," "intelligent," "hardworking," "goal-oriented," and "easy to get along with." They are also "energetic, outspoken, and generous." "Most aren't that into partying and just like to have fun with friends."

THE PRINCETON REVIEW SAYS

Admissions

Very important factors considered include: Application essay, academic GPA, recommendation(s), rigor of secondary school record, character/personal qualities. *Important factors considered include:* Class rank, standardized test scores, extracurricular activities, interview, talent/ability, volunteer work, work experience. *Other factors considered include:* Alumni/ae relation, first generation, level of applicant's interest. SAT or ACT required; TOEFL required of all international applicants. High school diploma is required and GED is accepted. *Academic units required:* 4 English, 3 mathematics, 2 science, (1 science labs), 2 foreign language, 2 social studies, 3 academic electives.

Financial Aid

Students should submit: FAFSA, institution's own financial aid form. The Princeton Review suggests that all financial aid forms be submitted as soon as possible after January 1. *Need-based scholarships/grants offered:* Federal Pell, SEOG, state scholarships/grants, private scholarships, the school's own gift aid, Federal Nursing Scholarships. *Loan aid offered:* Direct Subsidized Stafford, Direct Unsubsidized Stafford, Direct PLUS, Federal Perkins, Federal Nursing. Applicants will be notified of awards on a rolling basis beginning 3/15. Federal Work-Study Program available. Institutional employment available. Off-campus job opportunities are poor.

The Inside Word

In the words of one student, Regis is "a pretty easy school to get into." There are no cutoffs when it comes to standardized test scores. Decent grades in a solid college-prep curriculum ought to be enough to get you admitted without much of a problem. If you seek admission into the 3-year accelerated nursing program, though, you need a high school GPA of at least 3.4 and an 1100 or better on the Math and Critical Reading sections of the SAT.

THE SCHOOL SAYS "..."

From The Admissions Office

"Founded in 1927 by the Sisters of St. Joseph of Boston, Regis College is a four-year, coeducational, private liberal arts college. Regis College offers a place for young men and women to become individuals, through an innovative personal approach in the classroom and a strong spirit of friendship throughout the campus community. Regis students are educated to succeed in their careers and in their lives. From the start, they are encouraged to take a leadership role in their education. The college is uniquely designed to offer students academic support and flexibility as they complete their studies.

"Regis is located in Weston, Massachusetts, a residential community just 12 miles from metropolitan Boston. Our picturesque 132-acre campus has the best of both worlds: a suburban setting with quick and easy access to the cultural and social activities of the Boston area, as well as a multitude of internships and job opportunities. Our diverse student body benefits from a low student/faculty ratio, studies abroad in countless locations, and competes in NCAA Division III athletics.

"Whether participating in internships, cultivating academic partnerships that promote intellectual and social growth, or exploring the many attractions of the New England area, students will thrive in the 'Community of Learning' that is Regis College."

For even more information on this school, turn to page 517 of the "Stats" section.

RENSSELAER POLYTECHNIC INSTITUTE

110 EIGHTH STREET, TROY, NY 12180-3590 • ADMISSIONS: 518-276-6216 • FAX: 518-276-4072
FINANCIAL AID: 518-276-6813 • E-MAIL: ADMISSIONS@RPI.EDU • WEBSITE: WWW.RPI.EDU

RATINGS
Quality of Life: 68   Academic: 84   Admissions: 95   Financial Aid: 83

STUDENTS SAY ". . ."

Academics

Rensselaer Polytechnic Institute, which proud students declare "a small research institute making a large impact on the world," is "essentially a hard-core technical school; oriented toward engineering and the sciences, although the school is trying to expand its offerings" in the humanities and arts. The school has already made some headway; as one student points out, "There are a lot of students who are dedicated to their single major in a science or technology field here, which leads to a somewhat narrow-minded type of person...but RPI's saving grace is that it also offers rigorous degrees in architecture and the arts that make this technical institution more like a liberal arts college, as opposed to a strictly technical college." Students in all disciplines face "rigorous course loads" that provide "a lesson in perseverance and innovation to overcome future challenges." Most programs incorporate "a hands-on studio-based method" supplemented by "top-of-the-line facilities...and numerous resources for all students to use." RPI's identity as a research center helps here; according to one undergrad, "The greatest resource for students at RPI are the researchers. It's easy to go to any top-ranked school and take hard classes. It's much harder to find as many professors who are on the cutting edge of their disciplines and actively taking undergraduate students into their labs. RPI excels in this, and any RPI student who wants a research position can usually find one." RPI's co-op program and Career Development Center "are also outstanding, leading to a high placement rate in excellent jobs," although of the latter some warn that "many engineering firms are familiar with Rensselaer, but employers in other fields still have yet to learn of the students available."

Life

"The academics are challenging" at RPI, making life "stressful, but in a good way. Time management is a key to success here." A few students have trouble walking away from the books, but most "enjoy relaxing through various clubs and intramural sports" available to all. The Greek scene is popular, but it's not your stereotypical *Animal House* variety; sure, "there are definitely a bunch of parties every weekend if you're into that," but "they're all pretty much very responsible with sober bartenders and sober drivers." RPI's Greek organizations also "do a lot of community service in the area and philanthropy events on campus." Greek or not, many here agree that "one of the greatest things to do for fun is to head up to the field house on a Friday or Saturday night and watch some Division I men's hockey." For those who want something a little more active, "Intramural and inter-fraternity sports are a great way to unwind as well as just hanging out in our student-run union." Hometown Troy "is not the best town to live in, although it has a few cool things to do. But, Albany is only a 20-minute drive away (the bus is free), and there's always something to do there."

Student Body

"There are a lot of very, very nerdy kids here at RPI, as can be imagined at a school with primarily engineering students," but "there are a large number of 'normal' people as well, and each year, the percent of females in each incoming class increases." While the gender gap may be narrowing, it's still pretty wide, meaning that "there [may be] only one typical student at RPI: a white male. They might be into sports, video games, drinking, Greek life, computers, RPG, or whatever, but they're an overwhelming aspect of campus." The minority population includes "many Asian and Indian students." Nearly everyone "comes from the top of their class, so they are all very intelligent people" who are "driven and hardworking and think on a global level."

Admissions

Very important factors considered include: Class rank, academic GPA, rigor of secondary school record, standardized test scores. *Important factors considered include:* Application essay, recommendation(s), character/personal qualities, extracurricular activities, level of applicant's interest. *Other factors considered include:* Alumni/ae relation, geographical residence, interview, racial/ethnic status, talent/ability, volunteer work, work experience. SAT or ACT required; ACT with Writing component required. TOEFL required of all international applicants. High school diploma is required, and GED is accepted. *Academic units required:* 4 English, 4 mathematics, 3 science, 2 social studies. *Academic units recommended:* 4 science, 3 social studies.

Financial Aid

Students should submit: FAFSA, CSS/Financial Aid PROFILE. The Princeton Review suggests that all financial aid forms be submitted as soon as possible after January 1. *Need-based scholarships/grants offered:* Federal Pell, SEOG, state scholarships/grants, private scholarships, the school's own gift aid, Gates Millennium Scholarship, ACG, Smart Grants. *Loan aid offered:* Federal Perkins, state loans, college/university loans from institutional funds. Applicants will be notified of awards on or about 3/25. Federal Work-Study Program available. Institutional employment available. Off-campus job opportunities are good.

The Inside Word

Outstanding test scores and grades are pretty much a must for any applicant hopeful of impressing the RPI admissions committee. Underrepresented minorities and women—two demographics the school would like to augment—will get a little more leeway than others, but in all cases, the school is unlikely to admit anyone who lacks the skills and background to survive here. RPI offers many students January admission in order to allow them to pursue productive activities (work, travel, volunteering) in the fall semester following high school graduation.

THE SCHOOL SAYS "…"

From The Admissions Office

"The oldest degree-granting technological research university in North America, RPI or Rensselaer was founded in 1824 to instruct students to apply 'science to the common purposes of life.' Rensselaer offers more than 100 programs and 1,000 courses leading to bachelor's, master's, and doctoral degrees. Undergraduates pursue studies in architecture, engineering, humanities, arts, and social sciences, management and technology, science, and information technology (IT). A pioneer in interactive learning, Rensselaer provides real-world, hands-on educational opportunities that cut across academic disciplines. Students have ready access to laboratories and attend classes involving lively discussion, problem solving, and faculty mentoring. The Office of First-Year Experience provides programs for students and their primary support persons that begin even before students arrive on campus. Students are able to take full advantage of Rensselaer's three unique research platforms: the $80 million state-of-the-art Center for Biotechnology and Interdisciplinary Studies (CBIS); one of the world's most powerful academic supercomputers, the Computational Center for Nanotechnology Innovations (CCNI); and the newly opened Experimental Media and Performing Arts Center (EMPAC), which encourages students to explore the intersection of science, technology, and the arts. Newly renovated residence halls, wireless computing network, and studioclassrooms create a fertile environment for study and learning. Rensselaer offers recreational and fitness facilities plus numerous student-run organizations and activities, including fraternities and sororities, a newspaper, a radio station, drama and musical groups, and more than 160 clubs. In addition to intramural sports, NCAA varsity sports include Division I men's and women's ice hockey teams and 21 Division III men's and women's teams in 13 sports. The new East Campus Athletic Village, opened in 2009, raises the bar for student athletic facilities for varsity and non-varsity athletes alike, and includes a new football arena, basketball stadium, and sports medicine complex."

For even more information on this school, turn to page 518 of the "Stats" section.

THE RICHARD STOCKTON COLLEGE OF NEW JERSEY

JIM LEEDS ROAD, PO BOX 195, POMONA, NJ 08240 • ADMISSIONS: 609-652-4261 • FAX: 609-748-5541
E-MAIL: ADMISSIONS@STOCKTON.EDU • WEBSITE: WWW.STOCKTON.EDU

RATINGS
Quality of Life: 74   **Academic:** 69   **Admissions:** 81   **Financial Aid:** 75

STUDENTS SAY "..."

Academics

The Richard Stockton College of New Jersey is a midsized, "extremely affordable," "transfer-friendly" public school that "provides a very well-rounded liberal arts education." Classes are typically quite small and students tell us that the business programs here are excellent. There are also outstanding programs in marine science and solid programs in the visual and performing arts. The academic

> **SURVEY SAYS . . .**
> *Great computer facilities*
> *Students get along with local community*
> *Campus feels safe*
> *Student publications are popular*
> *Lots of beer drinking*

atmosphere at Stockton is different for different students. "If you want to receive a good education you can," says a math major, "but if you want to skate through, you can also do that." Professors come in "a huge variety." "Most of the professors are great teachers, prefer discussion-oriented classes instead of straight lecture, and are more than willing to help students succeed in and out of the classroom," says a computer science major. However, "there are a few" other faculty members that are "horrible." Registration at Stockton can be a pain. Some classes are reportedly "never available." Some students say that management is "very accessible and in touch." Others call the administration "cumbersome" and "generally a mess."

Life

"You need a strong stomach for campus food" and the parking situation is reportedly "pretty bad." Also, students say that the campus is located "in the sticks." However, an immediate benefit of that is that "the campus itself is right on the edge of New Jersey's Pine Barrens and it is absolutely gorgeous." Socially, "Stockton is a suitcase school that is bustling with commuters and residents during the week but is practically dead on the weekends." "There are plenty of clubs for people to join" and "all the generic stuff people usually do at college" is available here. The Greek system is small but pretty active. Intramural sports are popular and "real competitive." "There isn't much school pride" when it comes to intercollegiate sports, though. For students who stick around on the weekends, "there is the typical college party vibe," but nothing gets too crazy. There isn't a ton to do in the immediate area, but the campus is located "near the beach" and "Atlantic City is right around the corner." Students say that "it's pretty awesome to be so close to such a strong attraction."

Student Body

"There is great ethnic diversity on campus." Stockton has "a good mix" of "small-town kids" from south Jersey and kids from the areas around Philadelphia and New York City. There are lots of commuters. Only about one-third of all undergrads live in residence halls or other campus housing. "You have your hippies, but then you also have you sorority and fraternity members and athletes," observes a first-year student. You "see a lot of skateboarders," and the "Jersey Shore surfer" is pretty common as well. Students call themselves "environmentally conscious" and "beachy" and tell us they have an "overall laid-back demeanor." They are "interested in school but not obsessed with GPAs." Stockton is "somewhat cliquey" but "everyone is very friendly" and "and everyone generally gets along."

THE PRINCETON REVIEW SAYS

Admissions

Very important factors considered include: Class rank, academic GPA, rigor of secondary school record. *Important factors considered include:* Standardized test scores. *Other factors considered include:* Application essay, recommendation(s), alumni/ae relation, character/personal qualities, extracurricular activities, level of applicant's interest, talent/ability, volunteer work, work experience. SAT or ACT required; TOEFL required of all international applicants. High school diploma is required and GED is accepted. *Academic units required:* 4 English, 3 mathematics, 2 science, (2 science labs), 2 social studies, 5 academic electives. *Academic units recommended:* 4 English, 3 mathematics, 2 science, (2 science labs), 2 foreign language, 2 social studies, 5 academic electives.

Financial Aid

Students should submit: FAFSA. The Princeton Review suggests that all financial aid forms be submitted as soon as possible after January 1. *Need-based scholarships/grants offered:* Federal Pell, SEOG, state scholarships/grants, the school's own gift aid. *Loan aid offered:* Direct Subsidized Stafford, Direct Unsubsidized Stafford, Direct PLUS, Federal Perkins, state loans. Applicants will be notified of awards on a rolling basis beginning 4/1. Federal Work-Study Program available. Institutional employment available. Off-campus job opportunities are excellent.

The Inside Word

Admission at Stockton isn't terrifically competitive. If you can maintain a solid B average in a respectable college-bound high school curriculum and present average SAT scores, you should be fine. Your class rank is something that is very important as well. If your grades and test scores are below par, an on-campus interview is a wise idea.

THE SCHOOL SAYS "…"

From The Admissions Office

"Stockton College of New Jersey offers the atmosphere and rigorous academics of the very finest private institutions, at a surprisingly affordable cost. Stockton's outstanding faculty includes a Pulitzer Prize winner, two Fulbright Scholars, and the recipient of an Academy Award, several Emmy Awards, and a Grammy Award. Awards don't tell the whole story, though. Stockton's faculty is dedicated to teaching excellence and student success.

"Student life at Stockton is second to none. Our sports teams are nationally ranked, including the 2001 National Division III men's soccer champions. We recently opened a state-of-the-art, $17-million sports center that includes a fully equipped fitness center, and there are new arts and science, health science, and student housing buildings. Stockton's beautiful campus was voted one of the state's "Top 10 Architectural Treasures" by *New Jersey Monthly* magazine. Our pristine 1,600 acres are located within the Pinelands national preserves, including four lakes as well as trails for hiking and biking—all within a 10-minute drive to the popular southern New Jersey beach resorts. The numerous attractions of Philadelphia and New York City are easily accessible as well.

"Stockton features small class sizes, professors who are friendly and accessible, and student organizations to serve every interest. For the student seeking a total college experience at the most reasonable cost possible, Stockton College of New Jersey offers the best of both worlds. Stockton truly lives up to its slogan: 'An Environment for Excellence.'"

For even more information on this school, turn to page 518 of the "Stats" section.

RIDER UNIVERSITY

2083 LAWRENCEVILLE ROAD, LAWRENCEVILLE, NJ 08648-3099 ADMISSIONS: 800-257-9026 • FAX: 609-896-5042
E-MAIL: ADMISSIONS@RIDER.EDU • WEBSITE: WWW.RIDER.EDU

RATINGS
Quality of Life: 70   **Academic:** 72   **Admissions:** 77   **Financial Aid:** 73

STUDENTS SAY ". . ."

Academics

Rider University is a medium-sized suburban liberal arts school in New Jersey that offers internships galore and a wide variety of majors. Rider's Westminster Choir College (in nearby Princeton) is worth looking into if you can hum a tune exceptionally well, but the biggest draw is probably the "very good business program." Academically, "the classes aren't too big." "Last semester my biggest class had 17 kids in it," notes a public relations major. Coursework is generally "engaging." A few members of the faculty "should not be teaching," but most professors are "intelligent people with a lot to offer." They're "very interested and involved within their respective fields." "Professors are very easy to contact and are always excited to help answer a question even when you don't have them as a professor anymore," relates an accounting major. "It is easy to build close personal relationships with your professors, and that really helps students do well in the classroom." Views of the administration differ pretty radically. Some students call management "very efficient" and "simply wonderful;" other students say that the staff is "rude and very unhelpful." "It is very hard for me to get a straight answer," gripes an education major.

Life

Rider's main campus is "secluded from town" and full of too many "outdated and jail-like" buildings. Also, some dorms could stand to be "spruced up." The newer residence halls are "great" though, and the gleaming student recreation center is a big hit with many students. There's also a nice on-campus pub. Otherwise, "fun is a touchy topic." Disgruntled students tell us that life at Rider "is not amazingly exciting." It's "a suitcase school," they say, and "a ghost town on the weekends" because so many students drive home on Friday night. "Basically there's not a lot to do around here," laments a sophomore. Happier students report an "overwhelming" number of activities and a good amount of free food at weekend events. "One of the biggest perks about staying on the weekend is that you get a really good parking spot," says an optimistic sophomore. Many students who stick around also participate in the Greek system. "A lot of people party," too, but "the alcohol policies are extreme." As a result, there are "numerous parties off campus." Students also frequent "clubs and bars" in the area. While "there's nothing to do anywhere in Lawrenceville without having a car," Rider is situated "directly between" easily accessible Philadelphia and New York City.

Student Body

"Mostly, everyone is from New Jersey," but ethnic diversity is pretty laudable at Rider, and "students come from many different backgrounds." "It's not too hard to fit in." "There are a lot of students who take their work seriously." "There are the weird people who don't really socialize." There are also "slacker types" with "no sense of the real world" who are "trying to float through college" and "are more concerned with the party scene than academics." There are students "from middle-class homes" and wealthy students "with nice cars." You'll see quite a few women with "skinny jeans, Uggs, and poofy hair." There are "many clone students," too. "Your average student looks like your average kid." guesses a junior. "Overall, everyone has a niche" but "you have to join a group to make friends." "There are a lot of cliques," observes a senior. "The athletes stay with the athletes; the Greeks stay with the Greeks; and so on." Many people "stay connected to their high school friends."

THE PRINCETON REVIEW SAYS

Admissions

Very important factors considered include: Application essay, academic GPA, recommendation(s), rigor of secondary school record, standardized test scores. *Important factors considered include:* Level of applicant's interest. *Other factors considered include:* Class rank, alumni/ae relation, character/personal qualities, extracurricular activities, geographical residence, interview, state residency, talent/ability, volunteer work, work experience. SAT or ACT required. TOEFL required of all international applicants. High school diploma is required, and GED is accepted. *Academic units required:* 4 English, 3 mathematics. *Academic units recommended:* 4 mathematics, 4 science, (2 science labs), 2 foreign language, 2 social studies, 2 history.

Financial Aid

Students should submit: FAFSA. The Princeton Review suggests that all financial aid forms be submitted as soon as possible after January 1. *Need-based scholarships/grants offered:* Federal Pell, SEOG, state scholarships/grants, private scholarships, the school's own gift aid. *Loan aid offered:* Federal Perkins, state loans, college/university loans from institutional funds. Applicants will be notified of awards on a rolling basis beginning 2/20. Federal Work-Study Program available. Institutional employment available. Off-campus job opportunities are good.

The Inside Word

In the admissions world there are two all-important mandates: recruit the college's home state and recruit Jersey! As a school in the Garden State, Rider deserves some special attention for the diverse group of students it brings in each year. Students who wish to attend need to have a solid academic record and good test scores. A few bumps in your academic past, however, shouldn't pose too much of a threat.

THE SCHOOL SAYS "..."

From The Admissions Office

"Rider students are driven by their dreams of a fulfilling career and a desire to have an impact on the world around them. Rider is a place to apply your imagination, talents and aspirations in ways that will make a difference. A Rider education will prepare you as a leader and as a member of a team. When you graduate from Rider, you'll be a different person, confidently ready for your life's challenges and opportunities.

"We invite you to visit and experience Rider firsthand. Open Houses are offered in the fall and late spring, tours are available daily and Information Sessions are offered most weekends.

"Freshmen applicants are required to submit the results of either the SAT or ACT exam. The highest scores from either test will be considered for admission."

For even more information on this school, turn to page 519 of the "Stats" section.

ROBERTS WESLEYAN COLLEGE

2301 WESTSIDE DRIVE, ROCHESTER, NY 14624-1997 • ADMISSIONS: 585-594-6400 • FAX: 585-594-6371
E-MAIL: ADMISSIONS@ROBERTS.EDU • WEBSITE: WWW.ROBERTS.EDU

RATINGS
Quality of Life: 89   **Academic:** 84   **Admissions:** 82   **Financial Aid:** 73

STUDENTS SAY "..."

Academics

Roberts Wesleyan College in western New York is a "small" school with a pre-professional bent and a decidedly "Christian atmosphere." A few students tell us there's "too much religion and God stuff," but the vast majority of students love the "the integration of faith and learning" and the many opportunities to develop "personal character and

> **SURVEY SAYS . . .**
> *Students get along with local community*
> *Low cost of living*
> *Frats and sororities are unpopular or nonexistent*
> *Very little drug use*

spirituality." Roberts Wesleyan boasts "an excellent nursing program" with a "great reputation" in the local area. There's also a "solid" music program. Across the curriculum, classes are "small." "Not all the teachers here are amazing" but the faculty as a whole gets high marks. Professors are "passionate about their job and strong in their faith." "They aren't out to make your academic experience miserable," expounds a nursing major. "They want you to learn and they are tough, but all are very approachable and...want you to succeed." "All the teachers know their students by name," adds an education major. "Many of the professors will stop and talk on the path or whenever they see you." "The administration varies," says a criminal justice major. "Some are very easy to contact and others you have to jump [through] hoops to get to."

Life

The campus at Roberts Wesleyan is "really pretty and inviting." "Some of the buildings are very old," though, and "The food really isn't that good." The Christian aspects of the school play a dominant role in social life. "Chapel is three days a week for an hour," and you have to attend a little over half of them. The school is "alcohol and drug-free" (including nicotine). "There are visitation hours for males and females within each other's dorms." It isn't totally unheard of for students here to "get drunk," but most don't and "almost no one engages in premarital sex." For some students, "it's pretty much religion 24/7." They "get together a lot for Bible studies, or times to worship, or prayer." "A lot of people play intramural sports and participate in clubs." "We play a lot of games," adds a first-year student. "Snowball fights" and "deep conversations" are other popular pastimes. Off campus, the city of Rochester is a nice place that provides a decent amount of entertainment. This campus is in a "somewhat rural" area and "there is no public transportation from Roberts to anywhere," but if you have a car (or know someone with a car) it's easy to "go out to eat or go to coffee houses."

Student Body

At Roberts Wesleyan, it's basically "middle-class," "white" students "from New York State." "Atypical students are few and far between." "Generally, most kids grew up with some sort of Christian worldview" and were "raised in a Protestant church." They are "compassionate" people who "are looking for a good education along with spiritual growth." "We all commit to living our lives for Christ," relates a junior. Students also describe themselves as "conservative," "approachable, and nice." "Most people are really friendly and willing to help anyone." They are also "concerned about their academics." "The general Roberts student is pretty hard-working," observes a first-year student. "A lot of kids spend time doing schoolwork."

THE PRINCETON REVIEW SAYS

Admissions

Very important factors considered include: Academic GPA, rigor of secondary school record, standardized test scores, character/personal qualities, interview, religious affiliation/commitment. *Important factors considered include:* Application essay, recommendation(s), extracurricular activities. *Other factors considered include:* Class rank, alumni/ae relation, level of applicant's interest, talent/ability, volunteer work, SAT or ACT required; ACT with Writing component recommended. TOEFL required of all international applicants. High school diploma is required and GED is accepted. *Academic units required:* 4 English, 3 mathematics, 3 science, (1 science labs), 3 social studies. *Academic units recommended:* 4 mathematics, 4 science, (3 science labs), 3 foreign language.

Financial Aid

Students should submit: FAFSA, state aid form. The Princeton Review suggests that all financial aid forms be submitted as soon as possible after January 1. *Need-based scholarships/grants offered:* Federal Pell, SEOG, state scholarships/grants, private scholarships, the school's own gift aid. *Loan aid offered:* Direct Subsidized Stafford, Direct Unsubsidized Stafford, Direct PLUS, Federal Perkins. Applicants will be notified of awards on a rolling basis beginning 3/30. Federal Work-Study Program available. Institutional employment available. Off-campus job opportunities are fair.

The Inside Word

The grade-point averages of accepted applicants are often impressive, but standardized test scores are average. For marginal candidates, recommendations are vital. You want to show that you will fit well into this emphatically Christian environment. Additionally, note that Roberts Wesleyan accepts a large number of transfer students and makes transferring pretty easy to do.

THE SCHOOL SAYS "..."

From The Admissions Office

"A Roberts Wesleyan education is beneficial beyond just the first job—Roberts instills in students the knowledge and skills needed for a lifetime of learning and success. At Roberts Wesleyan College, we look for students who are interested in a Christian liberal arts education with plenty of professional opportunities. Students who would benefit from small class sizes, numerous internship options, a close-knit Christian community, and strong academic programs are encouraged to apply.

"Roberts Wesleyan College is a vital part of Rochester, N.Y.'s exceptional mix of educational opportunities. With nearly 2,000 students and a tradition of excellence since 1866, Roberts Wesleyan is a dynamic leader among American liberal arts colleges with a Christian worldview.

"Roberts Wesleyan offers more than 50 undergraduate programs, with graduate programs in education, school psychology and counseling, health administration, social work, management, marketing, Nursing Leadership & Administration, and Nursing Education. Roberts also offers undergraduate degree-completion programs for working adults in nursing (classroom-based) and organizational management (classroom and online). Northeastern Seminary on the Roberts campus offers Master of Divinity, Master of Arts in Theology and Transformational Leadership, and Doctor of Ministry degrees.

"Roberts Wesleyan is accredited by the Middle States Association of Colleges and Schools, the National Association of Schools of Music, the National Association of Schools of Art and Design, the Commission on Collegiate Nursing Education, the Council for Social Work Education, and the International Assembly for Collegiate Business Education (IACBE)."

For even more information on this school, turn to page 519 of the "Stats" section.

Rochester Institute of Technology

60 Lomb Memorial Drive, Rochester, NY 14623 • Admissions: 716-475-6631 • Fax: 716-475-7424
Financial Aid: 716-475-2186 • E-mail: admissions@rit.edu • Website: www.rit.edu

RATINGS
Quality of Life: 76   Academic: 77   Admissions: 85   Financial Aid: 92

STUDENTS SAY "..."

Academics

SURVEY SAYS . . .
Great computer facilities
Athletic facilities are great
Career services are great
Low cost of living

Uniting creativity, innovation, and applied knowledge, Rochester Institute of Technology is the place "where the technical left and artistic right brains collide." RIT offers a range of majors in technical fields—from game design to bioinformatics—as well as programs in art, engineering, and business. Across the board, there is an "emphasis on hands-on learning," and most majors require students to complete a cooperative work experience (basically, a paid internship), designed to "give you the opportunity to make connections in [an] industry within your field." On campus, undergraduates are encouraged to pursue research. Fortunately, "Funding is everywhere if a student takes the initiative to apply." The academic calendar at RIT is built around a "rigorous and fast-paced quarter system" that allows students to take more classes annually—but also keeps them burning the midnight oil. Not everyone is up to the challenge, and "The academic rigors of the school often force people to transfer or drop out." For those willing to put in the work, RIT offers all the tools for success: "All of the teachers I have had for problem-based classes (such as calculus and computer science) set up weekly office hours," and "Free tutoring is also widely available and excellent." In the classroom, "Professors are generally good, with the occasional whack-job or stellar teacher thrown in for good measure." Thanks to the "relatively small class sizes," teachers and students often develop personal relationships, and "even in the large lecture halls, [professors] try to get to know each student." Administrators get mixed reviews, but most students agree, "President Destler definitely shakes things up a bit (in a good way). He's all about the students and makes that very obvious."

Life

Thanks to RIT's demanding course work, "a lot of school life revolves around homework" and students are accustomed to "spending many nights in [the] lab working on an assignment." For fun, there are "huge campus events that happen once a year," and "[Division I] hockey is very popular" during the winter term. But, "For the most part, students don't really care about the clubs and organizations and simply do their own thing in their free time." In particular, students at RIT like to "play video games and drink"—though not necessarily in that order. RIT students also "go sledding in the winter, go to the movies," or make "late night diner runs." If you feel like taking a break from campus life, "There are many things to do on and off campus in the Rochester area. Museums and theaters are abundant, along with local festivals." However, not much lies within walking distance, so "a car is a necessity."

Student Body

With an unusual assortment of undergraduate majors on offer, RIT attracts a "wide variety" of people and personalities, including, "art students, engineers, computer geeks, ROTC guys, deaf students, GLBTQ students, [and] foreign students." A unique addition to the student population, "There are also many deaf/hard of hearing students, since RIT is home to the National Technical Institute for the Deaf (NTID)." Socially, students are divided into two major categories: "Half of the students play video games all the time and the other half socialize, go to the gym, and party." No matter what camp they fall into, "there's 15,000 undergrads, so everyone has a nook somewhere" and most students "find people like them and make friends easily." Given the school's technical focus, it's no surprise that, "most students are self proclaimed computer nerds," and "even the 'cool kids' have secret passions for Star Trek." A fortunate perk of attending school here is that "At any time, someone within 100 feet of you can fix your computer for you." Unfortunately, to the chagrin of many students, "women are still underrepresented on campus," ringing in at about 33 percent of the undergraduate population.

Admissions

Very important factors considered include: Academic GPA, rigor of secondary school record. *Important factors considered include:* Class rank, standardized test scores. *Other factors considered include:* Application essay, recommendation(s), character/personal qualities, extracurricular activities, first generation, interview, level of applicant's interest, talent/ability, volunteer work, w SAT or ACT required; TOEFL required of all non-English speaking applicants. High school diploma is required, and GED is accepted. *Academic units required:* 4 English, 2 mathematics, 2 science, (1 science labs), 4 social studies, 10 academic electives. *Academic units recommended:* 4 English, 3 mathematics, 3 science, (2 science labs), 3 foreign language, 4 social studies, 5 academic electives.

Financial Aid

Students should submit: FAFSA, institution's own financial aid form, state aid form. The Princeton Review suggests that all financial aid forms be submitted as soon as possible after January 1. *Need-based scholarships/grants offered:* Federal Pell, SEOG, state scholarships/grants, private scholarships, the school's own gift aid. *Loan aid offered:* Direct Subsidized Stafford, Direct Unsubsidized Stafford, Direct PLUS, Federal Perkins, alternative loans. Applicants will be notified of awards on a rolling basis beginning 3/15. Federal Work-Study Program available. Institutional employment available. Off-campus job opportunities are excellent.

The Inside Word

The RIT admissions department is wired. Through their website, you can live chat with admissions or other students, follow their Twitter feed, join their Facebook community, or read blogs written by current students. When applying to RIT, prospective students must indicate their intended major (as well as a second and third choice) on their applications. Admissions requirements vary based on a student's desired field of study, though a student's academic record, test scores, personal essay, and recommendations are usually the most important factors in an admissions decision.

THE SCHOOL SAYS "..."

From The Admissions Office

"RIT is among the world's leading career-oriented, technological institutions. Ambitious, creative, diverse, and career-oriented students from every state and more than 100 foreign countries find a home in RIT's innovative, vibrant living/learning community. The university's eight colleges offer undergraduate and graduate programs areas such as engineering, computing, information technology, engineering technology, business, hospitality, science, art, design, photography, biomedical sciences, game design and development, and the liberal arts including psychology, advertising and public relations, and public policy Distinctive academic offerings include microelectronic and software engineering, imaging science, film and animation, biotechnology, physician assistant, new media, international business, telecommunications, and the programs in the School for American Crafts. In addition, students may choose from more than 80 different minors to develop personal and professional interests that complement their academic program. As home of the National Technical Institute for the Deaf (NTID), RIT is a leader in providing educational opportunities and access services for deaf and hard-of-hearing students. Experiential learning has been a hallmark of an RIT education since 1912. Every academic program at RIT offers some form of experiential education opportunity which may include cooperative education, internships, study abroad, and undergraduate research. Students work hard, but learning is complemented with plenty of organized and spontaneous events and activities. RIT is a unique blend of rigor and fun, creativity and specialization, intellect and practice that prepares alumni for long-term career success in global society."

For even more information on this school, turn to page 520 of the "Stats" section.

ROGER WILLIAMS UNIVERSITY

One Old Ferry Road, Bristol, RI 02809 • Admissions: 401-254-3500 • Fax: 401-254-3557
E-mail: admit@rwu.edu • Website: www.rwu.edu

RATINGS
Quality of Life: 81   Academic: 77   Admissions: 82   Financial Aid: 78

STUDENTS SAY ". . ."
Academics

Roger Williams University is a "fairly small" private school in a suburban Rhode Island community "right on the water overlooking Mount Hope Bay" where the view "can't be beat." There's a nationally renowned program in marine biology, as well as a very demanding architecture program. Beyond the classroom, there are "endless opportunities" for

"hands-on" undergraduate research and study abroad. Some students say the administration is "top notch." Others charge that "registration is a complete pain" and call management "extremely, unnecessarily bureaucratic." The faculty is generally "wonderful," "except for one or two who are just boring." Most RWU professors are "always trying to engage students" and are "approachable." "If they can't teach it to you in class, they will try something different outside of class," one student explains. Classes are small and intimate, too. "I like being in small classes where the professor is on a first-name basis with every student," says an English literature major. "This school isn't a Harvard or a Caltech," concludes a biology major, "but it seems to serve its place in the education pecking order fairly well."

Life

RWU's "breathtaking" campus is "well kept" and "the new buildings are gorgeous." "The food is *incredible.*" "It's healthier than most food at other schools," too. Residence halls are "run down" and "filthy" or "very homey and cozy," presumably depending on where you live. Socially, Roger Williams is "a plethora of fun," where "intramural sports are incredibly popular." "There are nightly programs and guest lectures on campus." A few times each year, the old gym becomes "a nightclub with a theme." There are "tons" of activities—everything from squirrel watching to kayaking. Thanks to the "amazing waterfront location," "many students spend a great deal of time on or near the water." "Choosing not to be a part of [the party] scene does not condemn you to social death," either. However, "a lot of students frequent the local bars not necessarily to party or get drunk, but to be social." Off campus, nearby Providence and Newport are "very popular for evening activities" and "it's a reasonably decent drive up to Boston."

Student Body

Nearly 80 percent of the student body ventures to Roger Williams from out-of-state. "The typical student comes from a suburban New England town" or from the mid-Atlantic region. Many students note that RWU stands for "Rich White Underachievers." "The parking lot is full of BMWs and Volvos" and there is definitely a contingent of "astronomically rich" kids, but "there are many middle-class students" as well. These students "are usually preppy" and "dress fashionably." The architecture students consider themselves "a different breed from most of the students on campus" but virtually everyone comes "from the same mold." It's "a sea" of white "but very tan" students. "I grew up in affluent suburban Connecticut and when I got here I was like 'Wow, it's not very diverse here at all.'" To be sure, "minority students are fully accepted into the college community." It's just there aren't many of them. "It's so homogeneous here, it hurts."

Admissions

Very important factors considered include: Application essay, academic GPA, recommendation(s), rigor of secondary school record, standardized test scores. *Important factors considered include:* Class rank, extracurricular activities. *Other factors considered include:* Alumni/ae relation, first generation, level of applicant's interest, talent/ability, volunteer work, work experience. SAT or ACT required; ACT with Writing component recommended. High school diploma is required and GED is accepted. *Academic units required:* 4 English, 3 mathematics, 2 science, (2 science labs), 2 social studies, 2 history, 2 academic electives. *Academic units recommended:* 4 English, 4 mathematics, 4 science, (2 science labs), 2 foreign language, 3 social studies, 3 history, 3 academic electives.

Financial Aid

Students should submit: FAFSA, CSS/Financial Aid PROFILE Regular filing deadline is 2/1. The Princeton Review suggests that all financial aid forms be submitted as soon as possible after January 1. *Need-based scholarships/grants offered:* Federal Pell, SEOG, state scholarships/grants, private scholarships, the school's own gift aid. *Loan aid offered:* Federal Perkins. Applicants will be notified of awards on a rolling basis beginning 3/20. Federal Work-Study Program available. Institutional employment available. Off-campus job opportunities are excellent.

The Inside Word

Admission to the school's well-regarded architecture program is competitive; all other programs are much less so. Architecture candidates should apply early and would be well advised to spend considerable effort on their portfolios.

THE SCHOOL SAYS "..."

From The Admissions Office

"Looking for a beautiful, waterfront campus in historic New England? You've come to the right place! Welcome to Roger Williams University. Our 140-acre campus is complete with state-of-the-art facilities, brand new residence and academic halls and conveniently located midway between the historic seaside town of Newport, RI and the state's creative capital, Providence. RWU's campus is also only one hour from Boston and three hours from New York City.

"Ever heard of transdisciplinary education? Well you will. It's the education you'll receive at RWU, an innovator in the field of integrative education. Our aim is to educate citizen-scholars for the 21st century, which means outcome-based teaching. Yes, we want you to major in a subject you're interested in, but we want you to be able to apply that knowledge to complex problems you'll find in the real world, not just in your classes. A Roger Williams University education centers around personalized attention, a focus on community service and sustainability, student and faculty research and preparation for careers and future study.

"With 40 individual majors, RWU offers options unparalleled by many schools of similar size and more hands-on learning opportunities than many larger institutions. Still not convinced? Come to visit our campus and meet with our professors and deans."

For even more information on this school, turn to page 520 of the "Stats" section.

ROSEMONT COLLEGE

1400 MONTGOMERY AVENUE, ROSEMONT, PA 19010 • ADMISSIONS: 610-526-2966 • FAX: 610-520-4399
E-MAIL: ADMISSIONS@ROSEMONT.EDU • WEBSITE: WWW.ROSEMONT.EDU

RATINGS
Quality of Life: 78   Academic: 76   Admissions: 79   Financial Aid: 72

STUDENTS SAY "..."

Academics

Rosemont College, a newly coeducational liberal arts college just outside of Philadelphia, "is about providing the essential tools...to become active, independent, aware and analytical members of society, so that they may be successful in whichever path they choose to pursue." How are those tools conveyed? Reportedly through an "education centered around personal attention, leadership opportunities, and friendship." "The class sizes are small so there is more discussion in the classroom." "Overall, the professors are excellent, and they are very concerned about their students." One

student even describes having "gained confidence as a young woman just because the professors have invested themselves into showing me that they care about my individual success." Additionally, the college's "location and the natural beauty of the campus also help the students to feel safe." Students also really appreciate that the college "provides a lot of financial aid." Academic drawbacks include those typical of a small college: "All classes are only offered once a year, either always in the fall or always in the spring. Or they are offered every two years or only once." So if you are interested in a course, best to take it the first time you see it offered—it might not be offered again.

Life

"Rosemont is known as a 'suitcase college,'" meaning that "most students go home or leave campus for the weekends." Still, "there are activities on campus regularly" during the week, and for those who stick around on weekends. There is "movie night, casino night," and for those looking for a cause to support, "there are many special interest clubs." The Rosemont Activities Council also sponsors dance parties. "The most popular party is the Halloween party because it is the one party that serves free beer to the students who are over 21." And speaking of beer, "Admittedly, people like the bar scene." That common predilection, coupled with the "strict rules and regulations about alcohol" that Rosemont enforces, means that many "students find other colleges and places to have fun." Luckily for them, it's easy to get off campus. "The R5 train a few blocks from campus can take you into Philly or the movies or a grocery store (for real food)." In addition to the taste of city life Philadelphia has to offer, "many students like to go to the King of Prussia mall for shopping."

Student Body

Previously an all-women's college, Rosemont welcomed its first coeducational class in the fall of 2009. Thus, the student body admittedly underwent changes this past year! However, students from the once all female campus, characterize the student body thusly: "Typically everybody is very friendly...and pretty driven." "They understand that school comes first, but that it is also important to socialize." "They are seriously involved in one or two clubs on campus and may attend a couple of the several campus functions each semester." But beyond these common qualities, the student body is remarkably diverse, consisting "of many different ethnicities and religious backgrounds." "Some wear a hijab, some are running around in a little sundress. Then there are students who are changing their sexual identity." Atypical students are the commuters, who might describe their experience at Rosemont as feeling "a little left out."

Admissions

Very important factors considered include: Rigor of secondary school record, interview. *Important factors considered include:* Class rank, application essay, academic GPA, recommendation(s), standardized test scores, extracurricular activities, talent/ability, volunteer work. *Other factors considered include:* alumni/ae relation, character/personal qualities, work experience. SAT required; TOEFL required of all international applicants. High school diploma is required and GED is accepted. *Academic units required:* 4 English, 3 mathematics, 3 science, (2 science labs), 1 social studies, 1 history, 7 academic electives. *Academic units recommended:* 4 English, 3 mathematics, 3 science, (2 science labs), 2 foreign language, 2 social studies, 2 history, 4 academic electives.

Financial Aid

Students should submit: FAFSA. The Princeton Review suggests that all financial aid forms be submitted as soon as possible after January 1. *Need-based scholarships/grants offered:* Federal Pell, SEOG, state scholarships/grants, private scholarships, the school's own gift aid. *Loan aid offered:* Federal Perkins, other, alternative loans offered, payment plans offered. Applicants will be notified of awards on a rolling basis beginning 2/15. Federal Work-Study Program available. Institutional employment available. Off-campus job opportunities are good.

The Inside Word

Rosemont's Admissions Staff wants to ensure that its students are a perfect fit for both classroom and community. While high school transcript, standardized test scores, and letters of recommendation are all major considerations, pros here strongly suggest a campus visit and admissions interview.

THE SCHOOL SAYS "..."

From The Admissions Office

"Current Rosemont students tell us that the college provides them with an excellent education, that their experience is empowering, and that at Rosemont they meet friends they will keep for life. Rosemont has provided a unique educational experience for almost 85 years and continues to seek to enroll students interested in the liberal arts who have the capacity and desire to pursue a rigorous academic program. Students are considered without regard to race, religion, disability, or ethnic or national origin. A candidate for admission must present a satisfactory record of scholastic ability and personal integrity from an accredited high school as well as acceptable scores on the SAT or ACT. The student must have an official copy of his/her high school transcript sent to Rosemont's Office of Admissions. An applicant's secondary school preparation should include 16 college preparatory courses. Applicants are expected to carry a full academic program during their senior year of high school. Two recommendations are required in support of the student's application. Applications for admission are accepted on a rolling basis. A personal interview with a member of the Admissions Staff is strongly recommended as an important part of the application process.

"To arrange for an interview and a tour, or to receive additional information, students should contact the Office of Admissions."

For even more information on this school, turn to page 521 of the "Stats" section.

ROWAN UNIVERSITY

201 MULLICA HILL ROAD, GLASSBORO, NJ 08028 • ADMISSIONS: 856-256-4200 • FAX: 856-256-4430
E-MAIL: ADMISSIONS@ROWAN.EDU • WEBSITE: WWW.ROWAN.EDU

RATINGS
Quality of Life: 61   **Academic:** 71   **Admissions:** 84   **Financial Aid:** 70

STUDENTS SAY "..."
Academics

A New Jersey state school just southeast of Philadelphia, Rowan University is "dedicated to offering students a high quality education at an affordable price" as well as "a prodigious college experience through its many social, cultural and recreational organizations, events and activities." The school is perhaps best known for its "amazing education program that prepares future teachers in the best way possible," but students here tell us that offerings in engineering, music, business, history, and radio/television/film also shine. Rowan's science departments recently received an upgrade with "newer facilities" that are "very modern and have great equipment." Professors here receive good marks overall, although students warn that there is "too much variation in the quality of a course depending on the professor." "You could end up with great professors who are also tough, but you could also end up with professors whose courses aren't very challenging at all," explains a student. "For me, though, I have found the workload quite sizable and tough at times."

Life

"Campus life during the week tends to be pretty quiet" at Rowan, though most students are active within many of the campus' popular clubs and organizations. Others partake in bowling, shopping, laid back parties, and 50-cent movies (typically "the ones that came out of theaters but have not been released on DVD yet"). There are "plenty of parties to be found on weekends"—but be warned as the weekend starts on "Thursday night, and nearly everyone goes out." Things calm down a bit on Fridays and Saturdays when some students "go home to their families," but those who remain behind "usually end up having a lot of fun." Although drinking is popular, "Most people don't pressure other people into drinking," and nonalcoholic events are available. As one student explains, "There are a lot of options in terms of on-campus jobs, clubs, sports, and other organizations. If Rowan doesn't offer something you're interested in, you can get a few friends and start it on your own!" Many students choose to seek entertainment in nearby Philadelphia; the city is accessible by bus.

Student Body

The Rowan student body is "ethnically diverse but the majority are Caucasian and familiar with the region of south Jersey." Students are described as "very down-to-earth," "normal," and "average to high-middle class kids just trying to get an education." Many "get involved in several things on campus...have at least one job on-campus or are members of at least one club or organization." "Anyone can find a place to fit in at Rowan University because of the wide variety of students, events and organizations Rowan University offers." Some students "keep to themselves...[but] overall, students are very friendly and mannered. It's a more mature level of interaction," explains an undergrad.

Admissions

Very important factors considered include: Rigor of secondary school record. *Important factors considered include:* Class rank, academic GPA, standardized test scores. *Other factors considered include:* Recommendation(s), character/personal qualities, extracurricular activities, talent/ability, volunteer work, work experience. SAT or ACT required; TOEFL required of all international applicants. High school diploma is required and GED is accepted. *Academic units required:* 4 English, 3 mathematics, 2 science, (2 science labs), 2 social studies. *Academic units recommended:* 4 mathematics, 3 science, 2 foreign language.

Financial Aid

Students should submit: FAFSA. The Princeton Review suggests that all financial aid forms be submitted as soon as possible after January 1. *Need-based scholarships/grants offered:* Federal Pell, SEOG, state scholarships/grants, private scholarships, the school's own gift aid. Applicants will be notified of awards on a rolling basis beginning 3/15. Federal Work-Study Program available. Institutional employment available. Off-campus job opportunities are good.

The Inside Word

Low in-state tuition draws lots of applicants to Rowan, resulting in a pretty high rejection rate. Don't expect too personal an experience during this process. Admissions officers crunch numbers, then consider the balance of the application for marginal applicants, so a good letter of recommendation or an impressive slate of extracurriculars can really help out here. Solid high school students should encounter little difficulty gaining entry, though the school does grow more selective every year as its profile rises.

THE SCHOOL SAYS "..."

From The Admissions Office

"Rowan University is a selective, progressive public university with the funds and public support to transform itself into a top regional university. It is using these resources to improve the academic quality of the university while keeping tuition affordable. Because of its large endowment, the university is able to compete with private colleges and produce direct benefits for students. The university is in the midst of a $530-million 10-year plan to expand the campus, improve facilities, and hire more faculty. By implementing a comprehensive plan for enrollment management, Rowan University will maintain its reputation as a high-quality, moderate-price university.

"At Rowan, students have access to the resources of a large university without sacrificing the personal attention and small class size of a private college. All classes are taught by professors, not teaching assistants. The university enrolls more than 10,000 students among seven colleges (Business, Communication, Education, Engineering, Fine and Performing Arts, Liberal Arts and Sciences, and Professional & Continuing Education). Students can choose from 58 undergraduate majors and 29 graduate programs leading to master's and doctoral degrees."

For even more information on this school, turn to page 521 of the "Stats" section.

RUTGERS, THE STATE UNIVERSITY OF NEW JERSEY—NEW BRUNSWICK

65 DAVIDSON ROAD, PISCATAWAY, NJ 08854-8097 • ADMISSIONS: 732-932-4636 • FAX: 732-445-0237
FINANCIAL AID: 732-932-7057 • E-MAIL: ADMISSIONS@ASB-UGADM.RUTGERS.EDU • WEBSITE: WWW.RUTGERS.EDU

RATINGS
Quality of Life: 63   Academic: 66   Admissions: 87   Financial Aid: 73

STUDENTS SAY "..."

Academics

Rutgers, The State University of New Jersey—New Brunswick, "is the kind of university [at which], if you make the effort to create your niche and find opportunities to succeed, you will have one of the best experiences of your life." With "a great study-abroad program, solid academic departments and professors, the vast resources of a large research [school] and lots of scholarship money for honors students," Rutgers "offers boundless opportunity, both educational and professional, but you have to be willing to go out and seek it." Rutgers' immenseness is made

> **SURVEY SAYS . . .**
> Class discussions are rare
> Great computer facilities
> Athletic facilities are great
> Diverse student types on campus
> Everyone loves the Scarlet Knights
> Student publications are popular
> Lots of beer drinking
> Hard liquor is popular

more manageable by its subdivision into 13 colleges, "each with its own unique community and environment, all unified under one entity that can afford all the opportunities of a large university." Even so, the university's bureaucracy is legendary. One student writes, "The school seems to take pride in its web of red tape. The famous 'RU Screw' has become so notorious that the university president had to publicly denounce it." It's a good sign that Rutgers "is progressively changing its administrative policies under the administration of its relatively new president. There is a renewed focus on student service, and the changes are evident." As at many state schools, "Good things will not happen at Rutgers by sitting in the corner and waiting for opportunity to knock. It is a big school, so the more you put yourself out and make yourself known, the more likely you'll be able to find help in academics and administration." For self-starters, the rewards can be great. One writes, "I've had the opportunity to [conduct] my own research in the Rutgers facilities." Indeed, "there is a lot of research going on at Rutgers. The topics are numerous, and there are plenty of spots to fill if you look around well enough."

Life

"Weekdays are busy, and you can find places crowded at any time of the day" on the Rutgers campus. "There's always something going on: concerts, free movies, talks. It's all about diversity and going out to find what you want to do." Student government "is huge." Students say there are "always voter registration drives, and we even have Tent State University in the spring, during which a bunch of political student groups set up tents on the main courtyard and camp out for a week handing out literature, having fun stuff (concerts, etc.), and talking to people about what they do and how they can get involved." For some, "drinking is a big thing." One student writes, "If there was no such thing as getting inebriated, there would be nothing to do here." Many refute that position, noting "there are other things you can do as well. There are lots of places to eat and drink coffee...or going to a small discussion group with Jhumpa Lahiri, the Pulitzer Prize winning writer," to name a few. While weekdays are lively, weekends are another story. One student comments, "Life at Rutgers would feel more college-y if people didn't leave on weekends and it [didn't feel] so deserted."

Student Body

Rutgers "is huge, so there is just about every type of person you could think of here." One undergrad observes, "With so many students, it's hard not to find others with whom you fit in. But the drawback to such a large student body is that you need to go out and make friends; you can't expect them to come to you." Another student adds, "To be fair, sometimes it feels a bit like high school (there are 'skaters' and 'preps' and 'thugs' and all that), but once you're an upperclassmen you kind of learn to ignore it."

THE PRINCETON REVIEW SAYS

Admissions

Very important factors considered include: Class rank, academic GPA, rigor of secondary school record, standardized test scores. *Other factors considered include:* application essay, recommendation(s), extracurricular activities, first generation, geographical residence, interview, racial/ethnic status, state residency, talent/ability, volunteer work, work experience. SAT or ACT required; TOEFL required of all international applicants. High school diploma is required, and GED is accepted. *Academic units required:* 4 English, 3 mathematics, 2 science, 2 foreign language, 5 academic electives. *Academic units recommended:* 4 mathematics, 2 foreign language.

Financial Aid

Students should submit: FAFSA. The Princeton Review suggests that all financial aid forms be submitted as soon as possible after January 1. *Need-based scholarships/grants offered:* Federal Pell, SEOG, state scholarships/grants, private scholarships, the school's own gift aid, outside scholarships. *Loan aid offered:* Direct Subsidized Stafford, Direct Unsubsidized Stafford, Direct PLUS, Federal Perkins, state loans, college/university loans from institutional funds, other, other educational loans. Applicants will be notified of awards on a rolling basis beginning 2/1.

The Inside Word

With a literal mountain of applications to process each admissions season, Rutgers does not have the luxury of time. The school looks at your grades, the quality of your high school curriculum, your standardized test scores, and your essay to decide whether you can make the grade at Rutgers. Although the school grows more competitive each year, solid students should still find little difficulty getting in.

THE SCHOOL SAYS "..."

From The Admissions Office

"Rutgers, The State University of New Jersey, one of only 62 members of the Association of American Universities, is a research university that attracts students from across the nation and around the world. What does it take to be accepted for admission to Rutgers University? Our primary emphasis is on your past academic performance as indicated by your high school grades (particularly in required academic subjects), your class rank or cumulative average, the strength of your academic program, your standardized test scores on the SAT or ACT, any special talents you may have, and your participation in school and community activities. We seek students with a broad diversity of talents, interests, and backgrounds. Above all else, we're looking for students who will get the most out of a Rutgers education—students with the intellect, initiative, and motivation to make full use of the opportunities we have to offer.

"First-year applicants should take the SAT or the ACT (with Writing component). Test scores are not required for students who graduated high school more than two years ago or have completed more than 12 college credits since graduating."

For even more information on this school, turn to page 522 of the "Stats" section.

SACRED HEART UNIVERSITY

5151 Park Avenue, Fairfield, CT 06825 • Admissions: 203-371-7880 • Fax: 203-365-7607
E-mail: enroll@sacredheart.edu • Website: www.sacredheart.edu

RATINGS
Quality of Life: 77   **Academic:** 75   **Admissions:** 83   **Financial Aid:** 71

STUDENTS SAY "..."

Academics
Business is big business at Sacred Heart University, where one-third of a recent class graduated with an undergraduate business degree. The "up-and-coming" Welch College of Business (named for former General Electric CEO Jack Welch) utilizes the school's proximity to New York City to "enable students majoring in business, finance, media studies, etc., with tremendous opportunities" for internships. Nursing, physical therapy, and athletic training are among the school's other strong programs. "The surrounding towns provide amazing sites for...clinical experiences," so many members of SHU's career-minded student body leave here with solid experience under their belts to go along with course knowledge. However, pre-professional preparation is only part of the picture at this "small, Catholic university that prides itself [on] religion and faith." To ensure that students gain general knowledge along with expertise in their specialization (and to reinforce the school's commitment to the liberal-arts driven Catholic Intellectual Tradition), SHU recently introduced a Common Core Curriculum focusing on such lofty topics as justice and humanity's place in the cosmos. A number of students complain about the added requirements and deem the program "a waste of time," but most prefer to focus on the positives, telling us that SHU is "full of spirit along with great academics in a well-balanced manner that allows for the best and fullest college experience one could ask for."

Life
"People are heavily involved in community service, [with] Habitat for Humanity being the largest [service organization] on campus." "If you're into community service and volunteering"—and most students here are—"you'll be in your glory with the opportunities that are available for students." SHU undergrads take the school's mission of service seriously, although that doesn't mean they don't also know how to have a good time. "During the week the school is pretty laid back," but on weekends "a good portion of the student population goes out to clubs to drink." One student explains that "Sacred Heart isn't a party school so much as a bar school." Weekends are spent "frivolously" by many, although those who shun the alcohol scene say "the school does supply fun activities on campus" for them, including movie nights and concerts. Intercollegiate football, basketball, and hockey are all popular as well. Hometown Fairfield "offers shopping, good food, and the beach during warmer months" in addition to the clubs, and "The train is very close [to campus] so you can ride to New Haven or New York City for the day."

Student Body
The typical SHU undergrad "is pretty well-rounded [and is] involved in sports, community service, and clubs." She (two out of three students are female) is "preppy, friendly, and likes to have fun." The small size of the student body means that "everyone is involved in many different groups on campus" and that many "are student athletes. If they are not on one of the Division I sports teams then they are doing some type of club team." There are "a lot of people from Long Island" and an overall "strong Northeast presence (New York, New Jersey, Massachusetts in addition to Connecticut natives)." Many students (though hardly all) come from affluent families. As one student observes, "The parking lot says a lot. Lots of BMWs, Mercedes, and Audis." Other than their charitable undertakings, which are considerable, students tend not to look far beyond their daily lives and obligations. "The majority of students are not very active thinkers on world and political issues outside of their own lives," one student observes.

Admissions

Very important factors considered include: Academic GPA, rigor of secondary school record. *Important factors considered include:* Class rank, application essay, recommendation(s), character/personal qualities, extracurricular activities, interview, talent/ability, volunteer work, work experience. *Other factors considered include:* Standardized test scores (optional), alumni/ae relation, first generation, geographical residence, level of applicant's interest, racial/ethnic status, religious affiliation/commitment, state residency. TOEFL required of all international applicants. High school diploma is required, and GED is accepted. *Academic units required:* 4 English, 3 mathematics, 3 science, (1 science labs), 2 foreign language, 3 social studies, 3 history, 3 academic electives. *Academic units recommended:* 4 English, 4 mathematics, 4 science, (2 science labs), 4 foreign language, 4 social studies, 4 history, 4 academic electives.

Financial Aid

Students should submit: FAFSA, CSS/Financial Aid PROFILE, noncustodial PROFILE. The Princeton Review suggests that all financial aid forms be submitted as soon as possible after January 1. *Need-based scholarships/grants offered:* Federal Pell, SEOG, state scholarships/grants, private scholarships, the school's own gift aid. *Loan aid offered:* Direct Subsidized Stafford, Direct Unsubsidized Stafford, Direct PLUS, Federal Perkins, state loans, alternative loans. Applicants will be notified of awards on a rolling basis beginning 3/1. Federal Work-Study Program available. Institutional employment available. Off-campus job opportunities are excellent.

The Inside Word

Admissions officers at Sacred Heart take the time to consider each applicant on his or her own merits. There's no formula-crunching here; applicants have ample opportunity to make the case why they belong here on their applications. A campus visit is strongly recommended as a way of expressing your interest in the school and setting yourself apart from the crowd. SHU accepts the Common Application.

THE SCHOOL SAYS "…"

From The Admissions Office

"Sacred Heart University, distinguished by the personal attention it provides its students, is a thriving, dynamic university known for its commitment to academic excellence, cutting-edge technology, and community service. The second-largest Catholic university in New England, Sacred Heart continues to be innovative in its offerings to students; recently launched programs include Connecticut's first doctoral program in physical therapy, an MBA program for liberal arts undergraduates at the newly AACSB-accredited John F. Welch College of Business, and a campus in County Kerry, Ireland. The university's commitment to experiential learning incorporates concrete, real-life study for students in all majors. Drawing on the robust resources in New England and New York City, students are connected with research and internship opportunities ranging from co-ops at international advertising agencies to research with faculty on marine life in the Long Island Sound. These experiential learning opportunities are complemented by a rich student life program offering more than 80 student organizations including strong music programs, media clubs, and academic honor societies. Sacred Heart University is test-optional; SAT/ACT scores are not required but will be considered is submitted. For students taking the SAT more than once, the highest Math score and the highest Critical Reading score will be evaluated by the admissions committee. No current policy exists for the use of the SAT Writing component."

For even more information on this school, turn to page 522 of the "Stats" section.

SAINT ANSELM COLLEGE

100 SAINT ANSELM DRIVE, MANCHESTER, NH 03102-1310 • ADMISSIONS: 888-4ANSELM
FAX: 603-641-7550 • FINANCIAL AID: FINANCIAL_AID@ANSELM.EDU • WEBSITE: WWW.ANSELM.EDU

RATINGS
Quality of Life: 86   Academic: 84   Admissions: 84   Financial Aid: 77

STUDENTS SAY "..."

Academics

If you long for four years of "hard classes" and a faith-welcoming atmosphere, consider "wonderful, small" Saint Anselm College in Manchester, New Hampshire. The nursing program is reportedly "awesome," but Saint Anselm is best known for providing "a true liberal arts education." The college provides a liberal arts 'foundation' for all majors, but the biggest and best known programs are in nursing, business and criminal justice. In addition to comprehensive exams in every major, all students must complete courses in philosophy and theology, English courses, science courses, a foreign language, and four semesters of the College's well known humanities program. "Some people enjoy the humanities program." Others say "the lectures can be absolute torture." Depending on who you talk to, the administration either "functions smoothly" or is "too Catholic" and "takes its time with everything." Students almost universally gush about their "passionate" professors. "I get tons of individual attention," brags a nursing major. "They are always willing to set a time with you outside of class for help." However, "essays are numerous," and "classes are very difficult." "The library is always filled." There is something of a "crusade against grade inflation" on this campus as well. "Despite how hard you work, you may not see the results you want," warns an English major. Other students tell us "the work is not excruciatingly hard." "It's definitely not impossible," says a biochemistry major. "I'm no rocket scientist, and I'm taking in at least two A's this semester," agrees a classics major. "St. A's requires you to work very hard, but in a warm, friendly, and respectful atmosphere where there are plenty of opportunities to make your college years fantastic," reflects a business major.

Life

This "absolutely gorgeous" campus boasts "spectacular" food. A few students complain that Saint Anselm is "a suitcase school" but others say "you can be involved in numerous things." "It is a small, tight-knit school, where if you stick around on campus and get involved you will have the best time ever," declares a senior. "Community service is big." "I've never seen such a giving school," gloats a first-year student. There's mass every day (though student attendance is not required), and you'll always find a few Benedictine monks around campus. "The monks are awesome," says a junior. "For students who are interested, Saint Anselm is a haven for politics." The "really cool" New Hampshire Institute of Politics provides "a lot of speakers and political candidates," particularly when primary season rolls around. "It's a big deal to go to the hockey games." "Intramural sports are very popular," too. "The pub is a great place on campus for juniors and seniors who are 21 to grab a drink and relax." Various campus policies are "strict" though. First-year residence halls are not co-ed and visitation hours for members of the opposite sex are limited. "If you're looking for an intense party scene, Saint Anselm College isn't the place," advises a senior. Nevertheless, "the senior housing always has something going on" and "drinking is very prevalent" on the weekends, "though students must be sneaky." Nearby Boston is "a great option for the weekends" as well.

Student Body

The stereotype at Saint Anselm is definitely a "white, Catholic Red Sox fan." "Most students I've met here have Boston accents, and at least half are Irish and went to a private school," observes a freshman. "The student body is not the most diverse community but most people are very welcoming," adds a senior. "Social groups here tend to be well defined and yet somehow still permeable, or at least, amiable to one another." There are "sheltered, ignorant snobs," but "the majority of students is middle-class and receives some sort of financial aid." Students at Saint A's describe themselves as "smart, hardworking, involved in community service," and "very preppy." "There are a select few who are rebellious, artsy, and try to stand out but they generally get along with the preppy kids." "Most kids are on an athletic team of some type." Many are serious about religion, "but many are not." Politically, opinions "are surprisingly varied for a campus that is pretty conservative."

THE PRINCETON REVIEW SAYS

Admissions

Very important factors considered include: Application essay, academic GPA, recommendation(s), rigor of secondary school record, standardized test scores (optional for applicants to all but the nursing program). *Other factors considered include:* Class rank, alumni/ae relation, character/personal qualities, extracurricular activities, geographical residence, racial/ethnic status, state residency, talent/ability, volunteer work, work experience. SAT or ACT optional for applicants to all but the nursing program; TOEFL required of all international applicants. High school diploma is required, and GED is accepted. *Academic units required:* 4 English, 3 mathematics, 3 science, (2 science labs), 2 foreign language, 2 social studies. *Academic units recommended:* 4 mathematics, 4 science, 4 foreign language.

Financial Aid

Students should submit: FAFSA, CSS/Financial Aid PROFILE, noncustodial PROFILE, business/farm supplement. Regular filing deadline is 3/15. The Princeton Review suggests that all financial aid forms be submitted as soon as possible after January 1. *Need-based scholarships/grants offered:* Federal Pell, SEOG, state scholarships/grants, private scholarships, the school's own gift aid. *Loan aid offered:* Federal Perkins. Applicants will be notified of awards on a rolling basis beginning 3/1. Federal Work-Study Program available. Institutional employment available. Off-campus job opportunities are excellent.

The Inside Word

St. Anselm gets a predominately regional applicant pool, and Massachusetts is one of its biggest suppliers of students. An above-average academic record should be more than adequate to gain admission.

THE SCHOOL SAYS "…"

From The Admissions Office

"Saint Anselm is New England's only Benedictine College, a place where a 1,500 year tradition that values a love of learning and a balanced life is coupled with a very contemporary liberal arts education with strong professional preparation on a beautiful 400 acre campus. The college offers over 60 academic programs, but is particularly well known for nursing, criminal justice, business, politics and psychology. Located in the first-in the nation primary state, Saint Anselm is the home of the New Hampshire Institute of Politics which hosts national debates and provides countless opportunities for students of any major to engage with candidates, journalists, elected officials and scholars. A student who wants to meet the next President of the United States has a reasonably good chance of doing so here. Saint Anselm has been named a 'college with a conscience' by the Princeton Review, hailed by the Carnegie Foundation with Classification in both Curricular Engagement and Outreach and Partnerships, and has won federal grants to support its work in public advocacy and engagement with social problems. The college's Humanities Program, now in its third decade, has been hailed as a model of interdisciplinary study in philosophy, theology, science and art. Faculty from many departments teach in the seminar-based program where students contemplate the fundamental question of what it means to be great. The college's Dana Center for the Arts and Humanities, used by both students and the public, hosts a broad and eclectic range of theater programming including contemporary dance and music. Saint Anselm's Chapel Arts Center provides an extraordinary array of art exhibitions from classic to contemporary with recent acquisitions focused on the human form in art. 85 percent of the college's students participates in athletics, intramurals and club sports. New majors at Saint Anselm include Communication and Elementary Education. "

For even more information on this school, turn to page 523 of the "Stats" section.

SAINT JOSEPH'S UNIVERSITY (PA)

5600 CITY AVENUE, PHILADELPHIA, PA 19131 • ADMISSIONS: 888-BE-A-HAWK • FAX: 610-660-1314
E-MAIL: ADMIT@SJU.EDU • WEBSITE: WWW.SJU.EDU

RATINGS
Quality of Life: 78   Academic: 78   Admissions: 86   Financial Aid: 74

STUDENTS SAY "..."

Academics

"Saint Joseph's University is a tight-knit Jesuit school," which means that it is dedicated to "cura personalis," that is, "developing the whole person." To that end, students "have to take a number of general ed courses, such as theology and the like." Some students feel they "could definitely do without some of the GERs and have more electives," but others appreciate the more "rounded" academic experience that the general education requirements provide. Another component of a Jesuit education is a "commit-

ment to social justice," so students are encouraged to provide "service to others." Fortunately, students report, "a lot of our service projects are good." The undergraduate business school, which is "pretty well known," is the standout academic program here. "The study abroad center is also good." As far as professors go, they "make themselves wholly available to students—many give out their home/cell phone numbers—and are generally committed to high standards of personal and professional competence." On balance, the "administration is very polite," and students generally agree that "the president, Father Lannon, is brilliant and so cool." While "Saint Joe's has a gorgeous campus," students complain that some "academic facilities aren't as state-of-the-art as other universities."

Life

To say that school spirit at Saint Joseph's is overflowing is an understatement. "The Hawk will never die!" is not just a school cheer; for many, it's a mantra that captures the very gestalt of the student experience here. What are the main elements of that experience? First, in general, "sporting events are popular," and in particular, "basketball games are insane." Second, "service/volunteering is a big part of student life, and…often people are off building houses in the Appalachia region or tutoring kids in Camden, NJ." Then there are the more typical college pastimes that are also popular at Saint Joseph's. "The bar scene is…very big." "Parties are also a big scene, both during the week and on weekends." "SJU also provides a lot of weekend programming that is geared toward freshmen, but can be enjoyed by the entire student body. The programs are generally free or at a low cost to the students and take them off campus (to a New York Broadway show, a cultural event in the city of Philadelphia, or a concert right at SJU)." "Because SJU is so close to the city and other areas like Manayunk and the Main Line many people go into the city on weekends." "You are literally a five-minute train ride away." In addition, "King of Prussia Mall isn't far away, and neither is the Jersey shore." Students grouse that campus "security and cafeteria food could be a little better."

Student Body

"St. Joe's is heaven on Earth if you are a semi-preppy, middle-class student who has school-spirit," are "white," "went to a Catholic high school" "or top public school" in "New Jersey, Pennsylvania, Maryland, New York, or Connecticut," and are "looking for a job." The typical student here "works hard, plays hard, and has most likely done weekly community service." "Although not necessarily devoutly religious, students are, for the most part, somewhat religious." That is, the typical student here "loves the bars and parties on the weekends, then goes to Mass" on Sunday. "There are some minorities, but they still fit the middle-class Catholic school mold." If there is one uniting force for students here, it is that "school spirit is huge. Almost everyone takes a lot of pride in being a Hawk."

Admissions

Very important factors considered include: Academic GPA, rigor of secondary school record. *Important factors considered include:* Application essay, recommendation(s), character/personal qualities. *Other factors considered include:* Class rank, standardized test scores, alumni/ae relation, extracurricular activities, first generation, level of applicant's interest, talent/ability, volunteer work, work experience. SAT or ACT required; TOEFL required of all international applicants. High school diploma is required and GED is not accepted. *Academic units required:* 4 English, 3 mathematics, 2 science, (1 science labs), 2 foreign language, 1 history. *Academic units recommended:* 4 English, 3 mathematics, 2 science, (1 science labs), 2 foreign language, 1 history.

Financial Aid

Students should submit: FAFSA. The Princeton Review suggests that all financial aid forms be submitted as soon as possible after January 1. *Need-based scholarships/grants offered:* Federal Pell, SEOG, state scholarships/grants, private scholarships, the school's own gift aid. *Loan aid offered:* Direct Subsidized Stafford, Direct Unsubsidized Stafford, Direct PLUS, Federal Perkins, The Federal Direct Student Loan Program will be in effect beginning with the Fall 2010-2011 academic year. Applicants will be notified of awards on a rolling basis beginning 3/1. Federal Work-Study Program available. Institutional employment available. Off-campus job opportunities are excellent.

The Inside Word

Despite a growing applicant pool, the credentials that enrolled students generally bring to the table have not changed much in recent years. Those with GPAs above 3.5 and SAT scores above 1200 should not face many problems gaining admission as long as they take the application process seriously. The Jesuit ideals of educating the whole person and social justice are valued here, so students do well to highlight any community service experience they have during the application process.

THE SCHOOL SAYS "…"

From The Admissions Office

"For over 150 years, Saint Joseph's University has advanced the professional and personal ambitions of men and women by providing a rigorous Jesuit education-one that demands high achievement, expands knowledge, deepens understanding, stresses effective reasoning and communication, develops moral and spiritual character, and imparts enduring pride.

"As a Jesuit university, Saint Joseph's believes each student realizes his or her fullest potential through challenging classroom study, hands-on learning opportunities, and a commitment to excellence in all endeavors. The university also reinforces the individual's lifelong engagement with the wider world by offering study abroad opportunities on six continents and having student representation from 38 countries across the globe. Graduates of Saint Joseph's attain success in their careers with the help of an extensive network of alumni who have become leading figures in business, law, medicine, education, the arts, technology, government, and public service.

"A Saint Joseph's education encompasses all aspects of personal growth and development, reflecting the Ignatian credo of cura personalis-concern for the individual student. Guided by a faculty committed to both teaching and scholarship, students develop intellectually through an intense liberal arts curriculum and advanced study in a chosen discipline. Saint Joseph's University is "not for spectators," an attitude that is demonstrated by an exceptionally engaged student body, faculty and community that prefer doing to watching from the sidelines. Students grow personally by participating in Saint Joseph's campus life, noted for its rich variety of activities, infectious enthusiasm, and mutual respect. Students grow ethically and spiritually by living their own values in the larger society beyond campus.

"Located on the edge of metropolitan Philadelphia, Saint Joseph's University provides ready access to the vast career opportunities and cultural resources of America's sixth-largest city, while affording students a cohesive and intimate campus experience."

For even more information on this school, turn to page 523 of the "Stats" section.

SAINT MARY'S COLLEGE OF MARYLAND

ADMISSIONS OFFICE, 18952 EAST FISHER ROAD, ST. MARY'S CITY, MD 20686-3001 • ADMISSIONS: 800-492-7181 • FAX: 240-895-5001
FINANCIAL AID: 240-895-3000 • E-MAIL: ADMISSIONS@SMCM.EDU • WEBSITE: WWW.SMCM.EDU

RATINGS
Quality of Life: 94   **Academic:** 89   **Admissions:** 91   **Financial Aid:** 86

STUDENTS SAY "..."

Academics

Set on the "beautiful St. Mary's River," St. Mary's College of Maryland is a "humble oasis" that "has all of the intellectual stimulation of a private liberal arts school with none of the academic rivalry." The blissfully content students at SMCM throw around the word "community" like rice at a wedding, and they always precede it with some sort of positive lead-in: "small," "open-minded," "social justice minded, environmentally friendly, hippie-loving, and very diverse and accepting" are just some of the descriptors

> **SURVEY SAYS . . .**
> Athletic facilities are great
> Students are friendly
> Different types of students interact
> Great food on campus
> Campus feels safe
> Students are happy
> Frats and sororities are unpopular or nonexistent

used. Classes here are "rigorous" and "very engaging, requiring participation and input from all of the students," and the "amazing" professors are lauded for their brilliance, love of the material, and sheer accessibility. Students talk of having seen professors "at school events not related to their classes and students have been invited to class dinners at their houses." Not only does the small size of the school mean that the faculty knows each student's name—"you are NEVER a number"—but "you get to know your professors on a personal level, which is great when it comes time for them to write recommendations for scholarships, graduate school, or future jobs." The administration gets positive reviews with just a few naysayers. The deans are commended for being "everywhere, participating in athletics, music programs, etc." and making it clear " that the students are the first priority," but a few students still say that the administration "can be a little bit withdrawn from the student body." Although there are complaints of too much construction around the campus, most students know that improvements and growth are necessary for the growth of the college, though they do wish to see more immediate changes to the health services, which "need some serious work."

Life

The phrase "summer camp setting" doesn't just refer to how the campus looks; Frisbee golf, sailing, bonfires, sun tanning, and kayaking in the school-provided kayaks are some of the main activities for students taking a break from their studies (which often occur outside). The river seems to be the hub of student life, not only acting as a "tremendous stress reliever,"" but a sort of ad hoc campus center." Since the "very outdoorsy" campus is located in a remote location, "most of the fun that happens occurs on campus," and "the cold winter months are often difficult to bear and result in cabin fever." The lack of metropolitan areas (the nearest being Annapolis) means SMCM is "very residential," and "you really develop your own home and nest here with your friends as family." "There is a decent party scene on campus" with "parties on the weekends studying during the week," but "students are rarely pressured to drink [and] and many don't do it all." The plethora of clubs and other activities means no one goes home bored. "I couldn't ask for a better college experience," says a junior.

Student Body

The diversity rate here isn't all that high (though it's not expected to be at such a small school), but no one has any real complaints. Most here are very environmentally oriented, "both in terms of their leisure activities and in terms of their political leanings." Some affectionately refer to their "hippie" classmates, but the "very accepting" student body has plenty of "pearl-wearing preps" and jocks in its "big social mosh pit," so "even the non-tree huggers amongst us can find a comfortable niche with little trouble." "It's entirely acceptable to be a bit quirky," says a junior. SMCM "is truly its own place," and this extreme love of the campus and its surroundings creates a sort of communal understanding that those who don't contribute to the betterment of the campus community will find themselves answering to the angry masses. "Word gets around on a small campus, and if you are mean or vandalize or something, people will know and shun you for that bad action."

THE PRINCETON REVIEW SAYS

Admissions

Very important factors considered include: Academic GPA, rigor of secondary school record. *Important factors considered include:* Application essay, recommendation(s), standardized test scores, extracurricular activities, first generation, talent/ability, volunteer work. *Other factors considered include:* Alumni/ae relation, geographical residence, interview, racial/ethnic status, state residency, work experience. SAT or ACT required; TOEFL required of all international applicants. High school diploma is required, and GED is accepted. *Academic units required:* 4 English, 3 mathematics, 3 science, (2 science labs), 2 foreign language, 2 social studies, 1 history, 3 *Academic units recommended:* 4 mathematics, 4 foreign language, 2 history.

Financial Aid

Students should submit: FAFSA. Regular filing deadline is 3/1. The Princeton Review suggests that all financial aid forms be submitted as soon as possible after January 1. *Need-based scholarships/grants offered:* Federal Pell, SEOG, state scholarships/grants, private scholarships, the school's own gift aid. *Loan aid offered:* Federal Perkins. Applicants will be notified of awards on or about 4/1. Federal Work-Study Program available. Institutional employment available. Off-campus job opportunities are good.

The Inside Word

There are few better choices than St. Mary's for better-than-average students who are not likely to get admitted to extremely selective colleges in the country. It is likely that if funding for public colleges is able to stabilize, or even grow, that this place will soon be joining the ranks of the best. Now is the time to take advantage, before the academic expectations of the admissions committee start to soar.

THE SCHOOL SAYS "..."

From The Admissions Office

"St. Mary's College of Maryland occupies a distinctive niche and represents a real value in American higher education. It is a public college, dedicated to the ideal of affordable, accessible education and committed to quality teaching and excellent programs for undergraduate students. St. Mary's is designated by law the state of Maryland's 'public honors college,' one of only two public colleges in the nation to hold that distinction. It is this mix of honors and affordability that makes St. Mary's an education for the 21st Century."

For even more information on this school, turn to page 530 of the "Stats" section.

SAINT MICHAEL'S COLLEGE

ONE WINOOSKI PARK, COLCHESTER, VT 05439 • ADMISSIONS: 802-654-3000 • FAX: 802-654-2591
E-MAIL: ADMISSION@SMCVT.EDU • WEBSITE: WWW.SMCVT.EDU

RATINGS
Quality of Life: 98   Academic: 85   Admissions: 84   Financial Aid: 77

STUDENTS SAY "..."

Academics

Saint Michael's College is a Catholic liberal art college that
boasts "an absolutely unbeatable location" in the heart of
"prime" Vermont ski territory. A reasonably broad set of
core course requirements includes two mandatory religion
classes. Study abroad is "huge." "Sciences are very popular." "The education department, in general, is amazing."
Coursework at SMC "can be very challenging—by no
means is everything a breeze." However, classes tend to be

SURVEY SAYS...
Students are friendly
Students get along with local community
Students love Colchester, VT
Great off-campus food
Frats and sororities are unpopular or nonexistent
Student publications are popular

manageably small. "Rarely do you have a class larger than 30 students, which gives you a nice, intimate classroom experience." "The administration and professors at the school are all very open and welcoming to every
student," promises a junior. "Like any school, there are the good and the bad teachers." For the most part,
though, "professors are really passionate and devoted to the subjects that they teach." They are "available outside of class, open to lots of discussion in the classroom, and always are willing to help." The biggest academic gripe here is probably the "insufficient" course selection, since "the size of the college limits the overall variety of courses."

Life

Saint Mike's is lively. "It's my opinion that you cannot be bored on this campus," asserts one student. "The theater
kids, the sports kids, the campus ministry kids, the volunteer program kids, the fire and rescue kids—there are
groups for everyone." The community service program is "extremely popular." Rallies and demonstrations are
common. "Most people are moderately interested in the outdoors," and the wilderness program runs student-led
trips each weekend." Socially, SMC is "really close-knit." "The big family aspect of Saint Mike's makes it easy to
meet people and make friends. That boils down to awesome weekends." "Monday through Thursday, people tend
to really focus on classes." Thursday marks the beginning of the weekend, which continues until late Saturday
night. Mostly, "people get absolutely hammered in their rooms," then amble around campus to "various parties
and get-togethers." There's a drug scene, too, if that's your bag. If you choose not to partake in the festivities, it's
fine. Virtually all students "are required to live on campus all four years," and the students tell us "overcrowded"
dorms are "a mess." Also, the Vermont winters are "brutal." On the plus side, if you ski or snowboard, "several
great mountains" are nearby. (Smugglers' Notch offers ridiculously cheap season passes through a special offer to
Saint Mike's students.) In warmer weather, "many activities—even parties—happen outside in the beautiful
Vermont scenery." For a change of pace, students take the free bus to "artsy," "adorable" Burlington, "a hubbub of
fun."

Student Body

"We have little to no ethnic or racial diversity at our school," admits a senior. "For what it's worth, however, the
minorities here blend in with the rest of the student body." "A typical student is a solid B student in high school
who's really involved" and hails from "20 minutes outside Boston," observes one student. There are plenty of
"hockey/rugby player types," and many students are "involved in sports." Quite a few students grew up
wealthy. "New, expensive cars" dot the campus. "There is an abundance of preppy kids." You'll know them by
their "Ugg boots, North Face fleeces, and Vera Bradley bags." "Hippies" are around but not pervasive. "St Mike's
is painted as more of a hippie college than it really is," reports one student. Politically, there are conservatives,
but there are a lot more "left-wing liberals who care too much about the environment." Overall, there's an "open,
welcoming" vibe. "Everyone is pretty low-key about fitting in." "You can see a hippie hugging a preppie or a
Yankees fan and Red Sox fan eating lunch together," swears one student. "Everyone gets along here."

Admissions

Very important factors considered include: Class rank, academic GPA, rigor of secondary school record. *Important factors considered include:* Application essay, recommendation(s), standardized test scores, character/personal qualities, extracurricular activities, talent/ability. *Other factors considered include:* Alumni/ae relation, first generation, geographical residence, level of applicant's interest, racial/ethnic status, state residency, volunteer work, work experience. SAT or ACT required; ACT with Writing component required. TOEFL required of all international applicants. High school diploma is required, and GED is accepted. *Academic units required:* 4 English, 3 mathematics, 3 science, (2 science labs), 3 foreign language, 3 social studies. *Academic units recommended:* 4 English, 4 mathematics, 4 science, (3 science labs), 4 foreign language, 4 social studies.

Financial Aid

Students should submit: FAFSA, signed copies of parent's 2009 Federal Tax Return, parent's Federal W-2 forms, signed copies of student's 2009 Federal Tax Return, student's Federal W-2 forms, Dependent 2009–2010 Verification Worksheet (please check the Student Financial Services form). The Princeton Review suggests that all financial aid forms be submitted as soon as possible after January 1. *Need-based scholarships/grants offered:* Federal Pell, SEOG, state scholarships/grants, private scholarships, the school's own gift aid. *Loan aid offered:* Federal Perkins. Applicants will be notified of awards on a rolling basis beginning 1/15. Federal Work-Study Program available. Institutional employment available. Off-campus job opportunities are excellent.

Inside Word

Saint Mike's is a pretty easy admit if you've shown a reasonable level of consistency in solid college prep curriculum. Candidates who goofed around a little too much in high school would be well advised to strongly highlight their extracurricular activities.

THE SCHOOL SAYS "..."
From The Admissions Office

"Saint Michael's is a residential, Catholic, liberal arts college for students who want to make the world a better place. A Saint Michael's education will prepare you for life, as each of our 30 majors is grounded in our liberal studies core. Our superb faculty is committed first and foremost to teaching and is known for really caring about students while simultaneously challenging them to reach higher than they ever thought possible. Because of our holistic approach, Saint Michael's graduates are prepared for their entire careers, not just their first jobs out of college.

"With nearly 100% of students living on campus, our "24/7" learning environment means exceptional teaching goes beyond the classroom and into the living areas, which include three new suite-style residences, townhouse apartments, and traditional residence halls. The remarkable sense of community encourages students to get involved, take risks, and think differently. A unique passion for social justice issues on campus reflects the heritage of the Edmundite priests who founded Saint Michael's in 1904.

"Saint Michael's is situated just outside of Burlington, Vermont's largest city and a true college town. A unique Cultural Pass program allows students to see an array of music, dance, theater, and Broadway productions at the Flynn Center downtown. Students also take advantage of some of the best skiing in the East through an agreement with Smugglers' Notch ski resort—an all-access season pass is provided to any Saint Michael's student in good academic standing."

For even more information on this school, turn to page 524 of the "Stats" section.

SALISBURY UNIVERSITY

ADMISSIONS OFFICE, 1101 CAMDEN AVENUE, SALISBURY, MD 21801 • ADMISSIONS: 410-543-6161
FAX: 410-546-6016 • FINANCIAL AID: 410-543-6165 • E-MAIL: ADMISSIONS@SALISBURY.EDU • WEBSITE: WWW.SALISBURY.EDU

RATINGS
Quality of Life: 78   **Academic:** 69   **Admissions:** 86   **Financial Aid:** 69

STUDENTS SAY ". . ."

Academics

> **SURVEY SAYS . . .**
> Lab facilities are great
> Great computer facilities
> Great food on campus
> Intramural sports are popular
> Lots of beer drinking
> Hard liquor is popular

Salisbury University has come a long way since it first opened its doors in 1925. Originally a two-year college, Salisbury gradually grew into a four-year BA-conferring school, then it added graduate programs in education, business, and nursing. The pace of ascendance has quickened over the past decade, transforming Salisbury from a local school to a regional favorite to, most recently, a university with some national draw. As one student observes, SU is "rapidly gaining respect and a reputation as a challenging, high-level academic institution." Part of the school's allure has to do with cost; SU is extremely affordable for Maryland residents and not much more expensive for out-of-state students. Scale is another factor at this "laid-back, perfectly sized university" small enough to be "your home away from home," but large enough to "offer a top-notch education." Undergraduate business programs are the biggest draw here, attracting nearly 20 percent of all undergrads. Students love that the business curriculum prepares "well-rounded individuals" by "requiring us to have an internship to graduate, which forces one to get some real-world experience." The nursing, education, and communication programs also attract big crowds. In all programs, students enjoy "small class sizes, a compact campus, nice accessible professors, great majors, and fun trips." One student tells us that Salisbury "is about life learning, not just from textbooks and lectures, but from opportunity and diversity." Another adds that the university "is on its way to great things very soon."

Life

Life at SU "depends on what you are looking for. There is a club or organization for everything," and "all kinds of work, volunteer opportunities, and internships available through the school." The Student Office of Activity Programming (SOAP) "brings concerts, comedians, imitations of game shows, and open mic nights to campus and gives us students something fun and constructive to do!" The school's "amazing" Division III sports teams are well supported as well. Even so, many here tell us that life at SU "can get boring a lot of the time though because everything except bars and Taco Bell shuts down early, so many people end up going off campus or to bars and getting drunk." This does not sit well with the conservative rural locals, and as a result, "We have a bad reputation with the Salisbury community. We are known for being a drinking school." And indeed, "Students do drink here at SU. I mean, we are known to be a party school, and it's not a lie. But if you don't do that sort of thing then it's not a big deal. I had a hard time my freshman year first semester because I thought everyone on campus went to parties and that's all there was to do. However, I found people who didn't go to parties, to be friends with, and I started becoming more active in theater and the Honors Student Association, and I found my niche here at SU." As one student sums up, "basically anything you want, SU has."

Student Body

SU undergrads are typically "laid-back and like to hang out with friends, yet they know how and when to get work done when it needs to be done," although there are some here who "drink too much and complain when they don't get the grades they want even though they've skipped most classes due to hangovers. " Most of the latter are presumably gone by sophomore year. There are "a lot of student athletes" here as well as "a D&D crowd who are really nice. They sort of hang out with other Starnet (SciFi club) members." Insofar as diversity, SU apparently has "a department devoted to it."

THE PRINCETON REVIEW SAYS

Admissions

Very important factors considered include: Academic GPA, rigor of secondary school record, extracurricular activities, talent/ability. *Important factors considered include:* Class rank, standardized test scores, alumni/ae relation, geographical residence, volunteer work. *Other factors considered include:* Application essay, recommendation(s), character/personal qualities, racial/ethnic status, work experience. TOEFL required of all international applicants. High school diploma is required, and GED is accepted. *Academic units required:* 4 English, 3 mathematics, 3 science, (2 science labs), 2 foreign language, 3 social studies. *Academic units recommended:* 4 English, 4 mathematics, 4 science, (3 science labs), 3 foreign language, 3 social studies, 3 academic electives.

Financial Aid

Students should submit: FAFSA. Regular filing deadline is 12/31. The Princeton Review suggests that all financial aid forms be submitted as soon as possible after January 1. *Need-based scholarships/grants offered:* Federal Pell, SEOG, state scholarships/grants, private scholarships, the school's own gift aid. *Loan aid offered:* Direct Subsidized Stafford, Direct Unsubsidized Stafford, Federal Perkins. Applicants will be notified of awards on a rolling basis beginning 3/15. Federal Work-Study Program available. Institutional employment available. Off-campus job opportunities are fair.

The Inside Word

Salisbury has increased its undergraduate population by nearly 20 percent in the past few years, which hasn't made admission here any easier. On the contrary, the expansion was a reaction to a growing national profile and corresponding increase in the number of applications. Despite the trend, you can still expect a careful, personalized reading of your application here. It's about a lot more than just the numbers at Salisbury; prepare your application accordingly.

THE SCHOOL SAYS "..."

From The Admissions Office

"Friendly, convenient, safe, and beautiful are just a few of the words used to describe the campus of Salisbury University. The campus is a compact, self-contained community that offers the full range of student services. Beautiful, traditional-style architecture and impeccably landscaped grounds combine to create an atmosphere that inspires learning and fosters student pride. Located just 30 minutes from the beaches of Ocean City, Maryland, SU students enjoy a year-round resort social life as well as an inside track on summer jobs. Situated less than 2 hours from the urban excitement of Baltimore and Washington, D.C., greater Salisbury makes up for its lack of size—its population is about 80,000—by being strategically located. Within easy driving distance of a number of other major cities, including New York City, Philadelphia, and Norfolk, Salisbury is the hub of the Delmarva Peninsula, a mostly rural region flavored by the salty air of the Chesapeake Bay and Atlantic Ocean.

"Submission of SAT and/or ACT scores when applying would be optional to freshman applicants who present a weighted high school grade point average (GPA) of 3.5 or higher on a 4.0 scale. Any student applying with less than a 3.5 would still need to submit a standardized test score to supplement the official high school transcript. Additionally, an applicant may wish to submit a standardized test score subsequent to admission for full scholarship consideration as the majority of the university's scholarships include test scores as a requirement."

For even more information on this school, turn to page 524 of the "Stats" section.

SALVE REGINA UNIVERSITY

100 OCHRE POINT AVENUE, NEWPORT, RI 02840-4192 • ADMISSIONS: 401-341-2908 • FAX: 401-848-2823
E-MAIL: SRUADMIS@SALVE.EDU • WEBSITE: WWW.SALVE.EDU

RATINGS
Quality of Life: 76   **Academic:** 79   **Admissions:** 85   **Financial Aid:** 67

STUDENTS SAY ". . ."

Academics

Salve Regina offers "an excellent Catholic education" with a "focus on global issues combined with an unbelievably beautiful setting and small campus" to its 2,000 predominantly female students. The school "does an awesome job of tying the teachings of the Sisters of Mercy into every class" and "emphasizing the importance of community

service in conjunction with higher learning in a multitude of areas." Best of all for those outside the Catholic faith, the school is "very supportive and welcoming of other religions." "The nursing and teaching programs are very strong" here, and students in all disciplines receive an "education centered around the classic liberal arts" that helps students "become better speakers, writers, and thinkers." An "extremely accessible faculty and administration" creates "an atmosphere where your teachers really care about you and your classmates become your best friends." "By the time you're a senior here, the professors and dean will know your name, make no doubt about it," one student assures us. Most undergrads here "find the academic experience challenging, but not overwhelming." One student reports that "Even in the honors sector, it seems that the emphasis is placed on more work, like essays and research papers, rather than on open-mindedness and independent projects. But overall, you can tell the teachers try their hardest to make classes fun and interesting."

Life

Located alongside Newport's mansion-lined Cliff Walk, the Salve Regina campus is "an unbelievably beautiful setting." The location—"10 minutes from the beach" with "an ocean view" from student residences ("students get to live in mansions")—is optimal. The city is "easy to get to via the trolley, which runs from downtown Newport to several stops on campus every twenty minutes." Newport "is fun, especially in the early fall and late spring when the stores are open late for tourist season" and it's "also a great place for outdoor activities, like bike riding, hiking, and going to the beach." During the off-season, "Many people go to Providence on weekends because there are a lot of over-18 clubs." Students also point out that "Boston is fairly close and easy to get to." Closer to home, students find that their peers "are very involved in campus activities." "The school is very good about having fun things available to students on campus. There is a movie theatre, there are concerts, and there is also a game area with pool tables." Parties are infrequent due to the school's 'dry campus' policy; "There are not many parties on campus because it is so strict, but there are some in Newport at people's houses," one student explains.

Student Body

"Everyone is pretty much the same: preppy and white," notes one student. Others agree, "The typical student is a white, upper-class female who wears Uggs and Prada sunglasses everyday." There are "a lot of spoiled kids here" but "that is countered with a good amount of genuine, fun, artsy people. You just have to know where to find these people, and in general you will find your niche by sophomore year." "Salve is pretty homogenous," though there are "lots of transfer students" and the international population includes "lots of students from Japan."

Admissions

Very important factors considered include: Class rank, academic GPA, rigor of secondary school record. *Important factors considered include:* Application essay, recommendation(s), standardized test scores. *Other factors considered include:* Alumni/ae relation, character/personal qualities, extracurricular activities, level of applicant's interest, racial/ethnic status, talent/ability, volunteer work, work experience. SAT or ACT required; TOEFL required of all international applicants. High school diploma is required and GED is accepted. *Academic units required:* 4 English, 3 mathematics, 2 science, (2 science labs), 2 foreign language, 1 social studies, 4 academic electives.

Financial Aid

Students should submit: FAFSA, CSS/Financial Aid PROFILE, noncustodial PROFILE, business/farm supplement. Regular filing deadline is 5/15. The Princeton Review suggests that all financial aid forms be submitted as soon as possible after January 1. *Need-based scholarships/grants offered:* Federal Pell, SEOG, state scholarships/grants, private scholarships, the school's own gift aid. *Loan aid offered:* Federal Perkins, Federal Nursing, other, private loans. Applicants will be notified of awards on or about 4/1. Federal Work-Study Program available. Institutional employment available. Off-campus job opportunities are good.

The Inside Word

Salve Regina attracts many more applicants than it can accommodate in its freshman class, explaining why only about 65 percent of applicants are accepted. The school competes with many regional powerhouses for students, and as a result attracts few elite candidates. The profile of a typical admit here is a solid but not outstanding high school student with SAT scores in the mid-500s per section and a B-plus grade average. Admission to the university does not guarantee subsequent admission to such popular programs as nursing.

THE SCHOOL SAYS "..."

From The Admissions Office

"Salve Regina University is a small university with big opportunity. Located on one of the most beautiful campuses in the country, Salve Regina's historic oceanfront campus is a place where students feel at home. Students study and live in historic mansions, yet receive an education that prepares them for modern careers and a lifetime of serving their communities. Salve offers excellent professional and liberal arts programs (most popular are business, education, administration of justice, and biology). The classes are small and are all taught by professors (no grad assistants). Salve's small size also makes it easy for students to get involved on campus with clubs, activities, athletics, or intramurals. At Salve, it is easy to become a leader—even in your first year.

"Newport offers the perfect location for students who love history, sailing, and the outdoors. Students can surf and ocean kayak from First Beach, or bike ride on the famous Ocean Drive. Newport also hosts several festivals throughout the year. All students get a free statewide trolley/bus pass that takes them throughout Newport or to Providence, only 30 minutes away.

"Admission to Salve Regina is competitive. The Admissions Office looks at several factors in reviewing applications. Most important are applicants' day-to-day academic work and the level of the courses they have taken. Recommendation letters and test scores are also reviewed, as are leadership positions and community involvement."

For even more information on this school, turn to page 525 of the "Stats" section.

SARAH LAWRENCE COLLEGE

One Mead Way, Bronxville, NY 10708-5999 • Admissions: 914-395-2510 • Fax: 914-395-2676
Financial Aid: 914-395-2570 • E-mail: slcadmit@mail.slc.edu • Website: www.slc.edu

RATINGS
Quality of Life: 64   **Academic:** 95   **Admissions:** 90   **Financial Aid:** 85

STUDENTS SAY ". . ."

Academics

SURVEY SAYS . . .
Lots of liberal students
Class discussions encouraged
No one cheats
Students aren't religious

Offering a unique approach to liberal arts education, Sarah Lawrence College is a "serious academic and artistic environment where individual passion fuels learning." Through SLC's distinctive curriculum, students are the architects of their own educational experience and the school "places a great emphasis on personal research and personal responsibility." In their first year, undergrads meet with their advisors every week to discuss their academic plans, and "besides your don (permanent counselor), you have a slew of people who really want you to be the best that you can be." Of particular note, students benefit from "inordinate amounts of individual time with each professor," who are all "enormously educated, good teachers, and passionate about their subjects." Across disciplines, Sarah Lawrence professors "are generally willing to give over copious amounts of time to undergraduate research papers, projects, ideas, and extracurricular discussion." A student shares this noteworthy story: "I am in a lecture about Epic Poetry but I'm not really interested in poetry, so I talked to the professor and he was totally cool with all my papers being about anthropological elements of the text and not poetic ones." Among other innovations, SLC's unusual (but, some say, inefficient) course registration system allows students to interview teachers before signing up for classes. Fortunately, "all of the classes here are excellent, so if one doesn't get into a desired class, it isn't the end of the world." Unfortunately, many students feel SLC's administration can be bureaucratic and out-of-step with the school's dominant philosophy and culture. When discussing these shortcomings, however, students acknowledge that the administration faces many challenges in that the school is "expensive to run" and funds are more limited than at larger colleges.

Life

Whether you enjoy attending "study parties" or playing Frisbee in your underwear, "life at Sarah Lawrence is about as quirky as the college itself." Club meetings and school-sponsored activities are sometimes lightly attended; however, poetry readings, artistic pursuits, live music shows, and political organizing are widely popular, and "there is a growing athletic community on campus" as well. On campus, there are occasional dance parties, as well as casual get-togethers; however, on the whole, campus life is fairly subdued. A student claims, "The best way to relax is to get together with a few friends, put on some music, and just hang out. Conversations range from deep political or philosophical debates to discussing cartoons." Located near the village of Bronxville, "everybody enjoys the fact that we're a hop, skip and a jump away from wonderful Manhattan," and a majority of students head to the city on the weekend. For those who stay on campus, "weekends include a lot of wandering around, but mostly just sitting and talking in friends dorm rooms about typical stuff, you know, Nietzsche and the importance of green architecture." In addition, students might be found "playing music together, listening to music, throwing dinner parties, drinking beer, playing board games, playing drinking games, talking about music, going to the city, eating a lot of Chinese and Sushi take-out, [or] playing in the snow."

Student Body

With a motto like "we're different, so are you," it's not surprising that "Sarah Lawrence is like Mecca for creative, proactive, outrageous, and independent students who want ultimate freedom in designing their education." Bohemian attire and alternative music are culturally prevalent, and "writers, artists, eccentrics, musicians, academics, activists, and scientists all call Sarah Lawrence home." In fact, many students say that, "the typical Sarah Lawrence student looks like the atypical student at any mainstream university." Students agree that the SLC "environment is very inclusive of all people and walks of life;" however, many complain that the "indie" or bohemian veneer attracts students who are unfriendly, self-absorbed, or who are "so used to being the "different" ones that they can't deal with the fact that they aren't "special" here." While some would like a warmer and friendlier college atmosphere, students reassure us that "there is a wide spectrum of interests and lifestyles so almost everyone can find a crowd of friends that suits them."

Admissions

Very important factors considered include: Application essay, recommendation(s), rigor of secondary school record. *Important factors considered include:* Academic GPA, extracurricular activities, talent/ability. *Other factors considered include:* Class rank, alumni/ae relation, character/personal qualities, first generation, geographical residence, interview, level of applicant's interest, racial/ethnic status, volunteer work, work experience. TOEFL required of all international applicants. High school diploma is required, and GED is accepted. *Academic units required:* 4 English, 2 mathematics, 2 science, 2 foreign language, 2 history. *Academic units recommended:* 4 mathematics, 4 science, 4 foreign language, 4 social studies, 4 history.

Financial Aid

Students should submit: FAFSA, CSS/Financial Aid PROFILE, state aid form, noncustodial PROFILE. Regular filing deadline is 2/1. The Princeton Review suggests that all financial aid forms be submitted as soon as possible after January 1. *Need-based scholarships/grants offered:* Federal Pell, SEOG, state scholarships/grants, private scholarships, the school's own gift aid. *Loan aid offered:* Federal Perkins. Applicants will be notified of awards on or about 4/1. Federal Work-Study Program available. Institutional employment available. Off-campus job opportunities are good.

The Inside Word

In addition to two required essay questions, Sarah Lawrence College requests that candidates submit a graded, analytic writing sample. Students say you shouldn't underestimate the importance of this unusual requirement, as SLC's curriculum is writing-based and a good sample can make your application stand out. Sarah Lawrence College doesn't believe that standardized test scores accurately reflect a student's ability to succeed in their academic program, and therefore, they do not review ACT or SAT scores.

THE SCHOOL SAYS "..."

From The Admissions Office

"Students who come to Sarah Lawrence are curious about the world, and they have an ardent desire to satisfy that curiosity. Sarah Lawrence offers such students two innovative academic structures: the seminar/conference system and the arts components. Courses in the humanities, social sciences, natural sciences, and mathematics are taught in the seminar/conference style. The seminars enroll an average of 11 students and consist of lecture, discussion, readings, and assigned papers. For each seminar, students also meet one-on-one in biweekly conferences, for which they conceive of individualized projects and shape them under the direction of professors. Arts components let students combine history and theory with practice. Painters, printmakers, photographers, sculptors, filmmakers, composers, musicians, choreographers, dancers, actors, and directors work in readily available studios, editing facilities, and darkrooms, guided by accomplished professionals. The secure, wooded campus is 30 minutes from midtown Manhattan, and the diversity of people and ideas at Sarah Lawrence make it an extraordinary educational environment.

"Sarah Lawrence College no longer uses standardized test scores in the admission process. This decision reflects our conviction that overemphasis on test preparation can distort results and make the application process inordinately stressful, and that academic success is better predicted by the student's course rigor, their grades, recommendations, and writing ability."

For even more information on this school, turn to page 525 of the "Stats" section.

SETON HALL UNIVERSITY

400 SOUTH ORANGE AVENUE, SOUTH ORANGE, NJ 07079-2697 • ADMISSIONS: 973-761-9332
FAX: 973-275-2040 • FINANCIAL AID: 973-761-9332 • E-MAIL: THEHALL@SHU.EDU • WEBSITE: WWW.ADMISSIONS.SHU.EDU

RATINGS

Quality of Life: 66   **Academic:** 75   **Admissions:** 80   **Financial Aid:** 71

STUDENTS SAY " . . ."

Academics

"All the colleges within the university are well regarded" at Seton Hall, a prominent Catholic university just down the road from New York City, but the Stillman School of Business and the Whitehead School of Diplomacy and

> SURVEY SAYS . . .
> *Low cost of living*

International Relations "are considered the best schools on campus" and thus typically garner the most atten-tion, and understandably so. The former features "a great sports management program" and an attractive, five-year BA/Masters in accounting. Students benefit from proximity to New York, which creates the opportunity for valuable internships, especially in finance. The latter "is directly affiliated with the United Nations," a rela-tionship that "provides students with professors who have had experience with international relations, whether it be ambassadors or foreign correspondents." SHU also excels in nursing, and the university's commitment to keeping pace with technology gives all students a leg up in the modern job market. Indeed, the school works hard "to link the academic world with the real world" through "study abroad, internships, international speak-ers and events," but without forfeiting the benefits of a more traditional liberal arts education. "The core cur-riculum gives all students a great foundation beyond their majors so that students are well-rounded individu-als with a variety of experiences upon graduation," undergrads report. Students warn that administrative tasks can be onerous; one writes, "there is a lot of red tape at Seton Hall. The bills that are sent out at the end of the semester are never correct, and it takes several phone calls with financial aid to ascertain the correct balance."

Life

Social life at SHU fights an uphill battle. The school is located in South Orange, "a boring town for college-age students." A much more appealing town, New York City, is "a 20-minute train ride [from campus], so a lot of people go to the city for fun." Add to that the fact that "most of the student body lives in North Jersey, so it's easy for them to go home for the weekend," and many do just that. Under these circumstances, SHU does a pretty good job of offering on-campus attractions, students tell us. Greek life "is very popular," and the school's "big-time men's basketball program" is a huge draw, even though the team has not fared especially well in recent seasons. "Students are always attending basketball games" and "praying that the team does not suck." Intramurals "can be very competitive," "the athletic facilities are state-of-the-art," and "the campus lends itself to outdoor activities. Many students play sports outside when it is warm, and when it is cold there are plenty of indoor activities in which to participate."

Student Body

Seton Hall "is sort of a mishmash of different types. There are a lot of jocks who are definitely treated like stars by the administration, although not so much by the average professor," and "there are some very academic stu-dents who mostly try to ignore the actual school and focus on internships and study-abroad opportunities." And then there's "the average student, who is from New Jersey, has a major in the School of Arts and Sciences or Business, parties on Thursdays, goes home on weekends, and coasts through college on loans their parents have taken out." "While Seton Hall is a Catholic university, "it is not difficult to find students of other religions," and "the school is accepting of all religious beliefs." Indeed, SHU is big enough that "there are a lot of different kinds of people," and "everyone finds his place by sophomore year." Unfortunately "it also tends to be like high school, in that once you are in a group you're there for the rest of your four years." As one student puts it, "There are definitely cliques here, more so than in my high school. The athletes always sit together, as do peo-ple in certain clubs."

Admissions

Very important factors considered include: Application essay, academic GPA, recommendation(s), rigor of secondary school record, standardized test scores. *Important factors considered include:* Extracurricular activities, volunteer work, work experience. *Other factors considered include:* Class rank, character/personal qualities, interview, talent/ability. SAT or ACT required; ACT with Writing component required. TOEFL required of all international applicants. High school diploma is required, and GED is accepted. *Academic units required:* 4 English, 3 mathematics, 1 science, (1 science labs), 2 foreign language, 2 social studies, 4 academic electives.

Financial Aid

Students should submit: FAFSA. The Princeton Review suggests that all financial aid forms be submitted as soon as possible after January 1. *Need-based scholarships/grants offered:* Federal Pell, SEOG, state scholarships/grants, private scholarships, the school's own gift aid. *Loan aid offered:* Federal Perkins, state loans. Applicants will be notified of awards on a rolling basis beginning 3/1. Federal Work-Study Program available. Institutional employment available. Off-campus job opportunities are good.

The Inside Word

Students seeking a good school with solid, Catholic roots should consider Seton Hall, whose proximity to New York City helps the school draw prestigious faculty and affords students excellent access to educational, internship, and entertainment opportunities. Applicants who show decent grades in a college preparatory curriculum coupled with strong recommendations should have little trouble gaining admission here. Top students may be pleasantly surprised by the school's financial aid offers.

THE SCHOOL SAYS "…"

From The Admissions Office

"For more than 150 years, Seton Hall University has been a catalyst for leadership, developing the whole student—mind, heart and spirit. As a Catholic university that embraces students of all races and religions, Seton Hall combines the resources of a large university with the personal attention of a small liberal arts college. The University's attractive suburban campus is only 14 miles by train, bus or car to New York City, with the wealth of employment, internship, cultural and entertainment opportunities the city offers. Outstanding faculty, a technologically advanced campus, and a values-centered curriculum challenge Seton Hall students. Students are exposed to a world of ideas from great scholars, opening their minds to the perspectives, history and achievements of many cultures. Our new core curriculum focuses on the need for our students to have common experiences and encourages them to become thinking, caring, communicative and ethically responsible leaders while emphasizing practical proficiencies and intellectual development Our commitment to our students goes beyond textbooks and homework assignments, though. At Seton Hall, developing servant leaders who will make a difference in the world is a priority. That's why all students take classes in ethics and learn in a community informed by Catholic ideals and universal values. While Seton Hall certainly enjoys a big reputation, our campus community is close-knit and inclusive. Students, faculty and staff come from around the world, bringing with them a kaleidoscope of experiences and perspectives to create a diverse yet unified campus environment."

For even more information on this school, turn to page 525 of the "Stats" section.

SETON HILL UNIVERSITY

One Seton Hill Drive, Greensburg, PA 15601 • Admissions: 800-826-6234 • Fax: 724-830-1294
E-mail: admit@setonhill.edu • Website: www.setonhill.edu

RATINGS
Quality of Life: 79   Academic: 75   Admissions: 82   Financial Aid: 74

STUDENTS SAY ". . ."

Academics

Students come to Seton Hill University for a "quality liberal arts education" delivered in the context of a small and "supportive environment." At this Catholic institution, "personal help, education, and kindness are top priority," and "Faculty and staff genuinely care about the well-being

> **SURVEY SAYS . . .**
> *Low cost of living*
> *Frats and sororities are unpopular or nonexistent*
> *Theater is popular*

and success of each and every student." "Like any college, there are good professors and bad professors" at Seton Hill. Fortunately, most faculty members "take the time to know their students and become involved in their learning." If you are struggling, "the campus is small enough [to offer] individualized attention if you need additional help," and professors offer "a lot of out-of-class office hours." Some students feel the advising services could be improved, but they assure us that "The admissions office and registrar work very hard to make sure everyone gets where they need to go." Volunteerism, personal growth, and community involvement complement the academic experience; this school "empowers students with a liberal arts education and a foundation in Catholic Social Teaching to make meaningful contributions as productive members of society." On that note, students say that, "Seton Hill really lets the students become themselves. We have classes to help us deal with problems correctly, and clubs to express our feelings."

Life

Seton Hill's hilltop campus is an ideal setting for college life. "The campus is beautiful and clean" residents say, and "The dorm environments are wonderful and the staff is very friendly." On this small campus, "There's not a moment where nothing is going on. From academics to clubs, there is always something for students to take part in." Off campus, "there are a lot of bars and bistros in the area" and many students like to grab a bite or do homework in town. It helps that "Seton Hill is located a little bit outside of Pittsburgh and also not far away from attractions in the mountains (like ski lodges)." On that note, students warn us that you need a set of wheels to really enjoy life at Seton Hill. However, Seton Hill runs a shuttle from campus to downtown Greensburg. While some students say weekends can be quiet on campus, others point out "There are awesome activities coordinated by the Student Activities Council every week. We have concerts, game shows, comedians, and magicians on a regular basis." However, "most students simply hang out with friends on campus" for fun.

Student Body

Most Seton Hill undergraduates fall into one of two categories: "an athlete or an arts student." Despite these predominant groups, "there are many types of students" at Seton Hill, and "for the most part, everyone gets along." Blending work and play in equal measure, "A typical student at Seton Hill is active and social, [and] very focused on school work." Students generally describe their classmates as "nice, welcoming and very, very friendly." And even "those who are more introverted find quieter friends as well." Unlike the dynamics at other colleges, "The upperclassmen are usually very open to freshmen, and everyone has a fair chance to thrive." While the majority of students come from middle-class families in the Northeast, "there are a wide variety of students from various socio-economic statuses, cultures, and religions."

THE PRINCETON REVIEW SAYS
Admissions
Very important factors considered include: Academic GPA, rigor of secondary school record, interview. *Important factors considered include:* Class rank, standardized test scores, character/personal qualities, extracurricular activities, talent/ability. *Other factors considered include:* Application essay, recommendation(s), alumni/ae relation, level of applicant's interest, volunteer work, work experience. SAT or ACT recommended; ACT with Writing component recommended. TOEFL required of all international applicants. High school diploma is required and GED is accepted. *Academic units required:* 4 English, 2 mathematics, 1 science, (1 science labs), 2 social studies, 4 academic electives. *Academic units recommended:* 4 English, 2 mathematics, 1 science, (1 science labs), 2 foreign language, 2 social studies, 4 academic electives.

Financial Aid
Students should submit: FAFSA, institution's own financial aid form, state aid form. The Princeton Review suggests that all financial aid forms be submitted as soon as possible after January 1. *Need-based scholarships/grants offered:* Federal Pell, SEOG, state scholarships/grants, private scholarships, the school's own gift aid. *Loan aid offered:* Federal Perkins, college/university loans from institutional funds, other, Alternative. Applicants will be notified of awards on a rolling basis beginning 11/15. Federal Work-Study Program available. Institutional employment available. Off-campus job opportunities are good.

The Inside Word
For students who apply by the priority deadline, Seton Hill will offer an admissions decision in two weeks. In recent years, entering freshman students had a high school GPA that fell within the 3.0 to 3.5 range on a 4.0 scale.

THE SCHOOL SAYS "..."
From The Admissions Office
"Seton Hill University is an innovative center for learning, offering a variety of educational opportunities to diverse populations within and beyond the Southwestern Pennsylvania region. Seton Hill University produces graduates possessing the values and perspectives inherent in a Catholic education, capable of accomplishment and leadership in the workplace and their communities.

"Undergraduates choose from over 30 areas of study including the sciences, humanities, business, education, and visual and performing arts. At the graduate level, Seton Hill University grants master's degrees in art therapy, inclusive education, special education, writing popular fiction, marriage and family therapy, physician assistant, elementary education, and business administration. For working adults, Seton Hill University offers an adult degree program in which students can complete an undergraduate degree in 4 years or less by attending only on Saturdays. In addition, Seton Hill hosts over 50 international students from 20 different countries in both graduate and undergraduate study. It is the aim of Seton Hill University to do everything possible to provide each student with a complete and fulfilling academic experience that will serve as the foundation for a lifetime of learning.

"Seton Hill University, a member of the NCAA, Division II, offers basketball, cross country, equestrian, field hockey, track and field, golf, lacrosse, soccer, softball, tennis, and volleyball for women and baseball, basketball, cross-country, equestrian, football, lacrosse, soccer, tennis, track and field, and wrestling for men. Students benefit from both financial need-based aid, and merit-based aid, which includes both academic and athletic aid."

For even more information on this school, turn to page 526 of the "Stats" section.

SIENA COLLEGE

515 LOUDON ROAD, LOUDONVILLE, NY 12211 • ADMISSIONS: 518-783-2423 • FAX: 518-783-2436
FINANCIAL AID: 518-783-2427 • E-MAIL: ADMIT@SIENA.EDU • WEBSITE: WWW.SIENA.EDU

RATINGS
Quality of Life: 80   **Academic:** 79   **Admissions:** 86   **Financial Aid:** 73

STUDENTS SAY "..."

Academics

The Franciscan tradition "is all about community," and, at Siena College, a small school with "a strong Franciscan atmosphere," students benefit from a friendly community in which "there is always someone to lend a helping hand." That someone may be a professor, a tutor, or, on occasion, a Rollerblading friar in robes. No matter whose hand is extended, however, "Every student really has a lot of oppor-

> **SURVEY SAYS . . .**
> Lab facilities are great
> Students get along with local community
> Students love Loudonville, NY
> Frats and sororities are unpopular or nonexistent
> Hard liquor is popular

tunities to get any amount of personal academic attention or other scholastic opportunities that they want." Biology and other premedical disciplines are highly regarded, and students especially love the Siena College–Albany Medical College Program, a joint acceptance program that focuses on humanities and community service. In addition, the school's many business undergrads feel their program, which is enhanced by a loyal alumni base that helps newly minted grads quickly find jobs, is the school's "greatest strength." Regardless of discipline, Siena "teachers know who you are and do not just consider you a number, as opposed [to how it is at] larger colleges and universities." An honors program offers "even smaller classes, preferential registration, and seminars" to those seeking an extra challenge.

Life

For many students, recreation time at Siena means it's time for a beer or two, and lately that's become a point of contention with the administration. Students tell us that the administration, in its effort to crack down on underage drinking, has instituted security checkpoints at the townhouses (where upperclassmen live and, in previous years, had hosted parties) and limits on the amount of alcohol allowed in the rooms of students more than 21. Security can be aggressive, we're told, to the point that more than one undergraduate told us that students sometimes feel "like prisoners." Though this has driven the drinking crowd off campus to nearby clubs and the bars of Albany, on-campus drinking still occurs, but it's more often of the pre-gaming or small-quiet-party variety. The campus still bustles during the week, however, because "most people are involved in clubs" and at least "one sport, whether intramural or intercollegiate." Other diversions include a school-sponsored bus that takes students to the Crossgates Mall, which "is pretty large and houses a bunch of amazing stores," and "a whole strip of dining-out places." Still, an English major admits, "If you don't drink, I can see where weekends would be boring, especially in the winter." The school does sponsor activities on campus designed "to draw students away from the drinking scene," but "there is often a stigma about the 'coolness' of these events."

Student Body

There "isn't much diversity" on the Siena campus, where it seems just about everyone "is from an upper-middle-class Catholic family from Long Island" or "upstate New York." There are some who don't fit the mold, but not many; students speculate that they're mostly nontraditional or international students. Minority students tend to "stick together, but all seem well-liked." Many students "are involved either in D1 athletics, intramural teams, or clubs and Student Senate activities"; students in these groups tend to party together on the weekends "and generally create a strong group of friends easily." While there's a solid contingent of folks at Siena who "drink, party, and hardly ever study," there are also students, particularly in the sciences, who work hard but "don't socialize much outside of their departments, due to the nature of their programs."

THE PRINCETON REVIEW SAYS

Admissions

Very important factors considered include: Academic GPA, rigor of secondary school record. *Important factors considered include:* Recommendation(s), standardized test scores. *Other factors considered include:* Class rank, application essay, alumni/ae relation, character/personal qualities, extracurricular activities, first generation, interview, level of applicant's interest, racial/ethnic status, talent/ability, volunteer work, work experience. SAT or ACT required; ACT with Writing component required. TOEFL required of all international applicants. High school diploma is required, and GED is accepted. *Academic units required:* 4 English, 3 mathematics, 3 science, (3 science labs), 1 social studies, 2 history. *Academic units recommended:* 4 English, 4 mathematics, 4 science, (4 science labs), 3 foreign language, 1 social studies, 3 history.

Financial Aid

Students should submit: FAFSA, state aid form Regular filing deadline is 5/1. The Princeton Review suggests that all financial aid forms be submitted as soon as possible after January 1. *Need-based scholarships/grants offered:* Federal Pell, SEOG, state scholarships/grants, private scholarships, the school's own gift aid. *Loan aid offered:* Federal Perkins. Applicants will be notified of awards on or about 4/1.

The Inside Word

Siena's draw is still primarily regional, with the vast majority of students arriving from in state. Standards aren't especially high; the admit rate says as much about the applicant pool as it does about the school's selectivity. Expect to meet higher standards if you indicate an interest in the School of Science, as it is the gateway to the school's desirable premedical programs. The school does applicants a favor here—substandard students stand little chance of surviving the school's science regimen.

THE SCHOOL SAYS "..."

From The Admissions Office

"Siena, a liberal arts college with a Franciscan tradition offers 28 majors, 38 minors and nine certificates in three schools-liberal arts, science and business. Class sizes range between 15 and 35 students and the student/faculty ratio is 14:1. Siena's 174-acre campus is located in Loudonville, a suburban community within two miles of the New York State seat of government in Albany. With 15 colleges in the area, there is a wide variety of activities on weekends. Regional theater, performances by major concert artists and professional sports events compete with the activities on campus. The capital region's lifestyle is appealing to our students and many Siena graduates find their first jobs in upstate New York."

For even more information on this school, turn to page 526 of the "Stats" section.

SIMMONS COLLEGE

300 THE FENWAY, BOSTON, MA 02115 • ADMISSIONS: 617-521-2051 • FAX: 617-521-3190
FINANCIAL AID: 617-521-2001 • E-MAIL: UGADM@SIMMONS.EDU • WEBSITE: WWW.SIMMONS.EDU

RATINGS
Quality of Life: 86   Academic: 86   Admissions: 84   Financial Aid: 70

STUDENTS SAY "..."

Academics

Simmons College, an "all-women's college located in the Fenway area of Boston," provides students with "lots of opportunities to work closely with faculty and [to] interact with local Boston communities." The school excels in pre-professional programs in nursing and physical therapy, each of which capitalizes on the school's location to "give students opportunities to do internships/clinical placements at world-renowned hospitals that are only a few blocks away

(e.g. Children's Hospital Boston, Brigham and Women's, Mass General)." Students also rave about Simmons' offerings in psychology, biology, pre-dental sciences, economics, and management, and they praise the school's "excellent facilities, including an amazing new library" and the "large career resource department." Small classes here "allow great discussions, because those who want to participate have the opportunity to do so," which can be both a blessing and a curse. At Simmons "If you work hard, you get out of it what you put in." One drawback is the study-abroad program. One undergrad gripes, "There just aren't enough choices! And if there are, they are all usually around the same time, making it quite difficult to choose."

Life

Life at Simmons College "is more academic in nature: The classes are teaching-based, and life on campus revolves around schoolwork." One student agrees, "Simmons is pretty much where students go to school. We go elsewhere to have fun/party/live." With downtown Boston outside the school's front door, the options are plentiful. There are museums ("great things to do in the area" include "free gallery talks at the Museum of Fine Arts"), "shopping on Newbury Street," and "eating great food in the North End." Public transportation means "getting around is easy, and exploring the city is amazing." When students seek a party, they typically "go to other local colleges...like MIT, Harvard, Boston University, and Northeastern." On-campus fun is more subdued. There's "a lot of random friendly girl-time things going on, like decorating our doors for the holidays, making paper chains, or watching television. For entertainment here, you really have to turn to your friends, because almost nothing worth attending happens on campus," a female student notes. Most see this as a boon; writes one student, "What's nice about living at Simmons is that it is a peaceful and nice place to live, but when you want to go to a party, Northeastern and BU are just minutes away. After spending a night there, you realize how thankful you are for clean dorms and the lack of boys."

Student Body

The student body at Simmons is "mostly middle- to upper-class women who hail from all over the United States and many other countries. The school is predominately white, but a range of ethnicities are represented." One student reports that her study group consists of "an orthodox Jew, a Saudi Arabian, an African American, a Cambodian, an Indian, and two Caucasians. The UN could take lessons from us." Politically, "most students are liberal and involved with their community." Left-leaning politics dominates to the point that "it can be challenging to express conservative viewpoints." Sexual orientation "tends not to be a question, and it is very common for girls to be open about being straight, gay, or bisexual." While "there are a lot of lesbians here," they are "not at all the majority." Simmons hosts a conspicuous butch subculture. As one women explains, "Even though you know going into it that Simmons is an all-women's college, you may be shocked to see some guys walking around attending your classes...until you realize that they are girls! It's great that everyone is cool with everyone else, and the people who are narrow-minded stick to themselves."

THE PRINCETON REVIEW SAYS

Admissions

Very important factors considered include: Academic GPA, rigor of secondary school record. *Important factors considered include:* Class rank, application essay, recommendation(s), standardized test scores. *Other factors considered include:* Extracurricular activities, interview, talent/ability, volunteer work, work experience. SAT or ACT required; TOEFL required of all international applicants. High school diploma is required, and GED is accepted. *Academic units required:* 4 English, 3 mathematics, 3 science, 3 foreign language, 3 social studies, 3 history. *Academic units recommended:* 4 English, 4 mathematics, 3 science, 4 foreign language, 4 social studies, 3 history,

Financial Aid

Students should submit: FAFSA, institution's own financial aid form Regular filing deadline is 3/1. The Princeton Review suggests that all financial aid forms be submitted as soon as possible after January 1. *Need-based scholarships/grants offered:* Federal Pell, SEOG, state scholarships/grants, private scholarships, the school's own gift aid. *Loan aid offered:* Direct Subsidized Stafford, Direct Unsubsidized Stafford, Direct PLUS, state loans, college/university loans from institutional funds. Applicants will be notified of awards on a rolling basis beginning 3/15. Federal Work-Study Program available. Institutional employment available. Off-campus job opportunities are excellent.

The Inside Word

Most of the nation's best all-women's colleges are in the Northeast, including those Seven Sister schools (roughly the female equivalent of the formerly all-male Ivies) that remain single-sex institutions. The competition for students is intense, and although Simmons is a solid school, there are at least a half-dozen competitors more appealing to most candidates. Solid high school performers should have little need to worry here. The school's excellent academics and Boston location make Simmons a worthy option for any woman interested in single-sex education.

THE SCHOOL SAYS "..."

From The Admissions Office

"Simmons honors educational values that place students first and helps them build successful careers, lead meaningful lives, and realize a powerful return on their investment. Simmons delivers a quality education and measurable success through a singular approach to professional preparation, intellectual exploration, and community orientation.

"Simmons is a 100-year-old university in Boston, with a tradition of providing women with a collaborative environment that stimulates dialogue, enhances listening, catalyzes action, and spurs personal and professional growth.

"Simmons College accepts both the ACT with the Writing Section and SAT. Additionally, if English is not your native language a TOEFL is required."

For even more information on this school, turn to page 527 of the "Stats" section.

SKIDMORE COLLEGE

815 NORTH BROADWAY, SARATOGA SPRINGS, NY 12866-1632 • ADMISSIONS: 518-580-5570
FAX: 518-580-5584 • FINANCIAL AID: 518-580-5750 • E-MAIL: ADMISSIONS@SKIDMORE.EDU • WEBSITE: WWW.SKIDMORE.EDU

RATINGS
Quality of Life: 97   Academic: 94   Admissions: 94   Financial Aid: 94

STUDENTS SAY "..."

Academics

Both inside and outside the classroom, Skidmore College is a "school that values independence, creativity, and passion." At this unique, small college, "Creative approaches to learning and education are infused into the curriculum and daily life." Skidmore's strong majors in the liberal arts and sciences are complemented by top-rated programs in

art, theater, music, and dance. A senior tells us, "I couldn't decide between Ivy League academics or an arts conservatory, so this seemed to be the compromise." Ideal for students with diverse interests, Skidmore "allows students with a variety of interests to take classes that they are interested in," and "interdisciplinary courses and work are common" here. In the classroom, professors are "extremely enthusiastic about their subjects," and "All classes are really personal. You get to know everyone in the class, and the professors urge [you] to meet with them at least a few times one-on-one so that they can get to know you." A current student affirms, "I've been given many wonderful academic opportunities—I even started doing research as a first-semester freshman." Administrators are receptive to students, and "Every month or so the president will have fireside chats where students are open to discuss their issues with him." While Skidmore's financial aid programs are ample, excellence comes with a price. One sophomore explains, "Skidmore tries to offer the advantages of an Ivy League college with a far smaller endowment; as a result, tuition is astronomical."

Life

Fun, fulfilling, and a bit rowdy, life at Skidmore is "like summer camp for college students." On this busy campus, "Your typical student is a part of at least one club or extracurricular [activity], sometimes two or three or four." Thanks to the school's artistic inclinations, "Art openings, theater performances, student bands, a capella shows, and comedy shows are all really popular." In fact, a typical weekend night out would include "a performance and then the after-party." Here, "strong friendships and a great sense of community keep things interesting on campus," and students really like the fact that, "We don't have frats or sororities so there is no pressure to join or conform to anything." Students convene in the campus's central cafeteria, and "When the weather is nice out, students love to spend time outside talking, reading, playing tennis, or playing chess." You will also find "a network of hiking trails called 'Northwoods' that is a very popular place to exercise, talk, or have a bonfire on a Friday night." Described as "the perfect college town," Saratoga Springs is "extremely fun and accepting of college students" with "amazing restaurants" and tons of shops. In addition to recreational activities, "Skidmore students are very involved in the Saratoga community through everything from sustainability efforts to mentoring local children." Students rarely leave campus on the weekends, and you'll find "a mix of smaller parties on campus and larger ones in off-campus houses" on Friday and Saturday nights. For residents, dormitories are comfortable, and "The dining hall offers freshly made food which is delicious and gives students a variety, from vegetarian to full-out carnivor[ous]."

Student Body

With strong arts and athletics programs, "Skidmore's enduring stereotype is that there are two groups of students: the jocks and the hipsters." In reality, things aren't so black and white. "Most students are white, upper-middle-class" and hail from New England; however, "there is a wide range of racial and geographic backgrounds" within the student body. Whether it's music, dance, theater, or visual arts, "Most people are artistically inclined or at least interested in art." In fact, "The typical student here seems to be the atypical student elsewhere: super-liberal and socially conscious, 'creative' or artsy, weirdly dressed." Some undergraduates even claim, "You can't be a Skid kid unless you are a little weird." Whether you are weird or just unique, intellect and creativity are highly valued here: "If you can carry on an intelligent or quirky conversation you will have no trouble making friends." A student adds, "My group of friends in particular is always having discussions about what we are learning in classes, theoretical physics, political, and environmental issues."

Admissions

Very important factors considered include: Rigor of secondary school record and academic GPA. *Important factors considered include:* Recommendation(s), application essay, academic GPA, character/personal qualities, extracurricular activities, talent/ability, volunteer work, work experience. *Other factors considered include:* Standardized test scores, alumni/ae relation, first generation, geographical residence, interview, level of applicant's interest, racial/ethnic status, SAT Subject Tests recommended; SAT or ACT required; ACT with Writing component required. TOEFL required of all international applicants for whom English is not the first language. High school diploma is required, and GED is accepted. *Academic units recommended:* 4 English, 4 mathematics, 4 science (3 science labs), 4 foreign language, 4 social studies.

Financial Aid

Students should submit: FAFSA, CSS/Financial Aid PROFILE Regular filing deadline is 2/1. The Princeton Review suggests that all financial aid forms be submitted as soon as possible after January 1. *Need-based scholarships/grants offered:* Federal Pell, SEOG, state scholarships/grants, the school's own gift aid. *Loan aid offered:* Federal Perkins. Applicants will be notified of awards on or about 4/1. Federal Work-Study Program available. Institutional employment available. Off-campus job opportunities are fair.

The Inside Word

Admission to Skidmore is highly competitive, and the admissions staff carefully considers each applicant's academic background and standardized test scores. However, consistent with their motto—"creative thought matters"—Skidmore carefully reviews a student's extracurricular talents, achievements, and passions when making an admissions decision. While admissions interviews aren't a requirement for a Skidmore applicant, students may request a personal interview on campus or with an alumnus in their area.

THE SCHOOL SAYS "…"

From The Admissions Office

"At Skidmore, we believe a great education is about putting academic theory and creative expression into practice; hence, our belief that creative thought matters. It's a place where faculty and students work together, then figure out how to use what they've learned to make a difference. This often leads to multi-disciplinary approaches, where students carry more than one major, student-faculty research is common, most students study abroad, and internships and community service are standard. Skidmore students develop into independent, creative problem-solvers who aren't restricted to looking at things in traditional ways.

"This personal journey starts with the First-Year Experience-50 seminars from which to choose, faculty and peer mentors, and living in close proximity to seminar classmates in residence halls. It's meant to ensure that first-year students hit the ground running on day one, connected and involved. When it comes to your major, you can choose from 65 offerings in the sciences, social sciences, and humanities, as well as pre-professional fields like management and business.

"Since we have no fraternities or sororities, student life centers on the nearly 100 student clubs and organizations, which range from the Environmental Action Club to a capella groups to snowboarding. Add to this the prominence of the arts, which has long set Skidmore apart. Science classes collaborate on exhibits at the Tang Museum. Hundreds of students perform in music groups. Enroll in dance courses. Do theater performances. Most not even arts majors. At Skidmore, the arts don't dominate, they permeate.

"As for location, who wouldn't want to go to college in Saratoga Springs? A downtown brimming with shops, galleries, coffeehouses, and great restaurants. Boston, New York City, and Montreal are a three-hour car ride from campus. And the Adirondacks, Berkshires, and Green Mountains provide opportunities for skiing, mountain biking, hiking, rock-climbing, and kayaking."

For even more information on this school, turn to page 527 of the "Stats" section.

SLIPPERY ROCK UNIVERSITY OF PENNSYLVANIA

OFFICE OF UNDERGRADUATE ADMISSIONS, SLIPPERY ROCK, PA 16057 • ADMISSIONS: 724-738-2015 OR 800-929-4778
FAX: 724-738-2913 • E-MAIL: ASKTHEROCK@SRU.EDU • WEBSITE: WWW.SRU.EDU

RATINGS
Quality of Life: 76   **Academic:** 69   **Admissions:** 77   **Financial Aid:** 76

STUDENTS SAY ". . ."

> **SURVEY SAYS . . .**
> *Athletic facilities are great*
> *Dorms are like palaces*

Academics

Slippery Rock University is a medium-sized school in western Pennsylvania that is growing tremendously, yet, remains "fairly small compared to" other schools in the state. SRU has a "wonderful business school" and notable programs in music and physical therapy. The education majors are "excellent" as well. Academics at The Rock are solid but not overly demanding. "I don't feel like I'm wildly intelligent," muses a senior, "but when I hear that people have honest trouble making it through this school, I worry." Many professors are "very good teachers." Once you get into your major, "professors start to care about you." "I have been pleased with the availability of the professors, their willingness to work with students, and their reliability," reflects a senior. SRU's administration "rocks." "They are very personable and take the time to listen to students." However, some students note it can be hard to get into the classes you need.

Life

This "breathtakingly beautiful" campus "in the middle of nowhere" is rather enormous. "It is a hike to get to some classes" and the "hilly layout" doesn't help, particularly in the winter. ("The school is called 'Slippery Rock' for a reason.") The recreation center is excellent. Six out of eight campus dorms were built less than a year ago and the remaining were renovated. "I think some of the classrooms and buildings could be fixed up," says a sophomore. "I know [the administration is] trying to change the look and feel of the campus and that is great [because] it really is a beautiful place to be." Clubs and organized activities are abundant. Posters and sidewalk chalk describing various happenings are reportedly everywhere. "Intramural sports are huge." "Greek life is big enough to have an impact, but not too big where you can't have a social life without joining one." However, Slippery Rock is basically "a commuter school that is trying to become a stay-on-campus school." Students who remain on campus over the weekend "definitely tend to party" but "don't get too extreme." Some students call the surrounding community "quaint," but others say it's "a hick town." Whatever the case, there's "not a lot of action" except for a few bars. Without your own vehicle, "you will be stuck in your dorm or apartment. *A lot*." With a car, trips to larger nearby towns are possible. "The proximity to Pittsburgh" allows for an easy escape when the urge for a more serious road trip strikes.

Student Body

It's a "blue-collar" crowd, "not a bunch of spoiled rich kids." For the most part, "the people here are real people who have to actually work their way though college." "Most of the students come from the Pittsburgh area, or smaller towns" in the region and they "have a lot in common" with each other. Nontraditional students will find many kindred souls and so will students "straight out of high school." The Rock is "more diverse than a small farm town" but only by a little. "There are some foreign students" and some kids from different ethnic groups, but not many. "There is a variety of personalities on campus," though. "The stereotypical prep or jock" is well represented, but "cliques are pretty diverse, ranging from social partying crowds, to study groups, to tree-hugging hippies."

THE PRINCETON REVIEW SAYS

Admissions

Important factors considered include: Class rank, academic GPA, rigor of secondary school record, standardized test scores. *Other factors considered include:* Application essay, recommendation(s), talent/ability. SAT or ACT required; TOEFL required of all international applicants. High school diploma is required and GED is accepted. *Academic units recommended:* 4 English, 3 mathematics, 3 science, (1 science labs), 2 foreign language.

Financial Aid

Students should submit: FAFSA. The Princeton Review suggests that all financial aid forms be submitted as soon as possible after January 1. *Need-based scholarships/grants offered:* Federal Pell, SEOG, state scholarships/grants, private scholarships, the school's own gift aid. *Loan aid offered:* Federal Perkins. Applicants will be notified of awards on a rolling basis beginning 3/15. Federal Work-Study Program available. Institutional employment available. Off-campus job opportunities are good.

The Inside Word

If you earned decent grades in high school, you should have no problem gaining admittance to Slippery Rock. A 3.0 GPA and either a combined Math and Critical Reading score on the SAT of 950 or a 20 on the ACT will get you admitted automatically.

THE SCHOOL SAYS "..."

From The Admissions Office

"It's a great time to be at Slippery Rock University—Pennsylvania's premier public residential university. The evidence is everywhere. SRU is one of the top five "best value" public universities in America—and has the award to prove it. Enrollment and academic quality is at an all time high. And the campus is beaming with state-of-the-art academic and residence hall facilities.

"Slippery Rock's main campus is located on more than 650 acres in scenic western Pennsylvania, only 50 miles north of Pittsburgh and 35 miles east of Youngstown, Ohio. Founded in 1889, the SRU family is comprised of more than 8,500 students and 950 faculty and staff.

"SRU offers more than 60 undergraduate majors through our colleges of Education, Humanities, Fine and Performing Arts, Business, Information and Behavioral Sciences, and Health, Environment and Science. Our Honor's Program provides academically gifted students an opportunity to study with select faculty in small, highly interactive academic settings both here and abroad.

"The University has an accomplished faculty; over 91 percent have an earned doctorate or terminal degree. And, because our most common class size is only 20–29 students, faculty members have time to mentor students and provide the personal attention that has become a hallmark of a Slippery Rock University education.

"Our students do amazing things. Not surprising since SRU is student centered and intentionally combines academic with "hands-on" learning opportunities. At SRU you'll find opportunities to conduct undergraduate research, participate in service learning projects, volunteer or just have fun by participating in one or more of our 100 student organizations, intercollegiate athletics or intramural sports"

For even more information on this school, turn to page 528 of the "Stats" section.

SMITH COLLEGE

SEVEN COLLEGE LANE, NORTHAMPTON, MA 01063 • ADMISSIONS: 413-585-2500 • FAX: 413-585-2527
FINANCIAL AID: 413-585-2530 • E-MAIL: ADMISSIONS@SMITH.EDU • WEBSITE: WWW.SMITH.EDU

RATINGS
Quality of Life: 96   Academic: 96   Admissions: 96   Financial Aid: 96

STUDENTS SAY ". . ."

Academics

Smith College isn't for everyone. You have to be a woman to get in, for one, and a highly accomplished one at that—Smith is among the nation's most selective undergraduate institutions. More important still is a capacity for self-direction; Smith has an open curriculum ("no core requirements"), which means students "can make our schedules however we like, leaving lots of freedom to take interesting classes outside our majors." Those who thrive here are those who are "tired of being told that I needed to take things I wasn't interested in. I like being trusted with my own education, and Smith gave me that option," but students needing structure may find the freedom a bit overwhelming. Fortunately, Smith offers undergrads plenty of support; "Both the administration and the faculty at Smith are very invested in the success of students. It is very easy to get support and find someone to help navigate not only your academic career at Smith but also the continuation of a liberal arts education in the real world through internships, jobs, summer experiences, and other programs offered in conjunction with Smith." Students also enjoy "almost limitless resources in terms of libraries, funding, etc., all easily accessible," all in a "small community" setting; "From financial aid officers who've 'found' extra funds to professors who think of an internship you might be interested in, it really seems like everyone here is willing to go the extra mile for students."

> **SURVEY SAYS . . .**
> Great off-campus food
> Dorms are like palaces
> Frats and sororities are unpopular or nonexistent
> Student government is popular
> Political activism is popular

Life

Smith's unique housing system—students live in smaller houses rather than dorms—is a much-cherished tradition. Students crow that the system "provides for a strong campus community including friendly rivalries and close friendships. Your house is your lifeline, especially during the first few weeks of school." "Strong self-government within each household" reinforces Smith's academic emphasis on independence. Campus life "provides a variety of activities every night to keep their students entertained, including "great sports teams" and "an organization or group for just about everybody." Hometown Northampton "is a lively town with fun bars, restaurants, and theaters" and is surprisingly active given its size (approximately 30,000). Further opportunities arise from Smith's participation in the Five College Consortium; "Any event on any of the five campuses (Hampshire, UMass Amherst, Amherst, Mount Holyoke, and Smith) is open to all five college's students. Students are able to take classes at all the colleges, join clubs at all the colleges, get into parties at all colleges, and attend any performance or event at any of the colleges. Because of this, you can easily be involved in a wide variety of social engagements (e.g. frat parties at UMass, theater performances at Hampshire, or a night in your living room with housemates at Smith)."

Student Body

Smith fosters "an accepting and intellectual atmosphere" where "students actually enjoy their studies and happily talk about class work outside of class." The women here tend to be "overachievers…who take advantage of the many things Smith has to offer and tend to be constantly busy trying to manage school work and multiple extracurriculars. Smithies are always involved." As an elite school, Smith can attract students "from vastly different backgrounds who thus bring those differences with them to the Smith community," thereby exposing students "to people of different race, religion, socio-economic, cultural, social, gender, [and] sexual backgrounds" whom they might elsewhere not have encountered; undergrads appreciate the opportunity. The student body has a well-earned reputation for being "very open about and accepting of all types of sexual orientation, with active GLBTQ and transgender communities." They also tend to be "very environmentally aware and active," and "the large majority of students are liberal or very liberal politically."

THE PRINCETON REVIEW SAYS

Admissions

Very important factors considered include: Academic GPA, recommendation(s), rigor of secondary school record, character/personal qualities. *Important factors considered include:* Class rank, application essay, extracurricular activities, interview, talent/ability. *Other factors considered include:* Standardized test scores, alumni/ae relation, first generation, racial/ethnic status, volunteer work, work experience. TOEFL required of all international applicants. High school diploma or equivalent is not required. *Academic units recommended:* 4 English, 3 mathematics, 3 science, (3 science labs), 3 foreign language, 2 history,

Financial Aid

Students should submit: FAFSA, CSS/Financial Aid PROFILE, noncustodial PROFILE, business/farm supplement. Regular filing deadline is 2/15. The Princeton Review suggests that all financial aid forms be submitted as soon as possible after January 1. *Need-based scholarships/grants offered:* Federal Pell, SEOG, state scholarships/grants, the school's own gift aid. *Loan aid offered:* Direct Subsidized Stafford, Direct Unsubsidized Stafford, Federal Perkins, state loans, college/university loans from institutional funds. Applicants will be notified of awards on or about 4/1. Federal Work-Study Program available. Institutional employment available. Off-campus job opportunities are excellent.

The Inside Word

Applicants to Smith can expect a careful and thorough review of all application materials. Only students who have successfully pursued rigorous high school curricula and demonstrated unique and compelling talents or personal attributes are likely to get past the gatekeepers here. Standardized test scores are optional here; if yours are sub-par, don't submit them. If they're good, though, include them; they can't hurt.

THE SCHOOL SAYS "..."

From The Admissions Office

"Smith students choose from 1,000 courses in more than 50 areas of study. There are no specific course requirements outside the major; students meet individually with faculty advisers to plan a balanced curriculum. Smith programs offer unique opportunities, including the chance to study abroad, or at another college in the United States, and a semester in Washington, D.C. The Ada Comstock Scholars Program encourages women beyond the traditional age to return to college and complete their undergraduate studies. Smith is located in the scenic Connecticut River valley of western Massachusetts near a number of other outstanding educational institutions. Through the Five College Consortium, Smith, Amherst, Hampshire, and Mount Holyoke colleges, and the University of Massachusetts enrich their academic, social, and cultural offerings by means of joint faculty appointments, joint courses, student and faculty exchanges, shared facilities, and other cooperative arrangements. Smith is the only women's college to offer an accredited major in engineering; it's also the only college in the country that offers a guaranteed paid internship program ("Praxis")."

For even more information on this school, turn to page 528 of the "Stats" section.

St. Bonaventure University

PO Box D, Saint Bonaventure, NY 14778 • Admissions: 716-375-2400 • Fax: 716-375-4005
Financial Aid: 716-375-2528 • E-mail: admissions@sbu.edu • Website: www.sbu.edu

RATINGS

Quality of Life: 71   Academic: 74   Admissions: 73   Financial Aid: 81

STUDENTS SAY ". . ."

Academics

St. Bonaventure is "a small-town university with a lot to offer," including a "simply stellar" journalism and mass communications program that features "an amazing faculty" that "wants you to get the best job possible." SBU's business program is also "very strong," and its education department "has a good reputation." A new science building should bolster the university's small but growing biology, chemistry, and computer science departments. Regardless of major, all students must complete a core curriculum offered through SBU's Clare College. While a few here insist that "Clare College is not that bad, and a lot of the classes are interesting," the majority complain that the "required Catholic core curriculum" is "a complete drag and a waste of students' time and effort, in addition to being a GPA reducer." Somewhere in between are those pragmatists who tell us that "Clare College courses are annoying but not over demanding. If you didn't want to learn about Catholic heritage, you shouldn't come to a Catholic school." Amen! While SBU undergrads may not agree on the value of the core curriculum, nearly all concur that professors here "are easy to talk to and are always available after class and outside of class. They make students feel comfortable and want to get to know the students. We are not just numbers." They also agree that their degree provides them access to "great connections with alumni" and that, all things considered, SBU leaves them "as well equipped to take the jobs of their choosing out of college as students at any other college, period."

Life

"When the weekend arrives, the general consensus of the students is one thing: partying. Off-campus houses host triple keggers every weekends; and the four local bars begin to draw crowds on Wednesday nights." Almost everyone agrees that "Drinking is huge...and so are basketball games"—as one student explains it, "we all love love love basketball games; the entire student population will be at a basketball game on a Saturday night, without fail"—but undergrads add that "there are lots of other things to keep busy" for those outliers to whom neither beer nor hoops appeals. Winter sports such as snowboarding and skiing are quite popular, and students have access to numerous parks and trails for hiking during the warm months. Furthermore, "the radio station and Campus Activities Board work very hard to bring in an up-and-coming band probably once a week." Students add that "the radio station is also a great thing to do, it's very easy to get involved in." Finally, the school's many community-spirited undergrads can participate in "the oldest student-run soup kitchen in the country" or "a program called Bona Buddies that matches up students with underprivileged local kids to mentor them."

Student Body

The typical Bona undergrad "is white and Catholic, with a desire to do well and succeed but a stronger desire to have fun while doing so." Most "wear jeans and a North Face jacket or something very similar." Students are "trendy" but casual. A great number "hail from within three hours of the school, mostly in the Rochester and Buffalo area." Western New York is conservative terrain, so SBU "has a good number of conservative students." They are typically "involved, whether it be in our soup kitchen or radio station." While the demographic is largely white, "there are more and more minority students every year," and the school offers "a plethora of activities, groups and policies that seem to provide a soaring number of opportunities for minority students."

THE PRINCETON REVIEW SAYS

Admissions

Very important factors considered include: Academic GPA, recommendation(s), rigor of secondary school record, character/personal qualities, interview. *Important factors considered include:* Application essay, standardized test scores, extracurricular activities, level of applicant's interest, talent/ability, volunteer work. *Other factors considered include:* Class rank, alumni/ae relation, first generation, work experience. SAT recommended; SAT or ACT required; ACT recommended; TOEFL required of all international applicants. High school diploma is required, and GED is accepted. *Academic units required:* 4 English, 3 mathematics, 3 science, 2 foreign language, 4 social studies. *Academic units recommended:* 4 English, 3 mathematics, 3 science, (3 science labs), 2 foreign language, 4 social studies.

Financial Aid

Students should submit: FAFSA, institution's own financial aid form, state aid form. The Princeton Review suggests that all financial aid forms be submitted as soon as possible after January 1. *Need-based scholarships/grants offered:* Federal Pell, SEOG, state scholarships/grants, private scholarships, the school's own gift aid. *Loan aid offered:* Federal Perkins, college/university loans from institutional funds. Applicants will be notified of awards on a rolling basis beginning 4/1.

The Inside Word

Above-average students should meet little resistance from the St. Bonaventure admissions office; nearly nine in 10 applicants here are accepted, and the academic profile of the median admitted student is respectable but hardly overwhelming. A personal essay is required, and an interview is optional; barring a misstep of catastrophic proportions, both can only improve your chances of getting in.

THE SCHOOL SAYS "..."

From The Admissions Office

"The St. Bonaventure University family has been imparting an extraordinary Franciscan tradition to men and women of a rich diversity of backgrounds for more than 130 years. This tradition encourages all who become a part of it to face the world confidently, respect the earthly environment, and work for productive change in the world. The charm of our campus and the inspirational beauty of the surrounding hills provide a special place where growth in learning and living is abundantly realized. The Richter Student Fitness Center, which opened in 2004, provides all students with state-of-the-art facilities for athletics and wellness. Academics at St. Bonaventure are challenging. Small classes and personalized attention encourage individual growth and development. St. Bonaventure's nationally known Schools of Arts and Sciences, Business Administration, Journalism/Mass Communication, and Education offer majors in 31 disciplines. The School of Graduate Studies also offers several programs leading to the master's degree.

"Applicants can submit scores from either the SAT or the ACT. The biology Subject Test is required only for students applying to one of our dual-admission medical programs."

For even more information on this school, turn to page 529 of the "Stats" section.

ST. JOHN'S COLLEGE (MD)

PO BOX 2800, ANNAPOLIS, MD 21404 • ADMISSIONS: 410-626-2522 • FAX: 410-269-7916
FINANCIAL AID: 410-626-2502 • E-MAIL: ADMISSIONS@SJCA.EDU • WEBSITE: WWW.SJCA.EDU

RATINGS
Quality of Life: 92   **Academic:** 96   **Admissions:** 85   **Financial Aid:** 89

STUDENTS SAY "..."

> **SURVEY SAYS . . .**
> Class discussions encouraged
> No one cheats
> Registration is a breeze
> Frats and sororities are unpopular or nonexistent

Academics

Tiny St. John's College specializes in a four-year curriculum that is an "exhilarating and exhausting" survey of intellectual history, starting with ancient Greece and ending in modern times. Virtually all classes are required. There are no majors. There are no textbooks. And there are no tests, except for "occasional grammar and vocab quizzes" in ancient Greek and French. Grades are based on papers and class participation. Students encounter the works of "the greatest minds of Western Civilization" in their original, unadulterated form. While students at other schools may occasionally think outside the box, students at St. John's critically examine "the eternal questions of this world," namely "what it is to be a human." It's "certainly not the best education for everyone (especially students who want to learn certain technical skills)." For these students, though, it is a little slice of heaven. Classes are small—"never larger than 20 students"—and "discussion-based." Professors (called "tutors") are "deeply intelligent" and "can bounce from Newton to Leibniz to Baudelaire to Bach" with ease. They "do little or no lecturing," favoring instead to "facilitate discussion." Students engage in conversation, "instead of sitting through lectures on other people's interpretations." "There's a wonderful sense of camaraderie that develops in the classroom, as we wrestle with the great questions of the ages," enthuses one student.

Life

Despite the "overbearing" workload, "there is an almost snuggly feeling of community at St. John's." "The academic atmosphere is immersing and supportive, especially since everyone is in, or has had, or will have all the same classes." Social life is "alarmingly insular." "We at St. John's are removed from the world to a truly shocking degree," elaborates one student. "The campus feels not like a campus, but a miniature world, which actually is not very much like the real world." Extracurricular activities include "heaps of clubs." "Most everyone attends the Shakespeare plays and classical music concerts." Intramural sports are "incredibly fun" and a big part of Johnnie life. "Skill is optional but enthusiasm is required." "It is a great stress reliever," explains one student. "The books tear your soul apart," but sports here are a way of "pasting it back together." Campus-wide parties on the weekends include "raucous" reality dance parties as well as waltz and swing dancing parties. Drinking is popular. Coffee and cigarettes are big. Johnnies also "sail, watch movies," and play board games. Or they just hang out, "finding adventures where they pop up." Students also talk late into the night "about set theory, socks, art history, Moby Dick, why macaroni is so orange," and pretty much everything. While the food on campus "sucks," students find epicurean delights in "Annapolis, Baltimore, Washington, D.C., or New York."

Student Body

"St. John's is a unique program, and it takes a unique group of people to keep it going." "The one thing Johnnies have in common is their love of learning and their love for thought," says a junior. "A Johnnie is a bookworm, socially awkward in some fashion, and an intense thinker." Eyeglasses are common. "This campus may have the worst collective eyesight in America." "Many students are quite intelligent, and most are highly eccentric." "'Intellectual elitism' can be a problem." "Upperclassmen especially have an esprit de corps and traditionalist spirit that borders on crotchetiness." "Most people here are strange." Many are "brash and freakish." "There is definitely a certain type of person who picks St. John's, but how that quality reveals itself is different for every person," notes one student. "St. John's is entirely made up of atypical students, so none of them fit in, and they don't feel like they need to." Johnnies are "an amazing conglomeration of artists, mathematicians, jocks, role-playing enthusiasts, poets, iconoclasts, activists, and some who are all of these." That said, there's a serious lack of "ethnic diversity." However, intellectual diversity abounds. Students are "willing to assert opinions, and, more importantly, to reconsider them."

THE PRINCETON REVIEW SAYS

Admissions

Very important factors considered include: Application essay. *Important factors considered include:* Recommendation(s), rigor of secondary school record, character/personal qualities. *Other factors considered include:* Class rank, academic GPA, standardized test scores, alumni/ae relation, extracurricular activities, first generation, interview, racial/ethnic status, talent/ability, TOEFL required of all international applicants. High school diploma is required, and GED is accepted. *Academic units required:* 3 mathematics, 2 foreign language. *Academic units recommended:* 4 English, 4 mathematics, 3 science, (3 science labs), 4 foreign language, 2 social studies, 2 history.

Financial Aid

Students should submit: FAFSA, CSS/Financial Aid PROFILE, state aid form, noncustodial PROFILE, business/farm supplement. The Princeton Review suggests that all financial aid forms be submitted as soon as possible after January 1. *Need-based scholarships/grants offered:* Federal Pell, SEOG, state scholarships/grants, private scholarships, the school's own gift aid. *Loan aid offered:* Federal Perkins, college/university loans from institutional funds. Applicants will be notified of awards on a rolling basis beginning 12/1. Federal Work-Study Program available. Institutional employment available. Off-campus job opportunities are good.

The Inside Word

St. John's has one of the most personal admissions processes in the country. The applicant pool is highly self-selected and extremely bright, so don't be fooled by the high acceptance rate—every student who is offered admission deserves to be here. Candidates who don't give serious thought to the kind of match they make with the college and devote serious energy to their essays are not likely to be accepted.

THE SCHOOL SAYS "…"

From The Admissions Office

"The purpose of the admission process is to determine whether an applicant has the necessary preparation and ability to complete the St. John's program satisfactorily. The essays are designed to enable applicants to give a full account of themselves. They can tell the committee much more than statistical records reveal. Previous academic records show whether an applicant has the habits of study necessary at St. John's. Letters of reference, particularly those of teachers, are carefully read for indications that the applicant has the maturity, self-discipline, ability, energy, and initiative to succeed in the St. John's program. St. John's attaches little importance to 'objective' test scores, and no applicant is accepted or rejected because of such scores.

"St. John's College does not require the results of standardized tests, except in the case of international students, homeschooled students, and those who will not receive a high school diploma. Results of the ACT or SAT are sufficient for these students."

For even more information on this school, turn to page 529 of the "Stats" section.

ST. JOHN'S UNIVERSITY—QUEENS

8000 UTOPIA PARKWAY, JAMAICA, NY 11439 • ADMISSIONS: 718-990-2000 • FAX: 718-990-5728
E-MAIL: ADMISSIONS@STJOHNS.EDU • WEBSITE: WWW.STJOHNS.EDU

RATINGS
Quality of Life: 75   **Academic:** 68   **Admissions:** 86   **Financial Aid:** 70

STUDENTS SAY "..."

Academics

Like its hometown of Queens, New York, St. John's moves inexorably forward without forgetting its history and traditions. The school's administration is committed to constantly "updating the university's facilities." Recent improvements include "a state-of-the-art athletic training facility and revamped cafeterias," as well as an upgrade to science facilities, added townhouse residences for students, and a new 127,000

> **SURVEY SAYS . . .**
> *Great computer facilities*
> *Athletic facilities are great*
> *Diverse student types on campus*
> *Students get along with local community*
> *Students love Queens, NY*
> *Everyone loves the Red Storm*

square foot University Center. In addition, the school distributes "brand-new laptops to all incoming students" and has "done a tremendous job of implementing technology throughout the campus," which "is completely wireless except for a few athletic fields and parking lots." On the traditions side of the balance, the school maintains "a lot of policies and politics opposed by typical college students [such as] the visitor policies in the dorms." Many praise St. John's' study abroad programs and Institute for Writing Studies, which provides writing support to all students. When it comes to classroom experience, "professors are professors. Like [at] any school, some are better than others." Students report that "the experience you have at St. John's really depends on what you do with it. Don't take a professor just because he/she is easy—chances are that means they suck! If you are self-motivated...you will find challenging professors." Big-picture people will see that St. John's offers "a quality private education" and, in many instances, a "generous" financial aid package that translates to an overall "low cost."

Life

Students say "There are a lot of opportunities to get involved on campus," at St. John's. "Our student government works very hard on student engagement, creating popular events to foster the University community." Still, "Life for most St. John's students is not centered around the campus. We have NYC as our playground, so time not spent in classes is often [spent] off campus." For those who prefer off-campus activities in their spare time, the school helps to make that possible. There are "shuttles that can take us into the city [aka Manhattan, to those outside New York City] and on weekends...to the mall." In addition, the "school runs programs to see Broadway shows for free." Even without the school's help, however, New York is at students' fingertips; almost everything the city has to offer "is just a subway ride away." "Clubs, sports events, parties, restaurants"—you name it, NYC's got it, and St. John's students sample it. The faithful will be happy to know that "St. John's makes it easy to incorporate a spiritual life with an academic one." For the altruistic, there are "community-service initiatives galore."

Student Body

Because it is "located in Queens, the most diverse place on Earth," it's no surprise that St. John's itself is "very, very diverse." Though "everyone gets along exceptionally well," getting along well doesn't equal total integration. Each "ethnic group tends [to] hang around with itself. Yet students' external differences belie less visible similarities. Many are may be the first in their family to attend college, so a strong work ethic is pervasive. Everyone "wants to achieve something greater than their parents." The second major similarity stems from the first: "students here generally have many responsibilities outside of their schoolwork."

THE PRINCETON REVIEW SAYS

Admissions

Very important factors considered include: Academic GPA, standardized test scores. *Important factors considered include:* Rigor of secondary school record. *Other factors considered include:* Class rank, application essay, recommendation(s), alumni/ae relation, character/personal qualities, extracurricular activities, geographical residence, interview, level of applicant's interest, volunteer work, work experience. SAT or ACT required; TOEFL or IELTS required of international applicants from non-English speaking countries. High school diploma is required, and GED is accepted. *Academic units required:* 4 English. *Academic units recommended:* 3 mathematics, 2 science, (2 science labs), 2 foreign language, 2 history, 1 social studies/history units vary.

Financial Aid

Students should submit: FAFSA. The Princeton Review suggests that all financial aid forms be submitted as soon as possible after January 1. *Need-based scholarships/grants offered:* Federal Pell, SEOG, state scholarships/grants, private scholarships, the school's own gift aid. *Loan aid offered:* Direct Subsidized Stafford, Direct Unsubsidized Stafford, Direct PLUS, Federal Perkins. Applicants will be notified of awards on a rolling basis beginning 3/15. Federal Work-Study Program available. Institutional employment available. Off-campus job opportunities are good.

The Inside Word

The admissions process at St. John's doesn't include many surprises. High school grades and standardized test scores are undoubtedly the most important factors though volunteer work and extracurricular activities are also highly regarded. What is surprising is that this Catholic university doesn't consider religious affiliation at all when making admissions decisions; there are students of every religious stripe here (see the "Student Body" section).

THE SCHOOL SAYS "..."

From The Admissions Office

"Founded by the Vincentian Fathers in 1870, St. John's is a major Catholic university that prepares students for ethical leadership in today's global society. St. John's offers quality academics, high-tech resources and confidence-building service activities enlivened by the vast opportunities available only in exciting New York City. Representing 46 states and 111 foreign countries, students pursue more than 100 programs in the arts, sciences, business, education, pharmacy, and allied health. Professors are internationally respected scholars, 87% holding a Ph.D. or comparable degree. The 19:1 student-faculty ratio ensures personal attention in class.

"St. John's also offers these advantages:

- The new freshman Passport Program lets students study abroad in their very first year at St. John's, with two weeks at our Rome campus.
- Unique core courses like Discover New York use the city as a "living classroom."
- All entering students receive wireless laptop computers with access to our award-winning network.
- Reflecting our Vincentian heritage, course-related service activities provide real-world experience while serving those in need.
- Global studies programs like Discover the World allow students to earn 15 credits while studying in three foreign cities in a single semester.

"St. John's has three residential New York City campuses—our flagship campus in Queens; the wooded Staten Island campus; and a "vertical" campus in lower Manhattan. St. John's also has a campus in Oakdale, NY; a campus in Paris, France; and a campus in Rome, Italy."

For even more information on this school, turn to page 530 of the "Stats" section.

ST. LAWRENCE UNIVERSITY

PAYSON HALL, CANTON, NY 13617 • ADMISSIONS: 315-229-5261 • FAX: 315-229-5818
FINANCIAL AID: 315-229-5265 • E-MAIL: ADMISSIONS@STLAW.EDU • WEBSITE: WWW.STLAWU.EDU

RATINGS
Quality of Life: 83   Academic: 89   Admissions: 93   Financial Aid: 85

STUDENTS SAY "..."

Academics

Students at St. Lawrence love their professors. "All of my professors have been extremely accessible and willing to help out if I've ever had questions. The quality of the professors is very high;" "The professors for the most part are very receptive to feedback and love teaching their students," and "if you're showing effort, they will do everything they can to help you." "Showing effort" might be the operative phrase; "one could coast through…by choosing easy classes. However, there are plenty of opportunities to really challenge yourself and succeed with the support of grants, professors, and advisors." Students rave about the small class sizes, "even lectures, and not only does this contribute to a more comfortable, discussion-based learning experience, it ensures that every professor is available and interested, at almost any time." A few students admit that "as a first-year student it can be frustrating trying to get the classes of your choice," but others say, "if you talk to the teachers beforehand, you can usually get the classes you want if they are offered that semester." Regarding the administration, some students claim it "leaves a bit to be desired" and "is not always on the same page as the students." Most are very happy with the administration, though. "If you reach out to them, they will give you as much information as they can," and they "care a lot about our safety and make sure that all of our needs are well-met." "Some deans also teach classes—I had my first-year seminar with an academic dean, and it was great. They seem like they're always available if a student has an issue."

Life

Because Canton is small and the winter is long, "all of the fun and events happen on the campus [because] there is not much to do in town." "The student center is always full of people, and it's hard to not to stay there all day." "Theme houses," in which small groups of students focused on particular issues or activities live, receive high marks both from their residents and the students who come to the dorms for events. "The Java Barn is a small music venue located on campus that is completely run by 11 students that live together in a theme house on campus" and features popular live music events almost every weekend. Hockey games are huge, as are outdoor activities. "At St. Lawrence the natural world is our playground," "and there are lots of people and groups who carpool up to Whiteface in Lake Placid and go downhill skiing. During the warm months there is always something going on on the quad, and many people go on trips to the near by Adirondack Mountains for hiking and other outdoor activities." The rope swing on the Grasse River is also a popular destination, as are Ottawa and Montreal for day trips. If it's too cold to venture outside, students hit the gym: "Our athletic facilities are amazing with an indoor track, squash courts, gym, and climbing wall." As is typical for small schools in similar locales, drinking is popular on weekends. "There are many parties at St. Lawrence, but it is not the only thing to do on campus!" "People go to sporting, singing, and comedy events on campus," and "SLU students are creative with their fun."

Student Body

"A lot of students at St. Lawrence University are athletic and from the East Coast." "There are a lot of the classic Abercrombie & Fitch types…until you take a better look around." Though "preppy" seems to describe many students at St. Lawrence, "There are multitudes of clubs that provide a social scene for all students no matter their interests." "Everyone seems happy and has found some group [to] fit in with." "Most students join an extracurricular activity like art, music, sports, community service, etc." "A typical St. Lawrence student is easy-going, approachable, and likes to have a good time." "There are always a few atypical types, but they make the school more interesting. There's a place here for everyone."

Admissions

Very important factors considered include: Application essay, academic GPA, recommendation(s), character/personal qualities. *Important factors considered include:* Class rank, rigor of secondary school record, extracurricular activities, interview, racial/ethnic status. *Other factors considered include:* Standardized test scores, alumni/ae relation, first generation, geographical residence, level of applicant's interest, talent/ability, volunteer work, work experience. TOEFL required of all international applicants. High school diploma is required, and GED is accepted. *Academic units recommended:* 4 English, 4 mathematics, 4 science, (0 science labs), 4 foreign language, 2 social studies, 2 history.

Financial Aid

Students should submit: FAFSA, noncustodial PROFILE, business/farm supplement. Institution's own financial aid form OR CSS/Financial Aid PROFILE. Regular filing deadline is 2/1. The Princeton Review suggests that all financial aid forms be submitted as soon as possible after January 1. *Need-based scholarships/grants offered:* Federal Pell, SEOG, state scholarships/grants, private scholarships, the school's own gift aid. *Loan aid offered:* Direct Subsidized Stafford, Direct Unsubsidized Stafford, Direct PLUS, Federal Perkins, college/university loans from institutional funds. Applicants will be notified of awards on or about 3/30. Federal Work-Study Program available. Institutional employment available. Off-campus job opportunities are poor.

The Inside Word

St. Lawrence is "test-optional," which means you're not required to submit scores from the SAT or the ACT, but that means your high school transcript and teacher recommendations better be stellar. If you're an international student seeking financial aid, or a home-schooled student, it's probably a good idea to submit some standardized test scores. Scholarship selection is based on overall academic profile, so good scores can help.

THE SCHOOL SAYS "..."

From The Admissions Office

"In an ideal location, St. Lawrence is a diverse liberal arts learning community of inspiring faculty and talented students guided by tradition and focused on the future. The students who live and learn at St. Lawrence are interesting and interested; they enroll with myriad accomplishments and talents, as well as desire to explore new challenges. Our faculty has chosen St. Lawrence intentionally because they know that there is institutional commitment to support great teaching. They are dedicated to making each student's experience challenging and rewarding. Our graduates make up one of the strongest networks of support among any alumni body and are ready, willing, and able to connect with students and help them succeed.

"Which students are happiest at St. Lawrence? Students who like to be actively involved. Students who are open-minded and interested in meeting people with backgrounds different from their own. Students who value having a voice in decisions that affect them. Students who appreciate all that is available to them and cannot wait to take advantage of both the curriculum and the co-curricular options. Students who want to enjoy their college experience and are able to find joy in working hard.

"You can learn the facts about us from this guidebook: We have about 2,200 students; we offer more than 30 majors; the average class size is 16 students; a great new science center; close to 50 percent of our students study abroad; and we have an environmental consciousness that fits our natural setting between the Adirondack Mountains and St. Lawrence River. You must visit, meet students and faculty, and sense the energy on campus to begin to understand just how special St. Lawrence University is.

"The submission of standardized test scores (SAT or ACT) is optional. Students must indicate on the St. Lawrence Common Application supplement which scores, if any, they wish to have considered in the application process."

For even more information on this school, turn to page 530 of the "Stats" section.

STATE UNIVERSITY OF NEW YORK AT BINGHAMTON

PO Box 6000, Binghamton, NY 13902-6001 • Admissions: 607-777-2171 • Fax: 607-777-4445
Financial Aid: 607-777-2428 • E-mail: admit@binghamton.edu • Website: www.binghamton.edu

RATINGS
Quality of Life: 72   Academic: 74   Admissions: 94   Financial Aid: 81

STUDENTS SAY "..."

Academics

With fewer than 12,000 undergraduates, Binghamton University is "a decent sized school that doesn't feel that big." It's thanks to this that "you get to know people easily" here. Yet the school is also large enough to accommodate "a great education in a variety of fields, ranging from the liberal arts to engineering to business to education to nursing." Students report that "the school does the best it can to prepare its students at an Ivy level. It knows that it does not have the name recognition of others but teaches its students the values of hard work so that they can compete with Ivy students for jobs. Students aim for these jobs and are often successful getting them." Professional programs, which are among the most popular here, are "amazing" and "the connection with alumni is great," not to mention "the career development center is awesome," all huge pluses when it comes time for the job search. And the school accomplishes all this at a very reasonable cost. "Everyone here says value is a huge strength for this school," one student explains. In the past Binghamton students have complained that administrators "can sometimes be frustrating to deal with." Fortunately, Binghamton has addressed these issues by implementing an integrated student service system and creating a joint service area for registration, records, and financial aid.

> **SURVEY SAYS . . .**
> *Diverse student types on campus*
> *Campus feels safe*
> *Student publications are popular*

Life

Students tell us that "campus life is really great" at Binghamton, offering "tons of activities to participate in, including club or intramural sports, student government, fraternities/sororities (both social and professional), student groups, and more." Dorms are "convenient" and "clean" (although "living off-campus is less expensive"), and undergrads are kept busy "trying to balance classes, school work, jobs, volunteer work, and sports.... There's never enough time for everything you want to do." Some complain that "the weekends can get pretty dull on campus," which is why they opt for beer-soaked fraternity parties or "the bars downtown." According to the drinking crowd, "The weeks can be stressful with a lot of classes, papers and tests, so students tend to unwind on the weekends. Once the frats run out of alcohol, people generally walk about 10 minutes to the bars." However, the drinking scene is by no means the only weekend alternative. As one student explains, "For people not interested in that, there is Late Night Binghamton," which "shows movies; has hypnotists, magicians, or comedians come; [and] has crafts to do, and it's all free." Binghamton is also experiencing a resurgence, and students frequently patronize many of the cafes, restaurants, and galleries found downtown.

Student Body

The typical BU undergrad "is someone who was smart in high school"—they had to be to get in here—but was "well-rounded enough so as to not be only invested in academics. In general, although people are relatively smart, they have other things on their mind than pure academics." The campus is "very ethnically diverse," with "a lot of Jewish students and a lot of Asians" factoring into the mix. Geographically, Long Island and New York City are extremely well represented, "but there are many others from around the country and the world." Class background and local weather conspire to make "The North Face" a conspicuous brand on campus.

Admissions

Very important factors considered include: Academic GPA, rigor of secondary school record, standardized test scores. *Important factors considered include:* Class rank, application essay, recommendation(s), extracurricular activities. *Other factors considered include:* Alumni/ae relation, character/personal qualities, geographical residence, level of applicant's interest, racial/ethnic status, state residency, talent/ability, volunteer work, work experience, first generation. SAT or ACT required; ACT with Writing component required. TOEFL required of all international applicants. High school diploma is required, and GED is accepted. *Academic units required:* 4 English, 3 mathematics, 2 science, 3 foreign language, 2 social studies. *Academic units recommended:* 4 mathematics, 4 science, 3 foreign language, 4 social studies, 4 history.

Financial Aid

Students should submit: FAFSA. The Princeton Review suggests that all financial aid forms be submitted as soon as possible after January 1. *Need-based scholarships/grants offered:* Federal Pell, SEOG, state scholarships/grants, private scholarships, the school's own gift aid. *Loan aid offered:* Direct Subsidized Stafford, Direct Unsubsidized Stafford, Direct PLUS, Federal Perkins, Federal Nursing, college/university loans from institutional funds. Applicants will be notified of awards on a rolling basis beginning 4/1. Federal Work-Study Program available. Institutional employment available. Off-campus job opportunities are excellent.

The Inside Word

Binghamton receives nearly 11 applications for every slot in its freshman class. That's bad news for marginal candidates, who should probably start looking elsewhere in the SUNY system if they have their hearts set on attending one. With competition this stiff, you'll need solid test scores and high school grades just to get past the first winnowing stage.

THE SCHOOL SAYS "..."

From The Admissions Office

"Binghamton has established itself as the premier public university in the Northeast, because of our outstanding undergraduate programs, vibrant campus culture, and committed faculty. Students are academically motivated, but there is a great deal of mutual help as they compete against the standard of a class rather than each other. Faculty and students work side by side in research labs or on artistic pursuits. Achievement, exploration, and leadership are hallmarks of a Binghamton education. Add to that a campus wide commitment to internationalization that includes a robust study abroad program, cultural offerings, languages and international studies, and you have a place where graduates leave prepared for success. Binghamton University graduates lead the nation in top starting salaries among public universities, demonstrating that our students are recognized by employers and recruiters for having strong abilities to be leaders, critical thinkers, decision-makers, analysts and researchers in many fields and industries."

For even more information on this school, turn to page 531 of the "Stats" section.

State University of New York—The College at Brockport

350 New Campus Drive, Brockport, NY 14420 • Admissions: 585-395-2751 • Fax: 585-395-5452
E-mail: admit@brockport.edu • Website: www.brockport.edu

RATINGS

Quality of Life: 78   **Academic:** 70   **Admissions:** 83   **Financial Aid:** 73

STUDENTS SAY "..."

Academics

The College at Brockport is a selective, comprehensive liberal arts college which "specializes in producing nurses, PE teachers, and other teachers," but is still able to "accommodate students with a wide variety of interests." The school "has a unique atmosphere (especially in the Delta College Program [an interdisciplinary learning community]) in which students are able to come out of their comfort zone and blend with new people." "The professors are diverse," says one student. "Some are excellent teachers, others are simply extremely intelligent individuals. Most or all of them seem concerned students take something valuable away from their classes." Still, "everyone has the occasional bad professor." Students like that "class sizes are small for the most part" and the school offers "a great study-abroad program." "The administration that has recently come into place at Brockport is clearly trying to change the school for the better," notes one student. "It has put academics first and has aggressively lobbied for, and raised, money to expand programs and encourage positive intellectual growth within the college." Students also appreciate that the president is so visible and involved with the student body. "You will see him around campus a lot, at basketball and football games, and basically anywhere." All in all, Brockport seems a "good education for a good price!"

Life

Hometown Brockport, N.Y., is "a relatively small town" with an "inviting" community. "For entertainment students hang out in the dorms like other colleges, but also peruse the shops, restaurants, and bars of Brockport's quaint and thriving downtown. There is a regular bus schedule that makes rounds to the many malls, museums, cultural events, and landmarks of the Rochester, N.Y. area." "In the village there is a movie theater" that offers "$1 current midnight movies on Fridays," and also a bowling alley, where students enjoy "$1 bowling on Tuesdays and Thursdays." "Sports and fitness are very important here," and students are keen to both support and participate in them. "For the weekends drinking is pretty popular here," says one student. As "the school has become more academically focused during the last decade," "internships, studying abroad, and other academic experiences are becoming more popular." One on-campus perk several students cite is "the food is rated number one in all of SUNY schools for the past few years."

Students

While some think "the typical student here is your white, upstate, and western New York jock," others see a bit more diversity. "The student body varies from super athletic to super academic," notes one student. Still, most agree that the typical student here is "middle-class," "Christian," "and pretty moderate politically." And there is no question there are "a lot of physical education majors as well as nursing majors." One tool for categorizing these students might be the city/suburbs/rural divide. For example, "some people come from small towns and have that small-town something about them. Others come from Long Island, so they are opposite." While there are few atypical students, those who are "can fit in with other people with whom they identify." A student explains, "It can be difficult to find the right crowd for you at first, especially at a smaller school like Brockport, but once you find it, you're golden."

THE PRINCETON REVIEW SAYS

Admissions

Very important factors considered include: Academic GPA, rigor of secondary school record. *Important factors considered include:* Class rank, application essay, recommendation(s), standardized test scores, character/personal qualities, extracurricular activities, talent/ability, volunteer work, work experience. *Other factors considered include:* Interview, level of applicant's interest, racial/ethnic status. SAT or ACT required; ACT with Writing component recommended. TOEFL required of all international applicants. High school diploma is required and GED is accepted. *Academic units required:* 4 English, 3 mathematics, 3 science, (1 science labs), 4 social studies, 3 academic electives. *Academic units recommended:* 3 foreign language.

Financial Aid

Students should submit: FAFSA, state aid form. The Princeton Review suggests that all financial aid forms be submitted as soon as possible after January 1. *Need-based scholarships/grants offered:* Federal Pell, SEOG, state scholarships/grants, private scholarships, the school's own gift aid. *Loan aid offered:* Direct Subsidized Stafford, Direct Unsubsidized Stafford, Direct PLUS, Federal Perkins, Federal Nursing, other, private alternative loans. Applicants will be notified of awards on a rolling basis beginning 3/15. Federal Work-Study Program available. Institutional employment available. Off-campus job opportunities are good.

The Inside Word

Admission to Brockport is competitive, with less than half of all applicants gaining acceptance. Not surprisingly, it bases admissions decisions largely on the applicant's high school academic profile and standardized test results, along with some consideration of leadership, community service, and the like. The school uses the SUNY application, a standardized online application used by 50 of the 64 SUNY campuses. Admissions at Brockport are rolling, so as a general rule, the earlier you apply, the more likely a space in the freshman class will be available for you.

THE SCHOOL SAYS "..."

From The Admissions Office

"The College at Brockport "has the success of its students as its highest priority," asserts the college's mission statement.

"A selective comprehensive liberal arts college that can trace its roots back nearly 175 years to the opening of the Erie Canal, The College at Brockport, State University of New York, offers a multi-dimensional education that prepares students for success—personally and professionally.

"With a wealth of academic programs and co-curricular activities, our students explore their intellectual, creative and athletic potential, and pursue their talents. There are 49 undergraduate majors, 41 graduate programs and 23 areas of teacher certification. The College holds program accreditation in 12 areas. Each student at Brockport receives individual attention from our faculty—leading scholars in their own right—who also are dedicated advisors and mentors. Our students have access to one of the largest Study Abroad programs in the nation, a variety of internships with major corporations, 23 NCAA intercollegiate athletic teams, arts and cultural events and performance, and more than 70 clubs and organizations.

"Nearly 30 percent of undergraduates go on to graduate school, and 91 percent find jobs or are in graduate school within six months of graduation.

"Substantial investments on the 464-acre campus in recent years include renovation of Smith-Lennon Science Center, Hartwell Hall and Seymour College Union. New projects include the 208-bed townhome facility, renovation of Harrison Dining Hall, and plans for a $44-million Special Events Recreation Center.

"The College is located in the historic Village of Brockport, 16 miles west of Rochester with easy access to Buffalo and Lake Ontario. Students enjoy a small college-town atmosphere as well as easy access to Rochester's culture, shopping, professional sports and parks.

"To fully appreciate our outstanding academic programs, our beautiful campus, and our energetic student body, nothing compares to a personal visit. Schedule your visit online."

For even more information on this school, turn to page 535 of the "Stats" section.

STATE UNIVERSITY OF NEW YORK—COLLEGE OF ENVIRONMENTAL SCIENCE AND FORESTRY

OFFICE OF UNDERGRADUATE ADMISSIONS, SUNY-ESF, SYRACUSE, NY 13210 • ADMISSIONS: 315-470-6600 • FAX: 315-470-6933
E-MAIL: ESFINFO@ESF.EDU • WEBSITE: WWW.ESF.EDU

RATINGS
Quality of Life: 85   **Academic:** 75   **Admissions:** 83   **Financial Aid:** 93

STUDENTS SAY "..."

Academics

The motto is "Improve your world" at SUNY's nationally renowned College of Environmental Science and Forestry in Syracuse. ESF offers 22 various programs including environmental science and a bunch of different specialties in forestry, as well as fisheries science, landscape architecture, construction management, paper engineering, and wildlife science to name a few. It's "a small, personal school" (once you get past the often surprisingly large intro courses) with "tough" classes. "The courses here are very challenging but also very interesting and real," says a wildlife science major. "They connect real-life problems to all the course work." "Science is really strong." "Students are often very involved in research." "Field trips are prominent in most classes. There's always the opportunity to be outside." Faculty members are "not always great teachers," but they "can back up their teaching with real experiences" and "professors and students have a good relationship." "Registration is a mess" and there's some useless bureaucracy (this is a SUNY school, after all). Administrators are generally "flexible in their approach," and the "awesome" top brass is "very organized and on top of problems."

> **SURVEY SAYS . . .**
> *Great computer facilities*
> *School is well run*
> *Students are friendly*
> *Different types of students interact*
> *Great off-campus food*

Life

"Most activity focuses around the main quad" at ESF. "People are very involved in wildlife organizations and doing community service." "There are a lot of protests." "Winter is brutal because our campus is on a huge hill," notes a senior. Weather permitting, ultimate Frisbee is popular. The woodsmen's team competes in contests using old-fashioned lumberjack techniques with other schools in the Northeast and Canada. "ESF has one of the strictest drug and alcohol policies in the state" but drinking is nevertheless a pastime. Off campus, "downtown offers lots of culture and a lot of students spend weekends hiking (especially in the Adirondacks)." "No one here ever says no to going out for a hike." Syracuse University is "right next to the ESF campus," and "it easy to get involved there." "You can take their classes, use their facilities, and play their club sports and intramurals."

Student Body

Ethnic diversity at ESF is seriously lacking. It's an overwhelming white group of people from the state of New York. "Students generally don't put a lot of time into dressing for school and are generally very laidback" here. People universally "love the outdoors." To grossly generalize, "there are two loose groups at ESF." The "more populous" group is the "vegan, save-the-world" "tree huggers." For them, "tie-dye and green are the preferred colors to wear." "We're always taking the stairs instead of the elevators (even up to the eighth floor), using Tupperware instead of Styrofoam or plastic, and we love plants," explains a first-year hippie. Not surprisingly, these students "lean more toward the left." The other, smaller group is "fairly conservative" "hunters" and "rednecks" who have "a management view of the environment." They "often major in forestry resources management, construction management, paper science engineering, or some such thing." "Somehow," members of both groups manage to get along pretty well.

THE PRINCETON REVIEW SAYS

Admissions

Very important factors considered include: Application essay, academic GPA, rigor of secondary school record, standardized test scores, level of applicant's interest. *Important factors considered include:* Class rank, recommendation(s), character/personal qualities, extracurricular activities, talent/ability, volunteer work, work experience. *Other factors considered include:* Alumni/ae relation, first generation, geographical residence, interview, racial/ethnic status, state residency, SAT or ACT required; TOEFL required of all international applicants. High school diploma is required and GED is accepted. *Academic units required:* 4 English, 3 mathematics, 3 science, (3 science labs), 3 social studies. *Academic units recommended:* 4 mathematics, 4 science, (4 science labs), 3 social studies, 1 history.

Financial Aid

Students should submit: FAFSA, state aid form. The Princeton Review suggests that all financial aid forms be submitted as soon as possible after January 1. *Need-based scholarships/grants offered:* Federal Pell, SEOG, state scholarships/grants, private scholarships, the school's own gift aid Federal SMART Grants, Federal ACG Grants. *Loan aid offered:* Federal Perkins Applicants will be notified of awards on a rolling basis beginning 3/15. Federal Work-Study Program available. Institutional employment available. Off-campus job opportunities are excellent.

The Inside Word

Due to the highly specialized nature of the programs here, applicants to ESF are a highly self-selected group. Many high school students want to dedicate themselves to natural resources and the environment, so the admission is competitive. Serious candidates will devote thoughtful attention to the required essay.

THE SCHOOL SAYS "..."

From The Admissions Office

"The State University of New York College of Environmental Science and Forestry (SUNY—ESF) is the oldest and largest college in the nation focused on the science, design, engineering, and management of natural resources and the environment. ESF offers students 22 undergraduate and 30 graduate degree programs to choose from, and is consistently ranked among the nation's top universities based on value, class size, and student engagement in learning.

"Faculty members at ESF come from impressive backgrounds and are working on research that's at the forefront of solving many of the world's environmental problems. Students work side-by-side with faculty on research projects ranging from restoring polluted lakes to developing new sources of biofuels. ESF has more faculty and students engaged in academic programs focused on the environment than any other college in the United States, but our small-college atmosphere guarantees that faculty get to know students on a first-name basis. Outstanding teaching is the top priority for our faculty.

"ESF's special relationship with neighboring Syracuse University provides some truly unique advantages. Students at ESF can take classes at SU while paying SUNY tuition, use library and computing facilities, join more than 300 student organizations, and cheer on the Syracuse Orange sports teams. ESF students live in residence halls and apartments located on the Syracuse University campus, which is directly adjacent to ESF."

For even more information on this school, turn to page 532 of the "Stats" section.

STATE UNIVERSITY OF NEW YORK—FREDONIA

178 CENTRAL AVENUE, FREDONIA, NY 14063 • ADMISSIONS: 716-673-3251 • FAX: 716-673-3249
E-MAIL: ADMISSIONS.OFFICE@FREDONIA.EDU • WEBSITE: WWW.FREDONIA.EDU

RATINGS
Quality of Life: 76   **Academic:** 73   **Admissions:** 81   **Financial Aid:** 74

STUDENTS SAY "..."

Academics

> SURVEY SAYS . . .
> *Campus feels safe*
> *Theater is popular*
> *Lots of beer drinking*
> *Hard liquor is popular*

"Music and art are paramount" at this "beautiful, friendly, welcoming, and accepting," "small, liberal public arts school" in upstate New York. In addition to music and art, SUNY—Fredonia also offers "great degree programs" in "education, theatre, and communications." "Most if not all professors are masters of their craft" and "are welcoming and have open-door policies." "A lot of the professors could realistically be teaching at better schools, but they choose to be at Fredonia because the area is wonderful," says one student. Of course, "like anywhere else, there are always a few professors nobody can stand, but there is usually enough flexibility so you can avoid them when registering for classes if you put the effort into it." "The school's administration is great," agree students. "It really means something when you see President Hefner and other campus administrators walking around campus, eating in our dining halls, and attending nearly every campus event showing support." If there is any complaint about the administration, it's that it has a tendency to play favorites. "The administration focuses mainly on education, acting, and music majors." Still, such favoritism must go only so far, as "a new science building is being built" at this decidedly artsy school.

Life

"Besides attending classes and studying outside of class, life consists of attending various intercollegiate sports events including hockey and soccer," says one undergrad. Well, not entirely. In addition, there are "millions of clubs and organizations, a lot of which do community service," and also many "campus jobs that are not work study, so are open to everyone." As its academic reputation suggests, students also have numerous opportunities to take in "shows put on by the music and theater departments." Those seeking them will find "plenty of frat parties, if that's your idea of fun." Off-campus, "While the town of Fredonia is small and consists of mainly an older population, there is always something to do." For example, there are also "numerous bars in town that admit 18 and older to dance." Outdoorsy types appreciate that "there are beautiful parks to go walking around, including the New York State Lake Erie Park." Some "go fishing and take walks along the creek that runs through town." If you seek big-city excitement "you can easily drive to Erie, PA or to Buffalo." "Politics and diversity are strong topics for students at Fredonia."

Student Body

"The typical Fredonia student likes art and indie music and cares about environmental issues," however, there are also "a lot of the typical 'jock' and 'prep' type students." "Everyone at Fredonia parties a lot," says one student, "that includes drinking and drugs." "The average student is white, middle-class, and from upstate New York suburbia" and "is very friendly, outgoing, and has a smile on his or her face." In addition, he or she is "very open-minded." No surprise, then, that "there is a large LGBT population on our campus and they are treated without prejudice." Students are "often spiritual as opposed to religious and most show an appreciation for the arts." Politically, students are "typically left-wing liberal Democrats." As far as fashion goes, "Everyone is exactly the same in the way they try to be different: black clothes, weird hairdos, chains and pajama pants," or some combination thereof.

THE PRINCETON REVIEW SAYS

Admissions

Very important factors considered include: academic GPA, rigor of secondary school record. *Important factors considered include:* Class rank, recommendation(s), standardized test scores, extracurricular activities. *Other factors considered include:* Application essay, alumni/ae relation, character/personal qualities, first generation, level of applicant's interest, racial/ethnic status, talent/ability, volunteer work, work experience. SAT or ACT required; TOEFL required of all international applicants. High school diploma is required and GED is accepted. *Academic units required:* 4 English, 3 mathematics, 3 science, 3 foreign language, 4 social studies. *Academic units recommended:* 4 English, 4 mathematics, 4 science, 3 foreign language, 4 social studies.

Financial Aid

Students should submit: FAFSA, state aid form. The Princeton Review suggests that all financial aid forms be submitted as soon as possible after January 1. *Need-based scholarships/grants offered:* Federal Pell, SEOG, state scholarships/grants, private scholarships, the school's own gift aid. *Loan aid offered:* Federal Perkins. Applicants will be notified of awards on a rolling basis beginning 3/10. Federal Work-Study Program available. Off-campus job opportunities are good.

The Inside Word

Fredonia accepts about half of all applicants, making admission to the school competitive. The average freshman had a high B-plus average in high school, an SAT score over 1100, and an ACT score over 24. The school uses the SUNY application, a standardized online application used by 50 of the 64 SUNY campuses. To be considered for scholarships, applicants must complete a supplemental application after submitting the application for admission. Admissions at Fredonia are rolling, so as a general rule, the earlier you apply, the more likely you'll find a spot in the freshman class.

For even more information on this school, turn to page 532 of the "Stats" section.

STATE UNIVERSITY OF NEW YORK AT GENESEO

ONE COLLEGE CIRCLE, GENESEO, NY 14454-1401 • ADMISSIONS: 716-245-5571 • FAX: 716-245-5550
FINANCIAL AID: 716-245-5731 • E-MAIL: ADMISSIONS@GENESEO.EDU • WEBSITE: WWW.GENESEO.EDU

RATINGS

Quality of Life: 82   Academic: 79   Admissions: 94   Financial Aid: 85

STUDENTS SAY ". . ."

Academics

State University of New York—Geneseo, the school that considers itself the Honors College of the SUNY system, offers "challenging academics in a very home-like atmosphere" where "you don't get lost in the crowd like bigger schools." As one student puts it, "Geneseo is all about the classic college experience: a small town, rigorous academics, and having fun at the same time." One in five students pursues a teaching degree here, leading some to conclude that "Geneseo focuses mainly on training future teachers, but for the rest of us, they are preparing us for our next step into employment or further education." Nearly as many study business and marketing; the "best academic departments are by far the natural sciences," however, where "the students are the brightest, the courses are the toughest, and the professors really know their stuff." Geneseo also provides "great pre-professional (medical, dental, pharmacological) preparation in sciences." Students here enjoy a small-school experience that includes "superior academics, small, intimate classes, and professors who truly care about students and will offer them every opportunity to succeed" as well as "many study- abroad options (students are encouraged to explore the world)." They also point out that "leadership and research are also a great focus at SUNY Geneseo. If a student wants to do individual research, professors are more than willing to help students organize projects and carry them out." For these and other reasons, students describe Geneseo as a school "for the academically inclined non-rich citizen. It's the Harvard of the SUNY system."

Life

"The great thing about Geneseo is that there's always a party to go to if you want, but there's no pressure to go," and "it's perfectly acceptable to stay home and watch movies with friends on the weekends or even study on Saturday nights." Indeed, students tell us that "there is so much more to do than just party. The college always has amazing activities going on in the union. Every weekend there are crafts and games, and sometimes they bring in comedians or performers.... At the Halloween Monster Mash Bash, there is a costume ball and activities as well as a raffle for really great prizes. There are far too many activities to list here!" Intercollegiate hockey games "are a big hit, and lots of students go to them on weekends." There are "also many different organizations you can get involved in, including several volunteer organizations, intramural sports, and different hobbies." On the weekends, students "know how to party." The town of Geneseo provides little distraction; "There is nothing to do in town, and the closest city is a 45-minute drive away (Rochester, New York)."

Student Body

"The typical student here at SUNY Geneseo is much like that of the ordinary New York State public high school," except that "Most of the school is white (the college is making efforts to diversify). Despite the majority being white, there is still a wide diversity of student types, be it that they are from different backgrounds, economic classes, or simply around the nation." Undergrads "spend most of their time studying in Milne Library, and those who choose not to study usually don't make it to graduation." There are "a few minority and gay/lesbian/bisexual students" here, "but they really are the minority and often have difficulty adjusting. Many of these students feel like outsiders and transfer before graduating." Students tell us that "the two largest minorities are Asian and African American...the different ethnic groups tend to clump together."

THE PRINCETON REVIEW SAYS

Admissions

Very important factors considered include: Rigor of secondary school record, standardized test scores. *Important factors considered include:* Class rank, application essay, academic GPA, recommendation(s), extracurricular activities, racial/ethnic status, talent/ability. *Other factors considered include:* alumni/ae relation, character/personal qualities, first generation, level of applicant's interest, volunteer work, work experience. SAT or ACT required; TOEFL required of all international applicants. High school diploma is required, and GED is accepted. *Academic units recommended:* 4 English, 4 mathematics, 4 science, 4 foreign language, 4 social studies.

Financial Aid

Students should submit: FAFSA, state aid form. Regular filing deadline is 2/15. The Princeton Review suggests that all financial aid forms be submitted as soon as possible after January 1. *Need-based scholarships/grants offered:* Federal Pell, SEOG, state scholarships/grants. *Loan aid offered:* Federal Perkins. Applicants will be notified of awards on a rolling basis beginning 3/15. Federal Work-Study Program available. Institutional employment available. Off-campus job opportunities are poor.

The Inside Word

Geneseo is the most selective school in the SUNY system. No formulaic approach is used here. Expect a thorough review of your academic accomplishments (over half the student body graduated in the top 10 percent of their class) and your extracurricular/personal side. Admissions standards are tempered only by a somewhat low yield of admits who enroll. The school competes for students with some big-time schools, meaning it must admit many more students than it expects will attend.

THE SCHOOL SAYS "..."

From The Admissions Office

"Geneseo has carved a distinctive niche among the nation's premier public liberal arts colleges. Geneseo is the only undergraduate college in the state of New York system to be granted a chapter of Phi Beta Kappa. The college now competes for students with some of the nation's most selective private colleges, including Colgate, Vassar, Hamilton, and Boston College. Founded in 1871, the college occupies a 220-acre hillside campus in the historic Village of Geneseo, overlooking the scenic Genesee Valley. As a residential campus—with nearly two-thirds of the students living in college residence halls—it provides a rich and varied program of social, cultural, recreational, and scholarly activities. Geneseo is noted for its distinctive core curriculum and the extraordinary opportunities it offers undergraduates to pursue independent study and research with faculty who value close working relationships with talented students. Equally impressive is the remarkable success of its graduates, 41% of whom study at leading graduate and professional schools immediately following graduation.

"SUNY Geneseo will use either SAT or ACT test results in the admission selection process. The SAT Writing test result will not be used. SAT Subject Test results are not required but will be considered if the applicant submits the test results."

For even more information on this school, turn to page 533 of the "Stats" section.

STATE UNIVERSITY OF NEW YORK—MARITIME COLLEGE

ADMISSIONS OFFICE, SIX PENNYFIELD AVENUE, THROGGS NECK, NY 10465 • ADMISSIONS: 718-409-7200
FAX: 718-409-7465 • E-MAIL: ADMISSIONS@SUNYMARITIME.EDU • WEBSITE: WWW.SUNYMARITIME.EDU

RATINGS
Quality of Life: 74   Academic: 70   Admissions: 78   Financial Aid: 70

STUDENTS SAY ". . ."

Academics

SUNY Maritime, a college located on the edge of New York City is a "very unique," school that "prepares you to be a professional in the maritime industry," where starting salaries are impressive and—thanks to the school's "strong career placement"—jobs are easy to come by. "SUNY

> **SURVEY SAYS . . .**
> *Low cost of living*
> *Frats and sororities are unpopular or nonexistent*
> *Very little drug use*

Maritime takes regular kids and, at a reasonable price (especially when compared to other colleges), helps them become skilled professionals with knowledge that can take them to great careers with great companies around the world," beams a mechanical engineering major. "If you wish to work on ships or love the sea, this is the place for you." There's a broad core curriculum. Classes are small and the academic workload can "pile on if you're not careful," especially in the "excellent engineering program." The registration process is "terrible" but professors are "always accessible" and "usually fantastic." They frequently "come straight from the industry" and they "teach in-depth." "Hands-on training" is also an essential aspect of the curriculum. "Graduates are extremely prepared for their job and the real world," brags a naval architecture major. Each summer, for example, qualified students "get to tour foreign ports" as they cruise around the globe on Maritime's training vessel. "I have already gotten to see nine different countries," gloats an electrical engineering major.

Life

The civilian program at Maritime offers your basic undergraduate experience. The Regiment of Cadets program, on the other hand, requires you to wear a uniform and live a "quasi-military," "very structured" existence. About 75 percent of the students here choose the regiment. There's no military obligation after you graduate, but it's "four years of hell" just the same. Life is a "daily grind." Cadets "wake up super early" for "formation," for example, and they are subject to room inspections. Schoolwork is difficult and "takes up a lot of free time" for everyone. "During the week, most students do not have much of a personal life," explains a senior. The social scene is a mixed bag. When students are able, they take advantage of "the great city of New York," which is "only 20 minutes away." Sometimes, they "drink like sailors," but only off campus. On campus, most students participate in sports, "either intramural or varsity." Navy and marine ROTC are popular. "We have a gym and there are a bunch of clubs and activities," adds a junior. Life on campus is "pretty boring," though. "There is not much fun to be had," warns a senior. "It's like a *World of Warcraft* convention some days."

Student Body

"There's every different ethnicity and background as well as varied socioeconomic classes represented here." There is also a significant number of foreign students. There aren't very many women, though. The typical student at Maritime is a male "in uniform" with a "shaved head" who is looking for a "career on the water." Students at Maritime come primarily from the East Coast. They are "mostly conservative in their beliefs" and "in some sort of physical shape." They are "proud of the school and take pride in why they are here." Despite, "a shared spirit of apathy and loathing" at times, camaraderie remains high. "The uniform acts as an equalizer and people from various backgrounds and social strata tend to form friendships that might otherwise not have occurred," explains a junior.

Admissions

Very important factors considered include: Academic GPA, rigor of secondary school record, standardized test scores. *Important factors considered include:* Recommendation(s), talent/ability, volunteer work, work experience. *Other factors considered include:* Class rank, application essay, alumni/ae relation, extracurricular activities, first generation, interview, level of applicant's interest. SAT or ACT required; TOEFL required of all international applicants. High school diploma is required and GED is accepted. *Academic units required:* 3 English, 3 mathematics, 3 science, (1 science labs), 1 foreign language, 3 social studies, 3 history. *Academic units recommended:* 4 English, 4 mathematics, 4 science, 3 foreign language.

Financial Aid

Students should submit: FAFSA, institution's own financial aid form. Regular filing deadline is 7/15. The Princeton Review suggests that all financial aid forms be submitted as soon as possible after January 1. *Need-based scholarships/grants offered:* Federal Pell, SEOG, state scholarships/grants, private scholarships, the school's own gift aid. *Loan aid offered:* Federal Perkins, state loans. Applicants will be notified of awards on a rolling basis beginning 3/15. Federal Work-Study Program available. Institutional employment available. Off-campus job opportunities are fair.

The Inside Word

You need to have very exceptional credentials in math and science to get admitted here. Otherwise, though, standards are pretty reasonable. With a B average in a college preparatory curriculum and decent standardized test scores, you should be able to get in the door.

THE SCHOOL SAYS "..."

From The Admissions Office

"The world is open for business! In today's global market, SUNY—Maritime College prepares students for success—in the maritime industry, at sea, in the business world, in government—the choice is yours. SUNY—Maritime College undergraduates enjoy the best value of a public education while consistently earning the top undergraduate average starting salaries in the country. Seventy-nine percent of our student body receives financial aid. The average starting salary of our undergraduate Class of 2009 was $62,659. SUNY—Maritime College is nationally recognized as an Accreditation Board for Engineering and Technology (ABET)–accredited institution and home of the National Institute for Leadership and Ethics. We are one of only six colleges in the United States to offer a Naval Architecture degree. In 2007 SUNY—Maritime College received the Andrew Heiskell Award for Innovation in International Education by the Institute for International Education. Are you ready for an exciting 4 years of learning, discovery, and leadership development? To find out if a SUNY—Maritime College education can launch your life, contact our admissions office at 718-409-7221."

For even more information on this school, turn to page 533 of the "Stats" section.

STATE UNIVERSITY OF NEW YORK—OSWEGO

211 CULKIN HALL, OSWEGO, NY 13126 • ADMISSIONS: 315-312-2250 • FAX: 315-312-3260
E-MAIL: ADMISS@OSWEGO.EDU • WEBSITE: WWW.OSWEGO.EDU

RATINGS
Quality of Life: 77   **Academic:** 72   **Admissions:** 82   **Financial Aid:** 83

STUDENTS SAY "..."

Academics

> **SURVEY SAYS ...**
> *Students are happy*
> *Lots of beer drinking*
> *Hard liquor is popular*

An "excellent business program," a strong education program, a "successful honors program," and "good study-abroad options" highlight the academic offerings of SUNY—Oswego. Professors seem focused on creating a "personal and comfortable learning environment" for undergraduates. Oswego profs are "knowledgeable about their subject and excited to be in Oswego." They seem to "really care about what you do and want to help you in every way to make sure you do well." Students also appreciate that they "have a lot of opportunities to work with professors on research and other projects outside of the classroom to help build real-world experience." That makes sense to many students, as they view an Oswego education mainly as "preparation for the working world." That said, "some of the GE (general education) professors are not so great." But all-in-all, it's the "amazing professors" who make an Oswego bachelor's degree "a great education for the amount of money you pay." The administration gets only fair reviews. While it "has good intentions at heart," it is "pretty disorganized in many ways."

Life

Winter sport enthusiasts be advised, "Oswego offers some awesome winter activities due to the amount of snow we get." These include "one of the best" ice skating rinks, "so ice skating is always a fun activity." In addition, "snowball fights are a must." And of course, "one of everyone's favorite things is going to the home hockey games (we won the national championship in [2007])." "When the weather is nice we have bonfires down by the lake," and "in the summer and spring people will spread out beach towels and get some sun on the lakeside of campus." In addition, "there are also concerts and performers that come throughout the year to the school." "Some students go out on the weekends to parties and bars and others see a movie or go bowling," says one student. Some here think "the city of Oswego has seen better days," finding that because it is "a small city," it lacks the "excitement of big-city life."

Student Body

SUNY—Oswego's student body "consists mostly of middle-class to lower-middle-class students from upstate New York." That said, there are also many "from downstate like NYC and Long Island." How do you tell the difference between upstaters and downstaters? Word on campus is that upstaters aren't afraid to occasionally wear their flip flops outside in the winter, while downstaters keep their Uggs on. In addition to permanent residence somewhere in the Empire State, "the majority of students are white." Temperamentally, "the typical student is usually someone who is studious from Sunday to Wednesday, and parties on weekends. "There are some students who don't go to class, and those who don't party," explains an undergrad. "They are all accepted by the community and will have friends in different social cliques." "They normally fit in by finding a club that they enjoy," agrees another.

Admissions

Very important factors considered include: Academic GPA, rigor of secondary school record. *Important factors considered include:* Class rank, standardized test scores. *Other factors considered include:* Application essay, recommendation(s), character/personal qualities, extracurricular activities, first generation, interview, level of applicant's interest, racial/ethnic status, talent/ability, volunteer work, work experience. SAT or ACT required; TOEFL required of all international applicants. High school diploma is required and GED is accepted. *Academic units required:* 4 English, 3 mathematics, 3 science, (2 science labs), 2 foreign language, 4 social studies. *Academic units recommended:* 4 English, 4 mathematics, 4 science, (3 science labs), 4 foreign language, 4 social studies.

Financial Aid

Students should submit: FAFSA, state aid form. The Princeton Review suggests that all financial aid forms be submitted as soon as possible after January 1. *Need-based scholarships/grants offered:* Federal Pell, SEOG, state scholarships/grants, private scholarships, the school's own gift aid. *Loan aid offered:* Federal Perkins. Applicants will be notified of awards on a rolling basis beginning 3/1. Federal Work-Study Program available. Institutional employment available.

The Inside Word

About half of all applicants are accepted to Oswego, making admission here competitive. The school uses the Common Application and the SUNY application, a standardized online application used by 50 of the 64 SUNY campuses. However, Oswego does use a supplement for each of these applicants to find out more about you as a person, specifically about your extracurricular involvement, including work experience. Basically, the admissions office is interested in more than just numbers, so take this opportunity to shine. Oswego uses early admission, regular decision (Jan 15th) and rolling admissions, so as a general rule, the earlier you apply, the more likely a space in the freshman class will be available for you.

THE SCHOOL SAYS "..."

From The Admissions Office

"Oswego offers a great higher education value on a beautiful 696-acre lakeside campus in upstate New York, 35 miles northwest of Syracuse. Oswego is small enough to provide a friendly, welcoming environment and big enough to provide wide-ranging academic and social opportunities. The diverse selection of degree programs ranges from accounting to zoology and includes interdisciplinary options like cognitive science and international trade. The schools of education and business have each won the stamp of excellence from the premier accrediting organizations in their field. The weather makes the college popular with future meteorologists—one of Oswego's best-known alumni is the Today's Show's Al Roker. Oswego is noted for its honors program, internships, and international study. Ninety percent of students are full-time, one of the highest percentages among public colleges, and all courses are taught by faculty, not graduate assistants. More than $250 million dollars in campus construction has recently been completed and an additional $400 million of projects in construction or design. These projects include a 350 bed student townhouse village slated to open in fall of 2010 and work on a $110 million science complex. Students participate in 150 clubs and organizations and 24 intercollegiate sports. Over half of all students and 93 percent of freshmen live on campus, which has been named one of the safest in the country. More than $2.5 million in academic merit scholarships are awarded to 30 percent of the entering class in renewable awards, ranging from $500 to $4,400 per year. Many out-of-state students are also eligible for additional "residential" scholarships. More than $65 million in need-based financial aid is awarded. The Oswego Guarantee promises both that room and board costs will not increase during a student's four years on campus and that a student can complete a degree in that time."

For even more information on this school, turn to page 534 of the "Stats" section.

STATE UNIVERSITY OF NEW YORK—PURCHASE COLLEGE

ADMISSIONS OFFICE, 735 ANDERSON HILL ROAD, PURCHASE, NY 10577 • ADMISSIONS: 914-251-6300 • FAX: 914-251-6314
FINANCIAL AID: 914-251-6350 • E-MAIL: ADMISSIONS@PURCHASE.EDU • WEBSITE: WWW.PURCHASE.EDU

RATINGS
Quality of Life: 63   **Academic:** 74   **Admissions:** 85   **Financial Aid:** 64

STUDENTS SAY ". . ."

Academics

"Think Wide Open" is the motto at Purchase College, where "an eccentric environment…helps to fuel people's creativity and open-mindedness." "Purchase is about unapologetically being yourself," a place that "teaches real-world lessons with an 'against the grain' sort of approach." This unusual environment is due primarily to a large performing and creative arts program, in which just over one-third of all undergraduates are enrolled. These programs, which include dance, theater, music, film, and creative writing, benefit greatly from the school's proximity to New York City, an international leader in the arts. But while "the conservatories are the best known part of Purchase College," they are hardly the school's only assets. Students tell us "we do in fact have an almost equally strong liberal arts program," with excellent offerings in psychology, media studies, journalism, and premedical sciences, leading undergrads to praise "an artistic atmosphere with loads of academic opportunities." As a smaller school, Purchase can provide "the attention you need from caring professors" and can accommodate more student input; undergraduates tell us that "There is always the possibility of discussion in class, and teachers are tolerant of most thought." Professors "are very engaged, enthusiastic, and simply love learning and teaching."

> **SURVEY SAYS . . .**
> Diverse student types on campus
> Students aren't religious
> Frats and sororities are unpopular or nonexistent
> Musical organizations are popular
> Student publications are popular
> Student government is popular
> Political activism is popular
> Hard liquor is popular

Life

"Purchase is located in an area that is by no means a college town," meaning students need to rely on campus life for extracurricular fun. Fortunately, "each night there are opportunities to find something to do" without leaving the campus confines. The high concentration of creative and performing artists at Purchase means that "there's always something going on," including "concerts, plays, recitals" and "art exhibits." There are "fewer 'let's drink to drink' parties here" than at most state campuses, students believe. Instead, "Parties are organized around diversity and themes. Dance parties are common, celebrating African-American or Latino culture (there are two very active groups on campus: SOCA and a chapter of Latinos Unidos). Club activities such as Cheese Club or Hillel are [also] popular." In quieter moments, "Fun can range from hiking in the woods to playing video games, from playing music to smoking a cigarette and leaning on a brick wall." Or just shooting the breeze, as Purchase is home to "more philosophical people than you would expect at a state school. Not pretentiously, though. Even athletes are influenced by the community and begin to think in different ways." When all else fails, "New York City is a quick half-hour express train away on the Metro North, which has anything you could imagine available."

Student Body

"As one of the few public arts colleges that also integrates…reputable science and humanities departments," Purchase provides a home to a remarkably diverse student body. "We have athletes, cheerleaders, musicians, singers, dancers, and actors; this is just some of the diversity that is present at Purchase College," one undergrad reports. One thing many here share in common: They're likely to be a bit nerdy. As one student explains, "Imagine if you will, that you're back in grade school. Remember the last four students to be chosen [for teams in gym]? Those are Purchase College students, and the four of them are majoring in music composition, dance, biology, and literature. Or sociology, or printmaking, or gender studies." It's hardly wall-to-wall nerds, though; it's just that "The anime community is just as large as the athletic community or the premed students." As on many artsy campuses, "we have a lot of drag queens, hipsters, hippies…etc." but because "It is still a state school, students wanting to study science or language or anything…else also come here, and still fit in."

Admissions

Very important factors considered include: Application essay, academic GPA, talent/ability. *Important factors considered include:* Standardized test scores. *Other factors considered include:* Class rank, recommendation(s), rigor of secondary school record, character/personal qualities, extracurricular activities, interview. SAT recommended; SAT or ACT required; TOEFL required of all international applicants. High school diploma is required, and GED is accepted.

Financial Aid

Students should submit: FAFSA, state aid form. The Princeton Review suggests that all financial aid forms be submitted as soon as possible after January 1. *Need-based scholarships/grants offered:* Federal Pell, SEOG, state scholarships/grants, private scholarships, the school's own gift aid. *Loan aid offered:* Direct Subsidized Stafford, Direct Unsubsidized Stafford, Direct PLUS, Federal Perkins. Applicants will be notified of awards on a rolling basis beginning 3/1. Federal Work-Study Program available. Institutional employment available. Off-campus job opportunities are excellent.

The Inside Word

Just more than one-third of Purchase College undergraduates enroll in the School of the Arts. All must undergo either an audition or portfolio review as part of the application process; for such students, this is the most important part of the application. Traditional application components—such as high school transcript, test scores, and personal essay—are also considered, but figure less prominently. Applicants to the School of Liberal Arts and Sciences undergo a more conventional application review.

THE SCHOOL SAYS "..."

From The Admissions Office

"At Purchase College, you're encouraged to 'Think Wide Open.' The campus combines the energy and excitement of professional training in the performing and the visual arts with the intellectual traditions and spirit of discovery of the humanities and sciences. A Purchase College education emphasizes creativity, individual accomplishment, openness, and exploration. It culminates in a senior research or creative project that may focus on civic engagement or interdisciplinary work to become an excellent springboard to a career or to graduate or professional school. The Conservatories of Art and Design, Dance, Music, and Theatre Arts and Film that make up the School of the Arts deliver a cohort-based education with apprenticeships and other professional opportunities in nearby New York City.

"You'll find a unique and engaging atmosphere at Purchase, whether you are a student in the arts, humanities, natural sciences, or social sciences. You choose among a wide variety of programs, including arts management, journalism, creative writing, environmental science, new media, dramatic writing, premed, pre-law, and education. You'll attend performances by your friends, see world-renowned artists on stage at the Performing Arts Center, and experience the artworks on display in the Neuberger Museum of Art (one of the largest campus art museums in the country)—all without leaving campus. The new student services building, along with an enhanced student services website, is making Purchase a lot more user-friendly for its students.

"Admissions requirements vary with each program in the college and can include auditions, portfolio reviews, essays, writing samples, and interviews.

"In addition to individual program requirements, Purchase College requires SAT or ACT scores to complete your application."

For even more information on this school, turn to page 534 of the "Stats" section.

STATE UNIVERSITY OF NEW YORK—STONY BROOK UNIVERSITY

OFFICE OF ADMISSIONS, STONY BROOK, NY 11794-1901 • ADMISSIONS: 631-632-9898 • FAX: 631-632-9898
FINANCIAL AID: 631-632-6840 • E-MAIL: UGADMISSIONS@NOTES.CC.SUNYSB.EDU • WEBSITE: WWW.STONYBROOK.EDU

RATINGS
Quality of Life: 66   **Academic:** 68   **Admissions:** 91   **Financial Aid:** 71

STUDENTS SAY ". . ."

Academics

> **SURVEY SAYS . . .**
> *Diverse student types on campus*
> *Low cost of living*

Stony Brook University combines affordability and excellence with academic prestige, offering a "great academic reputation," ample research opportunities, and the chance to learn from "world-renowned professors for a great price." Don't let Stony Brook's "best value" reputation fool you; known as a "science powerhouse," the school is also a leader in pre-medical preparation. With over 150 academic programs on offer, "the breadth of the school's curriculum" is impressive, including "a wide variety of classes that you can take, ranging from [topics] such as theory of dance to nuclear physics." Academics are challenging and "Everyone lives in the library." In particular, "The science courses are no joke. They are large and hard, and you will most likely learn most of the material yourself." Fortunately, students paint a generally positive picture of the faculty, describing professors as "approachable and interested in their subject, making them good educators." Stony Brook is a research university, so while "it is relatively easy to find internships and research opportunities" as an undergraduate, you should also be aware that "Many professors feel their lab work is more important than their students." With almost 16,000 undergraduates, you'll end up in plenty of big lecture courses, making it more difficult to get to know your instructors personally. However, faculty maintains "reasonable office hours," and most are "very accessible" if you seek them out. In fact, Stony Brook students tell us that their "school is about taking initiative and taking advantage of opportunities that are available," rather than having your hand held—a happy condition for those who feel they are "too old to be spoon-fed." A current student explains, "Professors and staff are more than willing to help, but you have to ask for it…I feel that the balance between independence and assistance has prepared me well for entering a profession."

Life

Nothing at Stony Brook University will be handed to you on a silver platter, yet students reassure us that, "If you are willing to seek out activities and events, you will never be bored." On campus, there are almost 300 clubs and organizations, including sports teams, environmental groups, several student-run newspaper, and fraternities and sororities. In their downtime, students "hang out with friends," play video games or intramural sports, "head over to the University Café, or watch movies in their rooms." For additional distraction, "Each dorm building has its own ping-pong table and pool table in the basement." If you want to take a break from college life, "campus buses go to places like the mall and Walmart every weekend," and the surrounding community offers "movie theaters, bowling, Dave and Buster's, [and] countless restaurants." In addition, New York City is "fairly close," while nearby Southampton boasts "one of the top beaches in the United States." While people get together socially, SUNY Stony Brook is not a major party school, and "The campus is very quiet on weekends because many students live nearby and go home."

Student Body

Drawing a large crowd from the state of New York and a smattering of international students, Stony Brook University "combines the diversity of New York City with academic excellence to create a truly unique experience." At this large school, "Every personality type is represented…and it is easy to find a group to fit in with." Politically, "there are both strong right-wing and left-wing school newspapers," though "many more people support the liberal side." No matter what your persuasion, the community is generally open and accepting of different backgrounds, opinions, and interests. A current student elaborates, "I've never seen such a heterogeneous mixture of individuals in my life. And yet, despite the vast differences amongst students, everyone seems to get along." Across the board, academics are a priority, but most students strike a balance between work and play. At Stony Brook, "A typical student will go to class, spend a lot of their time studying, and try to have some fun on Thursday nights and the weekends."

THE PRINCETON REVIEW SAYS

Admissions

Very important factors considered include: Academic GPA, rigor of secondary school record, standardized test scores. *Important factors considered include:* Application essay, recommendations. *Other factors considered include:* Character/personal qualities, extracurricular activities, first generation, level of applicant's interest, geographical residence, talent/ability, volunteer work, work experience. SAT Subject Tests recommended; SAT or ACT required; ACT with Writing component required. TOEFL required of all international applicants. High school diploma is required, and GED is accepted. *Academic units required:* 4 English, 3 mathematics, 3 science, 2 foreign language, 4 social studies. *Academic units recommended:* 4 mathematics, 4 science, 3 foreign language.

Financial Aid

Students should submit: FAFSA, Program-specific Forms. The Princeton Review suggests that all financial aid forms be submitted as soon as possible after January 1. *Need-based scholarships/grants offered:* Federal Pell, SEOG, state scholarships/grants, the school's own gift aid. *Loan aid offered:* Direct Subsidized Stafford, Direct Unsubsidized Stafford, Direct PLUS, Federal Perkins. Applicants will be notified of awards on a rolling basis beginning 3/1. Federal Work-Study Program available. Institutional employment available. Off-campus job opportunities are excellent.

The Inside Word

Admission to Stony Brook University is competitive. Students with a particularly strong academic record may be considered for the university's special programs, including the Honors Program, the University Scholars program, and the Scholars in Medicine program. Admits to the Scholars in Medicine program can earn a bachelor's degree and M.D. through an integrated, eight-year curriculum; but applicants must meet high minimum GPA and test score requirements to be considered.

THE SCHOOL SAYS "..."

From The Admissions Office

"Our graduates include Carolyn Porco, the leader of the Imaging Team for the Cassini mission to Saturn; John Hennessy, the president of Stanford University; and Scott Higham, a Pulitzer Prize-winning investigative journalist for the Washington Post who has come to speak to students at our new School of Journalism. Situated on 1,100 wooded acres on the North Shore of Long Island, Stony Brook offers more than 150 majors, minors, and combined-degree programs for undergraduates, including our Fast Track MBA program, a thriving research environment, and a dynamic first-year experience in one of six small undergraduate communities. Faculty include four members of our School of Marine and Atmospheric Sciences who are recent co-winners of the Nobel Peace Prize. Students enjoy comfortable campus housing, outstanding recreational facilities that include an 8,800 seat stadium, modern student activities center, and indoor sports complex. In addition, the Staller Center for the Arts offers spectacular theatrical and musical performances throughout the year. We invite students who possess both intellectual curiosity and academic ability to explore the countless exciting opportunities available at Stony Brook. Freshmen applying for admission to the university are required to take the SAT (or the ACT with the Writing section). SAT Subject Test scores are recommended, but not required."

For even more information on this school, turn to page 535 of the "Stats" section.

State University of New York—University at Albany

1400 Washington Avenue, Albany, NY 12222 • Admissions: 518-442-5435 • Fax: 518-442-5383
Financial Aid: 518-442-5757 • E-mail: ugadmissions@albany.edu • Website: www.albany.edu

RATINGS
Quality of Life: 61   Academic: 61   Admissions: 86   Financial Aid: 69

STUDENTS SAY "..."

Academics

Is SUNY Albany (UAlbany to those in the know) the perfect-sized school? Many here think so. Students describe it as "a big school numbers-wise that feels small." Notes one student, "It has a very broad range of quality academic programs, which is very important for an undecided senior in high school." Another adds, "If you know what you want and are motivated, the sky is the limit." The school exploits its location in the state capital to bolster programs in political science, criminal justice, and business, and it "offers internship opportunities to college students that very few schools can." Other standout departments include psychology, Japanese studies, mathematics, and many of the hard sciences. Professors here vary widely in quality, but a surprising number "are receptive, active, and engaging"—in other words, "a lot more accessible than I would have thought for a school this big." Teachers are especially willing to "go out of their way to help students who are interested in learning, come to class regularly, and care about their academic work." The administration, as at most state-run schools, "is basically an over-bloated bureaucracy. Students are sent from department to department in each of their endeavors. It is advisable to avoid [the] administration if at all possible."

Life

There are three distinct social orbits on the Albany campus. Some students take the initiative "by joining one of the many clubs or groups or getting involved with the student government." Others "party for a good time," telling us that "any night of the week you can find people to go out to the bars and clubs with you" and that "the average night ends between 2:30–4:00 A.M." Both of these groups are likely to tell you that "there is a lot to do in Albany and the surrounding area," including "a great arts district, tons of awesome restaurants, museums, [and] a state park." A third, sizable group primarily complains about the cold weather and asserts that "there's nothing to do in Albany." The school works to excite these students with "fun programs and entertainers who come to the campus. We have had a series of comedians, rappers/singers, guests from MTV and VH1, authors, political figures, musical performances, sporting events, spirit events, and many other things around campus." School spirit is on the rise among all groups, we're told. The reason? "A few years ago, basketball team began winning, and everyone came out of the woodwork to support them—it was really a great thing to see."

Student Body

Undergrads here believe that the student body is very diverse in terms of ethnicity and also in terms of personality type; one student observes, "You have your motivated students [who] get good grades, are involved, and get amazing jobs in NYC after college. Then you have your unmotivated kids [who] complain, don't go to class, and blame a bad grade on the professor (when really it is because they crammed the night before and didn't go to class)." Geographically, the school is less diverse. Nearly everyone is a New York State resident, with many coming from "downstate New York"—Long Island, New York City, and Westchester County. There's a fair amount of upstate kids as well, and "a lot of people have certain stereotypes in their heads when they first come to Albany. The Long Islander has his idea about the upstater and vice versa. After a few weeks, though, people see that these aren't always true. I think people from anywhere get along pretty well." The international students, who form a small but noticeable contingent, "tend to keep to themselves," perhaps "due to a culture or language barrier." About one-quarter of the campus population is Jewish.

Admissions

Very important factors considered include: Class rank, academic GPA, recommendation(s), rigor of secondary school record, standardized test scores, character/personal qualities. *Important factors considered include:* application essay. *Other factors considered include:* alumni/ae relation, extracurricular activities, first generation, geographical residence, talent/ability, volunteer work, work experience. SAT or ACT required; ACT with Writing component required. TOEFL required of all international applicants. High school diploma is required, and GED is accepted. *Academic units required:* 4 English, 2 mathematics, 2 science, (2 science labs), 1 foreign language, 3 social studies, 2 history, 4 academic electives. *Academic units recommended:* 4 mathematics, 3 science, (3 science labs), 3 foreign language.

Financial Aid

Students should submit: FAFSA, NY State residents should apply for TAP on-line at www.tapweb.org. The Princeton Review suggests that all financial aid forms be submitted as soon as possible after January 1. *Need-based scholarships/grants offered:* Federal Pell, SEOG, state scholarships/grants, private scholarships, the school's own gift aid, NY State residents should apply for TAP on-line at www.tapweb.org. *Loan aid offered:* Federal Perkins. Applicants will be notified of awards on a rolling basis beginning 3/20. Federal Work-Study Program available. Institutional employment available. Off-campus job opportunities are good.

The Inside Word

The Wall Street Journal has noted a growing trend among students who, in the past, had limited their postsecondary options to high-end private schools: More such students, the paper reported, have broadened their vision to include prestigious state schools such as SUNY Albany. The driving force, unsurprisingly, is economic. In the event of an unlikely decline in the cost of private education, expect admissions at schools like UAlbany to grow more competitive in coming years.

THE SCHOOL SAYS "…"

From The Admissions Office

"Increasing numbers of well-prepared students are discovering the benefits of study in UAlbany's nationally ranked programs and are taking advantage of outstanding internship and employment opportunities in upstate New York's 'Tech Valley.' The already strong undergraduate program is being further enhanced by the recently established Honors College, a university-wide program for ambitious students. The Honors College offers enhanced honors courses and co-curricular options including honors housing.

"Ten schools and colleges, including the nation's first College of Nanoscale Science and Engineering, offer bachelor's, master's, and doctoral programs to more than nearly 13,000 undergraduates and 5,000 graduate students. An award-winning advisement program helps students take advantage of all these options by customizing the undergraduate experiences. More than two-thirds of Albany graduates go on for advanced degrees, and acceptance to law and medical school is above the national average.

"Student life on campus includes 200 clubs, honor societies, and other groups, and 19 Division I varsity teams. With 19 other colleges in the region, Albany is a great college town, adjacent to the spectacular natural and recreational centers of New York and New England.

"Freshmen are awarded more than $800,000 in merit scholarships each year and nearly three-quarters of our students receive financial aid."

For even more information on this school, turn to page 531 of the "Stats" section.

STATE UNIVERSITY OF NEW YORK—UNIVERSITY AT BUFFALO

15 CAPEN HALL, BUFFALO, NY 14260 • ADMISSIONS: 888-UB-ADMIT • FAX: 716-645-6411
FINANCIAL AID: 866-838-7257 • E-MAIL: UB-ADMISSIONS@BUFFALO.EDU • WEBSITE: WWW.BUFFALO.EDU

RATINGS

Quality of Life: 74   Academic: 69   Admissions: 87   Financial Aid: 83

STUDENTS SAY "..."

Academics

Offering "more academic programs per dollar than any other university in the state," SUNY Buffalo (UB for short) "is about choices. You can choose many different…combinations of academics and social activities with the support in place." Students brag that UB's "programs are all of the highest quality, translating [into] a best-value education for students." The

> **SURVEY SAYS . . .**
> *Diverse student types on campus*
> *Student publications are popular*
> *Lots of beer drinking*
> *Hard liquor is popular*

School of Engineering and Applied Science in particular "is well respected" and "works with corporate partners in a variety of ways that range from joint-research ventures to continuing education to co-op work arrangements for our students." Other stand-out offerings include: pharmacy, physical therapy, a popular business and management school "that is ranked highly," "a solid undergrad and grad architecture program," and "one of the top nursing programs in the state." Of course, a school with this much to offer is bound to be large, making it "easy not to attend class and fall through the cracks, so one must be self-motivated to do well." Administrative tasks are occasionally Kafkaesque, with "a lot of red tape to go through to get anything done. I feel like a pebble being kicked around when trying to get support or services," notes one student. Many students point out that support services and contact with professors improves during junior and senior years when students are pursuing their majors and forging stronger relationships within their departments.

Life

UB is divided into two campuses. Traditionally, South Campus in Northeast Buffalo has been where "the parties are," though students say, "it's much less safe than North Campus," which is located in the suburban enclave of Amherst. The recent closing of several bars near South Campus has made it less of a party destination than it was in years past; these days many students report going to downtown Buffalo "to go clubbing." Students living on North Campus describe it as "its own little city. We have food services, our own bus system, a highway, even our own zip codes. If you know how to play, North Campus is just as much fun as Main Street [which runs by South Campus]; you just need to know where to go." The North Campus, which features "a lake and a nice bike path for when you want to escape from the hectic [atmosphere]" of academic life, is the more populous of the two; the inter-campus bus system is "convenient," although a car is preferred. Students tell us that "between all of the clubs and organizations, the Office of Student Life, athletics, and the Student Association, there is always something to do" on campus. The school's Division I sports teams "are a big hit around here. Even if we are the worst in the division, we still cheer hard and go crazy for our guys and girls." Those who explore Buffalo extol its "amazing art and music scene."

Student Body

Because of UB's size, "You can find just about every kind of person there is here. Everyone has a place in this large and diverse student population." As one student notes, "Although the typical student is of traditional college age, there really isn't a 'typical' student—the student body is very diverse in terms of religion, ethnicity, nationality, age, gender, and orientation. 'Atypical' students fit in well because of the diversity of the student population." Another student adds, "There are a lot of foreign and minority students, to the point that the actual 'majority' is the minority here at UB." Geographically, UB draws "from urban areas, rural areas, NYC, Long Island, and most every country in the world." As a state school, "a lot of the students are from New York State, but with differing areas of the state, there are many different types of students."

THE PRINCETON REVIEW SAYS
Admissions
Very important factors considered include: Academic GPA, rigor of secondary school record, standardized test scores. *Important factors considered include:* Class rank, recommendation(s), interview. *Other factors considered include:* Application essay, character/personal qualities, extracurricular activities, first generation, geographical residence, racial/ethnic status, talent/ability, volunteer work, work experience. SAT or ACT required; ACT with Writing component required. TOEFL required of all international applicants. High school diploma is required, and GED is accepted. *Academic units recommended:* 4 English, 3 mathematics, 3 science, 3 foreign language, 4 social studies.

Financial Aid
Students should submit: FAFSA. The Princeton Review suggests that all financial aid forms be submitted as soon as possible after January 1. *Need-based scholarships/grants offered:* Federal Pell, SEOG, state scholarships/grants, private scholarships, the school's own gift aid, Federal Nursing Scholarships. *Loan aid offered:* Direct Subsidized Stafford, Direct Unsubsidized Stafford, Direct PLUS, Federal Perkins, Federal Nursing, college/university loans from institutional funds. Applicants will be notified of awards on a rolling basis beginning 2/1. Federal Work-Study Program available. Institutional employment available. Off-campus job opportunities are good.

The Inside Word
As students point out, UB "is famous for its architecture, nursing, and pharmacy schools," making those majors harder to get into. In fact, admissions standards at UB have grown more demanding across all programs in recent years. Despite the school's large applicant pool, it takes a close look at applications, searching for evidence of special talents and experiences that will enrich campus life.

THE SCHOOL SAYS "..."
From The Admissions Office
"The University at Buffalo (UB) is among the nation's finest public research universities—a learning community where you'll work side by side with world-renowned faculty, including Nobel, Pulitzer, National Medal of Science, and other award winners. As the largest, most comprehensive university center in the State University of New York (SUNY) system, UB offers more undergraduate majors than any public university in New York or New England. Through innovative resources like our Undergraduate Research and Creative Activities, Discovery Seminars, and Undergraduate Academics, you'll be free to chart an academic course that meets your individual goals. At UB you can even design your own major. Our unique University Honors College and University Scholars Program scholarship programs offer an enhanced academic experience, including opportunities for independent study, advanced research, and specialized advisement. The university is committed to providing the latest information technology—and is widely considered to be one of the most wired (and wireless) universities in the country. UB also places a high priority on offering an exciting campus environment. With nonstop festivals, Division I sporting events, concerts, and visiting lecturers, you'll have plenty to do outside of the classroom. We encourage you and your family to visit campus to see UB up close and in person. Our Visit UB campus tours and presentations are offered year-round.

"Freshman applicants must take the SAT (or the ACT with Writing component)."

For even more information on this school, turn to page 536 of the "Stats" section.

STERLING COLLEGE (VT)

PO Box 72, Craftsbury Common, VT 05827 • Admissions: 802-586-7711 • Fax: 802-586-2596
Financial Aid: 802-586-7711 • E-mail: admissions@sterlingcollege.edu • Website: www.sterlingcollege.edu

RATINGS

Quality of Life: 80   Academic: 65   Admissions: 65   Financial Aid: 74

STUDENTS SAY ". . ."

Academics

Sterling College offers an "amazing community dynamic" and a four-year program tucked in the woods of northern Vermont that has an emphasis on "real-life skills." Students earn a B.A. in one of four majors, including conservation ecology and outdoor education. The school also teaches its 105 students how to farm, survive in the wilderness, work with wood and metals, and become more self-reliant. In addition, students have the opportunity to self-design their own majors. "Sterling College, to me, is about connecting with the natural world and your community," one student says. Another adds, "I've learned more here at Sterling College in one semester than I ever learned in all four years of high school." During their first year, students learn at both the main 130-acre campus, which has a woodshop among its 14 buildings and at the 300-acre Center for Northern Studies in nearby Wolcott. During the second and third years, students do internships, leading up to a research project that is the centerpiece of their senior year. Some students complain classes "are not always very challenging" or some instructors are "unprepared." But virtually all students say the faculty and administrators are approachable and engage them in discussions, often over meals in the dining hall. Other students say the program has changed their lives in a profound way. "It has given me ways of directing my concern about the world's tenuous situation in positive ways and taught me the real power of community."

Life

Winters at Sterling, which is closer to Montreal than Boston, drag across most of the school year, so "Being in the middle of nowhere requires some creativity." When they're not in a structured class, students engage in any kind of game or activity that strikes their fancy: cross-country skiing, hiking, knitting, playing music, or dancing. Other pursuits are straight out of a Jeremiah Johnson diary entry: "For fun I tan hides and make baskets from the forest," one student says. There are spirited debates about every issue in the political constellation. There's a TV (although there's debate over whether it should be there) and plenty of movies, as well as a large supply of books. But sometimes there's just not much to do. "It can get boring and depressing with the short winter days. All students complete 80 hours of work each semester. Fifty through work college jobs and thirty through "chores" on campus. Students earn credit toward their tuition by participating in the Work College Job. We run the kitchen, the farm, and gardens, snow removal and landscaping, we work in the local community helping our elders and mentoring our youth."

Student Body

Who is the typical Sterling student? Probably someone from New England, that's certain. If they attended a more traditional college, they might be the ones who stand out, who get called "granolas" or "hippies." Descriptions tend to begin with the uniform: "Carhartts-and-flannel-wearing, hard-working, outdoor-loving, smelly, enthusiastic learners who actually [care] about the world we live in and want to change on a local and global level." Students say, "We do not care about our appearance and are comfortable with the way we are" and believe their ideas matter more than status and style. Nonconformity unites them, in a strange way. "Everyone who comes to Sterling is atypical in some way, so that makes us a college of misfits. No one is the weird kid or an outsider; we are all weird, just in different ways." Students who don't mind the cold and working hard, tend to do well and build strong bonds with their classmates. "Often they come from rural, farming, home-school or other non-typical backgrounds," one student says. "An atypical student is unfriendly, apathetic, and unwilling to help others."

THE PRINCETON REVIEW SAYS

Admissions

Very important factors considered include: Academic GPA, recommendation(s), rigor of secondary school record, level of applicant's interest. *Important factors considered include:* Class rank, application essay, character/personal qualities, extracurricular activities, interview, talent/ability, volunteer work. *Other factors considered include:* Standardized test scores, alumni/ae relation, geographical residence, work experience. TOEFL required of all international applicants. High school diploma is required and GED is accepted. *Academic units required:* 4 English, 3 mathematics, 2 science, (2 science labs), 2 social studies, 2 history. *Academic units recommended:* 4 English, 4 mathematics, 3 science, (3 science labs), 2 foreign language, 2 social studies, 2 history.

Financial Aid

Students should submit: FAFSA, institution's own financial aid form, state aid form. The Princeton Review suggests that all financial aid forms be submitted as soon as possible after January 1. *Need-based scholarships/grants offered:* Federal Pell, SEOG, state scholarships/grants, private scholarships, the school's own gift aid. Applicants will be notified of awards on a rolling basis beginning 2/1. Federal Work-Study Program available. Institutional employment available. Off-campus job opportunities are fair.

The Inside Word

Sterling admissions officers seek candidates who will weave seamlessly into the fabric of the college. Therefore, like many of their liberal arts contemporaries, the college strives to assess not only academic but personal criteria. Successful applicants will demonstrate intellectual curiosity and a desire to take control over one's own education. Students who display achievement in a standard college prep curriculum should find themselves in good standing with the admissions committee.

THE SCHOOL SAYS "…"

From The Admissions Office

"Sterling's programs are designed for those who are academically prepared for college studies, eager to embrace the demands of Sterling College, and willing to participate in all aspects of the curriculum. Our applicants include high school and home-school students, transfer students, adult students, and international students.

"The Admissions Committee looks most favorably upon applicants who express enthusiasm for experiential learning, in addition to intellectual curiosity and drive and desire to shape ones own education.

"We offer admission to first-year and transfer students who we feel are a good fit—students who will support our mission, prove to be academically engaged, and become successful members of the Sterling community. Prospective students are encouraged to initiate personal contact with admission counselors or others in the Sterling community. Schedule a visit to campus, write, call, or send an e-mail to make known your level of interest in attending Sterling College. An admissions interview is highly recommended."

For even more information on this school, turn to page 536 of the "Stats" section.

STEVENS INSTITUTE OF TECHNOLOGY

CASTLE POINT ON HUDSON, HOBOKEN, NJ 07030 • ADMISSIONS: 800-458-5323 • FAX: 201-216-8348
FINANCIAL AID: 201-216-5194 • E-MAIL: ADMISSIONS@STEVENS-TECH.EDU • WEBSITE: WWW.STEVENS-TECH.EDU

RATINGS
Quality of Life: 89   Academic: 71   Admissions: 94   Financial Aid: 72

STUDENTS SAY "..."

Academics

Stevens Institute of Technology "is all about preparing scientists and engineers for a real work experience through research, co-op, and hands-on classes." "Engineering dominates" the curriculum here—"almost every major is engineering, and those that aren't, they throw 'and engineering' on the end to make it sound like it is"—and "The course load is demanding in its math, physics and engineering classes." Just less than half of Stevens' undergraduates participate in the school's cooperative education program (co-op), which students brag is "one of the best in the country." The program places students in real-world work environments that "allow [them] to learn more outside the classroom than inside it." As one undergrad sees it, "Stevens prepares students to actually work in these advanced technical fields as opposed to other colleges that focus solely on book smarts." As a "smaller school," Stevens can address student needs and concerns with "a lot less bureaucracy, a lot less red tape, and more direct communication" than other schools. Professors, similarly, tend to be more accessible than at larger schools, making the educational experience "a lot less stressful than it could be." It's not all rosy, though; as at many tech schools, "Some professors and lab assistants speak English poorly, and are consequently difficult to understand." When students graduate, the school "really does try hard to increase job placement," and its "career fairs and workshops...are worth every minute."

> SURVEY SAYS . . .
> Career services are great
> Students love Hoboken, NJ
> Great off-campus food
> Campus feels safe
> Low cost of living

Life

"Academics are the main focus here at Stevens," but "there are also lots of activities available both on and off campus," and most students manage to find at least some time for them. The student-run entertainment committee "does a great job [of] bringing in a variety of shows," including "two big campus festivals offered in the fall and spring, known as Techfest and Boken respectively. There are lots of games, prizes, comedians, bands and much more...offered during this [event]." Many students "are very active in the 90+ RSOs (Registered Student Organizations) on campus," and "many play sports" as well ("The sports teams are very good overall in our conference and NCAA play"). "On Thursday, Friday, and Saturday nights, there are usually parties in dorm rooms and at the frats," but "if drinking and partying isn't your thing, there is still a lot for you to do," off campus as well as on. Hometown Hoboken "is a great place to walk around, go shopping, and hang out." It also has "a great social life and is filled with many bars to go to." And, "The train station is only a couple blocks away, making traveling into New York City easy and convenient." New York, of course, offers "endless possibilities for activities, no matter who the person is."

Student Body

Sure, there are "way too many people who are into anime" at Stevens, the kinds of kids who make jokes like "Stevens has 10 types of students: Those who know binary, and those who are hung over and forgot it." But students here insist that Stevens isn't all nerd, all the time. Most agree that "half of the students are obsessed with video games and are pretty nerdy," while the other half, "who are probably business and technology majors," "are so involved on campus it almost seems like they are running the entire school. Many of them have Blackberries and daily organizers to show just how busy they are." The student body includes "a huge proportion of athletes" as well as "great artists, great writers, great actors, and great singers." "There's absolutely a place for everyone to fit in. If you can't find a place, you must be doing something wrong," one student writes.

Admissions

Very important factors considered include: Application essay, academic GPA, recommendation(s), rigor of secondary school record, standardized test scores, character/personal qualities, extracurricular activities, interview, volunteer work, work experience. *Important factors considered include:* Class rank, talent/ability. *Other factors considered include:* Alumni/ae relation. SAT or ACT required; TOEFL required of all international applicants. High school diploma is required, and GED is not accepted. *Academic units required:* 4 English, 4 mathematics, 3 science, (3 science labs), 0 foreign language, 0 social studies, 0 history, 0 academic electives. *Academic units recommended:* 4 science, (4 science labs), 2 foreign language, 2 social studies, 2 history, 1 computer science, 4 academic electives.

Financial Aid

Students should submit: FAFSA and CSS/PROFILE. The Princeton Review suggests that all financial aid forms be submitted as soon as possible after January 1. *Need-based scholarships/grants offered:* Federal Pell, SEOG, state scholarships/grants, private scholarships, the school's own gift aid. *Loan aid offered:* Direct Subsidized Stafford, Direct Unsubsidized Stafford, Direct PLUS, Federal Perkins, state loans, Other, Signature Loans, TERI Loans, NJ CLASS, CitiAssist. Applicants will be notified of awards on a rolling basis beginning 3/30. Federal Work-Study Program available. Institutional employment available. Off-campus job opportunities are excellent.

The Inside Word

Stevens remains among the most desirable "second tier" engineering/science/math schools; its location and cachet with employers guarantee it will always rank fairly high. If you can handle the grueling curriculum of a top tech school but can't make the cut at MIT or Caltech—in other words, if you're merely mortal—Stevens is a solid alternative. The school waives its application fee for those who apply online.

THE SCHOOL SAYS "..."

From The Admissions Office

"Founded in 1870 as the first American college to devote itself exclusively to engineering education based on scientific principles, the Innovation University is a prestigious independent university for study and research. In past year, Stevens has been ranked by the Princeton Review as one of the nation's 'Most Entrepreneurial Campuses' for having tailored their undergraduate business and technology curricula to encourage young entrepreneurs, providing them with the training and guidance they need to start their own businesses. Stevens has also been ranked among the nation's top-20 'Most Wired Campuses' by *PC Magazine* and *The Princeton Review*.

"At the undergraduate level, Stevens' broad-based education leads to prestigious degrees in business, science, computer science, engineering, or humanities. Research activities are vital to the university's educational mission, thus Stevens attracts world-renowned faculty to complement its exceptional on-campus facilities. In addition, Stevens maintains an honor system that has been in existence since 1908. Stevens' more than 2,200 undergraduates come from more than 45 states and 47 countries, creating a diverse, dynamic environment. Stevens also boasts an outstanding campus life—students will find more than 150 student organizations and 26 NCAA Division III athletics teams.

"Stevens requires the SAT or ACT for all applicants. We recommend that all students take SAT Subject Tests to show their strength in English, math, and a science of their choice. Accelerated premed and pre-dentistry applicants must take the SAT as well as two SAT Subject Tests in math (Level I or II), and biology or chemistry. Accelerated law applicants must take two SAT Subject Tests of their choice."

For even more information on this school, turn to page 537 of the "Stats" section.

STONEHILL COLLEGE

320 WASHINGTON STREET, EASTON, MA 02357-5610 • ADMISSIONS: 508-565-1373 • FAX: 508-565-1545
E-MAIL: ADMISSIONS@STONEHILL.EDU • WEBSITE: WWW.STONEHILL.EDU

RATINGS
Quality of Life: 98   **Academic:** 89   **Admissions:** 92   **Financial Aid:** 72

STUDENTS SAY "..."

Academics

"Stonehill is a small liberal arts college" "focused on educating the mind and soul" in the Roman Catholic tradition. "With a great small, interactive classroom experience" and "amazing" professors who "will help you no matter what," the academic experience here is distinctly "personal." "You won't be lost in the crowd at Stonehill. Professors know who you are and want to help you succeed." (Dare we say they will also notice when you are absent and may call you

to find out why?) But that does not mean professors don't expect students to work hard. To the contrary, they "challenge you to question: question your readings, your professors, yourself." The whole point is to teach "how to be a critical thinker, and to look more in depth on ideas and topics." Faculty and administrators are extremely accessible."Many [faculty members] give students not only their school e-mail addresses, but their cell phone or home phone numbers as well as their AIM screen names if they have them!" Students also appreciate the learning opportunities off campus. "Stonehill has an amazing focus on internships and studying abroad and is known for having connections in the working world. The internships and opportunities given to students are pretty unique."

Life

"Being in the middle of Boston and Providence as well as having more than 70 clubs and organizations on campus that host two events a semester, there is always something to do" at Stonehill. "During the week, most people are considerate and allow you to get work done." "We have quiet hours at 10 P.M. on the weekdays and 1 A.M. on the weekends." But on the weekends, students cut loose. "For fun, people head into Boston a lot; the school has a shuttle to take us to the metro T station so it's very accessible if you don't have a car." On campus, "each night of the week there are different events sponsored by different groups on campus or by the Student Activities building. Some of the more widely attended events include our mixers (dances), which are held at various points throughout the year." "If you're looking for the frat/sorority party school, this isn't the place for you. It's much more laid-back, with drinking in the dorm rooms or in the 21-plus common rooms." And it should be noted that alcohol is taken seriously here; many call the school's alcohol policy "way too strict," though it's possible to "learn the ways around it." The dorms here "are beautiful, and you get to choose your housing based on a point system. You get points for being active in the school (sports, clubs, attending lectures, etc.), so the more you participate the better housing you get. You can lose points for misbehavior, so the best housing goes to the best students, which is a huge plus!"

Student Body

"Stonehill is a pretty homogeneous place." Most students are "Caucasian and from middle-class families in New England." They tend to be "preppy" and "love to party on the weekends." However, they "also know how to crack down during the week and excel in class." "The typical student at Stonehill is kind, considerate, friendly and smart. At Stonehill we hold doors, sometimes for an akwardly long time," but the friendly population makes everyone feel welcome." "There are some minorities, but the one thing that does not deviate from this mold is the expected college 'look'."

THE PRINCETON REVIEW SAYS

Admissions

Very important factors considered include: Class rank, academic GPA, rigor of secondary school record, character/personal qualities, talent/ability. *Important factors considered include:* Application essay, recommendation(s), extracurricular activities, level of applicant's interest, volunteer work, work experience. *Other factors considered include:* Standardized test scores, alumni/ae relation, first generation, geographical residence, interview, racial/ethnic status, religious affiliation/commitment, ACT with Writing component recommended. TOEFL required of all international applicants. High school diploma is required, and GED is accepted. *Academic units required:* 4 English, 3 mathematics, 1 science, (1 science labs), 2 foreign language, 3 history, 3 academic electives. *Academic units recommended:* 4 English, 4 mathematics, 3 science, (2 science labs), 3 foreign language, 3 history, 3 academic electives.

Financial Aid

Students should submit: FAFSA, CSS/Financial Aid PROFILE, noncustodial PROFILE, business/farm supplement. Regular filing deadline is 2/1. The Princeton Review suggests that all financial aid forms be submitted as soon as possible after January 1. *Need-based scholarships/grants offered:* Federal Pell, SEOG, state scholarships/grants, private scholarships, the school's own gift aid. *Loan aid offered:* Direct Subsidized Stafford, Direct Unsubsidized Stafford, Direct PLUS, Federal Perkins, state loans Applicants will be notified of awards on or about 4/1. Federal Work-Study Program available. Institutional employment available. Off-campus job opportunities are good.

The Inside Word

Though not nearly as selective as some of its fellow Boston-area colleges, Stonehill students are no dummies. Half of them graduated in the top 10 percent of their high school classes. Members of ethnic minorities may feel a bit isolated here.

THE SCHOOL SAYS "..."

From The Admissions Office

"Located 22 miles south of Boston, Stonehill is a selective Catholic college with an academically challenging, welcoming community on a beautiful, active campus. With an average class size of 20, Stonehill's dedicated and supportive faculty make personal connections with each of our 2,400 students and mentor them throughout all four years and beyond. Stonehill offers more than 70 diverse majors and minors in the liberal arts, sciences, and business. Nearly 90% of our students participate in enriching opportunities such as competitive international and U.S. internships; nationally ranked study abroad programs; and top-notch undergraduate research, practicum, and field work experiences. Our proximity to America's premier college town allows you to join a network of 250,000 students and offers easy access to theatres, museums, professional sports games, restaurants, and more. But most importantly, Stonehill is a vibrant community where many minds come together for one purpose: to educate students for lives that make a difference."

For even more information on this school, turn to page 537 of the "Stats" section.

SUFFOLK UNIVERSITY

8 ASHBURTON PLACE, BOSTON, MA 02108 • ADMISSIONS: 617-573-8460 • FAX: 617-742-4291
EMAIL: ADMISSION@ADMIN.SUFFLOLK.EDU • WEBSITE: WWW.SUFFOLK.EDU

RATINGS
Quality of Life: 80   Academic: 73   Admissions: 72   Financial Aid: 71

STUDENTS SAY "..."

Academics

Located in "the heart of downtown Boston," Suffolk University offers a "happy environment" for "anyone who wants to be at a school and still be directly in the city." The university offers "a wide selection of interesting majors" and small class sizes throughout its College of Arts and

> **SURVEY SAYS . . .**
> *Students love Boston, MA*
> *Great off-campus food*
> *Low cost of living*

Sciences and business school, giving this "united, diverse mass of students" a "global perspective in a real-world, urban setting." Students observe that depending on "[which] professor you have...you will like the class or not." Across the board, the teachers come across as being "very friendly" and genuine, and they "speak to you like an adult with respect." Some professors are "a bit dry;" however, "when you find [a great professor], they will be there for you through anything." Many here "wish the classes were more challenging," saying that coursework is "not as challenging as the school implies, but it is not easy." The school "offers students the resources they need should they want to put more effort into classes, job searching, and anything else, really;" students simply need to be self-motivated to take advantage of it. "Class participation comes naturally because class size is so small and the professor knows your name," says a freshman. "The administration is a little ridiculous sometimes with [its] rules," but overall it has "good relationships with the students."

Life

With the city as its "campus and playground," there is an "endless array of things to do" at Suffolk University, including shopping, museums, restaurants, and culture. "The students become part of the city," says a sophomore. "Suffolk doesn't really have a campus," though no one really seems to mind, as most students knew what they'd signed on for when they enrolled. Due to space constraints, not all upperclassmen can live on campus, and many happily choose to live in Boston apartments. "My classes require me to walk through the Common everyday," says one student. For those who do live on campus, the university offers freshman orientation activities that "students can participate [in] to ease the tensions of moving into a dorm and being on your own." Most students take their social lives off campus, choosing to hang out at other colleges and in the city itself. Suffolk's campus is dry, so "students have to find other places in which to party" on the weekends (weeknights are typically dedicated to homework). As for the commuters, most "don't interact directly with [resident] students as much." Unsurprisingly, "there's a lot of Boston pride among Suffolk students." "Everyone loves the Red Sox, the Celtics, and the Bruins."

Student Body

Most of the kids here come out of "a medium to high income family" and are from "some town in Massachusetts," though Suffolk has a lot of international students. "It is very easy for a student to blend in due to Suffolk being a very diverse campus." Cultures and beliefs do indeed vary greatly—"that is definitely a part of what makes Suffolk so unique"—but "most students are friendly and interact with one another regardless of where they are from." However, there is a slight—though not tense—divide between two other classifications of Suffolk students: the large commuter populations and those who live in on-campus housing. "Suffolk is not very successful at integrating the two, but everyone seems to get along okay," says a student. Luckily, classes also require several group projects, "forcing students to work together." Preppy seems to be what the Suffolk student body preaches, and button downs, polo shirts, and Uggs abound—"most would NEVER wear pajamas or sweatpants to class."

Admissions

Very important factors considered include: Rigor of secondary school record. *Important factors considered include:* Class rank, application essay, academic GPA, standardized test scores, character/personal qualities. *Other factors considered include:* Recommendation(s), alumni/ae relation, extracurricular activities, first generation, geographical residence, interview, level of applicant's interest, talent/ability, volunteer work, work experience. SAT or ACT required; TOEFL required of all international applicants. High school diploma is required, and GED is accepted. *Academic units required:* 4 English, 3 mathematics, 2 science, (1 science labs), 2 foreign language, 1 history, 4 academic electives. *Academic units recommended:* 4 English, 4 mathematics, 4 science, (1 science labs), 3 foreign language, 4 history, 4 academic electives.

Financial Aid

Students should submit: FAFSA, institution's own financial aid form regular filing deadline is 3/1. The Princeton Review suggests that all financial aid forms be submitted as soon as possible after January 1. *Need-based scholarships/grants offered:* Federal Pell, SEOG, state scholarships/grants, private scholarships, the school's own gift aid. *Loan aid offered:* Direct Subsidized Stafford, Direct Unsubsidized Stafford, Direct PLUS, Federal Perkins, state loans, college/university loans from institutional funds. Applicants will be notified of awards on a rolling basis beginning 2/5. Federal Work-Study Program available. Institutional employment available. Off-campus job opportunities are excellent. The President's Incentive Loan converts to a grant at graduation.

The Inside Word

Suffolk is unapologetic about its mission to provide access and opportunity to college-bound students. That said, test scores and high school GPA requirements are average. Applicants whose numbers are above-average have a good chance of gaining admission.

THE SCHOOL SAYS "..."

From The Admissions Office

"Ask any student, and they'll tell you: The best thing about Suffolk is the professors. They go the extra mile to help students to succeed. Suffolk faculty members are noted scholars and experienced professionals, but first and foremost, they are teachers and mentors. Suffolk's faculty is of the highest caliber. Ninety-four percent of the faculty hold PhDs. Suffolk maintains a 13:1 student/faculty ratio with an average class size of 19.

"Career preparation is a high priority at Suffolk. Many students work during the school year in paid internships, co-op jobs, or work-study positions. Suffolk has an excellent job placement record. More than 94 percent of recent graduates are either employed or enrolled in graduate school at the time of graduation.

"The university's academic programs emphasize quality teaching, small class size, real-world career applications, and an international experience. There are more than 50 study abroad sites available to students. The undergraduate academic program offers more than 70 majors and 1,000 courses.

"We require applicants to submit the SAT with the essay score or the ACT taken with the Writing component. Standardized tests are used for both placement and assessment. International students may submit any of the following tests for admission: the TOEFL or ELPT, IELTS, CPE, CAE, and FCE. The role of standardized testing is still a secondary role when considering admission to the university. The candidate's grades and the overall strength of curriculum are primary factors in the admission decision.

"Independent, eclectic, self-starters do best at Suffolk as do students who thrive in small classes and make the most of living in the city of Boston."

For even more information on this school, turn to page 538 of the "Stats" section.

SUSQUEHANNA UNIVERSITY

514 UNIVERSITY AVENUE, SELINSGROVE, PA 17870 • ADMISSIONS: 570-372-4260 • FAX: 570-372-2722
FINANCIAL AID: 570-372-4450 • E-MAIL: SUADMISS@SUSQU.EDU • WEBSITE: WWW.SUSQU.EDU

RATINGS
Quality of Life: 81   Academic: 82   Admissions: 80   Financial Aid: 80

STUDENTS SAY ". . ."

Academics

Students tell us that Susquehanna University's small size makes it "the perfect university to give students the opportunity to excel in all aspects of school—academics, research, athletics, clubs, and many other activities." Located in rural central Pennsylvania, SU is regarded by students as "an oasis of quirky in the middle of nowhere." This quirkiness

> **SURVEY SAYS . . .**
> *Great computer facilities*
> *Athletic facilities are great*
> *Dorms are like palaces*
> *Campus feels safe*

emanates from the school's strong programs in the fine arts (including a "big music program," solid departments in creative writing and graphic design, and an active theateer program). Less quirky and more populous is the school's popular School of Business—one in four students here pursues a business major. Students note that "This is a liberal arts university requiring you to take classes from many areas," meaning that all here receive a well-rounded education. They also point out that "It is understandable that you aren't going to be the best at all of those areas. The professors know this as well and are there to help." Indeed, what students love most about SU is the sense that "It is all about the student here. There are no graduate students teaching the undergraduates, the advisers want to make sure how you are doing, and the relationships formed with professors are priceless."

Life

SU's hometown of Selinsgrove "doesn't have the most exciting night life," but that "doesn't really matter" because students "don't have much money to spend on nightlife anyway" and "there's a ton of free stuff to do on campus." Popular campus options include TRAX, "a place were students can go and dance and have a few drinks if they are 21," and Charlie's Coffeehouse, a venue "that provides entertainment like live bands, movies, or games on Friday and Saturday nights." Students are also kept busy with the "abundance of student organizations and campus activities. Not only does it seem like students at Susquehanna are eager to get involved in probably more things than they realistically have time for, but the staff in our student life and campus activities office are amazing." As one student explains, "SU tries to provide as many options as it can because there is literally nothing to do around Selinsgrove." Well, maybe not exactly nothing. Some here concede that the town provides "close proximity to restaurants and stores" and a "decent-sized mall just a couple miles away, as well as everything else from Wall-Mart to every type of fast food restaurant you could think of, all within five miles of school." When small town life gets to be too much, students take advantage of "one-day bus trips to big cities like New York."

Student Body

While there is "a broad mix of students in the sense that there are those that relish in the fine arts, others that are greatly involved in the sciences, and others that enjoy the analytical business aspect of Susquehanna," SU undergrads concede that the typical student is "white and moderately well-off financially" and that "atypical students fit in because they hang out with other atypical students." Overall, students here are "somewhat preppy, but with their own style" and "are hard-working" individuals "who are involved in a ton of activities and sports, but still go out on the weekends."

THE PRINCETON REVIEW SAYS

Admissions

Very important factors considered include: Academic GPA, rigor of secondary school record. *Important factors considered include:* Class rank, application essay, recommendation(s), standardized test scores, alumni/ae relation, character/personal qualities, extracurricular activities, interview, level of applicant's interest, racial/ethnic status, talent/ability, volunteer work, work *Other factors considered include:* First generation, geographical residence, religious affiliation/commitment, state residency, TOEFL required of all international applicants. High school diploma is required, and GED is accepted. *Academic units required:* 4 English, 3 mathematics, 3 science, (2 science labs), 2 foreign language, 2 social studies, 2 history, 2 academic electives. *Academic units recommended:* 4 English, 4 mathematics, 4 science, (3 science labs), 4 foreign language, 4 social studies, 2 history, 3 academic electives.

Financial Aid

Students should submit: FAFSA, CSS/Financial Aid PROFILE, business/farm supplement. Prior year Federal tax return. Regular filing deadline is 5/1. The Princeton Review suggests that all financial aid forms be submitted as soon as possible after January 1. *Need-based scholarships/grants offered:* Federal Pell, SEOG, state scholarships/grants, private scholarships, the school's own gift aid. *Loan aid offered:* Federal Perkins, college/university loans from institutional funds. Applicants will be notified of awards on or about 3/1. Federal Work-Study Program available. Institutional employment available. Off-campus job opportunities are good.

The Inside Word

Susquehanna competes with a number of similar area schools for its student body, and as a result cannot afford to be as selective as it might like, thus creating an opportunity for high school underachievers to attend a challenging and prestigious school. Further improving the odds, Susquehanna does not require standardized test scores of applicants. Those who choose not to submit SAT/ACT scores must instead submit two graded writing samples.

THE SCHOOL SAYS "..."

From The Admissions Office

"Susquehanna University prepares its graduates to achieve, lead and serve in a diverse and interconnected world. Graduates consistently say their Susquehanna experiences give them a competitive edge over other recent graduates entering the workplace. Susquehanna's new central curriculum includes GO (Global Opportunities). This distinctive program allows every student to have a cross-cultural experience away from campus, either in the United States or abroad. A cross-cultural experience is designed to take students out of their everyday environment. It might include a traditional semester study-abroad program (GO Long), a short-term faculty/staff-led program (GO Short), a self-designed experience proposed and accepted in advance, or service in a cross-cultural setting."

"With more than 50 majors and minors, students find a fine balance of liberal arts and professional studies, and state-of-the-art facilities to support intellectual and personal growth. The Sigmund Weis School of Business is accredited by the Association to Advance Collegiate Schools of Business (AACSB). A new "green" science facility opened in spring of 2010. As the largest academic building on campus, it will include 19 teaching and research labs, 30 prep and support spaces and a rooftop greenhouse."

"Susquehanna's success is demonstrated by its graduation rate—80 percent of its students graduate within four years, a rate cited among the top in the nation, and far above the national average. And 96 percent of Susquehanna's graduates have a job or are attending graduate school within six months of graduation."

For even more information on this school, turn to page 538 of the "Stats" section.

SWARTHMORE COLLEGE

500 COLLEGE AVENUE, SWARTHMORE, PA 19081 • ADMISSIONS: 610-328-8300 • FAX: 610-328-8580
FINANCIAL AID: 610-328-8358 • E-MAIL: ADMISSIONS@SWARTHMORE.EDU • WEBSITE: WWW.SWARTHMORE.EDU

RATINGS
Quality of Life: 89   **Academic:** 99   **Admissions:** 99   **Financial Aid:** 99

STUDENTS SAY "..."

Academics

Swarthmore College "has a lovely campus, the people are almost unbelievably friendly, it's a safe environment, and it's really, really challenging academically," and "although it's not one of the most well-known schools, those who do know of it also know of its wonderful reputation. It's where to go for a real education—for learning for the sake of truly learning, rather than just for grades." Students warn that "academics here are definitely stressful, especially when you

> **SURVEY SAYS . . .**
> *No one cheats*
> *Lab facilities are great*
> *School is well run*
> *Low cost of living*
> *Musical organizations are popular*
> *Political activism is popular*

sign up for extracurricular activities that take up some more time—and almost everyone here's involved in something outside of just classes, because you don't want to just go to class, study, and sleep every day here." As a result, "Swarthmore is truly challenging. It teaches its students tough lessons not only about classes but about life, and though it may be extremely, almost unbearably difficult sometimes, it's totally worth it." Undergrads also note that "there are tons of resources to help you—professors, academic mentors, writing associates (who are really helpful to talk to when you have major papers), residential assistants, psychological counseling, multicultural support groups, queer/trans support groups—basically, whenever you need help with something, there's someone you can talk to." Swatties also love how "Swarthmore is amazingly flexible. The requirements are very limited, allowing you to explore whatever you are interested in and change your mind millions of times about your major and career path. If they don't offer a major you want, you can design your own with ease."

Life

The Swarthmore community is "a family of students who are engaged in academics, learning, politics, activism, and civic responsibility, with a work-hard, play-hard, intense mentality, who don't get enough sleep because they're too busy doing all they want to do in their time here, and who (this is kind of cheesy, but true) when you really think about it are really just smart students who care about the world and want to make it better." There "is a misconception that Swarthmore students do nothing but study, [but] while we certainly do a lot of it, we still find many ways to have fun." Not so much in hometown Swarthmore—"there isn't a lot to do right in the area"—but "with a train station on campus, Philly is very accessible." Additionally, "there are so many organizations and clubs on campus that you'd be pressed to find none of the activities interesting. Even then, you can start your own club, so that takes care of it." The small size of the school means that "opportunities to participate in many different programs" are usually available. On-campus activities "are varied, and there is almost always something to do on the weekend. There are student musical performances, drama performances, movies, speakers, and comedy shows," as well as "several parties every weekend, with and without alcohol, and a lot of pre-partying with friends." One student sums up, "While it is tough to generalize on the life of a Swarthmore student, one word definitely applies to us all: busy. All of us are either working on extracurriculars, studying, or fighting sleep to do more work."

Student Body

Students are "not sure if there is a typical Swattie" but suspect that "the defining feature among us is that each person is brilliant at something: maybe dance, maybe quantum physics, maybe philosophy. Each person here has at least one thing that [he or she does] extraordinarily well." A Swattie "is [typically] liberal, involved in some kind of activism group or multicultural group, talks about classes all the time, was labeled a nerd by people in high school, and is really smart—one of those people where you just have to wonder, how do they get all their homework done and manage their extracurriculars and still have time for parties?" The campus "is very diverse racially but not in terms of thought—in other words, pretty much everyone's liberal, you don't get many different points of view. Multicultural and queer issues are big here, but you don't have to be involved in that to enjoy Swarthmore. You just have to accept it."

Admissions

Very important factors considered include: Class rank, application essay, academic GPA, recommendation(s), rigor of secondary school record, character/personal qualities. *Important factors considered include:* Standardized test scores, extracurricular activities. *Other factors considered include:* Alumni/ae relation, first generation, geographical residence, interview, level of applicant's interest, racial/ethnic status, talent/ability, volunteer work, work experience. Applicants are required to submit scores for any one of the three following testing scenarios: 1) SAT and any two SAT Subject tests; 2) the ACT with Writing; or 3) SAT and ACT (with or without writing). Prospective engineers are encouraged to take the Mathematics Level 2 Subject Test, regardless of whether they opt for the SAT or ACT. High school diploma or equivalent is not required. *Academic units recommended:* 4 English, 3 mathematics, 3 science,

Financial Aid

Students should submit: FAFSA, institution's own financial aid form, CSS/Financial Aid PROFILE, state aid form, noncustodial PROFILE, business/farm supplement. Federal Tax Return, W-2 Statements, Year-end paycheck stub. Regular filing deadline is 2/15. The Princeton Review suggests that all financial aid forms be submitted as soon as possible after January 1. *Need-based scholarships/grants offered:* Federal Pell, SEOG, state scholarships/grants, private scholarships, the school's own gift aid. *Loan aid offered:* Federal Perkins, state loans, college/university loans from institutional funds. Applicants will be notified of awards on or about 4/1. Federal Work-Study Program available. Institutional employment available. Off-campus job opportunities are good.

The Inside Word

Competition for admission to Swarthmore remains fierce, as the school consistently receives applications from top students across the country. Applicants should understand that Swarthmore receives more than enough applications from well-qualified students to fill its classrooms. At some point, perfectly good candidates get rejected simply because there's no more room. Admissions officers comb applications carefully for evidence of intellectually curious, highly motivated, and creative-minded candidates.

THE SCHOOL SAYS "..."

From The Admissions Office

"Swarthmore College, a highly selective college of liberal arts and engineering, celebrates the life of the mind. Since its founding in 1864, Swarthmore has given students of uncommon intellectual ability the knowledge, insight, skills, and experience to become leaders for the common good. The College is private, yet open to all regardless of financial need; American, yet decidedly global in outlook and diversity, drawing students from around the world and all 50 states. So much of what Swarthmore stands for, from its commitment to curricular breadth and rigor to its demonstrated interest in facilitating discovery and fostering ethical intelligence among exceptional young people, lies in the quality and passion of its faculty. A student/faculty ratio of 8:1 ensures that students have close, meaningful engagement with their professors, preparing them to translate the skills and understanding gained at Swarthmore into the mark they want to make on the world. The College's Honors program features small groups of dedicated and accomplished students working closely with faculty; an emphasis on independent learning; students entering into a dialogue with peers, teachers, and examiners; a demanding program of study in major and minor fields; and an examination at the end of two years' study by outside scholars. Located 11 miles southwest of Philadelphia, Swarthmore's idyllic, 357-acre campus is a designated arboretum, complete with rolling lawns, creek, wooded hills, and hiking trails."

For even more information on this school, turn to page 539 of the "Stats" section.

SYRACUSE UNIVERSITY

201 TOLLEY, ADMINISTRATION BUILDING, SYRACUSE, NY 13244 • ADMISSIONS: 315-443-3611
FINANCIAL AID: 315-443-1513 • E-MAIL: ORANGE@SYR.EDU • WEBSITE: WWW.SYRACUSE.EDU

RATINGS
Quality of Life: 67   **Academic:** 80   **Admissions:** 92   **Financial Aid:** 89

STUDENTS SAY ". . ."

Academics

Syracuse University "is cold weather, good academics, and amazing sports," one student sums up, and that about captures the prevailing sentiment among SU undergrads. Sure, Syracuse students recognize and appreciate the "top-quality education" they receive, but they typically frame it in the totality of Syracuse living, which includes not only "an

SURVEY SAYS . . .

Low cost of living
Everyone loves the Orange
Frats and sororities dominate social scene
Student publications are popular

excellent academic experience" but also athletics and extracurriculars that together create "the perfect balance of a great education and an amazing social atmosphere, [making] for an excellent college experience." The result is a student body fiercely proud of its school. "Syracuse bleeds Orange," students inform us. On the basis of academics alone, they'd have just cause. Opportunities abound: "If you take advantage of all the great resources available to all students, it's impossible not to have a great college experience," one student observes. Most do. Syracuse students "are, for the most part, very serious about their work and know what they want to do in life after college." The school provides lots of choices. Its Newhouse School of Public Communications is "as good as it gets for journalism schools," students tell us. They're nearly as bullish on the school's separate colleges for citizenship and public affairs, architecture, engineering and computer science, and management. No wonder one student brags that "I'm a magazine journalism major with a specialization in fashion and a minor in theater. The best part about Syracuse is that it offers hundreds of specific programs that allow you to learn by doing."

Life

"People are very committed to their work Monday through Thursday" at SU, but "as soon as Thursday classes are over, people will start to party." Greek life attracts nearly one-fifth of the student body. The frats throw "a lot of parties, which are crowded, hot, noisy, and run out of alcohol frequently," but they are hardly the only game in town. "Social life is very well-rounded and consists of bars, fraternities/sororities, house parties, and apartment parties," students report. The perception that "there's not much to do off campus in Syracuse" amplifies the importance of the party scene. Students note, however, "There are many other options for students who don't drink." "During the winter, basketball season is huge, and we have one of the best student sections in the country. The school also provides free shuttles on the weekend to Carousel Mall, the country's fourth-largest mall." There are "easily accessible gyms" located "nearby both ends of the campus," and the school is home to "amazing musical groups" ranging from a cappella ensembles to jazz bands, an orchestra, and rock bands. In addition, "The university provides ways of having fun on the weekends as well, such as free movie screenings in lecture halls or activities such as water rafting (with a fee, of course)."

Student Body

Your standard issue Syracuse male "wears khakis, Polo, and Patagonias," while his female counterpart "wears American Apparel zip-ups, solid-colored v-neck tees, skinny jeans and leggings, Uggs, a North Face jacket, and a brand-name handbag" and "is glued to her Blackberry." Syracuse is a big university, though, with plenty of room for diversity, so pretty much everyone finds a comfortable niche here. There's "a huge population of hipsters…woodsy folk, city kids, and pretty average everyday people all over. It depends on what social scene you spend your time in." Dig deep enough and you'll find "students of every race, religion, and political background you can think of. There is a strong Asian and international student population as well as a noticeable percentage of gay, lesbian, and bisexual [students]." While groups "have their own cliques," there "is no animosity or unspoken status quo between different sorts of people."

THE PRINCETON REVIEW SAYS

Admissions

Very important factors considered include: Class rank, application essay, academic GPA, recommendation(s), rigor of secondary school record, standardized test scores, character/personal qualities, extracurricular activities, interview, talent/ability. *Important factors considered include:* First generation, volunteer work, work experience. *Other factors considered include:* Alumni/ae relation, racial/ethnic status. SAT or ACT required; ACT with Writing component required. TOEFL required of all international applicants. High school diploma is required, and GED is accepted. *Academic units required:* 4 English, 4 mathematics, 4 science, (4 science labs), 3 foreign language, 4 social studies.

Financial Aid

Students should submit: FAFSA, CSS/Financial Aid. PROFILE, noncustodial PROFILE Regular filing deadline is 2/2. The Princeton Review suggests that all financial aid forms be submitted as soon as possible after January 1. *Need-based scholarships/grants offered:* Federal Pell, SEOG, state scholarships/grants, private scholarships, the school's own gift aid. *Loan aid offered:* Direct Subsidized Stafford, Direct Unsubsidized Stafford, Direct PLUS, Federal Perkins. Applicants will be notified of awards on or about 3/21. Federal Work-Study Program available. Institutional employment available. Off-campus job opportunities are good.

The Inside Word

Syracuse University is divided into nine colleges, and applicants apply to the college in which they are interested. Some colleges make specific requirements of applicants (e.g., a portfolio, or an audition in addition to SU's general admission requirements. Applicants are allowed to indicate a second or third choice program, so you may still gain admission even if you don't get into your first-choice program.

THE SCHOOL SAYS "…"

From The Admissions Office

"Syracuse University provides a dynamic learning environment with a focus on scholarship in action, in which excellence is connected to ideas, problems, and professions in the world. Students at SU focus on interactive, collaborative, and interdisciplinary learning while choosing their course of study from more than 200 options. About half of undergraduates study abroad. SU operates centers in Beijing, Florence, Hong Kong, London, Madrid, Santiago, and Strasbourg. New facilities continue to expand scholarship in action opportunities for students. The Newhouse 3 building houses various facilities for public communications students, including research centers, a high-tech convergence lab, and meeting rooms for student activities. The new Life Sciences Complex promotes interdisciplinary research and education, signaling a new era in scientific research.

"A distinction of the SU education is the breadth of opportunity combined with individualized attention. Average class size is less than 20 students. Only 3 percent of all classes have more than 100 students. Faculty members are experts in their field, who are dedicated to teaching while conducting research, writing, and experiments they can share with students to aid in the learning process.

"Outside of the classroom, students are encouraged to immerse themselves in organizations and take advantage of the opportunities available in the city of Syracuse. The University community collaborates with city residents, organizations, and businesses in such areas as the arts, entrepreneurship and economic development, and scientific research. The Connective Corridor, a 3 mile pedestrian pathway and shuttle bus circuit, links SU and downtown Syracuse's arts institutions, entertainment venues, and public spaces."

For even more information on this school, turn to page 539 of the "Stats" section.

TEMPLE UNIVERSITY

1801 NORTH BROAD STREET, PHILADELPHIA, PA 19122-6096 • ADMISSIONS: 215-204-7200
FAX: 215-204-5694 • FINANCIAL AID: 215-204-8760 • E-MAIL: TUADM@MAIL.TEMPLE.EDU • WEBSITE: WWW.TEMPLE.EDU

RATINGS
Quality of Life: 74   Academic: 73   Admissions: 84   Financial Aid: 77

STUDENTS SAY ". . ."

Academics

Temple University is "a large school" that "makes you feel at home in the city of Philadelphia" and offers "rigorous academic classes and many outside activities." This "wonderful" school is "located right in the city," and students praise the campus as being "one of the most diverse in the country." "Temple University is a place where everyone fits

> **SURVEY SAYS . . .**
> *Great computer facilities*
> *Diverse student types on campus*
> *Low cost of living*
> *Very little drug use*

in and walks away with a little more knowledge than they had the day before," says one undergrad. This diversity also extends to classes. There's a "wide variety of classes" and "lots of awesome majors," all of which are supported by a "helpful and passionate set of professors who learn right along with students." There's also the "top-notch" honors program, which is a "favorite part of Temple by far," explains one student. "It's an outstanding program, and I feel very fortunate to be a part of it." Most here agree their academic experience has been "amazing." In the words of one undergrad, "Temple's standard of access and excellence is evident in its students' success." The "knowledgeable" professors "really want to see students succeed." While some feel that the administration "doesn't always run so smoothly," noting that "Temple is pretty much a small city, and it often runs like a bureaucracy," overall, students agree that administrators are "accessible at any time" and are "helpful when you need them."

Life

As you'd expect from a big school in a big city, "Temple has something for everyone." Whether you're looking for "city life," "friendly people," or "a million and one clubs or groups to join," you'll find it here at Temple. "There are tons of things to do," says one student. "If students get bored on campus, they were probably boring to begin with." Life on campus is "very interconnected," and "there's usually always something going on" thanks to "student organizations that appeal to every interest and social group." Most students keep busy during by "studying," "going to the gym," and "playing intramural sports," but even if nothing is happening on campus, "there's much to do in the city." Not surprisingly, Philadelphia plays a substantial part in students' social lives. "There are amazing bars in the city," says one undergrad. "The only nights that students do not go out for drinks are Sunday and Monday." That said, if imbibing isn't your cup of tea, not to worry—there's plenty more on offer than watering holes. "You can have tons of fun on campus without drinking," explains a student. "There are lots of fun things to do because of our close proximity to Center City Philadelphia." Some examples are "great clubs, shopping, hookah bars, and restaurants." Also, if you get tired of Temple's campus you can always check out another—"Drexel, LaSalle, and UPenn's campuses are close by."

Student Body

Diversity isn't just a word at Temple; it's a fact. "At Temple, the atypical students are the typical students," explains an undergrad. "The majority population is made up of ethnic minorities." The student body here is made up of "many different kinds of ethnicities, sexual orientations, and economic and political stances," all of whom "contribute to the overall sense of school spirit and pride." Students agree that everyone here is "unique," and that makes for a place where "everyone becomes comfortable with each other's differences." "Every student brings their own light to Temple, which is what makes the school shine so bright," says one student. Despite this "huge mixture of types," students here do share similarities, particularly in their "motivation" to do well. Students here fill their time with "studying" and "extracurricular activities," all while also "experiencing life in the city of Philadelphia." One thing that all students agree on is that "The typical student at Temple University is approachable and greatly accepts diversity." As one undergrad says, "Everyone just kind of fits in, which is why the students like Temple so much."

Admissions

Very important factors considered include: Academic GPA, rigor of secondary school record. *Important factors considered include:* Class rank, standardized test scores. *Other factors considered include:* Application essay, recommendation(s), alumni/ae relation, character/personal qualities, extracurricular activities, talent/ability, volunteer work, work experience. SAT or ACT required; ACT with Writing component required. TOEFL required of all international applicants. High school diploma is required, and GED is accepted. *Academic units required:* 4 English, 3 mathematics, 2 science, (1 science labs), 2 foreign language, 2 social studies, 1 history, 1 academic electives. *Academic units recommended:* 4 English, 4 mathematics, 3 science, (2 science labs), 2 foreign language, 2 social studies, 2 history, 3 academic electives,

Financial Aid

Students should submit: FAFSA. The Princeton Review suggests that all financial aid forms be submitted as soon as possible after January 1. *Need-based scholarships/grants offered:* Federal Pell, SEOG, state scholarships/grants, private scholarships, the school's own gift aid, Federal Nursing Scholarships. *Loan aid offered:* Federal Perkins, Federal Nursing, state loans, college/university loans from institutional funds. Applicants will be notified of awards on a rolling basis beginning 2/15. Federal Work-Study Program available. Institutional employment available. Off-campus job opportunities are excellent.

The Inside Word

Temple is a well-recognized name in higher education, and its location is one of the nation's most popular cities. Competition can be steep when it comes to admissions, particularly if you aren't a resident of Pennsylvania. Admissions officers are fairly objective about their approach to application assessment in that they focus primarily on the solid numbers: class rank, GPA, and standardized test scores. That said, keep in mind that there are no minimum requirements, so if you have skills and talents that can't be mathematically calculated, it would behoove you to point them out in your application.

THE SCHOOL SAYS "…"

From The Admissions Office

"Temple combines the academic resources and intellectual stimulation of a large research university with the intimacy of a small college. The university experienced record growth in attracting new students from all 50 states and more than 125 countries. Students choose from 134 undergraduate majors. Special academic programs include honors, learning communities for first-year undergraduates, co-op education, and study abroad. Temple has 7 regional campuses, including Main Campus and the Health Sciences Center in historic Philadelphia, suburban Temple University, Ambler, and overseas campuses in Tokyo and Rome. Main Campus is home to Alter Hall for the Fox School of Business, and the Tyler School of Art, both state-of-the-art facilities that opened in 2009. Our TECH Center has more than 600 computer workstations, 100 laptops, and a Starbucks. The Liacouras Center is a modern entertainment, recreation, and sports complex that hosts concerts, plays, trade shows, and college and professional athletics. It also includes the Independence Blue Cross Student Recreation Center, a major fitness facility for students now and in the future. Students can also take advantage of our Student Fieldhouse. The university is currently constructing a new residence hall, built to meet an unprecedented demand for main campus housing.

"Applicants are required to take the SAT (or the ACT with Writing). The best Critical Reading, Math and Writing scores from either test will be considered."

For even more information on this school, turn to page 540 of the "Stats" section.

TOWSON UNIVERSITY

8000 YORK ROAD, TOWSON, MD 21252-0001 • ADMISSIONS: 1-888-4TOWSON • FAX: 410-704-3030
E-MAIL: ADMISSIONS@TOWSON.EDU • WEBSITE: WWW.TOWSON.EDU/DISCOVER

RATINGS
Quality of Life: 77   **Academic:** 67   **Admissions:** 80   **Financial Aid:** 69

STUDENTS SAY ". . ."

Academics

Located only a stone's throw from Baltimore, Towson University offers "the perfect balance" between "academic and social life" with "tons of events on weekends and classes that you actually look forward to during the week." Indeed, students report classes are "interesting" and "challenging," which allows students "the opportunity to achieve academically in order to be successful both in the classroom and in the real world." "My experience at Towson has allowed me to expand my ideas and my mind," says one undergrad. "Friendly, insightful," and "resourceful" professors "want students to succeed." Another student says, they're "very easy to get in touch with" outside of class and "are open to answer[ing] any questions." Most students report their dealings with the administration have been "positive." "Whenever I have a question for them," says one student, "I receive an answer as soon as I call a particular office." That said, there are some concerns about housing. "They can't give on-campus housing to most students because (even though they are building more housing/parking), they keep accepting more and more students....You have to get to campus before 8 A.M. if you want a good space." When it comes to registration, students report "trouble signing up for their classes." This seems especially true for freshmen. "The classes fill up too quickly...Sometimes all the classes for a subject are gone by the time the freshmen enroll." However, most agree overall, being at Towson pays off. As one student explains, "I have found that if you work hard and are respectful here, you will be successful."

Life

Students praise Towson's location. "It's less than a mile from restaurants, movie theaters, bars, shops, etc.," says one student, "and about five miles from downtown Baltimore." Baltimore figures prominently in students' social lives. In addition, "the city of Towson is also a lot of fun." Keep in mind though, Towson students lead "very busy" lives thanks to "large work loads," meaning they're in classes "all day" and "studying at night." However, once Thursday rolls around students "start celebrating." For some, this might mean traveling "back home if they live close" (Towson does have a strong number of "commuters"). For others, this means everything from "partying" to "sports" to "frats and sororities." There's "plenty" to do without leaving the "beautiful" campus, including "Friday Night Live (a concert/lecture series)," "more than 200 student groups," and a gym with "a great rock climbing wall."

Student Body

What's the typical Towson student like in a word? According to nearly everyone here, it's "diverse." Though "There's a lot of Greek life," and "many students exemplify that stereotype," most students here struggle to describe any traits they share with their peers other than being "very social, outgoing, and committed to learning." "There are many different ethnicities, religious beliefs, and interests in the student body," says one undergrad. Or, more simply put, "Towson is so diverse that we cannot stereotype the students at Towson." This diversity is surely enhanced by the sizeable "international student" population, "particularly in the business college." The "good thing" about Towson is "no matter who you are or what your background there is a niche for you." Students here get involved in everything from campus organizations to "Greek life" to "ad hoc groups." And if you there isn't something that immediately suits your tastes, you and your pals can "start a new group."

Admissions

Very important factors considered include: Academic GPA. *Important factors considered include:* Rigor of secondary school record, standardized test scores. *Other factors considered include:* Class rank, application essay, recommendation(s), first generation, talent/ability. SAT or ACT required; ACT with Writing component required. TOEFL required of all international applicants. High school diploma is required and GED is accepted. *Academic units required:* 4 English, 3 mathematics, 3 science, (2 science labs), 2 foreign language, 3 social studies, 6 academic electives.

Financial Aid

Students should submit: FAFSA. The Princeton Review suggests that all financial aid forms be submitted as soon as possible after January 1. *Need-based scholarships/grants offered:* Federal Pell, SEOG, state scholarships/grants, private scholarships, the school's own gift aid. *Loan aid offered:* Direct Subsidized Stafford, Direct Unsubsidized Stafford, Direct PLUS, Federal Perkins. Applicants will be notified of awards on a rolling basis beginning 3/21. Federal Work-Study Program available. Institutional employment available. Off-campus job opportunities are excellent.

The Inside Word

With more than 17,000 undergraduates, there's no hyperbole involved when we say that Towson's big, so it's fair to expect the application process to be by the book. With this in mind, know grades will be the primary factor in admission, along with standardized test scores. At last count, the school admits, on average, just more than 60 percent of applicants, meaning that if you've got the grades you've got more than a good chance. But keep in mind that as the school's profile rises, so will its applicant pool.

THE SCHOOL SAYS " . . . "

From The Admissions Office

"Towson University is one of the most dynamic college communities in the country, offering academic programs that provide a solid liberal arts foundation and preparation for jobs and graduate school. Founded in 1866, Towson University today is nationally recognized for programs in the arts, sciences, business, communications, health professions, and education and computer science. *U.S. News & World Report* names Towson as one of the best regional public universities in the United States. Students choose from more than 60 undergraduate majors and 37 graduate programs. Towson offers a student-centered learning environment with big-school choices and small-school personal attention. We encourage students to pursue learning inside and outside the classroom—through internships, student organizations, extracurricular activities, and research projects with faculty.

"An NCAA Division I program, Towson fields intercollegiate athletic teams in 19 sports. Our 24-acre sports complex includes Johnny Unitas University Stadium, home of Tiger football, field hockey, track, and lacrosse. The Tiger basketball, volleyball, and gymnastics teams compete at the 5,000-seat Towson Center. Athletic and recreation facilities include an NCAA-regulation swimming pool, gymnasiums, a sand volleyball court, tennis courts, a fitness center, a climbing wall, and racquetball and squash courts.

"A member of the University System of Maryland, we enroll more than 21,000 students on our 328-acre campus located just eight miles north of downtown Baltimore. Local attractions include the National Aquarium, Oriole Park at Camden Yards, the Maryland Science Center, the Walters Art Museum, and historic Fells Point. The campus is a 10-minute walk to suburban shops, restaurants, movie theaters, and bookstores."

For even more information on this school, turn to page 540 of the "Stats" section.

TRINITY COLLEGE (CT)

300 Summit Street, Hartford, CT 06016 • Admissions: 860-297-2180 • Fax: 860-297-2287
Financial Aid: 860-297-2046 • E-mail: admissions.office@trincoll.edu • Website: www.trincoll.edu

RATINGS
Quality of Life: 62   Academic: 93   Admissions: 95   Financial Aid: 98

STUDENTS SAY "..."

Academics

"[It's all] about getting a top-notch education in small classes with professors who know you and being able to also have a good time outside of class" at Trinity College, a small and prestigious liberal arts school located in Connecticut's state capital. A "great political science department" exploits TC's location "about two blocks away from the state capitol, which is great for internships." Other social sciences, including economics and history, earn students' praises, as do offerings in engineering and education. Strength across the liberal arts bolsters the

school's Guided Studies Program, in which students undertake a fixed curriculum of interdisciplinary study to survey the entirety of Western civilization from the classical age to the present. In all disciplines, "small classes, very involved professors, and a very conscious student body" combine to provide "an excellent liberal arts education that will provide [students] with the skills to be thoughtful, independent adults." Professors "are always available to talk and offer help to students. They often invite students out to lunch." Likewise, administrators are easy to access. "Even the president of the school, James F. Jones, is accessible. He goes on the Quest Orientation hiking trip for first-year students and regularly attends various student events on campus." Students also appreciate that "the career services office is amazing" here.

Life

"The fraternity scene is the draw for the majority of campus" at Trinity College, where "On a typical weekend night, people go out to dinner, go back to their room and nap, get ready for the evening, and go meet up with a friend or two where they chill out and then go to someone's room for pre-gaming...Then when it's about 1 A.M. they go out and do some frat hopping. It's great for people who like their life to be predictable." The frats are hardly the only option, though; in fact, "There are a ton of underappreciated options on or near campus. Hartford has amazing restaurants, there are movie theaters and bowling alleys nearby, the Cinestudio is a 90-second walk from the main dining hall, and there are two dorms on campus devoted specifically to alcohol-free activities. Plus, plenty of student groups hold events" in such places as "the arts and cultural houses." Trinity's theater and dance department offer regular performances. Hometown Hartford "may be [an economically] depressed city, but it is still a city, and it affords benefits that tiny college towns just can't match."

Student Body

The stereotype about Trinity undergrads is that "most...are from the tri-state area and appear to have just stepped off a yacht or out of a country club," and students confirm that while "there are a lot of students who are not" in this crowd, the preppy contingent is "the main group" and "socially dominant" here. "There are definitely some very preppy girls and boys—blond hair, sunglasses, Chanel flats, a polo," one student concedes before adding that "sometimes people identify these students as typical Trinity students; however there are many students who are not like that at all." All students tend to be "well-rounded" and "very passionate," "intelligent but also social," with "good verbal skills." They "care deeply about their work and really like to have fun when they can," and while many gravitate to the Greek community for their fun, "There are [also] communities here for those who do not enjoy the frat scene, for people who are passionate about music and acting, and [for] those who want to spend their weekends giving back to the community."

Admissions

Very important factors considered include: Rigor of secondary school record. *Important factors considered include:* Class rank, application essay, academic GPA, recommendation(s), standardized test scores, character/personal qualities, extracurricular activities, interview, racial/ethnic status, talent/ability. *Other factors considered include:* Alumni/ae relation, first generation, geographical residence, level of applicant's interest, volunteer work, work experience. SAT or ACT required; ACT with Writing component recommended. High school diploma is required, and GED is accepted. *Academic units required:* 4 English, 3 mathematics, 2 science, (2 science labs), 3 foreign language, 2 history.

Financial Aid

Students should submit: FAFSA, CSS/Financial Aid PROFILE, noncustodial PROFILE, business/farm supplement. Federal Income tax returns. Regular filing deadline is 3/1. The Princeton Review suggests that all financial aid forms be submitted as soon as possible after January 1. *Need-based scholarships/grants offered:* Federal Pell, SEOG, state scholarships/grants, private scholarships, the school's own gift aid. *Loan aid offered:* Direct Subsidized Stafford, Direct Unsubsidized Stafford, Direct PLUS, Federal Perkins, college/university loans from institutional funds. Applicants will be notified of awards on or about 4/1. Federal Work-Study Program available. Institutional employment available. Off-campus job opportunities are good.

The Inside Word

Students describe Trinity as "the home of Yale rejects," an appraisal that accurately, if somewhat hyperbolically, characterizes the school's reputation as an Ivy safety. The hefty tuition and fees here ensure that a large percentage of the student body is made up of wealthy, preppy types, but the school does offer generous financial aid packages to top candidates who can't afford the considerable price of attending. The school would love to broaden its demographic, so competitive minority students should receive a very welcome reception here.

THE SCHOOL SAYS "..."

From The Admissions Office

"An array of distinctive curricular options—including an interdisciplinary neuroscience major and a professionally accredited engineering degree program, a unique Human Rights Program, a Health Fellows Program, and interdisciplinary programs such as the Cities Program, Interdisciplinary Science Program, and InterArts—is one reason record numbers of students are applying to Trinity. In fact, applications are up 80 percent over the past 5 years. In addition, the college has been recognized for its commitment to diversity; students of color have represented approximately 20 percent of the freshman class for the past 4 years, setting Trinity apart from many of its peers. Trinity's capital city location offers students unparalleled 'real-world' learning experiences to complement classroom learning. Students take advantage of extensive opportunities for internships for academic credit and community service, and these opportunities extend to Trinity's global learning sites in cities around the world. Trinity's faculty is a devoted and accomplished group of exceptional teacher-scholars; our 100-acre campus is beautiful; Hartford is an educational asset that differentiates Trinity from other liberal arts colleges; our global connections and foreign study opportunities prepare students to be good citizens of the world; and our graduates go on to excel in virtually every field. We invite you to learn more about why Trinity might be the best choice for you.

"Students applying for admission may submit the following testing options: SAT, ACT with Writing."

For even more information on this school, turn to page 541 of the "Stats" section.

TUFTS UNIVERSITY

BENDETSON HALL, MEDFORD, MA 02155 • ADMISSIONS: 617-627-3170 • FAX: 617-627-3860
FINANCIAL AID: 617-627-3528 • E-MAIL: ADMISSIONS.INQUIRY@ASE.TUFTS.EDU • WEBSITE: WWW.TUFTS.EDU

RATINGS
Quality of Life: 93   Academic: 94   Admissions: 98   Financial Aid: 95

STUDENTS SAY "..."

Academics

"Mid-sized" and "very internationally-focused," Tufts University boasts "an incredible blend of academics, extracurriculars, and athletics, and really emphasizes the impact an individual can have on his or her community." Tufts is probably best known for its world-class science programs (especially premed) and its prestigious international relations programs. Full-year and semester-long study abroad

options in places such as Chile, Ghana, and Oxford are so amazing that almost half the students here participate before heading off into the real world. Back on campus, students have a lot of latitude in their studies: "They do internships; they devise their own research projects; they assist professors on their work." Most faculty members are "brilliant," "dedicated to students," and "extremely accessible and friendly." A few, however, are "out of touch with reality." Classes, especially at the lower levels, can be "bigger than you think they'll be." The academic atmosphere is tough overall but it really varies by department. "Some classes are disproportionately easy, while others are disproportionately hard." "If you're premed, life is going to be miserable," warns a biomedical engineering major. "If you're an English or psych major, there are great professors in those departments and the majors are cake." "[In] some classes, you're forced to learn a lot," adds a computer science major. "[In others] you need to do a lot of the learning yourself." The administration at Tufts is "always there when you want them," but is otherwise "neither awful nor particularly noteworthy." "Some things could be smoother, but that is true almost everywhere."

Life

This "beautiful" campus offers a "great view of Boston" but some of the facilities "are not outstanding." Dorms in particular "can be a little gross." "Rooms are on the small side and the common areas are really subpar." Social life at Tufts can be "as big or small" as you want it to be. "Everyone loves to meet up in the dining halls and socialize," and "There is always so much going on around campus." "Fantastic extracurricular opportunities" proliferate. "Everyone is involved in something." "I ride on the equestrian team and I'm a member of the classics and archaeology club," declares a sophomore. Tufts also "holds a few social events each semester that most of the student body attends, which is a lot of fun." Students tend to "work hard" and stay "very focused on studying" during the week. They also "love to be ridiculous" on weekends. While "non-drinkers and moderate drinkers will be comfortable here," "alcoholic partygoers" will be happy, too. "There's kind of an expectation during freshman year that you go to fraternities on the weekend and get drunk." Older students "tend to be a little choosier and will have more exclusive off-campus gatherings, or go to the bars." "Going into Boston is always really fun" as well. Beantown is "a city full of opportunity and entertainment." Tufts runs a shuttle to public transportation in Somerville.

Student Body

Tufts is "an extremely liberal school" with a noticeably "politically correct" vibe. Some students tell us that this campus is a paradise of "cosmopolitanism and ethnic tolerance." Others tell us it's mostly "really rich" "white kids trying to make a difference in the world." "There is much less diversity than the administration touts," reports a senior, "especially socioeconomic diversity." Students at Tufts range from "preppy North Face and Ugg wearers to hipsters" to "self-aware dorky" types. "There are a lot of nerdy kids but it's great for them because they come here and find each other." "There are also a lot of international kids, which is great." Tufts students describe themselves as "generally very hard-working," "intellectually stimulating people." They are also "very real and unpretentious" and "very eclectic." "To be eccentrically passionate about something is absolutely necessary" here. "Some people are a little strange, but Tufts is known for that." "I have never met an un-quirky person associated with Tufts," swears a senior.

THE PRINCETON REVIEW SAYS

Admissions

Very important factors considered include: Application essay, academic GPA, rigor of secondary school record, character/personal qualities. *Important factors considered include:* Class rank, recommendation(s), standardized test scores, extracurricular activities, talent/ability, volunteer work, work experience. *Other factors considered include:* Alumni/ae relation, first generation, geographical residence, interview, racial/ethnic status, SAT and SAT Subject Tests or ACT required; ACT with Writing component required. TOEFL required of all international applicants. High school diploma is required, and GED is accepted. *Academic units recommended:* 4 English, 4 mathematics, 4 science, 4 foreign language, 4 social studies, 4 history.

Financial Aid

Students should submit: FAFSA, CSS/Financial Aid PROFILE, noncustodial PROFILE, parent and student Federal Income Tax Returns. Regular filing deadline is 2/15. The Princeton Review suggests that all financial aid forms be submitted as soon as possible after January 1. *Need-based scholarships/grants offered:* Federal Pell, SEOG, state scholarships/grants, the school's own gift aid. *Loan aid offered:* Direct Subsidized Stafford, Direct Unsubsidized Stafford, Federal Perkins, college/university loans from institutional funds. Applicants will be notified of awards on or about 4/1. Federal Work-Study Program available. Institutional employment available. Off-campus job opportunities are good.

The Inside Word

The admissions process is rigorous. Tufts rejects a little less than 75 percent of its applicants. You'll need to demonstrate fairly exceptional academic accomplishments and submit a thorough and well-prepared application in order to get admitted. On the bright side, Tufts is still a little bit of a safety school for aspiring Ivy Leaguers. Since many applicants will also get into an Ivy League school and will likely pass on Tufts, it has spots for "mere mortals" at the end of the day.

THE SCHOOL SAYS "..."

From The Admissions Office

"Tufts University, on the boundary between Medford and Somerville, sits on a hill overlooking Boston, five miles northwest of the city. The campus is a tranquil New England setting within easy access by subway and bus to the cultural, social, and entertainment resources of Boston and Somerville. Since its founding in 1852 by members of the Universalist church, Tufts has grown from a small liberal arts college into a nonsectarian university of more than 10,000 students with undergraduate programs in arts & sciences and engineering. By 1900 the college had added a medical school, a dental school, and graduate studies. The university now also includes the Fletcher School of Law and Diplomacy, the Graduate School of Arts & Sciences, the Cummings School of Veterinary Medicine, the Friedman School of Nutrition Science and Policy, the Sackler School of Graduate Biomedical Sciences, and the Gordon Institute of Engineering Management.

"Applicants are required to submit scores (including the Writing assessment) from either the SAT or ACT. If an applicant submits the SAT, SAT Subject Tests are also required (candidates for the School of Engineering are encouraged to submit math and either chemistry or physics)."

For even more information on this school, turn to page 541 of the "Stats" section.

UNION COLLEGE (NY)

GRANT HALL, SCHENECTADY, NY 12308 • ADMISSIONS: 518-388-6112 • FAX: 518-388-6986
FINANCIAL AID: 518-388-6123 • E-MAIL: ADMISSIONS@UNION.EDU • WEBSITE: WWW.UNION.EDU

RATINGS
Quality of Life: 74   Academic: 86   Admissions: Financial Aid: 60

STUDENTS SAY "..."

Academics

At Union College, challenging academic programs, friendly
faculty, and diverse co-curricular experiences are all rolled up
into one pretty little campus in upstate New York. Union "is
small in size, yet prestigious in nearly every major it offers,"

> SURVEY SAYS . . .
> *Low cost of living*
> *Frats and sororities dominate social scene*

making it a good choice for students interested in anything from the arts to engineering—or both! Here, "students
are encouraged to follow their passions and pursue all areas of interest." A current student chimes in, "As an engineering major, I am able to take courses that I would not normally take at a technical school, making the 'gen eds'
[general education requirements] and electives enjoyable." In addition to diverse courses, "Union has fantastic
research opportunities for undergraduate students (especially in the sciences)," and more than half the campus pursues studies or volunteer work overseas. Internships are also popular, and "Union has an awesome career center
that is always reaching out to students to help them with life after college." Across disciplines, "Professors are wonderful, extremely qualified, compassionate, and interested in their students." Teaching is taken seriously, and "All
of the professors do everything possible to engage their students and get discussions going." Relationships between
students and faculty often extend beyond the classroom, and "Professors can often be seen sitting with students at
lunch, literally bringing the classroom discussion into the lunchroom." You must be prepared to work at Union, as
academic standards are high. Fortunately, most students feel "the workload is very manageable as long as you don't
fall behind," not to mention "the rewards that come of those challenges make all the effort completely worthwhile."
As a small private school, all of this doesn't come cheap, but "Union College is very generous with its financial aid
and scholarship money" for qualified students.

Life

There are just 2,000 undergraduates at Union College, yet "there are always a million things to do" on the Union
campus. During the week, "the homework load is pretty heavy," but come the weekend, Union students "like to
go to a few off-campus bars on Wednesday nights and Thursday nights," while "Friday and Saturday are dominated by Greek life." For an alternative to parties, "Student activities and Minerva houses provide many non-
alcohol[ic] events," including concerts and speakers. Union students can also be found going to "campus movie
[screenings], going to [hear] a speaker, [attending] a hockey game, running around campus...going downtown
for a bite to eat." School spirit is healthy, and "In the winter, our [Division I] hockey team's home games are the
place to be." Hometown Schenectady draws few praises, and students would like to see the school promote
"more involvement in the local community." For a break from campus life, "Some of the clubs on campus also
organize ski trips or trips out of town such as to Montreal and New York City."

Student Body

On Union's small campus, "Students are always moving, always involved, always engaged," and most participate in "at least three organizations or clubs" on campus. Bright and motivated, students "are able to easily manage personal and professional time," and the typical student manages to "get great grades while volunteering
and balancing a busy schedule." Located in upstate New York, this school draws a lot of students from the
Northeast, and "the typical student is Caucasian, middle to upper-class, [and] from a private school or highly
regarded public school." However, the student population is evolving, and "The college is clearly becoming more
diverse, with more international and underrepresented student populations increasing by the year." Socially,
"everyone seems to find their niche." In addition to the visible preppy contingent, "There is also a pretty strong
indie scene that tends to be more involved in environmental awareness, community service, and the arts." In
addition, "There are a lot of athletes."

Admissions

Very important factors considered include: Class rank, academic GPA, rigor of secondary school record. *Important factors considered include:* Recommendation(s), standardized test scores, character/personal qualities, extracurricular activities, talent/ability. *Other factors considered include:* Application essay, alumni/ae relation, first generation, geographical residence, interview, level of applicant's interest, racial/ethnic status, state residency, volunteer work, work experience. TOEFL required of all international applicants. High school diploma is required, and GED is not accepted. *Academic units required:* 4 English, 3 mathematics, 2 science, (2 science labs), 2 foreign language, 1 social studies, 1 history. *Academic units recommended:* 4 English, 4 mathematics, 4 science, (4 science labs), 4 foreign language, 2 social studies, 2 history.

Financial Aid

Students should submit: FAFSA, CSS/Financial Aid PROFILE, state aid form, noncustodial PROFILE, business/farm supplement. Regular filing deadline is 2/1. The Princeton Review suggests that all financial aid forms be submitted as soon as possible after January 1. *Need-based scholarships/grants offered:* Federal Pell, SEOG, state scholarships/grants, private scholarships, the school's own gift aid. *Loan aid offered:* Direct Subsidized Stafford, Direct Unsubsidized Stafford, Direct PLUS, Federal Perkins, college/university loans from institutional funds. Federal Work-Study Program available. Institutional employment available. Off-campus job opportunities are good.

The Inside Word

Union College is an SAT-optional college. Students may simply indicate on their application if they would like the admissions committee to consider their test scores or not. However, applicants to the Leadership in Medicine Program (an eight-year M.D./M.B.A. program with Albany Medical College) and to the Law and Public Policy program (a combined B.A. and J.D.) must submit test scores for consideration. For students who know that Union is their first choice, the school offers two early-decision deadlines.

THE SCHOOL SAYS "..."

From The Admissions Office

"The Union academic program is characterized by breadth and flexibility across a range of disciplines and interdisciplinary programs in the liberal arts and engineering. With nearly 1,000 courses to choose from, Union students may major in a single field, combine work in two or more departments or create their own organizing-theme major. Opportunities for undergraduate research are robust and give students a chance to work closely with professors year-round, take part in professional-level conferences and use sophisticated scientific equipment. More than half of Union's students take advantage of the college's extensive international study program, with new opportunities created regularly. A rich array of service learning programs and strong athletic, cultural and social activities also enhance the overall Union experience. Union's seven student-run Minerva Houses are lively hubs for intellectual and social activities. They bring together students, faculty and staff for hundreds of events, from dinners with invited speakers, lectures, and live bands to trips to local attractions.

"The Union community welcomes talented and diverse students, and we work closely with each one to help identify and cultivate their passions. Admission to the College is based on excellent academic credentials as reflected in the high school transcript, quality of courses selected, teacher and counselor recommendations, personal essays and writing samples. Personal interviews are strongly recommended. All candidates who apply to Union receive a thorough and thoughtful review of their application. Submission of SAT and ACT scores is optional except for the law and medicine programs."

For even more information on this school, turn to page 541 of the "Stats" section.

UNITED STATES COAST GUARD ACADEMY

31 MOHEGAN AVENUE, NEW LONDON, CT 06320-8103 • ADMISSIONS: 800-883-8724 • FAX: 860-701-6700
E-MAIL: ADMISSIONS@CGA.USCG.MIL • WEBSITE: WWW.CGA.EDU

RATINGS
Quality of Life: 64   **Academic:** 88   **Admissions:** 95   **Financial Aid:** 60

STUDENTS SAY "..."

Academics

If you're ready to "deal with military rules and discipline along with a rigorous engineering education" so that "in four years you get the job you've always wanted" (provided that job involves military, maritime, or multi-mission humanitarian service), the United States Coast Guard Academy may be the place for you. "Rigorous academics and military training" prepare cadets "for success as junior officers in the [Coast Guard] as ship drivers, pilots, and marine safety officers." The workload is considerable. Students must take a minimum of 19 credits per semester while also handling military training and athletics. Cadets note that this regimen "builds character through intense physical and mental training," although some opine that "It's like a cup of boiling hot chocolate: It smells good, you know it tastes good, but you have wait a long time to let it cool down in order to enjoy it fully." Others simply say that the demands make USCGA "a great place to be from but not always the greatest place to be." The school offers eight majors, most heavily in science, technology, engineering, and math, including operations research, management, and government. In all disciplines, "The academic program is extremely difficult, but most instructors are willing to work with you one-on-one if necessary."

> **SURVEY SAYS . . .**
> *No one cheats*
> *Career services are great*
> *Campus feels safe*
> *Everyone loves the Bears*
> *Intramural sports are popular*
> *Frats and sororities are unpopular or nonexistent*
> *Political activism is unpopular or nonexistent*
> *Very little drug use*

Life

Life at USCGA, unsurprisingly, is highly regimented. One student sums it up: "We have to wake up at 0600 every day whether we have class or not. We have to have our doors open whether we're in our rooms or not from 0600 to 1600. They tell us exactly what we can and can't do and what we can wear and what we can't. We have military training period from 0700 to 0800 and class from 0800 to1600. We all eat lunch together at the same time in a family-style fashion. Sports period is from 1600 to 1800. Military training periods from 1900 to 2000. Study hour-from 2000 to 2200. We all have to stand duty and play sports and get a certain number of community-service hours. We can't drink on base, and we can't leave during the week. We have to make our own fun, which involves some creativity sometimes (and demerits), but our fun wouldn't appeal to most college students because it's silly and doesn't involve alcohol." Cadets warn that "The school can be very rigid with the rules. It hurts to see one of your friends get kicked out after having made a stupid decision, as almost all college students do," but students recognize that "that goes with the territory of being a military institution." Students "can only leave campus on the weekends." When they do "there is a bus system that takes cadets to familiar places in the New London area" as well as "a nearby Amtrak station that takes cadets to New York City or Boston when cadets are allowed to leave the Academy for an extended period of time (rare), usually holiday weekends."

Student Body

Service academies tend to attract students from particular demographics, and the USCGA is no exception. Most here are "fairly conservative," "extremely athletic," "very smart," and "were leaders of their schools while in high school." They tend to be "type-A personalities" who are "very disciplined or looking for discipline" in their lives. Students tell us that "although there are exceptions, almost everyone here is very selfless, and willing to take one for the team or to sacrifice to help out a buddy. As the saying goes, 'Ship, shipmates, self.' Along those same lines, everyone is held to a high standard by both comrades and superiors. Both have a low tolerance for slacking."

Admissions

Very important factors considered include: Class rank, academic GPA, rigor of secondary school record, standardized test scores, character/personal qualities, extracurricular activities. *Important factors considered include:* Application essay, recommendation(s), talent/ability. *Other factors considered include:* Alumni/ae relation, interview, level of applicant's interest, volunteer work, work experience. SAT or ACT required; ACT with Writing component required. TOEFL required of all international applicants. High school diploma is required, and GED is accepted. *Academic units required:* 4 English, 4 mathematics, 3 science, (3 science labs).

Financial Aid

Tuition, room, board, medical and dental care are paid by the U.S. Government. Each cadet receives a monthly salary to pay for uniforms, supplies and personal expenses. A government loan is advanced to each member of the freshman class.

The Inside Word

Though USCGA has a low level of public recognition, gaining admission is still a steep uphill climb. Candidates must go through the rigorous multi-step admissions process as do their other service-academy peers (although no congressional nomination is required) and will encounter a serious roadblock if they fall short on any step. Those who pass muster join a proud, if somewhat under-recognized, student body, virtually equal in accomplishment to those at other service academies.

THE SCHOOL SAYS "..."

From The Admissions Office

"Founded in 1876, the United States Coast Guard Academy enjoys a proud tradition of graduating leaders of character. The academy experience melds academic rigor, leadership development, and athletic participation to prepare you to graduate as a commissioned officer. Character development of cadets is founded on the core values of honor, respect, and devotion to duty. You build friendships that last a lifetime, study with inspiring professors in small classes, and train during the summer aboard America's tall ship Eagle, as well as the service's ships and aircraft. Top performers spend their senior summer traveling on exciting internships around the nation and overseas. Graduates serve for 5 years and have unmatched opportunities to attend flight school and graduate school, all funded by the Coast Guard.

"Appointments to the Academy are based on a selective admissions process; Congressional nominations are not required. Your leadership potential and desire to serve your country are what counts. Our student body reflects the best America has to offer—with all its potential and diversity!

"Applicants are required to take the SAT (or the ACT with the Writing section)."

For even more information on this school, turn to page 542 of the "Stats" section.

UNITED STATES MERCHANT MARINE ACADEMY

OFFICE OF ADMISSIONS, KINGS POINT, NY 11024-1699 • ADMISSIONS: 516-773-5391 • FAX: 516-773-5390
EMAIL: ADMISSIONS@USMMA.EDU • WEBSITE: WWW.USMMA.EDU

RATINGS
Quality of Life: 61   **Academic:** 69   **Admissions:** 93   **Financial Aid:** 95

STUDENTS SAY ". . ."

Academics

"The Merchant Marine Academy produces officers, leaders, and good citizens of honor and integrity to serve the economic and defense interests of the United States through the maritime industry and armed forces." A "prestigious academy, paid for by the federal government," has free tuition. With "strong alumni support," and "100 percent job placement," the USMMA offers "opportunities upon graduation [that] are endless." After gradation, students are automatically qualified to enter any branch of the armed forces as an officer, including: Army, Navy, Air Force, Marines, Coast Guard, or NOAA. Students who choose to pursue civilian jobs post graduation are quick to note that the school provides the "best marine engineering education available," chock full of skills that are "highly sought after in the engineering industry." Known for having "the hardest academics out of all the military academies," "the school is regimented and very disciplined. The class load is very rigorous." Beyond the regular course load, "spending a year studying at sea on merchant vessels gives the students a hands-on perspective that not many other engineering schools offer." Professors are "undoubtedly more than qualified in their fields of study (ranging from former NASA scientists to highly decorated and accomplished officers in the military). However, sometimes they experience difficulty in attempting to convey the subject matter." As one student notes, The United States Merchant Marine Academy "is academically challenging, which will push you far beyond what you thought you could do; it will also train you to assume a leadership role in any company."

> **SURVEY SAYS . . .**
> Class discussions are rare
> Career services are great
> Lousy food on campus
> Low cost of living
> Frats and sororities are unpopular or nonexistent
> Political activism is unpopular or nonexistent
> Very little drug use

Life

Life at the Merchant Marine Academy fosters "an environment that pushes you to the limit," and students say that it is "tough as hell, but worth every minute." Many midshipmen view "sea year" as the apex of their college experience because it is often considered "a gigantic study-abroad term" during which students spend their time "traveling the world on merchant ships." Because of the school's focus on "teaching time-management, integrity, leadership, and discipline," students are "getting the best education in the field, while making the best friends of your life, all under stressful [and] sometimes pain-staking conditions." For fun, students "will work out or play basketball or football." There are also "several clubs and activities to be involved in" and "several intramural tournaments held throughout the year." Because "New York City is 16 miles east of school…students take frequent trips on the weekends and enjoy the city life." With their sights set on the future, many say, The Merchant Marine Academy is "a tough place to be at but the best place to be from."

Student Body

Students are quick to form a "mutual bond with one another" and "get along very well." "Outgoing and focused," "everyone is strong-willed and generally respectful." The vast majority of students describe themselves as "white, male, intelligent, athletic, conservative, and competitive." Students are bonded by a fraternal patriotism and a strong work ethic. Regiments inspire an "esprit d'corps. "We are tight. We know everybody, and we are dedicated to everyone's success." Freshman year "is tough, both regimentally and academically." "As a plebe, a freshmen, you are an outcast from the rest of the regiment in order to build unity among their class. [Plebes] must complete a long series of steps before they become recognized." "Most time is spent doing: academics, sports, and regiment. The few remaining hours a week are spent socializing with friends outside of school at bars."

THE PRINCETON REVIEW SAYS

Admissions

Very important factors considered include: Rigor of secondary school record, standardized test scores, character/personal qualities. *Important factors considered include:* Class rank, application essay, academic GPA, recommendation(s), extracurricular activities, level of applicant's interest, talent/ability. *Other factors considered include:* Geographical residence, interview, racial/ethnic status, state residency, volunteer work, work experience. SAT or ACT required; TOEFL required of all international applicants. High school diploma is required, and GED is accepted. *Academic units required:* 4 English, 3 mathematics, 3 science, (1 science labs), 8 academic electives. *Academic units recommended:* 4 English, 4 mathematics, 4 science, (2 science labs), 2 foreign language, 4 social studies.

Financial Aid

Tuition, room, board, medical and dental care are paid by the U.S. Government. Each cadet receives a monthly salary to pay for uniforms, supplies and personal expenses. A government loan is advanced to each member of the freshman class.

The Inside Word

Prospective midshipmen face demanding admission requirements. The USMMA assesses scholastic achievement, strength of character, and stamina (applicants must meet specific physical standards). Candidates must also be nominated by a proper nominating authority, typically a state representative or senator.

THE SCHOOL SAYS "..."

From The Admissions Office

"What makes the U.S. Merchant Marine Academy different from the other federal service academies? The difference can be summarized in two phrases that appear in our publications. The first: 'The World Is Your Campus.' You will spend a year at sea—a third of your sophomore year and two-thirds of your junior year—teamed with a classmate aboard a U.S. merchant ship. You will visit an average of 18 foreign nations while you work and learn in a mariner's true environment. You will graduate with seafaring experience and as a citizen of the world. The second phrase is 'Options and Opportunities.' Unlike students at the other federal academies, who are required to enter the service connected to their academy, you have the option of working in the seagoing merchant marine and transportation industry or applying for active duty in the Navy, Coast Guard, Marine Corps, Air Force, or Army. Nearly 25 percent of our most recent graduating class entered various branches of the armed forces with an officer rank. As a graduate of the U.S. Merchant Marine Academy, you will receive a Bachelor of Science degree, a government-issued merchant marine officer's license, and a Naval Reserve commission (unless you have been accepted for active military duty). No other service academy offers so attractive a package.

"Applicants must take the SAT or the ACT with the Writing component. For homeschooled students, we recommend they also submit scores from SAT Subject Tests in Chemistry and/or Physics."

For even more information on this school, turn to page 542 of the "Stats" section.

UNITED STATES MILITARY ACADEMY

600 THAYER ROAD, WEST POINT, NY 10996-1797 • ADMISSIONS: 914-938-4041 • FAX: 914-938-3021
FINANCIAL AID: 914-938-3516 • E-MAIL: 8DAD@EXMAIL.USMA.ARMY.MIL • WEBSITE: WWW.USMA.EDU

RATINGS
Quality of Life: 83   **Academic:** 99   **Admissions:** 96   **Financial Aid:** 60

STUDENTS SAY ". . ."

Academics

West Point "is all about transforming a regular citizen into an intellectual soldier with unparalleled skills of leadership, fit to lead America's sons and daughters," a grueling process to be sure. The West Point experience entails "an intensive academic, physical, and military curriculum" in which students undergo "four years of breaking down to build up, unlearning to learn again, and narrowing purpose to open vast opportunities" in a highly regimented program in which "you need to be willing to put up with things you won't deal with anywhere else." Academics start with "a very large core curriculum" that some grouse about but most accept as "helping us become problem solvers...and critical thinkers" with "a broad base of knowledge to understand the world around us." The school employs the Thayer Method of instruction, "which means students prepare for class ahead of time and then discuss the material in class as opposed to the other way around." Cadets warn that it's "very difficult in some of the courses, particularly math and sciences," and also that there is often "not sufficient time to prepare for class" due to their busy academic and training schedules. Fortunately, professors are there to help cadets survive the grueling experience. They "are absolutely excellent" instructors who "put an incredible amount of effort and work into making sure the students succeed." "One-on-one tutoring from instructors is available on a daily basis," one grateful cadet reports.

> **SURVEY SAYS . . .**
> *No one cheats*
> *Athletic facilities are great*
> *Career services are great*
> *Different types of students interact*
> *Campus feels safe*
> *Low cost of living*
> *Very little drug use*

Life

Asked to describe life at West Point, one cadet quoted Winston Churchill: "If you're going through hell, keep on going!" Campus life "is very structured. Everything is planned out and executed," with most time consumed by "a heavy course load, military duties and physical fitness." Cadets "are able to have fun, but not in the ways typical college students have fun. [Even] weekends can be busy with mandatory sporting events or other obligations." The demands of the West Point experience can doubtless seem overwhelming at times, but "there are bright moments.... For fun, we have lots of athletic activities available and a surprisingly wide range of student clubs (ranging from a Korean-American relations seminar to the fly-fishing club) compared to the size of the student body." Alcohol and drugs are strictly forbidden on campus, and "penalties for breaking [the rules] are harsh." Once students are of age, they can drink "at designated locations on campus, which many take advantage of on Thursdays, as they often leave on Fridays." New York City is the most frequently mentioned getaway for those procuring precious leaves. In sum, life can be monotonous at West Point, "but it's worth it" because "more is accomplished at this school in one day than anywhere else. No other school has such great commitment to [developing] a well-rounded student."

Student Body

"Physically fit," "type A" "workaholics" fill the ranks at West Point, where "due to Army regulations, many people look the same in regards to facial hair and hair cuts. The uniform does not help either." There are a lot of "high school hero," "Captain America-type people" here. Not too many students stray from that prototype. "If there are any [atypical students], they are separated for failing to adapt," one student warns. Another adds, "Most people that do not eventually mold into the typical student do not make it through all four years. Cooperate and graduate." Although all students are "very competitive," there is a "great sense of duty to help out your classmates. Most students are very intelligent, polite, and professional." Other descriptors that pop up frequently include "patriotic," "religious," and "politically conservative." "While statistically the student body is probably mostly white and male," one student observes, "there is a good representation of all ethnic groups and both genders, and there are no discrimination issues that I have observed."

THE PRINCETON REVIEW SAYS

Admissions

Very important factors considered include: Class rank, application essay, academic GPA, recommendation(s), rigor of secondary school record, standardized test scores, character/personal qualities, extracurricular activities, talent/ability. *Important factors considered include:* Geographical residence, interview, level of applicant's interest, racial/ethnic status, volunteer work. *Other factors considered include:* Alumni/ae relation, state residency, work experience. SAT or ACT required; High school diploma is required, and GED is accepted. *Academic units recommended:* 4 English, 4 mathematics, 4 science, (2 science labs), 2 foreign language, 3 social studies, 1 history, 3 academic electives.

Financial Aid

The Princeton Review suggests that all financial aid forms be submitted as soon as possible after January 1. *Need-based scholarships/grants offered:* All students receive an annual salary of approximately $10,148. Room and board, medical and dental care is provided by the institution. A one-time deposit of $2,900 is required upon admission to pay for the initial issue of uniforms, books, supplies, equipment and fees. If needed, loans for the deposit are available for $100 to $2,400. *Loan aid offered:* Other, All students receive an annual salary of approximately $10,148. Room and board, medical and dental care is provided by the institution.

The Inside Word

The fact that you must be nominated by your Congressional representative in order to apply to West Point tells you all you need to know about the school's selectivity. Contact your district's Congressional representative to learn the deadline for nomination requests; typically these are made in the spring of your junior year. Successful candidates must demonstrate excellence in academics, physical conditioning, extracurricular involvement, and leadership. They must also be willing to commit to five years of active duty and three years of reserve duty upon graduation. The rigorous requirements and demanding commitments of a West Point education hardly dissuade applicants. Almost 11,000 applied for the 1,300 available slots.

THE SCHOOL SAYS "..."

From The Admissions Office

"Are you a physically fit, morally sound, adventurous high achiever? Are you looking for superior academics, top-notch faculty, and small classes? Do you dream of leading in the 21st century? Then West Point is for you. For more than 200 years our faculty and staff have had one goal: producing leaders of character. West Point isn't easy, but don't worry; if we accept you, you can succeed here. Our graduation rate, 80%, is among the nation's highest. Consistently rated in the top ten in the nation, our academic program has 31 core courses that provide a balanced education in the arts and sciences. You will graduate with a Bachelor of Science degree in one of more-than 40 majors ranging from electrical engineering to physics to history to philosophy. Every cadet participates in an intercollegiate, club, or intramural-level sport every semester, and every summer you will receive military training ranging from marksmanship to parachuting. The fully-funded four-year college education includes tuition, room, board, and full medical and dental care. In return, you will be commissioned as an Army officer with an 8-year commitment, five on active duty. As a new graduate you will have responsibilities your peers can only dream of—leading tens of Soldiers with millions of dollars worth of equipment and making decisions with worldwide implications. When you leave West Point you will be a member of the famed Long Gray Line, with friends and experiences to last a lifetime and prepared to fulfill your dreams."

For even more information on this school, turn to page 543 of the "Stats" section.

UNITED STATES NAVAL ACADEMY

117 DECATUR ROAD, ANNAPOLIS, MD 21402 • ADMISSIONS: 410-293-4361 • FAX: 410-295-1815
E-MAIL: WEBMAIL@GWMAIL.USNA.EDU • WEBSITE: WWW.USNA.EDU

RATINGS
Quality of Life: 84   **Academic:** 94   **Admissions:** 96   **Financial Aid:** 60

STUDENTS SAY ". . ."

Academics

The United States Naval Academy is "a rugged, in-your-face" "leadership laboratory" that "teaches you to think critically and develops your skills as a future combat leader." You'll find "the highest ideals of duty, honor, and loyalty" here. You'll find "unreal" facilities, too. Few colleges can boast a sub-critical nuclear reactor, just for example. All midshipmen get "a full-ride scholarship" that includes tuition, room and board, medical care, and a stipend. And you'll "have a guaranteed job when you graduate" as a Navy or Marine Corps officer. "Classes are extremely small." Academics "pile on fast." Regardless of major, you'll take a

ton of core courses in the humanities, the hard sciences, engineering, and naval science and weapons systems. Though the experience is "grueling," the professors at the Academy are "some of the most caring and well educated people in the world." They "are always accessible outside of class," and "they do whatever it takes for the students to understand the material." To put it mildly, the top brass "practices tough love." On one hand, "the administration has obligations to the military and the United States government" to train future officers. On the other hand, some students say "there are too many stupid policies." While the atmosphere "tends to brew cynicism," major reform is unlikely. "The administration is what it is," muses a chemistry major. "Deal with it."

Life

Ultimately, the Naval Academy "gives you a great education, a job, and financial security, but at the cost of your freedom for four years." "To quote a popular slogan: 'We're here to defend liberty, not enjoy it,'" quips one midshipman. During the summer before classes start, first-year students get indoctrinated with "yelling, physical training," and basic seamanship. The entire first year is a "stressful" "crucible-type experience," and it's "no fun." Older students have it slightly better as privileges increase every year. Life is "extremely micromanaged." "Each day begins for every student at 6:30 A.M. and ends well past 11:00 at night." "You have to wear a uniform almost all the time." There are "mandatory meals, formations," and sports and study periods. "Most people work out, watch movies, and play various videogames." "On weekends, you may or may not be allowed to leave for a night or two, depending on which class year you are." Older midshipmen often spend that time soaking up "the great bar scene" in Annapolis. "Catching up on sleep" is also popular. Graduates usually leave with "at least some degree of spite." "The food will always suck." Nevertheless, a "strong camaraderie" is pervasive. "Even though people complain, there is no place we'd rather be," declares a junior. "Nobody here was drafted."

Student Body

The overwhelmingly male population here represents "every state and a lot of foreign countries." "Everyone is 100 percent equal regardless of gender, race, or religion." "The only intolerance is that open homosexuals are not allowed in the military under federal law." Politically, there's "a fair share of liberals," but the majority is "conservative-minded." "You can usually point out a midshipman in a crowd." Students "are pretty much the same person" because they are "made to conform." Many midshipmen were "the best from where they came from." "The school is full of enormous egos." "Fiercely competitive," "type-A" personalities proliferate. "Almost everyone was a sports star in high school," and "everyone is in great physical condition." At the same time, "there are many students who play a lot of videogames and are socially awkward." Deep down, "everyone here is a dork or a geek, even the most macho of athletic commandos." they're "resilient," "hardworking," "intellectual," and "pretty straightedge." They have "a good sense of humor and a level head." The average midshipman is also "a little jaded," and, on some days, "a zombie that just tries to make it to the meals."

THE PRINCETON REVIEW SAYS

Admissions

Very important factors considered include: Class rank, application essay, academic GPA, recommendation(s), rigor of secondary school record, character/personal qualities, extracurricular activities, interview, level of applicant's interest. *Important factors considered include:* Standardized test scores, talent/ability. *Other factors considered include:* Alumni relation, first generation, geographical residence, state residency, volunteer work, work experience. SAT or ACT required; TOEFL required of all international applicants. High school diploma or equivalent is not required. *Academic units recommended:* 4 English, 4 mathematics, 2 science, (1 science labs), 2 foreign language, 2 history, and other honors/AP/IB courses.

Financial Aid

The Princeton Review suggests that all financial aid forms be submitted as soon as possible after 1/1.

The Inside Word

It doesn't take a genius to recognize that getting admitted to the USNA requires true strength of character; simply completing the arduous admissions process is an accomplishment worthy of remembrance. Those who have successful candidacies are strong, motivated students, and leaders in both school and community. Perseverance is an important character trait for anyone considering the life of a midshipman—the application process is only the beginning of a truly challenging and demanding experience.

THE SCHOOL SAYS "…"

From The Admissions Office

"The Naval Academy offers you a unique opportunity to associate with a broad cross-section of the country's finest young men and women. You will have the opportunity to pursue a 4-year program that develops you mentally, morally, and physically as no civilian college can. As you might expect, this program is demanding, but the opportunities are limitless and more than worth the effort. To receive an appointment to the academy, you need 4 years of high school preparation to develop the strong academic, athletic, and extracurricular background required to compete successfully for admission. You should begin preparing in your freshman year and apply for admission at the end of your junior year. Selection for appointment to the academy comes as a result of a complete evaluation of your admissions package and completion of the nomination process. Complete admissions guidance may be found online."

For even more information on this school, turn to page 543 of the "Stats" section.

THE UNIVERSITY OF THE ARTS

320 SOUTH BROAD STREET, PHILADELPHIA, PA 19102 • ADMISSIONS: 215-717-6049 • FAX: 215-717-6045
E-MAIL: ADMISSIONS@UARTS.EDU • WEBSITE: WWW.UARTS.EDU

RATINGS
Quality of Life: 81 **Academic:** 85 **Admissions:** 79 **Financial Aid:** 80

STUDENTS SAY "..."

Academics

The "fun," "accessible," and "learned" art professors at The University of the Arts "are all working artists" who "take it to the next level of teaching," infusing classes "with their own unique theories and techniques" and teaching students "what it is like to be a working professional." The "Theater and dance programs are arguably the most successful and popular" here, and dance professors "push you daily to make you a better dancer." In fact, all three colleges—Art and Design, Media and Communication, and Performing Arts—are very strong. Some students say that smaller programs deserve more attention and money—"The Communication Department is the only department in the school without studios for upperclassmen"—and that the school needs "a recreational center, parking lots, new studios, [and] renovated classrooms." However, the administration is "open," and "well-intentioned."

> **SURVEY SAYS ...**
> *Great off-campus food*
> *Intercollegiate sports are unpopular or nonexistent*
> *Intramural sports are unpopular or nonexistent*
> *Frats and sororities are unpopular or nonexistent*
> *Musical organizations are popular*

Life

Another art fix is always around the corner at UArts, which has "amazing connection[s] to real-life artists and the theater. There is always access to lectures and show openings." Since "Life at school is centered around what it takes to do your art," "Nine times out of ten, a conversation you'll overhear is about a project or production." Fun is disciplinary: Animation majors "watch cartoons with other animation majors," film and TV writers head to "the movies," and musicians "go to concert[s] and jazz clubs" and "get together and have jam sessions." Social divisions by medium are reinforced by the physical separation of the three schools and by unconventional living arrangements: "no meal plan, no 'campus,'" and no "student center." Philly is a more-than-adequate substitute: "The school is located right in the theater district...half a block from the Kimmel Center and other state-of-the-art performance halls. The nightlife is great" and the surrounding area is filled with "pool halls," "bars, movie theaters, theaters, South Street...it's a great time." Students agree that life here "is much better than the average college situation of going to a frat house and getting wasted." Anyway, partying isn't why UArts students are here. One student sums up the general attitude: "We work for the love of art, and that's fun for us."

Student Body

"All those crazy artists, actors, musicians, dancers, and computer geeks you knew in high school are all here." In fact, "Everyone is very accepted" and "You can act however you want, and nothing is crazy enough." While the typical undergrad is "White and from New Jersey," the African American community is much larger than at most other art schools, and many students are gay, lesbian, or bisexual. Personality types "run from extremely extroverted (the theater kids) to introverted until you get to know them. All are for the most part excited to be here, and while some stay in the cliques of their majors, most have a friends-circle that spans the university." The student body boasts that they are "overall nice people," and "Not only is it easy to find friends that you can relate to but they are [also] great friends that you will have for a long time." Students in all three schools are "very creative" and "focused on...career goals," but they "sometimes don't get all their work in on time...They do take classes seriously, though."

THE PRINCETON REVIEW SAYS

Admissions

Very important factors considered include: Rigor of secondary school record, interview, talent/ability. *Important factors considered include:* Class rank, application essay, standardized test scores, character/personal qualities, extracurricular activities. *Other factors considered include:* Recommendation(s), alumni/ae relation, racial/ethnic status, volunteer work, work experience. SAT or ACT required; TOEFL required of all international applicants. High school diploma is required and GED is accepted. *Academic units required:* 4 English. *Academic units recommended:* 3 mathematics, 2 science, 2 foreign language, 2 social studies, 2 history, 2 study in visual art, music, dance, drama, or creative writing.

Financial Aid

Students should submit: FAFSA Regular filing deadline is 3/1. The Princeton Review suggests that all financial aid forms be submitted as soon as possible after January 1. *Need-based scholarships/grants offered:* Federal Pell, SEOG, state scholarships/grants, private scholarships, the school's own gift aid, merit scholarships. *Loan aid offered:* Federal Perkins, alternative loans. Applicants will be notified of awards on a rolling basis beginning 3/15. Federal Work-Study Program available. Institutional employment available. Off-campus job opportunities are excellent.

The Inside Word

UArts recommends a GPA of 2.0 or better and requires the SAT or ACT, but does not place much emphasis on scores; applicants who received a C or better in a college-level English class can dodge the SAT requirement. The upshot? A selective admissions process that favors budding Picassos and Arbuses who spent more time in the studio than in the library. As at all art schools, the primary emphasis is on applicants' portfolios and auditions. If you are serious about admission to this or any other art college, strongly consider attending a National Portfolio Days event (during which Admissions Officers from various schools will give feedback on your portfolio) and look into intensive precollege summer programs (especially those offered by your school of choice).

THE SCHOOL SAYS " . . ."

From The Admissions Office

"'Art is central to our everyday lives,' says Barbara Elliott, Dean of Enrollment Management at the University of the Arts. "'It drives the media we consume, design of products we use, form of the buildings we frequent, layout of cities in which we live, and channels through which we communicate.'" As the only university in the nation dedicated exclusively to the visual, performing and communication arts, the University of the Arts is committed to advancing this notion by preparing students to apply their strengths to create a better society.

"Located in the heart of Philadelphia on the Avenue of the Arts, the University of the Arts offers 26 majors in a single environment where students inspire each other with their creativity, focus, and drive. Students learn through exposure to all the languages of imagination - sound, movement, words and form. The university offers traditional programs in painting, sculpture, printmaking and photography, as well new media programs in digital video, graphics, and multimedia communication. Its performing arts programs train dancers, musicians, actors, and directors. At the same time, UArts provides its 2,200 undergraduate students with an education grounded in the liberal arts through core courses in English, history and others.

"'We help students satisfy their need to create while preparing them to apply their talents and strengths to contribute to society as a whole,' says Elliott. 'These characteristics not only are important to success in the arts but to success in society in general.'"

For even more information on this school, turn to page 543 of the "Stats" section.

University of Connecticut

2131 Hillside Road, U-3088, Storrs, CT 06268-3088 • Admissions: 860-486-3137 • Fax: 860-486-1476
Financial Aid: 860-486-2819 • E-mail: beahusky@uconn.edu • Website: www.uconn.edu

RATINGS
Quality of Life: 71   Academic: 72   Admissions: 89   Financial Aid: 69

STUDENTS SAY ". . ."

> SURVEY SAYS . . .
> *Low cost of living*
> *Everyone loves the Huskies*
> *Student publications are popular*

Academics

Brimming with sincere Husky pride, students at the University of Connecticut eagerly dole out praise for their school's fabulous athletic programs, world-class academics, friendly atmosphere, and remarkable affordability. At this large research university, professors are "extremely in-tune with recent developments in their fields," and "research opportunities are outstanding," even on the undergraduate level. A political science major shares, "My professors are the ones invited to the White House to discuss the Middle East crisis, flying across the world to solve issues of border disputes, and more. The professors bring their life experiences to the classroom, and it brings the material to life." While most professors maintain their professional pursuits outside the classroom, teaching is taken seriously at UConn, and instructors and administrators "genuinely care and want you to succeed." By all accounts, faculty is easily accessible during office hours, and, "if you can't make those, they'll work out a different time for you." Like professors, UConn's leadership is surprising friendly, down-to-earth, and accessible. Well loved by all, "President Hogan rides the student bus to the football games, is always seen around campus, and even keeps a blog letting students know what he is up to." Even so, students remind us that UConn is a big school, and students must take responsibility for their own educations. A senior explains, "UConn doesn't spoon-feed you education. Students do have to take the initiative to communicate with professors and the other resources on campus." "You have to put into it what you want to get out of it."

Life

UConn's "vibrant school spirit" is one of the university's most distinctive qualities, and Huskies are enthusiastically involved in the campus community. Most UConn undergraduates are "in a million clubs, do community service, play sports, or simply have Husky pride and attend UConn events." Socially and academically, you'll find a mix: "Some students are all about academics, and they live in Babbidge Library, others are all about partying and can be found at the off-campus apartments or the bar throughout the week." In general, most students strike a balance between work and play. A sophomore elaborates, "From Sunday to Thursday, almost all students work diligently. Thursday nights bring some partying, followed by mass amounts of parties on Friday and Saturday nights." If you aren't interested in parties, there are plenty other options, "from athletics, to musical and theatrical performances, to events in the Student Union, UConn has so many different things to do!" In addition, there are more than "350 clubs and organizations," as well as an active intramural sports league, which is a great way to blow off steam. No summary of life at UConn would be complete without mentioning the competitive Division I athletics, which are the "heart of campus spirit." In their free time, UConn students (along with faculty and alumni) "love to go cheer on our nationally ranked UConn Huskies." In fact, student tickets for sporting events sell out months in advance.

Student Body

Considering the school's attractive in-state tuition, it's no surprise that 80 percent of UConn undergraduates come from Connecticut. While that fact may diminish the demographic diversity on campus, students reassure us that "there's a great mix at UConn. With more than 16,000 students enrolled, you're bound to run into just about every type of person." Students say you'll see a lot of students wearing North Face jackets and Ugg boots, but you'll also find an "animal science club, in which the students walk around with squirrel tails on." While UConn students exhibit varying degrees of academic seriousness, "the majority care about their grades, and the library is always packed during exams, midterms, and finals." More than anything else, "the real tie [among] students is the pride that we all have in our university." A senior insists, "I have not met one person who is unhappy and dislikes the university."

Admissions

Very important factors considered include: Class rank, academic GPA, rigor of secondary school record, standardized test scores. *Important factors considered include:* Application essay, recommendation(s), character/personal qualities, extracurricular activities, first generation, racial/ethnic status, talent/ability, volunteer work. *Other factors considered include:* Alumni/ae relation, geographical residence, level of applicant's interest, state residency, work experience. SAT or ACT required; ACT with Writing component required. TOEFL required of all international applicants. High school diploma is required, and GED is accepted. *Academic units required:* 4 English, 3 mathematics, 2 science, (2 science labs), 2 foreign language, 2 social studies, 3 academic electives. *Academic units recommended:* 3 foreign language.

Financial Aid

Students should submit: FAFSA. The Princeton Review suggests that all financial aid forms be submitted as soon as possible after January 1. *Need-based scholarships/grants offered:* Federal Pell, SEOG, state scholarships/grants, private scholarships, the school's own gift aid. *Loan aid offered:* Federal Perkins. Applicants will be notified of awards on a rolling basis beginning 3/1. Federal Work-Study Program available. Institutional employment available. Off-campus job opportunities are good.

The Inside Word

When reviewing applications, the UConn admissions committee evaluates students based on a wide range of factors, including standardized test scores, rigor of high school curriculum, classroom performance, extracurricular activities, and community involvement. Honors and AP classes are not required, but they are viewed favorably by the admissions committee. Competitive applicants have a cumulative grade point average of 3.3 on a 4.0 scale and usually rank in the top quarter of their high school class.

THE SCHOOL SAYS "..."

From The Admissions Office

"Thanks to a $2.8-billion construction program that is impacting every area of university life, the University of Connecticut provides students a high-quality and personalized education on one of the most attractive and technologically advanced college campuses in the United States. Applications are soaring nationally as an increasing number of high-achieving students from diverse backgrounds are making UConn their school of choice. From award-winning actors to governmental leaders, students enjoy an assortment of fascinating speakers each year, while performances by premier dance, jazz, and rock musicians enliven student life. Our beautiful New England campus is convenient and safe, and most students walk to class or ride university shuttle buses. State-of-the-art residential facilities include interest-based learning communities and honors housing as well as on-campus suite-style and apartment living. Championship Division I athletics have created fervor known as Huskymania among UConn students.

"Freshman applicants seeking admittance are required to submit official score reports from the SAT or ACT with Writing component."

For even more information on this school, turn to page 544 of the "Stats" section.

UNIVERSITY OF DELAWARE

116 HULLIHEN HALL, NEWARK, DE 19716 • ADMISSIONS: 302-831-8123 • FAX: 302-831-6905
FINANCIAL AID: 302-831-8761 • E-MAIL: ADMISSIONS@UDEL.EDU • WEBSITE: WWW.UDEL.EDU/VIEWBOOK

RATINGS
Quality of Life: 74   Academic: 76   Admissions: 93   Financial Aid: 78

STUDENTS SAY "..."

Academics

If you are looking for a "well-rounded" college experience, University of Delaware delivers on every front. According to the school's satisfied undergraduates, "the University of Delaware is everything college should be," from its "gorgeous campus" and "amazing school spirit," to "top notch" academics and "vibrant campus life." At UD, as at many public schools, "College is what you make it: If you take easy classes, college is a breeze; if you challenge yourself, classes will be more difficult." First-year courses are often large and impersonal; fortunately, major classes are usually smaller and "electives are interesting and engaging." Highly-qualified students may also apply to the school's "excellent" honors program, which provides access to "challenging, interesting classes taught by distinguished yet friendly professors." Through the touted undergraduate research program, students have access to "diverse research opportunities," and the school's extensive study abroad program is "one of the best in the nation." Overall, faculty get good reviews, though students warn it's a mixed bag: "Some professors shouldn't be allowed within 10 miles of a classroom; others will change your life. It's up to you to weed out the bad ones." While you won't have your hand held, professors are responsive to student needs: "If you ever need any help, a quick e-mail or a phone call usually solves your problem." On a similar note, "The administration is extremely approachable and talks to students on the same level."

> **SURVEY SAYS ...**
> Great computer facilities
> Great library
> Great off-campus food
> Students are happy
> Student publications are popular
> Lots of beer drinking
> Hard liquor is popular

Life

Work and play come together at the University of Delaware, an institution that offers "the perfect balance of academic intensity and excellent social life." Come the weekend (or even during the week), "UD kids like to have their share of fun," and "there is always a party happening." For an alternative to the party scene, students go to "movies in the student center or to ice-skating on Fridays," and "there are a lot of great guest speakers, bands, and cultural events on campus." In addition, "There are social groups for almost anything you can think of from the adventure club to organic cooking to ultimate Frisbee." While fraternities and sororities do exist, they do not dominate the social scene; still Greeks are "very spirited, have a ton of fun, and are widely supported by our campus community." Intramural and varsity sports are wildly popular, both for athletes and their raucous fans. In fact, "Homecoming is a university holiday where people wake up as early as 5 a.m. to start tailgating." What's more, the campus location can't be beat. Main Street, which runs right through campus, "is packed with great restaurants and shopping." For a fun day trip, "Philly is cheap and easy to get to by Septa train," and "the Chinatown bus costs $35 round trip into NYC."

Student Body

It's a largely East Coast crowd at University of Delaware, drawing the vast majority of its undergraduates from "around NYC, Philly, or Baltimore." Within that demographic, "Preppy sorority kids are probably the most common, but no matter who you are or what your into, the school population is big enough [that] you're bound to find a group that shares your interest." At UD, "You'll have your jocks and frat boys, but you'll also find skaters, rockers, artsy types, and everything else in between." However, most UD students share an incredible enthusiasm for their school community, and "A typical student is engaged in coursework and a multitude of various extracurricular [activities]." Despite its long-standing repute as a party school, "students here have become more focused on academics. Most students here really do have a passion for learning and study really hard in order to get those grades and graduate." Even so, UD's reputation for revelry isn't lost on undergraduates: "The typical UD student cares about their school work but loves to have fun on the weekends."

Admissions

Very important factors considered include: Academic GPA, rigor of secondary school record, state residency. *Important factors considered include:* Application essay, recommendation(s), standardized test scores, character/personal qualities, extracurricular activities, talent/ability, volunteer work, work experience. *Other factors considered include:* Class rank, alumni/ae relation, first generation, geographical residence, interview, level of applicant's interest, racial/ethnic status, SAT Subject Tests recommended; SAT or ACT required; ACT with Writing component required. TOEFL required of all international applicants. High school diploma is required, and GED is accepted. *Academic units required:* 4 English, 3 mathematics, 3 science, (2 science labs), 2 foreign language, 2 social studies, 2 history, 2 academic electives. *Academic units recommended:* 4 English, 4 mathematics, 4 science, (3 science labs), 4 foreign language, 2 social studies, 2 history.

Financial Aid

Students should submit: FAFSA. Regular filing deadline is 3/15. The Princeton Review suggests that all financial aid forms be submitted as soon as possible after January 1. *Need-based scholarships/grants offered:* Federal Pell, SEOG, state scholarships/grants, private scholarships, the school's own gift aid. *Loan aid offered:* Direct Subsidized Stafford, Direct Unsubsidized Stafford, Direct PLUS, Federal Perkins, Federal Nursing, college/university loans from institutional funds. Applicants will be notified of awards on a rolling basis beginning 3/15. Federal Work-Study Program available. Institutional employment available. Off-campus job opportunities are excellent.

Inside Word

Although UD is run by the state of Delaware, out-of-state students also benefit from the school's excellent academic and social offerings at a reasonable tuition. Even so, the school is expressly committed to supporting Delawarian students, who comprise about 70 percent of the student body. For Delaware natives who perform well in a high school college preparatory curriculum, UD promises acceptance to the undergraduate program. More details and samples of qualifying high school curriculums are available on the admissions department website. In all admissions decisions, UD considers the entirety of a student's application; there are no minimum test scores or grades.

THE SCHOOL SAYS "..."

From The Admissions Office

"The University of Delaware is a major national research university with a long-standing commitment to teaching and serving undergraduates. It is one of only a few universities in the country designated as a land-grant, sea-grant, urban-grant, and space-grant institution. The academic strength of this university is found in its highly selective honors program, nationally recognized Undergraduate Research Program, study abroad opportunities on all seven continents, and its successful alumni, including three Rhodes Scholars since 1998. The University of Delaware offers the wide range of majors and course offerings expected of a university but in spirit remains a small place where you can interact with your professors and feel at home. The beautiful green campus is ideally located at the very center of the East Coast 'megacity' that stretches from New York City to Washington, D.C. All of these elements, combined with an endowment approaching $1 billion and a spirited Division I athletics program, make the University of Delaware a tremendous value.

"Freshman applicants are required to take the SAT (or the ACT with the Writing section). Two SAT Subject Tests are recommended for applicants to the University Honors Program."

For even more information on this school, turn to page 544 of the "Stats" section.

THE UNIVERSITY OF MAINE

5713 CHADBOURNE HALL, ORONO, ME 04469-5713 • ADMISSIONS: 207-581-1561 • FAX: 207-581-1213
FINANCIAL AID: 207-581-1324 • E-MAIL: UM-ADMIT@MAINE.EDU • WEBSITE: WWW.UMAINE.EDU

RATINGS
Quality of Life: 74   Academic: 71   Admissions: 76   Financial Aid: 79

STUDENTS SAY ". . ."
Academics

SURVEY SAYS . . .
Athletic facilities are great
Everyone loves the Black Bears
Student publications are popular
Lots of beer drinking
Hard liquor is popular

The University of Maine boasts "a phenomenal engineering school" and notable programs in ecology, marine science, and forestry. "The campus is beautiful," says a sophomore, "melding scenery, history, and modernity." "The resources available through the library are quite staggering." There are also some "very fancy new labs." "It can be disheartening to see the beauty and grand scale of the engineering and science buildings, and then walk back to the buildings where most of your classes are held and see the lack of basic upkeep," gripes a history major. The academic atmosphere here is "challenging but not overwhelming." "Classes range in size from 20 to 200." "Professors can vary noticeably." There are "some rather dull professors." There are also plenty of "intelligent, kind, realistic human beings" on the faculty who are "quite flexible about meeting with and accommodating students." Some students say the top brass is "reasonable," "decently efficient," and "personable." Others see "layers of administration" and "terrible" management.

Life

Prepare for "bitter, arctic-like cold" and "a lot of snow" if you attend UMaine. Prepare for "unhealthy" food, too. "Ninety percent of it is deep-fried or covered in a dairy-based something," protests a junior. On the bright side, campus life is active. There are "tons of things to do." "Musicians, comedians, and other artists" perform frequently. Sports keep many students busy. "Intramurals are great." The recreation center is "state-of-the-art" and "hugely popular." Naturally, "hockey is crazy." "The campus is usually buzzing on game day," and the arena is "generally packed." Students are probably "too obsessed with the Red Sox" as well. "The party scene isn't too shabby." All in all, "consuming large quantities of cheap beer" is pretty common. There's a decent Greek presence, and, for some students, the frat houses are "the place to go on the weekends." There are also "house parties" and "a few local bars." More intimate get-togethers happen, too. "There's a tremendous amount of small-scale social drinking," notes a junior. The "rural community" of Orono "maintains that remote appeal" but it's "boring." "There is a ton of natural beauty around." though. "The extensive wilderness between campus and Canada" provides hiking, kayaking, and hunting opportunities galore. "Ventures to Sugarloaf are abundant."

Student Body

"Most of the students are Maine natives" or New Englanders. To put it diplomatically, the "minority percentage reflects that of the state." To put it bluntly, "this school is almost all white." "The typical student at UMaine is one who loves the outdoors, embraces the cold, is not too concerned with fashion, and lives in North Face or Patagonia clothes," reflects a sophomore. However, students report that you can find "every type of white person imaginable" on this campus. "There are tons of unique styles and groups that mix together." You've got "Carhartt-wearing, wood-chopping, straight-from-the-sticks, true-blue Mainers." There are "hockey rowdies" and "obnoxious frat boys." There are "a lot of hippies" and people who "care about the environment." There are "rare, wild-looking characters" and nontraditional students as well. The atmosphere is "relaxed" and "laid-back." "People are friendly up here." Some students tell us that "out-of-staters have a really hard time." Others disagree. "The in-state kids will totally accept you," promises a junior. "An out-of-stater can be distinguished from a Mainer fairly easily," explains a junior. "They can't drive, dress inappropriately for the weather, or wonder why school isn't cancelled during a blizzard. But we get used to them, and eventually, just maybe, by the time they graduate, part of them is Mainer, too."

Admissions

Very important factors considered include: Class rank, academic GPA, rigor of secondary school record, standardized test scores. *Important factors considered include:* Application essay, recommendation(s). *Other factors considered include:* Character/personal qualities, extracurricular activities, geographical residence, interview, talent/ability, volunteer work, work experience. SAT or ACT required; TOEFL required of all international applicants. High school diploma is required, and GED is accepted. *Academic units required:* 4 English, 3 mathematics, 2 science, (2 science labs), 2 foreign language, 2 social studies, 0 history, 4 academic electives, 1 physical education for Education Majors *Academic units recommended:* 4 English, 4 mathematics, 4 science, (3 science labs), 2 foreign language, 3 social studies, 1 history, 4 academic electives, 1 physical education for Education Majors.

Financial Aid

Students should submit: FAFSA. The Princeton Review suggests that all financial aid forms be submitted as soon as possible after January 1. *Need-based scholarships/grants offered:* Federal Pell, SEOG, state scholarships/grants, private scholarships, the school's own gift aid. *Loan aid offered:* Federal Perkins, state loans Applicants will be notified of awards on a rolling basis beginning 3/15. Federal Work-Study Program available. Institutional employment available. Off-campus job opportunities are good.

The Inside Word

The University of Maine is much smaller than most public flagship universities, and its admissions process reflects this; it is a much more personal approach than many others use. Candidates are reviewed carefully for fit with their choice of college and major, and the committee will contact students regarding a second choice if the first doesn't seem to be a good match. Prepare your application as if you are applying to a private university.

THE SCHOOL SAYS "..."

From The Admissions Office

"The University of Maine offers you the best of both worlds—the excitement, breadth and depth that are available at a land grant, sea grant, research university with the personal attention and community feel of a smaller college. Five academic colleges and an Honors College offer you the chance to belong to a supportive academic community, while providing the specialization, resources and opportunities for research, internships and scholarly activity you would expect at a major university. Academics are a priority at UMaine; most programs hold the highest level of accreditation possible, setting UMaine apart nationally.

"And at UMaine there is always something to do—there are more than 200 clubs and student organizations, lots of volunteer opportunities, an active student government, a new multi-million dollar student recreation center with an busy intramural schedule and Division I varsity athletics to keep you busy. A special First Year Residence Experience (FYRE) will help support your transitions to college—this unique program includes special activities and theme living communities. It is located between the new Student Recreation Center and the newly renovated Hilltop dining complex. Check out our website to learn more—or better yet, come visit us in person and see the campus for yourself!"

For even more information on this school, turn to page 545 of the "Stats" section.

UNIVERSITY OF MAINE—FORT KENT

23 UNIVERSITY DRIVE, FORT KENT, ME 04743 • ADMISSIONS: 207-834-7500 • FAX: 207-834-7609
E-MAIL: UMFKADM@MAINE.MAINE.EDU • WEBSITE: WWW.UMFK.MAINE.EDU

RATINGS

Quality of Life: 89   Academic: 74   Admissions: 64   Financial Aid: 84

STUDENTS SAY ". . ."

Academics

> **SURVEY SAYS . . .**
> *Students are friendly*
> *Different types of students interact*
> *Students get along with local community*
> *Low cost of living*

At the University of Maine—Fort Kent, undergraduates join "a close-knit community of educators and students working towards a common goal" to receive a "quality education in a small-town environment." Students typically have to pay private school prices to receive those perks, but not here; Fort Kent is a state school with very reasonable tuition and fees. Fort Kent's location makes it a natural choice for students of forestry, wildlife sciences, and environmental studies. "Not all schools can take the class on a field trip and within five minutes be completely submerged in hands-on experiences that will aid students when filling out their resumes." Business studies and nursing are also strong here. Of the latter, students brag that "The nursing program is one of the toughest in the state but the pass rate is very high. The professors are very good about assisting students in their work."

Life

Don't expect a big-college social scene at Fort Kent. The size of the student body and the school's remote location pretty much guarantee a low-key environment. Many arrive ready (even enthusiastic) for life in a place where "beautiful scenery" far outweighs any "large attractions" one might find elsewhere. Those comfortable with the slower pace assure us "There is always something to do here." Students "are big on soccer," and "you can ski in the winter at the local ski hill or go ice skating or cross-country skiing. You can also go snowmobiling on the greatest trail system on the East Coast." Traditions "become a big part of life" at Fort Kent; for many they include a Monday chicken wing night at a popular local restaurant, dollar movies on Sundays, and partying on Thursday nights ("It is usually a late night and is considered to replace the Friday and Saturday night, giving students who work weekends a night to relax and have a good time."). Undergrads also report that "trips to Canada to spend time with our friends from across the river are popular" and that "The city of Quebec is only four hours away."

Student Body

"Most everyone is from the surrounding area" at UM—Fort Kent, "which leads sometimes to lack of knowledge of other geographic areas or certain situations." The school's location on the border means lots of Canadian students and a substantial influence from "French and Acadian culture." The typical student here "hunts, goes outdoors, watches movies, and just likes to chill and hang out." He or she is also "either a part of athletics or other clubs and organizations" and "is Catholic because this is mainly a Catholic community. Those who are not Catholic have no problem fitting in because everyone is so friendly." The campus' large population of returning adults "fits in the crowd pretty well."

THE PRINCETON REVIEW SAYS

Admissions

Very important factors considered include: Level of applicant's interest. *Important factors considered include:* Class rank, application essay, academic GPA, recommendation(s), rigor of secondary school record, character/personal qualities, first generation, geographical residence, state residency, talent/ability, volunteer work. *Other factors considered include:* Standardized test scores, alumni/ae relation, extracurricular activities, interview, work experience. SAT and SAT Subject Tests or ACT recommended; TOEFL required of all international applicants. High school diploma is required and GED is accepted. *Academic units required:* 4 English, 2 mathematics, 2 science, (2 science labs). *Academic units recommended:* 2 foreign language.

Financial Aid

Students should submit: FAFSA, institution's own financial aid form, CSS/Financial Aid PROFILE, state aid form. The Princeton Review suggests that all financial aid forms be submitted as soon as possible after January 1. *Need-based scholarships/grants offered:* Federal Pell, SEOG, state scholarships/grants, private scholarships, the school's own gift aid, Federal Nursing Scholarships. *Loan aid offered:* Direct Subsidized Stafford, Direct Unsubsidized Stafford, Direct PLUS, Federal Perkins, Federal Nursing, state loans, college/university loans from institutional funds. Federal Work-Study Program available. Institutional employment available. Off-campus job opportunities are good.

The Inside Word

UM—Fort Kent is small enough to give each application a careful personal review. High school record and standardized test scores still weigh most heavily in admissions decisions here, but admissions officers can, and will, take the time to search the applications of borderline applicants for reasons to admit. Don't disappoint them.

THE SCHOOL SAYS "..."

From The Admissions Office

"The University of Maine at Fort Kent (UMFK) offers both a high-quality education and the personalized attention today's students are looking for. We take pride in the level of personal service and attention that we provide to our students. With a student-faculty ratio of 18:1 and a campus population of 1,100 professors know their students by name and provide many opportunities for interaction. At the same time, the University offers the benefits of a large university: a wide variety of academic and extracurricular opportunities. UMFK's students hail from small towns and big cities across North America, as well as Europe, Africa, South America, and Asia.

"We have a nationally recognized athletics program in men's and women's soccer and basketball as well as an outstanding list of intramural and club teams. We have an active campus community and lots of opportunity for student initiatives. Our co-curricular programs offer many student leadership opportunities.

"UMFK's unique rural, environmental, and cultural heritage as well as our long standing tradition of hands on learning sets us apart. Experiential learning is well integrated into many of our majors, giving students early preparation in their profession. The beauty and culture of the Saint John Valley, where UMFK is located, impacts everyone who lives and studies here. We expect all of our students to understand that they must take an active role in their communities, be socially responsible in their careers, and actively protect their environment."

For even more information on this school, turn to page 545 of the "Stats" section.

University of Maryland—Baltimore County

1000 Hilltop Circle, Baltimore, MD 21250 • Admissions: 410-455-2291 • Fax: 410-455-1094
Financial Aid: 410-455-2387 • E-mail: admissions@umbc.edu • Website: www.umbc.edu

RATINGS
Quality of Life: 69   Academic: 72   Admissions: 83   Financial Aid: 80

STUDENTS SAY "..."

Academics

Students agree that University of Maryland—Baltimore County "is a great school for scientific and information technology people" that boasts "very good programs in biology and mechanical engineering." Undergrads here find themselves immersed in "a science-y environment with some good departments and some not-so-good, but if you find the right niche you'll do fantastically." Provided, you can survive the "discouragingly difficult exams" and "very strict and/or too harsh grading of papers and exams" typically encountered in the school's trademark disciplines. Students of political science and government benefit from the fact that "The school is located near Baltimore and is a train ride from D.C., which opens up internship and learning opportunities. (One political science professor takes kids to embassies related to the class he's teaching every semester; I've met the Iraqi and Indonesian ambassadors to the USA.)" Students in the liberal arts, on the other hand, complain that "the school has no concern for us. All the money in the school only goes to the Science and Tech departments," which explains the "amazing technology" undergrads brag about. "There's a lot of focus on research" at UMBC, so "the professors and the library are a great strength" here. Professors "are required to do research in their fields, so they are always up-to-date on material they teach. Even if they are mean or difficult, they all know what they are talking about." The library "has a great deal of research assistance and access to a consortium of millions of books."

Life

"For the most part, campus is quiet" because "people take studying seriously," and "during the weekend many students go home." Add the large commuter population and the school's proximity to some attractive social destinations (downtown Baltimore, D.C., Columbia) and you begin to understand why "it may seem as if there's nothing going on" on the UMBC campus. Students assure us that, perceptions to the contrary, "someone is usually having a party or get together" on or around campus, most frequently in the apartment-style residences. Undergrads also enjoy about "200 clubs to join such as dancing, bike riding, football, and even juggling" as well as "the game room or the Sports Zone if a person just wants to relax." Mostly, though, students find their fun away from school grounds. The school sponsors "shuttle buses to go to the clubs in Baltimore, so it's great that they promote safety in regards to drinking and driving." Fells Point, a bar district near Baltimore's Inner Harbor, is a popular destination, as is the University of Maryland's College Park campus. All in all, this is not a highly social campus; "Everybody really dances to his own beat" we're told.

Student Body

"There is no typical student" on the "very diverse" UMBC campus. "Everyone varies, from preppy cheerleaders and jocks to antisocial art nerds to normal human beings to religious fanatics to animal rights activists to overachievers to underachievers to foreigners to truly gifted kids to how-did-they-pass-their-SATs kids to druggies to good people and everything in between." The campus is also "full of nontraditional students who are married/engaged, have kids, and work." The Asian population is so large at UMBC that "some folks describe UMBC as 'U Must Be Chinese,' but the majority are Caucasians, with minority black/African-Americans, and a noticeable number of Indian/Pakistani ethnic groups." The student body tends to form cliques along lines of background and academic field; this is hardly unusual for a predominantly commuter campus (only about one-third of students live on campus, more than half of whom are freshmen).

THE PRINCETON REVIEW SAYS

Admissions

Very important factors considered include: Academic GPA, rigor of secondary school record, standardized test scores. *Important factors considered include:* Class rank, application essay, recommendation(s), talent/ability. *Other factors considered include:* Character/personal qualities, extracurricular activities, SAT required; SAT or ACT required; ACT required; TOEFL required of all international applicants. High school diploma is required, and GED is accepted. *Academic units required:* 4 English, 3 mathematics, 3 science, 2 foreign language, 3 social studies, 3 social Studies & history. *Academic units recommended:* 4 mathematics.

Financial Aid

Students should submit: FAFSA. The Princeton Review suggests that all financial aid forms be submitted as soon as possible after January 1. *Need-based scholarships/grants offered:* Federal Pell, SEOG, state scholarships/grants, private scholarships, the school's own gift aid. *Loan aid offered:* Direct Subsidized Stafford, Direct Unsubsidized Stafford, Direct PLUS, Federal Perkins. Applicants will be notified of awards on a rolling basis beginning 3/15. Federal Work-Study Program available. Institutional employment available. Off-campus job opportunities are excellent.

The Inside Word

UMBC is an Honors College within the University of Maryland system. After the College Park campus, it is perhaps the most prestigious state-run undergraduate institution in Maryland. Selectivity is somewhat hampered by the school's inability to accommodate residents; about 70 percent of students commute. Even so, the densely populated Baltimore metropolitan area gives the school plenty of top-flight candidates to choose from. Your high school transcript must show a challenging curriculum (and success in your most demanding courses) if you hope to attend this school.

THE SCHOOL SAYS "..."

From The Admissions Office

"When it comes to universities, a mid-sized school can be just right. Some students want the resources of a large community. Others are looking for the attention found at a smaller one. With an undergraduate population of over 9,000, UMBC can offer the best of both. There are always new people to meet and things to do—from Division I sports to more than 170 student clubs. As a research university, we offer an abundance of programs, technology, and opportunities for hands-on experiences. Yet we are small enough that students don't get lost in the shuffle. More than 80 percent of our classes have fewer than 40 students. Among public research universities, UMBC is recognized for its success in placing students in the most competitive graduate programs and careers. Of course, much of the success of UMBC has to do with the students themselves—highly motivated students who get involved in their education."

"Freshman applicants are required to take the SAT or ACT."

For even more information on this school, turn to page 546 of the "Stats" section.

University of Maryland—College Park

Mitchell Building, College Park, MD 20742-5235 • Admissions: 301-314-8385 • Fax: 301-314-9693
Financial Aid: 301-314-9000 • E-mail: um-admit@uga.umd.edu • Website: www.maryland.edu

RATINGS
Quality of Life: 68   **Academic:** 72   **Admissions:** 95   **Financial Aid:** 64

STUDENTS SAY ". . ."

Academics

The University of Maryland—College Park is a grand mix of "20-minute walks to class across one of the country's most beautiful campuses, [an introduction] to high-level courses taught by the nation's top researchers, [and] a motivated 'green' campus" as well as "crowded, smelly frat parties, [and] living-learning communities that can make the gigantic campus much smaller." Students are quick to boast about sports, too, especially the school's titles as "the 2008 national champions in men's soccer and women's field hockey." In short: It's a quintessential large university, offering "a great experience with a variety of opportunities that are what you make of them." Students crow about Maryland's "nationally recognized business program," a "top-ranked criminology program," a solid engineering school, a great political science department that capitalizes on the school's proximity to Washington, D.C., and the "top-notch honors program." Most of all, they love the "great price. This school gives you a great education for a really cheap price." Low cost doesn't translate to budget accommodations. On the contrary, "the administration shows a desire to always upgrade facilities, as can be witnessed by the tremendous business school and the brand new engineering building." In conclusion, students applaud "the widely diverse opportunities available at UMD. You can never get bored because there is always something to do."

> **SURVEY SAYS . . .**
> *Athletic facilities are great*
> *Diverse student types on campus*
> *Everyone loves the Terrapins*
> *Student publications are popular*
> *Lots of beer drinking*

Life

"Life at UMD is awesome," with "a good mix of fun activities" including "school-sponsored parties, games," a "campus recreation center that has virtually everything you could wish for, including pools, an extensive gym, a rock wall, squash courts, an indoor track," and a student union "loaded with fun places like the arcade area, bowling alley," and "tons of places to eat as well." In addition, "there are always open games of soccer, football, or ultimate Frisbee being played on the mall and elsewhere." There are bars close to campus, and "students are always having parties," especially along College Park's raucous Frat Row. Terrapin sports are a passion for many. And if all that isn't enough, "the proximity to D.C., makes clubbing, nights out on the town, and general visits to D.C. frequent." With all this going on, no wonder students say that "the social life at UMD is unsurpassed." Some warn the surrounding area is dicey; "It's pretty annoying and scary to get crime alerts from the police informing us of incidents close to campus," one student explains. Undergrads also warn that parking regulations are brutal. "Bus transportation around campus provided by the university is great, but for students and visitors with cars, it's a huge hassle. Permits are expensive, and free parking for visitors is impossible to find. School officials are strict with violations, and tickets are $75. They are hard to refute and very costly."

Student Body

"The University of Maryland is a very large school," so "there is no 'typical' student here. Everyone will find that they can fit in somewhere." Better still, "different groups are very accepting of other groups. Students in Greek life are just as accepting of students in non-Greek life. Athletes blend in with non-athletes. UMD provides a great environment for students to meet people they would normally not know and helps to provide great connections with these people." UMD is "an especially diverse school," and this makes people "more tolerant and accepting of people from different backgrounds and cultures." A student from New Jersey explains it this way: "Coming from a very diverse area, I thought it was going to be hard to find a school that had that same representation of minority and atypical students until I found Maryland. I don't think I have ever learned so much about different religions, cultures, orientations, or lifestyles. All of them are accepted and even celebrated" at UMD.

THE PRINCETON REVIEW SAYS

Admissions

Very important factors considered include: Academic GPA, rigor of secondary school record, standardized test scores. *Important factors considered include:* Class rank, application essay, recommendation(s), first generation, state residency, talent/ability. *Other factors considered include:* Alumni/ae relation, character/personal qualities, extracurricular activities, geographical residence, racial/ethnic status, volunteer work, work experience. SAT or ACT required; ACT with Writing component required. TOEFL required of all international applicants. High school diploma is required, and GED is accepted. *Academic units required:* 4 English, 4 mathematics, 3 science, (2 science labs), 2 foreign language, 3 social studies.

Financial Aid

Students should submit: FAFSA. The Princeton Review suggests that all financial aid forms be submitted as soon as possible after January 1. *Need-based scholarships/grants offered:* Federal Pell, SEOG, state scholarships/grants, private scholarships, the school's own gift aid. *Loan aid offered:* Federal Perkins. Applicants will be notified of awards on a rolling basis beginning 4/1. Federal Work-Study Program available. Institutional employment available. Off-campus job opportunities are good.

The Inside Word

Maryland admissions officers don't simply crunch numbers and apply a formula. The school considers no fewer than 25 factors when determining who's in and who's out. Essays, recommendations, extracurricular activities, talents and skills, and demographic factors all figure into the mix along with high school transcript and standardized test scores. Give all aspects of your application your utmost attention; admissions are very competitive.

THE SCHOOL SAYS "..."

From The Admissions Office

"Commitment to excellence, to diversity, to learning—these are the hallmarks of a Maryland education. As the state's flagship campus and one of the nation's leading public universities, Maryland offers students and faculty the opportunity to come together to explore and create knowledge, to debate and discover our similarities and our differences, and to serve as a model of intellectual and cultural excellence for the state and the nation's capital. With leading programs in engineering, business, journalism, architecture, and the sciences, the university offers an outstanding educational value."

For even more information on this school, turn to page 546 of the "Stats" section.

UNIVERSITY OF MASSACHUSETTS—AMHERST

UNIVERSITY ADMISSIONS CENTER, AMHERST, MA 01003 • ADMISSIONS: 413-545-0222
FAX: 413-545-4312 • FINANCIAL AID: 413-545-0801 • E-MAIL: MAIL@ADMISSIONS.UMASS.EDU • WEBSITE: WWW.UMASS.EDU

RATINGS
Quality of Life: 88   Academic: 73   Admissions: 86   Financial Aid: 79

STUDENTS SAY ". . ."

Academics

It's all about "finding out where you fit in" at the University of Massachusetts—Amherst, where students say the experience is "all what you make of it. If you want to party, there is one available to you almost every night," but a pre-law

student warns that "academics are challenging," and other students agree, especially in the engineering program, the hard sciences, the sports management program ("one of the oldest and best in the country"), and at the Isenberg School of Management. As at many big schools, "It is easy to not go to class because they are so large, although many teachers now use the PRS [a handheld wireless interactive remote unit], which quizzes you and is a method of [taking] attendance during each class." You will also have the opportunity to get a degree with an "individual concentration" that allows you to design your own interdisciplinary majors. Students can also enroll—at no extra charge—in courses at Amherst, Hampshire, Mount Holyoke, and Smith colleges through the Five College Consortium. The consortium includes open library borrowing, a meal exchange, and a free bus system connecting the campuses. Unlike many major research institutions, UMass Amherst has a surprising number of professors who "show a passion for teaching. I have yet to see a professor who just teaches for money," a sports management major reports. By all accounts, "More than half of the professors are awesome." Students agree that "UMass Amherst has countless opportunities for one to get involved and improve his or her leadership and responsibilities."

Life

"There is so much to do on campus here that you rarely have to leave the school to find something," students report, pointing out that, in addition to attending one of the school's ubiquitous sporting events, "You can go ice skating on campus, go to a play, see bands play, see a movie, etc." Are you sitting down? "Most of these things are also free of charge, or available for a reduced fee." When the weather permits, "Numerous people are outside doing some sort of activity, whether it's playing catch, playing a sport with a bunch of people, or just laying out in the sun. In the Southwest Residential area, there is a horseshoe that people call Southwest Beach because on nice days it is packed with hundreds of people." If you're into socializing, "There is something going on every night of the week somewhere." One student says, "Drinking is big here but not totally out of control like some say." And another student assures us that, "It is more than possible to stay in on a Friday night, do your laundry, and watch a movie with friends. Parties are available, but not required." More students seem to want to live on campus now, lured perhaps by the new apartment style residence halls and dining services. Hometown Amherst provides "great restaurants and shows." Northampton and Holyoke, both close by, are "good places to go shopping."

Student Body

"There is no such thing as a typical student at UMass Amherst." An undergraduate population of moe than 20,000 makes that impossible; however, students do seem to fall into a few readily identified groups. There are "plenty of students who are here strictly for academics," people who are here for the party scene," and a "lot of people who came here for academics but fell into the party scene." Most learn to balance fun and work; those who don't exit long before graduation. Students also "tend to fit the mold of their residence," undergrads tell us. one student writes, "Southwest houses students of mainstream culture. Students there can be seen wearing everything from UMass—Amherst sweats to couture. Students in Central (especially Upper Central) tend to be the 'hippie' or scene type kids. Northeast houses...the more reserved types. Orchard Hill typically houses the more quiet types as well."

THE PRINCETON REVIEW SAYS

Admissions

Very important factors considered include: Academic GPA, rigor of secondary school record. *Important factors considered include:* Class rank, standardized test scores. *Other factors considered include:* Application essay, recommendation(s), character/personal qualities, extracurricular activities, first generation, geographical residence, level of applicant's interest, racial/ethnic status, state residency, talent/ability, volunteer work, work experience SAT or ACT required; ACT with Writing component recommended. TOEFL required of all international applicants. High school diploma is required, and GED is accepted. *Academic units required:* 4 English, 3 mathematics, 3 science, (2 science labs), 2 foreign language, 2 social studies, 2 academic electives.

Financial Aid

Students should submit: FAFSA. The Princeton Review suggests that all financial aid forms be submitted as soon as possible after January 1. *Need-based scholarships/grants offered:* Federal Pell, SEOG, state scholarships/grants, private scholarships, the school's own gift aid. *Loan aid offered:* Direct Subsidized Stafford, Direct Unsubsidized Stafford, Direct PLUS, Federal Perkins, state loans Applicants will be notified of awards on a rolling basis beginning 3/1. Federal Work-Study Program available. Institutional employment available. Off-campus job opportunities are good.

The Inside Word

University of Massachusetts—Amherst requires applicants to identify a first-choice and a second-choice major; admissions standards are tougher in the school's most prestigious programs (such as engineering, business, communications and journalism, economics, computer science, and sports management). It is possible to be admitted for your second-choice major but not your first; it is also possible to be admitted as an "undeclared" student if you fail to gain admission via your chosen majors. You can transfer into either major later, although doing so will require you to excel in your freshman and sophomore classes.

THE SCHOOL SAYS "..."

From The Admissions Office

"The University of Massachusetts—Amherst is the largest public university in New England, offering its students an almost limitless variety of academic programs and activities. Over 85 majors are offered, including a unique program called Bachelor's Degree with Individual Concentration (BDIC) in which students create their own program of study. (If you are a legal resident of Connecticut, Maine, New Hampshire, Rhode Island or Vermont, and the major you want at UMass—Amherst is not available at your public college, you may qualify for reduced tuition through the New England Regional Student Program.)The outstanding full-time faculty of over 1,100 is the best in their fields and they take teaching seriously. Students can take courses through the honors program and sample classes at nearby Amherst, Hampshire, Mount Holyoke, and Smith Colleges at no extra charge. First-year students participate in the Residential First-Year Year Experience with opportunities to explore every possible interest through residential life. The extensive library system is the largest at any public institution in the Northeast. The Center for Student Development brings together more than 200 clubs and organizations, fraternities and sororities, multicultural and religious centers. The campus completes in NCAA Division I sports for men and women, with teams winning national recognition. Award-winning student-operated businesses, the largest college daily newspaper in the region, and an active student government provide hands-on experience. About 5,000 students a year participate in the intramural sports program. The picturesque New England Town of Amherst offers shopping and dining, and the ski slopes of western Massachusetts and southern Vermont are close by. SAT or ACT scores are required for admission to the university. The school takes a holistic view of the student's application package and considers these scores as only part of the evaluation criteria. Additionally, any Advanced Placement, Honors, and SAT Subject Test scores are considered when reviewing each applicant. Increased applications in recent years have made admission more selective. "

For even more information on this school, turn to page 547 of the "Stats" section.

UNIVERSITY OF MASSACHUSETTS—BOSTON

100 MORRISSEY BOULEVARD, BOSTON, MA 02125-3393 • ADMISSIONS: 617-287-6000 • FAX: 617-287-5999
E-MAIL: ENROLLMENT.INFO@UMB.EDU • WEBSITE: WWW.UMB.EDU

RATINGS
Quality of Life: 72   Academic: 74   Admissions: 76   Financial Aid: 79

STUDENTS SAY "..."

Academics

SURVEY SAYS . . .
Diverse student types on campus
Different types of students interact
Students get along with local community
Frats and sororities are unpopular or nonexistent

The University of Massachusetts—Boston is an "afford-able" and "challenging" university "that cares about its students" and provides "a public education to all persons regardless of their walk of life." A "wide variety" of exemplary majors includes a "great nursing program." "At UMass Boston you get what you put in," explains a sopho-more. "If you put in the effort to get an Ivy League education you can get that, but if you only put in the effort to get a community college education, that's what you'll come away with." The faculty is "accomplished" and "very accessible outside of class." A few "awful" professors "can't teach," but most professors "will blow your mind with their intensity, passion, and commitment to your success." Administratively, "There are a lot of obnoxious bureaucratic obstacles." Class schedules are often "lousy." "If you want more guidance, you need to seek it out," warns a junior. "Otherwise, no one is going to help you." "Things generally sort themselves out," concludes another student. "There is a lot of red tape, but the academics are really great."

Life

UMass Boston's "urban" campus has "a beautiful location," being "precariously close to Boston Harbor." Students lament "the parking situation" and wish that "The buildings could be improved and renovated to look as nice as the Campus Center." Following that, the Campus Center "is a beautiful place with great food and places to hang out and study." "There are no residence halls" but "A lot of students live in an apartment complex called Harbor Point, next door to the school." There are "tons" of "fun and unique" organizations and activities here, though since "There are no dorms," "Most of the socializing happens off campus." "Students meet for classes without much interaction after classes." "UMB doesn't have a true student life," explains a senior. "It is quite possible to go through the day without interacting with other students, and to go through your college career without actually feeling that you are a part of the UMB community." "It's hard to meet people," agrees a nursing major. "They do their time and leave." That said, "There are parties" and "There is always something fun to do" in "the great and famous student city of Boston."

Student Body

"UMass Boston is the epitome of a diverse school," one student says. "Students come from suburbs and inner-city high schools with a huge range of perspectives." "Everyone brings with them unique experiences," says a junior, "just like the real world." "There are many international students" and "a significant number of older, adult, and elderly students . . . attend the school regularly between full-time and part-time jobs." "No student at the school is the same," so much so that "the only thing most students have in common is that they are from Massachusetts." UMass Boston is full of "uniquely determined," "individualistic" "career-seeking individuals." "We are, bar none, the hardest-working college students on the planet," boldly declares a sophomore. "We have to be, because we want to be lawyers, doctors, and leaders." "Except we have to do that and hold down full-time jobs," "raise families," and "run businesses."

THE PRINCETON REVIEW SAYS

Admissions

Very important factors considered include: Academic GPA, rigor of secondary school record, standardized test scores, character/personal qualities. *Important factors considered include:* Application essay, recommendation(s). *Other factors considered include:* Extracurricular activities, first generation, interview, level of applicant's interest, talent/ability, volunteer work, work experience. SAT required; SAT or ACT required; ACT required; TOEFL required of all international applicants. High school diploma is required and GED is accepted. *Academic units required:* 4 English, 3 mathematics, 3 science, (2 science labs), 2 foreign language, 1 social studies, 1 history, 2 academic electives.

Financial Aid

Students should submit: FAFSA. The Princeton Review suggests that all financial aid forms be submitted as soon as possible after January 1. *Need-based scholarships/grants offered:* Federal Pell, SEOG, state scholarships/grants, private scholarships, the school's own gift aid, Federal Nursing Scholarships. *Loan aid offered:* Direct Subsidized Stafford, Direct Unsubsidized Stafford, Direct PLUS, Federal Perkins. Applicants will be notified of awards on a rolling basis beginning 3/21. Off-campus job opportunities are excellent.

The Inside Word

Unless you want to be a part of the honors program, admission to UMass Boston is usually possible with solid high school grades and SAT or ACT scores (in some cases a GED can be enough). If you've been out of high school for three or more years, you don't have to submit standardized test scores. For all applicants, the 500-word essay plays a vital role in acceptance, so get typing!

THE SCHOOL SAYS " . . ."

From The Admissions Office

"The best advice we give out to any student considering us is simple: Just come see us for yourself. Visit us either for one of our year-round campus tours and info sessions. Or better yet, join us along with your friends and family for our annual fall Open House for prospective students, held on a Saturday at the end of every October—it's fun, informative, and you'll come away from it with a good idea of what life's like at UMass Boston.

"No matter when you decide to visit the campus, you'll get the opportunity to talk with one of our Admissions Counselors and current students about UMass Boston's academic programs, students services, student activities, and the application and financial aid process. Also, you'll get to check out the fitness center, library, computer labs, art gallery, sport facilities, bookstore, game room, food court, cafés, and classrooms. In addition, tours of the two apartment communities—located within steps of campus, where many students opt to live—can also be arranged.

"We also offer monthly Showcase Saturdays during most of the academic year for those who would prefer to visit us on the weekend for an in-depth information session and tour.

"Once you come to UMass Boston, you'll find a welcoming community. Every effort you make-to meet people, to get involved in activities, to share thoughts and projects with your professors-will be repaid in full.

"For more about the admissions process, and other aspects of UMass Boston—including the latest on campus visit options—please call 617-287-6000."

For even more information on this school, turn to page 547 of the "Stats" section.

UNIVERSITY OF NEW HAMPSHIRE

Four Garrison Avenue, Durham, NH 03824 • Admissions: 603-862-1360 • Fax: 603-862-0077
Financial Aid: 603-862-3600 • E-mail: admissions@unh.edu • Website: www.unh.edu

RATINGS

Quality of Life: 67   Academic: 68   Admissions: 80   Financial Aid: 73

STUDENTS SAY "..."

Academics

The benefits of going to a large, well-established state school, such as the University of New Hampshire, are exactly what one expects—its low in-state tuition, firmly established reputation, and place in the system allow it to offer "many resources to help students out in life." Located in tiny, beautiful Durham, the school "emphasizes research in every field, including non-science fields," and a lot of importance is placed "on the outdoors and the environment." The small town really fosters "lots of school spirit," and the laid-back denizens of UNH make it known that "having a good time" is a priority in their lives: "Weekends are for the Warriors."

Most professors "truly care" about the students' learning so that "you never feel like a number at the school but rather a respected student," and professors "will get down and dirty when it comes to experiencing what they're teaching first-hand." Though there are definitely complaints that some can be "subpar," a student "just needs to posses the initiative to go to their office hours" and they will get all the help they need. Some of the general education classes "are HUGE," and TAs can be difficult to understand, but for the most part, students report that they've had a "good experience" and that their academic careers has been "very successful." The Honors program is particularly challenging (in a very positive way) and offers "great seminar/inquiry classes that have about 15 students." Students universally pan the administration, claiming it "is a massive bureaucracy that gets little done," partially due to poor communication, or one student puts it that "the left hand has no idea what the right hand is doing." "The school is way more challenging than I thought it would be because the administration makes things harder than they need to be," says a sophomore.

Life

The school is just "15 minutes to the beach, one hour to the mountains, and one hour to Boston," making the world a Wildcat's oyster. Partying is big here, and the weekends are crazy; "Everyone goes out pretty much every Thursday, Friday, and Saturday night." The small number of bars in town "makes the age limit pretty well enforced." After a hard night out, "there are many late night convenience stores and food places to go to." In fact, it can be "difficult to find activities to do on the weekend that don't involve drinking," though UNH does a good job of bringing in "popular comedians, musicians, bands, political figures, etc.," and the school has tons of "amazing" a capella groups, so there is "almost always something to go see." Sports are also big here: "We love our hockey and football," says a student. Though there's a pretty big housing crunch, the oft-used athletic and recreational facilities here are both convenient and excellent, and since everything on this "beautiful" campus is only about 10 minutes away, "you walk pretty much everywhere," though public transportation and school-provided buses run often. Students do a lot of socializing over meals at the "eight cafés or in any of the three dining halls."

Student Body

This being New Hampshire, people are "very politically and socially aware." Students here are mostly middle-class and hail from New England (especially from New Hampshire, naturally), and a main point of contention among students is that there "is not a lot of ethnic/racial diversity," though the school is working on it. The size of UNH means that "even the most unique individual will find a group of friends," and even the most atypical students "fit in perfectly well." Most of these "laid-back" and "easy-to-get-along-with" Wildcats party, and it can be "hard to find one that doesn't." "EVERYONE skis or snowboards," and in the cold weather "Uggs and North Face fleece jackets abound."

THE PRINCETON REVIEW SAYS

Admissions

Very important factors considered include: Class rank, rigor of secondary school record. *Important factors considered include:* Academic GPA, recommendation(s). *Other factors considered include:* Application essay, standardized test scores, alumni/ae relation, character/personal qualities, extracurricular activities, first generation, geographical residence, racial/ethnic status, state residency, talent/ability, volunteer work, work experience. SAT or ACT required; ACT with Writing component required. TOEFL required of all international applicants. High school diploma is required, and GED is accepted. *Academic units required:* 4 English, 3 mathematics, 3 science, (2 science labs), 2 foreign language, 3 social studies. *Academic units recommended:* 4 English, 4 mathematics, 4 science, (3 science labs), 3 foreign language, 3 social studies, 1 academic electives.

Financial Aid

Students should submit: FAFSA. Regular filing deadline is 3/1. The Princeton Review suggests that all financial aid forms be submitted as soon as possible after January 1. *Need-based scholarships/grants offered:* Federal Pell, SEOG, state scholarships/grants, private scholarships, the school's own gift aid, Veterans Educational Benefits. *Loan aid offered:* Federal Perkins, college/university loans from institutional funds. Applicants will be notified of awards on a rolling basis beginning 3/1. Federal Work-Study Program available. Institutional employment available. Off-campus job opportunities are excellent.

The Inside Word

New Hampshire's emphasis on academic accomplishment in the admissions process makes it clear that the admissions committee is looking for students who have taken high school seriously. Standardized tests take as much of a backseat here as is possible at a large, public university.

THE SCHOOL SAYS "..."

From The Admissions Office

"The University of New Hampshire is an institution best defined by the students who take advantage of its opportunities. Enrolled students who are willing to engage in a high-quality academic community in some meaningful way, who have a genuine interest in discovering or developing new ideas, and who believe in each person's obligation to improve the community they live in typify the most successful students at UNH. Undergraduate students practice these three basic values in a variety of ways: by undertaking their own, independent research projects; by collaborating in faculty research; and by participating in study abroad, residential communities, community service, and other cultural programs.

"University of New Hampshire will require all high school graduates to submit results from the new SAT or the ACT (with the Writing component). The Writing portions will not be used for admissions decisions during the first 2–3 admissions cycles. Students graduating from high school prior to 2006 can submit results from the old SAT or ACT. The UNH admissions process does not require SAT Subject tests."

For even more information on this school, turn to page 547 of the "Stats" section.

UNIVERSITY OF PENNSYLVANIA

One College Hall, Philadelphia, PA 19104 • Admissions: 215-898-7507 • Fax: 215-898-9670
Financial Aid: 215-898-1988 • E-mail: info@admissions.ugao.upenn.edu • Website: www.upenn.edu

RATINGS
Quality of Life: 85   **Academic:** 91   **Admissions:** 99   **Financial Aid:** 95

STUDENTS SAY " . . ."

Academics

At the University of Pennsylvania, everyone shares an intellectual curiosity and top-notch resources but doesn't "buy into the stigma of being an Ivy League school." Still, no one turns down the opportunity to rave about the school's strong academic reputation or the large alumni network. Students here are also "very passionate about what they do outside the classroom" and the opportunities presented to them through attending UPenn. The university is composed of four undergraduate schools (and "a

> **SURVEY SAYS . . .**
> Athletic facilities are great
> Diverse student types on campus
> Great off-campus food
> Students are happy
> Student publications are popular
> Student government is popular
> Hard liquor is popular

library for pretty much any topic"), and students tend to focus on what they'll do with their degree pretty early on. Wharton, UPenn's "highly competitive undergraduate business school," creates a "tremendous pre-professional atmosphere" that keeps students competitive and somewhat stressed with their studies during the week. This "career-oriented" attitude spills over into other factions of the university, leaving some desiring more grounds for creativity and less climbing over each other. "It's when individuals' grades are on the line when the claws come out," says a student.

Professors can "sometimes seem to be caught up more in their research than their classes," but "there are very few other institutions where you can take every one of your classes with a professor who is setting the bar for research in his or her field." If you are willing to put in the time and effort, your professors "will be happy to reciprocate." In general, the instructors here are "very challenging academically," and one student says "some of them have been excellent, but all of them have at least been good." The administration is "very professional and efficient" and "truly interested in students' well being." "Academically, I have access to opportunities unparalleled elsewhere," says a student.

Life

Penn students don't mind getting into intellectual conversations during dinner, but "partying is a much higher priority here than it is at other Ivy League schools." Many students schedule their classes so as to not have class on Fridays, making the weekend "officially" start on Thursday night, and frat parties and Center City bars and clubs are popular destinations. However, when it comes down to midterms and finals, "people get really serious and...buckle down and study." Between weekend jaunts to New York and Philadelphia ("a city large enough to answer the needs of any type of person"), students have plenty of access to restaurants, shopping, concerts, and sports games, as well as plain old "hanging out with hallmates playing *Mario Kart*." The school provides plenty of guest speakers, cultural events, clubs, and organizations for students to channel their energies, and seniors can even attend "Feb Club" in the month of February, which is essentially an event every night. It's a busy life at UPenn, and "people are constantly trying to think about how they can balance getting good grades academically and their weekend plans."

Student Body

This "determined" bunch is very career-oriented, "takes classes pretty seriously," leans to the left, and "personality-wise tends to be type A." "There is always someone smarter than you are," says a chemical biomolecular engineering major. Everyone has "a strong sense of personal style and his or her own credo," but no group deviates too far from the more mainstream stereotypes. There's a definite lack of "emos" and hippies. There's "the career-driven Wharton kid who will stab you in the back to get your interview slot" and "the nursing kid who's practically non-existent," but on the whole, there is "tremendous school diversity," and whatever kind of person you are, "you will find a group of people like you."

Admissions

Very important factors considered include: Recommendation(s), rigor of secondary school record, character/personal qualities. *Important factors considered include:* Class rank, application essay, academic GPA, standardized test scores, extracurricular activities, work experience. *Other factors considered include:* Alumni/ae relation, first generation, geographical residence, interview, racial/ethnic status, talent/ability, volunteer work, SAT and SAT Subject Tests or ACT required; ACT with Writing component required. TOEFL required of all international applicants. High school diploma or equivalent is not required. *Academic units required:* 4 English, 4 mathematics, 3 science, (3 science labs), 4 foreign language, 3 history.

Financial Aid

Students should submit: FAFSA, institution's own financial aid form, CSS/Financial Aid PROFILE, noncustodial PROFILE, business/farm supplement, parents' and student's most recently completed income tax. The Princeton Review suggests that all financial aid forms be submitted as soon as possible after January 1. *Need-based scholarships/grants offered:* Federal Pell, SEOG, state scholarships/grants, private scholarships, the school's own gift aid. *Loan aid offered:* Federal Perkins, Federal Nursing, college/university loans from institutional funds, other, Supplemental 3rd Party Loans guaranteed by institution. Applicants will be notified of awards on or about 4/1. Federal Work-Study Program available. Institutional employment available. Off-campus job opportunities are excellent.

The Inside Word

After a small decline four cycles ago, applications are once again climbing at Penn—the fifth increase in six years. The competition in the applicant pool is formidable. Applicants can safely assume that they need to be one of the strongest students in their graduating class in order to be successful.

THE SCHOOL SAYS "…"

From The Admissions Office

"The nation's first university, the University of Pennsylvania, had its beginnings in 1740, some 36 years before Thomas Jefferson, Benjamin Franklin (Penn's founder), and their fellow revolutionaries went public in Philadelphia with incendiary notions about life, liberty and the pursuit of happiness. Today, Penn continues in the spirit of the Founding Fathers, developing the intellectual, discussion-oriented seminars that comprise the majority of our course offerings, shaping innovative new courses of study, and allowing a remarkable degree of academic flexibility to its undergraduate students. Penn is situated on a green, tree-lined, 260-acre urban campus, four blocks west of the Schuylkill River in Philadelphia. The broad lawns that connect Penn's stately halls embody a philosophy of academic freedom within our undergraduate schools. Newly developed interdisciplinary programs fusing classical disciplines with practical, professional options enable Penn to define cutting-edge academia in and out of the classroom. Students are encouraged to partake in study and research that may extend into many of the graduate and professional schools. Penn students are part of a dynamic community that includes a traditional campus, a lively neighborhood, and a city rich in culture and diversity. Whether your interests include artistic performance, community involvement, student government, athletics, fraternities and sororities, or cultural and religious organizations, you'll find many different options. Most importantly, students at Penn find that their lives in and out of the classroom compliment each other and are full, interesting and busy. We invite you to visit Penn in Philadelphia. You'll enjoy the revolutionary spirit of the campus and city. Penn requires either the SAT plus two SAT Subject Tests (in different fields) or the ACT."

For even more information on this school, turn to page 548 of the "Stats" section.

UNIVERSITY OF PITTSBURGH—BRADFORD

OFFICE OF ADMISSIONS—HANLEY LIBRARY, 300 CAMPUS DRIVE, BRADFORD, PA 16701 • ADMISSIONS: 814-362-7555 • FAX: 814-362-7578
E-MAIL: ADMISSIONS@WWW.UPB.PITT.EDU • WEBSITE: WWW.UPB.PITT.EDU

RATINGS
Quality of Life: 74   Academic: 70   Admissions: 71   Financial Aid: 89

STUDENTS SAY "..."

Academics

The University of Pittsburgh at Bradford is "a cozy gem in the middle of nowhere" that offers "small classes with individualized attention, professors who are always available, and a generally student-friendly atmosphere." The curriculum is largely career-oriented. Popular majors include business, education, and nursing. The athletic training major is reportedly excellent and "this school excels in the criminal justice area" as well. "Some professors are amazing and others are not very good," counsels a biology major. Overall though, faculty members are "personable" and they "have real life experiences to bring back to the classrooms." "Professors learn your name," adds an elementary education major, "and you are yourself instead of just a number." The administration is "very friendly and helpful," "or at least they try to be." "A lot of them are actually quite hilarious personally."

> **SURVEY SAYS . . .**
> *Different types of students interact*
> *Low cost of living*

Life

This campus in the "rural" upper reaches of Pennsylvania is very compact. "End to end, the campus is a 10-minute walk," estimates a first-year student, "if you walk slow." It's a good thing, too, because parking is "a struggle every day to even get a spot." "A lot of the students here at Bradford are involved in sports," either intramural or intercollegiate. "There are sororities and fraternities." "Campus-wide events"—"comedians and that sort of thing"—also "get students out of their dorms." Student opinion concerning the rustic location is split. Some students love the "absolutely beautiful," "peaceful location" and the "gorgeous view of mountains." "I love how it has that out-in-the-country feel," declares a senior. That good 'ole country feeling comes with plenty of outdoor activities, including "ice skating, tubing," and snowboarding and hunting a little farther afield. Other students complain that "it snows a lot" and tell us that "there is not much to do" in the "extremely boring" town of Bradford. A solid contingent of students enjoys "partying on the weekends" but the scene here is pretty tame. "If you require bars, clubs, and nightlife to be happy, this is not the place for you," advises a senior. "Many students return home or at least leave campus" when Friday classes are over.

Student Body

The typical undergrad is either "from a small town or from Pittsburgh." "There are a lot of commuter and adult learners" as well. Students describe themselves as "down-to-earth people" "who are easily approachable." The "friendly hello" is common here. "If you run short of money while doing laundry, don't be surprised if somebody throws you a dollar to help you get your laundry done," predicts a senior. "There are a handful of weird" students but nobody really strays too far in any direction away from the social median. "Everyone has friends." "Everyone fits in everywhere" and, "for the most part, everyone gets along with everybody else."

Admissions

Very important factors considered include: Level of applicant's interest. *Important factors considered include:* Academic GPA, rigor of secondary school record, standardized test scores, interview. *Other factors considered include:* Class rank, application essay, recommendation(s), character/personal qualities, extracurricular activities, talent/ability, volunteer work, work experience. SAT or ACT required; TOEFL required of all international applicants. High school diploma is required and GED is accepted. *Academic units required:* 4 English, 2 mathematics, 1 science, (1 science labs), 2 foreign language, 1 history, 5 academic electives. *Academic units recommended:* 4 English, 2 science, (2 science labs), 2 foreign language, 1 history, 5 academic electives.

Financial Aid

Students should submit: FAFSA. The Princeton Review suggests that all financial aid forms be submitted as soon as possible after January 1. *Need-based scholarships/grants offered:* Federal Pell, SEOG, state scholarships/grants, private scholarships, the school's own gift aid. *Loan aid offered:* Federal Perkins. Applicants will be notified of awards on a rolling basis beginning 4/1. Federal Work-Study Program available. Institutional employment available. Off-campus job opportunities are fair.

The Inside Word

The admit rate at Pitt-Bradford is not extraordinarily high but don't be deterred—admissions requirements are not out of reach. If you have a C-plus to B-minus average in high school and your standardized test scores are middling, you should have little problem getting accepted.

THE SCHOOL SAYS " . . ."

From The Admissions Office

"When it comes to picking a college, many students discover that they have to choose between a university where teachers know and care about their students or a world-renowned institution from which they can earn a reputable degree. At Pitt—Bradford, you don't have to choose. You can have both and so much more.

"You can go beyond: Go beyond the classroom by participating in one of the many internships and research opportunities. Go beyond the degree by taking advantage of our robust Career Services Office and our informal alumni network to help you find a satisfying career. Go beyond the typical 9-to-5 day by taking part in an active student life, a friendly residence life environment, and excellent athletic, cultural, and recreational opportunities. Go beyond place by receiving a liberal arts education that will expose you to the world and participating in one of several study abroad opportunities. And go beyond your expectations by receiving a college experience that will transform you.

"At Pitt—Bradford, you will live and learn on a safe, intimate campus where you will receive individual and personalized attention from committed professors who will work side by side with you. And you will earn a degree from the University of Pittsburgh, which commands respect around the world."

For even more information on this school, turn to page 548 of the "Stats" section.

UNIVERSITY OF PITTSBURGH—JOHNSTOWN

450 SCHOOLHOUSE ROAD, 157 BLACKINGTON HALL, JOHNSTOWN, PA 15904 • ADMISSIONS: 814-269-7050
FAX: 814-269-7044 • E-MAIL: UPJADMIT@PITT.EDU • WEBSITE: WWW.UPJ.PITT.EDU

RATINGS
Quality of Life: 73   **Academic:** 68   **Admissions:** 71   **Financial Aid:** 67

STUDENTS SAY ". . ."

Academics

Undergrads tell us that The University of Pittsburgh at Johnstown "is about having a good college experience at a small campus while growing as a student and person." The school offers "an excellent undergraduate campus to explore scientific fields," as well as engineering and education programs that "have a high success rate." Academics

focus on practical experience in most disciplines; as one student explains, "My professors have all worked in the field that they are teaching," which not only "adds validity to what they are teaching," but also means that "they can help students get internships and the experience that they need." Profs here "are generally very accessible," but their teaching can be "hit or miss." One student explains, "Some professors at UPJ are sensational, but others can be total bores. The academic experience in Johnstown is what you make of it. If you want to get the most out of it, you can." Those who succeed in doing so insist that UPJ offers "a small school feel with a big university name" that translates into "a very positive employment rate for graduating students."

Life

"The weekends can get pretty boring sometimes" at UPJ because "there isn't much to do in Johnstown" and "a lot of students go home on the weekends." As one student observes, "It's a rural atmosphere, so the social life reflects that. It's like choosing between living in the city and living in a small town. UPJ is the small-town choice. The safe and pleasant atmosphere compensates for the lack of nightlife." One perk of the location is that "We get a lot of snow, so many students enjoy going to local ski resorts or sled riding on campus." Students tell us that "there are parties every weekend," but "Although there is a majority of students who like to drink alcohol and party, it is easy to find other students that are not interested in those activities. Just because you don't drink, doesn't mean that you're not going to have any friends here." "The movies and bowling" are "always popular places for students" and it's "hard to go to either location without seeing another group of students from the university."

Student Body

UPJ undergrads are "hardworking, fun-loving individuals looking to make a difference on campus on way or another." They are "generally from western Pennsylvania," either "from the Pittsburgh or Johnstown-Somerset area," with many "who live nearby in small towns." The school is predominantly Caucasian "so ethnically, it's not very diverse," but this is something that the school is "working on." Additionally, "Many students here are engineering majors," so some find that the school also lacks diversity in terms of areas of interest. One student observes that "The typical student is a walking advertisement for Hollister. It is very preppy here. There aren't a lot of artsy, goth, or other types of people." That said, the atypical students here "fit in by banding in groups in which they recognize and celebrate each others uniqueness."

Admissions

Very important factors considered include: Class rank, academic GPA, rigor of secondary school record. *Important factors considered include:* Application essay, recommendation(s), standardized test scores, extracurricular activities, interview, level of applicant's interest, talent/ability, volunteer work, work experience. *Other factors considered include:* Character/personal qualities, racial/ethnic status. SAT or ACT required; ACT with Writing component recommended. TOEFL required of all international applicants. High school diploma is required and GED is accepted. *Academic units required:* 4 English, 2 mathematics, 2 science, (1 science labs), 2 foreign language, 4 social studies. *Academic units recommended:* 3 mathematics.

Financial Aid

Students should submit: FAFSA, state aid form. The Princeton Review suggests that all financial aid forms be submitted as soon as possible after January 1. *Need-based scholarships/grants offered:* Federal Pell, SEOG, state scholarships/grants, private scholarships, the school's own gift aid. *Loan aid offered:* Federal Perkins. Applicants will be notified of awards on a rolling basis beginning 3/15. Federal Work-Study Program available. Institutional employment available. Off-campus job opportunities are good.

The Inside Word

UPJ admits over 93 percent of all applicants. Essentially, the school admits everyone it believes has a chance to succeed in its academic programs. As a result of attrition through failure or transfer, just slightly over half of all students who enroll at UPJ graduate from the school within six years.

THE SCHOOL SAYS " . . ."

From The Admissions Office

"The University of Pittsburgh—Johnstown (UPJ) was established in 1927, one of the first regional campuses of a major university in the United States, and became a 4-year, degree-granting college of the university in 1970. As a regional campus of a public (state-related) university, it has the more affordable costs and the comprehensive range of programs (education, business, engineering technology, etc.) of a public institution. At the same time, it has many of the features found in a private college. It has a good reputation for academic rigor and quality programs. It's a relatively small enrollment (about 3,100 full- and part-time students); most students are full-time and of traditional age (18–24); it's entirely undergraduate—no graduate programs; all teachers are faculty, no graduate teaching assistants; the classes are typically small; the campus is largely residential (more than 60 percent of students reside in campus housing); and the campus itself is very attractive—suburban, wooded, with lots of room, a consistent fieldstone architecture, and peripheral parking.

"Students who choose the University of Pittsburgh—Johnstown feel that it offers a smaller setting and a beautiful campus, combined with most of the advantages of a large university. Students like the fact that most professors and administrators are accessible, and also see UPJ as offering a good variety of challenging classes. There is a strong emphasis on undergraduate research opportunities, a solid internship program, and good career guidance. Students often talk about finding a 'comfort zone' at UPJ."

For even more information on this school, turn to page 549 of the "Stats" section.

University of Pittsburgh—Pittsburgh Campus

Alumni Hall, 4227 Fifth Avenue, First Floor, Pittsburgh, PA 15260 • Admissions: 412-624-7488
Fax: 412-648-8815 • Financial Aid: 412-624-7488 • E-mail: oafa@pitt.edu • Website: www.pitt.edu

RATINGS

Quality of Life: 98   Academic: 83   Admissions: 92   Financial Aid: 78

STUDENTS SAY "..."

Academics

SURVEY SAYS . . .
Low cost of living
Student publications are popular

Students at the University of Pittsburgh—Pittsburgh Campus call their school an "under-recognized treasure of opportunity and scholasticism," with "brilliant professors doing fantastic things in their fields." As a large research university, some students say that "Administrators are generally unavailable for 'normal' students." However, others laud the effectiveness of the school's "Deans' Hours" where "students can ask questions and administrat[ors] can better learn of the needs of the student community" which "can help you get around the red tape." "The advising system isn't super strong, but is sufficient for someone [who is] relatively independent." Nevertheless, "Administrators and professors are both surprisingly eager to involve students and are sincerely interested in our happiness and success." In large lecture courses and in classes that meet general education requirements, "you have to go to office hours to get to know the professors"; however, if you reach out they will "push you to bring out the best of your abilities." In essence, "Pitt provides all the resources of a large research university (which it is), but [it] also retains a small college atmosphere with its Honors College to provide the best opportunities for its students." One of the benefits of being a major research university is that research opportunities abound and "there is definitely a professor willing to take on pretty much anyone." The in-class experience gets mixed reviews, with accolades for "brilliant" professors that are "passionate" about their fields coupled with concerns about those "who leave [students] behind" and aren't as focused about teaching. The key to avoiding the duds, "like at any other institution," "is to do your research."

Life

Pitt offers a great balance between a college environment "that offers a lot of opportunities for fun," and a medium-sized, affordable city "with a ton of places to eat and shop." As one student observes, "Something that unifies Pitt students is passion—be it [for] Pitt's renowned medical program, Division I athletics, copious quantities of clubs, or [for] the many internships available." On the weekends, "most students [go] to frat parties or house and apartment parties in Oakland." Oakland is also home to a "lively" college bar scene for Pitt students of age, and "There are a lot of informal get-togethers within the dorms." Even though "typical students study hard, party harder," "there are so many alternatives for things to do because of being in the city." Pitt (both the campus and the city) is home to "major sports teams [that] are also a big source of involvement and pride." So it's no surprise that participating in intramurals or watching sporting events—"college and professional"—are major pastimes. A "variety" of clubs and activities offer opportunities for any interest. Taking advantage of hometown Pittsburgh's many offerings is also easy, convenient, and free with a Pitt ID. "There are opportunities to do everything...for a reduced price," including attending professional sporting events. Moreover, "PittArts provides...free arts activities on weekends." As one sophomore sums up, "Pitt is the smallest big school, and the campus is truly the city."

Student Body

Roughly three-quarters of Pitt students are from Pennsylvania, and overall, students are "middle-class" and "personable and accepting." "You're going to find slackers at every school, but the majority of people [here] work very hard and have heavy workloads." Going to Pitt is about "being in the middle of everything with the greatest people you can find." Beyond that, Pitt's large size and diverse student body means "we're big enough that there's a group for everyone" and that students "can develop a group of friends" while still being "accepted with open arms" by the larger student community. Says one Pitt student, "There are many atypical students when considering backgrounds, ethnicity, and beliefs, but a common interest in positive academic pursuits and community development brings us all together." While "there are different cliques," "the interaction of so many cultures and student groups...leads to awesome exchanges and education for the student body.

THE PRINCETON REVIEW SAYS

Admissions

Very important factors considered include: Academic GPA, rigor of secondary school record. *Important factors considered include:* Standardized test scores. *Other factors considered include:* Class rank, application essay, recommendation(s), character/personal qualities, extracurricular activities, first generation, geographical residence, interview, level of applicant's interest, racial/ethnic status, talent/ability, volunteer work, work expe SAT or ACT required; TOEFL required of all international applicants. High school diploma is required, and GED is not accepted. *Academic units required:* 4 English, 3 mathematics, 3 science, (3 science labs), 2 foreign language, 2 social studies, 3 academic electives. *Academic units recommended:* 4 English, 4 mathematics, 4 science, (4 science labs), 3 foreign language, 3 social studies, 0 history, 0 visual/performing arts, 0 computer science, 5 academic electives.

Financial Aid

Students should submit: FAFSA. The Princeton Review suggests that all financial aid forms be submitted as soon as possible after January 1. *Need-based scholarships/grants offered:* Federal Pell, SEOG, state scholarships/grants, private scholarships, the school's own gift aid, Federal Nursing Scholarships. *Loan aid offered:* Federal Perkins, Federal Nursing, college/university loans from institutional funds. Applicants will be notified of awards on a rolling basis beginning 3/15. Federal Work-Study Program available. Institutional employment available. Off-campus job opportunities are excellent.

The Inside Word

Despite the large number of applications Pitt receives, admissions counselors review each application individually with a holistic perspective. Essays and recommendation are taken into consideration. That said, strong secondary school records and test scores rank high on the admit list. Applicants with honors classes, advanced placement classes, and solid grades have the best chance of admission.

THE SCHOOL SAYS "..."

From The Admissions Office

"The University of Pittsburgh is one of 62 members of the Association of American Universities, a prestigious group whose members include the major research universities of North America. There are nearly 400 degree programs available at the 16 Pittsburgh campus schools (two offering only undergraduate degree programs, four offering graduate degree programs, and ten offering both) and four regional campuses, allowing students a wide latitude of choices, both academically and in setting and style, size and pace of campus. Programs ranked nationally include philosophy, history and philosophy of science, chemistry, economics, English, history, physics, political science, and psychology. "Some of the company the University of Pittsburgh keeps: Pitt ranks in the very top cluster of U.S. public research universities according to the 2007 edition of The Top American Research Universities annual report, issued by The Center for Measuring University Performance, along with Berkeley, Illinois, Michigan, UCLA, UNC, Wisconsin; it has a notable record of high achieving graduates—since 1995 Pitt undergraduates have won two Rhodes, six Marshal, five Truman, four Udall, one Churchill, one Gates Cambridge, 33 Goldwater scholarships, and three Mellon Humanities Fellowships. In research, Pitt ranks sixth among all U.S. universities in terms of competitive grants awarded to faculty by the National Institutes of Health. In international education, only 17 American universities can claim four or more area studies programs that have been competitively designated National Resource Centers by the U.S. Department of Education. In intercollegiate athletics, Pitt's football and men's basketball teams are consistently considered among the finest."

For even more information on this school, turn to page 549 of the "Stats" section.

UNIVERSITY OF RHODE ISLAND

14 UPPER COLLEGE ROAD, KINGSTON, RI 02881-1391 • ADMISSIONS: 401-874-7000 • FAX: 401-874-5523
FINANCIAL AID: 401-874-9500 • E-MAIL: URIADMIT@ETA1.URI.EDU • WEBSITE: WWW.URI.EDU

RATINGS
Quality of Life: 66   Academic: 67   Admissions: 76   Financial Aid: 75

STUDENTS SAY ". . ."

Academics

The University of Rhode Island "is a pretty decent middle-sized school in a great location." Notable majors include "nursing, engineering, or anything science." Film media, languages and textiles program are also popular within the liberal arts fields. The "excellent" pharmacy program at URI is competitive and nationally recognized. Students also laud the great film media program. Many classes are "very

rigorous." Others are "wicked easy." For both, "there are many resources available to get help." The faculty really runs the gamut. "There are some really good ones, but some are just awful." The good profs "genuinely care about teaching" and "willingly offer their time" outside of class. "All of my teachers have had considerable experience in their field and bring a lot to the classroom," says an impressed freshman. As for the bad professors, "there are some serious horror stories." Some students think the subpar professors "cancel class almost too much," some bemoan the lack of outside help and the brief periods of time that qualify as office hours, and some have a hard time understanding the accents of foreign professors. URI's administration receives similarly mixed reviews. "I have had very few problems with administration," says one student. "They are happy to sit down and talk with you about any concerns that you have, and they will help solve your problems." Other students see "an ardent bureaucracy" "too obsessed with drinking policies to pay attention to what really matters."

Life

"URI is a gorgeous school—especially in the fall—on a big hill." It's located in a "safe" and "rural" area. "Parking is horrible," though the university has recently opened 1,400 new student parking space and set a shuttle bus system into place so as to make pedestrian traffic safer. The school has recently renovated 12 undergrad residence halls and added new suite and apartment style living quarters. For some students, URI is a "suitcase school." "A lot of students do go home on the weekends just because they live so close by." "If you get involved on campus you will love it," says a psychology major. "If not, you will want to transfer." Intramurals and varsity sports are popular. "Basketball is huge; so is hockey" "There are beautiful beaches right down the road from campus where you can surf, swim, or just sit and read," weather permitting. "Greek life is very popular, and if you live on campus it feels like everyone is part of it (but they're not)." The campus is ostensibly dry, but the alcohol policy certainly "hasn't stopped URI students from getting wasted." "One thing I didn't know coming to URI was how much of the social life happens off campus," discloses an English major. Parties occur 15 minutes away—"down the line," as students here say. On weekends, there are "house parties" in Narragansett by the beach. Bars are also popular. Students looking for more urban pursuits often travel 30 miles north to Providence.

Student Body

"The University of Rhode Island is an affordable option for in-state students." "Most out-of-state residents are from wealthy families or have scholarships." There are "a lot of generic college kids who go to college for the social aspect." "URI is mostly made up of guys that want to party and drive BMWs and girls that wear North Face jackets, Ugg boots, and big Dior sunglasses," stereotypes one student. Politically, it's a "pretty liberal" but mostly "apathetic" crowd. "However, if you search you can find some cool people who don't fit the mold." "There are many different students here," attests a nutrition major, "from jocks and jockettes to artists to frat boys and sorority girls." Ethnic diversity is not unreasonable but URI is cliquish. "People here do tend to hang out with people who are more similar to them." "Ethnicities mostly do not mix." Rhode Islanders often "stick to" high school friends.

THE PRINCETON REVIEW SAYS

Admissions

Very important factors considered include: Rigor of secondary school record. *Important factors considered include:* Class rank, application essay, academic GPA, standardized test scores. *Other factors considered include:* Recommendation(s), alumni/ae relation, character/personal qualities, extracurricular activities, first generation, geographical residence, level of applicant's interest, racial/ethnic status, state residency, talent/ability, volunteer work, work experienc SAT or ACT required; ACT with Writing component recommended. TOEFL required of all international applicants. High school diploma is required, and GED is accepted. *Academic units required:* 4 English, 3 mathematics, 2 science, (1 science labs), 2 foreign language, 2 social studies, 5 academic electives.

Financial Aid

Students should submit: FAFSA. The Princeton Review suggests that all financial aid forms be submitted as soon as possible after January 1. *Need-based scholarships/grants offered:* Federal Pell, SEOG, state scholarships/grants, private scholarships, the school's own gift aid. *Loan aid offered:* Direct Subsidized Stafford, Direct Unsubsidized Stafford, Direct PLUS, Federal Perkins, Federal Nursing, state loans, college/university loans from institutional funds. Applicants will be notified of awards on a rolling basis beginning 3/31. Federal Work-Study Program available. Institutional employment available. Off-campus job opportunities are good.

The Inside Word

Any candidate with solid grades is likely to find the university's Admissions Committee to be welcoming. The yield of admits who enroll is low and the state's population small. Out-of-state students are attractive to URI because they are sorely needed to fill out the student body. Students who graduate in the top 10 percent of their class are good scholarship bets. If you are a resident of a New England state other then Rhode Island, you get a tuition discount, but only if you enroll in certain degree programs.

THE SCHOOL SAYS "..."

From The Admissions Office

"Outstanding freshman candidates admission with a minimum SAT score of 1200 (combined Critical Reading and Math) or ACT composite score of 25 who rank in the top quarter of their high school class are eligible to be considered for a Centennial Scholarship. These merit-based scholarships range up to full tuition and are renewable each semester if the student maintains full-time continuous enrollment and a 3.0 average or better. In order to be eligible for consideration, all application materials must be received in the Admission Office by the December 1, early-action deadline. Applications are not considered complete until the application fee, completed application, official high school transcript, list of senior courses, personal essay, and SAT or ACT scores (sent directly from the testing agency) are received.

"If a student is awarded a Centennial Scholarship, and his or her residency status changes from out-of-state to regional or in-state, the amount of the award will be reduced to reflect the reduced tuition rate.

"The SAT Math and Critical Reading scores are used for admission evaluation and Centennial Scholarship consideration. The Writing score is not currently used for admission evaluation or Centennial Scholarship consideration."

For even more information on this school, turn to page 550 of the "Stats" section.

UNIVERSITY OF ROCHESTER

300 WILSON BOULEVARD, PO BOX 270251, ROCHESTER, NY 14627 • ADMISSIONS: 585-275-3221
FAX: 585-461-4595 • FINANCIAL AID: 585-275-3226 • E-MAIL: ADMIT@ADMISSIONS.ROCHESTER.EDU • WEBSITE: WWW.ROCHESTER.EDU

RATINGS

Quality of Life: 70   **Academic:** 87   **Admissions:** 96   **Financial Aid:** 90

STUDENTS SAY ". . ."

Academics

Students at the University of Rochester praise its "great atmosphere, superior academics," and "beautiful campus" by simply saying: "What more could you want?" Indeed, this college "couples strong academics without the cut-throat competitive atmosphere" meaning that students feel

"relaxed" while being "pushed to do their best and forge their own paths." As one undergrad explains, "Rochester balances the academic prestige of an Ivy League school with a small, close-knit community and the drive to ensure that every student reaches their full potential." The "intimate" classes allow students to get to know their "knowledgeable and enthusiastic" professors, who "on the whole" are "stellar in terms of their qualifications, their accessibility, and their ability to teach." The faculty is widely known for "making time for students," however some students note "most science professors are here to do research as a first priority, not to teach." Also worth mentioning are the "great" career center and study-abroad offices. The administration is "usually helpful," and most note that they have "open doors and ears to students." Others feel that while the administration "does a good job of running the university," they're a bit lacking when it comes to "communicating with the students." Despite this, students agree the "academic experience" at Rochester leaves "very little to be desired." After all, notes one student, "You cannot escape this place without learning a hell of a lot."

Life

At this "academic school" expect life to be "very busy" thanks to "a lot of studying," but don't worry: "There's always time for fun." Whether your interests involve "movies, music, parties," or "bars," you'll find something to occupy your time away from the books. "There's always something to do at school," says one undergrad, "which is in large part due to the student-run clubs. There are clubs in almost all areas of interest, and each club makes a true effort to organize interesting programs for the student population." When the weekend arrives "most people hang out at the frat quad," which is "generally bustling with parties." "There's drinking just like [at] any college," says one student, "but generally people are much more in control than at a big state school." For those less inclined to imbibe there are "bajillions of clubs and organizations" on campus, and then there's always the city of Rochester itself. The school has a "bus system" that provides free access for students to "various places around town." The city boasts a "pretty awesome" music scene, and "there's always a show or concert on the weekends." And while Rochester's notoriously brutal winters might make some stay indoors, outdoor enthusiasts will find plenty on offer in any season, including lots of "hiking" and "skiing."

Student Body

Most students at Rochester are hard-pressed to describe the "typical" student here. Expect a "very high level" of "ethnic, religious, and social" diversity here thanks to the "wide variety of opportunities" the school offers. However, despite differences the student body has many shared traits. "Rochester is all about smart, fun, and interesting people who take their classes and their work seriously but still know how to have a good time," says one undergrad. These "driven" and "hard-working" students often have "a unique set of interests and are dedicated to pursing them" within "the university and the outside community." Because of this wide range of interests "everyone finds their niche" here. Though this can yield a "sometimes cliquish" atmosphere, students note "there's plenty of opportunity for interaction between different groups."

Admissions

Very important factors considered include: Recommendation(s), rigor of secondary school record, character/personal qualities. *Important factors considered include:* Application essay, academic GPA, standardized test scores, extracurricular activities, interview, talent/ability. *Other factors considered include:* Class rank, alumni/ae relation, first generation, geographical residence, level of applicant's interest, racial/ethnic status, volunteer work, work experience. SAT or ACT required; TOEFL required of all international applicants. High school diploma is required, and GED is accepted.

Financial Aid

Students should submit: FAFSA, CSS/Financial Aid PROFILE, state aid form, noncustodial PROFILE, business/farm supplement. Regular filing deadline is 2/1. The Princeton Review suggests that all financial aid forms be submitted as soon as possible after January 1. *Need-based scholarships/grants offered:* Federal Pell, SEOG, state scholarships/grants, the school's own gift aid. *Loan aid offered:* Direct Subsidized Stafford, Direct Unsubsidized Stafford, Direct PLUS, Federal Perkins, Federal Nursing, college/university loans from institutional funds. Applicants will be notified of awards on or about 4/1. Federal Work-Study Program available. Institutional employment available. Off-campus job opportunities are excellent.

The Inside Word

With nearly 5,300 undergrads, applicants to Rochester can expect a highly individualized academic experience—something that not only makes this school a great place to learn, but also an increasingly competitive institution when it comes to admissions. The most important consideration for admission is grades and standardized test scores, followed closely by the rigor of class work and recommendations. Keep in mind that Rochester is looking for students who will fit well within the school's academic environment and demonstrate a true interest in attending—i.e., scheduling an interview could go a long way in increasing your odds.

THE SCHOOL SAYS "..."

From The Admissions Office

"Rochester believes that excellence requires freedom. In the Rochester Curriculum, students are free to select the courses that appeal to them most. There are no required subjects; students' interests drive their education. Students major in either sciences and engineering, humanities, or social sciences and complete a "cluster" of at least three related courses in each of the other two areas. Because Rochester is among America's smallest research universities, its students can pursue advanced studies and research in graduate courses, in arts and science or in any one of Rochester's nationally ranked schools of engineering, medicine, nursing, music, education, and business."

"Learning here takes place on a personal scale. Rochester remains one of the most collegiate among top research universities, with smaller classes and a 9:1 student-faculty ratio-all within a university setting that attracts more than $400 million in research funding each year. Rochester faculty publish articles across the globe, win awards for their work, and collaborate with undergraduate students on a level that is rare in higher education."

"The expectation is that each student will live up to Rochester's motto, "Meliora" (ever better), recognizing that they are future leaders in industry, education, and culture. Navigating through world-renowned facilities and resources, a day in the life of two Rochester students-or any two days in the life of a single student-is never the same."

For even more information on this school, turn to page 550 of the "Stats" section.

UNIVERSITY OF SCRANTON

800 LINDEN STREET, SCRANTON, PA 18510 • ADMISSIONS: 570-941-7540 • FAX: 570-941-5928
FINANCIAL AID: 570-941-7700 • E-MAIL: ADMISSIONS@SCRANTON.EDU • WEBSITE: WWW.SCRANTON.EDU

RATINGS
Quality of Life: 78   Academic: 77   Admissions: 85   Financial Aid: 70

STUDENTS SAY ". . ."
Academics

With "an outstanding record for admission to graduate programs, not only in law and medicine but also in several other fields," The University of Scranton is a good fit for ambitious students seeking "a Jesuit school in every sense of the word. If you come here, expect to be challenged to become a better person, to develop a strong concern for the poor and marginalized, and to grow spiritually and intel-

lectually." The school manages to accomplish this without "forcing religion upon you, which is nice." Undergraduates also approve of the mandatory liberal-arts-based curriculum that "forces you to learn about broader things than your own major." Strong majors here include "an amazing occupational therapy program, [an] excellent special education program," business, and biology. "This is a great place for premeds and other sciences," students agree. While the workload can be difficult, "a tutoring center provides free tutoring for any students who may need it, and also provides work-study positions for students who qualify to tutor." Need more help? Professors "are extremely accessible. They will go to any lengths to help you understand material and do well," while administrators "are here for the students, and show that every day inside and outside of the classroom." Community ties here are strong; as one student points out, "the Jesuits live in our dorms, creating an even greater sense of community, because we don't view them as just priests, we view them as real people who can relate on our level."

Life

"There is a whole range of activities to do on the weekends" at The University of Scranton, including "frequent trips, dances, and movies that are screened for free." Students tell us "the school and student organizations provide plenty of options, such as retreats, talent shows, and other various activities." There are also "many intramurals to become involved in, and the varsity sports (specifically the women's) are very successful." Furthermore, "being a Jesuit school, social justice issues are huge. They are taught in the classroom, and students spend a lot of time volunteering." Hometown Scranton is big enough to provide "movie theaters, two malls, parks, a zoo, a bowling alley, and a skiing/snowboarding mountain." In short, there are plenty of choices for the non-partier at Scranton. Many we heard from in our survey reported busy extracurricular schedules. But those seeking a party won't be disappointed here, either. Scranton undergrads "party a lot, but they balance it with studying. Parties are chances to go out, see people, dance, and drink if you want." You "can find a party any time of day, seven days a week" here, usually with a keg tapped and pouring. Few here feel the party scene is out of hand, however a typical student writes, "It's very different than at schools with Greek systems. It is a lot more laid-back, and all about everyone having a good time."

Student Body

While "the typical Scranton student is white, Catholic, and from the suburbs," students hasten to point out "within this sameness, there is much diversity. There are people who couldn't care at all about religion, and there are people who are deeply religious. Even in the Catholic atmosphere of the school, the school only requires that you learn about Catholicism as it stands. Theology classes…are prefaced with the idea that 'You do not have to believe this!'" Undergrads here are generally "friendly and welcoming. Cliques are pretty much nonexistent, and anyone who would be classified as 'popular' is only considered so because they are extremely friendly, outgoing, and seek out friendships with as many people as possible." Students tend to be on the Abercrombie-preppy side, with lots of undergrads of Italian, Irish, and Polish descent.

THE PRINCETON REVIEW SAYS

Admissions

Very important factors considered include: Class rank, academic GPA, rigor of secondary school record, standardized test scores. *Important factors considered include:* Extracurricular activities. *Other factors considered include:* Application essay, recommendation(s), alumni/ae relation, character/personal qualities, interview, level of applicant's interest, talent/ability, volunteer work, work experience. SAT or ACT required; TOEFL required of all international applicants. High school diploma is required, and GED is accepted. *Academic units required:* 4 English, 3 mathematics, 3 science, (1 science labs), 2 foreign language, 2 social studies, 2 history, 4 academic electives. *Academic units recommended:* 4 English, 4 mathematics, 3 science, (1 science labs), 2 foreign language, 3 social studies, 3 history, 4 academic electives.

Financial Aid

Students should submit: FAFSA. The Princeton Review suggests that all financial aid forms be submitted as soon as possible after January 1. *Need-based scholarships/grants offered:* Federal Pell, SEOG, state scholarships/grants, private scholarships, the school's own gift aid. *Loan aid offered:* Direct Subsidized Stafford, Direct Unsubsidized Stafford, Direct PLUS, Federal Perkins, Federal Nursing Applicants will be notified of awards on a rolling basis beginning 3/15. Federal Work-Study Program available. Institutional employment available. Off-campus job opportunities are good.

The Inside Word

Admission to Scranton gets harder each year. A steady stream of smart kids from the tristate area keeps classes full and the admit rate low. Successful applicants will need solid grades and test scores. As with many religiously affiliated schools, students should be a good match philosophically as well.

THE SCHOOL SAYS "..."

From The Admissions Office

"A Jesuit institution in Pennsylvania's Pocono Northeast, The University of Scranton is known for its outstanding academics, state-of-the art campus, and exceptional sense of community. Founded in 1888, the University offers more than 80 undergraduate and graduate academic programs of study through four colleges and schools.

"The Princeton Review included Scranton among *The Best Colleges* in the nation in past years. For years, Scranton was the only college in Pennsylvania and the only Jesuit university to have a student named to the first academic team.

"Freshman applicants are required to take the SAT or ACT exam. The writing scores will not be considered in the admissions decision process. Students are encouraged to apply early for admission and can do so online with no application fee."

For even more information on this school, turn to page 551 of the "Stats" section.

UNIVERSITY OF SOUTHERN MAINE

37 College Avenue, Gorham, ME 04038 • Admissions: 207-780-5670 • Fax: 207-780-5640
E-mail: usmadm@usm.maine.edu • Website: www.usm.maine.edu

RATINGS
Quality of Life: 70   **Academic:** 69   **Admissions:** 71   **Financial Aid:** 72

STUDENTS SAY "..."

Academics

The University of Southern Maine "provides the best bang for your buck for local and nontraditional students." The USM campus, with its hubs in Portland and Gorham, offers residence hall living on its Gorham hub. There are over 50 undergraduate majors here and USM is the largest of the seven campuses in the University of Maine System but it's

> **SURVEY SAYS . . .**
> Students get along with local community
> Students love Gorham and Portland, ME
> Great off-campus food
> Low cost of living

"not a gigantic university." "Lectures aren't that big" and upper-level courses tend to be pretty small. Some students tell us that classroom discussion is solid. Others contend that "the learning atmosphere is not at all lively." Whatever the case, USM's professors are often "passionate about the material" and sometimes "incredibly good." Students report that they are "very accommodating" outside of the classroom as well. The administration, on the other hand, receives mixed reviews. Students appreciate that "there are opportunities to meet with the President and discuss changes that should/could be made," but complain that "the times are completely inconvenient," and that sometimes the suggestions that are made are slow to be put into effect.

Life

In more ways than one, USM is largely "a commuter school." The majority of the "younger, traditional students" here live on the Gorham campus but many classes occur on the Portland campus, some 10 miles away. "It's quite frankly a pain to deal with two campuses," advises a weary senior. "Your freshman and sophomore year you spend a lot of time traveling between them." Also, "aesthetically, the campuses have some big eyesores." "The buildings are mostly old, cold, and outdated," though a state of the art green dorm has just opened and three new buildings forming a "university commons" on the Portland campus were recently completed. Students also complain about the "nauseating food." Socially, USM offers "a ton of things to do." Intercollegiate sports are strong and there are "dances, concerts, and game nights throughout the week." Quite a bit of social activity takes place in Portland. It's "a very nice city, the biggest in Maine," and it's reportedly "very much an epicenter for the arts, pubs, and eateries." Also, there are "two ski resorts within an hour away," and "winter sports are pretty much unlimited."

Students

"Most people who go to USM live in Maine or at least the New England area." Ethnic diversity is minimal. "Maine is not very diverse," points out a senior. "The student population reflects the overall population of Maine." Students describe themselves as "very laidback and polite." "Everyone seems to get along pretty well." Nevertheless, "USM lacks a cohesive, unified student body." "Many students work full time" and a sizeable segment of the population is either "slightly above traditional college age" or middle-aged and "in the midst of a total career change." Many nontraditional students are too busy with their own lives to really participate in campus activities. The traditionally college-aged students tend to stick to smaller groups. "It's kind of like high school with all the different clique types you see around campus," says a senior. "The range is from Abercrombie wannabe to eclectic nerd to gothic." There are the "left-wing liberal hippies," "the sorority girls, the frat guys," and the "music and theater kids." There is also "a big homosexual community."

THE PRINCETON REVIEW SAYS

Admissions

Very important factors considered include: Class rank, rigor of secondary school record, standardized test scores. *Important factors considered include:* Application essay, recommendation(s). *Other factors considered include:* Academic GPA, alumni/ae relation, character/personal qualities, extracurricular activities, geographical residence, interview, level of applicant's interest, racial/ethnic status, state residency, talent/ability, volunteer work, work experience. SAT or ACT required; ACT with Writing component required. TOEFL required of all international applicants. High school diploma is required and GED is accepted. *Academic units required:* 4 English, 3 mathematics, 2 science, (2 science labs), 2 foreign language, 2 social studies, 2 history. *Academic units recommended:* 4 mathematics, 3 science, (3 science labs), 3 foreign language, 3 social studies, 3 history.

Financial Aid

Students should submit: FAFSA. The Princeton Review suggests that all financial aid forms be submitted as soon as possible after January 1. *Need-based scholarships/grants offered:* Federal Pell, SEOG, state scholarships/grants, private scholarships, the school's own gift aid. *Loan aid offered:* Federal Perkins, Federal Nursing, state loans. Applicants will be notified of awards on a rolling basis beginning 3/15. Federal Work-Study Program available. Off-campus job opportunities are excellent.

The Inside Word

Admission at USM operates on a rolling basis, and it's basically uncompetitive. If you get your application in early and have remotely decent grades and standardized scores, you should have no problems getting in. It's also worth noting that applicants don't need to submit test scores if they have been out of high school for three years or have at least 30 hours of college credit.

THE SCHOOL SAYS " . . ."

From The Admissions Office

"At the center of the USM experience is a bustling campus with its hubs—only 12 miles apart—one in downtown Portland and the other in nearby Gorham. Students spend time at both hubs, living the Maine lifestyle to the fullest. The energy of the sophisticated city of Portland on the water, full of shopping, art, music, dining, and career opportunities, offer a living and learning experience that blends seamlessly from the classroom into the city.

"USM offers over 70 areas of study at the undergraduate level, 25 NCAA Division III athletic teams, and over 100 clubs and organizations. Students are given opportunities to uncover their hidden talents, and to take advantage of opportunities to get experience—whether it be through internships, volunteer projects, musical or theater performances, or any variety of experiences.

"USM gives students a motivating learning environment, with classmates whose varied experiences and cultures make discussion stimulating, and professors whose priority is teaching, USM is a place where not only knowledge is gained, but wisdom, too."

For even more information on this school, turn to page 551 of the "Stats" section.

UNIVERSITY OF VERMONT

OFFICE OF ADMISSIONS, 194 S. PROSPECT STREET, BURLINGTON, VT 05401-3596 • ADMISSIONS: 802-656-3370
FAX: 802-656-8611 • FINANCIAL AID: 802-656-3156 • E-MAIL: ADMISSIONS@UVM.EDU • WEBSITE: WWW.UVM.EDU

RATINGS
Quality of Life: 83   **Academic:** 73   **Admissions:** 83   **Financial Aid:** 72

STUDENTS SAY ". . ."

Academics

> **SURVEY SAYS . . .**
> Students are friendly
> Students love Burlington, VT
> Great off-campus food
> Political activism is popular
> Lots of beer drinking
> Hard liquor is popular

Quality of life issues are important to most University of Vermont undergrads; when discussing their reasons for choosing UVM, they're as likely to cite the "laid-back environment," the "proximity to skiing facilities," the "great parties," and their "amazing" hometown of Burlington as they are to mention the academics. But, students remind us, "That doesn't mean that there are not strong academics [at UVM]." On the contrary, UVM is made up of several well-established colleges and offers "a wide variety of majors." "You can jump around between majors, and then leave with a recognized diploma in hand for something you love to do." Students single out the business school, the "top-notch" education program, the psychology department, premedical sciences, and "the amazing animal science program" for praise, and are especially proud of The Rubenstein School of Natural Resources. It is home to UVM's environmental science majors; students tell us it "is a great college that feels like it's much smaller, [more] separate, and just cozier than the rest of the school." No matter which discipline, "you get out what you put in." "Teachers are readily available and are willing to help you do well in your classes. They encourage you to get help if you need it and are enthusiastic about what they teach. It's all there; you just have to take advantage of it." The size of the university, we're told, is just right. UVM is "a moderately-large school," and it allows undergrads "to feel at home while still offering just about any activity possible."

Life

"UVM is known to be a party school," "even though the university has cracked down on drinking." Indeed, students tell us that one can find "a good balance of having fun and academics" at UVM, "but it's tough, because there's always a party going on somewhere." Students who want to dodge the party scene will find "there is always something" happening in Burlington. The town has "lots of wonderful restaurants, a few movie theaters, a rockin' music scene, several bars, some dancing, and various environmental and social activities downtown." "On campus, there is typically at least one university-sponsored event each night, including interesting lectures, movies, games, or social events." Students love outdoor activities. "When it snows, it's very popular to go to the ski resorts around here and ski or snowboard for the day. When it's still warm out, going to the waterfront and swimming in Lake Champlain is popular too." UVM is an intercollegiate hockey powerhouse, and "in the fall and winter, hockey games are huge social events." They're so popular "that you have to get tickets to them the Monday before the game, or they will be sold out!"

Student Body

There's a "great variety of students" at UVM "because it's a big university," undergrads report, but they also note that "students at UVM are mostly white" and there's "a lot of money at this school." While the most prevalent UVM archetype is "the guitar-loving, earth-saving, relaxed hippie" who "care[s] strongly about the environment" and "social justice," the student body also includes "your athletic types, your artsy people, and a number of other groups" including "vocal LGBTQ and ALANA populations" who, "usually hang out in their own groups," but "are also active in all sorts of clubs across campus." Not surprisingly, there are many "New England types," "potheads," and "snow bums." Students report they "pretty much get along well with everyone." They either come here loving the outdoors or learn to love the outdoors by the time they leave.

THE PRINCETON REVIEW SAYS

Admissions

Very important factors considered include: Rigor of secondary school record. *Important factors considered include:* Class rank, application essay, academic GPA, standardized test scores, character/personal qualities, state residency. *Other factors considered include:* Recommendation(s), alumni/ae relation, extracurricular activities, first generation, geographical residence, interview, level of applicant's interest, racial/ethnic status, talent/ability, volunteer work, work experience. SAT or ACT required; ACT with Writing component required. TOEFL required of all international applicants. High school diploma is required, and GED is accepted. *Academic units required:* 4 English, 3 mathematics, 2 science, (1 science labs), 2 foreign language, 3 social studies.

Financial Aid

Students should submit: FAFSA. The Princeton Review suggests that all financial aid forms be submitted as soon as possible after January 1. *Need-based scholarships/grants offered:* Federal Pell, SEOG, state scholarships/grants, private scholarships, the school's own gift aid, Federal Nursing Scholarships. *Loan aid offered:* Federal Perkins, Federal Nursing, college/university loans from institutional funds. Applicants will be notified of awards on a rolling basis beginning 3/15. Federal Work-Study Program available. Institutional employment available. Off-campus job opportunities are good.

The Inside Word

UVM is a very popular choice among out-of-state students, whom the school welcomes; more than half the student body originates from outside of Vermont. While admissions standards are significantly more rigorous for out-of-staters, solid candidates (B-plus/A-minus average, about a 600 on each section of the SAT) should do fine here. The school assesses applications holistically, meaning students who are weak in one area may be able to make up for it with strengths or distinguishing skills and characteristics in other areas.

THE SCHOOL SAYS "..."

From The Admissions Office

"The University of Vermont blends the close faculty-student relationships most commonly found in a small liberal arts college with the dynamic exchange of knowledge associated with a research university. This is not surprising, because UVM is both. A comprehensive research university offering nearly 100 undergraduate majors and extensive offerings through its Graduate College and College of Medicine, UVM is one of the nation's premier public research universities. UVM prides itself on the richness of its undergraduate experience. Distinguished senior faculty teach introductory courses in their fields. They also advise not only juniors and seniors, but also first- and second-year students, and work collaboratively with undergraduates on research initiatives. Students find extensive opportunities to test classroom knowledge in field through practicums, academic internships, and community service. More than 100 student organizations (involving 80 percent of the student body), 18 Division I varsity teams, 15 intercollegiate club and 14 intramural sports programs, and a packed schedule of cultural events fill in where the classroom leaves off.

"Applicants for the entering class and beyond are required to take the SAT, or the ACT with the Writing section, and they must submit official test scores. SAT Subject Tests are neither required nor recommended for the admission application."

For even more information on this school, turn to page 552 of the "Stats" section.

Ursinus College

Ursinus College, Admissions Office, Collegeville, PA 19426 • Admissions: 610-409-3200
Fax: 610-409-3662 • Financial Aid: 610-409-3600 • E-mail: admissions@ursinus.edu • Website: www.ursinus.edu

RATINGS
Quality of Life: 82   Academic: 93   Admissions: 92   Financial Aid: 84

STUDENTS SAY ". . ."

Academics

Ursinus College, a small liberal arts school in aptly named Collegeville, PA. offers a wide array of courses and "has the facilities of a much larger school." "I truly believe that Ursinus is a transformative experience," declares an international relations major. "If you embrace the liberal arts education, this is the institution to be at." "Academic rigor is demanding." A required pair of first-year courses called "the Common Intellectual Experience" "create a bonding experience for the students, and it gets them to think about some extremely important issues." Beyond that, students must complete a host of core requirements in addition to their majors. You'll "do your fair share of 10- to 15-page term papers; usually a couple per semester." "But it pays off in the end." The small size allows for "discussion-based classes" and professors "really try to get students involved." "Some professors are full of themselves," admits a neuroscience major. However, they are "great teachers and certainly know what they're talking about." "I have loved all of my professors," gushes a math major. "They've been friendly, helpful, and knowledgeable. They're eager to get students involved in research." Management is "accessible" as well. The "down-to-earth" administrators "are often seen about the campus attending lectures, concerts, and sporting events." Strong majors here include biology and chemistry. Ursinus boasts an impressive 90-plus percent acceptance rate with medical schools. Students also laud the economics and arts programs.

Life

Ursinus boasts "a very beautiful campus." Some of the older dorms cry out for refurbishing, though, and newer ones are "faintly reminiscent of a hospital." The food isn't great, either. "They stop carting out the good food after the second week," warns a biology major. Also, wireless Internet is spotty. Despite these complaints, students tell us they are extremely happy. "People overall love the school," says a freshman. Ursinus students are proud of their ability to have fun. "There are parties almost every night," especially Thursday through Saturday." The administration tries to crack down, but students persevere, and the drinking scene remains rollicking. House parties or suite parties are options but the Greek system "rules campus life." "The keggers held by Greek organizations" are the most widely attended bashes. Not everyone drinks, of course, "not by a long shot." "The cool thing about Ursinus is that regardless of whether you drink or not, you can still go to the parties and have a great time." Some students warn that "Ursinus can be a little dull" if you insist on avoiding the party scene altogether. Others disagree saying, "there is an incredible availability of activities and clubs on campus." Intramural and varsity athletics are also very popular. Students "love to go to all the food places in Collegeville" as well. It is "difficult" to get too far off campus without a car, though. (And first-year students can't have them.) While "there is no shame inherent in taking the bus" to Philadelphia, few students do.

Student Body

By and large, while ethnic diversity isn't terrible for a small liberal arts school, Ursinus is "homogenous." "Most people come from wealthier families" and grew up in the comfortable suburbs of "New Jersey, Pennsylvania, and New York." Ursinus students are "very hardworking" and "have similar values." Politically, there's a mildly liberal slant. "Most students on this campus are active and highly involved, although those who do not engage in clubs and activities do seem to find each other." The prototypical Ursinus student is a "somewhat clean-cut, friendly, occasionally drunk," "Hollister-clad, Ugg-wearing" prepster. "Different cliques are evident," though. There are "smart jocks and wonderfully weird nerds." There are "stereotypical frat boys." "There are many weirdoes and there are many average Joes." "Ursinus somehow seems to provide a safe and comfortable environment for people of all different interests," remarks one student.

THE PRINCETON REVIEW SAYS

Admissions

Very important factors considered include: Class rank, rigor of secondary school record, extracurricular activities. *Important factors considered include:* Application essay, academic GPA, recommendation(s), alumni/ae relation, racial/ethnic status, talent/ability, volunteer work, work experience. *Other factors considered include:* Standardized test scores, character/personal qualities, first generation, geographical residence, interview, level of applicant's interest, ACT with Writing component recommended. TOEFL required of all international applicants. High school diploma is required, and GED is not accepted. *Academic units required:* 4 English, 3 mathematics, 1 science, (1 science labs), 2 foreign language, 1 social studies. *Academic units recommended:* 4 English, 4 mathematics, 4 science, (2 science labs), 4 foreign language, 4 social studies.

Financial Aid

Students should submit: FAFSA, institution's own financial aid form, CSS/Financial Aid PROFILE. Regular filing deadline is 2/15. The Princeton Review suggests that all financial aid forms be submitted as soon as possible after January 1. *Need-based scholarships/grants offered:* Federal Pell, SEOG, state scholarships/grants, private scholarships, the school's own gift aid. *Loan aid offered:* Federal Perkins. Applicants will be notified of awards on or about 4/1. Federal Work-Study Program available. Institutional employment available. Off-campus job opportunities are excellent.

The Inside Word

Grades, and class rank count for more than anything else, and unless you are academically inconsistent, you'll likely get good news. If you are hoping to snag a scholarship, it's really essential that you visit campus and get yourself interviewed. SAT and ACT test scores are now optional for all applicants.

THE SCHOOL SAYS "..."

From The Admissions Office

"Located a half-hour from center-city Philadelphia, the college boasts a beautiful 168-acre campus that includes the Residential Village (renovated Victorian-style homes that decorate the Main Street and house our students) and the nationally recognized Berman Museum of Art. Ursinus is a member of the Centennial Conference, competing both in academics and in intercollegiate athletics with institutions such as Dickinson, Franklin & Marshall, Gettysburg, and Muhlenberg. The academic environment is enhanced with such fine programs as a chapter of Phi Beta Kappa, an early assurance program to medical school with the Medical College of Pennsylvania, and myriad student exchanges both at home and abroad. A heavy emphasis is placed on student research—an emphasis that can only be carried out with the one-on-one attention Ursinus students receive from their professors.

"Ursinus will continue to ask applicants for writing samples—both a series of application essays and a graded high school paper."

For even more information on this school, turn to page 552 of the "Stats" section.

Vassar College

124 Raymond Avenue, Poughkeepsie, NY 12604 • Admissions: 845-437-7300 • Fax: 845-437-7063
Financial Aid: 845-437-5320 • E-mail: admissions@vassar.edu • Website: www.vassar.edu

RATINGS
Quality of Life: 79   **Academic:** 97   **Admissions:** 98   **Financial Aid:** 98

STUDENTS SAY "..."

Academics

Vassar College gives students "the chance to experiment with [their] life in an encouraging and stimulating environment," providing an unusual amount of academic freedom because "there's no real core curriculum. All you need in the way of requirements are one quantitative class and one foreign language credit. Plus, one-quarter of your credits must be outside of your major." This approach, students

> **SURVEY SAYS . . .**
> *No one cheats*
> *Students aren't religious*
> *Frats and sororities are unpopular or nonexistent*
> *Theater is popular*
> *Political activism is popular*

agree, "really encourages students to think creatively and pursue whatever they're passionate about, whether medieval tapestries, neuroscience, or unicycles. Not having a core curriculum is great because it gives students the opportunity to delve into many different interests." Of course, a system like this only works if students are motivated and teachers are dedicated. Fortunately, that's exactly how it shakes out at Vassar. The school boasts "world-class professors, small classes, and a faculty that really is interested in us as students. Every teacher and member of the faculty goes the extra mile to [be] available outside of class and [to] meet students for lunch or dinner." Vassar places "a real focus on the undergraduate students. There is big-time research just like at major universities, but there are no graduate students to fill all the spots. All assisting positions go to undergraduates." The school excels in the visual and performing arts—the "drama department is huge"—as well as in English, psychology, history, life sciences, and natural sciences.

Life

"Life is very campus-centered" at Vassar; the farthest off campus people regularly go is the 24-hour diner two blocks north of campus. This is partly because hometown Poughkeepsie "does not offer much in the way of entertainment." For whatever reason, insularity is a defining characteristic of life at Vassar, so much so that students speak of "The Vassar Bubble. This is a term any student will immediately become familiar with. Essentially, Vassar is an island closed off from the rest of the town and community. It would be entirely possible (and not even rare) for a student to not leave campus once in an entire semester. While this is good for some, others will likely go a little crazy stuck on campus." Some escape to New York City whenever possible, but unfortunately the trip to the city is a relatively "expensive endeavor for weekly entertainment; it's about $35 round-trip, and that doesn't include doing stuff once you get there." Fortunately, "there is a huge array of things to do every night on campus. Comedy shows, improv, an incredibly wide array of theater productions"—including "several shows a year and three student groups devoted to drama"—"four comedy groups, five a cappella groups," and "interesting lectures create numerous opportunities to get out of the dorms at night." Weekends are for parties; there's "no Greek life, so lots of parties are awesome, school-sponsored, theme events." There's also "lots of socializing at senior housing," and "Halloween is huge. People really go all out."

Student Body

There are "lots of hipsters" at Vassar including kids who are "very left-wing politically" and "very into the music scene." The school is "not entirely dominated by hipsters," however; there are "lots of different groups" on campus. "Walking around you'll see students who walked out of a thrift store next to students who walked out of a J.Crew catalog," one student tells us. Another adds that Vassar is a comfortable respite for "indie-chic students who revel in obscurity, some socially awkward archetypes, and some prep school pin-ups with their collars popped. But the majority of kids on campus are a mix of these people, which is why we mesh pretty well despite the cliques that inevitably form." What students share is having "an amazing talent or something they passionately believe in" that makes them distinctive. "Vassar admissions works tremendously hard to ensure every student at Vassar is unique and mold-breaking," students brag.

Admissions

Very important factors considered include: Rigor of secondary school record. *Important factors considered include:* Class rank, application essay, academic GPA, recommendation(s), standardized test scores, extracurricular activities, talent/ability. *Other factors considered include:* Alumni/ae relation, character/personal qualities, first generation, geographical residence, interview, level of applicant's interest, racial/ethnic status, volunteer work, work experience. SAT and SAT Subject Tests or ACT required; ACT with Writing component required. TOEFL required of all international applicants. High school diploma is required, and GED is accepted. *Academic units required:* 4 English, 4 mathematics, 4 science, (3 science labs), 3 foreign language, 2 social studies, 2 history, 4 academic electives. *Academic units recommended:* 4 English, 4 mathematics, 4 science, (3 science labs), 4 foreign language, 4 social studies, 2 history.

Financial Aid

Students should submit: FAFSA, CSS/Financial Aid PROFILE, noncustodial PROFILE, business/farm supplement. Regular filing deadline is 2/1. The Princeton Review suggests that all financial aid forms be submitted as soon as possible after January 1. *Need-based scholarships/grants offered:* Federal Pell, SEOG, state scholarships/grants, private scholarships, the school's own gift aid. *Loan aid offered:* Direct Subsidized Stafford, Direct Unsubsidized Stafford, Direct PLUS, Federal Perkins, Other, Loans for Non-citizens with need. Applicants will be notified of awards on or about 3/30. Federal Work-Study Program available. Institutional employment available. Off-campus job opportunities are fair.

The Inside Word

With acceptance rates hitting record lows, stellar academic credentials are a must for any serious Vassar candidate. Importantly, the college prides itself on selecting students who will add to the vitality of the campus. Once admissions officers see you meet their rigorous scholastic standards, they'll closely assess your personal essay, recommendations, and extracurricular activities. Demonstrating an intellectual curiosity that extends outside the classroom is as important as success within it.

THE SCHOOL SAYS "..."

From The Admissions Office

"Vassar presents a rich variety of social and cultural activities, clubs, sports, living arrangements, and regional attractions. Vassar is a vital, residential college community recognized for its respect for the rights and individuality of others.

"Candidates must submit either the SAT Reasoning Test and two SAT Subject Tests taken in different subject fields, or the ACT exam (the optional ACT writing component is recommended)."

For even more information on this school, turn to page 553 of the "Stats" section.

VILLANOVA UNIVERSITY

800 LANCASTER AVENUE, VILLANOVA, PA 19085-1672 • ADMISSIONS: 610-519-4000 • FAX: 610-519-6450
FINANCIAL AID: 610-519-4010 • E-MAIL: GOTOVU@EMAIL.VILLANOVA.EDU • WEBSITE: WWW.VILLANOVA.EDU

RATINGS
Quality of Life: 99   Academic: 88   Admissions: 95   Financial Aid: 70

STUDENTS SAY "..."

Academics

"Villanova emphasizes not only the importance of academics but also service and connection with the community," is
how one student sums up life at this Catholic university
just outside Philadelphia. Most students agree the school's
emphasis on community and "dedication to service" was

SURVEY SAYS . . .
School is well run
Low cost of living
Everyone loves the Wildcats

an important factor as was its excellent academic reputation. That said, Villanova's "well-rounded academic
focus," "excellent nursing and business school programs," and "outstanding" faculty are definitely strong
draws for students who choose to attend. Villanova "requires students to take classes based on a core curriculum, which [leads] to a well-rounded education." "You will work hard," warns one student, "but if you put in
the work, you will do well." "The professors at Villanova are fantastic!" says another. "I've had professors give
out e-mail addresses, cell, home and office numbers, even an AIM screenname in order to make contacting them
as easy as possible." The professors for the most part are "PhDs and love to teach. You are never taught by a
grad student." Even the harshest critique has an element of praise in it: "You either get someone you completely
click with and is very interactive with students, or you get a PhD who just has to teach a class and isn't very
good at teaching, but is really, really smart." The administration gets high marks as well. "If I wanted to meet
with Father Peter, the president of Villanova, I could go see him tomorrow. Everyone is accessible." Keep in
mind, though, that a little initiative is not a bad thing. "You need to be your own advocate—you can get anything you want if you ask nicely (or not so nicely, if need be), but nothing will happen if you don't ask."

Life

The "idea of community is extremely important" at Villanova, and student life, both on campus and off, tends
to reflect that. "The average student works hard four days a week, parties harder two days a week, and spends
the seventh day working for some cause," explains one student. "Life at Villanova seems to be a work hard during the day, play hard during the night atmosphere," says another. "People are serious about their schoolwork
and do many activities. However, once it becomes nighttime, especially Thursday through Saturday, many people drink and throw parties. People generally like to have a good time." "Basketball and frat parties" seem to
make up a majority of the social life. But, "there is always stuff to do for fun that does not involve partying."
"Sporting events are huge here at the school as our basketball program is fantastic." It's worth pointing out "if
you don't like basketball, you will learn to like it even if you never actually understand it." Villanova is only 12
miles and a short train ride away from Center City Philadelphia, where "many people go out to dinner or shopping," or to watch (of course) basketball at the Wachovia Center. The school also provides free shuttle buses to
the huge King of Prussia mall nearby. There is a Greek presence at Villanova, but because "there are no frat,
sorority, or sports houses on campus," much of the Greek life takes place at off-campus houses and apartments,
and "parties are usually hard to get to." Ultimately, "the community of students is very tight-knit," and "there
are always activities on campus that involve volunteer work or group projects in the surrounding areas."

Student Body

"Good-looking, white, over-achievers who like to have a good time" seems to be the prevailing consensus.
"However, that seems to be changing more and more every year," one student says. "We are starting to see
many more minorities, which obviously is a great and refreshing thing to see." "Villanova is not as preppy, conservative, or homogeneous as it was….The newer students seem a bit more liberal and academic than the students of years before." Regardless of race or politics, the typical Villanova student "is very service oriented and
excels academically," not to mention a "basketball fanatic." "In general, everyone gets along nicely, and the multitude of student organizations and trips foster school unity." Many people note, although Villanova is not a
huge university, "students outside the Villanova norm can easily find their own niche in the community."

THE PRINCETON REVIEW SAYS

Admissions

Very important factors considered include: Class rank, academic GPA, rigor of secondary school record, standardized test scores. *Important factors considered include:* Application essay, recommendation(s), character/personal qualities, extracurricular activities, talent/ability, volunteer work, work experience. *Other factors considered include:* Alumni/ae relation, first generation, geographical residence, level of applicant's interest, racial/ethnic status, state residency. SAT or ACT required; ACT with Writing component required. TOEFL required of all international applicants. High school diploma is required, and GED is accepted. *Academic units required:* 4 English, 4 mathematics, 4 science, (2 science labs), 2 foreign language, 2 academic electives. *Academic units recommended:* 4 English, 4 mathematics, 4 science, (3 science labs), 4 foreign language, 2 academic electives.

Financial Aid

Students should submit: FAFSA, institution's own financial aid form. Regular filing deadline is 2/7. The Princeton Review suggests that all financial aid forms be submitted as soon as possible after January 1. *Need-based scholarships/grants offered:* Federal Pell, SEOG, state scholarships/grants, private scholarships, the school's own gift aid. *Loan aid offered:* Federal Perkins, Federal Nursing Applicants will be notified of awards on or about 4/1. Federal Work-Study Program available. Institutional employment available. Off-campus job opportunities are excellent.

The Inside Word

Villanova's growing academic reputation means its application process is growing more competitive as well: 88 percent of the most recent freshman class ranked in the top 25 percent of their high school graduating class. But while academic achievement is important, the university looks at the whole package when considering applicants and expects candidates to do the same. As a private university, Villanova is not exactly cheap, but the school offers a wide variety of scholarships and aid to qualifying students.

THE SCHOOL SAYS "…"

From The Admissions Office

"Villanova is the oldest and largest Catholic university in Pennsylvania, founded in 1842 by the Order of Saint Augustine. Students of all faiths are welcome. The university tends to attract students who are interested in volunteerism. Villanovans provide more than 64,000 hours of service annually and host the largest student-run Special Olympics in the nation. Villanova's scenic campus is located 12 miles west of Philadelphia. The university offers programs through four undergraduate colleges: Liberal Arts and Sciences, Engineering, Nursing, and the Villanova School of Business. There are 250 student organizations and 32 National Honor Societies at Villanova. Incoming freshmen can opt to be part of a Learning Community, through which student groups live together in specially-designated residence halls and learn together in courses and co-curricular programs. The university offers Naval and Marine Reserve Officers Training Corps (ROTC) programs and hundreds of options for studying abroad. 'Nova's alumni body is comprised of 90,000 people. Some prominent grads *include:* Maria Bello, Golden Globe-Nominated Actress; Rear Admiral Christine Bruzek-Kohler, Director of the U.S. Navy Nurse Corps and Chief of Staff for the Navy Bureau of Medicine and Surgery; Nnenna Lynch, Olympian and Rhodes Scholar; Robert Moran, President and COO of PetSmart; James O'Donnell, CEO of American Eagle Outfitters; and Dianna Sugg, Pulitzer Prize Recipient for Journalism.

"If you're looking to join 'Nova Nation, be prepared: The competition for admission is getting tougher every year."

For even more information on this school, turn to page 553 of the "Stats" section.

WAGNER COLLEGE

ONE CAMPUS ROAD, STATEN ISLAND, NY 10301 • ADMISSIONS: 718-390-3411 • FAX: 718-390-3105
FINANCIAL AID: 718-390-3183 • E-MAIL: ADMISSIONS@WAGNER.EDU • WEBSITE: WWW.WAGNER.EDU

RATINGS
Quality of Life: 75   **Academic:** 78   **Admissions:** 88   **Financial Aid:** 80

STUDENTS SAY ". . ."

Academics

Wagner College on Staten Island boasts one of the most pastoral campuses New York City has to offer. The college is also a pioneer in "practical liberal arts education." All students here must complete a pretty broad curriculum. Interdisciplinary courses for first-year students focus on a unifying theme and include about 30 hours of course-related fieldwork. Seniors must complete a thesis or a big project within their major. Also, "Wagner requires senior-year internships" and "most" students end up working somewhere pretty cool in Manhattan. Classes "never really exceed 30 peo-

> **SURVEY SAYS . . .**
> Athletic facilities are great
> Students are friendly
> Campus feels safe
> Theater is popular
> Student publications are popular
> Student government is popular
> Lots of beer drinking
> Hard liquor is popular

ple." Some students tell us "this school is very strong academically." Others say Wagner's coursework is "absolutely cake." The difficulty level really varies from class to class. There are "very personable" professors who "really know what they're talking about," and there are "terrible ones." "It all depends on who you get." Virtually the entire faculty is "constantly available," though. "The administration, up to the president, is very accessible and conscious of students' needs," relates a biology major. "You can generally walk in without an appointment and get whatever help you need." However, the "mean old women" in the bursar's office are a problem. Also, advising can be hit or miss. "Make sure you get a good adviser," counsels an arts administration major, "because mine blows."

Life

Some students at Wagner contend "the dining hall is excellent." Others disagree. "The food here is terrible," gripes a sophomore. "I hate it." Critics also point out "there are really no fast food places" near campus. "Some of the facilities are a little out of date," too. "Campus maintenance and upkeep would be my biggest complaint," says a first-year student. "If they fixed things like clogged drains and broken lights faster, it would be nice." Also, while it's unquestionably "safe" around campus, that's only because "the overprotective security feels like a Gestapo." On the plus side, students relish their "gorgeous" dorm-room views of the Lower Manhattan skyline. They also love their location. "Wagner represents a unique mix of big city and small town." "Rumors are atrocious and spread quickly," but on the whole it's "a friendly and small campus where you pretty much know everyone." "There's always a sporting event of some kind going on." The coffeehouse on campus "is a great place to meet new people and play a game of pool or hear great local bands." Otherwise, "Greek life and the theater program seem to dominate." "Parties are really not too extensive on campus but we get it done," says a sophomore. Local bars and clubs on Staten Island are popular for students who are 21. When students tire of the local scene, there's always Manhattan. A free shuttle "runs to the ferry quite often" and "almost all of the students" take advantage frequently. "The city can sometimes be expensive," but "you're never bored."

Student Body

While there is clear and growing diversity in Wagner's numbers, one student notes there are "a lot of Staten Islanders and Jersey people." There are substantially more women than men here, and there's a decent gay population. As a result, "there just aren't that many guys who are actively pursuing girls." Overall, it's a "very cliquey" scene. There are "tanning princess types" and "spoiled rich kids" "who'd rather party than study." Other students "are your average go-to-class, hang-out-with-friends, and study kind of people." The biggest social divide is between thespians and jocks. "There are two main groups of students at Wagner," explains a senior. So expect some show tune humming mixed in with Sports Center recaps—and everything in between. Suprised? Didn't your mom tell ya New York City was a big melting pot?

THE PRINCETON REVIEW SAYS

Admissions

Very important factors considered include: Class rank, academic GPA, rigor of secondary school record. *Important factors considered include:* Application essay, recommendation(s), standardized test scores, extracurricular activities, interview. *Other factors considered include:* Character/personal qualities, geographical residence, level of applicant's interest, talent/ability, volunteer work, work experience. SAT or ACT required; TOEFL required of all international applicants. High school diploma is required, and GED is accepted. *Academic units required:* 4 English, 3 mathematics, 2 science, (1 science labs), 2 foreign language, 1 social studies, 3 history, 6 academic electives.

Financial Aid

Students should submit: FAFSA, institution's own financial aid form, state aid form. The Princeton Review suggests that all financial aid forms be submitted as soon as possible after January 1. *Need-based scholarships/grants offered:* Federal Pell, SEOG, state scholarships/grants, private scholarships *Loan aid offered:* Federal Perkins, Federal Nursing, Other, alternative loans. Applicants will be notified of awards on a rolling basis beginning 3/1. Federal Work-Study Program available. Institutional employment available. Off-campus job opportunities are good.

The Inside Word

As far as grades and test scores, the profile of the average freshman class at Wagner is solid but not spectacular. Don't take the application process too lightly, though. The admissions staff here is dedicated to finding the right students for their school. An interview is definitely a good idea.

THE SCHOOL SAYS "…"

From The Admissions Office

"At Wagner College, we attract and develop active learners and future leaders. Wagner College has received national acclaim (*Time* magazine, American Association of Colleges and Universities) for its innovative curriculum, The Wagner Plan for the Practical Liberal Arts. At Wagner, we capitalize on our unique geography; we are a traditional, scenic, residential campus, which happens to sit atop a hill on an island overlooking lower Manhattan. Our location allows us to offer a program that couples required off-campus experiences (experiential learning), with 'learning community' clusters of courses. This program begins in the first semester and continues through the senior capstone experience in the major. Fieldwork and internships, writing-intensive reflective tutorials, connected learning, 'reading, writing, and doing': At Wagner College our students truly discover 'the practical liberal arts in New York City.'"

For even more information on this school, turn to page 553 of the "Stats" section.

WASHINGTON COLLEGE

300 Washington Avenue, Chestertown, MD 21620 • Admissions: 410-778-7700 • Fax: 410-778-7287
E-mail: adm.off@washcoll.edu • Website: www.washcoll.edu

RATINGS

Quality of Life: 69   Academic: 83   Admissions: 86   Financial Aid: 82

STUDENTS SAY "..."

Academics

Students at Washington College enjoy "a great, small-school environment where everyone is always friendly and active," as well as "a lot of opportunities with not a lot of competition." ("The competition for these opportunities is lacking only because of the small school size, not because of the poor student body," one student explains). The school's location, while rural, is "great for jobs and internships after graduation" in nearby Baltimore, D.C., and

Philadelphia, and there are "a lot of opportunities to intern for a semester off campus" or to "study abroad." WC's proximity to several major cities and the big-name schools located therein, means that "famous guest lecturers often come to campus, and usually attend a dinner in their honor the evening before the lecture. Students are always invited to these and usually have great conversations with these lecturers." Undergraduates report that WC has "an exceptional premedical program," a "strong environmental studies program," and "a very good writing school." As at most quality, small schools, professors "are always available outside class and always willing to help or even just chat about daily life."

Life

Washington College "is located in a very rural area" where "there's not much [to do] off campus," so "most of the time people stay on campus and hang out here." (What downtown there is, however, is "very pretty by the Chester River.") A "staggering [25] percent of the student population is made up of athletes," and these students are "very busy juggling school and sports." "Everyone is willing to support each other at games," so attending sporting events is definitely high on many students' to-do lists. There's also an active theater department at WC, making the arts another big attraction on campus. Regardless of how they stay engaged, students caution that "You have to be actively involved in finding something to do on the weekends if you don't just want to party. However, it is very easy to be involved in a lot of activities because the school and campus are so small." Most manage well. As one explains, "The atmosphere is very good. Students on weekdays have a very good schedule [of] going to classes and getting their work done. During the weekends, students will go to parties for fun...attend school plays or performances...[or] dress up in Washington College attire and really get the crowds [going] at sports games." Many here believe that an automobile is a necessary lifeline to civilization-at-large. "Most people drive to Annapolis or Middletown, Delaware, on the weekends to go to the mall, the movies, or dinner," undergraduates here report.

Student Body

"The Washington College [stereotypical student] is middle/upper-middle class, athletic, fun-loving, apathetic, and probably a lacrosse player," according to WC undergraduates. "A preppy kid who attended one of the Baltimore prep schools" would find plenty of peers here. The main counter-current in the student body is provided by the kids from "the Lit House," where writers, "theater kids," and those who'd rather see a movie than a lacrosse game tend to gravitate. The international house, "with many different exchange students," provides another alternative nexus. The campus is "a 'live and let live' kind of deal." The different groups "mostly stick to themselves—and at such a small college it is for that reason that they (or any clique on campus) are so easily categorized—but [they] 'fit in' when they choose to mingle." Students add that everyone fits in "inside of the classroom."

THE PRINCETON REVIEW SAYS

Admissions

Very important factors considered include: Academic GPA, rigor of secondary school record, interview. *Important factors considered include:* Class rank, standardized test scores, level of applicant's interest, work experience. *Other factors considered include:* Application essay, recommendation(s), alumni/ae relation, character/personal qualities, extracurricular activities, first generation, geographical residence, racial/ethnic status, state residency, talent/ability, volunteer work. SAT or ACT required; High school diploma is required, and GED is accepted. *Academic units required:* 4 English, 3 mathematics, 3 science, (2 science labs), 2 foreign language, 2 social studies, 2 history. *Academic units recommended:* 4 English, 4 mathematics, 4 science, (3 science labs), 4 foreign language, 4 social studies.

Financial Aid

Students should submit: FAFSA, institution's own financial aid form. The Princeton Review suggests that all financial aid forms be submitted as soon as possible after January 1. *Need-based scholarships/grants offered:* Federal Pell, SEOG, state scholarships/grants, private scholarships, the school's own gift aid. *Loan aid offered:* Federal Perkins. Applicants will be notified of awards on a rolling basis beginning 2/15. Federal Work-Study Program available. Institutional employment available. Off-campus job opportunities are good.

The Inside Word

The profile of a typical successful applicant at Washington College is that of the solid but not exceptional high school student. Above-average standardized test scores and respectable grades in a college-prep high school curriculum should be enough to get you past the gatekeepers here. You might even be able to dispense with the standardized test scores; students who rank in the top 10 percent of their high school class or have a GPA above 3.5 can request a "score optional" admissions review, meaning they do not have to submit standardized test scores. WC is up front about its preference for students who visit campus and/or complete an interview; the school's website notes that such applicants "are processed and admitted before qualified non-visitors." Proceed accordingly.

THE SCHOOL SAYS "..."

From The Admissions Office

"We tell our students, 'Your revolution starts here,' because the person who graduates from Washington College is not the same one who matriculated four years earlier; and because through your experiences here, you can be empowered and emboldened to change the world. Your education reflects the maxims of our founder, George Washington: The strength of America's democracy depends on critical and independent thinkers who persevere in the face of challenge and assume the responsibilities and privileges of informed citizenship. We provide a truly personalized education that tests-and stretches-each student's talents and potentials. We create challenges and opportunities that expand your brainpower and creativity through collaborative research with faculty and through independent study."

"All this happens on a campus that has been through its own physical revolution in the past several years: some $70 million in improvements that include a brand new Commons with a food court, coffee shop, student center and game room; a totally renovated and expanded Arts Center; two new residence halls with geothermal heating, and dramatic landscape improvements. Beyond campus, a wonderfully distinct setting-historic Chestertown, on the Chester River, amid the ecological bounty of Maryland's Chesapeake Bay-helps define us and enriches our programs in history, literature and ecology."

"Admission to Washington College is selective; decisions are based primarily on a student's record of academic achievement. SAT/ACT scores are optional for students who rank in the top 10 percent of their class. Interviews are strongly recommended."

For even more information on this school, turn to page 554 of the "Stats" section.

WASHINGTON & JEFFERSON COLLEGE

60 SOUTH LINCOLN STREET, WASHINGTON, PA 15301 • ADMISSIONS: 724-223-6025 • FAX: 724-223-6534
E-MAIL: ADMISSION@WASHJEFF.EDU • WEBSITE: WWW.WASHJEFF.EDU

RATINGS
Quality of Life: 70   **Academic:** 84   **Admissions:** 92   **Financial Aid:** 74

STUDENTS SAY "..."

Academics

Washington & Jefferson College is an "intimate" and "prestigious" bastion of the liberal arts in western Pennsylvania. The 4-1-4 academic calendar here is fairly unique. In addition to two conventional semesters, a January term allows students to focus on a single course or to pursue an internship or study abroad in places like Japan, Germany, and Tanzania. A broad set of graduation requirements and "the liberal arts aspect creates well-rounded individuals." More than 40 majors and programs are available. W&J boasts "a great track record with law school admissions." Premed is also "excellent." The academic atmosphere is "wonderfully rigorous." "Small classes make for some good discussions." Coursework ranges from "intense" to "outrageously challenging." Students rarely miss class. "Absences are regarded as strange." The faculty receives high marks. "There are a few who really ought to retire," but most professors are "very knowledgeable and seem to fully enjoy the classes they are teaching." They are "dedicated" and "really personable." They "go out of their way to make themselves accessible" and "do whatever they can to help you." "They all care about me," says a satisfied econ major. "They want me to do well. They want me to learn a lot." The administration is "down-to-earth" and "always looking for student input." Career Services is "extremely helpful" as well. Employment placement is "impressive." "Great alumni connections" definitely help in this regard. "Alumni are always offering to take students under their wings," notes a biology major.

Life

"Someone once described W&J to me as a "mullet," remembers a sophomore. "Business in the front with a party in the back." During the week, students are "very busy." Academics are "pivotal." Scores of students play varsity, club, or intramural sports as well. "Almost everyone is involved in a couple different activities." "Sunday through Friday afternoon is all work, for sure," counsels a junior. "When the weekend rolls around," justifies a junior, "we deserve to have some fun." As such, "most of the students drink themselves into a stupor." "Going to the frats is the most common weekend fun." "It gets repetitive, but it's all we have," relates a sophomore. The Greek system here is the primary organizing force of social life, and it's "very popular." However, "If the party scene is not for a student, there are usually other forms of entertainment offered by the school." "If you don't drink, it's not hard to find things to do," says a first-year student. "But it's hard to find fun things to do." The hilly campus here is "beautiful" and traditional-looking. Several buildings need renovation, though. The dorms in particular "could be updated and made a lot nicer." "Other than the new dorms built a few years ago for seniors, living conditions are absolutely terrible." Also, the four-year residency requirement really rankles. "They force you to live on campus," explains a junior. "Getting off campus is like fighting your own personal war." Other complaints include "limited" wireless internet access and the meal plans, which are "a rip off." Off-campus, the surrounding town is "dull" at best and "scary" at worst. Pittsburgh is "only 30 minutes away," though, and expeditions there are "a frequent thing."

Student Body

W&J is "extremely homogenous." "We're pretty much all the same," admits a junior. "Although the school promotes diversity, there isn't a lot of it." "Mostly, the school consists of white students from relatively average or high socioeconomic backgrounds." You'll fit in especially well if you come from "suburban" "western Pennsylvania or Ohio." "If you are 'different' or eclectic in personal expression in some way and really want to develop that, then I would pick a different school," advises a senior. "If you like to wear sweats to class all the time but don't mind looking cute every now and then, then this is a good school for you." Students here are "fit" and "preppy." Many are "athletes who really break the dumb-jock mold." They are "laid-back but ambitious." They are "goal-oriented." They "take their academics fairly seriously" and have a "great work ethic." Some students tell us the campus is "close-knit." Others say "there are a lot of cliques." Whatever the case, "everyone seems to get along."

THE PRINCETON REVIEW SAYS

Admissions

Very important factors considered include: Class rank, application essay, academic GPA, recommendation(s), rigor of secondary school record, character/personal qualities, interview. *Important factors considered include:* Standardized test scores, extracurricular activities. *Other factors considered include:* Alumni/ae relation, geographical residence, level of applicant's interest, racial/ethnic status, state residency, talent/ability, volunteer work, work experience. TOEFL required of all international applicants. High school diploma is required, and GED is accepted. *Academic units required:* 3 English, 3 mathematics, 2 foreign language, 1 history, 6 or more academic courses from English, mathematics, foreign language, history (social or natural).

Financial Aid

Students should submit: FAFSA. The Princeton Review suggests that all financial aid forms be submitted as soon as possible after January 1. *Need-based scholarships/grants offered:* Federal Pell, SEOG, state scholarships/grants, private scholarships, the school's own gift aid, ACG and SMART Grants. *Loan aid offered:* Federal Perkins, college/university loans from institutional funds. Applicants will be notified of awards on a rolling basis beginning 3/1. Federal Work-Study Program available. Institutional employment available. Off-campus job opportunities are good.

The Inside Word

In a reflection of the students the school aims aim to admit, Washington & Jefferson College takes a well-rounded approach to admissions. Academic record, class rank, personal statement, and extracurricular activities are all thoroughly evaluated. Most prospective students work diligently to secure admittance. The lucky applicants who receive a fat letter in the mail are welcomed into a distinctive community that promises to broaden their horizons and to prepare them for a successful future.

THE SCHOOL SAYS "..."

From The Admissions Office

"There is a palpable sense of momentum and energy at Washington & Jefferson. Enrollment has grown significantly over the past 5 years. Additional faculty members have been hired, and academic programs have been added and expanded to accommodate the increased enrollment. The student-centered teaching and learning community that has always distinguished W&J remains our top priority. It is no surprise that 100 percent of our graduates who took the bar exam in the last three years passed, or that 90 percent of our graduates recommended for medical and law school are admitted. The college has added almost $100 million dollars in new facilities since 2002, including new residence halls, new athletic facilities, a state-of-the-art technology center, and the Howard J. Burnett Center, which houses our programs in accounting, business, economics, education, entrepreneurial studies, and modern languages. The new $33 million John A. Swanson Science Center, dedicated to the physical sciences, including physics, chemistry, biochemistry, and bioinformatics, is on track to open in 2010. Also, unique to W&J is the Magellan Project, which provides stipends for innovative internships, prestigious research fellowships, and independent study-travel programs either domestically or abroad. Despite an almost fourfold increase in applications in this time, the Admission Staff remains committed to reviewing each application individually. Our students are balanced, goal oriented, active, engaged and involved and we look for evidence of these traits in prospective students. We encourage students to use every aspect of the application process to demonstrate that they possess these qualities. If you are the kind of student who thrives on challenge, who wants a close personal relationship with top-notch faculty, and who values being a member of a true college community, then we encourage you to consider W&J. W&J recommends but does not require students to submit scores from the SAT (or ACT). We will use the student's best scores from either test."

For even more information on this school, turn to page 554 of the "Stats" section.

WEBB INSTITUTE

298 CRESCENT BEACH ROAD, OCEAN COVE, NY 11542 • ADMISSIONS: 516-674-9838
FINANCIAL AID: 516-671-2213 • E-MAIL: ADMISSIONS@WEBB-INSTITUTE.EDU • WEBSITE: WWW.WEBB-INSTITUTE.EDU

RATINGS
Quality of Life: 99   Academic: 95   Admissions: 97   Financial Aid: 86

STUDENTS SAY ". . ."

Academics

Webb Institute on Long Island is a very small school that
focuses on the complex field of ship design engineering. If
you feel destined to become one of "America's future ship
designers and engineers," enroll here. Every student receives
a four-year, full-tuition scholarship. The only costs are books
and supplies, room and board, and personal expenses.
Everyone majors in naval architecture and marine engineering, although non-engineering electives are available to juniors and seniors. Webbies are exposed to a smattering of the
liberal arts and a ton of advanced math and physics. Virtually

> **SURVEY SAYS . . .**
> Registration is a breeze
> Career services are great
> Different types of students interact
> Dorms are like palaces
> Frats and sororities are unpopular or nonexistent
> Student government is popular
> Political activism is unpopular or nonexistent
> Very little drug use

every other course involves ship design. There's also a senior thesis and a "required internship program." In January
and February, all students get real, paying jobs in the marine industry. Job prospects are phenomenal. Newly minted Webb graduates enjoy "a 100 percent placement rate in grad schools and careers." Coursework is "rigorous," but
the academic atmosphere is very intimate. "A huge plus of Webb's small size is that everyone knows everyone,"
relates a junior. "You're not just another number." "The administration, professors, and students all work in the same
building every day, every week." "The [President] can get carried away when he perceives a problem," but the faculty is "approachable," "always accessible," and "very dedicated to the school and students." "Professors have a
great deal of respect for the students and work closely with us to accomplish our goals," says a sophomore. "If you're
passionate about architecture and engineering, you cannot hope for a better learning environment."

Life

Webb has a "family-like atmosphere." It's "a tiny student body living, eating, sleeping, and learning ship design in
a mansion" "in a residential area overlooking the beautiful Long Island Sound." There's an honor code "that is
strictly adhered to by all students." Cheating and stealing just don't happen here. "You can leave your wallet lying
in the reception room, and if someone doesn't return it to you just because they know what your wallet looks like
compared to the other 90 wallets in the school, it will still be there the next day and even the next week." Life
at Webb "revolves around course load and the attempts to find distractions from it." "We average about five to
seven hours of homework per night," advises a freshman. At the end of the semesters, life [can get crazy] due
to a ton of projects." "People generally think about homework and spend most of their time discussing class
assignments." When students find some down time, movies and unorganized sports are common. Not surprisingly, "many people turn to the water" for amusement as well. "Sailing is popular." "The school has a skiff and
sailboats, which are frequently used during the warm months," says a sophomore. Annual whitewater rafting
and ski trips are well attended. New York City is a little less than an hour away, and "a bunch of people venture into" Manhattan on the weekends. "A lot of spontaneous and off-the-wall things occur" too, and "a fair
amount of partying goes on at least once a week."

Student Body

The average Webbie is a "middle-class, white male who enjoys engineering and sciences." "Everyone is motivated and works hard." Basically, you have your bookworms who "don't socialize as much" and your more
social students who get their work done but also play sports and "have a good time." "The differences in these
two groups are by far the most visible division within the student body." Camaraderie is reportedly easy due
to the academic stress and Webb's small size. Everyone interacts with everyone else, regardless of background.
With fewer than 100 students, it's "impossible to completely isolate yourself." "There are no social cliques, and
everyone is included in anything they'd like to be included in." As at most engineering schools, the ratio
between males and females is pretty severely lopsided here. "We want more women!" plead many students.

THE PRINCETON REVIEW SAYS

Admissions

Very important factors considered include: Class rank, academic GPA, rigor of secondary school record, standardized test scores, character/personal qualities, interview, level of applicant's interest. *Important factors considered include:* Recommendation(s), extracurricular activities. *Other factors considered include:* Talent/ability, volunteer work, work experience. SAT required; SAT Subject Tests required; High school diploma is required, and GED is not accepted. *Academic units required:* 4 English, 4 mathematics, 2 science, (2 science labs), 0 foreign language, 2 social studies, 4 academic electives.

Financial Aid

Students should submit: FAFSA. Regular filing deadline is 7/1. The Princeton Review suggests that all financial aid forms be submitted as soon as possible after January 1. *Need-based scholarships/grants offered:* Federal Pell, state scholarships/grants, private scholarships, the school's own gift aid. Applicants will be notified of awards on or about 8/1. Off-campus job opportunities are fair.

The Inside Word

Let's not mince words; admission to Webb is mega-tough. Webb's Admissions Counselors are out to find the right kid for their curriculum—one that can survive the school's rigorous academics. The applicant pool is highly self-selected because of the focused program of study: naval architecture and marine engineering.

THE SCHOOL SAYS "..."

From The Admissions Office

"Webb, the only college in the country that specializes in the engineering field of naval architecture and marine engineering, seeks young men and women of all races from all over the country who are interested in receiving an excellent engineering education with a full-tuition scholarship. Students don't have to know anything about ships, they just have to be motivated to study how mechanical, civil, structural, and electrical engineering come together with the design elements that make up a ship and all its systems. Being small and private has its major advantages. Every applicant is special and the President will interview all entering students personally. The student/faculty ratio is 8:1, and since there are no teaching assistants, interaction with the faculty occurs daily in class and labs at a level not found at most other colleges. The entire campus operates under the Student Organization's honor system that allows unsupervised exams and 24-hour access to the library, every classroom and laboratory, and the shop and gymnasium. Despite a total enrollment of between 85 and 90 students and a demanding workload, Webb manages to field six intercollegiate teams. Currently more than 60 percent of the members of the student body play on one or more intercollegiate teams. Work hard, play hard and the payoff is a job for every student upon graduation. The placement record of the college is 100 percent every year.

"Freshman applicants must take the SAT. We also require scores from two SAT Subject Tests: Math Level I or II and either physics or chemistry."

For even more information on this school, turn to page 555 of the "Stats" section.

WELLESLEY COLLEGE

BOARD OF ADMISSION, 106 CENTRAL STREET, WELLESLEY, MA 02481-8203 • ADMISSIONS: 781-283-2270
FAX: 781-283-3678 • FINANCIAL AID: 781-283-2360 • E-MAIL: ADMISSION@WELLESLEY.EDU • WEBSITE: WWW.WELLESLEY.EDU

RATINGS
Quality of Life: 96   **Academic:** 99   **Admissions:** 97   **Financial Aid:** 98

STUDENTS SAY ". . ."

Academics

> SURVEY SAYS . . .
> *No one cheats*
> *Lab facilities are great*
> *Great computer facilities*
> *School is well run*
> *Diverse student types on campus*
> *Dorms are like palaces*

Widely considered to be the top women's college in the nation, "Wellesley grooms its students to be strong leaders" through rigorous academic programs, "an intense intellectual environment," and "fierce commitment to social change." As a small college, Wellesley offers ample "personal attention" and a "comfortable environment;" however, choice and opportunity separate Wellesley from other similar institutions. While enrolling just 2,200 undergraduates, Wellesley offers a remarkable array of more than 1,000 courses and 50 major programs; plus, "You can cross-register at MIT (and to a limited extent at Brandeis, Babson, and Olin.)" From research to internships to overseas studies, Wellesley "provides great resources and opportunities to all its students." A senior shares, "I have had opportunities for research and independent study in both of my majors (and in at least one other field of interest.)" Attracting "fiercely driven and deeply passionate women," a Wellesley education "can be stressful and intense." At the same time, "It is a very friendly, respectful, intellectual environment where professors believe in your ability to do great things and the whole world seems to open up to you." When it comes to the teaching staff, "Not only are many of the professors notable in their fields, they are all excellent teachers. Classes in all departments are exciting, challenging, and engaging." And the benefits don't stop on your graduation day. Thanks to a "very strong alumni network" and a strong career placement program, Wellesley women are ready to enter the workplace. No matter what your field, "Wellesley women are everywhere. It's very helpful when you're looking for internships or jobs."

Life

Be prepared to burn the midnight oil at Wellesley. On this studious campus, "students tend to be very driven academically," and "Most of the weekday is spent in class or studying." Fortunately, no matter how busy they are, "People always try to make time for friends…whether it's a group study session or just dinner together." "Outspoken and well-informed," students are eager to engage in "insightful discussions about politics, religion, sexuality, etc., at the lunch table." In addition, "there are always seminars and panel discussions and cultural events to attend" on campus. Socially, the Wellesley campus is generally quiet, and "Private parties are often broken up due [to] the Draconian alcohol and party policies imposed by the administration." Therefore, when they want to blow off steam, many Wellesley students "go into Boston or Cambridge for parties, concerts, shopping, protests, or people-watching." For others, "The ideal night would [include having] a handful of friends clustered around the kitchen table in the Shakespeare house, debating, drinking, and laughing about politics, literature, and the latest celebrity events." For those concerned about meeting members of the opposite sex, Wellesley women assure us that, "You can interact with Harvard and MIT men, as well as men from the many institutions in Boston and the surrounding area, but, at the end of the day, you have a quiet, clean, and boy-free zone to come home to."

Student Body

While many students describe Wellesley as an "ethnically and financially diverse campus," a typical Wellesley undergraduate is "white, very liberal, very intelligent, [and] politically active, does a lot of community service, and has fashion sense like you wouldn't believe." Others describe their classmates as "intelligent, engaged, curious, quick-witted, articulate, politically-aware, outspoken, thoughtful, passionate, ambitious, and poised." While they share some impressive characteristics, Wellesley women come in a "variety of packages, from women who brag about showering in the Science Library to those who party [in] Cambridge every weekend to rugby players and Shakespearean actors to sorority-girl-esque 'society' members." Students also point out that "alternative gender expressions and sexual orientations are also quite common" on the Wellesley campus. Friendly and welcoming, "everyone is accepted" within the college community, though students note that "deeply religious students are less common and Republicans are quite the minority."

THE PRINCETON REVIEW SAYS

Admissions

Very important factors considered include: Application essay, academic GPA, recommendation(s), rigor of secondary school record, standardized test scores, character/personal qualities. *Important factors considered include:* Class rank, extracurricular activities. *Other factors considered include:* Alumni/ae relation, first generation, geographical residence, interview, level of applicant's interest, racial/ethnic status, state residency, talent/ability, volunteer work, work experience. SAT and SAT Subject Tests or ACT required; ACT with Writing component required. High school diploma or equivalent is not required. High school diploma is required, and GED is not accepted. *Academic units recommended:* 4 English, 4 mathematics, 3 science, (2 science labs), 4 foreign language, 4 social studies, 4 history.

Financial Aid

Students should submit: FAFSA, CSS/Financial Aid PROFILE, noncustodial PROFILE, business/farm supplement. Business taxes, if applicable. The Princeton Review suggests that all financial aid forms be submitted as soon as possible after January 1. *Need-based scholarships/grants offered:* Federal Pell, SEOG, state scholarships/grants, private scholarships, the school's own gift aid, ACG Grant and SMART Grant. *Loan aid offered:* Direct Subsidized Stafford, Direct Unsubsidized Stafford, Direct PLUS, Federal Perkins, state loans, college/university loans from institutional funds. Applicants will be notified of awards on or about 4/1. Federal Work-Study Program available. Institutional employment available. Off-campus job opportunities are excellent.

The Inside Word

When making an admissions decision, Wellesley considers a broad range of factors, including a student's academic record, the difficulty of her high school curriculum, participation in extracurricular activities, class rank, recommendations, personal essay, standardized test scores, leadership, and special talents (students may submit visual portfolios or audio tapes along with their application). Personal interviews are highly recommended, but not required, though they can be a useful way to help you stand out in Wellesley's extraordinary applicant pool.

THE SCHOOL SAYS "..."

From The Admissions Office

"Widely acknowledged as the nation's best women's college, Wellesley College provides students with numerous opportunities on campus and beyond. With a long-standing commitment to and established reputation for academic excellence, Wellesley offers more than 1,000 courses in 53 established majors and supports 180 clubs, organizations, and activities for its students. The college is easily accessible to Boston, a great city in which to meet other college students and to experience theater, art, sports, and entertainment. Considered one of the most diverse colleges in the nation, Wellesley students hail from 70 countries and all 50 states.

"As a community, we are looking for students who possess intellectual curiosity: the ability to think independently, ask challenging questions, and grapple with answers. Strong candidates demonstrate both academic achievement and an excitement for learning. They also display leadership, an appreciation for diverse perspectives, and an understanding of the college's mission to educate women who will make a difference in the world.

"The SAT and SAT Subject Tests or ACT with Writing component are required. Two SAT Subject Tests are required, one of which should be quantitative (Math or Science). We strongly recommend that students planning to apply early decision complete the tests before the end of their junior year and no later than October of their senior year."

For even more information on this school, turn to page 555 of the "Stats" section.

WELLS COLLEGE

ROUTE 90, AURORA, NY 13026 • ADMISSIONS: 315-364-3264 • FAX: 315-364-3327
FINANCIAL AID: 315-364-3289 • E-MAIL: ADMISSIONS@WELLS.EDU • WEBSITE: WWW.WELLS.EDU

RATINGS
Quality of Life: 77   Academic: 86   Admissions: 85   Financial Aid: 76

STUDENTS SAY ". . ."

Academics

Undergrads at Wells are full of praise for their academic experience. The "intimate" size of the college ensures a "personal" education that stresses "individual attention." The professors "genuinely care about their students" and often "form lasting friendships" with them. However, this doesn't mean the classroom is a cakewalk. One junior stressed the professors "set very high academic standards for their students." And a freshman revealed the workload, at times, can be "overwhelming." Indeed, it's "not a school where you will be able to get an easy A." Luckily, it's a supportive environment, and professors are "almost always willing to go the extra step to make sure you understand the material." Moreover, "they encourage you to explore beyond their own subject and connect your subjects with each other." It's clearly evident to these undergrads their profs "teach for the love it." While acclaim for the academics is virtually unanimous, opinions regarding the administrators definitely run the gamut. Some undergrads feel "the administration tend to do as they please with little regard for the students." And one senior adds that they "make it very obvious they are running a business." However, another undergrad counters by saying "students are allowed to have a voice, and can meet with the administration to discuss changes to controversial policies."

> **SURVEY SAYS . . .**
> No one cheats
> Lousy food on campus
> Low cost of living
> Frats and sororities are unpopular or nonexistent
> Very little drug use

Life

Wells students agree "there isn't a lot to do" in "rural" hometown Aurora. Fortunately, that just means entertainment is centered around the college. One junior reveals, "The traditions on campus are superior and amazing!" In turn, they foster "a great sense of community." The school sponsors a number of activities such as "concerts, parties, dances, and guest speakers." Additionally the college theater is pretty popular because the "performing arts are very high quality" at Wells. Of course many students love to simply "chill out with close friends, have an intellectual conversation, or host their own dance party." And a number of students "get creative" and "make their own fun." Indeed, an intrepid freshman regales with tales of "riding mattresses down stairs," and another shares that when it snows "students ride sleds or make snowmen or other types of sculptures." Though Aurora is "small," one sophomore gushes "the surrounding area is beautiful and there are lots of places to go hiking." When undergrads are itching to get a little farther away, they typically head to either "Ithaca or Auburn." Both towns offer ample opportunity for fun such as "movies, bowling, ice skating, a mall, [and] dining out."

Student Body

When Wells made the decision to go co-ed back in 2005, the college was forced to "restructure its student identity." Naturally, the transition was fraught with some growing pains. And while there's still some lingering tension, many undergrads assure us "one of the beautiful things about Wells is that, in general, everyone is welcome." A content English major expands upon this sentiment stating, "Everyone is important and has a place here." This can partly be attributed to the fact the college "has a strong emphasis on community." Additionally, Wells seems to attract "friendly, eccentric people" who are "socially and politically conscious, academic minded, and tolerant." And these "fun" students "aren't afraid to be different." Undergrads find common ground in that most everyone is "concerned about their education." Indeed, the "typical student at Wells is very studious [and] spends many hours studying or in the library." Perhaps this happy freshman sums up by sharing, "It is a diverse environment, but everyone can find someone that is like them. There is no such thing as not fitting in!"

THE PRINCETON REVIEW SAYS

Admissions

Very important factors considered include: Academic GPA, recommendation(s), rigor of secondary school record, standardized test scores, extracurricular activities. *Important factors considered include:* Application essay, interview. *Other factors considered include:* Class rank, alumni/ae relation, character/personal qualities, level of applicant's interest, talent/ability, volunteer work, work experience. SAT or ACT required; TOEFL required of all international applicants. High school diploma is required, and GED is accepted. *Academic units required:* 4 English, 3 mathematics, 2 science, (2 science labs), 1 social studies, 3 history, 2 academic electives. *Academic units recommended:* 4 mathematics, 3 science, (3 science labs), 2 foreign language, 2 social studies, 2 history, 3 academic electives, 2 music, art, computer science.

Financial Aid

Students should submit: FAFSACSS/Financial Aid Profile for Early Decision Applicants only. The Princeton Review suggests that all financial aid forms be submitted as soon as possible after January 1. *Need-based scholarships/grants offered:* Federal Pell, SEOG, state scholarships/grants, private scholarships, the school's own gift aid. *Loan aid offered:* Federal Perkins. Applicants will be notified of awards on a rolling basis beginning 3/1. Federal Work-Study Program available. Institutional employment available. Off-campus job opportunities are poor.

The Inside Word

Wells is engaged in that age-old admissions game called matchmaking. There are no minimums or cutoffs in the admissions process here. But don't be fooled by the high admit rate. The admissions committee will look closely at your academic accomplishments. However, they will also give attention to your essay, recommendations, and extracurricular pursuits. The committee also recommends an interview; we suggest taking them up on it.

THE SCHOOL SAYS "..."

From The Admissions Office

"Wells College believes the 21st century needs well-educated individuals with the ability, self-confidence, and vision to contribute to an ever-changing world. Wells offers an outstanding classroom experience and innovative liberal arts curriculum that prepares students for leadership in a variety of fields, including business, government, the arts, sciences, medicine, and education. By directly connecting the liberal arts curriculum to experience and career development through internships, off-campus study, study abroad, research with professors, and community service, each student has an ideal preparation for graduate and professional school as well as for the 21st century."

For even more information on this school, turn to page 556 of the "Stats" section.

WENTWORTH INSTITUTE OF TECHNOLOGY

550 HUNTINGTON AVENUE, ADMISSIONS OFFICE, BOSTON, MA 02115-5998 • ADMISSIONS: 617-989-4000 • FAX: 617-989-4010
E-MAIL: ADMISSIONS@WIT.EDU • WEBSITE: WWW.WIT.EDU

RATINGS
Quality of Life: 74   **Academic:** 75   **Admissions:** 77   **Financial Aid:** 65

STUDENTS SAY "..."

Academics

A technical school with strong design and architecture pro-grams, Wentworth Institute of Technology emphasizes "hands-on training" inside and outside the classroom. Practicality is WIT's strength: "This school is very focused on co-ops and career preparation," and "There are a lot of programs intended to help students network in their fields and know where they are heading." Bringing industry expertise to the classroom, "Many of the professors have valuable, real work experience in their fields, and use that to better teach their classes." WIT is best suited to students with clear career goals because students "have zero chance to explore any other interest," and "elective and humanities course selection is very narrow." At the same time, most WIT students "don't want to wallow in theory too long or be consumed by pointless humanities classes...people come to Wentworth to get a good job, period." With just over 3,000 full-time undergraduates, "Compact and small class sizes create a much better learning environment, and extensive lab experiences create students who are very practical in their related professions." Despite the importance of lab work, "The facilities need a lot of work." A junior warns, "If you want to come here to enjoy good food, working technology, and other luxurious pleasantries, then you should look elsewhere."

> **SURVEY SAYS . . .**
> Students love Boston, MA
> Great off-campus food
> Low cost of living
> Frats and sororities are unpopular or nonexistent
> Very little drug use

Life

On WIT's carrier-oriented campus, "everyone works hard," and "Most of the talk around this school is about class-es: what was taught, the professor, the next test, when to study." However, "On the weekend, it's completely dif-ferent. Kids party, drink, go out into Boston, bum around and joke in the dorms, go home—anything but work." The school's location is a major advantage, and "theaters, museums, skate parks, gyms, parks are the most pop-ular places to go" in Boston. Not to mention, "There are loads of good restaurants in the immediate area." While the cafeteria food is universally panned, "The dorms are very nice and all upperclassmen housing is apartment-style, with kitchens." Life is generally "low-key" but, if you want to blow off steam, "a party can always be found in the neighborhood, but not necessarily on campus. With so many students in Boston, there is always something to do, no matter what your interests are."

Student Body

One thing that really distinguishes the WIT student body is that "all of the students that come to Wentworth know from an early age what they want to do for their careers" and most are "extremely studious and care about getting top grades." Even so, there are many "regular, down-to-earth people who are serious about school but also about having a good time." While it's hard to generalize about the WIT student body as a whole, "Each major definitely has a certain look that is unique to it." For example, construction management students "are your typical 'frat' kids" whereas design majors are described as "artsy" types. Many students commute to school, and "There are a lot of non-traditional students, like students in their mid- to late-20's and transfer students." When it comes to offering a truly co-educational experience, students note that "There are way more boys than girls [on campus]; in a class of 40 there is sometimes only three girls." However, "The women that attend Wentworth are treated equally."

Admissions

Important factors considered include: Application essay, recommendation(s), rigor of secondary school record, standardized test scores. *Other factors considered include:* Academic GPA, alumni/ae relation, character/personal qualities, extracurricular activities, first generation, geographical residence, level of applicant's interest, talent/ability, volunteer work, work experience. SAT or ACT required; TOEFL required of all international applicants. High school diploma is required and GED is accepted. *Academic units required:* 4 English, 3 mathematics, 2 science, (1 science labs), 1 social studies, 3 college-preparatory math, 1 physics recommended for many programs, 4 years of math for some programs. *Academic units recommended:* 4 mathematics, 3 college-preparatory math, 1 physics recommended for many programs, 4 years of mathmematics for some programs.

Financial Aid

Students should submit: FAFSA. The Princeton Review suggests that all financial aid forms be submitted as soon as possible after January 1. *Need-based scholarships/grants offered:* Federal Pell, SEOG, state scholarships/grants, private scholarships, the school's own gift aid. *Loan aid offered:* Federal Perkins, state loans. Applicants will be notified of awards on a rolling basis beginning 3/15. Federal Work-Study Program available. Institutional employment available. Off-campus job opportunities are good.

The Inside Word

Wentworth accepts students on a rolling basis and responds to applications within two to five weeks. It behooves you to apply early before spots fill up, especially if you're applying to one of WIT's more popular programs. WIT greatly considers the rigor of the high school academic record, especially your performance in math and science courses. All applicants must have completed a mathematics course of study through Algebra II to be considered for admission. WIT expects the transcript to be supplemented by at least one recommendation from a guidance counselor or teacher; make sure it speaks to your preparation and passion for a technologically focused course of study.

THE SCHOOL SAYS " . . ."

From The Admissions Office

"One of the most affordable colleges in greater Boston, Wentworth Institute of Technology provides the tools today's career-oriented students need to succeed in the marketplace: strong academic programs, cutting-edge labs and studios, and a cooperative education program (co-op) that is one of the largest and most comprehensive of its kind.

"When you join the Wentworth community, you'll find energetic, can-do students from 36 states and 44 countries. You'll find individuals ready to roll up their sleeves and get to work. Most importantly, you'll find fellow students with a strong drive to succeed academically and professionally.

"At Wentworth you get the best of both worlds: small-college comforts and big-city excitement. You'll find a tree-lined quad, a food court cafeteria, traditional and modern residence halls, recreational facilities, and more on our 35-acre campus. You'll also enjoy easy access to Boston's exciting venues and New England's scenic wonders: walk to Fenway Park, the Museum of Fine Arts, or Copley Place; take a ferry to Cape Cod; hike the White Mountains. Whatever your destination, having the 'T' Green Line and the Ruggles Station stop on the commuter rail right beside campus means you can get into—or out of—Boston easily.

"Wentworth is also a member of the Colleges of the Fenway consortium. This consortium offers the benefits of cross registration and access to social events, professional activities, libraries, and campus facilities at six colleges within walking distance of one another. The other Colleges of the Fenway members are Emmanuel College, Massachusetts College of Art, Massachusetts College of Pharmacy and Health Sciences, Simmons College, and Wheelock College."

For even more information on this school, turn to page 556 of the "Stats" section.

WESLEYAN UNIVERSITY

THE STEWART M. REID HOUSE, 70 WYLLYS AVENUE, MIDDLETOWN, CT 06459-0265 • ADMISSIONS: 860-685-3000 • FAX: 860-685-3001
FINANCIAL AID: 860-685-2800 • E-MAIL: ADMISSIONS@WESLEYAN.EDU • WEBSITE: WWW.WESLEYAN.EDU

RATINGS
Quality of Life: 90   **Academic:** 96   **Admissions:** 98   **Financial Aid:** 98

STUDENTS SAY ". . ."

Academics

> **SURVEY SAYS . . .**
> *Low cost of living*
> *Students are happy*

Tucked away in Middletown, Connecticut, Wesleyan University is a dynamic institution "committed [to] catering to its undergraduates." The school certainly attracts those with a high level of "intellectual interest and curiosity" and students "really engage their education in a meaningful way." Fortunately, there's a "lack of...competitive cutthroat [behavior which] really promotes a community of learning." Undergrads at Wesleyan also appreciate "the lack of core curriculum," which gives students the flexibility to really "explore new areas" and "obtain a broad education." Academics here are "very challenging" but students find their classes immensely "rewarding." This is wholly due to professors that are "always available and eager to speak with students, and have a terrific passion for their work." Many of them maintain "intimate relationships with students" and a junior tells us that "having a meal with a professor at their home is not a rare occurrence." While a few students find that "the administration is full of red tape," others insist that they are "generally very responsive to student needs" and "very invested in the happiness of the students." As one senior concludes, "I feel that the administration as well as faculty work hard to make Wesleyan a strong community where everyone's voice matters."

Life

Wesleyan students have eclectic interests and passions and the social scene really reflects that. An intellectual group, undergrads can frequently be found deep in conversation with their peers, discussing anything from "the ethics of grading [or] the rendering of astrophysics into tangible graphics [to] the analysis of the feminist meanings of a Spanish worksheet." Of course, you shouldn't let this deceive you. These students also know how to kick back and have fun. "From the traditional frat party, to a gathering at a program house, [to] a performance or movie with friends in somebody's living room, Wesleyan offers a variety of social scenes for students to get involved in." Activities certainly run the gamut. An African-American studies major shares, "For fun, people go to performances, sporting events, lectures, protests, restaurants, open mics, parties, campus events, etc." On any given day these lucky students might enjoy "anything from an Indian dance festival to an open forum on the economic recession to a frat party that's also a charity event for a school in Kenya." Of course, Wesleyan students are also quite adept at making their own fun and they can be found "sledding on the snow, rolling down the hill, playing Duck Duck Goose, [and] having awesome corny dance parties."

Student Body

Undergrads at Wesleyan are fairly adamant about the fact that they cannot "be pigeon-holed." While many insist "there are no typical students," others concede that there "are a few traits that often connect [everyone]." Most people "are interested in engaging with the world around them, often in hopes of improving it." Indeed this is a "passionate" group who are very "socially-conscious, politically-aware, and [into] activism." Moreover, Wesleyan students are "driven," "intellectually curious" and "eager to learn and experience new things." These are kids who are "serious about academics" but also know how to "relax and have fun." They are also "very proud to be part of a diverse community" and are always excited to "meet new people." Another commonality is that undergrads here tend to "have a variety of interests." As a Spanish and film studies double major illustrates, "Your best friend might be captain of the football team and double majoring in chemistry and art studio." Perhaps most importantly, students at Wesleyan "aren't afraid to associate with many different kinds of people." A content senior sums up, "Students here are committed to creating a strong and close-knit community made up of open-minded people."

THE PRINCETON REVIEW SAYS

Admissions

Very important factors considered include: Rigor of secondary school record. *Important factors considered include:* Class rank, application essay, academic GPA, recommendation(s), standardized test scores, character/personal qualities, first generation, racial/ethnic status, talent/ability. *Other factors considered include:* Alumni/ae relation, extracurricular activities, geographical residence, interview, volunteer work, work experience. SAT and SAT Subject Tests or ACT required; ACT with Writing component recommended. TOEFL required of all international applicants. High school diploma is required, and GED is accepted. *Academic units recommended:* 4 English, 4 mathematics, 4 science, (3 science labs), 4 foreign language, 4 social studies, 4 history.

Financial Aid

Students should submit: FAFSA, CSS/Financial Aid PROFILE, state aid form, noncustodial PROFILE. Regular filing deadline is 2/15. The Princeton Review suggests that all financial aid forms be submitted as soon as possible after January 1. *Need-based scholarships/grants offered:* Federal Pell, SEOG, state scholarships/grants, private scholarships, the school's own gift aid. *Loan aid offered:* Direct Subsidized Stafford, Direct Unsubsidized Stafford, Direct PLUS, Federal Perkins, college/university loans from institutional funds. Applicants will be notified of awards on or about 4/1. Federal Work-Study Program available. Institutional employment available. Off-campus job opportunities are good.

The Inside Word

You want the inside word on Wesleyan admissions? Read *The Gatekeepers: Inside the Admissions Process at a Premier College*, by Jacques Steinberg. The author spent an entire admissions season at the Wesleyan admissions office. His book is a wonderfully detailed description of the Wesleyan admissions process (which is quite similar to processes at other private, highly selective colleges and universities).

THE SCHOOL SAYS "..."

From The Admissions Office

"Wesleyan faculty believe in an education that is flexible and affords individual freedom and that a strong liberal arts education is the best foundation for success in any endeavor. The broad curriculum focuses on essential communication skills and analytical abilities through course content and teaching methodology, allowing students to pursue their intellectual interests with passion while honing those capabilities. As a result, Wesleyan students achieve a very personalized but broad education. Wesleyan's Dean of Admission and Financial Aid, Nancy Hargrave Meislahn, describes the qualities Wesleyan seeks in its students: 'Our very holistic process seeks to identify academically accomplished and intellectually curious students who can thrive in Wesleyan's rigorous and vibrant academic environment; we look for personal strengths, accomplishments, and potential for real contribution to our diverse community.'

"Applicants will meet standardized testing requirements one of two ways: by taking the SAT plus two SAT Subject Tests of the student's choice or by taking the ACT (Writing component recommended)."

For even more information on this school, turn to page 557 of the "Stats" section.

WESTMINSTER COLLEGE (PA)

319 SOUTH MARKET STREET, NEW WILMINGTON, PA 16172 • ADMISSIONS: 800-942-8033
FAX: 724-946-7171 • FINANCIAL AID: 724-946-7102 • E-MAIL: ADMIS@WESTMINSTER.EDU • WEBSITE: WWW.WESTMINSTER.EDU

RATINGS

Quality of Life: 89   **Academic:** 82   **Admissions:** 79   **Financial Aid:** 62

STUDENTS SAY "..."

Academics

Students choose Westminster College, a small Presbyterian-affiliated liberal arts school north of Pittsburgh, for its cozy atmosphere and well-regarded pre-professional programs. Undergrads describe Westminster as "an extremely small school where everyone pretty much knows each other," where "professors are dedicated to helping students on all levels. From [within] the classroom and outside of class in fact professors are known to call students on the weekends at home to discuss coursework." and The community is like

> **SURVEY SAYS . . .**
> *Career services are great*
> *Students are friendly*
> *Campus feels safe*
> *Low cost of living*
> *Students are happy*
> *Frats and sororities dominate social scene*
> *Student government is popular*

"a family bound together with blue and white pride and a love for the people who are attending and those who have moved on." Indeed, "once you become a part of the Westminster tradition, it lasts for a lifetime!" The small class environment "creates opportunities above focused, by-rote study," facilitated by a "very hands-on" approach from both faculty and administrators. Premedical studies excel here. Students warn "being a biology major is much harder than some of the other majors, and even if you don't fail a class it is hard to graduate on time." However, this hard work pays off in Westminster's admit rate to medical schools, which is double the national average. Students also love the music, education, and public relations programs here. Other majors are "hit or miss...depending on the staff in the department." Where the school falls shortest, however, is in its facilities. Undergrads tell us that because Westminster is "a very old school that relies on alumni for donations, our building are terribly old and it shows." Westminster has spent $36 million on renovations in the last few years, however, and current renovations to McGill Library have just been completed.

Life

Westminster has "a very active Greek life in which the majority of our student population is involved." "Students have integrated Greek life as a positive force and influence in their school careers with many opportunities for leadership roles and future connections leading up to a week-long "Greek Week."" Weekends usually "involve going to the fraternities," which "gets old after a while," but since the school is located "in a very small town near an Amish community, there isn't much off campus to do besides go to fraternity houses." On-campus alternatives include "weekly events with a musician, comedian, etc. Also, there are two free movies offered each weekend." As one student warns, "If you're into the bar scene, clubs, or big-city life, don't go to Westminster. You'll be disappointed. If you like things more laid-back and prefer a slow-paced life, Westminster is probably going to fit you pretty well." Aesthetes will also find much to enjoy, as "the campus is the most beautiful [place]...There are so many wide open spaces with pastures, barns, acres of land and the trees are gorgeous in the fall." Among intercollegiate athletics, "Football is a big thing on campus as well as basketball. Many students come out to support their fellow teammates and friends."

Student Body

"Westminster does not have a lot of diversity," as "most students are local," meaning they tend to be "white and from a middle to upper middle class family." "Of course you have your various groups: the jocks, the gothic kids, the cheerleader types, the hippies that never bathe, etc., but the typical student here would have to be someone who is relatively laid back," explains one student. "They wear American Eagle jeans, vintage T-shirts, and flip-flops year round. They are moderately aware of the world around them, politically and environmentally. They play ultimate Frisbee and guitar, and have probably started or head some club on campus that is particular to their interests. In their free time they read poems, sing, practice an instrument, watch *Family Guy*, or catch up with some friends. Many on campus seem apathetic toward just about everything, but a surprising number actually take the responsibility and initiative to make a difference." Politically, the student body leans toward the "conservative."

Admissions

Very important factors considered include: Rigor of secondary school record, and standardized test scores. *Important factors considered include:* Class rank, application essay, recommendation(s), character/personal qualities. *Other factors considered include:* Alumni/ae relation, extracurricular activities, talent/ability, volunteer work, work experience. SAT or ACT required; TOEFL required of all international applicants. High school diploma is required, and GED is accepted. *Academic units required:* 4 English, 3 mathematics, 2 science, (2 science labs), 2 foreign language, 2 social studies, 1 history, 3 academic electives.

Financial Aid

Students should submit: FAFSA, institution's own financial aid form F. The Princeton Review suggests that all financial aid forms be submitted as soon as possible after January 1. *Need-based scholarships/grants offered:* Federal Pell, SEOG, state scholarships/grants, private scholarships, the school's own gift aid. *Loan aid offered:* Federal Perkins, Other, Resource Loans. Applicants will be notified of merit awards on a rolling basis beginning 10/1.

The Inside Word

Westminster College has grown increasingly more selective throughout the decade, the result of a 300+ percent increase in its applicant pool (without any corresponding increase in the size of its freshman class). The school has early action admissions September 1 through November 15 and admits on a rolling basis December 1–May 1. Westminster has implemented a waiting list in the past two years. Apply early to improve your chances.

THE SCHOOL SAYS "..."

From The Admissions Office

"Since its founding, Westminster has been dedicated to a solid foundation in today's most crucial social, cultural, and ethical issues. Related to the Presbyterian Church (U.S.A.), Westminster is home to people of many faiths. Our students and faculty, tradition of campus, and small-town setting all contribute to an enlightening educational experience.

"For purposes of admission and merit scholarships Westminster College will evaluate applicants using the composite score of the Math and Critical Reading sections of the SAT or the composite score of the ACT. Westminster will collect new Writing section scores and compare with national percentiles for possible inclusion in admission and scholarship criteria for the future."

For even more information on this school, turn to page 557 of the "Stats" section.

WHEATON COLLEGE (MA)

Office of Admission, Norton, MA 02766 • Admissions: 508-286-8251 • Fax: 508-286-8271
Financial Aid: 508-286-8232 • E-mail: admission@wheatoncollege.edu • Website: www.wheatoncollege.edu

RATINGS
Quality of Life: 64   **Academic:** 91   **Admissions:** 93   **Financial Aid:** 89

STUDENTS SAY "..."

Academics

A "small liberal arts school trying to break through and compete with the 'small Ivies' (Williams, Amherst, Colby etc.)," Wheaton College is "a true liberal arts college: People study what they are interested in for the sake of learning it and because it fascinates them". The school caters to students with eclectic interests through its Foundations requirements (which require at least one course in non-Western civilization) and its Connections curriculum (which requires students to take either two sets of two related courses or one set of three related courses across academic categories), leading students to crow that "Wheaton's curriculum is based on providing students with global awareness. It focuses on trying to get students to understand the dynamics of their own personal actions alongside that of those around the world." Undergrads also love the personal attention, "You can't get lost here. There's always someone you can talk to—your own age or a professor or administrator—if you're having problems. It's a really supportive and safe environment." And students love the "many opportunities to apply classroom knowledge outside of the class (whether through internships, research projects, fellowships, study abroad, etc.)." Many praise the school's new "absolutely amazing" Kollett Center, which houses "peer mentors, peer tutors for every subject, the academic advising office, and internship/career/job search," "the most useful college center on the face of the planet...because they help with you in writing resumes, finding internships, and preparing for life after college." Wheaton students also benefit from "a really active" alumni network "willing to help in any way."

Life

"From Monday through Wednesday, people are reserved and very focused" on the Wheaton campus. Thursday "usually starts the weekend where upperclassmen will head to the bars," while on "Friday and Saturday, most of the school will socialize by drinking at one of the on-campus houses or in groups in the dorms." Students explain that "because there are no frats, parties are held in houses (either on or off campus) or in dorm rooms." One student says, "It's actually a bit pathetic that that's the best they can do." There are also "college dances, which sometimes have free beer for those over 21," but many feel that "The dances are reminiscent of high school and usually suck except for the free beer." There are also "tons of musical and theatrical performances, club events, lectures, and other great things going on" around campus. Even so, students concede that the campus "gets a little boring at times." Hometown Norton "is very, very, very (did I say very yet?) small," the sort of place where "the biggest decision is whether you want to walk to Walgreens or CVS," so students seeking off-campus diversion must travel farther. That's why "A lot of students will go into Boston or Providence for a day on the weekends. Also, there are always home games or away games on the weekends, so many students attend one or the other."

Student Body

Wheaton "is made up of reasonably familiar subgroups. We have our jocks, and our über-nerds, slackers, and artists. There is, however, a large gray area, and most people don't limit themselves to one group." The predominant vibe is "a little bit preppy with a portion of hippie," with "the popped collar and pearls set" coexisting with "plenty of free spirits...Whether they choose to wear boat-shoes or Birks, they've got a place" here. Most students "are well-balanced...academically serious, but school is not the only activity in their lives." They "seem to generally be liberal, but everyone is so apathetic toward current events that it is difficult to inspire student activism." Undergrads estimate that "23 percent of us are varsity athletes;" and more than a few of the remaining 77 percent "do not like [the athletes] and feel like they get preferential treatment just because they are athletes."

> **SURVEY SAYS . . .**
> *rats and sororities are unpopular or nonexistent*
> *Student government is popular*
> *Lots of beer drinking*
> *Hard liquor is popular*

Admissions

Very important factors considered include: Application essay, academic GPA, rigor of secondary school record, character/personal qualities, extracurricular activities, first generation, talent/ability. *Important factors considered include:* Class rank, recommendation(s), alumni/ae relation, interview, volunteer work, work experience. *Other factors considered include:* Geographical residence, level of applicant's interest, racial/ethnic status, state residency, TOEFL required of all international applicants. High school diploma is required, and GED is accepted. *Academic units recommended:* 4 English, 4 mathematics, 3 science, (2 science labs), 4 foreign language, 3 social studies, 2 history.

Financial Aid

Students should submit: FAFSA, CSS/Financial Aid PROFILE, noncustodial PROFILE, business/farm supplement, parent and student Federal Tax Returns and W-2s. Regular filing deadline is 2/1. The Princeton Review suggests that all financial aid forms be submitted as soon as possible after January 1. *Need-based scholarships/grants offered:* Federal Pell, SEOG, state scholarships/grants, private scholarships, the school's own gift aid. *Loan aid offered:* Federal Perkins. Applicants will be notified of awards on or about 4/1. Federal Work-Study Program available. Institutional employment available. Off-campus job opportunities are good.

The Inside Word

Wheaton gives applicants the option of not submitting standardized test scores. The school also invites applicants to submit optional personal academic portfolios, collections of completed schoolwork that demonstrates talents the applicant wants to highlight. All applicants should seriously consider this option; for those who do not submit test scores, an academic portfolio is practically imperative, both as an indicator of the applicant's seriousness about Wheaton and as evidence of academic excellence (evidence that standardized test scores might otherwise provide).

THE SCHOOL SAYS "..."

From The Admissions Office

"What makes for a 'best college'? Is it merely the hard-to-define notions of prestige or image? We don't think so. We think what makes college 'best' and best for you is a school that will make you a first-rate thinker and writer, a pragmatic professional in your work, and an ethical practitioner in your life. To get you to all these places, Wheaton takes advantage of its great combinations: a beautiful, secluded New England campus combined with access to Boston and Providence; a high quality, classic liberal arts and sciences curriculum combined with award-winning internship, job, and community-service programs; and a campus that respects your individuality in the context of the larger community. What's the 'best' outcome of a Wheaton education? A start on life that combines meaningful work, significant relationships, and a commitment to your local and global community. Far more than for what they've studied or for what they've gone on to do for a living, we're most proud of Wheaton graduates for who they become.

"Wheaton does not require students to submit the results of any standardized testing. The only exception is the TOEFL for students for whom English is a second language. Students who choose to submit standardized testing may use results from the SAT or the ACT."

For even more information on this school, turn to page 558 of the "Stats" section.

WILKES UNIVERSITY

84 WEST SOUTH STREET, WILKES-BARRE, PA 18766 • ADMISSIONS: 570-408-4400 • FAX: 570-408-4904
E-MAIL: ADMISSIONS@WILKES.EDU • WEBSITE: WWW.WILKES.EDU

RATINGS
Quality of Life: 67   **Academic:** 70   **Admissions:** 73   **Financial Aid:** 71

STUDENTS SAY ". . ."

Academics

Students describe Wilkes as "a small campus focused on bringing out [each] student's best." The university boasts excellent pharmacy, engineering, and science programs. The school just received a generous grant from the Howard Hughes Medical Institute, "to improve our programs with a refocusing on student-professor research." "The professors are a mix," the students tell us. "Some professors are amazing. They're willing to meet with you outside of class

and eager to help you learn." Others, however, have "relied way too heavily on the texts and rarely started discussions." For the most part, though, classes are small, and "professors are always open to talk and willing to sit down to help you understand a lecture or lab." Students appreciate the development of practical skills in the classroom. "Almost all of the upper-level classes require the design and build of a project...it allows the student to get hands on and use the classroom knowledge on something he chose to design." "It has definitely put me on the right track for the future." Students are generally happy with the administration, although a few report problems with the bursar's office. "Most of the school's administration is available by appointment. They're generally always willing to help students." "Mentoring...is the heart and soul of this institution."

Life

Wilkes has a large commuter population, but this hasn't hindered the action on campus. "There's always something to do around campus, even if everyone just hangs out in a dorm lounge!" "Some dorms are actually old mansions, and they are beautiful." "RAs are really good at... encourag[ing] students to take up one of the 60 chartered Clubs of Student Government." There is some drinking but plenty of other activity as well. "When the weather permits, our intramural teams gather on our greenway, or you will find different organizations putting on different events throughout the semester." Everyone appreciates the size of the school, which gives it "a close-knit family feel." The surrounding area, Wilkes-Barre, "seems to be on the rise." Students seeking a break from campus can head to the mall, and "movies and bowling are popular activities for some down time." They also "hit the clubs/bars" or "check out bands play at a nearby café," and the school runs "cheap trips to the city [Philadelphia and New York] or entertainment venues for low or no cost."

Student Body

"Most of the students are from the Northeast region," and naturally the commuter population is local. The Wilkes community also has an international segment. "There is a sharing of culture. The university strives [to] bring everyone together." "There are different social groups...but you can pretty much talk to anybody and fit in wherever you want." "The typical student is outgoing and friendly." Students are pleased with the diversity of their interests. "There are all types of people, some are very political, and others care a lot about their sports teams." "Many students are very academic, especially those within the pharmacy program." "There is dedication toward service learning and helping others."

THE PRINCETON REVIEW SAYS

Admissions

Very important factors considered include: Class rank, rigor of secondary school record. *Important factors considered include:* Academic GPA, standardized test scores, character/personal qualities, extracurricular activities. *Other factors considered include:* Recommendation(s), alumni/ae relation, interview, talent/ability, volunteer work, work experience. SAT or ACT required; TOEFL required of all international applicants. High school diploma is required and GED is accepted. *Academic units recommended:* 4 English, 3 mathematics, 3 science, (2 science labs), 2 foreign language, 3 social studies, 1 computer science.

Financial Aid

Students should submit: FAFSA. The Princeton Review suggests that all financial aid forms be submitted as soon as possible after January 1. *Need-based scholarships/grants offered:* Federal Pell, SEOG, state scholarships/grants, private scholarships, the school's own gift aid. *Loan aid offered:* Federal Perkins, Federal Nursing, state loans, college/university loans from institutional funds. Applicants will be notified of awards on a rolling basis beginning 3/1. Federal Work-Study Program available. Institutional employment available. Off-campus job opportunities are good.

The Inside Word

The application process at Wilkes is fairly relaxed. Admissions officers rely mostly on hard data—essays and recommendations are optional. This allows them to make admit decisions and relay those decisions to applicants in only a few weeks. Wilkes processes applications on a rolling basis, so an early application will increase your chances.

THE SCHOOL SAYS " . . ."

From The Admissions Office

"As our students reported, 'People honestly care about [a student's] success at Wilkes.' This is the basis for deep and meaningful relationships between students and faculty members. Students conduct independent research under the direction of active, faculty scholars. Faculty members can be found interacting with their students in the cafeteria, at campus activities and sporting events, and in the hallways of the academic buildings, as well as in their offices and homes.

"These mentoring relationships, which extend from professional guidance to personal direction, blossom over 4 years, but don't end at graduation. Instead, alumni report that they stay in contact with their faculty members throughout their professional careers. Consider this recent event: During winter break, one professor drove two senior students to Boston to visit graduate schools. Upon arrival, they met with a Wilkes alumna, herself a former advisee of this professor, who shared her experiences with them. As our students say, "[Professors] really try to help you; they are here for you.'

"In choosing our students, we look for students who want to actively engage in their personal and professional development. To do so, we look at the entire individual: the academic record and strength of curriculum, community service and active extracurricular life, career goals and motivation for success. Successful students are those who want to learn in collaboration with their peers and professors. They also energetically participate in campus life because they know that learning takes place both in and outside the classroom."

For even more information on this school, turn to page 558 of the "Stats" section.

WILLIAMS COLLEGE

33 Stetson Court, Williamstown, MA 01267 • Admissions: 413-597-2211 • Fax: 413-597-4052
Financial Aid: 413-597-4181 • E-mail: admissions@williams.edu • Website: www.williams.edu

RATINGS
Quality of Life: 88   Academic: 99   Admissions: 99   Financial Aid: 99

STUDENTS SAY ". . ."

Academics

Williams College is a small bastion of the liberal arts "with a fantastic academic reputation." Administrators some-times "ignore student consensus in their misguided efforts to improve campus life," but they are "incredibly compas-sionate and accessible" and red tape is virtually unheard of. "Williams students tend to spend a lot of time com-plaining about how much work they have" but they say the

academic experience is "absolutely incomparable." Classes are "small" and "intense." "The facilities are absolutely top-notch in almost everything." Research opportunities are plentiful. A one-month January term offers study-abroad programs and a host of short pass/fail courses that are "a college student's dream come true." "The hard science departments are incredible." Economics, art history, and English are equally outstand-ing. Despite the occasional professor "who should not even be teaching at the high school level," the faculty at Williams is one of the best. Most professors "jump at every opportunity to help you love their subject." "They're here because they want to interact with undergrads." "If you complain about a Williams education then you would complain about education anywhere," wagers an economics major.

Life

Students at Williams enjoy a "stunning campus." "The Berkshire mountains are in the background every day as you walk to class" and opportunities for outdoor activity are numerous. The location is in "the boonies," though, and the surrounding "one-horse college town" is "quaint" at best. "There is no nearby place to buy necessities that is not ridiculously overpriced." Student life happens almost exclusively on campus. Dorm rooms are "large" and "well above par" but the housing system is "very weird." While some students like it, there is a general consensus that its creators "should be slapped and sent back to Amherst." Entertainment options include "lots of" performances, plays, and lectures. Some students are "obsessed with a capella groups." Intramurals are popular, especially broomball ("a sacred tradition involving a hockey rink, sneakers, a rubber ball, and paddles"). Intercollegiate sports are "a huge part of the social scene." For many students, the various varsity teams "are the basic social blocks at Williams." "Everyone for the most part gets along, but the sports teams seem to band together," explains a sophomore. Booze-laden parties" "and general disorder on weekends" are common. "A lot of people spend their lives between homework and practice and then just get completely smashed on weekends." Nothing gets out of hand, though. "We know how to unwind without being stupid," says a sophomore.

Student Body

The student population at Williams is not the most humble. They describe themselves as "interesting and beau-tiful" "geniuses of varying interests." They're "quirky, passionate, zany, and fun." They're "athletically awe-some." They're "freakishly unique" and at the same time "cookie-cutter amazing." Ethnic diversity is stellar and you'll find all kinds of different students including "the goth students," "nerdier students," "a ladle of envi-ronmentally conscious pseudo-vegetarians," and a few "west coast hippies." However, "a typical student looks like a rich white kid" who grew up "playing field hockey just outside Boston" and spends summers "vacation-ing on the Cape." Sporty students abound. "There definitely is segregation between the artsy kids and the ath-lete types but there is also a significant amount of crossover." "Williams is a place where normal social labels tend not to apply," reports a junior. "Everyone here got in for a reason. So that football player in your theater class has amazing insight on Chekhov and that outspoken environmental activist also specializes in improv comedy."

THE PRINCETON REVIEW SAYS

Admissions

Very important factors considered include: Application essay, academic GPA, recommendation(s), rigor of secondary school record, standardized test scores. *Important factors considered include:* Class rank, extracurricular activities, talent/ability. *Other factors considered include:* Alumni/ae relation, character/personal qualities, first generation, geographical residence, racial/ethnic status, volunteer work, work experience. SAT or ACT required; SAT and SAT Subject Tests or ACT required; ACT with Writing component required. High school diploma or equivalent is not required. *Academic units recommended:* 4 English, 4 mathematics, 3 science, (3 science labs), 4 foreign language, 3 social studies.

Financial Aid

Students should submit: FAFSA, CSS/Financial Aid PROFILE, noncustodial PROFILE, business/farm supplement, parent and student federal taxes and W-2s. Regular filing deadline is 2/1. The Princeton Review suggests that all financial aid forms be submitted as soon as possible after January 1. *Need-based scholarships/grants offered:* Federal Pell, SEOG, state scholarships/grants, private scholarships, the school's own gift aid. *Loan aid offered:* Direct Subsidized Stafford, Direct Unsubsidized Stafford, Direct PLUS, Federal Perkins, college/university loans from institutional funds. Applicants will be notified of awards on or about 4/1. Federal Work-Study Program available. Institutional employment available.

The Inside Word

As is typical of highly selective colleges, at Williams high grades and test scores work more as qualifiers than to determine admissibility. Beyond a strong record of achievement, evidence of intellectual curiosity, noteworthy non-academic talents, and a non-college family background are some aspects of a candidate's application that might make for an offer of admission. But there are no guarantees—the evaluation process here is rigorous. The admissions committee (the entire admissions staff) discusses each candidate in comparison to the entire applicant pool. The pool is divided alphabetically for individual reading; after weak candidates are eliminated, those who remain undergo additional evaluations by different members of the staff. Admission decisions must be confirmed by the agreement of a plurality of the committee. Such close scrutiny demands a well-prepared candidate and application.

THE SCHOOL SAYS "…"

From The Admissions Office

"Special course offerings at Williams include Oxford-style tutorials, where students (in teams of two) research and defend ideas, engaging in weekly debate with a faculty tutor. Annually 30 Williams students devote a full year to the tutorial method of study at Oxford; half of Williams students pursue overseas education. Four weeks of winter study each January provide time for individualized projects, research, and novel fields of study. Students compete in 32 Division III athletic teams, perform in 25 musical groups, stage 10 theatrical productions, and volunteer in 30 service organizations. The college receives several million dollars annually for undergraduate science research and equipment. The town offers two distinguished art museums, and 2,200 forest acres—complete with a treetop canopy walkway—for environmental research and recreation.

"Students are required to submit either the SAT or the ACT including the optional Writing section. Applicants should also submit scores from any two SAT Subject Tests."

"To limit the debt obligations of its graduates, Williams maintains one of the lowest loan expectations of any college or university in the country. Often the aid packages of students whose families demonstrate high financial need are made up entirely of grants and a campus job-and do not include any loans."

For even more information on this school, turn to page 558 of the "Stats" section.

WORCESTER POLYTECHNIC INSTITUTE

100 INSTITUTE ROAD, WORCESTER, MA 01609 • ADMISSIONS: 508-831-5286 • FAX: 508-831-5875
FINANCIAL AID: 508-831-5469 • E-MAIL: ADMISSIONS@WPI.EDU • WEBSITE: WWW.WPI.EDU

RATINGS
Quality of Life: 83   Academic: 87   Admissions: 93   Financial Aid: 77

STUDENTS SAY "..."

Academics

Learning "is project-based and very hands on" at Worcester Polytechnic Institute, a prestigious engineering, mathematics, and science university located in central Massachusetts. Here, "students are encouraged to do some hands-on work in almost every class" through a "project-based curriculum," in which "students are given the opportunity to work on projects with minimal guidance from their advisors." Students describe this approach as "a good and realistic experience that is helpful for future career plans." The project-based system "emphasizes the understanding of technical concepts, the practical implementation of these concepts, and also an appreciation for how technological advances can benefit mankind." WPI's unique grading system of A/B/C/NR—"fail a class and it won't show up on your transcript," one student explains—means "there is a lot of freedom to take riskier classes" and the school "promotes a culture of cooperation over competition." "Even though the curriculum is hard, [and] even though we have homework due every day, we are all happy because we know that failing is just another chance to try again. It's a good philosophy." A quarterly academic calendar "allows students to take a more diverse array of classes, and forces them to learn quickly or fall behind," but also means "if you're sick for two weeks, you have lots of make-up work to do." "Incredible technological resources" are the cherry on the sundae here.

Life

"Students are very involved with schoolwork, studying, and homework" during the week at WPI, where a heavy workload and rapid-paced academic calendar keep kids busy ("With classes that last only seven weeks, midterms hit fast, and then by the time they're over, it's already time to start up on finals," one student warns). Intense weeks are the rule of thumb at pretty much every top engineering school, but where WPI breaks rank with some of its peer institutions is that when the weekend rolls around, "the social life is unbeatable." The campus hosts "a very large amount of active clubs and organizations," including a student-run social committee that "is always holding really outrageous and fun events," including "concerts with really good and popular bands." WPI also has a well supported "sports scene—football and basketball are pretty popular," and intramurals draw plenty of participants as well. WPI's "awesome," "strong and very popular" Greek life, however, is probably the biggest factor. Parties "are really fun," drawing "people from all the neighboring schools," and students insist that the parties "are always fun-themed and not sketchy. You can have a fun time and not have to be concerned about your safety" due to "a driving service with a no-questions-asked policy" and "a detail cop so nothing goes wrong." Many here even find time for a little fun during the week; as one student explains, "On Tuesday nights, many people go out since there are typically only labs on Wednesdays and not everybody has labs."

Student Body

"We have a very nice mix of students here who do not fit the typical engineering student [profile]," which "stands us apart from other engineering schools," one student writes. Even so, most here concede that "the typical student is nerdy." "We're all nerdy in our own way, whether it be a love of calculus or getting excited over video games," one undergrad relates. Another student breaks down the population this way: "There are four groups of students at WPI. One group consists of the kids who are involved on campus, one consists of kids who never leave their rooms because they are playing video games, one consists of kids who spend all their time studying, and the final group consists of kids who go to class but just want to go to parties the rest of the time." Nearly everyone here is "very driven and self-motivated," because you can't survive WPI long without those qualities. The population includes "a lot of stereotypical Massachusetts or general New England people" and "lots of international students," with China and India especially well represented.

THE PRINCETON REVIEW SAYS

Admissions

Very important factors considered include: Academic GPA, rigor of secondary school record. *Important factors considered include:* Class rank, application essay, recommendation(s), standardized test scores, character/personal qualities, extracurricular activities. *Other factors considered include:* Alumni/ae relation, first generation, geographical residence, interview, level of applicant's interest, talent/ability, volunteer work, work experience. TOEFL required of all international applicants. High school diploma is required, and GED is accepted. *Academic units required:* 4 English, 4 mathematics, 2 science, (2 science labs). *Academic units recommended:* 4 science, 2 foreign language, 2 social studies, 1 history, 1 computer science.

Financial Aid

Students should submit: FAFSA, CSS/Financial Aid PROFILE, noncustodial PROFILE. Regular filing deadline is 2/1. The Princeton Review suggests that all financial aid forms be submitted as soon as possible after January 1. *Need-based scholarships/grants offered:* Federal Pell, SEOG, state scholarships/grants, private scholarships, the school's own gift aid. *Loan aid offered:* Federal Perkins, state loans, college/university loans from institutional funds. Applicants will be notified of awards on or about 4/1. Federal Work-Study Program available. Institutional employment available. Off-campus job opportunities are good.

The Inside Word

WPI's high admission rate is the result of a self-selecting applicant pool; those who don't have a decent chance of getting in here rarely bother to apply. The relatively low rate of conversion of accepted students to enrollees is due to the fact that WPI is a 'safety' school for many applicants. Those who get in here and at MIT, CalTech, Cornell, or Carnegie Mellon usually wind up elsewhere.

THE SCHOOL SAYS "..."

From The Admissions Office

"Projects and research enrich WPI's academic program. WPI believes that in these times simply passing courses and accumulating theoretical knowledge is not enough to truly educate tomorrow's leaders. Tomorrow's professionals ought to be involved in project work that prepares them today for future challenges. Projects at WPI come as close to professional experience as a college program can possibly achieve. In fact, WPI works with more than 200 companies, government agencies, and private organizations each year. These groups provide opportunities where students get a chance to work in real, professional settings. Students gain invaluable experience in planning, coordinating team efforts, meeting deadlines, writing proposals and reports, making oral presentations, doing cost analyses, and making decisions.

Applicants are required to submit SAT or ACT scores, or in lieu of test scores may submit supplemental materials through WPI's Flex Path program. Students who choose the Flex Path are encouraged to submit examples of academic work or extracurricular projects that reflect a high level of organization, motivation, creativity and problem-solving ability."

For even more information on this school, turn to page 559 of the "Stats" section.

WORCESTER STATE COLLEGE

486 CHANDLER STREET, DEPARTMENT OF ADMISSIONS, WORCESTER, MA 01602-2597 • ADMISSIONS: 508-929-8793 • FAX: 508-929-8183
E-MAIL: ADMISSIONS@WORCESTER.EDU • WEBSITE: WWW.WORCESTER.EDU

RATINGS
Quality of Life: 77   **Academic:** 75   **Admissions:** 76   **Financial Aid:** 84

STUDENTS SAY "..."

Academics

With small class sizes, friendly faculty, and low in-state tuition costs, Worcester State College "has the feel of a pricey, private university but the cost is very manageable." An excellent "investment," this school focuses on practical, career-oriented education, and "The professors have real

world knowledge and experience and that is a big plus to the learning process." Students praise the "intimate and learner-friendly" environment, where small classes make for "a much more comfortable" experience. A current student tells us, "I have also gotten to know many of my professors due to the small class sizes and their availability to meet with students after class." On that note, "the professors at Worcester State are very accessible and extremely helpful," and they "really just love to teach." Unfortunately, some administrative offices are "hard to work with" and when you have a paperwork problem, "everyone seems to forward you to someone else." At the same time, many top administrators are student-friendly and accessible. A current student shares, "I am…part of the honors program and we have had the chance to dine with the president of our school and talk to her about what we like and what we would like to improve. She truly takes into consideration what we say."

Life

On WSC's small but active campus, "there are different activities offered during most days, like massages, psychic fairs, and themed dinners," and when the weather is nice, "Students are frequently outside either throwing around a football or just sitting by the picnic tables." In their downtime, "people tend to go to dinner together or have movie nights" while other students "go out to bars and socialize." The campus is dry, yet "parties off campus are always big for the first two years," and many students go out Thursday, Friday, and Saturday night. In the residence halls, students "spend a lot of time playing video games and watching movies with friends," or they take advantage of "a few spots to hang out and play pool, ping pong, or video games" on campus. Working out is also common, and many students "like to play sports or go to a sports event at school" to blow off steam. For most commuters, "life at school consists of going to class and staying after class on occasion to complete homework assignments," though some also join clubs or hang out in the student center.

Student Body

A largely local crowd, most WSC students "come from any of the local cities or towns, both urban and rural," and "there's a decent mix of ethnicities" on campus. "The Massachusetts area is much more liberal than some states," and the student body follows suit. "Everyone fits in regardless of how they are," and "most seem to get along regardless of race, gender or sexual orientation." With a large commuter population (about 70 percent), "Tons of people are working part or full time while going to school, and many of the students are 'nontraditional' individuals who are going back to school years later." Even among traditional college-age students, the "Bulk of students have jobs, and juggle between paying bills and going to school." Adding a unique dynamic to the classroom, "The college welcomes elder students over 60 to attend, tuition free. This makes…for an interesting, age-diverse student body."

THE PRINCETON REVIEW SAYS

Admissions

Very important factors considered include: Academic GPA, rigor of secondary school record, standardized test scores. *Important factors considered include:* Class rank, character/personal qualities. *Other factors considered include:* Application essay, recommendation(s), alumni/ae relation, extracurricular activities, first generation, geographical residence, racial/ethnic status, state residency, talent/ability, volunteer work, work experience. SAT or ACT required; ACT with Writing component required. TOEFL required of all international applicants. High school diploma is required and GED is accepted. *Academic units required:* 4 English, 3 mathematics, 3 science, (1 science labs), 2 foreign language, 1 social studies, 1 history, 2 academic electives.

Financial Aid

Students should submit: FAFSA Regular filing deadline is 5/1. The Princeton Review suggests that all financial aid forms be submitted as soon as possible after January 1. *Need-based scholarships/grants offered:* Federal Pell, SEOG, state scholarships/grants, private scholarships, the school's own gift aid. *Loan aid offered:* Federal Perkins, state loans. Applicants will be notified of awards on a rolling basis beginning 3/1. Federal Work-Study Program available. Institutional employment available. Off-campus job opportunities are good.

The Inside Word

For Worcester State College, the single most important factor in an admissions decision is a student's academic record, including grade point average, grade trends, and the rigor of your high school coursework. When calculating your GPA, Worcester State awards extra points for honors and advanced placement courses.

THE SCHOOL SAYS " . . ."

From The Admissions Office

"Worcester State College is a four-year public college with 25 majors including traditional liberal arts and sciences, teacher education, business, visual and performing arts, biomedical sciences, and the health professions. Our students learn in small, friendly classes taught by committed, accessible faculty offering engaging research opportunities to graduate and undergraduate students alike. Worcester State College is the only Massachusetts State College to be named a Best Northeastern College by the Princeton Review seven years in a row and is nationally recognized for its community service, having been named two years in a row to the President's Higher Education Community Service Honor Roll. Worcester State College was named the "Best College in Worcester County" in Worcester Magazine's Readers Poll four out of the past six years.

"Worcester State College is dedicated to offering high quality, affordable undergraduate and graduate academic programs and to promoting the lifelong intellectual growth, global awareness, and career opportunities of our students. To this end, we value teaching excellence rooted in scholarship and community service; cooperate with the business, social, and cultural resources of Worcester County; collaborate with other institutions of higher learning in the region; and develop new programs responsive to emerging community needs.

"Set on 58 acres in the residential west side of Worcester, Massachusetts, Worcester State College is an attractive and safe campus within an hour's drive of all major population centers in New England."

For even more information on this school, turn to page 559 of the "Stats" section.

YALE UNIVERSITY

PO Box 208234, New Haven, CT 06520-8234 • Admissions: 203-432-9316 • Fax: 203-432-9392
Financial Aid: 203-432-2700 • E-mail: STUDENT.QUESTIONS@YALE.EDU • Website: WWW.YALE.EDU/ADMIT

RATINGS
Quality of Life: 95   **Academic:** 98   **Admissions:** 99   **Financial Aid:** 97

STUDENTS SAY "..."

Academics

Listening to Yale students wax rhapsodic about their school, one can be forgiven for wondering whether they aren't actually describing the platonic form of the university. By their own account, students here benefit not only from "amazing academics and extensive resources" that provide "phenomenal in- and out-of-class education," but also from participation in "a student body that is committed to learning and to each other." Unlike some other prestigious, prominent research universities, Yale "places unparalleled focus on undergraduate education," requiring all professors to teach at least one undergraduate course each year. "[You know] the professors actually love teaching, because if they just wanted to do their research, they could have easily gone elsewhere." A residential college system further personalizes the experience. Each residential college "has a Dean and a Master, each of which is only responsible for 300 to 500 students, so administrative attention is highly specialized and widely available." Students further enjoy access to "a seemingly never-ending supply of resources (they really just love throwing money at us)" that includes "the 12 million volumes in our libraries." In short, "The opportunities are truly endless." "The experiences you have here and the people that you meet will change your life and strengthen your dreams," says ones student. Looking for the flip side to all this? "If the weather were a bit nicer, that would be excellent," one student offers. Guess that will have to do.

> **SURVEY SAYS . . .**
> School is well run
> Musical organizations are popular
> Theater is popular
> Student publications are popular
> Political activism is popular

Life

Yale is, of course, extremely challenging academically, but students assure us that "Aside from the stress of midterms and finals, life at Yale is relatively carefree." Work doesn't keep undergrads from participating in "a huge variety of activities for fun. There are more than 300 student groups, including singing, dancing, juggling fire, theater...the list goes on. Because of all of these groups, there are shows on-campus all the time, which are a lot of fun and usually free or less than $5. On top of that, there are parties and events on campus and off campus, as well as many subsidized trips to New York City and Boston." Many here "are politically active (or at least politically aware)" and "a very large number of students either volunteer or try to get involved in some sort of organization to make a difference in the world." When the weekend comes around, "there are always parties to go to, whether at the frats or in rooms, but there's definitely no pressure to drink if you don't want to. A good friend of mine pledged a frat without drinking and that's definitely not unheard of (but still not common)." The relationship between Yale and the city of New Haven "sometimes leaves a little to be desired, but overall it's a great place to be for four years."

Student Body

A typical Yalie is "tough to define because so much of what makes Yale special is the unique convergence of different students to form one cohesive entity. Nonetheless, the one common characteristic of Yale students is passion—each Yalie is driven and dedicated to what he or she loves most, and it creates a palpable atmosphere of enthusiasm on campus." True enough, the student body represents a wide variety of ethnic, religious, economic, and academic backgrounds, but they all "thrive on learning, whether in a class, from a book, or from a conversation with a new friend." Students here also "tend to do a lot." "Everyone has many activities that they are a part of, which in turn fosters the closely connected feel of the campus." Undergrads tend to lean to the left politically, but for "those whose political views aren't as liberal as the rest of the campus...there are several campus organizations that cater to them."

Admissions

Very important factors considered include: Class rank, application essay, academic GPA, recommendation(s), rigor of secondary school record, standardized test scores, character/personal qualities, extracurricular activities, talent/ability, *Other factors considered include:* Alumni/ae relation, first generation, geographical residence, interview, level of applicant's interest, racial/ethnic status, state residency, volunteer work, work experience. SAT and SAT Subject Tests or ACT required; ACT with Writing component required. TOEFL required of all international applicants. High school diploma or equivalent is not required.

Financial Aid

Students should submit: FAFSA, CSS/Financial Aid PROFILE, noncustodial PROFILE, business/farm supplement, parent tax returns. Regular filing deadline is 3/1. The Princeton Review suggests that all financial aid forms be submitted as soon as possible after January 1. *Need-based scholarships/grants offered:* Federal Pell, SEOG, state scholarships/grants, private scholarships, the school's own gift aid, United Negro College Fund *Loan aid offered:* Federal Perkins, state loans, college/university loans from institutional funds. Applicants will be notified of awards on or about 4/1. Institutional employment available.

The Inside Word

Yale estimates that over three-quarters of all its applicants are qualified to attend the university, but less than ten percent get in. That adds up to a lot of broken hearts among kids who, if admitted, could probably handle the academic program. With so many qualified applicants to choose from, Yale can winnow to build an incoming class that is balanced in terms of income level, racial/ethnic background, geographic origin, and academic interest. For all but the most qualified, getting in typically hinges on offering just what an admissions officer is looking for to fill a specific slot. Legacies (descendents of Yale grads) gain some advantage—although they still need exceptionally strong credentials.

THE SCHOOL SAYS "..."

From The Admissions Office

"The most important questions the admissions committee must resolve are 'Who is likely to make the most of Yale's resources?' and 'Who will contribute significantly to the Yale community?' These questions suggest an approach to evaluating applicants that is more complex than whether Yale would rather admit well-rounded people or those with specialized talents. In selecting a class of 1,300 from more than 22,000 applicants, the admissions committee looks for academic ability and achievement combined with such personal characteristics as motivation, curiosity, energy, and leadership ability. The nature of these qualities is such that there is no simple profile of grades, scores, interests, and activities that will assure admission. Diversity within the student population is important, and the admissions committee selects a class of able and contributing individuals from a variety of backgrounds and with a broad range of interests and skills.

"Applicants for the entering class will be required to take the two SAT Subject Tests of their choice. Applicants may take the ACT, with the Writing component, as an alternative to the SAT and SAT Subject Tests."

For even more information on this school, turn to page 560 of the "Stats" section.

YORK COLLEGE OF PENNSYLVANIA

ADMISSIONS OFFICE, 441 COUNTRY CLUB ROAD, YORK, PA 17403-3651 • ADMISSIONS: 717-849-1600 OR 800-455-8018
FAX: 717-849-1607 • FINANCIAL AID: 717-815-1282 • WEBSITE: WWW.YCP.EDU/

RATINGS
Quality of Life: 73   Academic: 78   Admissions: 81   Financial Aid: 76

STUDENTS SAY "..."

Academics

It is easy to feel "right at home" at York College of
Pennsylvania, an affordable private school that attracts a
largely East Coast crowd. As many students note, this
small college is an "excellent size," with just over 4,600
undergraduates and uniformly small class sizes (in fact,
only a few York classes have more than 40 students). The

> **SURVEY SAYS . . .**
> *Great computer facilities*
> *Athletic facilities are great*
> *Low cost of living*

intimate campus atmosphere definitely enhances the learning experience, and "Each major is almost like a family. You get to meet students and benefit from a small institution setting." Many students choose York for its
"extremely competitive nursing program" and "stellar" engineering department, which are well known in the
region. No matter what your major, York professors "take their teaching job more seriously than their research,"
and through class discussion, "promote critical thinking and instill a sense of professionalism in their students."
Outside the classroom, professors "care about you as a person," and "are willing to help you if you have questions." A current student attests, "Whether it's finding a job on campus or preparing for a test, the faculty here
truly wants to help their students." For further assistance, "the tutoring services are also a big help," as are academic advisors. To top it all off, the reasonable tuition, large endowment, and generous financial aid packages
make York College "extremely affordable for a private college."

Life

Located on a "beautiful" campus in a small city, York College is "a relaxing and thought-provoking environment." Residence life is "safe" and comfortable, especially for upperclassmen: "After a student's freshman year
they live in apartment-style dorms which allow you to do your own cooking, have your own bathroom, and
feel more grown up." Working out is a popular way to blow off steam, and many students "like to play different intramural sports and go to the gym" or go "out on the lawn and throw around a Frisbee." Students also
enjoy getting off campus, and there are "outdoor roller rinks across town, plenty of malls, and some great places
to eat" in York—though, students admit, the campus could provide "better transportation around the surrounding town" for those who don't have a car. Socially, students often "go out and party on the weekends,"
or, if they are over 21, "go to the local bars in the city." Alternately, students can hang out in the dorms or participate in campus activities. For example, once a month, "a movie is played in the Life Science building with
free popcorn."

Student Body

Most students at York College are from the mid-Atlantic area—"usually from the York, Baltimore, Philadelphia,
or New York areas." Generally speaking, "students here come from middle-class families;" however, "There are
many student organizations that support diverse interests and backgrounds." In addition to traditional undergraduates, York attracts a "high population of commuters and non-traditional 'second degree' students." These
students are busy and efficient—"there to get a degree and get out." On the whole, "The people here are friendly,
and a strong camaraderie exists among students." At York, "There is always someone around that you know,
and someone is always saying hello or holding a door open for you." Academics are important, but York students "like to take advantage of social opportunities," too.

THE PRINCETON REVIEW SAYS

Admissions

Very important factors considered include: Academic GPA, rigor of secondary school record. *Important factors considered include:* Class rank, standardized test scores, character/personal qualities. *Other factors considered include:* Application essay, recommendation(s), alumni/ae relation, extracurricular activities, interview, level of applicant's interest, talent/ability, volunteer work, work experience. SAT or ACT required; ACT with Writing component required. TOEFL required of all international applicants. High school diploma is required and GED is accepted. *Academic units required:* 4 English, 3 mathematics, 3 science, 2 foreign language, 3 social studies. *Academic units recommended:* 4 mathematics.

Financial Aid

Students should submit: FAFSA. The Princeton Review suggests that all financial aid forms be submitted as soon as possible after January 1. *Need-based scholarships/grants offered:* Federal Pell, SEOG, state scholarships/grants, private scholarships, the school's own gift aid. *Loan aid offered:* Direct Subsidized Stafford, Direct Unsubsidized Stafford, Direct PLUS, Federal Perkins, Federal Nursing, college/university loans from institutional funds. Applicants will be notified of awards on a rolling basis beginning 2/1. Federal Work-Study Program available. Institutional employment available. Off-campus job opportunities are good.

The Inside Word

York College accepts students on a rolling basis after October 1 and continues to review applications until the incoming class is filled. If you apply online, the application fee is waived.

THE SCHOOL SAYS " . . ."

From The Admissions Office

"A private college in southcentral Pennsylvania, York offers more than 50 baccalaureate majors in professional programs, the sciences and humanities to its 4,600 students. York offers you what very few colleges can: an ideally sized, affordable private college, where students enjoy personal attention in the classroom while also enjoying a vibrant and diverse student life.

"York College prepares students to be professionals in demand in whatever career they pursue. Our students are taught these skills in the classroom by faculty who model and encourage professional behavior; through hands-on learning opportunities like internships and leadership activities, where students put into practice what they have learned in the classroom; and through the Center for Professional Excellence's seminars, which offer both theory and practical knowledge about being a highly regarded professional in today's workplace.

"Within the past few years, York has invested more than $160 million in new and enhanced facilities, including a certified "green" engineering building, stunning centers for sports and fitness, performing arts and humanities, and contemporary residence halls. We've transformed our campus while staying true to our mission of providing affordable academic excellence. York's annual tuition is half that of most other private colleges.

"If you are ready, York College offers you a world of opportunities in an environment where you are challenged and supported, and where your accomplishments are recognized and valued. Visit York College and your first impression will be 'Wow!'"

For even more information on this school, turn to page 560 of the "Stats" section.

PART 3: THE STATS

ADELPHI UNIVERSITY

CAMPUS LIFE
Fire Safety Rating	**99**
Green Rating	**87**
Type of school	private
Environment	metropolis

STUDENTS
Total undergrad enrollment	4,923
% male/female	29/71
% from out of state	8
% from public high school	73
# of fraternities	3
# of sororities	7
% African American	11
% Asian	6
% Caucasian	55
% Hispanic	7
% international	3
# of countries represented	63

ACADEMICS
Calendar	semester
Student/faculty ratio	9:1
Profs interesting rating	76
Profs accessible rating	74
Most common reg class size	10–19 students
Most common lab size	10–19 students

MOST POPULAR MAJORS
business/commerce
education
nursing

SELECTIVITY
# of applicants	7,359
% of applicants accepted	70
% of acceptees attending	20

FRESHMAN PROFILE
Range SAT Critical Reading	480–580
Range SAT Math	500–600
Range SAT Writing	498–590
Range ACT Composite	20–26
Minimum paper TOEFL	550
Minimum computer TOEFL	80
Average HS GPA	3.37
% graduated top 10% of class	24
% graduated top 25% of class	60
% graduated top 50% of class	87

DEADLINES
Early action	
Deadline	12/1
Notification	12/31
Regular	
Notification	rolling
Nonfall registration?	yes

FINANCIAL FACTS
Annual tuition	$24,100
Room and board	$10,500
Required fees	$1,200
Books and supplies	$1,000
% frosh rec. need-based scholarship or grant aid	54
% UG rec. need-based scholarship or grant aid	45
% frosh rec. non-need-based scholarship or grant aid	47
% UG rec. non-need-based scholarship or grant aid	43
% frosh rec. need-based self-help aid	62
% UG rec. need-based self-help aid	54
% frosh rec. athletic scholarships	2
% UG rec. athletic scholarships	2
% frosh rec. any financial aid	90
% UG rec. any financial aid	88
% UG borrow to pay for school	69
Average cumulative indebtedness	$28,307

ALBRIGHT COLLEGE

CAMPUS LIFE
Fire Safety Rating	**60***
Green Rating	**60***
Type of school	private
Affiliation	Methodist
Environment	suburban

STUDENTS
Total undergrad enrollment	2,074
% male/female	42/58
% from out of state	33
% from public high school	77
% live on campus	61
# of fraternities	4
# of sororities	3
% African American	9
% Asian	2
% Caucasian	78
% Hispanic	4
% international	8
# of countries represented	24

ACADEMICS
Calendar	4/1/4
Student/faculty ratio	13:1
Profs interesting rating	87
Profs accessible rating	87
Most common reg class size	10–19 students
Most common lab size	10–19 students

MOST POPULAR MAJORS
business/commerce
sociology

SELECTIVITY
# of applicants	6,135
% of applicants accepted	50
% of acceptees attending	21

FRESHMAN PROFILE
Range SAT Critical Reading	480–580
Range SAT Math	490–590
Average HS GPA	3.8
% graduated top 10% of class	23
% graduated top 25% of class	48
% graduated top 50% of class	79

DEADLINES
Regular	
Priority	3/1
Regular	
Notification	rolling
Nonfall registration?	yes

FINANCIAL FACTS
Annual tuition	$31,940
Room and board	$8,858
Required fees	$800
Books and supplies	$1,000
% frosh rec. need-based scholarship or grant aid	88
% UG rec. need-based scholarship or grant aid	82
% frosh rec. non-need-based scholarship or grant aid	7
% UG rec. non-need-based scholarship or grant aid	9
% frosh rec. need-based self-help aid	81
% UG rec. need-based self-help aid	73
% frosh rec. any financial aid	95
% UG rec. any financial aid	91
% UG borrow to pay for school	89
Average cumulative indebtedness	$31,845

ALFRED UNIVERSITY

CAMPUS LIFE
Fire Safety Rating	**60***
Green Rating	**72**
Type of school	private
Environment	rural

STUDENTS

Total undergrad enrollment	1,971
% male/female	51/49
% from out of state	35
% live on campus	67
% African American	4
% Asian	2
% Caucasian	64
% Hispanic	2
% international	3

ACADEMICS

Calendar	semester
Student/faculty ratio	12:1
Profs interesting rating	85
Profs accessible rating	84
Most common reg class size	10–19 students
Most common lab size	fewer than 10 students

MOST POPULAR MAJORS
business/commerce
ceramic sciences and engineering
fine/studio arts

SELECTIVITY

# of applicants	2,577
% of applicants accepted	70
% of acceptees attending	26
# of early decision applicants	53
% accepted early decision	83

FRESHMAN PROFILE

Range SAT Critical Reading	440–610
Range SAT Math	500–620
Range ACT Composite	22–27
Minimum paper TOEFL	550
Minimum computer TOEFL	213
% graduated top 10% of class	18
% graduated top 25% of class	46
% graduated top 50% of class	85

DEADLINES

Early decision	
Deadline	12/1
Notification	12/15
Regular	
Priority	2/1
Notification	rolling
Nonfall registration?	yes

FINANCIAL FACTS

Annual tuition	$25,246
Room and board	$11,174
Required fees	$850
Books and supplies	$900
% frosh rec. need-based scholarship or grant aid	74
% UG rec. need-based scholarship or grant aid	73
% frosh rec. non-need-based scholarship or grant aid	44

% UG rec. non-need-based scholarship or grant aid	39
% frosh rec. need-based self-help aid	66
% UG rec. need-based self-help aid	66
% frosh rec. any financial aid	92
% UG rec. any financial aid	90
% UG borrow to pay for school	83
Average cumulative indebtedness	$23,292

ALLEGHENY COLLEGE

CAMPUS LIFE

Fire Safety Rating	**79**
Green Rating	**93**
Type of school	private
Environment	town

STUDENTS

Total undergrad enrollment	2,099
% male/female	45/55
% from out of state	43
% from public high school	82
% live on campus	78
# of fraternities	5
# of sororities	5
% African American	4
% Asian	3
% Caucasian	89
% Hispanic	3
% international	1
# of countries represented	38

ACADEMICS

Calendar	semester
Student/faculty ratio	13:1
Profs interesting rating	92
Profs accessible rating	89
Most common reg class size	10–19 students
Most common lab size	10–19 students

MOST POPULAR MAJORS
biology/biological sciences
economics
psychology

SELECTIVITY

# of applicants	3,916
% of applicants accepted	66
% of acceptees attending	22
# accepting a place on wait list	327
% admitted from wait list	2
# of early decision applicants	92
% accepted early decision	66

FRESHMAN PROFILE

Range SAT Critical Reading	550–660
Range SAT Math	560–650
Range SAT Writing	550–640

Range ACT Composite	23–29
Minimum paper TOEFL	550
Minimum computer TOEFL	213
Minimum web-based TOEFL	80
Average HS GPA	3.75
% graduated top 10% of class	45
% graduated top 25% of class	76
% graduated top 50% of class	97

DEADLINES

Early decision	
Deadline	11/15
Notification	12/15
Regular	
Deadline	2/15
Notification	4/1
Nonfall registration?	yes

FINANCIAL FACTS

Annual tuition	$34,490
Room and board	$8,790
Required fees	$320
Books and supplies	$1,000
% frosh rec. need-based scholarship or grant aid	69
% UG rec. need-based scholarship or grant aid	69
% frosh rec. non-need-based scholarship or grant aid	12
% UG rec. non-need-based scholarship or grant aid	9
% frosh rec. need-based self-help aid	58
% UG rec. need-based self-help aid	61
% frosh rec. any financial aid	99
% UG rec. any financial aid	98

AMERICAN UNIVERSITY

CAMPUS LIFE

Fire Safety Rating	**91**
Green Rating	**86**
Type of school	private
Affiliation	Methodist
Environment	metropolis

STUDENTS

Total undergrad enrollment	6,430
% male/female	39/61
% from out of state	82
% live on campus	64
# of fraternities	11
# of sororities	12
% African American	4
% Asian	6
% Caucasian	61
% Hispanic	5
% international	6
# of countries represented	102

ACADEMICS

Calendar	semester
Student/faculty ratio	13:1
Profs interesting rating	86
Profs accessible rating	81

MOST POPULAR MAJORS
business/commerce
international relations and affairs
mass communication/media studies

SELECTIVITY

# of applicants	14,935
% of applicants accepted	53
% of acceptees attending	19
# accepting a place on wait list	205
# of early decision applicants	435
% accepted early decision	73

FRESHMAN PROFILE

Range SAT Critical Reading	590–700
Range SAT Math	580–670
Range SAT Writing	580–690
Range ACT Composite	26–30
Minimum paper TOEFL	550
Minimum web-based TOEFL	80
% graduated top 10% of class	50
% graduated top 25% of class	83
% graduated top 50% of class	98

DEADLINES

Early decision	
Deadline	11/15
Notification	12/31
Regular	
Deadline	1/15
Notification	4/1
Nonfall registration?	yes

FINANCIAL FACTS

Annual tuition	$36,180
Room and board	$13,468
Required fees	$517
% frosh rec. need-based scholarship or grant aid	3
% UG rec. need-based scholarship or grant aid	24
% frosh rec. non-need-based scholarship or grant aid	25
% UG rec. non-need-based scholarship or grant aid	22
% frosh rec. need-based self-help aid	46
% UG rec. need-based self-help aid	44
% frosh rec. athletic scholarships	2
% UG rec. athletic scholarships	2
% frosh rec. any financial aid	55
% UG rec. any financial aid	50

AMHERST COLLEGE

CAMPUS LIFE

Fire Safety Rating	**60***
Green Rating	**60***
Type of school	private
Environment	town

STUDENTS

Total undergrad enrollment	1,744
% male/female	50/50
% from out of state	89
% from public high school	58
% live on campus	97
% African American	11
% Asian	10
% Caucasian	39
% Hispanic	11
% international	8
# of countries represented	24

ACADEMICS

Calendar	semester
Student/faculty ratio	8:1
Profs interesting rating	87
Profs accessible rating	93
Most common reg class size	10–19 students
Most common lab size	fewer than 10 students

MOST POPULAR MAJORS
economics
political science and government
psychology

SELECTIVITY

# of applicants	7,679
% of applicants accepted	16
% of acceptees attending	38
# accepting a place on wait list	562
# of early decision applicants	444
% accepted early decision	30

FRESHMAN PROFILE

Range SAT Critical Reading	660–760
Range SAT Math	650–780
Range SAT Writing	660–770
Range ACT Composite	30–34
Minimum paper TOEFL	600
Minimum computer TOEFL	250
Minimum web-based TOEFL	100
% graduated top 10% of class	85
% graduated top 25% of class	94
% graduated top 50% of class	100

DEADLINES

Early decision	
Deadline	11/15
Notification	12/15
Regular	
Deadline	1/1
Notification	4/5
Nonfall registration?	no

FINANCIAL FACTS

Annual tuition	$38,250
Room and board	$10,150
Required fees	$678
Books and supplies	$1,000
% frosh rec. need-based scholarship or grant aid	53
% UG rec. need-based scholarship or grant aid	56
% UG rec. non-need-based scholarship or grant aid	56
% frosh rec. need-based self-help aid	45
% UG rec. need-based self-help aid	50
% frosh rec. any financial aid	44
% UG rec. any financial aid	54
% UG borrow to pay for school	41
Average cumulative indebtedness	$11,347

ARCADIA UNIVERSITY

CAMPUS LIFE

Fire Safety Rating	**60***
Green Rating	**60***
Type of school	private
Affiliation	Presbyterian
Environment	town

STUDENTS

Total undergrad enrollment	2,063
% male/female	27/73
% from out of state	36
% from public high school	72
% live on campus	68
% African American	8
% Asian	2
% Caucasian	81
% Hispanic	3
% international	1
# of countries represented	13

ACADEMICS

Calendar	semester
Student/faculty ratio	13:1
Profs interesting rating	78
Profs accessible rating	72
Most common reg class size	10–19 students
Most common lab size	10–19 students

MOST POPULAR MAJORS
business/commerce
education
psychology

SELECTIVITY

# of applicants	4,750
% of applicants accepted	67
% of acceptees attending	20

FRESHMAN PROFILE

Range SAT Critical Reading	510–610
Range SAT Math	500–590
Range SAT Writing	510–610
Range ACT Composite	21–27
Minimum paper TOEFL	550
Minimum computer TOEFL	213
% graduated top 10% of class	31
% graduated top 25% of class	62
% graduated top 50% of class	93

DEADLINES

Early decision	
Deadline	10/15
Notification	12/1
Regular	
Priority	6/1
Deadline	8/1
Notification	rolling
Nonfall registration?	yes

FINANCIAL FACTS

Annual tuition	$29,340
	$25,650
Room and board	$10,280
Required fees	$360
Books and supplies	$1,000
% frosh rec. any financial aid	97

THE ART INSTITUTE OF BOSTON AT LESLEY UNIVERSITY

CAMPUS LIFE

Fire Safety Rating	**88**
Green Rating	**72**
Type of school	private
Environment	metropolis

STUDENTS

Total undergrad enrollment	1,261
% male/female	25/75
% from out of state	44
% from public high school	84
% African American	4
% Asian	3
% Caucasian	63
% Hispanic	5
% international	3
# of countries represented	15

ACADEMICS

Calendar	semester
Student/faculty ratio	10:1
Profs interesting rating	89

Profs accessible rating	73
Most common reg class size 10–19 students	

MOST POPULAR MAJORS
graphic design
illustration
photography

SELECTIVITY

# of applicants	2,523
% of applicants accepted	65
% of acceptees attending	20
# accepting a place on wait list	32
% admitted from wait list	100

FRESHMAN PROFILE

Range SAT Critical Reading	490–600
Range SAT Math	460–560
Range SAT Writing	490–590
Range ACT Composite	19–26
Minimum paper TOEFL	500
Minimum computer TOEFL	173
Minimum web-based TOEFL	61
Average HS GPA	3
% graduated top 10% of class	12
% graduated top 25% of class	38
% graduated top 50% of class	70

DEADLINES

Regular	
Priority	2/15
Regular	
Notification	rolling
Nonfall registration?	yes

FINANCIAL FACTS

Annual tuition	$25,780
Required fees	$750
Books and supplies	$1,575
% frosh rec. need-based scholarship or grant aid	73
% UG rec. need-based scholarship or grant aid	51
% frosh rec. non-need-based scholarship or grant aid	18
% UG rec. non-need-based scholarship or grant aid	34
% frosh rec. need-based self-help aid	69
% UG rec. need-based self-help aid	63
% frosh rec. any financial aid	70
% UG rec. any financial aid	70
% UG borrow to pay for school	93
Average cumulative indebtedness	$17,000

ASSUMPTION COLLEGE

CAMPUS LIFE

Fire Safety Rating	**84**
Green Rating	**65**
Type of school	private
Affiliation	Roman Catholic
Environment	city

STUDENTS

Total undergrad enrollment	2,163
% male/female	41/59
% from out of state	32
% from public high school	68
% live on campus	89
% African American	2
% Asian	2
% Caucasian	76
% Hispanic	3
% international	1
# of countries represented	8

ACADEMICS

Calendar	semester
Student/faculty ratio	12:1
Profs interesting rating	82
Profs accessible rating	85
Most common reg class size 20–29 students	
Most common lab size	10–19 students

MOST POPULAR MAJORS
accounting
psychology
rehabilitation and therapeutic professions

SELECTIVITY

# of applicants	3,889
% of applicants accepted	71
% of acceptees attending	22
# accepting a place on wait list	146
% admitted from wait list	23

FRESHMAN PROFILE

Range SAT Critical Reading	470–580
Range SAT Math	480–580
Range ACT Composite	20–25
Minimum paper TOEFL	550
Minimum computer TOEFL	213
Minimum web-based TOEFL	80
Average HS GPA	3.44
% graduated top 10% of class	14
% graduated top 25% of class	43
% graduated top 50% of class	82

DEADLINES

Early action	
Deadline	11/15
Notification	12/15

Regular
Deadline 2/15
Nonfall registration? yes

FINANCIAL FACTS
Annual tuition $29,806
Room and board $10,070
Required fees $365
Books and supplies $1,000
% frosh rec. need-based
  scholarship or grant aid 74
% UG rec. need-based
  scholarship or grant aid 71
% frosh rec. non-need-based
  scholarship or grant aid 12
% UG rec. non-need-based
  scholarship or grant aid 8
% frosh rec. need-based self-help aid 59
% UG rec. need-based self-help aid 59
% frosh rec. athletic scholarships 1
% UG rec. athletic scholarships 1
% frosh rec. any financial aid 94
% UG rec. any financial aid 95
% UG borrow to pay for school 93
Average cumulative indebtedness $26,691

BABSON COLLEGE

CAMPUS LIFE
Fire Safety Rating 83
Green Rating 60*
Type of school private
Environment village

STUDENTS
Total undergrad enrollment 1,898
% male/female 57/45
% from out of state 46
% from public high school 50
% live on campus 85
# of fraternities 4
# of sororities 3
% African American 5
% Asian 13
% Caucasian 40
% Hispanic 9
% international 22
# of countries represented 66

ACADEMICS
Calendar semester
Student/faculty ratio 14:1
Profs interesting rating 88
Profs accessible rating 89
Most common
  reg class size 29 students

MOST POPULAR MAJORS
accounting
entrepreneurship
economics
marketing
finance

SELECTIVITY
of applicants 4,156
% of applicants accepted 40
% of acceptees attending 28
# accepting a place on wait list 342
% admitted from wait list 29
# of early decision applicants 166
% accepted early decision 57

FRESHMAN PROFILE
Range SAT Critical Reading 586–670
Range SAT Math 636–730
Range SAT Writing 600–640
Range ACT Composite 25–29
Minimum paper TOEFL 600
Minimum computer TOEFL 250
Minimum web-based TOEFL 100
% graduated top 10% of class 51
% graduated top 25% of class 87
% graduated top 50% of class 99

DEADLINES
Early decision
  Deadline 11/1
  Notification 12/15
Early action
  Deadline 11/1
  Notification 1/1
Regular
  Priority 11/15
  Deadline 1/15
  Notification 4/1
Nonfall registration? no

FINANCIAL FACTS
Annual tuition $39,040
% frosh rec. need-based
  scholarship or grant aid 41
% UG rec. need-based
  scholarship or grant aid 41
% frosh rec. non-need-based
  scholarship or grant aid 7
% UG rec. non-need-based
  scholarship or grant aid 6
% frosh rec. need-based
  self-help aid 45
% UG rec. need-based
  self-help aid 45
% frosh rec. any financial aid 51
% UG rec. any financial aid 51
% UG borrow to pay for school 49
Average cumulative
  indebtedness $28,164

BARD COLLEGE

CAMPUS LIFE
Fire Safety Rating 80
Green Rating 89
Type of school private
Environment rural

STUDENTS
Total undergrad enrollment 1,900
% male/female 43/57
% from out of state 67
% from public high school 64
% live on campus 64
% African American 2
% Asian 3
% Caucasian 55
% Hispanic 3
% Native American 1
% international 12
# of countries represented 57

ACADEMICS
Calendar semester
Student/faculty ratio 10:1
Profs interesting rating 88
Profs accessible rating 87

MOST POPULAR MAJORS
English language and literature
social sciences
visual and performing arts

SELECTIVITY
of applicants 5,510
% of applicants accepted 33
% of acceptees attending 28
# accepting a place on wait list 235
% admitted from wait list 4

FRESHMAN PROFILE
Range SAT Critical Reading 680–740
Range SAT Math 650–680
Minimum paper TOEFL 600
Minimum computer TOEFL 250
Average HS GPA 3.5
% graduated top 10% of class 64
% graduated top 25% of class 95
% graduated top 50% of class 100

DEADLINES
Early action
  Deadline 11/1
  Notification 1/1
Regular
  Deadline 1/15
  Notification 4/1
Nonfall registration? no

FINANCIAL FACTS
Annual tuition $40,840
Books and supplies $850

% frosh rec. need-based
scholarship or grant aid — 62
% UG rec. need-based
scholarship or grant aid — 56
% frosh rec. need-based
self-help aid — 51
% UG rec. need-based
self-help aid — 48
% frosh rec. any financial aid — 72
% UG rec. any financial aid — 66
% UG borrow to pay for school — 52
Average cumulative
indebtedness — $26,131

BARD COLLEGE
AT SIMON'S ROCK

CAMPUS LIFE
Fire Safety Rating	**60***
Green Rating	**60***
Type of school	private
Environment	village

STUDENTS
Total undergrad enrollment	432
% male/female	40/60
% from out of state	80
% live on campus	85
% African American	8
% Asian	7
% Caucasian	70
% Hispanic	4
% Native American	1
% international	4

ACADEMICS
Calendar	semester
Student/faculty ratio	9:1
Profs interesting rating	99
Profs accessible rating	97
Most common reg class size	10–15 students
Most common lab size	10–15 students

MOST POPULAR MAJORS
biology
pre-engineering
creative writing
psychology
photography

SELECTIVITY
# of applicants	257
% of applicants accepted	72
% of acceptees attending	67

FRESHMAN PROFILE
Range SAT Critical Reading	560–690
Range SAT Math	530–680
Range ACT Composite	25–30
Minimum paper TOEFL	550

Minimum computer TOEFL — 200
Average HS GPA — 3.36
% graduated top 10% of class — 60
% graduated top 25% of class — 82
% graduated top 50% of class — 94

DEADLINES
Regular
Priority	4/15
Deadline	5/31
Notification	rolling
Nonfall registration?	yes

FINANCIAL FACTS
Annual tuition	$39,380
Room and board	$10,960
Required fees	$790
Books and supplies	$1,000
% frosh rec. need-based scholarship or grant aid	51
% UG rec. need-based scholarship or grant aid	39
% frosh rec. non-need-based scholarship or grant aid	50
% UG rec. non-need-based scholarship or grant aid	33
% frosh rec. need-based self-help aid	47
% UG rec. need-based self-help aid	43
% frosh rec. any financial aid	92
% UG rec. any financial aid	89
% UG borrow to pay for school	70
Average cumulative indebtedness	$15,000

BARNARD COLLEGE

CAMPUS LIFE
Fire Safety Rating	**66**
Green Rating	**83**
Type of school	private
Environment	metropolis

STUDENTS
Total undergrad enrollment	2,417
% male/female	0/100
% from out of state	67
% from public high school	53
% live on campus	90
% African American	4
% Asian	16
% Caucasian	66
% Hispanic	9
% international	5
# of countries represented	32

ACADEMICS
Calendar	semester
Student/faculty ratio	9:1
Profs interesting rating	94
Profs accessible rating	91

Most common
reg class size — 10–19 students
Most common
lab size — 10–19 students

MOST POPULAR MAJORS
economics
English language and literature
psychology

SELECTIVITY
# of applicants	4,174
% of applicants accepted	31
% of acceptees attending	45
# accepting a place on wait list	482
% admitted from wait list	11
# of early decision applicants	409
% accepted early decision	52

FRESHMAN PROFILE
Range SAT Critical Reading	630–730
Range SAT Math	620–710
Range SAT Writing	660–740
Range ACT Composite	28–32
Minimum paper TOEFL	600
Minimum computer TOEFL	250
% graduated top 10% of class	75
% graduated top 25% of class	93
% graduated top 50% of class	98

DEADLINES
Early decision
Deadline	11/15
Notification	12/15

Regular
Deadline	1/1
Notification	4/1
Nonfall registration?	no

FINANCIAL FACTS
Annual tuition	$38,868
Room and board	$12,950
Required fees	$1,678
Books and supplies	$1,146
% frosh rec. need-based scholarship or grant aid	38
% UG rec. need-based scholarship or grant aid	42
% frosh rec. need-based self-help aid	40
% UG rec. need-based self-help aid	44
% frosh rec. any financial aid	53
% UG rec. any financial aid	51
% UG borrow to pay for school	44
Average cumulative indebtedness	$15,084

BATES COLLEGE

CAMPUS LIFE
Fire Safety Rating	**90**
Green Rating	**97**
Type of school	private
Environment	town

STUDENTS
Total undergrad enrollment	1,738
% male/female	47/53
% from out of state	90
% from public high school	55
% live on campus	93
% African American	5
% Asian	7
% Caucasian	75
% Hispanic	4
% international	6
# of countries represented	65

ACADEMICS
Calendar	4–4–1
Student/faculty ratio	10:1
Profs interesting rating	89
Profs accessible rating	95
Most common reg class size	2–9 students
Most common lab size	10–19 students

MOST POPULAR MAJORS
economics
political science and government
psychology

SELECTIVITY
# of applicants	4,767
% of applicants accepted	27
% of acceptees attending	37

FRESHMAN PROFILE
Range SAT Critical Reading	620–700
Range SAT Math	640–710
% graduated top 10% of class	63
% graduated top 25% of class	91
% graduated top 50% of class	99

DEADLINES
Early decision	
Deadline	11/15
Notification	12/20
Regular	
Deadline	1/1
Notification	3/31
Nonfall registration?	yes

FINANCIAL FACTS
Comprehensive fee	$51,300
Books and supplies	$1,750
% frosh rec. need-based scholarship or grant aid	40
% UG rec. need-based scholarship or grant aid	41
% frosh rec. need-based self-help aid	36
% UG rec. need-based self-help aid	40
% frosh rec. any financial aid	47
% UG rec. any financial aid	43
% UG borrow to pay for school	38
Average cumulative indebtedness	$17,945

BENNINGTON COLLEGE

CAMPUS LIFE
Fire Safety Rating	**79**
Green Rating	**83**
Type of school	private
Environment	town

STUDENTS
Total undergrad enrollment	664
% male/female	33/67
% from out of state	95
% from public high school	59
% live on campus	96
% African American	2
% Asian	2
% Caucasian	86
% Hispanic	2
% international	6
# of countries represented	29

ACADEMICS
Calendar	15 wk fall/spring, 7 wk winter work term
Student/faculty ratio	9:1
Profs interesting rating	97
Profs accessible rating	96
Most common reg class size	10–19 students
Most common lab size	10–19 students

MOST POPULAR MAJORS
English language and literature
visual and performing arts

SELECTIVITY
# of applicants	1,054
% of applicants accepted	66
% of acceptees attending	28
# accepting a place on wait list	78
% admitted from wait list	18
# of early decision applicants	93
% accepted early decision	47

FRESHMAN PROFILE
Range SAT Critical Reading	620–720
Range SAT Math	560–640
Range SAT Writing	610–710
Range ACT Composite	26–31
Minimum paper TOEFL	577
Minimum computer TOEFL	233
Average HS GPA	3.45
% graduated top 10% of class	31
% graduated top 25% of class	63
% graduated top 50% of class	85

DEADLINES
Early action	
Deadline	12/1
Notification	2/1
Regular	
Deadline	1/3
Notification	4/1
Nonfall registration?	yes

FINANCIAL FACTS
Annual tuition	$40,280
% frosh rec. need-based scholarship or grant aid	69
% UG rec. need-based scholarship or grant aid	67
% frosh rec. non-need-based scholarship or grant aid	10
% UG rec. non-need-based scholarship or grant aid	5
% frosh rec. need-based self-help aid	59
% UG rec. need-based self-help aid	63
% frosh rec. any financial aid	81
% UG rec. any financial aid	80
Average cumulative indebtedness	$22,402

BENTLEY UNIVERSITY

CAMPUS LIFE
Fire Safety Rating	**99**
Green Rating	**93**
Type of school	private
Environment	town

STUDENTS
Total undergrad enrollment	4,179
% male/female	60/40
% from out of state	52
% from public high school	73
% live on campus	83
# of fraternities	5
# of sororities	4
% African American	3
% Asian	7
% Caucasian	58
% Hispanic	5
% international	9
# of countries represented	89

ACADEMICS
Calendar	semester
Student/faculty ratio	14:1
Profs interesting rating	82
Profs accessible rating	83

Most common
reg class size   30–39 students

MOST POPULAR MAJORS
accounting
business administration and
management
marketing/marketing management

SELECTIVITY
# of applicants	6,675
% of applicants accepted	43
% of acceptees attending	33
# accepting a place on wait list	410
% admitted from wait list	29
# of early decision applicants	204
% accepted early decision	73

FRESHMAN PROFILE
Range SAT Critical Reading	540–630
Range SAT Math	600–680
Range SAT Writing	550–640
Range ACT Composite	25–28
Minimum paper TOEFL	550
Minimum computer TOEFL	213
Minimum web-based TOEFL	80
% graduated top 10% of class	38
% graduated top 25% of class	79
% graduated top 50% of class	97

DEADLINES
Early decision	
Deadline	11/1
Notification	12/15
Early action	
Deadline	11/15
Regular	
Deadline	1/15
Notification	4/1
Nonfall registration?	yes

FINANCIAL FACTS
Annual tuition	$34,360
Room and board	$11,740
Required fees	$1,468
Books and supplies	$1,050
% frosh rec. need-based scholarship or grant aid	40
% UG rec. need-based scholarship or grant aid	40
% frosh rec. non-need-based scholarship or grant aid	18
% UG rec. non-need-based scholarship or grant aid	15
% frosh rec. need-based self-help aid	42
% UG rec. need-based self-help aid	43
% frosh rec. athletic scholarships	1
% UG rec. athletic scholarships	1
% UG borrow to pay for school	64
Average cumulative indebtedness	$33,073

BOSTON COLLEGE

CAMPUS LIFE
Fire Safety Rating	**89**
Green Rating	**86**
Type of school	private
Affiliation	Roman Catholic/or Jesuit
Environment	city

STUDENTS
Total undergrad enrollment	9,171
% male/female	48/52
% from out of state	73
% from public high school	51
% live on campus	80
% African American	5
% Asian	10
% Caucasian	68
% Hispanic	8
% international	3
# of countries represented	96

ACADEMICS
Calendar	semester
Student/faculty ratio	13:1
Profs interesting rating	81
Profs accessible rating	83
Most common reg class size	10–19 students

MOST POPULAR MAJORS
communication and media studies
English language and literature
finance

SELECTIVITY
# of applicants	29,289
% of applicants accepted	30
% of acceptees attending	25
# accepting a place on wait list	2,677
% admitted from wait list	15

FRESHMAN PROFILE
Range SAT Critical Reading	610–700
Range SAT Math	640–730
Range SAT Writing	630–720
Range ACT Composite	29–32
Minimum paper TOEFL	600
Minimum computer TOEFL	250
Minimum web-based TOEFL	100
% graduated top 10% of class	79
% graduated top 25% of class	95
% graduated top 50% of class	99

DEADLINES
Early action	
Deadline	11/1
Notification	12/25
Regular	
Deadline	1/1
Notification	4/15
Nonfall registration?	yes

FINANCIAL FACTS
Annual tuition	$38,530
Room and board	$12,909
Required fees	$600
Books and supplies	$900
% frosh rec. need-based scholarship or grant aid	39
% UG rec. need-based scholarship or grant aid	35
% frosh rec. non-need-based scholarship or grant aid	1
% UG rec. non-need-based scholarship or grant aid	1
% frosh rec. need-based self-help aid	42
% UG rec. need-based self-help aid	40
% frosh rec. athletic scholarships	4
% UG rec. athletic scholarships	4
% frosh rec. any financial aid	63
% UG rec. any financial aid	69
% UG borrow to pay for school	52
Average cumulative indebtedness	$19,358

BOSTON UNIVERSITY

CAMPUS LIFE
Fire Safety Rating	**60***
Green Rating	**86**
Type of school	private
Environment	metropolis

STUDENTS
Total undergrad enrollment	16,295
% male/female	40/60
% from out of state	76
% from public high school	69
% live on campus	67
# of fraternities	14
# of sororities	9
% African American	4
% Asian	15
% Caucasian	43
% Hispanic	9
% international	11
# of countries represented	101

ACADEMICS
Calendar	semester
Student/faculty ratio	13:1
Profs interesting rating	78
Profs accessible rating	78
% classes taught by TAs	NA
Most common reg class size	10–19 students
Most common lab size	20–29 students

MOST POPULAR MAJORS
internal relations
communications
business management

SELECTIVITY

# of applicants	87,795
% of applicants accepted	58
% of acceptees attending	11
# accepting a place on wait list	1,104
% admitted from wait list	70
# of early decision applicants	966
% accepted early decision	40

FRESHMAN PROFILE

Range SAT Critical Reading	570–660
Range SAT Math	600–690
Range SAT Writing	590–680
Range ACT Composite	26–30
Minimum paper TOEFL	550/600
Average HS GPA	3.49
% graduated top 10% of class	51
% graduated top 25% of class	86
% graduated top 50% of class	99

DEADLINES

Early decision	
Deadline	11/1
Notification	12/15
Regular	
Deadline	1/1
Nonfall registration?	yes

FINANCIAL FACTS

Annual tuition	$39,314
Room and board	$12,260
Required fees	$550
Books and supplies	$940
% frosh rec. need-based scholarship or grant aid	47
% UG rec. need-based scholarship or grant aid	42
% frosh rec. non-need-based scholarship or grant aid	19
% UG rec. non-need-based scholarship or grant aid	12
% frosh rec. need-based self-help aid	44
% UG rec. need-based self-help aid	40
% frosh rec. athletic scholarships	2
% UG rec. athletic scholarships	2
% frosh rec. any financial aid	50
% UG rec. any financial aid	44
% UG borrow to pay for school	57
Average cumulative indebtedness	$30,998

BOWDOIN COLLEGE

CAMPUS LIFE

Fire Safety Rating	**95**
Green Rating	**97**
Type of school	private
Environment	village

STUDENTS

Total undergrad enrollment	1,772
% male/female	49/51
% from out of state	88
% from public high school	56
% live on campus	94
% African American	6
% Asian	12
% Caucasian	66
% Hispanic	10
% Native American	1
% international	3
# of countries represented	38

ACADEMICS

Calendar	semester
Student/faculty ratio	9:1
Profs interesting rating	96
Profs accessible rating	97
Most common reg class size	10–19 students
Most common lab size	10–19 students

MOST POPULAR MAJORS
biology/biological sciences
economics
political science and government

SELECTIVITY

# of applicants	5,940
% of applicants accepted	19
% of acceptees attending	43
# of early decision applicants	694
% accepted early decision	30

FRESHMAN PROFILE

Range SAT Critical Reading	660–750
Range SAT Math	660–750
Range SAT Writing	660–750
Range ACT Composite	30–33
Minimum paper TOEFL	600
Minimum computer TOEFL	250
Minimum web-based TOEFL	100
Average HS GPA	3.8
% graduated top 10% of class	81
% graduated top 25% of class	96
% graduated top 50% of class	100

DEADLINES

Early decision	
Deadline	11/15
Notification	12/31
Regular	
Deadline	1/1
Notification	4/5
Nonfall registration?	no

FINANCIAL FACTS

Annual tuition	$39,605
Room and board	$10,880
Required fees	$415
Books and supplies	$800
% frosh rec. need-based scholarship or grant aid	41

% UG rec. need-based scholarship or grant aid	43
% frosh rec. need-based self-help aid	32
% UG rec. need-based self-help aid	35
% frosh rec. any financial aid	45
% UG rec. any financial aid	47
% UG borrow to pay for school	45
Average cumulative indebtedness	$18,135

BRANDEIS UNIVERSITY

CAMPUS LIFE

Fire Safety Rating	**87**
Green Rating	**90**
Type of school	private
Environment	city

STUDENTS

Total undergrad enrollment	3,299
% male/female	44/56
% from out of state	74
% from public high school	70
% live on campus	83
% African American	5
% Asian	11
% Caucasian	47
% Hispanic	5
% international	10
# of countries represented	97

ACADEMICS

Calendar	semester
Student/faculty ratio	9:1
Profs interesting rating	83
Profs accessible rating	82
Most common reg class size	10–19 students

MOST POPULAR MAJORS
biology/biological sciences
economics
psychology

SELECTIVITY

# of applicants	6,815
% of applicants accepted	40
% of acceptees attending	28
# accepting a place on wait list	566
% admitted from wait list	33
# of early decision applicants	447
% accepted early decision	57

FRESHMAN PROFILE

Range SAT Critical Reading	620–730
Range SAT Math	640–730
Range SAT Writing	620–720
Range ACT Composite	27–31
Minimum paper TOEFL	600
Minimum computer TOEFL	250
Minimum web-based TOEFL	100

Average HS GPA 3.77
% graduated top 10% of class 79
% graduated top 25% of class 97
% graduated top 50% of class 100

DEADLINES
Early decision
Deadline 11/15
Notification 12/15
Regular
Deadline 1/15
Notification 4/1
Nonfall registration? yes

FINANCIAL FACTS
Annual tuition $37,530
Room and board $10,792
Required fees $1,232
Books and supplies $1,000
% frosh rec. need-based
scholarship or grant aid 53
% UG rec. need-based
scholarship or grant aid 48
% frosh rec. non-need-based
scholarship or grant aid 4
% UG rec. non-need-based
scholarship or grant aid 4
% frosh rec. need-based
self-help aid 52
% UG rec. need-based
self-help aid 45
% frosh rec. any financial aid 57
% UG rec. any financial aid 51
% UG borrow to pay for school 58
Average cumulative
indebtedness $26,078

BROWN UNIVERSITY

CAMPUS LIFE
Fire Safety Rating **86**
Green Rating **91**
Type of school private
Environment city

STUDENTS
Total undergrad enrollment 6,013
% male/female 48/52
% from out of state 95
% from public high school 56
% live on campus 79
# of fraternities 8
# of sororities 2
% African American 7
% Asian 16
% Caucasian 44
% Hispanic 9
% Native American 1
% international 9
# of countries represented 106

ACADEMICS
Calendar semester
Student/faculty ratio 8:1
Profs interesting rating 88
Profs accessible rating 89
Most common
reg class size 10–19 students

MOST POPULAR MAJORS
biology/biological sciences
economics
international relations and affairs

SELECTIVITY
of applicants 24,988
% of applicants accepted 11
% of acceptees attending 54
# accepting a place on wait list 500
% admitted from wait list 16
# of early decision applicants 2,404
% accepted early decision 24

FRESHMAN PROFILE
Range SAT Critical Reading 650–760
Range SAT Math 670–770
Range SAT Writing 670–770
Range ACT Composite 29–34
Minimum paper TOEFL 600
Minimum computer TOEFL 250
Minimum web-based TOEFL 100
% graduated top 10% of class 92
% graduated top 25% of class 99
% graduated top 50% of class 100

DEADLINES
Early decision
Deadline 11/1
Notification 12/15
Regular
Deadline 1/1
Notification 4/1
Nonfall registration? no

FINANCIAL FACTS
Annual tuition $38,048
% frosh rec. need-based
scholarship or grant aid 41
% UG rec. need-based
scholarship or grant aid 40
% frosh rec. need-based
self-help aid 35
% UG rec. need-based
self-help aid 39
% frosh rec. any financial aid 39
% UG rec. any financial aid 42
% UG borrow to pay for school 41
Average cumulative
indebtedness $21,858

BRYANT UNIVERSITY

CAMPUS LIFE
Fire Safety Rating **89**
Green Rating **77**
Type of school private
Environment village

STUDENTS
Total undergrad enrollment 3,367
% male/female 57/43
% from out of state 85
% live on campus 83
# of fraternities 6
# of sororities 3
% African American 4
% Asian 3
% Caucasian 82
% Hispanic 4
% international 5
# of countries represented 51

ACADEMICS
Calendar semester
Student/faculty ratio 18:1
Profs interesting rating 76
Profs accessible rating 80
Most common
reg class size 30–39 students
Most common
lab size fewer than 10 students

MOST POPULAR MAJORS
accounting
finance
marketing/marketing management

SELECTIVITY
of applicants 5,393
% of applicants accepted 53
% of acceptees attending 26
# accepting a place on wait list 480
% admitted from wait list 26
# of early decision applicants 280
% accepted early decision 71

FRESHMAN PROFILE
Range SAT Critical Reading 510–590
Range SAT Math 550–630
Range SAT Writing 510–600
Range ACT Composite 23–26.5
Minimum paper TOEFL 550
Minimum computer TOEFL 213
Minimum web-based TOEFL 80
Average HS GPA 3.35
% graduated top 10% of class 25
% graduated top 25% of class 58
% graduated top 50% of class 93

DEADLINES
Early decision
Deadline 11/16
Notification 12/16

Early action
Deadline 12/1
Notification 1/15
Regular
Deadline 2/1
Notification 3/21
Nonfall registration? yes

FINANCIAL FACTS
Annual tuition $33,033
Room and board $12,458
Required fees $324
Books and supplies $1,200
% frosh rec. need-based
scholarship or grant aid 56
% UG rec. need-based
scholarship or grant aid 57
% frosh rec. non-need-based
scholarship or grant aid 12
% UG rec. non-need-based
scholarship or grant aid 12
% frosh rec. need-based
self-help aid 55
% UG rec. need-based
self-help aid 60
% frosh rec. athletic scholarships 4
% UG rec. athletic scholarships 5
% frosh rec. any financial aid 76
% UG rec. any financial aid 78
% UG borrow to pay for school 75
Average cumulative
indebtedness $38,270

BRYN MAWR COLLEGE

CAMPUS LIFE
Fire Safety Rating **71**
Green Rating **80**
Type of school private
Environment metropolis

STUDENTS
Total undergrad enrollment 1,289
% male/female 0/100
% from out of state 84
% from public high school 64
% live on campus 95
% African American 6
% Asian 12
% Caucasian 42
% Hispanic 6
% international 10
# of countries represented 58

ACADEMICS
Calendar semester
Student/faculty ratio 8:1
Profs interesting rating 93
Profs accessible rating 96
Most common
reg class size 10–19 students

MOST POPULAR MAJORS
English language and literature
mathematics
psychology

SELECTIVITY
of applicants 2,276
% of applicants accepted 49
% of acceptees attending 33
# accepting a place on wait list 213
% admitted from wait list 18
# of early decision applicants 132
% accepted early decision 52

FRESHMAN PROFILE
Range SAT Critical Reading 606–706
Range SAT Math 580–680
Range SAT Writing 610–700
Range ACT Composite 26–30
Minimum paper TOEFL 600
Minimum computer TOEFL 250
Minimum web-based TOEFL 90
% graduated top 10% of class 61
% graduated top 25% of class 87
% graduated top 50% of class 99

DEADLINES
Early decision
Deadline 11/15
Notification 12/15
Regular
Deadline 1/15
Notification 4/1
Nonfall registration? no

FINANCIAL FACTS
Annual tuition $38,420
Room and board $12,420
Required fees $940
Books and supplies $1,000
% frosh rec. need-based
scholarship or grant aid 69
% UG rec. need-based
scholarship or grant aid 57
% frosh rec. non-need-based
scholarship or grant aid 0
% UG rec. non-need-based
scholarship or grant aid 2
% frosh rec. need-based
self-help aid 55
% UG rec. need-based
self-help aid 51
% frosh rec. any financial aid 80
% UG rec. any financial aid 68
% UG borrow to pay for school 54
Average cumulative
indebtedness $20,156

BUCKNELL UNIVERSITY

CAMPUS LIFE
Fire Safety Rating **87**
Green Rating **83**
Type of school private
Environment village

STUDENTS
Total undergrad enrollment 3,523
% male/female 49/51
% from out of state 76
% from public high school 63
% live on campus 87
# of fraternities 12
# of sororities 8
% African American 3
% Asian 4
% Caucasian 82
% Hispanic 3
% international 3
# of countries represented 52

ACADEMICS
Calendar semester
Student/faculty ratio 10:1
Profs interesting rating 87
Profs accessible rating 87
Most common
reg class size 10–19 students
Most common
lab size 10–19 students

MOST POPULAR MAJORS
business administration
and management
economics
English language and literature

SELECTIVITY
of applicants 7,572
% of applicants accepted 30
% of acceptees attending 41
# accepting a place on wait list 756
% admitted from wait list 3
# of early decision applicants 674
% accepted early decision 62

FRESHMAN PROFILE
Range SAT Critical Reading 600–680
Range SAT Math 630–720
Range SAT Writing 600–690
Range ACT Composite 27–31
Minimum paper TOEFL 550
Minimum computer TOEFL 213
Minimum web-based TOEFL 106
Average HS GPA 3.49
% graduated top 10% of class 59
% graduated top 25% of class 88
% graduated top 50% of class 99

DEADLINES

Early decision I
Deadline	11/15
Notification	12/15

Early decision II
Deadline	1/15
Notification	2/15

Regular
Deadline	1/15
Notification	4/1
Nonfall registration?	no

FINANCIAL FACTS

Annual tuition	$42,112
Room and board	$9,938
Required fees	$230
Books and supplies	$900
% frosh rec. need-based scholarship or grant aid	47
% UG rec. need-based scholarship or grant aid	46
% frosh rec. non-need-based scholarship or grant aid	6
% UG rec. non-need-based scholarship or grant aid	5
% frosh rec. need-based self-help aid	47
% UG rec. need-based self-help aid	46
% frosh rec. athletic scholarships	3
% UG rec. athletic scholarships	1
% UG rec. any financial aid	62
% UG borrow to pay for school	61
Average cumulative indebtedness	$18,800

CALIFORNIA UNIVERSITY OF PENNSYLVANIA

CAMPUS LIFE

Fire Safety Rating	**93**
Green Rating	**98**
Type of school	public
Environment	village

STUDENTS

Total undergrad enrollment	6,199
% male/female	48/52
% from out of state	6
% from public high school	80
% live on campus	34
# of fraternities	6
# of sororities	7
% African American	6
% Caucasian	67
% Hispanic	1
% international	1
# of countries represented	18

ACADEMICS

Calendar	semester
Student/faculty ratio	19:1
Profs interesting rating	71
Profs accessible rating	65
Most common reg class size	20–29 students
Most common lab size	20–29 students

MOST POPULAR MAJORS
business administration and management
criminal justice/safety studies
elementary education and teaching

SELECTIVITY

# of applicants	3,849
% of applicants accepted	68
% of acceptees attending	51

FRESHMAN PROFILE

Range SAT Critical Reading	460–536
Range SAT Math	460–540
Minimum paper TOEFL	450
Minimum computer TOEFL	133
Average HS GPA	3.3
% graduated top 10% of class	7
% graduated top 25% of class	28
% graduated top 50% of class	65

DEADLINES

Regular
Priority	5/1
Nonfall registration?	yes

FINANCIAL FACTS

Annual in-state tuition	$5,178
Annual out-of-state tuition	$8,284
Room and board	$8,466
Required fees	$1,673
Books and supplies	$875
% frosh rec. need-based scholarship or grant aid	45
% UG rec. need-based scholarship or grant aid	49
% frosh rec. non-need-based scholarship or grant aid	21
% UG rec. non-need-based scholarship or grant aid	13
% frosh rec. need-based self-help aid	55
% UG rec. need-based self-help aid	60
% frosh rec. athletic scholarships	2
% UG rec. athletic scholarships	3
% frosh rec. any financial aid	76
% UG rec. any financial aid	72
% UG borrow to pay for school	83
Average cumulative indebtedness	$21,860

CARNEGIE MELLON UNIVERSITY

CAMPUS LIFE

Fire Safety Rating	**75**
Green Rating	**95**
Type of school	private
Environment	metropolis

STUDENTS

Total undergrad enrollment	5,951
% male/female	59/41
% from out of state	79
% live on campus	64
# of fraternities	16
# of sororities	7
% African American	5
% Asian	24
% Caucasian	40
% Hispanic	5
% Native American	1
% international	15
# of countries represented	100

ACADEMICS

Calendar	semester
Student/faculty ratio	12:1
Profs interesting rating	70
Profs accessible rating	76
Most common reg class size	10–19 students
Most common lab size	20–29 students

MOST POPULAR MAJORS
computer science

SELECTIVITY

# of applicants	14,153
% of applicants accepted	36
% of acceptees attending	28
# accepting a place on wait list	645
% admitted from wait list	17
# of early decision applicants	1,110
% accepted early decision	24

FRESHMAN PROFILE

Range SAT Critical Reading	620–720
Range SAT Math	670–780
Range SAT Writing	620–720
Range ACT Composite	29–33
Minimum paper TOEFL	600
Minimum computer TOEFL	250
Average HS GPA	3.62
% graduated top 10% of class	75
% graduated top 25% of class	93
% graduated top 50% of class	99

DEADLINES

Early decision
Deadline	11/1
Notification	12/15

Regular
Deadline 1/1
Notification 4/15
Nonfall registration? no

FINANCIAL FACTS

Annual tuition $41,500
Room and board $10,750
Required fees $430
Books and supplies $1,000
% frosh rec. need-based
scholarship or grant aid 53
% UG rec. need-based
scholarship or grant aid 47
% frosh rec. non-need-based
scholarship or grant aid 21
% UG rec. non-need-based
scholarship or grant aid 18
% frosh rec. need-based
self-help aid 49
% UG rec. need-based
self-help aid 46
% UG borrow to pay for school 50
Average cumulative
indebtedness $29,546

CATHOLIC UNIVERSITY OF
AMERICA

CAMPUS LIFE
Fire Safety Rating **83**
Green Rating **87**
Type of school private
Affiliation Roman Catholic
Environment metropolis

STUDENTS
Total undergrad enrollment 3,422
% male/female 46/54
% from out of state 95
% from public high school 56
% live on campus 70
# of fraternities 1
# of sororities 1
% African American 5
% Asian 3
% Caucasian 64
% Hispanic 7
% international 3
# of countries represented 80

ACADEMICS
Calendar semester
Student/faculty ratio 10:1
Profs interesting rating 72
Profs accessible rating 74
% classes taught by TAs 11
Most common
reg class size 10–19 students
Most common
lab size 10–19 students

MOST POPULAR MAJORS
architecture
(BArch, BA/BS, MArch, MA/MS)
nursing/registered nurse
(RN, ASN, BSN, MSN, DNP, PhD)
political science and government

SELECTIVITY
of applicants 5,044
% of applicants accepted 86
% of acceptees attending 19

FRESHMAN PROFILE
Range SAT Critical Reading 510–610
Range SAT Math 500–600
Range ACT Composite 21–26
Minimum paper TOEFL 550
Minimum computer TOEFL 213
Minimum web-based TOEFL 80
Average HS GPA 3.25

DEADLINES
Early action
Deadline 11/15
Notification 12/15
Regular
Deadline 2/15
Notification rolling
Nonfall registration? yes

FINANCIAL FACTS
Annual tuition $31,740
% frosh rec. need-based
scholarship or grant aid 64
% UG rec. need-based
scholarship or grant aid 56
% frosh rec. need-based
self-help aid 59
% UG rec. need-based
self-help aid 54
% frosh rec. any financial aid 93
% UG rec. any financial aid 89

CENTRAL CONNECTICUT
STATE UNIVERSITY

CAMPUS LIFE
Fire Safety Rating **77**
Green Rating **86**
Type of school public
Environment town

STUDENTS
Total undergrad enrollment 9,570
% male/female 51/49
% from out of state 5
% from public high school 93
% live on campus 22
# of sororities 1
% African American 8

% Asian 3
% Caucasian 74
% Hispanic 7
% international 1
# of countries represented 64

ACADEMICS
Calendar semester
Student/faculty ratio 16:1
Profs interesting rating 66
Profs accessible rating 61
Most common reg class size 20–29 students
Most common lab size fewer than
10 students

MOST POPULAR MAJORS
accounting
criminology
psychology

SELECTIVITY
of applicants 6,791
% of applicants accepted 54
% of acceptees attending 35

FRESHMAN PROFILE
Range SAT Critical Reading 470–550
Range SAT Math 470–550
Range SAT Writing 460–550
Minimum paper TOEFL 500
% graduated top 10% of class 8
% graduated top 25% of class 30
% graduated top 50% of class 72

DEADLINES
Regular
Priority 10/1
Deadline 6/1
Notification rolling
Nonfall registration? yes

FINANCIAL FACTS
Annual in-state tuition $3,742
Annual out-of-state tuition $12,112
Room and board $9,122
Required fees $3,672
Books and supplies $1,100
% frosh rec. need-based
scholarship or grant aid 44
% UG rec. need-based
scholarship or grant aid 47
% frosh rec. non-need-based
scholarship or grant aid 7
% UG rec. non-need-based
scholarship or grant aid 5
% frosh rec. need-based self-help aid 43
% UG rec. need-based self-help aid 49
% frosh rec. athletic scholarships 1
% UG rec. athletic scholarships 2

% frosh rec. any financial aid	63
% UG rec. any financial aid	63
% UG borrow to pay for school	48
Average cumulative indebtedness	$19,205

CHATHAM UNIVERSITY

CAMPUS LIFE
Fire Safety Rating	**67**
Green Rating	**98**
Type of school	private
Environment	metropolis

STUDENTS
Total undergrad enrollment	771
% male/female	1/99
% from out of state	19
% live on campus	54
% African American	12
% Asian	2
% Caucasian	67
% Hispanic	2
% international	6
# of countries represented	26

ACADEMICS
Student/faculty ratio	10:1
Profs interesting rating	86
Profs accessible rating	88
Most common reg class size	10–19 students
Most common lab size	10–19 students

MOST POPULAR MAJORS
biology/biological sciences
English language and literature
psychology

SELECTIVITY
# of applicants	641
% of applicants accepted	68
% of acceptees attending	30

FRESHMAN PROFILE
Range SAT Critical Reading	478–600
Range SAT Math	458–583
Range SAT Writing	470–603
Range ACT Composite	22–25
Minimum paper TOEFL	550
Minimum computer TOEFL	210
Minimum web-based TOEFL	79
Average HS GPA	3.35
% graduated top 10% of class	15
% graduated top 25% of class	35
% graduated top 50% of class	73

DEADLINES
Regular
Priority	3/15
Deadline	8/1
Notification	rolling
Nonfall registration?	yes

FINANCIAL FACTS
Annual tuition	$27,006
Room and board	$8,700
Required fees	$1,020
Books and supplies	$860
% frosh rec. need-based scholarship or grant aid	67
% UG rec. need-based scholarship or grant aid	64
% frosh rec. non-need-based scholarship or grant aid	84
% UG rec. non-need-based scholarship or grant aid	75
% frosh rec. need-based self-help aid	76
% UG rec. need-based self-help aid	73
% frosh rec. any financial aid	98
% UG rec. any financial aid	98

CHESTNUT HILL COLLEGE

CAMPUS LIFE
Fire Safety Rating	**86**
Green Rating	**65**
Type of school	private
Affiliation	Roman Catholic
Environment	metropolis

STUDENTS
Total undergrad enrollment	1,277
% male/female	30/70
% from out of state	32
% from public high school	50
% live on campus	69
% African American	39
% Asian	2
% Caucasian	49
% Hispanic	5
% international	1
# of countries represented	24

ACADEMICS
Calendar	semester
Student/faculty ratio	10:1
Profs interesting rating	84
Profs accessible rating	86
Most common reg class size	10–19 students
Most common lab size	10–19 students

MOST POPULAR MAJORS
business administration and management
elementary education and teaching
human services

SELECTIVITY
# of applicants	1,589
% of applicants accepted	72
% of acceptees attending	17

FRESHMAN PROFILE
Range SAT Critical Reading	460–540
Range SAT Math	470–540
Range SAT Writing	440–530
Range ACT Composite	19–20
Minimum paper TOEFL	500
Average HS GPA	3.02
% graduated top 10% of class	9
% graduated top 25% of class	29
% graduated top 50% of class	67

DEADLINES
Early decision
Deadline	12/10
Notification	12/15

Regular
Priority	1/20
Notification	rolling
Nonfall registration?	yes

FINANCIAL FACTS
Annual tuition	$27,000
Room and board	$8,800
Required fees	$100
Books and supplies	$1,100
% frosh rec. need-based scholarship or grant aid	80
% UG rec. need-based scholarship or grant aid	59
% frosh rec. non-need-based scholarship or grant aid	12
% UG rec. non-need-based scholarship or grant aid	8
% frosh rec. need-based self-help aid	68
% UG rec. need-based self-help aid	50
% frosh rec. athletic scholarships	7
% UG rec. athletic scholarships	4
% frosh rec. any financial aid	80
% UG rec. any financial aid	60

CITY UNIVERSITY OF NEW YORK—BARUCH COLLEGE

CAMPUS LIFE
Fire Safety Rating	60*
Green Rating	64
Type of school	public
Environment	metropolis

STUDENTS
Total undergrad enrollment	12,080
% male/female	49/51
% from out of state	4
% from public high school	72
# of fraternities	9
# of sororities	7
% African American	10
% Asian	32
% Caucasian	30
% Hispanic	16
% international	12
# of countries represented	158

ACADEMICS
Calendar	semester
Student/faculty ratio	18:1
Profs interesting rating	64
Profs accessible rating	63
% classes taught by TAs	1
Most common reg class size	20–29 students
Most common lab size	20–29 students

MOST POPULAR MAJORS
accounting
finance

SELECTIVITY
# of applicants	19,775
% of applicants accepted	23
% of acceptees attending	32

FRESHMAN PROFILE
Range SAT Critical Reading	490–590
Range SAT Math	560–670
Minimum paper TOEFL	620
Minimum computer TOEFL	260
Average HS GPA	3.13
% graduated top 10% of class	37
% graduated top 25% of class	66
% graduated top 50% of class	90

DEADLINES
Early decision	
Deadline	12/13
Notification	1/7
Regular	
Priority	12/1
Deadline	2/1
Notification	rolling
Nonfall registration?	yes

FINANCIAL FACTS
Annual in-state tuition	$4,600
Annual out-of-state tuition	$12,450
Required fees	$340
% frosh rec. need-based scholarship or grant aid	58
% UG rec. need-based scholarship or grant aid	35
% frosh rec. non-need-based scholarship or grant aid	1
% UG rec. non-need-based scholarship or grant aid	1
% frosh rec. need-based self-help aid	46
% UG rec. need-based self-help aid	28
% frosh rec. any financial aid	72
% UG rec. any financial aid	57
% UG borrow to pay for school	22
Average cumulative indebtedness	$14,737

CITY UNIVERSITY OF NEW YORK—BROOKLYN COLLEGE

CAMPUS LIFE
Fire Safety Rating	60*
Green Rating	92
Type of school	public
Environment	metropolis

STUDENTS
Total undergrad enrollment	12,021
% male/female	41/59
% from out of state	2
# of fraternities	7
# of sororities	9
% African American	27
% Asian	15
% Caucasian	41
% Hispanic	13
% international	6

ACADEMICS
Calendar	semester
Student/faculty ratio	15:1
Profs interesting rating	61
Profs accessible rating	61
Most common reg class size	20–29 students

SELECTIVITY
# of applicants	17,497
% of applicants accepted	28
% of acceptees attending	20

FRESHMAN PROFILE
Range SAT Critical Reading	450–570
Range SAT Math	480–590
Minimum paper TOEFL	500
Minimum computer TOEFL	173
Average HS GPA	3.3
% graduated top 10% of class	14
% graduated top 25% of class	49
% graduated top 50% of class	79

DEADLINES
Regular	
Priority	2/1
Notification	rolling
Nonfall registration?	yes

FINANCIAL FACTS
Annual in-state tuition	$4,000
Annual out-of-state tuition	$10,800
Required fees	$431
% frosh rec. need-based scholarship or grant aid	74
% UG rec. need-based scholarship or grant aid	66
% frosh rec. non-need-based scholarship or grant aid	24
% UG rec. non-need-based scholarship or grant aid	20
% frosh rec. need-based self-help aid	72
% UG rec. need-based self-help aid	69
% frosh rec. any financial aid	74
% UG rec. any financial aid	70
% UG borrow to pay for school	45
Average cumulative indebtedness	$16,600

CITY UNIVERSITY OF NEW YORK—HUNTER COLLEGE

CAMPUS LIFE
Fire Safety Rating	93
Green Rating	84
Type of school	public
Environment	metropolis

STUDENTS
Total undergrad enrollment	14,806
% male/female	33/67
% from out of state	4
% from public high school	70
# of fraternities	2
# of sororities	2
% African American	12
% Asian	21
% Caucasian	39
% Hispanic	19
% international	9

ACADEMICS
Calendar	semester
Student/faculty ratio	15:1
Profs interesting rating	66
Profs accessible rating	62
Most common reg class size	20–29 students

MOST POPULAR MAJORS
accounting
English literature (British and Commonwealth)
psychology

SELECTIVITY
# of applicants	30,528
% of applicants accepted	26
% of acceptees attending	26

FRESHMAN PROFILE
Range SAT Critical Reading	510–610
Range SAT Math	520–620
Minimum paper TOEFL	500
Minimum computer TOEFL	173

DEADLINES
Regular	
Deadline	3/15
Notification	rolling
Nonfall registration?	yes

FINANCIAL FACTS
Financial Aid Rating	**78**
Annual out-of-state tuition	$12,450
Room and board	$3,726
Required fees	$399
% frosh rec. need-based scholarship or grant aid	61
% UG rec. need-based scholarship or grant aid	57
% frosh rec. non-need-based scholarship or grant aid	45
% UG rec. non-need-based scholarship or grant aid	21
% frosh rec. need-based self-help aid	8
% UG rec. need-based self-help aid	18
% frosh rec. any financial aid	91
% UG rec. any financial aid	94
% UG borrow to pay for school	48
Average cumulative indebtedness	$7,125

CITY UNIVERSITY OF NEW YORK—QUEENS COLLEGE

CAMPUS LIFE
Fire Safety Rating	**79**
Green Rating	**60***
Type of school	public
Environment	metropolis

STUDENTS
Total undergrad enrollment	15,270
% male/female	41/59
% from out of state	1
# of fraternities	4
# of sororities	3
# of countries represented	140

ACADEMICS
Calendar	semester
Student/faculty ratio	16:1
Profs interesting rating	66
Profs accessible rating	67
% classes taught by TAs	1
Most common reg class size	20–29 students

MOST POPULAR MAJORS
accounting
psychology
sociology

SELECTIVITY
# of applicants	18,028
% of applicants accepted	33
% of acceptees attending	29

FRESHMAN PROFILE
Range SAT Critical Reading	490–550
Range SAT Math	490–580
Range SAT Writing	490–550
Minimum paper TOEFL	500
Minimum computer TOEFL	173
Minimum web-based TOEFL	62

DEADLINES
Regular	
Priority	1/1
Notification	rolling
Nonfall registration?	yes

FINANCIAL FACTS
Annual in-state tuition	$4,600
Annual out-of-state tuition	$8,640
Required fees	$447
% frosh rec. need-based scholarship or grant aid	36
% UG rec. need-based scholarship or grant aid	46
% frosh rec. non-need-based scholarship or grant aid	27
% UG rec. non-need-based scholarship or grant aid	10
% frosh rec. need-based self-help aid	22
% UG rec. need-based self-help aid	15
% frosh rec. athletic scholarships	2
% UG rec. athletic scholarships	1
% frosh rec. any financial aid	52
% UG rec. any financial aid	46
% UG borrow to pay for school	41
Average cumulative indebtedness	$14,000

CLARK UNIVERSITY

CAMPUS LIFE
Fire Safety Rating	**95**
Green Rating	**85**
Type of school	private
Environment	city

STUDENTS
Total undergrad enrollment	2,293
% male/female	40/60
% from out of state	64
% from public high school	70
% live on campus	74
% African American	2
% Asian	4
% Caucasian	68
% Hispanic	2
% international	8
# of countries represented	72

ACADEMICS
Calendar	semester
Student/faculty ratio	10:1
Profs interesting rating	84
Profs accessible rating	85
Most common reg class size	10–19 students
Most common lab size	10–19 students

MOST POPULAR MAJORS
biology/biological sciences
political science and government
psychology

SELECTIVITY
# of applicants	5,299
% of applicants accepted	56
% of acceptees attending	20
# accepting a place on wait list	81
% admitted from wait list	19
# of early decision applicants	90
% accepted early decision	73

FRESHMAN PROFILE
Range SAT Critical Reading	550–660
Range SAT Math	540–650
Range SAT Writing	550–660
Range ACT Composite	24–28
Minimum paper TOEFL	550
Minimum computer TOEFL	213
Average HS GPA	3.47
% graduated top 10% of class	39
% graduated top 25% of class	76
% graduated top 50% of class	97

DEADLINES
Early decision	
Deadline	11/15
Notification	12/15

Regular
Deadline 1/15
Notification 4/1
Nonfall registration? yes

FINANCIAL FACTS
Annual tuition $34,900
Room and board $6,750
Required fees $320
Books and supplies $800
% frosh rec. need-based
scholarship or grant aid 51
% UG rec. need-based
scholarship or grant aid 51
% frosh rec. non-need-based
scholarship or grant aid 30
% UG rec. non-need-based
scholarship or grant aid 30
% frosh rec. need-based
self-help aid 45
% UG rec. need-based
self-help aid 45
% frosh rec. any financial aid 82
% UG rec. any financial aid 79
% UG borrow to pay for school 90
Average cumulative
indebtedness $22,250

CLARKSON UNIVERSITY

CAMPUS LIFE
Fire Safety Rating **80**
Green Rating **88**
Type of school private
Environment village

STUDENTS
Total undergrad enrollment 2,717
% male/female 73/27
% from out of state 29
% from public high school 88
% live on campus 80
# of fraternities 11
# of sororities 3
% African American 3
% Asian 4
% Caucasian 84
% Hispanic 3
% Native American 1
% international 3
# of countries represented 44

ACADEMICS
Calendar semester
Student/faculty ratio 15:1
Profs interesting rating 64
Profs accessible rating 73
Most common
reg class size 10–19 students
Most common
lab size 20–29 students

MOST POPULAR MAJORS
business/commerce
civil engineering
mechanical engineering

SELECTIVITY
of applicants 4,125
% of applicants accepted 73
% of acceptees attending 26
# accepting a place on wait list 20
% admitted from wait list 80
# of early decision applicants 153
% accepted early decision 68

FRESHMAN PROFILE
Range SAT Critical Reading 500–610
Range SAT Math 560–660
Range SAT Writing 490–580
Range ACT Composite 23–27
Minimum paper TOEFL 550
Minimum computer TOEFL 213
Average HS GPA 3.47
% graduated top 10% of class 34
% graduated top 25% of class 67
% graduated top 50% of class 94

DEADLINES
Early decision
Deadline 12/1
Notification 1/1
Regular
Deadline 1/15
Notification rolling
Nonfall registration? yes

FINANCIAL FACTS
Annual tuition $32,220
Room and board $11,518
Required fees $690
Books and supplies $1,100
% frosh rec. need-based
scholarship or grant aid 82
% UG rec. need-based
scholarship or grant aid 79
% frosh rec. non-need-based
scholarship or grant aid 22
% UG rec. non-need-based
scholarship or grant aid 17
% frosh rec. need-based
self-help aid 64
% UG rec. need-based
self-help aid 67
% frosh rec. athletic scholarships 1
% UG rec. athletic scholarships 1
% frosh rec. any financial aid 95
% UG rec. any financial aid 92
% UG borrow to pay for school 85
Average cumulative
indebtedness $32,125

COLBY COLLEGE

CAMPUS LIFE
Fire Safety Rating **92**
Green Rating **87**
Type of school private
Environment village

STUDENTS
Total undergrad enrollment 1,838
% male/female 46/54
% from out of state 87
% from public high school 54
% live on campus 94
% African American 3
% Asian 8
% Caucasian 62
% Hispanic 3
% Native American 1
% international 5
# of countries represented 64

ACADEMICS
Calendar 4/1/4
Student/faculty ratio 10:1
Profs interesting rating 92
Profs accessible rating 88
Most common
reg class size 10–19 students
Most common
lab size 10–19 students

MOST POPULAR MAJORS
biology/biological sciences
economics
political science and government

SELECTIVITY
of applicants 4,520
% of applicants accepted 34
% of acceptees attending 31
# accepting a place on wait list 477
% admitted from wait list 4
# of early decision applicants 456
% accepted early decision 50

FRESHMAN PROFILE
Range SAT Critical Reading 630–720
Range SAT Math 640–720
Range SAT Writing 630–710
Range ACT Composite 28–31
Minimum web-based TOEFL 100
% graduated top 10% of class 59
% graduated top 25% of class 89
% graduated top 50% of class 97

DEADLINES
Early decision
Deadline 11/15
Notification 12/15

Regular
Deadline 1/1
Notification 4/1
Nonfall registration? yes

FINANCIAL FACTS

Comprehensive fee $50,320
Books and supplies $700
% frosh rec. need-based
  scholarship or grant aid 41
% UG rec. need-based
  scholarship or grant aid 38
% frosh rec. non-need-based
  scholarship or grant aid 1
% UG rec. non-need-based
  scholarship or grant aid 1
% frosh rec. need-based
  self-help aid 32
% UG rec. need-based
  self-help aid 31
% frosh rec. any financial aid 46
% UG rec. any financial aid 43
% UG borrow to pay for school 41
Average cumulative
  indebtedness $21,697

COLGATE UNIVERSITY

CAMPUS LIFE

Fire Safety Rating **86**
Green Rating **85**
Type of school private
Environment rural

STUDENTS

Total undergrad enrollment 2,799
% male/female 47/53
% from out of state 72
% from public high school 62
% live on campus 91
# of fraternities 6
# of sororities 3
% African American 6
% Asian 5
% Caucasian 73
% Hispanic 6
% Native American 1
% international 5
# of countries represented 36

ACADEMICS

Calendar semester
Student/faculty ratio 10:1
Profs interesting rating 95
Profs accessible rating 98
Most common
  reg class size 10–19 students
Most common
  lab size 10–19 students

MOST POPULAR MAJORS
economics
English language and literature
history

SELECTIVITY

of applicants 7,816
% of applicants accepted 32
% of acceptees attending 30
# accepting a place on wait list 709
% admitted from wait list 3
# of early decision applicants 656
% accepted early decision 56

FRESHMAN PROFILE

Range SAT Critical Reading 630–710
Range SAT Math 640–730
Range ACT Composite 29–32
Average HS GPA 3.62
% graduated top 10% of class 66
% graduated top 25% of class 91
% graduated top 50% of class 100

DEADLINES

Early decision
  Deadline 11/15
  Notification 12/15
Regular
  Deadline 1/15
  Notification 4/1
Nonfall registration? no

FINANCIAL FACTS

Annual tuition $40,690
Room and board $9,970
Required fees $280
% frosh rec. need-based
  scholarship or grant aid 34
% UG rec. need-based
  scholarship or grant aid 35
% frosh rec. need-based
  self-help aid 26
% UG rec. need-based
  self-help aid 28
% frosh rec. athletic scholarships 6
% UG rec. athletic scholarships 6
% frosh rec. any financial aid 34
% UG rec. any financial aid 35
% UG borrow to pay for school 30
Average cumulative
  indebtedness $19,202

COLLEGE OF THE ATLANTIC

CAMPUS LIFE

Fire Safety Rating **95**
Green Rating **99**
Type of school private
Environment rural

STUDENTS

Total undergrad enrollment 321
% male/female 31/69

% from out of state 80
% from public high school 71
% live on campus 43
% African American 1
% Asian 2
% Caucasian 32
% Hispanic 1
% Native American 1
% international 15
# of countries represented 37

ACADEMICS

Calendar trimester
Student/faculty ratio 11:1
Profs interesting rating 95
Profs accessible rating 98
Most common
  reg class size 10–19 students
Most common
  lab size 10–19 students

MOST POPULAR MAJORS
biology/biological sciences
ecology
education

SELECTIVITY

of applicants 322
% of applicants accepted 75
% of acceptees attending 32
# of early decision applicants 39
% accepted early decision 79

FRESHMAN PROFILE

Range SAT Critical Reading 620–690
Range SAT Math 510–620
Range SAT Writing 570–670
Range ACT Composite 21–27
Minimum paper TOEFL 567
Minimum computer TOEFL 227
Minimum web-based TOEFL 86
% graduated top 10% of class 26
% graduated top 25% of class 63
% graduated top 50% of class 93

DEADLINES

Early decision
  Deadline 12/1
  Notification 12/15
Regular
  Deadline 2/15
  Notification 4/1
Nonfall registration? yes

FINANCIAL FACTS

Annual tuition $32,580
Room and board $8,490
Required fees $480
Books and supplies $600
% frosh rec. need-based
  scholarship or grant aid 80
% UG rec. need-based
  scholarship or grant aid 82

% frosh rec. need-based self-help aid	80
% UG rec. need-based self-help aid	79
% frosh rec. any financial aid	80
% UG rec. any financial aid	82
% UG borrow to pay for school	56
Average cumulative indebtedness	$23,762

COLLEGE OF THE HOLY CROSS

CAMPUS LIFE

Fire Safety Rating	**97**
Green Rating	**87**
Type of school	private
Affiliation	Roman Catholic/or Jesuit
Environment	city

STUDENTS

Total undergrad enrollment	2,897
% male/female	45/55
% from out of state	63
% from public high school	47
% live on campus	88
% African American	4
% Asian	6
% Caucasian	68
% Hispanic	8
% international	1
# of countries represented	18

ACADEMICS

Calendar	semester
Student/faculty ratio	11:1
Profs interesting rating	93
Profs accessible rating	93
Most common reg class size	10–19 students
Most common lab size	10–19 students

MOST POPULAR MAJORS
economics
English language and literature
political science and government

SELECTIVITY

# of applicants	6,652
% of applicants accepted	36
% of acceptees attending	31
# accepting a place on wait list	526
# of early decision applicants	488
% accepted early decision	73

FRESHMAN PROFILE

Range SAT Critical Reading	600–680
Range SAT Math	610–690
Range SAT Writing	600–690
Range ACT Composite	26–30
Minimum paper TOEFL	550

Minimum computer TOEFL	213
Minimum web-based TOEFL	79
Average HS GPA	3.79
% graduated top 10% of class	66
% graduated top 25% of class	93
% graduated top 50% of class	99

DEADLINES

Early decision Deadline	12/15
Regular Deadline	1/15
Nonfall registration?	no

FINANCIAL FACTS

Annual tuition	$39,330
Room and board	$10,940
Required fees	$562
Books and supplies	$700
% frosh rec. need-based scholarship or grant aid	45
% UG rec. need-based scholarship or grant aid	43
% frosh rec. non-need-based scholarship or grant aid	2
% UG rec. non-need-based scholarship or grant aid	1
% frosh rec. need-based self-help aid	41
% UG rec. need-based self-help aid	41
% frosh rec. athletic scholarships	4
% UG rec. athletic scholarships	2
% frosh rec. any financial aid	63
% UG rec. any financial aid	60
% UG borrow to pay for school	57
Average cumulative indebtedness	$23,785

THE COLLEGE OF NEW JERSEY

CAMPUS LIFE

Fire Safety Rating	**94**
Green Rating	**88**
Type of school	public
Environment	village

STUDENTS

Total undergrad enrollment	6,197
% male/female	41/59
% from out of state	6
% from public high school	70
% live on campus	58
# of fraternities	12
# of sororities	16
% African American	6
% Asian	6
% Caucasian	65
% Hispanic	9
% international	1
# of countries represented	17

ACADEMICS

Calendar	semester
Student/faculty ratio	13:1
Profs interesting rating	87
Profs accessible rating	86
Most common reg class size	20–29 students
Most common lab size	10–19 students

MOST POPULAR MAJORS
biology/biological sciences
business administration and management
psychology

SELECTIVITY

# of applicants	9,283
% of applicants accepted	46
% of acceptees attending	30
# accepting a place on wait list	550
% admitted from wait list	52
# of early decision applicants	611
% accepted early decision	47

FRESHMAN PROFILE

Range SAT Critical Reading	560–660
Range SAT Math	590–690
Range SAT Writing	570–670
Minimum paper TOEFL	550
Minimum computer TOEFL	213
Minimum web-based TOEFL	90
% graduated top 10% of class	61
% graduated top 25% of class	92
% graduated top 50% of class	99

DEADLINES

Early decision Deadline	11/15
Notification	12/15
Regular Priority	11/15
Deadline	1/15
Notification	rolling
Nonfall registration?	yes

FINANCIAL FACTS

Annual in-state tuition	$8,980
Annual out-of-state tuition	$17,666
Room and board	$9,612
Required fees	$3,742
Books and supplies	$1,000
% frosh rec. need-based scholarship or grant aid	22
% UG rec. need-based scholarship or grant aid	19
% frosh rec. non-need-based scholarship or grant aid	33
% UG rec. non-need-based scholarship or grant aid	19
% frosh rec. need-based self-help aid	29
% UG rec. need-based self-help aid	34

% frosh rec. any financial aid	86
% UG rec. any financial aid	72
% UG borrow to pay for school	58
Average cumulative	
indebtedness	$24,801

COLUMBIA UNIVERSITY

CAMPUS LIFE
Fire Safety Rating	**60***
Green Rating	**60***
Type of school	private
Environment	metropolis

STUDENTS
Total undergrad enrollment	5,766
% male/female	52/48
% from out of state	72
% from public high school	59
% live on campus	95
# of fraternities	10
# of sororities	10
% African American	11
% Asian	18
% Caucasian	36
% Hispanic	13
% Native American	1
% international	10
# of countries represented	87

ACADEMICS
Calendar	semester
Student/faculty ratio	6:1
Profs interesting rating	77
Profs accessible rating	74
Most common	
reg class size	10–19 students

MOST POPULAR MAJORS
engineering
English language and literature
political science and government

SELECTIVITY
# of applicants	25,427
% of applicants accepted	10
% of acceptees attending	60
# of early decision applicants	2,840
% accepted early decision	23

FRESHMAN PROFILE
Range SAT Critical Reading	680–770
Range SAT Math	690–780
Range SAT Writing	680–770
Range ACT Composite	31–34
Minimum paper TOEFL	600
Minimum computer TOEFL	250
Average HS GPA	NA
% graduated top 10% of class	97
% graduated top 25% of class	99
% graduated top 50% of class	100

DEADLINES
Early decision	
Deadline	11/1
Notification	12/15
Regular	
Deadline	1/1
Notification	4/1
Nonfall registration?	no

FINANCIAL FACTS
Annual tuition	$39,296
% frosh rec. need-based	
scholarship or grant aid	54
% UG rec. need-based	
scholarship or grant aid	49
% frosh rec. need-based	
self-help aid	42
% UG rec. need-based	
self-help aid	42
% frosh rec. any financial aid	60
% UG rec. any financial aid	55

CONNECTICUT COLLEGE

CAMPUS LIFE
Fire Safety Rating	**78**
Green Rating	**83**
Type of school	private
Environment	town

STUDENTS
Total undergrad enrollment	1,777
% male/female	39/61
% from out of state	85
% from public high school	55
% live on campus	99
% African American	4
% Asian	5
% Caucasian	75
% Hispanic	6
% international	4
# of countries represented	74

ACADEMICS
Calendar	semester
Student/faculty ratio	9:1
Profs interesting rating	94
Profs accessible rating	93
Most common	
reg class size	10–19 students
Most common	
lab size	10–19 students

MOST POPULAR MAJORS
economics
English language and literature
political science and government

SELECTIVITY
# of applicants	4,733
% of applicants accepted	37
% of acceptees attending	29
# accepting a place on wait list	367

% admitted from wait list	13
# of early decision applicants	318
% accepted early decision	7

FRESHMAN PROFILE
Range SAT Critical Reading	610–700
Range SAT Math	610–690
Range SAT Writing	620–710
Range ACT Composite	25–30
Minimum paper TOEFL	600
Minimum computer TOEFL	250
Minimum web-based TOEFL	100
% graduated top 10% of class	56
% graduated top 25% of class	93
% graduated top 50% of class	100

DEADLINES
Early decision	
Deadline	11/15
Notification	12/15
Regular	
Deadline	1/1
Notification	3/31
Nonfall registration?	no

FINANCIAL FACTS
Annual tuition	$53,110
(Includes room & board, and fees)	
% frosh rec. need-based	
scholarship or grant aid	43
% UG rec. need-based	
scholarship or grant aid	42
% frosh rec. need-based	
self-help aid	42
% UG rec. need-based	
self-help aid	41
% frosh rec. any financial aid	41
% UG borrow to pay for school	34
Average cumulative	
indebtedness	$22,038

THE COOPER UNION FOR THE ADVANCEMENT OF SCIENCE AND ART

CAMPUS LIFE
Fire Safety Rating	**97**
Green Rating	**79**
Type of school	private
Environment	metropolis

STUDENTS
Total undergrad enrollment	880
% male/female	63/38
% from out of state	40
% from public high school	65
% live on campus	20
# of fraternities	2
# of sororities	1
% African American	5
% Asian	19

% Caucasian 39
% Hispanic 8
% Native American 1
% international 15

ACADEMICS
Calendar semester
Student/faculty ratio 9:1
Profs interesting rating 64
Profs accessible rating 61
Most common
reg class size 10–19 students
Most common
lab size greater than 100 students

MOST POPULAR MAJORS
electrical, electronics and communications
engineering
fine arts and art studies
mechanical engineering

SELECTIVITY
of applicants 3,387
% of applicants accepted 7
% of acceptees attending 78
# accepting a place on wait list 85
% admitted from wait list 13
# of early decision applicants 627
% accepted early decision 13

FRESHMAN PROFILE
Range SAT Critical Reading 590–710
Range SAT Math 600–770
Range SAT Writing 600–770
Range ACT Composite 29–33
Minimum paper TOEFL 600
Minimum computer TOEFL 250
Minimum web-based TOEFL 100
Average HS GPA 3.6
% graduated top 10% of class 93
% graduated top 25% of class 98
% graduated top 50% of class 99

DEADLINES
Early decision
Deadline 12/1
Notification 12/23
Regular
Priority 12/1
Deadline 1/1
Notification 4/1
Nonfall registration? no

FINANCIAL FACTS
Annual tuition $35,000
Room and board $13,700
Required fees $1,650
Books and supplies $1,800
% frosh rec. need-based
scholarship or grant aid 37
% UG rec. need-based
scholarship or grant aid 25
% frosh rec. non-need-based
scholarship or grant aid 37

% UG rec. non-need-based
scholarship or grant aid 25
% frosh rec. need-based
self-help aid 22
% UG rec. need-based
self-help aid 20
% frosh rec. any financial aid 100
% UG rec. any financial aid 100
% UG borrow to pay for school 27
Average cumulative
indebtedness $12,717

CORNELL UNIVERSITY

CAMPUS LIFE
Fire Safety Rating **70**
Green Rating **97**
Type of school private
Environment town

STUDENTS
Total undergrad enrollment 13,882
% male/female 51/49
% from out of state 64
% from public high school 66
% live on campus 56
# of fraternities 50
# of sororities 19
% African American 5
% Asian 17
% Caucasian 46
% Hispanic 6
% international 8
# of countries represented 77

ACADEMICS
Calendar semester
Student/faculty ratio 9:1
Profs interesting rating 74
Profs accessible rating 78
Most common
reg class size 10–19 students
Most common
lab size 10–19 students

MOST POPULAR MAJORS
biology/biological sciences
hotel/motel administration/
management
labor and industrial relations

SELECTIVITY
of applicants 34,371
% of applicants accepted 19
% of acceptees attending .48
# accepting a place on wait list 1,949
# of early decision applicants 3,442
% accepted early decision 37

FRESHMAN PROFILE
Range SAT Critical Reading 630–730
Range SAT Math 660–770
Range ACT Composite 29–33

Minimum paper TOEFL 600
Minimum web-based TOEFL 100
% graduated top 10% of class 86
% graduated top 25% of class 98
% graduated top 50% of class 100

DEADLINES
Early decision
Deadline 11/1
Notification 12/15
Regular
Deadline 1/2
Notification 4/1
Nonfall registration? no

FINANCIAL FACTS
Annual tuition $39,450
% frosh rec. need-based
scholarship or grant aid 51
% UG rec. need-based
scholarship or grant aid 46
% frosh rec. need-based
self-help aid 46
% UG rec. need-based
self-help aid 43
% frosh rec. any financial aid 52
% UG rec. any financial aid 46
% UG borrow to pay for school 53
Average cumulative
indebtedness $21,549

DARTMOUTH COLLEGE

CAMPUS LIFE
Fire Safety Rating **60***
Green Rating **95**
Type of school private
Environment village

STUDENTS
Total undergrad enrollment 4,090
% male/female 50/50
% from out of state 95
% from public high school 60
% live on campus 87
# of fraternities 14
# of sororities 6
% African American 8
% Asian 15
% Caucasian 54
% Hispanic 7
% Native American 4
% international 7

ACADEMICS
Calendar quarter
Student/faculty ratio 8:1
Profs interesting rating 76
Profs accessible rating 82
Most common
reg class size 10–19 students

MOST POPULAR MAJORS
economics
political science and government
psychology

SELECTIVITY
# of applicants	18,132
% of applicants accepted	13
% of acceptees attending	48
# accepting a place on wait list	927
% admitted from wait list	9
# of early decision applicants	1,549
% accepted early decision	26

FRESHMAN PROFILE
Range SAT Critical Reading	660–770
Range SAT Math	680–780
Range SAT Writing	670–780
Range ACT Composite	30–34
% graduated top 10% of class	91
% graduated top 25% of class	99
% graduated top 50% of class	100

DEADLINES
Early decision
Deadline	11/1
Notification	12/15
Regular	
Deadline	1/1
Notification	4/1
Nonfall registration?	no

FINANCIAL FACTS
Annual tuition	$38,445
Room and board	$11,295
Required fees	$234
Books and supplies	$1,618
% frosh rec. need-based scholarship or grant aid	48
% UG rec. need-based scholarship or grant aid	51
% frosh rec. need-based self-help aid	40
% UG rec. need-based self-help aid	47
% frosh rec. any financial aid	50
% UG rec. any financial aid	52
% UG borrow to pay for school	48
Average cumulative indebtedness	$19,051

DELAWARE VALLEY COLLEGE

CAMPUS LIFE
Fire Safety Rating	**74**
Green Rating	**76**
Type of school	private
Environment	village

STUDENTS
Total undergrad enrollment	1,877
% male/female	42/58

% from out of state	39
% from public high school	86
% live on campus	67
# of fraternities	5
# of sororities	3
% African American	4
% Asian	1
% Caucasian	84
% Hispanic	2
# of countries represented	5

ACADEMICS
Calendar	semester
Student/faculty ratio	15:1
Profs interesting rating	72
Profs accessible rating	81
Most common reg class size	10–19 students
Most common lab size	10–19 students

MOST POPULAR MAJORS
animal science
animal sciences, general
business administration and management

SELECTIVITY
# of applicants	1,770
% of applicants accepted	71
% of acceptees attending	36

FRESHMAN PROFILE
Range SAT Critical Reading	450–550
Range SAT Math	460–560
Range SAT Writing	480–550
Range ACT Composite	20–25
Minimum paper TOEFL	500
Minimum computer TOEFL	173
Average HS GPA	3.47
% graduated top 10% of class	13
% graduated top 25% of class	37
% graduated top 50% of class	73

DEADLINES
Regular
Priority	5/1
Notification	rolling
Nonfall registration?	yes

FINANCIAL FACTS
Books and supplies	$1,000
% frosh rec. need-based scholarship or grant aid	82
% UG rec. need-based scholarship or grant aid	78
% frosh rec. non-need-based scholarship or grant aid	10
% UG rec. non-need-based scholarship or grant aid	8
% frosh rec. need-based self-help aid	66
% UG rec. need-based self-help aid	66

% frosh rec. any financial aid	97
% UG rec. any financial aid	86
% UG borrow to pay for school	63
Average cumulative indebtedness	$26,350

DICKINSON COLLEGE

CAMPUS LIFE
Fire Safety Rating	**77**
Green Rating	**98**
Type of school	private
Environment	city

STUDENTS
Total undergrad enrollment	2,330
% male/female	44/56
% from out of state	75
% from public high school	59
% live on campus	94
# of fraternities	6
# of sororities	6
% African American	4
% Asian	4
% Caucasian	77
% Hispanic	5
% international	6
# of countries represented	40

ACADEMICS
Calendar	semester
Student/faculty ratio	10:1
Profs interesting rating	84
Profs accessible rating	89
Most common reg class size	10–19 students

MOST POPULAR MAJORS
international business/trade/
commerce
political science and government
psychology

SELECTIVITY
# of applicants	5,026
% of applicants accepted	49
% of acceptees attending	24
# accepting a place on wait list	297
% admitted from wait list	22
# of early decision applicants	389
% accepted early decision	76

FRESHMAN PROFILE
Range SAT Critical Reading	600–690
Range SAT Math	590–680
Range SAT Writing	590–690
Range ACT Composite	26–30
Minimum paper TOEFL	600
Minimum computer TOEFL	250
Minimum web-based TOEFL	100
% graduated top 10% of class	37
% graduated top 25% of class	71
% graduated top 50% of class	95

DEADLINES

Early decision

Deadline	11/15
Notification	12/15

Early action

Deadline	12/1
Notification	2/1

Regular

Deadline	2/1
Notification	3/31
Nonfall registration?	no

FINANCIAL FACTS

Annual tuition	$39,780
Room and board	$10,080
Required fees	$334
Books and supplies	$1,000
% frosh rec. need-based scholarship or grant aid	54
% UG rec. need-based scholarship or grant aid	50
% frosh rec. non-need-based scholarship or grant aid	5
% UG rec. non-need-based scholarship or grant aid	3
% frosh rec. need-based self-help aid	48
% UG rec. need-based self-help aid	47
% frosh rec. any financial aid	59
% UG rec. any financial aid	57
% UG borrow to pay for school	55
Average cumulative indebtedness	$23,224

DREW UNIVERSITY

CAMPUS LIFE

Fire Safety Rating	**97**
Green Rating	**84**
Type of school	private
Affiliation	Methodist
Environment	village

STUDENTS

Total undergrad enrollment	1,739
% male/female	40/60
% from out of state	40
% from public high school	66
% live on campus	83
% African American	8
% Asian	6
% Caucasian	59
% Hispanic	10
% international	2
# of countries represented	18

ACADEMICS

Calendar	semester
Student/faculty ratio	11:1
Profs interesting rating	87
Profs accessible rating	85

Most common reg class size	10–19 students
Most common lab size	10–19 students

MOST POPULAR MAJORS
economics
political science and government
psychology

SELECTIVITY

# of applicants	5,392
% of applicants accepted	74
% of acceptees attending	13
# of early decision applicants	37
% accepted early decision	95

FRESHMAN PROFILE

Range SAT Critical Reading	510–630
Range SAT Math	500–610
Range SAT Writing	510–630
Range ACT Composite	21–27
Minimum paper TOEFL	550
Minimum computer TOEFL	213
Average HS GPA	3.27
% graduated top 10% of class	38
% graduated top 25% of class	67
% graduated top 50% of class	86

DEADLINES

Early decision

Deadline	12/1
Notification	12/24

Regular

Deadline	2/15
Notification	3/21
Nonfall registration?	yes

FINANCIAL FACTS

Annual tuition	$38,766
Room and board	$10,772
Required fees	$807
% UG rec. need-based scholarship or grant aid	52
% UG rec. non-need-based scholarship or grant aid	46
% UG rec. need-based self-help aid	44
% frosh rec. any financial aid	97
% UG rec. any financial aid	91
% UG borrow to pay for school	61
Average cumulative indebtedness	$17,444

DREXEL UNIVERSITY

CAMPUS LIFE

Fire Safety Rating	**75**
Green Rating	**94**
Type of school	private
Environment	metropolis

STUDENTS

Total undergrad enrollment	13,484
% male/female	55/45
% from out of state	49
% from public high school	70
% live on campus	34
# of fraternities	12
# of sororities	11
% African American	9
% Asian	13
% Caucasian	66
% Hispanic	4
% international	9
# of countries represented	119

ACADEMICS

Calendar	quarter for most, semester for College of Medicine
Profs interesting rating	65
Profs accessible rating	64
Most common reg class size	2–9 students

MOST POPULAR MAJORS
engineering
business administration
biological sciences
nursing
psychology

SELECTIVITY

# of applicants	39,827
% of applicants accepted	55
% of acceptees attending	11

FRESHMAN PROFILE

Range SAT Critical Reading	540–630
Range SAT Math	570–670
Range ACT Composite	23–28
Minimum paper TOEFL	550
Minimum computer TOEFL	213
Average HS GPA	3.47
% graduated top 10% of class	30
% graduated top 25% of class	63
% graduated top 50% of class	91

DEADLINES

Regular

Deadline	3/1
Nonfall registration?	yes

FINANCIAL FACTS

Annual tuition	$30,900
Room and board	$13,125
Required fees	$2,105
Books and supplies	$1,950
% frosh rec. need-based scholarship or grant aid	64
% UG rec. need-based scholarship or grant aid	61
% frosh rec. non-need-based scholarship or grant aid	10

% UG rec. non-need-based scholarship or grant aid	5
% frosh rec. need-based self-help aid	52
% UG rec. need-based self-help aid	59
% frosh rec. athletic scholarships	1
% UG rec. athletic scholarships	2
% frosh rec. any financial aid	94
% UG rec. any financial aid	89
% UG borrow to pay for school	73
Average cumulative indebtedness	$35,082

DUQUESNE UNIVERSITY

CAMPUS LIFE

Fire Safety Rating	**94**
Green Rating	**88**
Type of school	private
Affiliation	Roman Catholic
Environment	metropolis

STUDENTS

Total undergrad enrollment	5,735
% male/female	43/57
% from out of state	22
% live on campus	58
# of fraternities	10
# of sororities	7
% African American	4
% Asian	2
% Caucasian	83
% Hispanic	2
% international	2
# of countries represented	80

ACADEMICS

Calendar	semester
Student/faculty ratio	14:1
Profs interesting rating	73
Profs accessible rating	80
Most common reg class size	10–19 students
Most common lab size	fewer than 10 students

MOST POPULAR MAJORS
accounting
nursing/registered nurse
(RN, ASN, BSN, MSN)
pharmacy (PharmD [US], pharmd or
BS/BPharm [Canada])

SELECTIVITY

# of applicants	6,626
% of applicants accepted	76
% of acceptees attending	28
# of early decision applicants	435
% accepted early decision	57

FRESHMAN PROFILE

Range SAT Critical Reading	510–600
Range SAT Math	520–610
Range SAT Writing	510–600
Range ACT Composite	23–28
Minimum paper TOEFL	575
Minimum computer TOEFL	230
Minimum web-based TOEFL	90
Average HS GPA	3.57
% graduated top 10% of class	24
% graduated top 25% of class	55
% graduated top 50% of class	87

DEADLINES

Early decision	
Deadline	11/1
Notification	12/15
Early action	
Deadline	12/1
Notification	1/15
Regular	
Priority	11/1
Deadline	7/1
Notification	rolling
Nonfall registration?	yes

FINANCIAL FACTS

Annual tuition	$24,385
Room and board	$9,200
Required fees	$2,083
Books and supplies	$1,000
% frosh rec. need-based scholarship or grant aid	67
% UG rec. need-based scholarship or grant aid	67
% frosh rec. non-need-based scholarship or grant aid	66
% UG rec. non-need-based scholarship or grant aid	59
% frosh rec. need-based self-help aid	58
% UG rec. need-based self-help aid	58
% frosh rec. athletic scholarships	7
% UG rec. athletic scholarships	6
% frosh rec. any financial aid	100
% UG rec. any financial aid	96

EASTERN CONNECTICUT STATE UNIVERSITY

CAMPUS LIFE

Fire Safety Rating	**84**
Green Rating	**90**
Type of school	public
Environment	village

STUDENTS

Total undergrad enrollment	5,243
% male/female	45/55
% from out of state	8

% live on campus	62
% African American	6
% Asian	2
% Caucasian	64
% Hispanic	5
% Native American	1
% international	1
# of countries represented	48

ACADEMICS

Calendar	semester
Student/faculty ratio	16:1
Profs interesting rating	75
Profs accessible rating	76
Most common reg class size	20–29 students
Most common lab size	10–19 students

MOST POPULAR MAJORS
business/commerce
communication and media studies
psychology

SELECTIVITY

# of applicants	5,007
% of applicants accepted	67
% of acceptees attending	48

FRESHMAN PROFILE

Range SAT Critical Reading	470–550
Range SAT Math	480–560
Minimum paper TOEFL	550
Minimum computer TOEFL	213

DEADLINES

Regular	
Priority	5/1
Notification	rolling
Nonfall registration?	yes

FINANCIAL FACTS

Annual in-state tuition	$4,023
Annual out-of-state tuition	$13,020
Room and board	$10,048
Required fees	$4,327
Books and supplies	$1,500
% frosh rec. need-based scholarship or grant aid	40
% UG rec. need-based scholarship or grant aid	39
% frosh rec. non-need-based scholarship or grant aid	19
% UG rec. non-need-based scholarship or grant aid	7
% frosh rec. need-based self-help aid	47
% UG rec. need-based self-help aid	42
% frosh rec. any financial aid	56
% UG rec. any financial aid	75
% UG borrow to pay for school	61
Average cumulative indebtedness	$14,829

ELIZABETHTOWN COLLEGE

CAMPUS LIFE
Fire Safety Rating	**60***
Green Rating	**60***
Type of school	private
Affiliation	Church of Brethren
Environment	village

STUDENTS
Total undergrad enrollment	2,096
% male/female	35/65
% from out of state	34
% from public high school	80
% live on campus	85
% African American	1
% Asian	2
% Caucasian	82
% Hispanic	1
% international	2
# of countries represented	17

ACADEMICS
Calendar	semester
Student/faculty ratio	13:1
Profs interesting rating	83
Profs accessible rating	84
Most common reg class size	10–19 students
Most common lab size	10–19 students

MOST POPULAR MAJORS
biology
business/commerce
communication, journalism,
and related programs

SELECTIVITY
# of applicants	2,923
% of applicants accepted	64
% of acceptees attending	29

FRESHMAN PROFILE
Range SAT Critical Reading	510–610
Range SAT Math	510–630
Range ACT Composite	21–26
Minimum paper TOEFL	525
Minimum computer TOEFL	200
Average HS GPA	3.64
% graduated top 10% of class	30
% graduated top 25% of class	65
% graduated top 50% of class	93

DEADLINES
Regular	
Notification	rolling
Nonfall registration?	yes

FINANCIAL FACTS
Annual tuition	$26,950
Room and board	$7,300
Books and supplies	$700
% frosh rec. need-based scholarship or grant aid	71
% UG rec. need-based scholarship or grant aid	71
% frosh rec. non-need-based scholarship or grant aid	14
% UG rec. non-need-based scholarship or grant aid	9
% frosh rec. need-based self-help aid	59
% UG rec. need-based self-help aid	61
% frosh rec. any financial aid	96
% UG rec. any financial aid	94
% UG borrow to pay for school	78
Average cumulative indebtedness	$25,545

ELMIRA COLLEGE

CAMPUS LIFE
Fire Safety Rating	**60***
Green Rating	**60***
Type of school	private
Environment	town

STUDENTS
Total undergrad enrollment	1,363
% male/female	29/71
% from out of state	51
% from public high school	65
% live on campus	92
% African American	1
% Asian	1
% Caucasian	67
% Hispanic	1
% international	5
# of countries represented	20

ACADEMICS
Student/faculty ratio	12:1
Profs interesting rating	72
Profs accessible rating	74
Most common reg class size	10–19 students
Most common lab size	10–19 students

MOST POPULAR MAJORS
business/commerce
elementary education and teaching
psychology

SELECTIVITY
# of applicants	2,118
% of applicants accepted	68
% of acceptees attending	25
# accepting a place on wait list	55
% admitted from wait list	4
# of early decision applicants	108
% accepted early decision	62

FRESHMAN PROFILE
Range SAT Critical Reading	480–600
Range SAT Math	480–590
Range ACT Composite	19–26
Minimum paper TOEFL	500
Minimum computer TOEFL	173
Average HS GPA	3.4
% graduated top 10% of class	30
% graduated top 25% of class	65
% graduated top 50% of class	98

DEADLINES
Early decision	
Deadline	11/15
Notification	12/15
Regular	
Priority	2/1
Deadline	3/1
Notification	rolling
Nonfall registration?	yes

FINANCIAL FACTS
Annual tuition	$29,000
Room and board	$9,100
Required fees	$1,050
Books and supplies	$450
% frosh rec. need-based scholarship or grant aid	82
% UG rec. need-based scholarship or grant aid	78
% frosh rec. non-need-based scholarship or grant aid	10
% UG rec. non-need-based scholarship or grant aid	9
% frosh rec. need-based self-help aid	69
% UG rec. need-based self-help aid	65
% frosh rec. any financial aid	80
% UG rec. any financial aid	80
% UG borrow to pay for school	69
Average cumulative indebtedness	$25,347

EMERSON COLLEGE

CAMPUS LIFE
Fire Safety Rating	**71**
Green Rating	**73**
Type of school	private
Environment	metropolis

STUDENTS
Total undergrad enrollment	3,454
% male/female	41/59
% from out of state	75
% from public high school	70
% live on campus	48
# of fraternities	4
# of sororities	3
% African American	3

% Asian 5
% Caucasian 62
% Hispanic 8
% international 3
# of countries represented 48

ACADEMICS

Calendar semester
Student/faculty ratio 13:1
Profs interesting rating 80
Profs accessible rating 77
% classes taught by TAs 3
Most common
  reg class size 10–19 students
Most common
  lab size 10–19 students

MOST POPULAR MAJORS

cinematography and film/
video production
creative writing
theatre/theater

SELECTIVITY

of applicants 6,943
% of applicants accepted 42
% of acceptees attending 26
# accepting a place on wait list 798
% admitted from wait list 13

FRESHMAN PROFILE

Range SAT Critical Reading 570–670
Range SAT Math 540–640
Range SAT Writing 580–670
Range ACT Composite 24–29
Minimum paper TOEFL 550
Minimum computer TOEFL 213
Minimum web-based TOEFL 80
Average HS GPA 3.59
% graduated top 10% of class 42
% graduated top 25% of class 77
% graduated top 50% of class 98

DEADLINES

Early action
  Deadline 11/1
  Notification 12/15
Regular
  Deadline 1/5
  Notification 4/1
Nonfall registration? yes

FINANCIAL FACTS

Annual tuition $29,408
Room and board $12,280
Required fees $532
Books and supplies $800
% frosh rec. need-based
  scholarship or grant aid 53
% UG rec. need-based
  scholarship or grant aid 43
% frosh rec. non-need-based
  scholarship or grant aid 3

% UG rec. non-need-based
  scholarship or grant aid 1
% frosh rec. need-based
  self-help aid 53
% UG rec. need-based
  self-help aid 52
% frosh rec. any financial aid 85
% UG rec. any financial aid 71
% UG borrow to pay for school 59
Average cumulative
  indebtedness $15,262

EUGENE LANG COLLEGE

CAMPUS LIFE

Fire Safety Rating **73**
Green Rating **91**
Type of school private
Environment metropolis

STUDENTS

Total undergrad enrollment 1,439
% male/female 33/67
% from out of state 71
% live on campus 30
% African American 5
% Asian 5
% Caucasian 58
% Hispanic 9
% international 4
# of countries represented 35

ACADEMICS

Calendar semester
Student/faculty ratio 15:1
Profs interesting rating 81
Profs accessible rating 78
Most common
  reg class size 10–19 students
Most common
  lab size 10–19 students

SELECTIVITY

of applicants 1,682
% of applicants accepted 68
% of acceptees attending 26

FRESHMAN PROFILE

Range SAT Critical Reading 530–640
Range SAT Math 480–580
Range SAT Writing 540–640
Range ACT Composite 22–27
Minimum paper TOEFL 600
Minimum computer TOEFL 250
Minimum web-based TOEFL 100
Average HS GPA 3.2
% graduated top 10% of class 23
% graduated top 25% of class 63
% graduated top 50% of class 93

DEADLINES

Early decision
  Deadline 11/15
  Notification 12/15
Regular
  Priority 2/1
  Deadline 2/1
  Notification rolling
Nonfall registration? yes

FINANCIAL FACTS

Annual tuition $33,810
% frosh rec. need-based
  scholarship or grant aid 56
% UG rec. need-based
  scholarship or grant aid 54
% frosh rec. non-need-based
  scholarship or grant aid 7
% UG rec. non-need-based
  scholarship or grant aid 1
% frosh rec. need-based
  self-help aid 59
% UG rec. need-based
  self-help aid 55
% frosh rec. any financial aid 70
% UG rec. any financial aid 70
% UG borrow to pay for school 62
Average cumulative
  indebtedness $25,348

FAIRFIELD UNIVERSITY

CAMPUS LIFE

Fire Safety Rating **91**
Green Rating **82**
Type of school private
Affiliation Roman Catholic/or Jesuit
Environment town

STUDENTS

Total undergrad enrollment 3,623
% male/female 42/58
% from out of state 73
% from public high school 55
% live on campus 80
% African American 4
% Asian 3
% Caucasian 66
% Hispanic 8
% international 1
# of countries represented 58

ACADEMICS

Calendar semester
Student/faculty ratio 13:1
Profs interesting rating 83
Profs accessible rating 80
Most common
  reg class size 20–29 students

SELECTIVITY
# of applicants	8,316
% of applicants accepted	65
% of acceptees attending	16

FRESHMAN PROFILE
Range SAT Critical Reading	520–610
Range SAT Math	530–630
Range SAT Writing	530–630
Minimum paper TOEFL	550
Minimum computer TOEFL	213
Minimum web-based TOEFL	80
Average HS GPA	3.4
% graduated top 10% of class	41
% graduated top 25% of class	78
% graduated top 50% of class	95

DEADLINES
Early action	
Deadline	11/1
Notification	1/1
Regular	
Deadline	1/15
Notification	4/1
Nonfall registration?	no

FINANCIAL FACTS
Annual tuition	$36,900
Room and board	$11,270
Required fees	$590
Books and supplies	$900
% frosh rec. need-based	
scholarship or grant aid	49
% UG rec. need-based	
scholarship or grant aid	49
% frosh rec. non-need-based	
scholarship or grant aid	17
% UG rec. non-need-based	
scholarship or grant aid	15
% frosh rec. need-based	
self-help aid	48
% UG rec. need-based	
self-help aid	46
% frosh rec. athletic scholarships	6
% UG rec. athletic scholarships	7
% frosh rec. any financial aid	68
% UG rec. any financial aid	63
% UG borrow to pay for school	60
Average cumulative	
indebtedness	$35,161

FORDHAM UNIVERSITY

CAMPUS LIFE
Fire Safety Rating	**60***
Green Rating	**60***
Type of school	private
Affiliation	Roman Catholic/or Jesuit
Environment	metropolis

STUDENTS
Total undergrad enrollment	7,950
% male/female	47/53
% from out of state	45
% from public high school	47
% live on campus	55
% African American	5
% Asian	8
% Caucasian	73
% Hispanic	13
% international	2
# of countries represented	55

ACADEMICS
Calendar	semester
Student/faculty ratio	12:1
Profs interesting rating	75
Profs accessible rating	79
Most common	
reg class size	22 students
Most common	
lab size	10–19 students

SELECTIVITY
# of applicants	24,557
% of applicants accepted	49
% of acceptees attending	16
# accepting a place on wait list	1,490
% admitted from wait list	9

FRESHMAN PROFILE
Range SAT Critical Reading	570–670
Range SAT Math	570–670
Range SAT Writing	570–670
Range ACT Composite	26–30
Minimum paper TOEFL	575
Minimum computer TOEFL	231
Average HS GPA	3.7
% graduated top 10% of class	43
% graduated top 25% of class	73
% graduated top 50% of class	96

DEADLINES
Early action	
Deadline	11/1
Notification	12/25
Regular	
Priority	1/15
Deadline	1/15
Notification	4/1
Nonfall registration?	yes

FINANCIAL FACTS
Annual tuition	$35,825
Room and board	$13,716
Required fees	$1,057
Books and supplies	$880
% frosh rec. need-based	
scholarship or grant aid	66
% UG rec. need-based	
scholarship or grant aid	62
% frosh rec. non-need-based	
scholarship or grant aid	8
% UG rec. non-need-based	
scholarship or grant aid	5
% frosh rec. need-based	
self-help aid	51
% UG rec. need-based	
self-help aid	52
% frosh rec. athletic scholarships	2
% UG rec. athletic scholarships	2
% frosh rec. any financial aid	67
% UG rec. any financial aid	62

FRANKLIN & MARSHALL COLLEGE

CAMPUS LIFE
Fire Safety Rating	**93**
Green Rating	**97**
Type of school	private
Environment	town

STUDENTS
Total undergrad enrollment	2,137
% male/female	49/51
% from out of state	70
% from public high school	62
% live on campus	96
# of fraternities	7
# of sororities	3
% African American	4
% Asian	4
% Caucasian	67
% Hispanic	5
% Native American	1
% international	8
# of countries represented	41

ACADEMICS
Calendar	semester
Student/faculty ratio	10:1
Profs interesting rating	89
Profs accessible rating	95
Most common	
reg class size	10–19 students
Most common	
lab size	10–19 students

MOST POPULAR MAJORS
business/commerce
political science and government
psychology

SELECTIVITY

# of applicants	5,256
% of applicants accepted	48
% of acceptees attending	25
# accepting a place on wait list	596
% admitted from wait list	2
# of early decision applicants	487
% accepted early decision	71

FRESHMAN PROFILE

Range SAT Critical Reading	600–690
Range SAT Math	630–700
Range ACT Composite	28–31
Minimum paper TOEFL	600
Minimum computer TOEFL	250
% graduated top 10% of class	63
% graduated top 25% of class	86
% graduated top 50% of class	99

DEADLINES

Early decision	
Deadline	11/15
Notification	12/15
Regular	
Deadline	2/1
Notification	4/1
Nonfall registration?	yes

FINANCIAL FACTS

Annual tuition	$39,930
Room and board	$10,430
Required fees	$50
Books and supplies	$700
% frosh rec. need-based scholarship or grant aid	45
% UG rec. need-based scholarship or grant aid	41
% frosh rec. non-need-based scholarship or grant aid	3
% UG rec. non-need-based scholarship or grant aid	2
% frosh rec. need-based self-help aid	42
% UG rec. need-based self-help aid	41
% frosh rec. any financial aid	56
% UG rec. any financial aid	56
% UG borrow to pay for school	52
Average cumulative indebtedness	$27,162

FRANKLIN W. OLIN COLLEGE OF ENGINEERING

CAMPUS LIFE

Fire Safety Rating	**98**
Green Rating	**70**
Type of school	private
Environment	town

STUDENTS

Total undergrad enrollment	337
% male/female	55/45
% from out of state	90
% live on campus	99
% African American	2
% Asian	6
% Caucasian	37
% Hispanic	3
% international	4
# of countries represented	14

ACADEMICS

Calendar	semester
Student/faculty ratio	8:1
Profs interesting rating	99
Profs accessible rating	98
Most common reg class size	20–29 students

MOST POPULAR MAJORS
electrical, electronics and
communications engineering
engineering
mechanical engineering

SELECTIVITY

# of applicants	874
% of applicants accepted	16
% of acceptees attending	60
# accepting a place on wait list	17
% admitted from wait list	18

FRESHMAN PROFILE

Range SAT Critical Reading	685–765
Range SAT Math	725–790
Range SAT Writing	680–770
Range ACT Composite	32–35
Average HS GPA	3.9
% graduated top 10% of class	95
% graduated top 25% of class	100

DEADLINES

Regular	
Deadline	1/1
Notification	3/22
Nonfall registration?	no

FINANCIAL FACTS

Annual tuition	$36,400
Room and board	$13,230
Required fees	$1,645
Books and supplies	$750

% frosh rec. any financial aid	100
% UG rec. any financial aid	100

THE GEORGE WASHINGTON UNIVERSITY

CAMPUS LIFE

Fire Safety Rating	**60***
Green Rating	**90**
Type of school	private
Environment	metropolis

STUDENTS

Total undergrad enrollment	10,225
% male/female	44/56
% from out of state	99
% from public high school	70
% live on campus	67
# of fraternities	12
# of sororities	9
% African American	7
% Asian	11
% Caucasian	55
% Hispanic	7
% Native American	1
% international	6
# of countries represented	101

ACADEMICS

Calendar	semester
Student/faculty ratio	12:1
Profs interesting rating	74
Profs accessible rating	78
% classes taught by TAs	3
Most common reg class size	10–19 students
Most common lab size	20–29 students

MOST POPULAR MAJORS
business administration
and management
international relations and affairs
liberal arts and sciences/
liberal studies

SELECTIVITY

# of applicants	19,842
% of applicants accepted	37
% of acceptees attending	36
# of early decision applicants	1,893
% accepted early decision	47

FRESHMAN PROFILE

Range SAT Critical Reading	600–690
Range SAT Math	600–690
Range SAT Writing	600–690
Range ACT Composite	27–30
Minimum paper TOEFL	550
Minimum computer TOEFL	300
% graduated top 10% of class	67

% graduated top 25% of class	93
% graduated top 50% of class	100

DEADLINES
Early decision
Deadline	11/10
Notification	12/15

Regular
Priority	12/1
Deadline	1/10
Notification	4/1
Nonfall registration?	yes

FINANCIAL FACTS
Annual tuition	$41,610
% frosh rec. need-based	
scholarship or grant aid	38
% UG rec. need-based	
scholarship or grant aid	38
% frosh rec. non-need-based	
scholarship or grant aid	11
% UG rec. non-need-based	
scholarship or grant aid	9
% frosh rec. need-based	
self-help aid	33
% UG rec. need-based	
self-help aid	33
% frosh rec. athletic scholarships	2
% UG rec. athletic scholarships	2
% UG borrow to pay for school	47
Average cumulative	
indebtedness	$31,299

GEORGETOWN UNIVERSITY

CAMPUS LIFE
Fire Safety Rating	**91**
Green Rating	**90**
Type of school	private
Affiliation	Roman Catholic/or Jesuit
Environment	metropolis

STUDENTS
Total undergrad enrollment	6,692
% male/female	46/54
% from out of state	97
% from public high school	45.5
% live on campus	69
% African American	7
% Asian	10
% Caucasian	68
% Hispanic	7
% international	5
# of countries represented	138

ACADEMICS
Calendar	semester
Student/faculty ratio	11:1
Profs interesting rating	84
Profs accessible rating	81
% classes taught by TAs	8

MOST POPULAR MAJORS
English language and literature
international relations and affairs
political science and government

SELECTIVITY
# of applicants	18,696
% of applicants accepted	19
% of acceptees attending	45
# accepting a place on wait list	1,307
% admitted from wait list	11

FRESHMAN PROFILE
Range SAT Critical Reading	650–740
Range SAT Math	660–750
Range ACT Composite	26–33
Minimum paper TOEFL	200

DEADLINES
Early action
Deadline	11/1
Notification	12/15

Regular
Deadline	1/10
Notification	4/1
Nonfall registration?	no

FINANCIAL FACTS
Annual tuition	$38,616
Room and board	$13,125
Required fees	$420
Books and supplies	$1,160
% frosh rec. need-based	
scholarship or grant aid	40
% UG rec. need-based	
scholarship or grant aid	37
% frosh rec. non-need-based	
scholarship or grant aid	8
% UG rec. non-need-based	
scholarship or grant aid	7
% frosh rec. need-based	
self-help aid	38
% UG rec. need-based	
self-help aid	36
% frosh rec. athletic scholarships	5
% UG rec. athletic scholarships	4
% frosh rec. any financial aid	40
% UG rec. any financial aid	39
% UG borrow to pay for school	44
Average cumulative	
indebtedness	$23,333

GETTYSBURG COLLEGE

CAMPUS LIFE
Fire Safety Rating	**88**
Green Rating	**88**
Type of school	private
Affiliation	Lutheran
Environment	village

STUDENTS
Total undergrad enrollment	2,516
% male/female	49/51
% from out of state	75
% from public high school	70
% live on campus	94
# of fraternities	10
# of sororities	6
% African American	5
% Asian	2
% Caucasian	88
% Hispanic	3
% international	2
# of countries represented	27

ACADEMICS
Calendar	semester
Student/faculty ratio	11:1
Profs interesting rating	88
Profs accessible rating	94
Most common	
reg class size	10–19 students

MOST POPULAR MAJORS
business/commerce
political science and government
psychology

SELECTIVITY
# of applicants	5,448
% of applicants accepted	40
% of acceptees attending	34
# accepting a place on wait list	616
# of early decision applicants	472
% accepted early decision	65

FRESHMAN PROFILE
Range SAT Critical Reading	610–690
Range SAT Math	610–690
Minimum paper TOEFL	570
Minimum computer TOEFL	230
% graduated top 10% of class	68
% graduated top 25% of class	86
% graduated top 50% of class	99

DEADLINES
Early decision
Deadline	11/15
Notification	12/15

Regular
Priority	2/1
Deadline	2/1
Notification	4/1
Nonfall registration?	yes

FINANCIAL FACTS
Annual tuition	$38,690
Room and board	$9,360
Required fees	$410
Books and supplies	$500
% frosh rec. need-based	
scholarship or grant aid	58

% UG rec. need-based
scholarship or grant aid 52
% frosh rec. non-need-based
scholarship or grant aid 31
% UG rec. non-need-based
scholarship or grant aid 26
% frosh rec. need-based
self-help aid 55
% UG rec. need-based
self-help aid 47
% frosh rec. any financial aid 70
% UG rec. any financial aid 70
% UG borrow to pay for school 61
Average cumulative
indebtedness $23,258

GORDON COLLEGE

CAMPUS LIFE
Fire Safety Rating **84**
Green Rating **60***
Type of school private
Affiliation Protestant
Environment village

STUDENTS
Total undergrad enrollment 1,572
% male/female 38/62
% from out of state 71
% from public high school 70
% live on campus 89
% African American 2
% Asian 2
% Caucasian 84
% Hispanic 3
% international 4
# of countries represented 23

ACADEMICS
Calendar semester
Student/faculty ratio 14:1
Profs interesting rating 87
Profs accessible rating 83
Most common reg class size 10–19 students
Most common lab size 10–19 students

MOST POPULAR MAJORS
business/commerce
English language and literature
psychology

SELECTIVITY
of applicants 1,664
% of applicants accepted 66
% of acceptees attending 35
# of early decision applicants 30
% accepted early decision 93

FRESHMAN PROFILE
Range SAT Critical Reading 520–650
Range SAT Math 500–640
Range SAT Writing 560–640
Range ACT Composite 24–28
Minimum paper TOEFL 550
Minimum computer TOEFL 213
% graduated top 10% of class 32
% graduated top 25% of class 58
% graduated top 50% of class 86

DEADLINES
Early decision
  Deadline 11/15
  Notification 12/15
Early action
  Deadline 12/1
  Notification 1/1
Regular
  Priority 3/1
  Notification rolling
Nonfall registration? yes

FINANCIAL FACTS
Annual tuition $27,152
Room and board $7,720
Required fees $1,200
Books and supplies $800
% frosh rec. need-based
  scholarship or grant aid 63
% UG rec. need-based
  scholarship or grant aid 65
% frosh rec. non-need-based
  scholarship or grant aid 9
% UG rec. non-need-based
  scholarship or grant aid 7
% frosh rec. need-based self-help aid 53
% UG rec. need-based self-help aid 57
% frosh rec. any financial aid 96
% UG rec. any financial aid 91
% UG borrow to pay for school 81
Average cumulative indebtedness $33,332

GOUCHER COLLEGE

CAMPUS LIFE
Fire Safety Rating **86**
Green Rating **94**
Type of school private
Environment city

STUDENTS
Total undergrad enrollment 1,464
% male/female 31/69
% from out of state 72
% from public high school 63
% live on campus 84
% African American 8

% Asian 3
% Caucasian 66
% Hispanic 5
% Native American 1
% international 1
# of countries represented 30

ACADEMICS
Calendar semester
Student/faculty ratio 9:1
Profs interesting rating 87
Profs accessible rating 86
Most common
  reg class size 10–19 students

MOST POPULAR MAJORS
biological sciences
communication
dance
English
psychology

SELECTIVITY
of applicants 3,651
% of applicants accepted 73
% of acceptees attending 15
# accepting a place on wait list 192
% admitted from wait list 12

FRESHMAN PROFILE
Range SAT Critical Reading 550–670
Range SAT Math 510–630
Range SAT Writing 540–650
Range ACT Composite 23–29
Minimum paper TOEFL 550
Minimum computer TOEFL 213
Average HS GPA 3.17
% graduated top 10% of class 26
% graduated top 25% of class 52
% graduated top 50% of class 89

DEADLINES
Early decision
  Deadline 11/15
  Notification 12/15
Regular
  Priority 2/1
  Deadline 2/1
  Notification 4/1
Nonfall registration? yes

FINANCIAL FACTS
Annual tuition $34,626
% frosh rec. need-based
  scholarship or grant aid 60
% UG rec. need-based
  scholarship or grant aid 55
% frosh rec. non-need-based
  scholarship or grant aid 15
% UG rec. non-need-based
  scholarship or grant aid 20
% frosh rec. need-based
  self-help aid 56

% UG rec. need-based	
self-help aid	51
% frosh rec. any financial aid	75
% UG rec. any financial aid	81
% UG borrow to pay for school	65
Average cumulative	
indebtedness	$14,783

GREEN MOUNTAIN COLLEGE

CAMPUS LIFE
Fire Safety Rating	**60***
Green Rating	**98**
Type of school	private
Affiliation	Methodist
Environment	rural

STUDENTS
Total undergrad enrollment	759
% male/female	50/50
% from out of state	85
% from public high school	86
% live on campus	81
% African American	3
% Asian	1
% Caucasian	72
% Hispanic	2
% Native American	1
# of countries represented	24

ACADEMICS
Calendar	semester
Student/faculty ratio	14:1
Profs interesting rating	86
Profs accessible rating	83
Most common	
reg class size	10–19 students
Most common	
lab size	10–19 students

MOST POPULAR MAJORS
environmental studies
parks, recreation, and leisure studies
psychology

SELECTIVITY
Admissions Rating	**74**
# of applicants	1,500
% of applicants accepted	75
% of acceptees attending	24

FRESHMAN PROFILE
Range SAT Critical Reading	490–610
Range SAT Math	460–570
Range SAT Writing	480–600
Range ACT Composite	17–23
Minimum paper TOEFL	500
Minimum computer TOEFL	173
Average HS GPA	3.1
% graduated top 10% of class	11
% graduated top 25% of class	25
% graduated top 50% of class	58

DEADLINES
Regular	
Priority	4/1
Notification	rolling
Nonfall registration?	yes

FINANCIAL FACTS
Annual tuition	$25,910
Room and board	$9,670
Required fees	$989
Books and supplies	$1,100
% frosh rec. need-based	
scholarship or grant aid	77
% UG rec. need-based	
scholarship or grant aid	83
% frosh rec. non-need-based	
scholarship or grant aid	6
% UG rec. non-need-based	
scholarship or grant aid	6
% frosh rec. need-based	
self-help aid	64
% UG rec. need-based	
self-help aid	75
% frosh rec. any financial aid	84
% UG rec. any financial aid	86
% UG borrow to pay for school	78

GROVE CITY COLLEGE

CAMPUS LIFE
Fire Safety Rating	**82**
Green Rating	**61**
Type of school	private
Affiliation	Presbyterian
Environment	rural

STUDENTS
Total undergrad enrollment	2,530
% male/female	50/50
% from out of state	53
% from public high school	74
% live on campus	93
# of fraternities	8
# of sororities	8
% African American	1
% Asian	2
% Caucasian	94
% Hispanic	2
# of countries represented	9

ACADEMICS
Calendar	semester
Student/faculty ratio	16:1
Profs interesting rating	77
Profs accessible rating	88
Most common	
reg class size	20–29 students
Most common	
lab size	20–29 students

MOST POPULAR MAJORS
elementary education and teaching
English language and literature
mechanical engineering

SELECTIVITY
# of applicants	1,764
% of applicants accepted	64
% of acceptees attending	56
# accepting a place on wait list	176
% admitted from wait list	35
# of early decision applicants	550
% accepted early decision	60

FRESHMAN PROFILE
Range SAT Critical Reading	563–685
Range SAT Math	568–682
Range ACT Composite	25–30
Minimum paper TOEFL	550
Minimum computer TOEFL	213
Minimum web-based TOEFL	79
Average HS GPA	3.8
% graduated top 10% of class	51
% graduated top 25% of class	85
% graduated top 50% of class	97

DEADLINES
Early decision	
Deadline	11/15
Notification	12/15
Regular	
Deadline	2/1
Notification	3/15
Nonfall registration?	yes

FINANCIAL FACTS
Annual tuition	$13,088
Room and board	$7,132
Books and supplies	$1,000
% frosh rec. need-based	
scholarship or grant aid	42
% UG rec. need-based	
scholarship or grant aid	36
% frosh rec. non-need-based	
scholarship or grant aid	5
% UG rec. non-need-based	
scholarship or grant aid	3
% frosh rec. need-based	
self-help aid	20
% UG rec. need-based	
self-help aid	22
% frosh rec. any financial aid	42
% UG rec. any financial aid	38
% UG borrow to pay for school	45
Average cumulative	
indebtedness	$24,895

HAMILTON COLLEGE

CAMPUS LIFE
Fire Safety Rating	**82**
Green Rating	**95**
Type of school	private
Environment	rural

STUDENTS
Total undergrad enrollment	1,851
% male/female	47/53
% from out of state	67
% from public high school	57
% live on campus	97
# of fraternities	11
# of sororities	7
% African American	4
% Asian	8
% Caucasian	68
% Hispanic	5
% Native American	1
% international	5
# of countries represented	40

ACADEMICS
Academic Rating	**97**
Calendar	semester
Student/faculty ratio	10:1
Profs interesting rating	96
Profs accessible rating	97
Most common reg class size	10–19 students
Most common lab size	10–19 students

MOST POPULAR MAJORS
economics
political science and government
psychology

SELECTIVITY
# of applicants	4,661
% of applicants accepted	30
% of acceptees attending	34
# accepting a place on wait list	505
% admitted from wait list	3
# of early decision applicants	563
% accepted early decision	42

FRESHMAN PROFILE
Range SAT Critical Reading	660–740
Range SAT Math	650–730
Range SAT Writing	650–740
Range ACT Composite	28–31
% graduated top 10% of class	80
% graduated top 25% of class	97
% graduated top 50% of class	100

DEADLINES
Early decision	
Deadline	11/15
Notification	12/15
Regular	
Deadline	1/1
Notification	4/1
Nonfall registration?	yes

FINANCIAL FACTS
Annual tuition	$40,870
% frosh rec. need-based scholarship or grant aid	44
% UG rec. need-based scholarship or grant aid	41
% frosh rec. need-based self-help aid	36
% UG rec. need-based self-help aid	35
% frosh rec. any financial aid	56
% UG rec. any financial aid	57
% UG borrow to pay for school	46
Average cumulative indebtedness	$19,466

HAMPSHIRE COLLEGE

CAMPUS LIFE
Fire Safety Rating	**60***
Green Rating	**82**
Type of school	private
Environment	town

STUDENTS
Total undergrad enrollment	1,438
% male/female	40/60
% from out of state	82
% from public high school	44
% live on campus	89
% African American	4
% Asian	4
% Caucasian	68
% Hispanic	8
% Native American	1
% international	4
# of countries represented	31

ACADEMICS
Calendar	4/1/4
Student/faculty ratio	12:1
Profs interesting rating	86
Profs accessible rating	82
Most common reg class size	10–19 students
Most common lab size	10–19 students

MOST POPULAR MAJORS
creative writing
drama and dramatics/theatre arts
film/video and photographic arts

SELECTIVITY
# of applicants	2,515
% of applicants accepted	63
% of acceptees attending	24
# accepting a place on wait list	121

(continued, top right)
% admitted from wait list	2
# of early decision applicants	67
% accepted early decision	88

FRESHMAN PROFILE
Range SAT Critical Reading	600–710
Range SAT Math	530–660
Range SAT Writing	590–700
Range ACT Composite	25–29
Minimum paper TOEFL	577
Minimum computer TOEFL	233
Minimum web-based TOEFL	91
Average HS GPA	3.49
% graduated top 10% of class	27
% graduated top 25% of class	69
% graduated top 50% of class	89

DEADLINES
Early decision	
Deadline	11/15
Notification	12/15
Early action	
Deadline	12/1
Notification	2/1
Regular	
Priority	11/15
Deadline	1/1
Notification	4/1
Nonfall registration?	yes

FINANCIAL FACTS
Annual tuition	$39,112
% frosh rec. need-based scholarship or grant aid	69
% UG rec. need-based scholarship or grant aid	61
% frosh rec. non-need-based scholarship or grant aid	63
% UG rec. non-need-based scholarship or grant aid	53
% frosh rec. need-based self-help aid	69
% UG rec. need-based self-help aid	61
% frosh rec. any financial aid	86
% UG rec. any financial aid	77
% UG borrow to pay for school	51
Average cumulative indebtedness	$20,669

HARTWICK COLLEGE

CAMPUS LIFE
Fire Safety Rating	**86**
Green Rating	**71**
Type of school	private
Environment	village

STUDENTS
Total undergrad enrollment	1,455
% male/female	41/59
% from out of state	33

% from public high school 84
% live on campus 86
# of fraternities 3
# of sororities 3
% African American 4
% Asian 2
% Caucasian 61
% Hispanic 4
% international 3
# of countries represented 22

ACADEMICS
Student/faculty ratio 11:1
Profs interesting rating 84
Profs accessible rating 84
Most common reg class size 10–19 students
Most common lab size 30–39 students

MOST POPULAR MAJORS
business/commerce
nursing/registered nurse (RN, ASN, BSN, MSN)
psychology

SELECTIVITY
of applicants 2,385
% of applicants accepted 91
% of acceptees attending 18
# accepting a place on wait list 51
% admitted from wait list 73
# of early decision applicants 112
% accepted early decision 85

FRESHMAN PROFILE
Range SAT Critical Reading 480–598
Range SAT Math 490–600
Range SAT Writing 480–580
Range ACT Composite 23–27
Minimum paper TOEFL 550
Minimum computer TOEFL 213
% graduated top 10% of class 17
% graduated top 25% of class 42
% graduated top 50% of class 77

DEADLINES
Early decision
  Deadline 11/15
  Notification 12/1
Regular
  Deadline 2/15
Nonfall registration? yes

FINANCIAL FACTS
Books and supplies $700

HARVARD COLLEGE

CAMPUS LIFE
Fire Safety Rating **60***
Green Rating **99**
Type of school private
Environment city

STUDENTS
Total undergrad enrollment 6,655
% male/female 49/51
% from out of state 85
% African American 8
% Asian 17
% Caucasian 42
% Hispanic 7
% Native American 1
% international 11
# of countries represented 114

ACADEMICS
Calendar semester
Student/faculty ratio 7:1
Profs interesting rating 74
Profs accessible rating 69
Most common
  reg class size fewer than
  10 students

MOST POPULAR MAJORS
economics
political science and government
sociology

SELECTIVITY
of applicants 29,114
% of applicants accepted 7
% of acceptees attending 76

FRESHMAN PROFILE
Range SAT Critical Reading 690–780
Range SAT Math 690–790
Range SAT Writing 690–780
Range ACT Composite 31–34
% graduated top 10% of class 95
% graduated top 25% of class 100
% graduated top 50% of class 100

DEADLINES
Regular
  Priority 12/1
  Deadline 1/1
  Notification 4/1
Nonfall registration? no

FINANCIAL FACTS
Annual tuition $33,696
% frosh rec. need-based
  scholarship or grant aid 63
% UG rec. need-based
  scholarship or grant aid 60
% frosh rec. need-based
  self-help aid 39

% UG rec. need-based
  self-help aid 49
% frosh rec. any financial aid 70
% UG rec. any financial aid 70
% UG borrow to pay for school 38
Average cumulative
  indebtedness $11,059

HAVERFORD COLLEGE

CAMPUS LIFE
Fire Safety Rating **73**
Green Rating **92**
Type of school private
Environment town

STUDENTS
Total undergrad enrollment 1,190
% male/female 45/55
% from out of state 86
% from public high school 57
% live on campus 99
% African American 8
% Asian 9
% Caucasian 68
% Hispanic 8
% international 3
# of countries represented 35

ACADEMICS
Calendar semester
Student/faculty ratio 8:1
Profs interesting rating 87
Profs accessible rating 95
Most common
  reg class size fewer than
  10 students
Most common
  lab size fewer than 10 students

MOST POPULAR MAJORS
biology/biological sciences
economics
English language and literature

SELECTIVITY
of applicants 3,403
% of applicants accepted 25
% of acceptees attending 37
# accepting a place on wait list 311
% admitted from wait list 4
# of early decision applicants 247
% accepted early decision 49

FRESHMAN PROFILE
Range SAT Critical Reading 660–740
Range SAT Math 640–740
Range SAT Writing 660–750
Minimum paper TOEFL 600
Minimum computer TOEFL 250
% graduated top 10% of class 94
% graduated top 25% of class 99
% graduated top 50% of class 100

DEADLINES

Early decision

Deadline	11/15
Notification	12/15

Regular

Deadline	1/15
Notification	4/15
Nonfall registration?	no

FINANCIAL FACTS

Annual tuition	$38,735
Room and board	$11,890
Required fees	$350
Books and supplies	$1,194
% frosh rec. need-based scholarship or grant aid	47
% UG rec. need-based scholarship or grant aid	46
% frosh rec. need-based self-help aid	46
% UG rec. need-based self-help aid	44
% frosh rec. any financial aid	59
% UG rec. any financial aid	58
% UG borrow to pay for school	38
Average cumulative indebtedness	$16,500

HOBART AND WILLIAM SMITH COLLEGES

CAMPUS LIFE

Fire Safety Rating	**60***
Green Rating	**60***
Type of school	private
Environment	village

STUDENTS

Total undergrad enrollment	1,855
% male/female	46/54
% from out of state	55
% from public high school	65
% live on campus	90
# of fraternities	5
% African American	4
% Asian	2
% Caucasian	88
% Hispanic	4
% international	2
# of countries represented	18

ACADEMICS

Calendar	semester
Student/faculty ratio	11:1
Profs interesting rating	88
Profs accessible rating	91
Most common reg class size	10–19 students

MOST POPULAR MAJORS

economics
English language and literature
history

SELECTIVITY

# of applicants	3,410
% of applicants accepted	65
% of acceptees attending	25
# accepting a place on wait list	194
% admitted from wait list	16

FRESHMAN PROFILE

Range SAT Critical Reading	530–640
Range SAT Math	540–630
Range ACT Composite	24–27
Minimum paper TOEFL	550
Minimum computer TOEFL	220
Average HS GPA	3.22
% graduated top 10% of class	33
% graduated top 25% of class	67
% graduated top 50% of class	95

DEADLINES

Early decision

Deadline	11/15
Notification	12/15

Regular

Deadline	2/1
Notification	4/1
Nonfall registration?	no

FINANCIAL FACTS

Annual tuition	$31,850
Room and board	$8,386
Required fees	$887
Books and supplies	$850
% frosh rec. need-based scholarship or grant aid	58
% UG rec. need-based scholarship or grant aid	60
% frosh rec. non-need-based scholarship or grant aid	10
% UG rec. non-need-based scholarship or grant aid	7
% frosh rec. need-based self-help aid	48
% UG rec. need-based self-help aid	53
% frosh rec. any financial aid	74
% UG rec. any financial aid	64
% UG borrow to pay for school	65
Average cumulative indebtedness	$21,545

HOFSTRA UNIVERSITY

CAMPUS LIFE

Fire Safety Rating	**92**
Green Rating	**82**
Type of school	private
Environment	city

STUDENTS

Total undergrad enrollment	7,756
% male/female	48/52
% from out of state	36
% live on campus	46
# of fraternities	13
# of sororities	12
% African American	9
% Asian	5
% Caucasian	65
% Hispanic	9
% international	2
# of countries represented	70

ACADEMICS

Calendar	4/1/4
Student/faculty ratio	14:1
Profs interesting rating	74
Profs accessible rating	74
Most common reg class size	10–19 students
Most common lab size	10–19 students

MOST POPULAR MAJORS

business administration
and management
marketing/marketing management
psychology

SELECTIVITY

# of applicants	20,829
% of applicants accepted	57
% of acceptees attending	13
# accepting a place on wait list	269
% admitted from wait list	33

FRESHMAN PROFILE

Range SAT Critical Reading	540–630
Range SAT Math	560–640
Range ACT Composite	24–28
Minimum paper TOEFL	550
Minimum computer TOEFL	213
Minimum web-based TOEFL	80
Average HS GPA	3.4
% graduated top 10% of class	31
% graduated top 25% of class	59
% graduated top 50% of class	87

DEADLINES

Early action

Deadline	11/15
Notification	12/15

Regular

Notification	rolling
Nonfall registration?	yes

FINANCIAL FACTS

Annual tuition	$29,080
Room and board	$11,330
Required fees	$1,050
Books and supplies	$1,000

% frosh rec. need-based
scholarship or grant aid 56
% UG rec. need-based
scholarship or grant aid 49
% frosh rec. non-need-based
scholarship or grant aid 7
% UG rec. non-need-based
scholarship or grant aid 5
% frosh rec. need-based
self-help aid 52
% UG rec. need-based
self-help aid 49
% frosh rec. athletic scholarships 1
% UG rec. athletic scholarships 1
% frosh rec. any financial aid 91
% UG rec. any financial aid 84
% UG borrow to pay for school 64

HOOD COLLEGE

CAMPUS LIFE
Fire Safety Rating **82**
Green Rating **67**
Type of school private
Affiliation United Church of Christ
Environment town

STUDENTS
Total undergrad enrollment 1,363
% male/female 32/68
% from out of state 19
% from public high school 79
% live on campus 54
% African American 11
% Asian 2
% Caucasian 73
% Hispanic 4
% international 2
# of countries represented 40

ACADEMICS
Calendar semester
Student/faculty ratio 12:1
Profs interesting rating 89
Profs accessible rating 88
Most common reg class size 10–19 students
Most common lab size 10–19 students

MOST POPULAR MAJORS
biology/biological sciences
business administration and management
psychology

SELECTIVITY
of applicants 1,622
% of applicants accepted 72
% of acceptees attending 22

FRESHMAN PROFILE
Range SAT Critical Reading 490–600
Range SAT Math 470–590
Range SAT Writing 480–600
Range ACT Composite 20–25
Minimum paper TOEFL 550
Minimum computer TOEFL 213
Minimum web-based TOEFL 79
Average HS GPA 3.52
% graduated top 10% of class 20
% graduated top 25% of class 51
% graduated top 50% of class 85

DEADLINES
Early action
Deadline 12/1
Notification 12/15
Regular
Priority 2/15
Notification rolling
Nonfall registration? yes

FINANCIAL FACTS

% frosh rec. need-based
scholarship or grant aid 76
% UG rec. need-based
scholarship or grant aid 81
% frosh rec. non-need-based
scholarship or grant aid 20
% UG rec. non-need-based
scholarship or grant aid 18
% frosh rec. need-based self-help aid 58
% UG rec. need-based self-help aid 64
% frosh rec. any financial aid 98
% UG rec. any financial aid 97
% UG borrow to pay for school 64
Average cumulative indebtedness $17,382

HOUGHTON COLLEGE

CAMPUS LIFE
Fire Safety Rating **66**
Green Rating **85**
Type of school private
Affiliation Wesleyan
Environment rural

STUDENTS
Total undergrad enrollment 1,270
% male/female 34/66
% from out of state 40
% from public high school 67
% live on campus 89
% African American 2
% Asian 2
% Caucasian 89

% Hispanic 1
% international 4
# of countries represented 20

ACADEMICS
Calendar semester
Profs interesting rating 88
Profs accessible rating 89
Most common reg class size 10–19 students
Most common lab size 10–19 students

MOST POPULAR MAJORS
biology/biological sciences
business administration and management
elementary education and teaching

SELECTIVITY
of applicants 1,080
% of applicants accepted 82
% of acceptees attending 32

FRESHMAN PROFILE
Range SAT Critical Reading 520–660
Range SAT Math 510–640
Range SAT Writing 510–640
Range ACT Composite 22–29
Minimum paper TOEFL 550
Minimum computer TOEFL 213
Minimum web-based TOEFL 80
Average HS GPA 3.56
% graduated top 10% of class 36
% graduated top 25% of class 62
% graduated top 50% of class 89

DEADLINES
Early action
Deadline 11/15
Notification 1/1
Regular
Notification rolling
Nonfall registration? yes

FINANCIAL FACTS
Annual tuition $25,360
Room and board $7,330
Books and supplies $900
% frosh rec. need-based
scholarship or grant aid 81
% UG rec. need-based
scholarship or grant aid 81
% frosh rec. non-need-based
scholarship or grant aid 12
% UG rec. non-need-based
scholarship or grant aid 9
% frosh rec. need-based self-help aid 71
% UG rec. need-based self-help aid 73
% frosh rec. athletic scholarships 1
% UG rec. athletic scholarships 2
% frosh rec. any financial aid 100

% UG rec. any financial aid 99
% UG borrow to pay for school 81
Average cumulative indebtedness $28,334

HOWARD UNIVERSITY

CAMPUS LIFE
Fire Safety Rating **96**
Green Rating **60***
Type of school private
Environment metropolis

STUDENTS
Total undergrad enrollment 7,086
% male/female 34/66
% from out of state 97
% from public high school 80
% live on campus 56
# of fraternities 10
# of sororities 8
% African American 89
% Hispanic 1
% international 4
# of countries represented 86

ACADEMICS
Calendar semester
Student/faculty ratio 8:1
Profs interesting rating 63
Profs accessible rating 61
Most common
  reg class size fewer than
  10 students
Most common
  lab size 10–19 students

MOST POPULAR MAJORS
biology/biological sciences
journalism
radio and television

SELECTIVITY
of applicants 9,750
% of applicants accepted 49
% of acceptees attending 31

FRESHMAN PROFILE
Range SAT Critical Reading 470–670
Range SAT Math 460–680
Range SAT Writing 430–670
Range ACT Composite 19–29
Minimum paper TOEFL 550
Minimum computer TOEFL 213
Average HS GPA 3.2
% graduated top 10% of class 26
% graduated top 25% of class 55
% graduated top 50% of class 84

DEADLINES
Early action
  Deadline 11/1
  Notification 12/24

Regular
  Deadline 2/15
Nonfall registration? yes

FINANCIAL FACTS
Annual tuition $17,100
Room and board $9,804
Required fees $1,021
Books and supplies $2,240
% frosh rec. need-based
  scholarship or grant aid 32
% UG rec. need-based
  scholarship or grant aid 38
% frosh rec. non-need-based
  scholarship or grant aid 40
% UG rec. non-need-based
  scholarship or grant aid 15
% frosh rec. need-based
  self-help aid 24
% UG rec. need-based
  self-help aid 21
% frosh rec. athletic scholarships 5
% UG rec. athletic scholarships 3
% frosh rec. any financial aid 96
% UG rec. any financial aid 96
% UG borrow to pay for school 80
Average cumulative
  indebtedness $16,473

INDIANA UNIVERSITY OF PENNSYLVANIA

CAMPUS LIFE
Fire Safety Rating **88**
Green Rating **60***
Type of school public
Environment village

STUDENTS
Total undergrad enrollment 12,291
% male/female 44/56
% from out of state 5
% live on campus 33
# of fraternities 18
# of sororities 14
% African American 11
% Asian 1
% Caucasian 78
% Hispanic 2
% international 3
# of countries represented 47

ACADEMICS
Calendar semester
Student/faculty ratio 18:1
Profs interesting rating 76
Profs accessible rating 75
Most common
  reg class size 20–29 students
Most common
  lab size 10–19 students

MOST POPULAR MAJORS
criminology
communications, media
nursing/registered nurse
(RN, ASN, BSN, MSN)

SELECTIVITY
of applicants 11,669
% of applicants accepted 60
% of acceptees attending 43

FRESHMAN PROFILE
Range SAT Critical Reading 450–530
Range SAT Math 450–540
Range SAT Writing 440–530
Minimum paper TOEFL 500
Minimum computer TOEFL 173
% graduated top 10% of class 7
% graduated top 25% of class 26
% graduated top 50% of class 61

DEADLINES
Regular
  Notification rolling
Nonfall registration? yes

FINANCIAL FACTS
Annual in-state tuition $5,554
Annual out-of-state tuition $13,886
Room and board $8,558
Required fees $1,655
Books and supplies $1,100
% frosh rec. need-based
  scholarship or grant aid 47
% UG rec. need-based
  scholarship or grant aid 46
% frosh rec. non-need-based
  scholarship or grant aid 25
% UG rec. non-need-based
  scholarship or grant aid 15
% frosh rec. need-based
  self-help aid 65
% UG rec. need-based
  self-help aid 61
% frosh rec. athletic scholarships 2
% UG rec. athletic scholarships 2
% frosh rec. any financial aid 82
% UG rec. any financial aid 82
% UG borrow to pay for school 84
Average cumulative
  indebtedness $25,224

IONA COLLEGE

CAMPUS LIFE
Fire Safety Rating **91**
Green Rating **82**
Type of school private
Affiliation Roman Catholic
Environment suburban

STUDENTS

Total undergrad enrollment	3,314
% male/female	44/56
% from out of state	22
% from public high school	55
% live on campus	31
# of fraternities	4
# of sororities	6
% African American	5
% Asian	2
% Caucasian	67
% Hispanic	12
% international	1
# of countries represented	35

ACADEMICS

Calendar	semester
Student/faculty ratio	13:1
Profs interesting rating	75
Profs accessible rating	72
Most common reg class size	20–29 students
Most common lab size	10–19 students

MOST POPULAR MAJORS
finance
mass communication/media studies
psychology

SELECTIVITY

# of applicants	7,313
% of applicants accepted	58
% of acceptees attending	19
# accepting a place on wait list	246
% admitted from wait list	49

FRESHMAN PROFILE

Range SAT Critical Reading	541–642
Range SAT Math	553–651
Minimum paper TOEFL	550
Minimum computer TOEFL	213
Average HS GPA	3.5
% graduated top 10% of class	31
% graduated top 25% of class	54
% graduated top 50% of class	93

DEADLINES

Early action	
Deadline	12/1
Notification	12/21
Regular	
Deadline	2/15
Notification	3/20
Nonfall registration?	yes

FINANCIAL FACTS

Annual tuition	$26,850
Room and board	$11,800
Required fees	$2,000
Books and supplies	$1,800
% frosh rec. need-based scholarship or grant aid	67
% UG rec. need-based scholarship or grant aid	49
% frosh rec. non-need-based scholarship or grant aid	77
% UG rec. non-need-based scholarship or grant aid	72
% frosh rec. need-based self-help aid	62
% UG rec. need-based self-help aid	58
% frosh rec. athletic scholarships	8
% UG rec. athletic scholarships	7
% frosh rec. any financial aid	98
% UG rec. any financial aid	94
% UG borrow to pay for school	68
Average cumulative indebtedness	$24,213

ITHACA COLLEGE

CAMPUS LIFE

Fire Safety Rating	**75**
Green Rating	**98**
Type of school	private
Environment	town

STUDENTS

Total undergrad enrollment	6,400
% male/female	43/57
% from out of state	55
% from public high school	83
# of fraternities	3
# of sororities	1
% African American	3
% Asian	4
% Caucasian	69
% Hispanic	4
% Native American	1
% international	2
# of countries represented	80

ACADEMICS

Calendar	semester
Student/faculty ratio	12:1
Profs interesting rating	81
Profs accessible rating	87
% classes taught by TAs	1
Most common reg class size	10–19 students
Most common lab size	10–19 students

MOST POPULAR MAJORS
business/commerce
music
radio and television

SELECTIVITY

# of applicants	11,916
% of applicants accepted	79
% of acceptees attending	21

FRESHMAN PROFILE

Range SAT Critical Reading	530–630
Range SAT Math	530–640
Range SAT Writing	525–630
Minimum paper TOEFL	550
Minimum computer TOEFL	213
Minimum web-based TOEFL	80
% graduated top 10% of class	27
% graduated top 25% of class	67
% graduated top 50% of class	93

DEADLINES

Early decision	
Deadline	11/1
Notification	12/15
Regular	
Deadline	2/1
Notification	rolling
Nonfall registration?	yes

FINANCIAL FACTS

Annual tuition	$32,060
Room and board	$11,780
Books and supplies	$1,200
% frosh rec. need-based scholarship or grant aid	73
% UG rec. need-based scholarship or grant aid	67
% frosh rec. non-need-based scholarship or grant aid	23
% UG rec. non-need-based scholarship or grant aid	17
% frosh rec. need-based self-help aid	68
% UG rec. need-based self-help aid	64
% frosh rec. any financial aid	96
% UG rec. any financial aid	91

JOHNS HOPKINS UNIVERSITY

CAMPUS LIFE

Fire Safety Rating	**74**
Green Rating	**95**
Type of school	private
Environment	metropolis

STUDENTS

Total undergrad enrollment	4,970
% male/female	53/47
% from out of state	86
% from public high school	69
% live on campus	56
# of fraternities	12
# of sororities	7
% African American	7
% Asian	23
% Caucasian	47
% Hispanic	7
% international	7
# of countries represented	71

ACADEMICS

Calendar	4/1/4
Student/faculty ratio	12:1
Profs interesting rating	67
Profs accessible rating	72
Most common reg class size	10–19 students
Most common lab size	20–29 students

MOST POPULAR MAJORS
international relations and affairs
neuroscience
public health

SELECTIVITY

# of applicants	16,122
% of applicants accepted	27
% of acceptees attending	31
# accepting a place on wait list	3,006
# of early decision applicants	995
% accepted early decision	50

FRESHMAN PROFILE

Range SAT Critical Reading	630–730
Range SAT Math	670–770
Range SAT Writing	650–730
Range ACT Composite	29–33
Minimum paper TOEFL	600
Average HS GPA	3.68
% graduated top 10% of class	80
% graduated top 25% of class	95
% graduated top 50% of class	100

DEADLINES

Early decision	
Deadline	11/1
Notification	12/15
Regular	
Deadline	1/1
Notification	4/1
Nonfall registration?	no

FINANCIAL FACTS

Annual tuition	$39,150
Room and board	$12,040
Books and supplies	$1,200
% frosh rec. need-based scholarship or grant aid	34
% UG rec. need-based scholarship or grant aid	40
% frosh rec. non-need-based scholarship or grant aid	5
% UG rec. non-need-based scholarship or grant aid	5
% frosh rec. need-based self-help aid	40
% UG rec. need-based self-help aid	44
% frosh rec. athletic scholarships	1
% UG rec. athletic scholarships	1
% frosh rec. any financial aid	47
% UG rec. any financial aid	45
% UG borrow to pay for school	46
Average cumulative indebtedness	$21,859

JUNIATA COLLEGE

CAMPUS LIFE

Fire Safety Rating	**75**
Green Rating	**76**
Type of school	private
Environment	village

STUDENTS

Total undergrad enrollment	1,468
% male/female	44/56
% from out of state	32
% from public high school	83
% live on campus	82
% African American	2
% Asian	2
% Caucasian	87
% Hispanic	2
% international	7
# of countries represented	32

ACADEMICS

Calendar	semester
Student/faculty ratio	12:1
Profs interesting rating	84
Profs accessible rating	89
Most common reg class size	10–19 students
Most common lab size	10–19 students

MOST POPULAR MAJORS
biology/biological sciences
business/commerce
education

SELECTIVITY

# of applicants	1,964
% of applicants accepted	72
% of acceptees attending	26
# of early decision applicants	87
% accepted early decision	86

FRESHMAN PROFILE

Range SAT Critical Reading	550–650
Range SAT Math	550–660
Minimum paper TOEFL	550
Minimum computer TOEFL	213
Average HS GPA	3.75
% graduated top 10% of class	41
% graduated top 25% of class	74
% graduated top 50% of class	96

DEADLINES

Early decision	
Deadline	12/1
Notification	12/31
Early action	
Deadline	1/1
Notification	1/30
Regular	
Priority	12/1
Deadline	3/15
Notification	rolling
Nonfall registration?	yes

FINANCIAL FACTS

Annual tuition	$32,120
Room and board	$8,980
Required fees	$700
Books and supplies	$600
% frosh rec. need-based scholarship or grant aid	72
% UG rec. need-based scholarship or grant aid	71
% frosh rec. non-need-based scholarship or grant aid	10
% UG rec. non-need-based scholarship or grant aid	10
% frosh rec. need-based self-help aid	63
% UG rec. need-based self-help aid	60
% frosh rec. any financial aid	100
% UG rec. any financial aid	100
% UG borrow to pay for school	89
Average cumulative indebtedness	$23,618

KEENE STATE COLLEGE

CAMPUS LIFE

Fire Safety Rating	**95**
Green Rating	**83**
Type of school	public
Environment	village

STUDENTS

Total undergrad enrollment	4,990
% male/female	43/57
% from out of state	47
% live on campus	55
# of fraternities	4
# of sororities	5
% Caucasian	94
% Hispanic	1
# of countries represented	4

ACADEMICS

Calendar	semester
Student/faculty ratio	18:1
Profs interesting rating	73
Profs accessible rating	73
Most common reg class size	10–19 students

MOST POPULAR MAJORS
business administration and management
elementary education and teaching
occupational safety and health
technology/technician

SELECTIVITY
of applicants   4,997
% of applicants accepted   71
% of acceptees attending   34

FRESHMAN PROFILE
Range SAT Critical Reading   450–550
Range SAT Math   450–550
Range SAT Writing   450–540
Minimum paper TOEFL   550
Minimum computer TOEFL   173
Minimum web-based TOEFL   61
Average HS GPA   3.03
% graduated top 10% of class   5
% graduated top 25% of class   22
% graduated top 50% of class   67

DEADLINES
Regular
Deadline   4/1
Nonfall registration?   yes

FINANCIAL FACTS
Annual in-state tuition $7,000
Annual out-of-state tuition $15,170
Room and board $8,444
Required fees $2,334
Books and supplies $800
% frosh rec. need-based
   scholarship or grant aid   34
% UG rec. need-based
   scholarship or grant aid   32
% frosh rec. non-need-based
   scholarship or grant aid   13
% UG rec. non-need-based
   scholarship or grant aid   12
% frosh rec. need-based self-help aid   53
% UG rec. need-based self-help aid   49
% UG borrow to pay for school   78
Average cumulative indebtedness $27,785

KING'S COLLEGE (PA)

CAMPUS LIFE
Fire Safety Rating   **85**
Green Rating   **75**
Type of school   private
Affiliation   Roman Catholic
Environment   city

STUDENTS
Total undergrad enrollment   2,296
% male/female   50/50
% from out of state   28
% from public high school   78
% African American   2
% Asian   1

% Caucasian   82
% Hispanic   4
# of countries represented   5

ACADEMICS
Calendar   semester
Student/faculty ratio   13:1
Profs interesting rating   85
Profs accessible rating   81
Most common reg class size 10–19 students
Most common lab size   10–19 students

MOST POPULAR MAJORS
accounting
business administration and management
elementary education and teaching

SELECTIVITY
of applicants   2,172
% of applicants accepted   75
% of acceptees attending   30

FRESHMAN PROFILE
Range SAT Critical Reading   460–550
Range SAT Math   470–560
Range SAT Writing   450–550
Minimum paper TOEFL   530
Minimum computer TOEFL   197
Minimum web-based TOEFL   71
Average HS GPA   3.3
% graduated top 10% of class   15
% graduated top 25% of class   40
% graduated top 50% of class   75

DEADLINES
Regular
Notification   rolling
Nonfall registration?   yes

FINANCIAL FACTS
Annual tuition $25,644
Room and board $9,838
Books and supplies $1,220
% frosh rec. need-based
   scholarship or grant aid   86
% UG rec. need-based
   scholarship or grant aid   80
% frosh rec. non-need-based
   scholarship or grant aid   10
% UG rec. non-need-based
   scholarship or grant aid   8
% frosh rec. need-based self-help aid   76
% UG rec. need-based self-help aid   70
% frosh rec. any financial aid   97
% UG rec. any financial aid   95
% UG borrow to pay for school   84
Average cumulative indebtedness $30,843

KUTZTOWN UNIVERSITY OF PENNSYLVANIA

CAMPUS LIFE
Fire Safety Rating   **60***
Green Rating   **60***
Type of school   public
Environment   rural

STUDENTS
Total undergrad enrollment   9,181
% male/female   43/57
% from out of state   10
% from public high school   99
# of fraternities   9
# of sororities   8
% African American   6
% Asian   1
% Caucasian   86
% Hispanic   5
% international   1
# of countries represented   32

ACADEMICS
Calendar   semester
Student/faculty ratio   19:1
Profs interesting rating   70
Profs accessible rating   75
Most common reg class size 20–29 students
Most common lab size   20–29 students

MOST POPULAR MAJORS
business administration and management
criminal justice/safety studies
psychology

SELECTIVITY
of applicants   9,540
% of applicants accepted   66
% of acceptees attending   32

FRESHMAN PROFILE
Range SAT Critical Reading   440–530
Range SAT Math   430–530
Range SAT Writing   430–520
Range ACT Composite   17–22
Minimum paper TOEFL   550
Minimum web-based TOEFL   79
Average HS GPA   3.03
% graduated top 10% of class   6
% graduated top 25% of class   22
% graduated top 50% of class   63

DEADLINES
Regular
Priority   12/1
Notification   rolling
Nonfall registration?   yes

FINANCIAL FACTS

Annual in-state tuition	$5,554
Annual out-of-state tuition	$13,886
Room and board	$7,698
Required fees	$1,843
Books and supplies	$1,100
% frosh rec. need-based scholarship or grant aid	42
% UG rec. need-based scholarship or grant aid	39
% frosh rec. non-need-based scholarship or grant aid	2
% UG rec. non-need-based scholarship or grant aid	2
% frosh rec. need-based self-help aid	53
% UG rec. need-based self-help aid	50
% frosh rec. athletic scholarships	2
% UG rec. athletic scholarships	2
% frosh rec. any financial aid	82
% UG rec. any financial aid	76
% UG borrow to pay for school	86
Average cumulative indebtedness	$20,707

LA ROCHE COLLEGE

CAMPUS LIFE

Fire Safety Rating	**90**
Green Rating	**60***
Type of school	private
Affiliation	Roman Catholic
Environment	city

STUDENTS

Total undergrad enrollment	1,230
% male/female	36/64
% from out of state	7
% from public high school	88
% live on campus	37
% African American	6
% Asian	1
% Caucasian	66
% Hispanic	1
% international	11
# of countries represented	39

ACADEMICS

Calendar	semester
Student/faculty ratio	12:1
Profs interesting rating	76
Profs accessible rating	71
Most common reg class size	10–19 students
Most common lab size	10–19 students

MOST POPULAR MAJORS
design and visual communications
elementary education and teaching
interior architecture

SELECTIVITY

# of applicants	859
% of applicants accepted	68
% of acceptees attending	33

FRESHMAN PROFILE

Range SAT Critical Reading	380–500
Range SAT Math	390–500
Range SAT Writing	400–510
Range ACT Composite	17–22
Average HS GPA	3
% graduated top 10% of class	3
% graduated top 25% of class	21
% graduated top 50% of class	53

DEADLINES

Regular Notification	rolling
Nonfall registration?	yes

FINANCIAL FACTS

Annual in-state tuition	$20,938
Annual out-of-state tuition	$20,938
Room and board	$8,756
Required fees	$700
Books and supplies	$1,000
% frosh rec. need-based scholarship or grant aid	59
% UG rec. need-based scholarship or grant aid	53
% frosh rec. non-need-based scholarship or grant aid	77
% UG rec. non-need-based scholarship or grant aid	70
% frosh rec. need-based self-help aid	64
% UG rec. need-based self-help aid	62
% frosh rec. any financial aid	92
% UG rec. any financial aid	90
% UG borrow to pay for school	78
Average cumulative indebtedness	$69,494

LABORATORY INSTITUTE OF MERCHANDISING

CAMPUS LIFE

Fire Safety Rating	**60***
Green Rating	**60***
Type of school	proprietary
Environment	metropolis

STUDENTS

Total undergrad enrollment	1,357
% male/female	6/94
% from out of state	58
% from public high school	73
% live on campus	24
% African American	12

% Asian	5
% Caucasian	67
% Hispanic	15
% international	1
# of countries represented	13

ACADEMICS

Calendar	semester
Student/faculty ratio	18:1
Profs interesting rating	72
Profs accessible rating	68
Most common reg class size	10–19 students

MOST POPULAR MAJORS
fashion merchandising
marketing/marketing management

SELECTIVITY

# of applicants	1,110
% of applicants accepted	65
% of acceptees attending	36

FRESHMAN PROFILE

Range SAT Critical Reading	430–520
Range SAT Math	420–510
Range SAT Writing	450–540
Range ACT Composite	19–23
Minimum paper TOEFL	550
Minimum computer TOEFL	213
% graduated top 10% of class	2
% graduated top 25% of class	19
% graduated top 50% of class	50

DEADLINES

Early action Deadline	11/15
Notification	12/15
Regular Notification	rolling
Nonfall registration?	yes

FINANCIAL FACTS

Annual tuition	$20,900
Room and board	$19,874
Required fees	$525
% frosh rec. need-based scholarship or grant aid	50
% UG rec. need-based scholarship or grant aid	46
% frosh rec. non-need-based scholarship or grant aid	13
% UG rec. non-need-based scholarship or grant aid	9
% frosh rec. need-based self-help aid	58
% UG rec. need-based self-help aid	56
% frosh rec. any financial aid	83
% UG rec. any financial aid	83

% UG borrow to pay for school 56
Average cumulative indebtedness $27,505

LAFAYETTE COLLEGE

CAMPUS LIFE
Fire Safety Rating **60***
Green Rating **98**
Type of school private
Affiliation Presbyterian
Environment suburban

STUDENTS
Total undergrad enrollment 2,378
% male/female 53/47
% from out of state 76
% from public high school 68
% live on campus 94
# of fraternities 5
# of sororities 6
% African American 5
% Asian 4
% Caucasian 66
% Hispanic 5
% international 7
# of countries represented 46

ACADEMICS
Calendar semester
Student/faculty ratio 11:1
Profs interesting rating 86
Profs accessible rating 89
Most common
 reg class size 10–19 students
Most common
 lab size 10–19 students

SELECTIVITY
Admissions Rating **94**
# of applicants 5,635
% of applicants accepted 42
% of acceptees attending 26
# accepting a place on wait list 589
% admitted from wait list 13
# of early decision applicants 446
% accepted early decision 62

FRESHMAN PROFILE
Range SAT Critical Reading 570–670
Range SAT Math 600–710
Range SAT Writing 580–680
Range ACT Composite 26–30
Minimum paper TOEFL 550
Average HS GPA 3.46
% graduated top 10% of class 59
% graduated top 25% of class 87
% graduated top 50% of class 99

DEADLINES
Early decision
 Deadline 11/15
Regular
 Deadline 1/1
 Notification 4/1
Nonfall registration? yes

FINANCIAL FACTS
Annual tuition $38,810
Room and board $11,959
Required fees $295
Books and supplies $1,005
% frosh rec. need-based
 scholarship or grant aid 41
% UG rec. need-based
 scholarship or grant aid 45
% frosh rec. non-need-based
 scholarship or grant aid 11
% UG rec. non-need-based
 scholarship or grant aid 13
% frosh rec. need-based
 self-help aid 36
% UG rec. need-based
 self-help aid 38
% frosh rec. athletic scholarships 2
% UG rec. athletic scholarships 1
% UG borrow to pay for school 47
Average cumulative
 indebtedness $20,745

LANCASTER BIBLE COLLEGE

CAMPUS LIFE
Fire Safety Rating **60***
Green Rating **60***
Type of school private
Environment village

STUDENTS
Total undergrad enrollment 702
% male/female 53/47
% from out of state 26
% from public high school 60
% live on campus 51
% African American 3
% Asian 1
% Caucasian 71
% Hispanic 1
% international 1

ACADEMICS
Calendar semester
Student/faculty ratio 10:1
Profs interesting rating 87
Profs accessible rating 89
Most common reg
 class size fewer than 10 students
Most common lab size 10–19 students

MOST POPULAR MAJORS
bible/biblical studies
elementary education and teaching
theology and religious vocations

SELECTIVITY
of applicants 314
% of applicants accepted 97
% of acceptees attending 44

FRESHMAN PROFILE
Minimum paper TOEFL 550
Minimum computer TOEFL 213

DEADLINES
Regular
 Priority 8/1
 Notification rolling
Nonfall registration? yes

FINANCIAL FACTS
Annual tuition $15,240
Room and board $6,780
Required fees $600
Books and supplies $1,000
% frosh rec. need-based
 scholarship or grant aid 77
% UG rec. need-based
 scholarship or grant aid 74
% frosh rec. non-need-based
 scholarship or grant aid 75
% UG rec. non-need-based
 scholarship or grant aid 62
% frosh rec. need-based self-help aid 64
% UG rec. need-based self-help aid 70
% UG borrow to pay for school 27
Average cumulative indebtedness $19,579

LE MOYNE COLLEGE

CAMPUS LIFE
Fire Safety Rating **79**
Green Rating **79**
Type of school private
Affiliation Roman Catholic
Environment city

STUDENTS
Total undergrad enrollment 2,465
% male/female 39/61
% from out of state 5
% from public high school 82
% live on campus 60
% African American 4
% Asian 2
% Caucasian 82
% Hispanic 5
% Native American 1

% international 1
# of countries represented 33

ACADEMICS
Calendar semester
Student/faculty ratio 13:1
Profs interesting rating 79
Profs accessible rating 81
Most common reg class size 20–29 students
Most common lab size 10–19 students

MOST POPULAR MAJORS
accounting
biology/biological sciences
psychology

SELECTIVITY
of applicants 4,526
% of applicants accepted 67
% of acceptees attending 20
# accepting a place on wait list 49
% admitted from wait list 14
# of early decision applicants 52
% accepted early decision 85

FRESHMAN PROFILE
Range SAT Critical Reading 490–580
Range SAT Math 505–610
Range ACT Composite 20–26
Minimum paper TOEFL 550
Minimum computer TOEFL 213
Minimum web-based TOEFL 79
Average HS GPA 3.34
% graduated top 10% of class 22
% graduated top 25% of class 58
% graduated top 50% of class 88

DEADLINES
Early decision
  Deadline 12/1
  Notification 12/15
Regular
  Priority 2/1
  Notification rolling
Nonfall registration? yes

FINANCIAL FACTS
Annual tuition $25,110
Room and board $9,990
Required fees $670
Books and supplies $1,230
% frosh rec. need-based
  scholarship or grant aid 76
% UG rec. need-based
  scholarship or grant aid 76
% frosh rec. non-need-based
  scholarship or grant aid 24
% UG rec. non-need-based
  scholarship or grant aid 19

% frosh rec. need-based self-help aid 67
% UG rec. need-based self-help aid 69
% frosh rec. athletic scholarships 8
% UG rec. athletic scholarships 7
% frosh rec. any financial aid 88
% UG rec. any financial aid 90
% UG borrow to pay for school 84
Average cumulative indebtedness $27,483

LEBANON VALLEY COLLEGE

CAMPUS LIFE
Fire Safety Rating **83**
Green Rating **70**
Type of school private
Affiliation Methodist
Environment rural

STUDENTS
Total undergrad enrollment 1,650
% male/female 44/56
% from out of state 20
% from public high school 95
% live on campus 74
# of fraternities 4
# of sororities 4
% African American 2
% Asian 2
% Caucasian 89
% Hispanic 2
# of countries represented 3

ACADEMICS
Calendar semester
Student/faculty ratio 13:1
Profs interesting rating 74
Profs accessible rating 86
Most common reg class size 10–19 students
Most common lab size 10–19 students

MOST POPULAR MAJORS
business/commerce
elementary education and teaching
health services/allied health/health sciences

SELECTIVITY
of applicants 1,698
% of applicants accepted 81
% of acceptees attending 28

FRESHMAN PROFILE
Range SAT Critical Reading 480–590
Range SAT Math 500–620
Range SAT Writing 470–580
Range ACT Composite 19–25
Minimum paper TOEFL 550
Minimum computer TOEFL 213
Minimum web-based TOEFL 80
% graduated top 10% of class 34

% graduated top 25% of class 71
% graduated top 50% of class 93

DEADLINES
Regular
  Notification rolling
Nonfall registration? yes

FINANCIAL FACTS
Annual tuition $29,780
Room and board $8,080
Required fees $710
Books and supplies $1,000
% frosh rec. need-based
  scholarship or grant aid 85
% UG rec. need-based
  scholarship or grant aid 80
% frosh rec. non-need-based
  scholarship or grant aid 10
% UG rec. non-need-based
  scholarship or grant aid 8
% frosh rec. need-based self-help aid 74
% UG rec. need-based self-help aid 69
% frosh rec. any financial aid 99
% UG rec. any financial aid 99
% UG borrow to pay for school 82
Average cumulative indebtedness $33,348

LEHIGH UNIVERSITY

CAMPUS LIFE
Fire Safety Rating **92**
Green Rating **79**
Type of school private
Environment city

STUDENTS
Total undergrad enrollment 4,792
% male/female 59/41
% from out of state 75
% live on campus 68
# of fraternities 21
# of sororities 9
% African American 4
% Asian 6
% Caucasian 71
% Hispanic 6
% international 4
# of countries represented 51

ACADEMICS
Calendar semester
Student/faculty ratio 10:1
Profs interesting rating 77
Profs accessible rating 86
Most common
  reg class size 10–19 students
Most common
  lab size 10–19 students

MOST POPULAR MAJORS
accounting
finance
mechanical engineering

SELECTIVITY
# of applicants	11,170
% of applicants accepted	33
% of acceptees attending	33
# accepting a place on wait list	1,160
% admitted from wait list	4
# of early decision applicants	862
% accepted early decision	65

FRESHMAN PROFILE
Range SAT Critical Reading	590–630
Range SAT Math	630–710
Minimum paper TOEFL	570
Minimum computer TOEFL	230
Minimum web-based TOEFL	90
% graduated top 10% of class	93
% graduated top 25% of class	99
% graduated top 50% of class	100

DEADLINES
Early decision	
Deadline	11/15
Notification	12/15
Regular	
Deadline	1/1
Notification	4/1
Nonfall registration?	yes

FINANCIAL FACTS
Annual tuition	$39,480
% frosh rec. need-based	
scholarship or grant aid	45
% UG rec. need-based	
scholarship or grant aid	44
% frosh rec. non-need-based	
scholarship or grant aid	5
% UG rec. non-need-based	
scholarship or grant aid	5
% frosh rec. need-based	
self-help aid	44
% UG rec. need-based	
self-help aid	43
% frosh rec. athletic scholarships	1
% UG rec. athletic scholarships	1
% frosh rec. any financial aid	59
% UG rec. any financial aid	58
% UG borrow to pay for school	54
Average cumulative	
indebtedness	$31,123

LESLEY COLLEGE AT LESLEY UNIVERSITY

CAMPUS LIFE
Fire Safety Rating	**85**
Green Rating	**71**
Type of school	private
Environment	metropolis

STUDENTS
Total undergrad enrollment	1,377
% male/female	25/75
% from out of state	44
% from public high school	83
% African American	5
% Asian	3
% Caucasian	73
% Hispanic	4
% international	4
# of countries represented	30

ACADEMICS
Calendar	semester
Student/faculty ratio	10:1
Profs interesting rating	77
Profs accessible rating	80
Most common reg class size	10–19 students

MOST POPULAR MAJORS
counseling psychology
elementary education and teaching
marketing/marketing management

SELECTIVITY
# of applicants	2,611
% of applicants accepted	67
% of acceptees attending	22
# accepting a place on wait list	21
% admitted from wait list	14

FRESHMAN PROFILE
Range SAT Critical Reading	470–600
Range SAT Math	450–580
Range SAT Writing	470–600
Range ACT Composite	20–26
Minimum paper TOEFL	500
Minimum computer TOEFL	173
Minimum web-based TOEFL	61
Average HS GPA	2.9
% graduated top 10% of class	14
% graduated top 25% of class	43
% graduated top 50% of class	77

DEADLINES
Early action	
Deadline	12/1
Notification	12/31
Regular	
Priority	2/15
Notification	rolling
Nonfall registration?	yes

FINANCIAL FACTS
Annual tuition	$29,150
Room and board	$12,850
Required fees	$250
Books and supplies	$700
% frosh rec. need-based	
scholarship or grant aid	76
% UG rec. need-based	
scholarship or grant aid	69
% frosh rec. non-need-based	
scholarship or grant aid	18
% UG rec. non-need-based	
scholarship or grant aid	17
% frosh rec. need-based self-help aid	69
% UG rec. need-based self-help aid	61
% frosh rec. any financial aid	70
% UG rec. any financial aid	70
% UG borrow to pay for school	90
Average cumulative indebtedness	$18,000

LOYOLA UNIVERSITY— MARYLAND

CAMPUS LIFE
Fire Safety Rating	**83**
Green Rating	**76**
Type of school	private
Affiliation	Roman Catholic/or Jesuit
Environment	village

STUDENTS
Total undergrad enrollment	3,757
% male/female	41/59
% from out of state	82
% from public high school	51
% live on campus	84
% African American	4
% Asian	3
% Caucasian	85
% Hispanic	4
% Native American	1
% international	1
# of countries represented	15

ACADEMICS
Calendar	semester
Student/faculty ratio	12:1
Profs interesting rating	96
Profs accessible rating	94
Most common reg class size	20–29 students
Most common lab size	10–19 students

MOST POPULAR MAJORS
business
communications
psychology
social sciences
biological/life sciences

SELECTIVITY
# of applicants	9,117
% of applicants accepted	66
% of acceptees attending	16
# accepting a place on wait list	1,079
% admitted from wait list	85

FRESHMAN PROFILE
Range SAT Critical Reading	530–630
Range SAT Math	540–640
Range SAT Writing	550–640
Range ACT Composite	24–28
Minimum paper TOEFL	550
Minimum computer TOEFL	213
Average HS GPA	3.41
% graduated top 10% of class	31
% graduated top 25% of class	65
% graduated top 50% of class	94

DEADLINES
Early action	
Deadline	11/1
Notification	1/15
Regular	
Priority	11/1
Deadline	1/15
Nonfall registration?	yes

FINANCIAL FACTS
Annual tuition	$37,950
% frosh rec. need-based	
scholarship or grant aid	57
% UG rec. need-based	
scholarship or grant aid	49
% frosh rec. non-need-based	
scholarship or grant aid	10
% UG rec. non-need-based	
scholarship or grant aid	11
% frosh rec. need-based	
self-help aid	53
% UG rec. need-based	
self-help aid	46
% frosh rec. athletic scholarships	3
% UG rec. athletic scholarships	4
% frosh rec. any financial aid	57
% UG rec. any financial aid	49
% UG borrow to pay for school	72
Average cumulative	
indebtedness	$26,855

LYCOMING COLLEGE

CAMPUS LIFE
Fire Safety Rating	**72**
Green Rating	**76**
Type of school	private
Affiliation	Methodist
Environment	town

STUDENTS
Total undergrad enrollment	1,347
% male/female	48/52
% from out of state	35
% from public high school	90
% live on campus	85
# of fraternities	5
# of sororities	5
% African American	3
% Asian	1
% Caucasian	87
% Hispanic	2
% Native American	1
% international	1
# of countries represented	7

ACADEMICS
Calendar	semester
Student/faculty ratio	13:1
Profs interesting rating	78
Profs accessible rating	83
Most common reg class size	10–19 students
Most common lab size	10–19 students

MOST POPULAR MAJORS
biology/biological sciences
business administration and management
psychology

SELECTIVITY
# of applicants	1,601
% of applicants accepted	69
% of acceptees attending	31

FRESHMAN PROFILE
Range SAT Critical Reading	470–580
Range SAT Math	470–580
Range SAT Writing	460–570
Range ACT Composite	20–27
Minimum paper TOEFL	500
Minimum computer TOEFL	173
% graduated top 10% of class	19
% graduated top 25% of class	43
% graduated top 50% of class	80

DEADLINES
Regular	
Priority	4/1
Deadline	7/1
Notification	rolling
Nonfall registration?	yes

FINANCIAL FACTS
Annual tuition	$29,344
Room and board	$8,134
Required fees	$550
Books and supplies	$900
% frosh rec. need-based	
scholarship or grant aid	90
% UG rec. need-based	
scholarship or grant aid	85
% frosh rec. non-need-based	
scholarship or grant aid	8
% UG rec. non-need-based	
scholarship or grant aid	7
% frosh rec. need-based self-help aid	74
% UG rec. need-based self-help aid	73
% frosh rec. any financial aid	95
% UG rec. any financial aid	95
% UG borrow to pay for school	85
Average cumulative indebtedness	$29,478

MANHATTANVILLE COLLEGE

CAMPUS LIFE
Fire Safety Rating	**95**
Green Rating	**86**
Type of school	private
Environment	town

STUDENTS
Total undergrad enrollment	1,842
% male/female	35/65
% from out of state	47
% live on campus	80
% African American	8
% Asian	2
% Caucasian	45
% Hispanic	17
% international	13
# of countries represented	64

ACADEMICS
Calendar	semester
Student/faculty ratio	11:1
Profs interesting rating	84
Profs accessible rating	86
Most common	
reg class size	10–19 students

MOST POPULAR MAJORS
business/commerce
psychology
visual and performing arts

SELECTIVITY
# of applicants	4,502
% of applicants accepted	53
% of acceptees attending	21
# accepting a place on wait list	100
% admitted from wait list	20

FRESHMAN PROFILE
Minimum paper TOEFL	550
Minimum computer TOEFL	217
% graduated top 10% of class	22
% graduated top 25% of class	47
% graduated top 50% of class	80

DEADLINES
Early decision	
Deadline	12/1
Notification	12/31
Regular	
Priority	3/1
Deadline	3/1
Notification	rolling
Nonfall registration?	yes

FINANCIAL FACTS
Annual tuition	$33,030
Room and board	$13,920
Required fees	$1,320
Books and supplies	$800
% frosh rec. need-based scholarship or grant aid	68
% UG rec. need-based scholarship or grant aid	62
% frosh rec. non-need-based scholarship or grant aid	54
% UG rec. non-need-based scholarship or grant aid	50
% frosh rec. need-based self-help aid	64
% UG rec. need-based self-help aid	57
% frosh rec. any financial aid	75
% UG rec. any financial aid	70
% UG borrow to pay for school	53
Average cumulative indebtedness	$23,138

MARIST COLLEGE

CAMPUS LIFE
Fire Safety Rating	**88**
Green Rating	**75**
Type of school	private
Environment	town

STUDENTS
Total undergrad enrollment	4,837
% male/female	42/58
% from out of state	43
% from public high school	72
% live on campus	74
# of fraternities	3
# of sororities	4

(Students continued)
% African American	3
% Asian	2
% Caucasian	73
% Hispanic	6
# of countries represented	11

ACADEMICS
Calendar	semester
Student/faculty ratio	15:1
Profs interesting rating	77
Profs accessible rating	78
Most common reg class size	20–29 students
Most common lab size	20–29 students

MOST POPULAR MAJORS
business administration
and management
psychology
special education and teaching

SELECTIVITY
# of applicants	10,004
% of applicants accepted	36
% of acceptees attending	29
# accepting a place on wait list	746
% admitted from wait list	15
# of early decision applicants	208
% accepted early decision	85

FRESHMAN PROFILE
Range SAT Critical Reading	520–620
Range SAT Math	540–640
Range SAT Writing	530–640
Range ACT Composite	23–28
Minimum paper TOEFL	550
Minimum computer TOEFL	213
Minimum web-based TOEFL	80
Average HS GPA	3.2
% graduated top 10% of class	27
% graduated top 25% of class	70
% graduated top 50% of class	89

DEADLINES
Early decision	
Deadline	11/15
Notification	12/15
Early action	
Deadline	12/1
Notification	1/30
Regular	
Deadline	2/15
Notification	3/30
Nonfall registration?	yes

FINANCIAL FACTS
Annual tuition	$26,104
% frosh rec. need-based scholarship or grant aid	60
% UG rec. need-based scholarship or grant aid	57

(Financial facts continued)
% frosh rec. non-need-based scholarship or grant aid	39
% UG rec. non-need-based scholarship or grant aid	29
% frosh rec. need-based self-help aid	47
% UG rec. need-based self-help aid	52
% frosh rec. athletic scholarships	8
% UG rec. athletic scholarships	6
% frosh rec. any financial aid	89
% UG rec. any financial aid	90
% UG borrow to pay for school	76
Average cumulative indebtedness	$35,993

MARLBORO COLLEGE

CAMPUS LIFE
Fire Safety Rating	**67**
Green Rating	**73**
Type of school	private
Environment	rural

STUDENTS
Total undergrad enrollment	311
% male/female	52/48
% from out of state	88
% from public high school	70
% live on campus	80
% African American	1
% Asian	3
% Caucasian	61
% Hispanic	3
% international	1
# of countries represented	4

ACADEMICS
Calendar	semester
Student/faculty ratio	8:1
Profs interesting rating	97
Profs accessible rating	92
Most common reg class size	fewer than 10 students
Most common lab size	fewer than 10 students

MOST POPULAR MAJORS
English language and literature
social sciences
visual and performing arts

SELECTIVITY
# of early decision applicants	10
% accepted early decision	90

FRESHMAN PROFILE
Range SAT Critical Reading	590–690
Range SAT Math	510–650
Range SAT Writing	640–720
Range ACT Composite	24–32
Minimum paper TOEFL	550

Minimum computer TOEFL	213
Minimum web-based TOEFL	80
Average HS GPA	3.2
% graduated top 10% of class	40
% graduated top 25% of class	60
% graduated top 50% of class	95

DEADLINES
Early decision

Deadline	12/1
Notification	12/15

Early action

Deadline	2/1
Notification	2/15

Regular

Deadline	3/1
Notification	rolling
Nonfall registration?	yes

FINANCIAL FACTS
Annual tuition	$32,550
Room and board	$9,220
Required fees	$1,110
Books and supplies	$1,000
% frosh rec. need-based scholarship or grant aid	62
% UG rec. need-based scholarship or grant aid	63
% frosh rec. non-need-based scholarship or grant aid	73
% UG rec. non-need-based scholarship or grant aid	54
% frosh rec. need-based self-help aid	65
% UG rec. need-based self-help aid	68
% frosh rec. any financial aid	92
% UG rec. any financial aid	96
% UG borrow to pay for school	94
Average cumulative indebtedness	$6,631

MARYLAND INSTITUTE
COLLEGE OF ART

CAMPUS LIFE
Fire Safety Rating	**86**
Green Rating	**64**
Type of school	private
Environment	metropolis

STUDENTS
Total undergrad enrollment	1,702
% male/female	30/70
% from out of state	80
% from public high school	75
% live on campus	88
% African American	4
% Asian	11
% Caucasian	63

% Hispanic	4
% international	4
# of countries represented	46

ACADEMICS
Calendar	semester
Student/faculty ratio	10:1
Profs interesting rating	85
Profs accessible rating	74
Most common reg class size	10–19 students

MOST POPULAR MAJORS
illustration
graphic design
painting

SELECTIVITY
# of applicants	2,892
% of applicants accepted	47
% of acceptees attending	34

FRESHMAN PROFILE
Range SAT Critical Reading	530–660
Range SAT Math	510–620
Range SAT Writing	530–650
Minimum paper TOEFL	550
Minimum computer TOEFL	213
Average HS GPA	3.5
% graduated top 10% of class	30
% graduated top 25% of class	71
% graduated top 50% of class	93

DEADLINES
Early decision

Deadline	11/14
Notification	12/15

Regular

Deadline	2/13
Notification	3/13
Nonfall registration?	yes

FINANCIAL FACTS
Annual tuition	$34,550
Room and board	$9,850
Required fees	$1,140
Books and supplies	$1,450

MARYWOOD UNIVERSITY

CAMPUS LIFE
Fire Safety Rating	**90**
Green Rating	**73**
Type of school	private
Affiliation	Roman Catholic
Environment	city

STUDENTS
Total undergrad enrollment	2,147
% male/female	30/70
% from out of state	27

% from public high school	78
# of sororities	1
% African American	1
% Asian	2
% Caucasian	86
% Hispanic	3
% international	1
# of countries represented	20

ACADEMICS
Calendar	semester
Student/faculty ratio	13:1
Profs interesting rating	68
Profs accessible rating	65
Most common reg class size	10–19 students

MOST POPULAR MAJORS
elementary education and teaching
nursing/registered nurse
(RN, ASN, BSN, MSN)
psychology

SELECTIVITY
# of applicants	1,923
% of applicants accepted	72
% of acceptees attending	34

FRESHMAN PROFILE
Range SAT Critical Reading	480–570
Range SAT Math	480–570
Range SAT Writing	470–570
Range ACT Composite	20–23
Minimum paper TOEFL	530
Minimum computer TOEFL	197
Minimum web-based TOEFL	71
Average HS GPA	3.19
% graduated top 10% of class	22
% graduated top 25% of class	56
% graduated top 50% of class	84

DEADLINES
Regular

Notification	rolling
Nonfall registration?	yes

FINANCIAL FACTS
Annual tuition	$25,150
Room and board	$11,498
Required fees	$1,120
Books and supplies	$900
% frosh rec. any financial aid	98
% UG rec. any financial aid	98

MASSACHUSETTS INSTITUTE
OF TECHNOLOGY

CAMPUS LIFE
Fire Safety Rating	**75**
Green Rating	**90**
Type of school	private
Environment	city

STUDENTS

Total undergrad enrollment	4,218
% male/female	55/45
% from out of state	91
% from public high school	66
% live on campus	92
# of fraternities	27
# of sororities	6
% African American	8
% Asian	26
% Caucasian	36
% Hispanic	13
% Native American	1
% international	9
# of countries represented	93

ACADEMICS

Calendar	4/1/4
Student/faculty ratio	7:1
Profs interesting rating	70
Profs accessible rating	76
Most common reg class size	fewer than 10 students
Most common lab size	10–19 students

MOST POPULAR MAJORS
business/commerce
computer science
mechanical engineering

SELECTIVITY

# of applicants	15,663
% of applicants accepted	11
% of acceptees attending	64
# accepting a place on wait list	455
% admitted from wait list	17

FRESHMAN PROFILE

Range SAT Critical Reading	650–760
Range SAT Math	720–800
Range SAT Writing	660–760
Range ACT Composite	32–35
Minimum paper TOEFL	577
Minimum computer TOEFL	233
Minimum web-based TOEFL	90
% graduated top 10% of class	95
% graduated top 25% of class	100
% graduated top 50% of class	100

DEADLINES

Early action	
Deadline	11/1
Notification	12/20
Regular	
Deadline	1/1
Notification	3/20
Nonfall registration?	no

FINANCIAL FACTS

Annual tuition	$37,782
% frosh rec. need-based scholarship or grant aid	63
% UG rec. need-based scholarship or grant aid	60

MERRIMACK COLLEGE

CAMPUS LIFE

Fire Safety Rating	**60***
Green Rating	**60***
Type of school	private
Affiliation	Roman Catholic
Environment	town

STUDENTS

Total undergrad enrollment	2,064
% male/female	52/48
% from out of state	30
% from public high school	65
% live on campus	80
# of fraternities	2
# of sororities	3
% African American	2
% Asian	2
% Caucasian	62
% Hispanic	3
% international	2
# of countries represented	17

ACADEMICS

Calendar	semester
Student/faculty ratio	13:1
Profs interesting rating	79
Profs accessible rating	81
Most common reg class size	10–19 students

MOST POPULAR MAJORS
business administration and management
marketing/marketing management
psychology

SELECTIVITY

# of applicants	3,883
% of applicants accepted	79
% of acceptees attending	18
# accepting a place on wait list	60
% admitted from wait list	1

FRESHMAN PROFILE

Minimum paper TOEFL	550
Minimum computer TOEFL	230
Average HS GPA	3.2
% graduated top 10% of class	10
% graduated top 25% of class	36
% graduated top 50% of class	73

DEADLINES

Early action	
Deadline	11/15
Notification	12/15
Regular	
Deadline	2/1
Notification	4/1
Nonfall registration?	yes

FINANCIAL FACTS

Annual tuition	$29,310
Room and board	$10,190
Required fees	$600
Books and supplies	$800
% frosh rec. need-based scholarship or grant aid	80
% UG rec. need-based scholarship or grant aid	63
% frosh rec. non-need-based scholarship or grant aid	12
% UG rec. non-need-based scholarship or grant aid	19
% frosh rec. need-based self-help aid	53
% UG rec. need-based self-help aid	45
% frosh rec. athletic scholarships	13
% UG rec. athletic scholarships	13
% frosh rec. any financial aid	95
% UG rec. any financial aid	80
% UG borrow to pay for school	75
Average cumulative indebtedness	$19,680

MESSIAH COLLEGE

CAMPUS LIFE

Fire Safety Rating	**72**
Green Rating	**76**
Type of school	private
Environment	village

STUDENTS

Total undergrad enrollment	2,766
% male/female	37/63
% from out of state	41
% from public high school	75
% live on campus	87
% African American	2
% Asian	2
% Caucasian	84
% Hispanic	2
% international	3
# of countries represented	30

ACADEMICS

Calendar	semester
Student/faculty ratio	13:1
Profs interesting rating	82
Profs accessible rating	86

Most common reg class size 20–29 students
Most common lab size 10–19 students

MOST POPULAR MAJORS
elementary education and teaching
engineering
nursing/registered nurse
(RN, ASN, BSN, MSN)
psychology

SELECTIVITY
# of applicants	3,054
% of applicants accepted	68
% of acceptees attending	34
# accepting a place on wait list	2
% admitted from wait list	100

FRESHMAN PROFILE
Range SAT Critical Reading	510–620
Range SAT Math	510–640
Range SAT Writing	510–620
Range ACT Composite	23–28
Minimum paper TOEFL	550
Minimum computer TOEFL	213
Minimum web-based TOEFL	80
Average HS GPA	3.71
% graduated top 10% of class	35
% graduated top 25% of class	67
% graduated top 50% of class	94

DEADLINES
Regular	
Priority	5/1
Notification	rolling
Nonfall registration?	yes

FINANCIAL FACTS
Annual tuition	$25,900
Room and board	$7,880
Required fees	$800
Books and supplies	$1,050
% frosh rec. need-based scholarship or grant aid	75
% UG rec. need-based scholarship or grant aid	69
% frosh rec. non-need-based scholarship or grant aid	10
% UG rec. non-need-based scholarship or grant aid	6
% frosh rec. need-based self-help aid	61
% UG rec. need-based self-help aid	59
% frosh rec. any financial aid	99
% UG rec. any financial aid	97
% UG borrow to pay for school	76
Average cumulative indebtedness	$33,867

MIDDLEBURY COLLEGE

CAMPUS LIFE
Fire Safety Rating	**89**
Green Rating	**96**
Type of school	private
Environment	village

STUDENTS
Total undergrad enrollment	2,455
% male/female	49/51
% from out of state	94
% from public high school	52
% live on campus	97
% African American	4
% Asian	9
% Caucasian	65
% Hispanic	5
% international	10
# of countries represented	64

ACADEMICS
Calendar	4/1/4
Student/faculty ratio	99
Profs accessible rating	97
Most common reg class size	10–19 students

MOST POPULAR MAJORS
economics
English language and literature
psychology

SELECTIVITY
# of applicants	6,904
% of applicants accepted	20
% of acceptees attending	43
# accepting a place on wait list	756
% admitted from wait list	6
# of early decision applicants	969
% accepted early decision	29

FRESHMAN PROFILE
Range SAT Critical Reading	638–730
Range SAT Math	650–740
Range SAT Writing	650–740
Range ACT Composite	30–33
% graduated top 10% of class	87
% graduated top 25% of class	94
% graduated top 50% of class	100

DEADLINES
Early decision	
Deadline	11/1
Notification	12/15
Regular	
Deadline	1/1
Notification	4/1
Nonfall registration?	yes

FINANCIAL FACTS
Comprehensive fee	$52,500
Books and supplies	$1,000

% frosh rec. need-based scholarship or grant aid	43
% UG rec. need-based scholarship or grant aid	49
% frosh rec. need-based self-help aid	35
% UG rec. need-based self-help aid	42
% frosh rec. any financial aid	43
% UG rec. any financial aid	49
% UG borrow to pay for school	44
Average cumulative indebtedness	$21,458

MISERICORDIA UNIVERSITY

CAMPUS LIFE
Fire Safety Rating	**79**
Green Rating	**60***
Type of school	private
Affiliation	Roman Catholic
Environment	town

STUDENTS
Total undergrad enrollment	2,315
% male/female	29/71
% from out of state	16
% from public high school	86
% live on campus	37
% African American	1
% Asian	1
% Caucasian	95
% Hispanic	2
# of countries represented	1

ACADEMICS
Calendar	semester
Student/faculty ratio	13:1
Profs interesting rating	92
Profs accessible rating	83
Most common reg class size	10–19 students
Most common lab size	10–19 students

MOST POPULAR MAJORS
business/commerce
elementary education and teaching
nursing/registered nurse (RN, ASN, BSN, MSN)

SELECTIVITY
# of applicants	1,533
% of applicants accepted	69
% of acceptees attending	36
# accepting a place on wait list	50
% admitted from wait list	20

FRESHMAN PROFILE
Range SAT Critical Reading	470–550
Range SAT Math	480–570
Range ACT Composite	20–25

Minimum paper TOEFL	550
Minimum computer TOEFL	213
Minimum web-based TOEFL	79
Average HS GPA	3.2
% graduated top 10% of class	15
% graduated top 25% of class	49
% graduated top 50% of class	79

DEADLINES

Regular	
Notification	rolling
Nonfall registration?	yes

FINANCIAL FACTS

Annual tuition	$23,750
Room and board	$10,410
Required fees	$1,240
Books and supplies	$800
% frosh rec. need-based	
scholarship or grant aid	83
% UG rec. need-based	
scholarship or grant aid	82
% frosh rec. non-need-based	
scholarship or grant aid	9
% UG rec. non-need-based	
scholarship or grant aid	7
% frosh rec. need-based self-help aid	67
% UG rec. need-based self-help aid	70
% frosh rec. any financial aid	99
% UG rec. any financial aid	98
% UG borrow to pay for school	78
Average cumulative indebtedness	$33,641

MOLLOY COLLEGE

CAMPUS LIFE

Fire Safety Rating	**60***
Green Rating	**60***
Type of school	private
Affiliation	Roman Catholic
Environment	village

STUDENTS

Total undergrad enrollment	3,037
% male/female	22/78
% from public high school	70
% African American	15
% Asian	7
% Caucasian	63
% Hispanic	11
% international	1

ACADEMICS

Calendar	4/1/4
Student/faculty ratio	10:1
Profs interesting rating	67
Profs accessible rating	63

Most common reg class size	10–19 students
Most common lab size	10–19 students

MOST POPULAR MAJORS
business/commerce
education
nursing/registered nurse (RN, ASN, BSN, MSN)

SELECTIVITY

# of applicants	1,803
% of applicants accepted	59
% of acceptees attending	39

FRESHMAN PROFILE

Range SAT Critical Reading	460–560
Range SAT Math	480–570
Range SAT Writing	470–560
Range ACT Composite	22–27
Minimum paper TOEFL	500
Minimum computer TOEFL	175
Average HS GPA	2.9
% graduated top 10% of class	30
% graduated top 25% of class	50
% graduated top 50% of class	86

DEADLINES

Early action	
Deadline	11/15
Notification	11/30
Regular	
Notification	rolling
Nonfall registration?	yes

FINANCIAL FACTS

% frosh rec. need-based	
scholarship or grant aid	70
% UG rec. need-based	
scholarship or grant aid	71
% frosh rec. non-need-based	
scholarship or grant aid	10
% UG rec. non-need-based	
scholarship or grant aid	6
% frosh rec. need-based self-help aid	54
% UG rec. need-based self-help aid	70
% frosh rec. athletic scholarships	4
% UG rec. athletic scholarships	3
% frosh rec. any financial aid	94
% UG rec. any financial aid	75
% UG borrow to pay for school	77
Average cumulative indebtedness	$29,823

MONMOUTH UNIVERSITY (NJ)

CAMPUS LIFE

Fire Safety Rating	**95**
Green Rating	**79**
Type of school	private
Environment	village

STUDENTS

Total undergrad enrollment	4,633
% male/female	42/58
% from out of state	12
% from public high school	86
% live on campus	44
# of fraternities	7
# of sororities	6
% African American	4
% Asian	2
% Caucasian	77
% Hispanic	6
% international	1
# of countries represented	17

ACADEMICS

Calendar	semester
Student/faculty ratio	15:1
Profs interesting rating	75
Profs accessible rating	75
Most common	
reg class size	10–19 students

MOST POPULAR MAJORS
business administration
and management
communication studies/
speech communication and rhetoric
education

SELECTIVITY

# of applicants	6,738
% of applicants accepted	62
% of acceptees attending	120

FRESHMAN PROFILE

Range SAT Critical Reading	490–570
Range SAT Math	510–600
Range SAT Writing	490–570
Range ACT Composite	22–26
Minimum paper TOEFL	550
Minimum computer TOEFL	213
Minimum web-based TOEFL	79
Average HS GPA	3.31
% graduated top 10% of class	18
% graduated top 25% of class	46
% graduated top 50% of class	83

DEADLINES

Early action	
Deadline	12/1
Notification	1/15

Regular
Priority	12/1
Deadline	3/1
Nonfall registration?	yes

FINANCIAL FACTS

Annual tuition	$24,386
Room and board	$9,554
Required fees	$628
Books and supplies	$1,000
% frosh rec. need-based scholarship or grant aid	30
% UG rec. need-based scholarship or grant aid	26
% frosh rec. non-need-based scholarship or grant aid	70
% UG rec. non-need-based scholarship or grant aid	61
% frosh rec. need-based self-help aid	56
% UG rec. need-based self-help aid	53
% frosh rec. athletic scholarships	3
% UG rec. athletic scholarships	2
% frosh rec. any financial aid	99
% UG borrow to pay for school	73
Average cumulative indebtedness	$25,000

MOORE COLLEGE OF ART AND DESIGN

CAMPUS LIFE

Fire Safety Rating	**60***
Green Rating	**60***
Type of school	private
Environment	metropolis

STUDENTS

Total undergrad enrollment	525
% from out of state	41
% live on campus	23
% African American	12
% Asian	2
% Caucasian	74
% Hispanic	6
% Native American	1
% international	2
# of countries represented	15

ACADEMICS

Calendar	semester
Student/faculty ratio	8:1
Profs interesting rating	85
Profs accessible rating	61
Most common reg class size	10–19 students

MOST POPULAR MAJORS
fashion/apparel design
fine/studio arts
graphic design

SELECTIVITY

# of applicants	549
% of applicants accepted	59
% of acceptees attending	33

FRESHMAN PROFILE

Range SAT Critical Reading	450–570
Range SAT Math	430–550
Range ACT Composite	18–25
Minimum paper TOEFL	527
Minimum computer TOEFL	197
Average HS GPA	3.08

DEADLINES

Early decision	
Deadline	11/15
Notification	12/1
Regular	
Priority	3/1
Deadline	8/15
Notification	rolling
Nonfall registration?	yes

FINANCIAL FACTS

Annual tuition	$26,800
Room and board	$10,501
Required fees	$918
Books and supplies	$2,060
% frosh rec. need-based scholarship or grant aid	38
% UG rec. need-based scholarship or grant aid	53
% frosh rec. non-need-based scholarship or grant aid	57
% UG rec. non-need-based scholarship or grant aid	56
% frosh rec. need-based self-help aid	31
% UG rec. need-based self-help aid	31
% UG rec. any financial aid	97

MORAVIAN COLLEGE

CAMPUS LIFE

Fire Safety Rating	**80**
Green Rating	**75**
Type of school	private
Affiliation	Moravian
Environment	city

STUDENTS

Total undergrad enrollment	1,564
% male/female	42/58
% from out of state	37
% from public high school	69

% live on campus	71
# of fraternities	3
# of sororities	4
% African American	3
% Asian	2
% Caucasian	86
% Hispanic	5
% international	1
# of countries represented	14

ACADEMICS

Calendar	semester
Student/faculty ratio	10:1
Profs interesting rating	84
Profs accessible rating	84
Most common reg class size	20–29 students
Most common lab size	10–19 students

MOST POPULAR MAJORS
business/commerce
psychology
sociology

SELECTIVITY

# of applicants	2,021
% of applicants accepted	75
% of acceptees attending	25
# accepting a place on wait list	17
% admitted from wait list	53
# of early decision applicants	140
% accepted early decision	79

FRESHMAN PROFILE

Range SAT Critical Reading	490–590
Range SAT Math	490–600
Range SAT Writing	480–590
Range ACT Composite	20–22
Minimum computer TOEFL	79–80
% graduated top 10% of class	28
% graduated top 25% of class	51
% graduated top 50% of class	82

DEADLINES

Early action	
Deadline	12/1
Notification	12/1
Early decision	
Deadline	2/1
Notification	12/15
Regular	
Priority	3/1
Deadline	3/1
Notification	3/15
Nonfall registration?	yes

FINANCIAL FACTS

Annual tuition	$31,662
Room and board	$8,728
Required fees	$515
Books and supplies	$950
% frosh rec. need-based scholarship or grant aid	84

% UG rec. need-based
scholarship or grant aid 78
% frosh rec. non-need-based
scholarship or grant aid 6
% UG rec. non-need-based
scholarship or grant aid 6
% frosh rec. need-based
self-help aid 78
% UG rec. need-based
self-help aid 73
% frosh rec. any financial aid 84
% UG rec. any financial aid 79

MOUNT HOLYOKE COLLEGE

CAMPUS LIFE
Fire Safety Rating **79**
Green Rating **79**
Type of school private
Environment town

STUDENTS
Total undergrad enrollment 2,247
% male/female 0/100
% from out of state 73
% from public high school 59
% live on campus 93
% African American 7
% Asian 10
% Caucasian 47
% Hispanic 5
% international 20
# of countries represented 71

ACADEMICS
Calendar semester
Student/faculty ratio 9:1
Profs interesting rating 97
Profs accessible rating 96
Most common
reg class size 10–19 students
Most common
lab size 10–19 students

MOST POPULAR MAJORS
biology/biological sciences
English language and literature
international relations and affairs

SELECTIVITY
of applicants 3,061
% of applicants accepted 58
% of acceptees attending 32
# accepting a place on wait list 292
% admitted from wait list 0
# of early decision applicants 211
% accepted early decision 61

FRESHMAN PROFILE
Range SAT Critical Reading 610–730
Range SAT Math 600–720
Range SAT Writing 620–710
Range ACT Composite 27–31

Minimum paper TOEFL 600
Minimum computer TOEFL 250
Average HS GPA 3.66
% graduated top 10% of class 62
% graduated top 25% of class 87
% graduated top 50% of class 99

DEADLINES
Early decision
Deadline 11/15
Notification 1/1
Regular
Deadline 1/15
Notification 4/1
Nonfall registration? yes

FINANCIAL FACTS
Annual tuition $40,070
% frosh rec. need-based
scholarship or grant aid 71
% UG rec. need-based
scholarship or grant aid 65
% frosh rec. need-based
self-help aid 66
% UG rec. need-based
self-help aid 64
% frosh rec. any financial aid 84
% UG rec. any financial aid 76
% UG borrow to pay for school 61
Average cumulative
indebtedness $15,551

MUHLENBERG COLLEGE

CAMPUS LIFE
Fire Safety Rating **87**
Green Rating **73**
Type of school private
Affiliation Lutheran
Environment city

STUDENTS
Total undergrad enrollment 2,411
% male/female 42/58
% from out of state 71
% from public high school 70
% live on campus 92
# of fraternities 4
# of sororities 4
% African American 2
% Asian 2
% Caucasian 88
% Hispanic 3
# of countries represented 5

ACADEMICS
Calendar semester
Student/faculty ratio 12:1
Profs interesting rating 88
Profs accessible rating 89
Most common
reg class size 10–19 students

Most common
lab size 10–19 students

MOST POPULAR MAJORS
business/commerce
communication studies/
speech communication and rhetoric
psychology

SELECTIVITY
of applicants 4,410
% of applicants accepted 44
% of acceptees attending 31
# accepting a place on wait list 354
% admitted from wait list 6
# of early decision applicants 439
% accepted early decision 79

FRESHMAN PROFILE
Range SAT Critical Reading 560–660
Range SAT Math 560–660
Range SAT Writing 560–660
Range ACT Composite 25–31
Minimum paper TOEFL 550
Minimum computer TOEFL 213
% graduated top 10% of class 41
% graduated top 25% of class 43
% graduated top 50% of class 96

DEADLINES
Early decision
Deadline 2/1
Notification 12/1
Regular
Priority 2/15
Deadline 2/15
Notification 4/1
Nonfall registration? yes

FINANCIAL FACTS
Annual tuition $36,990
% frosh rec. need-based
scholarship or grant aid 46

NAZARETH COLLEGE

CAMPUS LIFE
Fire Safety Rating **60***
Green Rating **60***
Type of school private
Environment village

STUDENTS
Total undergrad enrollment 2,227
% male/female 24/76
% from out of state 8
% from public high school 90
% live on campus 53
% African American 4
% Asian 2
% Caucasian 76
% Hispanic 4

% international 1
# of countries represented 13

ACADEMICS

Calendar semester
Student/faculty ratio 12:1
Profs interesting rating 89
Profs accessible rating 88
Most common
reg class size 10–19 students
Most common
lab size 10–19 students

MOST POPULAR MAJORS

business administration, management and
operations
education
physical therapy/therapist

SELECTIVITY

of applicants 2,221
% of applicants accepted 77
% of acceptees attending 29
# accepting a place on wait list 61
% admitted from wait list 1
# of early decision applicants 52
% accepted early decision 85

FRESHMAN PROFILE

Range SAT Critical Reading 530–630
Range SAT Math 530–630
Range SAT Writing 510–610
Range ACT Composite 23–27
Minimum paper TOEFL 550
Minimum computer TOEFL 213
Minimum web-based TOEFL 79
Average HS GPA 3.3
% graduated top 10% of class 31
% graduated top 25% of class 64
% graduated top 50% of class 88

DEADLINES

Early decision
Deadline 11/15
Notification 12/15
Early action
Deadline 12/15
Notification 1/15
Regular
Priority 12/15
Deadline 2/15
Notification 3/1
Nonfall registration? yes

FINANCIAL FACTS

Annual tuition $25,046
% frosh rec. need-based
scholarship or grant aid 77
% UG rec. need-based
scholarship or grant aid 78
% frosh rec. non-need-based
scholarship or grant aid 23

% UG rec. non-need-based
scholarship or grant aid 20
% frosh rec. need-based
self-help aid 64
% UG rec. need-based
self-help aid 67
% UG borrow to pay for school 86
Average cumulative
indebtedness $36,911

NEUMANN UNIVERSITY

CAMPUS LIFE

Fire Safety Rating **97**
Green Rating **60***
Type of school private
Affiliation Roman Catholic
Environment town

STUDENTS

Total undergrad enrollment 2,484
% male/female 34/66
% from out of state 29
% from public high school 60
% live on campus 40
% African American 14
% Asian 1
% Caucasian 61
% Hispanic 2
% international 2
# of countries represented 20

ACADEMICS

Calendar semester
Student/faculty ratio 14:1
Profs interesting rating 76
Profs accessible rating 77
Most common reg class size 20–29 students
Most common lab size 10–19 students

MOST POPULAR MAJORS

criminal justice/law enforcement
administration
elementary education and teaching
nursing/registered nurse
(RN, ASN, BSN, MSN)

SELECTIVITY

of applicants 2,333
% of applicants accepted 95
% of acceptees attending 24

FRESHMAN PROFILE

Range SAT Critical Reading 400–490
Range SAT Math 400–490
Minimum paper TOEFL 550
Minimum computer TOEFL 213
Average HS GPA 3.25
% graduated top 10% of class 30

% graduated top 25% of class 50
% graduated top 50% of class 90

DEADLINES

Nonfall registration? yes

FINANCIAL FACTS

Annual tuition $19,742
Room and board $9,258
Required fees $660
Books and supplies $1,200
% frosh rec. need-based
scholarship or grant aid 84
% UG rec. need-based
scholarship or grant aid 75
% frosh rec. non-need-based
scholarship or grant aid 56
% UG rec. non-need-based
scholarship or grant aid 49
% frosh rec. need-based self-help aid 84
% UG rec. need-based self-help aid 75
% frosh rec. any financial aid 98
% UG rec. any financial aid 91
% UG borrow to pay for school 80
Average cumulative indebtedness $25,000

NEW JERSEY INSTITUTE OF TECHNOLOGY

CAMPUS LIFE

Fire Safety Rating **88**
Green Rating **83**
Type of school public
Environment metropolis

STUDENTS

Total undergrad enrollment 5,528
% male/female 80/20
% from out of state 4
% from public high school 80
% live on campus 27
# of fraternities 15
# of sororities 7
% African American 10
% Asian 21
% Caucasian 36
% Hispanic 20
% Native American 1
% international 4
# of countries represented 92

ACADEMICS

Calendar semester
Student/faculty ratio 15:1
Profs interesting rating 61
Profs accessible rating 61
Most common
reg class size 20–29 students

MOST POPULAR MAJORS
architecture (BArch, BA/BS, MArch,
MA/MS, PhD)
civil engineering
mechanical engineering

SELECTIVITY
# of applicants	4,315
% of applicants accepted	67
% of acceptees attending	34
# accepting a place on wait list	203
% admitted from wait list	25

FRESHMAN PROFILE
Range SAT Critical Reading	490–590
Range SAT Math	550–660
Range SAT Writing	480–580
Minimum paper TOEFL	550
Minimum computer TOEFL	213
Minimum web-based TOEFL	79
% graduated top 10% of class	26
% graduated top 25% of class	55
% graduated top 50% of class	83

DEADLINES
Regular	
Deadline	4/1
Notification	rolling
Nonfall registration?	yes

FINANCIAL FACTS
Annual in-state tuition	$10,816
Annual out-of-state tuition	$20,560
% frosh rec. need-based scholarship or grant aid	60
% UG rec. need-based scholarship or grant aid	38
% frosh rec. non-need-based scholarship or grant aid	49
% UG rec. non-need-based scholarship or grant aid	31
% frosh rec. need-based self-help aid	64
% UG rec. need-based self-help aid	44
% frosh rec. athletic scholarships	6
% UG rec. athletic scholarships	3
% frosh rec. any financial aid	70
% UG rec. any financial aid	70
% UG borrow to pay for school	40
Average cumulative indebtedness	$20,000

NEW YORK UNIVERSITY

CAMPUS LIFE
Fire Safety Rating	**82**
Green Rating	**95**
Type of school	private
Environment	metropolis

STUDENTS
Total undergrad enrollment	21,227
% male/female	39/61
% from out of state	65
% from public high school	65
% live on campus	51
# of fraternities	14
# of sororities	10
% African American	4
% Asian	20
% Caucasian	46
% Hispanic	8
% international	8
# of countries represented	133

ACADEMICS
Calendar	semester
Student/faculty ratio	11:1
Profs interesting rating	71
Profs accessible rating	62
Most common reg class size	10–19 students
Most common lab size	10–19 students

MOST POPULAR MAJORS
drama and dramatics/theatre arts
finance
liberal arts and sciences/
liberal studies

SELECTIVITY
# of applicants	37,462
% of applicants accepted	38
% of acceptees attending	35
# accepting a place on wait list	1,425
% admitted from wait list	21
# of early decision applicants	2,979
% accepted early decision	39

FRESHMAN PROFILE
Range SAT Critical Reading	610–710
Range SAT Math	600–720
Range SAT Writing	620–710
Range ACT Composite	27–31
Average HS GPA	3.6
% graduated top 10% of class	64
% graduated top 25% of class	92
% graduated top 50% of class	100

DEADLINES
Early decision	
Deadline	11/1
Notification	12/15
Regular	
Deadline	1/1
Notification	4/1
Nonfall registration?	no

FINANCIAL FACTS
Annual tuition	$37,866
% frosh rec. need-based scholarship or grant aid	51
% UG rec. need-based scholarship or grant aid	49
% frosh rec. need-based self-help aid	49
% UG rec. need-based self-help aid	47
% frosh rec. any financial aid	58
% UG rec. any financial aid	58
% UG borrow to pay for school	59
Average cumulative indebtedness	$33,487

NIAGARA UNIVERSITY

CAMPUS LIFE
Fire Safety Rating	**60***
Green Rating	**81**
Type of school	private
Affiliation	Roman Catholic
Environment	town

STUDENTS
Total undergrad enrollment	3,260
% male/female	37/63
% from out of state	7
% from public high school	95
% live on campus	52
# of fraternities	3
# of sororities	2
% African American	4
% Asian	1
% Caucasian	67
% Hispanic	2
% Native American	1
% international	15
# of countries represented	12

ACADEMICS
Calendar	semester
Student/faculty ratio	14:1
Profs interesting rating	81
Profs accessible rating	83
Most common reg class size	10–19 students
Most common lab size	10–19 students

MOST POPULAR MAJORS
criminal justice
hotel management
teacher education (multiple levels)
biology

SELECTIVITY
# of applicants	2,964
% of applicants accepted	80
% of acceptees attending	29

FRESHMAN PROFILE
Range SAT Critical Reading	490–590
Range SAT Math	470–570
Range ACT Composite	19–25

Minimum paper TOEFL	500
Minimum computer TOEFL	173
Average HS GPA	3.3
% graduated top 10% of class	13
% graduated top 25% of class	41
% graduated top 50% of class	78

DEADLINES
Early action
Deadline	12/10
Notification	12/10
Regular
Deadline	8/1
Nonfall registration?	yes

FINANCIAL FACTS
Annual tuition	$24,600
Room and board	$10,650
Required fees	$1,050
Books and supplies	$1,050
% frosh rec. need-based scholarship or grant aid	84
% UG rec. need-based scholarship or grant aid	70
% frosh rec. non-need-based scholarship or grant aid	14
% UG rec. non-need-based scholarship or grant aid	17
% frosh rec. need-based self-help aid	69
% UG rec. need-based self-help aid	57
% frosh rec. athletic scholarships	4
% UG rec. athletic scholarships	8
% frosh rec. any financial aid	99
% UG rec. any financial aid	88
% UG borrow to pay for school	78
Average cumulative indebtedness	$27,215

NORTHEASTERN UNIVERSITY

CAMPUS LIFE
Fire Safety Rating	**81**
Green Rating	**99**
Type of school	private
Environment	metropolis

STUDENTS
Total undergrad enrollment	15,699
% male/female	49/51
% from out of state	61
% live on campus	50
# of fraternities	9
# of sororities	8
% African American	4
% Asian	9
% Caucasian	52
% Hispanic	5
% international	8
# of countries represented	113

ACADEMICS
Calendar	semester
Student/faculty ratio	15:1
Profs interesting rating	67
Profs accessible rating	75
Most common reg class size	10–19 students

MOST POPULAR MAJORS
business/commerce
engineering
health services/allied health/
health sciences

SELECTIVITY
# of applicants	34,005
% of applicants accepted	41
% of acceptees attending	20
# accepting a place on wait list	2,216
% admitted from wait list	8

FRESHMAN PROFILE
Range SAT Critical Reading	580–670
Range SAT Math	620–700
Range SAT Writing	580–670
Range ACT Composite	27–31
Minimum paper TOEFL	550
Minimum computer TOEFL	213
Minimum web-based TOEFL	79
% graduated top 10% of class	50
% graduated top 25% of class	81
% graduated top 50% of class	96

DEADLINES
Early action
Deadline	11/1
Notification	12/31
Regular
Deadline	1/15
Nonfall registration?	yes

FINANCIAL FACTS
Annual tuition	$34,950
Room and board	$12,350
Required fees	$412
Books and supplies	$1,000

PACE UNIVERSITY

CAMPUS LIFE
Fire Safety Rating	**84**
Green Rating	**71**
Type of school	private
Environment	metropolis

STUDENTS
Total undergrad enrollment	7,971
% male/female	40/60
% from out of state	31
% from public high school	70
% live on campus	46

# of fraternities	11
# of sororities	9
% African American	10
% Asian	8
% Caucasian	42
% Hispanic	12
% international	6
# of countries represented	92

ACADEMICS
Calendar	semester
Student/faculty ratio	15:1
Profs interesting rating	67
Profs accessible rating	68
Most common reg class size	10–19 students
Most common lab size	10–19 students

MOST POPULAR MAJORS
accounting
finance
nursing/registered nurse
(RN, ASN, BSN, MSN)

SELECTIVITY
# of applicants	10,985
% of applicants accepted	78
% of acceptees attending	19

FRESHMAN PROFILE
Range SAT Critical Reading	490–590
Range SAT Math	500–600
Range ACT Composite	20–26
Minimum paper TOEFL	570
Minimum computer TOEFL	213
Average HS GPA	3.2
% graduated top 10% of class	14
% graduated top 25% of class	39
% graduated top 50% of class	76

DEADLINES
Early action
Deadline	11/30
Notification	1/1
Regular
Deadline	3/1
Notification	rolling
Nonfall registration?	yes

FINANCIAL FACTS
Annual tuition	$32,650
Room and board	$12,240
Required fees	$956
Books and supplies	$800
% frosh rec. need-based scholarship or grant aid	80
% UG rec. need-based scholarship or grant aid	73
% frosh rec. non-need-based scholarship or grant aid	6

% UG rec. non-need-based
scholarship or grant aid 5
% frosh rec. need-based self-help aid 68
% UG rec. need-based self-help aid 63
% frosh rec. athletic scholarships 1
% frosh rec. any financial aid 76
% UG rec. any financial aid 70
% UG borrow to pay for school 58
Average cumulative indebtedness $34,115

PENNSYLVANIA STATE UNIVERSITY— UNIVERSITY PARK

CAMPUS LIFE
Fire Safety Rating **95**
Green Rating **89**
Type of school public
Environment town

STUDENTS
Total undergrad enrollment 37,855
% male/female 55/45
% from out of state 25
% live on campus 37
# of fraternities 58
# of sororities 32
% African American 4
% Asian 5
% Caucasian 78
% Hispanic 4
# of countries represented 116

ACADEMICS
Calendar semester
Student/faculty ratio 17:1
Profs interesting rating 72
Profs accessible rating 85
Most common
reg class size 20–29 students
Most common
lab size 20–29 students

MOST POPULAR MAJORS
business administration
and management
engineering

SELECTIVITY
of applicants 40,714
% of applicants accepted 52
% of acceptees attending 31
# accepting a place on wait list 1,456
% admitted from wait list 100

FRESHMAN PROFILE
Range SAT Critical Reading 530–630
Range SAT Math 560–670
Range SAT Writing 540–640
Minimum paper TOEFL 550

Minimum computer TOEFL 213
Minimum web-based TOEFL 80
Average HS GPA 3.55
% graduated top 10% of class 50
% graduated top 25% of class 86
% graduated top 50% of class 98

DEADLINES
Regular
Priority 11/30
Notification rolling
Nonfall registration? yes

FINANCIAL FACTS
Annual in-state tuition $13,604
Annual out-of-state tuition $25,134
Room and board $8,790
Required fees $812
Books and supplies
% frosh rec. need-based
scholarship or grant aid 21
% UG rec. need-based
scholarship or grant aid 27
% frosh rec. non-need-based
scholarship or grant aid 20
% UG rec. non-need-based
scholarship or grant aid 16
% frosh rec. need-based
self-help aid 37
% UG rec. need-based
self-help aid 42
% frosh rec. athletic scholarships 2
% UG rec. athletic scholarships 1
% frosh rec. any financial aid 70
% UG rec. any financial aid 71
% UG borrow to pay for school 68
Average cumulative
indebtedness $28,680

POLYTECHNIC UNIVERSITY— BROOKLYN

CAMPUS LIFE
Fire Safety Rating **60***
Green Rating **81**
Type of school private
Environment metropolis

STUDENTS
Total undergrad enrollment 1,632
% male/female 80/20
% from out of state 12.7
% from public high school 82
% live on campus 26
# of fraternities 3
# of sororities 1
% African American 10
% Asian 28
% Caucasian 25
% Hispanic 11

% international 12
# of countries represented 45

ACADEMICS
Calendar semester
Student/faculty ratio 15:1
Profs interesting rating 64
Profs accessible rating 64
Most common reg class size 10–19 students
Most common lab size 10–19 students

MOST POPULAR MAJORS
civil engineering
electrical, electronics, and communications
engineering
mechanical engineering

SELECTIVITY
of applicants 3,947
% of applicants accepted 54
% of acceptees attending 17

FRESHMAN PROFILE
Range SAT Critical Reading 560–640
Range SAT Math 630–720
Range ACT Composite 31–36
Minimum paper TOEFL 550
Minimum computer TOEFL 217
Average HS GPA 3.36
% graduated top 10% of class 36
% graduated top 25% of class 69
% graduated top 50% of class 91

DEADLINES
Nonfall registration? yes

FINANCIAL FACTS
Annual tuition $32,643
Room and board $9,000
Required fees $1,147
Books and supplies $1,000
% frosh rec. need-based
scholarship or grant aid 66
% UG rec. need-based
scholarship or grant aid 60
% frosh rec. non-need-based
scholarship or grant aid 57
% UG rec. non-need-based
scholarship or grant aid 51
% frosh rec. need-based self-help aid 61
% UG rec. need-based self-help aid 59
% frosh rec. any financial aid 99
% UG rec. any financial aid 92
% UG borrow to pay for school 67
Average cumulative indebtedness $26,619

PRINCETON UNIVERSITY

CAMPUS LIFE
Fire Safety Rating	**99**
Green Rating	**97**
Type of school	private
Environment	town

STUDENTS
Total undergrad enrollment	5,029
% male/female	51/49
% from out of state	81
% from public high school	56
% live on campus	98
% African American	8
% Asian	16
% Caucasian	49
% Hispanic	8
% international	10
# of countries represented	115

ACADEMICS
Calendar	semester
Student/faculty ratio	6:1
Profs interesting rating	87
Profs accessible rating	96
Most common	
reg class size	10–19 students
Most common	
lab size	10–19 students

MOST POPULAR MAJORS
economics
history
political science and government

SELECTIVITY
# of applicants	21,963
% of applicants accepted	10
% of acceptees attending	60
# accepting a place on wait list	937
% admitted from wait list	6

FRESHMAN PROFILE
Range SAT Critical Reading	690–790
Range SAT Math	700–790
Range SAT Writing	700–780
Range ACT Composite	31–35
Minimum paper TOEFL	600
Minimum computer TOEFL	250
Average HS GPA	3.88
% graduated top 10% of class	95
% graduated top 25% of class	100
% graduated top 50% of class	100

DEADLINES
Regular	
Deadline	1/1
Notification	3/31
Nonfall registration?	no

FINANCIAL FACTS
Annual tuition	$36,640
Room and board	$11,940
Books and supplies	$1,200
% frosh rec. need-based	
scholarship or grant aid	56
% UG rec. need-based	
scholarship or grant aid	56
% frosh rec. need-based	
self-help aid	56
% UG rec. need-based	
self-help aid	56
% frosh rec. any financial aid	59
% UG rec. any financial aid	58
% UG borrow to pay for school	21
Average cumulative	
indebtedness	$4,957

PROVIDENCE COLLEGE

CAMPUS LIFE
Fire Safety Rating	**95**
Green Rating	**74**
Type of school	private
Affiliation	Roman Catholic
Environment	city

STUDENTS
Total undergrad enrollment	3,837
% male/female	43/57
% from out of state	87
% from public high school	57
% live on campus	78
% African American	2
% Asian	2
% Caucasian	77
% Hispanic	4
% international	1
# of countries represented	21

ACADEMICS
Calendar	semester
Student/faculty ratio	13:1
Profs interesting rating	71
Profs accessible rating	76
Most common	
reg class size	20–29 students
Most common	
lab size	20–29 students

MOST POPULAR MAJORS
biology/biological sciences
business administration
and management
marketing/marketing management

SELECTIVITY
# of applicants	8,376
% of applicants accepted	59
% of acceptees attending	19
# accepting a place on wait list	782
% admitted from wait list	82

FRESHMAN PROFILE
Range SAT Critical Reading	530–630
Range SAT Math	540–640
Range SAT Writing	540–640
Range ACT Composite	23–28
Minimum paper TOEFL	550
Minimum computer TOEFL	215
Minimum web-based TOEFL	80
Average HS GPA	3.49
% graduated top 10% of class	37
% graduated top 25% of class	72
% graduated top 50% of class	96

DEADLINES
Early action	
Deadline	11/1
Notification	1/1
Regular	
Deadline	1/15
Notification	4/1
Nonfall registration?	yes

FINANCIAL FACTS
Annual tuition	$38,610
Room and board	$11,690
Required fees	$825
Books and supplies	$900
% frosh rec. need-based	
scholarship or grant aid	52
% UG rec. need-based	
scholarship or grant aid	50
% frosh rec. non-need-based	
scholarship or grant aid	6
% UG rec. non-need-based	
scholarship or grant aid	5
% frosh rec. need-based	
self-help aid	50
% UG rec. need-based	
self-help aid	48
% frosh rec. athletic scholarships	4
% UG rec. athletic scholarships	4
% frosh rec. any financial aid	75
% UG rec. any financial aid	74
% UG borrow to pay for school	63
Average cumulative	
indebtedness	$34,927

QUINNIPIAC UNIVERSITY

CAMPUS LIFE
Fire Safety Rating	**94**
Green Rating	**79**
Type of school	private
Environment	town

STUDENTS
Total undergrad enrollment	5,888
% male/female	38/62
% from out of state	70
% from public high school	70
% live on campus	75
# of fraternities	2
# of sororities	3

% African American 3
% Asian 3
% Caucasian 80
% Hispanic 5
% international 1
# of countries represented 23

ACADEMICS

Calendar	semester
Student/faculty ratio	12:1
Profs interesting rating	73
Profs accessible rating	72
Most common reg class size	10–19 students
Most common lab size	10–19 students

MOST POPULAR MAJORS

business/commerce
physical therapy/therapist
psychology

SELECTIVITY

# of applicants	13,847
% of applicants accepted	69
% of acceptees attending	17
# accepting a place on wait list	980
% admitted from wait list	22

FRESHMAN PROFILE

Range SAT Critical Reading	540–610
Range SAT Math	560–630
Range ACT Composite	23–27
Minimum paper TOEFL	550
Minimum computer TOEFL	213
Minimum web-based TOEFL	77
Average HS GPA	3.4
% graduated top 10% of class	25
% graduated top 25% of class	66
% graduated top 50% of class	95

DEADLINES

Regular	
Priority	2/1
Notification	rolling
Nonfall registration?	yes

FINANCIAL FACTS

Annual tuition	$32,850
Room and board	$12,555
Required fees	$1,400
Books and supplies	$800
% frosh rec. need-based scholarship or grant aid	60
% UG rec. need-based scholarship or grant aid	57
% frosh rec. non-need-based scholarship or grant aid	27
% UG rec. non-need-based scholarship or grant aid	24
% frosh rec. need-based self-help aid	50
% UG rec. need-based self-help aid	50

% frosh rec. athletic scholarships 4
% UG rec. athletic scholarships 5
% frosh rec. any financial aid 72
% UG rec. any financial aid 68
% UG borrow to pay for school 69
Average cumulative indebtedness $34,621

RAMAPO COLLEGE OF NEW JERSEY

CAMPUS LIFE

Fire Safety Rating	**91**
Green Rating	**77**
Type of school	public
Environment	town

STUDENTS

Total undergrad enrollment	5,529
% male/female	42/58
% from out of state	5
% live on campus	53
# of fraternities	10
# of sororities	11
% African American	5
% Asian	5
% Caucasian	76
% Hispanic	9
% international	2
# of countries represented	42

ACADEMICS

Calendar	semester
Student/faculty ratio	18:1
Profs interesting rating	71
Profs accessible rating	68
Most common reg class size	20–29 students
Most common lab size	10–19 students

MOST POPULAR MAJORS

business administration and management
nursing science (MS, PhD)
psychology

SELECTIVITY

# of applicants	5,121
% of applicants accepted	51
% of acceptees attending	36
# accepting a place on wait list	314
% admitted from wait list	33

FRESHMAN PROFILE

Range SAT Critical Reading	520–600
Range SAT Math	550–630
Range SAT Writing	530–610
Minimum paper TOEFL	550
Minimum computer TOEFL	213
Minimum web-based TOEFL	90
Average HS GPA	3.39

% graduated top 10% of class 24
% graduated top 25% of class 62
% graduated top 50% of class 94

DEADLINES

Early action	
Deadline	11/15
Notification	12/15
Regular	
Deadline	3/1
Nonfall registration?	yes

FINANCIAL FACTS

Annual in-state tuition	$7,683
Annual out-of-state tuition	$15,366
Room and board	$11,290
Required fees	$3,733
Books and supplies	$1,200
% frosh rec. need-based scholarship or grant aid	23
% UG rec. need-based scholarship or grant aid	23
% frosh rec. non-need-based scholarship or grant aid	18
% UG rec. non-need-based scholarship or grant aid	17
% frosh rec. need-based self-help aid	44
% UG rec. need-based self-help aid	45
% frosh rec. any financial aid	73
% UG rec. any financial aid	71
% UG borrow to pay for school	55
Average cumulative indebtedness	$19,789

REGIS COLLEGE

CAMPUS LIFE

Fire Safety Rating	**80**
Green Rating	**77**
Type of school	private
Affiliation	Roman Catholic
Environment	village

STUDENTS

Total undergrad enrollment	972
% male/female	18/82
% from out of state	7
% from public high school	70
% live on campus	50
% African American	22
% Asian	5
% Caucasian	38
% Hispanic	9
% Native American	1
% international	1
# of countries represented	27

ACADEMICS

Calendar	semester
Student/faculty ratio	13:1
Profs interesting rating	79
Profs accessible rating	65
Most common reg class size	10–19 students

MOST POPULAR MAJORS
communication studies
speech communication and rhetoric
nursing/registered nurse
(RN, ASN, BSN, MSN)
political science and government

SELECTIVITY

# of applicants	1,735
% of applicants accepted	73
% of acceptees attending	19

FRESHMAN PROFILE

Range SAT Critical Reading	420–520
Range SAT Math	420–520
Range SAT Writing	420–520
Range ACT Composite	17–21
Minimum paper TOEFL	550
Minimum computer TOEFL	213
Average HS GPA	2.84
% graduated top 10% of class	10
% graduated top 25% of class	37
% graduated top 50% of class	73

DEADLINES

Regular	
Priority	2/15
Notification	rolling
Nonfall registration?	yes

FINANCIAL FACTS

Annual tuition	$28,900
Room and board	$12,190
% frosh rec. need-based	
scholarship or grant aid	78
% UG rec. need-based	
scholarship or grant aid	76
% frosh rec. non-need-based	
scholarship or grant aid	68
% UG rec. non-need-based	
scholarship or grant aid	57
% frosh rec. need-based self-help aid	83
% UG rec. need-based self-help aid	82
% frosh rec. any financial aid	86
% UG rec. any financial aid	85
% UG borrow to pay for school	88
Average cumulative indebtedness	$27,489

RENSSELAER POLYTECHNIC INSTITUTE

CAMPUS LIFE

Fire Safety Rating	**72**
Green Rating	**84**
Type of school	private
Environment	city

STUDENTS

Total undergrad enrollment	5,539
% male/female	72/28
% from out of state	58
% from public high school	73
% live on campus	59
# of fraternities	32
# of sororities	5
% African American	3
% Asian	11
% Caucasian	74
% Hispanic	6
% Native American	1
% international	3
# of countries represented	60

ACADEMICS

Calendar	semester
Student/faculty ratio	16:1
Profs interesting rating	62
Profs accessible rating	73
Most common reg class size	10–19 students
Most common lab size	10–19 students

MOST POPULAR MAJORS
business/commerce
computer engineering
electrical, electronics and communications engineering

SELECTIVITY

# of applicants	12,350
% of applicants accepted	43
% of acceptees attending	25
# accepting a place on wait list	276
% admitted from wait list	67
# of early decision applicants	1,268
% accepted early decision	39

FRESHMAN PROFILE

Range SAT Critical Reading	610–700
Range SAT Math	660–750
Range SAT Writing	580–680
Range ACT Composite	25–30
Minimum paper TOEFL	570
Minimum computer TOEFL	230
Minimum web-based TOEFL	88
Average HS GPA	3.67
% graduated top 10% of class	61
% graduated top 25% of class	90
% graduated top 50% of class	98

DEADLINES

Early decision	
Deadline	11/2
Notification	12/5
Regular	
Deadline	1/15
Notification	3/13
Nonfall registration?	yes

FINANCIAL FACTS

Annual tuition	$38,100
Room and board	$11,145
Required fees	$1,065
Books and supplies	$1,850
% frosh rec. need-based	
scholarship or grant aid	66
% UG rec. need-based	
scholarship or grant aid	65
% frosh rec. non-need-based	
scholarship or grant aid	17
% UG rec. non-need-based	
scholarship or grant aid	11
% frosh rec. need-based	
self-help aid	53
% UG rec. need-based	
self-help aid	53
% frosh rec. athletic scholarships	1
% UG rec. athletic scholarships	1
% frosh rec. any financial aid	100
% UG rec. any financial aid	97
% UG borrow to pay for school	71
Average cumulative indebtedness	$30,838

THE RICHARD STOCKTON COLLEGE OF NEW JERSEY

CAMPUS LIFE

Fire Safety Rating	**88**
Green Rating	**76**
Type of school	public
Environment	town

STUDENTS

Total undergrad enrollment	6,717
% male/female	43/57
% from out of state	1
% from public high school	74
% live on campus	37
# of fraternities	11
# of sororities	9
% African American	8
% Asian	5
% Caucasian	76
% Hispanic	6
% Native American	1
# of countries represented	14

ACADEMICS

Calendar	semester
Student/faculty ratio	19:1
Profs interesting rating	76
Profs accessible rating	74
Most common reg class size	30–39 students
Most common lab size	10–19 students

MOST POPULAR MAJORS
biology/biological sciences
business administration and management
psychology

SELECTIVITY

# of applicants	4,547
% of applicants accepted	61
% of acceptees attending	31
# accepting a place on wait list	418
% admitted from wait list	25

FRESHMAN PROFILE

Range SAT Critical Reading	490–590
Range SAT Math	510–610
Range SAT Writing	480–580
Range ACT Composite	19–23
Minimum paper TOEFL	550
Minimum computer TOEFL	217
% graduated top 10% of class	26
% graduated top 25% of class	60
% graduated top 50% of class	96

DEADLINES
Regular

Deadline	5/1
Notification	rolling
Nonfall registration?	yes

FINANCIAL FACTS

Annual in-state tuition	$7,067
Annual out-of-state tuition	$12,750
Room and board	$10,189
Required fees	$3,873
Books and supplies	$1,500
% frosh rec. need-based scholarship or grant aid	35
% UG rec. need-based scholarship or grant aid	33
% frosh rec. non-need-based scholarship or grant aid	30
% UG rec. non-need-based scholarship or grant aid	16
% frosh rec. need-based self-help aid	57
% UG rec. need-based self-help aid	55
% frosh rec. any financial aid	84
% UG rec. any financial aid	77
% UG borrow to pay for school	69
Average cumulative indebtedness	$27,847

RIDER UNIVERSITY

CAMPUS LIFE

Fire Safety Rating	**60***
Green Rating	**93**
Type of school	private
Environment	village

STUDENTS

Total undergrad enrollment	4,712
% male/female	39/61
% from out of state	22
% from public high school	80
% live on campus	56
# of fraternities	4
# of sororities	8
% African American	10
% Asian	3
% Caucasian	68
% Hispanic	6
% international	3
# of countries represented	50

ACADEMICS

Calendar	semester
Student/faculty ratio	13:1
Profs interesting rating	73
Profs accessible rating	75
Most common reg class size	10–19 students
Most common lab size	10–19 students

MOST POPULAR MAJORS
accounting
communication
elementary education and teaching

SELECTIVITY

# of applicants	7,372
% of applicants accepted	75
% of acceptees attending	19
# accepting a place on wait list	16
% admitted from wait list	25
# of early decision applicants	30
% accepted early decision	97

FRESHMAN PROFILE

Range SAT Critical Reading	460–560
Range SAT Math	470–580
Range SAT Writing	470–580
Range ACT Composite	19–24
Minimum paper TOEFL	550
Minimum computer TOEFL	213
Minimum web-based TOEFL	80
Average HS GPA	3.27
% graduated top 10% of class	16
% graduated top 25% of class	45
% graduated top 50% of class	79

DEADLINES
Early decision

Deadline	11/15
Notification	12/15

Early action

Deadline	11/15
Notification	12/15

Regular

Priority	1/15
Notification	rolling
Nonfall registration?	yes

FINANCIAL FACTS

Annual tuition	$28,470
Room and board	$10,720
Required fees	$590
Books and supplies	$1,500
% frosh rec. need-based scholarship or grant aid	76
% UG rec. need-based scholarship or grant aid	68
% frosh rec. non-need-based scholarship or grant aid	14
% UG rec. non-need-based scholarship or grant aid	11
% frosh rec. need-based self-help aid	57
% UG rec. need-based self-help aid	51
% frosh rec. athletic scholarships	7
% UG rec. athletic scholarships	6
% frosh rec. any financial aid	77
% UG rec. any financial aid	70
% UG borrow to pay for school	72
Average cumulative indebtedness	$35,042

ROBERTS WESLEYAN COLLEGE

CAMPUS LIFE

Fire Safety Rating	**60***
Green Rating	**60***
Type of school	private
Environment	city

STUDENTS

Total undergrad enrollment	1,388
% male/female	31/69
% from out of state	8
% live on campus	62
% African American	10
% Asian	1
% Caucasian	78
% Hispanic	4
% international	1
# of countries represented	18

ACADEMICS

Calendar	semester
Student/faculty ratio	11:1
Profs interesting rating	89
Profs accessible rating	85
Most common reg class size	10–19 students
Most common lab size	10–19 students

MOST POPULAR MAJORS
elementary education and teaching
music teacher education
nursing

SELECTIVITY

# of applicants	1,358
% of applicants accepted	65
% of acceptees attending	30

FRESHMAN PROFILE

Range SAT Critical Reading	470–590
Range SAT Math	480–610
Range SAT Writing	450–560
Range ACT Composite	21–27
Minimum paper TOEFL	550
Minimum computer TOEFL	213
Minimum web-based TOEFL	79
Average HS GPA	3.3
% graduated top 10% of class	28
% graduated top 25% of class	56
% graduated top 50% of class	80

DEADLINES

Regular	
Priority	2/1
Notification	rolling
Nonfall registration?	yes

FINANCIAL FACTS

Annual tuition	$22,580
Room and board	$8,520
Required fees	$866
Books and supplies	$1,000
% frosh rec. need-based scholarship or grant aid	83
% UG rec. need-based scholarship or grant aid	82
% frosh rec. non-need-based scholarship or grant aid	5
% UG rec. non-need-based scholarship or grant aid	4
% frosh rec. need-based self-help aid	77
% UG rec. need-based self-help aid	78
% frosh rec. athletic scholarships	3
% UG rec. athletic scholarships	2
% frosh rec. any financial aid	97
% UG rec. any financial aid	92
% UG borrow to pay for school	96
Average cumulative indebtedness	$22,619

ROCHESTER INSTITUTE OF TECHNOLOGY

CAMPUS LIFE

Fire Safety Rating	**60***
Green Rating	**96**
Type of school	private
Environment	city

STUDENTS

Total undergrad enrollment	13,258
% male/female	67/33
% from out of state	50
% from public high school	85
% live on campus	68
# of fraternities	19
# of sororities	10
# of countries represented	102

ACADEMICS

Calendar	quarter
Student/faculty ratio	14:1
Profs interesting rating	70
Profs accessible rating	75
Most common reg class size	10–19 students
Most common lab size	10–19 students

MOST POPULAR MAJORS
engineering
information technology
photography

SELECTIVITY

# of applicants	12,994
% of applicants accepted	61
% of acceptees attending	33
# accepting a place on wait list	344
% admitted from wait list	100
# of early decision applicants	1,461
% accepted early decision	66

FRESHMAN PROFILE

Range SAT Critical Reading	530–640
Range SAT Math	560–670
Range SAT Writing	520–620
Range ACT Composite	25–30
Minimum paper TOEFL	550
Minimum computer TOEFL	215
Minimum web-based TOEFL	79
% graduated top 10% of class	33
% graduated top 25% of class	67
% graduated top 50% of class	92

DEADLINES

Early decision	
Deadline	12/1
Notification	1/15

Regular	
Priority	2/1
Deadline	2/1
Notification	rolling
Nonfall registration?	yes

FINANCIAL FACTS

Annual tuition	$30,282
Room and board	$10,044
Required fees	$435
Books and supplies	$1,050
% frosh rec. need-based scholarship or grant aid	71
% UG rec. need-based scholarship or grant aid	65
% frosh rec. non-need-based scholarship or grant aid	20
% UG rec. non-need-based scholarship or grant aid	20
% frosh rec. need-based self-help aid	64
% UG rec. need-based self-help aid	61
% frosh rec. any financial aid	88
% UG rec. any financial aid	80
% UG borrow to pay for school	77
Average cumulative indebtedness	$23,800

ROGER WILLIAMS UNIVERSITY

CAMPUS LIFE

Fire Safety Rating	**88**
Green Rating	**91**
Type of school	private
Environment	village

STUDENTS

Total undergrad enrollment	4,267
% male/female	51/49
% from out of state	82
% from public high school	85
% live on campus	66
% African American	2
% Asian	1
% Caucasian	87
% Hispanic	4
% international	2
# of countries represented	47

ACADEMICS

Calendar	semester
Student/faculty ratio	12:1
Profs interesting rating	72
Profs accessible rating	75
Most common reg class size	10–19 students
Most common lab size	10–19 students

MOST POPULAR MAJORS
architecture (BArch, BA/BS, MArch,
MA/MS, PhD)
business/commerce
psychology

SELECTIVITY
# of applicants	8,220
% of applicants accepted	77
% of acceptees attending	17

FRESHMAN PROFILE
Range SAT Critical Reading	495–580
Range SAT Math	510–600
Range SAT Writing	480–580
Range ACT Composite	21–25
Average HS GPA	3.17
% graduated top 10% of class	15
% graduated top 25% of class	39
% graduated top 50% of class	76

DEADLINES
Early action	
Deadline	11/1
Notification	1/15
Regular	
Priority	2/1
Deadline	2/1
Notification	3/15
Nonfall registration?	yes

FINANCIAL FACTS
Annual tuition	$27,840
Room and board	$12,740
Required fees	$1,878
Books and supplies	$900
% frosh rec. need-based scholarship or grant aid	31
% UG rec. need-based scholarship or grant aid	35
% frosh rec. non-need-based scholarship or grant aid	60
% UG rec. non-need-based scholarship or grant aid	39
% frosh rec. need-based self-help aid	45
% UG rec. need-based self-help aid	47
% frosh rec. any financial aid	91
% UG rec. any financial aid	84
% UG borrow to pay for school	71
Average cumulative indebtedness	$32,856

ROSEMONT COLLEGE

CAMPUS LIFE
Fire Safety Rating	**81**
Green Rating	**76**
Type of school	private
Affiliation	Roman Catholic
Environment	village

STUDENTS
Total undergrad enrollment	556
% male/female	20/80
% from out of state	21
% from public high school	61
% live on campus	70
% African American	47
% Asian	5
% Caucasian	33
% Hispanic	8
% international	1
# of countries represented	14

ACADEMICS
Calendar	semester
Student/faculty ratio	10:1
Profs interesting rating	85
Profs accessible rating	87
Most common reg class size	10–19 students

MOST POPULAR MAJORS
art/art studies
biology/biological sciences
social services

SELECTIVITY
# of applicants	1,104
% of applicants accepted	54
% of acceptees attending	30

FRESHMAN PROFILE
Range SAT Critical Reading	430–573
Range SAT Math	418–520
Range SAT Writing	435–555
Minimum paper TOEFL	500
Minimum computer TOEFL	213
Average HS GPA	3
% graduated top 10% of class	25
% graduated top 25% of class	45
% graduated top 50% of class	70

DEADLINES
Regular	
Priority	8/1
Deadline	8/1
Notification	rolling
Nonfall registration?	yes

FINANCIAL FACTS
% frosh rec. need-based scholarship or grant aid	94
% UG rec. need-based scholarship or grant aid	92
% frosh rec. non-need-based scholarship or grant aid	7
% UG rec. non-need-based scholarship or grant aid	6
% frosh rec. need-based self-help aid	92
% UG rec. need-based self-help aid	89
% frosh rec. any financial aid	99
% UG rec. any financial aid	98
% UG borrow to pay for school	86
Average cumulative indebtedness	$21,338

ROWAN UNIVERSITY

CAMPUS LIFE
Fire Safety Rating	**86**
Green Rating	**90**
Type of school	public
Environment	town

STUDENTS
Total undergrad enrollment	9,282
% male/female	48/52
% from out of state	2
% live on campus	34
# of fraternities	10
# of sororities	10
% African American	9
% Asian	4
% Caucasian	77
% Hispanic	7
# of countries represented	17

ACADEMICS
Calendar	semester
Student/faculty ratio	15:1
Profs interesting rating	69
Profs accessible rating	69
Most common reg class size	20–29 students

MOST POPULAR MAJORS
criminal justice/police science
elementary education and teaching
multi-/interdisciplinary studies

SELECTIVITY
# of applicants	7,696
% of applicants accepted	66
% of acceptees attending	32

FRESHMAN PROFILE
Range SAT Critical Reading	470–570
Range SAT Math	490–600
Range SAT Writing	470–570
Minimum paper TOEFL	550
Minimum computer TOEFL	213
Minimum web-based TOEFL	79
Average HS GPA	3.35

% graduated top 10% of class	16
% graduated top 25% of class	45
% graduated top 50% of class	86

DEADLINES
Regular
Priority	1/1
Deadline	3/1
Notification	rolling
Nonfall registration?	yes

FINANCIAL FACTS
Annual in-state tuition	$8,074
Annual out-of-state tuition	$15,148
Room and board	$9,958
Required fees	$3,160
Books and supplies	$1,500
% frosh rec. need-based scholarship or grant aid	19
% UG rec. need-based scholarship or grant aid	28
% frosh rec. non-need-based scholarship or grant aid	11
% UG rec. non-need-based scholarship or grant aid	8
% frosh rec. need-based self-help aid	43
% UG rec. need-based self-help aid	49
% frosh rec. any financial aid	81
% UG rec. any financial aid	61
% UG borrow to pay for school	73
Average cumulative indebtedness	$26,092

RUTGERS, THE STATE UNIVERSITY OF NEW JERSEY—NEW BRUNSWICK

CAMPUS LIFE
Fire Safety Rating	**78**
Green Rating	**60***
Type of school	public
Environment	town

STUDENTS
Total undergrad enrollment	28,817
% male/female	52/48
% from out of state	7
% live on campus	50
# of fraternities	29
# of sororities	15
% African American	8
% Asian	25
% Caucasian	51
% Hispanic	10
% international	2
# of countries represented	117

ACADEMICS
Calendar	semester
Student/faculty ratio	14:1
Profs interesting rating	61
Profs accessible rating	61
% classes taught by TAs	20

MOST POPULAR MAJORS
biology/biological sciences
engineering

SELECTIVITY
Admissions Rating	**87**
# of applicants	28,624
% of applicants accepted	61
% of acceptees attending	27

FRESHMAN PROFILE
Range SAT Critical Reading	530–630
Range SAT Math	560–680
Range SAT Writing	540–640
Minimum paper TOEFL	550
Minimum computer TOEFL	213
% graduated top 10% of class	42
% graduated top 25% of class	38
% graduated top 50% of class	18

DEADLINES
Regular
Priority	12/1
Notification	3/1
Nonfall registration?	yes

FINANCIAL FACTS
Annual in-state tuition	$9,546
Annual out-of-state tuition	$20,178
Room and board	$10,676
Required fees	$2,340
Books and supplies	$1,431
% frosh rec. need-based scholarship or grant aid	27
% UG rec. need-based scholarship or grant aid	31
% frosh rec. non-need-based scholarship or grant aid	27
% UG rec. non-need-based scholarship or grant aid	26
% frosh rec. need-based self-help aid	38
% UG rec. need-based self-help aid	43
% frosh rec. athletic scholarships	1
% UG rec. athletic scholarships	1
% frosh rec. any financial aid	67
% UG rec. any financial aid	69
% UG borrow to pay for school	74
Average cumulative indebtedness	$16,300

SACRED HEART UNIVERSITY

CAMPUS LIFE
Fire Safety Rating	**80**
Green Rating	**70**
Type of school	private
Affiliation	Roman Catholic
Environment	town

STUDENTS
Total undergrad enrollment	4,123
% male/female	39/61
% from out of state	68
% from public high school	70
% live on campus	60
# of fraternities	4
# of sororities	6
% African American	4
% Asian	2
% Caucasian	80
% Hispanic	7
% international	1
# of countries represented	34

ACADEMICS
Calendar	semester
Student/faculty ratio	13:1
Profs interesting rating	78
Profs accessible rating	79
Most common reg class size	20–29 students

MOST POPULAR MAJORS
business/commerce
nursing (BSN)
psychology
exercise science

SELECTIVITY
# of applicants	7,343
% of applicants accepted	66
% of acceptees attending	19
# of early decision applicants	167
% accepted early decision	71

FRESHMAN PROFILE
Range SAT Critical Reading	460–570
Range SAT Math	490–580
Minimum paper TOEFL	550
Minimum computer TOEFL	213
Minimum web-based TOEFL	70
Average HS GPA	3.3
% graduated top 10% of class	18
% graduated top 25% of class	54
% graduated top 50% of class	83

DEADLINES
Early decision
Deadline	12/1
Notification	12/15

Regular
  Priority   1/15
  Notification   rolling
Nonfall registration?   yes

FINANCIAL FACTS
Annual tuition $30,090
Room and board $11,860
Required fees $208
Books and supplies $1,000
% frosh rec. need-based
  scholarship or grant aid   70
% UG rec. need-based
  scholarship or grant aid   68
% frosh rec. non-need-based
  scholarship or grant aid   7
% UG rec. non-need-based
  scholarship or grant aid   5
% frosh rec. need-based
  self-help aid   59
% UG rec. need-based
  self-help aid   59
% frosh rec. athletic scholarships   7
% UG rec. athletic scholarships   6
% frosh rec. any financial aid   70
% UG rec. any financial aid   70
Average cumulative
  indebtedness $18,819

SAINT ANSELM COLLEGE

CAMPUS LIFE
Fire Safety Rating   **60***
Green Rating   **60***
Type of school   private
Affiliation   Roman Catholic
Environment   city

STUDENTS
Total undergrad enrollment   1,889
% male/female   43/57
% from out of state   79
% from public high school   65
% live on campus   91
% African American   1
% Asian   1
% Caucasian   87
% Hispanic   2
% Native American   1
# of countries represented   20

ACADEMICS
Calendar   semester
Student/faculty ratio   11:1
Profs interesting rating   89
Profs accessible rating   87
Most common
  reg class size   10–19 students
Most common
  lab size   10–19 students

SELECTIVITY
of applicants   3,664
% of applicants accepted   77
% of acceptees attending   19
# accepting a place on wait list   356
% admitted from wait list   49
# of early decision applicants   82
% accepted early decision   71

FRESHMAN PROFILE
Range SAT Critical Reading   500–590
Range SAT Math   510–580
Range SAT Writing   490–590
Range ACT Composite   20–26
Minimum paper TOEFL   550
Minimum computer TOEFL   213
Minimum web-based TOEFL   80
Average HS GPA   3.13

DEADLINES
Early decision
  Deadline   11/15
  Notification   12/1
Early action
  Deadline   11/15
  Notification   1/15
Regular
  Priority   3/1
  Deadline   3/1
  Notification   rolling
Nonfall registration?   yes

FINANCIAL FACTS
Annual tuition $29,720
Room and board $11,240
Required fees $795
% frosh rec. need-based
  scholarship or grant aid   74
% UG rec. need-based
  scholarship or grant aid   72
% frosh rec. non-need-based
  scholarship or grant aid   7
% UG rec. non-need-based
  scholarship or grant aid   6
% frosh rec. need-based
  self-help aid   65
% UG rec. need-based
  self-help aid   65
% frosh rec. athletic scholarships   1
% UG rec. athletic scholarships   1
% UG borrow to pay for school   75
Average cumulative
  indebtedness $36,823

SAINT JOSEPH'S UNIVERSITY
(PA)

CAMPUS LIFE
Fire Safety Rating   **98**
Green Rating   **78**
Type of school   private
Affiliation   Roman Catholic-Jesuit
Environment   metropolis

STUDENTS
Total undergrad enrollment   5,188
% male/female   48/52
% from out of state   52
% from public high school   49
% live on campus   59
# of fraternities   4
# of sororities   4
% African American   7
% Asian   2
% Caucasian   82
% Hispanic   4
% international   1
# of countries represented   56

ACADEMICS
Calendar   semester
Student/faculty ratio   14:1
Profs interesting rating   85
Profs accessible rating   87
Most common reg class size 20–29 students
Most common lab size   10–19 students

MOST POPULAR MAJORS
accounting
finance
marketing/marketing management

SELECTIVITY
of applicants   6,520
% of applicants accepted   82
% of acceptees attending   22
# accepting a place on wait list   234
% admitted from wait list   49

FRESHMAN PROFILE
Range SAT Critical Reading   510–600
Range SAT Math   510–620
Range SAT Writing   510–610
Range ACT Composite   21–26
Minimum paper TOEFL   550
Minimum computer TOEFL   213
Minimum web-based TOEFL   79
Average HS GPA   3.39
% graduated top 10% of class   23
% graduated top 25% of class   55
% graduated top 50% of class   86

DEADLINES
Early action
| Deadline | 11/15 |
| Notification | 12/25 |

Regular
Deadline	2/1
Notification	3/15
Nonfall registration?	yes

FINANCIAL FACTS
Annual tuition	$33,940
Room and board	$11,575
Required fees	$150
Books and supplies	$1,500
% frosh rec. need-based scholarship or grant aid	54
% UG rec. need-based scholarship or grant aid	48
% frosh rec. non-need-based scholarship or grant aid	51
% UG rec. non-need-based scholarship or grant aid	46
% frosh rec. need-based self-help aid	37
% UG rec. need-based self-help aid	37
% frosh rec. athletic scholarships	2
% UG rec. athletic scholarships	3
% frosh rec. any financial aid	93
% UG rec. any financial aid	91

SAINT MICHAEL'S COLLEGE

CAMPUS LIFE
Fire Safety Rating	**74**
Green Rating	**85**
Type of school	private
Affiliation	Roman Catholic
Environment	city

STUDENTS
Total undergrad enrollment	1,915
% male/female	48/52
% from out of state	81
% from public high school	69
% African American	1
% Asian	1
% Caucasian	93
% Hispanic	2
% international	2
# of countries represented	30

ACADEMICS
Calendar	semester
Student/faculty ratio	12:1
Profs interesting rating	90
Profs accessible rating	92
Most common reg class size	10–19 students
Most common lab size	20–29 students

MOST POPULAR MAJORS
biology/biological sciences
business/commerce
psychology

SELECTIVITY
# of applicants	3,228
% of applicants accepted	81
% of acceptees attending	18
# accepting a place on wait list	129
% admitted from wait list	73

FRESHMAN PROFILE
Range SAT Critical Reading	520–630
Range SAT Math	520–620
Range SAT Writing	510–620
Range ACT Composite	22–27
Minimum paper TOEFL	550
Minimum computer TOEFL	213
Average HS GPA	3.44
% graduated top 10% of class	24
% graduated top 25% of class	54
% graduated top 50% of class	81

DEADLINES
Regular
Priority	11/1
Deadline	2/1
Notification	4/1
Nonfall registration?	yes

FINANCIAL FACTS
Annual tuition	$34,555
% frosh rec. need-based scholarship or grant aid	66
% UG rec. need-based scholarship or grant aid	60
% frosh rec. non-need-based scholarship or grant aid	12
% UG rec. non-need-based scholarship or grant aid	8
% frosh rec. need-based self-help aid	55
% UG rec. need-based self-help aid	52
% UG rec. athletic scholarships	1
% frosh rec. any financial aid	96
% UG rec. any financial aid	93
% UG borrow to pay for school	76
Average cumulative indebtedness	$30,742

SALISBURY UNIVERSITY

CAMPUS LIFE
Fire Safety Rating	**70**
Green Rating	**87**
Type of school	public
Environment	town

STUDENTS
Total undergrad enrollment	7,285
% male/female	45/55
% from out of state	12
% live on campus	36
# of fraternities	8
# of sororities	4
% African American	11
% Asian	3
% Caucasian	82
% Hispanic	3
% Native American	1
% international	1
# of countries represented	54

ACADEMICS
Calendar	4/1/4
Student/faculty ratio	17:1
Profs interesting rating	72
Profs accessible rating	75
Most common reg class size	20–29 students
Most common lab size	20–29 students

MOST POPULAR MAJORS
biology/biological sciences
business administration and management
communication studies/
speech communication and rhetoric

SELECTIVITY
# of applicants	7,525
% of applicants accepted	54
% of acceptees attending	32

FRESHMAN PROFILE
Range SAT Critical Reading	520–600
Range SAT Math	520–620
Range SAT Writing	530–600
Range ACT Composite	21–26
Minimum paper TOEFL	550
Minimum computer TOEFL	213
Average HS GPA	3.59
% graduated top 10% of class	23
% graduated top 25% of class	58
% graduated top 50% of class	91

DEADLINES
Early action
| Deadline | 12/1 |
| Notification | 1/15 |

Regular
Priority	1/15
Notification	3/15
Nonfall registration?	yes

FINANCIAL FACTS
Annual in-state tuition	$4,814
Annual out-of-state tuition	$13,310
Room and board	$8,070

Required fees	$1,804
Books and supplies	$1,300
% frosh rec. need-based scholarship or grant aid	35
% UG rec. need-based scholarship or grant aid	31
% frosh rec. need-based self-help aid	30
% UG rec. need-based self-help aid	33
% frosh rec. any financial aid	79
% UG rec. any financial aid	73
% UG borrow to pay for school	56
Average cumulative indebtedness	$17,521

SALVE REGINA UNIVERSITY

CAMPUS LIFE

Fire Safety Rating	**86**
Green Rating	**78**
Type of school	private
Affiliation	Roman Catholic
Environment	town

STUDENTS

Total undergrad enrollment	1,976
% male/female	31/69
% from out of state	84
% from public high school	65
% live on campus	60
% African American	2
% Asian	1
% Caucasian	77
% Hispanic	3
% Native American	1
% international	1
# of countries represented	17

ACADEMICS

Calendar	semester
Student/faculty ratio	14:1
Profs interesting rating	72
Profs accessible rating	77
Most common reg class size	10–19 students
Most common lab size	20–29 students

MOST POPULAR MAJORS
criminal justice/law enforcement administration
elementary education and teaching
nursing/registered nurse
(RN, ASN, BSN, MSN)

SELECTIVITY

# of applicants	5,256
% of applicants accepted	64
% of acceptees attending	15

FRESHMAN PROFILE

Range SAT Critical Reading	500–585
Range SAT Math	500–590
Range SAT Writing	500–590
Range ACT Composite	22–26
Minimum paper TOEFL	500
Minimum computer TOEFL	173
Minimum web-based TOEFL	61
Average HS GPA	3.34
% graduated top 10% of class	21
% graduated top 25% of class	57
% graduated top 50% of class	88

DEADLINES

Early action	
Deadline	11/1
Notification	12/25
Regular	
Priority	2/1
Notification	rolling
Nonfall registration?	yes

FINANCIAL FACTS

Books and supplies	$900
% frosh rec. need-based scholarship or grant aid	75
% UG rec. need-based scholarship or grant aid	68
% frosh rec. non-need-based scholarship or grant aid	4
% UG rec. non-need-based scholarship or grant aid	2
% frosh rec. need-based self-help aid	73
% UG rec. need-based self-help aid	68
% frosh rec. any financial aid	68
% UG rec. any financial aid	71
% UG borrow to pay for school	80.93
Average cumulative indebtedness	$35,394

SARAH LAWRENCE COLLEGE

CAMPUS LIFE

Fire Safety Rating	**90**
Green Rating	**81**
Type of school	private
Environment	metropolis

STUDENTS

Total undergrad enrollment	1,295
% male/female	27/73
% from out of state	77
% from public high school	51
% live on campus	83
% African American	3
% Asian	5
% Caucasian	58
% Hispanic	5

% international	3
# of countries represented	32

ACADEMICS

Calendar	semester
Student/faculty ratio	9:1
Profs interesting rating	97
Profs accessible rating	89
Most common reg class size	10–19 students

SELECTIVITY

Admissions Rating	**90**
# of applicants	2,126
% of applicants accepted	58
% of acceptees attending	29
# of early decision applicants	151
% accepted early decision	63

FRESHMAN PROFILE

Minimum paper TOEFL	600
Minimum computer TOEFL	250
Average HS GPA	3.6
% graduated top 10% of class	46
% graduated top 25% of class	79
% graduated top 50% of class	97

DEADLINES

Early decision	
Deadline	11/1
Notification	12/15
Regular	
Deadline	1/1
Notification	4/1
Nonfall registration?	no

FINANCIAL FACTS

Annual tuition	$41,040
Room and board	$13,820
Required fees	$928
Books and supplies	$600
% frosh rec. need-based scholarship or grant aid	61
% UG rec. need-based scholarship or grant aid	54
% frosh rec. need-based self-help aid	59
% UG rec. need-based self-help aid	56
% frosh rec. any financial aid	65
% UG rec. any financial aid	58
% UG borrow to pay for school	52
Average cumulative indebtedness	$17,246

SETON HALL UNIVERSITY

CAMPUS LIFE

Fire Safety Rating	**81**
Green Rating	**60***
Type of school	private
Affiliation	Roman Catholic
Environment	village

STUDENTS

Total undergrad enrollment	4,972
% male/female	42/58
% from out of state	25
% from public high school	70
% live on campus	43
% African American	14
% Asian	7
% Caucasian	53
% Hispanic	12
% international	2
# of countries represented	54

ACADEMICS

Calendar	semester
Student/faculty ratio	14:1
Profs interesting rating	76
Profs accessible rating	72
% classes taught by TAs	4
Most common reg class size	10–19 students
Most common lab size	10–19 students

MOST POPULAR MAJORS
biology
communication
nursing

SELECTIVITY

# of applicants	10,851
% of applicants accepted	79
% of acceptees attending	13

FRESHMAN PROFILE

Range SAT Critical Reading	470–570
Range SAT Math	470–580
Minimum paper TOEFL	550
Minimum computer TOEFL	213
Average HS GPA	3.13
% graduated top 10% of class	22
% graduated top 25% of class	50
% graduated top 50% of class	83

DEADLINES

Regular Priority	3/1
Notification	rolling
Nonfall registration?	yes

FINANCIAL FACTS

Annual tuition	$29,940
Room and board	$12,050
Required fees	$1,950
% frosh rec. need-based scholarship or grant aid	54
% UG rec. need-based scholarship or grant aid	38
% frosh rec. non-need-based scholarship or grant aid	47
% UG rec. non-need-based scholarship or grant aid	33
% frosh rec. need-based self-help aid	45
% UG rec. need-based self-help aid	45
% frosh rec. athletic scholarships	4
% UG rec. athletic scholarships	4
% frosh rec. any financial aid	91
% UG rec. any financial aid	86
% UG borrow to pay for school	6
Average cumulative indebtedness	$16,160

SETON HILL UNIVERSITY

CAMPUS LIFE

Fire Safety Rating	**76**
Green Rating	**60***
Type of school	private
Affiliation	Roman Catholic
Environment	town

STUDENTS

Total undergrad enrollment	1,483
% male/female	38/62
% from out of state	20
% live on campus	56
% African American	9
% Asian	1
% Caucasian	82
% Hispanic	1
% international	2
# of countries represented	23

ACADEMICS

Calendar	semester
Student/faculty ratio	15:1
Profs interesting rating	74
Profs accessible rating	74
Most common reg class size	10–19 students

MOST POPULAR MAJORS
business/commerce
fine/studio arts
psychology

SELECTIVITY

# of applicants	1,729
% of applicants accepted	66
% of acceptees attending	26

FRESHMAN PROFILE

Range SAT Critical Reading	420–540
Range SAT Math	430–560
Range SAT Writing	420–540
Range ACT Composite	17–24
Minimum paper TOEFL	600
Minimum computer TOEFL	250
Minimum web-based TOEFL	100
Average HS GPA	3.24
% graduated top 10% of class	18
% graduated top 25% of class	44
% graduated top 50% of class	71

DEADLINES

Regular Priority	5/1
Deadline	8/15
Notification	rolling
Nonfall registration?	yes

FINANCIAL FACTS

% frosh rec. need-based scholarship or grant aid	79
% UG rec. need-based scholarship or grant aid	78
% frosh rec. non-need-based scholarship or grant aid	12
% UG rec. non-need-based scholarship or grant aid	10
% frosh rec. need-based self-help aid	65
% UG rec. need-based self-help aid	65
% frosh rec. athletic scholarships	10
% UG rec. athletic scholarships	8
% frosh rec. any financial aid	98
% UG rec. any financial aid	90
% UG borrow to pay for school	91
Average cumulative indebtedness	$25,807

SIENA COLLEGE

CAMPUS LIFE

Fire Safety Rating	**60***
Green Rating	**60***
Type of school	private
Affiliation	Roman Catholic
Environment	town

STUDENTS

Total undergrad enrollment	3,220
% male/female	47/53
% from out of state	16
% live on campus	76
% African American	2
% Asian	3
% Caucasian	81
% Hispanic	4
# of countries represented	6

ACADEMICS

Calendar	semester
Student/faculty ratio	13:1
Profs interesting rating	82
Profs accessible rating	86
Most common reg class size	20–29 students
Most common lab size	10–19 students

MOST POPULAR MAJORS
finance
marketing/marketing management
psychology

SELECTIVITY

# of applicants	7,282
% of applicants accepted	53
% of acceptees attending	20
# accepting a place on wait list	341
% admitted from wait list	7
# of early decision applicants	160
% accepted early decision	34

FRESHMAN PROFILE

Range SAT Critical Reading	500–600
Range SAT Math	530–630
Range SAT Writing	500–600
Range ACT Composite	22–27
Minimum paper TOEFL	550
Minimum computer TOEFL	213
Minimum web-based TOEFL	79
% graduated top 10% of class	28
% graduated top 25% of class	61
% graduated top 50% of class	93

DEADLINES

Early decision	
Deadline	12/1
Notification	12/15
Early action	
Deadline	12/1
Notification	1/1
Regular	
Priority	3/1
Deadline	3/1
Notification	3/15
Nonfall registration?	yes

FINANCIAL FACTS

Annual tuition	$26,500
Room and board	$10,375
Required fees	$225
Books and supplies	$1,080
% frosh rec. need-based scholarship or grant aid	68
% UG rec. need-based scholarship or grant aid	65
% frosh rec. non-need-based scholarship or grant aid	48
% UG rec. non-need-based scholarship or grant aid	44
% frosh rec. need-based self-help aid	53
% UG rec. need-based self-help aid	53
% frosh rec. athletic scholarships	9
% UG rec. athletic scholarships	8
% frosh rec. any financial aid	96
% UG rec. any financial aid	95

SIMMONS COLLEGE

CAMPUS LIFE

Fire Safety Rating	**90**
Green Rating	**85**
Type of school	private
Environment	city

STUDENTS

Total undergrad enrollment	1,934
% male/female	0/100
% from out of state	39
% live on campus	48
% African American	6
% Asian	7
% Caucasian	69
% Hispanic	4
% international	3
# of countries represented	46

ACADEMICS

Calendar	semester
Student/faculty ratio	13:1
Profs interesting rating	84
Profs accessible rating	83
Most common reg class size	10–19 students

MOST POPULAR MAJORS
nursing/registered nurse
(RN, ASN, BSN, MSN)
psychology

SELECTIVITY

# of applicants	3,522
% of applicants accepted	57
% of acceptees attending	18

FRESHMAN PROFILE

Range SAT Critical Reading	500–590
Range SAT Math	490–600
Range SAT Writing	510–610
Range ACT Composite	22–26
Minimum paper TOEFL	560
Minimum computer TOEFL	220
Minimum web-based TOEFL	83
Average HS GPA	3.15
% graduated top 10% of class	19
% graduated top 25% of class	55
% graduated top 50% of class	89

DEADLINES

Early action	
Deadline	12/1
Notification	1/20
Regular	
Deadline	2/1
Notification	4/15
Nonfall registration?	yes

FINANCIAL FACTS

Annual tuition	$30,520
Room and board	$12,050
Required fees	$930
Books and supplies	$1,280
% frosh rec. need-based scholarship or grant aid	78
% UG rec. need-based scholarship or grant aid	70
% frosh rec. non-need-based scholarship or grant aid	4
% UG rec. non-need-based scholarship or grant aid	3
% frosh rec. need-based self-help aid	73
% UG rec. need-based self-help aid	67
% frosh rec. any financial aid	94
% UG rec. any financial aid	85
% UG borrow to pay for school	78
Average cumulative indebtedness	$45,237

SKIDMORE COLLEGE

CAMPUS LIFE

Fire Safety Rating	**60***
Green Rating	**60***
Type of school	private
Environment	town

STUDENTS

Total undergrad enrollment	2,632
% male/female	40/60
% from out of state	67
% from public high school	61
% live on campus	85
% African American	4
% Asian	9
% Caucasian	67
% Hispanic	5
% Native American	1
% international	3
# of countries represented	48

ACADEMICS

Calendar	semester
Student/faculty ratio	9:1
Profs interesting rating	91
Profs accessible rating	97
Most common reg class size	10–19 students
Most common lab size	10–19 students

MOST POPULAR MAJORS
business/commerce
English language and literature
psychology

SELECTIVITY

# of applicants	6,371
% of applicants accepted	41
% of acceptees attending	25
# accepting a place on wait list	334
% admitted from wait list	20
# of early decision applicants	414
% accepted early decision	71

FRESHMAN PROFILE

Range SAT Critical Reading	570–680
Range SAT Math	580–670
Range SAT Writing	580–680
Range ACT Composite	26–30
Minimum paper TOEFL	NA
Minimum computer TOEFL	NA
Minimum web-based TOEFL	53

Average HS GPA	3.355
% graduated top 10% of class	39
% graduated top 25% of class	74
% graduated top 50% of class	94

DEADLINES
Early decision

Deadline	11/15
Notification	12/15
Regular	
Deadline	1/15
Notification	4/1
Nonfall registration?	no

FINANCIAL FACTS

Annual tuition	$39,600
Room and board	$10,776
Required fees	$820
Books and supplies	$1,304
% frosh rec. need-based scholarship or grant aid	40
% UG rec. need-based scholarship or grant aid	42
% frosh rec. non-need-based scholarship or grant aid	10
% UG rec. non-need-based scholarship or grant aid	9
% frosh rec. need-based self-help aid	37
% UG rec. need-based self-help aid	38
% frosh rec. any financial aid	40
% UG rec. any financial aid	42
% UG borrow to pay for school	51
Average cumulative indebtedness	$18,303

SLIPPERY ROCK UNIVERSITY OF PENNSYLVANIA

CAMPUS LIFE

Fire Safety Rating	**98**
Green Rating	**78**
Type of school	public
Environment	rural

STUDENTS

Total undergrad enrollment	7,703
% male/female	44/56
% from out of state	9
% from public high school	80
% live on campus	36
# of fraternities	9
# of sororities	8
% African American	5
% Asian	1
% Caucasian	85
% Hispanic	1
% international	1
# of countries represented	38

ACADEMICS

Calendar	semester
Student/faculty ratio	20:1
Profs interesting rating	69
Profs accessible rating	73
Most common reg class size	20–29 students
Most common lab size	fewer than 10 students

MOST POPULAR MAJORS
business administration and management
elementary education and teaching
kinesiology and exercise science

SELECTIVITY

# of applicants	5,928
% of applicants accepted	63
% of acceptees attending	42
# accepting a place on wait list	1,279
% admitted from wait list	36

FRESHMAN PROFILE

Range SAT Critical Reading	460–550
Range SAT Math	470–560
Range SAT Writing	450–540
Range ACT Composite	19–24
Minimum paper TOEFL	500
Minimum computer TOEFL	173
Average HS GPA	3.39
% graduated top 10% of class	12
% graduated top 25% of class	42
% graduated top 50% of class	84

DEADLINES

Regular	
Notification	rolling
Nonfall registration?	yes

FINANCIAL FACTS

Annual in-state tuition	$5,554
Annual out-of-state tuition	$8,331
Room and board	$8,454
Required fees	$1,681
Books and supplies	$1,363
% frosh rec. need-based scholarship or grant aid	49
% UG rec. need-based scholarship or grant aid	45
% frosh rec. non-need-based scholarship or grant aid	29
% UG rec. non-need-based scholarship or grant aid	18
% frosh rec. need-based self-help aid	66
% UG rec. need-based self-help aid	61
% frosh rec. athletic scholarships	4
% UG rec. athletic scholarships	3
% frosh rec. any financial aid	93
% UG rec. any financial aid	85

% UG borrow to pay for school	81
Average cumulative indebtedness	$23,879

SMITH COLLEGE

CAMPUS LIFE

Fire Safety Rating	**71**
Green Rating	**96**
Type of school	private
Environment	town

STUDENTS

Total undergrad enrollment	2,614
% male/female	0/100
% from out of state	78
% from public high school	67
% live on campus	94
% African American	7
% Asian	13
% Caucasian	41
% Hispanic	7
% Native American	1
% international	8
# of countries represented	72

ACADEMICS

Calendar	semester
Student/faculty ratio	9:1
Profs interesting rating	93
Profs accessible rating	89
Most common reg class size	10–19 students

MOST POPULAR MAJORS
economics
political science and government
psychology

SELECTIVITY

# of applicants	4,011
% of applicants accepted	47
% of acceptees attending	35
# accepting a place on wait list	312
% admitted from wait list	31
# of early decision applicants	297
% accepted early decision	56

FRESHMAN PROFILE

Range SAT Critical Reading	610–710
Range SAT Math	580–690
Range SAT Writing	610–710
Range ACT Composite	27–30
Minimum paper TOEFL	600
Minimum computer TOEFL	250
Minimum web-based TOEFL	95
Average HS GPA	3.9
% graduated top 10% of class	66
% graduated top 25% of class	94
% graduated top 50% of class	100

DEADLINES
Early decision
Deadline 11/15
Notification 12/15
Regular
Deadline 1/15
Notification 4/1
Nonfall registration? no

FINANCIAL FACTS
Annual tuition $38,640
% frosh rec. need-based
scholarship or grant aid 57
% UG rec. need-based
scholarship or grant aid 60
% frosh rec. non-need-based
scholarship or grant aid 5
% UG rec. non-need-based
scholarship or grant aid 5
% frosh rec. need-based
self-help aid 59
% UG rec. need-based
self-help aid 62
% frosh rec. any financial aid 70
% UG rec. any financial aid 72
% UG borrow to pay for school 62
Average cumulative
indebtedness $21,573

ST. BONAVENTURE UNIVERSITY

CAMPUS LIFE
Fire Safety Rating **60***
Green Rating **60***
Type of school private
Affiliation Roman Catholic
Environment village

STUDENTS
Total undergrad enrollment 1,905
% male/female 50/50
% from out of state 24
% from public high school 70
% live on campus 77
% African American 4
% Asian 2
% Caucasian 18
% Hispanic 2
% international 2
# of countries represented 24

ACADEMICS
Calendar semester
Student/faculty ratio 14:1
Profs interesting rating 78
Profs accessible rating 81
Most common
reg class size 10–19 students
Most common
lab size 10–19 students

MOST POPULAR MAJORS
business/commerce
elementary education and teaching
journalism

SELECTIVITY
of applicants 1,730
% of applicants accepted 86
% of acceptees attending 32

FRESHMAN PROFILE
Range SAT Critical Reading 480–570
Range SAT Math 480–500
Range ACT Composite 19–23
Minimum paper TOEFL 550
Minimum computer TOEFL 213
Average HS GPA 3.13
% graduated top 10% of class 12
% graduated top 25% of class 32
% graduated top 50% of class 66

DEADLINES
Regular
Priority 2/1
Deadline 4/15
Notification rolling
Nonfall registration? yes

FINANCIAL FACTS
Annual tuition $24,928
Room and board $9,100
Required fees $865
Books and supplies $709
% frosh rec. need-based
scholarship or grant aid 73
% UG rec. need-based
scholarship or grant aid 71
% frosh rec. non-need-based
scholarship or grant aid 13
% UG rec. non-need-based
scholarship or grant aid 12
% frosh rec. need-based
self-help aid 60
% UG rec. need-based
self-help aid 59
% frosh rec. athletic scholarships 3
% UG rec. athletic scholarships 4
% UG borrow to pay for school 72
Average cumulative
indebtedness $16,900

ST. JOHN'S COLLEGE (MD)

CAMPUS LIFE
Fire Safety Rating **84**
Green Rating **72**
Type of school private
Environment town

STUDENTS
Total undergrad enrollment 464
% male/female 53/47
% from out of state 87

% from public high school 87
% live on campus 80
% African American 1
% Asian 1
% Caucasian 85
% Hispanic 4
% international 4
# of countries represented 11

ACADEMICS
Calendar semester
Student/faculty ratio 8:1
Profs interesting rating 98
Profs accessible rating 97
Most common
reg class size 14–21 students

MOST POPULAR MAJORS
liberal arts and sciences studies
and humanities

SELECTIVITY
of applicants 390
% of applicants accepted 81
% of acceptees attending 44

FRESHMAN PROFILE
Range SAT Critical Reading 630–730
Range SAT Math 570–670
Minimum paper TOEFL 600
Minimum computer TOEFL 270
Minimum web-based TOEFL 100
% graduated top 10% of class 34
% graduated top 25% of class 66
% graduated top 50% of class 71

DEADLINES
Regular
Priority 3/1
Nonfall registration? yes

FINANCIAL FACTS
Annual tuition $41,792
Room and board $9,984
Required fees $400
Books and supplies $630
% frosh rec. need-based
scholarship or grant aid 63
% UG rec. need-based
scholarship or grant aid 62
% frosh rec. non-need-based
scholarship or grant aid 1
% UG rec. non-need-based
scholarship or grant aid 2
% frosh rec. need-based
self-help aid 58
% UG rec. need-based
self-help aid 57
% frosh rec. any financial aid 79
% UG rec. any financial aid 71

ST. JOHN'S UNIVERSITY

CAMPUS LIFE
Fire Safety Rating	**86**
Green Rating	**86**
Type of school	private
Affiliation	Roman Catholic
Environment	metropolis

STUDENTS
Total undergrad enrollment	14,808
% male/female	42/58
% from out of state	23
% from public high school	65
% live on campus	30
% African American	17
% Asian	18
% Caucasian	37
% Hispanic	15
% international	5
# of countries represented	111

ACADEMICS
Calendar	semester
Student/faculty ratio	19:1
Profs interesting rating	65
Profs accessible rating	62
Most common reg class size	20–29 students
Most common lab size	20–29 students

MOST POPULAR MAJORS
accounting
finance
liberal arts and sciences/
liberal studies
pharmacy (Pharmd [USA], Pharmd or
BS/BPharm Canada])
psychology

SELECTIVITY
# of applicants	52,980
% of applicants accepted	43
% of acceptees attending	14

FRESHMAN PROFILE
Range SAT Critical Reading	480–590
Range SAT Math	490–620
Minimum paper TOEFL	500
Minimum computer TOEFL	173
Minimum web-based TOEFL	61
Average HS GPA	3.3
% graduated top 10% of class	24
% graduated top 25% of class	50
% graduated top 50% of class	79

DEADLINES
Regular Notification	rolling
Nonfall registration?	yes

FINANCIAL FACTS
Annual tuition	$29,350
Room and board	$13,140
Required fees	$690
Books and supplies	$1,000
% frosh rec. need-based scholarship or grant aid	72
% UG rec. need-based scholarship or grant aid	68
% frosh rec. non-need-based scholarship or grant aid	65
% UG rec. non-need-based scholarship or grant aid	56
% frosh rec. need-based self-help aid	61
% UG rec. need-based self-help aid	63
% frosh rec. athletic scholarships	1
% UG rec. athletic scholarships	2
% frosh rec. any financial aid	97
% UG rec. any financial aid	97
% UG borrow to pay for school	70
Average cumulative indebtedness	$30,692

ST. LAWRENCE UNIVERSITY

CAMPUS LIFE
Fire Safety Rating	**67**
Green Rating	**80**
Type of school	private
Environment	village

STUDENTS
Total undergrad enrollment	2,274
% male/female	45/55
% from out of state	57
% from public high school	67
% live on campus	98
# of fraternities	2
# of sororities	4
% African American	3
% Asian	2
% Caucasian	82
% Hispanic	4
% Native American	1
% international	6
# of countries represented	44

ACADEMICS
Calendar	semester
Student/faculty ratio	11:1
Profs interesting rating	92
Profs accessible rating	88
Most common reg class size	10–19 students
Most common lab size	10–19 students

MOST POPULAR MAJORS
economics
political science and government
psychology

SELECTIVITY
# of applicants	4,715
% of applicants accepted	39
% of acceptees attending	31
# accepting a place on wait list	122
% admitted from wait list	30
# of early decision applicants	242
% accepted early decision	79

FRESHMAN PROFILE
Range SAT Critical Reading	570–640
Range SAT Math	570–650
Range SAT Writing	560–640
Range ACT Composite	26–29
Minimum paper TOEFL	600
Minimum computer TOEFL	250
Average HS GPA	3.46
% graduated top 10% of class	41
% graduated top 25% of class	81
% graduated top 50% of class	96

DEADLINES
Early decision Deadline	11/15
Notification	12/15
Regular Deadline	2/1
Nonfall registration?	yes

FINANCIAL FACTS
Annual tuition	$40,905
Books and supplies	$750
% frosh rec. need-based scholarship or grant aid	66
% UG rec. need-based scholarship or grant aid	62
% frosh rec. non-need-based scholarship or grant aid	11
% UG rec. non-need-based scholarship or grant aid	9
% frosh rec. need-based self-help aid	49
% UG rec. need-based self-help aid	49
% frosh rec. athletic scholarships	1
% UG rec. athletic scholarships	2
% frosh rec. any financial aid	85
% UG rec. any financial aid	83
% UG borrow to pay for school	74
Average cumulative indebtedness	$31,653

ST. MARY'S COLLEGE OF MARYLAND

CAMPUS LIFE
Fire Safety Rating	**77**
Green Rating	**89**
Type of school	public
Environment	rural

STUDENTS

Total undergrad enrollment	1,978
% male/female	43/57
% from out of state	19
% from public high school	70
% live on campus	85
% African American	8
% Asian	4
% Caucasian	77
% Hispanic	4
% Native American	1
% international	2
# of countries represented	38

ACADEMICS

Calendar	semester
Student/faculty ratio	12:1
Profs interesting rating	96
Profs accessible rating	97
Most common reg class size	10–19 students
Most common lab size	10–19 students

MOST POPULAR MAJORS
biology/biological sciences
English language and literature
psychology

SELECTIVITY

# of applicants	2,411
% of applicants accepted	57
% of acceptees attending	35
# accepting a place on wait list	148
% admitted from wait list	47
# of early decision applicants	221
% accepted early decision	78

FRESHMAN PROFILE

Range SAT Critical Reading	580–690
Range SAT Math	550–650
Range SAT Writing	560–670
Range ACT Composite	24–29
Minimum paper TOEFL	550
Minimum computer TOEFL	250
Minimum web-based TOEFL	90
Average HS GPA	3.78
% graduated top 10% of class	47
% graduated top 25% of class	78
% graduated top 50% of class	95

DEADLINES

Early decision	
Deadline	11/1
Notification	12/1
Regular	
Deadline	1/1
Notification	4/1
Nonfall registration?	yes

FINANCIAL FACTS

Annual in-state tuition	$11,325
Annual out-of-state tuition	$22,718
Room and board	$10,245
Required fees	$2,305
Books and supplies	$1,000
% frosh rec. need-based scholarship or grant aid	17
% UG rec. need-based scholarship or grant aid	19
% frosh rec. non-need-based scholarship or grant aid	17
% UG rec. non-need-based scholarship or grant aid	19
% frosh rec. need-based self-help aid	17
% UG rec. need-based self-help aid	19
% frosh rec. any financial aid	59
% UG rec. any financial aid	61
% UG borrow to pay for school	70
Average cumulative indebtedness	$17,125

STATE UNIVERSITY OF NEW YORK AT ALBANY

CAMPUS LIFE

Fire Safety Rating	**80**
Green Rating	**88**
Type of school	public
Environment	city

STUDENTS

Total undergrad enrollment	12,797
% male/female	52/48
% from out of state	5
% live on campus	57
# of fraternities	11
# of sororities	18
% African American	10
% Asian	6
% Caucasian	57
% Hispanic	9
% international	3
# of countries represented	84

ACADEMICS

Calendar	semester
Student/faculty ratio	19:1
Profs interesting rating	61
Profs accessible rating	61
% classes taught by TAs	11
Most common reg class size	20–29 students
Most common lab size	20–29 students

MOST POPULAR MAJORS
business administration
and management
English language and literature
psychology

SELECTIVITY

# of applicants	22,188
% of applicants accepted	47
% of acceptees attending	22

FRESHMAN PROFILE

Range SAT Critical Reading	500–590
Range SAT Math	530–620
Minimum paper TOEFL	550
Minimum computer TOEFL	213
Minimum web-based TOEFL	79
Average HS GPA	3.4
% graduated top 10% of class	21
% graduated top 25% of class	60
% graduated top 50% of class	94

DEADLINES

Early action	
Deadline	11/15
Notification	1/1
Regular	
Priority	3/1
Deadline	3/1
Notification	rolling
Nonfall registration?	yes

FINANCIAL FACTS

Annual in-state tuition	$4,970
Annual out-of-state tuition	$12,870
Room and board	$10,238
Required fees	$1,778
Books and supplies	$1,600
% frosh rec. need-based scholarship or grant aid	49
% UG rec. need-based scholarship or grant aid	50
% frosh rec. non-need-based scholarship or grant aid	2
% UG rec. non-need-based scholarship or grant aid	1
% frosh rec. need-based self-help aid	46
% UG rec. need-based self-help aid	46
% frosh rec. athletic scholarships	2
% UG rec. athletic scholarships	2
% frosh rec. any financial aid	64
% UG rec. any financial aid	62
Average cumulative indebtedness	$22,092

STATE UNIVERSITY OF NEW YORK AT BINGHAMTON

CAMPUS LIFE

Fire Safety Rating	**76**
Green Rating	**99**
Type of school	public
Environment	city

STUDENTS

Total undergrad enrollment	11,704
% male/female	53/47
% from out of state	10
% from public high school	89
% live on campus	61
# of fraternities	23

# of sororities 23
% African American 5
% Asian 12
% Caucasian 43
% Hispanic 7
% international 10
# of countries represented 98

ACADEMICS

Calendar semester
Student/faculty ratio 20:1
Profs interesting rating 63
Profs accessible rating 68
% classes taught by TAs 7
Most common
  reg class size 20–29 students
Most common
  lab size 20–29 students

MOST POPULAR MAJORS
biology/biological sciences
business administration
and management
engineering

SELECTIVITY

of applicants 29,061
% of applicants accepted 33
% of acceptees attending 22
# accepting a place on wait list 735
% admitted from wait list 6

FRESHMAN PROFILE

Range SAT Critical Reading 580–670
Range SAT Math 620–710
Range ACT Composite 27–30
Minimum paper TOEFL 550
Minimum computer TOEFL 213
Minimum web-based TOEFL 80
Average HS GPA 3.6
% graduated top 10% of class 51
% graduated top 25% of class 84
% graduated top 50% of class 97

DEADLINES

Early action
  Notification 1/15
Regular
  Priority 1/15
  Notification 4/1
Nonfall registration? yes

FINANCIAL FACTS

Annual in-state tuition $4,970
Annual out-of-state tuition $12,870
Room and board $10,614
Required fees $1,791
Books and supplies $800
% frosh rec. need-based
  scholarship or grant aid 36
% UG rec. need-based
  scholarship or grant aid 40
% frosh rec. non-need-based
  scholarship or grant aid 6

% UG rec. non-need-based
  scholarship or grant aid 5
% frosh rec. need-based
  self-help aid 44
% UG rec. need-based
  self-help aid 45
% frosh rec. athletic scholarships 4
% UG rec. athletic scholarships 3
% frosh rec. any financial aid 77
% UG rec. any financial aid 68
% UG borrow to pay for school 49
Average cumulative
  indebtedness $14,560

STATE UNIVERSITY OF NEW YORK—COLLEGE OF ENVIRONMENTAL SCIENCE AND FORESTRY

CAMPUS LIFE

Fire Safety Rating **92**
Green Rating **97**
Type of school public
Environment city

STUDENTS

Total undergrad enrollment 1,541
% male/female 59/41
% from out of state 16
% from public high school 90
% live on campus 33
# of fraternities 26
# of sororities 21
% African American 1
% Asian 3
% Caucasian 91
% Hispanic 3
% Native American 1
% international 1
# of countries represented 30

ACADEMICS

Calendar semester
Student/faculty ratio 12:1
Profs interesting rating 78
Profs accessible rating 81
Most common reg class size 10–19 students
Most common lab size 10–19 students

MOST POPULAR MAJORS
environmental biology
environmental science
landscape architecture
(BS, BSLA, BLA, MSLA, MLA, PhD)

SELECTIVITY

of applicants 1,682
% of applicants accepted 43

% of acceptees attending 39
# accepting a place on wait list 50
% admitted from wait list 10

FRESHMAN PROFILE

Range SAT Critical Reading 530–620
Range SAT Math 540–640
Range ACT Composite 23–27
Minimum paper TOEFL 550
Minimum computer TOEFL 213
Minimum web-based TOEFL 79
% graduated top 10% of class 40
% graduated top 25% of class 77
% graduated top 50% of class 96

DEADLINES

Early action
  Deadline 12/1
  Notification 1/1
Regular
  Priority 12/1
  Notification rolling
Nonfall registration? yes

FINANCIAL FACTS

Annual in-state tuition $4,970
Annual out-of-state tuition $12,870
Room and board $12,460
Required fees $849
Books and supplies $1,200
% frosh rec. need-based
  scholarship or grant aid 63
% UG rec. need-based
  scholarship or grant aid 59
% frosh rec. non-need-based
  scholarship or grant aid 41
% UG rec. non-need-based
  scholarship or grant aid 16
% frosh rec. need-based self-help aid 63
% UG rec. need-based self-help aid 59
% frosh rec. any financial aid 80
% UG rec. any financial aid 82
% UG borrow to pay for school 80
Average cumulative indebtedness $23,000

STATE UNIVERSITY OF NEW YORK—FREDONIA

CAMPUS LIFE

Fire Safety Rating **74**
Green Rating **60***
Type of school public
Environment village

STUDENTS

Total undergrad enrollment 5,375
% male/female 44/56

% from out of state	2
% from public high school	75
% live on campus	52
# of fraternities	3
# of sororities	3
% African American	3
% Asian	1
% Caucasian	68
% Hispanic	3
% international	1
# of countries represented	18

ACADEMICS

Calendar	semester
Student/faculty ratio	16:1
Profs interesting rating	68
Profs accessible rating	71
Most common reg class size	10–19 students
Most common lab size	20–29 students

MOST POPULAR MAJORS
business/commerce
elementary education and teaching
music

SELECTIVITY

# of applicants	6,632
% of applicants accepted	49
% of acceptees attending	35
# of early decision applicants	92
% accepted early decision	81

FRESHMAN PROFILE

Range SAT Critical Reading	500–590
Range SAT Math	510–600
Range ACT Composite	21–26
Minimum paper TOEFL	500
Minimum computer TOEFL	177
Minimum web-based TOEFL	62
Average HS GPA	3.45
% graduated top 10% of class	15
% graduated top 25% of class	49
% graduated top 50% of class	90

DEADLINES

Early decision	
Deadline	11/1
Notification	12/1
Regular	
Notification	rolling
Nonfall registration?	yes

FINANCIAL FACTS

Annual in-state tuition	$4,970
Annual out-of-state tuition	$12,870
Room and board	$9,140
Required fees	$1,288
Books and supplies	$1,000

% frosh rec. need-based scholarship or grant aid	52
% UG rec. need-based scholarship or grant aid	53
% frosh rec. non-need-based scholarship or grant aid	15
% UG rec. non-need-based scholarship or grant aid	10
% frosh rec. need-based self-help aid	53
% UG rec. need-based self-help aid	54
% frosh rec. any financial aid	81
% UG rec. any financial aid	86
% UG borrow to pay for school	88
Average cumulative indebtedness	$19,338

STATE UNIVERSITY OF NEW YORK AT GENESEO

CAMPUS LIFE

Fire Safety Rating	**87**
Green Rating	**87**
Type of school	public
Environment	village

STUDENTS

Total undergrad enrollment	5,495
% male/female	43/57
% from out of state	2
% from public high school	79
% live on campus	55
# of fraternities	8
# of sororities	11
% African American	3
% Asian	8
% Caucasian	74
% Hispanic	2
% Native American	1
# of countries represented	24

ACADEMICS

Calendar	semester
Student/faculty ratio	19:1
Profs interesting rating	73
Profs accessible rating	80
Most common reg class size	20–29 students
Most common lab size	10–19 students

MOST POPULAR MAJORS
biology/biological sciences
business administration
and management
psychology

SELECTIVITY

# of applicants	10,412
% of applicants accepted	35
% of acceptees attending	26
# accepting a place on wait list	295

# of early decision applicants	319
% accepted early decision	43

FRESHMAN PROFILE

Range SAT Critical Reading	610–700
Range SAT Math	630–690
Range ACT Composite	28–30
Minimum paper TOEFL	525
Minimum computer TOEFL	197
Minimum web-based TOEFL	71
Average HS GPA	3.75
% graduated top 10% of class	56
% graduated top 25% of class	88
% graduated top 50% of class	99

DEADLINES

Early decision	
Deadline	11/15
Notification	12/15
Regular	
Deadline	1/1
Notification	3/1
Nonfall registration?	yes

FINANCIAL FACTS

Annual in-state tuition	$2,485
Annual out-of-state tuition	$6,435
Books and supplies	$900
% frosh rec. need-based scholarship or grant aid	20
% UG rec. need-based scholarship or grant aid	44
% frosh rec. non-need-based scholarship or grant aid	20
% UG rec. non-need-based scholarship or grant aid	15
% frosh rec. need-based self-help aid	21
% UG rec. need-based self-help aid	36
% frosh rec. any financial aid	62
% UG rec. any financial aid	72
% UG borrow to pay for school	63
Average cumulative indebtedness	$21,000

STATE UNIVERSITY OF NEW YORK—MARITIME COLLEGE

CAMPUS LIFE

Fire Safety Rating	**77**
Green Rating	**77**
Type of school	public
Environment	metropolis

STUDENTS

Total undergrad enrollment	1,562
% male/female	90/10
% from out of state	27
% live on campus	80
% African American	6

% Asian 4
% Caucasian 72
% Hispanic 9
% international 7

ACADEMICS

Calendar semester
Student/faculty ratio 17:1
Profs interesting rating 71
Profs accessible rating 75
Most common reg class size 20–29 students
Most common lab size 20–29 students

MOST POPULAR MAJORS
engineering
transportation/transportation management

SELECTIVITY

of applicants 1,386
% of applicants accepted 63
% of acceptees attending 41
# accepting a place on wait list 20
% admitted from wait list 25

FRESHMAN PROFILE

Range SAT Critical Reading 460–550
Range SAT Math 510–600
Range ACT Composite 20–24
Minimum paper TOEFL 550
Minimum computer TOEFL 213
Minimum web-based TOEFL 79
Average HS GPA 2.95
% graduated top 10% of class 12
% graduated top 25% of class 60
% graduated top 50% of class 92

DEADLINES

Regular
  Priority 3/15
  Notification rolling
Nonfall registration? yes

FINANCIAL FACTS

Annual in-state tuition $4,970
Annual out-of-state tuition $12,870
Room and board $9,930
Required fees $1,120
Books and supplies $1,260
% frosh rec. need-based
  scholarship or grant aid 30
% UG rec. need-based
  scholarship or grant aid 31
% frosh rec. non-need-based
  scholarship or grant aid 16
% UG rec. non-need-based
  scholarship or grant aid 16
% frosh rec. need-based self-help aid 44
% UG rec. need-based self-help aid 40

% UG borrow to pay for school 73
Average cumulative indebtedness $30,244

STATE UNIVERSITY OF NEW YORK—OSWEGO

CAMPUS LIFE

Fire Safety Rating 66
Green Rating 75
Type of school public
Environment village

STUDENTS

Total undergrad enrollment 7,200
% male/female 48/52
% from out of state 2
% live on campus 59
# of fraternities 13
# of sororities 10
% African American 4
% Asian 2
% Caucasian 87
% Hispanic 5
% international 1
# of countries represented 15

ACADEMICS

Calendar semester
Student/faculty ratio 18:1
Profs interesting rating 74
Profs accessible rating 73
Most common reg class size 20–29 students
Most common lab size 10–19 students

MOST POPULAR MAJORS
business/commerce
elementary education and teaching

SELECTIVITY

of applicants 10,464
% of applicants accepted 47
% of acceptees attending 28
# of early decision applicants 150
% accepted early decision 53

FRESHMAN PROFILE

Range SAT Critical Reading 530–590
Range SAT Math 520–600
Range ACT Composite 21–25
Minimum paper TOEFL 550
Minimum computer TOEFL 213
Minimum web-based TOEFL 80
Average HS GPA 3.3
% graduated top 10% of class 15
% graduated top 25% of class 54
% graduated top 50% of class 89

DEADLINES

Early decision
  Deadline 11/15
  Notification 12/15
Regular
  Priority 1/15
  Notification rolling
Nonfall registration? yes

FINANCIAL FACTS

Annual in-state tuition $4,970
Annual out-of-state tuition $12,870
Room and board $10,870
Required fees $1,186
Books and supplies $800
% frosh rec. need-based
  scholarship or grant aid 56
% UG rec. need-based
  scholarship or grant aid 56
% frosh rec. non-need-based
  scholarship or grant aid 10
% UG rec. non-need-based
  scholarship or grant aid 5
% frosh rec. need-based self-help aid 56
% UG rec. need-based self-help aid 56
% frosh rec. any financial aid 84
% UG rec. any financial aid 85
% UG borrow to pay for school 86
Average cumulative indebtedness $25,488

STATE UNIVERSITY OF NEW YORK—PURCHASE COLLEGE

CAMPUS LIFE

Fire Safety Rating 60*
Green Rating 85
Type of school public
Environment town

STUDENTS

Total undergrad enrollment 3,830
% male/female 44/56
% from out of state 19
% live on campus 67
% African American 7
% Asian 3
% Caucasian 55
% Hispanic 12
% international 2
# of countries represented 21

ACADEMICS

Calendar semester
Student/faculty ratio 16:1
Profs interesting rating 78
Profs accessible rating 65
% classes taught by TAs 1
Most common
  reg class size 10–19 students

Most common
lab size   fewer than 10 students

MOST POPULAR MAJORS
journalism
literature
psychology
biology
new media
visual and performing arts

SELECTIVITY
# of applicants	8,620
% of applicants accepted	27
% of acceptees attending	30
# of early decision applicants	32
% accepted early decision	47

FRESHMAN PROFILE
Range SAT Critical Reading	510–630
Range SAT Math	490–580
Range SAT Writing	500–620
Range ACT Composite	21–25
Minimum paper TOEFL	550
Minimum computer TOEFL	213
Average HS GPA	3.2
% graduated top 10% of class	11
% graduated top 25% of class	38
% graduated top 50% of class	81

DEADLINES
Early decision	
Deadline	11/1
Notification	12/5
Regular	
Priority	3/1
Deadline	7/15
Notification	5/1
Nonfall registration?	yes

FINANCIAL FACTS
Annual in-state tuition	$4,970
Annual out-of-state tuition	$12,870
Room and board	$9,908
Required fees	$1,461
Books and supplies	$1,100
% frosh rec. need-based	
scholarship or grant aid	42
% UG rec. need-based	
scholarship or grant aid	46
% frosh rec. non-need-based	
scholarship or grant aid	1
% UG rec. non-need-based	
scholarship or grant aid	1
% frosh rec. need-based	
self-help aid	53
% UG rec. need-based	
self-help aid	55
% UG borrow to pay for school	58
Average cumulative	
indebtedness	$26,275

STATE UNIVERSITY OF NEW YORK—STONY BROOK UNIVERSITY

CAMPUS LIFE
Fire Safety Rating	**60***
Green Rating	**92**
Type of school	public
Environment	town

STUDENTS
Total undergrad enrollment	16,034
% male/female	52/48
% from out of state	7
% from public high school	90
% live on campus	51
# of fraternities	17
# of sororities	16
% African American	7
% Asian	23
% Caucasian	37
% Hispanic	9
% international	7
# of countries represented	100

ACADEMICS
Calendar	semester
Student/faculty ratio	19:1
Profs interesting rating	61
Profs accessible rating	62
Most common	
reg class size	20–29 students
Most common	
lab size	20–29 students

MOST POPULAR MAJORS
biology/biological sciences
business/commerce
psychology

SELECTIVITY
# of applicants	28,587
% of applicants accepted	40
% of acceptees attending	25
# accepting a place on wait list	949
% admitted from wait list	14

FRESHMAN PROFILE
Range SAT Critical Reading	520–620
Range SAT Math	580–670
Range SAT Writing	520–620
Range ACT Composite	24–28
Minimum paper TOEFL	550
Minimum computer TOEFL	213
Minimum web-based TOEFL	80
Average HS GPA	3.6
% graduated top 10% of class	38
% graduated top 25% of class	72
% graduated top 50% of class	95

DEADLINES
Regular	
Deadline	1/15
Notification	4/1
Nonfall registration?	yes

FINANCIAL FACTS
Annual in-state tuition	$4,970
Annual out-of-state tuition	$12,870
Room and board	$10,070
Required fees	$1,608
Books and supplies	$900
% frosh rec. need-based	
scholarship or grant aid	48
% UG rec. need-based	
scholarship or grant aid	48
% frosh rec. non-need-based	
scholarship or grant aid	2
% UG rec. non-need-based	
scholarship or grant aid	1
% frosh rec. need-based	
self-help aid	36
% UG rec. need-based	
self-help aid	39
% frosh rec. athletic scholarships	1
% UG rec. athletic scholarships	1
% frosh rec. any financial aid	74
% UG rec. any financial aid	65
% UG borrow to pay for school	63
Average cumulative	
indebtedness	$17,502

STATE UNIVERSITY OF NEW YORK—THE COLLEGE AT BROCKPORT

CAMPUS LIFE
Fire Safety Rating	**79**
Green Rating	**83**
Type of school	public
Environment	village

STUDENTS
% from out of state	1.1
% live on campus	38
# of fraternities	6
# of sororities	3
# of countries represented	21

ACADEMICS
Calendar	semester
Student/faculty ratio	18:1
Profs interesting rating	71
Profs accessible rating	70
Most common reg class size	20–29 students
Most common lab size	10–19 students

MOST POPULAR MAJORS

business administration and management
health professions and related
clinical sciences
physical education teaching and coaching

SELECTIVITY

# of applicants	8,671
% of applicants accepted	45
% of acceptees attending	28
# accepting a place on wait list	29

FRESHMAN PROFILE

Range SAT Critical Reading	470–560
Range SAT Math	500–590
Range SAT Writing	450–560
Range ACT Composite	21–25
Minimum paper TOEFL	530
Minimum computer TOEFL	197
Minimum web-based TOEFL	71
Average HS GPA	3.5
% graduated top 10% of class	14.7
% graduated top 25% of class	50
% graduated top 50% of class	88

DEADLINES

Regular	
Notification	rolling
Nonfall registration?	yes

FINANCIAL FACTS

Annual in-state tuition	$4,970
Annual out-of-state tuition	$12,870
Room and board	$9,200
Required fees	$1,138
Books and supplies	$1,000
% frosh rec. need-based	
scholarship or grant aid	57
% UG rec. need-based	
scholarship or grant aid	58
% frosh rec. non-need-based	
scholarship or grant aid	21
% UG rec. non-need-based	
scholarship or grant aid	13
% frosh rec. need-based self-help aid	52
% UG rec. need-based self-help aid	57
% frosh rec. any financial aid	91
% UG rec. any financial aid	84
% UG borrow to pay for school	81
Average cumulative indebtedness	$26,086

STATE UNIVERSITY OF NEW YORK—UNIVERSITY AT BUFFALO

CAMPUS LIFE

Fire Safety Rating	**60***
Green Rating	**60***
Type of school	public
Environment	city

STUDENTS

Total undergrad enrollment	19,149
% male/female	54/46
% from out of state	4
% live on campus	34
# of fraternities	22
# of sororities	17
% African American	7
% Asian	10
% Caucasian	58
% Hispanic	3
% international	13
# of countries represented	108

ACADEMICS

Calendar	semester
Student/faculty ratio	16:1
Profs interesting rating	62
Profs accessible rating	67
% classes taught by TAs	11
Most common reg class size	20–29 students
Most common lab size	20–29 students

MOST POPULAR MAJORS

business/commerce
engineering
social sciences

SELECTIVITY

# of applicants	21,137
% of applicants accepted	52
% of acceptees attending	29
# accepting a place on wait list	443
% admitted from wait list	52
# of early decision applicants	504
% accepted early decision	72

FRESHMAN PROFILE

Range SAT Critical Reading	510–600
Range SAT Math	550–650
Range ACT Composite	23–28
Minimum paper TOEFL	550
Minimum web-based TOEFL	79
Average HS GPA	3.3
% graduated top 10% of class	28
% graduated top 25% of class	65
% graduated top 50% of class	95

DEADLINES

Early decision	
Deadline	11/1
Notification	12/15
Regular	
Priority	11/1
Notification	rolling
Nonfall registration?	yes

FINANCIAL FACTS

Annual in-state tuition	$4,970
Annual out-of-state tuition	$12,870
Room and board	$9,648
Required fees	$2,043
Books and supplies	$975
% frosh rec. need-based	
scholarship or grant aid	26
% UG rec. need-based	
scholarship or grant aid	13
% frosh rec. non-need-based	
scholarship or grant aid	3
% UG rec. non-need-based	
scholarship or grant aid	4
% frosh rec. need-based	
self-help aid	12
% UG rec. need-based	
self-help aid	24
% frosh rec. athletic scholarships	2
% UG rec. athletic scholarships	1
% frosh rec. any financial aid	50
% UG rec. any financial aid	52
% UG borrow to pay for school	44
Average cumulative indebtedness	$15,911

STERLING COLLEGE (VT)

CAMPUS LIFE

Fire Safety Rating	**60***
Green Rating	**60***
Type of school	private
Environment	rural

STUDENTS

Total undergrad enrollment	98
% male/female	57/43
% from out of state	77
% from public high school	70
% live on campus	82
% Asian	1
% Caucasian	76
% Hispanic	1
# of countries represented	1

ACADEMICS

Calendar	semester
Student/faculty ratio	5:1
Profs interesting rating	62
Profs accessible rating	78
Most common reg class size	10–19 students

MOST POPULAR MAJORS
agriculture, agriculture operations,
and related sciences
natural resources conservation and research,
parks, recreation and leisure studies

SELECTIVITY
# of applicants	104
% of applicants accepted	78
% of acceptees attending	33

FRESHMAN PROFILE
Minimum paper TOEFL	500
Minimum computer TOEFL	173
Minimum web-based TOEFL	61
Average HS GPA	3
% graduated top 10% of class	11
% graduated top 25% of class	21
% graduated top 50% of class	79

DEADLINES
Early action	
Deadline	12/15
Notification	1/15
Regular	
Priority	2/15
Deadline	2/15
Notification	4/1
Nonfall registration?	yes

FINANCIAL FACTS
Annual tuition	$23,196
Room and board	$7,554
Required fees	$400
Books and supplies	$900
% frosh rec. need-based scholarship or grant aid	71
% UG rec. need-based scholarship or grant aid	74
% UG rec. non-need-based scholarship or grant aid	16
% frosh rec. need-based self-help aid	71
% UG rec. need-based self-help aid	74
% frosh rec. any financial aid	71
% UG rec. any financial aid	74
% UG borrow to pay for school	40
Average cumulative indebtedness	$15,880

STEVENS INSTITUTE OF
TECHNOLOGY

CAMPUS LIFE
Fire Safety Rating	**98**
Green Rating	**70**
Type of school	private
Environment	city

STUDENTS
Total undergrad enrollment	2,234
% male/female	72/28
% from out of state	40
% from public high school	80
% live on campus	90
# of fraternities	12
# of sororities	5
% African American	3
% Asian	11
% Caucasian	54
% Hispanic	10
% international	4
# of countries represented	47

ACADEMICS
Calendar	semester
Student/faculty ratio	7:1
Profs interesting rating	61
Profs accessible rating	64

MOST POPULAR MAJORS
business administration
and management
computer/information technology
mechanical engineering

SELECTIVITY
# of applicants	3,233
% of applicants accepted	50
% of acceptees attending	37
# of early decision applicants	506
% accepted early decision	67

FRESHMAN PROFILE
Range SAT Critical Reading	550–650
Range SAT Math	620–710
Range SAT Writing	540–650
Range ACT Composite	24–29
Minimum paper TOEFL	550
Minimum computer TOEFL	213
Minimum web-based TOEFL	83
Average HS GPA	3.8
% graduated top 10% of class	58
% graduated top 25% of class	85
% graduated top 50% of class	98

DEADLINES
Early decision	
Deadline	11/15
Notification	12/15
Regular	
Priority	11/15
Deadline	2/1
Notification	3/15
Nonfall registration?	yes

FINANCIAL FACTS
Annual tuition	$36,600
Room and board	$12,150
Required fees	$1,380
Books and supplies	$900
% frosh rec. need-based scholarship or grant aid	66

% UG rec. need-based scholarship or grant aid	54
% frosh rec. non-need-based scholarship or grant aid	62
% UG rec. non-need-based scholarship or grant aid	55
% frosh rec. need-based self-help aid	65
% UG rec. need-based self-help aid	57
% frosh rec. any financial aid	82
% UG rec. any financial aid	93
% UG borrow to pay for school	66
Average cumulative indebtedness	$17,885

STONEHILL COLLEGE

CAMPUS LIFE
Fire Safety Rating	**90**
Green Rating	**76**
Type of school	private
Affiliation	Roman Catholic
Environment	village

STUDENTS
Total undergrad enrollment	2,448
% male/female	40/60
% from out of state	47
% from public high school	64
% live on campus	88
% African American	3
% Asian	1
% Caucasian	92
% Hispanic	4
# of countries represented	10

ACADEMICS
Calendar	semester
Student/faculty ratio	13:1
Profs interesting rating	97
Profs accessible rating	98
Most common reg class size	20–29 students
Most common lab size	10–19 students

MOST POPULAR MAJORS
biology/biological sciences
English language and literature
psychology

SELECTIVITY
# of applicants	5,871
% of applicants accepted	56
% of acceptees attending	21
# accepting a place on wait list	412
% admitted from wait list	2
# of early decision applicants	59
% accepted early decision	85

FRESHMAN PROFILE
Range SAT Critical Reading	550–630
Range SAT Math	570–650

Range ACT Composite | 24–28
Minimum paper TOEFL | 550
Minimum computer TOEFL | 213
Minimum web-based TOEFL | 79
Average HS GPA | 3.49
% graduated top 10% of class | 50
% graduated top 25% of class | 87
% graduated top 50% of class | 99

DEADLINES
Early decision
  Deadline | 11/1
  Notification | 12/25
Early action
  Deadline | 11/1
  Notification | 1/15
Regular
  Deadline | 1/15
  Notification | 3/15
Nonfall registration? | yes

FINANCIAL FACTS
% frosh rec. need-based
  scholarship or grant aid | 70
% UG rec. need-based
  scholarship or grant aid | 64
% frosh rec. non-need-based
  scholarship or grant aid | 10
% UG rec. non-need-based
  scholarship or grant aid | 8
% frosh rec. need-based
  self-help aid | 60
% UG rec. need-based
  self-help aid | 60
% frosh rec. athletic scholarships | 3
% UG rec. athletic scholarships | 3
% frosh rec. any financial aid | 98
% UG rec. any financial aid | 88
% UG borrow to pay for school | 73
Average cumulative
  indebtedness | $29,163

SUFFOLK UNIVERSITY

CAMPUS LIFE
Fire Safety Rating | **92**
Green Rating | **89**
Type of school | private
Environment | metropolis

STUDENTS
Total undergrad enrollment | 5,617
% male/female | 44/56
% from out of state | 32
% from public high school | 70
% live on campus | 23
# of fraternities | 1
# of sororities | 1
% African American | 4
% Asian | 7
% Caucasian | 53
% Hispanic | 7

% international | 10
# of countries represented | 105

ACADEMICS
Calendar | semester
Student/faculty ratio | 13:1
Profs interesting rating | 75
Profs accessible rating | 72
Most common
  reg class size | 10–19 students
Most common
  lab size | 10–19 students

MOST POPULAR MAJORS
business/corporate communications
interior design
sociology

SELECTIVITY
of applicants | 9,036
% of applicants accepted | 85
% of acceptees attending | 16
# accepting a place on wait list | 94
% admitted from wait list | 84

FRESHMAN PROFILE
Range SAT Critical Reading | 450–560
Range SAT Math | 450–560
Range SAT Writing | 450–560
Range ACT Composite | 19–24
Minimum paper TOEFL | 525
Minimum computer TOEFL | 197
Minimum web-based TOEFL | 71
Average HS GPA | 3.02
% graduated top 10% of class | 12
% graduated top 25% of class | 38
% graduated top 50% of class | 73

DEADLINES
Early action
  Deadline | 11/15
  Notification | 12/20
Regular
  Deadline | 3/1
  Notification | rolling
Nonfall registration? | yes

FINANCIAL FACTS
Annual tuition | $28,414
Room and board | $16,957
Required fees | $112
Books and supplies | $11,200
% frosh rec. need-based
  scholarship or grant aid | 81
% UG rec. need-based
  scholarship or grant aid | 80
% frosh rec. non-need-based
  scholarship or grant aid | 22
% UG rec. non-need-based
  scholarship or grant aid | 28
% frosh rec. need-based
  self-help aid | 81
% UG rec. need-based
  self-help aid | 81

% frosh rec. any financial aid | 85
% UG rec. any financial aid | 86

SUSQUEHANNA UNIVERSITY

CAMPUS LIFE
Fire Safety Rating | **87**
Green Rating | **71**
Type of school | private
Affiliation | Lutheran
Environment | town

STUDENTS
Total undergrad enrollment | 2,231
% male/female | 47/53
% from out of state | 46.1
% from public high school | 81
% live on campus | 77
# of fraternities | 5
# of sororities | 6
% African American | 3
% Asian | 2
% Caucasian | 91
% Hispanic | 3
% international | 1
# of countries represented | 13

ACADEMICS
Calendar | semester
Student/faculty ratio | 13:1
Profs interesting rating | 82
Profs accessible rating | 88
Most common
  reg class size | 10–19 students
Most common
  lab size | 10–19 students

MOST POPULAR MAJORS
business administration
and management
communication studies/
speech communication and rhetoric
creative writing

SELECTIVITY
of applicants | 2,954
% of applicants accepted | 75
% of acceptees attending | 28
# accepting a place on wait list | 90
% admitted from wait list | 5
# of early decision applicants | 117
% accepted early decision | 84

FRESHMAN PROFILE
Range SAT Critical Reading | 500–600
Range SAT Math | 510–610
Range SAT Writing | 500–600
Range ACT Composite | 23–27
Minimum paper TOEFL | 550
Minimum computer TOEFL | 213
Minimum web-based TOEFL | 81
Average HS GPA | 3.24
% graduated top 10% of class | 23

% graduated top 25% of class 51
% graduated top 50% of class 86

DEADLINES
Early decision
Deadline 11/15
Notification 12/1
Regular
Priority 3/1
Deadline 3/1
Notification rolling
Nonfall registration? yes

FINANCIAL FACTS
Annual tuition $33,650
Room and board $9,230
Required fees $420
Books and supplies $850
% frosh rec. need-based
scholarship or grant aid 66
% UG rec. need-based
scholarship or grant aid 67
% frosh rec. non-need-based
scholarship or grant aid 11
% UG rec. non-need-based
scholarship or grant aid 8
% frosh rec. need-based
self-help aid 55
% UG rec. need-based
self-help aid 59
% frosh rec. any financial aid 95
% UG rec. any financial aid 93

SWARTHMORE COLLEGE

CAMPUS LIFE
Fire Safety Rating **87**
Green Rating **77**
Type of school private
Environment village

STUDENTS
Total undergrad enrollment 1,505
% male/female 48/52
% from out of state 87
% from public high school 59
% live on campus 95
# of fraternities 2
% African American 10
% Asian 16
% Caucasian 44
% Hispanic 11
% Native American 1
% international 7
# of countries represented 57

ACADEMICS
Calendar semester
Student/faculty ratio 8:1
Profs interesting rating 97
Profs accessible rating 96
Most common
reg class size 10–19 students

Most common
lab size fewer than 10 students

MOST POPULAR MAJORS
biology/biological sciences
economics
political science and government

SELECTIVITY
# of applicants 5,575
% of applicants accepted 17
% of acceptees attending 41
# of early decision applicants 497
% accepted early decision 33

FRESHMAN PROFILE
Range SAT Critical Reading 670–760
Range SAT Math 670–770
Range SAT Writing 670–760
Range ACT Composite 29.5–33
% graduated top 10% of class 87
% graduated top 25% of class 99
% graduated top 50% of class 100

DEADLINES
Early decision
Deadline 11/15
Notification 12/15
Regular
Deadline 1/2
Notification 4/1
Nonfall registration? no

FINANCIAL FACTS
Annual tuition $37,510
Room and board $11,740
Required fees $350
Books and supplies $1,150
% frosh rec. need-based
scholarship or grant aid 55
% UG rec. need-based
scholarship or grant aid 49
% frosh rec. need-based
self-help aid 54
% UG rec. need-based
self-help aid 48
% frosh rec. any financial aid 55
% UG rec. any financial aid 57

SYRACUSE UNIVERSITY

CAMPUS LIFE
Fire Safety Rating **89**
Green Rating **93**
Type of school private
Environment metropolis

STUDENTS
Total undergrad enrollment 13,243
% male/female 44/56
% from out of state 53
% from public high school 72
% live on campus 75
# of fraternities 29

# of sororities 19
% African American 8
% Asian 9
% Caucasian 57
% Hispanic 7
% Native American 1
% international 5
# of countries represented 124

ACADEMICS
Calendar semester
Student/faculty ratio 15:1
Profs interesting rating 72
Profs accessible rating 73
Most common
reg class size 10–19 students
Most common
lab size 20–29 students

MOST POPULAR MAJORS
commercial and advertising art
psychology
marketing/marketing management

SELECTIVITY
# of applicants 20,951
% of applicants accepted 60
% of acceptees attending 26
# accepting a place on wait list 1,550
% admitted from wait list 33
# of early decision applicants 859
% accepted early decision 77

FRESHMAN PROFILE
Range SAT Critical Reading 510–620
Range SAT Math 540–650
Range SAT Writing 520–630
Range ACT Composite 23–28
Minimum paper TOEFL 550
Minimum web-based TOEFL 80
Average HS GPA 3.6
% graduated top 10% of class 39
% graduated top 25% of class 73
% graduated top 50% of class 96

DEADLINES
Early decision
Deadline 11/15
Notification 12/15
Regular
Deadline 1/1
Notification rolling
Nonfall registration? yes

FINANCIAL FACTS
Annual tuition $33,630
Room and board $12,374
Required fees $1,296
Books and supplies $1,306
% frosh rec. need-based
scholarship or grant aid 57
% UG rec. need-based
scholarship or grant aid 54
% frosh rec. non-need-based
scholarship or grant aid 3

% UG rec. non-need-based scholarship or grant aid	3
% frosh rec. need-based self-help aid	61
% UG rec. need-based self-help aid	59
% frosh rec. athletic scholarships	2
% UG rec. athletic scholarships	3
% frosh rec. any financial aid	80
% UG rec. any financial aid	80
% UG borrow to pay for school	65
Average cumulative indebtedness	$28,358

TEMPLE UNIVERSITY

CAMPUS LIFE
Fire Safety Rating	**94**
Green Rating	**88**
Type of school	public
Environment	metropolis

STUDENTS
Total undergrad enrollment	26,244
% male/female	47/53
% from out of state	20
% from public high school	72
% live on campus	19
# of fraternities	11
# of sororities	9
% African American	16
% Asian	10
% Caucasian	58
% Hispanic	4
% international	3
# of countries represented	117

ACADEMICS
Calendar	semester
Student/faculty ratio	17:1
Profs interesting rating	67
Profs accessible rating	71
Most common reg class size	20–29 students
Most common lab size	20–29 students

MOST POPULAR MAJORS
elementary education and teaching
marketing/marketing management
psychology

SELECTIVITY
# of applicants	18,574
% of applicants accepted	61
% of acceptees attending	37
# accepting a place on wait list	642
% admitted from wait list	45

FRESHMAN PROFILE
Range SAT Critical Reading	490–600
Range SAT Math	510–610
Range SAT Writing	500–600
Range ACT Composite	21–26

Minimum paper TOEFL	550
Minimum computer TOEFL	213
Minimum web-based TOEFL	79
Average HS GPA	3.41
% graduated top 10% of class	21
% graduated top 25% of class	57
% graduated top 50% of class	94

DEADLINES
Regular Deadline	3/1
Notification	rolling
Nonfall registration?	yes

FINANCIAL FACTS
Annual in-state tuition	$11,174
Annual out-of-state tuition	$20,454
Room and board	$9,198
Required fees	$590
Books and supplies	$1,000
% frosh rec. need-based scholarship or grant aid	65
% UG rec. need-based scholarship or grant aid	64
% frosh rec. non-need-based scholarship or grant aid	38
% UG rec. non-need-based scholarship or grant aid	31
% frosh rec. need-based self-help aid	55
% UG rec. need-based self-help aid	56
% frosh rec. athletic scholarships	1
% UG rec. athletic scholarships	1
% frosh rec. any financial aid	72
% UG rec. any financial aid	63
% UG borrow to pay for school	75
Average cumulative indebtedness	$29,886

TOWSON UNIVERSITY

CAMPUS LIFE
Fire Safety Rating	**95**
Green Rating	**84**
Type of school	public
Environment	metropolis

STUDENTS
Total undergrad enrollment	16,598
% male/female	40/60
% from out of state	18
# of fraternities	12
# of sororities	10
% African American	12
% Asian	4
% Caucasian	68
% Hispanic	3
% international	3
# of countries represented	94

ACADEMICS
Calendar	semester
Student/faculty ratio	17:1
Profs interesting rating	74
Profs accessible rating	71
Most common reg class size	20–29 students
Most common lab size	10–19 students

MOST POPULAR MAJORS
business administration, management and operations,
elementary education and teaching
social sciences

SELECTIVITY
# of applicants	15,423
% of applicants accepted	63
% of acceptees attending	25
# accepting a place on wait list	185
% admitted from wait list	203

FRESHMAN PROFILE
Range SAT Critical Reading	490–580
Range SAT Math	490–590
Range SAT Writing	500–580
Range ACT Composite	21–24
Minimum paper TOEFL	500
Minimum computer TOEFL	173
Minimum web-based TOEFL	61
Average HS GPA	3.55
% graduated top 10% of class	9
% graduated top 25% of class	23
% graduated top 50% of class	40

DEADLINES
Regular Priority	12/1
Deadline	2/15
Notification	rolling
Nonfall registration?	yes

FINANCIAL FACTS
Annual in-state tuition	$5,180
Annual out-of-state tuition	$15,994
Room and board	$8,670
Required fees	$2,238
Books and supplies	$984
% frosh rec. need-based scholarship or grant aid	32
% UG rec. need-based scholarship or grant aid	31
% frosh rec. non-need-based scholarship or grant aid	22
% UG rec. non-need-based scholarship or grant aid	13
% frosh rec. need-based self-help aid	38
% UG rec. need-based self-help aid	34
% UG rec. athletic scholarships	1

% frosh rec. any financial aid 76
% UG rec. any financial aid 68
% UG borrow to pay for school 23
Average cumulative indebtedness $13,245

TRINITY COLLEGE (CT)

CAMPUS LIFE
Fire Safety Rating **86**
Green Rating **60***
Type of school private
Environment metropolis

STUDENTS
Total undergrad enrollment 2,341
% male/female 51/49
% from out of state 82
% from public high school 40
% live on campus 95
# of fraternities 7
# of sororities 3
% African American 6
% Asian 6
% Caucasian 61
% Hispanic 6
% international 5
# of countries represented 48

ACADEMICS
Calendar semester
Student/faculty ratio 9:1
Profs interesting rating 83
Profs accessible rating 82
Most common
  reg class size 10–19 students
Most common
  lab size 10–19 students

MOST POPULAR MAJORS
economics
English language and literature
political science and government

SELECTIVITY
of applicants 4,532
% of applicants accepted 41
% of acceptees attending 31
# accepting a place on wait list 433
% admitted from wait list 24
# of early decision applicants 386
% accepted early decision 73

FRESHMAN PROFILE
Range SAT Critical Reading 590–680
Range SAT Math 610–690
Range SAT Writing 610–710
Range ACT Composite 26–30
% graduated top 10% of class 68
% graduated top 25% of class 93
% graduated top 50% of class 99

DEADLINES
Early decision
  Deadline 11/15
  Notification 12/15
Regular
  Deadline 1/1
  Notification 4/1
Nonfall registration? no

FINANCIAL FACTS
Annual tuition $40,360
Room and board $10,960
Required fees $2,010
Books and supplies $1,000
% frosh rec. need-based
  scholarship or grant aid 41
% UG rec. need-based
  scholarship or grant aid 39
% frosh rec. non-need-based
  scholarship or grant aid 10
% UG rec. non-need-based
  scholarship or grant aid 10
% frosh rec. need-based
  self-help aid 35
% UG rec. need-based
  self-help aid 32
% frosh rec. any financial aid 53
% UG rec. any financial aid 52
% UG borrow to pay for school 42
Average cumulative
  indebtedness $20,174

TUFTS UNIVERSITY

CAMPUS LIFE
Fire Safety Rating **96**
Green Rating **86**
Type of school private
Environment town

STUDENTS
Total undergrad enrollment 5,164
% male/female 49/51
% from out of state 76
% from public high school 59
# of fraternities 11
# of sororities 3
% African American 5
% Asian 13
% Caucasian 58
% Hispanic 6
% international 6
# of countries represented 93

ACADEMICS
Calendar semester
Student/faculty ratio 9:1
Profs interesting rating 86
Profs accessible rating 85
% classes taught by TAs 1
Most common
  reg class size 10–19 students
Most common
  lab size 10–19 students

MOST POPULAR MAJORS
economics
English language and literature
international relations and affairs

SELECTIVITY
of applicants 15,042
% of applicants accepted 27
% of acceptees attending 33

FRESHMAN PROFILE
Range SAT Critical Reading 680–750
Range SAT Math 680–750
Range SAT Writing 680–760
Range ACT Composite 30–33
Minimum paper TOEFL 600
Minimum computer TOEFL 100
% graduated top 10% of class 85
% graduated top 25% of class 98
% graduated top 50% of class 100

DEADLINES
Early decision
  Deadline 11/1
  Notification 12/15
Regular
  Deadline 1/1
  Notification 4/1
Nonfall registration? no

FINANCIAL FACTS
Annual tuition $39,432
% frosh rec. need-based
  scholarship or grant aid 37
% UG rec. need-based
  scholarship or grant aid 36
% frosh rec. non-need-based
  scholarship or grant aid 2
% UG rec. non-need-based
  scholarship or grant aid 1
% frosh rec. need-based
  self-help aid 36
% UG rec. need-based
  self-help aid 37
% frosh rec. any financial aid 40
% UG rec. any financial aid 40
% UG borrow to pay for school 41
Average cumulative
  indebtedness $23,731

UNION COLLEGE (NY)

CAMPUS LIFE
Fire Safety Rating **60***
Green Rating **60***
Type of school private
Environment town

STUDENTS
Total undergrad enrollment 2,141
% male/female 51/49
% from out of state 59
% from public high school 74

% live on campus	87
# of fraternities	12
# of sororities	5
% African American	5
% Asian	7
% Caucasian	79
% Hispanic	5
% international	3
# of countries represented	32

ACADEMICS

Calendar	trimester
Student/faculty ratio	10:1
Profs interesting rating	90
Profs accessible rating	92
Most common reg class size	10–19 students
Most common lab size	10–19 students

MOST POPULAR MAJORS
economics
English language and literature
political science and government

SELECTIVITY

# of applicants	4,829
% of applicants accepted	41
% of acceptees attending	26
# accepting a place on wait list	255
% admitted from wait list	43
# of early decision applicants	308
% accepted early decision	72

FRESHMAN PROFILE

Range SAT Critical Reading	590–670
Range SAT Math	620–700
Range SAT Writing	580–670
Range ACT Composite	27–30
Minimum paper TOEFL	600
Minimum computer TOEFL	250
Minimum web-based TOEFL	90
Average HS GPA	3.56
% graduated top 10% of class	58
% graduated top 25% of class	84
% graduated top 50% of class	99

DEADLINES

Early decision	
Deadline	11/15
Notification	12/15
Regular	
Deadline	1/15
Notification	4/1
Nonfall registration?	no

FINANCIAL FACTS

Comprehensive fee	$50,439
% frosh rec. need-based scholarship or grant aid	51
% UG rec. need-based scholarship or grant aid	46
% frosh rec. non-need-based scholarship or grant aid	2
% UG rec. non-need-based scholarship or grant aid	2
% frosh rec. need-based self-help aid	51
% UG rec. need-based self-help aid	45
% frosh rec. any financial aid	69
% UG rec. any financial aid	68
% UG borrow to pay for school	61
Average cumulative indebtedness	$24,739

UNITED STATES COAST GUARD ACADEMY

CAMPUS LIFE

Fire Safety Rating	**72**
Green Rating	**82**
Type of school	public
Environment	city

STUDENTS

Total undergrad enrollment	973
% male/female	73/27
% from out of state	94
% from public high school	81
% live on campus	100
% African American	3
% Asian	4
% Caucasian	82
% Hispanic	7
% Native American	1
% international	2
# of countries represented	10

ACADEMICS

Calendar	semester
Student/faculty ratio	7:1
Profs interesting rating	72
Profs accessible rating	98
Most common reg class size	10–19 students
Most common lab size	fewer than 10 students

MOST POPULAR MAJORS
business administration
and management
civil engineering
political science and government

SELECTIVITY

# of applicants	1,672
% of applicants accepted	25
% of acceptees attending	70

FRESHMAN PROFILE

Range SAT Critical Reading	560–660
Range SAT Math	600–680
Range ACT Composite	24–30
Minimum paper TOEFL	560
Minimum computer TOEFL	220
Average HS GPA	3.7
% graduated top 10% of class	49
% graduated top 25% of class	83
% graduated top 50% of class	99

DEADLINES

Early action	
Deadline	11/1
Notification	12/24
Regular	
Priority	11/1
Deadline	2/1
Notification	rolling
Nonfall registration?	no

FINANCIAL FACTS
Tuition covered by full scholarship

UNITED STATES MERCHANT MARINE ACADEMY

CAMPUS LIFE

Fire Safety Rating	**60***
Green Rating	**60***
Type of school	public
Environment	village

STUDENTS

Total undergrad enrollment	985
% male/female	88/12
% from out of state	86
% from public high school	71
% live on campus	100
% African American	3
% Asian	5
% Caucasian	84
% Hispanic	5
% Native American	1
% international	3
# of countries represented	5

ACADEMICS

Calendar	trimester
Student/faculty ratio	11:1
Profs interesting rating	61
Profs accessible rating	69
Most common reg class size	10–19 students
Most common lab size	10–19 students

MOST POPULAR MAJORS
engineering
naval architecture and
marine engineering
transportation and materials moving

SELECTIVITY

# of applicants	1,734
% of applicants accepted	18
% of acceptees attending	100

FRESHMAN PROFILE

Range SAT Critical Reading	540–640
Range SAT Math	600–660
Range ACT Composite	25–29
Minimum paper TOEFL	533
Minimum computer TOEFL	200
Minimum web-based TOEFL	73
Average HS GPA	3.6
% graduated top 10% of class	18
% graduated top 25% of class	23
% graduated top 50% of class	85

DEADLINES

Regular
Deadline	3/1
Notification	rolling
Nonfall registration?	no

FINANCIAL FACTS

Required fees	$2,843

Tuition covered by full scholarship

UNITED STATES MILITARY ACADEMY

CAMPUS LIFE

Fire Safety Rating	**83**
Green Rating	**60***
Type of school	public
Environment	village

STUDENTS

Total undergrad enrollment	4,553
% male/female	85/15
% from out of state	93
% from public high school	86
% live on campus	100
% African American	6
% Asian	7
% Caucasian	75
% Hispanic	8
% Native American	1
% international	1
# of countries represented	35

ACADEMICS

Calendar	semester
Student/faculty ratio	7:1
Profs interesting rating	96
Profs accessible rating	99
Most common reg class size	10–19 students
Most common lab size	10–19 students

MOST POPULAR MAJORS

business administration
and management
economics
engineering/industrial management

SELECTIVITY

# of applicants	10,778
% of applicants accepted	14
% of acceptees attending	77

FRESHMAN PROFILE

Range SAT Critical Reading	570–670
Range SAT Math	600–690
Range ACT Composite	21–36
Average HS GPA	3.75
% graduated top 10% of class	43
% graduated top 25% of class	75
% graduated top 50% of class	96

DEADLINES

Regular
Deadline	2/28
Notification	rolling
Nonfall registration?	no

FINANCIAL FACTS

Tuition covered by full scholarship

UNITED STATES NAVAL ACADEMY

CAMPUS LIFE

Fire Safety Rating	**60***
Green Rating	**60***
Type of school	public
Environment	town

STUDENTS

Total undergrad enrollment	4,552
% male/female	80/20
% from out of state	96
% from public high school	60
% live on campus	100
% African American	5
% Asian	4
% Caucasian	71
% Hispanic	12
% international	1
# of countries represented	28

ACADEMICS

Calendar	semester
Student/faculty ratio	9:1
Profs interesting rating	82
Profs accessible rating	99
Most common reg class size	10–19 students

MOST POPULAR MAJORS

economics
political science and government
systems engineering

SELECTIVITY

# of applicants	15,342
% of applicants accepted	8
% of acceptees attending	85

# accepting a place on wait list	127
% admitted from wait list	30

FRESHMAN PROFILE

Range SAT Critical Reading	560–700
Range SAT Math	600–700
% graduated top 20% of class	76
% graduated top 40% of class	91

DEADLINES

Regular
Deadline	1/31
Notification	rolling
Nonfall registration?	no

FINANCIAL FACTS

Tuition covered by full scholarship

UNIVERSITY OF THE ARTS

CAMPUS LIFE

Fire Safety Rating	**60***
Green Rating	**60***
Type of school	private
Environment	metropolis

STUDENTS

Total undergrad enrollment	2,139
% male/female	42/58
% from out of state	63
% from public high school	85
% live on campus	35
% African American	11
% Asian	7
% Caucasian	64
% Hispanic	6
% international	5
# of countries represented	25

ACADEMICS

Calendar	semester
Student/faculty ratio	10:1
Profs interesting rating	90
Profs accessible rating	65
Most common reg class size	10–19 students

MOST POPULAR MAJORS

illustration
photography
jazz dance
theater arts

SELECTIVITY

# of applicants	2,928
% of applicants accepted	50
% of acceptees attending	42

FRESHMAN PROFILE

Range SAT Critical Reading	470–580
Range SAT Math	450–570
Range SAT Writing	460–580

Range ACT Composite	19–26
Minimum paper TOEFL	550
Minimum computer TOEFL	80
Average HS GPA	2.86
% graduated top 10% of class	10
% graduated top 25% of class	27
% graduated top 50% of class	64

DEADLINES

Regular	
Priority	3/1
Notification	rolling
Nonfall registration?	yes

FINANCIAL FACTS

Annual tuition	$30,700
Room and board	$7,200
Required fees	$990
Books and supplies	$2,100

UNIVERSITY OF CONNECTICUT

CAMPUS LIFE

Fire Safety Rating	**86**
Green Rating	**95**
Type of school	public
Environment	town

STUDENTS

Total undergrad enrollment	16,691
% male/female	50/50
% from out of state	23
% from public high school	95
% live on campus	73
# of fraternities	14
# of sororities	12
% African American	5
% Asian	8
% Caucasian	64
% Hispanic	5
% international	1
# of countries represented	109

ACADEMICS

Calendar	semester
Student/faculty ratio	18:1
Profs interesting rating	64
Profs accessible rating	71
% classes taught by TAs	24
Most common	
reg class size	10–19 students
Most common	
lab size	10–19 students

MOST POPULAR MAJORS

business/commerce
political science and government
psychology

SELECTIVITY

# of applicants	21,999
% of applicants accepted	50
% of acceptees attending	29
# accepting a place on wait list	1,667
% admitted from wait list	26

FRESHMAN PROFILE

Range SAT Critical Reading	550–640
Range SAT Math	570–670
Range SAT Writing	550–650
Range ACT Composite	24–29
Minimum paper TOEFL	550
Minimum computer TOEFL	213
Minimum web-based TOEFL	79
% graduated top 10% of class	44
% graduated top 25% of class	83
% graduated top 50% of class	99

DEADLINES

Early action	
Deadline	12/1
Notification	2/1
Regular	
Deadline	2/1
Notification	rolling
Nonfall registration?	yes

FINANCIAL FACTS

Annual in-state tuition	$7,632
Annual out-of-state tuition	$23,232
Room and board	$10,120
Required fees	$2,254
Books and supplies	$800
% frosh rec. need-based scholarship or grant aid	37
% UG rec. need-based scholarship or grant aid	34
% frosh rec. non-need-based scholarship or grant aid	37
% UG rec. non-need-based scholarship or grant aid	24
% frosh rec. need-based self-help aid	36
% UG rec. need-based self-help aid	38
% frosh rec. athletic scholarships	2
% UG rec. athletic scholarships	2
% frosh rec. any financial aid	49
% UG rec. any financial aid	48
% UG borrow to pay for school	61
Average cumulative indebtedness	$21,521

UNIVERSITY OF DELAWARE

CAMPUS LIFE

Fire Safety Rating	**96**
Green Rating	**88**
Type of school	public
Environment	town

STUDENTS

Total undergrad enrollment	15,757
% male/female	42/58
% from out of state	64
% from public high school	80
% live on campus	46
# of fraternities	22
# of sororities	15
% African American	5
% Asian	5
% Caucasian	4
% Hispanic	6
% international	2
# of countries represented	91

ACADEMICS

Calendar	4/1/4
Student/faculty ratio	12:1
Profs interesting rating	74
Profs accessible rating	77
% classes taught by TAs	5
Most common	
reg class size	20–29 students
Most common	
lab size	10–19 students

MOST POPULAR MAJORS

biology/biological sciences
nursing/registered nurse
(RN, ASN, BSN, MSN)
psychology

SELECTIVITY

# of applicants	24,744
% of applicants accepted	57
% of acceptees attending	30
# accepting a place on wait list	669
% admitted from wait list	29

FRESHMAN PROFILE

Range SAT Critical Reading	520–630
Range SAT Math	540–650
Range SAT Writing	520–640
Range ACT Composite	24–28
Minimum paper TOEFL	550
Minimum computer TOEFL	213
Minimum web-based TOEFL	80
Average HS GPA	3.5
% graduated top 10% of class	37
% graduated top 25% of class	74
% graduated top 50% of class	96

DEADLINES

Regular	
Priority	12/1
Deadline	1/15
Notification	3/15
Nonfall registration?	yes

FINANCIAL FACTS

Annual in-state tuition	$8,540
Annual out-of-state tuition	$22,240
Room and board	$9,066
Required fees	$946
Books and supplies	$800

% frosh rec. need-based
scholarship or grant aid 36
% UG rec. need-based
scholarship or grant aid 39
% frosh rec. non-need-based
scholarship or grant aid 22
% UG rec. non-need-based
scholarship or grant aid 16
% frosh rec. need-based
self-help aid 39
% UG rec. need-based
self-help aid 48
% frosh rec. athletic scholarships 4
% UG rec. athletic scholarships 4
% frosh rec. any financial aid 57
% UG rec. any financial aid 55
% UG borrow to pay for school 44
Average cumulative
indebtedness $17,200

UNIVERSITY OF MAINE

CAMPUS LIFE
Fire Safety Rating **86**
Green Rating **99**
Type of school public
Environment village

STUDENTS
Total undergrad enrollment 8,759
% male/female 52/48
% from out of state 15
% live on campus 40
# of fraternities 13
# of sororities 6
% African American 1
% Asian 1
% Caucasian 81
% Hispanic 1
% Native American 2
% international 2
# of countries represented 67

ACADEMICS
Calendar semester
Student/faculty ratio 15:1
Profs Interesting rating 69
Profs accessible rating 70
% classes taught by TAs 17
Most common
reg class size 10–19 students
Most common
lab size 10–19 students

MOST POPULAR MAJORS
business/commerce
education
engineering

SELECTIVITY
of applicants 6,786
% of applicants accepted 80
% of acceptees attending 32

FRESHMAN PROFILE
Range SAT Critical Reading 470–580
Range SAT Math 480–590
Range SAT Writing 460–560
Range ACT Composite 20–26
Minimum paper TOEFL 530
Minimum computer TOEFL 197
Minimum web-based TOEFL 71
Average HS GPA 3.18
% graduated top 10% of class 20
% graduated top 25% of class 49
% graduated top 50% of class 85

DEADLINES
Early action
Deadline 12/15
Notification 1/31
Regular
Priority 2/1
Notification rolling
Nonfall registration? yes

FINANCIAL FACTS
Annual in-state tuition $7,170
Annual out-of-state tuition $20,580
% frosh rec. need-based
scholarship or grant aid 53
% UG rec. need-based
scholarship or grant aid 46
% frosh rec. non-need-based
scholarship or grant aid 4
% UG rec. non-need-based
scholarship or grant aid 3
% frosh rec. need-based
self-help aid 52
% UG rec. need-based
self-help aid 52
% frosh rec. any financial aid 76
% UG rec. any financial aid 93
% UG borrow to pay for school 76
Average cumulative
indebtedness $22,630

UNIVERSITY OF MAINE—FORT KENT

CAMPUS LIFE
Fire Safety Rating **95**
Green Rating **78**
Type of school public
Environment rural

STUDENTS
Total undergrad enrollment 1,063
% male/female 34/66
% from out of state 4
% from public high school 96
% live on campus 30
# of sororities 1
% African American 2
% Caucasian 52

% Native American 1
% international 12

ACADEMICS
Calendar semester
Student/faculty ratio 17:1
Profs interesting rating 82
Profs accessible rating 85
Most common reg class size 10–19 students
Most common lab size fewer than
10 students

MOST POPULAR MAJORS
business/commerce
elementary education and teaching
nursing/registered nurse
(RN, ASN, BSN, MSN)

SELECTIVITY
of applicants 280
% of applicants accepted 78
% of acceptees attending 58

FRESHMAN PROFILE
Range SAT Critical Reading 350–482
Range SAT Math 350–465
Range SAT Writing 324–471
Range ACT Composite 18–22
Minimum paper TOEFL 500
Minimum computer TOEFL 175
Average HS GPA 2.64
% graduated top 10% of class 2
% graduated top 25% of class 19
% graduated top 50% of class 62

DEADLINES
Regular
Priority 8/15
Notification rolling
Nonfall registration? yes

FINANCIAL FACTS
Annual in-state tuition $6,030
Annual out-of-state tuition $15,180
Room and board $7,080
Required fees $773
Books and supplies $1,100
% frosh rec. need-based
scholarship or grant aid 47
% UG rec. need-based
scholarship or grant aid 35
% frosh rec. non-need-based
scholarship or grant aid 81
% UG rec. non-need-based
scholarship or grant aid 56
% frosh rec. need-based self-help aid 62
% UG rec. need-based self-help aid 46
% frosh rec. any financial aid 86
% UG rec. any financial aid 80

UNIVERSITY OF MARYLAND—
BALTIMORE COUNTY

CAMPUS LIFE
Fire Safety Rating	**85**
Green Rating	**91**
Type of school	public
Environment	metropolis

STUDENTS
Total undergrad enrollment	9,815
% male/female	54/46
% from out of state	6.7
# of fraternities	11
# of sororities	12
% African American	17
% Asian	21
% Caucasian	52
% Hispanic	4
% Native American	1
% international	4
# of countries represented	92

ACADEMICS
Calendar	4/1/4
Student/faculty ratio	19:1
Profs interesting rating	68
Profs accessible rating	66
% classes taught by TAs	2
Most common	
reg class size	20–29 students
Most common	
lab size	10–19 students

MOST POPULAR MAJORS
biology/biological sciences
computer and information sciences
psychology

SELECTIVITY
# of applicants	6,047
% of applicants accepted	69
% of acceptees attending	37
# accepting a place on wait list	246
% admitted from wait list	46

FRESHMAN PROFILE
Range SAT Critical Reading	530–630
Range SAT Math	550–660
Range SAT Writing	530–630
Range ACT Composite	22–29
Minimum paper TOEFL	460
Minimum computer TOEFL	140
Minimum web-based TOEFL	48
Average HS GPA	3.61
% graduated top 10% of class	24.2
% graduated top 25% of class	52
% graduated top 50% of class	84

DEADLINES
Early action	
Deadline	11/1
Notification	12/15
Regular	
Priority	11/1
Deadline	2/1
Notification	rolling
Nonfall registration?	yes

FINANCIAL FACTS
Annual in-state tuition	$8,872
Annual out-of-state tuition	$18,213
Room and board	$9,050
Books and supplies	$1,200
% frosh rec. need-based	
scholarship or grant aid	38
% UG rec. need-based	
scholarship or grant aid	39
% frosh rec. non-need-based	
scholarship or grant aid	7
% UG rec. non-need-based	
scholarship or grant aid	4
% frosh rec. need-based	
self-help aid	38
% UG rec. need-based	
self-help aid	43
% frosh rec. athletic scholarships	5
% UG rec. athletic scholarships	4
% frosh rec. any financial aid	70
% UG rec. any financial aid	61
% UG borrow to pay for school	51
Average cumulative	
indebtedness	$19,353

UNIVERSITY OF MARYLAND—
COLLEGE PARK

CAMPUS LIFE
Fire Safety Rating	**76**
Green Rating	**99**
Type of school	public
Environment	metropolis

STUDENTS
Total undergrad enrollment	25,898
% male/female	53/47
% from out of state	24
% live on campus	42
# of fraternities	36
# of sororities	27
% African American	12
% Asian	15
% Caucasian	58
% Hispanic	6
% international	2
# of countries represented	135

ACADEMICS
Calendar	semester
Student/faculty ratio	18:1
Profs interesting rating	71
Profs accessible rating	67
% classes taught by TAs	15
Most common	
reg class size	20–29 students
Most common	
lab size	20–29 students

MOST POPULAR MAJORS
criminology
economics
political science and government

SELECTIVITY
# of applicants	28,331
% of applicants accepted	42
% of acceptees attending	35
# accepting a place on wait list	857
% admitted from wait list	9

FRESHMAN PROFILE
Range SAT Critical Reading	580–680
Range SAT Math	620–710
Minimum paper TOEFL	575
Average HS GPA	3.93
% graduated top 10% of class	71
% graduated top 25% of class	91
% graduated top 50% of class	99

DEADLINES
Early action	
Deadline	11/1
Notification	1/31
Regular	
Priority	11/1
Deadline	1/20
Nonfall registration?	yes

FINANCIAL FACTS
Annual in-state tuition	$6,556
Annual out-of-state tuition	$22,503
Room and board	$9,377
Required fees	$1,487
Books and supplies	$1,025
% frosh rec. need-based	
scholarship or grant aid	25
% UG rec. need-based	
scholarship or grant aid	26
% frosh rec. non-need-based	
scholarship or grant aid	21
% UG rec. non-need-based	
scholarship or grant aid	14
% frosh rec. need-based	
self-help aid	23
% UG rec. need-based	
self-help aid	26
% frosh rec. athletic scholarships	1
% UG rec. athletic scholarships	1
% frosh rec. any financial aid	68
% UG rec. any financial aid	60
% UG borrow to pay for school	44
Average cumulative	
indebtedness	$20,091

UNIVERSITY OF
MASSACHUSETTS—AMHERST

CAMPUS LIFE
Fire Safety Rating **80**
Green Rating **89**
Type of school public
Environment town

STUDENTS
Total undergrad enrollment 20,873
% male/female 50/50
% from out of state 17
% live on campus 63
# of fraternities 21
# of sororities 15
% African American 5
% Asian 8
% Caucasian 70
% Hispanic 4
% international 1
# of countries represented 44

ACADEMICS
Calendar semester
Student/faculty ratio 18:1
Profs interesting rating 68
Profs accessible rating 71
Most common
reg class size 20–29 students
Most common
lab size 20–29 students

MOST POPULAR MAJORS
biology/biological sciences
business administration
and management
psychology

SELECTIVITY
of applicants 29,452
% of applicants accepted 67
% of acceptees attending 21
# accepting a place on wait list 214
% admitted from wait list 79

FRESHMAN PROFILE
Range SAT Critical Reading 520–630
Range SAT Math 540–650
Range ACT Composite 23–28
Minimum paper TOEFL 550
Minimum computer TOEFL 213
Average HS GPA 3.6
% graduated top 10% of class 27
% graduated top 25% of class 67
% graduated top 50% of class 97

DEADLINES
Early action
Deadline 11/1
Notification 12/15

Regular
Deadline 1/15
Nonfall registration? yes

FINANCIAL FACTS
Annual in-state tuition $11,732
Annual out-of-state tuition $23,229
% frosh rec. need-based
scholarship or grant aid 43
% UG rec. need-based
scholarship or grant aid 41
% frosh rec. non-need-based
scholarship or grant aid 3
% UG rec. non-need-based
scholarship or grant aid 3
% frosh rec. need-based
self-help aid 45
% UG rec. need-based
self-help aid 46
% frosh rec. athletic scholarships 1
% UG rec. athletic scholarships 1
% frosh rec. any financial aid 84
% UG rec. any financial aid 89
% UG borrow to pay for school 67
Average cumulative
indebtedness $23,614

UNIVERSITY OF
MASSACHUSETTS—BOSTON

CAMPUS LIFE
Fire Safety Rating **60***
Green Rating **96**
Type of school public
Environment metropolis

STUDENTS
Total undergrad enrollment 10,130
% male/female 42/58
% from out of state 5
% African American 16
% Asian 13
% Caucasian 48
% Hispanic 9
% international 4
# of countries represented 139

ACADEMICS
Calendar semester
Student/faculty ratio 16:1
Profs interesting rating 78
Profs accessible rating 69
Most common reg class size 20–29 students
Most common lab size fewer than
10 students

MOST POPULAR MAJORS
management science
nursing/registered nurse
(RN, ASN, BSN, MSN)
psychology

SELECTIVITY
of applicants 6,050
% of applicants accepted 61
% of acceptees attending 27

FRESHMAN PROFILE
Range SAT Critical Reading 460–570
Range SAT Math 480–580
Minimum paper TOEFL 550
Minimum computer TOEFL 213
Minimum web-based TOEFL 79
Average HS GPA 3

DEADLINES
Regular
Priority 3/1
Deadline 6/1
Nonfall registration? yes

FINANCIAL FACTS
Annual in-state tuition $1,714
Annual out-of-state tuition $9,758
Required fees $8,897
% frosh rec. need-based
scholarship or grant aid 58
% UG rec. need-based
scholarship or grant aid 52
% frosh rec. non-need-based
scholarship or grant aid 3
% UG rec. non-need-based
scholarship or grant aid 2
% frosh rec. need-based self-help aid 57
% UG rec. need-based self-help aid 58
% UG borrow to pay for school 67
Average cumulative indebtedness $19,327

UNIVERSITY OF NEW
HAMPSHIRE

CAMPUS LIFE
Fire Safety Rating **96**
Green Rating **97**
Type of school public
Environment village

STUDENTS
Total undergrad enrollment 12,226
% male/female 44/56
% from out of state 42
% from public high school 81
% live on campus 59
# of fraternities 10
# of sororities 7
% African American 2
% Asian 2
% Caucasian 77
% Hispanic 2

% international	1
# of countries represented	52

ACADEMICS

Calendar	semester
Student/faculty ratio	19:1
Profs interesting rating	62
Profs accessible rating	62
% classes taught by TAs	1
Most common	
reg class size	20–29 students
Most common	
lab size	20–29 students

MOST POPULAR MAJORS
business administration
and management
English language and literature
psychology

SELECTIVITY

# of applicants	16,132
% of applicants accepted	72
% of acceptees attending	25

FRESHMAN PROFILE

Range SAT Critical Reading	510–610
Range SAT Math	520–630
Minimum paper TOEFL	550
Minimum computer TOEFL	213
Minimum web-based TOEFL	80
% graduated top 10% of class	25
% graduated top 25% of class	71
% graduated top 50% of class	97

DEADLINES

Early action	
Deadline	11/15
Notification	1/15
Regular	
Deadline	2/1
Notification	rolling
Nonfall registration?	yes

FINANCIAL FACTS

Annual in-state tuition	$10,080
Annual out-of-state tuition	$24,050
Room and board	$8,874
Required fees	$2,663
Books and supplies	$1,200
% frosh rec. need-based	
scholarship or grant aid	39
% UG rec. need-based	
scholarship or grant aid	37
% frosh rec. non-need-based	
scholarship or grant aid	6
% UG rec. non-need-based	
scholarship or grant aid	4
% frosh rec. need-based	
self-help aid	58
% UG rec. need-based	
self-help aid	57
% frosh rec. athletic scholarships	2
% UG rec. athletic scholarships	2
% frosh rec. any financial aid	84

% UG rec. any financial aid	79
% UG borrow to pay for school	74
Average cumulative	
indebtedness	$30,760

UNIVERSITY OF PENNSYLVANIA

CAMPUS LIFE

Fire Safety Rating	**70**
Green Rating	**90**
Type of school	private
Environment	metropolis

STUDENTS

Total undergrad enrollment	9,756
% male/female	50/50
% from out of state	83
% from public high school	55
% live on campus	62
# of fraternities	35
# of sororities	13
% African American	8
% Asian	18
% Caucasian	43
% Hispanic	6
% international	10
# of countries represented	103

ACADEMICS

Calendar	semester
Student/faculty ratio	6:1
Profs interesting rating	73
Profs accessible rating	79
% classes taught by TAs	5
Most common	
reg class size	10–19 students

MOST POPULAR MAJORS
business administration
and management
finance
nursing/registered nurse
(RN, ASN, BSN, MSN)

SELECTIVITY

# of applicants	22,935
% of applicants accepted	17
% of acceptees attending	63
# accepting a place on wait list	2,381
% admitted from wait list	7
# of early decision applicants	3,912
% accepted early decision	29

FRESHMAN PROFILE

Range SAT Critical Reading	650–740
Range SAT Math	680–780
Range SAT Writing	670–760
Range ACT Composite	30–33
Minimum paper TOEFL	600
Minimum computer TOEFL	220
Minimum web-based TOEFL	100
Average HS GPA	3.83

% graduated top 10% of class	99
% graduated top 25% of class	100
% graduated top 50% of class	100

DEADLINES

Early decision	
Deadline	11/1
Notification	12/15
Regular	
Deadline	1/1
Notification	4/1
Nonfall registration?	no

FINANCIAL FACTS

Annual tuition	$34,868
Room and board	$11,016
Required fees	$4,102
Books and supplies	$1,094
% frosh rec. need-based	
scholarship or grant aid	37
% UG rec. need-based	
scholarship or grant aid	39
% frosh rec. need-based	
self-help aid	38
% UG rec. need-based	
self-help aid	41
% frosh rec. any financial aid	60
% UG rec. any financial aid	55
% UG borrow to pay for school	41
Average cumulative	
indebtedness	$19,085

UNIVERSITY OF PITTSBURGH AT BRADFORD

CAMPUS LIFE

Fire Safety Rating	**81**
Green Rating	**75**
Type of school	public
Environment	village

STUDENTS

Total undergrad enrollment	1,705
% male/female	50/50
% from out of state	14
% from public high school	94
% live on campus	52
# of fraternities	3
# of sororities	3
% African American	6
% Asian	2
% Caucasian	85
% Hispanic	2
% Native American	1
# of countries represented	8

ACADEMICS

Calendar	semester
Student/faculty ratio	18:1
Profs interesting rating	78

Profs accessible rating 75
Most common reg class size 20–29 students
Most common lab size 10–19 students

MOST POPULAR MAJORS
elementary education
business management
criminal justice
nursing
sports medicine

SELECTIVITY
# of applicants	987
% of applicants accepted	83
% of acceptees attending	51
# accepting a place on wait list	10
% admitted from wait list	100

FRESHMAN PROFILE
Range SAT Critical Reading	440–520
Range SAT Math	450–550
Range SAT Writing	430–530
Range ACT Composite	19–22
Minimum paper TOEFL	550
Minimum computer TOEFL	213
Average HS GPA	3.11
% graduated top 10% of class	0.29
% graduated top 25% of class	6.47
% graduated top 50% of class	42.06

DEADLINES
Regular	
Priority	5/1
Notification	rolling
Nonfall registration?	yes

FINANCIAL FACTS
Annual in-state tuition	$11,012
Annual out-of-state tuition	$20,572
Room and board	$7,480
Required fees	$710
Books and supplies	$1,050
% frosh rec. need-based scholarship or grant aid	56
% UG rec. need-based scholarship or grant aid	36
% frosh rec. non-need-based scholarship or grant aid	61
% UG rec. non-need-based scholarship or grant aid	31
% frosh rec. need-based self-help aid	86
% UG rec. need-based self-help aid	57
% frosh rec. any financial aid	86
% UG rec. any financial aid	89
% UG borrow to pay for school	82
Average cumulative indebtedness	$21,683

UNIVERSITY OF PITTSBURGH AT JOHNSTOWN

CAMPUS LIFE
Fire Safety Rating	**60***
Green Rating	**60***
Type of school	public
Environment	city

STUDENTS
Total undergrad enrollment	3,043
% male/female	54/46
% from out of state	2
% live on campus	56
# of fraternities	5
# of sororities	3
% African American	2
% Asian	2
% Caucasian	92
% Hispanic	1
% international	1
# of countries represented	20

ACADEMICS
Calendar	semester
Student/faculty ratio	18:1
Profs interesting rating	77
Profs accessible rating	78
Most common reg class size	20–29 students
Most common lab size	10–19 students

SELECTIVITY
# of applicants	1,652
% of applicants accepted	89
% of acceptees attending	56

FRESHMAN PROFILE
Range SAT Critical Reading	450–540
Range SAT Math	460–570
Range SAT Writing	440–540
Range ACT Composite	18–23
Minimum paper TOEFL	550
Minimum computer TOEFL	213
Minimum web-based TOEFL	80
Average HS GPA	3.36
% graduated top 10% of class	10
% graduated top 25% of class	35
% graduated top 50% of class	73

DEADLINES
Regular	
Notification	rolling
Nonfall registration?	yes

FINANCIAL FACTS
Annual in-state tuition	$11,012
Annual out-of-state tuition	$20,572
Room and board	$7,530

Required fees	$836
Books and supplies	$1,030
% frosh rec. need-based scholarship or grant aid	55
% UG rec. need-based scholarship or grant aid	51
% frosh rec. non-need-based scholarship or grant aid	22
% UG rec. non-need-based scholarship or grant aid	19
% frosh rec. need-based self-help aid	69
% UG rec. need-based self-help aid	64
% frosh rec. athletic scholarships	5
% UG rec. athletic scholarships	4
% frosh rec. any financial aid	80
% UG rec. any financial aid	80
% UG borrow to pay for school	85
Average cumulative indebtedness	$23,243

UNIVERSITY OF PITTSBURGH— PITTSBURGH CAMPUS

CAMPUS LIFE
Fire Safety Rating	**82**
Green Rating	**80**
Type of school	public
Environment	metropolis

STUDENTS
Total undergrad enrollment	17,682
% male/female	49/51
% from out of state	19
% live on campus	45
# of fraternities	20
# of sororities	16
% African American	8
% Asian	5
% Caucasian	79
% Hispanic	1
% international	1
# of countries represented	48

ACADEMICS
Calendar	semester
Profs interesting rating	77
Profs accessible rating	81
Most common reg class size	10–19 students
Most common lab size	20–29 students

MOST POPULAR MAJORS
marketing/marketing management
psychology
speech and rhetorical studies

SELECTIVITY
# of applicants	21,737
% of applicants accepted	59

% of acceptees attending	29
# accepting a place on wait list	186
% admitted from wait list	12

FRESHMAN PROFILE

Range SAT Critical Reading	570–680
Range SAT Math	590–680
Range SAT Writing	560–660
Range ACT Composite	25–30
Minimum paper TOEFL	550
Minimum computer TOEFL	213
Minimum web-based TOEFL	80
Average HS GPA	3.87
% graduated top 10% of class	49
% graduated top 25% of class	86
% graduated top 50% of class	99

DEADLINES

Regular	
Notification	rolling
Nonfall registration?	yes

FINANCIAL FACTS

Annual in-state tuition	$13,344
Annual out-of-state tuition	$23,042
Room and board	$8,900
Required fees	$810
Books and supplies	$1,050
% frosh rec. need-based scholarship or grant aid	41
% UG rec. need-based scholarship or grant aid	38
% frosh rec. non-need-based scholarship or grant aid	22
% UG rec. non-need-based scholarship or grant aid	16
% frosh rec. need-based self-help aid	43
% UG rec. need-based self-help aid	45
% frosh rec. athletic scholarships	1
% UG rec. athletic scholarships	1
% frosh rec. any financial aid	64
% UG rec. any financial aid	63

UNIVERSITY OF RHODE ISLAND

CAMPUS LIFE

Fire Safety Rating	**80**
Green Rating	**93**
Type of school	public
Environment	village

STUDENTS

Total undergrad enrollment	13,234
% male/female	45/55
% from out of state	38
% live on campus	45
# of fraternities	12
# of sororities	10
% African American	5

% Asian	3
% Caucasian	73
% Hispanic	6
# of countries represented	41

ACADEMICS

Calendar	semester
Student/faculty ratio	15:1
Profs interesting rating	62
Profs accessible rating	63
% classes taught by TAs	2.8
Most common reg class size	20–29 students
Most common lab size	10–19 students

MOST POPULAR MAJORS
communication studies/
speech communication and rhetoric
nursing/registered nurse
(RN, ASN, BSN, MSN)
psychology

SELECTIVITY

# of applicants	16,126
% of applicants accepted	84
% of acceptees attending	23

FRESHMAN PROFILE

Range SAT Critical Reading	480–580
Range SAT Math	490–600
Minimum paper TOEFL	550
Minimum computer TOEFL	213
Minimum web-based TOEFL	79
Average HS GPA	3.2
% graduated top 10% of class	17

DEADLINES

Early action	
Deadline	12/1
Notification	1/31
Regular	
Deadline	2/1
Notification	rolling
Nonfall registration?	yes

FINANCIAL FACTS

Annual in-state tuition	$8,238
Annual out-of-state tuition	$24,736
Room and board	$10,334
Required fees	$1,290
Books and supplies	$1,200
% frosh rec. need-based scholarship or grant aid	60
% UG rec. need-based scholarship or grant aid	60
% frosh rec. non-need-based scholarship or grant aid	5
% UG rec. non-need-based scholarship or grant aid	4
% frosh rec. need-based self-help aid	59
% UG rec. need-based self-help aid	59
% frosh rec. any financial aid	60

% UG rec. any financial aid	60
% UG borrow to pay for school	69
Average cumulative indebtedness	$22,500

UNIVERSITY OF ROCHESTER

CAMPUS LIFE

Fire Safety Rating	**70**
Green Rating	**88**
Type of school	private
Environment	metropolis

STUDENTS

Total undergrad enrollment	5,291
% male/female	49/51
% from out of state	50
% from public high school	75
% live on campus	83
# of fraternities	19
# of sororities	14
% African American	4
% Asian	10
% Caucasian	54
% Hispanic	4
% international	8
# of countries represented	92

ACADEMICS

Calendar	semester
Student/faculty ratio	9:1
Profs interesting rating	72
Profs accessible rating	77
Most common reg class size	10–19 students

MOST POPULAR MAJORS
biology/biological sciences
economics
psychology

SELECTIVITY

# of applicants	12,111
% of applicants accepted	39
% of acceptees attending	23
# accepting a place on wait list	357
% admitted from wait list	20
# of early decision applicants	765
% accepted early decision	39

FRESHMAN PROFILE

Range SAT Critical Reading	590–690
Range SAT Math	640–720
Range SAT Writing	590–690
Range ACT Composite	28–33
Minimum paper TOEFL	600
Minimum computer TOEFL	250
Minimum web-based TOEFL	100
Average HS GPA	3.8
% graduated top 10% of class	76
% graduated top 25% of class	91
% graduated top 50% of class	99

DEADLINES
Early decision
Deadline	11/1
Notification	12/15

Regular
Deadline	1/1
Notification	4/1
Nonfall registration?	yes

FINANCIAL FACTS
Annual tuition	$37,870
Room and board	$11,200
Required fees	$820
Books and supplies	$1,250
% frosh rec. need-based scholarship or grant aid	61
% UG rec. need-based scholarship or grant aid	57
% frosh rec. non-need-based scholarship or grant aid	7
% UG rec. non-need-based scholarship or grant aid	5
% frosh rec. need-based self-help aid	53
% UG rec. need-based self-help aid	51
% frosh rec. any financial aid	88
% UG rec. any financial aid	88
% UG borrow to pay for school	55
Average cumulative indebtedness	$27,121

UNIVERSITY OF SCRANTON

CAMPUS LIFE
Fire Safety Rating	80
Green Rating	71
Type of school	private
Affiliation	Roman Catholic/or Jesuit
Environment	city

STUDENTS
Total undergrad enrollment	4,154
% male/female	43/57
% from out of state	53
% live on campus	53
% African American	1
% Asian	3
% Caucasian	80
% Hispanic	4
% international	1
# of countries represented	25

ACADEMICS
Calendar	semester
Student/faculty ratio	12:1
Profs interesting rating	77
Profs accessible rating	81
Most common reg class size	10–19 students
Most common lab size	10–19 students

MOST POPULAR MAJORS
biology/biological sciences
elementary education and teaching
marketing/marketing management

SELECTIVITY
# of applicants	8,254
% of applicants accepted	70
% of acceptees attending	18
# accepting a place on wait list	405
% admitted from wait list	9

FRESHMAN PROFILE
Range SAT Critical Reading	510–600
Range SAT Math	520–620
Minimum paper TOEFL	500
Minimum computer TOEFL	173
Average HS GPA	3.36
% graduated top 10% of class	27
% graduated top 25% of class	62
% graduated top 50% of class	90

DEADLINES
Early action
Deadline	11/15
Notification	12/15

Regular
Priority	3/1
Deadline	3/1
Notification	rolling
Nonfall registration?	yes

FINANCIAL FACTS
Annual tuition	$34,236
Room and board	$12,264
Required fees	$300
Books and supplies	$1,150
% frosh rec. need-based scholarship or grant aid	68
% UG rec. need-based scholarship or grant aid	63
% frosh rec. non-need-based scholarship or grant aid	7
% UG rec. non-need-based scholarship or grant aid	5
% frosh rec. need-based self-help aid	59
% UG rec. need-based self-help aid	56
% frosh rec. any financial aid	85
% UG rec. any financial aid	82
% UG borrow to pay for school	77
Average cumulative indebtedness	$30,920

UNIVERSITY OF SOUTHERN MAINE

CAMPUS LIFE
Fire Safety Rating	60*
Green Rating	60*
Type of school	public
Environment	town

STUDENTS
Total undergrad enrollment	6,548
% male/female	43/57
# of fraternities	4
# of sororities	4
% African American	2
% Asian	2
% Caucasian	92
% Hispanic	1
% Native American	2
% international	2
# of countries represented	40

ACADEMICS
Calendar	semester
Profs interesting rating	71
Profs accessible rating	64

MOST POPULAR MAJORS
perioperative/operating room and surgical nurse/nursing
psychology

SELECTIVITY
# of applicants	4,141
% of applicants accepted	84
% of acceptees attending	27

FRESHMAN PROFILE
Range SAT Critical Reading	450–560
Range SAT Math	450–560
Range SAT Writing	440–550
Range ACT Composite	18–23
Minimum paper TOEFL	550
Minimum computer TOEFL	213
Average HS GPA	3.04
% graduated top 10% of class	8
% graduated top 25% of class	29
% graduated top 50% of class	66

DEADLINES
Regular
Priority	2/15
Notification	rolling
Nonfall registration?	yes

FINANCIAL FACTS
Annual in-state tuition	$6,930
Annual out-of-state tuition	$19,140
Room and board	$8,762

Required fees	$884
Books and supplies	$1,000
% frosh rec. any financial aid	70
% UG rec. any financial aid	79

UNIVERSITY OF VERMONT

CAMPUS LIFE

Fire Safety Rating	**89**
Green Rating	**93**
Type of school	public
Environment	town

STUDENTS

Total undergrad enrollment	10,371
% male/female	44/56
% from out of state	65
% from public high school	70
% live on campus	51
# of fraternities	9
# of sororities	6
% African American	1
% Asian	2
% Caucasian	91
% Hispanic	2
% international	1
# of countries represented	54

ACADEMICS

Calendar	semester
Student/faculty ratio	17:1
Profs interesting rating	75
Profs accessible rating	76
% classes taught by TAs	2
Most common reg class size	10–19 students
Most common lab size	20–29 students

MOST POPULAR MAJORS
biology/biological sciences
business administration
and management
psychology

SELECTIVITY

# of applicants	22,365
% of applicants accepted	71
% of acceptees attending	17
# accepting a place on wait list	1,173
% admitted from wait list	19

FRESHMAN PROFILE

Range SAT Critical Reading	540–640
Range SAT Math	550–640
Range SAT Writing	540–640
Range ACT Composite	24–28
Minimum paper TOEFL	550
Minimum computer TOEFL	213
% graduated top 10% of class	29
% graduated top 25% of class	66
% graduated top 50% of class	96

DEADLINES

Early action	
Deadline	11/1
Notification	12/15
Regular	
Deadline	1/15
Notification	3/31
Nonfall registration?	yes

FINANCIAL FACTS

Annual in-state tuition	$11,712
Annual out-of-state tuition	$29,568
Room and board	$8,996
Required fees	$1,842
Books and supplies	$1,050
% frosh rec. need-based scholarship or grant aid	55
% UG rec. need-based scholarship or grant aid	50
% frosh rec. non-need-based scholarship or grant aid	4
% UG rec. non-need-based scholarship or grant aid	3
% frosh rec. need-based self-help aid	48
% UG rec. need-based self-help aid	47
% frosh rec. athletic scholarships	2
% UG rec. athletic scholarships	2
% frosh rec. any financial aid	90
% UG rec. any financial aid	84
% UG borrow to pay for school	63
Average cumulative indebtedness	$27,682

URSINUS COLLEGE

CAMPUS LIFE

Fire Safety Rating	**87**
Green Rating	**85**
Type of school	private
Environment	suburb

STUDENTS

Total undergrad enrollment	1,700
% male/female	45/55
% from out of state	42
% from public high school	61
% live on campus	95
# of fraternities	7
# of sororities	8
% African American	6
% Asian	4
% Caucasian	73
% Hispanic	3
% international	1
# of countries represented	13

ACADEMICS

Calendar	semester
Student/faculty ratio	12:1
Profs interesting rating	83
Profs accessible rating	87

Most common reg class size	fewer than 10 students
Most common lab size	10–19 students

MOST POPULAR MAJORS
biology/biological sciences
economics
psychology

SELECTIVITY

# of applicants	6,192
% of applicants accepted	55
% of acceptees attending	32
# accepting a place on wait list	260
% admitted from wait list	3
# of early decision applicants	197
% accepted early decision	62

FRESHMAN PROFILE

Range SAT Critical Reading	570–680
Range SAT Math	570–670
Range SAT Writing	560–660
Range ACT Composite	25–29
Minimum paper TOEFL	500
Minimum computer TOEFL	173
Average HS GPA	3.67
% graduated top 10% of class	48
% graduated top 25% of class	78
% graduated top 50% of class	96

DEADLINES

Early decision	
Deadline	1/15
Notification	2/15
Early action	
Deadline	12/1
Regular	
Priority	2/15
Deadline	2/15
Notification	4/1
Nonfall registration?	yes

FINANCIAL FACTS

Annual tuition	$38,500
Books and supplies	$1,000
% frosh rec. need-based scholarship or grant aid	64
% UG rec. need-based scholarship or grant aid	66
% frosh rec. non-need-based scholarship or grant aid	17
% UG rec. non-need-based scholarship or grant aid	16
% frosh rec. need-based self-help aid	50
% UG rec. need-based self-help aid	55
% frosh rec. any financial aid	92
% UG rec. any financial aid	91
% UG borrow to pay for school	75
Average cumulative indebtedness	$21,171

VASSAR COLLEGE

CAMPUS LIFE
Fire Safety Rating	**81**
Green Rating	**90**
Type of school	private
Environment	town

STUDENTS
Total undergrad enrollment	2,394
% male/female	41/59
% from out of state	73
% from public high school	61
% live on campus	95
% African American	5
% Asian	11
% Caucasian	70
% Hispanic	7
% international	6
# of countries represented	43

ACADEMICS
Calendar	semester
Student/faculty ratio	8:1
Profs interesting rating	91
Profs accessible rating	89
Most common reg class size	10–19 students
Most common lab size	10–19 students

MOST POPULAR MAJORS
English language and literature
political science and government
psychology

SELECTIVITY
# of applicants	7,577
% of applicants accepted	25
% of acceptees attending	35
# accepting a place on wait list	608
% admitted from wait list	9
# of early decision applicants	599
% accepted early decision	43

FRESHMAN PROFILE
Range SAT Critical Reading	660–750
Range SAT Math	640–720
Range SAT Writing	660–750
Range ACT Composite	29–32
Minimum paper TOEFL	600
Minimum computer TOEFL	250
Minimum web-based TOEFL	100
Average HS GPA	3.77
% graduated top 10% of class	67
% graduated top 25% of class	95
% graduated top 50% of class	99

DEADLINES
Early decision	
Deadline	11/15
Notification	12/15
Regular	
Deadline	1/1
Notification	4/1
Nonfall registration?	no

FINANCIAL FACTS
Annual tuition	$41,335
Room and board	$9,370
Required fees	$595
Books and supplies	$860
% frosh rec. need-based scholarship or grant aid	60
% UG rec. need-based scholarship or grant aid	56
% frosh rec. need-based self-help aid	60
% UG rec. need-based self-help aid	56
% frosh rec. any financial aid	61
% UG rec. any financial aid	56
% UG borrow to pay for school	49
Average cumulative indebtedness	$18,876

VILLANOVA UNIVERSITY

CAMPUS LIFE
Fire Safety Rating	**85**
Green Rating	**86**
Type of school	private
Affiliation	Roman Catholic
Environment	village

STUDENTS
Total undergrad enrollment	6,897
% male/female	49/51
% from out of state	70
% from public high school	56
% live on campus	70
# of fraternities	9
# of sororities	9
% African American	5
% Asian	7
% Caucasian	76
% Hispanic	7
% international	3
# of countries represented	53

ACADEMICS
Calendar	semester
Student/faculty ratio	11:1
Profs interesting rating	85
Profs accessible rating	92
Most common reg class size	10–19 students
Most common lab size	10–19 students

MOST POPULAR MAJORS
communication studies/
speech communication and rhetoric
finance
nursing/registered nurse
(RN, ASN, BSN, MSN)

SELECTIVITY
# of applicants	13,098
% of applicants accepted	46
% of acceptees attending	27
# accepting a place on wait list	1,922
% admitted from wait list	4

FRESHMAN PROFILE
Range SAT Critical Reading	580–680
Range SAT Math	620–710
Range ACT Composite	28–31
Minimum paper TOEFL	550
Minimum computer TOEFL	213
Average HS GPA	3.76
% graduated top 10% of class	58
% graduated top 25% of class	88
% graduated top 50% of class	98

DEADLINES
Early action	
Deadline	11/1
Notification	12/20
Regular	
Priority	12/15
Deadline	1/7
Notification	4/1
Nonfall registration?	no

FINANCIAL FACTS
Annual tuition	$37,210
Room and board	$10,320
Required fees	$580
Books and supplies	$950
% frosh rec. need-based scholarship or grant aid	49
% UG rec. need-based scholarship or grant aid	42
% frosh rec. non-need-based scholarship or grant aid	16
% UG rec. non-need-based scholarship or grant aid	13
% frosh rec. need-based self-help aid	50
% UG rec. need-based self-help aid	45
% frosh rec. athletic scholarships	2
% UG rec. athletic scholarships	2
% frosh rec. any financial aid	53
% UG rec. any financial aid	48
% UG borrow to pay for school	55
Average cumulative indebtedness	$31,048

WAGNER COLLEGE

CAMPUS LIFE
Fire Safety Rating	**96**
Green Rating	**74**
Type of school	private
Environment	metropolis

STUDENTS

Total undergrad enrollment	1,911
% male/female	38/62
% from out of state	52
% live on campus	71
# of fraternities	5
# of sororities	4
% African American	5
% Asian	2
% Caucasian	83
% Hispanic	6
% international	1
# of countries represented	19

ACADEMICS

Calendar	semester
Student/faculty ratio	14:1
Profs interesting rating	73
Profs accessible rating	76
Most common reg class size	10–19 students
Most common lab size	10–19 students

MOST POPULAR MAJORS
biology/biological sciences
business/commerce
psychology

SELECTIVITY

# of applicants	3,012
% of applicants accepted	61
% of acceptees attending	26
# accepting a place on wait list	120
% admitted from wait list	53
# of early decision applicants	90
% accepted early decision	63

FRESHMAN PROFILE

Range SAT Critical Reading	530–640
Range SAT Math	530–650
Range SAT Writing	520–650
Range ACT Composite	23–28
Minimum paper TOEFL	550
Minimum computer TOEFL	217
Minimum web-based TOEFL	17
Average HS GPA	89
% graduated top 10% of class	17
% graduated top 25% of class	70
% graduated top 50% of class	92

DEADLINES

Early decision	
Deadline	1/1
Notification	1/15
Regular	
Priority	2/15
Deadline	2/15
Notification	3/1
Nonfall registration?	yes

FINANCIAL FACTS

Annual tuition	$32,430
Room and board	$9,700
Required fees	$150
Books and supplies	$745
% frosh rec. need-based scholarship or grant aid	63
% UG rec. need-based scholarship or grant aid	55
% frosh rec. need-based self-help aid	48
% UG rec. need-based self-help aid	44
% frosh rec. athletic scholarships	6
% UG rec. athletic scholarships	6
% frosh rec. any financial aid	92
% UG rec. any financial aid	90
% UG borrow to pay for school	56
Average cumulative indebtedness	$34,326

WASHINGTON & JEFFERSON COLLEGE

CAMPUS LIFE

Fire Safety Rating	85
Green Rating	82
Type of school	private
Environment	village

STUDENTS

Total undergrad enrollment	1,479
% male/female	53/47
% from out of state	24
% from public high school	82
% live on campus	92
# of fraternities	6
# of sororities	4
% African American	3
% Asian	1
% Caucasian	84
% Hispanic	1
# of countries represented	11

ACADEMICS

Calendar	4/1/4
Student/faculty ratio	12:1
Profs interesting rating	89
Profs accessible rating	88
Most common reg class size	10–19 students
Most common lab size	10–19 students

MOST POPULAR MAJORS
accounting
business/commerce
psychology

SELECTIVITY

# of applicants	6,658
% of applicants accepted	42
% of acceptees attending	14
# accepting a place on wait list	18
% admitted from wait list	22

FRESHMAN PROFILE

Range SAT Critical Reading	510–610
Range SAT Math	520–620
Range ACT Composite	22–28
Minimum paper TOEFL	567
Minimum computer TOEFL	227
Minimum web-based TOEFL	86
Average HS GPA	3.34
% graduated top 10% of class	38
% graduated top 25% of class	71
% graduated top 50% of class	94

DEADLINES

Early decision	
Deadline	12/1
Notification	12/15
Early action	
Deadline	1/15
Notification	2/15
Regular	
Priority	1/15
Deadline	3/1
Notification	rolling
Nonfall registration?	yes

FINANCIAL FACTS

Annual tuition	$34,150
Books and supplies	$800
% frosh rec. need-based scholarship or grant aid	65
% UG rec. need-based scholarship or grant aid	65
% frosh rec. non-need-based scholarship or grant aid	71
% UG rec. non-need-based scholarship or grant aid	65
% frosh rec. need-based self-help aid	69
% UG rec. need-based self-help aid	68
% frosh rec. any financial aid	100
% UG rec. any financial aid	98
% UG borrow to pay for school	75
Average cumulative indebtedness	$23

WAHINGTON COLLEGE

CAMPUS LIFE

Fire Safety Rating	95
Green Rating	60*
Type of school	private
Environment	rural

STUDENTS

Total undergrad enrollment	1,268
% male/female	41/59
% from out of state	48
% from public high school	65
% live on campus	86
# of fraternities	4
# of sororities	3
% African American	5

% Asian | 2
% Caucasian | 86
% Hispanic | 1
% international | 2
# of countries represented | 25

ACADEMICS
Calendar | semester
Student/faculty ratio | 12:1
Profs interesting rating | 87
Profs accessible rating | 87
Most common
reg class size | 10–19 students
Most common
lab size | fewer than 10 students

MOST POPULAR MAJORS
business administration
and management
English language and literature
psychology

SELECTIVITY
of applicants | 4,498
% of applicants accepted | 72
% of acceptees attending | 12
# accepting a place on wait list | 120
% admitted from wait list | 50
# of early decision applicants | 262
% accepted early decision | 76

FRESHMAN PROFILE
Range SAT Critical Reading | 520–620
Range SAT Math | 510–610
Range SAT Writing | 520–620
Range ACT Composite | 22–29
Average HS GPA | 3.44
% graduated top 10% of class | 30
% graduated top 25% of class | 71
% graduated top 50% of class | 92

DEADLINES
Early decision
Deadline | 11/1
Notification | 12/1
Early action
Deadline | 11/15
Notification | 12/15
Regular
Priority | 2/15
Deadline | 3/1
Notification | rolling
Nonfall registration? | yes

FINANCIAL FACTS
Annual tuition | $34,690
Room and board | $7,460
Required fees | $660
Books and supplies | $1,250
% frosh rec. need-based
scholarship or grant aid | 57
% UG rec. need-based
scholarship or grant aid | 53
% frosh rec. non-need-based
scholarship or grant aid | 30

% UG rec. non-need-based
scholarship or grant aid | 27
% frosh rec. need-based
self-help aid | 50
% UG rec. need-based
self-help aid | 47
% frosh rec. any financial aid | 88
% UG rec. any financial aid | 82
% UG borrow to pay for school | 58
Average cumulative
indebtedness | $28,727

WEBB INSTITUTE

CAMPUS LIFE
Fire Safety Rating | **63**
Green Rating | **60***
Type of school | private
Environment | village

STUDENTS
Total undergrad enrollment | 89
% male/female | 87/13
% from out of state | 72
% from public high school | 73
% live on campus | 100
% Asian | 8
% Caucasian | 85
% Hispanic | 4

ACADEMICS
Calendar | semester
Profs interesting rating | 89
Profs accessible rating | 99
Most common
reg class size | 20–29 students

SELECTIVITY
of applicants | 74
% of applicants accepted | 36
% of acceptees attending | 61
# of early decision applicants | 10
% accepted early decision | 20

FRESHMAN PROFILE
Range SAT Critical Reading | 640–680
Range SAT Math | 700–740
Range SAT Writing | 610–670
Average HS GPA | 3.8
% graduated top 10% of class | 67
% graduated top 25% of class | 83
% graduated top 50% of class | 100

DEADLINES
Early decision
Deadline | 10/15
Notification | 12/15
Regular
Priority | 10/15
Deadline | 2/15
Notification | rolling
Nonfall registration? | no

FINANCIAL FACTS
Annual tuition | $0
Room and board | $10,200
Books and supplies | $750
% frosh rec. need-based
scholarship or grant aid | 8
% UG rec. need-based
scholarship or grant aid | 14
% frosh rec. non-need-based
scholarship or grant aid | 4
% UG rec. non-need-based
scholarship or grant aid | 10
% frosh rec. need-based
self-help aid | 21
% UG rec. need-based
self-help aid | 11
% frosh rec. any financial aid | 25
% UG rec. any financial aid | 20
% UG borrow to pay for school | 20
Average cumulative
indebtedness | $7,303

WELLESLEY COLLEGE

CAMPUS LIFE
Fire Safety Rating | **83**
Green Rating | **88**
Type of school | private
Environment | town

STUDENTS
Total undergrad enrollment | 2,193
% male/female | 0/100
% from out of state | 84
% from public high school | 63
% live on campus | 92
% African American | 7
% Asian | 26
% Caucasian | 43
% Hispanic | 8
% Native American | 1
% international | 10
# of countries represented | 70

ACADEMICS
Calendar | semester
Student/faculty ratio | 8:1
Profs interesting rating | 99
Profs accessible rating | 98
Most common
reg class size | 10–19 students
Most common
lab size | 10–19 students

MOST POPULAR MAJORS
economics
political science and government
psychology

SELECTIVITY
of applicants | 4,156
% of applicants accepted | 35
% of acceptees attending | 40
# accepting a place on wait list | 543

% admitted from wait list | 6
# of early decision applicants | 204
% accepted early decision | 59

FRESHMAN PROFILE
Range SAT Critical Reading | 640–740
Range SAT Math | 640–730
Range SAT Writing | 650–740
Range ACT Composite | 29–32
% graduated top 10% of class | 78
% graduated top 25% of class | 96
% graduated top 50% of class | 100

DEADLINES
Early decision
Deadline | 11/1
Notification | 12/15
Regular
Deadline | 1/15
Notification | 4/1
Nonfall registration? | no

FINANCIAL FACTS
Annual tuition | $38,062
% frosh rec. need-based
scholarship or grant aid | 57
% UG rec. need-based
scholarship or grant aid | 60
% frosh rec. need-based
self-help aid | 51
% UG rec. need-based
self-help aid | 56
% frosh rec. any financial aid | 58
% UG rec. any financial aid | 62
% UG borrow to pay for school | 56
Average cumulative
indebtedness | $13,324

WELLS COLLEGE

CAMPUS LIFE
Fire Safety Rating | **81**
Green Rating | **75**
Type of school | private
Environment | rural

STUDENTS
Total undergrad enrollment | 568
% male/female | 29/71
% from out of state | 32
% from public high school | 88
% live on campus | 86
% African American | 6
% Asian | 2
% Caucasian | 67
% Hispanic | 4
% Native American | 1
% international | 2
# of countries represented | 13

ACADEMICS
Calendar | semester
Student/faculty ratio | 10:1
Profs interesting rating | 94

Profs accessible rating | 93
Most common
reg class size | 14–20 students

MOST POPULAR MAJORS
English language and literature
molecular biology
psychology

SELECTIVITY
of applicants | 1,673
% of applicants accepted | 71
% of acceptees attending | 12
# accepting a place on wait list | 56
% admitted from wait list | 102
# of early decision applicants | 15
% accepted early decision | 27

FRESHMAN PROFILE
Range SAT Critical Reading | 500–630
Range SAT Math | 480–600
Range SAT Writing | 480–590
Range ACT Composite | 22–27
Minimum paper TOEFL | 550
Minimum computer TOEFL | 213
Average HS GPA | 3.5
% graduated top 10% of class | 31
% graduated top 25% of class | 65
% graduated top 50% of class | 91

DEADLINES
Early decision
Deadline | 12/15
Notification | 1/15
Early action
Deadline | 12/15
Notification | 2/1
Regular
Priority | 12/15
Deadline | 3/1
Notification | 4/1
Nonfall registration? | yes

FINANCIAL FACTS
Annual tuition | $30,680
Room and board | $11,000
Required fees | $1,500
Books and supplies | $800
% frosh rec. need-based
scholarship or grant aid | 86
% UG rec. need-based
scholarship or grant aid | 83
% frosh rec. non-need-based
scholarship or grant aid | 57
% UG rec. non-need-based
scholarship or grant aid | 49
% frosh rec. need-based
self-help aid | 78
% UG rec. need-based
self-help aid | 80
% frosh rec. any financial aid | 96
% UG rec. any financial aid | 95
% UG borrow to pay for school | 82

Average cumulative
indebtedness | $24,182

WENTWORTH INSTITUTE OF TECHNOLOGY

CAMPUS LIFE
Fire Safety Rating | **84**
Green Rating | **87**
Type of school | private
Environment | metropolis

STUDENTS
Total undergrad enrollment | 3,816
% male/female | 81/19
% from out of state | 42
% from public high school | 65
% live on campus | 51
% African American | 4
% Asian | 5
% Caucasian | 70
% Hispanic | 4
% international | 3
# of countries represented | 46

ACADEMICS
Calendar | semester
Student/faculty ratio | 15:1
Profs interesting rating | 71
Profs accessible rating | 73
Most common reg class size | 20–29 students
Most common lab size | 10–19 students

MOST POPULAR MAJORS
architecture (BArch, BA/BS, MArch,
MA/MS, PhD)
construction management
mechanical engineering/mechanical
technology/technician

SELECTIVITY
of applicants | 4,845
% of applicants accepted | 67
% of acceptees attending | 26

FRESHMAN PROFILE
Range SAT Critical Reading | 460–560
Range SAT Math | 500–610
Range SAT Writing | 450–550
Range ACT Composite | 20–25
Minimum paper TOEFL | 525
Minimum computer TOEFL | 197
Average HS GPA | 3

DEADLINES
Regular
Priority	5/1
Notification	rolling
Nonfall registration?	yes

FINANCIAL FACTS
Annual tuition	$22,870
Room and board	$11,000
Books and supplies	$1,500
% frosh rec. need-based scholarship or grant aid	23
% UG rec. need-based scholarship or grant aid	23
% frosh rec. non-need-based scholarship or grant aid	70
% UG rec. non-need-based scholarship or grant aid	57
% frosh rec. need-based self-help aid	68
% UG rec. need-based self-help aid	63
% frosh rec. any financial aid	67
% UG rec. any financial aid	75
% UG borrow to pay for school	83
Average cumulative indebtedness	$22,000

WESLEYAN UNIVERSITY

CAMPUS LIFE
Fire Safety Rating	**86**
Green Rating	**86**
Type of school	private
Environment	town

STUDENTS
Total undergrad enrollment	2,766
% male/female	50/50
% from out of state	92
% from public high school	57
% live on campus	98
# of fraternities	8
# of sororities	2
% African American	7
% Asian	10
% Caucasian	58
% Hispanic	9
% Native American	1
% international	7
# of countries represented	53

ACADEMICS
Calendar	semester
Student/faculty ratio	9:1
Profs interesting rating	86
Profs accessible rating	91
Most common reg class size	10–19 students
Most common lab size	20–29 students

MOST POPULAR MAJORS
English language and literature
political science and government
psychology

SELECTIVITY
# of applicants	10,068
% of applicants accepted	22
% of acceptees attending	34
# accepting a place on wait list	688
% admitted from wait list	6
# of early decision applicants	854
% accepted early decision	41

FRESHMAN PROFILE
Range SAT Critical Reading	640–750
Range SAT Math	650–750
Range SAT Writing	640–740
Range ACT Composite	29–33
Minimum paper TOEFL	600
Minimum computer TOEFL	250
Minimum web-based TOEFL	100
Average HS GPA	3.82
% graduated top 10% of class	70
% graduated top 25% of class	90
% graduated top 50% of class	100

DEADLINES
Early decision
| Deadline | 11/15 |
| Notification | 12/15 |
Regular
Deadline	1/1
Notification	4/1
Nonfall registration?	no

FINANCIAL FACTS
Annual tuition	$41,814
% frosh rec. need-based scholarship or grant aid	43
% UG rec. need-based scholarship or grant aid	42
% frosh rec. need-based self-help aid	47
% UG rec. need-based self-help aid	47
% frosh rec. any financial aid	47
% UG rec. any financial aid	47
% UG borrow to pay for school	44
Average cumulative indebtedness	$29,174

WESTMINSTER COLLEGE (PA)

CAMPUS LIFE
Fire Safety Rating	**97**
Green Rating	**60***
Type of school	private
Affiliation	Presbyterian
Environment	village

STUDENTS
Total undergrad enrollment	1,431
% male/female	41/59
% from out of state	23
% from public high school	90
% live on campus	78
# of fraternities	5
# of sororities	5
% African American	3
% Caucasian	80
% Hispanic	1
# of countries represented	4

ACADEMICS
Calendar	semester
Student/faculty ratio	12:1
Profs interesting rating	89
Profs accessible rating	88
Most common reg class size	10–19 students
Most common lab size	10–19 students

MOST POPULAR MAJORS
biology/biological sciences
business/commerce
education

SELECTIVITY
# of applicants	4,262
% of applicants accepted	58
% of acceptees attending	20

FRESHMAN PROFILE
Range SAT Critical Reading	490–590
Range SAT Math	500–600
Range ACT Composite	21–26
Minimum paper TOEFL	550
Minimum computer TOEFL	80
Average HS GPA	3.4
% graduated top 10% of class	29
% graduated top 25% of class	60
% graduated top 50% of class	93

DEADLINES
Early action
| Deadline | 11/15 |
| Notification | 11/15 |
Regular
Deadline	4/15
Notification	rolling
Nonfall registration?	no

FINANCIAL FACTS
Annual tuition	$28,020
Room and board	$8,840
Required fees	$1,130
Books and supplies	$1,000
% frosh rec. need-based scholarship or grant aid	84
% UG rec. need-based scholarship or grant aid	83
% frosh rec. non-need-based scholarship or grant aid	97

% UG rec. non-need-based scholarship or grant aid	97
% frosh rec. need-based self-help aid	65
% UG rec. need-based self-help aid	67
% UG borrow to pay for school	80
Average cumulative indebtedness	$23,262

WHEATON COLLEGE (MA)

CAMPUS LIFE
Fire Safety Rating	**78**
Green Rating	**81**
Type of school	private
Environment	village

STUDENTS
Total undergrad enrollment	1,632
% male/female	38/62
% from out of state	67
% from public high school	62
% live on campus	93
% African American	5
% Asian	2
% Caucasian	76
% Hispanic	4
% international	5
# of countries represented	38

ACADEMICS
Calendar	semester
Student/faculty ratio	11:1
Profs interesting rating	88
Profs accessible rating	88
Most common reg class size	30 students
Most common lab size	32 students

MOST POPULAR MAJORS
economics
English language and literature
psychology

SELECTIVITY
# of applicants	3,304
% of applicants accepted	59
% of acceptees attending	22
# accepting a place on wait list	146
% admitted from wait list	12
# of early decision applicants	169
% accepted early decision	83

FRESHMAN PROFILE
Range SAT Critical Reading	570–680
Range SAT Math	560–670
Range ACT Composite	27–30
Minimum paper TOEFL	580
Minimum computer TOEFL	243
Minimum web-based TOEFL	90
Average HS GPA	3.5
% graduated top 10% of class	42

% graduated top 25% of class	40
% graduated top 50% of class	98

DEADLINES
Early decision	
Deadline	11/15
Notification	12/15
Regular	
Deadline	1/15
Notification	4/1
Nonfall registration?	yes

FINANCIAL FACTS
Annual tuition	$40,790
Room and board	$10,180
Required fees	$294
Books and supplies	$940
% frosh rec. need-based scholarship or grant aid	59
% UG rec. need-based scholarship or grant aid	53
% frosh rec. non-need-based scholarship or grant aid	16
% UG rec. non-need-based scholarship or grant aid	13
% frosh rec. need-based self-help aid	59
% UG rec. need-based self-help aid	55
% frosh rec. any financial aid	76
% UG rec. any financial aid	68
% UG borrow to pay for school	53
Average cumulative indebtedness	$25,540

WILKES UNIVERSITY

CAMPUS LIFE
Fire Safety Rating	**60***
Green Rating	**71**
Type of school	private
Environment	city

STUDENTS
Total undergrad enrollment	2,240
% male/female	52/48
% from out of state	20
% live on campus	40
% African American	3
% Asian	2
% Caucasian	83
% Hispanic	2
% international	3
# of countries represented	12

ACADEMICS
Calendar	semester
Student/faculty ratio	15:1
Profs interesting rating	73
Profs accessible rating	81

Most common reg class size	10–19 students
Most common lab size	10–19 students

MOST POPULAR MAJORS
business administration and management
nursing/registered nurse
(RN, ASN, BSN, MSN)
pharmacy (PharmD [US], PharmD or
BS/BPharm [canada])

SELECTIVITY
# of applicants	2,641
% of applicants accepted	76
% of acceptees attending	27

FRESHMAN PROFILE
Range SAT Critical Reading	460–580
Range SAT Math	480–600
Range SAT Writing	450–570
Minimum paper TOEFL	500
Minimum computer TOEFL	173
Minimum web-based TOEFL	60
% graduated top 10% of class	35
% graduated top 25% of class	63
% graduated top 50% of class	96

DEADLINES
Regular	
Notification	rolling
Nonfall registration?	yes

FINANCIAL FACTS
Annual tuition	$24,690
Room and board	$11,100
Required fees	$1,320
Books and supplies	$1,100
% frosh rec. need-based scholarship or grant aid	68
% UG rec. need-based scholarship or grant aid	59
% frosh rec. non-need-based scholarship or grant aid	75
% UG rec. non-need-based scholarship or grant aid	63
% frosh rec. need-based self-help aid	90
% UG rec. need-based self-help aid	83
% frosh rec. any financial aid	99
% UG rec. any financial aid	96
% UG borrow to pay for school	87
Average cumulative indebtedness	$34,775

WILLIAMS COLLEGE

CAMPUS LIFE
Fire Safety Rating	**60***
Green Rating	**92**
Type of school	private
Environment	village

STUDENTS

Total undergrad enrollment	2,032
% male/female	48/52
% from out of state	86
% from public high school	58
% live on campus	93
% African American	10
% Asian	12
% Caucasian	61
% Hispanic	10
% international	7
# of countries represented	73

ACADEMICS

Calendar	4/1/4
Student/faculty ratio	7:1
Profs interesting rating	94
Profs accessible rating	99
Most common reg class size	fewer than 10 students
Most common lab size	10–19 students

MOST POPULAR MAJORS
economics
English language and literature/ letters
visual and performing arts

SELECTIVITY

# of applicants	6,017
% of applicants accepted	20
% of acceptees attending	44
# accepting a place on wait list	492
% admitted from wait list	2
# of early decision applicants	614
% accepted early decision	38

FRESHMAN PROFILE

Range SAT Critical Reading	660–760
Range SAT Math	650–760
Range ACT Composite	30–34
% graduated top 10% of class	88
% graduated top 25% of class	99
% graduated top 50% of class	100

DEADLINES

Early decision	
Deadline	11/10
Notification	12/15
Regular	
Deadline	1/1
Notification	4/1
Nonfall registration?	no

FINANCIAL FACTS

Annual tuition	$39,250
Room and board	$10,390
Required fees	$240
Books and supplies	$800
% frosh rec. need-based scholarship or grant aid	53
% UG rec. need-based scholarship or grant aid	52
% frosh rec. need-based self-help aid	53
% UG rec. need-based self-help aid	52
% frosh rec. any financial aid	53
% UG rec. any financial aid	50
% UG borrow to pay for school	43
Average cumulative indebtedness	$8,103

WORCESTER POLYTECHNIC INSTITUTE

CAMPUS LIFE

Fire Safety Rating	**81**
Green Rating	**89**
Type of school	private
Environment	city

STUDENTS

Total undergrad enrollment	3,391
% male/female	72/28
% from out of state	49
% from public high school	66
% live on campus	50
# of fraternities	13
# of sororities	3
% African American	3
% Asian	6
% Caucasian	74
% Hispanic	6
% Native American	1
% international	9
# of countries represented	83

ACADEMICS

Calendar	semester
Student/faculty ratio	14:1
Profs interesting rating	76
Profs accessible rating	89
Most common reg class size	fewer than 10 students
Most common lab size	20–29 students

MOST POPULAR MAJORS
computer science
electrical, electronics and communications engineering
mechanical engineering

SELECTIVITY

# of applicants	6,284
% of applicants accepted	63
% of acceptees attending	23
# accepting a place on wait list	288
% admitted from wait list	1

FRESHMAN PROFILE

Range SAT Critical Reading	560–660
Range SAT Math	630–720
Range SAT Writing	560–660

Range ACT Composite	26–31
Minimum paper TOEFL	550
Minimum computer TOEFL	213
Minimum web-based TOEFL	79
Average HS GPA	3.8
% graduated top 10% of class	55
% graduated top 25% of class	88
% graduated top 50% of class	99

DEADLINES

Early action	
Deadline	11/10
Notification	12/20
Regular	
Deadline	2/1
Notification	4/1
Nonfall registration?	yes

FINANCIAL FACTS

Annual tuition	$38,360
Room and board	$11,610
Required fees	$560
Books and supplies	$1,000
% frosh rec. need-based scholarship or grant aid	70
% UG rec. need-based scholarship or grant aid	64
% frosh rec. non-need-based scholarship or grant aid	27
% UG rec. non-need-based scholarship or grant aid	17
% frosh rec. need-based self-help aid	46
% UG rec. need-based self-help aid	51
% frosh rec. any financial aid	99
% UG rec. any financial aid	95
% UG borrow to pay for school	74
Average cumulative indebtedness	$44,340

WORCESTER STATE COLLEGE

CAMPUS LIFE

Fire Safety Rating	**81**
Green Rating	**89**
Type of school	public
Environment	city

STUDENTS

Total undergrad enrollment	4,211
% male/female	41/59
% from out of state	3
% live on campus	24
% African American	6
% Asian	3
% Caucasian	80
% Hispanic	6
% Native American	1
% international	1
# of countries represented	20

ACADEMICS

Calendar	semester
Student/faculty ratio	17:1
Profs interesting rating	76
Profs accessible rating	89
Most common reg class size	20–29 students
Most common lab size	10–19 students

MOST POPULAR MAJORS
business administration and management
criminal justice/safety studies
psychology

SELECTIVITY

# of applicants	3,559
% of applicants accepted	59
% of acceptees attending	33

FRESHMAN PROFILE

Range SAT Critical Reading	460–550
Range SAT Math	470–560
Range SAT Writing	450–550
Range ACT Composite	19–24
Minimum paper TOEFL	550
Minimum computer TOEFL	213
Minimum web-based TOEFL	79
Average HS GPA	3.06

DEADLINES

Regular	
Priority	2/1
Deadline	5/1
Notification	rolling
Nonfall registration?	yes

FINANCIAL FACTS

% frosh rec. need-based scholarship or grant aid	49
% UG rec. need-based scholarship or grant aid	36
% frosh rec. non-need-based scholarship or grant aid	28
% UG rec. non-need-based scholarship or grant aid	16
% frosh rec. need-based self-help aid	55
% UG rec. need-based self-help aid	45
% frosh rec. any financial aid	57
% UG rec. any financial aid	49
% UG borrow to pay for school	42
Average cumulative indebtedness	$17,819

YALE UNIVERSITY

CAMPUS LIFE

Fire Safety Rating	**60***
Green Rating	**99**
Type of school	private
Environment	city

STUDENTS

Total undergrad enrollment	5,258
% male/female	50/50
% from out of state	94
% from public high school	55
% live on campus	88
% African American	9
% Asian	14
% Caucasian	42
% Hispanic	9
% Native American	1
% international	9
# of countries represented	108

ACADEMICS

Calendar	semester
Student/faculty ratio	6:1
Profs interesting rating	84
Profs accessible rating	83
% classes taught by TAs	3
Most common reg class size	10–19 students

MOST POPULAR MAJORS
economics
history
political science and government

SELECTIVITY

# of applicants	26,003
% of applicants accepted	8
% of acceptees attending	67
# accepting a place on wait list	600
% admitted from wait list	1

FRESHMAN PROFILE

Range SAT Critical Reading	700–800
Range SAT Math	700–780
Range SAT Writing	700–790
Range ACT Composite	30–34
Minimum paper TOEFL	600
Minimum computer TOEFL	250
Minimum web-based TOEFL	100
% graduated top 10% of class	96
% graduated top 25% of class	100
% graduated top 50% of class	100

DEADLINES

Early action	
Deadline	11/1
Notification	12/15
Regular	
Deadline	12/31
Notification	4/1
Nonfall registration?	no

FINANCIAL FACTS

Annual tuition	$36,500
Room and board	$11,000
Books and supplies	$950
% frosh rec. need-based scholarship or grant aid	58
% UG rec. need-based scholarship or grant aid	51

% frosh rec. need-based self-help aid	34
% UG rec. need-based self-help aid	39
% frosh rec. any financial aid	58
% UG rec. any financial aid	52
% UG borrow to pay for school	33
Average cumulative indebtedness	$12,297

YORK COLLEGE OF PENNSYLVANIA

CAMPUS LIFE

Fire Safety Rating	**91**
Green Rating	**60***
Type of school	private
Environment	city

STUDENTS

Total undergrad enrollment	5,281
% male/female	45/55
% from out of state	36
% from public high school	80
% live on campus	45
# of fraternities	9
# of sororities	7
% African American	4
% Asian	2
% Caucasian	87
% Hispanic	1
# of countries represented	52

ACADEMICS

Calendar	semester
Student/faculty ratio	18:1
Profs interesting rating	78
Profs accessible rating	75
Most common reg class size	20–29 students
Most common lab size	10–19 students

MOST POPULAR MAJORS
biology/biological sciences
business administration and management
nursing/registered nurse
(RN, ASN, BSN, MSN)

SELECTIVITY

# of applicants	11,048
% of applicants accepted	56
% of acceptees attending	18

FRESHMAN PROFILE

Range SAT Critical Reading	510–600
Range SAT Math	490–570
Range SAT Writing	470–560
Range ACT Composite	20–24
Minimum paper TOEFL	530
Minimum computer TOEFL	200

Average HS GPA	3.51
% graduated top 10% of class	13
% graduated top 25% of class	41
% graduated top 50% of class	77

DEADLINES
Regular Notification	rolling
Nonfall registration?	yes

FINANCIAL FACTS
Annual tuition	$13,640
Room and board	$8,530
Required fees	$1,500
Books and supplies	$1,200
% frosh rec. need-based scholarship or grant aid	50
% UG rec. need-based scholarship or grant aid	44
% frosh rec. non-need-based scholarship or grant aid	37
% UG rec. non-need-based scholarship or grant aid	20
% frosh rec. need-based self-help aid	60
% UG rec. need-based self-help aid	57
% frosh rec. any financial aid	64
% UG rec. any financial aid	61
% UG borrow to pay for school	75
Average cumulative indebtedness	$27,583

PART 4: INDEX
ALPHABETICAL INDEX

Index By Location

INDEX BY TUITION

MORE THAN $30,000

ABOUT THE AUTHORS

Robert Franek is a graduate of Drew University and has been a member of The Princeton Review staff since 1999. Robert comes to The Princeton Review with an extensive admissions background, most recently at Wagner College in Staten Island, New York. In addition, he owns a walking tour business and leads historically driven, yet not boring, tours of his home town.

Tom Meltzer is a graduate of Columbia University. He has taught for The Princeton Review since 1986 and is the author or co-author of seven TPR titles, the most recent of which is *Illustrated Word Smart*, which Tom co-wrote with his wife, Lisa. He is also a professional musician and songwriter. A native of Baltimore, Tom now lives in Hillsborough, North Carolina.

Christopher Maier is a graduate of Dickinson College. During the past five years, he's lived variously in New York City, coastal Maine, western Oregon, central Pennsylvania, and eastern England. Now he's at an oasis somewhere in the Midwestern cornfields—the University of Illinois—where he's earning his MFA in fiction. Aside from writing for magazines, newspapers, and The Princeton Review, he's worked as a radio disc jockey, a helping hand in a bakery, and a laborer on a highway construction crew. He's trying to avoid highway construction these days.

Julie Doherty is a freelance writer, Web designer, and preschool teacher. She lives in Mexico City.

Andrew Friedman graduated in 2003 from Stanford University where he was a President's Scholar. He lives in New York City.

NOTES

NOTES

NOTES

NOTES

NOTES

NOTES

Notes

NOTES

Funding It

**Paying for College Without
Going Broke, 2010 Edition**
978-0-375-42942-2 • $20.00/C$24.95

Ace the APs

**Cracking the AP Biology Exam,
2011 Edition**
978-0-375-42996-5 • $18.99/C$20.99

**Cracking the AP Calculus AB & BC Exams,
2011 Edition**
978-0-375-42988-0 • $19.99/C$22.99

**Cracking the AP Chemistry Exam,
2011 Edition**
978-0-375-42989-7 • $18.99/C$20.99

**Cracking the AP Economics
Macro & Micro Exams, 2011 Edition**
978-0-375-42997-2 • $18.00/C$20.00

**Cracking the AP English Language &
Composition Exam, 2011 Edition**
978-0-375-42998-9 • $18.00 /C$20.00

**Cracking the AP English Literature &
Composition Exam, 2011 Edition**
978-0-375-42999-6 • $18.00/C$20.00

**Cracking the AP Environmental Science
Exam, 2011 Edition**
978-0-375-42776-3 • $18.00/C$20.00

**Cracking the AP European History Exam,
2011 Edition**
978-0-375-42990-3 • $18.99/C$20.99

**Cracking the AP Human Geography Exam,
2011 Edition**
978-0-375-42777-0 • $18.00/C$20.00 ·

**Cracking the AP Physics B Exam,
2011 Edition**
978-0-375-42778-7 • $18.00/C$20.00

**Cracking the AP Physics C Exam,
2011 Edition**
978-0-375-42779-4 • $18.00/C$20.00

**Cracking the AP Psychology Exam,
2011 Edition**
978-0-375-42780-0 • $18.00/C$20.00

**Cracking the AP Spanish Exam with Audio
CD, 2011 Edition**
978-0-375-42781-7 • $24.99/C$27.99

**Cracking the AP Statistics Exam,
2011 Edition**
978-0-375-42782-4 • $19.99/C$22.99

**Cracking the AP U.S. Government &
Politics Exam, 2011 Edition**
978-0-375-42783-1 • $18.99/C$20.99

**Cracking the AP U.S. History Exam,
2011 Edition**
978-0-375-42991-0 • $18.99/C$20.99

**Cracking the AP World History Exam,
2011 Edition**
978-0-375-42995-8 • $18.99/C$20.99

**Available everywhere books are sold and at
PrincetonReviewBooks.com**